Developmental Psychology

Developmental Psychology

Kenneth O. McGraw
University of Mississippi

Harcourt Brace Jovanovich, Publishers
and its subsidiary, Academic Press

San Diego   New York   Chicago   Austin   Washington, D.C.
London   Sydney   Tokyo   Toronto

To the teachers who taught me
and the schools
where I learned

Cover illustration by Jamie Fidler

ISBN: 0-15-517623-4
Library of Congress Catalog Card Number: 86-80761
Printed in the United States of America

Preface

We know best those things that we know in their origins, a historian once said. Every developmentalist would agree, because a fundamental belief in all developmental science is that a sound understanding of things is based on a knowledge of their beginnings and of the processes by which they have come to be. This textbook provides an introduction to the branch of science that applies this belief to the study of human behavior and mental processes. The name of the science is developmental psychology.

The potential audience for a developmental psychology textbook includes not only psychologists but nurses, pediatricians, psychiatrists, educators, and parents as well. Given the diversity of interests represented by these groups, authors must choose the particular portion of the audience they wish to address. My decision was to write for students who are drawn to the field more by their intellectual interests than by their practical needs. Consequently, I have tried to represent the field of developmental psychology in a way that makes clear its past and its future. Also, I have attempted to show students the interrelationship between developmental psychology and other sciences, its position within the larger field of psychology, and the unique contributions it can make to a liberal arts education. But most of all I wanted to make the field conceptually interesting. To do that, I have focused on issues.

Although I strive to maintain theoretical neutrality while dealing with issues, I do give heavy emphasis to the epigenetic point of view, which today represents the dominant view among developmentalists. Human development from this perspective is basically open-ended, characterized by potential and the ever-present possibility for addition, deletion, and correction. At the same time, epigeneticists acknowledge that there are important constraints on an individual's overall developmental freedom. For example, the evolutionary past of our species, the unique genetic constitution of each individual, and the unique environmental circumstances of individuals are factors that shape and mold development in predictable ways.

In addition to the emphasis on issues, the conceptual treatment, and the use of the epigenetic point of view as a recurring theme, students will find that this book provides complete, up-to-date coverage of the research and theories that deal with age-related changes in the lives of human beings. The book is organized topically with one chapter on physical development, three on cognitive development, one on language development, and three on social development. These chapters, which comprise Part III of the text, are preceded by two chapters that deal with introductory material (Part I) and three that introduce the epigenetic approach (Part II). Each chapter begins with an outline and concludes with a summary. A glossary at the back of the book contains definitions of all of the key words that appear in boldface type throughout the text and many of those that appear in italics.

Whatever success this book may ultimately achieve as an introduction to the field of developmental psychology will be attributable in part to the help and support that I have been given in writing it. In particular I want to thank Warren Abraham, who signed the book, and Sue Miller, Marcus Boggs, Andrea McCarrick, Rick Roehrich, and Jon Preimesberger, who have been invaluable in putting it together. While these editors were working hard to help me get the words right, Robin Risque and Cheryl Solheid were preparing the artwork and design. From the start I was concerned that the art in the book be used to educate rather than decorate, and they have done a marvelous job in ensuring that this goal was met. Schamber Richardson, the production manager, kept everyone on schedule.

As important as the technical assistance from editors has been, a textbook's success rests ultimately on the quality of the scholarship that supports it. I have been fortunate in having the help of some true scholars in the field. Joseph Campos, Robbie Case, Adele Diamond, Joseph Fagan III, Richard Galbraith, John Locke, Craig Ramey, Carolyn Rovee-Collier, Sandra Scarr, Robert Selman, Albert

Yonas, and Robert Zajonc volunteered to read and critique portions of the manuscript. Nelson Cowan, University of Missouri; David Dodd, University of Utah; David Englund, California Polytechnic State University; Mary Gauvain, University of Pennsylvania; Janet Kistner, Florida State University; Edward Lonky, SUNY-Oswego; Barbara E. Moely, Tulane University; Evelyn Oka, Michigan State University; Robert Plomin, Pennsylvania State University; Margaret Schadler, University of Kansas; Thomas Spenser, San Francisco State University; Ellen Strommen, Michigan State University; and Marsha Walton, Rhodes College, made detailed comments on the work as a whole. I am sincerely grateful to these reviewers for their many helpful suggestions.

One does not write a textbook without a substantial amount of support from one's colleagues, friends, and family. I wish to thank the staff of the John D. Williams Library at the University of Mississippi, especially Jim Butler, Laura Harper, Emma Rogers, Sherrie Sam, and Martha Swan, for their extraordinary patience in tracking down resources for me. My colleagues in the psychology department have been extremely indulgent, understanding, and supportive of my efforts. Steve Fowler, Mary Jeanne Kallman, Dan Landis, Jan St. Lawrence, and Stan O'Dell offered help not only as friends but as reader/critics. I thank them for their encouragement and frank feedback.

The most supportive colleague and all-around, single most important person in my life during the development of this book has been my wife, Jo Ann O'Quin, whose clinical skills have been brought into play at considerable advantage to us both over the last several years. My final thanks I reserve for those who are most responsible for this work, Bernice and Lee.

Contents

PART I

An Introduction to the Science of Developmental Psychology

CHAPTER OUTLINE

A DEFINITION OF DEVELOPMENTAL PSYCHOLOGY

DIVISIONS OF THE LIFE SPAN

THE ORIGINS OF DEVELOPMENTAL PSYCHOLOGY

The Emergence of Psychology in the Late Nineteenth Century

The Roots of Developmental Psychology in Evolutionary Science

The Roots of Developmental Psychology in the Child-Study Movement

REASONS FOR CONTINUED INTEREST IN DEVELOPMENTAL PSYCHOLOGY IN THIS CENTURY

Relevance of Child Study to the Nature–Nurture Issue

Child Study as a Means of Uncovering Continuities and Connections in Development: The Roots Motive

Simplicity of Psychological Processes in Children

Evolutionary Interests in Child Development

SUMMARY

CHAPTER 1

Developmental Psychology: Past and Present

When students are asked on their first day in class to define developmental psychology, they generally say that it is the study of children. The more sophisticated ones say that it is the study of behavior and mental processes of children. Both definitions reflect the view that developmental psychology is *about* children. This is not surprising given that developmental psychologists belong to an organization known as the Society for Research in Child Development, they publish articles in journals with "child" in their titles such as the *Journal of Experimental Child Psychology* and *Child Development,* they teach sophomore- and junior-level courses in child psychology at the universities where they work, and when they become authorities in their field, they get invited to write a chapter for what was once called the *Manual of Child Psychology* (Carmichael, 1946, 1954; Mussen, 1970) and is now called the *Handbook of Child Psychology* (Mussen, 1983). But you must not let all this emphasis on children fool you.

Developmental psychology is not actually about children; it is about learning, memory, perception, personality, and all the other topics in which psychologists share an interest. What makes developmental psychologists unique is their approach to these topics. Whereas a physiological psychologist would ask about the physiological basis of memory and a social psychologist would ask about social influences on memory, a developmental psychologist would ask how and why memory changes with age. (Chapter 9 will address this particular question.) Developmental psychology, there-

fore, is *about* psychology, and its association with children is achieved only because the phenomena psychologists are interested in generally undergo important changes during the early years of human life.

A DEFINITION OF DEVELOPMENTAL PSYCHOLOGY

As a first step in developing a proper definition of developmental psychology we need to eliminate explicit reference to children and to make reference to developmental psychology's close association with the interests of general psychology. One way to do this is to say that developmental psychology is concerned with age-related changes in behavior and mental processes. The study of behavior and mental-processes is what ties developmental psychology to psychology at large. By specifying age-related change as the principal concern, we indicate that the discipline does not focus on children exclusively. People of any age can be of interest and, indeed, not just people but animals as well. Animal research, in fact, plays a very important role in developmental psychology. The work of developmental psychologists with unusual animals such as ambystoma (a type of salamander) and more conventional ones such as mice and rats has been a mainstay of the discipline since its inception. Today the menagerie of animals used in research on issues central to the discipline has grown to include sheep, stickleback fish, greylag geese, rhesus monkeys, chow dogs, chimpanzees, and many other species. The reason for this, which will become evident later in this chapter, has to do with the historical and current connections between developmental psychology and evolutionary biology.

A key word in any proper definition of developmental psychology is the word "science." To say that a discipline qualifies as a science means, in part, that its goals are *description* and *explanation*. Thus, every science you have ever studied has included the goals of description and explanation as part of its definition. In the history of sciences, description and explanation do not always proceed side by side. More often, the former precedes the latter. For example, careful descriptions of the motion of the planet Mars by Tycho Brahe preceded Johannes Kepler's explanation for the peculiar motions of that planet (and all the others that orbit the sun); biologists' classifications of the varieties of animal life preceded Charles Darwin's explanation for that variety; and geographers' descriptions of the land masses on the planet preceded the plate-tectonics explanations of how those masses got to where they are. In the same way, we will see that description precedes explanation in developmental psychology. Sometimes it precedes it by quite a bit, because we often have far more interesting descriptions than we have explanations. But progress is being made. Quoting from editor Paul Mussen's preface to the 1970 edition of the *Manual of Child Psychology*:

> Until approximately 25 years ago, developmental psychologists were primarily concerned with precise descriptions of children's capabilities at various ages and reliable determination of age changes in psychological functions. . . . The major contemporary . . . emphases in the field of developmental psychology, however, seem to be on *explanations* of the psychological changes that occur. (p. vii)

That emphasis continues today.

Where we do have explanations for psychological development, the explanations involve explanatory variables that are divisible into variables of *nature* and variables of *nurture*. Under the term nature, developmental psychologists lump all those variables that are primarily biological variables. Examples are neurological and muscular maturation, gene expression, and hormone release. Nurture variables are primarily experiential variables (that is, those based on experience). Examples are nutrition, education, and home environment. As we will see in Chapters 3 and 4, the forces of nature and nurture are tightly wound in a causal chain, which makes it impossible to pull out either the nature or nurture strand and say, "here, this is the cause of this development we have observed." If developmental psychologists have learned anything over the past 50 years, it is the folly of this approach to explanation in their science.

All that has been said about developmental psychology to this point can be summed up in the following definition: **developmental psychology** *is the scientific discipline concerned with describing age-related changes in the behavior and mental processes of both humans and animals and then explaining how nature and nurture through their interaction produce these changes.* Given the actual breadth of the field encompassed by this definition, one must be a bit exclusive in selecting topics to include in an introductory text on the subject. The selection of topics for the present text is weighted toward child development and toward descriptions. Where animal data can serve to illustrate important developmental principles, however, they are used liberally; and enough theory is given so that you can gain a good understanding of the major theoretical approaches taken by developmental psychologists. Though the emphasis is on development in children, we will also cover a number of developmental topics from outside of childhood. For example, developments from the prenatal period will prove to be important at several points in the book, as will developments from adolescence. Also, we will have occasion in the next chapter to discuss research on intellectual changes in old age.

DIVISIONS OF THE LIFE SPAN

When referring to development across the life span in this book, the technical term for this process—ontogenesis—will frequently be used. **Ontogenesis,** which refers to the development of individuals, is contrasted with the term **phylogenesis,** which refers to the development of species (see Figures 1-1 and 1-2). Human phylogenesis, like the phylogenesis of every other species that now shares the earth with us, extends back in time nearly three billion years. Human ontogenesis, on the other hand, extends over just the time of an individual life, which in contemporary America should last about 71 years for men and 78 years for women.

The normal human life span during which ontogenesis occurs can be segmented in any number of ways. Some of these divisions are "natural" ones based on major anatomical, physiological, or behavioral changes that occur during the life span. For frogs there is a natural division into egg, embryo, and adult stages; and for some insects (moths, butterflies, beetles, and bees) there is a division into egg, larva, pupa, and adult stages. For mammals there is an obvious division between the prenatal and postnatal

When man is born he in a cradle lyes,
At one times seven a hoby-horse devise,
At two times seven a book to read withall,
At three times seven a bandy and a ball,
At four times seven a wife he seeks to know,
At five times seven the horn of strength he blow,
At six times seven Time standeth by him still,
At seven times seven his bag begins to fill,
At eight times seven his bags are fill'd each nuke,
At nine times seven he to the earth doe stoop,
At ten times seven his glasse and time is run,
Into the earth man falls, and so he's gone.

FIGURE 1-1
Ontogenesis
Ontogenesis refers to the development of individuals from conception to death.
Milestones in human ontogeny are artfully portrayed in this seventeenth-century
woodcut.

periods, as well as between the sexually immature (prepubertal) and mature (postpubertal) periods. For mammals also the behavioral event known
as *weaning*—leaving the breast and beginning to feed on other foods—
provides a natural segmentation of the early years. Later, the attainment of
permanent teeth can be used as another stage or segment boundary. Seg-
menting the life span in this way is merely a matter of observing development closely to see at what points there seem to be significant changes in
the nature of the organism.

The divisions of the human life span that are most frequently used
today are given in Table 1-1. Because the factors that mark the divisions in
this table are a hodgepodge of anatomical, physiological, behavioral, and
social factors, the divisions are not necessarily natural ones. But they do
provide a useful segmentation of the life span, if for no reason other than

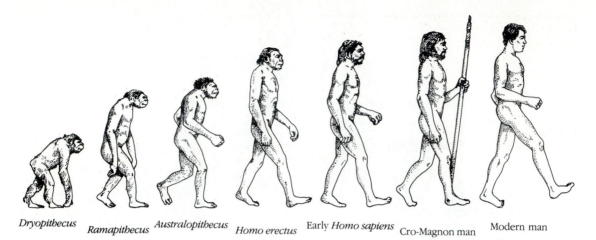

Dryopithecus   *Ramapithecus*   *Australopithecus*   *Homo erectus*   Early *Homo sapiens*   Cro-Magnon man   Modern man

FIGURE 1-2
Phylogenesis
Phylogenesis refers to the development of individual species during evolution. These drawings show an artist's conception of recent developments in human phylogeny.

the fact that it is easier to write "infant" than it is to write "child under age two," or to write "early childhood" than to write "childhood between the ages of two and seven."

The terms in Table 1-1 will be more meaningful if accompanied by some comments on the distinctions among the terms. For example, the distinction in the prenatal period between the **period of the embryo** and the **period of the fetus** is a distinction between the time during which the human organism is relatively formless (an embryo) and the time during which it is relatively well-formed (a fetus). This distinction goes back at least to the early eighteenth century (Boyd, 1980). In humans, the term fetus should be applied to the developing organism from the eighth week after conception. As shown in Figure 1-3, the developing organism is recognizably human at this point, down to its fingers and toes.

A terminological distinction that is historically more recent than that between embryonic and fetal stages of development is the distinction between the embryonic and preembryonic stages. Prior to the clear emergence of the embryo, there is just a mass of cells (the blastocyst), only a few of which will go on to become the embryo. The others lead to the development of the placenta and chorion, the support system for the developing human. The preembryonic period goes by various names including the *germinal stage* and the **period of the ovum.**

For the first month following birth, babies can be referred to as *neonates* or *newborns.* In the psychological literature, however, this particular

TABLE 1-1
Divisions of the Human Life Span Commonly Used
by Developmental Psychologists Today

	CONCEPTION (Zygote)	
Prenatal period	Germinal stage Period of the ovum	0 to 2 weeks
	Period of the embryo (Embryo)	2 to 8 weeks
	Period of the fetus (Fetus)	8 weeks to birth
	BIRTH	
Infancy	Neonatal period (neonate, newborn)	0 to 4 weeks
	Infancy proper	4 weeks to 18–24 months
Childhood	Early Childhood Preschool period	2 years to 6 years
	Middle childhood	6 years to 9–10 years
	Later childhood	9–10 years to 12–14 years
	PUBERTY (12 years for females, 14 years for males)	
Adolescence	Early adolescence	to 14–16 years
	Late adolescence	to 20 years
	MATURITY	
Adulthood	Young adulthood Middle adulthood Later adulthood or Period of old age	
	DEATH	

division of the life span is not especially important. Of far greater importance is the division called *infancy,* of which the neonatal period is part. The terms infant and infancy have been in the language for a very long time and stem originally from the Latin terms *infans* (infant) and *infantia* (infancy). Literally the term infancy means "period of not speaking," so you might think that it refers just to the stage of life prior to the acquisition of speech. For the use of the term infant in this text, this literal definition is a fairly good definition, but in fact the term infancy has been used over the years to refer to widely varying periods of developmental time. The Romans

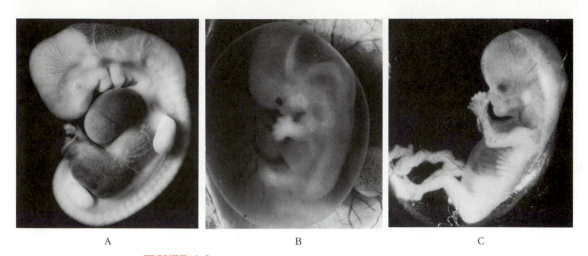

A   B   C

FIGURE 1-3
The Transition from Embryo to Fetus
These photographs show the transition from an embryonic human (A and B) to a
fetal human (C). The fetus is recognizably human, whereas the embryo is not.

used it to refer to the first 7 years of life, the time prior to the attainment
of permanent teeth. In later usage the term infancy designated just the first
14 months of life, the time until babies were able to walk erect (see, for
example, Scammon, 1942). In conjunction with this use of the word infant,
the term *toddler* was also used. Toddlers are babies who walk, but not well.
Toddlerhood, therefore, is the period from about 14 months to 2 ½ years.
In this book the term toddler will not be used because developmental psychologists today do not usually focus on walking as a behavior that divides
one stage of development from another. Instead they focus on the cognitive
advances that come with the ability to think and to speak as providing the
more important division. Because these abilities emerge in the period 18 to
24 months, developmental psychologists generally use the term infancy to
refer to the first 2 years of life.

Beyond infancy, the term *child* is used to designate the developing
human, and the term is appropriate until puberty begins. This rather long
period can be subdivided into early, middle, and late childhood. Early childhood corresponds to the years from about 2 to 6, which are the preschool
years in our society; middle childhood refers to the first years of elementary
school; and late childhood refers to the years 10 to about 12 or whenever
a child's body begins to go through the masculinization or feminization
processes of *puberty.* When puberty begins the term child is no longer appropriate. We say that the person is an *adolescent.* Adolescence then continues until *adulthood,* the point at which growth and puberty have ended.

The divisions of adulthood are marked primarily by social factors.
Young adults are relatively free of societal responsibilities. They are child-

less, in junior positions at work, and not leaders in the society. They are just establishing themselves in the adult world. By *middle adulthood,* there has been a shift toward far greater societal responsibilities in the family, in the community, and at work. *Late adulthood* begins with the relinquishing of responsibilities, as occurs for parents when the children leave home, and then continues with retirement and the eventual physical loss of the abilities to function as a healthy adult. This period may also be called the *period of old age*.

The terms introduced here for referring to various portions of the life span will be used throughout the text. Keep in mind, however, that the age boundaries on these terms are in many cases loose and in every case a matter of convention. That is, there is nothing "real" about these particular divisions. They just happen to be useful. In fact, the stream of life that constitutes the life span is continuous, and any divisions we put on that stream are primarily for convenience of reference.

THE ORIGINS OF DEVELOPMENTAL PSYCHOLOGY

Before getting into the substantive matters that constitute the knowledge base of developmental psychology, there is a final introductory matter to be considered. It is summarized in the question, Why should there be a developmental psychology? The historical answer to this question lies in intellectual and societal influences of the late nineteenth century. These initial influences only partially overlap with the influences that operate today to perpetuate an interest in the field.

The Emergence of Developmental Psychology in the Late Nineteenth Century

When a science has a short history, as developmental psychology does, the usual reason is that its subject matter was only recently discovered. The science of genetics, for example, dates only from Gregor Johann Mendel's discovery of the genetic mode of inheritance, a discovery that came to light in 1900. The science of immunology is but slightly older, beginning in earnest with Louis Pasteur's discovery of the immune response to cholera in chickens in 1879. In the case of developmental psychology, however, lack of a subject to study was not the factor causing a delay. After all, the development of children has been available as a subject for study for as long as human societies have existed.

Why then should a science of developmental psychology have been delayed until the late 1800s? There are two answers to this question. First, developmental studies depend on an interest in change and transition, called **evolutionism.** A spirit of evolutionism did not develop in science until the mid-nineteenth century with the work that culminated in Darwin's *Origin of Species.* Prior to the mid-nineteenth century, *stasis,* or being, was the concern of science, not development, or becoming; and this was true in the many branches of science. There was no developmental study of the earth, nor of the species on the earth, nor of the individuals in a species. With the publication of Charles Lyell's geological evidence (1830) that the topography of the earth—its mountains and seas, its valleys and plains—evolved over time, and with Darwin's evidence (1859) that species did too, an evolutionary approach to scientific studies was opened up for the first time. The evolutionary approach invented many new fields of study. Among these was developmental psychology.

Equally important in explaining the delayed beginnings of developmental psychology was the fact that prior to the latter half of the nineteenth century, children were not generally recognized to be different from adults and, therefore, worthy of study in their own right. During the second half of the nineteenth century, however, the Western industrialized world for the first time officially recognized childhood to be a unique and important period of life, according it a legal and social status it had never before held. Concurrent with this social change, there developed a scientific movement known as the **child-study movement,** which was dedicated to gathering whatever information it could about the age-to-age differences among children. These two factors—evolutionism, with its interest in humans' evolutionary past, and the child-study movement, with its interest in children per se—were the principal influences that led to the establishment of a science of developmental psychology.

The Roots of Developmental Psychology in Evolutionary Science

The evolutionary influence on developmental psychology was clearly evident in the first names applied to this new field: *evolutionary psychology* and, more popularly, *genetic psychology.* A genetic psychologist was interested in the origins (or genesis) of mental characteristics in individuals and then in their subsequent "descent" through the various stages of life. This meant that genetic psychologists were interested in how mental characteristics evolved during the life history of individuals. To make their studies, genetic psychologists examined the development of contemporary animals and children—particularly children. Commenting on the flood of post-Darwin child-development research, Sigmund Freud in 1897 wrote in a letter, "It is interesting that writers are now turning so much to child psychology. Today I received another book on the subject" (in Sulloway, 1979, p. 251).

From what has just been said about genetic psychology, you can deduce that the early genetic psychologists saw themselves as the counterparts to evolutionary biologists. The one was interested in the genesis and descent of mental characteristics during the life history of an individual; the other was concerned with the genesis and descent of morphological characteristics during the development of a species. In more technical language, genetic psychologists studied ontogeny (or ontogenesis) and evolutionary biologists studied phylogeny (or phylogenesis).

Even today, it is appropriate to view developmental psychology's concern with ontogeny as analogous to evolutionary biology's concern with phylogeny. At the outset, however, genetic psychology was based on more than just an analogy with the biological discipline that gave rise to it. More than just being complementary disciplines, the two were thought to overlap in some respects. Today, it puzzles us to imagine how this could be so. What could possibly be found in ontogenetic development to overlap with phylogenetic development? Had you been part of the intellectual *zeitgeist* at the end of the nineteenth century, however, you would not have asked this question. You would have accepted as fact that individual development was linked to the development of the species of which it was a member. How? By the law of recapitulation.

Ontogeny, Phylogeny, and the Law of Recapitulation

To recapitulate something means to summarize or retrace it briefly. The **law of recapitulation,** or the *biogenetic law* as it was also called, held that individual development was lawfully compelled to provide a brief summary of the entire phylogenetic past that preceded the individual. This law, formulated by the German evolutionist and natural philosopher Ernst Haeckel, was summarized in the still famous phrase, "ontogeny recapitulates phylogeny."

Though called a law, recapitulation should really have been labeled a theory. The fact that it was not indicates something about the uncritical acceptance it enjoyed at the close of the last century and the start of this one. Stephen Jay Gould, in his book *Ontogeny and Phylogeny,* tells an anecdote illustrative of the exalted status that the "law" attained in the minds of many of the early evolutionists. The story is that when a young paleontologist (Bernhard Kummel) expressed some reservations about the doctrine of recapitulation to the classical paleontologist R. C. Moore, Moore banged down his fist on the dinner table and said, "Bernie, do you deny the law of gravity!" (p. 116).

To give a quick illustration of the alleged lawful relationship between ontogeny and phylogeny, we can take Louis Agassiz's example (1857) of how the tails of phylogenetically advanced fish, such as bass and salmon (technically called teleost fish), go through changes in shape during development that directly parallel the changes in shape that appear in the fossil

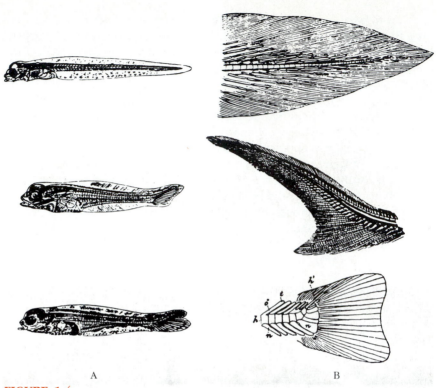

A   B

FIGURE 1-4
The Relationship Between Ontogeny and Phylogeny
Going from top to bottom, the drawings in Panel A represent an ontogenetic
sequence; those in B represent a phylogenetic sequence. Note that there is a
distinct parallel between the ontogenetic and phylogenetic sequences evident in
the development of the tails of the fish represented here. The fish on the left is a
flatfish *(Pleuronectes)* of the teleost order. In its larval form, its tail has the shape of
evolutionarily primitive fish; as a juvenile, its tail has a shape that corresponds to
fish of more-recent evolutionary origin; as an adult, it has a tail with a shape like
that found only among the most recently evolved fish. (From Gould, 1977)

(or geological) record for fish from ancient to modern times. Figure 1-4
clearly shows the parallel that exists in teleost fish between ontogeny (A)
and phylogeny (B).

In what is perhaps a more stunning example, Figure 1-5A shows an
artist's reconstruction of *Archaeopteryx,* the famous fossil bird that is
thought to be the evolutionary link between reptiles and birds. The feature
to notice is that *Archaeopteryx's* wings have claws, which is exactly what one
would expect to occur at the point in history when forelimbs of reptiles
were becoming functional wings. Figure 1-5B shows a photograph of a contemporary bird—a hoatzin—in its juvenile stage. This juvenile bird, like the

FIGURE 1-5
The Phylogeny of Birds and the Ontogeny of the Hoatzin
Archaeopteryx (A), shown here in an artist's reconstruction, represents the
evolutionary link between reptiles and birds, as evidenced by the reptilelike claws
on the end of its feathered forelimbs. The hoatzin (B)—pronounced *wattzin*—is a
contemporary bird that in its juvenile stage (shown here) has two claws on the
front edge of each wing. These claws, which are used for climbing, disappear as
the bird matures. The ontogeny of hoatzins, therefore, coincides in interesting ways
with the phylogeny of their species.

adult *Archaeopteryx,* has two claws on the front side of its wings. But in keeping with the view that the claws appear in ontogeny only as a recapitulatory vestige of the past, the claws do not last long during the hoatzin's ontogeny. They disappear by adulthood.

In addition to the physical evidence that the hoatzin's development maps its evolutionary past, there is behavioral evidence too. In evolution, swimming preceded flying as a means of locomotion. It precedes it, too, in the ontogeny of hoatzins. To escape danger, adult hoatzins fly away, as we would expect birds to do; but young hoatzins dive into the water next to where their nests are built and swim underwater to safety. Where would this behavior come from if not from recapitulation of a behavior present in ancestral amphibians that was lost in more recently evolved birds?

A host of instances can be found once one begins to look for examples in which ontogeny recapitulates phylogeny. For example, if you examine a 3-week-old embryo you will find what appears to be a gill slit in the location where an ear will eventually develop. The significance of this ontogenetic development from gill slit to ear is that it corresponds to a phylogenetic development. According to students of comparative anatomy and the fossil record, the structure that is the gill slit in fish has been transformed through evolution into portions of the external ear and eardrum in humans. Thus, the ontogeny of the human ear corresponds to its phylogeny. Other examples of human ontogeny recapitulating phylogeny include the fact that the embryonic human develops body hair and a tail, but then loses them before birth (except in very unusual cases; see Figure 1-6). Moving into postnatal life, there are some developmental patterns that seem to be in close accordance with phylogenetic sequences. Take for example the pattern in which adult locomotion (that is, walking) appears. First the infant locomotes by crawling, then by creeping about on all fours, and finally by walking upright. Similarly, infants often use their feet in a prehensile fashion and sleep in crouched, animal-like positions (see Figure 1-7). Early developmental psychologists delighted at such examples and took them as proof of the law of recapitulation.

Recapitulation's Influence

It would be hard to overestimate the influence that the doctrine of recapitulation had on the development of biology, psychology, and related disciplines in the late nineteenth and early twentieth centuries. Stephen Jay Gould, in his excellent book on the subject (1977), estimates that recapitulation was second only to natural selection as the most influential new idea of that period.

To understand the impact of the doctrine of recapitulation one must first realize that the fossil record that contains the major paleontological

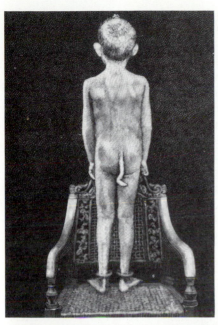

A

FIGURE 1-6
The Human Tail
It is quite rare that a child is born
with a tail. But it does happen as
shown in photograph A. As embryonic
humans we have a tail (B) but it never
fully develops in most of us;
nonetheless, we retain the vestiges of
a tail in the bone and muscle
structure at the base of the spine.

B

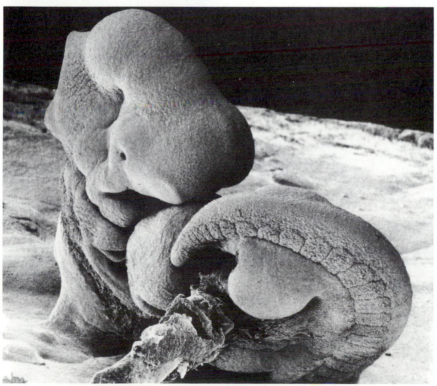

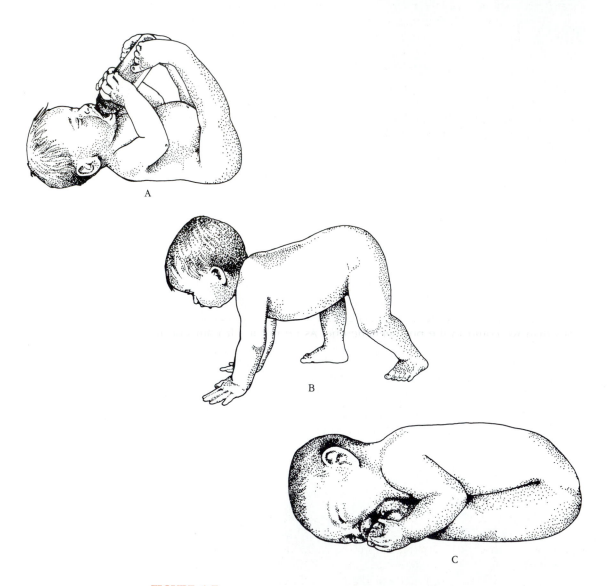

FIGURE 1-7
Is Human Phylogeny Evident in Human Ontogeny?
Early evolutionists eagerly sought evidence of recapitulation in the motor
development of children. These drawings show an infant using its feet in
prehensile fashion (A), crawling about on all fours (B), and sleeping in an
animal-like crouch (C). (After Hrdlicka, 1931)

evidence for evolution is a record with many gaps. Much that one would like to know about evolution is simply not there. This is true of morphological development certainly, but it is all the more true of behavior. We can get nothing from the fossil record about behavior except what we can infer from reconstructions of extinct life forms and the habitats in which they lived. As you might imagine, this is in no way a certain science. But what if it were true that individuals in their development reenact their phylogenetic past? If so, the past could be made forever new with each individual's reenactment of it. What a marvelous tool! We could peek in on the ponderously slow process of evolution by watching it replayed high speed in individual development. As Conklin said in a postmortem written to the biogenetic law in 1928:

> Here was a method which promised to reveal more secrets of the past than would the unearthing of all the buried monuments of antiquity— in fact nothing less than a complete genealogical tree of all the diversified forms of life which inhabit the earth. It promised to reveal not only the animal ancestry of man and the line of his descent *but also the method of origin of his mental, social, and ethical faculties.* (in Gould, 1977, p. 116; italics added)

To obtain all this, all one had to do was observe development. Agassiz even believed we could find better models of past forms in the ontogenetic record than we could in the phylogenetic one. As he put it, "If I am not mistaken, we shall obtain from sketches of those embryonic forms more correct figures of fossil animals than have been acquired by actual restoration" (in Gould, 1977, p. 66).

It was not just the chroniclers of physical evolution, however, who expected to make phylogenetic profit from ontogenetic studies. As indicated in the Conklin quote above, students of social and mental evolution—all of whom were classed as genetic psychologists—expected to gain as much.

The Influence on Psychology

To document the direct influence that the doctrine of recapitulation had on developmental psychology at its outset we need only to turn to the words and work of three principal figures in developmental psychology: G. Stanley Hall (1844–1924), Sigmund Freud (1856–1939), and Jean Piaget (1896–1980), all of whom were founders of the discipline.

Hall   G. Stanley Hall, the first president of the American Psychological Association (APA) and the founder of developmental studies in this country, began his studies of children in 1880 not because of an interest in children per se but rather because of his interest in social evolution. In the words of

G. Stanley Hall

John McCullers (1969), who made a study of Hall's influence on developmental psychology,

> Hall was an ardent evolutionist, and the abiding question to which he addressed himself was that of social evolution, the development of civilization. This question carried him not only into child study and psychology but also into biology, anthropology, history, Greek philosophy, and theology in search of answers. (p. 1110)

The major work for which Hall is known is his two-volume study of adolescence. He chose this topic because adolescence was in his view the point at which developing humans ceased to recapitulate their phylogenetic past and began to live their human present. In Hall's words, "Adolescence is a new birth, for the higher and more completely human traits are now born. The qualities of body and soul that now emerge are far newer. The child [on the other hand] comes from and harks back to a remoter past" (Hall, 1904, p. xiii).

Not only was Hall's selection of subject guided by the doctrine of recapitulation, but the message that he derived from his studies was as well. Unlike many a retiring academician, Hall was not reticent to express his opinion on the social relevance of his research. Thus, he argued vehemently that youth in their development from childhood to adolescence must be allowed to participate in activities suited to the phylogenetic stage through which they were passing.

> The child revels in savagery, and if its tribal, predatory, hunting, fishing, fighting, roving, idle, playing proclivities could be indulged in the country and under conditions that now, alas! seem hopelessly ideal, they would conceivably be . . . far more truly humanistic. . . .

The deep and strong cravings in the individual to revive the ancestral experiences and occupations of the race can and must be met. (Hall, 1904, pp. x–xi)

The Boy Scout movement, which came along at this time, shows no direct influence of the philosophy of G. Stanley Hall, but it was certainly in line with his thinking, a fact that was discussed at length in an article by M. Jane Reaney, which was published in 1914 in a journal edited by none other than the ubiquitous G. Stanley Hall.

Freud   As a medical student in Austria in the 1880s, Sigmund Freud received a very strong dose of evolutionary thought in general and recapitulation in particular as part of his formal training. This training influenced Freud's subsequent work in psychology far more than has been generally acknowledged. Frank Sulloway, Freud's most recent biographer, sets the record straight on this point (1979, see chapter 12 in particular). According to Sulloway, "Freud's implicit endorsement of [the biogenetic law] constitutes perhaps the least appreciated source of a priori biological influence in all of psychoanalysis" (1979, p. 251). No one short of G. Stanley Hall, Sulloway says, applied evolutionary theory and the biogenetic law to psychology as extensively as did Freud.

Sulloway carefully documents the pervasive influence that the biogenetic law had on Freud's views on topics ranging from individual and societal development to sexual perversion and neurotic development. According to Sulloway, knowledge of the role of the biogenetic law in Freud's thinking is crucial to understanding his theory.

Take for example Freud's interpretation of nursing in infancy and defecation in early childhood as sexual acts. Where would anyone possibly get such notions? They came from Freud's interpretation of the biogenetic law. First Freud decided that if individuals recapitulate the history of their species, they recapitulate its sexual history as well. Therefore, children must pass through stages in which the antiquated forms of sexual pleasure—all of those that lie on the phylogenetic road to the adult human sexual pleasure of heterosexual genital contact—are reexperienced. What are these early forms of pleasure? Freud identified two: oral and anal.

In the case of the development of the libido [or sexuality] this phylogenetic origin is, I venture to think, immediately obvious. Consider how in one class of animals the genital apparatus is brought into the closest relation to the mouth, while in another it cannot be distinguished from the excretory apparatus, and yet in others it is linked to the motor organs. (1963, vol. 16, p. 354)

Thus, one goes through the oral and anal stages of psychosexual development in which real sexual pleasure is derived from oral and anal activities because these were once the reproductive regions. Having gone through these stages, sexual pleasure in these regions should extinguish. Thus, when Freud said that adult anal and oral sex was perverse, he was not being moralistic; he was simply applying the logic of recapitulation: adult humans should have evolved beyond these interests.

Piaget   Jean Piaget, whose work on cognitive development takes up all of Chapter 8 in the present text, began his career in psychology in 1921 after studying zoology. No less than Freud, Piaget was a product of his times and thus had a substantial faith in the general validity of the law of recapitulation. In fact he used it as his justification for choosing the development of logical thought in children as his field of study. To understand this statement requires a little background.

Throughout Piaget's long career, his principal interest was in the adaptation of organisms to their environments. He began by doing original research on how mollusks in Lake Geneva achieve important adaptations in their lifetimes through structural changes, and he ended by studying how humans do the same through intellectual changes. This latter study, which extended over 60 years of his life, is a field of study known as **genetic epistemology:** genetic because it deals with the origins (or genesis) of thought and knowledge; epistemology because it is the conventional term from philosophy to refer to the study of knowledge.

If one is to study the development of logical thought as the evolutionary biologist would study it, however, one would need to have access to some record of this development in human and prehuman history. No such record exists. What then is one to do? Piaget's answer was to study children. That Piaget's choice of children in fact came about in this way is made quite clear in the following passage from a lecture he gave at Columbia University in 1969.

> The fundamental hypothesis of genetic epistemology is that there is a parallelism between the progress made in the logical and rational organization of knowledge and the corresponding formative psychological processes. With that hypothesis, the most fruitful, most obvious field of study would be the reconstituting of human history— the history of human thinking in prehistoric man. Unfortunately, we are not very well informed in the psychology of primitive man, but there are children all around us, and it is in studying children that we have the best chance of studying the development of logical knowledge, mathematical knowledge, physical knowledge, and so forth. (1969, p. 4)

In an interview conducted with Piaget four years after the Columbia lecture, Richard Evans asked Piaget whether the preceding passage accurately expressed his reason for studying children. Piaget's answer was "Yes, of course, that is quite right. . . . I am doing what biologists do when they cannot constitute a phylogenetic series, they study ontogenesis" (Evans, 1973, p. 48).

In brief, it is probably safe to say that except for his belief in the law of recapitulation, Piaget, who is by all accounts the premiere developmental psychologist in the field to date, would never have become a developmental psychologist. By the same token, without the law of recapitulation, Hall's research with children and adolescents would have lost its focus and purpose, and Freud's theory as we know it would never have been. The theory of evolution and the law of recapitulation that was associated with it, therefore, played a crucial part in the history of developmental psychology. Their influence was to make developmental psychologists out of a number of young scientists by providing them with a rationale for child study and a means of interpreting the results.

Despite the fact that the law of recapitulation had such an important role to play at the start of the field of developmental psychology, its influence waned quickly in the twentieth century. One reason was that the theory was built on selective evidence. The law of recapitulation simply did not work as a general rule for the ordering of events in human and animal ontogeny. There were instances of it of course, but there were also counterinstances (see the discussion of neoteny in Chapter 6). An even more important reason for the decline of recapitulation's influence in fields such as psychology is that the theory died at its source in biology. This occurred because the theory depended on a mechanism that ceased to make sense when people learned about the genetic mode of inheritance.

The mechanism that had made recapitulation feasible was the mechanism of *terminal addition*. According to this mechanism, once an animal had recapitulated its past, it was then possible for it to add on its own novel life stages through adaptations to whatever unique life circumstances the animal faced. If it did make adaptations, instructions for making these same adaptations would then get transmitted—somehow—back to the offspring so that they too and all their descendants would now have these novel life stages built into their own recapitulatory life pattern. Darwin himself had accepted this mechanism as a possibility because he had believed that the hereditary material that parents pass to offspring might be continually altered. But this notion makes no sense in terms of Mendelian genetic theory. In the Mendelian view, which today has become dogma, the genetic material that we pass on to our offspring is fixed at our own conception. Therefore, the facts of our individual lives are irrelevant in determining the genetic information we pass to our offspring. The conclusion, then, is that even if an individual animal did "evolve" beyond its recapitulated past, there would be no way for that evolutionary message to be passed on to offspring. In light of this fact, the biogenetic law became just an important footnote in the history of science, and those who chose to make a science of child study had to look elsewhere to find a general scientific justification for their work.

The Roots of Developmental Psychology in the Child-Study Movement

Darwin's theory of evolution by natural selection and the law of recapitulation, despite their wide impact, were strictly scientific developments, not tied in any clear way to developments in the society at large. The second influence that led to a science of developmental psychology, however, involved developments in the entire culture. Among these were industrialization and the growth of cities, sharp reductions in infant and child mortality, and the expansion of the middle class coupled with a generally improved standard of living. Together these developments brought the last touches to a new conception of childhood, a conception that had begun to develop following the Middle Ages but was only completed in the latter part of the nineteenth century. Because the new conception of childhood was one that put great value in the child and set aside childhood as a special time of life, it was natural that societies holding that conception would invest resources in children. In the nineteenth century, they did so for the first time in history, particularly in the United States. Much of the societal investment was in social programs, but part of it was in research. The research effort became known as the child-study movement (see Siegel & White, 1982).

Changing Conceptions of Childhood

According to social historians who have studied the history of childhood, the conception of childhood that we hold today is a modern invention. Whereas today we consider childhood to encompass many years of life (extending in effect to the age of 18 or 21), historically it has been viewed as a short period of life (extending in many cases only to the age of 6 or 7). In addition, both the family and the culture invest heavily in childhood today, whereas in previous centuries childhood was thought to merit little in the way of family or societal investment. The result is that if visitors from any previous century could visit industrialized nations of the twentieth century, they would be as surprised by the way these nations treat their children as by the way they treat their pets. The surprise would be that children, like pets, have a place in the culture and a share of the resources they have never before enjoyed. Children, for example, have their own special schools, doctors, clothes, books, laws, playgrounds, and civil rights. The degree of child-focus that we express in these and other ways is unprecedented in history.

Two essential changes have occurred in the general conception of childhood that have made possible the historically unique developments we observe today. First, we no longer expect children to be little adults. Second, we no longer expect them to have utilitarian value for their parents. With the elimination of these two expectations, the way was opened for children to receive special status in society.

Children as Little Adults   Beliefs that characterize cultures can be either implicit or explicit. For example, the belief that all people are created equal is explicit in that it is recorded in our Constitution and frequently stated as an explicit belief by members of the society. Other beliefs, such as the belief that bigger and faster is also better, are implicit beliefs. People who hold them act in a way that manifests the belief without their ever having to express it explicitly. They may not even be expressly aware of the belief; it is just one of those things that "goes without saying." The belief that children are just little adults was held in this implicit fashion by many pre-nineteenth century societies.

In the Middle Ages in Europe, for example, little distinction was drawn between adults and children. This is amply demonstrated in one of the seminal works on child history, Phillipe Ariès' *Centuries of Childhood* (1962). According to Ariès, as soon as children outgrew their swaddling clothes—the bands of cloth that were wrapped tightly round their bodies in baby-

FIGURE 1-8

Children as Little Adults

In Duccio's *Madonna and Child* (A) we see a good example of Medieval artists' convention of drawing children as scaled-down adults. Representations of children in art that showed them to have proportions that were different from adults did not appear until the Renaissance. One of the first artists to portray children with reasonable accuracy was Albrecht Dürer, who composed a study of children's proportions as shown in panel B.

A   B

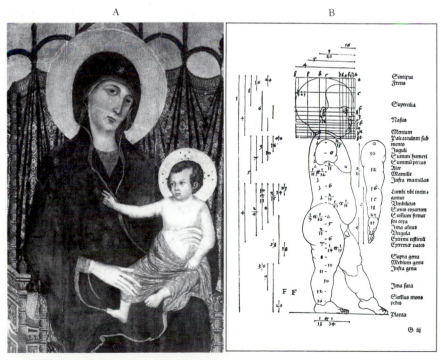

hood—they were dressed just like the other men and women of their class. Similarly, children's games and pastimes were those of adults; there was no attempt made to protect their innocence in sexual or other matters; and in a surprising expression of the implicit belief that children were just little adults, when children were depicted in art, they were depicted as scaled-down adults not as children whose body proportions differ greatly from those of an adult (see Figure 1-8).

The belief that children were but little adults did not die following the Middle Ages. It persisted for some time in one form or another. For example, science once held that all life was preformed. One aspect of the preformationist doctrine was that the embryonic human was not different in kind from the adult human: all that was to be found in the adult was to be found in the embryo. This belief received "confirmation" from early microscopists who thought they saw little humans, like those depicted in Figure 1-9, inside sperm cells. The microscopists were, of course, wrong; but the very fact that they could make this mistake illustrates how strongly the notion of preformed humans was held.

Perhaps more convincing than any of the foregoing facts in establishing that children were once thought to be but little adults and, therefore, not inherently different from anyone else is the history of child-labor practices. Today, the use of child labor is an abhorrent practice that ranks on a par with cruelty to animals and slavery. Most of us do not realize, therefore, that the use of child labor was once an accepted societal practice. In ancient Sparta, male children entered the military barracks at age 7. In Europe during the Middle Ages, they were farmed out as apprentices at this age. The same was true in Japan. The worst practices, however, may have taken place

FIGURE 1-9

Conceptions of the Homunculus
Had you been a student of development in the late seventeenth century, you would have found drawings like these in your textbook. The drawings are of the homunculi (little humans) that were alleged to be present in sperm cells.

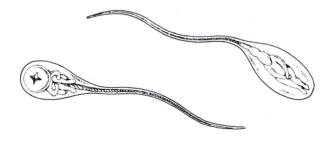

during the industrial development of the late eighteenth and early nine-teenth centuries when children were routinely employed in mills, factories, and mines.

The work that children did in cottage industries and agriculture may have made few allowances for childhood, but at least these jobs were at home and in the open air. Industrial jobs were different. They were boring, dirty, repetitive, and unhealthy, yet children as young as 4 and 5 years of age were placed in them. They crawled behind the looms in textile mills to retie broken threads, a job for which their small bodies and hands were suited; and they worked the same hours as adults in the factories doing jobs that required them to be on their feet the entire day.

Although there are horror stories to be told about the way children were treated in all industrial jobs, their treatment can be exemplified with a brief description of life in the coal mines. Mining was a 6-days-a-week, 12-hours-a-day job, with workers descending into the mines at dawn and not coming out until dusk. The youngest children in the mines (5 and 6 years of age) were given the job of minding the doors that were used to seal off the shafts. For this job they would sit alone for 12 hours a day in one of the narrow dark passages of the mine. Older children worked as "hurriers." Their job was to haul coal about in the narrow tunnels. To achieve this there was a harness-and-sledge system like that depicted in Figure 1-10, which forced the children to pull the coal like draft animals (Bready, 1926). One child who performed this task described his work as follows:

> I went into a pit at seven years of age. When I drew with the girdle and chain the skin was broken and blood ran down. . . . If we said anything they would beat us. I have seen many draw at six [years]. They must do it or be beat. They cannot straighten their backs during the day. I have sometimes pulled till my hips have hurt me so that I have not known what to do with myself. (Bready, 1926, p. 273)

Work done by adult miners was, of course, just as difficult and unpleasant as the work given to children, but the point is that children were given no special treatment: they were treated just like little adults.

Significant social protest to the use of child labor in the mills, facto-ries, and mines did not develop until well into the nineteenth century. En-gland, which was the pioneer in child-labor laws (and perhaps the worst abuser of children prior to the passage of the laws), first passed legislation regulating the use of children in factories and mills in 1832. A decade later, further legislation was passed to regulate the use of children in the mines. One must not think, however, that these laws eliminated child labor. For example, the coal-mining law only eliminated the worst abuses. It forbade the use of girls altogether in underground jobs (primarily for moral rea-sons) and required that boys be at least 10 years of age. Thus, even after

FIGURE 1-10

Children at Work in the Mines

A British royal commission in 1840 investigated the use of children in the coal mines. The commission's report described the general conditions in the mines and the work that children performed there. The most gruesome job of all was said to be that of a "hurrier" (illustrated in the top and bottom panels).

the English reforms in child-labor practices, it is still not clear that the concept of childhood had evolved to the point that it has in industrialized countries of today.

To sum up this section in brief, it seems clear that whether the activity was work, war, or play, children—particularly those of the lower and middle classes—were fully integrated with adults throughout most of history. Such practices are shocking only to people who have adopted the belief that childhood up to and perhaps through adolescence is a special time of life, a time that ought to be free of adult cares and responsibilities and dedicated to education, play, and leisure. It is precisely this notion, however, that is new and that, when it developed, contributed to the formation of developmental psychology.

The Utility of Children   The second aspect of the change in our conception of childhood is that children have become less useful to their families over the past 100 years. For example, children today generally do not add to the family income; rather they subtract from it—and quite substantially. Current U.S. government figures put the cost of raising and educating a single child to age 18 at between $90,000 and $100,000 if one does not figure in inflation (see Table 1-2). If inflation is added, the cost rises considerably. This makes children a luxury item; they cost but don't pay. Moreover, children are no longer a form of old-age insurance. It used to be that caring for aged parents was expected of children. Now governments have taken on that function and children have abandoned it. Even in Japan, where traditionally the first-born male had an obligation to stay at home and care for the parents, the old ways are changing. Having children today is not even a good way for men to show off their virility. Siring ten children or more used to be a source of male pride, particularly in the Muslim world where multiple wives were allowed. However, given the economic and social circumstances of the twentieth century, this reason for having children is also disappearing. Thus, today's children have no clear economic or social utility for the adults who conceive and raise them. This situation is historically unique; in the past the utility of children was a major argument for having them. There is no better evidence of this fact than the widespread and much used practices of abandonment and infanticide that were used in the past to get rid of children whenever they were inconvenient or a drain on family resources.

Abandonment and Infanticide   The means that societies have used to get rid of children of "no value" have varied over the years. The most direct means was simply to kill unwanted children or abandon them, leaving them to the elements. Less direct practices were sending infants away from the home to be wet-nursed in the country or housing them in an orphanage where they were almost sure to die.

TABLE 1-2 Updated Estimates of the Cost of Raising a Child

The Cost of Raising Urban Children: June 1985; Moderate-Cost Level[1]

Region and Age of Child (Years)	Total	Food at Home[2]	Food Away from Home	Clothing
Midwest[5]				
Under 1	$ 4,429	$ 570	$ 0	$ 140
1	4,558	699	0	140
2-3	4,240	699	0	228
4-5	4,490	803	146	228
6	4,692	777	146	316
7-9	4,873	958	146	316
10-11	5,055	1,140	146	316
12	5,396	1,166	175	456
13-15	5,525	1,295	175	456
16-17	6,059	1,450	175	632
Total	89,957	18,155	2,218	6,176
Northeast				
Under 1	4,386	673	0	140
1	4,542	829	0	140
2-3	4,422	803	0	246
4-5	4,672	907	146	246
6	5,021	907	175	333
7-9	5,202	1,088	175	333
10-11	5,435	1,321	175	333
12	5,766	1,321	175	491
13-15	5,921	1,476	175	491
16-17	6,345	1,632	204	614
Total	94,832	20,748	2,450	6,454
South				
Under 1	4,823	622	0	158
1	4,952	751	0	158
2-3	4,640	725	0	246
4-5	4,864	803	146	246
6	5,159	803	175	333
7-9	5,314	958	175	333
10-11	5,522	1,166	175	333
12	5,883	1,166	204	491
13-15	6,038	1,321	204	491
16-17	6,482	1,450	204	632
Total	97,889	18,467	2,566	6,526
West				
Under 1	4,751	622	0	140
1	4,906	777	0	140
2-3	4,652	751	0	228
4-5	4,931	855	175	228
6	5,300	829	204	333
7-9	5,481	1,010	204	333
10-11	5,714	1,243	204	333
12	6,028	1,243	204	474
13-15	6,158	1,373	204	474
16-17	6,754	1,554	234	597
Total	100,004	19,426	2,858	6,280

[1]Annual cost of raising a child from birth to age 18, by age, in a husband–wife family with no more than 5 children. For more information on these and additional child-cost estimates, see USDA Miscellaneous Publication No. 1411, "USDA Estimates of the Cost of Raising a Child: A Guide to Their Use and Interpretation," by Carolyn S. Edwards, Family Economics Research Group, Agricultural Service, USDA.

[2]Includes home-produced food and school lunches.

Housing[3]	Medical Care	Education	Transportation	All Other[4]
$ 1,909	$ 298	$ 0	$ 890	$ 622
1,909	298	0	890	622
1,678	298	0	775	562
1,678	298	0	775	562
1,591	298	138	775	651
1,591	298	138	775	651
1,591	298	138	775	651
1,649	298	138	833	681
1,649	298	138	833	681
1,707	298	138	919	740
30,086	5,364	1,656	14,700	11,602
1,938	298	0	775	562
1,938	298	0	775	562
1,765	298	0	718	592
1,765	298	0	718	592
1,736	298	173	718	681
1,736	298	173	718	681
1,736	298	173	718	681
1,794	298	173	804	710
1,794	298	173	804	710
1,823	298	173	861	740
32,174	5,364	2,076	13,668	11,898
2,054	332	0	947	710
2,054	332	0	947	710
1,823	332	0	833	681
1,823	332	0	833	681
1,736	332	207	833	740
1,736	332	207	833	740
1,736	332	207	833	740
1,794	332	207	890	799
1,794	332	207	890	799
1,852	332	207	976	829
32,696	5,976	2,484	15,736	13,438
1,996	365	0	947	681
1,996	365	0	947	681
1,794	365	0	833	681
1,794	365	0	833	681
1,765	365	173	861	770
1,765	365	173	861	770
1,765	365	173	861	770
1,823	365	173	947	799
1,823	365	173	947	799
1,909	365	173	1,034	888
32,868	6,570	2,076	16,248	13,678

[3]Includes shelter, fuel, utilities, household operations, furnishings, and equipment.

[4]Includes personal care, recreation, reading, and other miscellaneous expenditures.

[5]Formerly the North Central Region.

SOURCE: *Family Economics Review,* 1985, no. 4, p. 26. Published by the United States Department of Agriculture: Agricultural Research Service.

The practice of killing unwanted children is called *infanticide,* and the practice has quite a history (Piers, 1978). Its use is illustrated by the warring culture of Sparta in ancient Greece where a panel of elders was given responsibility for deciding whether infants were to be allowed to live. Infants who appeared weak or cried too much were not tolerated.

Information on infanticide in Europe during the Middle Ages and later is not easy to come by because it was technically a crime. According to Maria Piers (1978), however, it was probably the most frequent crime in all of Europe from the Middle Ages until about 1800. Unwanted babies were left by the roadside, like an unwanted pet might be today. They were also drowned—sometimes in rivers and sometimes in latrines. In fact, the first foundling home was begun in Italy in the 1300s when Pope Innocent III became so upset by the sight of infant bodies floating in the Tiber River that he decided to do something about it. Foundling homes (or orphanages) were a good idea, but in practice they just became a more acceptable form of infanticide. Survival rates for infants confined to them were incredibly low. One Irish orphanage in the nineteenth century had only 45 survivors of 10,272 children admitted (Thompson & Grusec, 1970, p. 603). Figures as incredible have been reported from Russia. Even in this country in the early part of this century infants reared in institutions were more likely to die than not. For example, a 1915 study in Baltimore, Maryland, found that 90 percent of the infants admitted to orphanages and foundling homes in that city died within one year of their admission (Gardner, 1972).

The practices of infanticide, abandonment, and wet-nursing that were so prevalent in the past should not be conceived of as acts performed by a species of humans somehow crueler and more vicious than the one we know today. The practices were a result of certain facts of life (for example, extreme economic hardship and no birth control) and the fact that children were not given the same privileged place in society as they are today.

A number of historical documents support the notion that the very people who acted in what we view to be a criminal way toward children were not people who were satanic, cruel, or compassionless. One of the most moving is an account of a "killing nurse" of eastern Europe, a woman who took in unwanted infants and arranged for them to die. Holding an infant who was fated to die, she said, "You poor, poor little one! . . . fruit of sin through no fault of your own, but sinless in yourself . . . soon you will be gone, soon, soon, my poor one . . . and going now, you will not go to hell as you would if you lived and grew up to become a sinner" (in DeMause, 1974, p. 30). This woman apparently viewed the act she was about to commit as a mercy killing. Is this not our attitude today when we abandon a pet or "arrange" for it to die? The only difference between us today and the killing nurse of over a century ago is the beliefs that we hold as a society. Her society had not yet sanctified infant life.

If abandonment is no longer a problem today, our changed conception of childhood is in part responsible. The children who were abandoned in the past were those who would not be useful—the illegitimate child, the female who would require a dowry, the child with a birth defect. Today since we no longer expect children to have utility, the lack of it does not deprive a child of a place in the family. Just what factors led to this change are not clear. Certainly economic improvements are among them, along with vaguer factors such as a raised consciousness regarding children as human beings. Whatever the causes, the fact is that today's attitudes toward "useless" children are altogether different from what they were a century or two ago. Whereas the Spartans judged the worthiness of infants on whether they could be predicted to be good warriors, members of our society go to heroic efforts to preserve the lives of even the least promising infants. Infants born three months premature or with genetic defects or with physical deformities all get the best chance at life that we can give them (see Figure 1-11), all because of some implicit beliefs we hold about the inherent value of life. These beliefs overshadow any concern for utility.

The Child-Study Movement

The changed conception of childhood in the culture at large spawned a wealth of social programs designed to improve the lot of children. These were children's aid societies, societies for the prevention of cruelty to children, juvenile courts, orphanages, schools, and numerous child health programs. The establishment of these and other social programs meant that "tens of thousands of adults had jobs that involved them with child care, protection, training, and rehabilitation" (Siegel & White, 1982, p. 248). In the words of Alexander Siegel and Sheldon White, these people employed in the service of children, along with the parents of the late nineteenth century, formed a "social juggernaut" that bore down on academia asking for answers to child-related questions. At this time, however, there were no answers. The child-study movement had only just begun.

Though it may seem surprising that little was known about children prior to 1880, it is true. This is documented, for example, by Sara Wiltse, first secretary to the section of the National Education Association for child study. In her history of the child-study movement, Wiltse (1894) begins by saying that child study really began in America. She then goes on to say that, "previous to 1880 practically no scientific observations of child life had been undertaken in America. . . . One searched libraries in vain to find what the average child could either know or do at a given age" (p. 191). Likewise, Margaret Schallenberger of Stanford University, another leader in the child-study movement, wrote in 1894 that children were

> among the last of nature's productions to become the privileged subjects of scientific study. We have thought it worthwhile to give careful attention and deep thought to the movements of stars, the lives of plants, and the formation of stones. Meanwhile many a Topsy has come into the world and has "just growed." (p. 87)

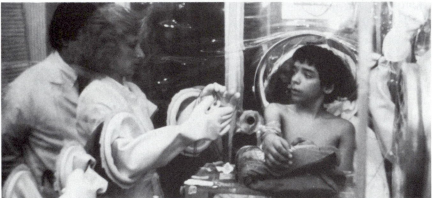

FIGURE 1-11

Immune-Deficient Children

Both of the children pictured here serve to illustrate the lengths that parents and society at large will go to preserve the lives of children today. Jared Reisman (top photo), shown here with his mother, had such severe allergic reactions to the normal levels of pollen and dust in the air that his life was threatened. A special air-purifier system in his home plus this "space suit" have alleviated Jared's problem, and he is now adapting well. A child known only as David (bottom photo), of Houston, Texas, was 12 years old when this picture of him in his isolation bubble was taken. He lived from birth to age 12 in this special bubble home because of an immune deficiency that left him defenseless against bacterial and viral infection. In the fall of 1983, he was removed from the bubble in order to attempt a bone-marrow transplant that doctors hoped would give him sufficient resistance to live outside the bubble, but the operation failed and he died in the spring of 1984.

Further documenting the paucity of information available to educators and others regarding child development in the late nineteenth century is the following quote from John A. Hancock (1894), a colleague of G. Stanley Hall at Clark University. This quote also serves to confirm the point made earlier that the new child studies stemmed from the discovery that children and adults were different.

> The enormous difference in ability between the child and the adult, both physically and mentally, is fully realized by few. . . . Pedagogy is based on the psychology of the adult mind, and the conditions of school-room work are generally adapted to the adult. It is obvious that instruction and discipline should be adjusted to the mental and physical stages of development of children; and that we need to know just what the ability of children of each age is in order to plan a fitting course of education. (p. 9)

In order to meet the goal of knowing "just what the ability of children of each age is," participants in the child-study movement embarked on a host of studies that are best described as *normative*. Normative studies, quite simply, seek to determine what is normal and, therefore, to be expected in development. As pointed out in the preceding quotes by Schallenberger and Wiltse, however, knowledge of developmental *norms* was so abysmal in the late nineteenth century that teachers did not even know what to expect from their students. This was because the only studies that had been done up to this point were principally studies of individuals. Charles Darwin, for example, made a study of his son's development. Unfortunately, data from such "baby biographies" hardly enabled parents and teachers to know what to expect from children who were probably more average than the sons and daughters of the likes of Charles Darwin.

Members of the child-study movement worked hard to correct the deficiency by making studies of huge numbers of children in which they measured everything from physical growth and strength to the ability to imagine. Although these studies were generally methodological disasters that yielded little in the way of reliable knowledge, they were a start. G. Stanley Hall's massive study (1883) of the "contents of children's minds" provides a good example of the type of studies that were part of the movement.

The purpose of Hall's study was to determine what Massachusetts' 5- and 6-year-olds knew on entering school. To measure this, he had teachers administer a long list of questions that assessed children's knowledge of natural phenomena (for example, the seasons, rainbows, stars), animals (bees, snails, robins, and so on), body parts (such as ribs, lungs, ankles), and other matters (for example, Where do leathern things come from?). He found that children knew less than one might think and that they had many misconceptions. "The high rate of ignorance here indicated may surprise most who will be likely to read this report . . . ," Hall wrote. "Skeins and spools of thread were said to grow on the sheep's back or on bushes, stockings on trees, butter to come from buttercups, flour to be made of beans, oats to grow on oaks, bread to be swelled yeast, trees to be stuck in the ground by God and rootless, meat to be dug from the ground, and potatoes to be picked from trees" (in Dennis, 1972, p. 122).

In other studies of the day, John Hancock undertook a study of the motor ability in children in which he determined that a curriculum requiring fine motor movements by kindergarten children was inappropriate. "Kindergarten work generally is too fine," Hancock reported. "Occupations and games for young children should be of a nature that will involve large muscles and movements" (1894, pp. 26–27). The nature and purpose of other studies can be judged from their titles: "The Growth of Memory in School Children" (Bolton, 1892), "The Language of Childhood" (Tracy, 1893), "The Hearing of Children" (Chrisman, 1893), and "Individual Differences in the Imagination of Children" (Burnham, 1893). The rush of such studies that appeared in the late nineteenth century gives clear evidence to the sociohistorical fact that the people of that time had taken a sudden interest in child development. This interest in scientific studies of the child served to culminate the large social movement of which it was a part, the post-Renaissance movement described by Ariès as the "discovery" of childhood. By the end of the nineteenth century, childhood had been fully discovered. With the discovery came the realization that children were different from the miniature adults that society had long thought them to be. Describing and explaining those differences became a goal of the new science of developmental psychology.

REASONS FOR CONTINUED INTEREST IN DEVELOPMENTAL PSYCHOLOGY IN THIS CENTURY

By the turn of the century, the scientific study of children had gained considerable momentum. In 1910, for example, G. Stanley Hall wrote that

> child study has now so many departments, medical, hygienic, criminological, legal, religious, pedagogic, linguistic, social and the rest and its literature is so vast, the academic chairs and journals and sciences devoted to it are so numerous that no one can master all its fields. (1910, p. 497)

Thus, by 1910 we had gone from being a society ignorant of children to one that knew more about them than any one person could assimilate. Of course, not all the information was collected, analyzed, or reported in a way that ensured its reliability, but nonetheless there was a tremendous momentum to child studies in particular and to developmental studies in general.

The momentum of child studies was greatly assisted in the years following World War I by a public and private commitment to child research. Public commitment began with the Iowa legislature, which in 1917 budgeted $50,000 for the Iowa Child Welfare Research Station. The legislature's pacesetting move was prompted by the persuasive Mrs. Cora Bussey Hillis who argued that "if research could improve corn and hogs it could also improve children" (Sears, 1975, p. 19). Though the Iowa station was the first of its kind, it was quickly followed by many others. The principal ones were the Teachers College Child Development Institute (at Columbia University), the University of Minnesota Institute of Child Welfare, Yale University's Psycho-Clinic (later called the Clinic of Child Development), and the University of California (at Berkeley) Institute of Child Welfare.

Major private funding for the child-research institutes was provided through the Laura Spelman Rockefeller Memorial Fund, a sizable fund that according to John E. Anderson, first director of the Minnesota Institute, "advanced work in the area of child study by several decades" (Anderson, 1956, p. 185). The major reason was that substantial federal funds did not become available for child research until after World War II. This was not because the federal government was uninterested in child-development research. To the contrary, beginning in 1909, a tradition of national conferences on children (originally called the White House Conferences on Child Health and Protection) was begun. In that year and about every ten years thereafter, a White House conference was convened to discuss child-development issues. The conferences have been important for identifying needed legislation and for prompting government programs. For example, the first White House conference led to the establishment in 1912 of the U.S. Children's Bureau (McCullers & Love, 1976).

Although child research became a booming scientific enterprise as a result of the child-research institutes and the public attention children were getting, most of the research conducted was in the tradition of the child-study movement. This is to say the focus was on issues of child health, education, and welfare. With this being the case, you might well ask whether this research was truly developmental in nature. Much of it in fact was not. The research had no wider purpose than to establish certain basic facts about child development: How many words does the average 3-year-old know? (Answer: about 896.) At what age do the permanent teeth first erupt? (Answer: at about 6 years.) These questions are very much *about* children, and as you know from the discussion with which this chapter began, developmental psychology is *not about* children. To qualify as developmental psychology, research must use the data collected on children (or adults, or animals) to illuminate larger issues relevant to psychology in general. The "larger issues" to which child data were first applied came from the evolutionary concerns, such as recapitulation, that were of intellectual interest in the late nineteenth century. Since then, a great many other issues have arisen. Collectively, they serve to answer the question of why developmental psychology continues to be a viable and intellectually exciting discipline today and why children continue to play such a large part in this discipline. Children, it turns out, provide the key for answering many fascinating questions.

Relevance of Child Study to the Nature–Nurture Issue

Of all the general theoretical motives for child study in this century, the single most important has been provided by the **nature–nurture issue.** Richard Lerner (1978) calls it "the core conceptual issue" in developmental psychology. As originally formulated in the late nineteenth century, the nature–nurture issue manifested itself in the form of a debate between those who held that development occurs as the inevitable consequence of biological factors (for example, genetic condition, hormonal condition, maturation) and those who held the opposite to be true, namely, that the environment and experience determine development by overwhelming the significance of whatever biological differences exist among us. Questions such as, "Are criminals born or made?" or "Does smoking stunt your growth?" or "Would Plato have been a genius even if he had not studied with Socrates?" were nature–nurture questions. They were appropriate to the original debate because they asked whether an outcome of development was due to inborn biological factors or externally imposed factors such as social history, smoking habits, and the quality of one's education.

The nature–nurture question in its original either–or form led directly to studies of childhood and infancy. The reason is that children and infants have had little to no experience. Therefore, they seemed to provide the ideal subjects for many studies in which researchers wanted to know whether a particular phenomenon was acquired through experience or was inborn. The logic for this type of research can be summed up as follows: children have been relatively untouched by nurture, therefore, they reveal nature directly. An early example of this rationale for studying children comes from work by C. W. Valentine (1930), who was interested in the origins of fear. "The question of the innate bases of fear . . . can hardly be settled," he wrote, "except by a careful study of early childhood. . . . We must turn, then, to the very first months of life" (p. 394).

The same logic that led Valentine to choose infant humans as his subject for study has led countless others to choose them as well. The result has been that the reactions and characteristics of children, which formerly might have been of interest only to parents, became of interest to theoretical scientists. As we will see in Chapter 7, the original studies of infant perception were motivated by a concern with the nature–nurture issue in perception. Early studies of infant motor development, discussed in Chapter 6, had a similar motive. Even today, studies of intellectual development, language, and personality development routinely address the nature–nurture issue. An important proviso, however, is that when contemporary studies address the nature–nurture issue, the issue gets expressed in a much more sophisticated way than it originally did. Explaining this more sophisticated view is the goal of Chapters 3, 4, and 5, which make up Part 2 of this text, titled "The Epigenetic View of Development."

Child Study As a Means of Uncovering Continuities and Connections in Development: The Roots Motive

A fundamental assumption in Western science is that our knowledge and understanding of events is enhanced by knowing their origins. When applied to psychology this assumption leads us to search for the origins of adult psychology in the early days of childhood. The search for "roots," therefore, is a second motive that developmentalists have had for child study.

As Jerome Kagan (1980, 1983) has pointed out, the search for roots in development has been dominated by the twin assumptions of continuity and connectedness. The first of these assumptions holds that structures are stable. The second holds that when events occur in a temporal sequence, early events play a causal role in the development of later events. The two together are part of an intellectual tradition begun by ancient Greek and Roman philosophers. In perfect keeping with this tradition, when developmental psychologists at the child-research institutes first began studies of the life spans of individuals by following them over time, they did not look for differences between 12-year-olds and 2-year-olds. They looked instead for continuities and connections. The continuities were sought in what Kagan called "the slim threads of sameness" that were assumed to extend from the past to the present. The causal connections were sought by sifting through life's many events to find those that formed a causal thread, or at least a set of events that were part of a common developmental course.

Studying Threads of Sameness

The search for threads of sameness is frequently invoked by the discovery of great talent, genius, or villainy. The developmental question that is asked when such discoveries are made is whether there were any signs of the "greatness" early in life. Biographers pore over the lives of people such as Adolph Hitler, Amadeus Mozart, and Albert Einstein, for example, seeking in their early lives evidence for some constancy. The type of questions they ask are familiar: Did Mozart show musical promise early in life? (he did); Was Einstein a child genius? (he was not); Was Hitler a leader in his school days? (he was not).

The same motive found among biographers of exceptional individuals is found among psychologists who are interested in the lives of more common people. The motive is to find whether there is constancy or stability on some personal attribute from early to later life.

One way to measure the stability of an attribute (more commonly called a *trait*) is to measure its **ipsative stability.** The hallmark of this type of stability is that it does not require any comparisons with other people. One simply notes whether a trait that is present in later life was also present in earlier life. Jerome Kagan (1980, p. 34) illustrates this type of stability with the parental claim that a child has been shy all his life. The parents do not necessarily mean by this that the child is more shy than other children or that the child is equally shy now as when he was two or three. All that they mean is that in choice situations in which the child could be socially outgoing or withdrawn, the stable tendency has been to withdraw.

A second means of measuring stability, and the one that is favored by developmentalists, is to measure **normative stability** (Kagan, 1980; McCall, 1977). Normative stability can be relabeled as the stability of individual differences. Labeling it this way indicates that normative stability has to do with continuity in a person's ranking on a trait relative to peers. Our concern, then, is not simply with whether a person manifests the same trait over time, but rather with the degree to which that trait is manifested, as assessed through peer comparisons. The search for normative stability has motivated a great deal of developmental research involving traits such as intelligence, body size, physical attractiveness, and even aggressiveness. Recently, for example, it has been reported that aggressiveness in males is about as stable a personality trait as is intelligence (Olweus, 1979). Such findings raise intellectually interesting questions about the basis for the stability.

Studies of the Causal Thread

If we can explain why a person becomes an engineer by saying, "She's always been a tinkerer," or answer why she chooses the cheesecake over the cheese by saying, "She's always had a sweet tooth," then we have in some sense explained the current behavior. We explained it in terms of its continuity with the past (its ipsative stability, actually). But the roots motive is satisfied more clearly when we explain not just by continuity but by causality.

The influence that the search for causal threads can have on child study is nowhere more evident than in the lifework of Freud and Piaget. By virtue of the influence of recapitulation alone, both Freud and Piaget believed that contemporary behavior had developmental connections to phylogeny, but far more central to their theories was their belief in developmental connections within ontogeny. Much of the intellectual excitement created by Freudian theory, for example, stemmed from the fact that it offered coherent connections between the experiences of infancy and the personalities of adults. It did so by linking such adult personality attributes as stinginess and generosity with dispositions established at the time these adults were toilet trained. Piaget's theory contains equally bold assertions of connectedness, linking, for example, the trial-and-error play of infants with the experimental science of adulthood.

The search for causal connections among life events that typified the work of Freud and Piaget has not abated. According to Kagan, it "continues to be one of the most important rationales for the study of children" (1983, p. 37). In the present, however, researchers may not be as willing to accept the premise of distant connectivity as they have been in the past. To use Kagan's helpful metaphor (see Kagan, 1980, p. 36), a tangled ball of string has both long and short segments. Some wind their way back to the center, but others begin and end at the surface. Kagan urges developmentalists to acknowledge, therefore, that lengthy connections from past to present are not a foregone conclusion. As he points out, "Although [historical] explanations are often the most compelling, some phenomena are not best understood through consideration of early history. Increasing rates of suicide and pregnancy among adolescents in the United States are not likely to be clarified by knowledge of the opening years of life" (1980, p. 69). Nor, he says, would it be wise to seek an explanation for children's poor reading skills by "poring over a complete diary of the first three years of life." These phenomena are principally controlled by more current events such as the values of the peer group and the quality of education. Thus, while historically the roots motive has led psychologists to seek distant connections among developmental events, we should not be blind to the possibility that some developments may have only proximate causation.

Simplicity of Psychological Processes in Children

A third reason that broad-scale theoretical scientists from this century have continued to turn to child studies is that in some cases children can be presumed to be psychologically simpler than adults. This motive of finding a simple model in which to study complex phenomena frequently guides scientists in their choice of subjects. It has led geneticists to study the fruit fly, neurologists to study the squid, and psychologists to study not only the child but also the white rat.

A perfect example of how child subjects can make a phenomenon simpler and easier to study comes from recent research on the link between facial expressions and human emotion (see Ekman, 1982). Adult subjects pose problems for aspects of this research. One reason is that adults are quite good at both faking and hiding emotions. Another is that the cultures adults grow up in have sizable effects on the intensity and manner with which they express emotions (for example, Japanese can hide grief with a smile, but Arabs are likely to display it passionately by weeping and tearing at their hair and skin). In light of the cultural diversity and individual differences of adults, infants can be quite useful subjects for the simple reason that they are far more likely than adults to display a pure, unadulterated facial expression of joy, sadness, or surprise.

Evolutionary Interests in Child Development

The final entry in our list of reasons for why child study has continued to be of interest to the larger scientific community in this century harks back to the past in that it concerns an evolutionary interest in developmental psychology. This interest did not come, however, from the doctrine of recapitulation. By the start of the twentieth century, the theory of recapitulation had lost favor in biology (as mentioned earlier), and though its death came more slowly in the other disciplines that had adopted it, it did die. With the demise of recapitulation as an organizing principle for the events in ontogeny, evolutionists found little of direct interest for them in developmental studies for a number of years. Beginning in the 1930s, however, with the founding of a new discipline called ethology, evolutionists again turned to developmental psychology. The interest of evolutionists in developmental psychology has been further strengthened recently with the development of a second new discipline, sociobiology. Because of the importance of the evolutionary perspective on developmental studies provided by these two disciplines, we will take time to introduce them here.

Ethology

Ethology, the scientific discipline founded by 1973 Nobel prizewinners Konrad Lorenz and Niko Tinbergen, is considered a branch of psychology because, like the larger field of psychology, ethology concerns itself with human and animal behavior. However, it is distinguished from the larger field of psychological studies by two features. First, ethologists conduct their studies in natural settings. Second, and more important for our purposes, they study behavior largely from the perspective of evolutionary science. This perspective is found in the four major questions asked by the field (see Hinde, 1983): (1) What causes this behavior? (2) How did it develop? (3) What is its biological function? and (4) How did it evolve? With this perspective on the facts of child behavior, one can gain a whole new intellectual interest in them. Take, for example, the fact that children begin smiling at around 4 weeks of age. From the ethological perspective we can wonder why this would be so. What role might it play in the child's current life and how might it have played a role in the human child's ancestral past? Could the role have been one of enhancing *biological fitness* by enhancing the probability that the smiler's genes would survive into future generations? If so, the behavior may have been subject to natural selection during evolution.

Sociobiology

Sociobiology, founded by E. O. Wilson of Harvard (see Wilson, 1975), has also added evolutionary concerns to developmental studies. It has done so by showing that the concept of biological fitness can be used to explain a number of human social behaviors that otherwise would seem to be cut off from any evolutionary explanation. As sociobiologists explain it, biological fitness is not synonomous with individual survival. In fact, there are many times when animals, acting to save themselves, may reduce their fitness. Assume, for example, that an animal abandons its family to a predator. By failing to defend its family, the animal saves itself but sacrifices its fitness. The reason is that it leaves far more reproductive potential behind in the nest or den than it manages to carry away. To understand how this is so, you need only to count the number of a parent's genes that are present in the offspring. When there are more of a parent's genes present in its offspring than in the parent itself, the parent's best survival strategy is to fight to the death for its offspring. Although this sounds paradoxical, it is not, so long as you distinguish between an individual's survival and the survival of an individual's genes. Sociobiologists are careful to make this important distinction. Using the concept of fitness as they do, they have been able to offer an explanation for how self-sacrificing or *altruistic* acts could have evolved in both humans and animals.

Sociobiologists have used their principles to explain more than just altruism. To demonstrate the broader application of the sociobiological perspective, we can consider the sociobiological explanation for the mother–offspring conflicts that occur among mammals during weaning. According to zoologist Robert Trivers (1974), weaning brings a mother's overall fitness into conflict with that of her offspring. The fundamental reason is that nursing is a cost to the mother and a benefit to the offspring, at least in terms of individual fitness. It is in the mother's interest to bear the cost so long as her offspring have not reached an age of viability. Once they can survive on their own, however, it is in the mother's interest to cut her losses. Of course, it is also in the interest of offspring that their mother get on with the business of producing brothers and sisters (because this serves to perpetuate their genes, too), so they should be somewhat willing to accept her refusal to nurse. The problem is that, according to Trivers' calculations, the interests of offspring and mother in having additional offspring do not develop simultaneously. Thus there will inevitably be conflict, but particularly in animals where subsequent offspring are likely to be fathered by a new male. When this is the case, the new offspring will only be half brothers and sisters to those that currently exist. This reduces the sociobiological benefit of a new brother or sister by half. Under these circumstances, it should take even longer for offspring to willingly give up the right to nurse. One species in which there is good evidence of a protracted conflict over weaning is baboons. As expected, this is a nonmonogamous primate species, which means that multiple males will have fathered the offspring of a single female.

SUMMARY

This chapter began with a definition of developmental psychology and a list of the terms that developmental psychologists use to refer to periods of the human life span. The definition of developmental psychology stressed that the discipline is *not about* children, even though it is quite true that ever since developmental psychology was founded in the late nineteenth century, children have been the principal subjects studied by developmental (or genetic) psychologists. There were two reasons that science turned to child studies in the late nineteenth century. One was the movement labeled evolutionism, which, for the first time in science, placed a focus on change and transition as opposed to stasis. In psychology, the spirit of evolutionism led to ontogenetic studies. These were given added zest because, according to Haeckel's law of recapitulation, ontogeny recapitulates phylogeny. This meant that early genetic psychologists such as Hall, Freud, and Piaget could find evolutionary importance in their studies of ontogenetic development.

The second movement that inspired scientists to take a close look at childhood was the child-study movement. Unlike the evolutionary movement, which resulted from a rather abrupt scientific development, the child-study movement was the result of gradual changes that had been taking place in society from the Middle Ages. These changes resulted in a new conception of childhood so that by the end of the nineteenth century the consensus view was that children were different from adults and that they had inherent, as opposed to just utilitarian, value. Prior to this time the opposite view had been held.

Developmental psychology has remained a viable and exciting discipline throughout this century for many reasons. One reason is that the same societal forces that established the child-study movement in the first place have continued to be felt. The difference is that they have become institutionalized through the liberal use of private, state, and federal funding for research institutes and research programs. Although much of the research produced in response to societal forces has been aimed at questions that are asked by parents, teachers, and pediatricians, pure developmentalists have found ample reason to maintain their interests in child studies too. The reasons given here were that child studies are relevant to the nature–nurture issue, they are essential in the search for the developmental roots of behavior, they focus on individuals who can be presumed to be psychologically simpler than adults, and when viewed from the perspective of ethology and sociobiology, child studies even have relevance for evolutionary theorists.

SUGGESTIONS FOR FURTHER READING

Bateson, P. (1985). Problems and possibilities of fusing developmental and evolutionary thought. In G. Butterworth, J. Rutkowska, & M. Scaife (Eds.), *Evolution and developmental psychology*. New York: St. Martin's Press.

deMause, L. (Ed.) (1974). *The history of childhood*. New York: Psychohistory Press. A collection of articles dealing with the social treatment of children from late-Roman to modern times.

Gould, S. J. (1977). *Ontogeny and phylogeny*. Cambridge, MA: The Belknap Press. An intellectually exciting account of the relation between ontogeny and phylogeny and the scientific history associated with the study of this topic.

Kagan, J. (1984). Chapter 3: Connectedness. In *The nature of the child*. New York: Basic Books. This is a very readable yet sophisticated treatment of the concept of connectedness in development. Advanced students who wish to read a somewhat broader essay on the concept of connectedness should consider Kagan's 1983 essay "Developmental categories and the premise of connectivity" in R. M. Lerner (Ed.), *Developmental psychology: Historical and philosophical perspectives*, Hillsdale, NJ: Lawrence Erlbaum.

Kessen, W. (1965). *The child*. New York: Wiley. A well-edited volume that includes writings of historical importance to contemporary developmental psychology.

Siegel, A. W. & White, S. H. (1982). The child study movement: Early growth and development of the symbolized child. In H. W. Reese (Ed.), *Advances in child development and behavior,* (Vol. 17). New York: Academic Press. An account of the social forces that came together under the banner of the child study movement.

CHAPTER OUTLINE

CHAPTER 2

Consequences of Being a Science

We saw in Chapter 1 that developmental psychology is a science and that its goal is to describe and explain age-related changes in behavior and mental processes. In this chapter we will explore the consequences that scientific membership has on the types of descriptions and explanations that developmental psychologists are able to offer. First we will pursue the consequences for the descriptive side of the science, then for the theoretical or explanatory side.

It will be important to realize throughout this chapter that science is not an activity that is limited to laboratories, and it is not practiced solely by PhDs. Science can be practiced anywhere by anyone who wants to think scientifically. Garage mechanics, bakers, and journalists can all practice science if they want to. They merely have to adopt some basic rules. As we will see when the rules of science are explained later in this chapter, they are rather demanding with regard to what is and is not admissible as science. They are, in fact, quite limiting, and often we would like to know more than we can ever know scientifically. When this is the case, intuition, faith, logic, and even what is popularly known as common sense become alternatives to science.

WHAT MAKES A DESCRIPTION SCIENTIFIC?

A description is scientific to the extent that it is an accurate (or valid) report of an objective and reliable phenomenon. The key words in this definition are *objective, reliable,* and *valid.* On the basis of these three criteria, scientific descriptions can be distinguished from unscientific ones.

Objectivity

A phenomenon is **objective** when it is measurable and available for all to see. Making phenomena objective can be difficult in all the sciences, but none more so than psychology. The reason is that so many of the phenomena of interest to psychologists involve covert, invisible events. Perceptual processes, memories, emotions, motives, and thoughts are all events of this type. For psychologists to be scientific in their descriptive work on these phenomena, they have had to focus on objective behavioral measures of the covert phenomena that interest them. Thus, sweat-gland activity in the hand has become a measure of anxiety, and verbal interpretations of ink blots have become measures of distorted thought processes.

Because of the need for objectivity, progress in the descriptive science of psychology is frequently tied to progress in our methods for making psychological phenomena objective and, thereby, available to study. In developmental psychology, for example, we once had little to say about infants. The only things we knew about them were the most observable things, such as how size or motor behavior changed with age. Now developmental psychologists talk freely about what they judge to go on inside infants' heads. Developmental psychologists also study such seemingly subjective phenomena as the quality of infant–mother attachment and differences in infant temperaments. They do so because they have found objective behavioral measures for these otherwise unobservable psychological characteristics.

Reliability

In addition to being objective, the phenomena studied in science must be reliable. There are two types of **reliability** that scientifically observable phenomena must have. One is *interobserver reliability,* which means that all the observers must be able to agree on what they see. The second type of reliability is across-time reliability or, more simply, *replicability.* Scientific observations must be ones that we can make again and again as often as we like.

To achieve interobserver reliability, scientific studies generally require that more than one person record the data. If the data records of the observers agree, then the interobserver-reliability criterion has been met. If they do not, then the data are unacceptable as science. One of the reasons that objectivity is so important in science is that interobserver reliability cannot be achieved in the absence of objectivity. If, for example, observers were given the task of determining whether a child became anxious in the presence of a stranger, it would be unlikely that they could agree unless they established some objective criterion for what constituted anxiety, such as the behavioral criterion of "averts eyes after looking at stranger, looks to mother, and cries."

Just because a phenomenon achieves an acceptable level of interobserver reliability is no guarantee that it will also be replicable. In fact, it often happens in science that the painstakingly collected observations of one research team will go unreplicated by others. Frequently there is no good explanation for why the replication is not possible, but nonetheless, a failure to replicate—by the rules of science—means that the phenomenon observed in the original research cannot be accepted as science. To illustrate, in the 1970s infant researchers became excited by research conducted on newborn infants that led to the conclusion that neonates were far more knowledgeable about the world than anyone had previously thought (Bower, Broughton, & Moore, 1970b). The research implied that neonates would reach toward visible objects under suitable conditions and that they would be upset if the objects could not be found where they appeared to be. (The research involved some optical trickery.) In the years since 1970, persistent failure to replicate this research has led to the original research being dropped from textbooks (for reviews see Fox, 1981, p. 365, and Gibson & Spelke, 1983, pp. 7 and 33). There is a good reason for this. Science concerns itself with knowing those things that are generally true. Special cases that do not represent general phenomena fall outside of the realm of science.

Validity

Validity, the third criterion to use in judging the merit of scientific descriptions, concerns the truth value of these descriptions. Are they, in fact, accurate? There are at least three senses in which a description can be accurate, or valid. One is that it is internally valid, another that it is externally valid, and a third that it is ecologically valid.

Internal validity is achieved when our descriptive statements are an accurate representation of what we in fact have seen. To achieve internal validity, scientists must be careful to report nothing more than what they in fact observe. Despite their best efforts, however, scientists may occasionally go beyond the information given. This can come about quite innocently. We have already seen a good example in the case of the microscopists who first peered through their microscopes at sperm cells and reported seeing little homunculi inside. This turned out to be a somewhat fanciful report that lacked validity. The microscopists should have exercised greater caution. Only in this regard, however, were they behaving unscientifically. The phenomena they were studying were objective enough. After all, the alleged homunculi could be touched, probed, weighed, and measured. Also, the existence of homunculi in sperm cells was not based on one person's report. It was reliably observed by multiple microscopists using multiple sperm cells. This means that homunculi met the criteria of interobserver reliability and replicability. The microscopists' only failing as scientists was that they let their expectations affect their perceptions. This is a particularly common source of invalid descriptions.

A modern example comes from the research of T. G. R. Bower (reviewed in Bower, 1982, pp. 83–84). Interested in determining the age at which infants can first detect that an expanding visual image is a signal of an approaching object, Bower moved a large cube slowly toward 1- to 2-week-old infants as shown in Figure 2-1. He then watched to see how the infants would react. He was particularly interested in any signs that the infants might try to protect themselves from the object. Bower observed that when the cube got close to the infants' faces, their heads fell back and they put their hands between their faces and the approaching cube. Bower described this as an "obvious defensive reaction" (Bower, 1982). Had he stopped with the statement that the infants' heads fell back and their hands came up when the cube was at its closest point (8 centimeters), his description would have been perfectly valid. But by calling the reaction defensive, Bower—who is a very talented and creative developmental psychologist—made an apparent mistake. It turns out that the reaction is not defensive at all. According to Albert Yonas (1981, pp. 322–28), it is nothing more than a postural reflex caused by loss of balance. What has happened is that the infants are looking at the upper edge of the approaching cube and as it gets closer they have to tip their heads ever farther back. Lacking the muscular control of older infants, these 1-week-olds eventually can no longer hold their heads upright. As their heads fall back, their arms come up automatically as part of a righting reflex. We know that the reaction is not in fact defensive because infants make the same reaction when tracking an object that rises ever-higher in their visual field without actually approaching.

Whereas internal validity has to do with the relationship between what one has actually observed and what one reports to have observed, *external validity* has to do with the generality of the report. Is it true in general or only in this specific case? Psychologist Harry Harlow, for example, performed some very interesting developmental research using rhesus monkeys. One of the many things he discovered about these animals was that they became severely depressed when separated from their mothers (Seay, Hansen, & Harlow, 1962). This conclusion was quite valid for rhesus monkeys under the conditions that Harlow observed, but should we conclude

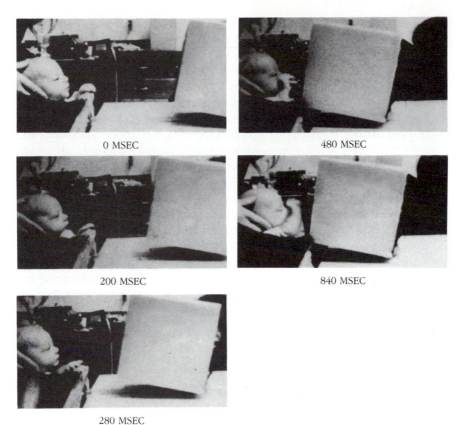

0 MSEC   480 MSEC

200 MSEC   840 MSEC

280 MSEC

FIGURE 2-1
Alleged Defensive Reaction
This 10-day-old infant responds to the approach of an object. But does the
response reflect a defensive reaction or simply a loss of balance?

that rhesus monkeys are representative of all monkeys or that Harlow's
means of separating mother and infant was representative of all means of
separation? This is a question of the external validity of Harlow's observation that separation leads to severe depression. It turns out that Harlow's
observation is not completely generalizable. Animals of different species do
not all become equally depressed following separation, and the manner in
which the separation is executed is important (see Hinde, 1983, pp. 72–73).
These considerations limit the generalizability and, hence, the external validity of Harlow's conclusion.

   Ecological validity becomes an issue whenever scientific observations
are made in a setting that is contrived, artificial, and unfamiliar to subjects.
It is always possible that the observations obtained in such a setting may

have little relevance to the real world in which humans and animals live. Only when observations do apply to the real world are they said to have ecological validity (Vasta, 1982).

To illustrate the relevance of the concept of ecological validity, we might consider the frequently cited finding that lower-class children are less creative in their pretend and fantasy play than are middle-class children (Rubin, Fein, & Vandenberg, 1983, p. 737). Although the observations on which this finding is based are probably reliable, we need to consider the context in which the observations have been made. In nearly all of the research, the context has been a toy-filled laboratory or classroom setting. Critics (for example, McLoyd, 1982) point out that the toy-filled rooms used in the research may be so unlike the usual play settings for most lower-class children that the children are either intimidated or overwhelmed. Others suggest that the novel toys that are available might entice them to spend more time in pure object play, thereby limiting the time they have to spend in more social forms of imaginative play (Rubin, Fein, & Vandenberg, 1983, pp. 736–37.) These considerations make us wonder whether the conclusion that lower-class children are less creative in their play is valid for the real world in which children live. To know for sure, we would have to observe children in ecologically valid settings such as their own playgrounds and homes.

METHODS USED TO MAKE SCIENTIFIC OBSERVATIONS

Thus far we have only considered general criteria that can be used to judge if descriptions are scientific; we have not considered the means by which observations—the objects of our descriptions—are made. That is as it should be because methods are secondary to the objectivity, reliability, and validity of the data they produce.

Despite what you may have once been told, there is no "best" method in science. One method cannot be judged better than another any more than a hammer can be judged better than a screwdriver or a drill better than a saw. Like tools, methods are designed in response to specific needs and, therefore, until one knows the job to be done, there is no way to say whether a method is a "good" method or not. The particular methods discussed here are the principal methods—what might be called the basic data gathering tools—of developmental psychology: *case studies, naturalistic studies, clinical interviews, correlational studies,* and *experiments*. In presenting these procedures for data gathering, definitions are given first, followed by some of the strengths and weaknesses associated with each of the methods. If you have had a good introduction to these methods in a previous course, you may skip this material and go on to the section on measuring change over time.

Case Studies

Case studies are studies of unique events, typically from the lives of individuals. The data from them are recorded as a simple narrative or story. Sigmund Freud built his entire theory of human personality development on such studies by collecting observations on particular individuals and then inducing from these observations the general principles that underlay them. With the exception of his early medical research, Freud never used any other method of data collection. Modern researchers also find case studies to be a useful means of data collection. In Chapter 4, for example, we will see that Anke Ehrhardt and John Money have collected case-history data on a number of children who were raised as if they were one sex when, in fact, they were biologically the other sex. From these case histories (Money & Ehrhardt, 1972), they have been able to make statements about factors in sexual development that could have been made in no other way.

One of the great benefits of case-study approaches is that they are what Victoria Seitz has called *open methods* (1984, p. 38). This means that when making observations on a case history, everything is admitted as data. Some of the other methods used by developmental psychologists record only a minute portion of what is actually observed. These methods presume that investigators know exactly what they are looking for so that they can specify in advance just those data that will be relevant. This is fine if you do know what you are looking for, but if you do not, a more open method such as a case history can be quite appropriate.

The two major methodological problems associated with case studies concern the reliability of the observations and the external validity of conclusions. Reliability is a problem because frequently case histories are recorded by a single individual. This means that there is no check on the investigator's use of indiosyncratic and subjective judgments about the "facts" of the case. Contemporary critics of Freud, for example, find the facts on which his theory is based to be one of the most questionable aspects of the theory (see, for example, Miller, 1983). Freud claimed it to be a fact, for example, that a little boy he studied named Hans wanted his father to die so that he, Hans, could marry his own mother (Freud, 1909/1955). Many wonder about the reliability of the evidence used to support this alleged fact.

External validity is a problem for case studies simply because they deal with unique events. Consequently, we cannot be sure about the generalizability of conclusions drawn from them. To illustrate, one of the most famous case histories in all of developmental psychology comes from Dr. Jean Marc Gaspard Itard's detailed nineteenth-century account of the discovery and subsequent development of a 9- or 10-year-old boy who allegedly had been raised in the wild (Itard, 1806/1962). The child, named Victor by Itard but popularly known as the Wild Boy of Aveyron, was reported in Itard's case history to have been "indifferent" toward women during the time that he was going through the physical changes associated with "a very pronounced puberty" (in Dennis, 1972, pp. 47–48). Assuming that this description of Victor as indifferent is both reliable and valid, can we take it to be true in any general sense? Can we conclude that, unlike the ordinary adolescent who responds to puberty's changes by taking an interest in the opposite sex, socially isolated males reared like Victor will show no automatic or "instinctive" affinity toward women? We may be tempted to draw this conclusion, but it is totally unwarranted by the data. Victor, like the subjects of all case studies, was a special case. We do not even know that he was in fact socially isolated. It could have been that he was just a retarded boy abandoned by his unloving parents a month or so before he was found. To go from observations on such special cases to statements about the general case is an easy trap to fall into, but it is not good science. Case studies, therefore, no matter how carefully conducted, can only lead to guesses regarding the general truth of what we have observed.

Naturalistic Studies

Naturalistic studies are marked by the lack of intervention and manipulation. Researchers using this method attempt to avoid any involvement with the natural course of events they are studying. This feature more than any other serves to distinguish naturalistic observations from other research methods. In a typical naturalistic study, the researcher might show up in the home or the school with a notepad, tape recorder, or video camera and proceed to record what goes on. Later these observations are analyzed in an attempt to discover important generalizations. These might range from generalizations about the frequency with which children spontaneously correct the grammar of their own incorrect utterances to descriptions of developmental changes in children's attention span. The data from naturalistic studies are valued because they are real and true to life. This feature enhances the ecological validity of whatever conclusions we draw from them.

Naturalistic observation is the preferred method of data collection for the behavioral scientists known as ethologists. As you will recall from Chapter 1, the science of ethology is concerned with the behavior of animals (and humans) in natural settings. Because of this, ethologists spend far more time in the field than in the laboratory. Their field settings can be anywhere from Niko Tinbergen's backyard pond to Jane Goodall's chimpanzee research station in Tanzania. Wherever they are, the goal is to make objective recordings of reliable data without intervention, though occasionally some minimal tampering with the ways of nature is a necessity (for example, setting up a feeding station for wild animals so that they can be observed regularly).

As an example of a naturalistic study, we can take Roger Brown's study (Brown, Cazden, & Bellugi, 1969) of the language development of three children—Adam, Eve, and Sarah. Whereas a scientist with a nonnaturalistic approach might have chosen to study language development by giving periodic tests or by setting up contrived interviews during which adults would try to entice the children into revealing the full extent of their linguistic knowledge, Brown's naturalistic approach was simply to sit in on normal mother–child conversations. Following the children over time, Brown was able to describe their natural course of language development.

The lack of artificiality in naturalistic data is the biggest asset of the naturalistic approach. After all, if we want to make valid statements about the behavior of chimpanzees, it only makes sense to study them in the wild rather than in zoos. Caged animals, like caged humans, can behave in ways that do not reflect their behavior in their more typical habitats. Likewise, parent–child interactions, when they occur in a university laboratory setting, may provide a very poor simulation of what actually happens in the home. For these reasons, naturalistic observations are often preferred.

The late naturalist Dian Fossey with two of her research subjects in their southern African habitat.

As you would suspect, however, the benefits of naturalistic study are not obtained without some disadvantages. One of the disadvantages is that naturalistic studies are a poor way of obtaining data regarding *competence*. Developmentalists use the word competence in contrast with the word *performance*. The distinction is between what one does (performance) and what one can do (competence). To see how naturalistic studies are apt to yield invalid statements regarding competence, consider what would be likely to happen if Roger Brown were to assess your linguistic competence in a naturalistic study. His naturalistic observations might very well lead to an unflattering conclusion regarding your knowledge of grammar, particularly if you were talking informally to a friend. The point, therefore, is that while naturalistic studies can lead to quite valid assessments of how people actually behave, they are less useful for telling us how people are capable of behaving (or, in this case, speaking).

Another disadvantage of naturalistic observations is that they often make it difficult to compare cases. This is not a problem if the study is restricted to a single pond, jungle, classroom, or home, but it is a problem if observations are made in multiple settings. Let us say, for example, that we are making a naturalistic study of aggression in preschool children. To conduct the study we visit nursery-school settings during a free-play period. Some nursery schools have more group-play toys, some have more individual-play toys, some are crowded, others are less crowded, some have close teacher supervision of play, some have little supervision. All of these factors can have an impact on the likelihood that we will observe instances of aggression, as well as on the types of aggression we are likely to observe. With all this variability from setting to setting, it will be impossible for us to make any general statements regarding the causes, the consequences, or even the frequency of aggression in free-playing preschoolers.

Clinical Interviews

Whereas naturalistic observations are characterized by the maintenance of distance between researcher and subject, **clinical interviews** are characterized by an intense, probing interaction between researcher and subject. The goal is to use a verbal interview to get at what subjects know or think without affecting what they know or think. This can be extremely difficult to do because there is a frequent tendency for people, especially young children, to tell you what they think you want to hear. Also, interviewers have a tendency to talk too much. For these reasons, Jean Piaget, who used the clinical–interview method as exclusively as Freud used case studies, believed that to conduct useful clinical interviews "at least a year of daily practice is necessary before passing beyond the inevitable fumbling stage of the beginner" (in Flavell, 1963, p. 29).

Because the clinical-interview technique is so closely associated with Piaget's name, his work will be used to illustrate the method. Piaget's general research interest was the development of reasoning in children. In the following interviews, Piaget attempts to gain information about children's understanding of age. In the first interview, he discovers that a 7-year-old male subject does not know that age is related to order of birth.

PIAGET:	How old are you?
7-YEAR-OLD:	Seven and a half.
PIAGET:	Have you any brothers or sisters?
7-YEAR-OLD:	No.
PIAGET:	Any friends?
7-YEAR-OLD:	Yes, Gerald.
PIAGET:	Is he older or younger than you?
7-YEAR-OLD:	A little older. He's 12 years old.
PIAGET:	How much older is he than you?
7-YEAR-OLD:	Five years.
PIAGET:	Was he born before or after you?
7-YEAR-OLD:	I don't know.
PIAGET:	But think about it, haven't you just told me his age? Was he born before you or after you?
7-YEAR-OLD:	He didn't tell me.
PIAGET:	But is there no way of finding out whether he was born before you or after you?
7-YEAR-OLD:	I could ask him.
PIAGET:	But couldn't you tell without asking?
7-YEAR-OLD:	No. (Piaget, 1946/1969, p. 209)

In an interview with a 9-year-old girl, Piaget finds the same phenomenon. The interview begins with the discovery that the girl has a younger sister and then proceeds as follows:

PIAGET:	How many years younger than you [is your sister]?
9-YEAR-OLD:	Two years.
PIAGET:	When you will be a big lady, will she be the same age as you?
9-YEAR-OLD:	No, she'll always be younger than me.
PIAGET:	By how much?
9-YEAR-OLD:	Two years.
PIAGET:	Are you absolutely certain?
9-YEAR-OLD:	By 21 months.
PIAGET:	Why?
9-YEAR-OLD:	Because it will be the same as today.
PIAGET:	And when you are very old?
9-YEAR-OLD:	It will always be the same.
PIAGET:	Well then, tell me, which of you was born first?
9-YEAR-OLD:	I don't know. (Piaget, 1946/1969, p. 209)

One thing to note about clinical interviews from these two examples is that clinical interviews have some of the same openness that case studies have. Lots of information is obtained, some of it relevant and some irrelevant. The openness of interviews can be quite valuable for researchers who have not come to any prior decisions about just what they are looking for. At the same time, however, interviews are far more focused than pure case histories. The interviewer has a precise question in mind and uses this question to guide the interview.

One of the drawbacks associated with the use of interviews is that the validity of conclusions may be affected by the verbal abilities of the children being interviewed. In interviewing children about their conceptual understanding, for example, the danger is that the interviewer might conclude that a child does not understand some particular concept when in fact the only difficulty is in the child's ability to adequately express his or her understanding of the concept. If this mistake were made, it would confuse performance with competence.

A second potential drawback in using clinical interviews relates to the fact that these interviews are not standardized. This means that no two children ever get quite the same set of questions posed in quite the same way. Such a procedure poses problems if the goal is to make comparisons among individual children. Piaget was never concerned with this goal, so this particular shortcoming of the interview procedure was not a problem for him. But if we were to take interview data and try to make a descriptive statement such as "Twenty percent of all 4-year-olds believe in _____ ," the validity of this statement would be in doubt because not all children would have been assessed in the same way.

Correlational Studies

A fourth general method used by developmental psychology and a host of other scientific disciplines is the **correlational method.** Unlike the methods discussed earlier, the correlational method has nothing to do with how we collect our observations—whether through case histories, naturalistic observations, or interviews. It has to do with what we do with the observations once we get them. In everyday terms, correlation is the method of finding out what goes with what. Do blue eyes go with blond hair? A correlational study will tell us. Do authoritarian parents have more obedient children than permissive parents? Again, a correlational study will tell us. Our goal in each of these cases is to make a descriptive statement about the relationship that exists between two variables.

The best way to gain an intuitive appreciation for what is meant by correlation is to draw a picture called a **scatterplot.** For a simple but useful example of this method, imagine that we have collected height and weight data on a sample of 60 ten-year-old boys. The individual values for height and weight for the boys in our sample are given in Table 2-1, but in this tabular form it is impossible to detect any particular relationship. We need to order the data in a more meaningful way, and scatterplots provide a means of doing that.

To produce a scatterplot, we begin at a single point and draw two lines at right angles to one another. One of these lines can be used to represent height and the other weight. It does not matter which line is used for which variable. Now we transfer the data from the table to the space between the two lines by using a single point to represent each boy's height–weight combination. The first boy in Table 2-1, for example, had a height of 54.7 inches and a weight of 94 pounds. This information can be represented in the scatterplot using the single point shown in Figure 2-2A. Figure 2-2B shows what happens when we add the data for the other 59 boys in this same way. The result is a set of 60 points—one for each of our 60 subjects. If these points are scattered randomly, we can conclude that there is no relationship between the height and weight of 10-year-olds. If the points are not scattered randomly, then there is a relationship.

TABLE 2-1
Heights (in inches) and Weights (in pounds) of 60 Ten-year-old Boys

HEIGHT	WEIGHT	HEIGHT	WEIGHT	HEIGHT	WEIGHT
54.7	94	54.3	89	52.4	66
50.9	59	51.1	56	55.1	63
50.8	59	51.3	63	54.9	86
53.0	68	52.3	67	55.1	61
55.5	66	54.4	73	56.1	72
56.9	88	50.2	58	51.1	54
52.0	68	49.4	54	55.1	74
51.3	62	53.2	71	56.4	84
55.9	78	55.4	72	49.3	55
54.0	70	53.8	70	52.5	68
53.4	70	54.1	68	51.8	59
51.1	52	53.3	85	53.6	62
52.5	71	50.1	58	52.9	87
56.1	67	53.1	56	50.5	60
53.1	71	52.3	60	51.4	58
50.4	57	54.3	70	51.4	70
55.7	86	57.6	80	51.7	64
52.8	78	55.9	81	58.4	86
50.9	64	54.9	82	56.3	90
54.8	67	58.9	82	56.4	96

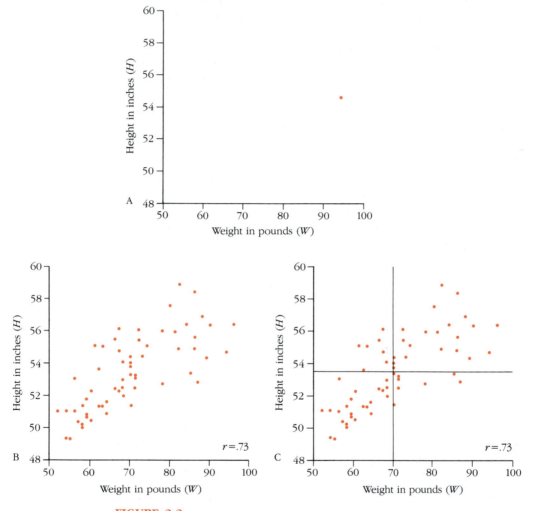

FIGURE 2-2
Scatterplot Representation of the Data in Table 2-1
(A) The plot shows the single point representing a boy who is 54.7 inches tall and weighs 94 pounds. (B) The scatterplot shows the points for all 50 boys whose data were listed in Table 2-1. (C) By dividing the scatterplot into quadrants, it is clear that the points are not distributed randomly; rather, they cluster in the lower-left and upper-right quadrants, which is a sign of a positive linear relationship between the variables.

In our sample data, the scatter is far from being totally random. If you cannot see this immediately, you might perform a simple test for nonrandom scatter, which is to divide the space in Figure 2-2B into four quadrants as show in Figure 2-2C. Now count the number of points per quadrant. Obviously, the upper left and the bottom right quadrants are deficient in points relative to the others. This is clear evidence that the scatter is a nonrandom pattern known as a *linear* (linelike) pattern.

Though a scatterplot provides a clear and intuitively appealing picture of a correlation, scientists do not often use scatterplots for depicting the relationship between variables. Usually they describe a relationship using a single number called a **correlation coefficient,** which they refer to with the letter r. This coefficient is nothing more than a measure of the extent of linearity that exists among the points in a scatterplot. If the points all fall on a perfect line, the correlation's value is 1.00. If there is no linearity at all, the value is 0.00. For values between 0 and 1, interpretation is not so easy.

To get some idea of the amount of linearity indicated by various values of the correlation coefficient, you can refer to Figure 2-3, which shows the scatterplots associated with different values of the correlation coefficient. As you can see there, correlation coefficients are not ratio measures of the extent of linearity. This means that a correlation of .80, say, is not twice as great as one of .40. In fact it is four times as great. You need not worry over why this is so; just remember that correlation coefficients cannot be treated as simple multiples of one another and that the degree of linearity indicated by a correlation coefficient increases with the value of the coefficient.

As you have noted in examining Figure 2-3, correlation coefficients can be negative as well as positive. A large negative value signals the same degree of linearity as a large positive value. It just means that the linearity runs in the other direction: high scores on one variable are associated with low scores on the other variable. In terms of scatterplots divided into quarters (as in Figure 2-2C and 2-3), this means that points will cluster in the upper-left and lower-right quadrants.

The reason we have delved so deeply into correlations and the relationship of scatterplots to correlation coefficients is that this information will prove vital to an understanding of the data of developmental psychology presented elsewhere in this text. Mastering the technical details of the concept at the outset will definitely pay off in terms of later understanding. Using correlations, we can determine, for example, whether traits such as intelligence, temperament, aggressiveness, and sociability are in any way related to each other and whether each is stable across time. Such information is vital to the study of continuity and discontinuity in development. Correlations are also used to relate child-development variables, such as children's intelligence or self-control, to factors that are descriptive of the environments in which children develop, such as parental discipline tech-

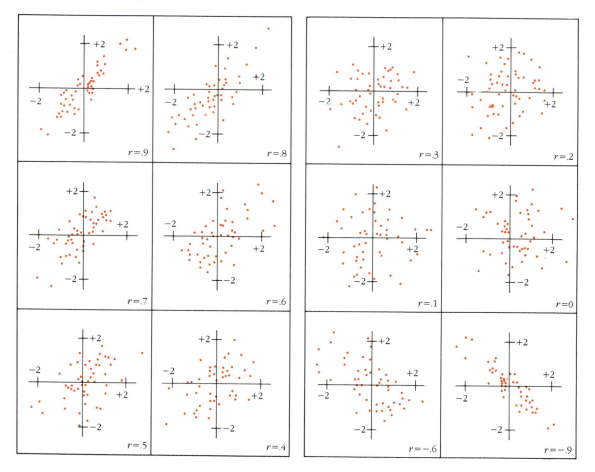

FIGURE 2-3

Scatterplots and Correlation Coefficients

You can gain an intuitive understanding for the degree of relationship signaled by different values of the correlation coefficient *(r)* by studying the *r* values associated with the scatterplots in this figure. Note that *r* can be both positive and negative with maximum values of $+1.00$ and -1.00. When there is no relationship between the variables, the value is 0.

niques or parents' education. In the study of behavioral genetics (see Chapter 5), correlations are a primary tool for understanding genetic and environmental influences in development. In brief, correlations are an indispensable tool in developmental analyses. Thus, even introductory students need to know a good bit about them.

In addition to knowing the technical aspects regarding how correlations are represented, you need to know what we can conclude when two variables—*A* and *B*—are correlated. It turns out that even sophisticated investigators sometimes slip up and interpret correlations in a way that is not necessarily valid.

A correlation of *A* and *B* has three possible explanations: *A* may have caused *B, B* may have caused *A,* or *A* and *B* may both be the common product of some third variable, *C.* The primary danger in using correlations is that an investigator will select one of these explanations as correct without first ruling out the other possibilities. Take the case of a correlational study that demonstrates that mothers who use positive discipline techniques (that is, highly verbal discipline that employs reasoning and explanations) tend to have children who have higher IQs, $r = .26$, and better communication skills, $r = .22$ (the data are from Scarr, 1985). If these findings lead you to believe that the positive discipline techniques are in part responsible for the development of IQ and communication skills in children, you are falling into the trap of believing that *A* causes *B* when in fact you have insufficient evidence for this conclusion. It could be, for example, that *A* and *B* are correlated not because *A* causes *B* but because *B* causes *A.* This would be the case, for example, if children with high IQs and good communication skills inspired their parents to use positive discipline techniques. A further possibility is that *A* and *B* are correlated simply because mothers with high IQs and good communication skills tend to use positive discipline techniques and tend to have children who, like themselves, are intelligent and skilled in communicating. This is the alternative in which *C* causes both *A* and *B.* A single correlation gives us absolutely no way of choosing among these alternatives. In order to know which is correct, we need to use the experimental method in lieu of the correlational method.

Experiments

Experiments are a major tool of developmental psychologists and all other scientists for the simple reason that they provide the most direct and convincing means of determining what causes what. Does watching violent television programs create violent individuals? Does Head Start boost IQ? Does visual experience affect maturation within the visual system in the brain? Only experiments can answer these questions unambiguously.

Control is the reason that experiments allow us to make causal inferences. Experiments give us the control we need to create observations and judge which of many variables may have caused these observations to come out as they did. The simplest experiment consists of a single variable that we are interested in measuring. For the sake of an example we will say that it is the degree of maturation within the visual system of the brain. Because this is the variable we plan to observe, it is known as the **dependent variable.** Now we might suspect that visual experience would affect this variable. If so, we need to make visual experience an **independent variable** in our experiment by manipulating this variable. Our manipulation might consist of putting blindfolds on one group of kittens while leaving others to develop normally. To be sure that we are not inadvertently manipulating some other variable at the same time, we need to be sure that our decision to blindfold a kitten or raise it normally is random and that the kittens used in our experiment are equal in every way except that one group has blindfolds and the other does not. Once this is done, we are ready to make observations regarding differences in brain maturation between blindfolded and nonblindfolded kittens. If we find maturational differences, we can conclude that visual experience matters: it is a causal factor in brain maturation. If there are no differences as a function of the blindfold variable, we can conclude that visual experience does not matter.

To be sure you understand the difference between correlational studies and experiments, you should now ask yourself why it is that a relationship between two variables such as the discipline techniques used by mothers and the communication skills of their children does not allow a causal inference, whereas a relationship between an independent and dependent variable does allow a causal inference. The reason goes back to control. In correlational studies we have no control. This means, to use the example above, that we did not assign some mothers to use positive discipline techniques and others to use nonpositive techniques. We took the mothers as they came. As a result, the explanation that A causes B is only one of several possible explanations for the relationship. The control that we have in experiments, however, allows us to rule out every explanation for the relationship other than the A causes B explanation.

Along with the benefits of experiments for determining causality come some drawbacks. A primary drawback is that to conduct an experiment, one has to intervene in the normal course of events. Frequently, this leads to the creation of artificial experimental worlds that have little in common with real-life, naturalistic settings. This can cause problems for the ecological validity of conclusions drawn from experiments. Edwin Willems and James Alexander (1982) provide a good illustration of this. They cite an experimental study (Gump & Sutton-Smith, 1955) that showed that poorly skilled, slow-running boys made defeatist and distress comments and were teased by other children when they were put into the principal role in a game of tag (that is, the role of tagger). It turns out, however, that it takes an experiment to be able to make such observations. In real life, boys avoid roles in games they are not good at, and if a poorly skilled boy winds up as the "tagger," the most likely real-life outcome is that one of the better players will arrange to get caught in order to become the "tagger." (Gump & Kounin, 1959–1960). In this tag-game experiment, then, observations were created that could not have been created otherwise. This does not make the experiment less interesting, but it does limit the ecological validity of its conclusions.

A second problem with using experiments in developmental psychology is that it is difficult to conduct a long-term experiment. Given the need for stringent control, most experiments are short-term. This means that if we were to conduct an experiment on the effects of television on children, we would control children's television viewing for a single experimental session or perhaps for as long as a week if we got the cooperation of parents, but it is unlikely that we could control children's television viewing for any longer than this. As a result, we are invariably limited to making statements about the short-term effects of television (or whatever the independent variable happens to be). It may or may not be safe to assume that short-term effects are the same as long-term effects.

The methods reviewed thus far are methods common to all of science. They are among the all-purpose tools that scientists use for making observations. Each method has particular strengths and weaknesses that are related to the method's ability to satisfy the reliability and validity criteria of descriptive science. The strengths and weaknesses of each method are summarized in Table 2-2. In the next section we will turn from these general

TABLE 2-2

Strengths and Weaknesses of Some General Methods
for Making Scientific Observations

METHOD	STRENGTHS	WEAKNESSES
Case Study	Open method that admits all potentially relevant data; deals with rare, infrequent events.	Difficult to check the reliability of observations; also, validity of conclusions is questionable because case studies involve unique events.
Naturalistic Study	Requires no intervention or manipulation; likely to have good ecological validity.	May be inadequate for judging competence; lack of control makes it impossible to compare data across settings.
Clinical Interview	Yields observations for judging what a person thinks and believes; freedom to probe makes method relatively open.	Can only be used with highly verbal subjects; nonstandardized interviews may make conclusions unreliable.
Correlational Study	Yields a quantitative measure of the degree of linear relationship between two variables.	Cannot be used to determine causal relationships among variables.
Experiment	Allows a determination of causal relationships among variables.	Control required may lead to observations with little ecological validity; difficult to conduct long-term studies.

methods to methods that are unique to developmental psychology. These are *longitudinal, cross-sectional, sequential,* and *retrospective methods.*

MEASURING CHANGE OVER TIME

Developmental psychologists are not alone among psychologists in studying changes in psychological processes over time. What is unique, however, is that the time course of the changes developmental psychologists are interested in can be quite long. The psychologist concerned with sensory processes might study phenomena with a time course of, say, 30 minutes. An example would be the process of dark adaptation. The psychologist interested in learning might study the acquisition and extinction of conditioned responses, which might have a time course of a few days to a few weeks. But many phenomena of interest to developmental psychologists extend over months, years, and sometimes decades. The special problem of developmental psychology is how to collect data that yield reliable and valid assessments of development over these time periods.

Longitudinal and Cross-Sectional Designs

There are two principal research methods for making observations of age-related change. One is called the longitudinal method and the other, the cross-sectional method. The **longitudinal research design** involves taking repeated measurements on the same individuals or set of individuals across time. You are conducting a longitudinal study, for example, if you put marks on the wall (most families use doorways) to keep track of how much a child has grown from one birthday to the next. Longitudinal research is convenient so long as the time period during which we make our observations is relatively brief. It is not so convenient, however, when the observations we want to make are months and years apart. The reason is that the method requires waiting.

To avoid the wait involved in longitudinal research, there is a simple solution. You can turn to an independent-groups design known as the **cross-sectional research design.** The groups in the design represent different age groups. Each can be measured in the present to know how the different ages compare. If, for example, you are interested in knowing how height changes over the years 0 to 18, and you do not want to wait 18 years to find out, all you have to do is go out today and measure samples of people representing all the ages you are interested in. Voilà! You have completed your study of age-related changes in height.

It might seem to one who is naive to the practical considerations and problems of research that the choice of a cross-sectional or longitudinal design would be merely a matter of convenience. It is not. The two can lead to quite different conclusions, neither of which is necessarily a valid conclusion regarding age-related change. The reason is that each has its own set of hazards that can mislead a naive researcher into reporting results that are not in fact true. To illustrate this important point, we can turn to the case history of research on the question of the relationship of age to intelligence.

The question of when developing humans are at the height of their intellectual powers and when, if at all, a decline ensues has been a question of interest for a long time. When intelligence tests for both adults and children were developed in the early part of this century, developmental psychologists had for the first time a means of answering the question. They pursued it with vigor.

The initial answer was provided by cross-sectional studies in which the test performances of people at 5-year intervals were compared. David Wechsler (1944) interpreted the data from such studies as providing clear evidence of a decline. "Every human intellectual capacity," he wrote, "after attaining a maximum begins an immediate decline. The decline is very slow but after a while increases perceptibly. The age at which the maximum is attained varies from ability to ability but seldom occurs beyond 30 and in most cases somewhere in the early 20s. Once the decline begins, it progresses continually" (p. 55). Figure 2-4 is a presentation of the data on

FIGURE 2-4
Cross-Sectional Data Showing Relationship of Age to IQ
Data from Wechsler show a progressive decline in adult intelligence. This same trend has been found in every cross-sectional study in this century. (After Wechsler, 1944).

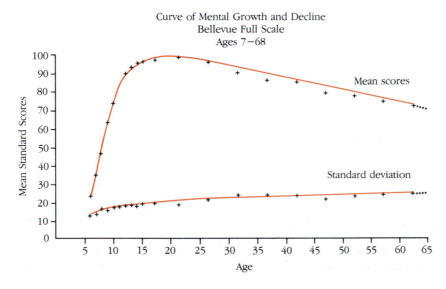

which Wechsler based these conclusions regarding developmental change in adult intelligence.

When one turns to longitudinal studies for an answer to the same question of how intelligence changes with age, a different answer emerges. Not only is there no slow, progressive decline, for many abilities there is an actual increase with age. William Owens (1966), for example, reported intelligence test scores obtained from 96 men who were first tested as college freshmen at Iowa State University and later tested at the ages of 50 and 61. From the time they were freshmen to the age of 50, the scores of these men on the Army Alpha Examination, a group intelligence test developed for World War I draftees, increased. This was particularly true of the "verbal" component of intelligence, which was determined by scores on subtests labeled Synonyms–Antonyms, Disarranged Sentences, General Information, and Number Series Completion. From age 50 to 61, their intelligence remained stable. Bayley (1970), in a second longitudinal study that was influential in getting psychologists to rethink their conclusions regarding the relationship of age and intelligence, showed that people performed better on intelligence tests in their mid-30s than in adolescence. Again the biggest gain came in verbal abilities. The results of longitudinal studies, therefore, conflicted with those of cross-sectional studies.

To resolve the discrepancies between longitudinal and cross-sectional research designs regarding the relationship of age and intelligence, we need to examine the potential biases that are inherent in each of the two approaches.

Generational Differences and Cohort Effects

A potential source of bias in the cross-sectional method is that it compares individuals who were born and raised in different historical periods. In the language of the field, the independent groups in a cross-sectional design are different **cohorts.** A cohort can be defined as a unique birth group.

Because cohorts have unique birthdates, it is possible that political, technological, or social changes in the society might make cohorts different from one another in ways that are totally independent of age. However, since cross-sectional studies involve people of different ages and different cohorts, there is no way to determine whether differences are due to age or cohort effects. In other words, age and cohort are *confounded;* that is, both vary together, and there is no simple way to disentangle the relative influence of each. The likelihood of cohort effects being confounded with developmental effects is increased, of course, when the cohorts are far apart in years.

To illustrate the problem that cohort effects can pose for cross-sectional studies, consider a simple cross-sectional study designed to provide valid statements of how height changes with age. For simplicity, let us assume that we are only interested in changes in adult height. If we conducted our study using cohorts that are 20, 30, 40, 50, 60, and 70 years of age, we would find that there is a decline of about 6 centimeters in height over the years represented (U.S. Bureau of the Census, 1986.) We might be tempted to conclude from this that people shrink by this much during their adult years (due to thinning of the cartilage that separates the bones of the vertebral column). This conclusion, however, would not be valid because cohort differences are in part responsible for the height differences. As anyone knows who has ever gone to a museum and seen the armor worn by medieval combatants or the uniforms worn by soldiers in more recent wars, people today are taller than their predecessors. This trend toward increases in height is still going on and has been present in every decade of the present century. Because there are cohort differences in height, a cross-sectional study becomes an uninterpretable means of assessing developmental change in this variable. The reason is that we can never know from the cross-sectional method alone how much of the height difference between cohorts is due to development (for example, thinning cartilage) and how much is due to unique characteristics of the cohorts (such as differences in general health and nutrition during their growing years).

With the thought in mind that the presence of cohort effects can destroy the logic of a cross-sectional design, we can return to the issue of developmental changes in adult intelligence and ask whether cohort differences could account for the apparent decline in intelligence evident in cross-sectional data such as Wechsler's. Indeed they could, if we assume that education for the masses has been steadily improving throughout this century. Certainly more people are going to school and staying for a longer time than earlier in this century. When one adds to this greater exposure to formal education the impact of the greater informal education one gets through television, travel, and the benefits of an enhanced standard of living, the assumption of improved education across generations is hard to deny. Thus just as people have grown taller in each decade, they have grown smarter too. In cases such as this where cohort effects are known to exist, a cross-sectional design leads to confusion because it confounds cohort with developmental effects, making it impossible to know which is which. Wechsler's cross-sectional study of age-related changes in adult intelligence is a case in point. The decline he observed in his cross-sectional data is as likely to be due to cohort differences as age differences.

Nondevelopmental Effects in Longitudinal Data

To get rid of the age and cohort confound potentially present in cross-sectional designs, we can turn to longitudinal studies. The data from longitudinal studies, however, are themselves subject to some nondevelopmental influences. Potential confounds in longitudinal designs are, in fact, more numerous than in cross-sectional designs.

First, when longitudinal studies require administering the same tests to individuals at different points in their lives, we must be wary of the *effects of retesting* as an explanation for age-related changes in scores. In studying the development of intelligence, for example, it is easy to see that some longitudinal improvement could be due to the practice one gets from taking the same or similar tests again and again.

A second problem potentially present in longitudinal studies—especially when they are conducted over long periods of time—is *selective attrition*. Following individuals longitudinally in this highly mobile society is difficult and requires considerable cooperation from the subjects. Not all subjects agree to cooperate at first, and of those who do, some will drop out. Unfortunately for the validity of conclusions drawn from longitudinal studies, those who drop out are seldom a random sample from the entire longitudinal research group. Often, for example, those who drop out will be less well-off and have less education than those who remain. This would mean that in a developmental study of intelligence, selective attrition alone might serve to increase the average intelligence of the group over time.

As a final caution regarding the interpretation of longitudinal data, one should note that such studies are as susceptible to historical influences as are cross-sectional studies. When such influences are present, they are known as *time-of-measurement effects*. Time-of-measurement effects on track and field performance provide a good example. Athletes today are jumping farther and higher and running faster than ever before, but we would not want to conclude from this that today's athletes are necessarily better; some of their improvement is due simply to improved equipment. The shoes are lighter, the running surfaces are better, the poles are springier, and so on. Whatever improvement is due to these is a time-of-measurement effect. A psychological example of such an effect comes from John Nesselroade and Paul Baltes (1974), who studied personality changes in adolescence. They found declines with age in measures of super-ego strength, anxiety, and achievement. These declines might have been seen as developmental changes had they not included multiple cohorts in their study. The multiple-cohort feature to the design revealed that subjects who were followed from age 13 to 15 in the years 1970 to 1972 showed the same decline as subjects followed from age 16 to 18 during the same period. Nesselroade and Baltes concluded that what would have appeared to be a longitudinal effect if they had included only one cohort was in fact a time-of-measurement effect because all of their adolescents, regardless of age, shifted in the same direction during the years 1970 to 1972 (see Figure 2-5). In the words of Nesselroade and Baltes (1974), the personalities of the adolescents they studied were "more influenced by the cultural moment than by age sequences."

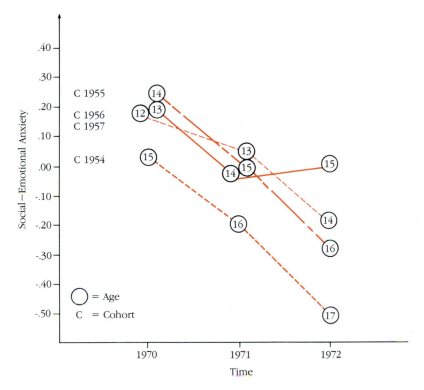

FIGURE 2-5
A Time of Measurement Effect
Data from John Nesselroade and Paul Baltes show that regardless of the age of the adolescents being studied, social–emotional anxiety scores fell over the period 1970 to 1972. (The one exception is the slight increase for 15-year-olds in the 1957 cohort.) This means that time of measurement was a major variable in this study. If multiple cohorts had not been used, there would have been no way to know this. (After Nesselroade & Baltes, 1974).

We have now reached the point of realizing that there are potential pitfalls in the use of developmental psychologists' two approaches to measuring psychological change over time, especially when the time period is a long one. This means that neither cross-sectional nor longitudinal methods can be blindly applied or blindly interpreted, because each requires certain assumptions. To interpret cross-sectional differences as developmental differences requires that we assume the absence of cohort effects. To interpret longitudinal change in a single cohort as evidence of a developmental change requires that we assume the absence of effects due to repeated measurement, selective attrition, and time of measurement. In some cases, these assumptions may be reasonable. It all depends on what we are measuring. In cases where we cannot safely assume that these effects will be absent, something must be done to separate true developmental effects from the various effects that are potentially confounded with them. The way to do this is to use what is known as a sequential research design (Schaie, 1965).

Sequential Research Designs

There are in fact three different sequential designs, but for the sake of simplicity, we will discuss just one of these—the **cohort-sequential research design.** A cohort-sequential design combines features of cross-sectional and longitudinal research in that a researcher begins with a simple cross-sectional study but then follows longitudinally each of the cohorts represented in the cross-sectional design. In following the cohorts longitudinally, the researcher can either use the same subjects over and over (which is the usual longitudinal approach) or use independent samples of subjects from the cohort at each measurement date. The advantage of the latter approach is that it eliminates repeated measures and selective attrition as sources of bias. Repeated measures provide no bias because each individual is tested only once (even though the cohort is tested repeatedly). Selective attrition is not a bias because there is no attrition—the full sample is replenished at each measurement date.

The advantage of the sequential-design approach is that it gives a researcher sufficient data, so that with the help of statistics a true developmental effect can be separated from other effects that might be confounded with it. Because the method involves statistics, we will not go into it in detail. However, one can begin to get a feel for the method by examining a cohort-sequential study directed by K. Warner Schaie, the principal authority in the field of intelligence and aging and the inventor of sequential-research methods as well. This study, which was begun in 1957 (see Schaie & Hertzog, 1983), provides us with the best data yet for evaluating whether intelligence declines with age.

Schaie's research began with samples of individuals who ranged in age from 32 to 67. He gave them all a test that measures a number of different intellectual abilities. Every 7 years thereafter—in 1963, 1970, and most recently in 1977—Schaie collected new samples of individuals from the old cohorts (1889 to 1931). He also added a 1938 cohort of individuals first tested at the age of 25. Figure 2-6, which shows the overall design for Schaie's study, reveals that by 1977 Schaie had developmental data on individuals who ranged in age from 25 to 81 and who represented cohorts from 1889 to 1938. Collectively these data represent seven different cohort-sequential designs, each of which is marked by a rectangle in the figure. The first design enabled Schaie to determine if there was a difference in intellectual functioning between the 1931 and 1938 cohorts and to determine if there was a developmental difference in intellectual functioning between the ages 25 and 39. The analysis on design II tested for a 1924 to 1931 cohort difference and a developmental change from age 32 to 46. Each of the analyses for the remaining designs was conducted in the same way. The outcome of all of these analyses is what appears to be the definitive assessment of cohort and developmental effects on intellectual functioning. This assessment shows that while cohort effects in this century have been more important than developmental differences, developmental differences do exist. For most aspects of overall intellectual functioning, a decline begins in the 50s on average and then becomes quite noticeable after age 60 (Schaie & Hertzog, 1983).

While Schaie's conclusion that intellectual functioning, on average, begins to decline in the 50s appears to be valid, it is extremely important to remember that what is true of the average person is not necessarily true of every person. One must never equate averages with individuals, because an average will change by the same absolute amount whether there is a large shift in the scores of a few people, a small shift in the scores of everybody, or some combination of these. The change in the average alone gives us no way of knowing which has happened. This means that if we are going to attempt to explain developmental data, it is crucial that we know how representative the average is of the individual. In the case of intellectual decline

FIGURE 2-6
Schaie's Seven Cohort-Sequential Design

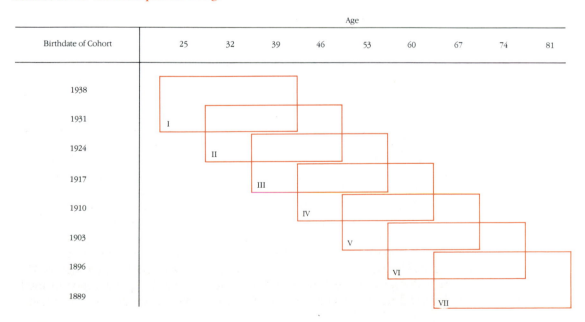

with age, for example, an average decline that is truly reflective of individuals (that is, all individuals show a decline approximately equal in size to the average decline) might lead us to believe that the loss of intellectual ability is the result of a biological process that none of us can hope to escape. If, however, the average drop is not really reflective of changes in individuals, we might suspect that individual differences in factors such as health and activity could create the age-related declines.

The need to understand the relationship between the average and the individual raises an important methodological point. Our discussion of research methods has led to the conclusion that sequential research designs provide the best basis for valid descriptions of developmental change. This does not mean, however, that simple cross-sectional or one-cohort longitudinal studies are necessarily second-class studies. The problems that have been discussed are potential problems, but they need not exist in every case. When a reseacher has reason to doubt their relevance, it is perfectly appropriate to proceed with the simpler research strategy. For example, in the case of declines in intellectual functioning, if we are to understand the basis of individual differences we need to employ a research methodology that to this point has seemed fraught with problems—the single-cohort longitudinal design. For all of its problems of interpretation, this method is the only one that does not obscure the individual. Because it enables us to track changes in individuals and not just in averages, this method can provide valuable insights into the causes of developmental change. For example, examination of individual longitudinal data has been crucial in convincing Schaie that the cause of intellectual decline with age is more likely to lie in the social, environmental, and health conditions associated with aging than in aging of the brain and nervous system per se. The following is a passage reflecting this view:

> Our longitudinal studies of individuals show that we have some remarkable individuals who gained in level of performance into their 70s; others have declined by their 30s. What can account for these individual differences? Two major classes of variables may be important. First, we suspect the role of cumulative health trauma, which may vary widely across individuals. In other words, individuals who have had significant and accumulative physical illness may be at a disadvantage. . . . Secondly, we know that young children function at the upper limits of their intellectual capability in terms of intelligence if they have been raised in a rich and complex environment. The maintenance and growth of intelligence of an adult may also have much to do with the complexity of his or her environment. . . . Results of these studies show that people who live in a varied environment are often the ones who show continued growth throughout life, while those who live in a static environment may be the ones who most likely show some decrement. (Schaie, 1983, pp. 145–46)

Schaie's conclusion that there is nothing inevitable about intellectual decline means that the individual should be able to beat the averages. The important point, however, is that this optimistic theoretical conclusion was totally dependent on having data on individual change from longitudinal studies. With averages alone to work from, one could never know whether changes in the average reflect changes in all, or even most, individuals. Without this knowledge, theoretical work in developmental psychology can be quite hazardous.

Retrospective Research Designs

We have now found in sequential research designs a means of isolating developmental effects, even in cases where they are confounded with a lot of other effects, and we have found in longitudinal studies a means of gaining insight into the possible causes of developmental effects. We are still faced, however, with the problem posed by the long timespan of some developmental change. Collecting developmental data takes a considerable amount of time, most of which is spent waiting for people to age. As we have seen, one way around this problem is to use a cross-sectional design, but in using this method one has to be careful of cohort effects. A second way around the problem would be to use people's memories to restore the past. In this way, just as in a cross-sectional study, one could collect longitudinal data with just a short-term time investment.

Because of its time-saving benefits, developmental psychologists have frequently employed the **retrospective method** as a way to fill out longitudinal designs. A particularly popular use of retrospective, or after-the-fact, data has been to compare the present behavior of a child or adult with parental retrospective reports of that person's early development. Robert Sears's studies (Sears, Whiting, Nowlis, & Sears, 1953; Sears, Maccoby, & Levin, 1957) of the relation between a mother's report of childrearing practices and her children's behavior are classic studies of this type. Unfortunately, studies that rely on a person's memory for data are notoriously subject to distortion. This has become ever-clearer since the 1950s when Sears did his research with the hope that mothers' reports would be reasonably accurate. Today, studies based on retrospective reports are usually not published unless the author can present some evidence that the retrospective reports are accurate.

An interesting illustration of the problems involved in retrospective data collection is provided by a case history involving a mother's statements in 1950 regarding her 3½-year-old boy, Peter, and her statements during an interview in 1978 (Rampling, 1980). The first statements come from a letter to a clinic physician asking him to set up a diagnostic session for her son about whom she was worried.

Mother's Letter, 1950

> I was pleased to say that Mary [daughter] has improved greatly; she eats her meals without any effort now, and her bowels are much regular [sic]. I only hope she keeps it up. Joan [daughter] who is six years old, doesn't eat well, she mostly just picks, but Peter who is 3½ years is the one I am most concerned about now. He seems most dreadfully highly strung, eats at the wrong time, can't coax or force him to eat at meal time, an hour or so later he wants a sandwich or cake, he sleeps very little, he stammers his words when he's nervy, when things don't go exactly the way he wants them to, he screeches and dances and tosses things in all directions. (p. 502)

Here's what the mother said in the interview 28 years later in response to questions from a psychiatrist.

PSYCHIATRIST: Did you have any worries with Peter as a small boy?
MOTHER: No. Not that I know of. I suppose I would remember.
PSYCHIATRIST: How did he compare with his sisters for example?
MOTHER: I'm not sure, what do you mean, in his ways?
PSYCHIATRIST: Yes, was he more difficult to bring up than his sisters?
MOTHER: Oh, no, nothing at all, no. He always wanted to be with us. . . .
PSYCHIATRIST: So you can't recall any problems in his upbringing?
MOTHER: No. . . . (Rampling, 1980, p. 502)

This case history illustrates that even events we would predict to be highly salient can get lost or distorted in memory. Elizabeh Loftus reinforces this point with reports of people who have misremembered such significant events as where they were or who they were with at key moments in history, such as the day President John F. Kennedy was assassinated (Loftus, 1980, pp. 125–26).

Inaccurate stories we have heard or told so often that we begin to believe them are one frequent source of inaccurate memories. Even the most astute person can be subject to this type of error as is illustrated in the inaccurate recall of Jean Piaget, one of the premier developmental psychologists of this century. In the passage quoted here, Piaget (1946/1962) recalls a childhood memory:

> I was sitting in my pram, which my nurse was pushing in the Champs Elysées, when a man tried to kidnap me. I was held in by the strap fastened round me while my nurse bravely tried to stand between me and the thief. She received various scratches, and I can still see vaguely those on her face. Then a crowd gathered, a policeman with a short cloak and a white baton came up, and the man took to his heels. I can still see the whole scene, and can even place it near the tube station. (p. 188n)

Despite the clarity and vividness of this memory from the past, nothing like it ever occurred, as Piaget learned later when his childhood nurse confessed her past sins, one of which was fabricating this story. Piaget was forced to conclude that his memory was created from an account of the story that he had heard during his childhood and "projected into the past in the form of a visual memory" (Piaget, 1946/1962, p. 188n).

The examples given so far are vivid evidence that memory can be a highly invalid source of information for the developmental researcher. One might still feel, however, that the memory errors illustrated above are relatively rare and would not jeopardize the conclusions from studies using retrospective data so long as large numbers of people were included in the studies. Using large numbers of people presumably would overcome the problem of a "few" errors. Unfortunately, there are more than just a few errors. The average person has trouble recalling the past accurately. Stella Chess and Alexander Thomas (1984, p. 7), for example, found significant distortions of memory in better than one third of the 119 subjects whom they followed longitudinally from birth to adulthood. G. E. Vaillant (1977) found a similar degree of distortion in the retrospective recall of adults. He concluded that "maturation makes liars of us all" (in Chess & Thomas, 1984, p. 7). In a more detailed analysis of the inaccuracy of adult memories, Lillian Cukier Robbins (1963) obtained retrospective reports from parents regarding their childrearing practices. She found that these retrospective reports differed from initial reports taken from 1 to 3 years earlier on each of 19 items. Parents were most consistent in reporting whether their child had been breast-fed or not, but even here 2 of 44 mothers and 1 of 39 fathers gave a retrospective report different from their initial report. For quantitative questions like "When did bowel training begin?" or "When did the child first walk alone?" somewhere from 70 to 90 percent of the mothers and from 75 to 100 percent of the fathers gave retrospective reports that differed from their initial reports. The magnitude of the errors was in some cases considerable. Mothers misremembered the age when they began bowel training by an average of 14.2 weeks and fathers by 22.7 weeks. For bladder training, the differences were 22.3 and 25.5 weeks, respectively.

Although the study by Robbins showed discrepancies between initial and retrospective reports on each of 19 items, we must consider these discrepancies to be an underestimate of what occurs in most settings. The reason is that the parents Robbins studied were exceptional. They were far above average in intelligence, in income, and in interest in parenting. Furthermore, the period of recall was just from 1 to 3 years—far shorter than in most studies; the information was information they had provided previously, and so it was something they had thought about before; and, finally, the parents knew the accuracy of their recollections could be checked, a factor that also should have led to greater accuracy.

The conclusion from this discussion on the use of retrospective data in developmental research is that we simply cannot trust it to be accurate enough for most research purposes. This is unfortunate in that it adds to the cost of doing developmental research.

To this point we have been concerned solely with issues that face developmental psychologists in their role as descriptive, or empirical, scientists. Their primary responsibility in this role is judging their work by the criteria of objectivity, reliability, and validity. As we have seen, a concern for reliability must encompass both interobserver reliability and across-time reliability (that is, replicability). The concern for validity should cause scientists to question the internal validity, external validity, and ecological validity of whatever conclusions they draw from their data. Scientists can best do these things if they are fully aware of the inherent strengths and weaknesses of their data-gathering and data-analysis procedures. For this reason, the strengths and weaknesses of case studies, naturalistic studies, clinical interviews, correlational studies, and experiments were discussed at length. Following the review of general methods, we turned to a consideration of the strengths and weaknesses inherent in the methods that developmental psychologists use to measure change over time. These are longitudinal, cross-sectional, sequential, and retrospective studies.

WHAT MAKES A THEORY SCIENTIFIC?

Having seen some of the issues developmental psychologists must concern themselves with in order to be good descriptive scientists, we can now turn to the flip side of the coin and view the issues that concern them in their role as theoretical scientists.

Theoretical scientists (or theorists) differ from descriptive scientists (or empiricists) in that theorists go beyond a mere description of what has been observed to an explanation of what has been observed. Gregor Mendel, the Austrian monk who was the founder of modern genetics, provides a good illustration of this distinction. If Mendel had only been an empiricist, he would have been content to report the results of his pea-plant breeding experiments without speculation as to why he obtained those particular results. Thus, he would have reported that when plants with yellow, round seeds were crossed with plants with green, wrinkled seeds the hybrid plants produced 100 percent yellow, round seeds but that when these hybrids were allowed to self-pollinate to produce a new generation of plants, about one-sixteenth (more specifically, 32 of 556) of the seeds from the new plants were green and wrinkled. A purely empirical scientist would have stopped there. But Gregor Mendel, good empiricist that he was, was also a theorist, and so went on to speculate about the causal role of unobserved hereditary material (which today we call genes) in producing these results. Our concern in this section of the chapter is how we can evaluate the scientific usefulness of theoretical contributions such as Mendel's. That is, given that a researcher or other observer has made novel observations that can be reported to us, how valuable are the researcher's further comments as to why the observations took the form that they did. Interestingly, validity, which is such an important consideration for descriptive science, plays no role in the evaluation of theories.

General Criteria for Evaluating Theories

To evaluate the scientific usefulness of a theory, any number of criteria might be applied. The set of criteria actually chosen depends on one's purposes and preferences. The important point is that before one can say whether a theory is scientifically useful or useless, the criteria on which the evaluation is being made need to be made explicit. The criteria we will apply here are among those most frequently used in evaluating "scientific" theories. They are *parsimony, falsifiability,* and *heuristic value*.

Parsimony refers to the economy of a theoretical explanation: the best theory is one that requires the fewest assumptions or explanatory entities. As William of Ockham, the fourteenth-century logician who first discussed the principle of parsimony put it, "What can be done with fewer assumptions is done in vain with more" (in Moody, 1972, p. 307). A frequently used example illustrating the sort of parsimony that can be achieved by scientific theories is Newton's formulation of the principle of universal gravitation. This single theoretical principle explains a whole host of empirical observations, including both terrestrial phenomena such as the movement of the tides and celestial phenomena such as the movement of planets.

Falsifiability is a criterion of importance for evaluating scientific theories, because one does not advance theory by seeking evidence consistent with the theory; one advances theory only by seeking evidence inconsistent with it. The philosopher of science best associated with this criterion is the Austrian, Karl Popper.

Popper became intuitively aware of the importance of falsifiability when he was still a young man. He commented, for example, that when he was a student, he was attracted to the theories of Sigmund Freud and Alfred Adler as explanations for aspects of human behavior; but, then, he became aware that there was no behavior that these theories could not explain. "I could not think," he said, "of any human behavior which could not be interpreted in terms of either theory. . . . They always fitted, . . . they were always confirmed" (Popper, 1968, p. 35). Whereas this feature of the theories was their strongest attraction to many, Popper saw it as their greatest weakness. By explaining everything, the theories became untestable. No data could challenge their validity. When such is the case, a theory can still be "interesting," but it cannot be "scientific." Science expands its knowledge by testing its explanations and then modifying the explanations in light of the tests. Untestable theories rule out this crucial activity, thereby putting such theories outside the boundaries of science.

Whereas the first two criteria—parsimony and falsifiability—can be justified on philosophical grounds, the third—**heuristic value**—can be justified on simple pragmatic grounds: Does the theory, whether true or false, help us to learn or to discover anything of value? This question is answered differently depending on the applications one finds for a theory.

One heuristic use of theory is as a guide to research. Scientific theories, as we have just seen, are testable, and there is nothing scientists like to do more than test them. The research that this entails guarantees that there will be new observations made, perhaps of new variables, perhaps using novel methods. All of these are part of the heuristic fallout from theories.

Because of their heuristic value in stimulating thought and research, theories that are wrong can be just as valuable as ones that are right. Speaking of the theory of recapitulation, for example, Ernst Mayr (1982) has said that, "The theory is now known to be invalid, but it was nevertheless a most heuristic theory, having given rise to comparative embryology and having generated many spectacular discoveries" (p. 215). Another fine example of an invalid theory that led to valuable ends is Camillo Golgi's nineteenth-century theory that the nervous system is a continuous network of nerve fibers (see Brazier, 1959). In the early years of this century, we learned that this theory was incorrect. The nervous system is made up of individual nerve cells called neurons, which are not physically connected to each other. The only reason we learned this, however, was that in pursuing his own incorrect theory, Camillo Golgi developed a procedure for staining nervous tissue with silver nitrate in a way that made its fine features visible under a microscope. This staining procedure, in the hands of Santiago Ramon y Cajal, revealed distinct gaps between individual nerve cells. Activities associated with Golgi's inadequate theory, therefore, were instrumental in the development of a better one, a fact that was acknowledged when Golgi was asked to share the 1906 Nobel Prize in Physiology and Medicine with Cajal.*

In addition to the fact that even invalid theories can lead to the discovery of new observations and new scientific methods, theories can be valuable by suggesting applications that prove to be valuable. A theory's value in this regard is that it may lead to applications that "work." Correct theories are more likely to do so than incorrect theories, but again, even incorrect theories can be useful. The general rule among practitioners is that it is better to have some theory than no theory at all. The theory that malaria is caused by gases in the night air, for example, led to the recommendation that people in malaria-prone areas keep their windows closed at

*I would like to thank Dr. Mary Jeanne Kallman for suggesting this example.

night. This recommendation worked in reducing the number of malaria cases, even if for the wrong reasons (that is, it worked by keeping malaria-bearing mosquitoes out). To take an example from psychology, Freud's Oedipus complex is a theoretical principle with no empirical support; however, many psychoanalytically oriented therapists would give testimony that interpreting the behavior of their clients in terms of the Oedipus complex has given them valuable insights into the emotional lives of their clients and thereby resulted in more effective therapy.

Applying the Criteria to an Actual Theory

In order to explicate the three basic criteria beyond this point, it will be helpful to apply the criteria to an actual instance of a theory. The theory we will use is one developed by Robert Zajonc and Gregory Markus, reseachers at the University of Michigan's Research Center for Group Dynamics.

The Zajonc and Markus Theory

The Zajonc and Markus theory, first published in 1975, was designed to explain a number of empirical relationships that had been observed in studies of intellectual development, but particularly the relationships between birth order, family size, and intellectual development presented in Figure 2-7.

The data of Figure 2-7 are from a study by Lillian Belmont and Francis Marolla (1973). In Zajonc and Markus's original presentation of their theory (1975), they focused on five features of these data. First they noted that in general, intelligence was higher for the children from smaller families than for children from larger families (the *family-size effect*). Second, within any family size, earlier-born children performed better than later-born children (the *birth-order effect*). Third, there was a precipitous drop in intelligence from the next to last to the last child (the *last-child effect*). Fourth, only-children are an exception to the family-size and birth-order effects (the *only-child effect*). Fifth, if last-born children are excluded, the rate of decline in intelligence for higher birth orders is less than that for lower birth orders (the *declining-rate effect*).

It might seem risky to develop a theory on a single set of data that could be subject to idiosyncratic influences; however, Zajonc and Markus had good reason to believe that the effects in the Belmont–Marolla data of Figure 2-7 were real (that is, replicable) effects. First, Figure 2-7 is a summary of data from 386,114 people! These people constitute the *entire* population of male 19-year-olds who were born in the Netherlands in the years 1944 to 1947 and tested in the years 1963 to 1966. Furthermore, the Belmont–Marolla data were not alone in indicating the effects that Zajonc and

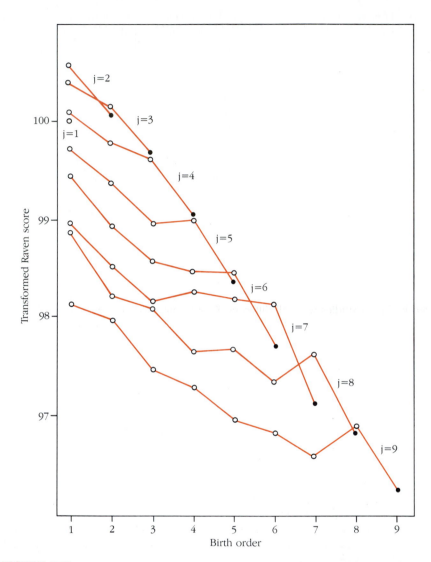

FIGURE 2-7
The Belmont and Marolla Data
These data from Belmont and Marolla (1973) show the five features of intelligence-test data that Zajonc and Markus (1975) wanted to explain. The numbers on the ordinate (or y axis) are rescaled raw scores from a relatively culture-free test of intelligence known as Raven's Progressive Matrices. The lines that relate these scores to birth order are for families with from 1 to 9 children (indicated as j = 1 to j = 9). (After Belmont & Marolla, 1973)

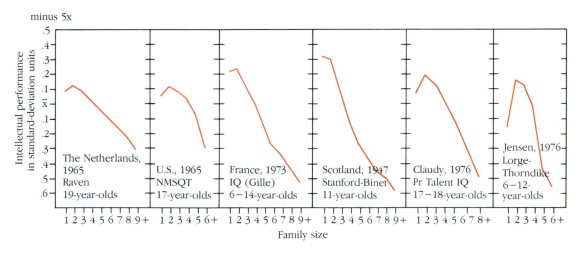

FIGURE 2-8
Other Large Data Sets
Data from Zajonc, Markus, and Markus (1979) show the relationship between family size and intelligence in six large-scale studies. Because the intelligence tests used in the six studies were all different, Zajonc converted all the scores to the common metric of standard deviation units or z scores. (After Zajonc, Markus, & Markus, 1979)

Markus wished to explain. Figure 2-8, for example, shows the family-size effect and the only-child exception to this effect to be common findings in large data sets. Data from 800,000 National Merit Scholarship applicants provide an even more complete replication of the Belmont–Marolla data. As shown in Table 2-3, when the National Merit Scholarship Qualification Test (NMSQT) scores for these 800,000 students were averaged by birth order and family size, there was clear evidence of a family-size effect, a birth-order effect, an only-child effect, and a declining-rate effect.

The model that Zajonc and Markus developed in 1975 to explain their data is labeled the **confluence model.** It postulates that the causal factors working to produce the data are the mutual influences (hence, confluence) that family members have on each other's intellectual development. The most important of the influences comes from a variable known as the family's *intellectual climate;* this variable is also known as the intellectual environment.

The intellectual climate of the family is defined as the collective mental maturity of the family. It is a kind of composite mental age. Adults contribute a maximum value to the family's intellectual climate, newborns a minimum value, and children in between contribute a value that is related to their age by a *sigmoidal* (s-shaped) function. The intellectual growth curves in Figure 2-9 follow such a function. Use of a sigmoidal function (rather than, say, a linear function) to describe intellectual development is based on the assumption that intellectual growth begins slowly in the early years, picks up rapidly in the preschool and school years, and then tapers

TABLE 2-3
Mean Scores on the NMSQT, 1965, by Place in Family Configuration

FAMILY SIZE	BIRTH ORDER				
	1	2	3	4	5
1	103.76				
2	106.21	104.44			
3	106.14	103.89	102.71		
4	105.59	103.05	101.30	100.18	
5	104.39	101.71	99.37	97.69	96.87
Twins	98.04				

SOURCE: From "Family Configuration and Intelligence" by R. Zajonc, 1976, *Science, 192,* p. 228.

off by adulthood. This part of the theory is not particularly controversial, and, in fact, there are data to support the assumption of a sigmoidal growth function (Zajonc, 1983, p. 459). The controversial part of the theory comes from the claim that the intellectual climate within a family is a crucial variable in determining how elevated or depressed an individual's growth function will be.

How Intellectual Climate Affects Growth Toward Mental Maturity   To determine the intellectual climate in a family, the individual contributions of family members—as determined by their own position on their individual sigmoidal mental growth curve—must be combined. The mathematical means of doing so (see Zajonc, Markus, & Markus, 1979, p. 1341) results in a single, family-wide value for the intellectual climate that is weighted toward the contributions of the more mature members. This family-wide value then serves to predict the intellectual growth of the children in the family at the time the value is obtained. Of course, because the mental maturity of children in a family is undergoing constant growth and because families add and lose members, the intellectual climate is not a constant. It changes as family members are added or lost and as existing members age. To see how changes in intellectual climate serve to elevate or depress mental growth curves, we can again turn to Figure 2-9.

The data in Figure 2-9 are purely hypothetical, but they show clearly the type of predictions that result from an application of the intellectual-climate principle as spelled out in the confluence model. The two sigmoidal curves in the figure are intellectual growth curves for two separate individuals growing up in the same family. For illustrative purposes we will assume they are a sister and brother who are spaced 4 years apart. That is, we are assuming that the first-born, a girl, was 4-years-old when her brother was born.

The first thing to notice about the two curves is that the girl's growth curve takes her to a higher level of achievement than does the boy's at the

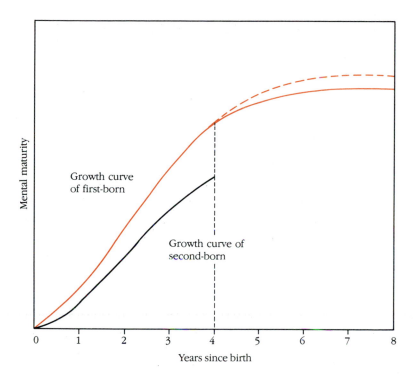

FIGURE 2-9

Confluence-Model Predictions

These hypothetical data show confluence model predictions for the growth in mental maturity of children in a two-child family up until the time the second-born reaches the age of 4. The top function is the confluence-model prediction for the intellectual growth of the first-born child who is 4 years old when the second child is born. The decline in growth rate of this function beginning at age 4 reflects the fact that the intellectual climate in the family has been reduced by the addition of a newborn. Had this second child not been born, the first-born would have continued to develop along the dashed portion of the top function. The lower function represents the intellectual growth function for the second-born child at the same ages. It has a lower slope than the first-born's growth curve because the intellectual climate for this second child is worse than it was for the older child during the first 4 years. (After Zajonc, Markus, & Markus, 1979)

same age. That is, the curve is relatively elevated. Why is this? The reason is that the intellectual climate for the girl at any point before age 4 is superior to that for her brother. This automatically elevates her curve. Take 1 year of age as an example. At this age the infant girl was alone in her family with two adults. But the boy, when he reached 1, was not alone. He had a 5-year-old sister whose intellectual immaturity dragged down the family average. His development at age 1 lags behind his sister's at age 1 because he has a less favorable intellectual climate at this age than his sister had.

In addition to the fact that one curve is more elevated than the other, a second thing to notice about the intellectual growth curves in Figure 2-9 is what happens to the girl's curve at age 4 when her brother is born: her rate of development slows. To make this clear, a dashed continuation to the original curve shows the expected growth had a sibling not been born. Actual growth is quite depressed from this original expectation. The reason is that there has been an important change in the intellectual climate that causes a recalculation of her growth rate. The 4-year-old now has a newly born brother whose mental maturity score of 0 (the score shared by all neonates) brings down the intellectual climate, thereby causing an adjustment in the growth curve that was calculated based on the intellectual climate before the brother was born.

The Importance of Birth Interval   In the example used above to illustrate the principle of intellectual climate and its effect on intellectual development, the sister and brother were spaced 4 years apart. What if they had been spaced farther apart? How would this have affected their sigmoidal growth trajectories in both absolute and relative terms? The answer is that both the sister and the brother would have benefited. The first-born would have benefited by being farther along on her original growth trajectory before the sibling came along to suppress that trajectory. The second-born would have benefited by getting to start life with an even older sister, a difference that would translate into a trajectory elevated from its current level. The elevation would be due, of course, to the improved intellectual climate: older siblings contribute more than younger ones, thus for families of a fixed size, the greater the age differences between siblings, the more mature the intellectual climate for each of the siblings.

If we switch the scenario and ask what would happen if the children had been spaced closer together, we would get an opposite prediction. Both children would develop along trajectories depressed from the levels shown in Figure 2-9. For the first-born, this would occur because she would experience her depression earlier than at present (the "present" being at 4 years); for the second-born, the depression would occur because he would be starting life with a sibling even younger than at present (perhaps a 2-year-old sibling rather than a 4-year-old).

The extreme in close spacing occurs when twins are born. Twin data, therefore, gives us a quick way of testing the prediction that spacing is important. We can compare twins to nontwins to see if in fact they have lower scores. Indeed they do. If you will look back to Table 2-3 you will see the data for twins who took the NMSQT. Their composite score of 98.04 was considerably lower than the composite score for all nontwins except the fourth- and fifth-born in 5-child families. The data from twins, therefore, tend to confirm the spacing hypothesis. (In case you are thinking that there might be other ways to explain the twin deficit, it is interesting to note that children born as twins whose twin died at birth *do not show* a twin deficit

[Record, McKeown, & Edwards, 1970]. This fact rules out any hypothesis involving prenatal effects.)

Thus far in the discussion of spacing, we have only seen that spacing affects the overall levels of achievement. This is not, however, the most important consequence of spacing. The most important consequence is that birth-order effects are totally dependent on relatively close spacing. To see why, consider the effects of extreme spacing as occurs, for example, when a new child is added to the family when the older sibling is in adolescence. In this case, the average intellectual climate will be greater for the second-born than it was for the first-born because the first-born had only two adult intellects in the family at her birth, while the second-born has three. This would lead to a reversal of the usual birth-order effect. Now the second-born should develop to a higher level than the first-born.

The point that the usual birth-order effect is dependent on close spacing is extremely important. To make the point with a more fully developed example, consider the hypothetical data in Table 2-4. This table shows the

TABLE 2-4
Intellectual Environment at Birth

		INTELLECTUAL LEVEL OF SIBLING									INTELLECTUAL ENVIRONMENT
MOTHER	FATHER	1	2	3	4	5	6	7	8	9	
					Family A—1-Year Gap						
100	100	0									66.7
100	100	1	0								50.2
100	100	4	1	0							41.0
100	100	9	4	1	0						35.7
100	100	15	9	4	1	0					32.7
100	100	22	15	9	4	1	0				31.4
100	100	30	22	15	9	4	1	0			31.2
100	100	39	30	22	15	9	4	1	0		32.0
100	100	47	39	30	22	15	9	4	1	0	33.4
					Family B—2-Year Gap						
100	100	0									66.7
100	100	4	0								51.0
100	100	15	4	0							43.8
100	100	30	15	4	0						41.5
100	100	47	30	15	4	0					42.3
100	100	63	47	30	15	4	0				44.9
100	100	76	63	47	30	15	4	0			48.3
100	100	86	76	63	47	30	15	4	0		52.1
100	100	92	86	76	63	47	30	15	4	0	56.6

SOURCE: From "Birth Order and Intellectual Development" by R. Zajonc and G. Markus, 1975, *Psychological Review, 82,* p. 80. Copyright 1975 by the American Psychological Association.

average intellectual climate (in the far right column) that exists at the birth of each successive child in two 9-child families. In Family A there is a 1-year gap between children, and in Family B there is a 2-year gap. As can be seen, the intellectual climate at birth for the second-born to ninth-born in Family B is higher than that for the corresponding child in Family A, and the ninth-born child in Family B starts life in an environment superior to that of any of his siblings except the first-born. This makes it clear that the confluence model does not invariably predict that first-borns will outstrip second-borns, second-borns outstrip third-borns, and so on. It all depends. It depends on spacing, as we see here. But it also depends on a second factor—the age of the children at testing (see Zajonc, Markus, & Markus, 1979). This requires a bit of explanation.

You can begin to see why age is an important factor in the prediction of birth-order effects if we go back to our example of the sister and brother spaced 4 years apart. It is quite clear from this example that the first-born sister will show more rapid mental development during her first 4 years than the second-born brother will during his first 4 years. But what will happen after this point? At age 4, the sister suddenly had a neonatal brother who had a detrimental effect on her growth trajectory via the intellectual-climate principle. But now let us consider the brother at age 4. Up until this age he was handicapped relative to his sister, but now he will experience an advantage. The reason is that while his sister at age 4 (and ever thereafter) has a younger brother, the boy at age 4 (and ever thereafter) has an older sister. This means that the second-born's disadvantage will begin to disappear at 4 years of age, because via the intellectual climate principle, he will be in a superior intellectual climate in relation to his sister in all the years after age 4. By virtue of this fact, his growth curve gets elevated relative to hers, causing him to eventually catch up and surpass her (see Figure 2-10).

We can summarize what has been said of the confluence model thus far by discussing which of the effects in the Belmont–Marolla data it can explain. Using the intellectual-climate principle, we have a good way of understanding both family-size effects and declining-rate effects. The family-size effect is a necessary consequence of the fact that adding children serves to drag down the intellectual climate for all the family. With each new birth, a mental maturity score of zero must get averaged into the family's intellectual environment. This lowers the intellectual climate, causing everyone's growth curve to be suppressed from what it would have been without the birth of the new child. The declining-rate effect can be understood as a simple consequence of the fact that the first zeros to be averaged in have a larger effect on the average than do later zeros. Just as an average grows stabler as more numbers contribute to it, so, too, an intellectual climate grows stabler as ever-more individuals contribute to it. Thus, each extra child has less of an effect on the intellectual climate than does the previous one. To confirm this fact just look at the child-to-child changes in intellectual climate that are given in Table 2-4.

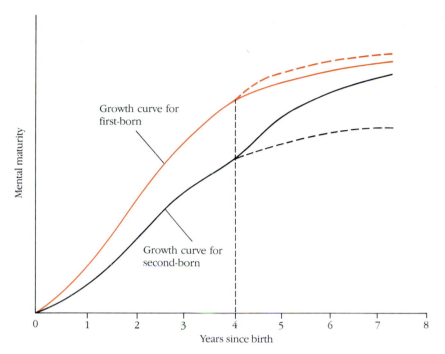

FIGURE 2-10

The Importance of Age in Confluence-Model Predictions.

Whereas the second-born child in our hypothetical two-child family was in an inferior intellectual climate for the first 4 years, this changes after age 4. Relative to the first-born at this age, the second-born has a better intellectual climate (by virtue of having an older, not a younger, sibling.) This puts the second-born onto a trajectory that would enable him to catch up to the first-born if the confluence model were defined solely by the factor known as intellectual climate.

Although intellectual climate alone can explain some of the effects in the Belmont–Marolla data, it falls considerably short of explaining them all. One obvious problem is with the birth-order effect. The Belmont–Marolla data were collected on late adolescents. According to our calculations, there should be a first-born advantage only during the years of early childhood. In adolescence we would expect for the early first-born advantage to be wiped out completely and replaced by a second-born advantage, because— in terms of intellectual climate alone—it is better to grow up with older brothers and sisters than with younger ones. A second problem with a confluence model based only on the principle of intellectual climate is that it gives us no way to explain either the only-child effect or the last-child effect. Reasoning from intellectual climate alone, only-children should exceed all others in intellectual development because their growth curve would never get suppressed. Likewise, last-borns should not be an exception to the declining-rate effect; rather than experience the largest birth-order decrement, they should experience the smallest. These considerations make it clear that a model based on intellectual climate alone is too simple to explain the Belmont–Marolla data. For this reason, Zajonc and Markus added a second major factor to the model. They call it the *teaching factor*.

The Importance of the Teaching Factor   The teaching factor is in essence quite simple. It is based on the premise that instructing others is good for one's own mental growth. Thus, everyone in a family who has the privilege of teaching others will experience a boost in the trajectories of their mental growth curves. The only children who do not get to teach are only-children and last-borns. Both experience what is referred to as the *last-born's handicap*. Zajonc and Markus explain it this way: "If a child does not know how to solve a particular problem, he is not likely to ask the youngest; if he is missing a word, it is not the youngest who will supply it; if there is an ambiguity about the rules of a game or a pattern of play, it will not be resolved by the youngest. In short the last-born is not a 'teacher' and neither is the only child" (1975, p. 82). For this reason they are handicapped relative to all other children.

The teaching factor in conjunction with the intellectual-climate principle serves to explain not only the last-child and only-child effects, it also serves to explain the presence of birth-order effects in adolescent data. As we just saw, the intellectual-climate factor acting alone should begin to wipe out the early-born's advantage sometime during early childhood. With the teaching factor added, however, there is a way for the first-born to regain an advantage later in development. The advantage will come from the opportunities that a younger sibling offers for teaching. This benefit that a younger sibling offers to an older sibling eventually wipes out the disadvantage created when younger children dilute the family's intellectual climate.

Evaluation of the Zajonc and Markus Theory

With the five explanations offered by the confluence model for the Belmont–Marolla data now in place, we can proceed to evaluate the theory in terms of our three criteria: parsimony, falsifiability, and heuristic value.

Parsimony   The Zajonc and Markus confluence model lost considerable parsimony when the teaching function had to be added to account for the last-child, only-child, and adolescent birth-order data. The model would have been far more parsimonious without this added factor. Nonetheless, with just two factors Zajonc and Markus are able to account for an impressive number of facts. We have considered just five (or six if you include the twin data). To these, Zajonc (1976) has added a number of others including racial, ethnic, and regional differences in intelligence, sex differences in intelligence, and the fact that intelligence-test performance is lower for children from single-parent homes than for children from two-parent homes. Altogether, then, the theory provides a lot of explanation for little in the way of theoretical assumptions and, therefore, is a commendably parsimonious theory.

Falsifiability   A theory increases in falsifiability by the extent to which it is precise in its predictions. The sort of precision of prediction that can be achieved using the Zajonc and Markus model is quite good. Consider, for example, a precise prediction that follows from our previous discussion of intellectual climate. According to this principle, there should be a short-term drop in the rate of intellectual growth for all older siblings when a younger sibling is born. We might even predict that this decrement should last for about 2 years, which is the time it would take before the teaching factor could come into play. In case you find this prediction at all confusing, you need only refer back to Figure 2-10. The predicted short-term drop is the gap between the first-born's previous growth trajectory (dashed line) and the actual growth trajectory (solid line). In a test of this specific prediction, Robert McCall (1984) found it to be accurate. Using longitudinal data collected every 6 months throughout childhood, he showed that in the 2 years following the birth of a sibling, older siblings dipped in their intellectual growth relative to children who had not had siblings born in this period.

The prediction of a short-term drop in mental growth following the birth of a sibling is but one of many precise predictions that can be derived from the theory. Others are given in a 1979 article by Zajonc, Markus, and Markus. A prediction not listed there, which is nonetheless quite interesting is Zajonc's 1976 prediction that Scholastic Aptitude Test (SAT) scores would begin to rise in this country in the early to mid-1980s.

Zajonc's prediction of rising SAT scores was based on a correlation of two factors—family size in America in the years 1939 to 1957 and SAT scores in the 18-year period 1956–1957 to 1974–1975. As shown in Figure 2-11, the rise and fall in SAT scores over the 18-year period correspond to the rise and fall in family size in the years the students taking a given exam were born. This covariation appears too remarkable to be a mere coincidence, and, of course, Zajonc did not see it as coincidence. Therefore, he predicted that the relationship would continue into the future (see shaded portion of Figure 2-11). The turnaround in scores should come, he said, in the early 1980s. In partial fulfillment of this prediction, the beginnings of a turnaround did occur in 1981. In that year, for the first time in 18 years, the mathematics and verbal scores that make up the SAT did not fall. In 1982 the scores went up for the first time. Headlines began to appear such as "The Seniors' Slump May Be Over" (*Time,* 1982). The results for 1983 were mixed. Although the mathematics scores continued to increase, the verbal scores fell a point. In 1984, mathematics scores rose 3 points and verbal scores 1 point for a combined increase of 4 points. In 1985 the combined increase was 9 points, but in 1986 scores held steady. Overall, these data are in com-

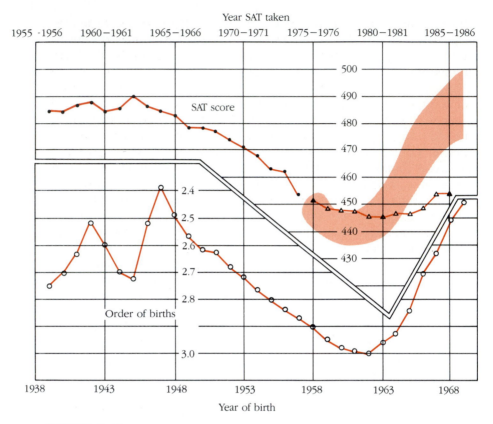

FIGURE 2-11

Relationship of SAT Scores and Family Size

The 18-year time-lag correlation between family size (as represented by average "order of births") is dramatically presented in this figure. The SAT data through 1975 were known to Zajonc at the time the relationship was discovered. Data points for 1976 to 1986 have been added. These fall outside the zone of scores predicted by Zajonc (shaded area in the figure), but they do mark the predicted turnaround in test scores. (After Zajonc, 1976)

plete keeping with the 1975 prediction of a turnaround in college-entrance-exam scores; however, the actual upswing has been far more modest than predicted.

Although he was off the mark in predicting the magnitude of the turn-around in SAT scores, the fact that Zajonc was able to predict a reversal of the downward trend constitutes a significant theoretical achievement, as does his prediction of a dip in mental growth following the birth of a sibling. Not every test of the model has turned out so well. For example, Zajonc himself (Zajonc & Bargh, 1980) has shown that intellectual climate as related to family size alone is insufficient to explain much of the total SAT decline in that it accounts for only a small percentage (8 to 16 percent depending on the method of estimation) of the actual 34.5 point decline in SAT scores that occurred between 1963 and 1975. This means that there are factors more important than those specified by Zajonc that contributed to the decline. Other problems are posed by recently collected data that do not fit the confluence model. Richard Galbraith, for example, collected birth-order and family-size data on better than 10,000 students at Brigham Young University (Galbraith, 1982). Students at this university are primarily Mormons and many come from large families, yet there is no family-size effect in the data. Zajonc (1983) suspects this was true because in Mormon families socioeconomic status is not related to family size in the same way that it is for non-Mormon families. Michael Berbaum, a former student of Zajonc and Markus, suggests that the absence of a family-size effect was due to a cultural peculiarity of Mormons: the "close parental attention to and interaction with children in the home, even in their often large families" (Berbaum et al., 1982, p. 178). Galbraith's (1983) reaction to this is that if the confluence modelers think that it is family-interaction variables that are important, they should emphasize these variables rather than the impersonally determined variables of spacing, birth order, and climate. Other problems have developed for the confluence model with regard to its prediction that the spacing between children is an important variable. Both Galbraith's (1982) data and data from a study by Yvonne Brackbill and Paul Nichols (1982) failed to support the importance of spacing.

Heuristic Value   Regardless of its future role among explanations for population trends in data on intellectual development, the Zajonc and Markus model has already proved valuable in generating research. Before Zajonc and Markus, for example, researchers did not concern themselves with the spacing of children when considering birth-order effects. The new data being collected include this variable for evaluation. Also prior to Zajonc and Markus, investigators ignored a person's age at testing as a variable. Now they do not because, in the Zajonc and Markus view, age at testing is an important variable (Zajonc, Markus, & Markus, 1979). Consideration of these new variables enriches the empirical data that theories have to explain, so that even if the Zajonc and Markus confluence model itself turns out to be an inadequate explanation, whatever theory supplants it will be in its debt. From the point of view of a basic scientist, therefore, the Zajonc and Markus theory has been quite valuable. It provided an explanation for certain empirical relations that had gone unexplained, and it has directed researchers to examine new variables that they ignored previously.

As was stated at the outset of the chapter, however, heuristic value is a somewhat relative matter. Whereas the Zajonc and Markus model might influence the research and scholarly activities of some basic scientists, it has not yet inspired much that is new among scientists with more applied interests. The problem these scientists would note with the theory is that, for them, it seems to have no practical uses. In particular, it does nothing to suggest how to extend the intellectual potential of individuals nor does it adequately predict individual differences in intelligence.

To understand why the Zajonc and Markus model is poor at predicting individual differences, you need to know the magnitude of the "effects" on intelligence we have been talking about. They are miniscule. The birth-order effect, for example, amounts to just 6 percent of a standard deviation per birth rank, which converts to about 6 SAT points or less than 1 point of IQ. Such differences do not make for meaningful differences in the functioning of individual children. In the language of statistics, the confluence model in fact can account for only 1 or 2 percent of the variance in individual scores (see, for example, Galbraith, 1982; Grotevant, Scarr, & Weinberg, 1977; Svanum & Bringle, 1980). For this reason, scientists interested in predicting or controlling individual development find the theory to be of little value.

Zajonc himself finds the dismissal of his theory's practical value to be short-sighted. Personally, he believes that the variables in the confluence model can account for as many as 5 points difference in the IQ of individuals (personal communication), and while he notes that a 5-point increase or decrease would not produce noticeable changes in an individual, it would produce noticeable changes in an aggregate of individuals. If the aggregate defined an entire society, that society would be brighter and less handicapped by low-functioning members. Therefore, Zajonc believes that the intelligence of the aggregate, which his theory predicts better than any other, is a very practical matter.

SUMMARY

As scientists, developmental psychologists have two different but related roles to play. One is to describe the age-related changes in behavior that are of interest to their discipline, and the other is to explain them. The acceptability of their work as science can be judged by applying a number of criteria. In this chapter we first dealt with the criteria that specify that scientific descriptions must be objective, reliable, and valid. Each of the methods used within science has some interpretational hazards associated with it. Case-study results may lack both reliability and generality; naturalistic studies offer no means of control, and they may underestimate a person's true ability; clinical interviews require highly verbal subjects, and their lack of standardization may make the results unreliable; correlational results do not show causality; and the results of experiments may lack real-world validity. A particular problem for developmental scientists is how to make valid statements about change over long periods of time. Cross-sectional and longitudinal studies each pose hazards to interpretation that are corrected only by using an expensive and time-consuming sequential design. The validity of retrospective studies is suspect whenever there is no way to check subjects' recall for accuracy.

The problem of validity, which looms so large on the descriptive side of science, is not so important on the theoretical side. Here scientists are concerned with developing parsimonious and falsifiable theories with clear heuristic value. To illustrate the use of these criteria, they were applied to the Zajonc and Markus confluence model, a theory designed to explain a number of facts regarding the relationship between birth order (or spacing), family size, and intelligence. This theory is precise enough in its predictions that investigators can easily design studies to falsify the theory. Also, it is relatively parsimonious in that it explains a number of diverse facts with but two assumptions: one involving the variable labeled intellectual climate and the other involving the variable known as the teaching factor. The heuristic value of the theory has been substantial for the basic scientist interested in understanding large-scale patterns, but the value has been limited for more practically minded educators, who find the size of the effects explained by the model to be disappointingly small.

SUGGESTIONS FOR FURTHER READING

Achenbach, T. M. (1978). *Research in developmental psychology: Concepts, strategies, methods*. New York: The Free Press. A general source that can serve as a reference for specifics on the use of correlational research, experimentation, data analysis, and research design in developmental psychology.

Goodall, J. (1971). *In the shadow of man*. Boston: Houghton Mifflin. A popular account of Jane Goodall's achievements in conducting extensive naturalistic observations of wild chimpanzees. Both the merits and limitations of naturalistic observations are evident in this enthralling account of the daily lives and habits of the closest animal relative to humans.

Mednick, S. A., Harway, M, & Finello, K. M. (1984). *Handbook of longitudinal research: Vol. 1. Birth and childhood cohorts*. New York: Praeger. This compilation of longitudinal projects conducted in the United States contains descriptions of classic studies along with more recent ones. It is an excellent source book.

Schaie, K. W. (1983). The Seattle longitudinal study: A twenty-one year exploration of psychometric intelligence in adulthood. In K. W. Schaie, *Longitudinal studies of adult psychological development*. New York: Guilford. Schaie's definitive work on the development of intelligence in adulthood is described in his own words.

Vasta, R. (1979). *Studying children: An introduction to research methods*. San Francisco: W. H. Freeman. Topics covered range from the broad (for example, the nature of scientific explanation) to the specific (for example, the use of the habituation procedure in infant studies.)

PART II

The Epigenetic View of Development

CHAPTER OUTLINE

CHAPTER 3

The Epigenetic View: A Solution to the Nature–Nurture Controversy

In preparation for the study of the details of human development beginning in Part 3, this section will deal with general developmental principles as they apply to all animals. The first point to establish is that all development—human or animal, psychological or biological—is **epigenetic.** In brief, this means that none of the characteristics of animals are preformed and few are predetermined. Instead, psychological and biological development are characterized by emergence. During the emergence, there are many possible paths that development can take. Just how many depends on the process and the animal; but in general, the development of the physical and behavioral characteristics of animals is far more open-ended, or **plastic,** than one would imagine.

ENVIRONMENTALISTS, NATIVISTS, AND EPIGENETICISTS

The epigenetic view of development that characterizes contemporary developmental psychology stands as a relatively recent alternative to two views that dominated historically. These were the *environmentalist* and *nativist* views. Referring to them in the past tense is not completely appropriate because even today it is possible to take one or the other view.

From the environmentalist view, nurture, not nature, is the all-determining force in shaping development. The boldest statement ever made of this belief came from the founder of behaviorism, John B. Watson. His famous declaration, made in 1925, was that if he were given control over a person's environment from birth, he could shape that person in whatever direction he chose. The declaration reads as follows:

> Give me a dozen healthy infants, well-formed, and my own specified world to bring them up in and I'll guarantee to take any one at random and train him to become any type of specialist I might select—doctor, lawyer, artist, merchant-chief and, yes, even beggarman and thief, regardless of his talents, penchants, tendencies, abilities, vocations, and race of his ancestors. (1924/1930, p. 104)

Usually this is all of the Watson quote that is given, because most authors prefer a straw-man environmentalist to a real one. The real Watson acknowledged the extremity of his view by adding, "I am going beyond my facts and I admit it, but so have the advocates of the contrary and they have been doing it for many thousands of years" (p. 104). Nonetheless, whether fair or not, Watson has gone down in history as an uncompromising environmentalist, the arch-proponent of nurture as the sole determinant of developmental outcomes.

Historically in opposition to the Watsonian environmentalist view was the nativist view, which held that there is a genetically determined destiny in development that cannot be denied. The view is expressed clearly in the following quote taken from Albert E. Wiggam, a contemporary of John B. Watson, who in the early part of this century lectured widely that societies could improve the human race by "improving" the human gene pool. According to Wiggam, "Heredity and not environment is the chief maker of men. . . . Nearly all of the misery and nearly all of the happiness in the world are due not to environment, . . . the differences among men are, in the main, due to differences in the germ cells from which they are born" (1923, p. 42).

Lying between the extreme environmentalist and nativist views captured here in the Watson and Wiggam quotes is a philosophical, scientific, and occasionally political battlefield where advocates of one polar position or another engage in debates known variously as the *nature–nurture debate,* the *heredity–environment debate,* the *maturation–learning debate,* and the *nativist–empiricist controversy.* Contemporary developmental psychologists do not take sides in these debates when they are waged in an either–or fashion, because today we recognize that development is due not to nature or nurture, but to nature *and* nurture. The two are inseparable.

THE INSEPARABILITY OF NATURE AND NURTURE

The inseparability of nature and nurture can be demonstrated in a variety of ways. First, there is the readily apparent fact that biological entities must have ongoing interactions with an environment for life to exist. This demonstration, though, is a trivial one because it is self-evident. A more revealing demonstration comes from studies of development that show nature and nurture variables to have reciprocal effects on one another. In these cases, there is an interplay between the nature-and-nurture variable sets such that an animal's nature in part determines its nurture and its nurture then has a reciprocal effect, altering the animal's nature. Nature–nurture interplay of this sort provides the firmest basis for denying the separability of nature and nurture in development.

Discoveries made by University of Wisconsin psychologist Robert Ressler (1962, 1963, and 1966) in a series of experiments on mice will serve to illustrate the type of intricate interplay that can occur between environmental and hereditary factors. Keep in mind while reading about the research that the point it makes is as valid for humans and all other species as it is for mice: nature and nurture do not operate as independent factors in development; rather they interact in a dynamic way that makes it impossible to separate the one from the other.

The mice that Ressler used in his research were from two genetically different laboratory strains, which will be labeled the albino and pigmented strains for simplicity. (Their actual names involve a relatively meaningless alphanumeric code.) Raised under standard laboratory conditions, mice of the albino strain grow to be both heavier and more exploratory in their behavior than mice of the pigmented strain. Under standard laboratory conditions, therefore, genetic differences make for physical and behavioral differences. The way in which they do, however, shows that genetics is in no way independent of the environment. Ressler (1963) discovered this by performing a *cross-fostering study* in which albino pups (that is, baby mice) were foster-reared by pigmented mothers and pigmented pups were foster-reared by albino mothers. The result was that the albino-reared pups, regardless of the genetic strain from which they came, were heavier and more exploratory than pups reared by pigmented mice. Mothering made a difference! The reason, according to Ressler, is that albino mothers tend to lick, groom, and handle their offspring more than pigmented mothers, and this difference in care results in hormonal and metabolic changes that in turn affect weight and exploration habits. Ressler's example shows, then, that in mice, nature affects nurture in that mothers of genetically different strains provide different degrees of care for their offspring. Beyond that, the nurture received affects the nature of the animal, in this case via hormones and metabolism.

Can you see in this research any implications for human development? You might if we examine a concrete example. For illustrative purposes, then, let us consider the aspect of personality that is summed up by people's basic behavioral preferences; such preferences are expressed in decisions on whether to stay at home or got out, be impetuous or prudent, meet new people or see old friends, dance until three or go to bed early. Now assume, as most do, that the genes parents pass on to their children have some direct influence on the development of their children's preferences (see, for example, Eysenck, 1970). But remember, too, that parents who pass on their preference-influencing genes also provide the environment in which these preferences develop. Not only do the parents determine all the particulars of their children's lives (discipline, diet, books, television, music, whether or not they have pets, playmates, or outings to the zoo), they also serve as models for their children's behavior. Through both their genetic and environmental contributions, therefore, parents could conceivably affect the development of their children's preferences. We must not think of these contributions as independent, however. Thinking in terms of Ressler's mice leads us to realize that just as the genetic characteristics of mice affect the amount of licking and grooming mothers provide their pups, the genetic characteristics of parents can affect the environments they create for their children. The reason is that parents' own genetically influenced preferences are expressed in the behavioral models they provide their children and in the other environmental particulars that are under parental control. The environment parents provide, therefore, is not independent of their own genetics, and it may well be that in humans, as well as mice, the environment that parents provide is coded into the nature of the offspring.

We can carry the story on interactions in mice and humans a bit further, because there was a second important interaction in Ressler's data. Overall, albino pups received more licking, grooming, and handling than did pigmented pups, regardless of the genetic strain of the parent. It appears that coat color of the pups—a nature variable in the pups but an environmental variable in its influence on the mother—had an effect of its own on the maternal behavior of mice. For the human parallel to this we need only to assume that infants, through their own genetically influenced personalities, have important effects on the parents. As we will see more clearly in Chapter 12, this is not a hard assumption to make. Infants through their own behavioral differences elicit varying degrees of nurturance from their parents.

In conclusion, Ressler's experimental demonstration and the human example developed here clearly show that nature and nurture do not operate independently as causal factors in development. The effects of one are invariably felt on the other, making it impossible to separate out a nature from a nurture effect. If you need a final bit of convincing, simply try to answer the question whether the weight and exploratory behavior of mice or your own behavioral preferences are due to nature or to nurture. The answer is undeniably and indisputably *both,* with the really interesting part of the answer being the actual dynamics by which the interaction occurs.

THE EPIGENETIC MODEL

Once you realize that nature and nurture cannot be separated from each other in their effects on an individual's development, you are in a position to see that the old nature–nurture debate was based on a false premise. That premise, quite simply, was that there could be an effect due purely to genetics (and other nature factors) or purely to nurture. Today these purist views are completely untenable.

The demise of the either–or version of the nature–nurture debate has been extremely important to the advancement of our theoretical understanding of development. In its place, we have a better model of development in what Gilbert Gottlieb (1970) and Richard Lerner (1976) have called the "probabilistic epigenetic model" or, more simply, the *epigenetic model.* Rather than view development as determined by either nature or nurture, the epigenetic model sees development as an interactive process in which the influence of both sets of forces are experienced in an inseparable tangle.

In biology, epigenesis is a theory of development that holds that anatomical structures emerge with development; they are not all present in the embryo. The contrary view, once held by preformationists, was that all the structures present in the adult were present in miniature in the embryo (see Figure 1-10). This theory, popular until late in the nineteenth century, was part of the basis for the implicit societal belief that children were little adults (see Figure 1-9). The theory was refuted by experiments that showed that frog eggs could be split in half (at the two-cell stage) and then, from the halves, produce two whole frogs, not two half frogs as the preformationists would predict. Obviously, the biological structures that define a frog were not present at the frog's conception. They emerged in development as the theory of epigenesis held.

When psychologists say that development is epigenetic, they are using the term epigenesis in somewhat the same way as biologists, because they mean that behavior and mental processes (which we can refer to loosely as psychological structures) emerge in development. Beyond this, however, they mean that neither heredity through predetermination nor the environment through current determination completely predicts developmental outcomes. This emphasis in the use of the term stems from the fact that in psychology epigenesis is the alternative not to preformationism but to "either-orism." Either-orism sees the causes of development in a one-sided way. Epigenesis is a superordinate point of view (Lerner, 1978) that resolves the conflict between nature and nurture advocates.

Waddington's Landscape Metaphor

A helpful way of seeing how the epigenetic approach resolves the conflict between the nature and nurture approaches is to imagine what the celebrated embryologist Conrad Hal Waddington (1957) has called an *epigenetic landscape* (see Figure 3-1). This landscape provides a convenient way of picturing the interaction of nature and nurture forces as they combine to affect development. In this visual metaphor, heredity is responsible for canals inscribed on the landscape's surface. These represent the paths development is likely to take. They are what Waddington calls "canalized" aspects of development. These paths become all the more probable when they are deeply canalized. Development, represented by a ball in Waddington's metaphor, rolls down this landscape, top to bottom. The ball can represent a single developing structure, a system, or an entire individual. As it proceeds down the canals on the landscape, it reaches choice points. At each point, it is most likely to take the most deeply canalized route, but whatever is happening in the ball's environment at the moment can act to push the ball

FIGURE 3-1
Epigenetic Landscape

An epigenetic landscape can be used as a convenient means of conceptualizing the joint roles that nature and nurture play in determining developmental outcomes. This figure shows a small portion of such a landscape.

from its expected path, putting it onto an alternate path. The ball can be pushed from shallow canals most easily, but even the developments along the most canalized paths are susceptible to influence, as we will soon see.

Waddington's model is far too loose in its predictions to be considered in any sense a theory of development. Moreover, the key term in Waddington's model—canalization—is far better defined in embryology than in psychology. Nonetheless, psychologists have found the model useful for depicting some of the essentials of their epigenetic view. It captures their belief (1) that there are a number of possible paths along which any one individual can develop, (2) that some of these paths—by virtue both of an individual's heredity and past history—are more likely to be taken than others, (3) that nature and nurture combine to determine the paths actually taken, and (4) that while development is quite plastic, there are still some limits to this plasticity. Although this fourth point is represented in Waddington's model by the limited number of paths on the epigenetic landscape, the point is perhaps better made using Irving Gottesman's (1963) concept of a reaction range.

The Concept of Reaction Range

The reaction-range concept concerns the developmental fates of genotypes. In reality, there are no genotypes, only individuals; but ideally at least we can separate the genetic component of individuals from all else, and when we do, we have a *genotype*—the pure genetic component to an individual. The value of the reaction-range model as developed by Gottesman is that it shows the different degrees of reaction that one gets from different genotypes when they are exposed to identical environments (see Figure 3-2). In doing so, the model makes the important point that there are limits to plasticity and that the limits vary as a function of the genetic differences among individuals. This makes the reaction-range concept a useful adjunct to the concept of an epigenetic landscape, particularly when thinking about plasticity in quantitative traits such as IQ, height, and amount of pigmentation in the skin. According to the reaction-range concept, the genotype for any such characteristic will be expressed differently, depending on the conditions in which it develops. The extent of the potential differences is what is known as the reaction range. This concept is illustrated in Figure 3-2 using ranges of reaction in skin color as an example.

As Figure 3-2 shows, an environmental change (represented here by varying degrees of exposure to ultraviolet light) does not necessarily have the same effect on all genotypes. In the skin-color example, a Negroid genotype would show a very narrow range of reaction to changes in ultraviolet radiation, whereas a Caucasoid genotype would show a broad range of reaction. A Mongoloid genotype would show a somewhat intermediate range of reaction. In the case of most psychological characteristics, we can assume

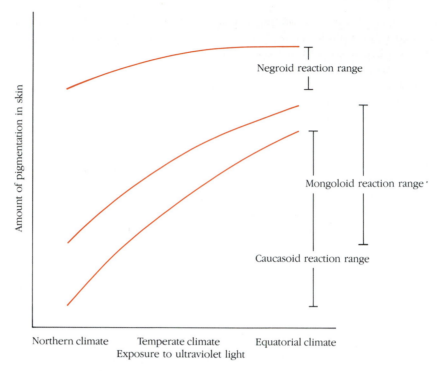

FIGURE 3-2
Reaction Range
The concept of a reaction range for individual genotypes is illustrated here using the trait of skin color. The genotype for skin color present in Negroids would lead to relatively heavy pigmentation regardless of exposure to ultraviolet light, and, therefore, this genotype would show a very limited range of reaction. Mongoloids would show a substantially greater reaction to changes in exposure, and Caucasoids would show the greatest reaction of all.

that normal human genotypes have broad reaction ranges, somewhat like that of Caucasoids for skin color. A reasonable estimate of the reaction range for the expression of IQ in humans with normal (that is, not severely retarded) genotypes is 25 points (Scarr, 1981). This means that by varying the circumstances in one's life, a person's IQ might go from a retarded level to a normal level, or from a normal level to a gifted level.

DEMONSTRATIONS OF PLASTICITY IN THE DEVELOPMENT OF HUMANS AND ANIMALS

If you were to object to the epigenetic model on some grounds, it might be from the belief that some developments in human and animal behavior are so "instinctive," or canalized, that they are not subject to alteration. One of the principal findings of developmental psychology, however, is that no *behaviors* meet the criterion of inalterability. All are subject to some change. Take whatever example you want—the swarming of bees, the migration of birds, the territoriality of Alaskan wolves, or the rutting of male elk in mating season—and the contemporary developmental psychologist will argue that the behavior is alterable by changing the way the animals are reared. The grounds for this assertion are that whenever a supposed case of instinctual, predetermined behavior has been examined carefully, it has been found that specific rearing conditions were prerequisite to the appearance of the "instinct." Alter the rearing conditions and you alter the behavior. In light of this finding, we no longer use the term instinct. In its place we substitute the term **species-typical behavior.** This term emphasizes that what we casually call instincts are typical, but not inevitable behavioral outcomes. Without species-typical rearing in a species-typical environment, the so-called instincts do not appear.

Zing Yang Kuo's Research

The psychologist who has had the greatest role in developing the hypothesis that species-typical environments are crucial for the development of species-typical behaviors is Zing Yang Kuo. Back in the 1920s when Kuo had just finished graduate school at the University of California, Berkeley, he entered the heredity–environment fray with articles (1921, 1922) such as "Giving Up Instincts in Psychology" and "How Are Instincts Acquired?" He was an extremely careful observer and made the observation that even motor patterns such as walking, pecking, and preening by young chicks are dependent on a normal embryonic life (that is, a species-typical environment). Specifically, these patterns were dependent on the position of the embryonic chick relative to the yolk sac in the egg. When Kuo altered the position, thereby creating an atypical environment, he altered the nature of the postnatal movement patterns.

Kuo's more telling research has been with mammals, principally cats and dogs. By conducting rearing studies on these animals, Kuo has shown that the rodent- and bird-killing tendencies of cats can be completely eliminated by rearing them with rodents and birds. Also, he has shown that normally vicious dogs can be brought up to be docile and that dogs that normally take to the water can be made water-phobic. Even the diet of animals is subject to much change. As Kuo (1967) puts it: "There is no genetic basis in the central neural organization that determines the kinds of food which the young of a given species will eat. . . . Animals eat what they eat not because of what they are born with but because of what they are fed with" (p. 71). This statement is a bit strong, because Kuo (1967) elsewhere clearly acknowledges what we all know to be true: there are limits to the plasticity of behavior. As he says, for example, an epigeneticist "cannot make a horse take wing and fly" (p. 127). Still, his principal point is an extremely important one, which today is undeniable: there are far more developmental possibilities open to all developing animals than will ever be realized. In Kuo's words, a log

> can be used as firewood, molded into a part of furniture, burnt into charcoal, ground into pulp for paper, buried underground and after millions of years turned into coal, carved into a statue, or innumerable other possibilities. By the same token; a newborn kitten has no genetic factor that makes it a rat killer, but it does possess the *potentialities* for becoming both a rat killer and a rat lover. (1967, p. 126)

Both potentialities are within the reaction range of feline genotypes.

What is true regarding the plasticity of the particular animal behaviors we erroneously call instincts is true also of broad categories of human development such as physical development, motor development, cognitive development, and the development of psychoses. In the remainder of the chapter, we will take each of these topics and demonstrate through examples the plasticity present in these areas of human development. In each case, genetics sets some limits on the number and range of potential outcomes, but as development proceeds from the formation of the initial fertilized egg to the formation of the infant, child, adolescent, and then the adult, a great amount of variability is possible depending on the environment to which the developing person is exposed.

Physical Development

Physical development is generally taken to be a process that is primarily biological in nature. After all, one is a dwarf or a giant by virtue of one's genes, with the action of the genes being mediated through the amount and timing of growth hormones (see Figure 3-3). Normally we tend to think that all the environment needs to supply is adequate nutrients. A number of examples can be used to show that this is not the total picture, however. In fact, the psychological environment in which one develops can on occasion override all the other variables affecting physical growth, at least in the short run (Tanner, 1978, chap. 9). Two examples can be used to illustrate this. Both show that emotional factors stemming from stress in the psychological environment are capable of disrupting the growth process.

Psychosocial Dwarfism

Psychosocial dwarfism is a specific instance of what is more generally known as the *failure-to-thrive syndrome*. In all failure-to-thrive cases there is stunted growth in young infants, but in the case of psychosocial dwarfism

FIGURE 3-3
Genetics as a Source of Individual Differences
Former jockey Eddie Arcaro (left) and former basketball star Wilt Chamberlain
(right) represent extremes in human growth. Height differences such as theirs are
due primarily to genetic effects on pituitary gland activity; however, not all growth
differences are due to genetic factors.

the effect is specifically due to parenting failure (Green, Campbell, & David,
1984). One such case, reported by Lytt Gardner (1972), is depicted in Figure
3-4. Here the male (on the right) is clearly stunted in his growth relative to
his twin sister (on the left). The label of psychosocial dwarfism is appropriate for this case of stunting because the cause of the child's growth problem
was an unloving and punitive parent. According to the case record, the parents of these children began to have marital problems 4 months after the
children were born. Shortly thereafter, the father lost his job and left home.
The mother then took out her hostile feelings on the son, but not the
daughter, Presumably, the son reminded her of the husband who had des-
erted her.

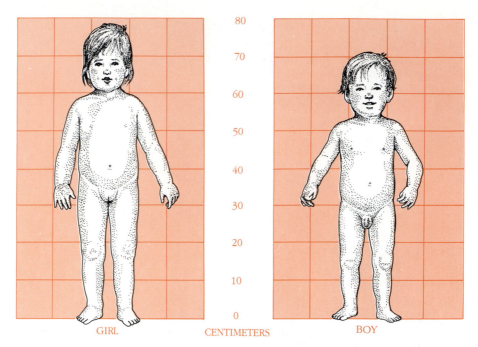

80

70

60

50

40

30

20

10

0

GIRL   CENTIMETERS   BOY

FIGURE 3-4
Psychosocial Dwarfism
This girl and boy are 13-month-old twins. The girl (on the left) is of normal size, but the boy (on the right) is 6 months behind in height and weight. The apparent cause of the boy's stunted growth was the lack of love shown by his mother. (After Gardner, 1972)

Although this case of twins may be sufficient to convince you that psychological stress can cause arrested growth in young children, it is hardly conclusive. It may be, for example, that the mother expressed her hostility toward her son by simply not feeding him. If so, it would not be the psychological environment that caused the arrested growth, not directly anyway. To counter such objections and to argue that the psychological environment can indeed by the cause of growth defects, we can take a second case history reported by Gardner. This one is somewhat better documented than the first and points clearly to the psychological environment as the direct cause of some growth problems.

In this case, a mother gave birth to a daughter with an underdeveloped esophagus that prevented the baby girl from ingesting her food in the normal way. To correct the problem, an operation was performed to install a tube in the child's stomach through which the mother could inject a special nutrient formula on which the baby was to be maintained. The presence of this tube, however, made the mother very fearful that she might dislodge it, thereby endangering her baby. Her solution was to avoid handling the baby. She neither held nor played with her for the first 15 months of life. This had a devastating effect on the child's development, and at the age of 15 months she had to be hospitalized.

The effects of the girl's deprivation, which were assessed at the time she entered the hospital, included both behavioral and biological effects.

> Her facial expression was sad and her muscles flaccid. She was inactive and withdrawn; the withdrawal frequently led to abnormally long periods of sleep. Her stomach secretions were deficient in pepsin and hydrochloric acid. Doses of histamine that ordinarily stimulate a profuse outpouring of acid by the stomach lining failed to elicit the normal response. (Gardner, 1972, p. 77)

Within a short time in the hospital, however, the girl was on the road to full recovery. The recovery in the hospital was not due to a change in diet, because precisely the same schedule of food injections was maintained in the hospital as had been used in the home. The only difference was that this child, who had been left untouched in her crib at home, now received an immense amount of tactile stimulation in the form of touching and holding from the nursing staff. This single change proved sufficient to alter her physical development dramatically, because the child quickly began to thrive. The recovery evident in this particular case is not unusual. In fact, it is the norm. A recent review of cases of psychosocial dwarfism reports that the literature is "almost unanimous in agreeing" that replacing a child's unfavorable psychosocial environment with a positive, loving one will cause growth to return to its normal course, even without any hormonal or medical treatment (Green, Campbell, & David, 1984).

The Case of the Despotic Director

A second example of the effect of psychological stress on the physical process of growth involves young children, not infants. The example comes from a study conducted by Cambridge University nutritionist Elsie Widdowson when she was in Germany following World War II (Widdowson, 1951). The study was designed to determine the impact of dietary supplements on growth and was carried out on groups of children living in two orphanages. Only inadvertently did the study turn into one of psychological effects on growth.

The design of Widdowson's study was quite straightforward. It called for the children in one orphanage to be the experimental group, which would receive a dietary supplement, and the children in other to be a control group, which would be maintained on the standard orphanage diet. The plan was facilitated by the fact that the children in both orphanages received the same standard diet and because there was no chance for the children to supplement their diet with food obtained elsewhere.

Being a good experimentalist, Widdowson began her study by collecting 6 months of baseline data on the children's growth patterns. The baseline data collected prior to the initiation of the improved diet gave Widdowson a way to determine whether the growth patterns in her two groups of children were the same before the introduction of the improved diet. If not, she would have to take these preexperimental differences into account when assessing the effect of her treatment.

It turned out that there were indeed preexperimental differences in the growth rates of the children in the two orphanages. The children in one orphanage, referred to here as Orphanage A, were growing more rapidly than children in Orphanage B. With these data in hand, Widdowson began the experimental portion of her study. She gave the children in Orphanage A unlimited access to bread, jam, and juice at mealtime. The extra food gave the children a means of always satisfying their appetites. What Widdowson, of course, expected to happen at this point was for the growth rate in Orphanage A to be accelerated over its baseline rate, whereas children in Orphanage B were expected to continue at the preexperimental rate. To her great surprise she found the opposite to be true. As you can see in Figure 3-5, in the second 6 months of the study—the experimental period—the weight gain of children in Orphanage A slowed somewhat relative to baseline, whereas the weight gain of children in Orphanage B—children who had experienced no dietary change—was greatly increased. These results made no sense. It was obvious that some variable more important than diet was affecting the children's growth.

After much effort, Widdowson located what she believed to be the factor of principal importance in accounting for the results of her growth study. The factor was Fräulein Schwarz, director of Orphanage B during the first 6 months of the study and director of Orphanage A during the second 6 months. This woman, it turns out, was particularly severe in her discipline of the children, often choosing the mealtime to mete out her punishments. Also, she was inconsistent in her punishments. One child was scolded one day for wearing gloves and the next day for not wearing them. Her severe and inconsistent manner apparently created a stressful environment for the children. As fate would have it, at the very time that Widdowson was introducing the improved diet into Orphanage A, Fräulein Schwarz was transferred there. Thus, along with their bread and jam, the children of Orphanage A got a heavy dose of daily stress. The latter proved to be the more important variable, so that even though their diet was improved, their growth rate was suppressed.

In confirmation of her belief that the director variable in fact accounted for her bizarre results, Widdowson reported in her study the data for eight children who showed a different growth pattern from all the others. These eight children, it turns out, were the favorites of the director.

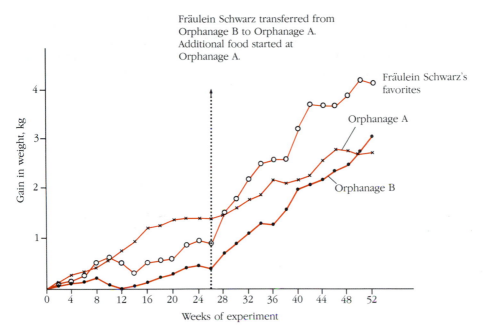

FIGURE 3-5
Case of the Despotic Director
Shown here are the weight gains of the children in Orphanages A and B and of the eight favorites of Fräulein Schwarz for the first 6 months of baseline and for the 6 months during which dietary supplements were available to children in Orphanage A. These results show that Fräulein Schwarz was a more important variable in determining weight gain than was diet. (After Widdowson, 1951)

They were initially with her in Orphanage B, and, as is shown in Figure 3-5 by the dotted line, their growth rate was accelerated over that of other children in the orphanage. Because these children were favorites of hers, Fräulein Schwarz took them with her when she transferred to Orphanage A. The acceleration in the growth of these children in the second 6 months, the months during which they were receiving the dietary supplement along with the other children in Orphanage A, shows the true effect of diet when it is not confounded with psychological stress. Clearly, the pattern of physical growth in children is insufficiently canalized to protect it from environmental effects.

Motor Development

Motor development refers to the development of abilities such as reaching, grasping, crawling, walking, throwing, and catching (see Figure 3-6). These

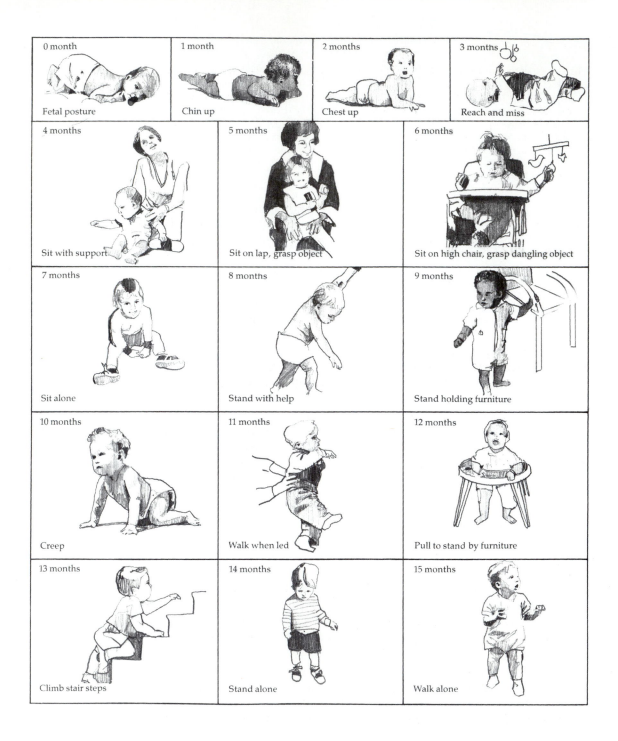

0 month — Fetal posture	1 month — Chin up	2 months — Chest up	3 months — Reach and miss
4 months — Sit with support	5 months — Sit on lap, grasp object	6 months — Sit on high chair, grasp dangling object	
7 months — Sit alone	8 months — Stand with help	9 months — Stand holding furniture	
10 months — Creep	11 months — Walk when led	12 months — Pull to stand by furniture	
13 months — Climb stair steps	14 months — Stand alone	15 months — Walk alone	

FIGURE 3-6
Motor Development
This set of drawings (at left) shows some major motor-skill developments from the first year of life. The ages given for each development are the averages that Mary Shirley (1933) obtained for 25 infants whom she studied. Because she had only 25 infants, Shirley's norms differ somewhat from norms based on larger and more representative samples of infants. Nonetheless, as the text makes clear, one should always expect considerable variability around any norm for motor development, no matter how carefully it is calculated. Individual differences in experience, which arise from the differences in the way children are raised, will affect the age at which motor skills are achieved.

are motor abilities because they involve the coordinated use of muscles that are controlled by *motor neurons*. Such neurons control all the voluntary muscles in our bodies. (Some muscles like heart muscle and muscles that control the opening of the pupil of the eye are involuntary and are controlled by sympathetic and parasympathetic neurons, not motor neurons.)

At one time psychologists thought that the development of motor abilities in humans and animals was totally dependent on maturation of the nervous system and that the process was relatively immune to external influence. Naturally enough, the psychologists espousing this view were known as *maturationists* (see Figure 3-7). The best known of them was Arnold Gesell, a psychologist trained at Clark University when G. Stanley Hall was serving as president of that university. Gesell believed that "the factors of maturation work with considerable force" in motor development and that while there are individual differences in development, "many of these seem to arise out of variations in the original growth equipment rather than in the physical environment" (Gesell, 1933, p. 222). In fact, however, motor development, like every other aspect of development, is far more plastic than Gesell and the other maturationists thought it was. Examples of development being both slowed and hastened by environmental circumstances will serve to demonstrate that plasticity.

Retarded Motor Development as a Function of Experience

One of the maturationists who, along with Gesell, felt that maturation independent of experience was chiefly responsible for motor development was Wayne Dennis. In confirmation of this view, Dennis (1935, 1940) conducted a number of celebrated studies in which it appeared that despite differences in experience, motor development occurred on a predetermined course not altered by experience. One such study was conducted among Hopi Indians (Dennis, 1940). Hopi Indians, when reared in the way traditional to their culture, spend much of their first year of life strapped to a cradleboard that their mothers carry about as they work (see Figure 3-8).

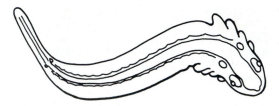

FIGURE 3-7
Maturation of Swimming Movements in Ambystoma
In a study that today is remarkable only for the historical impact it has had, Leonard Carmichael (1926) showed that the development of the swimming movement of salamander larvae (shown here) does not depend on any particular experience. He showed this by immobilizing an experimental group of larvae with the drug chloretone until a control group of larvae had begun to swim. He then removed the chloretone and observed that the experimental larvae began to swim in the time that it took for the drug to wear off. Apparently, their previous immobility had not blocked the maturation of their swimming movements. At the time the experiment was performed, the relatively "experience-free" instance of motor development in ambystoma was taken to be evidence for the general validity of the maturationist's view.

Dennis's study involved comparing Hopi infants reared in this traditional way with Hopi infants reared in the way that is traditional in contemporary American society. The rationale for the study was that the two groups differed greatly in the degree to which their prewalking motor movements were restricted. Thus, if external factors like practice and exercise were important to the development of a motor ability like walking, the Hopis reared on cradleboards would be retarded relative to the Hopis not reared on cradleboards. This is not what Dennis found. The two groups did not differ. Thus Dennis concluded that the maturation of motor abilities operated independently of experience.

Much later in his career, Dennis had occasion to alter his views. The occasion was provided by a year's leave of absence from his teaching duties at Brooklyn College to go to Beirut, Lebanon, and while there conduct a study in orphanages in both Lebanon and Iran. We will focus here on the study conducted in the Iranian orphanages (Dennis, 1960) because it dealt with the widest age range of children, 1 to 4 years.

Orphanages were a dying institution at the time that Dennis was studying motor development among children. Established as we have seen as society's response to the problem of infanticide, orphanages had become the target of social criticism of their own. One reason, of course, was the very high death rate for children in orphanages that resulted from overcrowding and poor care. In most countries, orphanages were being re-

FIGURE 3-8
Cradleboards and the Development of Walking
Hopi infants studied by Dennis (1940b) spent much of their early life strapped on a cradleboard like that shown here. Because they nonetheless were able to walk at the same age as Hopi infants who had not been reared in this restrictive fashion, Dennis concluded that maturation alone controlled the appearance of motor developments.

placed by other means of caring for dependent children such as foster care. Thus the situation in Iran was a unique one that provided Dennis the chance to make observations that are not likely to be repeated.

Three orphanages were used in Dennis's study. Two were public institutions, and one was private. The children in Institution A ranged from 0 to 3 years of age, with most (47 percent) in the range 0 to 1 year. Institution B took in the "graduates" of Institution A and, therefore, housed slightly older children, but it was otherwise the same type of institution. Institution C was the private facility. It was an attempt to provide model institutional care. Most of the children in this institution were infants selected from Institution A.

Five standard tests of motor development were made on a sample of children from all three institutions. These consisted of testing for the ability to sit alone, to locomote a distance of 6 feet by either creeping or scooting, to stand by holding, to walk by holding, and to walk alone. On all these measures the Iranian children were grossly retarded relative to home-reared infants in the United States. For example, according to the Denver Developmental Screening Test, which is a standardized measure of development used in this country, 90 percent of all babies can sit alone before 8 months of age. Dennis's Institution A children, however, did not achieve this level of success until they were in their third year of life, somewhere between the ages of 2 and 3. Children in Institution C, the private institution, progressed a bit more rapidly. They reached the 90 percent level of success by age 2, but this still reflects motor retardation relative to American children. The last item on the brief test that Dennis administered, walking alone, showed an even greater retardation, which is to be expected if deficits are cumulative. In this country, 90 percent of infants can walk alone by the age of 1 year 3 months. In contrast, not a single one of the Iranian orphans could walk alone at this age. Orphans in the private institution were more than a year behind in achieving the 90 percent level of success. Orphans in the public institutions did not begin walking alone until around 4 years of age, at which time just 15 pecent were successful.

How is one to explain these deficits? Dennis entertained several hypotheses. For example, he considered whether the retardation might be due to malnutrition. There was no evidence, however, that the children were malnourished. For one thing, the children's activity level denied that they were malnourished. Malnourished children are lethargic. These children were not. They were motorically active; it was just that their motor acts were retarded. Dennis also wondered whether the apparent retardation might just be due to inborn differences between American and Iranian babies in maturation rate. If this were true, however, then the Iranians should only have differed from the Americans and not from each other. As we have seen, though, Iranian infants reared in the private institution had more advanced motor development than children in the public institutions. Thus Dennis was forced to conclude that the differences between home-reared Americans and institutionalized Iranians and the differences between Iranian children in public and private orphanages had to be due to environmental differences.

In searching for the environmental variable that could account for these differences, Dennis hit upon one that seems to have some explanatory merit. The variable was whether or not children got to spend time on their stomachs (in a prone position). He had noted that the Institution A children were left in their cribs all day long until the time when they were able to sit up alone. At this point, they were given some out-of-crib time on the floor. Up until this point, though, they just lay in their cribs on their backs. Why on their backs? Because, first of all, that was the way they were placed in the cribs and, second, because the mattresses were so soft that when infants tried to turn over it was literally an uphill battle.

To account for the importance of spending time in the prone position during early development, Dennis hypothesized a chain of developments that led in a causal sequence from being on one's stomach, to creeping, to standing by holding, to standing alone, and then to walking alone. In the prone position, Dennis (1960) argued, the infant can

> raise his head from the surface, push with his arms, raise his chest, pull his arms and legs beneath his body—in other words, he can practice acts that are employed in creeping. . . . The child who can creep can go to a piece of furniture, grasp it and pull to his knees. This may lead to walking on his knees while holding to furniture . . . and thence to walking alone. (p. 55)

Deprived of the opportunity to spend time on one's stomach, however, none of this would come to be because the chain would be broken at its very start. This, Dennis believed, was the cause of the retarded motor development of his young Iranians.

Adding credibility to Dennis's explanation for the motor retardation that he observed is the fact that it seems to explain an additional aspect of his data. This is the curious fact that children in Institutions A and B chose scooting as their preferred method of locomotion on the creeping and scooting test, whereas children in Institution C chose creeping—a precursor to walking—as their preferred method. Dennis believed this fact was in accordance with his theory. If the retardation were due to general factors that merely slowed the rate of development, then one would not expect for development to take a different course in the two Iranian groups. But it did. One group scooted and the other creeped when they went to get the cookie that was used as the incentive on the scooting and creeping test. As Dennis (1960) says, "It is difficult to believe that malnutrition can lead to scooting rather than creeping" (p. 54). Far more likely is the hypothesis that the children took different developmental courses because of what Dennis called "different learning situations."

Because of his experiences in Iran and Lebanon, Dennis moved well away from the maturationist position that he had taken early in his career, as evidenced by the following quote:

> The results of the [Iranian orphanages] study challenge the widely held view that motor development consists in the emergence of a

behavioral sequence based primarily upon maturation. . . . These facts seen to indicate clearly that experience affects not only the ages at which motor items appear but also their very form. No doubt, the maturation of certain structures . . . is necessary before certain responses can be learned, but learning is also necessary. Maturation alone is insufficient to bring about most post-natal developments in behavior. (1960, p. 57)

Accelerated Motor Development as a Function of Experience

In the previous example, the generally slow progress toward walking of all the children and the fact that some of the children preferred scooting to creeping were said to result from the absence of a specific experience—the chance to spend time in the prone position, both in the crib and on the floor. In the next example, we will see that when specific experiences are provided earlier than they usually occur, motor development can be accelerated. The first example we will use is one provided by Burton White of Harvard University. It deals with the onset of visually guided reaching in infancy. The second has to do with the effects of practicing reflexes.

Visually guided reaching is a behavior that is prerequisite to the development of one of the most important behavioral capacities of humans—the ability to take things into the hands so that they can be transported, manipulated, shaped, and studied. The general name for this grasping ability is *prehension,* an ability in which humans excel over all other creatures. In evolution the behavior was made possible when the animals who were ancestral to us first began to walk on two legs, thereby freeing the forelimbs (or arms) for functions other than locomotion.

Partly because of the critical importance of prehension to both the phylogenesis and the ontogenesis of human beings, White chose it for his studies of the plasticity of motor development (White, Castle, & Held, 1964; White & Held, 1966). Rather than look at aspects of the grasp per se, however, White looked at what preceded the grasp, that is, the visually guided reach that brings hand and object together.

White began his studies by making careful observations of the sequence of behaviors from birth to 5 months of age that are part of the natural sequence leading to accurate visually guided reaching (White, Castle, & Held, 1964). The sequence begins with eye and hand behaving independently. At around 2 months of age, however, infants begin making unilateral, close-fisted swipes at objects that they see. This at least was the first object-oriented arm movement that White was able to observe. The one-armed swipe gives way to bilateral responses in the third month. An important consequence of these bilateral movements of the arms in the field of vision is that one hand becomes an object that can be grasped by the other. Anyone who has been around infants of this age knows that children find watching their hands interact a fascinating activity. More than just being a temporary pleasure, however, this activity leads to permanent knowledge that is vitally important, namely, things that can be seen can also be touched. All one must do is get the hand to them. Once children have learned this, reaching and grasping become a dominant mode of interacting with the world. Initially, this is achieved by a reach that requires lots of visual monitoring (looking from the hand to the object and back to the hand). By the fifth month, however, it has become a smooth act, which White labeled the *top-level reach.* Top-level reaches can be initiated even when the hand is outside of the field of vision.

Although ages were given in the above discussion of the principal developments in the attainment of visually guided reaching, the whole point of White's experimental studies was to show that there is great plasticity in the actual time at which the behaviors are acquired. For example, after collecting normative data on the development of this sequence in infants, all of whom shared the same hospital environment for the first 6 months of their lives, White and his colleague Richard Held (White & Held, 1966) introduced two experimental conditions. One was a "massive-enrichment" condition and the other a "modified-enrichment" condition. For the massive-enrichment condition, attractive objects were hung above the cribs so that the children could look at them while lying on their backs. Also, three times each day from the age of 37 days to 124 days, the nursing staff raised the crib liners and placed the massive-enrichment-condition infants on their stomachs so that they could look out at the ward in which they were housed. Normally they would have been left supine like Dennis's infants and without a view of the activities on the ward. Finally, the liners to the cribs were made colorful and attractive so that even when the liners were down the infants had something interesting to look at.

Infants in the modified-enrichment condition were treated somewhat differently. First, the attractive toys were not hung overhead until Day 69. Second, the infants were not placed on their stomachs at all, and the liners on their cribs were left plain. They did, however, get a little extra visual stimulation from Days 37 to 68. During this period two attractively mounted pacifiers were placed near each infant's head (see Figure 3-9). These were designed to elicit both looking and grasping.

Both the massive- and modified-enrichment groups showed rapid development of the top-level reach relative to control infants—infants who received the same amount of extra handling as the experimental infants but who otherwise were not given any extra visual enrichment. Overall, the top-level reach was achieved about 2 months early in the experimental groups. This is quite an advance over a behavior that under normal circumstances would not appear until 5 months. Clearly, the development of the eye–hand coordination required for top-level reaching is not strictly a function of maturation.

To explain this effect, White and Held focused on visual–motor responses as the crucial variable. Looking alone, they argued, is not sufficient to promote normal development. Looking must be coupled with self-initi-

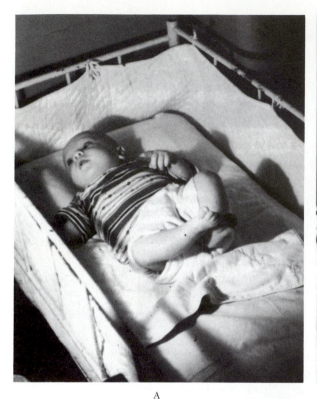

A

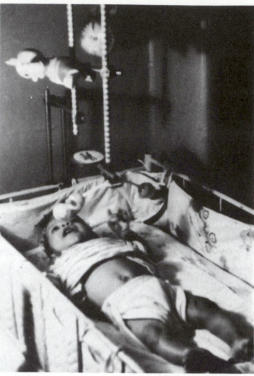

B

FIGURE 3-9
Conditions That Affect the
Development of Reaching
These photographs show the normal
visual environment (A), the massively
enriched environment (B), and the
moderately enriched environment (C)
that were experienced by the groups of
children in the White and Held (1966)
study. The accompanying table (on p.
123) describes more precisely the way
in which the experimental conditions
differed. (After White & Held, 1966)

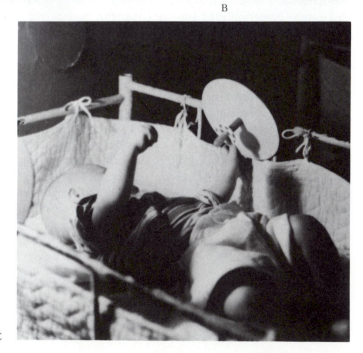

C

GROUP	DAYS		
	6–36	37–68	69–124
Control	20 minutes extra handling by nurse	No treatment	No treatment
Massive Enrichment	20 minutes extra handling by nurse	Prone position after feeding; crib liners removed; multicolored sheets; special mobiles placed over crib	These treatments continued until day 124
Moderate Enrichment	20 minutes extra handling by nurse	Two pacifiers attached to crib rail	Special mobiles placed over crib

SOURCE: Adapted from "Plasticity of Sensorimotor Development in the Human Infant" by B. L. White and R. Held, in *The Causes of Behavior,* Vol. 2, by J. F. Rosenblith and W. Allinsmith (Eds.), 1966, Boston: Allyn & Bacon, Inc. Copyright © 1966 by Allyn & Bacon, Inc. Reprinted by permission.

ated actions directed at the things one is looking at. Thus White and Held were not surprised that the massive-enrichment group did not develop the top-level reach sooner than the modified-enrichment group. The reason is that the first group had more to look at, but not more to visually and manually interact with. In fact, White and Held argued that the moderately enriched environment was better for eliciting visual–motor acts, because in this condition the two targets were directly in the child's line of sight and reach when the infant was lying in the crib in the postural position created by the asymmetrical *tonic neck reflex* (see Figure 3-10). This position dominates among the postures that young infants assume while they are lying on their backs; thus, in the moderately enriched condition, infants had their eyes, extended hand, and target all in line, ready to interact and thereby promote optimal development.

Though White and Held's enrichment study indicated that self-initiated visual–motor action might be crucial in stimulating the onset of the top-level reach, the study was inadequate to demonstrate actual causality. The authors acknowledged this limitation. "Our initial studies were designed," they said, "to assess the modifiability of [the rates of motor development] by introducing relatively gross environmental alterations. Future research . . . will become more analytical, with the identification of specific experimental factors as their goal" (White & Held, 1966, p. 60). What they mean by "analytical" will become clear in the next example, which by virtue of its "analytical design" is able to clearly identify exercise of the stepping reflex as a factor that leads to accelerated walking in a group of infants.

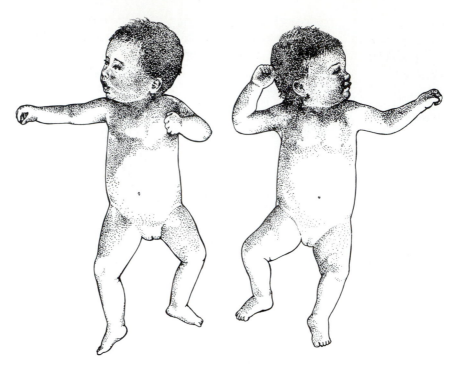

FIGURE 3-10
The Tonic Neck Reflex
When young infants (ages 0 to 3 months) are on their back, their head is usually to one side. In addition, it is characteristic for the arm and leg on the side to which the head is turned to be extended and for the contralateral arm and leg to be flexed. This posture is caused by the tonic neck reflex.

According to norms that have been developed for use with the Denver Developmental Screening Test, the ability to walk alone appears on average at 11.7 months of age. The maturationists thought that whatever variability existed around this average value was due to individual differences in rates of maturation, but not to experience. We already know from the earlier example of Dennis's research in Lebanon and Iran that this is not so. The present example will further show the error in thinking that maturation alone explains development.

Figure 3-11 shows the stepping reflex and the procedure for eliciting it in infants under 8 weeks of age. The infant is held under the arms with his or her bare feet resting on a flat surface. The touch of the feet to the surface will stimulate the stepping movements. Until recently the stepping reflex was thought to be a rather useless bit of behavior in that it served no function in the infant's life. It still is not thought of as important to future motor development, but University of Minnesota psychologist Phillip Zelazo has made the interesting observation that exercising this reflex can have a functional out-come: it speeds up the development of walking. Zelazo and his colleagues (Zelazo, Zelazo, & Kolb, 1972) showed this in an experiment that narrowed the possible explanations for accelerated walking to just practice.

For their experiment, Zelazo and his colleagues randomly divided twenty-four infants into four groups of six infants each. Only one of these groups (the active-exercise group) was given a regular opportunity to prac-tice the stepping reflex. This opportunity came in 3-minute practice sessions that took place four times daily. The sessions were continued until the chil-dren were 8 weeks old, the age at which the reflex usually disappears. The other three groups in the study were used as control groups. In one, the passive-exercise group, the infants were exercised four times daily just like

FIGURE 3-11
The Stepping Reflex
The stepping reflex shown here can be easily elicited up until about 8 weeks of age by supporting an infant in an upright position with his or her feet touching a flat surface.

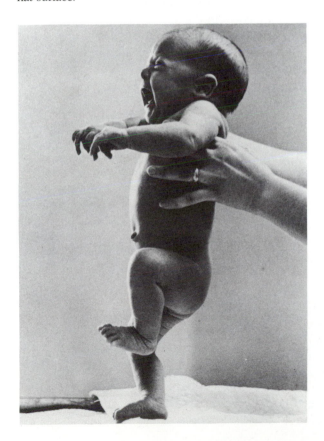

the experimental infants, but they were not given a chance to exercise the stepping reflex. For example, infants in this group might have their arms and legs pumped while lying on their backs. A second control group, the no-exercise group, was given no exercise but was tested on the same schedule as the infants in the first two groups. These tests occurred weekly. The infants were placed in the position shown in Figure 3-11 and the number of stepping movements made were counted. The third control group was not tested until the eighth week of the study, the point at which the experimental interventions ceased. The performance of this group at this session gave a way of assessing the influence that the test sessions alone might have had on prolonging the stepping reflex. This group was referred to as the 8-week control.

As you can see in Figure 3-12, there were large differences among the groups in the number of stepping responses made in the test sessions. For example, infants in the active-exercise group made an average of 30 stepping responses per minute at the 8-week point. Passive- and no-exercise subjects made only 3. The 8-week control group made 0. One conclusion to be drawn from these results is that the strength of the stepping reflex at 8 weeks is purely a function of practice. In the absence of practice, it drops out—the species-typical outcome. With practice, the reflex is still strong and getting stronger at the 8-week point in development. Zelazo and his colleagues went on to show that there may be some practical interest in this

FIGURE 3-12

Preserving the Stepping Reflex

Data from Zelazo, Zelazo, and Kolb (1972) show that the strength of the stepping reflex is a function of age and of exercise. As this graph shows, it is only the active-exercise group in which the stepping reflex is still strong and getting stronger at 8 weeks—the point at which this reflex normally disappears. (After Zelazo, Zelazo, & Kolb, 1972)

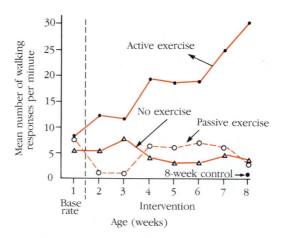

phenomenon. They showed this by tracking their infants until they began walking. Infants who had received the active practice sessions until their eighth week walked sooner on average (10.12 months) than infants in any of the other groups, with the 8-week control group being the last to walk (12.35 months on average).

Although no one doubts Zelazo's results, there is some recent debate over their explanation. Zelazo (1976) attributed his results regarding both the prolonged reflex and the accelerated walking to learning—**instrumental learning** to be exact, the same learning that results in a rat pressing a bar in a Skinner box. Esther Thelen of the University of Missouri contests this view with data that show that the "stepping reflex" is motorically the same as the leg kicks infants make spontaneously when on their backs and active (Thelen & Fisher, 1982). This leads her to believe that the stepping reflex is really just a vertical leg kick. The reason it drops out at 8 weeks of age in the absence of training is that the legs have become too heavy to lift. Practicing the reflex promotes muscle development, which thereby accounts not only for the presence of the vertical-kick/stepping-response beyond 8 weeks of age but also for the accelerated walking. The effects Zelazo observed are due, therefore, not to learning, but to simple muscular development brought on by the species-atypical activity of daily practice in moving the legs against gravity.

Taken together, the studies discussed in this section clearly show the plasticity of motor development. Far from being purely a function of internally controlled maturation, motor development can be both slowed and accelerated through relevant experience. Dennis's work indicated, for example, that infants who do not have the chance to spend time on their stomachs do not engage in some of the motor acts that are precursors to walking. Thus, they are slower to walk and, for reasons that are not clearly specified, may prefer a not-so-typical form of locomotion such as scooting. White and Held argued that visual–motor experiences in combination are crucial to the development of such behaviors as visually guided reaching. Their data were certainly consistent with this argument. Taking a more analytical approach, Zelazo and his colleagues showed clearly that practice of the stepping reflex altered not only the strength of that reflex at 8 weeks of age but also the age at which children first began to walk. Whether Zelazo's results are due to learning in the central nervous system or simply to muscle growth, the point remains that there is considerable plasticity for the time at which motor patterns appear and disappear.

Cognitive Development

Just as motor development can be accelerated or retarded as a result of experience, so too can cognitive development, an aspect of development that involves mental activities in general. Observations of children reared in orphanages and other unstimulating surroundings have always emphasized the detrimental effect of these environments on cognitive development. The observations of Rene Spitz (1945) and Howard Skeels (1966) are particularly well known in this regard. More recently, Jerome Kagan of Harvard University (Kagan & Klein, 1973) has shown that children reared in the unstimulating world of rural villages in Guatemala are slower in their initial cognitive development than children reared in Kagan's hometown of Cambridge, Massachusetts. Moreover, the children from a particular village—San Marcos—were especially slow. The aparent reason was that in this village it is the custom to leave infants in dark huts for the first year of their lives for fear they will be exposed to the "evil eye." To these observations we can add the further evidence supplied by data on deaf children. These children progress cognitively along the same path as hearing children, but they do so more slowly (Furth, 1966). There can be no doubt, then, that cognitive development can be slowed in the absence of adequate stimulation.

By the same token, enriched environments can accelerate cognitive development. David Feldman of Tufts University has pointed out, for example, a discrepancy between folkore and fact regarding the development of child prodigies. The folklore on child prodigies is that they are able to perform dazzling feats at an early age with little instruction or practice. This is wrong. "It is clear," writes Feldman, "that early prodigious achievement does not occur without extensive and often formal instruction" (1980, p. 146). Backing up such statements are the experiences of two of the best known child prodigies in this century—William James Sidis and Norbert Wiener. The fathers of both of these prodigies strongly disagreed with the educators of the day who believed that the mind of a child should be allowed to lie fallow for its first 6 years. Consequently they made extensive efforts to educate their children, beginning even in the crib years. Their efforts were rewarded. William Sidis was enrolled at Harvard at the age of 11. Norbert Wiener took his PhD from that institution at the age of 18. In the previous century, the efforts of Karl Witte's father to provide his son with a superior education resulted in Karl's starting college at 10, receiving a PhD at age 14, a Doctor of Laws degree at age 16, and then going on to become an important legal and literary scholar (Bruce, 1914). Although these case histories in no way demonstrate that training alone makes a Sidis, Weiner, or Witte, they are persuasive in arguing that cognitive development can be enhanced through enrichment programs.

The discovery of the plasticity of intellect is an important one for developmental psychology to have made. One reason is that it leads to the conclusion that the incidence of mental retardation can be reduced. Not all retardation can be eliminated, because some retardation is *organically* based. This means that there is a fundamental abnormality in the nervous system that limits cognitive potential. Such cases, though, make up a small portion of the total population of individuals who, because of low intelligence, cannot function on their own. The rest are appropriate targets for intervention programs that have as their goal the elimination of the most frequent type of retardation, *cultural–familial retardation* (see Chapter 10).

In the early 1960s, Project Head Start was begun in this country with the explicit goal of raising the cognitive abilities of that portion of our youth who experienced the greatest environmental blocks to achieving reasonable levels of intelligence. Head Start has had only limited success in meeting this goal, but the reasons may have more to do with politics than with the actual plasticity of intelligence (Caruso, Taylor, & Detterman, 1982). Smaller-scale intervention programs have been quite successful (Lazar, Darlington, Murray, Royce, & Snipper, 1982). One of the best examples of a small-scale (but nonetheless expensive) intervention program is the Carolina Abecedarian Project, which was conducted by Craig Ramey and his colleagues at the University of North Carolina (see Ramey, Bryant, & Suarez, 1985; Ramey & Campbell, 1984; Ramey & Haskins, 1981). This project exemplifies the type of changes that can be produced in cognition through early education programs.

The Abecedarian Project was conducted with children from families that were considered to be at high risk for producing retarded children. For example, all of the families were welfare families, and most were single-parent families. Moreover, the parents themselves were of low intelligence (with IQ's of 70 to 85), unemployed, and uneducated.

The children selected for the Abecedarian Project all began in the program between their sixth and twelfth week of life. This very early intervention was considered crucial by the project directors in order to forestall the forces that might work to retard the children. All told, there were four cohorts of about 28 children each to enter the program. In each cohort, half of the children were assigned to an experimental group that attended a special educational day-care program, which was offered from 7:15 A.M. to 5:15 P.M. daily, 5 days a week, and 50 weeks a year. The student-to-teacher ratio was low, and the educational programs were carefully planned to facilitate cognitive growth. The second half of each cohort was assigned to a control group. The control group was like the experimental group in every way except children in this group did not attend the day-care program. Both groups got free pediatric care, dietary supplements, and social services. The reason was that the investigators wanted to be sure that any increases in intelligence in the experimental group were due to their educational program and not incidental factors like better diet or health care.

Data are available on the IQs of children in the Abecedarian Project through 60 months of age (Ramey, Bryant, & Suarez, 1985). These are given in Figure 3-13. As is apparent in this chart, educational day care made a consistent difference in the *test scores* of the children. Whether this represents a change in adaptive intelligence that is as large as the test score difference is a matter of some debate. To be on the conservative side in interpreting the Abecedarian results, therefore, one should perhaps just say that the experimental group has scored higher on standardized tests than the control group at every age they have been tested; that the true absolute difference in test-taking performance probably lies somewhere in the range of 7 to 15 IQ points; and that this difference has been resistant to changes in type of test, sample size, and some vagaries in group membership. The potential importance of such differences, however, is staggering when you consider that an average gain of as few as 5 points of IQ, if experienced

FIGURE 3-13

The Abecedarian Project

Results from the Abecedarian Project show that the experimental-group children have consistently scored higher on standardized tests of intelligence than have the control-group children. A score of 100 reflects performance at the national average on each of the tests. The various tests that have been used—the Bayley, the Binet, and the Wechsler—will be described in Chapter 10.

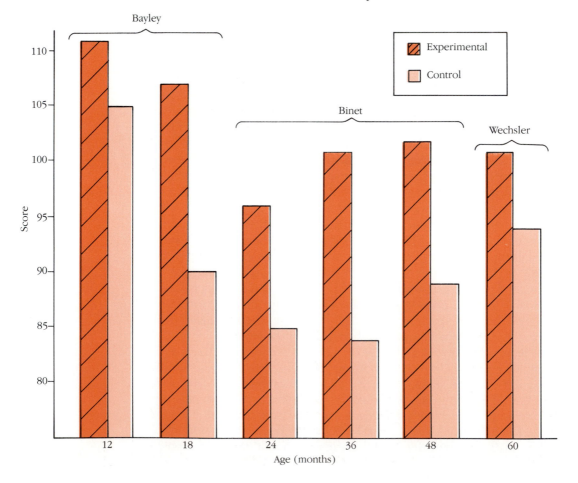

across the full range of IQs and if reflective of true changes in intellectual competence, would double the percentage of people in the population at large who, by current standards, are considered gifted (IQ of 130 or above) and halve the number of individuals who are considered retarded (IQ of 69 or below).

Although not all psychologists are convinced that data such as those produced by the Abecedarian Project really promise a mass reduction of retardation through environmental programs (see, for example, Jensen, 1981), even the strongest critic would acknowledge that cognitive potential and cognitive achievement can be altered. The only question surrounds the issue of how much they can be changed. At present, we need only to understand that cognitive development as reflected in intelligence is a plastic trait. Kagan's data from Guatemala, the case histories of child prodigies, and careful studies such as the Abecedarian Project provide evidence that this is the case, because they show that retardation, normality, and genius are all in part explained by the different environments in which people are reared.

Psychopathology

As a final example of a large-scale developmental process in which rearing makes a difference, we can take the example of the development of mental illness. Since Freud, it has been widely accepted that the causes of mental illness are not always organic (that is, biological). Environmental factors— either specific traumas or chronic experiences in our total life histories— have been widely accepted as causal factors in mental illness. More recently, however, the organic factors have been receiving renewed emphasis with the discovery that genetic differences among people are highly associated with specific disorders such as schizophrenia, depression, and alcoholism (see Chapter 5). The point to make here is that even though biological factors surely play a large role in the development of mental illness, so too do environmental variables. Therefore, mental illness is no more determined by biological variables alone than is physical development, motor development, or cognitive development.

There can be no better evidence that a developmental model of mental illness will always require environmental components than the fact that identical twins do not always share mental illness. In fact, for schizophrenia, which is the form of mental illness thought to be most strongly influenced by biological factors, identical twins are no more likely to share the disease than a coin is to come up tails. That is to say, there is only about a 50 percent chance of an individual being (or becoming) schizophrenic if he or she has an identical twin who has already been diagnosed as schizophrenic (see Gottesman & Shields, 1982, tabs. 6-1 and 6-2). This, of course, is far greater than the odds of someone being schizophrenic given that a neighbor or some other unrelated person has the disease. (The odds of this are only 1 in 100.) Nonetheless, a 50–50 chance of schizophrenia in someone who is the genetic copy of a schizophrenic is a far cry from biological determinism. In fact, it is a clear argument for the epigenetic interaction of nature and nurture.

The case for interactionism in psychopathology is enhanced further when we examine the case histories of individual twins who have been jointly diagnosed schizophrenic. Even when the twins share the disease, they often do not share the exact symptoms, time of onset, or severity. A vivid example of this is provided in the case history of the Genain sisters—quadruplets, all of whom became schizophrenic (see Figure 3-14).

Hester was the first of the Genain sisters to show clear evidence of mental illness, and to this day she is the most severely affected. Her clinical record states that around age 18 she became very irritable and destructive. She knocked out her sister Nora for no reason, she kicked her mother in the shins, she broke light bulbs, and tore buttons from her clothes. Her apparent emotional disturbance led to her being withdrawn from school prior to the start of the twelfth grade. The other three girls—Nora, Iris, and Myra—went on to finish school and take jobs as secretaries in their hometown.

The next to become ill was Nora. By age 20 she had become exceedingly "nervous" and a year later was unable to continue working. She stayed home, where she behaved in odd ways such as standing on her knees and elbows until her elbows began to bleed. She would also moan aloud at meals.

Iris was 22 when she left work. Like Nora, she too had become extremely nervous at work and was totally unable to accept criticism, whether real or implied. There were other symptoms as well. One was "stomach trouble." According to a supervisor at work, "She would sit [in the grill] at lunch time and eat lunch and she'd vomit up her food right on the counter. Then dazed she'd just look at it, order another meal, and wouldn't even attempt to move and clean it up" (Rosenthal, 1963, p. 121).

Throughout her childhood, Myra had been the best adjusted of the Genain sisters, but with three sick sisters and an increasingly deranged father who fought constantly to keep her from having social contacts outside the family, the strain began to show. At 24, Myra, too, left work. The precipitating incident occurred when an older man scared her while she was working alone in her office. "That evening, Myra came home from work at the usual time, crying and feeling very nervous, and immediately ran up to her bedroom" (Rosenthal, 1963, p. 141). During that night and subsequent nights she awoke screaming, "Mama, help me." According to the doctor who treated her at this time, she was having a "partial" psychotic episode.

At about this time in their lives, the Genain sisters came to the attention of researchers at the National Institute of Mental Health (NIMH) where they went for treatment. Today, their case histories are still being followed by researchers there. At last report (Hamer, 1982), Iris, Nora, and Hester

FIGURE 3-14
The Genain Sisters
Nora, Iris, Myra, and Hester are not the real names of these quadruplets. Nor is
Genain their real family name. The first names were made up to correspond to the
letters in the acronym for the National Institute of Mental Health (NIMH). The last
name is a neologism constructed to mean "unfortunate gene."

are living with their mother and must take antipsychotic medication. Myra, however, is married and apparently cured of her schizophrenia.

It is, of course, impossible to say what factors in the Genain sisters' development account for the different courses taken by their disease. Rosenthal, in his compilation of all the data available on the Genain sisters (1963), offers some suggestions: differences in the girls' success in establishing friendships outside the home, differences in the extent to which the girls identified with their father, and differences in the levels of stress to which they were exposed. These, however, are nothing more than suggestions of possible causes. All that can be said with any certitude is that these girls, with the same genotype who grew up together in the same family, still had remarkably different life experiences and, furthermore, that these differences affected the way in which their genetic propensity for schizophrenia expressed itself.

SUMMARY

Although developmental psychologists historically have been inclined to view development as controlled by either nature or nurture, contemporary developmental psychologists view it as an emergent process in which neither nature nor nurture is all-controlling. This makes contemporary developmental psychologists epigeneticists rather than nativists or environmentalists. To explain development, epigeneticists appeal not to nature or nurture alone, but to their interaction. Examples of development, such as the one involving the development of weight and exploratory behavior in mice, make it clear why this approach is necessary.

The epigenetic view of development can be pictorially represented using Waddington's epigenetic landscape. Heredity gives initial shape to this landscape by laying out a great variety of developmental paths that are within the genetic potential of the animal to achieve. The actual paths taken, however, are determined through the interaction of nature and nurture over time. An important feature of Waddington's landscape is that the paths are drawn with varying degrees of canalization. This captures the epigenetic belief that though there are a great number of paths open to development, not all the paths are equally probable.

Canalization, though it enhances the probability that a particular path will be taken, is not equivalent to predetermination. This became evident in the examples of research by Zing Yang Kuo, which showed that even the most deeply canalized routes, such as those leading to species-typical behaviors (instincts), are not invariably followed. Development, therefore, must be conceived of as a plastic process, malleable through alterations in the environment, with the extent of malleability being a function of the genotype.

In the years since Kuo first showed the plasticity of instincts, psychologists have shown that there is plasticity even in those broad areas of human development where one might naively expect little malleability. The ones covered here were motor development, physical growth, cognitive development, and psychopathology. As was shown in the cases of psychosocial dwarfism and Widdowson's despotic director, physical development, for example, is plastic due to variations in diet and, more interestingly, psychological stress. Motor development, despite the beliefs of early maturationists, can be speeded up, slowed down, and even changed somewhat in form (for example, scooting rather than creeping among Iranian orphans). Cognitive development is susceptible to similar environmentally induced changes. Society's greatest interest in this fact lies in the hope that familial retardation can be reduced significantly through early intervention programs like the Carolina Abecedarian Project. Plasticity in psychopathology was illustrated using the case of the Genain sisters, genetically identical quadruplets living in the same family who nevertheless achieved different case histories with regard to onset, symptoms, and severity of their schizophrenia.

SUGGESTIONS FOR FURTHER READING

Anastasi, A. (1958). Heredity, environment, and the question "how?" *Psychological Review, 65,* 197–208. This address to the Division of General Psychology at the meeting of the American Psychological Association in 1957 marked the beginning of the end for the either–or version of the nature–nurture debate.

Kuo, Z. Y. (1967). *The dynamics of behavior development: An epigenetic view.* New York: Random House. A classic treatment of the contemporary epigenetic view in developmental psychology by a Chinese scholar who helped forge this view through his careful studies of animal development.

Lerner, R. M. (1984). *On the nature of human plasticitiy.* Cambridge: Cambridge University Press. A difficult but rewarding text for the advanced student.

Rosenthal, D. (Ed.). (1963). *The Genain quadruplets: A case study and theoretical analysis of heredity and environment in schizophrenia.* New York: Basic Books. A fascinating case history full of rich detail regarding the lives of the Genain sisters and their parents.

CHAPTER OUTLINE

CHAPTER 4

Development as an Epigenetic Process: The Importance of Timing

The epigenetic view of development presented in the last chapter contained no assumptions about the role that maturational state plays in the interactions of nature and nurture. It turns out, however, that in both human and animal development, maturational state can be quite important. This notion is probably not foreign to you. Old sayings such as "You can't teach an old dog new tricks" and "Strike while the iron is hot" embody the belief that some moments in development are more propitious than others. In these particular instances, for example, the state of the dog and the state of the iron have a lot to do with the changes that will occur when the one is taught and the other is struck. To switch from adages to developmental data, consider the effects that a vitamin-A overdose can have on the development of rat pups. If the overdose is given on Days 8–10 of a rat's 23-day pregnancy, the rat pups will have no cortex development in their brains, a condition known as *anencephaly*. They will also have eye defects. If the overdose comes during Days 11–13, the rats will have normal brains and eyes but be afflicted with a cleft palate. An overdose between Days 18–20 has yet another effect: it produces cataracts on the eyes (see Goldstein, Aronow, & Kalman, 1974, p. 710).

The consideration of embryonic rats, old dogs, and hot irons raises an interesting question that the first part of this chapter will serve to answer: To what extent is the plasticity of animal and human development constrained by temporal considerations? In other words, is development organized such that there are brief moments in which development gets routed along one path or another and that beyond these moments plasticity yields to fixity? As we will see, for some animals there are periods of special developmental importance that put permanent constraints on the plasticity of some developments. In these special time periods, called **critical periods,** development is easily influenced by factors that in another time period would have a different influence, less of an influence, or perhaps no influence at all.

CRITICAL PERIODS IN EMBRYOLOGICAL DEVELOPMENT

The relevance of the critical-period concept to both animal and human development is most clearly evident in the prenatal months during the period of **organogenesis.** This period, which lies at the very start of prenatal development (see Figure 4-1), derives its name from the fact that during this time the various organs of the body and the specialized tissues that make them up differentiate out of previously undifferentiated tissue and cell masses. For example, shortly after a mammalian embryo first attaches itself to the wall of the uterus, it consists of just three types of tissue—ectoderm, mesoderm, and endoderm. These three types, arranged in layers, make up the whole animal organism. No matter how closely you examine any one of these layers, you will not see in it any of the organs that it will eventually form. But out of each will arise all the specialized organs and tissues that make up the mature animal (Moore, 1977, p. 63). In the ectoderm, for example, are cells that will lead to the development of the entire brain and nervous system. In the mesoderm are cells that will give rise to all of the muscles and the bones to which they attach. In the endoderm are cells that

FIGURE 4-1

Susceptibility to Teratogens During Organogenesis

Sensitivity to teratogenic agents is highest during the period of organogenesis and then tapers off during later periods of prenatal development. (Graph by Tom Shepard of the University of Washington School of Medicine.)

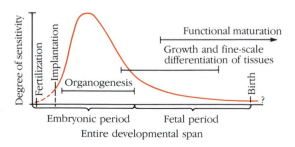

are precursors to all of the cells that will make up the elaborate structures of the alimentary canal.

Given the fact that the development of tissues, organs, and organ systems proceeds epigenetically from formlessness to form, from lack of differentiation to differentiation, and from little organization to elaborate organization, critical periods for embryological development are a necessity. The reason is that biophysical choices must be made as one proceeds down the epigenetic landscape, and some of these choices are final (for example, whether a particular undifferentiated cell will become a bone cell or a muscle cell). Because there is but one developmental moment at which some choices are made, events occurring at these choice times determine whether development is routed along one or another of the several possible paths. Somewhat earlier or later the same events would have a different effect, a fact that gives further testimony to the need for an interactionist perspective on the workings of nature and nurture.

A crucial question to be answered is whether an epigenetic model featuring final choices made during critical periods has any relevance for animal and human psychological development in the postnatal period. First, however, we will examine the relevance of this epigenetic model in embryological development, where it helps us to understand some of the data on birth defects.

We have already seen in the example of vitamin-A overdose effects on rats the importance of the critical-period concept to an understanding of birth defects. In that example, it was clear that anencephaly, cataracts, and cleft palate were not caused by the vitamin A alone. They were caused by the vitamin A acting at a *specific time* in the organ development of rats. Many human birth defects develop in precisely the same way. Some environmental agent is the cause, but the effect cannot be understood independently of the time when the agent appears.

The environmental agents that can cause disruptions of organogenesis include drugs, hormones, viruses, and radiation. When they do in fact lead to birth defects, these agents are labeled as **teratogens,** which in literal translation means "monster maker." One well known human teratogen is rubella, the virus responsible for the disease known as German measles. If a woman contracts this disease while she is pregnant, the virus will pass from the woman's bloodstream through a tissue barrier, called the *placenta,* into the developing child's blood supply. There, like all teratogens, its exact effects will be a function of the developments taking place at that time. If the virus is present in strength during the first trimester of development (the first 12 weeks), the effects will be quite different from the effects—if any—that the virus produces at later points in development.

The principal observable characteristics of the infant exposed to the rubella virus during the first trimester are threefold: cataracts on the eyes, abnormalities of the heart, and deafness. If a woman is infected by the ru-

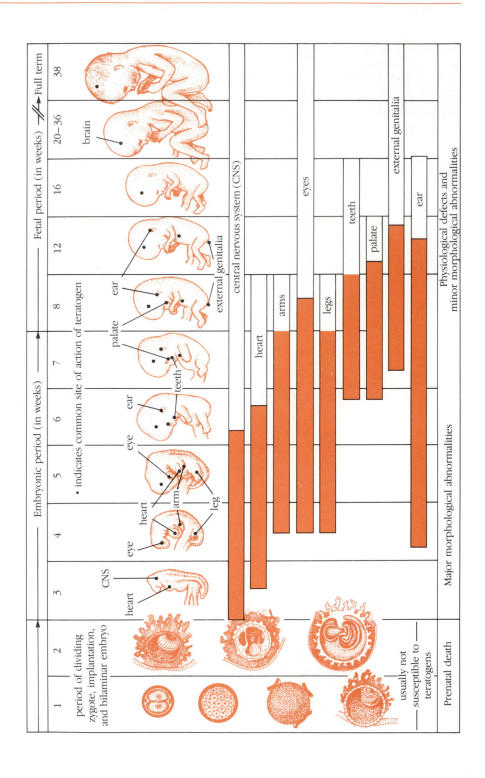

FIGURE 4-2 (Opposite)
Prenatal Development
Pictures of the embryo and fetus at the top of the chart indicate the developmental regions most subject to teratogenic effects at different points in prenatal development. Bar graphs at the bottom show the length of time that susceptibility lasts for the different regions. Black indicates the period of greatest susceptibility. Overall, the chart shows that the critical period for major anatomical development in humans lies between the 3rd and 12th week (the first trimester). Weeks 1 and 2 are not included in the critical period because adverse environmental events during this period are so detrimental that they usually result in abortion. (After Moore, 1977)

bella virus later in her pregnancy than the first trimester, this classic trilogy of symptoms will not be present and the overall risk for any congenital malformations will be low (Moore, 1977, p. 139). One can infer from this that teratogens do not create their damage by attacking existing structures; rather they have their effect by interfering with the developments taking place at the time the teratogen is introduced. Figure 4-2 shows a time chart of human prenatal development that features the most likely sites for teratogenic effects as a function of the time at which teratogens are introduced.

A second well-known teratogen, which has brought home in a horrifying way the developmental principle that there are critical periods during embryonic development, is the tranquilizing drug thalidomide. This drug was taken widely in Europe during the mid to late 1950s and was later associated with a rash of congenital defects involving the extremities (McBride, 1961). The defects in these so-called thalidomide babies occurred when their mothers had taken the drug between the 21st and 36th day of their pregnancies. Depending on when the drug was taken during this interval, the babies had stunted ears, arms, and legs or some combination of the three (see Figure 4-3). Interestingly, testing on rats had initially failed to turn up an indication that the drug could be teratogenic, and this was partly responsible for the tragedy in the first place. Later testing showed that rats were indeed susceptible—but only on the 12th day of gestation (Goldstein, Aronow, & Kalman, 1974, p. 718).

In addition to the rubella virus and thalidomide, a host of other teratogenic agents are known to exist. Some, like radiation or physical trauma (which might result from a severe blow), act directly. Most teratogenic effects, however, are created when the teratogen gets into the developing child's bloodstream. Prior to the thalidomide tragedy, it was thought that few substances crossed the placental barrier; now it is assumed that most do. Infectious agents, hormones, and drugs of all kinds (including alcohol and nicotine) can get into the baby's bloodstream, and when they do, they can have potentially damaging effects, depending on the developments occurring at the time they are introduced (see Figure 4-4).

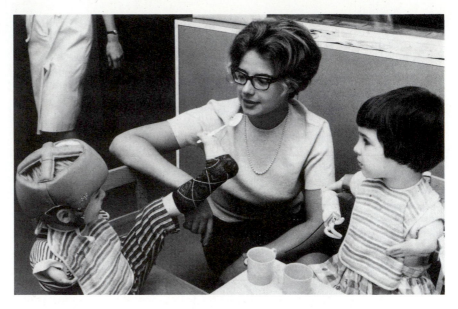

FIGURE 4-3
Effects of Thalidomide
These children show some of the typical effects that thalidomide had on development when mothers took the drug somewhere between the 21st and 36th days of their pregnancies.

EXTENDING THE CRITICAL-PERIOD CONCEPT TO PSYCHOLOGICAL DEVELOPMENT

The embryonic developments considered thus far—teratogenic effects on the physical development of humans and rats—are appropriately called critical-period effects because the effects are irreversible. Later interventions and influences can do nothing to alter the developmental consequences of these periods. The important question to ask now is whether the concept of critical periods is restricted to prenatal embryological development of the type we have been considering or whether it might have some applicability in the field of psychological epigenesis as well. Might it be that the nascent intellect, personality, and emotional system could be in some sense analogous to the developing endoderm, mesoderm, and ectoderm—initially formless and undetermined but taking on form and determination during specific developmental periods?

Psychologists from Freud until the present have led us to think that psychological and embryological development might have parallels by theorizing that behavior patterns established during critical periods of infancy and early childhood can become so firmly entrenched that subsequent

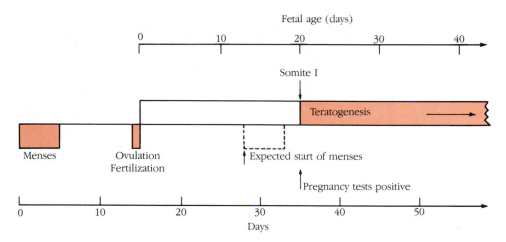

FIGURE 4-4
Relationship of Teratogenic Susceptibility and Pregnancy Diagnosis
This diagram illustrates an important fact that all potential mothers should be aware of. The critical period for teratogenesis extends from the 3rd to the 12th week of pregnancy. However, even the most regular of women would not suspect she was pregnant until the embryo was 2 weeks old. This leaves just 1 week during which a mother who is taking drugs can cease taking them before they have the potential of producing birth defects. The lesson in this is clear: sexually active women who are late in their period should assume they are pregnant and cease taking all drugs until they know otherwise. (After Goldstein, Aronow, & Kalman, 1974)

events in an individual's life are virtually powerless to change them. Freud (1949) for example, wrote "that neuroses are only acquired during early childhood (up to the age of 6), even though their symptoms may not make their appearance until much later." John B. Watson (1928) was equally adamant about the role of the early years in determining aspects of one's life course: "At three years of age," he wrote, "the child's whole emotional life plan has been laid down, his emotional disposition set." John Bowlby (1951) felt that poor maternal care during a child's early years could "have grave and far-reaching effects in his character and so on the whole of his future life." And Burton White (1971a) has stated "that much of the basic quality of the entire life of an individual is determined" during the years from 1 to 3.

While most modern developmentalists feel that the views of these theorists are overly pessimistic regarding the human potential for change (see, for example, Clarke & Clarke, 1976), a brief history of research on critical periods in development reveals why this fatalistic attitude toward the human potential for change was able to develop.

Early Research on Critical Periods in the Psychological Development of Animals

When the critical-period concept was first brought from embryology into psychology in the 1930s by ethologist Konrad Lorenz, it was with the thought that the development of an animal's behavior, like the development of its anatomy, might indeed be subject to critical periods, periods during which future status would be established by whatever was ongoing in the developmental environment of the moment. **Psychogenesis** in this view was seen as analogous to organogenesis, at least in the sense that critical events at critical times might leave as permanent an impression on the thoughts and perceptions of the mind as rubella leaves on the structure of the heart.

Providing the initial fuel for speculation that there might be organogenic and psychogenic parallels was Lorenz's excellent example of a parallel in the development of certain lifelong behavioral preferences in many species of birds (Lorenz, 1935/1970). According to Lorenz, these preferences were stamped into the developing brain, or "imprinted," during time periods every bit as critical as those for prenatal organ development. One preference involved the object of a young bird's *filial* (child-to-parent) affections; the other, the object of its adult sexual attractions. Not all birds showed a similar developmental pattern, but most of those that were ground-nesters and precocious in their motor development did. These birds, known as precocial birds, provide countless illustrations of the learning process that has come to be known as **imprinting.**

Imprinting

The premier example of imprinting in precocial birds is called *filial imprinting* because it serves to establish the affectional bond between a fledgling bird and its mother. The species-typical outcome for this process is for a young bird to establish an attachment to its *own* mother. What Lorenz and a few investigators before him showed, however, was that this attachment for one's own mother was not innate. Young birds could become attached to a great variety of other animals and even inanimate objects (for example, moving boxes and motor-driven decoys; see Figure 4-5). The crucial factor was exposure, usually in the hours just after hatching. Research showed that in most species of precocial birds, the first mobile object that young birds saw after hatching became the object of their imprinting. They would follow it and show distress whenever they became separated from it. This is illustrated in the experience of a German scientist, Oskar Heinroth, who raised some goose eggs in an incubator and then became the first animate object the newly hatched goslings saw when the incubator was opened.

FIGURE 4-5
Imprinting
These pictures show some of the wide variety of objects to which birds have been imprinted. They include Konrad Lorenz (A), some colored balls (B), and a mallard decoy (C).

Without any display of fear, they stare calmly at human beings and do not resist handling. If one spends just a little time with them, it is not so easy to get rid of them afterwards. They pipe piteously if left behind and soon follow reliably. It has happened to me that such a gosling, a few hours after removal from the incubator, was content as long as it could settle under the chair on which I sat. If such a gosling is carried to a goose family . . . the gosling runs off, piping, and attaches itself to the first human being that happens to come past; it regards the human being as its parent. (in Lorenz, 1935/1970, p. 126)

The second instance of imprinting in precocial birds is known as *sexual imprinting* because it serves to establish the sexual attraction between adult birds and opposite-sex members of their own species. Interestingly, this development is a by-product of filial imprinting. Thus if a young bird is imprinted on an adult of an alien species, the misimprinted bird will be attracted to opposite-sex members of the alien species as an adult. This is evident when misimprinted birds are observed during their first mating season. Rather than copulate with available members of their own species, they choose members of the alien species. Lorenz (1955) listed parrots, cockatoos, eagles, owls, and Andean geese as species in which this reaction has been observed. In some cases of cross-species imprinting, the alien species has even been dramatically different from the bird's own species. In one of the more bizarre cases of cross-species sexual imprinting, for example, a white peacock at the Schonbrunn Zoo in Vienna, Austria, was imprinted on a giant Galápagos tortoise. Annually, during the mating season, this peacock performed its mating dance exclusively for the tortoise and attempted to mate with it (Sluckin, 1965, p. 55–56). Other bizarre outcomes result when cross-species imprinting involves animals of disproportionate size. In these cases, the small animal will select but a portion of the larger animal as its object of affection. For example, in one instance of this phenomenon, a group of domestic roosters made a sexual fetish out of their keeper's yellow glove and performed their mating rituals for it and it alone (Guiton, 1966).

Other Critical-Period Developments

Following on the heels of the study of imprinting in birds were studies on the formation of social relations in a number of other animals, many of which seemed to be subject to the same critical-period effects.

Social Relations in Dogs   In a series of studies on dogs, for example, J. P. Scott (see Scott & Fuller, 1965), working at the Jackson Laboratory in Bar Harbor, Maine, found that the period from 3 to 12 weeks following birth is a very important time period in the social development of dogs. Dogs kept isolated from humans during this period were later fearful of them. Even when this fear was overcome through forced contact, the isolated dogs never became as affec-

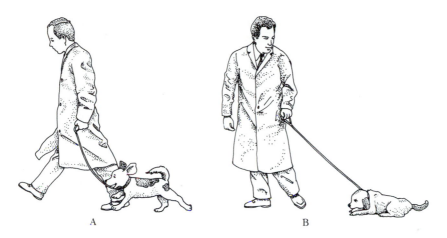

A   B

FIGURE 4-6

Effects of Different Critical-Period Experiences on Socialization

Dogs of the same species react quite differently to leash training when their experiences during the critical period for primary socialization are different. The puppy in panel A had contact with people for a week during the most sensitive phase of the critical period. The puppy in panel B spent the critical period with other dogs. One of the consequences of this difference in early experience was that Dog A was easily leash trained because he was already prone to follow humans. Dog B, however, was fearful and refused to follow.

tionate as dogs that were exposed to humans during the period from 3 to 12 weeks (see Figure 4-6). What was true of contact with humans was true of contact with other species, as well. The period from 3 to 12 weeks, therefore, seemed to be a period for what Scott called *primary socialization,* and the events of this period had lifelong implications.

Social Relations in Rhesus Monkeys   At the same time that the Bar Harbor work on dogs was being conducted, Harry Harlow of the University of Wisconsin was working with infant monkeys. Part of his research involved isolating the monkeys from all social contact with other monkeys. What he found was that monkeys left in isolation less than 6 months could later adapt to normal social life in a monkey troop, but monkeys kept isolated longer than 6 months never adapted (Harlow, Dodsworth, & Harlow, 1965). This finding implied that there is a critical period in the social development of monkeys just as there is in dogs and some birds. Social contacts during this period, it appeared, are essential to normal development. When they are omitted, the prospects for social development are permanently altered.

Maternal Bonding   In yet other research that was being conducted at roughly the same point in history, investigators were finding evidence that maternal responses to infants in the minutes and hours following birth were essential in establishing a **maternal bond,** without which a mother would simply ignore her young. In cats, for example, the tie binding mother to her kittens was shown to be influenced by the odor of birth fluids (Schneirla & Rosenblatt, 1961). Birth fluids also play a part in the establishment of a bond between female goats (called dams) and their offspring (Blauvelt, 1955). When exposed to any young goat in the 5 minutes just after birth, dams spend their time licking and grooming the young animal. Following this brief 5-minute exposure, the young goat can be separated from the dam without consequence for the attachment relation. Reunited as much as 4 hours later, the dam will recognize her "offspring" (even if it is not her own) and respond lovingly to it. When dams are not given 5 minutes of bonding time, an entirely different reaction occurs. A dam's own offspring and alien goats alike are butted away when they come to nurse (Klopfer, 1971; see Figure 4-7). Similar observations were made on sheep (Collias, 1956).

FIGURE 4-7
Maternal Bonding in Goats
Dams will be unaccepting of any kid that they have not been exposed to within 5 minutes following birth. The explanation is that goat mothers are hormonally primed in these first minutes to form a bond with their offspring. Kept from doing so during the critical period, dams will then butt away any young kid that comes to nurse, even their own.

Rat mothers also go through a period immediately after birth that is crucial to the successful rearing of offspring. Unlike the same period in goats, however, this period in rats does not serve as a time for mothers to form specific bonds to specific individuals. Rather it is a time for eliciting maternal behaviors (such as, nest building, retrieving pups that stray from the nest, and proper posturing for nursing) without which the pups could not survive (Rosenblatt & Lehrman, 1963; Rosenblatt & Siegel, 1981). Separation of rat mothers from their offspring in the immediate postpartum period leads to inadequate parenting and the eventual death of the offspring. Rats, goats, and sheep provide the best known instances of critical periods in the development of mothering behavior, but a few other mammalian species (for example, flying squirrels and primiparous rhesus monkeys) may have some parenting behaviors and dispositions triggered by the events of the immediate postpartum period as well.

The discovery in the 1950s and 1960s that early social experiences were critical to later social development in animals served as scientific confirmation of the longstanding belief, promulgated by Freud and others, that the same was true in humans. This sense of scientific confirmation was only enhanced by discoveries in other areas of animal learning. Though this learning is distinct from the learning involved in filial and sexual imprinting, it nonetheless can be described—metaphorically anyway—as a kind of imprinting, because it involves a process whereby the experiences of a particular period in development seem to imprint themselves on the animal brain in an indelible way. One good example is the process by which some migratory birds develop the ability to use a star compass to orient themselves when flying at night.

Learning to Use a Star Compass   Not all migratory birds learn to use a star compass, but those that do learn to use this compass in the autumn of their first migration. Exposed to the night sky during the weeks that precede the migration, indigo buntings, for example, will later be able to maintain a southerly course in the fall and a northerly course in the spring using information from the night sky alone (see Figure 4-8). According to Cornell ornithologist Stephen Emlen, their navigational ability is based on recognition of the fact that all the stars in the sky rotate around a north–south axis that is anchored (approximately) by the North Star (see Emlen, 1975). (This rotation is evident if you look at the north sky throughout the night. The entire pattern of stars seems to spin about the North Star, which itself maintains a fairly constant position.) Learning to navigate by the North Star appears to be limited to a critical period in the bunting's development, because if young indigo buntings, ready for their first autumn migration, are not allowed to see the sky until after the migratory season has begun, they never learn to use a star compass no matter how often they see the night sky after that (Keeton, 1981).

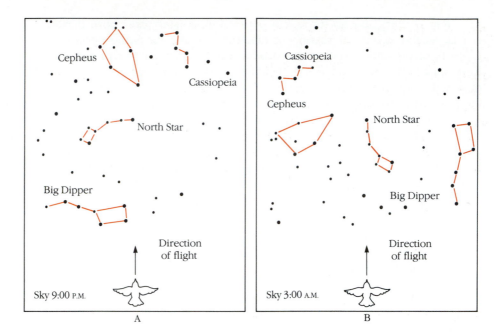

FIGURE 4-8
The Star Compass
The North Star is a convenient guide to direction because its position in the night sky is relatively invariant. The other stars appear to rotate about it. Indigo buntings and other migratory birds can locate the north–south axis that is anchored by the North Star and use it as a guide when flying at night. The development of this ability, however, seems to be restricted to a critical period in development.

Learning Birdsongs   A second example of lifelong learning that takes place through an imprintinglike process early in life is the learning of birdsongs (see Grier, 1984, for an overview). This learning, which has been studied extensively by Peter Marler, Fernando Nottebohm, and others at Rockefeller University, is characteristic of birds known as Passeriformes. Most birds in this order—which includes canaries, wrens, sparrows, and others—begin song learning in the summer they are hatched. During this time they are exposed to adult versions of their species' song—the one males produce to attract females and the one females respond to. The exposure serves to imprint key aspects of the song into their brain. Usually this process takes place only in the first summer, but songbirds born late in the hatching year may retain some impressionability into the next spring (Kroodsma & Pickert, 1980). In any event, once songbirds have been exposed to their song, this is all that is required for them later to be able to recognize it in the case of females and to produce it in the case of males. The data show, for example, that when testosterone levels begin to build in males the spring following their hatching year, song production begins. At first, the song is incomplete, consisting simply of subsong components. Through a trial-and-errorlike process in which they compare their own productions to the song in their memories, a correct adult song is eventually produced. We know this song is not "innate" because birds exposed initially to an incorrect song will wind up producing this incorrect song (or some version of it.)

Conclusion

With these examples before us of the type of research that was emanating from research sites all over Europe, England, and America in the 1950s and 1960s, you can appreciate some of the excitement that the critical-period concept produced. Indeed it did seem that the power of specific environmental events to shape behavior would wax, wane, and even disappear as a function of the maturational state of animals (Scott, 1962). This realization had sobering implications for human development. It implied that humans who underwent some species-atypical experience early in their development might be forever marked by the experience. They might not even be able to compensate for their deficits.

Are There Critical Periods in the Psychological Development of Humans?

The discovery that psychological developments in birds, goats, monkeys, rats, and dogs could be permanently influenced by events early in life led many investigators to jump to the conclusion that these time-constrained animal developments would find their parallels in human developments. The greatest concerns involved social development. Human mothers, like all others, need to love their infants for development to be optimal, and human infants need to be strongly attached to their mothers (and fathers) if socialization is to be most effective. What if the bonds and attachments did not develop at their appointed time? What if, for example, a human infant was isolated from his or her mother by being orphaned, hospitalized, or born prematurely? Might not these events, along with other deviations from the species-typical pattern, have long-term social implications? Many investigators thought so. Hence they warned that dire consequences, such as enhanced risk for social deviancy and child abuse, could result whenever infant development was left either incomplete or malformed at the time a critical-period door closed.

Evaluating the Evidence

In considering the relevance of the data on imprinting, bonding, and learning for humans, there are a number of factors to take into account. The first is that *analogy* is not *homology.* This is a biologist's way of saying that just because two things look alike does not mean that they are alike, not in any functional or evolutionary sense anyway. We must keep the biologist's admonition in mind, because there is a seductive tendency to think that resemblance implies functional and evolutionary relatedness. The seductiveness of this fallacious form of logic can be quite strong. For example, once young birds have imprinted on their mother, they will gather under their mother's wing when they are frightened. This behavior bears a resemblance to the behavior of young children who hide in their mother's skirt. We are apt to think that if the one is led to do this through imprinting, then the other is too. Likewise, goats and rats who abuse or neglect their offspring provide a powerful visual metaphor for human mothers who neglect and abuse their children. This can lead us to believe—quite unjustifiably—that if a bonding failure can account for the animal abuse, then perhaps it accounts for the human abuse as well. Such reasoning is known as reasoning by analogy. It has absolutely no claim on validity unless independent evidence can be obtained to show that similar mechanisms underlie the similar behaviors. To think otherwise—to believe from resemblance alone that there is a functional or evolutionary connection—is to make as fundamental an error in biological thinking as the correlation-implies-causation error is in statistical thinking.

To determine whether imprinting and bonding have their **homologs** in human development, we need to seek scientific evidence that the events in fact have similar functional characteristics or common evolutionary antecedents. As we will see in the following review of the evidence, there is no reason to believe that humans go through an imprintinglike process to establish their initial caretaker attachment. Nor is there evidence of a critical period during which the primary socialization of humans must take place. Critics are highly skeptical at best of the suggestion that human mothers form a special emotional bond with their infants homologous to the bond formed by sheep and goats.

Evaluating the Evidence for a Human Homolog to Imprinting   In the heyday of imprinting studies in the 1950s, the formation of an infant–mother attachment was thought to be restricted to a critical period, just as imprinting appeared to be (shortly we will see that not even imprinting is a truly critical-period affair). In the boldest statement of its type, Phillip Gray (1958) wrote, "It is reasonable to place the critical period for imprinting in humans from about six weeks to about six months. It begins with the onset of learning ability, continues with the smiling response, and ends with the fear of strangers" (p. 161). Others were more oblique. They did not say that humans imprinted necessarily but that there was, nonetheless, a period of primary socialization, much like the period in Scott's dogs, during which a one-on-one infant-to-adult attachment had to take place. John Bowlby (1951), the most influential proponent of this view, put the end of this period at about 12 months of age. Drawing on the embryological metaphor that was so prevalent at the time, Bowlby (1951, p. 54) wrote that beyond 12 months of age the character of the psychic tissues becomes fixed and is no longer susceptible to the effects of a "maternal organizer."

Taking up Bowlby's position first, a problem arises in that scientific studies fail to reveal that maternal deprivation in the first year has an unvarying and irreversible effect on later development. Bowlby had predicted that maternal deprivations as mild as those created by day care and group rearing (such as that practiced in hospitals, orphanages, and the Israeli kibbutzim) would have detrimental effects, but none have been found (Rutter, 1972). Even the severe deprivations suffered by motherless children have failed to yield evidence of long-term effects that can be attributed to the deprivation per se (Thompson & Grusec, 1970, p. 607). A study of children adopted into American homes out of refugee camps in Korea and Greece, for example, reported an amazing resiliency on the part of most of these children, a resiliency that was attributed to their ability to form meaningful relationships (Rathbun, McLaughlin, Bennett, & Garland, 1965). And even one of Bowlby's own studies, conducted on 60 children who spent from 6 months to 2 years in a tuberculosis sanitarium prior to age 4, failed to support his initial critical-period position. Children in this institution, for example, did not give evidence of being "affectionless characters." Thus Bowlby—who had once proclaimed in a report to the World Health Organization (Bowlby, 1951) that the failure to establish an affectionate, one-on-one human attachment in the infant years would make it impossible to form affectionate relationships later—was forced to admit that he had overstated his case (Bowlby, Ainsworth, Boston, & Rosenbluth, 1956). Humans, it appears, are not so time-bound or rigid as birds and dogs with regard to the development of their affectional systems. Such data serve to falsify a belief in the homology of the two systems.

Turning to the more specific hypothesis that filial attachments in humans are directly homologous to those in birds, we again find little scientific evidence to encourage a belief in the homology. One compelling argument from comparative psychology is that while imprinting does occur in birds, other animals much closer to us phylogenetically than birds show no evidence of this phenomenon. Rhesus monkeys, for example, are easily able to form new attachments when separated from their mothers. They can be quite versatile in doing so. In one experiment by University of California scientists (Mason & Kenney, 1974), monkeys that had been attached to their mothers formed new attachments to mongrel dogs (see Figure 4-9). When the monkeys were first placed in cages with a dog, they were frightened.

But within 4 hours, seven of the eight rhesus infants used in the experiment were clinging to their canine cagemates. In the days and weeks that followed, the rhesus infants formed filial attachments to the dogs that were equally as strong as the attachments they originally had to their own mothers. Thus the formation of primary attachments in rhesus monkeys is not

FIGURE 4-9
Forming Attachments Is Not a Time-Limited Process for Monkeys
The formation of a filial attachment may be a critical-period development in precocial birds, but in rhesus monkeys it is not. This monkey and seven others were separated from their own mothers after forming attachments to them. Given a chance to form new attachments, all did so. This particular monkey became attached to the dog that she shared an outdoor kennel with. Tests showed the attachment to be "strong, specific, and exclusive" in the same way as the monkey's initial mother attachment. The two animals went on walks together, slept together, and groomed each other.

restricted to one critical period. The consensus opinion is that the formation of attachments in humans is also flexible with regard to the time in which it can occur.

Evaluating the Evidence for a Human Homolog to Maternal Bonding

Although the hypothesis that a human form of imprinting occurs in a critical period has been dropped by all its former adherents, there is still a great deal of discussion regarding the proposal of pediatricians Marshall Klaus and John Kennell (Klaus & Kennell, 1976) that there is a critical period for human maternal bonding (Chess & Thomas, 1982; Myers, 1984; Sluckin, Herbert, & Sluckin, 1983). Most discussion is negative, at least as regards the scientific merit of the Klaus and Kennell claim.

Klaus and Kennell's (1976, pp. 67–80) claim is that there is a brief window of time following birth during which human mothers can form a very special emotional bond with their infants. Beyond this time, they can surely come to love and care for their infants, but they will be missing out on the unique mother–infant bond that has been prepared through biological evolution.

When the bonding hypothesis was first proposed, it gained immediate acceptance in the medical community, an acceptance that has gone a long way toward humanizing maternity stays. This is evident in the dramatic changes that have occurred in hospital maternity care in the last 10 years. It is now routine, for example, for mothers to be given extended contact with their babies in the first hours and days following birth. During this period, skin-to-skin contact and nursing are encouraged. The reason is that these experiences are thought to optimize bonding.

Though Klaus and Kennell (1982) have cited some scientific studies that they feel are consistent with their bonding hypothesis, the bulk of the evidence is against them. For example, some of the studies favoring the hypothesis show that mothers who roomed-in with their newborns while in the hospital were later found to be more sensitive and competent mothers (on some measures anyway) than those who did not (Greenberg, Rosenberg, & Lind, 1973). Critics point out, though, that the effects of rooming-in tend to be short-term at best. Reviewer Wladyslaw Sluckin and his colleagues (1983) conclude, therefore, that

> there may be short-term and *general* advantages in giving mother and baby the opportunity to get familiar with each other, as happens in the rooming-in tradition. All relationships have to have a beginning point and require a framework within which mutual awareness and familiarity can grow. . . . But, is it necessarily a disaster if and when [early contact] does not occur? The evidence suggests the answer is "No"! (p. 40)

In addition to noting that the beneficial effects of early contact, when found, tend to be short-term, critics also point out that the best controlled

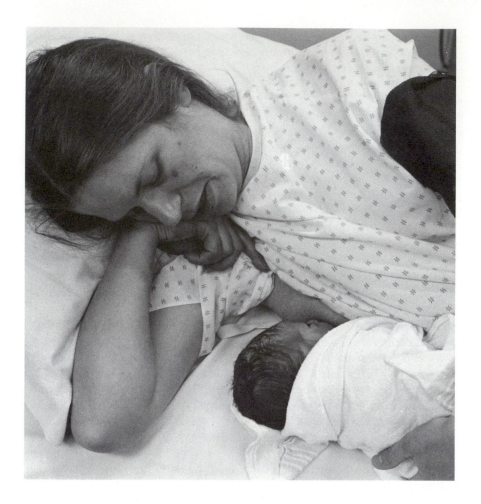

and most carefully conducted studies fail to find differences of any kind between early-contact and late-contact mothers (see Myers, 1984). Referring to the many inconsistent results now present in the scientific literature on bonding, Michael Lamb and Carl-Philip Hwang (1982) comment quite reasonably that "If early [mother–infant] contact tapped some important biological process, we would expect greater consistency" (p. 28). We would also expect that variables such as a mother's previous history of births, social status, age, education, and other purely social factors should be rendered relatively unimportant if there were a biological basis for bonding. As Sluckin and his colleagues (1983) point out, however, these social variables are very predictive of the nature of the mother–infant bond. The mere fact that social variables are important does not, of course, deny that a tiny portion of the mother–infant bond might still be due to a mechanical critical-period process, but it does greatly diminish our concern for the relevance of that alleged process to healthy human development.

Using Logic to Evaluate Critical-Period Hypotheses   Having looked at the scientific evidence for critical periods in the establishment of early parent–child relations, we can back off and ask a more philosophical question: Would it make sense that there would be critical periods for the formation of human parent–child relations as described by the imprinting and bonding phenomena or any other? This is a question not of science but of logic. It is nonetheless relevant to an evaluation of critical-period hypotheses because hypotheses gain or lose credibility by the extent to which they are consistent or inconsistent with larger bodies of knowledge. Thus we could more readily accept a critical-period hypothesis if it fit with something else we happen to know about humans.

One thing we know about humans is that the factors that control their behavior are incredibly complex, more complex certainly than the controls on any other creatures. Freud referred to the diversity of human controls with the terms **id,** which represents biological factors, **ego,** which represents rational factors, and **superego,** which represents societal factors. Psychologists are not all agreed on the extent to which id, ego, and superego controls enter into daily human lives. Some argue that the id component is stronger than we would like to believe (Freud held this position as do contemporary sociobiologists); others argue that the id has been relegated to a position of near irrelevance, because the human ego (reason) and superego (the societal values reflected in an individual's conscience) can overpower any simple biological motive. Be that as it may, we can all agree that behaviors or dispositions such as the love of human mothers for their children or of human children for their mothers will be a far more complex affair than in any nonhuman animal. Thus, whereas one can accept that behaviors that ensure responsible mothering in rats may be mediated by an idlike factor and that it may be that this factor becomes activated by some maturational event like the release of maternal hormones, it is very difficult to accept such an argument for humans. Speaking of the mother–infant bond, Stanford's P. Herbert Leiderman (1981) has said, "It is unlikely, for such a complex organism as man, that fixing of an essential bond would occur only in the brief period following childbirth" (p. 464). He could have said as much for the likelihood of all other claims that the establishment and maintenance of human affections would be given over to single developmental moments and single control systems.

In addition to evaluating the logic of critical-period hypotheses against what we know of behavioral controls in humans, we can also evaluate these hypotheses against what we know of human evolution. The theory of evolution is relevant because if we are to believe that there are critical periods in human social development, it would help to believe that evolution found such periods to be in the adaptive interests of the humans who first evolved from our more apelike ancestors. Applying logic to instances of critical-period developments reveals that many of them do make good evolutionary sense. The bunting's star compass, for example, made perfectly good sense to Cornell ornithologist William Keeton (1981), who argued that there has been evolutionary selection of a brief learning period for the star compass "to avoid the acquisition of wrong information at a later time when the bird has left its breeding ground" (p. 510). The same argument for early critical-period learning applies to salmon, which must remember for up to 7 years the chemical cues that distinguish the water in which they were hatched from all the other water through which they have swum (Hasler, Scholz, & Horrall, 1978). Similarly, early-life sexual imprinting and song learning make sense for birds that will soon leave their family nests and then live in habitats that are home to a variety of species similar to their own. If the songs and sexual preferences of these birds were not fixed prior to dispersal, the survival of their species would be in jeopardy. This same early learning would be disastrous, however, for a parsitic nester like the cowbird, which leaves its eggs to be hatched and raised in the nests of at least 100 different species of birds. If young cowbirds learned the song of their foster parents and sexually imprinted on them, the cowbird species would not long survive. It is not surprising to learn, then, that cowbirds are an exception to the usual imprinting rule (West, King, & Eastzer, 1981).

What then is the case for humans? Would it make evolutionary sense for parent–child relations to be fixed automatically by critical-period developments in early infancy? To make this argument one must be able to show that such periods could have been in the adaptive interests of the humans who first evolved from our more apelike ancestors. This is a hard argument to make. Imprinting, bonding, and other critical-period strategies would seem to be poor survival strategies for our human ancestors, if what we know of them is true. In small hunter–gatherer bands of genetically related individuals, there were relatively few infants at any one time, and these infants had a long period of dependency. To have any mechanisms, such as imprinting or bonding, that guaranteed exclusivity in the infant–mother relation could have been quite detrimental. What if the mother died, for example? Exclusivity in the mother–child relationship and time constraints on its formation would mean that a mother's infants would die with her, and this could occur at any time in the 4- or 5-year period of dependency. For caribou living in vast herds or geese living in large flocks, the payoff from imprinting, bonding, or both in terms of guaranteed protection and identification appears to be worth the sacrifice in plasticity, particularly given that the period of mother dependency is only months long in these animals. But in human evolution, any strategy designed to promote exclusivity would seem to be a disastrous strategy. We can reason, then, that evolutionary developments that allowed for greater shared responsibilities in childrearing and for adoption were the developments providing the greatest selective advantage, not developments that led to exclusivity and narrowness in human relations. Indeed, if you look to contemporary primate groups to gain a better perspective on our humanity, you again find that adoption and sharing of infant responsibilities is quite characteristic of primates as a whole.

The empirical and logical considerations put forth here add up to quite a strong case against a belief that there are critical periods that constrain human social development. With regard to the specific hypotheses that humans go through an imprinting and bonding period, critics find no evidence for the one and little for the other. In addition, the complexity of behavior controls in humans makes it unlikely that the events of a single period of development could have permanent and overwhelming importance. Also, if there were such periods, they presumably would have been built into the developmental sequence by a process of evolutionary selection. Again, with regard to the dependency and protection pact among parents and children, it would make no sense for evolution to have taken this course. Human and other primate interests seem to have been in the direction of maintaining flexibility in one's social relations and affectional ties.

In light of these considerations, we can safely dismiss the specific hypotheses for critical periods in parent–child relations. But what about the broader question of time-constrained developments in human psychological development? Can we dismiss the relevance of this concept altogether? The answer is no, but first we must make some distinctions between critical periods and some related developmental phenomena. We also must shift from a concern with description to a concern with explanation. The explanatory question to be answered is how events, early in a developmental sequence, might attain permanency in their effects; because despite all that has been said here, no one doubts the potential importance of early experience for starting development along one path or another. All that has been called into question is the finality of this experience.

Distinguishing Sensitive and Foundational Periods from Critical Periods

Experiences at one point in life can have an apparent determining influence on later events for a variety of reasons. To this point we have considered but one—the embryological mechanism by which tissues and organs become "fixed" during their emergence from an undifferentiated and unorganized state. But now, to close out our consideration of how early experience might tend to fix the developmental path that is taken, we need to consider other mechanisms by which experience early in a developmental sequence might acquire—or appear to acquire—permanent significance.

The one mechanism considered thus far for achieving fixity is known in embryology as **induction** (Spemann, 1938). It brings about irreversible and inalterable changes in the developing organism, because induction itself is an irreversible process. But how good is the inductive mechanism for explaining how early experience gains its permanent effects outside the domain of actual tissue differentiation?

Shortly after the first evidence for imprinting and imprintinglike phenomena began to appear, researchers checked the validity of induction as an explanation by asking whether the results of imprinting (and imprintinglike phenomena) were permanent. They found that they were not. Work by Klaus Immelmann (see Immelmann & Suomi, 1981) on the phenomenon of sexual imprinting showed, for example, that misimprinted birds (ones raised with foster parents from a different species) could still establish a sexual preference for their own species if their postweaning experiences were properly arranged. In the case of filial imprinting, researchers also found that the original learning could be modified. The reversibility of object preference was evident in data that showed that chicks that are imprinted to one object can have that preference reversed when the originally imprinted object is no longer available (Salzen & Meyer, 1968).

Countless other studies over the years have been equally persuasive in demonstrating the reversibility of imprinting. The method common to these studies has been to force an already imprinted bird to come into contact with an alien bird or species. The forced contact tends to wear down the behavioral incompatibilities (such as avoidance and fear), which otherwise would serve to protect the old learning from any alteration. This same procedure can work to overcome the detrimental effects of mother–infant separation in goats. Normally, as we have seen, a dam separated from her kid at birth will not later accept it. But the reason turns out to be a function of smell. In the hours after birth, dams learn to identify their offspring by smell. They can do the same thing later if they are given time to adapt to the initially novel odor of their young (Hersher, Richmond, & Moore, 1963).

Sensitive Periods   In light of the new data, it is evident that Konrad Lorenz misled us back in 1935 when he attributed imprinting to induction. How he came to do so is understandable, however, when you consider that 1935, the year of Lorenz's first publications on imprinting, was also the year that Hans Spemann—an Austrian compatriot of Lorenz—received the Nobel Prize for his discovery of induction. Now, more than half a century later, we see clearly that the only reason that imprinting experiences ever appeared inalterable is that the original learning has built-in behavioral protection. As explained by Cambridge University psychologist Patrick Bateson, imprinted birds are not unable to acquire new filial and sexual preferences, they are simply unwilling (1979, p. 482). This is a very important distinction to make. The critical periods in embryology, which led off our discussion of time-constrained development, resulted in the inability to bring about change. This is what merited them the name *critical period*. Now we see that imprinting does not occur in a critical period in this sense. It occurs in what is better described as a **sensitive period,** which is a period of heightened susceptibility but not of permanent determination.

It is eye-opening to realize that some developments, like imprinting and bonding, may attain their permanence only by virtue of the fact that in the natural state, animals seldom have experiences to challenge their initial learning. It was first assumed that when early-established behaviors persisted across time the reason had to be that something internal and structural had been permanently fixed. Now we see that this does not need to be the case, and even if it is the case to some extent (as in the case of a permanently inscribed memory for one's initial imprinting object), it still does not limit the opportunity for altering and extending the early learning. Thus Bateson (1979) summarizes the value of work done on the mechanisms of imprinting by saying the major virtue of the work is that "it indicates that the notion of the powerful determining influence of early experience can co-exist with that of subsequent rehabilitation" (p. 476). Faith in plasticity, therefore, is completely compatible with the existence of sensitive periods in development. All one must do to change these developments is invest the energy to reroute development from its previously chosen path.

Foundational Periods   The mechanisms of protected learning and induction do not exhaust the means whereby the events of an early period in life can either rob or appear to rob development of its plasticity. A third mechanism is that of missed foundations. In this case, experience early in a developmental sequence gains its importance because it is foundational to later experience. When this mechanism is at work, development is not only alterable, it is reversible. For a person who misses out on a foundational experience, all that is necessary is to correct the deficiency.

The concept of **foundational periods** is illustrated in the theoretical work of Glen Doman and Carl Delacato, who have jointly developed a theory of neural organization called *patterning* (Delacato, 1966). According to this controversial theory, ontogenetic development within the nervous system must follow a phylogenetic sequence if later difficulties are to be avoided. Recent societal practices, however, have served to alter the sequence for some individuals. For example, many children today never spend much time crawling or creeping because their parents give them "walkers" to stroll about in. Allegedly this causes aberrations in neural organization that can then affect reading and vision. While one might think that failing to crawl and creep during the period for these motor activities would put neural development on an irreversible and inalterable course, according to Doman and Delacato, phylogenetic experiences such as crawling are merely foundational. This means that people can correct any problems in their neural organization by making up for their deficiency. Thus the therapy for adult reading problems might be to crawl and creep about for several hours a day until the nervous system gets organized according to the original phylogenetic plan. In a quite similar expression of the belief that early experience can be foundational rather than critical, therapists who use psychoanalysis attempt to take patients back to the developmental moment when their lives first went awry and "work through" that moment in a different way than occurred initially. According to Freudian theory, which is the basis of psychoanalysis, working through the past in this manner can undo the effects of the past and thereby establish a foundation for a healthier life.

Though both the Freudian and Doman–Delacato theories express a belief in a foundational and, therefore, reversible past, there is no direct evidence that the theories are correct. In fact, the American Academy of Pediatrics has denounced the Doman–Delacato theory as oversimplified and unscientific (Herbert, 1982). For clear empirical evidence of a reversible past, therefore, we need to go elsewhere. One good example comes from a development reviewed earlier: the effects of social isolation on monkeys. As you will recall, the initial conclusion from this research was that the period from birth to 6 months constituted a critical period for the development of normal social relations among monkeys. The evidence was that monkeys that spent their first 6 months in isolation were later unable to integrate themselves into a normal social group. Subsequent research showed, however, that the first 6 months were merely foundational. This was discovered in a research project that involved putting 6-month-isolate monkeys into a group of 3-month-old monkeys (Suomi & Harlow, 1972). The 3-month-olds proved to be successful therapists. The apparent reason for the success is that rhesus monkeys first begin social play around 3 months of age. When the 6-month-isolates were placed with 3-month-olds (rather than 6-month-old age-mates), the isolates were able to learn social relations from the beginning. By doing so, they were able to reverse the effects of their early isolation.

A Final Assessment

The major thrust of the discussion throughout this section on the role of timing in psychological development has been to show that the timing of events, though relevant, is not in fact critical for most of human psychological development. This serves to correct the fatalistic attitude adopted by many in the past (see, for example, earlier quotes from Freud, Watson, Bowlby, and White) that a missed experience or a traumatic event in psychological development could be as permanently crippling as a missed experience or trauma in embryological development. However, it is quite important that we not dismiss entirely the concept of critical periods or the mechanism of induction from the domain of psychological development. They do have their place. That place is in the brain.

Human behavior, like the behavior of all animals, is ultimately directed by events in the brain. In fact, some psychological functions—perception and language are among them—are even localized in the brain. This means that there are specific brain sites associated with these psychological functions. The time period during which these functions are undergoing localization appears to be critical and, apparently, for reasons having to do with induction. For some aspects of perception, the period from birth to about 3 years of age may mark a critical period (see Chapter 7). For language it may extend from about 2 to 12 years of age, though there is little hard data on this point (see Chapter 11). Another alleged critical period occurs in the period from birth to 2 years of age that marks the brain's postnatal growth spurt. Malnutrition in this period, along with the lethargy and inactivity that accompany malnutrition, are known to have long-lasting effects on general intellectual functioning (Evans, Bowie, Hansen, Moodie, & Vander Spuy, 1980). Given these facts of brain development and their relevance to human psychological development, the critical-period concept continues to be an important one in the science of developmental psychology.

THE DEVELOPMENT OF SEXUAL DIFFERENCES IN BIOLOGY AND BEHAVIOR: AN EXAMPLE OF EPIGENETIC DEVELOPMENT

The goal of the previous chapter and the present one has been to present the epigenetic point of view currently held by developmental psychologists. In the last chapter, the plasticity of development was emphasized, along with the point that developmental potential is realized through the interactions of nature and nurture. In this chapter, we have explored the extent to which the timing of nature–nurture interactions alters their outcomes and limits—or fails to limit—plasticity within particular systems. Now in final fulfillment of the goals of both the present chapter and the previous one, all the developmental principles covered so far will be reviewed in the context of a single example. The example is the development of sexual or gender differences in human biology and behavior.

The story of human sexual development will be told in three parts. The first part deals with the prenatal physical development of humans. The second deals with the development of how one thinks of oneself **(gender identity)** and the third with how one behaves **(gender role).** In species-typical development, little boys are identified at birth by their penis and little girls by their vagina. Once identified as boys and girls, social forces conspire to direct little boys and little girls down gender-appropriate paths of development. Along the way, a masculine or feminine gender identity develops to coincide with one's anatomy and behavior. As we will see, however, there are a great number of possible variations in the species-typical pattern. When these occur, nature, nurture, and time must all be invoked as contributing factors.

The Physical Development of Males and Females

You may have once thought—or even been taught—that the determination of maleness or femaleness was a relatively simple matter. If the sperm that fertilized the egg from which you developed had an X chromosome, you became female. If it had a Y chromosome, you became male. This single coin-toss model for the development of sexuality is, in fact, very misleading. The actual process is both far more complex and far more interesting than a case of simple genetic determination.

Rather than being a single-stage process with but two outcomes, the determination of sexual characteristics is a multistage epigenetic process with a variety of potential outcomes. Prenatally, it involves the determination of genotype (either XX, XY, or some variant), gonadal type (testes, ovaries, or some variant), internal anatomical features (for example, fallopian tubes for females or the vas deferens for males), external anatomical features (male or female genitals), and it involves a process whereby parts of the brain become either masculine or feminine in their structure and function. Postnatally, it involves the release of brain-based pituitary hormones, which begin puberty. These stimulate the production of large amounts of sex hormones in both males and females. The relative amounts of the various hormones that are present determine all the many primary and secondary sexual characteristics associated with adolescence. These include among other changes the growth of body hair, voice changes, fat distribution, bone development in the hips and shoulders, and breast development (see Figure 4-10).

Genotype

An individual's **genotype** is determined when a sperm cell from the male penetrates the wall of the female sex cell—the ovum—thereby fertilizing it. Figure 4-11 is a photograph of this event. If the penetrating sperm cell is normal, it has 23 chromosomes in its nucleus, 22 of which are indifferent to the eventual sex of the individual. The 23rd, however, is sex-determining and is known in humans as either an X (female) chromosome or a Y (male) chromosome. In each ejaculation, the number of sperm cells bearing an X chromosome equals the number bearing a Y chromosome, but the Y-bearing sperm cells—perhaps because they have less mass than X bearing sperm cells—are 1.2 to 1.6 times more likely to fertilize the ovum (Moseley & Stan, 1984, p. 149). The ovum itself is not sex-determining because it invariably carries an X chromosome.

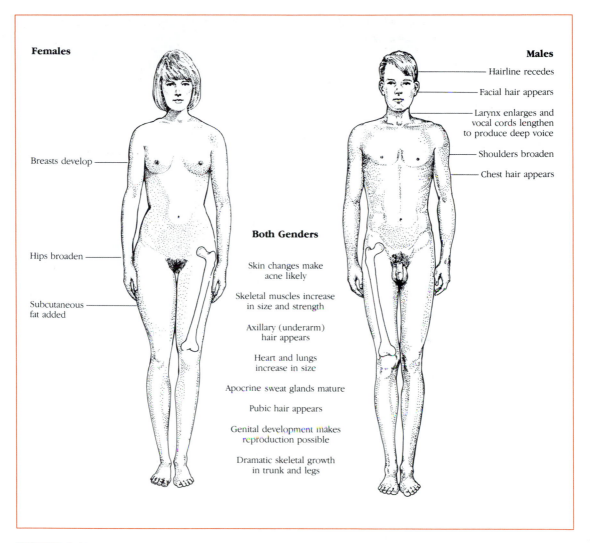

FIGURE 4-10
Male–Female Differences at Puberty
This figure shows the sex differences that appear at puberty and the physical
changes that both sexes share.

Like the sperm cell, a normal ovum has a total of 23 chromosomes.
These are said to be *homologous* to the sperm's 23 chromosomes because
each of the 23 chromosomes in the one type of sex cell has structural features that match it up with one of the 23 chromosomes in the other. Once
the sperm has penetrated the ovum, the 23 chromosomes in the sperm

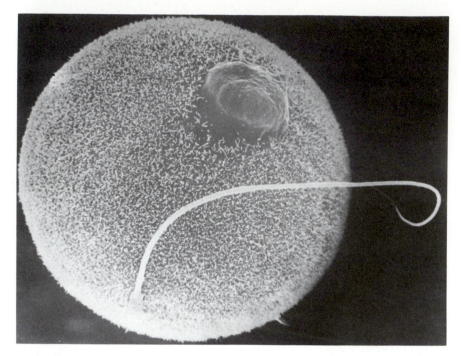

FIGURE 4-11
Human Conception
This electron-microscope photograph shows the moment of conception when the tiny sperm with its 23 chromosomes enters the egg cell and combines its chromosomes with those of the egg.

combine with the homologous chromosomes in the ovum to form a single 46-chromosome cell called a **zygote.** Approximately 30 hours later, the zygote begins to duplicate itself (Moore, 1977, p. 27). Development has begun, and so has the individual.

Although a 46-chromosome zygote is the typical outcome following fertilization, other outcomes are possible. Each represents what can be called a *chromosomal anomaly.* Most, but not all, involve the sex chromosomes. They are of interest because of the light they shed on the role of genetics in sexual differentiation. They are also of interest because they illustrate the plasticity available in human development even at the level of genetics.

Two relatively frequent anomalies occur in individuals who look male. These are the XXY genotype, which leads to *Klinefelter's syndrome,* and the XYY genotype. Each occurs in about 1 out of every 1,000 male births. The most frequent anomaly in individuals who look female is the XO genotype, which is shorthand for saying that in place of two sex chromosomes the individual has only one. Invariably this one is an X. The mechanisms through which individuals can come to have a single sex chromosome in the nucleus of their cells should lead to individuals with a YO genotype as well, but no such individual has survived until birth. Presumably, absence of an X chromosome makes survival impossible. The XO condition we have been discussing leads to the condition known as *Turner's syndrome.* The incidence rate for Turner's is about 1 in every 3,000 female births.

Gonadal Determination

Following the determination of an individual's male, female, or anomalous genotype at the very start of development, the next important step in sexual development is taken at a gestational age of about 6 weeks when gonadal determination occurs. *Gonads* are organs with the responsibility of producing both sexual hormones and reproductive cells (that is, sperm cells and ova). The gonads come in pairs, one on each side of the body. The male gonads are known as *testes.* The female gonads are *ovaries.* Both types of gonads produce the three categories of sex hormones—androgens, estrogens, and progestins. They differ, however, in the relative amounts of each that are produced. Androgens dominate among the hormonal output of the testes and estrogens dominate among the hormonal output of the ovaries.

Despite the fact that testes and ovaries are quite different organs in their final form, the two types of gonads arise from a single structure developmentally. This structure has both a central (or medullary) and an outer (or cortical) component. To become a testis, the medullary component must be induced to develop and the cortical component to wither away. To become an ovary, the opposite must occur. There is nothing in the primitive gonadal tissue itself that predetermines it to develop in one direction or the other. Rather, in pure epigenetic fashion, there is a critical period for determining the fate of the gonads. This period lasts in humans from the fifth to the seventh week of gestation. If during this period the Y chromosome produces a particular protein—as yet unidentified, but probably an H-Y antigen (Ohno, 1979)—the primitive gonadal tissue will develop in the direction of testes. If the necessary protein is not present (as in the case of XX individuals), the developing tissue loses its capacity to become testicular tissue. In that case, the alternative path of ovary development is chosen.

As in the case of chromosomal determination, some anomalies are possible during gonadal determination. In some rare cases, for example, the primitive gonadal tissue gets a mixed message. This can result in individuals who have *ovotestes,* structures that consist of both ovarian and testicular tissue, or even individuals who have an ovary on one side of the body and a testis on the other. Though rare, these outcomes are among the epigenetic possibilities for gonadal development in humans and other mammals.

Up until the time of testicular differentiation at 6 weeks, human embryos are unisex as best we can tell (see Figure 4-12). Their tissues, organs,

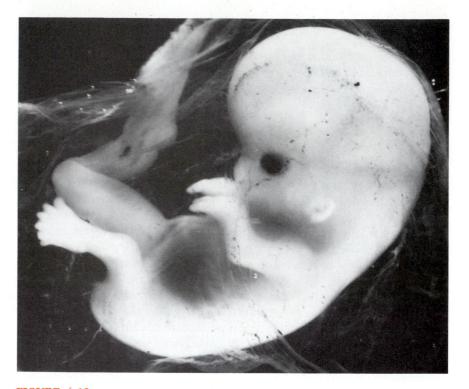

FIGURE 4-12
The Sexually Undifferentiated Human Embryo
At 6 weeks, the developing human embryo is a unisex individual except for its genotype. Regardless of whether the genotype is male or female, however, the embryo still has the potential of becoming either sex.

and size are the same regardless of genotype. The gonadal difference that occurs at 6 weeks, therefore, is the first indication of a physical difference between the sexes. There will be many to come—body size and shape, muscle strength, distribution of hair, and so on—but the gonadal distinction is the first. The gonadal difference at 6 weeks soon leads to a hormonal difference, a hormonal difference that makes all the difference.

The hormonal choice involves whether the male hormone *testosterone* (an androgen) or the female hormone *estradiol* (an estrogen) will dominate during the rest of development. Large amounts of testosterone are produced in about the eighth week by the gonads-turned-testes. Estradiol is produced at the same time by the nontestis gonads (which eventually will become ovaries with the appearance of the ovarian follicles in the second trimester). As regards sexual development, however, it is only the testosterone that matters. This is because development will take the female course at each epigenetic choice point, even in the absence of estradiol, but it will not take the male course except when testosterone—or some other androgen—is present in quantity. Subsequent masculine development, therefore, depends on androgens. If present in the proper strength at the proper time, normal male development occurs. If not, normal female development occurs.

As you might expect from the discussion of developmental anomalies possible at the first two choice points in gender development, anomalies will also be possible at each subsequent choice point (see Figure 4-13). In each case the anomalies will result from the abnormal presence of androgens in individuals with ovaries and the abnormal absence of them in individuals with testes. The former case is the more common. It occurs because nature did not make the testes the only source of androgens. Androgens can enter a fetus's blood stream from a tumor in the mother, from a drug she has taken, or from the fetus's own malfunctioning adrenal gland. Regardless of their source—testis, tumor, drug, or malfunctioning adrenal—their effect on development is the same: they channel it down the masculine path, an effect called **masculinization.**

Internal Reproductive Anatomy

Once hormonal activity begins, the reproductive anatomy of males and females begins to differentiate. The structures involved can be conveniently divided into two parts—the internal reproductive anatomy and the external genitalia. Internal development begins in the second month, slightly before the onset of development of the external genitalia.

The prenatal development of the internal reproductive anatomy is pictured in Figure 4-14. As shown there, the internal portions develop from one of two structures, which are both present in the unisex embryo of Figure 4-12. These are the **Wolffian structure** (or duct) and the **Müllerian structure** (or duct). If one is to be a normal male, the Müllerian structure will degenerate completely and the Wolffian structure will develop into the structures for carrying sperm from the testes and semen from the prostate. The technical names for the structures involved are the epididymis, vas deferens, and seminal vesicles. If one is to be a normal female, the Müllerian structure will differentiate into fallopian tubes, uterus, and the upper portion of the vagina, and the Wolffian structure will degenerate.

The factor that leads to Wolffian development in males is the presence of androgens in the eighth week of gestation. In the presence of androgens the Wolffian structure develops; in their absence the Müllerian structure develops. This makes the development of the internal reproductive anatomy of males and females appear to be a relatively simple matter. There is a complication, however, which stems from nature's developmental design of beginning with two structures. When you have two structures, one must be eliminated. Elimination of the Wolffian structure appears not to be a problem in the typical development of females, because degeneration of the

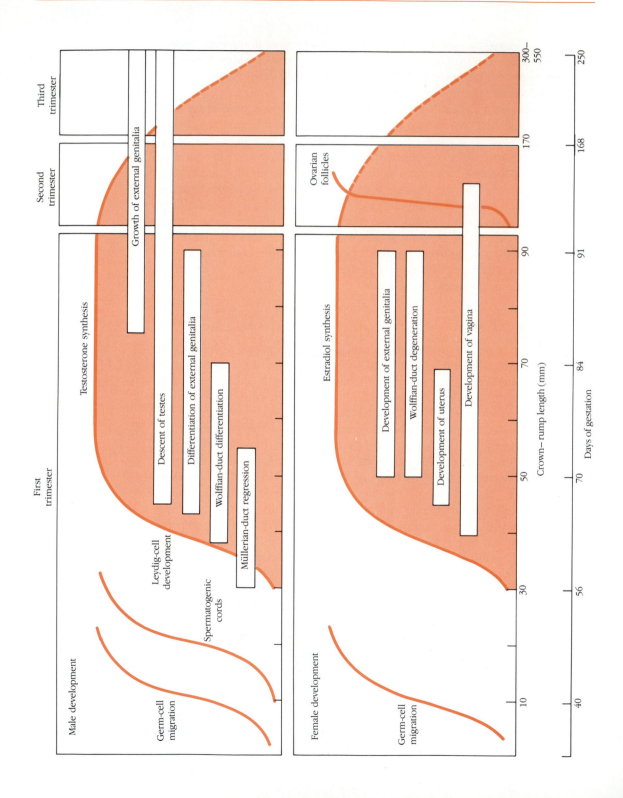

FIGURE 4-13 (Opposite)
Critical Periods for Sexual Differentiation
This time chart shows the critical periods for prenatal
sexual development in humans.

Wolffian structure occurs as a natural consequence of the development of the Müllerian structure. The same is not true, however, in typical male development. In this case the fetal testes must not only produce testosterone, which leads to the development of the Wolffian structure, but they must also produce a substance, as yet unidentified, that serves to inhibit the development of the Müllerian structure. For lack of a better name, this substance has been labeled **Müllerian inhibiting substance** or **MIS.**

FIGURE 4-14
Wolffian and Müllerian Development
Differentiation of the internal reproductive anatomy of males and females begins with two structures, the Wolffian duct and the Müllerian duct. The Wolffian duct has the potential of becoming the male epididymis, vas deferens, and seminal vesicles. The Müllerian duct has the potential of becoming the female fallopian tubes, uterus, and upper vagina. Under the influence of testosterone, the Wolffian duct develops. In the absence of testosterone, the Müllerian duct develops.

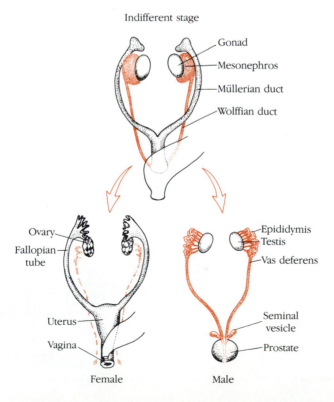

Two bits of evidence tend to confirm the existence of MIS. Both come from individuals who experience abnormal prenatal sexual development. In one, neither the Müllerian nor Wolffian structures develop. In the other, both develop. The former case results when XY individuals have a genetic condition that makes it impossible for their cells to metabolize testosterone. The condition is known as **androgen insensitivity.** Individuals with this condition have testes that produce testosterone, but the developing cells that come in contact with this testosterone are not affected. To the developing cells in the Wolffian structure and elsewhere, it is as if the testosterone did not exist (see Figure 4-15).

If the development of the internal reproductive anatomy were totally determined by the presence or absence of androgens, we would expect for androgen-insensitive individuals to develop internally as females, because as far as the Wolffian structure is concerned, no androgens are present. This should signal this structure to atrophy and for the Müllerian structure to develop along the usual path for females. What we in fact find in the case of androgen-insensitive males, however, is that neither the Wolffian nor the Müllerian structures develop. This means that the testes must be producing

FIGURE 4-15
Consequences of Androgen Insensitivity
This woman lacks any internal female organs, and she has a male genotype (XY) and male gonads (testes). Nonetheless, she is very female in appearance—obviously. She is also very female in her behavior and self-concept (gender identity).

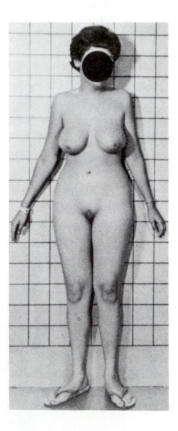

something to actively inhibit the expected feminine development. That "something" is what we have labeled as MIS.

The other instance of atypical development that argues for the existence of MIS is the case in which individuals develop with the full complement of male and female internal organs. This occurs when both the Müllerian and Wolffian structures are induced to follow their normal courses of development. Individuals in which this development occurs are genotypically XY. Their testes provide the testosterone needed to promote the Wolffian development, but either they fail to produce MIS or the Müllerian tissue is insensitive to the substance. If testosterone alone were responsible for both promoting Wolffian development and inhibiting Müllerian development, we would not find individuals with this "persistent Müllerian duct syndrome" (Sloan & Walsh, 1976). But such individuals do exist. In one case, for example, a very masculine ex-marine was found during abdominal surgery to have a uterus and fallopian tubes.

External Reproductive Anatomy

Unlike the internal anatomy, which develops from separate male and female structures, the external reproductive anatomy develops—like the gonads—from structures that are unisex at the outset (see Figure 4-16). These structures are the genital tubercle, genital fold, and genital swelling. When these structures develop in the presence of androgen, they become the male penis and scrotum. When they develop in the absence of androgen, they become the female clitoris and labia. The timetable for these developments is given in Figure 4-13, which shows that masculinization of the genital tubercle, genital fold, and genital swelling begins just shortly after the Wolffian duct begins to develop in males.

The direction taken in the development of the genitals is of greater psychological importance than any of the developments we have discussed thus far. Genes, hormones, and internal anatomy are, after all, invisible both to us and to those who rear us. The genitals are not. The ex-marine mentioned earlier, for example, did not have his male identity challenged by the fact that he had a uterus, because neither he nor anyone else was aware of it until he had the operation. This is never the case, however, when the anomalies involve the external manifestations of masculinity and femininity, because from birth on, the genitalia provide society with its principal means of classifying us as male or female.

Anomalies can occur in the development of the genitals in both XY and XX individuals. A genotypic male, for example, might be born with an undersized penis with a urinary opening at its base rather than at the tip. This can occur when there is a partial androgen insensitivity. Such a male might be interpreted to be female. Likewise, a genotypic female can be born with full Müllerian development but with an enlarged clitoris and fused

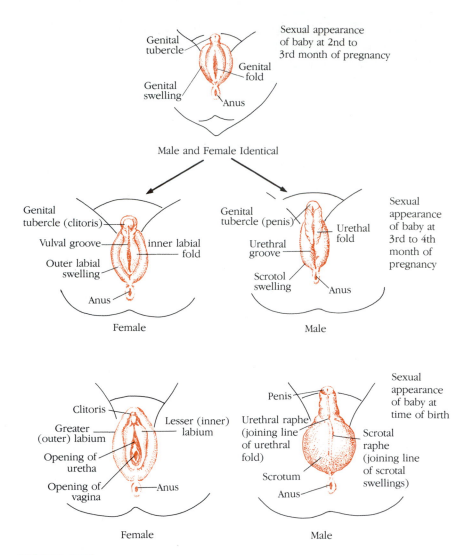

FIGURE 4-16
Development of the External Genitalia
Differentiation of the external genitalia in males and females begins with a set of structures that are common to both. Under the influence of testosterone or some other androgen, these structures develop into the male penis and scrotum. In the absence of androgens, they become the female labia and clitoris.

labia, which might lead the obstetrician and others to believe that she was a boy with undescended testes. Masculinized genital development of this sort can occur in females when androgens are introduced into their blood. As mentioned earlier, the three androgen sources are tumors in the mother, drugs taken by the mother, and the fetus's own adrenal glands (if they have the defect known as *adreno-cortical hyperplasia*).

Brain Differentiation

For a long time, investigators have been reluctant to say that the brains of males and females might be different, because somehow this seems to go against our notions of equality and egalitarianism. After all, behavior, thought, and personality stem from the brain, and once one admits to physical differences, there is the danger of supplying the ignorant with an argument for practicing discrimination. But now it is becoming quite probable that there are significant physical differences between the brains of males and females. In a summary of research on sex differences in animal brains, for example, Arthur Arnold (1980) of UCLA's Brain Research Institute wrote that "the question . . . is no longer whether or not sex differences in neural organization exist, but rather what sequence of developmental events leads to the *pervasive* sex differences observed" (p. 172, italics added). Human research is not as advanced in this area as animal research, but even in humans some differences are being uncovered (see, for example, LaCoste-Utamsing & Holloway, 1982).

The mechanism by which differences in animals (and presumably humans) is achieved is the same as for the other male and female differences reviewed here. That is, the presence of androgens during a critical period causes development to take a masculine course. In their absence, development takes a feminine course.

Direct observation of hormone effects on brain development was first made by Dominique Toran-Allerand (1976). She put very thin slices of brain tissue from the hypothalamuses of sexually undifferentiated fetal mice into petri dishes. She then treated these tissue samples with various steroid hormones, among them testosterone. The testosterone-treated tissue became different from the others. This observation confirmed the long-suspected connection between testosterone in the prenatal period and differentiation in key brain structures such as the hypothalamus.

The hypothalamus was suspected as a likely site for male–female differentiation because signals from the hypothalamus signal the pituitary gland, which lies just below it, to release chemicals known as *gonadotropins*. These, in turn, are responsible for the cyclic production of gonadal hormones in the female, which accounts for the 28-day menstrual cycle, and the acyclic pattern in males, which accounts for the constant production of testosterone. These differences do not appear until adolescence, but they were known to be attributable to prenatal influences as long ago as 1936. In that year, C. A. Pfeiffer conducted a classic set of studies in which he castrated male rats prior to brain differentiation and implanted testosterone in female rats. The result was that the castrated males developed the female cyclic pattern for gonadotropin release and the females developed the male acyclic pattern. Subsequent researchers have shown that behavior is also affected by these hormonal manipulations. Rats castrated during the critical period for sexual differentiation in the brain become more feminine in their behavior, and testosterone-treated females become more masculine (Hines, 1982, p. 56–57). Rhesus monkeys, which are much closer to humans than are rats, show similar effects. In one especially interesting study, Robert Goy (1978) of the University of Michigan exposed female rhesus monkeys to testosterone during the critical period for hypothalamic development. He later observed the social behavior of these prenatally exposed females as they interacted with other monkeys—both males and females. What he found was that his experimental females were decidedly more rough and tumble in their play than normal females. They were not as rough and tumble as average males, but their play patterns had definitely been masculinized.

Summary of Prenatal Sexual Development

As emphasized in the preceding discussion, the process by which males and females become physically different from one another is a gradual, epigenetic process. Rather than being inherently different from the start, males and females are inherently the same and remain so for 6 weeks. In the absence of either of two masculinizing factors—the Y-chromosome-related protein, or androgens—development will choose the female path at every epigenetic choice point. If, however, masculinizing factors are present during the critical periods for development of the gonads, reproductive organs, and brain, development takes the masculine course. Because there are so many choice points and because androgens can be obtained from sources other than males testes, the potential developmental outcomes are far more numerous than just the two outcomes—male and female—that you may have initially envisioned. In fact, you may now find the possibilities to be so rich that you find the single terms male and female to be rather imprecise. The options in the development of gender identity and role are even richer.

Armed with our knowledge of prenatal sexual development, we can turn now to a topic of even greater interest, the postnatal development of sexual differences in behavior and personality. The first difference to concern us will be gender identity, the extent to which people think of themselves as male, female, or ambivalent. The second will be differences in the gender roles people take on.

Gender Identity

The simplest test for gender identity is to have someone fill out the standard item that appears on nearly all application forms—Sex: Male   Female

(Circle one). If people could answer this question in private, it would tell us about their self-identities as male or female, which is all that is meant by the gender-identity concept. For most people, gender identity becomes part of their self-identity beginning around 3 years of age (Kohlberg, 1966). By this time they have learned to state whether they are male or female, and they have begun to develop the realization that sexual identity is a permanent, inalterable attribute (see Chapter 14).

Our concerns regarding the development of gender identity are summed up in a pair of questions: Is gender identity determined by biological events? and Is identity alterable outside of the period of childhood during which it is normally established? The first question, in that it asks about biological determination, asks whether the general principle of nature–nurture interactions is going to be violated by the facts of identity development. The second, in that it asks about the alterability of identity, concerns whether this development is constrained by a critical or sensitive period. Relevant data for answering both questions come from a carefully studied set of case histories.

Do Biological Factors Determine Gender Identity?

As regards gender identity, the biological factors of prenatal history and current hormonal state appear to have little if any impact. This, at least, is the conclusion of John Money of Johns Hopkins University and Anke Ehrhardt (see Ehrhardt & Meyer-Bahlburg, 1981; Money-Ehrhardt, 1972). From a mass of case history data, they have developed a persuasive argument for their point of view.

One of the most compelling case histories is of twins, both born as males. During circumcision in which a cauterization technique was used, one of the boys was burned to the point that a normal penis could not be reconstructed. Because of this, the doctor recommended a sex-change operation, and the parents agreed. The operation took place, and hormone therapy was begun so that the boy-turned-girl would have a proper feminine hormone balance. The last clinical report of her progress (Money & Tucker, 1975) was that she was a quite normal young girl, quite confident of her femininity. Her mother in fact wrote that she was amazed by her little girl's feminine ways:

> I've never seen a little girl so neat and tidy as she can be when she wants to be. . . . She is very proud of herself, when she puts on a new dress, or I set her hair. She just loves to have her hair set; she could sit under the drier all day long to have her hair set. She just loves it. (Money & Ehrhardt, 1972, p. 119-20).

None of these things were true of the twin brother. He was quite the little man in his behavior.

Because the "girl" in Money and Ehrhardt's case history was castrated and placed on feminine hormones as part of her medical treatment, a critic who wanted to maintain a biological explanation for gender identity could say that her hormonal condition accounted for her feminine identity. For this argument, however, Money and Ehrhardt have other case histories. The most convincing are case histories of individuals whose genitals at birth did not clearly qualify them as male or female in the eyes of the family or the medical staff attending the delivery. These individuals' ambiguous state meant that they were *hermaphrodites,* a word formed from the names Hermes and Aphrodite, who, in Greek mythology, were parents to a child of mixed sexual properties. The medical practice appropriate at hermaphroditic births is for the physician to assign a sex. Money and Ehrhardt examined case histories involving both male and female assignments and discovered that if the assignment was made at a young age, gender identity was completely plastic, regardless of the amount of testosterone, progesterone, and estrogen present in the blood.

In one of the Money and Ehrhardt (1972) case histories, for example, a child with adrenocortical hyperplasia (the condition in which the adrenal glands become a source of masculinizing androgens) was assigned at birth to be a boy and was reared unambiguously as a boy until the age of 12. At this age, when he expected to experience the masculinizing effect of the male hormones associated with puberty, a shocking discovery was made. Except for the boy's penis and empty scrotum, he was a female. That is, he had an XX genotype and had functioning ovaries. The estrogen production of these ovaries had been stepped up due to the events of puberty, with the result that this boy was experiencing breast development and other feminine changes that were discordant with his belief that he was male. The extent to which he was feminized by the onset of puberty is clearly evident in the picture of him shown in Figure 4-17A.

When the boy was 13 years old and strongly feminized in his appearance, he was referred to Johns Hopkins for the purpose of obtaining a sex-change operation. The decision was made, however, not to perform this operation. Money and Ehrhardt report that the reason for not recommending the operation was the same as would be given for any 13-year-old boy. In identity he was a psychological male, not a female. He enjoyed hunting and fishing with his dad, and he raced motorbikes. His mother reported, "He has a sister, and they are completely different. He does not think like a girl, and he does not have the same interests" (Money & Ehrhardt, 1972, p. 156). For his mother, the "clincher" that her boy was not a girl was that he had a girlfriend. Not only that, he became erotically aroused experiencing "a slow secretion of genital moistness" when he was with his girlfriend and when girl watching. In this one case it is clear, then, that the boy's gender identity stood firm in the face of a lot of discrepant information from both his physical and hormonal state.

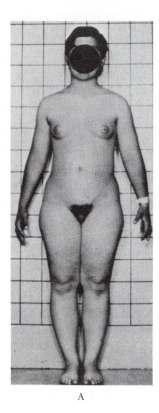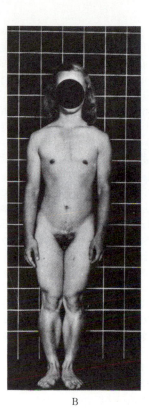

A   B

FIGURE 4-17
Individuals Discordant for Body Type and Gender Identity
The individual in panel A has a male gender identity despite his body, which has
been feminized by the hormonal output of the ovaries he does not know he has.
The individual in panel B has a female gender identity despite the masculinization
of her body, which has occurred as a result of an output of adrenal androgens that
has gone unchecked.

Just as there are case histories of boys whose masculine identity has
not been shaken by the feminizing effects of ovarian hormones, so too are
there cases of females whose feminine identities have not been shaken by
the masculinizing effects of male hormones. For example, the individual
shown in Figure 4-17B, like the one in 4-17A, had adrenocortical hyperplasia. The masculinity of her appearance stems from the fact that her hyperplasia had gone untreated. This meant that throughout childhood, the malfunctioning adrenal glands continued to be a source of excess androgens.
These androgens led to the masculinization seen in the photograph, as well
as to characteristics that the photograph cannot show, such as a deep voice.
Despite the discordant physical and hormonal condition, she strongly main-

tained a feminine gender identity. When her hyperplasia was detected at age 12, she began cortisone therapy to correct her abnormal hormone condition. The cortisone treatment led her to develop the normal secondary sexual characteristics of females, and she underwent surgery to complete her feminine appearance. Today she maintains her feminine gender identity and, at last report, is married and enjoys a normal heterosexual sex life.

The total collection of Money and Ehrhardt case histories makes a compelling argument that nature, as represented in one's physical, genetic, and hormonal condition, has little to do with gender identity. But can we conclude that nature has nothing to do with it? If so, we will have found a case in which the interaction rule does not apply. Rather than being the joint outcome of nature and nurture in interaction, gender identity will be a personality attribute shaped in Watson-like fashion by the environment alone. From this purely environmentalist perspective, which is in fact the perspective taken by Money, Ehrhardt, and others (see, for example, Hoyenga & Hoyenga, 1979), a child's gender identity is putty in the hands of those who rear the child.

While compelling, the environmentalist view is probably too extreme. The best argument against it is the phenomenon of transsexualism. Transsexuals are individuals with a gender identity opposite both to their biological gender and gender of rearing. Although some investigators argue that transsexuals develop their gender-identity conflict because they are reared in a confusing way (for example, a mother who wanted her boy to be a girl or a father who wanted his girl to be a boy), this argument is pure speculation, and some case histories offer no evidence for it at all. In one recently reported case (Shore, 1984) a boy, Michael, chose to become a girl, Micki, even though he had been highly successful as a male. In high school, for example, he had been the president of his class and the captain of the football team. In his early childhood there was no evidence that his parents had induced any gender confusion. The father, a truck driver, and the mother, a homemaker, had treated him like a normal boy, including having him sleep with his older brother whom he admired. Nonetheless, Michael knew from early childhood that his body was "wrong," and he began secretly dressing in his twin sister's clothes.

Michael's case history is not unusual for transsexuals. Many case studies are equally impossible to understand from a purely environmental perspective. This has led John Hoenig of the Gender Identity Institute in Toronto to declare that transsexuals provide a very clear exception to the Money and Ehrhardt rule that the environment alone determines gender identity (Hoenig, 1985). "Whatever the merits of [Money and Ehrhardt's] views in relation to hermaphrodites," he writes, "it is obvious that they do not have any application to the origin of abnormal gender identity in transsexuals." The reason, he says, is that transsexuals have no physical abnormalities in their genitals, no ambiguity at birth, no improper assignment or rearing, and yet "in spite of all this and often in the face of harsh efforts by their parents and peers to correct or prevent this, they show, usually from the earliest age, a paradoxical gender identity" (p. 33). Such data have caused researchers to restore an interest in "biological forces" that might contribute to a gender-identity preference. Despite promising leads (Eicher, 1984), no specific factors have yet been identified.

Although there is no conclusive evidence yet that nature factors play a role in the development of gender identity, the data on transsexuals do call into question the validity of an extreme environmentalist position. It is quite possible, therefore, that biological factors will eventually be found that interact with environmental factors in the development of gender identity just as they do in every other domain or behavior. For example, it is interesting to note that a question has been raised about the gender adjustment of the boy who became a girl following the circumcision accident. According to some psychiatrists who examined her at age 13, she is not as comfortable with her female gender identity as Money last claimed (Diamond, 1982).

Is There a Critical Period for Establishing Gender Identity?

The belief that there might be a critical period for the establishment of gender identity stems from the early work of John Money (Money, Hampson, & Hampson, 1955) in which he speculated that the period of childhood lasting from 18 to 30 months was the period during which a person would normally be "imprinted" with a gender identity. Once established, this identity was considered to be irreversible. The initial evidence for this position was the fate of children who were given sex-change operations. Operations undertaken after age 2½ were successful in altering the anatomy of the children, but their identities were confused. The implication was that these children already had begun to form a firm identity, and the effects of that early identity formation could not then be reversed. Only by operating prior to identity formation, could there be a successful psychological outcome.

Some of the Money and Ehrhardt case histories do point to gender confusion in children with childhood sex changes, but it is never clear that the confusion stems from the children themselves. An alternative hypothesis is that the confusion stems from the child's social environment. If the parents, for example, are confused about the "true" sex of their child, it is not surprising that the child would be confused. Another of the Money and Ehrhardt case histories in fact shows how the social environment could make it difficult for a child to adjust to a new self-identity. In this case, a "girl" was registered on her birth certificate as a boy, but during 2½ years of hospitalization caused by complications resulting from her adrenocortical hyperplasia, she was called by a girl's name and was treated as a girl. Despite being treated as a girl, corrective surgery to demasculinize her genitals was not initiated, and for some unknown reason she was taken off cortisone.

This caused her to begin a "precocious and strongly masculinizing puberty." Her parents accepted all this with the belief that the Creator had meant her to live this way. Although the parents now accepted her as a girl, people in the neighborhood thought she was a boy. When finally referred for medical help, the "girl" elected to receive masculinizing surgery, but she was clearly confused about her gender.

Money and Ehrhardt present cases of uncertain gender identity such as this as evidence in favor of their hypothesis that there is a critical period from 18 to 30 months of age for the establishment of gender identity. They believe that an identity established during this period cannot be successfully altered and that an identity that is confused during this period will be forever confused. As we have seen, however, an equally plausible explanation for gender confusion is that the confusion exists because of perpetuated confusion in the social environment, not because a critical period has been exceeded. To test this hypothesis, we would need to have evidence from cases in which the social environment conspires to go along with a post-critical-period gender change. Such data in fact exist. They come from work conducted in the Dominican Republic by Cornell University endocrinologist Julianne Imperato-McGinley and colleagues (1979). The generalization to be drawn from her work is that the critical-period hypothesis is wrong.

Imperato-McGinley's data concerned 18 Dominicans, all of whom had had firm female gender identities throughout childhood. They had been raised as females because their external genitals were female in appearance at birth. In fact, however, they were males with a form of androgen insensitivity that left their external genitals unmasculinized. Thus each had a penis that was clitorislike in appearance and an apparent vaginal opening. The amazing part of the story is that in adolescence all of these individuals experienced near complete masculinization of their genitals. The clitorislike penis grew, the apparent labia fused to form a scrotal sack, and the testicles descended into this sack. The reason for these oddities was due to a genetic defect whereby the tissue that makes up the prenatal genital structures did not respond to the presence of testosterone. Pubertal hormones from the testes, however, were able to correct the defect, with the result that persons who thought themselves to be a female were discovered in adolescence to be male. The condition is now so frequent in the areas of the Dominican Republic where Imperato-McGinley did her work that the natives even have names for it. They call it *guevedoce,* penis at twelve, and *machihembra,* first woman then man.

It is truly astounding to believe that individuals who have been raised to be female–particularly in a rigidly sexually divided culture such as that in rural areas of the Dominican Republic—could make an easy adjustment to becoming males, but that is what Imperato-McGinley and her colleagues claim. In their view, however, the community's laissez-faire acceptance of the change played an important role. The community accepted the sex change by giving the "girls" boys' names and treating them accordingly. With no confusion in the community, there was little confusion in the individuals. Imperato-McGinley and her colleagues in fact claim that 17 of the 18 individuals whom they studied made a successful adjustment to a male gender identity. A more conservative estimate puts the number of successful readjustments at 13 (Rubin, Reinisch, & Haskett, 1981), but nonetheless even one successful readjustment, if indeed it occurred following a childhood of totally unambiguous rearing as a female, would make the point that such changes do lie within the epigenetic potential of human beings, thereby falsifying the critical-period hypothesis.

Gender Roles

Gender roles vary from culture to culture and from time to time, but at any one time in any one culture there have traditionally been fairly clear notions of the roles that should be reserved for males and those that should be reserved for females. Frequently, for example, males are cast in the role of warrior–provider and females in the role of homemaker–childrearer. Personality attributes also become part of societies' definitions of the male and female roles. Males are frequently characterized as aggressive, arrogant, and independent; females, as gentle, understanding, and subordinate. The question to be answered here is whether sex roles such as these are ever determined by nature alone.

To begin answering our question, we can consider some data on male and female behavior in animals, because animals, like humans, have some sex-specific behaviors. The first thing to note about these data is that hormones in animals seem to have fairly direct control over the stereotyped behaviors of males and females. Through programs of pre- and postnatal hormone regulation, female birds can be induced to sing male songs, female dogs will lift their legs to urinate, and female monkeys will refuse to "present" themselves to males who wish to copulate. By the same token, prenatal castration of male animals and later estrogen and progesterone treatment can bring out in males behaviors that are typically female. Male rats, for example, who have been given progesterone following castration early in life will build nests and care for the young.

Although human behavior is far less responsive to hormone levels than is nonhuman behavior, there is some interesting evidence that links prenatal exposure to androgens with malelike behavioral choices in humans. Much of this evidence has been compiled by Anke Ehrhardt (reported in Money & Ehrhardt, 1972) using data collected on some of the Money and Ehrhardt case histories of women with feminine gender identities yet prenatal histories of androgen exposure.

The women studied by Ehrhardt were of two clinical types. One type was women who had adrenocortical hyperplasia, the condition that causes unavoidable prenatal exposure to androgens (and postnatal exposure, as well, in women who do not obtain regular cortisone injections). The second type was women whose mothers had taken the drug progestin during their pregnancies, a drug whose androgenlike effects result in the same prenatal genital and brain masculinization as occurs with adrenocortical hyperplasia.

In comparing women from the two clinical categories with normal women who had been matched with the clinical subjects on race, age, IQ, and socioeconomic status, Ehrhardt examined a number of areas in which males and females typically differ: tomboyism, energy expenditure in recreation and aggression, clothing and adornment, toy preference, interest in infant caretaking, and orientation toward marriage or career. The results of the study, obtained from interviews and sex-role preference tests, give strong support to the hypothesis that prenatal exposure to androgens has a masculinizing effect on behavior, because the women in both clinical groups tended to be more masculine on average than their matched controls among the normal women. This is not to say, of course, that all of the subjects exposed to prenatal androgens had a male profile of behaviors and interests. Far from it. What it means is simply that women with adrenocortical hyperplasia were somewhat more likely than normal women to have a male profile, and the same was true of women exposed to progestin prenatally.

The specific areas in which women exposed to androgens prenatally were most likely to differ from normal women were in the areas of tomboyism and energy expenditure in play and aggression. Also, they tended to prefer male toys (such as cars and guns) to female toys (such as dolls) and to consider career ahead of marriage. These findings were not at all unexpected, because Money and Ehrhardt had found frequent reference in their case histories to the tomboyism of girls with a history of prenatal androgen exposure. Ehrhardt's studies only confirmed what they had already suspected to be the case. In this regard you may recall the study of prenatal androgen exposure in female monkeys and the later discovery that they were more rough and tumble in their play than normal females. A number of related laboratory and case-history observations support the general validity of the hypothesis that prenatal androgen exposure is associated with the development of later sex-related behaviors. Interestingly, this does not extend to sexual preferences. Prenatal exposure to androgens is unrelated to lesbianism and bisexuality (Hines, 1982).

Given that Ehrhardt's data showed that prenatal exposure to androgens was related to subsequent masculine role development, we must wonder why. What was the developmental course by which this was achieved? One way would be through biological means alone. This nativist view, however, simply does not fit with all that we know of development. To hold a nativist view regarding Ehrhardt's data, one would have to assume that once programmed prenatally, behavior would be on an inalterable track toward masculine roles. This seems preposterous. If Zing Yang Kuo could alter such species-typical behaviors as rat- and bird-killing by cats, surely it is within the environment's power to rechannel sex-typical behaviors in humans. What is more likely is that prenatal androgen exposure has some specific effect that only tips the developmental landscape in the masculine direction. A possibility, for example, is that prenatal exposure, through its effects on the brain, could establish a broad behavioral preference for high levels of activity. Girls who preferred more active play would find it more pleasurable to play the games usually associated with males. To play them, they would have to socialize more with males, thereby gaining greater exposure to male peers and their values. In normal females with higher activity levels, a preference for vigorous games and male playmates might be subtly or overtly discouraged as unfeminine; but consider the case of women who were hermaphroditic at birth. Not only would these girls themselves know of their hermaphroditism, but their parents would too. It is easy to imagine that a parent, knowing of a daughter's prenatal masculinization, might accept masculine role choices by this girl as "normal" and, therefore, tolerate in her what would not be tolerated in other daughters. If so, then the development of the ultimate sex-role preferences of hermaphroditic women would clearly be due not to biology alone or to the social environment alone but to the intricate interaction of the two.

SUMMARY

This chapter began with the question of whether the plasticity of human development might be compromised somewhat by the existence of critical periods in development. The concept of a critical period comes from embryology, where it refers to the brief periods of time during which structures are rapidly emerging and first forming themselves into systems. In this embryological context, the critical-period concept helps us understand why teratogenic effects differ as a function of when the teratogen is introduced into the environment of the developing organism. Konrad Lorenz was the first to suggest that the critical periods in embryological development might find their parallels in psychological development. Lorenz's example of filial and sexual imprinting did indeed seem to fit the critical-period model. Other developments were later found that also appeared to fit the model. Among them are the learning of star maps and birdsongs in some birds and the formation of mother–infant bonds in goats and rats.

The discovery that some aspects of psychological development in some animals seemed to be organized according to the critical-period model led investigators to wonder whether the model might not also apply to aspects of human psychological development. Of particular concern was the development of human social relations. Research has now alleviated most of the fear that human children who have abnormal social experiences (for example, separation from their mothers, inadequate mothering, or no opportunity to form a primary attachment) will be marked for life by virtue of the early experience alone. The reason is that the critical-period concept does not apply in the case of human social development. Thinking that it did in the first place was based primarily on reasoning by analogy. The scientific data show no evidence that imprinting has any direct human parallels and precious little evidence that maternal bonding does. Moreover, evaluating the critical-period hypothesis in human social development from a purely logical point of view reveals it to have no merit. For one thing, the controls regulating human social behavior are far, far more complex than in the animals to which humans are compared whenever the critical-period hypothesis is invoked. Also, the critical-period hypothesis makes no sense in light of what we know of human evolution.

A further reason to discount the earlier concern that the critical-period model might have wide-scale application in human psychological development is that it is not even widespread in animal psychological development. Some of the developments originally thought to occur in critical periods have now been shown to occur in either sensitive or foundational periods. This means that many effects of early experience are at least alterable and perhaps reversible. Thus the only real relevance of the critical-period model in human psychological development is for behaviors that depend on specific brain structures. If these brain structures have a time-limited period of plasticity, then the behaviors will, too.

The chapter concluded with a discussion of the development of sexual differences in human anatomy, gender identity, and sex-role behavior. The reason for this discussion was that what we know of the development of sexual differences vividly illustrates the major points from both this chapter and the previous one. In a way that can be visualized using Waddington's epigenetic landscape, the process of sexual development begins with a set of vast potentialities, all of which are inherent in the initial genetic constitution. During ontogeny, environmental and biological factors act on development to channel it toward certain of these potentialities. In some cases it matters greatly when these factors act (for example, in determining aspects of one's sexual anatomy); in other cases it matters less or perhaps not at all (for example, in determining gender identity). Even when there are specific timing effects, however, as in the critical period during which androgen can affect the developing brain, they apply to structure but not behavior. Critical-period developments—particularly those in the brain—may tilt behavior in a certain direction, but they hardly rob it of its plasticity. This extended example of epigenesis provided by sexual development makes clear, as did the miniexamples that preceded it in both this chapter and the previous one, that development is not an either–or process that features nature and nurture as independent causal agents. Instead it is a complex interactive process in which current developments are conditioned by past history, maturational state, genetic potential, and current environmental forces.

SUGGESTIONS FOR FURTHER READING

Bateson, P. (1979). How do sensitive periods arise and what are they for? *Animal Behaviour, 27,* 470–86.

Clarke, A. M. & Clarke, A. D. B. (1976). *Early experience: Myth and evidence.* New York: The Free Press. This is a classic text that was the first major work to challenge the assumption that early experience might serve to lock social, cognitive, or personality development onto an inalterable course.

Immelmann, K., Barlow, G. W., Petrinovich, L., & Main, M. (Eds.). (1981). *Behavioral development: The Bielefeld interdisciplinary project.* Cambridge: Cambridge University Press. This remarkably good collection of papers by psychologists and biologists who participated in a 9-month-long interdisciplinary conference held at Bielefeld, West Germany, will be of interest to advanced students. The epigenetic view of development is represented throughout the collection.

Money, J. & Ehrhardt, A. A. (1972). *Man & woman boy & girl.* Baltimore: Johns Hopkins University Press. The seminal work on the development of gender identity from conception to maturity. Contains valuable case history data. A follow-up volume of interest is J. Money and P. Tucker's 1975 text, *Sexual signatures: On being a man or a woman,* Toronto: Little, Brown.

Sluckin, W. (1965). *Imprinting and early learning.* Chicago: Aldine. This scholarly text serves to explain why the concept of imprinting was originally of such interest to developmental psychologists.

Tavris, C. & Wade, C. (1984). *The longest war: Sex differences in perspective* (2nd ed.). San Diego, CA: Harcourt Brace Jovanovich. An entertaining and lively presentation of the data on sex differences and the various approaches that scientists have taken to explain these differences.

CHAPTER 5

Behavioral Genetics

THE FOCUS ON INDIVIDUAL DIFFERENCES

As we saw in Chapters 3 and 4, the value of the concept of epigenesis to developmental psychology is that it conceptualizes the mutual influences of nature and nurture on development in a way that avoids the either–or view of development. Thus, as shown in the example of sexual development, neither the biological nor psychological aspects of our sexuality are predetermined at conception. The epigenetic process by which they emerge is an interactive one in which nature and nurture have reciprocal effects on one another, making the two indistinguishable as causal factors.

Because the epigenetic nature of development has been emphasized so strongly to this point, it may now come as a surprise to you that we are about to spend a whole chapter on the topic of behavioral genetics, a discipline dedicated to measuring and understanding genetic influences on behavior. As you will soon see, behavioral geneticists talk in terms of the *independent* roles of genetics and environment. On the surface, such language seems to be absolutely antithetical to the epigenetic view that we have been developing. Could it be that the behavioral geneticists are out of touch? Not at all. No psychologists are more aware of the epigenetic nature of individual development than are behavioral geneticists such as Sandra Scarr (see, for example, Scarr & Weinberg, 1983) of the University of Virginia or Robert Plomin (see, for example, Plomin, 1981) of the University of Colorado.

The key to understanding how Scarr, Plomin, and others can talk of the independent roles of genetics and environment and yet be epigeneticists lies in understanding that behavioral genetics is concerned with explaining the *differences* between people in their development. The either–or question we have ruled out as meaningless applies to the development of individuals. This either–or question cannot be answered, because an individual cannot be broken down into genetic and environmental components. Individuals are inseparable entities. The differences *between* individuals, on the other hand, can be broken down in this way. Some portion of the difference is attributable to the fact that people differ genetically and some portion to the fact that they have different life histories.

To take the simplest of all examples, consider the case of identical twins who are different in height and weight (see Figure 5-1). The height and weight of either one of them alone is due neither to genes nor environment nor any quantifiable combination of the two, such as two-thirds genes and one-third environment. The reason is that the height and weight of an individual are epigenetic phenomena to which both genes and environment contribute. But if the two twins are different in height and

FIGURE 5-1

Individual Differences Due to the Environment

Although these MZ twins are remarkably similar in their body shape and facial characteristics, they are remarkably different in overall height and weight. These differences are due to differences in their life histories. The differences occurred because the twins were separated at birth and reared apart. The twin on the left was reared by a relative who, according to Tanner, was "neurotic and cruel" (1978, p. 119). The twin on the right was raised by "sympathetic" parents.

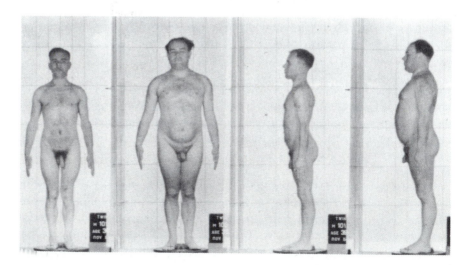

weight—as those in Figure 5-1 are—we can say unequivocally that the difference is due solely to environmental factors. The difference must be environmental in origin because the individuals are *monozygotic* twins: they developed from a single fertilized egg and, therefore, are genetically the same. By the same token, if we have biologically unrelated individuals who differ in height and weight after being reared in identical environments (in practice, of course, identical environments can never be completely realized, not even with laboratory animals), we can be sure that the source of the difference lies in their genes.

The logic of behavioral genetics for separating environmental from genetic sources of variability, revealed in the examples above, is really quite simple: find a character on which people differ and then break down their difference into genetic and environmental components. While this logic is simple, the methods behavioral geneticists use for determining whether differences among individuals are genetic or environmental in origin (and particularly the methods for quantifying the extent to which differences are genetic or environmental) can become quite complex. We will begin, therefore, with a consideration of the methods of behavioral genetics. Following this presentation of the methods, we will present some interesting findings from behavioral genetics regarding differences among us in intelligence, personality, and mental health. The chapter will conclude with a consideration of the means through which genetic differences can produce psychological differences.

METHODS

Data from three sources are used to answer questions regarding whether and to what extent the psychological differences among individuals are rooted in their genetic differences. The sources are *controlled breeding studies, family studies,* and *natural experiments.* The data from these three sources differ in the extent to which they can be used to separate genetic from environmental effects on individuals. **Controlled breeding studies** separate heredity and environment best. The results from these studies lead to statements regarding the effects of heredity and environment that have the best claim to validity. The shortcoming of controlled breeding studies is that, for ethical reasons, they cannot be used to dissect the genetic and environmental contributions to differences in human behavior. **Family studies,** on the other hand, are perfectly usable with humans. The only problem is that they are purely correlational in nature: they examine which traits run in which families but do not separate the effects of shared environments from the effects of shared genes. **Natural experiments** are the best compromise between the ethical constraints on the study of humans and the scientific need to separate genetic from environmental influences.

They take advantage of the biological phenomenon of twinning and the social phenomenon of adoption.

Controlled Breeding Studies

Controlled breeding studies can involve either inbreeding or selective breeding. The difference lies in whether mating partners are selected on the basis of kinship **(inbreeding)** or physical/behavioral resemblance **(selective breeding).** Though the experimental use of these methods is restricted to animals for ethical reasons, and to fast-breeding animals for practical reasons, there are some naturally occurring instances of both inbreeding and selective breeding in human populations. Inbreeding, for example, was the procedure used by royal families in Egypt and Europe for maintaining "pure" bloodlines. Some selective breeding occurs in all human populations by virtue of the fact that matings are not random events. We select our mates, and when we do, we tend to select mates who are more similar to us than they are different. Human mates tend to be alike, for example, in intelligence, height, and personality. (This phenomenon is known as *assortative mating.)*

Inbreeding

When inbreeding is used experimentally, the result is a whole race of animals—called a **strain**—which are virtual genetic clones of one another. To attain such strains, geneticists begin with a single pair of animals—usually a brother–sister pair. When these animals produce offspring (called the F_1 or *first filial generation),* a second brother–sister pair is selected. These animals mate to produce the F_2 generation from which we again select a single brother–sister pair. Continuing in this way results in offspring that are ever-more like one another genetically. In theory, if this process were continued long enough, we would eventually obtain offspring all of which were genetically identical. In practice, we would probably just get very, very close to attaining total genetic identity.

    Inbreeding achieves near genetic identity among strain members by eliminating what are called *heterozygotic* gene combinations. These are combinations in which the pair of genes at a particular site (or *locus)* on homologous chromosomes are different forms *(alleles)* of the same gene. In Mendelian notation, the alleles of a particular gene are designated using capital and lowercase letters. So if one has an Aa gene pair at some chromosomal locus, that individual is said to be heterozygotic for that locus because the alleles are different. AA or aa individuals, on the other hand, are *homozygotic* for that locus.

    By inbreeding brother and sister pairs, we can reduce by one fourth the number of heterozygotic loci in each successive generation. Thus if we begin with 50 percent homozygosity in a sibling pair, then their offspring will be 62.5 percent homozygous on average. When we continue in this way for 20 generations, we wind up with offspring in which 98 percent of all gene pairs are homozygotic. Continuing beyond 20 generations, we get ever-closer to 100 percent. The importance of this is that it reveals the way in which the offspring of *inbred strains* (technically 20 generations plus of inbreeding) maintain their genetic identities: the gene pool has become restricted to a single allelic form for each chromosomal locus. Thus, when both the father and mother are identical homozygotes (for example, AA and AA), the offspring will also be AA. If the parents had been heterozygotes (Aa), however, the offspring could have been any one of three genotypes— AA, aa, or Aa. The rate at which homozygosity is achieved is solely determined by the number of alleles that the breeding animals share at the outset, and this is determined by their kinship. The rates at which homozygosity is achieved for different kinships is shown in Figure 5-2.

Answering Questions with Data from Inbred Strains   Inbred strains can be used to answer any number of behavioral-genetics questions. The most

FIGURE 5-2

Inbreeding Leads to Homozygosity

This graph shows the rate at which homozygosity is achieved under different inbreeding programs. The brother–sister method is the one normally used to produce inbred strains of animals.

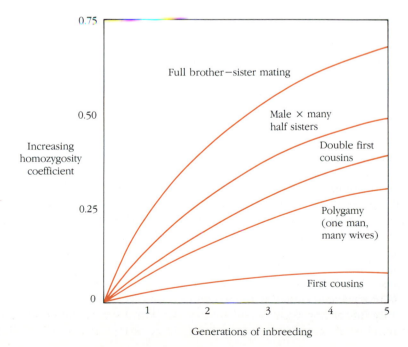

basic, is Do the animals of different strains differ in their behavior, even when they are raised under identical conditions? Answering this question involves using the method known as *strain comparison*. The strains of interest are selected, and offspring from each strain are put into identical environments—same cages, same food, same lighting, and even same mothers. They are then observed for any differences in their behavior. Whatever the behavioral differences are, they can be presumed to exist because of genetic differences. The logic—and limitations—of this approach can be understood by using the example of Ressler's study of cross-fostered mice (see Chapter 3). As you will recall from Ressler's study, pigmented mice raised by albino mothers differed from albino pups raised by albino mothers (and vice versa). This result clearly implicates the pigmented–albino genetic difference as one source of the differences in weight and exploratory behavior—the two traits studied by Ressler. This is a valuable contribution to knowledge, but please note that it does not tell us why genetics is important (for example, that albino mice get more licking and grooming); it just tells us that genetic differences make a difference. The exact reason must be worked out from developmental studies, a point to which we will return at the conclusion of this chapter.

Richard L. Sprott and Joan Staats of the Jackson Laboratory at Bar Harbor, Maine, have been keeping track of the studies in which behavioral comparisons have been made between animals from different inbred strains. As of 1980 (see Sprott & Staats, 1981), there were better than 2,000 of these. The general conclusion to be drawn from all these strain comparisons is that strains can be expected to differ on just about any behavior you measure them on. Inbred strains of mice, for example, differ in their susceptibility for seizures, ability to learn, taste preferences, activity levels, anxiety shown in novel environments, alcohol preference, and a host of other behaviorally relevant dimensions. We can conclude that not all mice are born equal; given the same environment in which to develop, they nonetheless develop differently. What is true here of mice is true of humans as well.

Because of the relative ease with which strain differences can be found, it has become almost trivial to produce them. Today, therefore, strain-comparison studies go beyond the simple question, Is there a difference? For our purposes, though, we do not need to know anything about the more complex strain studies, ones that involve *hybrid* strains and *backcrosses*. It is sufficient for us to know that the outcome of strain-comparison studies has been to show that it is far harder to find an animal behavior that is not affected by genetics than it is to find one that is.

Selective Breeding

In inbreeding, mating partners are selected merely on the basis of kinship or genotypic similarity; in selective breeding they are selected on the basis of their physical/behavioral, or *phenotypic,* similarity. This makes selective breeding a procedure of great practical importance. An individual's genotype after all is of interest only to geneticists and genealogists. But the **phenotype**—the sum total of an individual's physical and behavioral attributes—is of practical concern because it represents what becomes of genetic potential.

Long before anyone knew the mechanism by which "like begets like," farmers, hunters, and sportsmen practiced selective breeding as a means of improving their crops, cows, hunting dogs, and horses. They used selective breeding as a practical tool. For behavioral geneticists, on the other hand, selective breeding is a theoretical tool, because mating individuals similar on a trait provides a direct means of determining whether or not that trait is influenced by genetics. If the trait responds to selective breeding, that is, if the offspring tend to resemble their parents, we can conclude that genetics does indeed play a role in creating the similarity.

When selective breeding is employed in behavioral-genetics studies, the selection is usually done bidirectionally. This means that investigators simultaneously breed for highs and lows on the trait in question. Edward Tolman and Robert Tryon of the University of California at Berkeley used this procedure in some famous studies of maze-learning ability in rats. The trait they were concerned with was labeled "maze brightness." Animals high on the trait were known as *maze bright* and those low on the trait were known as *maze dull.*

The Tolman–Tryon studies lacked some methodological perfections, due to the fact that theirs was pioneer work in the field; nonetheless, they demonstrated to everyone's satisfaction that a rat's propensity to enter blind

alleys in a complex 17-choice maze is a behavioral trait that can be bred for. You can increase or decrease the tendency merely by selectively breeding maze-bright animals in each generation with other maze-bright animals, and maze-dull animals with other maze-dull animals. After 7 generations of this type of selection (which in Tryon's studies was unfortunately combined with inbreeding), Tryon (1942) obtained the distribution-of-error scores

FIGURE 5-3
Maze-Bright and Maze-Dull Rats
These data from Tryon show how selective breeding affected the maze-learning performance of rats. The top of graph A shows the distribution of errors in the parent (P) generation. Animals on the lower end of this distribution are the "bright" animals. Those on the upper end are the dull animals. Bright animals were then bred to bright animals and dull to dull to produce the F_1 generation at the bottom of graph A. Here there are two distribution-of-error scores that show how the first-generation bright animals (B_1) differed from the first-generation dull animals (D_1). As you can see, there was not much difference at this point. After 7 generations of continuous selective breeding, however, there was almost no overlap in the error scores of brights (B_7) and dulls (D_7). This is shown in graph B. (After Tryon, 1942)

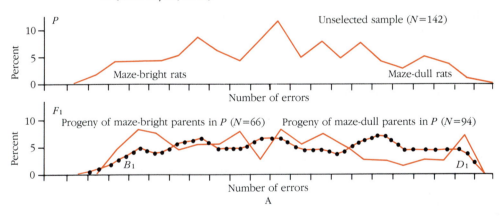

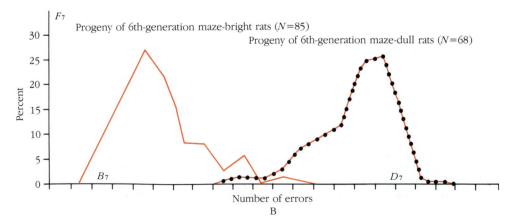

shown in Figure 5-3. What you should notice in this figure is that after the 7 generations of selective breeding, rats bred from maze-bright rats were completely distinguishable on the basis of their phenotype (in this case, maze performance) from rats bred from maze-dull rats. In a more modern selective-breeding study, Gerald McClearn (1976) has shown that the rate at which mice sleep off an inebriating dose of alcohol responds well to selection. Figure 5-4 shows that after 15 generations in which the mice were bred to be either long or short sleepers, there was a complete separation of long-sleep from short-sleep mice in their phenotypes.

As in the case of inbreeding, the use of selective breeding merely to demonstrate genetic influence on a behavioral trait has become almost trivial, because nearly every trait that has been studied in whatever species (for example, open-field activity level in mice, geotaxis in fruit flies, learning in blowflies, visual preferences in quail, and brooding in chickens) has been shown to respond to selection. One of the very few traits found not to respond to selection is paw preference in mice. In a study by Robert L. Collins (1968), for example, after 4 generations of breeding for left- and right-pawed individuals, the original 50–50 odds of being one or the other had not changed. These data probably have no implications for humans

FIGURE 5-4

Effects of Alcohol Respond to Selection

McClearn's data on the amount of time it takes for mice to sleep off an injection of ethanol show that this trait—sleep time—responds well to selection. Mice selectively bred to be short sleepers showed progressive differentiation from mice bred to be long sleepers. Although the data here do not indicate the degree of variability in sleep times that surrounded the group averages, McClearn reports elsewhere (Plomin, DeFries, & McClearn, 1980, p. 272) that after the 15 generations of selective breeding (selection was suspended in Generations 6 through 8), there was total separation of long sleepers from short sleepers. (After Plomin, DeFries, & McClearn, 1980)

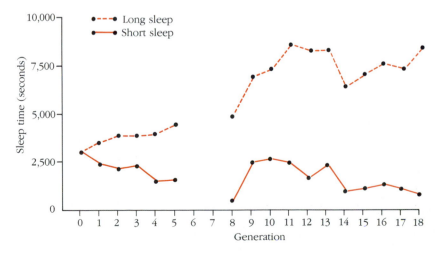

though, because recent data indicate that human hand preference would respond to selective breeding (Carter-Saltzman, 1980).

As methods, inbreeding and selective breeding are of vital importance to the behavioral geneticist, because when coupled with other breeding procedures (for example, crosses and backcrosses of strains and breeds) they yield some rather precise information. Using procedures not reviewed here, they allow the determination of whether a trait is controlled by one major gene (a **monogenic trait)** or by more than one (a **polygenic trait).** Moreover, in some cases, even the chromosomes on which the genes are located can be determined, along with linkages that exist among some genes. Furthermore, data from breeding studies can be analyzed statistically to yield estimates of the extent of genetic as opposed to environmental influence on a trait. The reason it is not necessary for us to delve too deeply into these procedures is that they cannot be used with humans. Currently we allow ourselves liberties in the study of animals that are ethically forbidden in the study of humans. In the study of human behavioral genetics, therefore, animal studies are of interest only in so far as we can draw conclusions from them that are relevant to humans. For the direct study of humans, behavioral geneticists must rely on nonexperimental techniques, such as family studies, and quasi-experimental techniques, such as twin and adoption studies.

Family Studies: The Sins of the Past

Family studies, also known as *consanguinity* (same blood) *studies,* examine the phenotypic similarities of family members for evidence of genetic inheritance. They are not experiments, because the investigators do not exercise any control over the breeding of the individuals whom they study (or the environments in which these individuals are raised).

The fact that there is no experimental control greatly limits the conclusions that can be drawn from family studies. For example, family studies of the Fore tribe in New Guinea (see Ehrman & Parsons, 1981) led to the belief that the neurological disease *kuru,* which once afflicted these people, was genetically transmitted. It turned out, however, to be due to a viral infection that was transmitted within families by the practice of eating the brains of dead relatives. In this country, a disease known as *pellagra* was similarly thought to be a genetic disorder until it was shown to be due to a dietary deficiency.

Despite the problems that stem from the lack of experimental control in family studies, a great deal of information can be obtained from them when they are used properly. Unfortunately, the field of human behavioral genetics began with the injudicious use of these studies, and the field still suffers from this legacy. Before going on to the examples of the judicious use of family studies, we will digress briefly to illustrate the sins of the past, because it can be a lesson to us all to be slow in judging genetic influence merely from family resemblance. The examples to be used are two of the most famous: Francis Galton's studies of hereditary genius and Henry Goddard's study of the Kallikaks.

Galton's Hereditary-Genius Studies

The title of Francis Galton's famous collection of family studies, *Hereditary Genius,* is a bit of a misnomer because the book is not so much about the inheritance of genius in intellect as it is about the inheritance of eminence in reputation and ability. The term eminence is used throughout the book and means "a position that is attained by only 250 persons in each million of men, or by one person in 4,000" (1881, p. 10). Galton selected for his studies approximately 1,000 men (no women) who met the criterion of eminence in their respective fields—the law, politics, religion, literature, art, the military, and sports (rowing and wrestling). He then examined the extent of eminence in the *first-, second-,* and *third-degree relatives* of these eminent people. The first category consisted of fathers, brothers, and sons (those whom today we know share one half of their genes on average); the second, of grandfathers, uncles, nephews, and grandsons (those who share one fourth of their genes on average); and the third, great-grandfathers, great-uncles, first cousins, great-nephews, and great-grandsons (those who share but one eighth of their genes on average). The results of the study were quite clear (see Table 5-1). Regardless of the field of eminence, first-degree relatives of eminent people were more likely to be eminent themselves than were second-degree relatives, and second-degree relatives of eminent people were more likely to be eminent than were third-degree relatives. Even third-degree relatives, however, stood a far better chance of being eminent than men taken at random.

The data obtained from Galton's large collection of family studies was quite consistent with his hereditary hypothesis, because as degree of kinship diminished so did the frequency of eminence. This is just what one would expect if eminence is primarily influenced by genetics. The problem is, of course, that it is also what you would expect if eminence is primarily influenced by environmental factors. Each view—the hereditary one and the environmental one—is an equally parsimonious explanation of the data, because just as genetic similarity decreases from first- to second- to third-degree relatives, so too does environmental similarity. We have in these data, then, a hopeless confound, which Galton did little to resolve.

Galton's primary treatment of the environmental hypothesis was merely to assert that it could not possibly account for the extent to which he had found eminence to run in families. In making this assertion, Galton did present some data, but basically he relied on a few case histories of eminent men who had come from allegedly humble backgrounds and on data from individuals who had had favored lives (for example, the adopted children of popes) and yet had failed to achieve eminence at a rate better

TABLE 5-1
Galton's Data on the Inheritance of Eminence in First-, Second- and Third-Degree Relatives

	SEPARATE GROUPS								ALL GROUPS TOGETHER
Number of families, each containing more than one eminent man	85	39	27	33	43	20	28	25	300
Total number of eminent men in all the families	262	130	89	119	148	57	97	75	977
	Judges	Statesmen	Commanders	Literary	Scientific	Poets	Artists	Divines	Illustrious and Eminent Men of all Classes
Father	26	33	47	48	26	20	32	28	31
Brother	35	39	50	42	47	40	50	36	41
Son	36	49	31	51	60	45	89	40	48
Grandfather	15	28	16	24	14	5	7	20	17
Uncle	18	18	8	24	16	5	14	40	18
Nephew	19	18	35	24	23	50	18	4	22
Grandson	19	10	12	9	14	5	18	16	14
Great-grandfather	2	8	8	3	0	0	0	4	3
Great-uncle	4	5	8	6	5	5	7	4	5
First cousin	11	21	20	18	16	0	1	8	13
Great-nephew	17	5	8	6	16	10	0	0	10
Great-grandson	6	0	0	3	7	0	0	0	3
All more remote	14	37	44	15	23	5	18	16	31

Note: Numbers in the lower portion of the table show the percentage of relatives of each type who themselves were eminent.

SOURCE: *Hereditary Genius* (p. 317) by Francis Galton, 1881, New York: Appleton.

than the chance rate of 1 in 4,000. In addition, he argued that if social-class differences such as access to an education were responsible for the fact that eminence ran in families, then the removal of social-class advantages should increase the number of eminent men to some number well beyond 1 in 4,000. Yet he noted that in America, where the barriers to an education had been removed to a greater extent than in England, there was no evidence of a great unleashing of previously untapped eminence. To the contrary,

Galton (1881) noted that "America certainly does not beat us in first-class works of literature, philosophy, or art." In fact, he wrote, "the number of their really eminent authors is more limited even than with us" (p. 40). On such grounds, Galton was satisfied in dismissing entirely the environmental explanation for his data.

Galton's work, despite its interest as a family study, has had a regrettable impact historically because of its overly adamant and unwarranted conclusion that the raw stuff of human talent is transmitted more through genes than the environment. Anyone who would read Galton's work today would see how thin his argument is, but in his own day readers were more willing to accept a hereditary argument, and so this work went on to become part of the "scientific" basis for an English–American movement known as the *eugenics movement*. The movement was dedicated to improving the human race by influencing breeding practices. The movement won great favor among racists, social and religious bigots, and the likes of Adolf Hitler.

The responsibility for the eugenics movement does not rest solely on the shoulders of the English upper class of which Galton—later Sir Galton—was a member. Prominent American scientists contributed as much if not more. One good example is the work of Henry Goddard, whose study of the Kallikak family did much to convince people in this country that genetics contributed more to individual differences in the important traits of talent and character than did the environment. As in the case of Galton's study, the problem here lies not with the study itself but with the unwarranted and prejudicial conclusions that were drawn from it (see Smith, 1985).

The Kallikaks

In 1912, Henry Goddard, psychologist at the Vineland Training School for the "feebleminded," as the retarded were then called, published a study in which he traced the ancestral ties of an 8-year-old resident of his school, Deborah Kallikak (a fictitious name). Six generations back in her past, Goddard and his field workers found a man whom they named Martin Kallikak (see Figure 5-5).

Martin, it turned out, had produced two family lines, one by way of a feebleminded barmaid he met during the revolutionary war and the other by way of an upstanding Quaker lady he married after the war. This dual lineage provided Goddard with what he judged to be data from which irrefutable conclusions could be drawn. "The biologist," Goddard wrote, "could hardly plan and carry out a more rigid experiment and one from which the conclusions would follow more inevitably" (1912, p. 69).

The "inevitable" conclusion that Goddard drew from his research was that Deborah's feeblemindedness was inherited. As evidence, he pointed to the high incidence of feeblemindedness on her entire side of the Martin

MARTIN KALLIKAK

He dallied with a feeble-minded tavern girl

He married a worthy Quakeress

She bore a son known as "Old Horror" who had ten children

She bore seven upright worthy children

From "Old Horror's" ten children came hundreds of the lowest types of human beings

From these seven worthy children came hundreds of the highest types of human beings

FIGURE 5-5

Two sides to the Kallikaks

Pedigree data collected in Henry Goddard's study of the Kallikaks led him to conclude that heredity alone was responsible for the high incidence of feeblemindedness on the illegitimate side of Martin Kallikak's line. Despite the obvious logical fallacy in this conclusion, the study had a tremendous impact in gaining popular and even legislative support for eugenics early in this century.

Kallikak family. The illicit product of the union of Martin Kallikak with his barmaid consort was a boy who grew up to be known by his neighbors as Old Horror. Although he was not feebleminded himself, Old Horror had 480 descendants, of whom only 46 could be unambiguously judged to be normal in intelligence and 147 were clearly feebleminded. This lack of intellect in the family led, according to Goddard, to general depravity. Thus there were 37 prostitutes uncovered in the research, 24 alcoholics, and 3 criminals. On the other side of the Kallikak family, no evidence of such degeneracy was found except for 2 individuals with an "appetite for strong drink." Otherwise, the lineage consisted solely of doctors, lawyers, judges, educators, and generally fine citizens. While it is amazing to us today that Goddard could view his conclusion as inevitable, it is even more amazing that his readers could have been as blind as he was to the alternative hypothesis that social conditions might be better breeders of social problems than genes are. Nonetheless, Goddard's work was added to the scientific base for the eugenics movement and, thus, further damaged the reputation of the field of human behavioral genetics as a dispassionate scientific enterprise.

Today, those who produce and consume research on the role of genetics in creating behavioral differences among humans surely have their moments of illogic, illusion, and idealogical influence, but at least we can say that they are no longer guilty of the sins of their intellectual fathers. Today, therefore, no investigator would ignore environmental explanations for the family resemblances revealed in family studies.

Modern Use of Family Studies

Because, as we have already seen, heredity and environment are hopelessly confounded in simple family studies, the use of these studies today has had to become more sophisticated. We will consider two sorts of studies here. The first will be *pedigree studies,* like those conducted by Galton and Goddard. The second will be *statistical studies* of family relationships.

Pedigree Studies

In a **pedigree study,** one begins with an *index case* or **proband.** This is a person who has the characteristic that you wish to study. In Galton's case it was each of the eminent people whom he studied. In Goddard's study it was Deborah. Through interviews with the proband and through public and private records, one then searches as extensively as possible among relatives of the proband to determine which, if any, have the same characteristic. The result of this investigation can be represented formally in a pedigree chart. A common procedure for preparing such a chart is to represent all of the individuals in a family with a circle, square, or diamond. Circles are for females, squares for males, and diamonds for people whose gender we do not know. When a person is discovered to have the trait under study, the figure representing that person is blackened in. When the trait is absent, the figure is left open. Lines that are drawn between the figures show the relationship that exists among the individuals. Mates are connected by horizontal lines like this:

Children are connected to their parents by vertical lines that fork into as many branches as there are children. Thus a two child family would look like this:

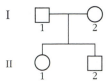

To enable us to refer to each of these symbols individually, they are numbered. The Roman numerals on the left indicate the generation; the Arabic numerals indicate the order of birth for offspring. With this representational system, we can speak of individuals using designations such as I-2 or II-1. One more convention in pedigree charts is a space-saving convention. Since we are interested primarily in people who have the trait under question and because there are usually far more people in a family without the trait than with it, we can abbreviate symbols such as:

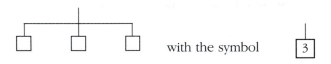

Rather than draw in the three unaffected males, we simply enlarge the usual male square and write a number inside it to represent the number of individuals of this type.

Modern pedigree studies differ in a couple of ways from those conducted by Galton and Goddard. First, pedigree studies are only done for what are called *threshold traits*. These are traits or characteristics that can be reliably judged to be either present or absent in each relative studied. Blue eyes is a trait of this sort and so is schizophrenia. The traits studied by Galton and Goddard—eminence and feeblemindedness—were *continuous*, not threshold traits, because they are characteristics that come in degrees. The possibility that such traits are influenced by heredity cannot appropriately be examined in a pedigree study. Other statistical methods, which we will review shortly, must be used. One of the reasons is that for continuous traits, there is frequently a problem in determining just how an individual is to be classed. Depending on the whims of the investigator, a given individual might be classified as exhibiting the trait and another not, when in fact there is at best a hair's difference between them. You get the impression, for example, that Goddard was guilty of some selective placement when he found "drunkards" on one side of the Kallikak family but on the other merely individuals with an "appetite for strong drink." In modern pedigree studies, any potential for ambiguity in trait measurement is resolved at the outset in an impartial way.

A second way in which the modern pedigree studies differ is that they are conducted with full knowledge of the Mendelian theory of genetic inheritance. This theory was not available at all in Galton's time and in Goddard's it was only beginning to be known. The value of Mendelian theory in judging pedigrees for genetic influence on trait expression is that the theory makes clear predictions about the patterns that should appear when traits are transmitted via single genes that are located either in the sex chromosomes (the X and Y) or in the autosomes (the other 22 chromosome pairs). The three most frequent single-gene (monogenic) transmission patterns to appear are those created by *autosomal recessive alleles, autosomal dominant alleles,* and *X-linked recessive alleles.*

Recessive, Dominant, and X-linked Genes   To understand the three most frequent modes of monogenic transmission of traits, you need to remember that genes come in pairs, each pair-member being referred to as an allele. An allele then is an individual form of a gene. Sometimes the two alleles combine in an *additive* fashion to determine the phenotype. When this is the case, both alleles can be said to express themselves in the phenotype. At some gene sites, however, one allele will completely mask the other. When this occurs, the allele that expresses itself is said to be **dominant.** The other is described as **recessive.** For a recessive allele to express itself, it must be either alone at a gene locus or matched at a locus by a second recessive allele. Matching, in the terminology developed earlier, is referred to as homozygosity. Recessive genes express themselves when they are in the homozygous state. The other time they express themselves is when they are alone. Sometimes, for example, there are chromosomal aberrations that result in lone chromosomal bodies, a condition referred to as monosomy (see p. 248). Turner's XO genotype is a good example. There is one X chromosome but no corresponding Y. This means that whatever genes are on the single X will express themselves.

Although the monosomic Turner's genotype is an aberration, even in the normal XY state, there will be gene loci on the X that are unmatched by gene loci on the Y. You can see why by examining Figure 5-6, which shows the 46 chromosomes of a normal human male arranged by size. Whereas the usual arrangement for paired chromosomes is for corresponding genes to exist at corresponding loci, this is not the case for the X and Y chromosome pair of genotypic males. Some genes on the X chromosome (transmitted to the XY individual by his mother) have no corresponding genes on the Y chromosome (transmitted by the father). This means that the traits governed by the unpaired genes transmitted from the mother—which are referred to as **X-linked** traits—will be expressed in the male phenotype. In females where every X-linked allele is matched with a corre-

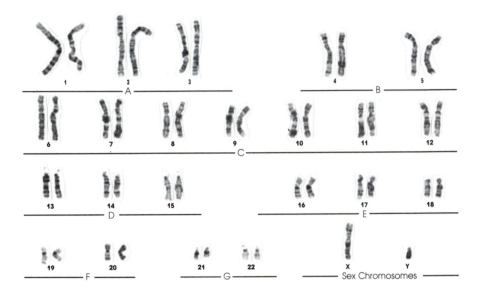

FIGURE 5-6
Chromosomal Structures in the Cells of Human Males
A normal male karyotype shows 22 pairs of autosomes with two sex chromosomes in each somatic cell. Note that all the pairs are identical in size except the sex chromosomes. This indicates that there is genetic information on the X chromosome that is unique. These unique genes will be expressed in males, even if they normally would be recessive.

sponding X-linked allele, trait expression follows the usual rules for dominance, recessivity, or additivity. This explains why X-linked recessive traits are expressed so much more often in males than in females. Take, for example, the case of color blindness, which males are 12.5 times more likely to have than females. This occurs because when a female carries the color-blind trait in one of her X chromosomes, it is passed on to half of her male offspring and expressed in these offspring. Although the trait is also passed to half of the female offspring, its expression in these females is not automatic. Because the allele for color blindness is recessive, females only express the trait when they get a second allele for color blindness from their father, thereby making them homozygous for the recessive allele.

Testing Mendelian Hypotheses Using Pedigree Data   Once one has a pedigree, testing Mendelian hypotheses is purely an exercise in logic, as is illustrated in Box 5-1. The reason is that Mendelian theory makes precise predictions about the frequency with which traits associated with single genes will appear. It makes these predictions for the offspring of parents who are known to either have the trait or to be *carriers* of the trait. (A parent is a carrier when he or she has an unexpressed recessive allele for the trait.) When the pedigree data fit the hypothesis, that is, when the pedigree matches what one would expect from Mendelian theory, the hypothesis is *confirmed.* When the data do not match theoretical expectancies, the hypothesis is *falsified.* Pedigrees, therefore, are an important testing ground for Mendelian, single-gene hypotheses for how traits might be transmitted. With the cases of kuru and pellagra (mentioned earlier) to remind us, however, we need to remember that genetic hypotheses are not the only ones to be considered when examining pedigrees. One should always keep in mind that environmental hypotheses deserve equal weight, because it is certainly possible that the pattern of resemblance in a pedigree could be due solely to environmental factors. Imagine, for example, what a pedigree for religious preference might look like!

Using pedigree analysis of the type illustrated in Box 5-1, a great deal has been learned about the transmission of many threshold traits that are of psychological importance to humans. One such trait is the inability to metabolize a protein called *phenylalanine,* which is normally present in the human diet. This disease is named *phenylketonuria* and abbreviated as PKU. When untreated, it leads to severe mental retardation. Pedigree analysis shows that this disorder appears in children whose parents do not have the disease and that about one fourth of the children in affected families have the disease. In addition, the incidence of PKU is enhanced when there is inbreeding in families. These three factors are all consistent with the hypothesis that PKU is inherited via a single recessive gene located on one of the autosomes. A pedigree is given as Figure 5-7.

FIGURE 5-7

Pedigree for Phenylketonuria

The disease known as PKU is transmitted via a recessive allele. The "outbreak" of PKU phenotypes in the fourth generation of this pedigree was due to the marriage of heterozygotic carriers of the recessive allele. Such marriages occur most often when there is inbreeding as occurred among these people, all of whom lived in an isolated group of islands in Norway. (The individuals marked with a cross were probably affected. They died young.) (After Følling, Mohr, & Rudd, 1945)

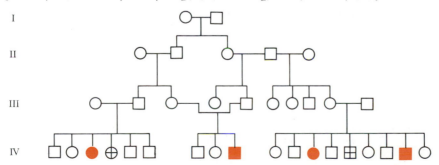

BOX 5-1
Pedigree Analysis of Testicular Feminization

For an introduction to the type of genetic analysis that can be performed using pedigrees, we can return to a disorder discussed in Chapter 4—androgen insensitivity. As you will recall, some XY individuals with functioning testes are insensitive during the prenatal and postnatal periods to the effects of testosterone. This means that they develop physically (and behaviorally) as females (see Figure 4-13). Another name for this disorder is *testicular feminization*.

The figure below presents the pedigrees for families in which testicular feminization has appeared. The first thing to notice is that only males have the disorder. Of course, we already knew this; testicular feminization is by defnition a male disorder. When a geneticist sees a pedigree in which just males are affected, however, two hypotheses pop to mind immediately regarding the mode of inheritance. One hypothesis would be that the trait is *sex-linked;* the other, that it is *sex-limited*.

A **sex-linked trait,** according to Mendelian theory, is usually an X-linked trait, which means that it is produced by an allele in that portion of the X chromosome that is unique to the X. A **sex-limited trait** is produced when an allele has consequences for one sex but not the other. In cattle, for example, the genes that control milk production are present in both bulls and cows, but, obviously, they are only expressed in cows.

From the pedigree information available at present, it is impossible to say whether testicular feminization is a sex-linked or sex-limited trait. Either hypothesis is plausible given the data. For the purpose of further analysis, however, let us assume that testicular feminization is due to the sex-limited expression of an allele that appears not in the X-chromosome but in one of the autosomes. This assumption of a sex-limited autosomal gene will enable us to go a few steps further in forming—and rejecting—hypotheses about the way in which the trait may be transmitted. We can, for example, attempt to determine whether the testicular-feminizing allele acts as a dominant or a recessive gene.

In order to determine whether

Pedigrees of Testicular Feminization
(Panel A: after Petterson & Bonnier, 1937   Panel B: after Burgermeister, 1953)

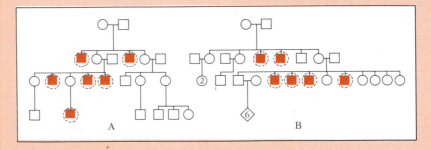

A   B

the testicular-feminizing allele is acting as a dominant or recessive gene, we need to test the hypothesis that it acts in one or the other of these ways against the data available in the two pedigrees below. To follow this exercise, which is merely an exercise in if–then logic, you will need to refer to the table below, which shows all the possible combinations of parental genotypes.

Taking the recessive hypothesis first, we know that children who have the trait must be homozygous for the recessive allele which we will designate as t. The

Expected Outcomes Due to Different Parental Genotypes and Modes of Transmission for Testicular Feminization

ALL POSSIBLE PARENTAL GENOTYPES		
Male	Female	RECESSIVE HYPOTHESIS
TT	TT	Impossible. These parents would not have children with the *tt* genotype.
TT	Tt	
TT	tt	
Tt	TT	
Tt	Tt	Possible. But only ¼ of children would have the *tt* genotype.
Tt	tt	Possible. But the trait would be very unlikely in the third generation.
tt	TT	Impossible. Father would be phenotypic female and could not mate.
tt	Tt	
tt	tt	
		DOMINANCE HYPOTHESIS
TT	TT	Impossible. The TT genotype is impossible. This would require the mating of two phenotypic females.
TT	Tt	
TT	tt	
Tt	TT	
Tt	Tt	Impossible. The father would be a phenotypic female and could not mate.
Tt	tt	
tt	TT	Impossible. The TT genotype is impossible.
tt	Tt	Possible. Provides best fit to data in figure to the left.
tt	tt	Impossible. These parents would not have children with the dominant *T* allele.

BOX 5-1 Continued

children must have the genotype tt to have the disorder. This means that both parents must carry the rare allele. Carrier parents would have the genotype Tt, T representing the normal allele that dominates the testicular-feminizing recessive. But we know from Mendelian theory that only one fourth of the children from heterozygotic parents (Tt) will be homozygotic for the recessive allele. Our pedigreees indicate that far better than one fourth of the male children in the affected families express the trait. We can eliminate as unlikely, therefore, the hypothesis that our pedigrees resulted from the mating of parents both of whom were heterozygotic carriers for the trait-determining allele.

What if, however, one of the parents—it would have to be the female—was a homozygotic carrier of the trait. This genotype when combined with the genotype of a heterozygotic carrier husband would yield children one half of whom would have the tt genotype needed by males to express the trait. This hypothesis fits the data for the affected families except that there is a greater than 50 percent incidence of the disease among male offspring in the affected families. We need not worry about this too much, however, because the data collection procedures in pedigree studies often lead to a greater than expected

incidence rate. What is a problem, though, is that the disease continues to appear in successive generations of the family. This is an unlikely outcome if it is transmitted as a recessive gene. The reason is that heterozygotic males need to keep marrying into the family. Specifically, in order for testicular feminization to appear in the third generation of pedigrees A and B of the figure, the females II-2 in pedigree A and II-8 in pedigree B would have had to marry husbands with the heterozygotic carrier genotype Tt. Because the t allele is carried by only a few people in the population (we know this because the disorder is extremely rare), it is very unlikely in the absence of inbreeding that two of the five men who marry into this family would be carriers of the testicular-feminizing allele. We can conclude, therefore, that if testicular feminization is transmitted as an autosomal recessive, it is highly unlikely that we would have obtained the data that we did in the two pedigrees. How about, then, transmission via an autosomal dominant allele?

Because a dominant allele always expresses itself when present, we know that the males of the first generation in our pedigrees are homozygous for the normal allele that we will now designate as t. The normal genotype, therefore, is the

Pedigrees for *Huntington's chorea*—a fatal neural disease—show that one half of the children of a parent with the disease have the disease themselves (see Figure 5-8). This is the expected pattern of inheritance for single autosomal genes that are dominant. Because the disease is fatal, one would ordinarily expect for the disease-determining allele to disappear from the population. In the case of Huntington's chorea, however, the gene does not homozygotic one, tt. For the trait to appear in the offspring of such males, the females must be the trait carriers. In theory the females could carry either a single dose of the testicular-feminizing gene with a heterozygotic Tt genotype or a double dose with a homozygotic TT genotype. In fact, however, the TT genotype in females becomes an impossibility when you realize that the only way to obtain this genotype is to have parents who both have the T allele in their genotypes. The problem with this is that males with the T allele, under our current hypothesis of dominance, have the disease and therefore do not mate. We can safely conclude from this that if the disease is transmitted via an autosomal dominant gene the gentoypes of the parents would have to be tt males and Tt females.

Matings between parents with the tt male and Tt female genotypes would produce, according to Mendelian theory, children half of whom would have the Tt genotype. The males with this genotype would have the disease and therefore develop as females. The females with this genotype would be carriers of the trait. When we return to the pedigree data we find that this hypothesis fits the data fairly well. Of the five females in the second generation, two did prove to be carriers. The only discrepancy from

expectation is that the trait shows up more often in the male offspring of affected families than chance would predict. It would be expected to show up in half the males of affected families but, in fact, shows up in 85 percent of the males in these families. Nonetheless, given the potential problems of bias in our methods of data collection, plus the very small data set, we can be reasonably satisfied with our hypothesis that the testicular-feminizing gene acts as a dominant, not a recessive gene, if it is in fact located in one of the autosomes.

It is important that you realize that the above analysis does not prove anything. Although we were able to narrow the probable mode of transmission down to an autosomal dominant, this was only when we assumed that the gene was not X-linked. X-linkage is very much a possibility. Also we had to assume that only a single gene was involved in transmission of the trait. We do not know that this is the case either. This single-gene assumption, however, is more easily defended than our assumption that the gene is located in one of the autosomes. The defense is provided by the criterion of parsimony discussed in Chapter 2. If a single-gene model appears to account for the data, why seek a more complicated theoretical explanation?

express itself until the person carrying it is between 40 and 45 years of age on average. This means that there is plenty of time to pass on the gene before it has its fatal effect on the individual who bears it.

In all, pedigree analyses to date have led to the identification of 1,637 characters that are transmitted in what appears to be a simple Mendelian fashion. Of these, 934 fit the pattern of autosomal dominants, 528 fit the

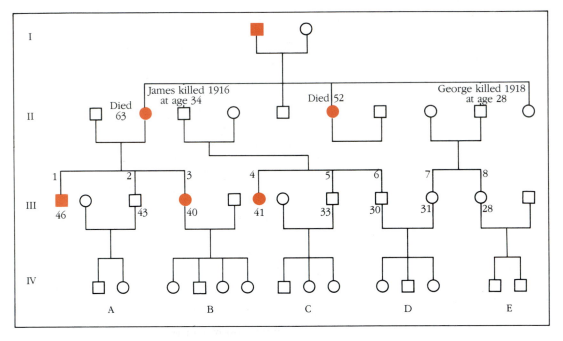

FIGURE 5-8
Pedigree for Huntington's Disease

This pedigree shows the autosomal dominant transmission pattern that is characteristic of Huntington's chorea. Ages of the individuals at the time the pedigree was compiled are given in small numbers, except for those marked died or killed. The ages of these individuals are their ages at death. We can infer that the male from the second generation who was killed at age 34 would have developed Huntington's disease had he lived, because the disease showed up in his daughter. The actual incidence expected for Huntington's disease in this pedigree is much greater than the incidence shown. The reason is the disease's late onset. Some of the third-generation individuals were still at risk when the pedigree data were collected, as were all of their fourth-generation children, none of whom was older than 15 at the time the pedigree was done.

pattern of autosomal recessives, and 115 appear to be X-linked (McKusick, 1983). Examination of the pedigrees for other traits has revealed that they most probably are not transmitted in a simple Mendelian way. This may be because they are polygenic traits and it may be because there is a substantial contribution from the environment in determining whether or not a trait will appear. Two good examples of how pedigree study has led to a rejection of simple Mendelian hypotheses are schizophrenia (Faraone & Tsuang, 1985) and stuttering (Scarr & Kidd, 1983). The pedigrees for these show clear genetic influence, but the mode of inheritance is complex.

Statistical Analysis of Family Study Data

As we have seen pedigree studies for all their value are only useful to test for Mendelian patterns of inheritance for threshold traits—those traits that we either have or do not have. The other category of traits is the category of continuous traits, those that we measure by degree rather than presence or absence. To test hypotheses regarding the inheritance of these, statistical analyses must replace pedigrees.

Goddard and Galton both dealt with traits that should have been treated as continuous traits—feeblemindedness and eminence—but they reduced them to discontinuous ones and treated them in pedigrees, because the mathematics for more sophisticated use of their data had not been developed. Today the mathematics is readily available to anyone who would like to use it, so statistical studies of family resemblance have totally replaced pedigrees for studying genetic influence on continuous traits. The mathematics that is required is that of *correlation* and *regression*. To keep our discussion as simple as possible, we will deal with research results in terms of just one of these—correlation, a mathematical concept with which you are already familiar (see Chapter 2).

Correlation   Until now, when speaking of family resemblance we have been able to get by with a very simple measure of resemblance. We have not labeled it, but the measure is one of *concordance*. This is merely a measure of whether two people share a trait. When they do, they are said to be concordant for the trait. When dealing with continuous traits, however—like one's degree of introversion, anxiety, or intelligence—a more sophisticated measure of resemblance is required. Everyone, after all, has some intelligence. So how do we measure whether family members resemble one another in intelligence more than they resemble nonfamily members? The answer is to use the statistical measure of association known as *correlation*.

Correlational data can be used to test hypotheses regarding major gene effects, as is demonstrated in Box 5-2. But, in fact, this use of correlations is not typical. One reason is that most continuous traits are not suspected to show major gene effects. Major gene effects occur when one gene alone has a dramatic effect on the expression of a trait. Continuous traits are generally thought not to show such monogenic influence; rather, many genes acting together—primarily in an additive fashion—are thought to be responsible for any genetic influence that is expressed in a continuous trait. From the collective effect of these *polygenes,* the effect of any one gene cannot be sorted out using correlations or any other procedure. When it is the case that traits are influenced by many genes whose individual effects are indistinguishable, we can no longer test hypotheses regarding specific modes of inheritance; so we turn to a separate issue in behavioral genetics—the determination of *heritability.*

BOX 5-2
The Spatial Gene Hypothesis

Spatial reasoning is contrasted with verbal or analytic reasoning and is measured in a variety of ways. One way is to present subjects with a two-dimensional drawing, like that in the figure below and ask them to select one of a series of drawings that is a representation from a different perspective of the same object. This test is a mental-rotation test of spatial reasoning. On such tests (see below), males score better than females on average.

The general superiority of males on not just mental-rotation tests but on all spatial-reasoning tests has led some people to suspect that there might be an X-linked recessive allele that, when expressed in the phenotype, would serve to enhance spatial ability (see, for example, Hartlage, 1970; Stafford, 1961). This would lead to overall male superiority on this trait because the allele—by virtue of its X-linkage—would express itself when present in a single dose in the male genotype (XY), but only when present in a

double dose in the female genotype (XX). If the ability-enhancing allele was as likely as its alternative to be inherited, this would mean that half of the males would express an enhanced spatial-reasoning trait while only one fourth of the females would express an enhanced trait. The rationale for this prediction is summarized in the table on p. 215.

To test the hypothesis that male superiority in spatial reasoning is due to a common allele that is X-linked and recessive, a pedigree would be of no use. The reason is that there is no way to identify affected cases. The best we could do would be to draw a pedigree, put a value in each person's square or circle to represent the person's spatial-reasoning ability, and then attempt in a subjective way to estimate whether the pattern of values reflected X-linkage. We would never be very successful in this. We need another approach. The alternative has been to replace small-scale pedigree studies of spatial test

Mental-Rotation Test

Which of the four figures in the box at the right is the same as the figure at the left?

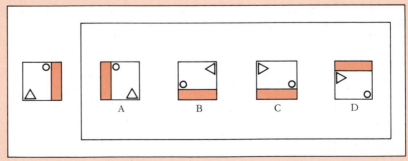

performance, which involve only a few families, with large-scale correlational studies involving many families. By virtue of being large-scale these studies overcome a particular problem for correlational studies, which is the unreliability of the correlation coefficient when it is based on small samples.

In correlational tests of the spatial gene hypothesis, the correlations of interest are those calculated for parent–child pairs (mother–daughter, mother–son, father–daughter, and father–son). These are of interest because, according to the reasoning used by investigators to date, these correlations should be rank-ordered with the father–son correlation being the smallest. Their reasoning is as follows: fathers cannot transmit their X chromosome to their sons; thus, whether a son has the X-linked ability-enhancing allele or not will be totally independent of whether the father has it. The father–daughter relation is quite different, however. For this relation, if the father has the ability-enhancing allele, his daughters are guaranteed to inherit it from him. Thus there should be some relationship between fathers and daughters in their scores on spatial-reasoning tests. The same should be true for mothers and daughters and mothers and sons, because both sons and daughters are guaranteed to inherit one of their mother's X chromosomes.

Since 1970, when the spatial gene hypothesis was first introduced, a number of family studies have used the rationale described above to test the spatial gene hypothesis. Most of these studies have failed to find evidence in support of the hypothesis (for a review, see Vandenberg & Kuse, 1979; McGee, 1979). A good example of a family study that has used this procedure to disconfirm the hypothesis was

---

Rationale for the Spatial Gene Hypothesis

A. Allele for enhancing spatial ability is present in one half of all X chromosomes in the population.

↓ ↓

B. One half of all X chromosomes transmitted to males will have the ability-enhancing allele.

B. One half of all X chromosomes transmitted to females will have the ability-enhancing allele.

↓ ↓

C. The ability-enhancing allele will be expressed in all males who have the allele (that is, one half of all males) because the allele is at a locus unique to the X.

C. The ability enhancing allele will only be expressed in women who are homozygous for the allele. This will be one fourth of all females. ($\frac{1}{2} \times \frac{1}{2} = \frac{1}{4}$)

BOX 5-2 Continued

conducted by J. C. DeFries and other researchers at the University of Colorado.

The data that DeFries and his colleagues used to test the X-linked spatial gene hypothesis (DeFries et al., 1976) came from a large-scale project known as the Hawaii Family Study of Cognition, which includes Americans of both Japanese and European ancestry. In the Japanese sample of 138 families, the father–son correlation for spatial ability was .33. Contrary to the prediction that this relation should be the weakest of the parent–child relations, it was in fact the strongest. For fathers and daughters the correlation was .31, for mothers and sons .21, and for mothers and daughters .13. In the European sample of 434 families, the father–son correlation was the weakest—as predicted—but not by much. The father–son correlation of .23 compared closely to the mother–son correlation of .28. The other correlations were .32 for father–daughter pairs and .41 for mother–daughter pairs. These results are in poor agreement with what we would expect if there were indeed a recessive gene in the X chromosome that served to enhance spatial abilities. In fact, if we collapsed the data from the two populations into one data set, all the parent–child correlations would be about equal, a result that is clearly contrary to predictions. We can conclude, therefore, that if the statistical test that has been used is valid, the spatial gene hypothesis has been falsified. Currently, however, there is some debate over whether comparing parent–child correlations does in fact provide an adequate test of the hypothesis (see Thomas, 1983, and Loehlin's rebuttal, 1984.)

Heritability   Most people naively think that **heritability** serves as an index of whether traits can be inherited by individuals. Thus they think that the common cold is something that is not heritable but that the number of arms and legs we have is. Such conceptions of heritability are grossly in error. In fact, what we will come to call the *heritability coefficient* is probably fairly substantial for number of colds whereas the heritability coefficient for number of human limbs is 0. To understand why, it is vital that you recall what was said at the outset of this chapter: behavioral genetics is concerned with genetic influence on the differences that exist among people in a trait. The *only* reasons people would differ in the number of arms and legs they have would be environmental reasons, like land mines and car accidents. This makes the **environmentality** (Fuller & Thompson, 1978) of the trait 1.00 but the heritability 0. The number of colds people have per year, on the other hand, would have to do not just with environmental factors like climate and exposure but also with genetic factors that contribute to people's general resistance level. When we say, therefore, that a trait has some degree of heritability, we mean that polygenic factors account for some of the differences that exist among people.

Statisticians represent the differences among people—or differences among other entities that they measure—in one of two ways. One is to represent the differences in a figure called a *frequency distribution,* which provides a "picture" of the differences (see Figure 5-9). The other is to use a number called a **variance.** This number is a measure of how spread out the scores in a frequency distribution are. For the sake of simplicity, let us say that the variance on some trait is 100. (This would mean that the people in the sample that we measured had scores that differed on average by 10 points—the square root of 100—from the mean, or average, score for the entire sample.) Now we can define heritability as that portion of the total variance that is attributable to genetic factors, and environmentality as that portion that is due to nongenetic factors. If, then, the genetic variance is 60 and the environmental variance 40, the heritability of the trait is .60, meaning that 60 percent of the total variance is genetic variance. You can think of this number as a measure of the potency of genetic factors relative to all others in producing phenotypic differences among people.

Although dividing a total variance into genetic and environmental components is easy to do conceptually, in practice the trick is to come up with quantitative measures of the independent contributions of genetics and the environment to the total variance. This can be quite a problem. As we have seen in family studies, for example, genetics and environments *covary.* This is a statistician's way of saying that changes in one variable are associated with changes in the other. In the particular case of family studies, as relatives become more distant genetically, they also become more environmentally distant. That is, as relatives diminish in the extent to which they

FIGURE 5-9

Representing Individual Differences Using a Frequency Distribution
Bell-shaped frequency distributions such as these can be described using just two numbers. One is the number that represents the mean, or average, value in the distribution. The second is the number that represents the variance, or "spread," of the distribution. Both general cognitive ability and specific cognitive abilities (for example, spatial reasoning) are distributed in this way, and so are the personality variables of neuroticism and extraversion.

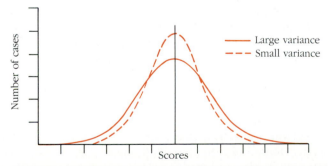

Frequency Distributions with the Same Mean but Different Variability.

share genes, they also diminish in the extent to which they share environments. How then are we to get estimates of the independent contributions of each? One way is to use a powerful set of statistical procedures that allow us to "analyze" a variance into its various parts. Fortunately, correlations can be used as a tool in some of these analyses of variance (Falconer, 1960), so we already have at our disposal the mathematical means of analyzing some variances.

It turns out, for example, that if you take the correlation of parents with their children on a trait and then double it, you have an estimate of the *maximum* value possible for the heritability coefficient (the proportion of the total variance that is genetic variance). This may not be much, but it is a start. Consider, for example, the question of the heritability of spatial-reasoning ability that was discussed in Box 5-2. The conclusion to that discussion was that the male superiority that is found in tests of spatial reasoning is probably not due to contributions from an X-linked recessive allele. Now we are in a position to ask a further question about the possible role of genes in the determination of spatial-reasoning ability. The question is, What proportion of the differences that exist among people in spatial ability is potentially due to polygenic factors? One sample of people in which family relationships in spatial ability have been studied is a Hawaiian group included in the Hawaii Family Study of Cognition (DeFries, Kuse, & Vandenberg, 1979). We will base our initial estimate of the heritability of spatial reasoning ability on them, but remember that the estimate is valid for this group and this group alone until we have in fact shown that it is more general.

There were eight single-parent child correlations reported in the Hawaii Family Study for the families of Japanese and European ancestry that made up the subject population for the study. The correlations were .33, .31, .21, .13, .23, .32, .28, and .41. If we double each of these and then take the average, or median, value as our "best guess" of the maximum heritability for spatial reasoning, we get a value of .59. This means that, at most, 59 percent of the variance in spatial-reasoning ability among the Hawaiians in the study could be due to genetic differences among them. Perhaps more importantly, it means that at least 41 percent of the variance is due to environmental differences.

You may sense that this practice of computing maximum-heritability estimates from parent–child correlations is a rather crude business. All we get from it is an estimate of the maximum heritability. This means that the actual heritability for this population could range from 0 to the value obtained. We have done nothing to confirm that the trait is indeed heritable; we have only set an upper limit on the extent to which it might be heritable. If you do feel some dissatisfaction with the lack of conclusiveness in this exercise so far, you are being appropriately critical. However, please remember that correlations applied to family-study data are but one way to get heritability estimates, and in fact they are far from the best way. For family studies a more satisfactory way is to use a slightly different statistical procedure called regression, but a better way yet is to collect some different data.

The data that are needed are those that will allow us to separate the effects of the environment from the effects of heredity. Working with animals, we can obtain such data by doing experiments. For example, animals of different genotypes can be assigned in equal numbers to different rearing conditions. We can then see how animals of Genotype 1 react in Environments A to Z, how animals of Genotype 2 react in these same environments, and so on. In this way, we gain the data needed to state how environmental variation alone affects the phenotype and how genotypic variation alone affects the phenotype.

With humans we are completely unwilling to attempt any experiment so manipulative as this, but we are fortunate because there are some naturally occurring human conditions that produce comparable data. One is twinning and the other is adoption. These two "naturally" occurring events give us data that can be used to separate the effects of heredity from the effects of the environment.

Natural Experiments

Twin Studies

The potential value of **twin studies** for separating the variance-producing effects of heredity from those of the environment was first realized by Francis Galton (1876). Useful applications of twin data were not made until the mid-1920s, however, with a study by C. Merriman (1924) of the intellectual resemblance of "duplicate" as opposed to fraternal twins. Methodological and statistical improvements in these applications have been made ever since.

Heritability and Environmentality Estimates from Monozygotic–Dizygotic Comparisons   Identical twins come from a single (mono-) fertilized egg (zygote) that has split into two at some point very early in gestation. Because of the manner in which these twins develop, we call them **monozygotic (MZ) twins.** They are assured to be genetic copies of one another. Aside from having twin genotypes, MZ twins raised in the same family have twin experiences throughout most of their early development. They share the same womb, birthdate, birth order in the family, parents, siblings, diet, schools, religion, social class, friends, and probably trips to the zoo. In addition, they are of the same sex and race. From an objective point of view, therefore, MZ twins have early life histories that are as similar as the life histories of two human beings can ever be.

In contrast to MZ twins, who are genetic copies of one another, **dizygotic (DZ) twins,** also called fraternal twins, share only half their genes on average. This is the same proportion of genes as normal brothers and sisters would share. But while they are only half twins genetically, they are full twins from the environmental point of view. Like their MZ twin counterparts, DZ twins also share the same womb, birth order, social class, parents, siblings, diet, friends, and so forth. Though only half share the same sex, we can restrict our studies to just those DZ twins who are of the same sex. In this way we can obtain a group of DZ twins that because of the impact of the shared environment should be just as similar as MZ twins under conditions where genetics plays no part. This is an assumption, called the *equal-environments assumption* (for a discussion see DeFries & Plomin, 1978, p. 480; Scarr & Kidd, 1983, pp. 395-98).

By assuming that the shared environments of MZ and DZ twins operate with equal potency to make twins like one another, we open the door to obtaining a heritability estimate through a comparison of MZ resemblance on a trait to DZ resemblance. Here is how it works. Assume we find a trait that produces equal MZ and DZ correlations. We can conclude that because MZ twins are no more similar than DZ twins, genetics accounts for none of the variance in the trait. The heritability, therefore, is 0. What if we find, however, that the MZ correlation is greater than the DZ correlation. This would mean that MZs are more similar than DZs, a finding that would indicate that the greater trait similarity has to be due to greater genetic similarity.

Once we have an MZ correlation that is in fact greater than a DZ correlation, the methods of quantitative genetics provide a means of estimating the percent of the total variance due to genetics (that is, the heritability of the trait). The particular method to be illustrated here is known as *Falconer's estimate of broad sense heritability* (see Falconer, 1960, 183-85). There are other procedures that can be used and that under different circumstances yield different estimates (for example, Holzinger's method; see Plomin, DeFries, & McClearn, 1980, pp. 301-302), but we hardly need to involve ourselves with the technical distinctions among these.

To estimate the heritability of a trait using Falconer's method, you subtract the DZ from the MZ correlation and multiply the result by 2. Thus if r MZ is .60 and r DZ is .40, then the heritability of the trait is .20 $\times$ 2 = .40; 40 percent of the variance is estimated to be due to genetic differences. For an intuitive understanding of why this is so, think of the MZ correlation as the percent of variance due to all the factors (both genetic and environmental) that conspire to make twins alike. Likewise, the DZ correlation represents the variance due to all the factors (both genetic and environmental) that conspire to make DZ twins alike. We have made the assumption, though, that the environmental contributions to the DZ and MZ twin variances are equal. This equal-environments assumption enables us to conclude that any differences are due to the genetic-variance component. The genetic component present in MZ–DZ differences is one-half the total ge-

netic component in the variance, because DZ twins share one half of their genes. Performing the r MZ $-$ r DZ operation, therefore, gives us half the heritability, and multiplying by 2 gives us the full heritability. With a heritability estimate in hand, we can turn to the problem of obtaining an environmentality estimate.

Until now we have been content to talk of environmental variance as a single unanalyzed entity, but with our MZ twin data we can break it down a bit to speak of *within-twin* and *between-twin* environmental variances. Between-twin environmental variance is a concept we have already discussed. This is the variance that stems from the environmental factors that, for example, make a twin pair born on a farm in Iowa different from a twin pair born and raised in urban Atlanta. These then are factors that make Twin Pair 1 different from Twin Pair 2, but that make individual twins (for example, the pair in Iowa) like one another. Within-twin environmental variance stems from all those environmental factors that operate to make the members of individual twin-pairs unlike one another. What are these? They are all the subtle factors that operate in life to make even two identical twins different from one another. One twin might have an illness that the other does not have. One might make a friend the other does not make. One might gain confidence by taking a risk and succeeding; the other might become fearful by having tried and failed. If you simply recall the case of the Genain sisters (see Chapter 3), you will realize that even same sex, same age, same genotype children in a single family cannot be said to have identical life experiences. Their lives are somewhat unique, and the importance of that uniqueness to their development is expressed in the within-twin environmental variance.

To estimate the within-twin environmental variance, you subtract the MZ correlation from 1.00. The remainder is the variance due to the environmental factors operating within twin pairs. To understand this operation, you need to remember that the MZ correlation represents the variance due to all the factors that operate to make MZ twins like one another. Whatever is left over, therefore, is the variance due to within-twin environmental differences. With this estimate and a heritability estimate we now have two of the three parts to the total variance. The only part not yet estimated is the between-twin environmental variance. To get it we subtract the heritability (.40, using the example value from p. 220) and the within-twin environmentality (1.00 − .60 = .40) from 1.00 (1.00 − .40 − .40 = .20). This provides the estimate that 20 percent of the variance in the trait is due to the environmental factors that vary between twins.

To give but a quick indication of the type of values produced using the estimation procedure just introduced, we can return to the trait used for illustrative purposes previously—spatial–reasoning ability. In a study conducted in Finland that employed 157 MZ pairs and 189 DZ pairs, Brunn, Markkanen, and Partanen (1966) obtained an MZ correlation of .59 and a DZ correlation of .36 for spatial ability. This yields a heritability estimate of .46 (2 × [.59 − .36] = .46) meaning that 46 percent of the variance in spatial ability among people in the population represented by the twins is estimated to be genetic variance. By the same token, 41 percent of the variance (1.00 minus the MZ correlation of .59) can be estimated to be due to factors that operate within twins and the remaining 13 percent to factors that operate between twins (that is, all those factors that would make twins in Family A different from twins in Family B). Data from a comparison of MZ and DZ twins conducted in this country by Schoenfeldt (1968) produced similar estimates. The heritability of spatial ability was estimated to be .52, the within-twin environmentality to be .33, and the between-twin environmentality to be .15.

The relatively small between-twin difference found in the above two studies is of particular interest, because sex is one of the factors that varies between twin pairs in twin studies. This follows from the fact that we only use same-sex pairs of twins. If males score higher than females, therefore, it contributes to between-twin differences, not within-twin differences. This result contributes further to our belief (see Box 5-2) that sex is not a potent variable in producing differences among people in spatial reasoning. We can draw this conclusion because sex—in combination with other potentially important between-twin factors such as socioeconomic status, parents' education and occupations, and family size—accounts for just 13 to 15 percent of the total variance in spatial-reasoning ability. This tells us that if the genetics of sex (XX versus XY) is a factor at all in influencing spatial reasoning, it is not a very important factor.

The example above indicates what an advance can be made in estimating heritability and environmentality by switching from family studies to twin studies. Not only do we get an estimate of the heritability as opposed to just an estimate of the maximum possible heritability, but also we can break down the environmentality estimates to distinguish between factors that operate between and within sets of twins.

MZ Twins Reared Apart   The comparison of MZ and DZ correlations is not the only use that can be made of twin data by behavioral geneticists, but it is the only use that we will consider in detail. Other methods do deserve mention however. One very obvious method is to collect data on MZ twins who have been reared apart. If the twins were separated early enough and placed in environments at random, then any correlation between them on a trait would be genetic in origin. As of 1973 (Farber, 1981), there were 121 cases of MZ twins reared apart (MZAs) reported in the literature, and the correlations among these on many traits were extremely high. Methodological problems have plagued MZA studies to date, however, making the obtained correlations untrustworthy (see Kamin, 1974). One of the principal problems is that most MZAs do not meet the criterion of random assignment to environments. Adoption agencies, which have been responsible for most of the MZ twin separations, have tended in the past to place family members in similar environments. This means that much of the high correlation between MZAs that has been reported may be due to environmental similarity after all. Furthermore, the methods used by investigators in selecting cases have led to the inclusion of some late separated MZ pairs among the MZAs and even, in one case, the inclusion of an MZ pair that had grown up in houses that were next door to each other (Kamin, 1974).

Today there is a renewed interest in MZAs as reflected in the work of Thomas Bouchard of the University of Minnesota. This newer work has been undertaken with full awareness of the problems that have plagued the research in the past, so we may yet see some compelling evidence for heritability in data from MZAs. It is doubtful, however, that the actual evidence will meet the advance billings it has received in the popular press. Press reporters have been fascinated by the fact that some of the twins share uncanny resemblances (see Figure 5-10). For example, twins known as the Jim twins have wives, children, and pets all with the same name. They also drive the same make of car, drink the same brand of beer, and live in similar houses with similar structures built around the trees in their front

FIGURE 5-10
MZ Triplets Reared Apart
Monozygotic twins and triplets separated at birth through adoption provide one approach to distinguishing between environmental and genetic effects in twin studies. The triplets pictured here lived apart for 19 years before discovering they had twin brothers. When such cases are brought to light, the popular press generally emphasizes the "amazing" similarities said to exist among them. These triplets, for example, all smoked the same brand of cigarettes and flunked a mathematics course. In evaluating the importance of such facts as evidence for genetic influence, you should remember that if you examined closely you would find that any three people taken at random would share many characteristics. They may not all smoke the same brand of cigarettes and score poorly in math but they might all three read poetry for pleasure, go to the beach for vacation, or own shares in AT&T. Unless one specifies in advance the specific traits on which twins (or triplets) reared apart are expected to be similar, there is nothing at all amazing about finding similarities.

yards. These reporters have not learned apparently that science is advanced by efforts to falsify, not confirm, theories (see Chapter 2). If we took any two individuals at random and examined every aspect of their lives, it would be quite easy to find a large set of "uncanny" resemblances. Both may have had orthodontic treatment beginning at age 9, both may part their hair on the same side, and vacation at the same out-of-the-way resort. By looking only for resemblances we would be led to the foolish conclusion that two strangers are in fact quite alike. Thus it is important for us to know not just in what ways the MZAs are similar, but in what ways they are different.

Families of MZ Twins   A second twin method that deserves mention for its future promise more than its past achievements is a newly developed method called the *families-of-identical-twins method* (Plomin, DeFries, & McClearn, 1980, p. 304). The method takes advantage of the fact that when identical twins marry and have children, there are some between-family genetic relationships that are as strong as the usual within-family genetic relations. For example, if MZ twin sisters marry, then the sons and daughters of Twin 1 share the same genetic relationship with their mother as they do with their aunt (see Figure 5-11). Furthermore, their cousins are half siblings genetically. These between-family genetic relations offer new opportunities for estimating genetic and environmental sources of variance. It is interesting that in one of the first uses of the family-of-identical-twins method, psychologist Richard Rose from the University of Indiana and his geneticist colleagues obtained heritability estimates for spatial-reasoning ability using data from the families of 65 MZ twins (Rose, Harris, Christian, & Nance, 1979). The estimates ranged from .40 to .56 with a median value of .48. This value is in keeping with the values obtained previously using the single parent–child correlations from the Hawaii Family Study of Cognition (which produced an upper limit value of .59) and MZ–DZ twin comparison (which produced values of .46 and .52 in the two available studies).

Adoption Studies

The final method to be considered is the **adoption-study method.** In many ways it is the best. Writing in a general review of behavioral genetics research, for example, J. C. DeFries and Robert Plomin (1978) had this to

FIGURE 5-11
Families-of-Identical-Twins Design
The families-of-identical-twins design shows how individuals in different families have the same genetic similarities as individuals in the same family.

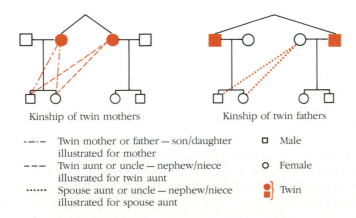

Kinship of twin mothers   Kinship of twin fathers

--·-- Twin mother or father — son/daughter   ☐ Male
       illustrated for mother
- - - Twin aunt or uncle — nephew/niece   ○ Female
       illustrated for twin aunt
······ Spouse aunt or uncle — nephew/niece   ⬤} Twin
       illustrated for spouse aunt

say of the method, "Although we do not wish to denigrate the usefulness of family study and twin study methods, it is our opinion that adoption studies provide a more convincing demonstration of genetic influence upon human behavioral characters" (p. 481).

The strength of the adoption-study method is that it offers the closest parallel we have yet seen to true experimental separation of genetic from environmental influences. Adopted children share genes with their biological parents, but not environments (except insofar as adoption agencies may attempt through selective placement to match characteristics of the biological parents with the adoptive parents). And they share environments with their adoptive parents and siblings, but not genes. This fortuitous set of genetic and environmental relations can be analyzed statistically to estimate once again the heritability of traits.

THE RESULTS OF INVESTIGATIONS INTO BEHAVIORAL GENETICS

Until now in this chapter we have concerned ourselves almost exclusively with methods—specifically, animal-breeding-study methods, family-study methods, twin-study methods, and adoption-study methods. So far, results obtained using these methods have only been included for illustrative purposes. Now we will shift the focus entirely to results.

Two Preliminary Cautions

Before attempting to summarize what we currently know about the extent to which genetic influences create psychological differences among people, two cautions need to be inserted. Both regard the interpretation of behavioral genetics research. The first caution is that a trait's heritability must not be confused with its plasticity. Plasticity and heritability are in fact independent. A trait with a heritability of 1.00 can still be quite malleable.

To illustrate the importance of this first point, we can consider some data from Joseph Horn's Texas Adoption Project, a massive investigation involving 300 families with adopted children. The data showed that there is a greater correlation in intelligence between biological mothers and their adopted-away children ($r = .32$) than there is between these adopted children and the adoptive parents who raise them ($r = .17$ for fathers and $r = .19$ for mothers). What you are apt to conclude from this is that biological parents, through the influence of their genes, make a greater contribution to their children's intelligence than do the adoptive parents who provide the environment in which the children's intelligence develops. This is wrong.

The Texas Adoption Project and others (see, for example, Scarr & Weinberg, 1976; Skodak & Skeels, 1949) clearly show that adopted children have *higher* IQs than their biological parents. This means that adoption improves the intellectual abilities of adopted children. The accepted explanation is that the families that society allows to adopt children generally provide quite favorable environments for the development of intelligence, far more favorable usually than the environments the biological parents could have provided. These adoption data, therefore, clearly underscore the conclusion we came to in Chapter 3 after discussing retardation in orphans, genius in Norbert Wiener, and the results of the Abecedarian Project: intelligence is a plastic trait subject to environmental influence. The data from the Texas Adoption Project do nothing to deny this fact. They do, however, add to it. They show that intelligence is heritable at the same time that it is plastic.

Understanding how a trait can be both heritable and plastic depends on the realization that people can correlate on a trait without being equal on that trait. Take height as an example. In Japan, as elsewhere in the world, relatively tall parents have relatively tall children. This correlation continues to hold, despite the fact Japanese adults are taller today than they were before World War II. The children are growing taller because there are dairy products in the postwar diet that were not part of the prewar diet, but

that does nothing to affect parent–child correlations or heritability. The increasing heights do not affect the parent–child correlation, because a parent's position in the distribution of parent heights still serves to predict the child's position in the distribution of child heights, regardless of the height differences that exist between parents and their children. The increasing heights do not affect heritability, because changes in the overall height of a population do not necessarily affect the variance in the height of that population, and heritability—as we learned above—is based on variances.

The example of height changes in Japan is a direct parallel with what we find in the case of adopted children and their biological mothers. Adopted children with higher IQs tend to have biological mothers with higher IQs, even though the level of intelligence achieved by all the adopted children is generally higher than that achieved by their biological mothers. The increase in level of IQ is a sign of the plasticity of intelligence. The existence of a biological-parent/child correlation is evidence of its heritability. Quite clearly, a trait can be heritable and plastic at the same time.

The second caution regarding the interpretation of behavioral genetics research also concerns the meaning of heritability. Some people tend to think of heritability coefficients as once-and-for-all figures that reflect an immutable relation between genotypes and phenotypes. Thus, after determining the heritability of a trait to be .50, they assume that 50 percent of the phenotypic variance in the trait will always be accounted for by genetic differences. Not so. As Arthur Jensen (1969) has pointed out, heritability is not a constant like *pi* or the speed of light. The estimates of the extent of genetic influence on a trait are specific to the population on which the estimate is calculated. Consider what would happen, for example, if we calculated the heritability of a trait in a highly inbred population. As we know already, inbreeding produces greater genetic homogeneity. With each successive generation of inbreeding, the heritability of traits would drop and their environmentality would be increased. On the other hand, if we were to raise a genetically diverse set of animals in a completely common environment, the heritability of every trait expressed in these animals' phenotypes would be increased. Heritability, therefore, is a variable—not a constant—and it varies as the environment and the genotypes in the population we are considering become more or less homogeneous.

With these two cautions in mind regarding the interpretation of behavioral genetics claims regarding the heritability of traits, we can begin to examine the results of studies aimed at determining the extent to which the genetic differences among people produce differences among them in psychological traits. The first traits we will consider are general intelligence, specific cognitive abilities, and personality traits. Following a presentation of the results dealing with these continuous traits, we will examine behavioral genetics research on the discontinuous traits of alcoholism, schizophrenia, and affective disorders.

The Heritability of Continuous Traits

Intelligence

Intelligence as measured by IQ tests, or other measures of general cognitive ability, has historically been the most widely studied trait in behavioral genetics. In 1969 when Arthur Jensen of the University of California at Berkeley reviewed all the behavioral genetics research on intelligence to that time, he concluded that the heritability coefficient for IQ in contemporary American society was about .81. "This represents," he wrote, "probably the best single overall estimate of the heritability of measured intelligence we can make" (Jensen, 1969, p. 51). Unfortunately, some of the evidence that Jensen relied on heavily—namely the twin studies of Cyril Burt—have since been shown to be fraudulent (see Gould, 1981). Today, most estimates of the heritability for general cognitive ability are considerably less than Jensen's .81. A good rule-of-thumb estimate is about .50.

The contemporary view that about half of the variance in IQ in this country is genetic variance is based on a host of individual studies. These studies include each of the types we have discussed. Rather than attempt to summarize them all, we will take selected cases.

Family Studies   A good family study to use in estimating the heritability of intelligence is the Hawaii Family Study of Cognition, which for its Caucasian sample had data on 830 families. In this study, when a relatively culture-free measure of intelligence (Raven's Progressive Matrices) was used as the measure of general intelligence, the within-family relations in the 830 Caucasian families indicated a heritability of .52. (This was not a maximum estimate, because it was based on a midparent–child regression, a statistical procedure that yields an estimate of the actual heritability.) When a second measure of general intelligence was used—a composite score based on a number of individual tests—the estimate was .60. Interestingly, both of these heritability estimates for the Caucasian population of Hawaii were greater than the comparable estimates for the Japanese population of Hawaii. This reminds us that, until proven otherwise, we must assume that a heritability estimate applies only to the specific population in which it was obtained.

Twin Studies   Using twin studies to estimate the heritability of intelligence, we get a very similar result. The median MZ correlation obtained from tests of general cognitive ability in 19 relatively large twin studies compiled in 1976 by John Loehlin and Robert Nichols (see Table 5-3) was .86, and it was .62 for DZ twins. The remarkable thing about the MZ correlation in these data is that it reflects about the same degree of resemblance that you would find if you compared individuals to themselves. The same per-

TABLE 5-3
Identical and Fraternal Twin Correlations for Measures of General Cognitive Ability

TEST	CORRELATION		NUMBER OF PAIRS		SOURCE
	Identical	Fraternal	Identical	Fraternal	
National and Multi-Mental	0.85	0.26	45	57	Wingfield and Sandiford (1928)
Otis	0.84	0.47	65	96	Herrman and Hogben (1933)
Binet	0.88	0.90	34	28	Stocks (1933)
Binet and Otis	0.92	0.63	50	50	Newman, Freeman, and Holzinger (1937)
I-Test	0.87	0.55	36	71	Husen (1947)
Simplex and C-Test	0.88	0.72	128	141	Wictorin (1952)
Intelligence factor	0.76	0.44	26	26	Blewett (1954)
JPQ-12	0.62	0.28	52	32	Cattell, Blewett, and Beloff (1955)
I-Test	0.90	0.70	215	416	Husen (1959)
Otis	0.83	0.59	34	34	Gottesman (1963)
Various group tests	0.94	0.55	95	127	Burt (1966)
PMA IQ	0.79	0.45	33	30	Koch (1966)
Vocabulary composite	0.83	0.66	85	135	Huntley (1966)
PMA total score	0.88	0.67	123	75	Loehlin and Vandenberg (1968)
General ability factor	0.80	0.48	337	156	Schoenfeldt (1968)
ITPA total	0.90	0.62	28	33	Mittler (1969)
Tanaka B	0.81	0.66	81	32	Kamitake (1971)
NMSQT total score:					
1962	0.87	0.63	687	482	Nichols (1965)
1965	0.86	0.62	1,300	864	Loehlin and Nichols (1976)

SOURCE: Adapted from *Heredity, Environment, and Personality: A Study of 850 Sets of Twins* by J. C. Loehlin and R. Nichols, 1976, Austin: University of Texas Press.

sons retested on an IQ test might get scores that differed by about 4 points (a median value) from their first scores. That is roughly the same difference that is found between MZ twins. DZ twins show considerable resemblance, but still, their scores will differ by at least twice as much as the scores of MZ twins. That is, DZ twins will differ by 8 points or more (again, a median value).

Combining the MZ and DZ correlations to make a heritability estimate yields the value, .48. Heritability estimates obtained from a totally different twin procedure—the families-of-identical-twins method—are quite comparable. For example, Richard Rose of the University of Indiana (Rose, Harris, Christian, & Nance, 1979) obtained heritability estimates ranging from .40 to .56 in a study of 550 members of 65 MZ kinships.

Adoption Studies   Turning to adoption studies for a final estimate of the heritability of intelligence, we again find support for the view that in the portion of the American society represented in our studies to date, about half of the variation in intelligence is genetic variation. The best example of this comes from an adoption study conducted in Minnesota by Sandra Scarr and Richard Weinberg (Scarr & Weinberg, 1977). Their heritability estimate for IQ was .61, based on a procedure that compares the correlations of adoptive brothers and sisters to biological brothers and sisters. This finding from Scarr and Weinberg's Minnesota adoption study comes as no surpirse given what we already know of the results of the Texas Adoption Project: the adopted children in the Texas study correlated more closely with their biological mothers than their adoptive mothers. This result is prima facie evidence of heritability, because it shows that genetic differences among the adoptees contributed more to their differences in intelligence than did differences in the family environments in which they were raised.

Changes in Heritability over Time   Apart from the discovery of the fundamental fact that intelligence is a highly heritable trait, behavioral geneticists are now uncovering some interesting information regarding changes in the heritability of intelligence during development. The major source of data on this topic comes from a longitudinal twin study begun in Louisville in 1955 (see Wilson, 1983). Briefly summarized, data from the Louisville Twin Study showed that the heritability of intelligence increased from late infancy to adolescence. The result was due to the fact that while MZ twins maintained a close relationship in measured intelligence throughout their development, DZ twins grew apart (see Figure 5-12). Specifically, MZ twins were found to have correlations of around .80 or higher for intelligence no matter when it was measured. DZ twins, on the other hand, though they began life resembling each other as closely as MZ twins, wound up resembling each other no more than ordinary brothers and sisters! Their correlation for intelligence was only about .50 at age 15. The Louisville results indicate, then, that genetic differences become progressively more important for explaining intelligence differences as development proceeds. They also indicate that the extraordinary environmental commonality shared by twins has an effect early in development, but by school age, the twin experience (for example, shared womb and entry into the family at the same time) is no longer an important factor as regards the development of intelligence. From about age 6 onwards, then, DZ twins do not resemble their co-twins any more closely than they resemble other siblings (see sib–twin correlation in Figure 5-12).

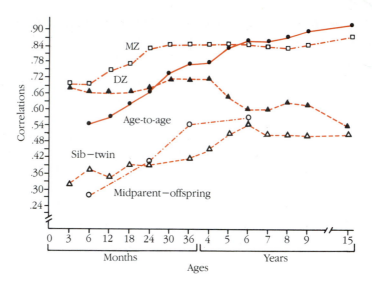

FIGURE 5-12
Louisville Twin Study
Longitudinal data from the Louisville Twin Study show that DZ resemblance in intelligence declines relative to MZ resemblance. In fact, by age 15, the DZ resemblance is no greater than the resemblance found between nontwin brothers and sisters. (The nontwin resemblance is represented here by the "sib–twin" correlation, which is an average of the correlations of each member of the DZ pair with the others siblings in the family.) (After Wilson, 1983)

Though the Louisville Twin Study provides the best data for studying developmental trends in heritability, it is not the only source of data on which to base the inference that the heritability of intelligence increases with age. A longitudinal adoption study conducted by Marie Skodak and Howard Skeels (1949) found that the biological-parent/adopted-away-child correlation increased from age 2, not reaching its peak until the children were in school (see Figure 5-13). This result is completely consistent with the twin-study data. Like the MZ-DZ data, it indicates that the relative importance of genes increases over the early years of development. During the same years, however, the contribution of the family environment to individual differences in intelligence remains at a constant low level as judged by the adopted-child/adoptive-mother correlation (see Figure 5-13).

It is too early yet to interpret the meaning of the shifting heritability of IQ. On the one hand, it may simply reflect that children in schools have more homogeneous environments for the development of IQ than children not in schools. After all, children in schools share a curriculum and experiences that are not shared by children outside of schools. Homogeneity in the environment, as we have seen, always acts to enhance heritability. With environmental differences playing less of a role, genes by default play more of a role. It is equally possible, however, that the heritability of IQ increases for reasons having to do with how and when genes express themselves. Ronald Wilson, Director of the Louisville Twin Study, for example, argues that behavioral development no less than biological development is guided by a genetic strategy. From this view, the fact that MZ twins remain remarkably alike while DZ twins become less so can be accounted for by the *progressive actualization* of this genetic strategy.

Wilson's progressive-actualization hypothesis leads to the prediction that the effects of similarities or differences in family environment should wash out over time as genetic differences have the chance to express themselves fully. By adolescence, then, if you want to know how closely correlated two people will be in intelligence, the absolute best predictor will be

FIGURE 5-13

Longitudinal Studies of Mother–Child Correlations

The dashed lines in this figure show the results of Skodak and Skeels's (1949) longitudinal study of the relationship of children's IQs to their biological mother's and adoptive mother's intelligence (as estimated by level of education). Also included in this graph are data from Marjorie Honzik's (1957) longitudinal study of natural child/mother pairs. Because the relationship of the biological mother to her child is the same whether the child lives with the mother (Honzik's study) or not (Skodak & Skeels's study), these data would indicate that the mother's presence in the child's environment does nothing to enhance the mother–child correlation in IQ. (After Honzik, 1957)

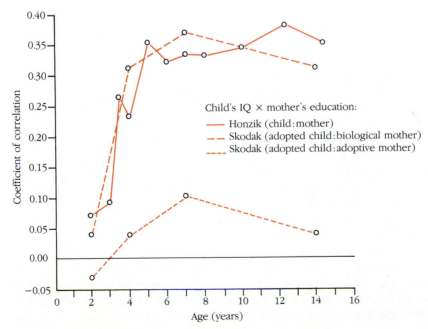

Child's IQ × mother's education:
— Honzik (child:mother)
-- Skodak (adopted child:biological mother)
---- Skodak (adopted child:adoptive mother)

genetic relatedness. This view is receiving support. Take, for example, the case of adopted children who have grown up with their adoptive siblings in a common family environment. One would think that this would lead to some resemblance in intelligence. It does not. According to the results of the Minnesota adoption study (Scarr & Weinberg, 1978), adolescent adoptees do not resemble their family-mates at all. Sandra Scarr draws a straightforward conclusion from this result: "The effects of being reared in the same household, neighborhood, and schools are negligible unless one is genetically related to one's brother or sister" (Scarr & Kidd, 1983, p. 407). This means that you can basically ignore the shared aspects of the family environment when predicting how much resemblance in intelligence there will be between parents and children, brothers and sisters, or even uncles and nephews. Wilson (1983) concurs completely. For example, in answer to the question of why children resemble their parents in intelligence, he concludes that "the principal link between parental intelligence and offspring intelligence is genetic in origin" (p. 311). These statements sound inflammatory in that one could read them to mean that the environment plays no role in the development of intelligence. In fact, the statements are not inflammatory at all. They make perfectly good sense.

Shared Versus Nonshared Environment   To see the "sense" in Scarr and Wilson's views, you need to think of environmental variance as divided into its two parts—*between-family variance* and *within-family variance*. The former variance is due to all those environmental factors that act to make family members more similar on a trait than individuals taken at random. If, for example, social-class differences in a society tend to make the individuals in one class different from individuals in a different class, then social class would be a factor that contributed to making families different. The reason is that family members *share* class membership. This tends to make them like one another and different from the members of families from other social classes. Within-family environmental variance is created by environmental influences *not shared* by family members. When Scarr and Wilson denigrate the importance of environmental differences in producing differences in intelligence, they are talking about between-family factors—the factors shared within families but not between families. This means that those factors, such as socioeconomic status, which psychologists and sociologists have focused on for so long as particularly important to psychological development, turn out to be far less "psychoactive" than was once believed. Environmental factors are important in establishing individual differences, but the really important environmental factors—the ones that turn out to be most psychoactive—operate within, not between, families. David Rowe and Robert Plomin have provided the useful service of listing some of the potential sources of within-family environmental variation in tabular form (see Table 5-4).

TABLE 5-4
Specific Sources of Within-Family Environmental Variance

| | SOURCES | | | | |
Measurement	Accidental Factors	Sibling Interaction	Family Structure	Parental Treatment	Extrafamilial Networks
Error of measurement	Teratogenic agents Physical illness Prenatal and postnatal trauma Separation	Differential treatment Deidentification	Birth order Sibling spacing	Differential treatment of children Interactions of parent and child characteristics	Peer-group members not shared by siblings Relatives Teachers Television

SOURCE: The Importance of Nonshared (E_1) Environmental Influences in Behavioral Development" by D. C. Rowe and R. Plomin, 1981, *Developmental Psychology, 17,* p. 524.

Two provisos should be noted for Scarr and Wilson's argument that the aspects of the environment that are shared by family members do little to create similarities in the intelligence of children growing up in those families. The first proviso is that Scarr and Wilson's argument applies to the role of between-family (that is, shared) factors *in the long run.* The kind of between-family variables represented in the Minnesota and Louisville families definitely create major sibling–sibling and parent–child resemblance in intelligence in the short run. But as the children enter the school system and come under both school and peer control, the influence of the immediate family environment washes out.

The second proviso needed to understand Scarr and Wilson's conclusions is that the conclusions do not rule out the importance of all between-family variables. They only rule out the particular between-family factors represented in their studies. As they point out, these factors did *not* include the full range of between-family factors that exists in human societies. They did not even include the full range that exists in the American society. The families were drawn from the white, majority culture in America and did not include families that were abusive, neglectful, or indigent. Thus, even though there were families of different socioeconomic status, different degrees of stress, different religious preferences, and different childrearing philosophies, they were all basically loving families, able to care for the minimal needs of their children. The Louisville twin families were somewhat more representative of the breadth of American culture, but still, severely deprived families and children were not included in the sample. Despite these sampling restrictions, the Minnesota and Louisville results are still extremely important. They serve to falsify the hypothesis that the particular factors separating normal working-class families from normal upper-class families in America lead to systematic differences in intelligence among the children growing up in these families. Rather than being a startling revelation of genetic control on intelligence, however, this finding is a glorious affirmation of the essential equality that exists in our society for the development of intelligence. The environmental variance for most of us is within-family variance created by nonshared experiences that are unrelated to our family membership. This is precisely what a democratic society would hope to be the case.

Specific Cognitive Abilities

Although people who score high in one area of cognitive ability generally score high in other areas, the correspondence is not perfect. It makes sense, therefore, to speak of specific cognitive abilities as well as a general cognitive ability. The theoretical problem is to determine just how many unique abilities there are. J. P. Guilford and his students believe there are 120, Louis Thurstone believed that there were 7, and almost everyone agrees that there are at least 2.

Regardless of the number of unique abilities that exist in theory, in practice we can make up test questions all of a single type and detemine whether there is more or less family similarity on these specific tests than there is on the general test. For example, we might give an exclusively verbal test that employs analogies, a purely spatial test that consists of mental-rotation problems, a purely perceptual-speed test that consists of problems like finding all the vowels on a page of letters, or a test that just taps one's ability to memorize. When specific tests like these are given, the overall heritability is about the same as for tests of general intelligence. The one difference is that the specific within-family factors known as within-twin factors (see p. 221) contribute more to the overall variance. This is reflected in the fact that MZ correlations for specific traits are generally lower than for general intelligence. Loehlin and Nichols (1976), for example, who estimated that MZ correlation for IQ to be about .86, estimated the correlation on specific abilities to be only about .68. This indicates that the unique experiences of twins growing up in the same family serve to separate them more on specific cognitive abilities than on general intelligence (Plomin, DeFries, & McClearn, 1980).

Scarr has offered a reasonable explanation for why within-family environmentality might be greater for traits such as specific cognitive abilities than for general cognitive abilities. Parents, she suggests, are not likely to dissuade children from following whatever special bent might interest them. Parents are not likely to insist, for example, that all their children excel at mechanical skills or that all of them excel at musical skills. They will be perfectly tolerant for one child to go one way and a second child another way. But, when it comes to overall intelligence, the parental effect should be uniform. This would mean that the environments in families would be more insistent on uniformity in overall intelligence than in specific abilities. Thus MZ twins and DZ twins alike would be expected to show less resemblance in specific areas of cognitive ability than in general cognitive ability. Shifts in the source of environmental variation, however, would have no implications for heritability. Thus the heritability for specific abilities could remain constant while the importance of within-twin factors increased.

Personality

Psychology does not have the means to measure many aspects of personality with the same reliability and validity as it can measure aspects of intelligence. This measurement problem is a fundamental block to behavioral genetics investigations of a broad number of personality traits. Investigators have been restricted, therefore, to those few traits that can be measured reasonably well. One of these is a trait known as *neuroticism*. As measured by Hans Eysenck's personality inventory (the EPI), people who are high in neuroticism are those who are generally displeased with themselves and with life. People who are low in neuroticism are well adjusted and generally happy. Measures of neuroticism are interpreted as overall measures of emotional stability.

The second trait that personality theorists can measure reasonably well is *sociability* or *extraversion*. To again use the EPI definition of this trait, people high on sociability are known as *extraverts,* and those low on the trait are known as *introverts*. Extraverts are just what you would expect them to be—outgoing people who have a high need for external stimulation. They are sociable and enjoy large get-togethers. Introverts, on the other hand, depend less on external stimulation in their everyday lives, and when it comes to socializing, they prefer smaller, more intimate groups.

The tests such as the EPI that are used to obtain measures of neuroticism and sociability consist of a number of statements that people mark *true* or *false*. Here are some examples; these particular items are used to measure neuroticism:

> I wake up fresh and rested most mornings.
> I wish I could be as happy as others seem to be.
> I have very few fears as compared with my friends.

The pattern of responses for neurotics on the above items would have been *false, true, false*. The next statements are sampled from those that could be used to measure sociability:

> Talking with strangers doesn't bother me at all.
> I like to be with a crowd of people.
> I really prefer to do things by myself.

An extravert's responses to these items would follow the pattern *true, true, false;* an introvert's would follow the opposite pattern.

Twin Studies If you believe that the behavioral preferences associated with neuroticism and extraversion are influenced by genetic differences among people, you will find support for your belief in twin studies. In one Swedish study of 12,898 twin pairs (Floderus-Myrhed, Pederson, & Rasmuson, 1980), the MZ correlation for neuroticism was .48 and for extraversion .50. The DZ correlations for these traits were .23 and .21, thus yielding heritability estimates of .50 and .58. These data indicate that although the overall twin resemblance in personality is far less than for intelligence, the heritability is still about 50 percent. Other studies agree. In a review of twin research not just on sociability and neuroticism but on a host of other traits as well (dominance, authoritarianism, vocational preferences), Robert Nichols (1978) found that MZ correlations on average have hovered around .50 while the DZ correlations have been only about half that.

Robert Plomin and his colleagues (see Buss & Plomin, 1984), who have worked not with adult personality differences but with differences in infants and children, have come to similar conclusions. Twin studies using ratings on the traits of emotionality, activity, and sociability show substantial heritability for what Plomin calls temperament, which is a composite of the emotionality, activity, and sociability variables.

Adoption Studies and Family Studies With the completion of a number of adoption and family studies on personality, it is now possible to compare the results of these studies to those of twin studies. The conclusion is they do not match. Adoption and family studies show some heritability for sociability, neuroticism, and a few other traits, but not nearly so much as twin studies (Scarr & Kidd, 1983, pp. 416-17). For example, whereas twin studies generally estimate the neuroticism and sociability heritabilities to be around .50, studies not based on twin data yield estimates only half as large. Plomin's family studies of childhood temperaments (Buss & Plomin, 1984) show the maximum heritability estimates to be .40 for emotionality, .20 for activity, and .30 for sociability.

At present no one knows why twin studies differ so much from family and adoption studies in their estimates of the genetic influence on personality. There are, however, a number of suggestions. One suggestion is that genetics and environments interact in the development of personality (Loehlin, Willerman, & Horn, 1982). The term "interact" here has a special meaning. It means that an environment that affects one genotype one way will affect another genotype a different way. Thus, an experience that might promote a pleasure in "talking to strangers" for people of one genotype could promote a fear of strangers (xenophobia) in people of another genotype. If there is interaction of this sort, it could account for the current discrepancies in heritability estimates for personality. The reason is that twin studies include interaction variance as genetic variance. Twin studies, therefore, would yield inflated heritability estimates for those personality traits that are subject to genotype–environment interactions. Family and adoption studies do not have this bias, so their heritability estimates are more valid in cases where interaction variance is indeed present.

We have not considered interaction variance previously because there was never any evidence of it. In the case of intelligence, for example, all the data indicate that environmental events that facilitate the intellectual development of one person facilitate the development of all people. In the case of personality, however, it is easy to imagine that children could respond very differently to identical developmental experiences. One person's trauma, for example, can be another person's "growth experience."

Environmentality of Personality Traits   Although we do not know as much as we would like about the heritability of neuroticism and extraversion, we know a good deal about their environmentality. The most surprising thing we know is that nearly all the environmental variance is within-family variance. This means that after we subtract the effects of genetic relatedness, people within families are as variable in personality as people between families. This comes through most clearly in the adoption studies, which show that adopted children do not resemble either their adoptive parents or their brothers and sisters (Loehlin, Willerman, & Horn, 1982; Scarr, Webber, Weinberg, & Wittig, 1981). In brief, when family members do not share genes, they do not share personalities. Brothers and sisters who share half their genes do share personalities to some extent, but the reason probably has little to do with their shared family environment. This is an extremely important finding because it challenges the cherished belief of some psychologists that children learn their personalities by modeling their behavior on those around them. This does not seem to be the case. As Sandra Scarr puts it, "Individuals within families are vastly different in [their] personality characteristics . . . , and psychology has no theory to explain that individuality" (Scarr et al., p. 897). In the case of personality, therefore, even more so than in the case of intelligence, the full range of psychoactive environmental factors are completely available within families.

The Heritability of Discontinuous Traits

Studying the genetic effects on traits such as alcoholism, schizophrenia, and depression (technically, an affective disorder) is simpler than studying cognitive and personality traits because the statistics are simpler. For what remains to be discussed in this chapter we need two statistics—an *incidence* or *risk* figure and a *probandwise concordance rate*.

Incidence is a measure of the percent of people in a population who develop the trait in question over the course of their lifetime. Risk is a probability estimate based on incidence. Just to give a quick example, the population incidence of schizophrenia is about 1 percent. This means that individuals taken at random from the population have about a 1 percent risk of being diagnosed as schizophrenic at some point during their lifetime.

A probandwise concordance rate is a statistic that reflects the extent to which pairs of relatives share a trait. We will illustrate it using pairs of twins. If we know of 30 twins who have a trait of interest and 15 of their co-twins happen to share the trait, then the concordance rate in this set of twins is 66 percent. This is calculated by counting the total number of twins who are in concordant pairs, which in our case is 15×2, or 30 individuals, and dividing that by the total number of affected individuals, which is 45 in our case (the 30 individuals in concordant twin pairs plus the 15 probands with a nonconcordant co-twin.) This gives us the concordance rate of 66 percent, which is the percent of all the affected individuals (or probands) who share their trait with a co-twin.

With the information on incidence, risk, and probandwise concordance in mind, we are now ready to examine the data on alcoholism, schizophrenia, and affective disorders for evidence of the heritability of these. As you might suspect, genetics plays a clear role in the development of each. It is important to remember, however, that in these areas of development, as in all others, a genetic influence does not preclude an environmental influence, nor does it predetermine an outcome. An influence is only that, an influence. As a consequence of the many influences that act on us, we take the developmental courses that we eventually take. It would be an extreme error to take any of what follows fatalistically. Remember what was said of schizophrenia in Chapter 3. Schizophrenia is a highly heritable trait. Nonetheless, even if you have a schizophrenic MZ co-twin with whom you have lived since birth, you still have about a 50 percent chance of being normal.

Alcoholism

The data from family studies show clearly that alcoholism runs in families. Incidence figures from five countries show that the average male has a 3 to 5 percent chance of becoming alcoholic, but this risk is enhanced to 25 percent in first-degree male relatives of alcoholics. Although the actual incidence of alcoholism in females is far less than in males, the increased risk for first-degree female relatives of alcoholics is about the same. The average female has a risk that ranges from 0.1 to 1.0 percent, but this rises to from 5 to 10 percent when there is a first-degree relative who is alcoholic (data reported in Goodwin, 1979). Of course, as we are now quite aware, family-study data can be explained as easily by environmental as by genetic factors. The data from twin and adoption studies are needed, therefore, to clarify the relative influences of each.

Twin and Adoption Studies   In four twin studies, the concordance rate for MZ twins has been considerably higher than the rate for DZ twins. In the most frequently cited of these studies (Kaij, 1957), there was an 84.5 percent MZ concordance and a 66.7 percent DZ concordance. These data alone are evidence that genetics plays a role in the development of alcholism. Adoption studies make the relation even clearer.

In the largest adoption study of alcoholism to date, Michael Bohman and his associates gathered the names of all persons born out of wedlock and placed for adoption in Stockholm, Sweden, in the years 1930 to 1949 (Bohman, 1978). The list came to 2,324 people. The list was then pared down to eliminate any children who were placed with relatives and any who spent more than 6 months with their biological mother before being adopted away. This left 1,775 names. Public registers were then searched to see which of these individuals had subsequent alcohol problems and whether their biological or adoptive parents had problems. (Yes, the public records in Sweden are in fact this complete!) The alcohol problems these people might have had ranged from mild to severe. On the mild end was a single episode of drunkenness that led to a violation of Sweden's temperance act. On the severe end was hospitalization and treatment. Bohman and his colleagues (Bohman, Sigvardsson, & Cloninger, 1981; Cloninger, Bohman, & Sigvardsson, 1981) have distinguished mild, moderate, and severe cases of alcohol abuse in their analyses, but their three categories will be collapsed for the purposes of this introductory treatment.

Table 5-5 is a reconstruction of data presented in Bohman's reports (see Cloninger, 1983). It breaks the 1,775 total adoptees into the categories of those whose biological parents had a record of alcohol abuse (father, mother, or both) and those who did not. It then shows the number of adoptees who went on to have records of alcohol abuse themselves. Collapsing across both male and female adoptees, we find that 13 percent (82 out of 627) of the adoptees with one or more biological parents who were alcohol abusers were alcohol abusers themselves, whereas just 8.7 percent (100 out of 1,148) of the adoptees with nonabusive biological parents became abusers themselves. Having one or more biological parents who are alcohol abusers definitely increases the risk of a child being an alcohol abuser, even when the child is separated at birth and reared apart. Because the biological relation includes fathers as well as mothers, we can be sure that this is indeed a genetic effect and not just an intrauterine effect.

Of the 1,775 adopted children, 58 were raised in homes where there was evidence of alcohol abuse. The incidence of alcohol abuse in the adopted children raised in these homes was just 8.6 percent (5 out of 58). This incidence rate is less than the 10.3 percent rate (177 out of 1,717) for children raised by nonabusing parents. Bohman's data indicate, therefore, that exposure to alcohol abuse in the home does not contribute to alcohol abuse in children who are genetically unrelated to the abusers. Exposure to abuse, in fact, may even serve as a mild preventitive.

TABLE 5-5
Percent of Adoptees with Alcohol Problems Classified by Sex
and by Alcohol Abuse in the Biological Parents

ADOPTEES	ALCOHOL ABUSERS			
	Father Only	Mother Only	Both	Neither
Females				
Number	285	29	22	577
Number of alcoholics	10	3	2	16
Percent of alcoholics	3.5%	10.3%	9.1%	2.8%
Males				
Number	259	23	9	571
Number of alcoholics	58	6	3	84
Percent of alcoholics	22.4%	26.0%	33.3%	14.7%
Total				
Number	544	52	31	1148
Number of alcoholics	70	9	5	100
Percent of alcoholics	12.9%	17.3%	16.1%	8.7%

SOURCE: "Genetic and Environmental Factors in the Development of Alcoholism" by C. R. Cloninger, 1983, *Journal of Psychiatric Treatment and Evaluation, 5,* p. 489.

Schizophrenia

In number, the behavioral genetics studies of schizophrenia rank second only to studies of general cognitive ability. In a word, the literature is vast. Fortunately, it is also in high agreement so that it is easy to draw general conclusions. The principal conclusion to be drawn is that some genotypes are far more likely than others to produce a schizophrenic phenotype. Beyond that there are other facts of interest.

Family Studies   Family studies yield the interesting information that a schizophrenic is about as likely to have a schizophrenic parent as a schizophrenic sibling. The risk for both types of relatives is between 7 and 10 percent, after we correct for the fact that schizophrenics are less likely to have children than nonschizophrenics. These data argue that the factors that are important in the development of schizophrenia are ones that children share with their parents to the same extent that they share them with their siblings. Genes are shared equally between siblings and between children and parents; therefore, the data support the role of genes in the development of schizophrenia. But the data do not support explanations for schizophrenia that depend on sharing a particular family environment. If particular family environments were important, we would expect for the incidence of schizophrenia in the siblings of schizophrenics to be greater than in the parents of schizophrenics. After all, parents and their children grow up in different generations in different homes. In spite of this, the incidence of schizophrenia is the same in parents as in siblings. This means that the environmental factors that are important must be ones that generalize across generations and homes.

A second fact to be derived from family-study data is that it does not matter if the schizophrenic parent is the father or the mother; the incidence in children is the same. This fact indicates that neither a sex-linked hypothesis nor an intrauterine hypothesis is likely to have any merit in explaining why one person develops schizophrenia and another does not.

Twin Studies   Twin studies have been a mainstay for behavioral genetics research on schizophrenia for some time. As a result, data are now available on quite a large number of twins. This means that averaging the concordance rates across the many studies that have been conducted yields concordance values that are probably quite stable. Irving Gottesman and James Shields (1982) have used this procedure to obtain an overall probandwise concordance of 46 percent for MZ twins and 14 percent for DZ twins. Although these results indicate strong genetic influence, they also indicate a strong within-twin environmental effect, because 54 percent of the schizophrenic probands do not have schizophrenic co-twins.

Several twin studies have indicated that the MZ concordance rate for schizophrenia is increased if only chronic cases of schizophrenia are included. For example, Gottesman and Shields (1977) found a 27 percent MZ concordance rate for probands who had been hospitalized for less than 2 years, but a 77 percent concordance for probands hospitalized for more than 2 years. This indicates that the genetic influence is stronger in the more-severe cases than it is in the less-severe ones. It also indicates, of course, that how one defines schizophrenia will determine the concordance rate that is produced. For this reason, the overall estimates of twin concordance given above (MZ = 46 percent and DZ = 14 percent) were from studies with fairly homogeneous criteria for defining schizophrenia.

Adoption Studies   Adoption studies were introduced to the behavioral genetics literature on schizophrenia in 1966 with the publication of a study by Leonard Heston, who was then a psychiatry resident at a hospital in Oregon. This study was important, because at that time, many professionals doubted the validity of the conclusions from twin and family studies. Consequently, they had not yet accepted the fact that schizophrenia is to some extent heritable. Heston's adoption study made that conclusion unavoidable and, thus, bolstered people's confidence in twin-and family-study data.

In Heston's original study, the hospital records from 1915 to 1945 were searched to find instances of chronically schizophrenic women who had had children who were placed in foundling or foster homes. There was a total of 74 such cases, of which 47 were usable. These 47 offspring were matched with 50 control children on the basis of age, sex, type of final placement, and quality of early life. By tracing all 97 adopted children into adulthood, Heston found that 5 of the 47 children with schizophrenic mothers became schizophrenics themselves. In contrast, none of the 50 control group children became schizophrenics. Beyond this major finding, there was also evidence that the children of schizophrenics were at higher risk for disorders that are part of the "schizophrenia spectrum" (see Kendler & Gruenberg, 1984). These disorders are not as disabling as schizophrenia, but they can still affect a person's ability to behave in socially appropriate ways. Job performance could also be affected. Symptoms might include mild paranoia, delusional thinking, social withdrawal, and inappropriate emotions. The importance of this result is that it conforms to the result found in some twin studies (Rosenthal, 1970) that the genetic influence on schizophrenia is not specific to schizophrenia. Rather, it may include a tendency for a wide range of related, but milder disorders. These do not include other forms of psychosis, however. The genetic risk for schizophrenia is specific to schizophrenia and schizophrenia-spectrum disorders; it does not include affective disorders like depression or character disorders like extreme aggressiveness, alcoholism, or sociopathy (Kendler & Gruenberg, 1984).

Since Heston's initial work, a number of other adoption studies have been conducted. Today there are data on 211 adoptees from schizophrenic mothers and 185 control adoptees. The overall incidence rate for schizophrenia is 13 percent in the first group and 1.6 percent in the second (Plomin, DeFries, & McClearn, 1980, p. 350). We can compare the 13 percent risk in the adopted-away children of schizophrenics to the risk in children who are not adopted but rather live, like the Genain sisters, in a schizophrenic household. With the comparison, we can determine whether being reared by a schizophrenic parent as well as sired by one adds anything to the risk of a child's being schizophrenic.

The figure we need to make our comparison has already been presented in the data for family studies. Those data showed that there is no greater than a 10 percent risk for schizophrenia in the children of schizophrenics who are reared with their parents. The risk then is 13 percent in children reared apart from their parents and 10 percent in those reared with them. Clearly, living with a schizophrenic parent does nothing to increase one's risk! This is a surprising conclusion that runs counter not only to common sense but also to a popular theory of but a few years ago. The popular theory was that schizophrenia breeds schizophrenia because of the "schizophrenogenic" atmosphere in the home. The data now force us to believe otherwise. Gottesman and Shields (1982), for example, have written that

> the adoption studies . . . show that sharing an environment with a schizophrenic does not account for the familial aggregation of cases. Furthermore such factors as the presence of schizophrenia or related illnesses in the rearing family are *ruled out* as primary environmental causes of schizophrenia. (p. 145)

Affective Disorders

We did not need to distinguish the different "types" of schizophrenic disorders because there is no compelling evidence to indicate differential heritability for the different types (for example, paranoid, catatonic, and disorganized types). There is, however, in the case of affective disorders, also known as *depressive disorders*. There are two major subtypes, and their heritabilities may differ.

The two types of affective disorders are *unipolar* and *biopolar*. Both involve depression as a major symptom. Individuals with the bipolar type constitute one fourth of all cases and are commonly known as manic-depressives because their mood can change without warning from a depressed state to a manic, animated state of euphoria and optimism. Unipolar depressives (three fourths of all cases) just cycle between severe depression and normality. They never become manic.

Family Studies   Family studies provided the initial basis for the hypothesis that an affective disturbance was heritable and that the mechanism for inheritance varied somewhat for the two types. David Rosenthal (1970) calculated risk figures on the basis of family-study data that show that the risk for the two types combined in the population at large is about 0.7 percent. It is far greater, however, in first-degree relatives of affectively disturbed individuals. In parents of probands the incidence is 7.6 percent, in siblings it is 8.8 percent, and in children it is 11.2 percent. The evidence for the unipolar and bipolar distinction in these family-study data is that "unipolar depressive probands tend to have unipolar relatives, and bipolars, to a lesser extent, tend to have bipolar relatives" (Plomin, DeFries, & McClearn, 1980, p. 286). Although the results here are not terribly clear-cut, there is definitely the suggestion of a difference.

Twin Studies   Twin studies are consistent with family studies in supporting the general heritability for affective disturbance. The overall MZ concordance rate as estimated by Rosenthal (1970) is 71 percent, a good bit higher than the concordance for schizophrenia, and for DZ twins it is 19 percent, about the same as for schizophrenia. The hypothesis that there may be genetic involvement in the unipolar–biopolar distinction also receives some support from twin studies. If unipolar and biopolar depression were just different phenotypic expressions of the same genotypic state then we would expect for mixed pairs (one biopolar and one unipolar twin) to be relatively frequent among the concordant pairs. In fact, if we could assume that within-family environmental factors were solely responsible for differentiating the bipolar from the unipolar phenotype (which is implied by the large separation in MZ and DZ concordance) then we would expect the frequency for bipolar, unipolar, and mixed bipolar–unipolar concordance to be in the ratio of 1 to 1 to 2. We would expect this for the same reason that when tossing two coins we expect to get 1 pair of heads and 1 pair of tails for every 2 head–tail combinations. The result of studies of MZ concordance shows exactly the opposite relationship, however. Pure pairs are about twice as frequent as mixed pairs.

Adoption Studies   The few adoption studies available do not add evidence to the hypothesis that bipolar and unipolar depression are differentiated genotypically. They do, however, show that being born of a depressive parent increases one's risk for depression far more than does being reared by a depressive. This argues that a genetic link to mood disturbance has greater potential consequences than an environmental link. In a study by J. Mendlewicz and John D. Rainer (1977), for example, the biological parents and adoptive parents for 29 bipolar manic-depressive probands and 22 normal adoptee controls were interviewed. The clinical condition of the adopted children (normal or affected) did not predict at all whether the adoptive parents would have manic-depressive-type symptoms. The opposite, however, was true for the biological parents. An affected adoptee predicted an affected parent, because 14 of the 58 biological parents of the 29 manic-depressive adoptees included in the study (31 percent) had a clinical history of manic-depression. In contrast, only 1 of the 44 parents of the 22 control adoptees had a clinical history of bipolar depression. To add to the strength of the conclusion that being reared by a manic-depressive does not enhance the chance that a person will become manic depressive, Mendlewicz and Rainer also collected a sample of 31 bipolar manic-depressive probands who were reared by their biological parents. The incidence of manic-depression among these parents was 26 percent, less than the 31 percent incidence rate among parents whose children were reared apart from them. This means that there is nothing about the environment created in the family by manic-depressive parents that heightens the chance of this disorder in the children who live with them. This, of course, is the same conclusion we reached with regard to schizophrenia.

FROM GENES TO BEHAVIOR

As you have been learning about the evidence for genetic influence on a variety of human traits over the last several pages, you may have begun to wonder just how it is that genes can exert their influence. After all, the hallucinations and disordered thought of schizophrenics, the behavioral choices of an extravert, the inferential ability of a person with a high IQ, and the drinking of an alcoholic are all very complex events. How can variations in the chemical structure of our genes produce differences in behaviors such as these? The answer, unfortunately, is that we do not know. To be able to answer the question would require a great deal more information about biochemistry and the causes of behavior than we currently possess. The only genetic influences that we truly understand at a biochemical level at present are a few major gene conditions that lead to metabolic errors. Phenylketonuria is a prime example of this.

Examples of Metabolic Errors with Behavioral Consequences

Phenylketonuria, or PKU, results when a person is unable to metabolize phenylalanine, one of the essential amino acids and a compound found in almost all the foods we consume—including mother's milk. When this substance is not fully metabolized, the kidneys are unable to excrete the excess and so there is a toxic buildup of unmetabolized phenylalanine. This toxicity is expressed on the developing nervous system, so the most striking characteristic of people with PKU is profound mental retardation. In addition there are other effects. PKU victims, for example, are lightly pigmented and have larger than average heads. It is important to remember these additional effects, because it is a mistake to ever think in terms of a one-gene-one-effect model. Although the one biochemical effect of the PKU gene when it expresses itself is to produce a deficient enzyme—the enzyme that is responsible for transforming phenylalanine into tyrosine—the ultimate consequences of this defect are felt in many different areas. The technical term for this fact is **pleiotropy.** Genes have pleiotropic effects.

Although PKU was the first behavioral condition whose biochemical causes could be traced and then linked to a specific gene, others have followed. *Sickle-cell anemia,* for example, is caused when the single gene responsible for constructing the hemoglobin molecule (responsible for carrying oxygen in the blood) substitutes a single amino acid in the usual hemoglobin structure. Such a small change has surprisingly large consequences. The principal consequence is that under low-oxygen conditions the sickle-cell hemoglobin causes red blood cells to change in shape. The shape change causes them to clog capillaries, thereby reducing the blood flow to specific areas. When blood flow is restricted there are dramatic consequences for whatever organs or tissues are affected. Common consequences are mild retardation, heart problems, kidney malfunction, and chronic muscle pain. These again are pleiotropic effects.

Chromosomal Abnormalities with Behavioral Consequences

In addition to the genetic conditions that we understand biochemically, there are others that we do not understand biochemically but nonetheless can distinguish as due to a specific genotype. These conditions all go under the name of chromosomal abnormalities because they involve some major variation on the usual 46-chromosome condition as shown in Figure 5-14. One common abnormality is **trisomy:** in addition to the pair of homologous chromosomes that are included in the normal genotype, there is a third chromosome present. Theoretically, trisomy could occur for any of the 23 chromosome pairs, but most trisomies are lethal and result in spontaneous abortion. The only ones that appear with any frequency among humans who survive birth are trisomy of the small chromosomes that make up the 21st pair and trisomy of the sex chromosomes. The former condition results in a collection of mental and physical effects that collectively are known as **Down's syndrome,** once known as *mongolism* (see Figure 5-14A). The latter trisomies include the XXY genotype of Klinefelter's syndrome (see Figure 5-14B) and the XYY genotype.

In addition to trisomic genotypes, there is also a monosomic (one-chromosomal body) condition that is relatively frequent. This is the XO genotype of Turner's syndrome. Also there are conditions in which a portion of a chromosome gets deleted by being broken off during cell division. The best known of these cases occurs when a small portion of one of the 5th pair of chromosomes is deleted and results in the condition known as *cri-du-chat.* Occasionally the piece that breaks off will attach itself elsewhere. Thus the genetic information is not lost, just misplaced. Nonetheless the developmental consequences are severe. Infants with cri-du-chat are retarded and physically deformed. They also produce an eerie catlike cry in infancy. This cat cry *(cri du chat* in French) accounts for the name of the disorder.

The Impossibility of Linking Normal Trait Variation with Specific Genotypes

Locating the source of genetic variation in traits such as intelligence and personality constitutes a problem that is quite different from locating the genetic or chromosomal conditions that underlie Turner's syndrome, cri-

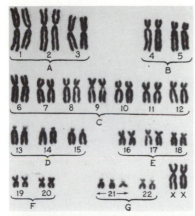

FIGURE 5-14
Trisomic Conditions
Karyotypes for Down's syndrome (A), also
called trisomy-21, and Klinefelter's
syndrome (B).

A

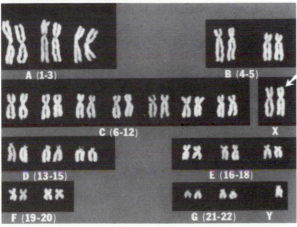

B

du-chat, or other well-defined disorders. In fact, we will probably never be
in a position to identify the source of normal trait variation in actual genotypes or in biochemical processes. One reason is that there is no such thing
as a specific genotype for an IQ of 100 or for an extraverted personality. To
make this point we might return to the Tolman–Tryon rats that were selectively bred to make as few errors as possible in running a complex maze.
If you ask yourself why it might be that one rat would make fewer errors
than another, you might think that one just had a better memory. But what
if keen vision or olfaction (the ability to smell) led to additional information
that was helpful in learning the maze. In this case, rats with better vision or
better olfaction might make fewer errors even with a mediocre memory.
Or consider how a rat might fare in the maze if it was of a type that became
extremely anxious and excited when placed in a novel environment. Even
with superior senses, it would probably make more errors than a less-
aroused animal. It could also be that one type of rat would be inherently
slower than another to make a decision at any of the choice points and that

slowness in maze running had as its side effect fewer errors. This bit of armchair speculation should be sufficient to alert you to the fact that there are many reasons why one rat might make more errors than another in running a maze, and all of these are no doubt heritable. Thus, while there is a specific genotype that we can associate with Turner's syndrome or PKU, there is no such single genotype for maze brightness or for maze dullness. What is true of a trait as specific as number of maze errors in rats is all the more true of traits as general as human intelligence and personality. For this reason and others, we can hardly expect to ever explain much of the normal variation in human beings with specific genetic or biochemical theories.

Even if we are never able to tie individual variation in psychological traits to specific genetic conditions, we can still make considerable progress in understanding the process by which epigenetic development occurs. A theory recently proposed by Sandra Scarr and Kathleen McCartney (1983) shows how this is so. Scarr and McCartney's theory ties genetic variations to environmental variations by arguing that genetic differences set people onto inherently different experiential paths. As these people live their experientially different lives, they come to be distinct from one another, even if they happen to live in the same family.

Scarr and McCartney's Theory of Gene–Environment Interaction

According to the theory, different gentoypes experience substantially different environments because genes and environments are correlated (see Plomin, DeFries, & Loehlin, 1977). These correlations arise in three different ways. One is *passive,* one *reactive,* and one *active.* The passive gene–environment correlation is one we have acknowledged all along as the factor that makes family studies uninterpretable. Children inherit genes from their parents, but they also inherit environments. If we assume that the environments parents offer their children are linked to the parents' genotypes, then we see that the children's genes and environments will invariably be linked. To use a concrete example, consider the case of parents who have become quite musical, partly through the influence of their own genetic predispositions. When they give birth to a child, that child will carry some of the same genetic predisposition. In addition, however, the child will be raised in a musical environment, one that complements his predisposition. This kind of correlation is passive because it comes about with no effort on the child's part. It is a birthright. Though this kind of correlation is well known to us by now, Scarr and McCartney advance our understanding of this correlation somewhat by pointing out that this correlation has its major impact on development early, during the time that the parentally controlled environment serves to define a child's world.

The reactive gene–environment correlation occurs when the responses children evoke in others are in part a function of the child's genotype. Take again the case of musical ability. If parents and others react to a child's signs of musical interest by buying a piano or giving the child a harmonica for Christmas, they are reacting in a way that serves to correlate the environment (in this case having an instrument to play) with the child's genetic predisposition. This particular correlation would be positive, because the reaction is one that enhances the tendency. Negative reactions are also possible, however. A negative reaction would involve attempts to suppress a child's interest. In either case, however, people's reactions would be related to the child's genotype. Reactive gene–environment correlations, therefore, provide a further way for genes to gain importance in human development.

Although the first two types of correlation are certainly important ones, the most important type of gene-environment correlation is the one that remains—the active type. Scarr and McCartney call this type *niche-picking* and *niche-building* because it develops when people have sufficient independence to "seek out the environments they find compatible and stimulating." Because people can play such a large role in building their own environments (or niches), the effect that genes have on environment selection becomes "the most powerful connection between people and their environments and the most direct expression of the genotype in experience" (Scarr & McCartney, 1983 p. 427).

To demonstrate the usefulness of their theory, Scarr and McCartney have applied it to a few of the curious facts derived from behavioral genetics studies. One of these regards the declining resemblance of DZ twins over time. As you will recall, MZ and DZ twins begin life with nearly the same level of resemblance, but by adolescence, DZ twins have declined in similarity to a level equivalent to that of nontwin siblings. According to the theory, DZ twins begin life with as close a resemblance as MZ twins, because early in development parental reactions to infants—even of different genotypes—should be fairly uniform. Also, early in development the twin experience will ensure identity in the passive environment to which the twins are exposed. But when niche-building begins, the genetic differences of DZ twins will lead them to different niches within their otherwise "twin environment," thereby reducing there resemblance. The same would not apply to MZ twins. MZ twins, because they have the same genotype, will tend to pick the same niches. Their resemblance, therefore, will not change over time.

With a similar appeal to the differential effects over time of the three sources of gene–environment correlation, Scarr and McCartney explain two other surprising facts. One is the failure of adopted children to resemble their adoptive brothers and sisters beyond early childhood. The second is the failure of separate rearing to greatly diminish the similarity of some adult MZ twins, who, despite separate rearing from birth, become amazingly alike.

The most important fact of all to be explained by the theory, however, is how within-family factors could account for so much of the environmentality of traits. As we have seen throughout this section, the genetic differences among people along with their within-family environmental differences account for most of the differences in psychological phenotypes. This means that those aspects of the environment that vary between families but not within families are just not a very important source of individual differences. Thus, variations in such factors as parenting style, social class, parental values, wealth, ethnic group, and all those other factors that separate one family from another just do not make much difference in determining the psychological outcomes of children raised in those families. This conclusion—which we have come to again and again throughout this section—is perfectly consistent with the developmental theory of Scarr and McCartney. According to the theory, between-family environmental factors would only be important when they serve to restrict the environmental opportunities available to people. However, when there is no restriction of opportunity, "most differences among people [will] arise from genetically determined differences in the experiences to which they are attracted and which they evoke from their environments" (Scarr & McCartney, 1983, p. 433). These differences are fully achievable within families.

Besides its help in explaining some troubling facts, another reason that the Scarr and McCartney theory is important in the study of behavioral genetics is that it directs us away from a consideration of just heritability, or just environmentality, to a consideration of the actual epigenetic process by which genes and environments interact in development. If behavioral genetics was concerned only with establishing data on heritability, it would not be a very useful part of developmental psychology. Heritability, after all, is something that we are interested to know but can do nothing about. Knowing about the environmentality of traits is more useful, because it enables us to determine which environmental factors are important and which are not. Still, environmentality, like heritability, provides only a static view of how individual differences evolve. The Scarr and McCartney theory on the other hand offers a first attempt at explaining some of the essentials in the actual process by which genetic differences are translated into psychological differences. Their theory provides, then, a dynamic view of gene–environment interaction. This is precisely what we need.

SUMMARY

Behavioral genetics does not tell us about the development of individuals per se. Rather, it tells us about how individuals come to be different from one another. Because of this, behavioral geneticists are justified in talking of the independent contributions of genetic and environmental factors in creating these differences.

Studies in behavioral genetics involve both humans and animals, but only with animals can we use the experimental methodologies known as selective breeding and inbreeding. Inability to use experimental methods on humans limits but does not preclude our ability to gain important insights into the role that genes and the environment play in creating human differences. When the traits we wish to study are threshold traits, pedigree data allow us to test the hypothesis that the trait is transmitted on a single major gene with the mode of inheritance being sex-linked or autosomal, recessive or dominant. In the case of continuous traits, pedigrees are of no use, but they can be replaced by family studies in which we examine the degree to which family members resemble one another. The statistical procedures known as correlation and regression provide useful measures of the degree of this resemblance.

The principal problem with family studies is that they confound genetics and environment in such a way that we can never be quite sure the extent to which resemblance is due to one or the other. Twin studies and adoption studies provide us a way out of this difficulty. This is reflected in the fact that while family studies yield only a maximum possible value for a trait's heritability, twin and adoption studies provide direct estimates of this statistic.

Use of the various methods available to behavioral geneticists has led to a number of interesting conclusions. First, the experimental animal data show that genetic differences between animals contribute to differences on most if not all behavioral traits. Second, approximately half of the variance among humans in general intellectual ability appears to be due to their genetic differences. This leaves about half that is due to environmental differences. Most of the environmentality in intellectual ability scores, however, is due not to the environmental variables that operate between families but rather to the environmental variables that operate within families. Breaking the environmental variance down further, we can say that most of it is between-twin not within-twin variance. The heritability of specific cognitive abilities such as verbal abilities or spatial-reasoning abilities are equally as heritable as overall intellectual ability, but the environmentality is more heavily influenced by within-twin factors. A third major finding is that personality variables such as neuroticism and extraversion in adults and temperament in children are heritable, but not to the extent that general intellectual ability is. Again, the environmental variables that serve to make people different tend to be the variables that operate within, not between, families. A final set of findings involves the threshold traits of alcoholism, schizophrenia, and affective disorders. For these, between-family factors are again surprisingly unimportant in the development of these disorders. Thus, living with an alcoholic, schizophrenic, or clinically depressed person does not predispose people to develop these conditions. There is, however, a definite genetic predisposition. This is reflected most clearly in the increased risks for these disorders experienced by children adopted from affected parents.

The data from behavioral genetics to date give little insight into the mechanisms through which genetic influences are expressed. We know in the case of a few monogenic conditions, such as PKU, how gene products result in behavioral differences between people, but these cases are limited. Given that most psychological conditions will not have single genotypes associated with them, it is unrealistic to think that we will ever completely understand behavioral variability at the genetic level. We will, however, make advances in understanding the dynamic relationship of genes and environments in development. The Scarr and McCartney theory is an initial step in this direction.

SUGGESTIONS FOR FURTHER READING

Behavior Genetics. New York: Plenum. This international journal, founded in 1970, is a primary source for recent research on the inheritance of behavior. Although all of the articles are written by and for professionals in the field, introductory students can still profit by browsing through a bound volume of recent issues of the journal.

Kamin, L. (1974). *The science and politics of IQ*. Hillsdale, NJ: Lawrence Erlbaum. This first-rate work attacks the methods and conclusions of many of the scientists who have promoted a belief in the inheritability of intelligence.

Plomin, R. DeFries, J. C., & McClearn, G. E. (1980). *Behavioral genetics: A primer*. San Francisco: W. H. Freeman. An excellent introduction to the field of behavior genetics.

Smith, D. J. (1985). *Minds made feeble: The myth and legacy of the Kallikaks*. Rockville, MD: Aspen Systems Corporation.

Wilson, J. Q. & Hernstein, R. (1985). *Crime and human nature*. New York: Simon & Schuster. A controversial book that argues for the importance of constitutional factors in the causation of crime.

Description and Explanations of Ontogenetic Change

CHAPTER OUTLINE

CHAPTER 6

Physical Development

Physical development is a good place to begin a study of human ontogenesis, because as James Tanner, the world's leading authority on human growth, has said, "All the skills, aptitudes, and emotions of the growing child are rooted in or conditioned by . . . bodily structure" (1970, p. 77). In this chapter, the phenomena of physical development will be summarized using five inductive generalizations that apply, with some exceptions, to physical development within each of the physical systems, both separately and collectively—the skeletal system, nervous system, reproductive system, and so forth. In addition, there will be a detailed presentation of the facts of brain development. But first, Tanner's claim that psychological development is "rooted in and conditioned by" physical development will be justified using an example from adolescence that links general social and personality development to rate of maturation.

THE PSYCHOSOCIAL IMPORTANCE OF MATURATIONAL STATUS

Rate of maturation is but one of the many ways in which the physical development of individuals can differ, yet it is a variable of particular interest because of its potential for influencing psychological development. This potential is captured in the following conversation between two 14-year-old boys who were participants in a longitudinal study begun in 1932, known as the Oakland Growth Study. The boys have just completed an annual examination of growth and development that has made one of them quite proud. He said, "I'm going to tell my father about my gain in strength. I've got plenty of power on the pull. I beat myself in everything. And I grew two and a half inches. They said it was a spurt or something. Next year I'll have hair on my chest. How about you?" The second boy, who was a late maturer, had not shown much progress in physical development since his last visit. His less exuberant response was, "It's hormones. I've always been small and skinny. Some kids grow when they're young but the average boy grows when he's sixteen" (Jones, Bayley, MacFarlane, & Honzik, 1971, p. 267).

As suggested by this anecdote, rate of maturation alone, apart from any other differences in physical development, can be an important factor in influencing the particular developmental paths one will take. In the example above, the more mature boy may have chosen to develop his skill in sports requiring size and strength. The less mature boy may have chosen other sports or, perhaps, no sport at all. Debating might have seemed a more appealing competitive activity. We can also imagine that the relative maturational status of the two boys might have had an impact on such factors as their self-confidence and self-consciousness, which leads to the speculation that personality differences might be found to correlate with differences in the rate of maturation. The available scientific data tend to support what anecdotes and speculation suggest: systematic differences in overall psychological development do appear between early- and late-maturing adolescents, at least among males.

Early- and Late-Maturing Males

The earliest correlational research on the relationship of age of maturation to overall psychological development was conducted by Mary Cover Jones and Nancy Bayley (1950) in conjunction with the Oakland Growth Study. They selected the 16 earliest-maturing males and the 16 latest-maturing males from a sample of some 90 boys in the study. They then compared them in a variety of ways over the ages 13 to 17 years, using both adult raters and classmates. Overall, the late maturers had more negative traits: they were more attention-getting, bossy, restless, and talkative than were the early maturers. The early maturers were more self-assured and sociable. Indicative of the overall differences that existed between the two groups are data on their social success among peers. Of the 16 early maturers, 2 were class presidents, 1 was a boys' club president (second in status to class president), several were elected to committee chairmanships, and 4 were known as outstanding athletes. Of the 16 late maturers, only 1 was an officeholder and only 1 an athlete.

When a follow-up study was conducted some 20 years later (Jones, 1965), the 12 early maturers and the 15 late maturers who could be located still differed in some ways that suggested that the timing of their puberty might have had a long-lasting impact on their developmental outcomes. For example, the early maturers achieved via conformity more so than the late maturers and were more concerned with making a good impression. They also scored higher on measures of poise and self-assurance and had a be-low-average level of neuroticism (a trait described in Chapter 5 as reflecting one's general level of happiness and self-satisfaction). Late maturers, on the other hand, had their own strengths. They were less rigid than early matur-ers and showed greater overall insight into their behavior. These measures reflect psychological strengths in late-maturing males that were not evident in the measures taken during adolescence.

Although the personality and behavioral differences found among early- and late-maturing males in the Oakland Growth Study are intriguing, the small sample of early and late maturers makes the data suspect. Can we really trust these data to reflect general trends? Probably we can, at least to the point of expecting systematic differences between early- and late-matur-ing males on *some* variables of psychological importance. Confidence on this point is enhanced by a study conducted at the Stanford University Med-ical School by Paula Duke and a number of her colleagues (Duke et al., 1982). Taking advantage of data collected on a sample of 5,735 males and females aged 12 to 17, who were specifically chosen to represent the entire adolescent population in this country, Duke and her colleagues determined that late-maturing males were indeed different from early- and mid-matur-ing males. The variables on which they were measured involved educational aspirations and achievement, parental expectations, and intelligence test scores (see Figure 6-1). Late-maturing males were relatively low on all three, particularly in the later years of adolescence (ages 16 and 17). Moreover, the disparity in educational aspirations, expectations, and achievement was not due to differences in intelligence or the socioeconomic status of the families from which the adolescents came.

An interactional hypothesis that focuses on the relations among phys-ical, social, and psychological variables provides one way to explain the correlational evidence linking individual differences among males to their rates of maturation. According to this hypothesis, a mature masculine phy-sique serves as a social signal, both to oneself and others, that has a great many implications for how one acts and how one is treated. The plausibility of this hypothesis stems from the fact that males who achieve the physical signs of manhood early would seem to have a number of social advantages over males who preserve a childish body during this period (see Figure 6-2 for a dramatic portrayal of the differences that can exist). After all, who is more likely to quarterback the team, to receive the attention of older chil-dren and adults, and to get the lead in the high-school play?

FIGURE 6-1
Differences Among Early, Mid-, and Late-Maturing Males
These data indicate that late-maturing males by the time they are 16 or 17 years of age are different from early- and mid-maturing males in terms of educational aspirations for themselves, the educational aspirations their parents have for them, their educational achievement, and their general intelligence, as measured using the WISC and WRAT tests of intelligence. (After Duke et al., 1982)

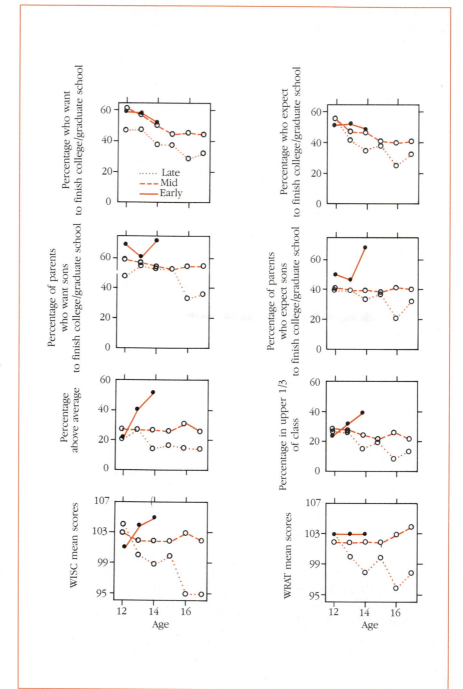

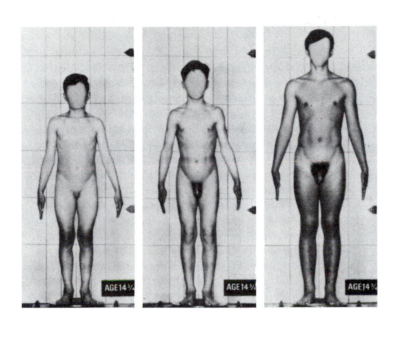

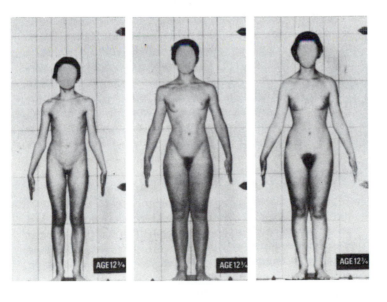

FIGURE 6-2
Differences in
Maturational Status
Among Adolescents
of the Same Age
All three males are
14¾ years of age, yet
there is a vast
difference among
them in terms of
physical
development. The
same is true of the
three females, each
of whom is 12¾
years of age. The
dramatic difference
among the same-sex
individuals in stature
and development
points clearly to the
importance that
physical development
during adolescence
can have for many
aspects of
psychological
development.

Early- and Late-Maturing Females

One of the attractive features of the interactional hypothesis is that it does not predict the same advantages for early-maturing females as for males. To understand why, you need to know that females, on average, go through puberty 2 years in advance of males. This sex difference means that an early-maturing female would be 1 to 2 years in advance of other females in her age group and 3 to 4 years in advance of most of the males! This would put her far in front of the rest of her age group, thus the early-maturing female is more likely to feel conspicuous than proud. This is nowhere better illustrated than in the case of 9- and 10-year-old girls who because of an early growth spurt find themselves to be taller than the boys in their class. Theirs is not an enviable position. Thus, as John Conger and Anne Petersen (1984) point out, the social advantages that seem quite clearly present for a male who enters puberty early are not so clearly present for a female who enters puberty early:

> . . . Society's expectations for adolescent boys tend to be clearer and less ambiguous than for girls. In boys, early maturing means greater strength and physical prowess—and, eventually, active sexual behavior. In girls, the expectations are less clearly defined. Is early sexual maturity a help or a hindrance? Is sexual activity at an earlier age than peers good or bad? Is the girl's adjustment aided by having to deal with the complex feelings aroused by the onset of menstruation and the adaptations it requires, when most of her peers are still more like little girls? (p. 121)

In keeping with the view that early maturation in females might be socially and psychologically undesirable, one study by Harold Jones (1971) found that early-maturing females were more likely than their peers to be "below the average in prestige, sociability, and leadership; below the average in popularity; below the average in cheerfulness, poise, and expressiveness" (p. 258). This study is a bit of an exception, however. The previously mentioned study by Paula Duke and her colleagues (1982), which examined intellectual differences as a function of early versus late maturation, found no differences among early- and late-maturing females. The same was true for a large-scale study conducted in Australia that examined prestige (Harper & Colins, 1972). Only Margaret Faust (1960) has in any way replicated Jones's results, and she found that the association between early maturation and low prestige was short-lived, lasting only as long as the early maturer's physical uniqueness. When the rest of the peer group caught up with the early maturers, there was an enhancement in the prestige of early maturers. Given this mixed bag of results, drawing any definitive conclusions regarding the relationship of early and late maturation to overall psychological development in females is impossible. All we can say is that the relationship between rate of maturation and psychosocial development appears to be different than for males, which is what we would expect from the interactional hypothesis that links maturational status to psychological and social consequences.

The data on early and late maturation have served the purpose of awakening us to the overall relevance of physical development to psychological development. With this point firmly established, we can proceed to a presentation of the phenomena of physical development. First, however, two brief issues merit discussion. One involves the distinction between physical growth and development; the other concerns the use of chronological age as an index of maturation.

A DISTINCTION BETWEEN PHYSICAL GROWTH AND DEVELOPMENT

In speaking of physical development, a distinction is often made between growth and development. *Growth* refers to increases in size, and *development* refers to changes in the structure, complexity, and degree of integration of organisms. The important point to note in the distinction is that development can occur in the absence of growth. A good example of this occurs in the physical development of the human zygote. When the zygote goes from being a one-celled to a two- and then a four-celled organism, it does not increase in size. In fact, it shrinks somewhat. Another example, to be discussed in detail later in this chapter, is that development in the nervous system is accompanied by a *loss* of nerve cells. As these examples show, growth and development are not synonymous, even though the two do frequently occur together.

The distinction between growth and development, which has been made here for the convenience of our discussion of physical development, is not restricted to physical development. The distinction applies to other aspects of development as well. Significant language or mental development can occur, for example, without growth in vocabulary and general knowledge.

PROBLEMS WITH CHRONOLOGICAL AGE AS AN INDEX OF PHYSICAL DEVELOPMENT

Though heavily influenced by environmental factors (see Chapter 3), the process of physical development is directly due to biochemical processes that lead to the development of age-related changes in the cells, tissues, and organs of the body. These age-related changes are referred to collectively as *maturation*. Time since birth, the conventional measure of **chronolog-**

ical age, provides a rough index of overall maturation, but it is far from perfect. The reason is that an external clock like chronological age runs at the same speed for all people, whereas maturational clocks run at different speeds for different people. This means that people at the same chronological age can be quite different developmentally. This is a general principle, applying throughout the life span; however, it is particularly well illustrated by the often dramatic developmental differences among adolescents of the same age (see again Figure 6-2).

To get a better measure of maturation than just chronological age, we need a measure that is directly tied to physical maturation itself. Measures of growth can fulfill this need, and societies have frequently turned to them, particularly in the days when birth records were not kept reliably. To measure school readiness, for example, some societies have used the age at which a child could reach across his or her head and touch the opposite ear (Tanner, 1970). Bartenders, in the days before the establishment of legal drinking ages, judged a person's right to drink by the ability to "stand up to the bar." Today, we have a better measure of the internal clock's progress than either of these growth-based measures. It is known as skeletal age.

Skeletal Age

Skeletal age, also known as *bone age,* is a measure of the extent to which the cartilage, with which the human skeleton begins, has become bone. The maturational process that turns cartilage into bone is called *ossification.* This process produces a highly regular set of changes in the number, shape, and positions of the skeletal bones.

To determine skeletal age all you need is an X ray of the left hand and wrist. (Use of the left is merely conventional. The hand and wrist are used because there are lots of bones here and radiation poses no threat). This X ray for an individual can then be compared to a set of standard X rays (see, for example, Greulich & Pyle, 1959) to determine whether the individual is advanced, retarded, or normal in development for his or her chronological age. Figure 6-3 shows how different the skeletal development can be in children of the same chronological age.

There are several advantages to using skeletal age as a measure of developmental age. First, we will all eventually achieve the same level of skeletal maturity (namely, complete ossification and fusion of the growth centers in bone known as *epiphyses*). Had we used some other "direct" measure of physical maturation—such as dental development, weight gain, growth in height, or changes in body proportions—this would not have been true. Second, though ossification is only one maturational process, the clock that runs it seems to be fairly well synchronized with the clock that runs other maturational events. This can be seen, for example, in data that show how well skeletal age corresponds to the age at which girls experi-

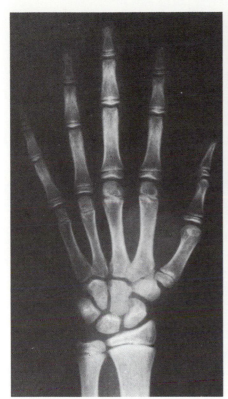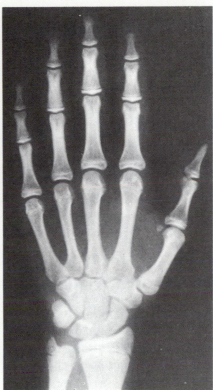

FIGURE 6-3
Skeletal Age
X-rays of the hand can be used to obtain a measure of skeletal age. Here, the hand on the left yields a skeletal-age estimate of 12 years, and the hand on the right yields a skeletal-age estimate of 16 years. Both hands are from males with a chronological age of 14 years.

ence their first menstrual period, an event known as *menarche*. In a 1974 study by W. A. Marshall of the University of London (see Figure 6-4), 65 percent of the females studied had the same skeletal age at menarche. This compares to only a 27 percent correspondence between chronological age and menarche. Obviously, the maturational clock controlling ossification is much better synchronized with puberty than the chronological-age clock is.

Conceptual Age

Although skeletal age is quite useful as an index of development, it is not as sensitive a measure as we would like for the earliest period of develop-

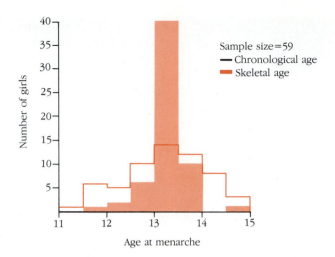

FIGURE 6-4
Comparing Skeletal to Chronological Age
As this graph shows, there is a better relationship between skeletal age and menarche in females than there is between chronological age and menarche. (After Marshall, 1974)

ment—the first year of life. In fact, X rays of the hand and wrist in the first year offer no way of reliably scoring developmental age, because there is not sufficient change during this period. For the first year, then, a different measure is needed. One that is often used is conceptual age.

Conceptual age is like chronological age in that it is determined using an external clock (a calendar) rather than an internal clock (one's own rate of physiological maturation). It differs, however, in that conceptual age, also called *gestational age,* is a measure of the calendar time since conception rather than the calendar time since birth. You might wonder why we would resort to a calendar-based clock to measure development when we have just seen that calendar time can be an invalid measure of developmental status (see again Figure 6-2). The reason is that the validity of calendar time as a measure declines with age. For the prenatal and early postnatal period, calendar time is quite valid because there is little variability in individual maturation rates. It was this fact, for example, that allowed us in Chapter 4 to specify "critical periods" in development using an external clock.

There are several ways of calculating conceptual age, none of which are exact. The most common is to begin with the date of the last menstrual period. This *post-menstrual age* adds about two weeks to the actual time since conception, because ovulation occurs at the midpoint of the 28-day menstrual cycle. Thus, a full-term infant would have a post-menstrual age of 40 weeks at birth and a conceptual or gestational age of 38 weeks. The inexactness in calculating conceptual age is due to the fact that conception is a private event that occurs in the fallopian tubes of the woman. Even if we knew when intercourse took place, the time of conception could not be determined exactly because sperm can survive up to 72 hours in the female reproductive tract (Schuster & Ashburn, 1980).

Despite the inexactness of our conceptual-age estimate, conceptual age is still a far better index of development in the first year of life than is time-since-birth because it correlates better with behavioral change in the first year. Thus, if we want to judge whether an infant is retarded, accelerated, or normal in development, we can best judge by knowing the conceptual age.

One indication that conceptual age has a closer relationship to development during the first year than does time-since-birth is provided in a study of infant visual attention by Robert Fantz and Joseph Fagan (1975) at Case Western Reserve University. The infants in their study had chronological ages of 5 to 25 weeks. Some, however, had been born prematurely, so that all infants of the same chronological age were not of the same conceptual age. When Fantz and Fagan compared the attention scores of the premature versus the full-term infants with the two being equated on chronological age (see Figure 6-5), there were large differences between the groups. With the two being equated on conceptual age, there were no differences between the groups. Obviously in this case as in others, in the first year of life conceptual age is a better predictor of behavioral change than is chronological age.

With the introduction of skeletal age and conceptual age as alternatives to chronological age, you have become aware that maturation does not run on a clock that starts at birth and then runs at the same speed for all people.

FIGURE 6-5

Comparing Conceptual to Chronological Age
Data from Fantz and Fagan show that visual attention as measured by fixation time is better predicted in infancy by conceptual age than by chronological age. (After Fantz & Fagan, 1975)

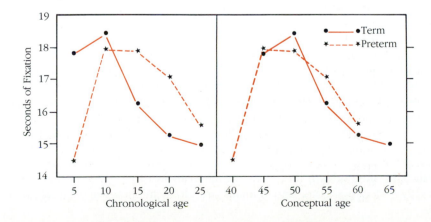

Maturation really starts at conception; and beyond the first 18 months or so (9 prenatal months plus the first 9 postnatal months), a great many factors— both genetic and environmental—can affect the rate at which it runs.

Having established the distinction between growth and development, and having established, as well, that chronological age gives only a crude measure of developmental status, we can proceed to the first three of the five general growth principles that are to be discussed in this chapter. The first three describe aspects of growth and development within individuals.

PRINCIPLES OF PHYSICAL DEVELOPMENT IN INDIVIDUALS

There are three general descriptive principles that we can apply with some success to individual physical development. First, the clock that runs development within individuals does not run at a uniform rate. For this reason, there are speedups and slowdowns in development that occur in an irregular—though predictable—manner. Second, as development proceeds within a system, it tends to occur along a physical gradient. Third, growth and development are designed in such a way that there is some room for *catch-up*.

Physical Development Is Not Uniform

Uniform development is illustrated by the growth of organisms such as sponges and oak trees. They start slow, speed up, and then taper off. This is to say that they follow a simple s-shaped or sigmoidal growth function. You may recall that this was the same pattern that Zajonc and Markus felt characterized the development of one's intellectual growth (see Chapter 2). The growth function for human physical development is not nearly so regular as these growth functions. Rather than start slow, the human growth curve starts fast. Then it straightens out until adolescence when suddenly it takes off again. This is shown in Figure 6-6A. A better way of portraying the non-uniform features of the human growth curve, however, is given in Figure 6-6B. This curve, known as a *velocity curve,* shows the rate of change at any point in development. When growth is depicted in this way, the rapid early growth, juvenile deceleration, and adolescent growth spurt become even more apparent.

The nonuniform changes in the linear growth rates of humans are shared somewhat by other primates but not by mammals in other orders. The usual pattern is for mammals to grow rapidly after birth and then gradually slow their growth rate as they reach maturity (Weisfeld & Berger, 1983, p. 122). Monkeys, apes, and humans are alone in showing the pattern of

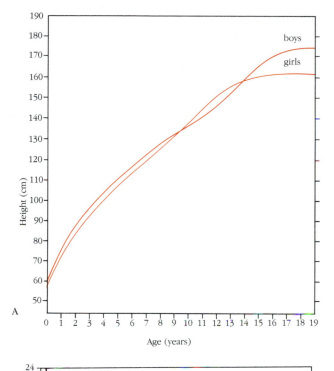

A

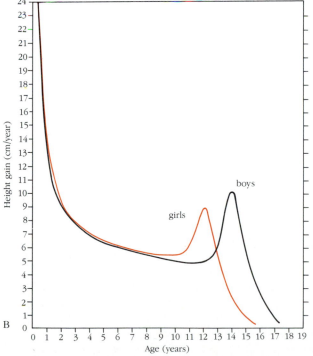

B

FIGURE 6-6
Growth Curves
A cumulative growth curve (A) and a velocity curve (B) show the nonuniform growth pattern in height that is characteristic of human males and females. (After Tanner, Whitehouse, & Takaishi, 1966)

juvenile deceleration and subsequent adolescent acceleration. Even among primates, however, there are important differences in the pattern. In female rhesus monkeys, for example, the adolescent growth spurt comes after maturation of sexual functions whereas in human females it comes before (Watts & Gavan, 1982).

The nonuniform growth pattern that is reflected in linear growth is reflected in other growth measures, as well. For example, the relative size of the various body parts changes dramatically over time in humans. This results in body proportions that are quite different for infants, children, and adults. Artists and clothing manufacturers need to be acutely aware of these differences. Others of us are likely to be less explicitly aware that these differences exist. Figure 6-7 will give you a good idea of the type of changes we are talking about. As you can see in the figure, the changes are indeed quite dramatic. The head, for example, makes for one fourth of the total body length at birth, but in adulthood it will be only about one eighth of the total body length.

So far in examining the nonuniformity of human development, we have restricted ourselves to the surface features of body length, weight, and the relative size and shape of body parts. We can also go inside the skin to find illustrations of nonuniformity. Take, for example, the different rates at which the parts of the reproductive system, nervous system, and lymphatic system achieve their full adult size. As shown in Figure 6-8, there is considerable variability.

FIGURE 6-7
Maturational Changes in Body Proportions
The body proportions of human beings change dramatically over the growth years as shown in this series of drawings.

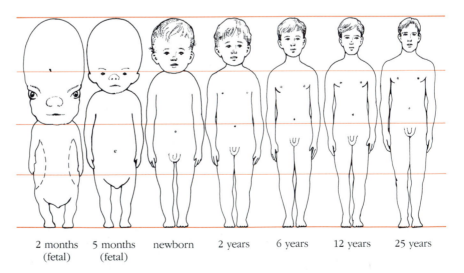

| 2 months (fetal) | 5 months (fetal) | newborn | 2 years | 6 years | 12 years | 25 years |

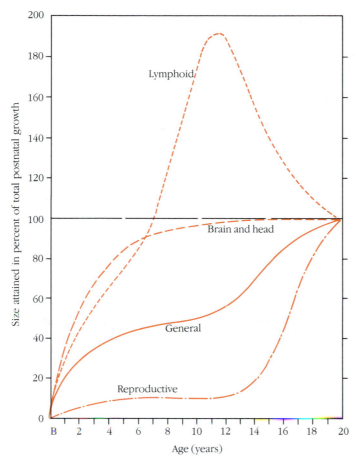

FIGURE 6-8

Nonuniform Growth of Tissues

Growth curves differ for tissues in different organ systems. Note that lymphoid tissue, the producer of antibodies, enlarges during childhood and then shrinks in the postpubertal years. The childhood increase is evident on examination of the adenoids and tonsils, both of which can become so enlarged that they interfere with breathing. Because enlargement, or *hypertrophy,* is normal for the development of organs in the lymphatic system, the growth curve exceeds 100 percent for all of middle childhood, late childhood, and adolescence. (After Scammon, 1930)

Developmental Gradients

Although growth and development are not uniform processes, they none-theless have a pattern. The pattern is a spatial one known as a gradient. Development in the brain provides one example of this. The example comes from development within the largest and most important part of the human brain, the **cerebrum.** This is a large structure that sits on top of the brain stem like a massive mushroom cap. The surface of the cerebrum is covered by a *cortex* (literally an outer rind). Maturation of this cortex follows spatial patterns or gradients. The first areas to mature on the human cortex are the *projection areas,* areas that receive input from the body's senses and then send messages out to the muscles (see Figure 6-9). These areas are the *primary motor area,* the *somatosensory* or body-sense area, the *primary visual area,* and the *primary auditory area.* From these areas development spreads out into the *association areas* of the brain, which adjoin the projection areas. Tanner describes this spread as wavelike: "Gradually the waves of development spread out . . . from the primary areas. Thus in the frontal lobe the parts immediately in front of the motor cortex develop [first] and the tip of the lobe develops last" (Tanner, 1978, p. 108).

Within the individual areas of the brain there are further gradients. Within the primary motor area, for example, the neurons that control movement of the trunk and arms develop ahead of those in the control of the legs. The same developmental gradient appears in the somatosensory area.

Though the connection has not been demonstrated between gradients of neural maturation and gradients of behavioral development, it is reasonable to suspect that the gradient in the motor area of the brain will acount for two major patterns in behavioral development—the **cephalocaudal** and **proximodistal** sequences. The former term derives from the Greek words for head and tail and means that we can expect for the headmost regions of an animal to be under muscular control before the rump or tail regions. The latter term is from the Latin words for near and far and means that we can expect for neuromuscular development to occur close to the central axis of the body before proceeding out into the peripheral limbs of the body. The reason is that behavioral development is not possible until we gain control of the muscles responsible for the behavior. Voluntary muscle control in turn is dependent on neuromuscular maturation.

Neuromuscular maturation refers to the development of the ability to control voluntarily the contraction of skeletal muscles in the body and thereby control movement. The cephalocaudal and proximodistal sequences for this development are plainly evident in a chronology of human motor development such as that in Table 6-1.

Table 6-1 lists some of the major milestones in motor development that occur during infancy. The ages listed beside the motor milestones are the ages at which 50 percent of unimpaired American children become capable of the behavior as judged by a sample of infants collected in Denver, Colorado (Frankenburg & Dodds, 1967). Examining this table will convince you that a cephalocaudal principle does indeed apply to these developments, because children achieve mastery of their heads before their trunks and legs, and they achieve mastery of their hands before their feet.

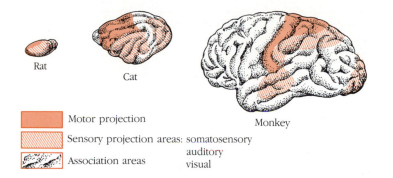

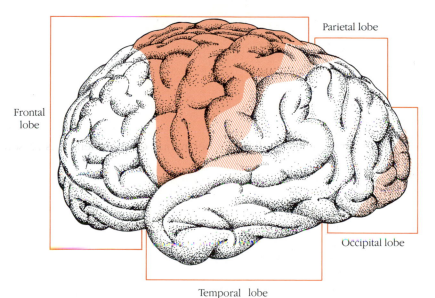

FIGURE 6-9
The Mammalian Brain
These drawings indicate the primary projection areas in the human brain and the comparable areas in the brains of some other mammals. The dark area in each of the brains is the motor projection area. This area is included within the frontal lobe of the brain, a portion of the brain that will be discussed later in this chapter. The areas marked with diagonal stripes are sensory projection areas. The one just to the rear of the motor area is the somatosensory area (touch and pain project here), the one in the occipital lobe of the brain is the visual area, and the one in the temporal lobe bordering on the somatosensory area is the auditory projection area. The unmarked areas are association areas of the brain. Note that these association areas are far more prominent in the human brain than in those of the other mammals. (After R. F. Thompson, 1975)

TABLE 6-1
Cephalocaudal and Proximodistal Gradients in Neuromuscular Maturation As Evidenced by Age Norms for Motor Developments

BEHAVIOR[1]	MEDIAN AGE (MONTHS)[1]
Prone, head up 90 degrees	2.2
Rolls over	2.8
Sits—head steady	2.9
Prone, chest up, arm support	3.0
Reaches for object	3.6
Bears some weight on legs	4.2
Pulls to sit, no head lag	4.2
Sits without support	5.5
Stands holding on	5.8
Pulls self to stand	7.6
Thumb–finger grasp	8.3
Walks holding on furniture	9.2
Stands momentarily	9.8
Stands alone well	11.5
Walks well	12.1
Tower of 2 cubes	14.1
Walks backward	14.3
Throws ball overhand	19.8
Kicks ball forward	20.0
Tower of 8 cubes	23.8

[1]Behaviors and median ages for their attainment are taken from the Denver Developmental Screening Test.

SOURCE: "The Denver Developmental Screening Test" by W. K. Frankenburg and J. B. Dodds, 1967, *The Journal of Pediatrics, 71,* 181-91.

The proximodistal, or near-to-far, sequence in neuromuscular maturation is equally well illustrated by the order in which motor developments occur in infancy. For example, motor control in the limbs begins in the upper limb area and proceeds out to the digits (fingers and toes) at the ends of the limbs. Thus the children can reach well for objects (3.6 months) long before they can grasp the objects using a deft finger–thumb pincer grasp (8.3 months).

Sometimes developmentalists state that the cephalocaudal and proximodistal patterns apply to growth as well as neuromuscular development (see, for example, Schell & Hall, 1983, p. 134). This is not generally true, however. Many growth facts violate the principles in some way. For example, the contribution that growth in the legs makes to the adolescent growth spurt is completed *before* trunk growth is complete. This is in contrast to the cephalocaudal principle. In contrast to the proximodistal principle, foot growth terminates before calf growth, which in turn terminates before thigh growth. Growth in the arms follows the same reverse pattern: the adolescent hand reaches its full mature size before the forearm, and the forearm, before the upper arm. Such development is distoproximal, not proximodistal.

Catch-up

A third descriptive principle that applies widely in the study of physical development is the principle of catch-up. We can be grateful for this growth principle, because it means quite literally that if you undergo a period during which an aspect of your physical development is depressed for some reason, you can expect to catch up. There are many illustrations of this phenomenon.

One illustration is a universal of development known as **birth catch-up.** If you examine human growth closely in the *perinatal period* (the weeks surrounding birth), you find an interesting nonuniformity. Growth slows down just prior to birth and then speeds up just after. This can be seen clearly in a velocity curve like that in Figure 6-10. The explanation for the decrease in growth rate in the month prior to birth is that the uterus has run out of room into which the fetus can expand. Like the wrappings that in ancient China were used to prevent foot growth in upper-class Mandarin women, the womb binds the fetus and prevents its growth. If this is the case, then the increase in rate of growth that accompanies birth demonstrates catch-up.

One reason that the growth pattern in Figure 6-10 is said to be a case of catch-up rather than just a case of programmed nonuniformity (like the adolescent growth spurt) is that the actual pattern appears to be a deviation from a much simpler "plan." The growth plan is indicated in Figure 6-10 by the dashed line. This line is pure speculation based on the now-familiar principle of parsimony. There is more to indicate the validity of the concept of birth catch-up, however, than just parsimonious speculation. One bit of data to indicate that the irregularity in the perinatal growth curve is a deviation from what would be obtained if growth were not fettered is the fact that there is a negative correlation between the size of infants at birth and their growth in the first 6 months. The smallest babies grow most rapidly— as if they were indeed catching up. More convincing yet is the fact that mating large Shire horses with small Shetland ponies yields offspring (foals) that vary in size at birth depending on whether the mother was the horse or the pony. Regardless, however, the foals are all the same size after a few months (Tanner, 1978, p. 43). Apparently, the foals carried by ponies are

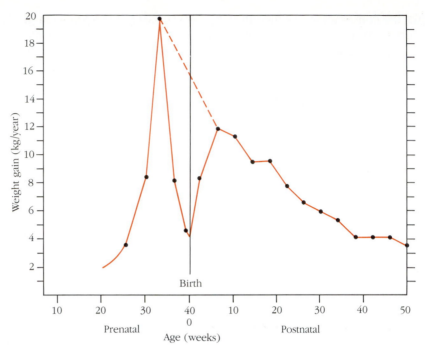

FIGURE 6-10

Birth Catch-up

Birth catch-up is shown in this velocity curve for weight gain in the perinatal period. The period of catch-up extends over about the first 8 weeks of postnatal life. During this time, weight gain accelerates rapidly as if to compensate for the extreme slowdown that occurred prenatally. The dashed line indicates the growth curve that humans would probably follow if the womb were less physically restricting. (After McKeown & Record, 1959; Ministry of Health, 1959; and Tanner, 1963)

undersized at birth but catch up postnatally on the growth that was denied them prenatally.

To demonstrate that catch-up is not limited just to catch-up from prenatal restriction in growth, Tanner offers a number of individual growth curves that indicate that catch-up is common following a growth-restricting illness or emotional experience. For example, the data in Figure 6-11 show the growth of a single child relative to a normal growth curve. Note that there were two periods of *anorexia*—periods during which the child stopped eating. During these periods, the child's growth deviated from the normal pattern, but when the anorexia ended, there was a rapid acceleration in growth that helped the child to catch up to the average. For a second example of individual catch-up, we can return to one of the cases of psycho-

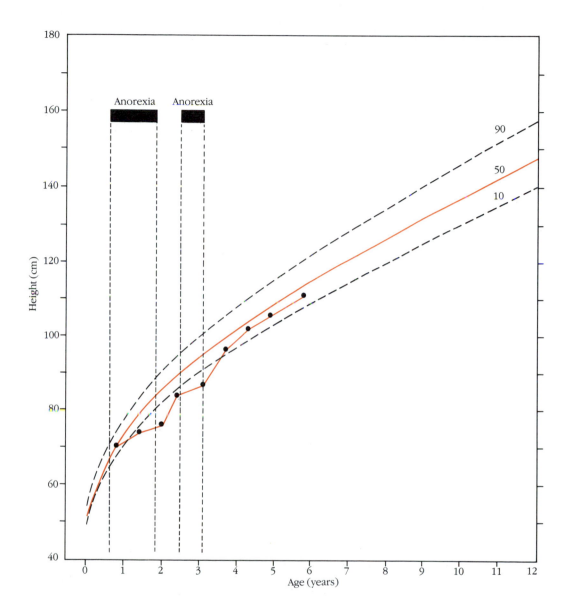

FIGURE 6-11

Individual Catch-up

Individual catch-up is illustrated here by the growth curve of a young girl who went through two periods during which she stopped eating (anorexia). Following each bout of anorexia, her rate of growth accelerated relative to the average (marked by the 50th percentile line). Lines representing the 10th and 90th percentiles in height are included to show that the girl was well within the normal range. (After Prader, Tanner, & Von Harnack, 1963)

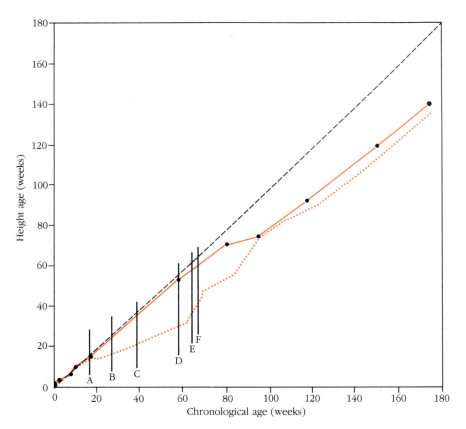

FIGURE 6-12

Catch-up Following Deprivation Dwarfism

This graph shows the growth in height of the twins pictured in Figure 3-4 relative to the expected height for children of their age (represented here by the dashed line). The solid line shows the growth in height of the twin girl; the dotted line represents the growth of her twin brother. The vertical lines A through F mark the events in the family that are alleged to have affected the boy's height. At A, the mother became pregnant. At B, the father lost his job. At C, the father left home. Catch-up began at D when the boy was admitted to the hospital suffering from deprivation dwarfism. Catch-up continued when the boy was returned to his mother at F, following his father's return home at E. (After Gardner, 1972)

social dwarfism discussed in Chapter 3. A cumulative growth curve for the dwarfed male of Figure 3-4 and his twin sister is given in Figure 6-12. You can see there that the dwarfed male caught up to his sister in growth around age 2, following hospitalization and the return of his father to the home.

The phenomenon of catch-up indicates that, in Waddington's terms, physical growth is well canalized (see Chapter 3). Momentarily deflect an individual's growth from its appointed course and the person recovers to catch up to his or her growth plan. In light of the canalization of individual growth, we might expect population growth norms to remain stable over time. Human growth in the 1980s, then, should proceed at pretty much the same rate toward the same end results as it did in the 1880s. This, however, has not been the case. Instead there has been a secular trend toward greater size and more rapid maturation over the past 100 years. Thus the principle of individual catch-up in growth stands in apparent contradiction to the principle of secular trends in growth.

SECULAR TRENDS: SYSTEMATIC CHANGES IN POPULATION GROWTH NORMS OVER TIME

The principle of **secular trends** in growth, the fourth of the growth principles to be discussed here, is illustrated by systematic changes in growth norms over historical time. If the spans of historical time over which we see change are long enough, the change might be due to genetic changes in the population. In fact, however, the secular trends that have been identified occur over very short periods of time (100 years or less) and so could not be due to genetic trends in the population. Rather, they appear to be due to societal changes. The secular trends set off by changes such as these are a principal reason that cross-sectional studies cannot always be trusted to yield purely developmental data as discussed in Chapter 2. What looks like a developmental effect in a cross-sectional design could just be a secular-trend effect on the different cohorts.

Figure 6-13 illustrates what is meant by a secular trend. The particular trend it illustrates is for height and rate of growth. The secular trend in adult height is evidenced in the fact that there are differences in the heights of 22-year-olds depending on the year of their birth. Those born in 1925 are shorter at age 22 than those born in each of the years after that. The secular trend in rate of growth is evident in the fact that differences at 17 are much greater than at 22. This means that the final adult height of the French university students represented in the data of Figure 6-13 was achieved at an ever-earlier age across the period of time that was sampled. Such data are not unique. Data comparable to these can be found in every industrialized nation from about 1900 to the present (Tanner, 1978, p. 150). The average person not only attains a greater terminal size but also attains that size more quickly.

The increase in rate of maturity that is seen in height data for the last 100 years is seen even more dramatically in data on the age at which women experience menarche. According to James Tanner, the age of menarche in women of western Europe has been dropping at the rate of about 4 months per decade for the years 1880 to 1960, and today it is at its lowest

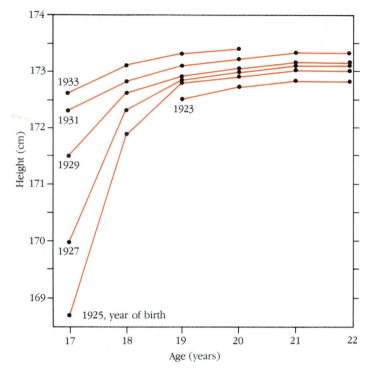

FIGURE 6-13

Secular Trend in Height

These data show the height of different cohorts of French university students at ages 17 to 22. Although each cohort from 1923 to 1933 was taller at age 22 than the one that followed, the height difference was greatest at age 17. These data reflect two secular trends therefore: one is a secular trend in adult heights; the other is a secular trend in the rate of maturation. (After Aubenque, 1957)

point ever, about 12.6 years. This precipitous drop is shown in Figure 6-14. The actual secular trend in age of menarche over the last 100 years may not be quite so precipitous as this figure implies, because Tanner's data for the nineteenth century may be inflated (Bullough, 1981). Nonetheless, there is definitely a downward trend over this period of history. Males have shown a comparable decline in the age of their puberty and thus have consistently remained at 2 years behind females in whatever decade one considers. Male data are generally not plotted with female data, however, because there is no good single index of pubescence in males.

The reasons for the decline in age of maturity are unknown, though it is generally concluded that the decline is due to the elimination of negative factors that inhibited development rather than the addition of positive fac-

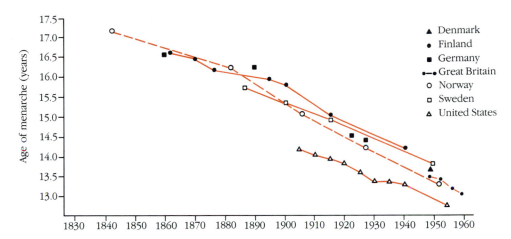

FIGURE 6-14
Decline in the Age of Menarche
This graph shows the decline in age of menarche in various Western countries over the past 100 years. (After Tanner, 1962)

tors that stimulated it. Robert Malina (1979) of the University of Texas, for example, has suggested that the key factor is the reduction in the number of infectious diseases that children must suffer through during their development. "With a reduced incidence of infectious disease," he writes, "children . . . experience fewer insults that drain the organism's reserves" (pp. 88-89). Others have pointed to factors such as improved nutrition, more stimulating environments, increases in body fat, reductions in overall family size, and increased outbreeding (the opposite of inbreeding) as possible causes. As Malina notes, however, these are "more speculation than confirmed hypotheses" (p. 60).

Reconciling Individual Catch-up with Secular Trends

With both individual catch-up and secular trends in the population as established phenomena, we can return to the problem of reconciling the two. How can growth be canalized in the individual and yet show steady changes over brief periods of history? To answer this question, we need first to look at a more complete explanation for the control of individual growth than just "canalization." The explanation is provided by Tanner's concept of target seeking.

Target seeking is Tanner's conceptualization of the way in which physical development might be regulated over the growth years. It is best explained in Tanner's own words:

> It is thought that the processes of growth are self-stabilizing, or, to take another analogy, 'target seeking.' Children, no less than rockets, have their trajectories, governed by the control systems of their genetical constitution and powered by energy absorbed from the natural environment. Deflect the child from its growth trajectory by *acute* malnutrition or illness, and a restoring force develops so that as soon as the missing food is supplied or the illness terminated, the child catches up toward its original curve. (1970, p. 125; italics added)

The word acute is emphasized in Tanner's explanation because this is the key to reconciling secular trends with individual catch-up. Individual catch-up occurs following relatively brief (or acute) postnatal exposure to adverse environmental conditions (such as malnutrition, disease, emotional distress). Full catch-up may be prevented, however, when the adverse conditions are chronic. "The evidence leads us to suppose," Tanner writes, "that it is both the duration of the malnutrition and the magnitude of the normal rate of growth at the time the malnutrition is applied that determine whether a full catch-up is possible" (1970, p. 127). If this is true, we can reconcile the phenomenon of individual catch-up with the historical phenomenon of secular trends by supposing that the conditions that depressed growth in the decades prior to the mid-twentieth century were chronic conditions. It would not be the elimination of a single disease or the avoidance of a single drought or famine, therefore, that could explain an average increase in size in a population.

Tanner's concept of target seeking has been presented here simply because it is the only explanation of long-term growth regulation available. You should realize, however, that the target-seeking hypothesis is not at all precise in the predictions it makes and, therefore, would be difficult to falsify. One reason is that the meaning of the terms acute and chronic are left completely open. If full catch-up occurs, then the conditions were only acute. If not, then the conditions were chronic. Such definitions as these are scientifically useless. Logicians call them *circular definitions*. The only reasonably precise prediction one could make would be to hypothesize that for points on the growth curve that are matched for velocity, adverse conditions of fixed durations at later points should have a greater effect on adult stature. No one has yet attempted to test Tanner's hypothesis in this way.

Beyond the fact that Tanner's hypothesis lacks the precision needed to make it easily falsifiable, it relies on some elaborate assumptions for which we have no evidence. One is that the genetical constitution has a growth trajectory inherent in it that will be realized when growing conditions are optimal. Despite there being no direct evidence of this, it is an assumption that is compatible with our general view that the genotype lays down the initial contours on our individual epigenetic landscapes. A second assumption, however, is a bit more fanciful. This assumption is that somewhere in our brains is a mechanism that operates like a thermostat to turn development on and to turn it off, to speed it up and to slow it down, all in response to the expectations of our genetical constitution. This "sizostat," as Tanner calls it, would have to be able not only to sense our current size but also to change its expectation for size on a time course that is in congruence with the expectations of our genetical constitution. This would be quite a device! Fanciful though it may be, however, one would surely not want to say that it is beyond the power of the central nervous system to perform such complex control. After all, it is now known that there are a number of homeostats in the brain that monitor our temperature, the amount of glucose in our blood, and our water needs, all for the purpose of maintaining *homeostasis* in our internal environment. Tanner's proposal goes but one step beyond these known devices by hypothesizing a "homeorhet" in place of a homeostat. The difference is that a homeostat has a fixed set point (for example, 98.6 degrees), whereas the "homeorhet"—in order to maintain "homeorhesis"—must constantly be adjusted upward.

HETEROCHRONY: AN ORIGIN OF SPECIES

The four general principles of physical development listed thus far are the nonuniformity of growth, the gradient phenomenon as illustrated in cephalocaudal and proximodistal patterns, the phenomenon of catch-up, and the secular-trend phenomenon. The first three were descriptive of individual patterns of physical development; the fourth was descriptive of growth patterns in societies over time. A fifth principle, which we will now add to these, extends our concern for growth beyond ontogeny and beyond local historical trends (like the past 100 years) to the evolutionary time scale and phylogeny. The principle is that of heterochrony, a word that Stephen Jay Gould (1977) uses to refer to an important source of evolutionary change.

The literal meaning of **heterochrony** is "different timing." The timing referred to is that which controls the appearance and rate of development of the various structures and systems that make up organisms. The possibility for making substantial changes in a life form by simply altering the schedule according to which its various parts grow can be seen clearly by examining facial differencess among primates. Figure 6-15, for example, shows that humans and chimpanzees begin with a head that is very much alike in structure that is then transformed more dramatically in the chimp than in the human. We get the impression from this comparison that the primary reasons that adult human skulls differ from those of chimpanzees is that the program for their development from a relatively common initial form is different. Specifically, the various bones and bone groups that make up the skull grow at different rates and for different times in the two species.

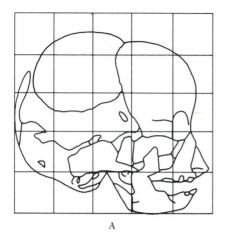

A

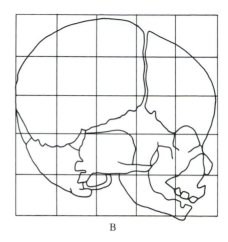

B

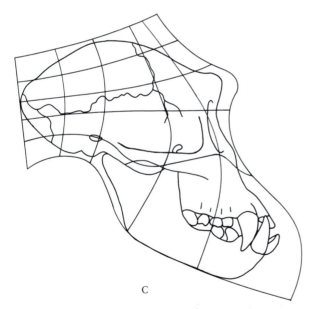

C

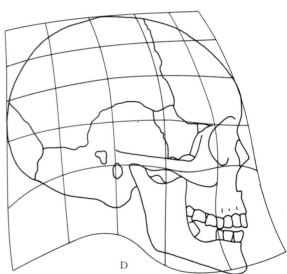

D

FIGURE 6-15

Neoteny of the Human Skull

The skulls of humans and chimpanzees are far more alike in their fetal than in their adult stages of development. It is thought that the growth of the chimp skull (A and C) represents a phylogentically older pattern of skull development and that the development of the human skull (B and D) is a neotenic variation on that older pattern.

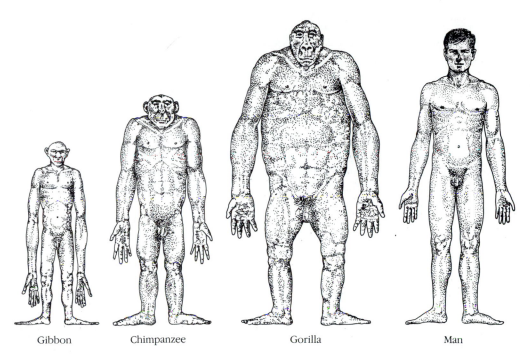

Gibbon   Chimpanzee   Gorilla   Man

FIGURE 6-16
Comparison of Primate Proportions
Contemporary primates in upright posture reveal that many of their differences
may stem from heterochronic growth changes.

The very same point can be made using not just skulls but whole
bodies. As shown in Figure 6-16, the major anatomical differences among
primates are differences in proportions. This makes it easy to think of the
various primate species as different heterochronic variations on a common
theme. In evolutionary terms, the common theme would have been the
common ancestor from which apes and humans derived. The heterochronic
variations would be the changes in growth rates of parts (for example, digits
relative to limbs, brow relative to jaw, or trunk relative to head) that would
have led to the selective enlargement of one body part over another or the
premature curtailment of growth in one dimension coupled with the pro-
longation of growth in another.

It is fine to make a comparative anatomy study among primates and
then imagine that one could create many of their differences simply through
stretching a body part here and compacting one there, but without a mechanism for achieving differential growth patterns on common growth materials, our thoughts are pure fancy. This is one reason the discovery of regulator genes (Jacob & Monod, 1961) has been so exciting. **Regulator**

genes provide a mechanism for heterochrony because they are single genes that can have large effects on patterns of physical growth.

To use a simple analogy, regulator genes stand in relation to structural genes like an orchestra leader to an orchestra. The structural genes do most of the work. They control the manufacture of the enzymatic proteins and structural proteins involved in all our biochemical processes. But the regulator genes can turn them on and off. Because of this, according to one especially bold theorist, "If it were possible to take judiciously chosen structural genes and put them together in the right relationship with regulatory elements, it should be possible to make any primate, with some small variations, out of human genes" (Zuckerkandl, quoted in Gould, 1977, p. 408). With the mechanism of mutations in regulatory genes, then, we have a somewhat less than fanciful means of attaining evolutionary control over aspects of growth. We also have a means of explaining how two species such as humans and chimps can be so alike genetically (Bruce & Ayala, 1978) and yet so distinct in the way their genes express themselves.

Recapitulation and Neoteny: Two Manifestations of Heterochronic Change

If heterochrony has in fact played a role in the evolution of humans from ancestral primates, there are two general directions this evolution might have taken. One is toward recapitulation (see Chapter 1). In this mode, the evolution of the human form would have occurred by a genetic change that allowed us to evolve beyond the terminal point of physical development in the ancestral species that preceded us. Had the human form evolved through recapitulation, we would expect to find evidence showing that juvenile humans resemble adult members of ancestral species more closely than adult humans do. The logic for this prediction is that when heterochrony leads to recapitulation, the adult form of the transformed species will be an evolutionary novelty, unlike anything that has preceded it. The juvenile forms, however, will be evolutionarily old and represent adult stages of ancestral development.

The second direction heterochronic change can take is toward **neoteny** which is often described as evolutionary juvenilization. Via the neotenic mode of heterochronic change, rather than passing through all the adult stages of ancestors, animals cease their physical development in a juvenile stage of ancestral development. Via neoteny, therefore, the adult human should resemble the juvenile members of ancestral species more closely than the adult members.

In some forms of life, heterochronic change has led to recapitulation. Examples come from the evolutionary history of scallops and mollusks of the Pecten order (Miyazaki & Mickevich, 1982). In humans, however, if heterochrony has played any role at all in our recent evolution, it is most surely through neoteny, not recapitulation.

Support for the belief that humans diverged from their more apelike ancestors via neotenic change is reflected in many measures. For example, unlike our adult ancestors, but like the juvenile forms of these ancestors, we have a large forehead and a flat face. Also, our bodies are relatively hairless and the ratio of brain weight to body size is large. A neotenic mode of evolution is further evidenced in humans by the fact that adult humans diverge from their infant forms less radically than other adult primates do (see again Figure 6-15). Konrad Lorenz sees the playfulness and curiosity of human adults to be a sign of their neotenous evolution, because in most contemporary species (and presumably in our ancestral species) these characteristics are only characteristic of juveniles (Lorenz, 1971). All told, the theory of neotenic evolution in humans is a fairly parsimonious explanation for many facts regarding our physical and psychological development and the relationship of our development to that of primate relatives. As developed by Stephen Jay Gould (1977), the theory holds that there were genetic changes in members of an ancestral species that caused these individuals to mature more slowly and terminate their physical development in a more juvenile form than any of their fellow species members. Their slowed development and juvenile form then proved to be adaptive so that those who developed in this way had a selective advantage over those who did not.

The Importance of Heterochrony to Psychology

The reason we need to know about phylogenetic growth principles as well as ontogenetic ones is that changes in physical development that have occurred during phylogeny—no less than those that occur during ontogeny—have psychological implications (see Belsky, Lerner, & Spanier, 1984, chap. 2). In fact, it is generally concluded that many of the unique behavioral and cultural characteristics of humans have emerged because of our neotenous development (Gould, 1977, pp. 400-404). Consider, for example, some potential consequences of our slowed development. One consequence is that we remain infants and children—and therefore dependent—much longer than our immediate ancestors did. This prolonged dependence would have put selective pressure on both humans themselves and their cultural institutions to evolve in the direction of providing greater nurturance. One result of the individual selective pressure may have been an increase in the dispositions toward infant–mother attachment. A result of the cultural pressure may have been an increase in the likelihood of multiple-adult family structures, such as the husband-and-wife family structure that is species-typical for humans. With this structure, one adult can provide for the needs of the child while the other provides for the needs of the family. Only within the last 100 years have cultural developments freed humans—some of them anyway—from the age-old need for two-parent families. (The extent to which culture has eliminated some of the biological imperatives that formerly regulated human existence is quite dramatic in the case of our own society. By 1990, one half of all U.S. families will be headed by a single adult [Newsweek, 1985].)

In addition to the role that neoteny may have played in shaping characteristics of the human family structure and the parent–child relationships within the family, the long childhood that our neotenous development has afforded us seems perfectly designed to facilitate learning. Childhood is the time for learning, and humans have a longer childhood than any other species. As will be noted in the next section, brain developments that take place prenatally in other mammalian species, take place postnatally in humans. This delayed brain development may well enhance the extent to which we can take advantage of opportunities to learn.

If infant–mother attachment, the structure of the human family, and the period of time for learning have all been influenced by our neotenous evolution, then they are important consequences, but an even more significant consequence is the attainment of a skull large enough to house a human brain. The sloped skulls of our adult ancestors could not have held a contemporary human brain. With our neotenic skulls, which are shaped more like the juvenile skulls of our ancestors, we have a larger cranial vault and thus more room to house a brain with an enlarged cerebrum. As you already know, the evolution of the brain within the large cranial vault has been the key factor in human development. What has been true in the evolution of humans is true in their ontogeny as well. The brain is again the key. Given the central importance of the brain in our overall development as humans, we will conclude this chapter by examining aspects of its development in some detail.

DEVELOPMENT OF THE BRAIN

The brain is the most precociously developed organ in the human body (see Figure 6-17). At birth the brain is already at 25 percent of its full adult weight. This puts it far in advance of other organs. The heart and the liver, for example, are only at about 5 percent of their full adult weight, and the gonads are proportionately even smaller. In fact, the brain is so large at birth relative to the rest of the body that it accounts for about 12 percent of our birth weight. By adulthood it will account for only about 2 percent of our weight. Not only is the brain large at birth, it continues to get larger faster than other organs in the body. By 6 months of age, the brain will have doubled in weight, and by age 3 it will have tripled. Throughout development, then, the brain will be in advance of all the other body parts.

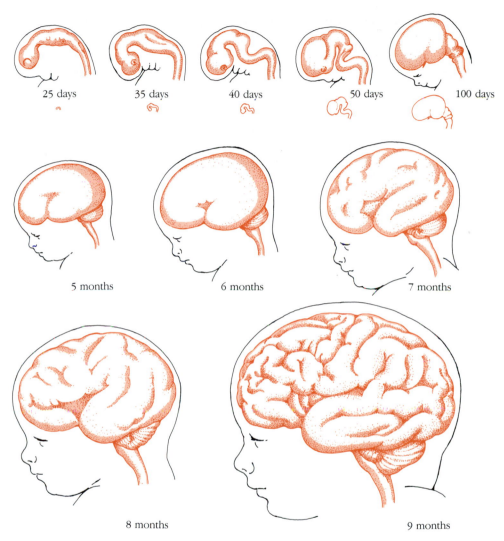

25 days   35 days   40 days   50 days   100 days

5 months   6 months   7 months

8 months   9 months

FIGURE 6-17
The Developing Human Brain
Developmental changes in size and appearance of the brain.

With regard to its large-scale structure, the neonatal brain is just like the adult brain. It consists of two cerebral hemispheres, plus a complete set of "lower" brain structures. To see these other structures, we have to cut away one of the hemispheres, as shown in Figure 6-18. Once exposed, the other brain structures—thalamus, hypothalamus, cerebellum, pons, medulla, and so on—are revealed to have exactly the same anatomical arrangement as in adults, though their relative sizes may differ somewhat. Particularly notable in this regard are the undersized corpus callosum (the band

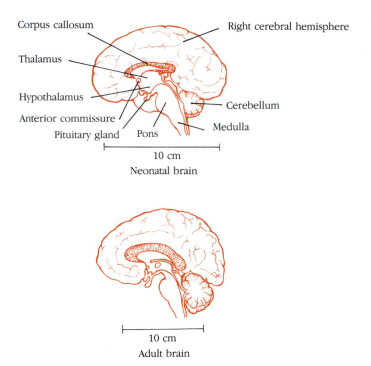

Corpus callosum
Thalamus
Hypothalamus
Anterior commissure
Pituitary gland   Pons
Right cerebral hemisphere
Cerebellum
Medulla

10 cm
Neonatal brain

10 cm
Adult brain

FIGURE 6-18
Comparing Structures in the Neonatal and Adult Brains
Cutting away the left hemisphere of the brain reveals a number of important
"lower" structures not visible when the left hemisphere is in place. As shown here,
every structure present in the adult brain is present in the neonatal brain; however,
there are some size differences. (After Trevarthan, 1974)

of nerve fibers joining the two hemispheres) and cerebellum (the bulbous
structure strapped to the brain stem that is vital in regulating coordinated
movement). However, despite the fact that some brain structures will grow
relative to others during development, the overall similarity in gross anatomy between the neonatal and adult brains might lead you to believe that
the human brain is basically complete at birth. It is not. In fact, it is extremely immature.

The Immaturity of the Brain at Birth

The immaturity of the human brain is evident in comparative, behavioral,
and anatomical measures. The comparative measures are taken from studies
of brain development in our closest mammal relatives, the nonhuman primates (monkeys and apes). These measures show that if we were to gauge

the maturity of the human brain at birth using a maturity scale set by the brains of other primates, the human brain would appear to be in a fetal state. For example, whereas our brains at birth weigh 25 percent of their full adult weight, the brains of monkeys and apes are far more advanced. They weigh from 40 to 60 percent of their full adult weight.

Not only is the human brain comparatively small at birth, it is relatively nonfunctional as well. This is quite evident in behavior. Neonatal humans are capable of almost no functional motor behaviors. This means that they can do little beyond what is provided by reflex actions to aid in their own survival. Behaviorally, then, humans are quite helpless at birth. In fact, they are the most helpless of all the primates.

An anatomical measure of the brain's immaturity at birth is provided by fine-scale studies involving microscopic examination of tissues. As background for a discussion of the anatomical immaturity that exists at the level of fine-scale structure, you need to know that brain tissue consists chiefly of two types of cells—neurons and glial cells. **Neurons** are nerve cells that are responsible for the transmission of messages throughout the nervous system (brain, spinal cord, and peripheral nervous system). **Glial cells** provide a variety of support functions. Of the two types of cells, neurons are clearly the ones of greatest concern to us. The production of neurons within the developing brain is complete at birth (Dobbing & Sands, 1973; Rakic, 1985), but the production of glial cells continues at least for the first two postnatal years.

By one current estimate there are about 100 billion neurons in the neonate's brain (Cowan, 1979). Averaging out the production of 100 billion neurons over the 9-month gestational period reveals that neurons have been produced at an average rate of 250,000 per minute. This will give you some appreciation for just how big a number 100 billion is. Although these neurons are located throughout the brain, the bulk of them are in the six cell layers of the **cerebral cortex,** a structure previously described as the "rind" that covers the two massive cerebral hemispheres. Because the cerebral cortex is the single most important anatomical feature for distinguishing the human brain from all others (see Figure 6-19), we will focus on the neurons here to detect signs of immaturity.

Two features of the neonatal cortex stand out as signs of its general immaturity. One is that the individual neurons are relatively undeveloped structurally. Second, the cells lack a coating of *myelin,* a fatty covering—supplied by glial cells—that serves to insulate them and speed nerve conduction.

The Structural Immaturity of Cortical Neurons

Structurally, mature neurons have cell bodies from which a number of *processes* extend. This makes these cells look like the roots, trunk, and limbs

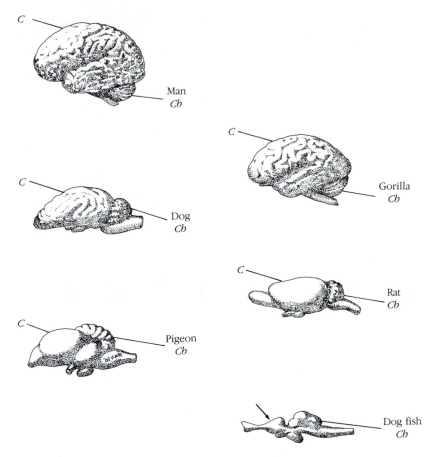

FIGURE 6-19

Species Differences in the Size of the Cerebrum

The cerebrum (*C*), with its six-layered cortex, is the most recent evolutionary development in the brain of vertebrates. Here we see that if we compare contemporary species, their brains differ dramatically in cerebral size. The human cerebrum is massive, dwarfing all the other brain parts, but in the lowly dogfish there is only the beginnings of a cerebrum (marked by an arrow in this figure). Note also that not all brain structures show the same dramatic differences between humans and other animals. The human cerebellum (*Cb*), for example, is much more comparable to that in the other animals represented here than is the cerebrum.

of trees or bushes (see Figure 6-20A). The roots are called *dendrites,* the trunk an *axon,* and the limbs are called *axonal branches.* When neurons are immature they have very limited dendritic and axonal branching. Functionally this translates into an inability to communicate extensively with other neurons in the nervous system, because communication occurs when dendrites receive messages and axons pass them on (see Figure 6-20B).

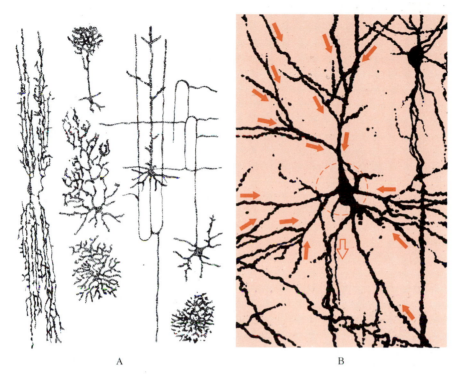

A   B

FIGURE 6-20
The Structure of Neurons
Panel A shows structural differences that exist among some of the cortical neurons.
Despite their differences in appearance, they all work in the same way as shown in
panel B. Incoming messages are picked up at synaptic sites located on the
dendrites and cell body. When these messages are sufficiently strong, a signal will
be sent along the axon of this neuron out to the synaptic sites located along axonal
branches. This outgoing message will serve to stimulate other neurons.

At birth, the neurons in the cerebral cortex are in a relatively undeveloped state as indicated by the actual pictures of some of the neurons in
one part of the cortex that are given in Figure 6-21. These pictures show
that the brains of neonates, when compared to those of older infants, are
structurally impoverished. The nerve cells are all in place in the brains of
neonates, but these nerve cells are yet to produce the elaborate interconnections that are the sign of mature, well-developed brains. By one current
estimate (Kandel & Schwartz, 1981), the number of interconnections that
will be present in normal adult brains is 10 to the 15th power! That translates into 1,000 trillion contact points—called *synapses*—where the dendrites of some nerve cells can receive the electrochemical messages transmitted from the axonal branches of others. Because a nerve cell can only

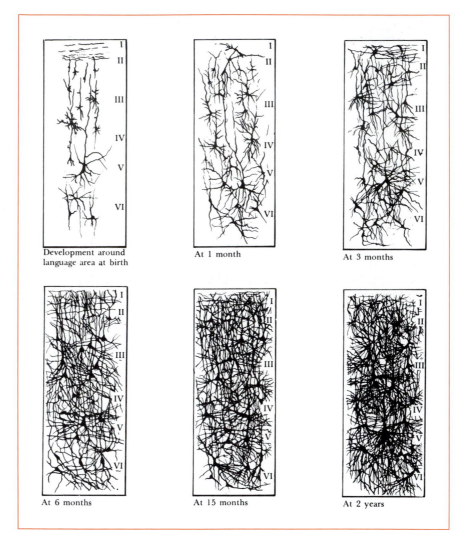

Development around
language area at birth

At 1 month

At 3 months

At 6 months

At 15 months

At 2 years

FIGURE 6-21

Developmental Enrichments in the Structure of the Cortex

By using a cell staining procedure known as the *Golgi stain,* it is possible to get pictures of individual neurons and their dendritic and axonal branches. The developmental sequence here shows the dendritic and axonal development of neurons in the six cortical layers of a region of the cortex known to be involved in language production. The sequence begins in the neonatal period and ends at 2 years of age, the time when language has become functional for most children. Because the Golgi stain, for unknown reasons, stains only some of the neurons that are actually present, these pictures do not accurately represent the number of neurons present in the cortex. There are many more than are shown here. (After photographs of Conel, 1939-1963, and graphs of Schadé & Van Groenigen, 1961, and Lenneberg, 1967) influence others through its synapses, the relative paucity of synapses in the neonatal brain (which is evidenced by the lack of dendritic and axonal development in Figure 6-21) is a clear sign of its limited capacity. The first result of histological examination of neuronal tissue in the neonatal brain, therefore, is to reveal that, at birth, a lot of wiring remains to be done.

Myelinization

The second feature of the cerebral cortex of the neonate that makes its immaturity evident is the lack of **myelinization.** Myelin, as we just mentioned, is a fatty covering that serves to insulate the axons of many neurons. Although it is *not* the case, as was once thought, that a neuron cannot conduct a nerve signal along its axon in the absence of myelin, it is the case that neurons are more efficient in conducting signals with the myelin in place. For one thing, the signals transmitted by myelinated axons are faster than those transmitted by unmyelinated axons. This means that myelinization will be particularly important for long-range transmissions. Since there are no long-range signals to be communicated within the brain itself, it is not clear how the lack of myelin affects functioning there (see Kinsbourne & Hiscock, 1983, p. 217). Nonetheless, in terms of anatomy alone, the lack of myelin in the neonatal brain is a striking feature that clearly marks it as immature. By the end of infancy, the process of myelinization will be well advanced, but it will continue even out into adolescence.

Maturational Processes in the Development of the Cortex

Two important generalizations can be made about neural development within the cortex. First, it involves both progressive and regressive events. Second, these events are under epigenetic control. Among the important epigenetic influences are experiential factors.

Progressive and Regressive Processses in Neural Development

The progressive processes in neural development are those that lead to dendritic and axonal growth, the interconnections of neurons, and the myelinization of axons. These are progressive processses in the sense that something is being built up. Equally important as these progressive processes are some regressive processes by which excess neurons and synapses are eliminated.

The best understood and most dramatic of the regressive processes is the massive cell death that accompanies normal development. Whereas cell death was once thought to be a consequence only of disease, it is now known to be an essential part of normal brain development (Kandel, 1981; Miller, 1982). Loss of some synaptic connections is also normal. The nervous system begins by establishing more contacts than are needed and then improves on its organization by eliminating the least efficient of these. For example, whereas the adult rule for the junction of nerve cells to muscle cells is that there be one nerve synapse per muscle cell, life begins with more contacts than this. Rather than the one-to-one adult ratio of synapses to muscle cells (or fibers) the ratio may be as high as five or six to one (Cowan, Fawcett, O'Leary, & Stanfield, 1984, p. 1263).

The regulation of regressive and progressive processes in brain development appears to be quite Darwinian in that the success of individual nerve cells depends on survival of the fittest. According to neurobiologist Gordon M. Shepherd, for example, "The competition of organisms for survival in the external world mirrors a competition in the inner world among neurons to fashion the circuits that will be the most effective. . . ." (in Restak, 1984, p. 47). In this competition, some cells survive and prosper in the sense that they develop elaborate dendritic and axonal branching. Others lose synapses they have already formed, and many die.

Knowing that the normal course of neural development involves neuronal regression and cell death should make you feel far better about the fact that we do not produce new neurons beyond birth. The developmental strategy for not just the brain but for the nervous system as a whole appears to be one of building up selected units while weeding out all that is superfluous (Miller, 1982). One consequence of this is that the actual number of cells in the brain is a relatively unimportant statistic. Underscoring this conclusion is the fact that the number of neurons in a brain is not a good measure of its ability and the fact that the overall size of a human brain does nothing to predict its success in intellectual matters (Stott, 1983). French writer Anatole France had a brain that at just 1,000 cubic centimeters in volume was only half the size of the 2,000-cubic-centimeter brain that was housed in the skull of England's lord protector Oliver Cromwell. France, however, was no less a man of intellect. By the same token, Karl F. Gauss, one of the greatest mathematicians of all time, had a very average brain weight of 1,492 grams. Many an ignorant scoundrel has had a brain as big.

Neural Development is Epigenetically Determined

The processes that lead to the success of some neurons and the regression and death of others are not fully understood at present, but we do know that they are epigenetic both in the sense that there is no predetermination and in the sense that both nature and nurture interact in determining a neuron's fate. Specialists Dale Purves and Jeff Lichtman place special emphasis on the nature–nurture interaction. In their words, this feature of neural development cannot be overemphasized (1985, p. 35). Nonetheless, even though there is neither pure nature nor pure nurture to be found in the processes that lead to neural development, we can still classify the factors in neural development according to whether their immediate origin happens to be internal or external.

Internal Factors Controlling Neural Growth and Development   We have already seen in Chapter 4 evidence of one internal factor affecting brain development. The factor was hormones. The presence of these during critical periods of brain development causes the brain to take on some sex-specific structural characteristics as documented in Figure 6-22. The sex hormones are not alone in affecting brain development, however. Insufficient levels of thyroxin, which result from the condition known as hypothyroidism, cause abnormalities that can lead to mental retardation and poor motor control (Purves & Lichtman, 1985, p. 143).

Of the internal factors that influence the interconnections among neurons, the most important during the earliest stages of brain organization are *trophic agents* (Cowan, Fawcett, O'Leary, & Stanfield, 1984). These are chemicals secreted by nerve-cell targets such as muscles, glands, and other nerve cells. Nerve cells grow (via their axons) toward these chemicals in much the same way that tree roots grow toward water. The only such trophic agent that is well understood at present is one called **nerve growth factor.** It is not secreted in the brain, but when it is put there experimentally, nerve cells outside the brain will grow into the brain to seek it out (research by Levi-Montalcini, cited in Kandel, 1981, p. 531). We can assume that there are similar trophic agents in the brain itself and that these help nerve cells to find appropriate neuronal targets with which to form synapses.

In the initial period during which nerve cells are extending their axons to sources of whatever trophic agents they need, there are far more cells sending out axons than will ever survive. Depending on the area of the brain involved, death rates are estimated to range from 15 to 85 percent (Cowan, Fawcett, O'Leary, & Stanfield, 1984, p. 1258). Survival is achieved only by forming synapses with whatever surface—be it gland, muscle, or neuron—is the source of the trophic agent. This process is illustrated in the development of motor neurons—ones that extend their axons toward skeletal muscles. These neurons die when they fail to actually establish synaptic connections with a muscle. In one "dirty trick" type experiment that demonstrates this, a chick embryo's wing bud (the structure from which a wing will develop) was removed before motor neurons had made contact with it. As a result, those neurons that under ordinary circumstances would have controlled the movements of muscles in the missing wing died. In a reverse experiment, an extra wing bud was added, with the result that a far greater number of motor neurons survived (see Kandel, 1981, p. 524). Research such as this has led to the general rule that the number of neuron targets controls the number of neurons that survive. We keep as many as we need.

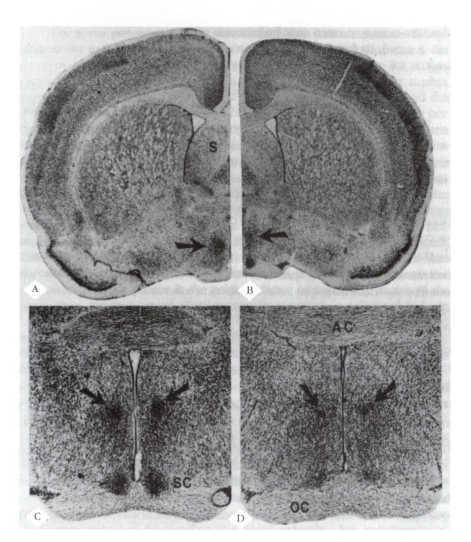

FIGURE 6-22

Gender-Related Differences in the Brain

Anatomical differences between the brains of males and females result from the presence of different concentrations of hormones during the prenatal period. The arrows in the photographs point to visible differences in the brains of male (A) and female (B) rats. The top photographs were taken at low power; the bottom ones at high power. No one knows what implications the anatomical differences have for behavior. (From Gorski, 1979)

External Factors Controlling Neural Growth and Development Experience and nutrition are two external factors that play a part in neural growth and development. Individual differences in these can lead to differences in brain development.

1. **Experience Effects.** An example of an experimental factor that is known to affect the fate of neurons is "use." When neurons are used, they survive; when they are not, they degenerate. This use-it-or-lose-it principle in neural development is well illustrated by events in the development of the visual system of mammals.

Getting nerve signals from the eye to the visual cortex is a two-stage process (see Figure 6–23). First the signals are sent via the *optic nerve* to a midway station in the brain called the *lateral geniculate nucleus*. There are two of these, one on each side of the brain. From there a different set of nerve cells project back to the visual cortex at the back of the brain (in the occipital lobe) where other cells await their input. Nerve cells throughout this system will degenerate without use, as in the case of people who are blinded or animals that live in dark caves.

In addition to having an influence on nerve cell survival, experience plays a part in determining the specialized role that some neurons will play within the brain. This can also be illustrated using data from the development of the visual system. As shown by Nobel Prize winners David Hubel and Torsten Wiesel, there are cells in the visual cortex of the brain that have highly specialized functions. Some of these cells are specialized in the sense that they respond differentially to the input from the two eyes. They are also

FIGURE 6-23
Pathways from the Eye to the Brain
Neural pathways from the eyes to the visual cortex via the lateral geniculate nucleus.

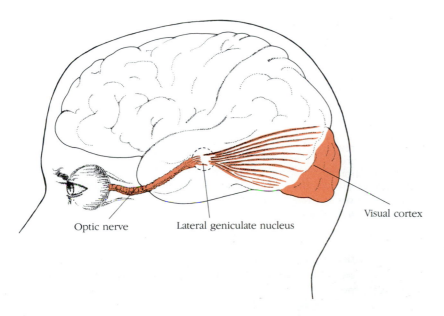

Optic nerve   Lateral geniculate nucleus   Visual cortex

specialized in the sense that only certain visual features excite them. Experiments on cats and monkeys have shown that both of these aspects of a cell's role—the eye that dominates it and the visual features that stimulate it—are determined by visual experiences in the first months. Up until this time, the cells are uncommitted with regard to their future role in perception.

The role of experience in the specialization of cells in the visual cortex has been made evident through two different types of experiments. In one, experimenters deprive an animal of sight in one eye for the duration of the sensitive period for experience effects (approximately 4 weeks to 4 months in cats). This results in a dramatic change in the usual pattern of *ocular dominance,* which is the technical term for referring to the specificity of a neuron's responsiveness to one eye or the other (Wiesel & Hubel), 1965). Figure 6-24 shows the kind of changes that are observed when input from one of the eyes is totally absent. Almost all of the cells are shifted toward sensitivity for inputs from the one-sighted eye.

In the other type of experiment, animals have their visual input restricted to lines of a particular orientation for the duration of the sensitive period. This affects their ability to respond to lines of a different orientation. In a study by Colin Blakemore and G. F. Cooper (1970), for example, kittens spent 5 hours a day from 2 weeks to 5 months of age in a chamber with only vertical or horizontal lines (see Figure 6-25). As a consequence of this experience, the experimental cats were, in the words of Blakemore and Cooper (1970), "virtually blind for contours perpendicular to the orientation they had experienced" (p. 478). This means that the kittens exposed to horizontals did not see verticals well (they would bump into chair legs), and the kittens exposed to verticals did not see horizontals well (they would bump into the rungs connecting chair legs).

Further evidence of the role of experience in the development of the brain comes from a long series of experiments begun in the late 1950s by Mark Rosenzweig and his colleagues at the University of California at Berkeley (see Rosenzweig, 1984, for a review). The independent variable in all of this research has been the type of environments in which animals are reared. Some are raised in "enriched" environments and perhaps given training. Others are raised in "impoverished" environments.

Figure 6-26 gives a good idea of what an enriched environment might consist of for rats, the species of animal most frequently used by both Rosenzweig and others. Basically, it is an environment providing lots of social contact and a great many objects to manipulate. An impoverished environment is best described as the standard laboratory condition—a bare cage, no cage-mate, uniform lighting, and nothing to do but sleep, eat, and drink. The results of such rearing studies are absolutely unequivocal. Animals reared in the enriched environments have heavier, thicker cortexes than do animals reared in the usual impoverished conditions (first shown by Rosen-

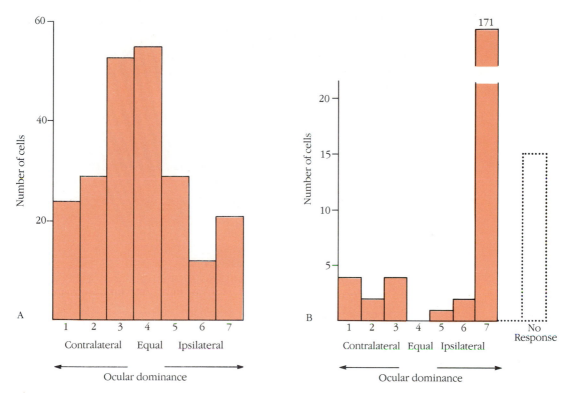

FIGURE 6-24
Plasticity in Ocular-Dominance Patterns
Graph A shows the expected distribution for the ocular dominance of cells in the visual cortex of cats. Most cells are binocularly driven (cell types 2 through 6), but some are driven exclusively by one eye (cell types 1 and 7). The eye that drives a cell can be on the same side of the brain as the cell (the ipsilateral condition) or the opposite side (the contralateral condition). Binocularly driven cells are labeled as equal. When a cat is reared through the period 4 weeks to 4 months with only monocular experience, the ocular preference of cells is shifted to the pattern shown in graph B. Nearly all of the cells have become monocular cells, dedicated to the functioning eye, which in this case is ipsilateral to the cells that were sampled. (After Hubel & Wiesel, 1962; Wiesel & Hubel, 1965)

zweig, Krech, Bennett, & Diamond, 1962). Also, microscopic analysis of the neural tissue in the cerebral cortexes of the two types of rats shows that the rats that have had enriched experiences have a richer neuronal structure (that is, more dendritic branching) and a larger neuron-to-glial-cell ratio. A recent finding from this line of research is that the effects of enriched experiences on the structure of the brain are not limited to a critical or sensitive period. Similar effects can be achieved throughout the life spans of

FIGURE 6-25
Blakemore and Cooper's Apparatus for Restricting Visual Experience
to Lines of a Single Orientation
(After Blakemore & Cooper, 1970)

rats, with even very aged rats showing a measurable anatomical response to increased stimulation (Rosenzweig, 1984, p. 368). For a given dose of enrichment, the response is often not as great as for younger rats, but the mere demonstration of continued plasticity has been extremely important to our understanding of brain development.

2. **Nutritional Effects.** A final external factor important to neural growth and development is nutrition. There is a commonsense belief that starvation during a period of rapid brain growth and development might serve to permanently stunt the brain's development. The period of greatest concern is the first 2 years of development, the years during which glial-cell production is at its peak and during which neurons are rapidly developing. Evidence favoring the commonsense view comes from any number of studies that have found that children undernourished in infancy are later intellectually deficient when compared to well-fed peers (Warren, 1973). The problem with these studies in showing that malnutrition is the causal factor, however, is that malnutrition is invariably associated with a host of other factors that might cause poor intellectual development. Emotional problems, child abuse, and family instability are among them.

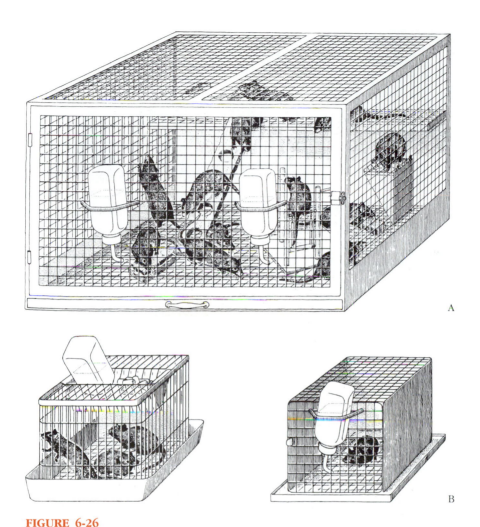

A

B

FIGURE 6-26
Enriched Versus Impoverished Environments
Rats who grow up in "enriched" environments (A) have brains that are quite different from those of rats reared in the impoverished environment of standard laboratory cages (B).

In an experiment conducted in South Africa (Evans Bowie, Hansen, Moodie, & Vander Spuy, 1980), investigators managed to separate malnutrition from some of its usual correlates by comparing the intellectual development of malnourished children with that of adequately fed children from the same family. The results showed that adequately fed children were intellectually superior to their malnourished siblings at the age of 9. However, even in this study it was not obvious that the improved performance was due to improved nutrition directly. An equally likely explanation, as the authors of the study were careful to point out, is that adequately nourished

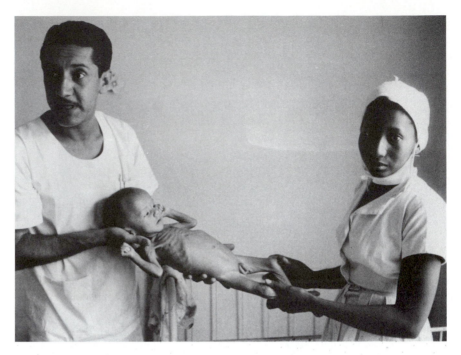

Malnutrition affects behavior and social relations, not just growth.

children are more active, more inquisitive, and more alert. In addition to the effect that these factors can have on "enriching" a child's intellectual environment, a more alert child stimulates more maternal attention, thereby increasing the level of stimulation. In fact in experiments on rats, when malnutrition coincides with a program of enrichment, no major brain deficits in brain development are found (Crnic, 1984).

At present, therefore, we cannot say for sure that prolonged deprivation from essential nutrients in and of itself has a permanent effect on the brain's development. It surely does not help, but the capacity of the brain to recover from insult—or at least to compensate— is impressive. We can say for sure, however, that when prolonged deprivation from essential nutrients leads to a diseased, inactive, listless existence, it will quite definitely have long-term effects. These will be manifested in both the structure and function of the brain, and some may be completely irreversible.

Functional Plasticity Within the Brain

One of the most interesting aspects of large-scale brain organization is the left–right division of the hemispheres. This division is interesting because it has functional significance. For some functions the left and right hemispheres cooperate, with the left brain controlling the function on the right side of the body and the right brain controlling the function of the left side. For other functions, there is asymmetrical control of the function, which means that a single hemisphere dominates in controlling the function. The classic examples of this organizational principle occur in the case of language, which is a left-hemisphere function, and spatial reasoning, which is a right-hemisphere function.

The Equipotentiality Hypothesis

Given the asymmetry of the hemispheres, an important developmental question is raised regarding how functions come to be lateralized. Some psychologists such as Eric Lenneberg have argued that the two hemispheres of the brain begin as unspecialized organs that become lateralized progressively (Lenneberg, 1967). Others argue that the lateralization has already been determined at birth, with the implication being that there will be a limitation on the brain's ability to adapt to unexpected glitches in the species-typical plan for brain development (Kinsbourne & Hiscock, 1983; Woods, 1983).

Most of the evidence at present tends to disconfirm Lenneberg's equipotentiality hypothesis. From birth there seems to be a bias for the hemispheres to develop along separate paths. Some of the evidence for this view comes from studies that show that the right and left hemispheres of neonates respond differently when presented with different sensory events. For example, when brain waves are recorded in response to speech sounds, the brain activity in the left hemisphere is more pronounced than in the right in most infants (Molfese, 1977). This fact is significant in light of the fact that better than 90 percent of all people have their speech functions localized in the left hemisphere (95 percent of all right handers and 70 percent of all left handers). The degree of localization is such that damage to the speech areas of the left hemisphere would cause one to lose some key aspect of linguistic functioning, a loss referred to as *aphasia*.

The same research that shows preferential processing of speech sounds in the left brains of neonates shows a preference for music sounds in the right. The significance of this stems from the fact that adults also hear musical sounds presented to their right hemispheres better than similar sounds presented to the left. Additional evidence for an early existing brain asymmetry comes from data that show that a lot of infant motor activity is asymmetrical. The asymmetrical posture created by the tonic neck reflex (see Figure 3-10) is an example. The right-oriented posture is the dominant posture assumed by almost all infants. Moreover, children show a unilateral hand preference as early as 7 months of age. This occurs on tests designed to determine which hand infants reach with (Ramsay, 1980a). By 12 months of age, the hand preference manifests itself reliably on bimanual tests (Ramsay, 1980b). For these, infants are given an object that must be held by one hand while being manipulated by the other. The hand that does the manipulating is judged to be dominant.

Evidence for asymmetries in behavior in the first year of life are backed up by some studies that even show asymmetries in the structure of the two hemispheres at birth (Springer & Deutsch, 1981, 135-36). In light of all this evidence of early-existing asymmetries, researchers today generally accept the belief that, by birth, the potentials for development in the two hemispheres have diverged somewhat. There is not, then, complete equipotentiality.

The Lack of Equipotentiality Does Not Imply a Lack of Plasticity

The fact that there is a bias in development for different paths of development in the two cerebral hemispheres at birth should not overshadow the fact that a great deal of plasticity is still present in the anatomical and functional development of the hemispheres. Children, for example, who suffer irreversible left-brain damage prior to the acquisition of language will use their right hemisphere to acquire language. Even if the left-brain damage occurs after speech has become localized in the left hemisphere, recovery will occur. The reason is not that the left hemisphere repairs itself. Rather, speech is regained because the right hemisphere takes over the function originally performed by the left.

One of the most amazing instances of one hemisphere developing so as to fill in for the other occurs in the case of individuals who have had an entire hemisphere removed. This surgical procedure known as *hemidecortication* is used to correct life-threatening seizures (and, in adults, as a surgical cure for some types of brain cancer). When the operation is performed on children under age 2, the one surviving hemisphere is capable of performing remarkably like a "whole" brain. For example, individuals who undergo hemidecortication early in life can go on to develop near "normal" IQs. Although there are hemisphere-specific deficits (some language deficits for left hemidecorticates and some spatial deficits for right hemidecorticates; see Dennis & Whitaker, 1976), the extent to which the one hemisphere can operate alone is incredible.

Time Limitations on Functional Plasticity

The data on the development of hemispheric asymmetries leads us to conclude that although there may not be complete equipotentiality, there is nonetheless a considerable capacity for compensation. For most functions, however, this compensatory ability will be time-limited. With regard to language, for example, left-brain damage beyond age 5 results in a poor prognosis that substantial language abilities can be recovered by the undamaged right hemisphere (Krashen, 1973).

Though the time limitation on the functional plasticity of the hemispheres is widely acknowledged, most authors do not speculate on why this might be the case. In light of the general absence of hypothesized mechanisms for the loss of plasticity, a recent suggestion by Peter Huttenlocher (1984) takes on special interest. Huttenlocher's suggestion is that plasticity will be lost as excess synaptic connections are eliminated. This suggestion is based on the well-known fact that, in the early period of synapse formation, more synapses are formed than will in fact be used (see p. 296). Huttenlocher's own data, for example, show that the density of synaptic connections in the frontal area of the cortex is 60 percent less in adults than in 2-year-olds. His interpretation of this is that the excess of synapses available early in development provides a buffer against just such eventualities as brain damage. Thus the explanation for the successful language recovery in cases of early left-brain damage is that backup language-functional synapses in the right hemisphere are still available. Over time, however, these extra synapses are depleted through disuse, making recovery ever-less likely.

Inhibitory Controls in the Nervous System and the Development of Behavior

Though we most often think of neural development in terms of expanded synaptic connections that enable one neuron to "fire" or "excite" many others, the fact is that inhibiting neuronal activity can be as important as stimulating it (Cotman & McGaugh, 1979, p. 218). You can understand why by considering any number of commonsense observations. Take the case of the normal action of skeletal muscles, the ones that are attached to limbs. For these muscles to work properly there must be excitation on either the extensor or the flexor side, coupled with inhibition on the opposite side. If the neurons controlling extensor and flexor muscles were simultaneously sending excitatory messages, the limb would not work. Epileptic seizures provide a dramatic instance of what happens when excitation within the nervous system is not balanced by inhibition. In an epileptic seizure there is massive, uncontrolled neural discharging throughout the brain. Some suspect that even everyday, normal psychological problems such as a loss of attention or an inability to keep one's thoughts on target are due to lapses in inhibitory control somewhere within the brain (see Taylor, 1980).

Despite the acknowledged importance of inhibition as a general mechanism within the nervous system, little is known about it except at the neuronal level. *Neural inhibition,* however, is fairly well understood. Specific chemicals and neurons have been identified that serve the inhibitory function. Within the visual system, for example, the neural-inhibitory mechanism is completely responsible for the fine detail with which we can see. We can guess that similar mechanisms are involved when the initially clumsy, diffuse movements of infants are transformed into pinpoint-accurate motor acts, but that is yet to be demonstrated.

The second way in which inhibition is achieved within the nervous system involves entire regions within the brain. This form of inhibitory control is apparently quite important in the development of behavior. One indication of this comes from research on the phenomenon known as *cortical inhibition.* Other evidence comes from research on the relationship between behavioral development in infants and maturation within the frontal lobe, the forward-most cortical region in the brain (see Figure 6-9).

Cortical Inhibition As an Explanation for the Fate of the Vestigial Reflexes

Hughlings Jackson, a self-trained nineteenth-century neurologist, was the first to promote the still popular notion that during development certain regions of the cortex come to dominate and control the activity of lower regions of the brain (see Taylor, 1958). This notion, known as cortical inhibition, is particularly well illustrated in the developmental fate of a set of behaviors known as vestigial reflexes.

The **vestigial reflexes,** like most other neonatal reflexes (such as sucking, gagging, and breathing), are controlled by neural circuits located in the brain stem. They differ, however, in that the vestigial reflexes are only a temporary part of behavior. Most will have disappeared completely by 6 months of age. This makes them quite curious. One question raised by their disappearance is why they should ever have been present in the first place. The general answer is that they are just "vestiges" of our evolutionary past that appear in a brief recapitulatory moment. A second question is what

FIGURE 6-27
The Rooting Reflex

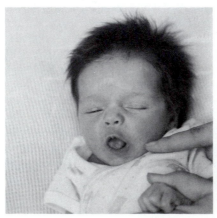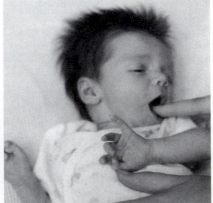

causes them to disappear. The general answer to this question is inhibition —inhibition that stems from the evolutionarily newer regions of the cortex.

Though one might think that neural degeneration would be as likely an explanation for the disappearance of the vestigial reflexes as inhibition, this is not so. Degeneration is ruled out by the fact that vestigial reflexes can reappear following damage to the cortex. This fact, which makes the vestigial reflexes clinically important in diagnosing brain damage, argues strongly that their initial disappearance is only due to inhibition.

One of the primitive vestigial reflexes that becomes inhibited is the *rooting reflex* (see Figure 6-27). It can be produced by touching the neonate on the cheek near the mouth with a finger or a nipple. The neonate will then turn in the direction of the touch and begin to suck. This reflex disappears somewhere around 4 months of age and only reappears in cases of severe cortical degeneration such as occurs in the late stages of *Alzheimer's disease*.

Other reflexes that are included in the set of short-lived vestigial reflexes are the hand- and foot-grasp reflexes, which are known as the *palmar-grasp* and *plantar* reflexes respectively. With these reflexes infants can hang on (much like little monkeys) to thin strings (see Figure 6-28) or fingers. A fourth vestigial reflex is the swimming reflex. It is sufficiently strong so that neonates can actually propel themselves through water. Accompanying this reflex is a breathing reflex that keeps the infant from taking

FIGURE 6-28

Reflexive Grasps of Hand and Foot

The reflex that enables the human hand and foot to grasp is present at birth but disappears completely by 4 months of age. The same is true of the rooting reflex in Figure 6-27. The presence of these and other vestigial reflexes is a sign of the immaturity of the human brain at birth.

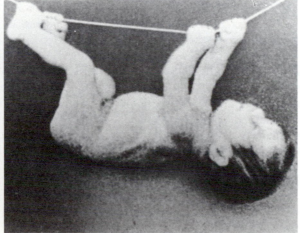

water into the lungs. Unfortunately, parents cannot completely count on these reflexes to protect a baby turned loose in the family pool.

In addition to the vestigial rooting, palmar-grasp, plantar, and swimming reflexes, there are a couple of other well-known vestigial reflexes. These are the *Moro* and *Babinski* reflexes. The Moro reflex is initiated by loss of head support. It is a whole-body response, but its most visible component involves spreading the arms and then returning them to the midline. The Babinski reflex involves fanning the toes in response to a stroke on the sole of the foot.

Inhibitory Mechanisms Within the Frontal Lobe

Inhibition is important not only for the suppression of primitive reflexes. It is also important in the emergence of some of the highest cognitive functions of which humans are capable: abstract thinking, planning, intentionality, and selective attention. The region of the brain essential to achieving this inhibitory control is the *frontal lobe,* which includes the motor cortex and all of the association area that lies in front of the motor cortex (see Figure 6-9). This region, which constitutes one quarter of the entire human cortex, has increased dramatically in size during primate evolution, a factor that contributes further to our belief that it plays an essential role in the emergence of some of the distinctive cognitive attributes of humans.

Evidence for the inhibitory role that the frontal lobe plays in high-level cognitive functioning comes from both clinical and developmental data. The clinical data have been collected on adults with frontal-lobe brain damage. Inhibition failures are among the most common symptoms observed in these individuals. For example, if frontal-lobe patients are given a set of color names that are printed in ink of a different color (for example, "red" is printed in blue ink, "green" in orange ink, and so on), they find it difficult to name the color ink (Perret, 1974). Instead, when instructed to report the color of the ink, they read the color name. The tendency to read the color name rather than name the color ink is strong in anyone who takes the color-naming test (known as the Stroop test), but in the absence of frontal-lobe damage, people are able to inhibit the reading tendency. Those with frontal-lobe damage lack this inhibitory ability. They also have difficulty in suppressing old habits. For example, once frontal-lobe patients have learned to sort a set of cards using one criterion, such as the number of elements pictured in the design of the card, they find it very difficult to switch to some new criterion, such as the shape (square, cross, or triangle) of the elements in the design (Milner, 1963, pp. 90–100; Milner, 1964, pp. 313–34). Instead of making the switch, they continue to sort according to the old criterion, even when they know that it is wrong to do so.

Developmental data also support the view that the frontal cortex plays an inhibitory role in normal human cognition. The developmental data come from research conducted by Adele Diamond and her colleagues (Diamond & Goldman-Rakic, 1985). Working with two separate response errors that human infants make between 7½ and 9 months of age, Diamond and her colleagues found evidence that the disappearance of these errors by 12 months of age may be attributable to maturation within the frontal lobe.

One of the response errors that young infants make occurs in a simple game of hide and seek (Diamond & Goldman-Rakic, 1985). In the game, called the AAB problem, the experimenter hides a toy at one of two locations either at Well A or Well B (see Figure 6-29). When the toy is hidden repeatedly at Well A, 7½- to 9-month-olds are quite good at going to Well A to retrieve it. But when the toy is then hidden at Well B, even when infants see the toy being placed there, they go back to Well A. This marks a failure to inhibit what Diamond calls the "prepotent" response of going to Well A.

FIGURE 6-29
The AAB Error
An 8-month-old infant watches as a toy is hidden in Well A. Wells A and B are then covered, and the infant is allowed to reach for the object, which he finds in Well A. After repeating this procedure two times, the toy is hidden in Well B. Both wells are again covered, the infant's visual fixation on Well B is broken, and then he is observed to see which well he will go to in search of the toy. In this case, he goes to A, thus making the typical AB error. (From Diamond, 1985)

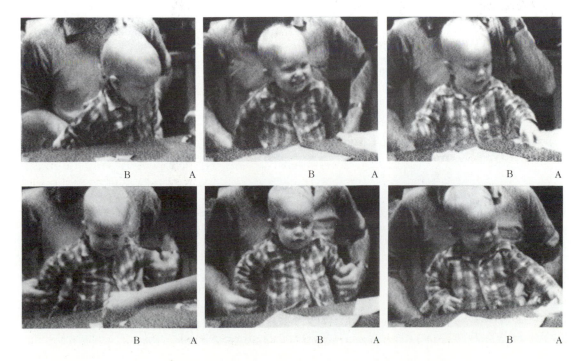

In this sense the young infants behave similarly to frontal-lobe patients, who fail to inhibit their prepotent responses on card-sorting and color-naming tasks.

Another example of the tendency for 7½- to 9-month-olds to make response errors occurs in a second toy-retrieval task (Diamond, 1982). In this case, the toy is not placed out of sight. It is simply put in a see-through plastic box. One side of the box is open so that all one has to do to get the toy is to reach through the open side. What Diamond finds with 7½- to 9-month-old infants, however, is a persistent tendency to reach only along the line of sight. This means that if infants are allowed to see the toy via an open side, they reach along their line of sight and succeed in retrieving the toy. But if their line of sight passes through one of the box's clear plastic sides, they will again reach along their line of sight and therefore fail to retrieve the toy. They fail because the side of the box blocks their reach. The extent to which the reach-along-the-line-of-sight rule is adhered to is remarkable. As shown in Figure 6-30, an infant who is allowed to begin reaching along a line of sight that passes through the open side of the box

FIGURE 6-30
Persistence in Reaching Along the Line of Sight
The subject can see the toy through the clear plastic topic of the box but he cannot get the toy because he persists in reaching along his line of sight, which is through the closed top. The experimenter then raises the box so that the toy is visible through the open front of the box. With the open front in his line of sight, the subject reaches along this line and is quite near grasping the toy when the experimenter lowers the box so that the line of sight is again through the closed top. The subject responds by withdrawing his hand and trying again to reach "through" the top. This behavior is characteristic of young infants between 7½ and 9 months of age. (From Diamond, 1981)

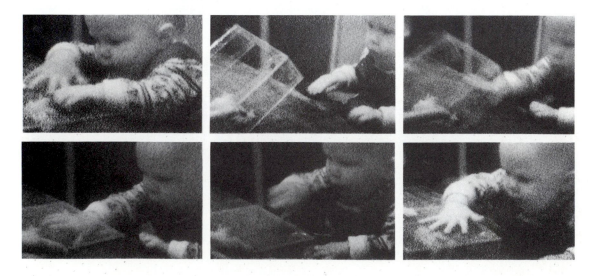

will then give up this reach when the box is moved in such a way that the new line of sight is via the closed top of the box. They give up even when their hand is already through the opening and quite near the toy! Apparently, then, achieving success on the toy-in-the-box problem requires inhibiting a rather strong infant tendency to reach only along the line of sight. This makes the toy-in-the-box problem conceptually similar to the AAB problem, which requires infants to inhibit their prepotent tendency to search in the usual place.

Human infants are not alone in making the AAB and reaching errors described above. Rhesus monkeys make them too, though in the period 1½ to 2½ months of age rather than 7½ to 9 months. Like humans also, rhesus monkeys cease making these errors as a part of their normal developmental progression—by 4 months for rhesus monkeys and 12 months for humans. What is interesting, however, is that when Diamond lesioned portions of the frontal cortex in the brains of three adult rhesus monkeys, the errors returned (Diamond & Goldman-Rakic, 1985). The three brain-damaged adults looked just like infants in that they made the AAB error and they reached only along the line of sight in the toy-in-the-box problem. An obvious implication of this research is that the normal mechanism that leads to the disappearance of the errors involves the development of inhibitory control via the maturation in the frontal lobe.

SUMMARY

To make the point that the skills, aptitudes, and emotions of growing children are rooted in their physical development, we began the chapter with a discussion of the relationship of early and late maturation to the psychological development of adolescents. Other introductory matters dealt with the fact that growth and development are not synonymous and the fact that chronological age is only a rough index of maturational state. For some purposes, skeletal age and conceptual age are more useful.

Five separate growth principles were used to organize the material on general physical development. The first three applied to individual growth. These were the nonuniformity of growth, developmental gradients, and growth catch-up. The fourth applied to growth in populations and the fact that there are local historical trends, called secular trends, in the average growth values in a population. Such trends were illustrated using the examples of changes in height and age of menarche that have occurred in industrialized nations over the past 100 years. The fifth phenomenon—heterochrony—applies to changes in growth patterns over the phylogenetic time span. Such changes could account for the emergence of new species during phylogenesis. Species-creating heterochronic changes are made plausible by the existence of regulator genes, because mutations in these single genes could have dramatic effects on the rate and timing of physical development. Changes in some genes could slow development or terminate it early, thereby producing neoteny. Changes in other genes could speed up development or prolong it, thereby producing recapitulation. Assuming that heterochronic changes are in fact a possibility in evolution, it seems apparent that humans have evolved from their ancestors via neotenic changes in the developmental pattern.

Because the nervous system is the organ system of greatest overall importance to psychological development, the physical development of the brain and nervous system was discussed at length. The discussion was organized around the facts that the brain is precocious at birth relative to other human organ systems but that, in absolute terms, it is quite immature. The immaturity is reflected in comparative data, behavioral data, and data that stem from fine-scale examination of neural tissue in the cortex of the brain.

As the brain matures, both regressive and progressive processes can be noted. The progressive processes involve dendritic and axonal growth, the formation of synapses, and the myelinization of individual nerve fibers. The regressive processes involve the massive death of cells and the loss of nonfunctional synapses. Whether an individual nerve cell progresses or regresses is under epigenetic control. Among the important epigenetic factors are internal factors such as hormones and trophic agents. Among the external factors are use, experience, and nutrition.

An important characteristic of the adult brain is that some psychological functions are asymmetrically localized in the two cerebral hemispheres. Though psychologists once thought that there was equipotentiality in the two hemispheres at birth to take on these functions, it now appears that this is not the case. One of the hemispheres (the left one in 90 percent of the cases) will already have differentiated in a way that makes it the best hemisphere in which to acquire language; the other will have gone through a similar process making it superior for spatial and visual reasoning. Despite this early differentiation, there is still a great deal of plasticity present. The right hemisphere can serve the language function and the left can serve the spatial function. This plasticity declines with age, however, so that the brain is better able to compensate for brain damage in infancy and early childhood than for comparable damage later in life.

The brain is not just an instrument for exciting action in nerves, muscles, and glands. It is also an instrument for inhibiting action in these. The inhibitory function is found to operate at both the neuronal level (neural inhibition) and the regional level. One good example of regional inhibition is found in the phenomenon of cortical inhibition, which has been used to explain the disappearance (and occasional reappearance) of the vestigial reflexes. Another is found in data on the function of the frontal lobe in high-level human cognition. Apparently, the frontal lobe allows us to inhibit pre-potent-response tendencies, thereby gaining a level of behavioral flexibility that is not available to young infants whose frontal lobes are not fully matured and to adults with frontal-lobe brain damage. Evidence for the immaturity of the frontal lobes in 7½ to 9-month-old infants comes from data that show that infants at this age make the same errors on object retrieval tasks as do monkeys with surgically created frontal-lobe damage.

SUGGESTIONS FOR FURTHER READING

Belsky, J., Lerner, R. M., & Spanier, G. B. (1984). The evolutionary basis of the child in the family. Chapter 2 in *The child in the family*. Reading, MA: Addison-Wesley. This brief chapter reinforces the view that the story of human evolution can help to explain the origins of some of the psychological and social characteristics of contemporary humans.

Greenough, W. T. (1975). Experimental modification of the developing brain. *American Scientist, 63,* 37–46. A review of research on the effects of enriched and impoverished environments on the structural development of the brain.

Katchadourian, H. (1977). *The biology of adolescence.* San Francisco: W. H. Freeman.

Stanley, S. M. (1981). *The new evolutionary timetable: Fossils, genes, and the origin of species.* New York: Basic Books. An easy-to-read introduction to the exciting new view that evolution has occurred through rapid jumps as well as through gradual change. The chapters of greatest interest are Chapter 6, entitled "On the rapid origin of species," and Chapter 7, "Human origins."

Tanner, J. M. (1968). Earlier maturation in man. *Scientific American, 218* (1), 21–27. This article discusses the secular trend that has occurred for body size and age of maturation over the past 100 years.

Tanner, J. M. (1978). *Foetus into man: Physical growth from conception to maturity.* London: Open Books, 1978. The most interesting and the most authoritative introductory text on physical development that is available.

CHAPTER OUTLINE

CHAPTER 7

Cognitive Development: The Dawning of Perceptual Awareness

In this chapter and the two that follow, we will focus on developments in the human capacity for intelligent action. These are called cognitive developments because they deal overall with thinking, learning, remembering, and perceiving, all of which are aspects of cognition. In this first chapter, we will meet cognition only in its humblest form—rudimentary perceptual knowledge. Such knowledge is expressed in knowing when to duck an approaching object or when to dodge, in knowing that a distant oak is no smaller than one close by, and in knowing that sounds diminish in volume as the objects making them get farther away. Such knowledge is fundamental to all humans; it is manifested even by otherwise severely retarded individuals.

THE ONSET OF SENSORY EXPERIENCE

As we learned in the discussion of the brain and its development in the last chapter, there are sensory projection areas on the human cerebral cortex to which the body's senses project their neural messages (see Figure 6-9). This means that neural messages from senses such as pressure, pain, vision, and audition are passed on to cells in the cortex, and when they are we experience pressure, pain, visual, or auditory **sensations.** Once there, further processing in the association areas of the cortex leads to **perceptions,** which are meaningful interpretations of sensory events. (See Figure 7-1 for a demonstration of the distinction between sensations and perceptions.)

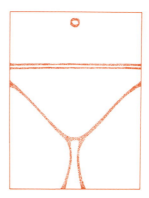

FIGURE 7-1
The Distinction Between Sensation and Perception
Everyone who looks at this figure experiences the same sensory event, but perceptions of the event differ. Some perceive a martini; some, a bikini. (After Shepard, 1978)

Most of the human senses begin functioning prior to birth (vision may be the only exception), but with birth the variety and intensity of their messages increase enormously. The first question to concern us is how well neonates can understand the flood of new sensory information that occurs at birth. Do they perceive people to be people, do they perceive objects to be objects, and do they perceive either of these as located in space and as the source of the sounds that they hear? Philosophers and and psychologists of the *empiricist* school have long argued that they do not. According to the empiricists, the meaning of individual sensory experiences and the meaning of the interrelationships among experiences have to be learned. Learning is required, they say, because the perceptual world of newborns is nothing more than a kaleidoscopic pattern of sound and light in which no one part can be differentiated from the rest. In William James's memorable phrase, the neonate's world is "one great blooming, buzzing confusion" (1890, vol. 1, p. 488). The empiricists historically have been countered in their arguments by *nativists.* According to the philosophers and psychologists of the nativist school, the ability to make meaningful interpretations of sensory experiences is not learned, it is native to us, which is to say inborn.

THE HISTORY OF THE NATURE–NURTURE ISSUE IN THE STUDY OF PERCEPTUAL DEVELOPMENT

By asking whether the knowledge that underlies perception is innate or acquired, the nativists and empiricists made perceptual development an important concern of the nature–nurture debate. The nativist–empiricist component to this debate began in the late seventeenth century with the publication of the first edition of John Locke's *Essay Concerning Human Understanding* (1690). In keeping with the nondevelopmental spirit of those preevolutionary days, the question of whether perception was innate or acquired was applied not to the child's initial acquisition of perceptual knowledge, but to the adult's. The area of knowledge to which it was applied is called **intersensory knowledge** because the question dealt with whether what one learned from one sense (for example, touch) would lead to automatic knowledge in another (for example, vision). That is, would knowledge of the *tactile* (touch) properties of an object lead one to know "innately" how the object would look? As William Molyneux put it in a letter to his philosopher friend John Locke:

> Suppose a man born blind, and now adult, and taught by touch to distinguish between a cube and a sphere . . . so as to tell, when he felt one and the other, which is the cube, which the sphere. Suppose then the cube and sphere placed on a table, and the blind man be made to see: *quaere,* whether by his sight, before he touched them, he could not distinguish and tell which is the globe, which the cube? (in Klein, 1970, p. 390)

The answer that John Locke and others in his empiricist school of philosophy gave to this *quaere,* or question, was a resounding no. All knowledge, they believed, is built up out of experience. Without direct visual experience, one could have no visual knowledge, not even to the point of recognizing a sphere and a cube by sight once they were known to touch. Bishop Berkeley, one of Locke's strong proponents, extended this view to other aspects of perceptual knowledge. His major concern was an aspect of *space perception*—the knowledge of distance through vision.

You may never have given much thought to the fact that the visual perception of distance (or depth) requires any knowledge at all. But it does. As Berkeley is quite correct in telling us "*distance* of itself . . . cannot be seen." His reason for saying this is irrefutable: "*distance* being a line directed end-wise to the eye . . . projects only one point in the fund of the eye. Which point remains invariably the same, whether the distance be longer or shorter" (Berkeley, 1709, as quoted in Klein, 1970, p. 514; italics in original). A second way of saying the same thing is to say that the sensory surface of the eye—the retina—is a two-dimensional surface. Depth or distance is a third dimension that cannot be portrayed directly in two-dimensional representations. To know about depth, one must have some knowledge that goes beyond the information given. Berkeley's conclusion was that this knowledge was learned.

> . . . a man born blind, being made to see, would, at first, have no idea of distance by sight; the sun and stars, the remotest objects as well as

the nearer, would all seem to be in his eye, rather in his mind. The objects . . . would seem . . . as near to him, as the perceptions of pain or pleasure, or the most inward passions of his soul. (Berkeley, 1709, as quoted in Klein, 1970, p. 520)

SCIENTIFIC ATTEMPTS TO RESOLVE THE NATURE–NURTURE ISSUE IN PERCEPTION

When Locke and his fellow philosophers first established the empiricist point of view in the study of perceptual development, they did not use scientific research to support their position. They used instead the philosopher's tools of logical analysis and thought experiments. You have had a small sample of these in their arguments regarding a man born blind being made to see. Interestingly, however, when science first turned to the question of the origins of perceptual knowledge, it was with subjects who were the embodiment of the imaginary subjects of the philosophers. They were people born with *cataracts* (opaque or clouded lenses)—and therefore blind—who were later given sight through surgery. The experiences of congenital cataract victims with restored sight were reported with relish in the late nineteenth and early twentieth centuries (see M. Von Senden, 1932, translated in Heath, 1960). The conclusion from these studies was that, in general, the perceptual ability of adults with surgically restored vision was quite poor (thereby supporting the empiricist view). A number of problems arose in interpreting the data, however. These problems made the validity of any conclusions regarding the nature–nurture issue quite suspect.

Later in the twentieth century, science turned to studies of chimpanzees and other animals that had been experimentally deprived of vision (see Riesen, 1950). It was hoped that the ability to experiment on these animals would alleviate the methodological problems of the cataract-victim studies. Again, however, there were problems in interpreting the data. The primary problem was the discovery that light deprivation of any kind can alter the normal maturational process in both the eye and the brain (Rasch, Swift, Riesen, & Chow, 1961; see also Chapter 6). The assumption of the research had been that vision-deprived subjects, once they were put into the light, would have completely normal visual experiences. When this assumption was found to be false, it meant that one could never be sure whether the absence of perceptual knowledge in a vision-deprived subject was due to the lack of experience or to the lack of a species-typical visual system. The concerns of nativists and empiricists, therefore, could not be resolved with work on animals reared in visually deprived environments.

Given that it was impossible to make meaningful interpretations of the data from animals and humans raised in abnormal ways, science at last turned to normally reared human infants to obtain the perceptually naive subjects it needed for research on perceptual development. One reason infants were not used any earlier for research on the nature–nurture issue in perception was that no one knew much about their ability to see. Because of the general immaturity of their visual system, they were presumed to have extremely poor vision, perhaps even worse than that of light-deprived subjects. Some baby books in fact informed parents that newborn infants were functionally blind (and deaf as well).

A second reason infants had not been used much by science to this point was methodological. Young infants sleep and drowse for much of the day, making it difficult to assure their alertness. Also, they have poor control over their movements, except for the movements of their head, mouth and eyes. These characteristics make it difficult to study infant cognitions scientifically. But the problems are not insurmountable, as shown by the wealth of methods that are available today for studying infant cognition. Using these methods, all of which have been developed within the last 25 to 30 years, psychologists can collect data that lead to reasonable inferences regarding the sensory acuity and perceptual understanding of even very young infants.

Infant-Research Methods

Four of the more useful methods for studying the sensory and perceptual experiences of infants are the *preference method, habituation method, high-amplitude sucking method,* and the *method of evoked potentials.* The first three involve behavioral measures. The fourth involves measuring brain activity. Each of these methods allows us to make inferences about what is happening inside an infant brain. Never before in history have we had "windows" on the infant mind that are as clear as these.

Preference Method

The **preference method** involves presenting two stimuli simultaneously in order to see whether infants will attend more to the one than the other. Although simple in concept, the method generally requires some ingenuity to execute if it is to lead to valid conclusions. The first person to apply preference methods to infant perception in a methodologically sound way was Robert Fantz (see, for example, Fantz, 1961) at Western Reserve University (now Case Western Reserve). Fantz used the preference method for obtaining information on the visual ability of infants—even neonates—to see.

His particular method required that subjects be placed on their backs, in the chamber shown in Figure 7-2. The infant then was presented with a pair of visual stimuli simultaneously. In Fantz's chamber these were a pair of cards inserted near the ceiling of the chamber. A variety of cards was used, each with a different design. The question was whether infants would show a preference among them.

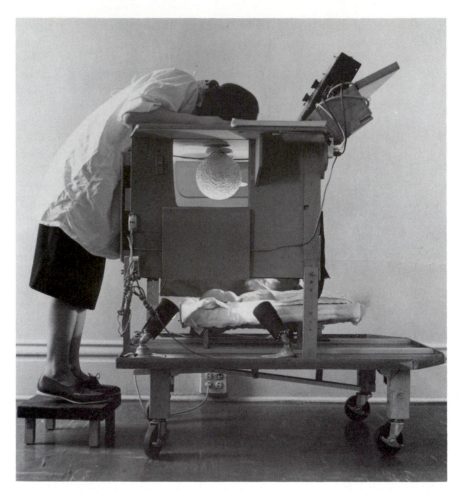

FIGURE 7-2
Visual Preference Apparatus
This is a photograph of Fantz's original visual-preference apparatus, which was used to determine whether infants could discriminate visual stimuli by determining if they preferred one stimulus over another.

The method of determining preference was quite simple. An adult peeked into the chamber through a hole in the top and watched the subject's eyes. When one of the targets was reflected from the corneal surface directly over the pupil of the eye, the infant was judged to be fixating the target. The time of each fixation was recorded. If infants were indeed functionally blind as some suspected, they would be unable to discriminate among the patterns and so they should look at one no longer than another. What Fantz found, however, was that even neonates just hours old had preferences among the patterns. For example, the neonates preferred a bull's-eye pattern to a pattern of horizontal stripes. Also, they preferred patterns of any kind (bull's-eye, horizontal stripes, or just newsprint) to no pattern (target cards of a uniform color—red, yellow, or gray). Fantz's preference method produced clear evidence, therefore, that even neonates can see.

Today's preference studies no longer use Fantz's chamber. Investigators have found that it is better to have infants seated than lying down. (They are more likely to be alert in this position.) Also, in the study of vision, rear-projected slides have replaced manually inserted cards. Nonetheless, the logic is the same. If there is a preference, we can infer that the infant discriminates whatever stimuli (visual, auditory, or olfactory) are being compared. If there is no preference, our inference is not so easy. It may be that the two stimuli are judged to be different but of equal interest, or it may be that the two are judged to be the same.

Habituation Method

Once stimuli become old and familiar, we attend to them less than when they were new and novel. This phenomenon is known as **habituation,** and it is easily demonstrated in infants as young as 8 to 10 weeks of age (Cohen & Gelber, 1975, p. 378ff). To measure habituation, any number of general attentional responses can be used. These include heart-rate changes, changes in respiration, and visual looking. For visual stimuli, however, the time spent looking *(fixation time)* is the most frequently used measure of habituation.

In a typical habituation study, the investigator begins by presenting a visual stimulus that can be predicted to capture the infant's attention. The time the infant spends examining this stimulus is then recorded. As you can well imagine, on the first presentation of an attractive stimulus, infants spend a large amount of time looking at the stimulus. On subsequent presentations, they look at it ever less.

The decline in attention that marks habituation sets the stage for measuring the capacity of the infant visual system to differentiate among stimuli. The reason is that we can now transform the stimulus used to produce habituation. If the transformation is detected it should produce a dramatic increase in attention. When this occurs, we can conclude that the infant sensory system is capable of discriminating the transformation. When it does not, we can assume that the transformation was too subtle to be detected. Typical data from a study using the habituation method are given in Figure 7-3.

High-Amplitude Sucking Method

In addition to looking, one of the few things newborn infants do well is suck. They can suck up a storm and do so whenever a nipple is placed in

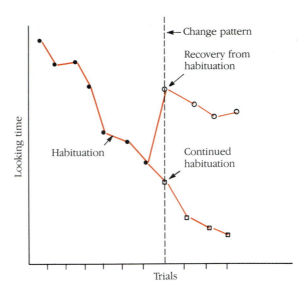

FIGURE 7-3
Habituation
Typical data from a study using the habituation method. (After Goldstein, 1984)

their mouths. Investigators, beginning with Einar Siqueland and Clement DeLucia in 1969, have taken advantage of this fact to produce yet another procedure for determining young infants' abilities to discriminate stimuli. This particular procedure is most useful with auditory stimuli, though visual and other stimuli can also be used.

The **high-amplitude sucking** procedure is based on the fact that infants will work to make interesting spectacles last (Piaget, 1936/1963). Learning theorists attribute this to *conjugate reinforcement*. What it all comes down to is that if we hook up some electronic circuitry to enable infants, through their sucking, to exert some control over their sensory world, they will work hard to maintain those sensations they find interesting and cease working when they become uninteresting. Work, in this context, is measured as the strength (or amplitude) of each sucking movement. In a typical application, the strength of these movements would control the volume on a tape recorder, allowing the sound to fade as the sucking became less vigorous and maintaining an optimal volume when the sucking was at some predetermined level of strength. To maintain the volume at optimal level, for example, an infant might have to produce two or three particularly strong sucking movements per second. If fewer high-amplitude sucks were made, the volume would begin to fade. Investigators using this procedure to study the auditory discriminations that infants can make would allow the rate of high-amplitude sucks to diminish to the point where it was safe to conclude that the infant no longer found the sound interesting (or reinforcing.) At this point a transformed sound would be introduced. If the infant detected the transformation, we would expect for the rate of high-amplitude sucks to increase dramatically in order to make the interesting spectacle last. If the transformation was not detected, we would expect no change in the rate of sucking. Just as in the habituation procedure, therefore, a sudden change in behavior would reflect discrimination.

Method of Evoked Potentials

The last of the four principal methods for investigating the sensory and perceptual experiences of infants involves brain-wave measurements. Recording devices are placed on the scalp above the brain sites where the infant is known to process sensory information. This would be on the back of the head (above the occipital lobe) for visual stimuli and on the side of the head (above the temporal lobe) for auditory stimuli. We, then, would present a brief visual or auditory stimulus and look for the reaction on a device that can record changes in electrical activity in the brain. Such a device is known as an *electroencephalograph* or *EEG.* Through multiple stimulus presentations, a specific, event-related response can be detected. This is known as the **evoked potential.** Because it is usually obtained by averaging across multiple stimulus presentations, it is also called the *average evoked potential.* In any event, stimuli that are sensed by the brain should produce such an event-related response. Those that are not sensed should produce no response. And two stimuli that are differentiated one from the other should produce two different responses.

THE SENSORY AND PERCEPTUAL WORLD OF INFANCY

With methods such as the four listed above, scientists have obtained a wealth of information useful in answering questions regarding infants' earliest perceptual experiences. This information has served not so much to resolve the old nativist–empiricist debate as to dissolve it. The dissolution of the debate has come as we have learned that the facts of perceptual development can only be portrayed using a developmental model, such as Waddington's epigenetic landscape, that acknowledges the joint, interactive, and inseparable roles of nature and nurture. This will become evident with the first of our topics—the taste and smell senses in infants. We begin with this topic because it is brief and leads to a clear epigenetic conclusion. The topics of visual, auditory, and intersensory perception will follow.

Taste and Smell

In adults, the sense of smell is quite keen. A single molecule of odorant will stimulate an adult olfactory receptor. The minimum stimulus needed to trigger comparable sensations in infants has not been determined, but we do know that a capacity for detecting odors is present very early in life. In one case a premature infant with a conceptual age of just 28 weeks was able to detect "peppermint extract" in the air. It was a strong dose of peppermint, but nonetheless the chemical receptors in the nose and their neural connections with the brain would have had to be functional at least by this age (Sarnat, 1978). Somewhat older infants (with chronological ages of 2 weeks) have demonstrated a capacity for discriminating their mothers from strangers on the basis of odor alone (MacFarlane, 1975).

With regard to taste, again, little is known about the actual degree of sensitivity, but qualitatively infants seem to experience the same sensations as adults. The fundamental distinctions that adults make are between sweet, sour, salt, and bitter. Even neonates make the same distinctions. Not only that, they also show a definite behavioral preference for sweet liquids over all others, and there is a definite aversion for sour and bitter solutions.

One reason that olfaction and taste would be functioning sensory systems early in an infant's life is that the brain's olfactory and taste centers are not on the cerebral cortex. They are in the lower, older part of the brain. This explains why *anencephalic* infants (born without a cortex and destined to live but a few months) show the same responses to tastes and smells as infants with normal cerebral development (Steiner, 1979).

The Ability to Interpret Olfactory and Taste Sensations

If we were to take the nativist–empiricist approach to the study of taste and smell, we would begin with the belief that either the meaning of certain odors and tastes would be inherent in the functioning human nervous system, or it would have to be acquired slowly by building up associations between sensations on the tongue or in the nose and later experiences in the gut. Thus from a nativist view, bad food would smell bad innately. From the empiricist view, bad food would smell bad because we had been made sick by it in the past. Good food would smell good because it had proved nutritious in the past.

Prior to ever ingesting foods, however, infants show the same responses to bitter foods and rotten odors as adults do; and they show the same preferences for sweet food and pleasant food smells as adults do. It is an established fact, therefore, that neonates have some taste and smell knowledge in the sense that they have the ability to interpret some taste and smell sensations. Namely, they interpret some as desirable and others as undesirable. Evidence for this comes from research by Jacob Steiner (1979).

Steiner's primary evidence that tastes and smells are interpreted meaningfully comes from facial expressions (see Figure 7-4). "Sweet stimulation," according to Steiner (1979), "induces facial relaxation and an expression of enjoyment resembling a smile." Sour tastes, on the other hand, produce "typical lip pursing," and bitter tastes produce "depressed mouth angles expressive of disgust" (Steiner, 1979, p. 262). The neonate's clear capacity for discriminating pleasant from unpleasant tastes has led reviewers Linda Acredolo and Janet Hake (1982) to conclude that "savoring one's food is apparently one of life's earliest pleasures."

The full range of odors to which neonates can respond has not been established, but, as in the case of taste, there seem to be clear preferences. "Fishy" and "rotten egg" smells are not among them. "Banana", however, is a big favorite. Steiner (1979) established these preferences by choosing smells that for adults ranged from pleasant to unpleasant. He then observed neonates' facial responses when presented with the test odors. The neonates' responses, a sample of which are shown in Figure 7-4B, indicate that they respond in the same way as adults.

From the theoretical view offered by the nativists and empiricists, we would have to conclude from neonates' responses to odors that their nervous systems, educated through evolution, "know innately" what is disgusting and putrid from what is good and wholesome. As soon as we arrived at such a conclusion, however, some modern-day Z. Y. Kuo (see Chapter 3) would be apt to come along to show that the neonate's response to tastes and smells at birth is dependent on some fetal experience such as the ingestion of amniotic fluid, which begins to take place in the 13th week (Hofer, 1981). This hypothetical investigator might even be able to show experimentally that by altering the taste of the amniotic fluid we could alter the postnatal responses observed by Steiner. Though this statement is speculative, there are some data to support it. Research with rats shows clearly that flavoring the amniotic fluid with mint, apple, or lemon has strong effects on the postnatal behavior of rats. In a study by Elliott Blass and Patricia Peterson (in Kolata, 1984), for example, rat pups that had spent part of their fetal period in lemon-flavored amniotic fluid sought out mothers whose breasts had been swabbed with a lemon-scented solution. Normal rats avoided these mothers. Does this mean that we should reverse our theoretical position and conclude that rudimentary taste and smell knowledge are not really innate but acquired after all, a product not of evolution but of ontogeny? The answer, of course, is no.

Rather than allow the new data to induce a reversal in our theoretical position, the wiser course is never to think of nature and nurture as independent in the first place. From this point of view, we would merely conclude that adaptive responses to some tastes and smells are present at least by birth and, then, search for the developmental events—morphological, physiological, or behavioral—that makes this possible (see Kuo, 1967, p.

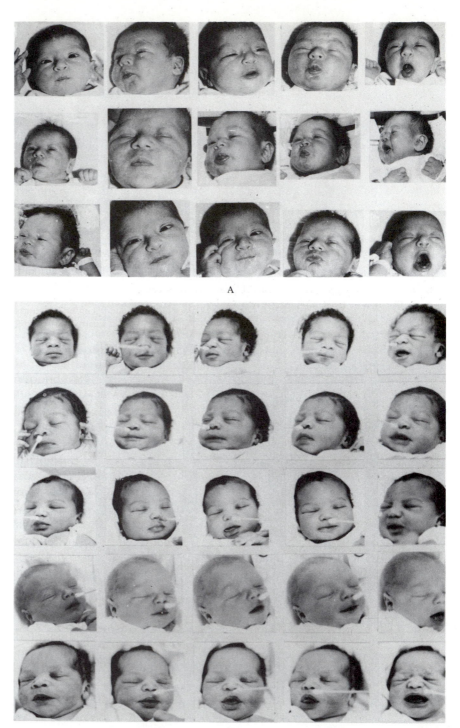

A

B

FIGURE 7-4
Neonatal Responses to Olfactory and Taste Sensations
The pictures in the left to right rows of panel A show the faces of three different neonates, none of whom have ever ingested food. Column 1 (on the left) shows the neonates in a resting state; column 2 shows them after getting a taste of distilled water. The three remaining faces were produced by either bitter, sour, or sweet tastes. You can probably tell the columns that correspond to these. Sweet is 3, sour is 4, and bitter is 5. Panel B, again, contains rows of pictures of individual neonates, showing the faces they made in response to different odors. Column 2 shows the response to banana and vanilla odors; column 3, a fishy smell; column 4, a milky odor; and column 5, rotten eggs. Column 1 (resting state) is for comparison.

117). For the most part, this is the approach that has been adopted by current students of early perceptual development. Rather than attempt to determine whether some bit of perceptual knowledge is innate, their goal has been to determine what knowledge infants have, when they first have it, and how it develops. This research plan typifies recent research on vision and audition, the topics that follow.

Vision

As we learned earlier in this chapter, Robert Fantz used a visual-preference apparatus to determine that even newborns prefer patterned visual stimuli to nonpatterned ones (see p. 322). This discovery gave science its first means of measuring the quality of infant vision. Fantz himself performed the first studies. In them, he measured the capacity of the infant visual system for discriminating fine detail. This capacity is known as *visual acuity.*

Visual Acuity Under Conditions of Maximal Contrast

When you or I want our acuity checked, we go to an optometrist who has us read letters off a Snellen eye chart at a distance of 20 feet. Such a method takes advantage of our age, education, and ability to speak. Fantz's method for measuring visual acuity required far less of subjects. While they were on their backs in the visual-preference apparatus, targets were placed in front of their eyes. One of these was a black-and-white striped pattern. The other was a solid-gray card carefully matched for average brightness with the striped card. The rationale for this procedure was that when the stripes on the patterned card were so thin that they were blurred by the infant visual system, the infant would see just two gray cards and, therefore, have no grounds for preference. (Black and white mixed yield gray.) As long as there was a preference though, it was safe to assume that vision was clear, not blurred.

Using his procedure, Fantz determined that neonate vision—though limited—is still far better than anyone ever expected before. From a distance of 10 inches, Fantz's infant subjects showed a preference for striped cards, even when the stripes were as thin as ⅛ of an inch. Other studies, some of which have used the method of evoked potentials, have found that the ability to discriminate maximally contrasted black–white patterns may permit the discimination of stripes slightly thinner than 1/16 of an inch (Cohen, DeLoache, & Strauss, 1979). This would be equivalent to having 20/300 vision, a value that reflects visual impairment but certainly not blindness.

Whatever the acuity of normal neonate vision might be, it rapidly improves. By 6 months of age, Fantz's subjects could discriminate stripes that were just 1/64 of an inch in width. This is an eightfold increase in acuity from just 6 months prior and converts to a Snellen measure of 20/100. The normal adult acuity of 20/20 is achieved after 1 year of age (Banks & Salapatek, 1983). Because acuity improves according to conceptual age rather than chronological age (see Banks & Salapatek, 1983, p. 488), we can assume that neurological development is the primary factor in improving acuity. At the same time, for this neural development to proceed in a normal fashion, infants must have normal visual experiences. One infant, who had a cataract in one eye for a period of 25 days following birth, never achieved the same degree of acuity in this bad eye as he did in the one that functioned properly from birth (Enoch & Rabinowicz, 1976).

Contrast Sensitivity: A More Complete View of the Capacity for Pattern Vision

Although the ability to discriminate black–white patterns provides an important measure of how well one can see, it is in fact a very incomplete measure. All we learn from a test of black–white discrimination is the fineness of visual detail that can be discriminated under conditions of maximal contrast. Real-life vision involves some black–white contrasts—the letter discrimination required for reading is a good example—but it primarily involves discriminating contours that are marked by less than maximal contrast. A nose, for example, is an image a great deal wider than ⅛ of an inch (which we just learned may be about the limit of neonate acuity at 10 inches distance), but it is low in contrast relative to the face. Lips are the same way. Can an infant make these out at a distance of 10 inches? An acuity measure alone gives us no way of knowing. We need a wider set of measures. We need to know the fineness of detail that can be detected for all the conditions of less than perfect contrast. A full set of these values (thresholds for image detection at all possible contrast values) can be obtained from a *contrast sensitivity function* (CSF).

Figure 7-5 shows the CSF for a typical adult along with the CSFs generated for infants of 1, 2, and 3 months of age. The information needed to understand these curves is given in the caption to the figure. Suffice it to

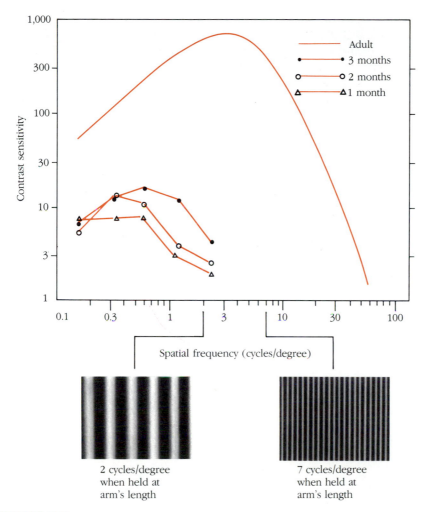

FIGURE 7-5

Contrast Sensitivity Function

A typical CSF for an adult is contrasted with the CSFs for 1-, 2-, and 3-month-old infants. To produce such functions, subjects are presented with a set of sine-wave gratings like those along the horizontal axis. As you can see, these are simply patterns made up of fuzzy stripes. The amount of contrast in these gratings is then decreased to the point where the pattern becomes just barely visible. That degree of contrast marks the threshold sensitivity for that particular grating. Continuing in this way, investigators can determine the entire CSF. In interpreting the functions shown here you need to note that higher values on the horizontal axis indicate ever-thinner stripes, and higher values on the vertical axis indicate ever-less contrast. The application of such functions to understanding infant and adult vision is given in the text. One interesting aspect of the CSFs not mentioned there is that a CSF provides a measure of acuity. Acuity is the point where the CSF meets the horizontal axis. The adult acuity shown here converts to a Snellen value somewhat better than 20/20. That is because measuring acuity in different ways yields different threshold values. (After Banks & Salapatek, 1978)

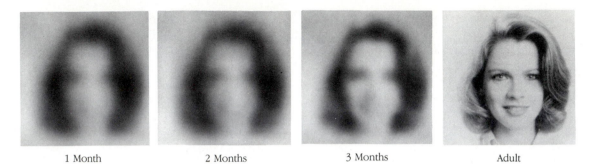

| 1 Month | 2 Months | 3 Months | Adult |

FIGURE 7-6
Simulations of Infant Contrast Sensitivity
Using the data in Figure 7-5, Arthur P. Ginsburg simulated the overall quality of infant vision by showing how well infants would be able to see the photograph on the far right at ages 1, 2, and 3 months.

say here that with these curves to guide us, predictions can be made about how good pattern vision will be for images of ever-decreasing size across all degrees of contrast. What the infant curves show is that on average it takes far more contrast for young infants to be able to discriminate images than it does for adults.

One of the values of knowing the CSF for infants at various ages is that it enables us to stimulate their ability to see real-life patterns. In Figure 7-6, for example, the CSFs of Figure 7-5 are used to indicate what a 1-, 2-, and 3-month-old would see when looking at a woman's face from 6 inches away. Initially they see only the grossest detail of the pattern, but this improves rapidly. Although the data are not shown here, we know that by 6 months of age, the CSF is much more adultlike (Pirchio, Spinelli, Fiorentini, & Maffei, 1978)

Optical Factors That Affect Pattern Vision

In addition to the limited acuity and contrast sensitivity of infants, a second factor that limits the clarity of vision in infants, particularly during their first 6 months, is *astigmatism.* The fact that most infants are astigmatic to some degree is evident in the fact that if you rotate the maximally contrasted black-and-white striped patterns used to obtain acuity measures to some new orientation, patterns that were visible may become invisible. Losing visual resolution at different line orientations defines astigmatism. In normal vision, acuity is equally good for all orientations. To get some idea of how astigmatism would affect vision, you can examine Figure 7-7, which simulates the vision of an astigmat who sees verticals sharply but loses acuity as the vertical line is transformed into a horizontal line. By 18 months of age, all the astigmatism associated with infancy is gone so that the percentage of astigmats among 18-month-olds is no larger than it is among adults (Atkinson & Braddick, 1981, pp. 267-68).

Astigmatism occurs when the cornea, the transparent structure that covers the pupil of the eye, is less than perfectly spherical. This causes images lying in some orientations to be distorted. Distortion due to astigmatism is an *optical error,* because the cause of the poor vision lies in the optics of the eye itself—its ability to produce a sharp image on the retina. A second cause of poor optics is failure of the eye to accommodate to the distance of an image from the eye. As you know if you have ever tried to focus a camera, you must adjust the lens of the camera in order to get a sharp image on the photographic film. Close subjects require a different adjustment than more distant subjects. The lens in the eye is no different; it, too, must be adjusted for changing distances. The adjustment is known as *accommodation.* At one time it was thought that human newborns had no accommodative power at all (Haynes, White, & Held, 1965). Instead, they were thought to have a fixed focus that was optimal only for objects at a distance of about 8 inches. As objects came closer than 8 inches or moved farther away, infants were presumed powerless to keep them in focus. Now we know that this is not true. Even newborns can make adjustments—within a range of from 4 to 60 inches—for changes in the distance of things they are looking at. By 6 months of age, their accommodative adjustments are errorless in this range so that the lens always adjusts properly to form a completely sharp image on the retina (Atkinson & Braddick, 1981).

The introduction of optical factors (shape of the cornea and accommodative power of the lens) into our discussion of acuity and contrast sensitivity raises the question whether the limited acuity of young infants might be due to these optical factors alone. That is, the limitations on infant vision might be purely in the eye. The alternative is that they lie in the brain,

FIGURE 7-7

An Astigmatic Fan

Astigmats do not see lines in all orientations with equal acuity. Thus, if shown the set of lines arranged in a fan on the left, an astigmat whose preferred line orientation was vertical would see ever-more blur in the lines as they diverged from the full vertical position. This is portrayed in the figure to the right.

which, as we know from Chapter 6, has the job of interpreting the eye's neural messages. The evidence on this point is entirely negative. Although astigmatism and somewhat limited accommodation do affect the clarity of vision, the major limitation to infant vision is in the brain. Even given a sharp visual image, the brain will be unable to represent that sharpness. This is due to immaturity both in the occipital cortex and in the connections between the occipital cortex and the retina (Banks & Salapatek, 1983, p. 487).

Color Vision

Thus far we have dealt exclusively with the infant capacity for detecting patterns in a visual world in which brightness is the only variable. How about color? Color vision is based on visual responsiveness to differences in the wavelengths of light (hue) rather than the amplitude of these waves (brightness). Do infants have color vision the same as adults? Earlier investigators were as pessimistic on this point as they were on visual acuity, but again they were wrong. Even 1- and 2-month-olds do see in color as evidenced by their looking behavior in carefully controlled preference studies (Oster, 1975; Peeples & Teller, 1975). However there is some dispute over whether they have the same *trichromatic,* or three-color, vision as adults. That is, they might be color blind to some degree, even though they can make many hue discriminations.

To determine if 4-month-old infants in fact have trichromatic vision, Marc Bornstein (1976) performed a rather elaborate experiment using the habituation method. The 3-month-old infants in his study sat at a distance of 51 centimeters from a display panel on which lights of precisely controlled properties could be shown. An observer, placed behind the panel, could record the fixation time of infants looking at a light when it was presented. Because the research was designed to determine whether infants had normal trichromatic color vision (the ability to see the three colors red, blue-green, and yellow), Bornstein habituated the infants to a stimulus light that was blue-green in color. He chose this particular stimulus because *only trichromats* can see it as having color. People with defective color vision (dichromats) see this color as an achromatic white. The particular shade of white depends on the brightness of the color, and brightness was varied randomly in Bornstein's study.

After habituating his subjects to the blue-green light by presenting it 12 times in a row for 15 seconds each time, Bornstein changed the light to a white. If the infant subjects had been deficient in color vision, they would have seen the blue-green light as white all along, so that this "new" stimulus would look just the same to them. Infants with trichromatic vision, however, would see the light on Trials 13 and 14 as different from the ones before and, therefore, would show a recovery of attention. Figure 7-8 shows clearly that this is what happened. Fixation times increased dramatically when the chromatic blue-green was changed to an achromatic white in the same

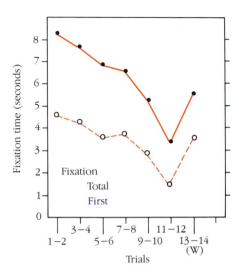

FIGURE 7-8

Evidence for Trichromatic Color Vision

Bornstein's data show that fixation times declined steadily for the trials on which the blue-green light was presented. This is evidence of habituation. When the light was changed to a white light on Trials 13 and 14, however, there was an increase in fixation time, which indicates recovery from habituation. The recovery would only have occurred on Trials 13 and 14 if the infants had trichromatic color vision. (After Bornstein, 1976)

brightness range. Bornstein concluded that human infants, at least by 3 months of age, have adultlike trichromatic color vision. There has been some criticism of this conclusion on the grounds that it does not demonstrate that adult and infant color vision are exactly alike (see Banks & Salapatek, 1983, p. 530). But even if color vision in 3-month-old infants is based on something less than a perfect three-color process, this does nothing to take away from the conclusion that they see in rich, living color. It only means that their color experience may not be quite that of a normal adult.

In summary of this section on the sensory capacity of the infant visual system, research has shown that there is some acuity and contrast sensitivity present at birth. This makes it possible even for newborns to detect visual patterns, at least in the immediate visual world. By 6 months of age, acuity and contrast sensitivity have advanced to quite high levels so that it is safe to assume that 6-month-olds have basically the same pattern vision as adults. The advance in acuity and contrast sensitivity over the first 6 months is due primarily to maturation within the brain. But during the same period there are some optical improvements that also serve to enhance the quality of pattern perception. These are a loss of astigmatism and improved accommodation. Not only do neonates have some pattern vision, but they also see patterns that vary in color. By 3 months of age, the color vision may be qualitatively identical to adult color vision in the sense that it is based on the same trichromatic system as adult color vision. The ultimate conclusion to be drawn from these facts is that the visual capacity of young infants is far better than classical texts on the subject implied. Also, it means that young infants can be quite useful in research directed at determining the origins of perceptual knowledge.

Visual Knowledge

Given that infants can in fact see, even from birth, we are led to ask the question with which the chapter began: What sense do they make of what they see? Given that they make out contours to some extent, do they judge these to be the contours that mark the boundaries of objects, or do they just take them to be lines in an otherwise meaningless array of lines? If they do see objects, can they judge the relative distances of objects? And when an object is moving, can the infant judge from visual cues alone whether it is moving closer or farther away? Can infants distinguish, for example, between objects that are actually changing in size (like a balloon that is being blown up) and objects that are staying the same size but moving closer? And when an object presents a new angle to the infant's eye (such as a door that goes from being closed to one slightly ajar), will the infant brain judge it to be a new and different object? All these are questions that have been asked of infant visual perception. To understand the answers to them, we need to learn a bit more about the psychophysics of vision. In particular, we need to know about the information that the brain receives from the eye that would enable it to perceive distance relations. The reason is that until one sees the world in depth (that is, as existing in three dimensions), there is no point asking about more esoteric aspects of visual knowledge, such as whether an infant knows that as an object moves away it does not become smaller in actual size.

Visual Information from the Third Dimension

As you will recall from Bishop Berkeley's argument that the perception of depth requires knowledge, the distance of objects is not represented any more directly on the retina of the eye than it is on the surfaces of pictures or paintings. To "see" depth, we must infer the distance of objects from some indirect cues.

The most important visual cues to depth stem from the graded sensory information that the brain experiences whenever an object or an eye moves. Because it takes movement to create these cues, they are known as **dynamic cues.** An example is *retinal expansion*. As an object approaches the eye on a "hit path," its image expands symmetrically. When it is on a "miss path," the image expands asymmetrically, but it expands nonetheless. Retinal expansion of object images can be a cue that objects are getting closer.

(Of course, it might also mean that they are staying in place but growing bigger. We would not know which without additional cues.)

A second dynamic cue is *motion parallax*. As you drive down a highway, the fence posts and telephone poles next to the road whip past while the trees on a hill in the distance move more slowly across your visual field. The relatively rapid motion of objects is a clear cue that they are close; relatively slower motion is a clear cue of distance.

A third dynamic cue is *accretion and deletion of texture* (Gibson, 1965). This cue comes into play whenever an object moves through space, thereby blocking and unblocking our view of whatever lies behind it. When it unblocks some of the background, we experience accretion of texture. When it blocks background, there is deletion of texture. Accretion and deletion working together produce the clear impression that an object is moving relative to its background. To isolate this depth cue from all others, it can be presented using a computer screen and a pattern of random dots. As long as the dots are not in motion, an observer sees nothing but a depthless field of dots. But if the dots are placed in motion so that one set moves over and tends to block out another set, an adult viewer will suddenly perceive the dots to lie on two surfaces. One surface will be perceived as foreground; the other, as background. Figure 7-9 demonstrates how sets of dots can be manipulated to create this effect.

In addition to the dynamic cues to depth, which require movement, there are a host of static cues, which do not. Because these cues are present even in motionless pictures, they are generally referred to as **pictorial cues.** One such cue is illustrated in Figure 7-10.

FIGURE 7-9

Accretion and Deletion of Texture

The accretion and deletion of texture that occurs when one surface moves relative to another is a dynamic cue to depth. To create this cue on a computer screen, randomly arranged dots are set in motion in a nonrandom way. One set of dots moves together and gradually occludes another set of dots. This creates the illusion that is displayed here. Viewers see a foreground and a background surface, even though all the dots are in fact located in the same two-dimensional space. The accretion and deletion display depicted here is one used in research by Carl Granrud and his colleagues. The three drawings are used to simulate what happens over time in the display. The one surface is drawn in front of the second because that is what subjects report seeing. (After Granrud et al., 1984)

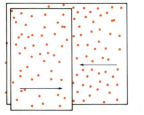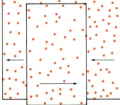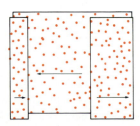

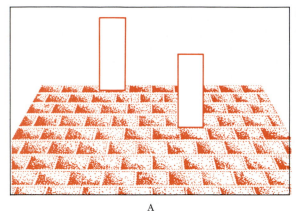
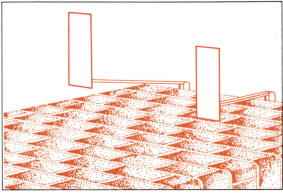

A   B

FIGURE 7-10
Height in the Field as a Cue to Depth
If you look just at panel A, you will interpret the higher rectangle to be farther away and, therefore, judge it to be larger than the rectangle that is lower in your visual field. In fact, the two rectangles are the same size, as shown in panel B. This illusion works by disrupting what is normally a reliable relationship between height and distance—namely, the object higher in the visual field is usually farther away.

If you examined Figure 7-10A without suspecting a trick, you would judge the rectangular shape on the left to be farther away, but you might not know why. The reason is that it is higher in the visual field. This becomes apparent when you see in Figure 7-10B how the illusion of greater distance is created. All else being equal, particularly when a distance relation is plausible, we judge the higher of two objects to be farther away. (Look at the objects that are around you right now and you will probably find height in the field to be a pretty valid cue for relative distance. Is not the higher object the farther in most instances?)

The visual cue known as *height in the field* is but one instance of a pictorial cue that is available to the brain for determining depth and distance. Other pictorial cues are *overlay* (or interposition), *linear perspective, image size, texture gradient,* and *shading.* These are illustrated in Figure 7-11.

Binocular disparity, a final cue to depth, results from the fact that each of our two eyes has a slightly different perspective on the visual world. Normally we are not aware of the difference in perspective because, through a process known as *stereopsis,* our brain fuses the images from the two eyes into a single image. However, when we examine the two images separately, we discover that the two are not duplicates (see Figure 7-12). For objects close to the fixation point, there is a slight difference in the location of objects within the two images (see Figure 7-12). This positional difference is referred to as disparity. For objects farther away, the disparity becomes greater. Because of this relationship between the magnitude of the disparity and the distance of objects from the fixation point, binocular disparity serves as a cue to depth. The brain uses these disparity cues when it forms the stereoscopic or three-dimensional view that we have of the world.

Discovering that there are so many cues to depth available to us takes some of the mystery out of how it is that we see in three dimensions. But

FIGURE 7-11
Pictorial Cues to Depth
In addition to height in the visual field (see Figure 7-10), there are a number of other pictorial cues to distance. They are image size of familiar objects, overlay, linear perspective, texture gradient, and shading.

Image

Image size of familiar objects

Overlay

Linear perspective

Texture gradient

Shading

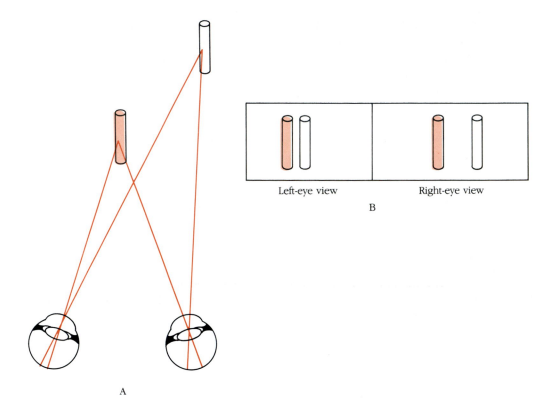

Left-eye view   Right-eye view

B

A

FIGURE 7-12
Binocular Disparity
Binocular disparity is created because our eyes give us two separate views of the visual field. With eyes focused on the cylinders in panel A, two views, represented in panel B, are produced. The size of the disparity in the two views is a cue to how much farther away one cylinder is than the other.

it does not remove all the mystery, because we must still wonder how it is we come to use these cues.

Developing the Ability to Interpret Depth and Distance Cues

The first contemporary investigations of visual knowledge in infants dealt with knowledge of depth. Still today, an infant's ability to judge depth from the various cues that are available remains a topic of interest.

Research Using the Visual Cliff

In the late 1950s Eleanor Gibson was helping to deliver baby goats. One had just been delivered and a second was on the way. Troubled by what to do with the first, the farm manager whom she was helping suggested that she put it on a nearby camera platform 5 feet from the ground. She did, and the goat stayed where it was put. Gibson was amazed that the animal had not fallen from its perch. The event had no real impact on her, though, until later when she and her colleague, Richard Walk, decided to study infant perceptual knowledge. Walk was just returning from working with military recruits in parachute training. This parachute-training experience combined with Gibson's goat led them to conceive of the *visual-cliff apparatus* (see Figure 7-13) as an interesting way to test animals for knowledge of depth (Gibson, 1980).

The visual cliff is called that because the drop-off, or cliff, is only apparent. In reality, there is a sheet of clear plexiglass covering the apparatus. On one side—the shallow side—fabric is placed directly under the glass. On the other side—the deep side—an identical piece of fabric is placed at some distance below the glass. A centerboard, which is raised slightly above the glass, ensures that animals placed on the centerboard will have to look down before stepping off to one side or the other. With the apparatus, Gibson and Walk could determine whether any animal that could walk or crawl could detect a drop-off on the basis of visual cues.

The earliest human infants begin to crawl is around 6 months of age, so 6-month-olds were the youngest humans that could be tested on the visual cliff. To urge them off the centerboard during the tests, the children's mothers stood either on the deep or the shallow side and called to their infants. "All of the 27 infants who moved off the board crawled out on the shallow side . . . ; only three of these crept off the brink. . . . " (Gibson & Walk, 1960, p. 64). In addition to infant humans, a variety of young animals were tested on the visual cliff. The list included rats, chicks, lambs, kids, piglets, kittens, puppies, and a snow leopard. Like the infants, they avoided the cliff. The only animals willing to venture onto the deep side with any frequency at all were—not surprisingly—aquatic turtles and ducklings. Gibson and Walk concluded that by the time animals can move about, they are able to detect depth from visual cues. Determining which visual cues played a role in depth detection became the next goal of their research.

Gibson and Walk first determined that binocular vision was not crucial, because even a one-eyed infant, as well as animals with little binocular vision (such as rats and chicks), were able to detect depth. Thus, if there was a cue that was common to all their subjects, it had to be a monocular cue. Of the monocular cues, the only pictorial cue present was the different texture (or pattern) densities on the two sides. The pattern on the shallow side was larger (to the eye anyway) than the pattern on the deep side. Looking from the one side to the other would produce a "jump in the density of the optical texture" that could signal the drop-off. Gibson and Walk eliminated this "jump" by using fabric with small checks on the shallow side and large checks on the deep side. Thus, there would be no difference in texture density from the point of view of an animal on the center board.

FIGURE 7-13
The Visual Cliff
These photos illustrate the visual-cliff apparatus developed by Gibson and Walk, which is used to test subjects for knowledge of depth. As illustrated here, infants who avoid the cliff, even when mother calls to them, are picking up visual information that tells them of the drop-off.

Judging from the pattern densities alone, the two sides should appear continuous. Still, however, the young animals and infants refused to venture onto the deep side.

By a process of elimination, motion parallax was judged to be the one cue that all the animals had to be able to interpret meaningfully. No other cue could have been common to all the subjects. As the animals moved along the center board or as they just moved their heads, the pattern on the deep side was displaced less on their retinas than the pattern on the shallow side. This differential motion of near and far patterns was sufficient to inform them of the relative depth of the two sides. When there was no pattern but just a uniform gray cloth underlying the deep and shallow sides, the subjects were no longer able to judge depth.

The Use of Motion Parallax as a Cue to Depth

Because motion parallax is produced whenever we move our eyes by moving our heads, it is a cue that even neonates could potentially use to judge depth. Neonates, after all, have sufficient control over their neck muscles to move their heads from side to side. Apparently, however, the meaning of the motion parallax cue is not immediately available to them. This at least is the conclusion that has been drawn from research by Joseph Campos and his colleagues.

Campos's initial contribution to the study of perceptual development was to show that 2- and 3-month-old infants do not become distressed when they are placed on the deep side of a visual cliff (Campos, Langer, & Krowitz, 1970). The best indicator of this in Campos's study was that laying the young infants face down over the deep side led to a decline in heart rate—an indication of interest, not fear. The decline on the deep side coupled with no change on the shallow side meant that the infants did detect a difference between the sides. But they did not know what to make of it. When animals and older infants with depth perception are placed on the deep side, they become visibly upset and their heart rates increase (Campos, Hiatt, Ramsay, Henderson, & Svejda, 1978). It appears, then, that the older infants know something that the younger ones do not. What they know is that the relative motion of surfaces in the visual field tells you whether you are firmly planted on a surface or hovering dangerously above it. How do they develop this knowledge?

The Role of Locomotion in the Development of Visual Knowledge

The infants that Campos first used were what he called "prelocomotor" infants because they were not yet capable of locomotion by crawling. He later discovered that the extent of locomotor experience infants have had will predict how fearful they become when placed on the deep side of the cliff (see Bertenthal, Campos, & Barrett, 1984; Lamb & Campos, 1982). Infants who learn to crawl early develop the fear response early. Those who learn to crawl late develop the fear response late. Campos has produced this result experimentally, thus demonstrating that locomotion is in fact the key factor (see Lamb & Campos, 1982, p. 80). Some infants who were not yet able to crawl on their own were given walkers to assist them in moving about. These infants developed the fear response to heights sooner than infants who did not have walkers.

We can conclude that something in the experience of moving about on one's own in space leads to correct interpretation of the movement-produced parallax cue. This view is strongly supported by a classic study in perceptual development done by Richard Held and Alan Hein (1963) using kittens reared in a controlled visual environment. In all there were ten pairs of kittens. One member of each pair had visual experiences associated with

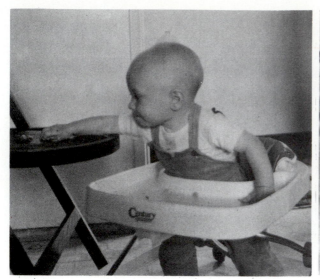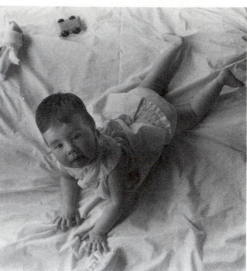

Infants in walkers develop perceptual knowledge more rapidly than prelocomotor age-mates.

self-movement. The other pair member had the same visual experiences but without self-movement. This was achieved by using the apparatus and chamber shown in Figure 7-14. The pair members spent 3 hours a day in the chamber, with one kitten walking and the other riding. When they were not in the chamber, the kittens were kept with their mothers and litter-mates in a darkened cage. After from 3 to 21 days of visual experience, the pair members were tested for their knowledge of depth. One of the tests used was the visual cliff. The results were quite clear. The "active" kittens chose the shallow side of the cliff on 12 out of 12 trials. The "passive" kittens, however, were as apt to wander off onto the deep side as the shallow side. Even when the passive kittens were given as many as 42 days in the chamber, they were still unable to detect depth.

Held and Hein, as well as Campos, believe, therefore, that without the chance to move about in space under one's own power, the ability to detect depth from motion parallax will not develop. Richard Walk has a slightly different view. He believes that self-controlled movement is only important as a developmental experience, because it leads us to attend to the motion cues, and in attending to them we discover their meaning (Walk, 1981, p. 99). Work by Linda Acredolo and her colleagues at the University of California (Acredolo, Adams, & Goodwyn, 1984) supports the view that it is attention to cues, not locomotion per se, that leads to discovering the meaning of motion cues to depth. Regardless of the actual means by which the knowledge is obtained, however, we can conclude with some certainty that

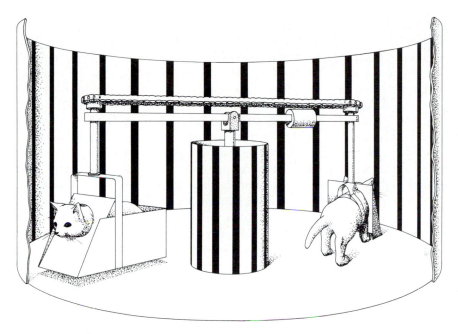

FIGURE 7-14
The Role of Self-locomotion in Perceptual Development.
The "active" and "passive" kittens in Held and Hein's apparatus received the same visual stimulation, but the perceptual knowledge they derived from this was quite different. The "active" kittens, whose visual experiences were associated with self-locomotion, demonstrated a knowledge of depth. The "passive" kittens, whose visual experience was associated with riding rather than walking, did not. (After Held & Hein, 1963)

neonates do not initially use the parallax cues that are available to them through head movements. Rather, this ability emerges during the first 6 months as a natural consequence of the species-typical experiences infants undergo as they begin to negotiate in space on their own.

The Use of Retinal Expansion to Infer Object Approach

Because the ability to use motion parallax to interpret depth does not develop until infants begin to crawl (or stroll about in a walker), we might suspect that the ability to interpret depth from a second motion-related cue—the retinal expansion of an object's image as it approaches—likewise would be correlated with the development of self-controlled movement. This may well be the case.

One bit of evidence suggesting the importance of self-produced motion for learning to interpret retinal expansion comes from the Held and Hein study mentioned earlier. In that study of perceptual differences between kittens that had had active and passive visual experiences, one of the tests of depth perception involved lowering the kittens to a surface. This test is one that produces retinal-expansion cues. Kittens with depth perception prepare to land when nearing the surface by making a *placing response* with their paws. Held and Hein's passive kittens did not make this response, which could mean that retinal expansion was no more meaningful to them as a cue for depth than was motion parallax. According to Albert Yonas of the University of Minnesota (Pettersen, Yonas, & Fisch, 1980), however, there is more than just visual experience involved in learning the meaning of retinal expansion. He holds this view because of observations of what makes infants blink or, more accurately, of what does not make them blink.

Unlike you and me, newborn infants do not blink when an object approaches them. They will only blink if there is direct stimulation of the eye, as with a puff of air. This would seem to indicate that they do not know that an expanding retinal image is a sign that an object is drawing near. Blinking to real and simulated object approach only begins around 1 month of age, and it does not become reliable until about 4 months of age (White, 1971b; Yonas, 1981). This, of course, is quite consistent with the view that retinal expansion as a cue to object approach must be learned through experience. However, Yonas holds that neurological maturation plays a part in this learning (Pettersen, Yonas, & Fisch, 1980). His reason for saying so is that the blinking response to real and simulated approach is better associated with conceptual age than chronological age. Thus, term, preterm, and postterm infants with the same conceptual age behave alike on tests to determine when they will blink at a visual stimulus, whereas those matched on chronological age show large differences in behavior. These data do seem to indicate that a certain amount of neural maturation must precede the occurrence of whatever species-typical experiences give us our sense of depth from the expansion cue.

The Use of Accretion and Deletion of Texture as a Cue to Depth

The final dynamic cue to depth for which we have any infant data is accretion and deletion of texture. Use of this cue has been studied using random-dot displays on computer screens. When the dot displays are not in motion, there is no apparent depth. Even an adult would only see a 2-dimensional display of dots. Set in motion, however, the dots suddenly appear to lie on two surfaces separated in depth. One set appears to lie on a foreground surface that passes over and occludes a background surface. Figure 7-11, used earlier to illustrate the accretion–deletion cue, represents this visual phenomenon. In research by Carl Granrud and his colleagues at the University of Minnesota, infants 5 and 7 months of age were placed in front of a computer screen on which such a display was generated to see what their reaction would be (Granrud et al., 1984). In both age groups there was good evidence that the three-dimensional (3-D) illusion was effective, because the infants reached out as if to grab the "nearer" of the two surfaces. Infants younger than 5 months have not been tested, but Granrud believes that their sensitivity to the accretion–deletion cue would follow the same developmental course as their sensitivity to other dynamic cues—motion parallax and retinal expansion. This, of course, would mean that an infant's correct interpretation of the cue would only come following some experience in the visual world.

Binocular Disparity as a Cue to Depth

Switching from the dynamic cues to the binocular-disparity cue, we can wonder again whether experience would seem to be important. One might suspect not, since binocular vision is wired into the nervous system. Barring any experiences such as monocular deprivation or misalignment of the eyes, our brains fuse the images from the two eyes into the one, stereoscopic image that we all experience. This one image is a 3-D image. The 3-D effect comes about because of our brain's interpretation of the disparity cues available in the two images. Background objects (objects more distant than the one we are looking at) produce what is known as *uncrossed disparity* and thereby are perceived as more distant. Foreground objects produce *crossed disparity* and thereby appear closer than the object we are focused on. Because there is evidence that the brain has disparity detectors as part of its design, you might believe that neonates on first opening their eyes would experience the third dimension in the same vivid way as 3-D movie patrons. It turns out, however, that this speculation is wrong. Neonates do not have 3-D, stereoscopic vision; however, the reason for this may have more to do with maturation than with experience.

Convergence of the eyes improves gradually over the first 6 months.

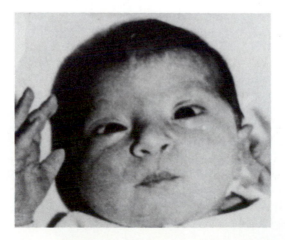

One of the limitations on the ability of young infants to see the world stereoscopically is that their eyes do not converge accurately when they look at something. Without accurate convergence the brain cannot fuse the two images. Adults experience the visual world in a single image because their eyes rotate in their sockets together. When one turns the other turns, and they stay focused on the same point in space. Neonates, however, lack this coordination. Their eyes are yoked together somewhat in their movements, but they do not always look at the same thing. Lyn Wickelgren of Yale University found that when neonates were tested using the Fantz visual-preference apparatus, one eye would be on one target and the other eye on the other target 22 percent of the time. More often still, the second eye would be looking somewhere between the two patterns. From further research, Wickelgren (1969) concluded that there is usually a 4- to 5-inch separation in the point of fixation for neonates' eyes when they are looking at patterns just 20 inches away.

Convergence of the two eyes on a single point improves slowly over the first 6 months. Richard Aslin (1977) for example, has measured the ability of infants from 1 to 6 months of age to converge and "diverge" their eyes as objects approach and recede from them: 1-month-olds had accurate convergence on just 37 percent of the trials; 2-month-olds improved to 52 percent; and 3-month-olds, to 69 percent of the trials. This indicates, along with other evidence, that infants in their first 3 months spend much of their time seeing double. One consequence of the fact that double vision is the norm for early infancy is that infants with misaligned eyes (a condition called *squint* or *strabismus*) can have the condition corrected some time during their first 6 months without there being any danger of long-term consequences for visual development. Beyond 6 months, however, surgically corrected strabismus may still not produce stereoscopic vision. The reason is that prolonged strabismus has the same effect on ocular dominance as monocular deprivation: It leads to a reduction in the number of binocularly driven cells in the visual cortex (Goldstein, 1984). Such cells are crucial to the ability to detect disparity.

The fact that young infants' eyes do not converge with perfect accuracy is a limitation to the use of disparity cues for depth, but there is still some depth information available. Some studies, therefore, have looked directly at the ability of very young infants to interpret disparity information. This research has provided direct tests of the ability to see stereoscopically. The conclusion is that stereoscopic vision is not present in the first months of life. The ability is measured by having infants wear special glasses—like those used at 3-D movies—that enable the experimenter to feed one image to one eye and a second, slightly displaced image to the other eye. Except for one unreplicated study (Bower, Broughton, & Moore, 1970b), there is no evidence that infants under 3½ months of age see single images when presented with two (Fox, Aslin, Shea, & Dumais, 1980). The failure to see 3-D images when they are presented has to be due in part to the lack of convergence. But it is also due to the inability of the brain at this young age to fuse two images even when the eyes converge. The consensus view at present is that the necessary neural maturation is not complete until somewhere around 4 months of age (Birch, Shimojo, & Held, 1985).

The Use of Pictorial Cues to Depth

So far we have examined the development of depth perception using four separate depth cues. The first three—motion parallax, retinal expansion, and accretion and deletion of texture—are dynamic cues available to each eye when either the world or the viewer is in motion. The fourth is binocular disparity, a cue available from both dynamic and static views of a three-dimensional world when input to the two eyes is compared. All of these cues are available at birth, but knowledgeable use of them is not. The cues to which we turn next—the pictorial cues—are also available at birth. Even when looking with just one eye, the pictorial cues to depth are all present. The emerging view, however, is that pictorial cues may be the last depth cues to be interpreted accurately.

The studies that are the basis for this view are being conducted by Albert Yonas and a number of his colleagues (Granrud & Yonas, 1984; Kaufmann, Maland, & Yonas, 1981; Yonas, Cleaves, & Pettersen, 1978; Yonas, Pettersen, & Granrud, 1982). The first studies in this series showed that the texture-gradient and perspective cues in a photograph of a window turned at a 45 degree angle are interpreted correctly by 6- and 7-month-old infants, but not by 5-month-olds. This was demonstrated using the experimental procedure shown in Figure 7-15. Infants sat within reaching distance of a window that had been constructed by pasting a window photograph (with its window panes cut out) onto a piece of metal. Seen against a blue felt background, adults perceive a rectangular window rotated at a 45 degree angle. The 7-month-olds in Yonas's research apparently saw the same thing, because they reached out as if the right edge were nearer to them than the left. This, however, is a misjudgment created by the pictorial cues that are present (see Figure 7-15A). In reality, the two edges of the window are equidistant, as demonstrated in the overhead view of the window-reaching task shown in Figure 7-15B. Unlike the older infants, 5-month-olds were not taken in by the illusion of nearness that the pictorial cues created. By inference, then, these 5-month-olds were not able to interpret the pictorial cues to depth that were present. Of course, for Yonas's window illusion to work, infants must not only know about the meaning of pictorial cues, they must also know that windows are rectangular. It is possible that ignorance of the usual geometric properties of windows and not ignorance of the pictorial cues could account for the age differences in reaching on Yonas's test.

Subsequent research, however, using other pictorial cues tends to confirm the view that the period between 5 and 7 months of age is when children first become sensitive to pictorial information for depth. Sensitivity

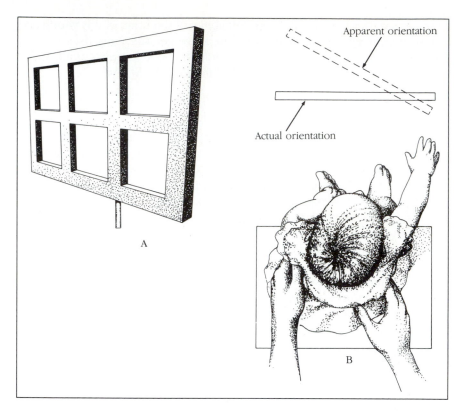

FIGURE 7-15
A Test for Knowledge of Pictorial Cues
When a picture of a window taken at a 45 degree angle is presented directly in front of infants at a 0 degree angle (that is, in the frontolateral plane), the two edges of the window are, in fact, equally distant from the infant (panel A). Infants who are influenced by the pictorial cues in the photograph, however, perceive the right edge as being nearer. In research at the University of Minnesota, 6- and 7-month-old infants, but not 5-month-olds, have been fooled by this illusion into thinking that the right side of the window is nearer (panel B).

to relative size as a cue develops during this period (Yonas, Granrud, & Pettersen, 1985), as does sensitivity to interposition as a cue (Granrud & Yonas, 1984). Both of these results were obtained using the same reaching-study methodology as was just described. Infants were placed in front of visual stimuli containing the pictorial information (either size or interposition), and they were observed to see whether they would reach to the part of the display that, on the basis of pictorial information, appeared to be nearer. Though both groups reached out to the display, the older infants showed a clear preference for the part of the display that was "nearer." The younger infants showed no such preference and, therefore, probably did not judge that one part was any closer than another.

Additional Visual Knowledge

Knowledge of Size Constancy

An important consequence of our ability to judge depth visually is that we can distinguish between objects that are shrinking in size and those that are just moving farther away. Because we can make this distinction, we are able to maintain **size constancy.** This means simply that our psychological interpretations of an object's size remain constant even though the image size of an object varies. An interesting consequence of this bit of knowledge can be seen in Figure 7-16A. Try to ignore size constancy and judge just the image size of the two men. In your mind's eye, cut out the image of the man who is farther down the walk and move him to the same level in the photograph as the man in the foreground. Now, what is their relative size? After making your judgment turn the page to find Figure 7-16B. If you are

FIGURE 7-16A
Size Constancy Confounds Estimates of Image Size
Because of size constancy, you will overestimate the size of the image of the man in the background. Look on the next page to see his true size.

FIGURE 7-16B
This picture shows the actual size relation between the two images that appeared in perspective in Figure 7-16A.

like every other adult who attempts this exercise, you overestimated the image size of the farther man. Your knowledge of his true size (made possible by size constancy) led you to overestimate his image size. Perception here has clearly added something to sensation.

On logical grounds alone, we can conclude that infants cannot have size constancy until they can judge distance. Because there has been a rough consensus in the work reviewed thus far that the dynamic, pictorial, and binocular cues to depth are not used effectively to infer depth until some time between 4 and 6 months, it is unlikely that infants younger than this would know about size constancy. The evidence to date is consistent with this expectation.

In two studies using the habituation paradigm, Australian psychologists Ross Day and Beryl McKenzie have sought evidence of a knowledge of size constancy in 4- to 8-month-old infants. When familiar objects were displayed at familiar distances of about 1 to 6 feet, even the 4-month-olds gave some evidence of size constancy (Day & McKenzie, 1981). The procedure was to habituate the visual fixations of the infants to a model of a human head and then to change either the size of the head, its distance from the subject, or both. Infants dishabituated when the head size was changed but not when the same size head was just moved to a new distance. This is just the result that would be expected for infants with knowledge of size constancy. It implies that they would know if their mother's head suddenly doubled in size and that they would not confuse this true change in size with the apparent change created when their mother moved closer or farther away. For some unknown reason, however, the evidence of size constancy in the younger infants was restricted to the case in which they were habituated to a moving head. When they were habituated to a stationary head, only the 6- and 8-month-olds demonstrated a knowledge of size constancy (McKenzie, Tootell, & Day, 1980).

An important qualifier to be remembered about the Day and McKenzie results is that they apply only to familiar objects at familiar distances. Most students of perception believe that size constancy is not in all-or-none phenomenon but rather that we extend our belief in size constancy gradually outwards as we get more experience with objects and their movements in space. Indeed there is anecdotal evidence that even children and adults can experience a failure of size constancy when objects are viewed at an uncommonly great distance. Herman von Helmholtz reported, for example, that when he first saw people high up in the belfry of a church tower in Potsdam, he took them to be dolls (in Gibson, 1966). Hayne Reese and Lewis Lipsitt (1970, p. 384) report the story of a boy on his first plane trip who asked his dad just after takeoff, "How come we aren't getting any littler yet?" It may be, therefore, that size constancy does not immediately apply to all objects at all distances.

Knowledge of Shape Constancy

Just as we know that the actual size of objects does not change as they move closer to us or farther from us, so too we know that the actual shape of objects does not change as they are rotated or tilted. We judge, then, that even when the shape of the image made by an object is transformed by spatial changes, the true shape of the object is the same. This bit of knowledge is called **shape constancy.** To understand clearly what is meant by this, take a circular object and turn it about in space. As soon as it is tilted or rotated the least bit, it no longer makes a circular image on your eye. Rather it makes an elliptical image that gets ever flatter as you continue to turn the circle (see Figure 7-17). The reason that you nonetheless see the circle to be a circle is that you have shape constancy.

Because the methods of testing for shape constancy are basically the same as those for size constancy, we can proceed directly to the conclusions to be drawn from the research. These have been summed up clearly in an authoritative review (Cohen, DeLoache, & Strauss, 1979): "No clear-cut experimental evidence supports the existence of shape constancy in infants under 7 months of age" (p. 421). Once again, then, we are drawn to the same conclusion that we have been drawn to previously in this section on

FIGURE 7-17
Shape Constancy
When a circular object is rotated, the image it projects becomes elliptical.
Nonetheless, because of shape constancy, you still perceive the object to be
circular.

the development of depth perception: use of the various cues to depth to
produce knowledge of depth and to produce related bits of knowledge such
as size and shape constancy is not well developed until the middle of the
first year of life, the time when infants are first able to move about on their
own to explore the spatial world in which they live. The one bit of visual
knowledge that we can clearly say is present earlier than this, and perhaps
is even present at birth, is knowledge of the color categories.

Knowledge of the Color Categories

The naive empiricist would think that even though infants have trichromatic
color vision, they would not know that a blue and an aqua are both blue or
that a green and an olive are both green. How after all could they know
such a thing? Color (or *hue*) is a continuous phenomenon created by the
effects of different wavelengths of light on the color receptors in the retina
of the eye. Color categories, however, are discontinuous, because psychologically there is a point in the continuous change of wavelength where one
color stops and another begins. One would think that these boundaries
between categories would be mere conventions in a language community.
Children would learn the boundaries by being corrected whenever they
misjudged the boundaries, for example by calling a red "orange" or an
orange "red." In a surprising discovery, however, it has been determined
that the boundaries are not arbitrary conventions. Speakers of different languages agree on what the boundaries are (Berlin & Kay, 1969) and so do
infants who are yet to learn a language.

Marc Bornstein was the first to show that infants divide the color spectrum into the same categories as adult language users. His procedure was
to habituate 4-month-old infants to a color of a specified wavelength, say
480 nanometers (billionths of a meter, abbreviated as nm), and then to
change this stimulus either to 510 nm or 450 nm. In physical terms these

shifts are equivalent shifts of 30 nm. In psychological terms, however, the 480-nm-to-510-nm shift moves across the blue-green boundary. A 510-nm light is viewed as primarily green by adults, but a 480-nm light is viewed as primarily blue. So is a 450-nm light. This means that adults would say that going from 480 nm to 510 nm produces a color change but that going from 480 nm to 450 nm does not. Infants who make the same judgments would show a much greater increase in fixation time when the 480-nm stimulus was changed to 510 nm than when it was changed to 450 nm. This is precisely what happened (Bornstein, Kessen, & Weiskopf, 1976). Not only did they respond this way for the blue-to-green shift but also for a green-to-yellow shift and a yellow-to-red shift. We can conclude then that "human infants group visible wavelengths into hue categories much like the adult's" (Bornstein, Kessen, & Weiskopf, 1976, p. 202).

Knowledge of the Meaning of Facial Expressions

Our study of perceptual knowledge thus far has been restricted to what could be called nonsocial perception, which is to say perception of the objective properties of things in the visual world. Studies of infant perception are not restricted to nonsocial perception, however. Recently, for example, investigators have begun to ask about social perception in infants. This has led to interesting data on the development of infants' abilities to interpret human facial expressions.

Perceiving the Meaning of Facial Expressions   Ever since Charles Darwin (1872/1965) originated work on the evolutionary significance of facial expressions in humans, researchers have held the view that facial expressions are "innately" meaningful. Certainly facial expressions are a key source of social information, and the young of many animals are capable of reading them to some extent. Rhesus monkeys, for example, raised in isolation from all other rhesus monkeys can recognize the meaning of a rhesus "threat face" even though they have never see one (Sackett, 1966). The evidence for this is that around 2½ months of age they begin to respond to threat faces with fear. They withdraw, rock, and huddle in their cage even though the threat face they are looking at is nothing more than a photograph of a threatening monkey that has been projected onto one of the walls of their cage. We can infer from the monkeys' behavior that they have made a meaningful interpretation of a social stimulus. This is social perception in a quite literal sense. They have perceived threat in a set of facial cues in a way analogous to perceiving distance in a set of dynamic, pictorial, and stereoscopic cues. The fact that these monkeys can correctly interpret a threat face, even in the absence of any chance to learn its social significance (see also Kenney, Mason, & Hill, 1979), raises the question of whether human infants might be similarly sensitive to the meaning inherent in facial expressions.

One reason we might suspect that the interpretation of facial expressions would not depend solely on experience with others is that there is a remarkable universality in the meaning of human facial expressions. The facial expressions, for example, that signal happiness, disgust, surprise, sadness, anger, and fear are the same the globe over (see, for example, Ekman, 1973; see Figure 7-18). Even blind children conform to the human norms. This indicates that the emotions experienced in our brains are expressed through our faces in a universal human language. It might be, then, that infants do not need special training in seeing emotional expressions in others in order to be able to interpret their meaning.

Infants' reactions to a variety of emotional expressions have been studied in an attempt to determine if accurate interpretation of the emotional messages in faces might be part of the young infant's perceptual capacities. In these studies there has been no indication that any human emotions are discriminated before 5 months of age. In a classic study conducted by Rene Spitz and K. M. Wolf (1946), for example, infants younger than 5 months smiled as often at angry faces as at friendly ones. Other studies show a similar indifference to changes in emotional expression (see, for example, Kreutzer & Charlesworth, 1973). These results are contrary to, the hypothesis that human infants do not need special training in order to be able to read the faces of others correctly.

Harriet Oster (1981) feels that it is in the best interests of young primates—humans and monkeys alike—that they be indifferent to adult emotional states. Oster points out that altricial animals (animals born in a relatively immature and helpless condition, such as humans) only have reflexive behaviors at birth to aid in their survival. Becoming fearful in the presence of threat or depressed in the presence of nonloving, hostile faces would serve no end. To the contrary, a constancy of response—independent of the emotional states of others—might be the best strategy. Specifically, says Oster, until an infant gains some degree of motoric independence, its interests are best served by trying to "win" the nurturence of others. It can do this by being cute, cuddly, and lovable despite whatever threats and rebuffs it might receive from the social world. Oster's hypothesis implies a maturationally timed period during which infant primates would be ignorant of the emotional states of others. This period would last until about 2½ months in monkeys (based on Sackett's [1966] data) and until around 5 months in humans.

FIGURE 7-18
Human Facial Expressions
The universality of emotional expression was determined by presenting faces showing the basic human emotions and having adults in different cultures state the emotion that they expressed. As shown in these data, there is considerable cross-cultural agreement in the emotional meaning of the various facial expressions.

	United States (Sample size = 99)	Brazil (Sample size = 40)	Chile (Sample size = 119)	Argentina (Sample size = 168)	Japan (Sample size = 29)
	97% Happiness	95% Happiness	95% Happiness	98% Happiness	100% Happiness
	92% Disgust	97% Disgust	92% Disgust	92% Disgust	90% Disgust
	95% Surprise	87% Surprise	93% Surprise	95% Surprise	100% Surprise
	84% Sadness	59% Sadness	88% Sadness	78% Sadness	62% Sadness
	67% Anger	90% Anger	94% Anger	90% Anger	90% Anger
	85% Fear	67% Fear	68% Fear	54% Fear	66% Fear

Oster illustrates the potential advantage of infantile indifference to the emotional states of others with the case history of Ned S. (originally reported by Sander, 1969). Ned, like all human infants was smiling beautifully in social situations beginning in his second month. The fact is, however, that Ned had little to smile about because his mother, due to depression and anxiety, had been avoiding him. According to Oster, if Ned had not begun smiling indiscriminately at his mother in complete ignorance of her own bad humor, the mother might have continued to ignore him. As it was, however, the smile and his delightful ways won the mother over so that she became nurturant.

Though highly speculative, Oster's argument for the value of emotional indifference in infants has some support from data on monkeys, much of which shows that very young monkeys have a remarkable indifference to the emotional states of others. For example, when infant rhesus monkeys were reared by physically abusive mothers, the infants accepted the abuse and continued to approach their mothers in an attempt to establish a nurturant relationship. Artificial mothers who were equally abusive (Harlow, Harlow, & Suomi, 1971) were equally ineffective in altering the infants' tendency to approach and cling.

Though Oster's hypothesis is an interesting one, it is not the only way to explain young infants' apparent inability to perceive basic emotions such as anger, threat, and happiness. In fact there is a far more parsimonious explanation, which does not involve the assumption of evolutionary factors and maturational timing. This more parsimonious explanation is that children and young rhesus monkeys are initially unresponsive to the emotional expressions of others simply because they cannot see them. Two visual factors could be important: one is the lack of adequate contrast sensitivity (see pp. 330–32); the other is a scanning pattern inadequate for the "whole-face" perception that is needed to see a facially expressed emotion.

To perceive an emotion expressed in the face, infants must take in the eyes, forehead, cheeks, and mouth simultaneously. When infants under 5 months scan faces, however, their attention locks onto individual parts of the face. Data from 1- and 2-month-olds dramatically illustrate the general problem. The data, taken from research by Daphne Maurer and Phillip Salapatek (1976), show with line tracings the actual pattern of eye movements that accompany facial viewing (see Figure 7-19). The 1-month-olds scan only the exterior of the face, particularly the hair line. The 2-month-olds focus on the eye region and corners of the mouth. In either case, it is obvious from the scanning pattern that the infants are not taking in the whole face. With age, children do an ever-better job of scanning, but most investigators find that scanning patterns are inadequate to create whole-form (or in this case, whole-face) perception until around 5 months of age. Data other than the facial data support this conclusion. For example, infants do not perceive

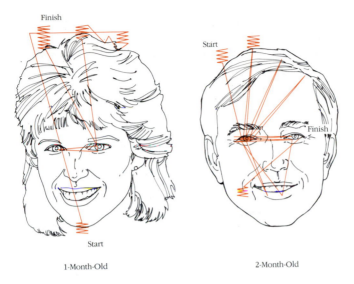

FIGURE 7-19
Visual Scanning
The scanning patterns of 1- and 2-month-old infants are restricted just to high contrast areas of the face. These patterns are incompatible with the whole-face perception needed to see emotion in the human face. (After Maurer & Salapatek, 1976)

illusory *subjective contours* until the period 5 to 7 months (Bertenthal, Campos, & Haith, 1980). What is interesting about this is that perceiving subjective contours (see Figure 7-20) depends on whole-form perception. This is explained briefly in the caption for Figure 7-20.

Regardless of whether the infant's initial insensitivity to facial expressions is a consequence of evolution, poor vision, or both, infants beyond 5 months of age begin to read other people's faces quite well. This is becoming clear from research on the infant behavior known as social referencing.

Social Referencing   The term **social referencing** was coined by a team of Denver psychologists led by Joseph Campos (see Campos & Stenberg, 1981). It refers to the use of the emotional expressions of others to resolve the meaning of otherwise ambiguous situations.

The mechanism by which social referencing occurs is simple. Infants simply look at the faces of their mothers. The mother's reaction then serves to regulate the infant's reaction. This has been shown quite convincingly using a visual cliff. With the cliff adjusted to a not-so-deep level, infants can be put into doubt about the threat apparent in the drop-off. In this situation, they look to their mothers to see if they should venture off. Mothers who

FIGURE 7-20
Subjective Contours

If you examine Figure 7-20A, you will see what is meant by a subjective contour. The objective contours present are those that separate the four three-quarter circles from the white background. But subjectively, we impose another set of contours. These are the contours of a square that seems to overlay the four circles and the white background. These contours are not present at all, yet we perceive them whenever we view the four three-quarter circles arranged as they are on the left. Arrange them differently, (B), and no subjective contours are present. The importance of subjective contours for the present discussion is that seeing subjective contours depends on whole-figure perception. An infant must process all parts simultaneously and integrate them into a whole before the contour will appear. The fact that infants do not see subjective contours prior to the period 5 to 7 months is further evidence that they would not see faces as a whole either.

respond to their infants with a smiling, happy face provide reassurance that the drop-off is not a danger. The infants, then, are highly likely to venture out onto the deep side in order to reach an attractive toy. When the mothers respond with a fearful face, their infants are deterred from crossing the cliff and in fact back up, as if recoiling from the now fearful cliff. Mothers displaying an angry face are also successful in deterring their infants from crossing the cliff and in getting them to retreat. The emotional response from the mother must be a response relevant to the situation, however. When infants look to their mothers for information and see her with a sad face, it serves neither to increase nor decrease the infants' willingness to venture onto the deep side of the visual-cliff apparatus.

It is plain to see that social referencing is an ingenious means of learning. Infants who recognize their own inability to make perfect sense of social and nonsocial stimuli can look to others who are more experienced to determine what their reaction should be. According to Campos and Stenberg (1981), infants first begin using this means of learning in the period 5 to 9 months. Laboratory studies of infant reactions to strangers back up this speculation. When strangers approach while their mother is present, infants—beginning around 5 months of age—look quickly to their mother and then may continue to look from mother to stranger to mother for some time.

Audition

After vision, the second-most studied sensory modality is audition. The onset of auditory sensations occurs prenatally (Busnel & Granier-Deferre, 1983). Fetuses in the womb can hear a bit of what is going on in the outside world and a lot of what is going on inside mother. We have no idea, however, what interpretation, if any, the fetal brain has for these sensations. Nor do we know if there is any functional consequence of prenatal auditory experiences. In precocial birds such as ducks, hearing a mother's call prenatally leads to auditory imprinting. To recognize mother's call after hatching, ducks must hear it while they are still in the shell (Gottlieb, 1981). At least for ducks, therefore, prenatal audition plays a vital role in later development. Whether prenatal auditory experiences play any functional role in human development is not known. There are scattered reports that suggest that hearing their mother's voice prenatally may give infants the ability to discriminate their mother's voice from that of a stranger (see, for example, DeCasper & Fifer, 1980). It is unlikely, however, that a prenatal head start in learning to make this discrimination is of any real use to humans.

Following birth, hearing is quite good in humans. Using measures that involve recording neural activity in the auditory areas of the brain along with measures of behavioral responses, research in the 1960s established that infants can hear a wide variety of sounds (Acredelo & Hake, 1982). Since then we have learned more about the qualitative properties of these auditory experiences. For neonates, hearing requires greater sound volume than it does for older children and adults; the added volume is generally estimated at anywhere from 10 to 20 decibels. John Flavell (1985) has pointed out that this means that neonates detect sound about as well as an adult with a head cold. In addition to their slight insensitivity to sounds low in volume, neonates may also be deficient in their ability to sense high frequency sounds. The evidence on this, however, is not completely clear at present (see Aslin, Pisoni, & Jusczyx, 1983).

Given the generally good quality of infant audition from birth, investigators have been more interested in what infants can use their hearing to do than in the actual properties of sounds they detect. One of the most important things they can do is discriminate among sounds. Sounds such as those made when doors open as opposed to when drawers open are rich in information about what is happening outside the child's field of vision. We need have no worry about their ability to discriminate such sounds from each other. Infant auditory discrimination is extremely acute. In fact, in some cases infants can make discriminations that even adults fail to make. This has been demonstrated using pairs of speech sounds that differ in subtle ways that are linguistically unimportant (Lasky, Syrdal-Lasky, & Klein, 1975; Werker, Gilbert, Humphrey, & Tees, 1981). Infants hear the subtle differences even when adults do not. Such results lead to the overall conclusion that audition is a far more developed sense at birth than vision.

Auditory Knowledge

The clearest example of auditory knowledge that neonates possess is the ability to localize a sound. That is, when hearing a sound, they know whether it is to the left, to the right, or straight ahead. They indicate this knowledge by turning either their head or their eyes in the direction of sounds they hear. No one knows just how discriminating this knowledge is, because there is no way from head or eye movements to know precisely where the infant judges the sound to be. But just knowing direction in a gross way is no minor achievement. It depends on being able to interpret some rather subtle binaural (two-ear) cues. One is based on an intensity (or volume) difference between the two ears. For laterally presented sounds, the lead ear will hear a louder version of the sound than will the second ear. The second cue is the time difference between the sound signal in the lead ear and the second ear. The second ear, being more distant, picks up the sound signal later in time than the first ear. Though the difference is only a few milliseconds, a perceptually mature brain is able to use this time difference to judge the location of the sound.

The first evidence that neonates could use one or both of the binaural cues to judge whether sounds come from the left, right, or middle was obtained by Michael Wertheimer in a delivery room. Using a toy "cricket," he presented clicks to the right and left of a newborn girl. "As soon as the first click was made, the neonate, who had been crying with eyes closed, stopped crying, opened her eyes, and turned them in the direction of the click" (Wertheimer, 1961, p. 1692). Fifty-one clicks later, Wertheimer and his observers were convinced that the baby's first response was no accident. She really knew where the sound was coming from. Subsequent observers using methods that are less subject to criticism have confirmed this ability in neonates (see, for example, Muir & Field, 1979). Interestingly, however, this neonatal ability to locate sounds reliably is lost in the second and third postnatal months only to return again in the fourth month (Muir, Abraham, Forbes, & Harris, 1979). No one knows why this should be so, but it has led Rachel Clifton and her colleagues to suspect that neonatal sound localization is really just a reflex (Clifton, Morrongiello, Kulig, & Dowd, 1981). This would mean that the neonatal localization of sound is basically an involuntary response requiring far less "understanding" than later localization. It would also mean that the neurological organization of the head-turn response in neonates would be different from the same response in older infants. Four-month-olds would be using their cortex to direct the head turn, but neonates would be using a more primitive, subcortical area of the brain.

The Precedence Effect

Although neonates are capable (perhaps reflexively) of localizing a sound that comes from a single source, they become confused when the sound comes from multiple sources. We can show this by adding a second sound to the original localization experiment. The second sound is just like the first, except that it comes from the opposite direction. Also it is delayed slightly in time (somewhere from 7 to 50 milliseconds) in order to produce a localization cue. Under these circumstances, neonates fail to locate either sound correctly. They turn neither to the first sound nor to its time-delayed echo. Instead, for time-delayed sounds that come from the right and left respectively, neonates behave as if they have heard a single sound coming from directly in front of them (Clifton, Morrongiello, Kulig, & Dowd, 1981). That is, they fuse the two sounds into one, with no appreciation for the time difference. Adults have an altogether different perception. They, too, fuse the sound into one, but not by averaging. Instead they ignore (psychologically, anyway) the second sound. All they hear is the first sound. Therefore, if asked if a second sound was present, they would say no. This phenomenon is known as the **precedence effect** in adult auditory perception (see Figure 7-21). The sound with precedence is heard in its proper location, and subsequent competing sounds are ignored.

The precedence effect is quite important to accurate auditory perception. Without it, every sound we heard would have a series of trailing

FIGURE 7-21

The Precedence Effect

Onset of an auditory signal is marked in this figure by a rise in the horizontal time line. The figure shows how the time of onset differs for the two ears, both when a sound is first heard (T1) and when it echoes back (T3). In this particular case a sound was heard first in the left ear and then, a short time later, in the right ear. These two sounds are heard as one sound and the interaural time difference (T1) is our cue to the sound's lateral position. When the sound echoes back after the period designated T2, first to the right ear and then to the left ear, adults and 6-month-old infants still perceive just the one sound to the left (the precedence effect). They ignore the echo information in situations like this where T2 is short. Neonates, however, are unable to locate a sound's source under these conditions.

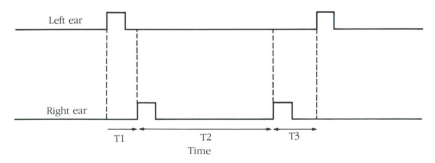

echoes after it. These would be created by reflections of the sound as they bounced back off of walls, floors, and ceilings. Not only would this be distracting, it would be confusing as well. Whereas in reality there would be but a single sound to hear, our auditory system would be hearing multiple sounds coming from multiple directions. It is clearly important for our accurate perception of the auditory world, therefore, that the brain suppress all secondary sound information. In neonates, as we have seen, this does not happen. The secondary sound information disrupts neonates' ability to localize the source of sounds.

Though no one knows what factors contribute to this disruption, the ability to locate sounds accurately when there is competing secondary sound information develops over the first few months of life. By 5 months of age, interpreting precedence is no longer a problem. The only difference between adult and infant responses is in the length of the time delay during which the precedence effect is experienced; 5-month-olds experience the effect over longer delays than do adults (Morrongiello, Kulig, & Clifton, 1984). That is, with delays that would create the perception of two distinct sounds for adults, 5-month-olds are still hearing just the sound with precedence.

Categorical Perception of Sounds

As we just learned, the acuity of infant audition is quite good. Though this discussion was not documented with evidence from research on infant speech perception, it could have been. Speech perception involves distinctions among some rather subtle sound differences, and infants' ability to make these distinctions is part of the evidence for their auditory acuity. Work in the area of infant speech perception, however, has revealed something much more amazing than the fact that infant hearing has good acuity. It has demonstrated that infants make the same *categorical distinctions* among speech sounds that you and I make. To understand why this is amazing, you need a little background on the properties of speech sound.

The distinctions that you and I make among speech sounds are between categories of sounds called *phonemes*. Though we perceive these as categories of sounds, the categories are distinguished by some very thin borders. Take the sounds [d] (as in "dot") and [t] (as in "tot"), for example. Psychologically, these are quite distinct, but if you were measuring the difference between them, not with a human ear and brain but with a sound spectrograph, you would find only a minute difference. The difference is created by a continuous variable called *voice onset time* or VOT. This has to do with the time relation between the release of air pressure and the start of the vocal-cord activity needed to produce the sound. For adult speakers of English, a VOT of about 35 milliseconds (msec) marks the boundary between [d] and [t]. If voicing begins earlier than this, we hear a [d] sound. If it begins later, we hear a [t]. Once across the border, VOT can vary by 60 or 70 msec without affecting our interpretation of the sound we hear. VOT is but one of several speech sound variables that operate this way. Point of articulation, nasality, and laterality are others. Defining each of these would take us further into the physics of speech production than we need to go. Suffice it to say that variation in these variables is continuous, but listeners do not hear the variation except when certain borders are crossed.

With this background to the properties of speech sounds, you can understand that the phonemes of speech are perceptual categories imposed on what is in physical terms a set of continuously varying events. In every case, there is a border somewhere along the physical dimension that separates one sound from another. Phoneme perception, therefore, is quite similar to color perception. In both cases, our perceptual systems impose psychologically distinct borders at places where, physically, there is no border at all. Thus, green becomes blue at wavelengths of 470 nm and [d] becomes [t] at VOTs in excess of 35 msec.

Research on infant knowledge of speech sound boundaries (see, for example, Eimas, Siqueland, Jusczyk, & Vigorito, 1971) has been similar to that on infant knowledge of color boundaries. Infants are first habituated to a sound that lies near a phoneme boundary. Then one of two other sounds is presented. Both comparison sounds are equidistant from the first in physical terms, but one is across the boundary and the other is not. If infants respond to the change when the shift is across a border but not when the shift is on the same side of the border, we can infer that they know the importance of the border. The response that we look for is a change in the rate of high-amplitude sucks. Using the HAS procedure, it has been shown that 2- and 3-month-old infants know the location of almost every phonemic border that has been tested.

Researchers became excited over infants' preverbal knowledge of speech sound boundaries because they believed that it might be evidence that the human brain is specialized for the auditory reception and production of speech sounds long before speech begins. Such evidence would contribute to the general view that language functions are not just tacked onto phylogenetically old brain structures. Rather, special—perhaps uniquely human—adaptations are required. Speech then would be a special type of auditory signal recognized as such by the human brain. Some of the initial excitement over this possibility has waned with the discovery that chinchillas and rhesus monkeys also categorize human speech sounds at VOT and point-of-articulation borders (Passingham, 1982). One conclusion from this is that categorical classification of all sounds—not just speech sounds—is a fundamental aspect of the mammalian auditory system.

Although the categories that infants impose on speech sound variation are basically the same as the categories that adults impose, experience with a language has some interesting effects on speech sound perception. These effects can be variously described as enhancement, attenuation, sharpening, broadening, and realignment (Aslin, Pisoni, & Jusczyx, 1983), but in every case they demonstrate the now-familiar fact that development is an epigenetic process in which nature and nurture play a constantly interactive role. This means that although infants have an innate ability to impose some language-relevant discriminations on continuous sound variation, the actual language learning experience will markedly affect the discriminations that in fact are made.

As a simple illustration of one of the possible effects, consider the case of a Japanese infant who will be introduced to a language in which the boundary between the [r] and [l] sounds is not honored as a linguistically significant one. This means that the infant begins language learning with a perceptual apparatus that is ready to perceive *r*amen noodles and *l*amen noodles as separate linguistic messages. The infant quickly learns, however, that adults say both when referring to the very same thing. They also talk about Sappo*r*o, Japan, and Sappo*l*o, Japan, as the same place. Thus, the [r]–[l] difference, though perceptually discriminable, is not linguistically important. This means that the infant will cease to attend to this difference when processing speech sounds and, eventually, will even cease to hear the difference!

In other cases, experience can enhance phoneme differences. The English language and many others, for example, do not discriminate among what are called prevoiced and voiced consonants. Other languages such as Spanish and Kikuyu do. It is of interest, then, that the only infants who have been clearly shown to discriminate between voiced and prevoiced consonants are those who have been exposed to the Spanish and Kikuyu languages (see Aslin, Pisoni, & Jusczyx, 1983, p. 639).

Intersensory Knowledge

Early in our discussion of perceptual knowledge, William Molyneaux's question regarding intersensory knowledge was posed: Would a man born blind and then made to see be able to recognize objects on sight that he had previously only known from touch? To end our discussion, we will take up this question and related ones that involve the integration of the senses.

Touch and Vision

Molyneaux's question regarding whether visual knowledge can be obtained from tactile experience alone has been answered affirmatively for infants. At least by 6 to 8 months of age, and perhaps as early as 1 month of age (Gibson & Walker, 1984), infants can visually recognize objects that they have only touched, or sucked on, previously (see also Harris, 1983, p. 743).

For example, one study with 6-month-olds showed that an egg-shaped object that had been handled previously was recognized when it was first seen (Ruff & Kohler, 1978). The evidence was that the 6-month-olds looked longer at the previously handled object than at one that was new to both sight and touch. Eleanor Gibson and Arlene Walker (1984) found similar evidence for intersensory perception among 1-month-olds who had become familiar with novel objects by sucking on them. Apparently, therefore, infants develop the ability to form accurate visual hypotheses from tactile experiences quite early in life. We can suspect that the combined tactile and visual experiences of infants (that is, simultaneously looking at and handling a single object) are important experiences in this rapid development, but what is interesting is that these experiences generalize. In other words, infants apparently learn not just about the tactile–visual correspondences of individual objects but about the tactile–visual correspondences for all objects of a given class (for example, spongy objects or hard wooden objects.)

Vision and Audition

We saw in the case of sound localization (p. 362) that even neonates will turn their heads to the source of a sound. The purpose of this action, perhaps in neonates but certainly in 4-month-olds, is to bring the eyes into contact with whatever is making the noise. This implies that there is at least the implicit knowledge in young infants that things that make noise can be seen in the same place that the noise originated from. Further evidence that sights and sounds are known to go together comes from research in which mothers speak to their infants from the front while their voices are projected from a speaker on the side (Aronson & Rosenbloom, 1971). This dislocation of face and voice causes infants to become upset. Apparently the infants know the voice and face should be together in space. Beyond that, do they know anything else? Do they know what sights and sounds are likely to go together? Recent evidence shows that they do.

Elizabeth Spelke has shown, for example, that 4-month-old infants can match sound tracks and visual displays. She showed this initially by presenting infants with two films of simple actions to watch (Spelke, 1976). One was a peekaboo game; the other showed percussion instruments being played. The films were accompanied by just one sound track—either the peekaboo-game sound track or the percussion-instrument sound track. Spelke's subjects preferred to watch the film that matched the sound track. It appears, therefore, that infants—at least by 4 months—know something about the kinds of sounds that should accompany particular objects and actions. This is shown even more clearly in a study in which Spelke presented two films: one of a toy kangaroo and the other of a toy donkey, with each animal attached to puppet strings (Spelke, 1979). The films showed the same simple actions: the toys were lifted into the air and let fall. Sound

Infants know when sound tracks fail to match movements.

tracks for the two films differed however. In one case a noise (either a thump or a gong) was made each time the animal came down. In the other case, noises failed to correspond with the animal hitting the floor. Spelke's infant subjects had a clear preference for the film in which the sound track matched the action. This implies a knowledge that some action–noise combinations make more sense than others.

Not only can 4-month-olds match simple actions and sound patterns, they can match complex ones as well. Using the preference design just described, Spelke has shown that when two talking faces are presented, the face that is in synchrony with its voice recording is preferred over the one in which the mouth movements and voice recording do not match (Spelke & Cortelyou, 1981). Though it would seem that this ability might be based on some primitive recognition that sound changes should keep time with mouth movements, there is additional evidence that implies an even more analytic ability than this. According to data from Patricia Kuhl and Andrew Meltzoff (1982), infants 4½ to 5 months of age know the particular mouth shape that should go with particular sounds. Thus, in their experiment, when infants heard an [a] (as in "pot") sound, they looked to the motion picture of a mouth making that sound. When an [i] (as in "Pete") sound was produced, they looked to the mouth making the [i] sound.

An additional example of infants' knowledge of what sights and sounds should go together comes from research showing that 5-month-olds know that the noises objects make should increase as objects approach and diminish as they recede (Walker-Andrews & Lennon, 1985). This was shown using films of approaching and receding automobiles. Infants preferred watching a film that had a matched sound track (for example, a receding car and diminishing automobile noise) to one that had a mismatched sound track.

Vision and Proprioception

A sense that we have not yet had occasion to mention is the *proprioceptive sense,* which brings us feedback from our muscles about their state of contraction. This sense is made relevant, however, by some rather startling data regarding the capacity of neonates to match their own facial expressions to the expressions made by others. A very influential research report from Andrew Meltzoff indicated that even neonates can imitate adult facial expressions (Meltzoff & Moore, 1977; see Figure 7-22A). A later report from Tiffany Field and her colleagues (Field, Woodson, Greenberg, & Cohen, 1982) indicated that neonates can imitate emotional expressions as well (see Figure 7-22B). Such research is startling because it goes against observations extending back at least 60 years (Guillaume, 1926/1971) that indicate that infants do not begin to imitate facial expressions until toward the end of their first year. The Meltzoff and Field reports are startling also because they seem to go against the general trend for other perceptual and intersensory skills, which is for them to emerge slowly during the first year. One certainly wonders how facial imitations could be possible. To imitate, one must be able to recognize an equivalence between visual information from a model's face and proprioceptive feedback from one's own face. Where could such equivalence information possibly come from?

In keeping with the startling nature of the Meltzoff and Field results, a lot of research into infant imitative abilities has been initiated. Some of this research has failed to replicate the original findings (see, for example, McKenzie & Over, 1983). Other reports have replicated imitation of a single facial movement—tongue protrusion—but not the others shown in Figure 7-22 (Abravanel & Sigafoos, 1984). In addition to producing new data, these subsequent studies have clarified a number of issues that make the claim for imitation somewhat less startling than it was initially. First, when evidence for imitation is found, it is found only under some very special conditions. In Meltzoff's laboratory (Meltzoff & Moore, 1983), for example, lights are dimmed and the adult model's face is illuminated. A videotape camera is zoomed in to pick up detailed facial movements of the infant subjects as the adult goes through a long series of burst-and-pause presentations of the expression to be imitated. During this time the infants are quite active, and their facial expressions change rapidly. It is never the case, therefore, that one adult expression produces one imitation. Quite to the contrary, evidence of imitation comes only from a statistical analysis of the data that seeks to show that the expression that was to be imitated was in

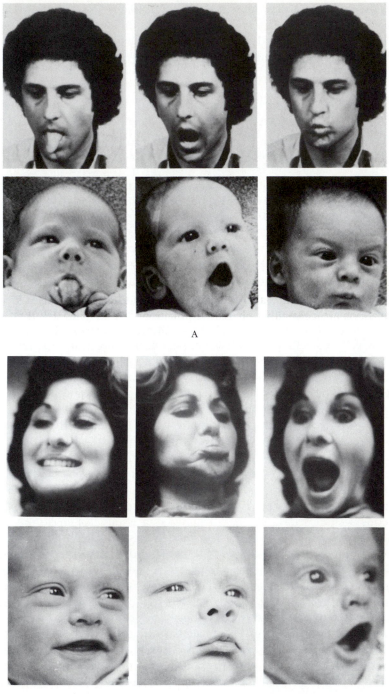

A

B

FIGURE 7-22
Imitating Adult Facial Expressions
Imitating someone else's facial expression requires matching information from vision with information from proprioception and determining that the two are equivalent. These pictures of 2- and 3-week-old infants give the impression that even neonates are capable of such an elaborate cognitive act. However, many critics disagree. They point out that the infant expressions shown here are part of the neonate's normal repertoire of expressions that are made even in nonimitative situations. This means that the matches could have been fortuitous. Also, whereas the photos give the impression that a modeled face produces an imitative face in a one-to-one fashion, this is far from true. Infants make many faces during the imitative sessions, and statistical analysis is required to show an enhanced frequency for the modeled face. For these and other reasons, many infant researchers believe that if neonates do in fact imitate some expresssions, the mechanism that underlies their imitations is more likely to be reflexive than cognitive. Certainly there does seem to be a substantial difference between the alleged facial imitations of neonates and those of infants who are nearing 1 year of age.

fact produced somewhat more often than others during the imitation period. Two other facts are also relevant. First, infant facial responses scored as imitations are generally only partial imitations. This means that the near-perfect imitations shown in Figure 7-22 are quite exceptional. Second, there is no evidence from anyone that infants' imitative expressions are any different from the expressions that make up their normal repertoire of facial movements. In light of these considerations, what is meant by imitation in neonates is very different from what is meant by imitation in 8- to 12-month-olds. These latter infants are quite good at matching proprioceptive feedback from their own facial muscles to what they see in someone else's face. Neonates may be able to do something similar, at least for a limited number of expressions (such as tongue protrusion), but it is too early to say that their mechanism for doing this is the same as in older infants. That is, the occasional matches by neonates may not require the same knowledge as is required for matches by older infants. Eugene Abravanel and Ann Sigafoos (1984) suggest, for example, that the neonatal matches—when they occur—may be reflexive rather than cognitive.

To sum up our current knowledge of infant intersensory knowledge, it is quite clear that early in their first year infants start becoming perceptually astute regarding what auditory, visual, and tactile experiences go together. They know about the relationship of perceived form and felt shape, they know that objects emit noises, they know how these noises should be synchronized to the movements of objects, and they even know how different object movements (such as mouth movements and the movements of cars) should affect the sounds they produce. Toward the end of their first year, they will be able to use proprioceptive feedback to create on their own faces a great variety of facial expressions seen on the faces of others.

Research has not yet revealed how all this knowledge is acquired. We can only assume that infants learn what goes with what from the experience of directing their multiple senses onto single events and then discovering reliable relationships among the sensations that are produced (for example, as cars get more distant, they make less noise). What is amazing about this learning, however, is that individual intersensory experiences seem to lead to general intersensory rules. We have no theory yet to explain how such learning is possible.

How Plastic Is the Human Capacity for Forming Intersensory Associations?

If our intersensory knowledge is in fact learned from individual intersensory experiences, we can wonder just how plastic this learning might be. A discovery regarding association learning in animals is that frequently there are serious constraints on just what can be learned. Rats and other mammals, for example, can readily learn to identify poisons by taste, but they are very slow in learning to identify poisons by appearance or sound. This phenomenon has been labeled **preparedness** (Seligman & Hager, 1972, pp. 3–5). It alerts us to the fact that learning, like other animal characteristics, has been shaped by evolution. As a result, animals are better prepared to learn relevant associations that are a natural part of the world in which they live than they are to learn associations that only exist in some psychologist's laboratory, such as the association between "bright, noisy water" and illness, which was invented by psychologist John Garcia in his studies on the preparedness of taste-aversion learning in rats (Garcia & Koelling, 1966).

Given that preparedness is a general phenomenon characterizing associational learning throughout the animal kingdom, we might expect that some human perceptual learning is also prepared. Thus, for reasons having to do with the evolution of our brain and nervous system, some intra- and intersensory associations might be easier for us to form than others. In the intrasensory domain, for example, it might be easier for us to learn that an expanding retinal pattern signals an approaching object than that it signals a receding object. In the intersensory domain, it might be easier to learn to look to the right to find an object heard on the right than it would be to learn to look to the left under the same circumstances.

Though preparedness in human intersensory learning is a distinct possibility, it is also possible that—at least for humans—the brain is so plastic in the associations that it can make, that even a totally disarranged perceptual world—one in which the normal sight–sound–touch correspondences were completely altered—might be as easy for infants to learn as the usual associations. This is a highly speculative view, but there is some limited evidence for it from research on the use of auditory feedback from a sonar device to teach blind infants about objects in space. Evolution has had no chance to prepare the human auditory system for such feedback, yet the brain seems to be able to make use of it.

Visual Information from Novel Auditory Information

Normally audition tells us little about the distance, size, and texture of objects. Such knowledge must come from vision. T. G. R. Bower has reported, however, that when blind infants are provided with an auditory signal that contains distance, size, and texture information, they can interpret it (Bower, 1982; Aitken & Bower, 1982).

Bower's technique employs a device developed by Leslie Kay (1974), an engineer from New Zealand. Conceptually the device is rather simple (see Humphrey & Humphrey, 1986). It works like any sound-navigation system (sonar). An ultrasound signal is sent from a device on the infant's forehead, and an auditory signal is produced when the ultrasound echoes come back to the "sonic guide" receiver/amplifier. The auditory signal from the sonic guide, like all auditory signals, varies in volume, pitch, and purity. The trick in making the sonic guide was to tie variation in the volume, pitch, and purity dimensions to information about the object at which the ultrasound signal was aimed. Through clever engineering, the information to which volume, pitch, and purity are tied are object distance, size, and texture. Farther objects produce lower-pitched sounds, bigger objects produce louder sounds, and harder, smoother objects produce purer sounds (see Figure 7-23). With this device, Bower has provided his blind infant subjects with some novel auditory information that corresponds to object properties in the spatial world. What is absolutely stunning is not just that blind infants have been able to interpret the meaning of their new sensory information but that they have done so quite readily.

Bower's first blind subject was a 16-week-old boy. After the sonic guide was mounted on him, a silent object was moved to and from the infant's face. On the approach, the object was brought close enough to "tap him on the nose" (Bower, 1982, p. 103). After just four trials, Bower and his fellow observers noted that the boy's blind eyes converged a bit as the object came closer. After just seven trials, he was putting his hands in front of his face when the object got close. Shortly thereafter he was swiping at small toy blocks that were moved left and right in front of him.

When the first tests were completed, the boy's mother put him on her knee at arm's length and began telling him what a clever boy he was.

The infant was facing her and wearing the sonic guide. He slowly turned his head to remove her from the sound field, then slowly turned back to bring her in again. This behavior was repeated several times to the accompaniment of immense smiles from the infant. All

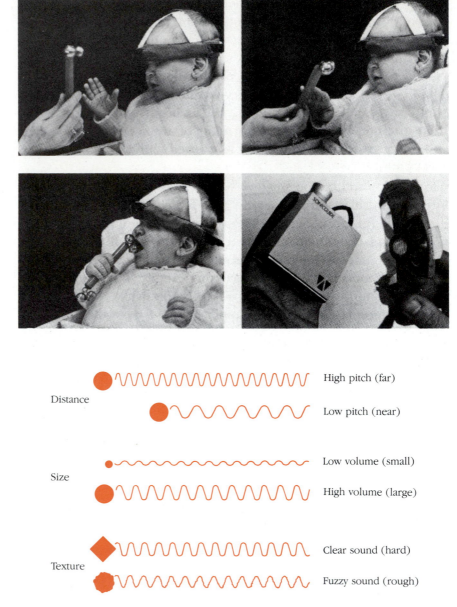

FIGURE 7-23
Using Sound to "See"
The sonic guide is a sonar device that converts ultrasound echos into information about the objects to which the ultrasound is directed. The pitch of the sonic-guide signal tells the blind "viewer" about the distance of objects that are in the ultrasound path; the volume indicates object size; and the purity of the tone is a cue to texture.

three observers had the impression that he was playing a kind of peekaboo with his mother, and deriving immense pleasure from it. (Bower, 1982, p. 103)

According to Bower, then, understanding the meaning of the novel auditory signal was no problem for this young boy. Soon after he first experienced the object-related changes in volume, pitch, and purity of an auditory signal, he knew that they contained spatial information.

Whether we can have complete confidence in Bower's conclusions has been questioned by the inventor of the sonar device, Leslie Kay (1984). His doubt primarily concerns the immediacy of this learning. Nonetheless, Kay does not doubt that such learning is possible, at least after extended use of the device. He notes, for example, that blind adults have learned to move about in their world more easily once they have learned to use the device.

Bower has now tried the sonic-guide device on a number of congenitally blind infants (Aitken & Bower, 1982). One theoretical claim to emerge from this not-so-large data set is that age is an important variable in determining the ease with which the sonic-guide cues are converted to interpretable information. Bower states that the fastest learners are infants 4 to 6 months of age. This would imply that there may be a sensitive period associated with the development of the ability to extract spatial information from species-atypical cues (and perhaps from species-typical cues as well). It may be true then, as Bower has suggested, that young infants are ready by age 4 or 5 months to interpret any neural auditory or visual signal as having spatial meaning. It would not matter, then, the particular mode (auditory or visual) in which it was experienced.

With Bower's bold start, future research on the capacities of developing animals to learn to use atypical perceptual cues is guaranteed to be exciting. Even with Bower's findings alone, however, there is much to titillate developmentalists. Bower's results imply that the ability to "see" from sound—which is a typical developmental outcome in bats—is also among the potential human developments. If so, it is further evidence for the amazing plasticity provided to humans by their capacity to learn.

SUMMARY

We have obviously come a long way in our knowledge of perceptual development since the 1700s, when empiricist philosophers first began speculating about the role of experience in perceptual development. Our progress has been marked not only by what we have learned but by the questions we ask. No longer do we ask the naive nativist–empiricist question with which we first began. Perceptual development, like all other aspects of development, is an epigenetic process that is neither totally preformed nor totally acquired. Now we simply ask what the species-typical developmental course is and what variables affect this developmental course. We also seek to know what the full range of potential development is.

When the nativist–empiricist debate was still raging, the best way to answer the questions that most interested investigators seemed to be to interrogate adults who had just had their sight restored through cataract surgery. It turned out, however, that the perceptual development of cataract victims is abnormal. Science then turned to infants. Methodological advances such as visual-preference methods, the habituation method, and the high-amplitude sucking method made "interrogation" of very young infants possible. In the last 25 years, therefore, we have made great progress in learning about the normal course of perceptual development.

As regards the development of sensation per se, infants are now known to have all their senses intact and functioning from birth. With regard to the two most-studied senses—vision and audition—audition is the better developed at birth. Visual development is slower and must wait on neurological development of the brain. This process occurs rapidly so that by about 6 months of age infant acuity and contrast sensitivity are approaching adultlike levels. Also, between 4 and 6 months of age, binocular convergence and the development of binocularly driven cells in the visual cortex provide the binocular parallax and disparity information needed for stereopsis. There is every reason to believe that infants see in color from birth, though here, too, there may be some improvements over the first 6 months.

Neonates give some limited evidence of being born with some perceptual knowledge. For example, some of their responses to tastes and smells seem knowledgeable. Also they turn their heads to sounds. A great deal of fundamental visual knowledge is absent at birth, however, and does not fully develop until around 6 months. This includes the ability to use dynamic, binocular, and pictorial information to judge depth and to maintain shape and size constancy. It also includes the ability to judge people's emotions from their facial expressions. Another perceptual ability not fully present until around 6 months is the ability to respond appropriately to precedence in auditory information. By 2 to 3 months of age, which is the earliest some tests can be conducted, infants make the same categorical distinctions among speech sounds and colors as adults do. Also, they have begun to make a number of intersensory associations.

Relatively little is known at present about the variables that affect these developments. Neurological development—particularly in the case of binocular vision and the auditory precedence effect—is surely important. But experience will also be important for some developments. Even though it may not be completely necessary, self-controlled movement, for example, plays a role in the development of species-typical visual knowledge in both humans and cats. The experiences (prenatal or postnatal) that are important for the development of other aspects of our perceptual knowledge are unknown. We are also still poorly informed about the range of potential developmental outcomes. Would it be within our developmental capacity, for example, to learn that a diminishing auditory signal was to be interpreted as an approaching object or that a sweet taste should produce disgust? Is our perceptual learning ability in fact this plastic? Such questions remain to be answered.

SUGGESTIONS FOR FURTHER READING

Bower, T. G. R. (1982). *Development in infancy* (2nd ed.). San Francisco: W. H. Freeman. Written as an introductory text, this intellectually stimulating work gives extensive coverage to Bower's clever but controversial research on the development of infant perception.

Goldstein, E. B. (1984). *Sensation and perception* (2nd ed.). Belmont, CA: Wadsworth. Because the study of perception involves some technical matters, some students may want to refer to a general text on sensation and perception rather than to one that deals just with developmental issues and data. Goldstein's book is the best for this purpose.

Hochberg, J. E. (1962). *Nativism and empiricism in perception*. In L. Postman (Ed.), *Psychology in the making: Histories of selected research problems*. New York: Alfred A. Knopf. An interesting and thorough history that explains how the nativist-empiricist question served to shape the initial research conducted on perceptual development.

Siegler, R. S. (1986). *Children's thinking*. Englewood Cliffs, NJ: Prentice-Hall. This text on children's thinking is relevant not just to the present chapter on perceptual development but to the subsequent chapters on cognitive development as well.

Walk, R. D. (1981). *Perceptual development*. Monterey, CA: Brooks/Cole. This text serves as a valuable primer for the introductory student.

CHAPTER OUTLINE

CHAPTER 8

Cognitive Development: The Piagetian View

Though it is clear by now that there is a lot of knowledge in perception, perceiving is not what most people think of when considering acts of cognition. Thought, reason, and problem solving are more likely to come to mind. Swiss psychologist Jean Piaget (1896–1980) made a monumental contribution to developmental psychology by providing a descriptive and theoretical account of developments in these areas of cognition. His account, which was developed in conjunction with other Swiss psychologists such as Bärbel Inhelder, portrays the universals of cognitive development and gives a complete, total view of the emergence of the human intellect from the earliest days of infancy until late in adolescence.

Today it is impossible to ignore that there are some chinks in a few of Piaget's descriptive generalizations and some flaws in his theoretical work. Nonetheless, the Piagetian view continues to dominate in the field of cognitive development. Each year, many research articles in the major developmental journals are addressed directly or indirectly to issues raised by Piaget's research and theory, and countless more articles cite his name. There is even a professional society dedicated to Piagetian research—the Jean Piaget Society. In brief, Piaget's dominance over the field that is the topic of this chapter makes it clear why one must begin a study of cognitive development with his work. As Rochel Gelman, a well-known critic of Piaget, has said, "He picked the right problems to work on. So he's going to live forever. We who are called anti-Piagetian today are really neo-Piagetian.

Jean Piaget

We're only trying to articulate better . . . the way the mind develops" (in Hunt, 1982, p. 211–12).

The plan for the chapter is to begin with the facts of development, as interpreted by Piaget. This presentation will be divided into four major sections that correspond to the four major periods of development identified by Piaget: the *sensorimotor period* (birth to age 2 approximately), the *preoperational period* (ages 2 to 7), the *concrete-operational period* (ages 7 to 11/12), and the *formal-operational period* (ages 11/12 and beyond). Collectively, the observations in these sections will give us an integrated view of how children change in their ability to think and reason during development. Although Piaget's observations of development within these periods have proven to be remarkably reliable, we will see that some of his interpretations require qualification. The most important of the qualifications will be handled in a Critique and Evaluation section appended to each of the four period sections. At the end of the chapter, following the presentation of the basic facts of development as interpreted by Piaget—and reinterpreted by some of his critics—the essentials of Piaget's theory will be presented. As we will see, this theory is troubled at present by facts that tend to invalidate some of its key assumptions.

FORMAL-OPERATIONAL THOUGHT: THE END POINT OF DEVELOPMENT

To understand the four periods of cognitive development portrayed by Piaget, it is best to begin our study with a brief description of the last of Piaget's periods—the **formal-operational period.** Although adolescents who can think in terms of what Piaget called formal operations can do many things that younger children cannot (they can theorize, find analogies, generalize, compare proportions and probabilities, and plan experiments), the chief characteristic distinguishing this last period from the ones that precede it is that formal thought involves an act of imagination known as pure conception.

To know what is meant by pure conception you might refer to some of the concepts you have developed in science and mathematics courses. Take, for example, your conceptualizations of phenomena such as black holes, objects that travel at the speed of light, frictionless space, and infinite divisions of an interval. These are not phenomena that you have experienced directly. To know them and to be able to reason about them you must be able to create them in your mind alone. This is what is meant by pure conception. When we are thinking using the formal-operational structures envisioned by Piaget, such conceptions are both the objects and the products of our thought.

Although it is a mistake to equate Piaget's use of the term formal thought with the thought required in science and mathematics, you can begin to get an understanding of the term by considering examples from these disciplines. A particularly good example comes from the biologist J. B. S. Haldane (1928) who described a highly formal act of thought he used to develop an understanding of a very other-worldly form of geometry. The geometry is that of German mathematician Georg Friedrich Riemann. The description involves Haldane "imagining himself into an elliptical space" and from there gaining an intuitive understanding of propositions in Riemann's geometry, one of which is that parallel lines meet. This required the highly nonconcrete experience of looking up from inside this space and seeing the bottom of his own boots. The full quote is as follows:

> I remember convincing myself of the arbitrary character of Euclid's parallel postulate by imagining myself into a . . . elliptical space, in which all coplanar lines meet once. I was standing on a transparent plane. I could see it as I looked down. If I looked up I saw the other side of it, and through it the soles of my boots, pointing backwards. By

looking round I could see every point on the plane, and most of them from both sides. I soon began to get intuitive proofs of many of the more elementary propositions in that rather bizarre geometry. (Haldane, 1928, p. 273)

To be classified as a formal thinker you fortunately do not need to master Riemann's geometry or any other for that matter. You need only demonstrate that you are capable of divorcing your thought from reality (while at the same time maintaining logic and consistency in your thinking). There is a quick test you can use to see if people can do this: select a chip from a collection of chips and place it in your hand without showing it to the person you are testing. Then say, "Tell me whether the following statement is true or false: the chip in my hand is either green or it is not green." A formal thinker will respond that the statement is true and perhaps be puzzled that you have asked such a silly question. Concrete thinkers, on the other hand, will surprise you by saying, "There's no way to tell until I look" (Osherson & Markman, 1975). The concrete thinkers are described as concrete because they want to appeal to concrete sensory data to test the statement. Formal thinkers on the other hand appeal only to the statement itself, which they know to be unequivocally true regardless of the color chip you hold in your hand.

An illustration of the formal–concrete distinction used by Piaget involves the use of nonsense sentences (Piaget, 1957, p. 18). An example is the sentence, "I am very glad I do not eat onions, for if I liked them I would always be eating them, and I hate eating unpleasant things." Concrete thinkers object to the sentence on other than logical grounds. They say, "Onions are not unpleasant" or, "It is wrong not to like onions." Formal thinkers object on the purely formal grounds that it is a contradiction to say that onions are unpleasant when operating under the hypothesis "if I liked them."

Now that you have a beginning understanding of what is meant by Piaget's term formal-operational thought, you can probably recognize the developmental importance of it. Prior to achieving formal-operational thought we are restricted to thinking about reality and *what is;* with formal thought, we can consider possibility and *what if.* This puts formal thought at the pinnacle of human intellectual achievement. Without it, human culture might not be far removed from that of chimpanzees; with it, however, we are free to create wholly new worlds in our imaginations, worlds that, once conceived, can be realized through our actions.

THE LONG ROAD TO FORMAL THOUGHT

The long road to formal thought is in part a vertical road that takes one up ever higher through an ascending series of improvements in the ability to think and to conceptualize. It is also, however, a horizontal road, or at least a road with an important horizontal dimension. This means that intelligence not only moves up, it spreads out. No area of the child's life goes untouched. Thus, when a child makes discoveries about causality, it affects the child's understanding of causality not just in one domain but in all domains. Social causation is understood differently, physical causation is understood differently, and children can begin to use words like because and expressions like "in order to" with meaning. In each of the "period sections" to follow, we will note not just the heights to which intelligence has risen but some of the breadth to which it is applied. A full appreciation of the breadth, however, will not be attained until we have completed a study of language development in Chapter 11 and social cognition in Chapter 14.

The Sensorimotor Period: The Origins of Formal Thought in the Actions of Infancy

The story of the development of formal thought is a long one that begins not even with concrete thought but well before that, in the first days of human life when there is no thought, just action. In this period, which extends from birth to the end of infancy (between 18 and 24 months), humans do not "figure things out" at the purely mental level; they work them out in actions, and—if Piaget is correct—for the first 6 months of this period, they work them out totally in the here and now, without the aid of mental images for either restoring the past or anticipating the future. Piaget called this period of life the sensorimotor period.

The **sensorimotor period** takes its name from Piaget's belief that in this period of development, one can only "know" and act on the world through sensory (vision, touch, smell, and hearing) and motor (reaching, grasping, tracking, and pulling) behavior. For example, an object passes from left to right across a 2-month-old's field of vision. The child's eyes orient to, focus on, and then track the object. For this brief period of time, the object has a psychological existence, but once it is no longer a part of the child's ongoing sensory and motor experience, the object loses its psychological existence. In the course of sensorimotor development, thought independent of action (for example, mentally foreseeing and recalling actions in the absence of the action and considering objects that are not now present) will gradually emerge. The ability to think and conceive independent of action marks the height to which intelligence rises in the first 2 years of life. The breadth of this achievement is marked by parallel developments occurring in several domains (Piaget, 1936/1963). The first regards an infant's behavior toward objects that have disappeared; the second, an infant's behavior in solving sensorimotor problems such as how to insert a section of chain into a matchbox or how to get a stick through the bars on one's crib; the third, an infant's behavior that is an imitation of the behavior of a model. These three areas—*object knowledge, means–end behavior, and imitation*—all provide evidence that thought first emerges as a useful tool for guiding behavior around 18 months of age.

Object Knowledge

For approximately the first half of the first year, infants behave in a very surprising way toward objects that disappear—they seem to forget all about

FIGURE 8-1
Reactions to Hidden Objects
The test shown here for object knowledge is appropriate for infants under 6 months of age. The experimenter first gains the infant's attention using an attractive object. Then a screen is slowly moved in front of the object. Eye movements and emotional responses are observed for any indication that the infant's interest in the object lasts beyond the time that it is actually visible. Four-month-old Adam, shown here, looks away from the attractive toy as soon as it is occluded and shows no signs of upset or arousal. This observation is consistent with Piaget's belief that "out of sight is out of mind" for infants of this age. (Photographs by S. L. O'Dell.)

them. For example, if you take an object out of an infant's hand or mouth at this early age, there will be no crying or protest. Piaget would claim that infants of this age are not just being agreeable; instead, they very literally do not know what they are missing. This proposition can be tested by hiding objects from children and observing their reactions.

Piaget used a long series of hiding tasks in order to assess infants' understanding of objects. The general procedure for all of the tasks was to interest infants in some toylike object before placing it out of sight, usually under or behind something such as a small piece of cloth or cardboard. Today, those who replicate Piaget's work generally seat infants in their mothers' lap at the edge of a table where objects can be displayed before hiding (see Figure 8-1). Three hiding tasks used by Piaget have become of particular interest: a *simple hiding task,* an *AAB hiding task,* and an *invisible-displacement task* (see Figure 8-2). Infants can start being tested on these tasks beginning around 4 months of age, the age at which children first begin to reach out for objects that are in sight.

Using the three tasks illustrated in Figure 8-2, a steady progression can be observed in infants' ability to retrieve the hidden object. Data from a normative study by Jennifer Wishart and T. G. R. Bower (1984), which used

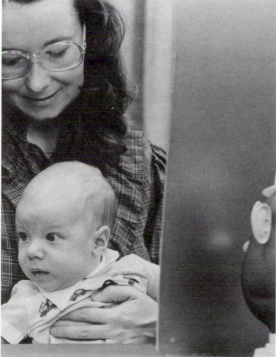

the tasks of Figure 8-2, show this clearly. Measuring success by the ability to retrieve the hidden object within 2 minutes after it was hidden, Wishart and Bower found that Task-1 success preceded Task-2 success developmentally, and Task-2 success preceded Task-3. What are we to make of this age-related growth in success?

According to Piaget infants who fail at simple hiding tasks such as Task 1 do so because their only way of representing objects to themselves is with sensorimotor actions. This means that when an object is not part of ongoing actions—looking, mouthing, manipulating, and so forth—it does not exist for the infant. Covering an object, therefore, which is all that one does on simple hiding tasks, is sufficient to remove the object from an infant's con-

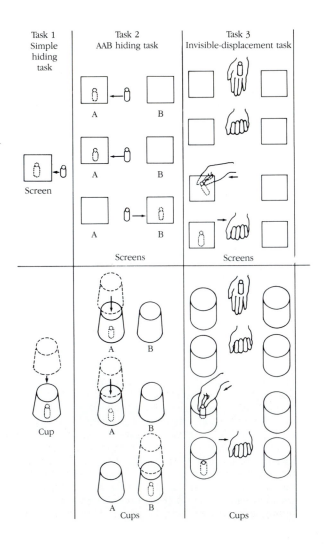

sciousness. This occurs even when infants are already reaching out to the object when it is covered. They cease reaching immediately and look away. You might think that infants behave this way when objects are hidden only because they believe themselves to be helpless to remove the cover. This is not the case, however. When objects are covered with clear rather than opaque coverings, children continue to show an interest in them, and they remove the cover to get the still-visible object (Bower, 1974; Gratch, 1972). The only reason they stop reaching on the standard hiding task, therefore, is that in their mind's eye, there is nothing to reach for (except an uninteresting cup or cloth). The original object no longer exists for them once it is out of sight. In Piaget's words, "out of sight is out of mind" for infants in

Developmental data for Tasks 1, 2, and 3

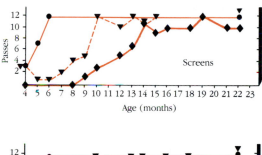

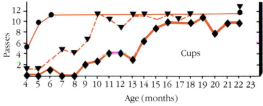

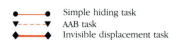

FIGURE 8-2

Tests of Object Permanence

The three tasks shown at left are tasks designed to test an infant's understanding that objects have a permanent existence independent of the infant's actions on them. The first is a simple hiding task. While the infant is seated in mother's lap (see Figure 8-1), an object that the infant is looking at and perhaps reaching for is occluded by either a cup or a screen. The second is an AAB task. After being allowed to find the object twice at location A, the child sees the object hidden at location B. The third task is an invisible-displacement task. Before the object is hidden in either the A or B location, the experimenter closes his or her hand over the object, so that the child must follow the object to its hiding place not with the eyes but with the mind. The graphs above show how performance on the three hiding tasks changes with age. (After Wishart & Bower, 1984)

BOX 8-1

Piaget's Descriptions of Developments in Object Knowledge, Means–End Behavior, and Imitation During the Six Stages of the Sensorimotor Period

Stage 1 (0-1 month*)

Object Knowledge: Infants have no knowledge that objects exist independent of themselves.

Means–End Behavior: Behaviors are ends in themselves, and they are not preceded by any intentions. Thus, it is impossible to speak of neonates' behaviors as having a goal.

Imitation: Some of the neonates' behaviors may look like imitations but they are not. At best, they are pseudoimitations such as crying when someone else cries.

Stage 2 (1-4 months)

Object Knowledge: Infants track objects when they move, but they show no ability to anticipate their movements. When objects disappear, infants will continue to look at the place where they disappear, but they do not search. Out of sight is out of mind.

Means–End Behavior: Behaviors still are not goal oriented, and their effects are not intentional; however, when a behavior produces interesting and enjoyable results, the infant is able to reinstate the behavior. This leads to the appearance of *primary circular reactions.* The goal of a primary circular reaction is not specific except insofar as it is intended to make an interesting spectacle last.

Imitation: A model who imitates an infant's own actions can trigger continued activity in the infant. Though this makes it appear that the infant is imitating the model, the imitations are really pseudoimitations.

Stage 3 (4-8 months)

Object Knowledge: Infants will search for objects that are only partially hidden but not for objects that are completely hidden.

Means–End Behavior: Circular reactions become secondary, because they expand to include objects outside the self (such as pulling on things, pushing, and hitting). Toward the end of Stage 3, there is a clear indication that infants foresee the effects their behaviors will have when repeated. Thus, for the first time there is a specific goal in mind when a behavior is begun.

this early stage of object knowledge, which lasts at least for the first 4 to 6 months. (Piaget himself extended the out-of-sight-out-of-mind period to 8 months, but Wishart and Bower's normative data show somewhat earlier development.)

In the second half of the first year, during what Piaget called Stage 4 of the 6-staged sensorimotor period, infants begin to search for objects that have disappeared (see Box 8-1 for a description of the behaviors associated with all 6 stages). They do so as long as the object is part of an ongoing

Imitation: Infants begin to imitate successfully but only when they can see their own movements (for example, they can imitate hand movements).

Stage 4 (8–12 months)

Object Knowledge: Infants find completely hidden objects on simple hiding tasks but make the AAB and invisible-displacement errors.

Means–End Behavior: Infants initiate behavior with a goal in mind, and for the first time they can employ a detour behavior to reach their goal.

Imitation: Successful imitations expand to include unseen body parts (such as the face), but only familiar behaviors are imitated. Infants will make an effort to reproduce new behaviors (for example, hitting two blocks together after seeing an adult perform this action), but they generally fail.

Stage 5 (12–18 months)

Object Knowledge: Infants no longer make the AAB error but persist in making the invisible-displacement error.

Means–End Behavior: Infants are no longer interested in achieving goals per se. They show an interest in experimenting with novel means of achieving goals.

Imitation: New, never-before seen movements can now be imitated regardless of what body parts are involved.

Stage 6 (18–24 months)

Object Knowledge: Objects can be located on hiding tasks even when their disappearance involves an invisible displacement.

Means–End Behavior: Previously, the means of attaining behavioral goals were discovered only through trial and error. Now, they can be discovered through insight.

Imitation: Previously, successful imitations were limited to imitations of a model that was present. Now the imitations can be deferred to some time when the model is no longer present.

*The ages given for each of the stages are Piaget's. The consensus today is that these are not good estimates of the actual norms for infants.

action when it disappears. If they are shaking a toy, for example, and drop it, they will reach around for it; if they are following it with their eyes when it goes behind a screen, they will look for it; and if they are reaching for it when it is covered, they will continue reaching. Even if they are forced to delay for a few seconds before being allowed to reach, Stage-4 infants can still solve hidden-object problems like the Task-1 problem from the Wishart and Bower study. But when objects are not part of ongoing activities, they are not searched for and presumably not thought of.

One might infer that Stage-4 infants' ability to find out-of-sight objects that have just disappeared signals the emergence of a new ability that enables them to picture objects in the mind's eye, at least for a while. This may be the case, but we must not think that this mental knowledge of objects is in any way equivalent to an adult's. There are serious limitations. The limitations of the Stage-4 mental knowledge become quite evident on AAB tasks and on invisible-displacement tasks. Because there are problems with Piaget's interpretation of the AAB task performance, however, we will move straight to the invisible-displacement task performance to see what these limitations are. (The AAB performance will be discussed in the Critique and Evaluation section.)

The only difference between the simple hiding task (Task 1) and the invisible-displacement task (Task 3) is that in Task 1 infants see the object disappear under the cup, whereas in Task 3 it disappears first in the hand. One would hardly think that such a small change in the hiding procedure would make any difference at all, but as we have already seen in the developmental data of Figure 8-2, infants who perform impeccably on Wishart and Bower's Task 1 fail miserably on Task 3. The general tendency is for infants to search in the experimenter's hand for the toy and, on not finding the toy there, to begin searching randomly. Wishart and Bower's observation was that infants' random searches included such acts as "looking under the table or glancing appealingly to the Experimenter for help" (1984, p. 72). This behavior makes it clear that infants who solve simple hiding tasks may be able to conceive of objects in their absence, but they are still not able to manipulate them in thought. They cannot even perform so simple a mental manipulation as mentally tracking an invisible object from one location to another. For this reason, the very small change in procedure from a simple hiding task to an invisible-hiding task makes a huge difference in performance. The former task requires tracking objects with the eyes; the latter requires tracking them with the mind. Infants are well into their second year before they can do this.

Means–End Behavior

The mental capacity that enables infants to begin representing objects starting in Stage 4 of the sensorimotor period is reflected in behaviors other than object searches. It is reflected also in the emergence of the ability to keep a goal in mind while intermediary actions instrumental to reaching the goal are undertaken. We will begin with a very simple example of this which comes from observations Piaget made on Laurent, one of his three children (Piaget, 1936/1963, pp. 217-18). Laurent's goal in this particular observation was a simple one of reaching out and grasping an attractive toy. Piaget kept blocking his path to the object by putting his hand or a cushion in the way. What Piaget found interesting was that when these observations began at 6 months of age, Laurent's response was never to attack the obstacle. He tried instead to go straight to his goal, even though this approach was unsuccessful. By the time Laurent was 7½ months of age, his behavior had changed. Instead of going straight at the object, Laurent would first remove Piaget's hand or mash down the cushion. Many a parent has probably made observations similar to this. Piaget's genius shows in the enlightening explanation he placed on this simple developmental advance.

In Piaget's view, the reason Laurent did not attack the meddlesome barrier at first was that, had he done so, he would have lost track of what it was he was trying to do. Remember that in the early days of the sensorimotor period thought is action. If Laurent found himself acting on the barrier, this would be all that he was thinking of. The goal would have been lost. But with the emergence of the ability to represent objects mentally, Laurent had the wherewithal to keep his goal in mind while engaging in a behavior to unblock the goal (called *detour behavior*). This explanation not only fits the simple observation of Laurent's behavior, it is consistent, too, with the emergence of success on simple hiding tasks, which require infants to keep an object in mind while searching for it. It is also consistent with the fact that all infants at about this same age (8 to 12 months) begin to engage in activities that are clearly subordinate to the achievement of goals. For example, they will use strings and sticks to retrieve out-of-reach objects (Gesell & Amatruda, 1947), and they will do things to get adults to entertain them (like giving Daddy a whistle they want him to blow). This is means–end, problem-solving behavior. The infants have no interest in sticks or strings or Daddy per se; instead, they want to see the effects of these on the ends they have in mind.

Although infants become problem solvers by 1 year of age, there is a shortcoming to their problem solving at this age because their problems are solved through actions, not thought. The problem solving is best described as *trial and error,* and it typifies problem-solving activity from the time it first emerges in Stage 4 of the sensorimotor period until the end of Stage 5 (around 16 months of age.) Not until the last half of the second year is there clear evidence of thought preceding actions. This is an important advance, because it enables infants to anticipate or foresee the effect of their planned actions and to find the means for solving problems quickly through *insight* rather than laboriously—and sometimes dangerously—through trial and error.

Two of Piaget's own observations can be used to illustrate the kind of insightful discovery of means that appears near the end of infancy. In one, Jacqueline (Piaget's first daughter) was carrying a blade of grass in each hand but had to put one down in order to open a door (Piaget 1936/1963, p. 339). She did so, but as she went to open the door, she realized that the grass she had put down would be in the way of the opening door. Therefore, she moved the grass out of the way and then opened the door. What is so interesting about this? you may wonder. The interest lies in the fact that at an earlier stage of development Jacqueline would have come to her realization only after opening the door and actually seeing it run over the blade of grass. But at 20 months of age, which was her age when this observation was made, she was able to foresee what would happen. She did not need to play out the action in real time and real space. She could solve her simple problem in her head. Her sister Lucienne was observed doing something similar at 16 months of age (Piaget, 1936/1963, p. 336). Lucienne's problem was how to get a length of chain into a matchbox. Piaget was holding the matchbox in the air in front of her, and Lucienne was shoving segments of chain into the box. No sooner, however, would she get one segment in than the weight of the chain still outside the box would cause the whole thing to fall out again. After failing on three attempts to fit the chain into the box in this trial-and-error way, she paused, placed the chain on a flat surface, rolled it into a ball, grasped the ball of chain, and placed the whole thing safely inside the box. You can imagine Piaget's excitement on seeing this. Lucienne, like Jacqueline before her, had advanced to a stage of mental development where she could not only carry out simple actions in her head but she could compare the effects of these actions to a goal she had in mind to see whether they would be successful. When capacities such as this have emerged, infants are clearly on the road to formal operations.

Imitation

The final area of achievement in the sensorimotor period is imitation, a process whereby novel behaviors may be acquired without the need for either trial and error or insightful discovery. One just needs to observe and do. But as we saw in the last chapter on perceptual development, observing involves one sensory system (for example, vision or audition) whereas doing involves some other system. We have an immediate problem, then, in how to get the information from the observing modality into the performing modality, and, in particular, we have a problem if the information must be stored over time as is the case when we perform *deferred imitations*.

According to Piaget, imitation proper, as opposed to just pseudoimitation (for example, crying because others are crying or repeating one's own actions), does not emerge until Stage 4 of the sensorimotor period. This is one of the reasons that claims of neonatal facial imitation (see Figure 7-22) have created such a clamor. Facial imitations are true imitations in the sense that the act of another suggests an act to the child, and the child's goal in executing the act is to match what he or she has seen. Most observers agree, however, that if there is any validity to the claim that neonates do imitate facial expressions, this imitative capacity is quite isolated, reflecting a specific imitative capacity rather than a general one. Most agree with Piaget that infants do not begin to imitate actions of others—facial or otherwise—until the latter part of the first year. At the same time, therefore, that infants begin to pursue goals and to retrieve hidden objects on simple hiding tasks, they also begin to imitate.

The initial imitations of infants often seem to be laboriously constructed, somewhat like their solutions to simple sensorimotor problems. Piaget, for example, gave daughter Jacqueline the task of imitating a simple finger movement at 9 months of age (Piaget, 1946/1962, pp. 46–47), and it was two weeks later that she finally perfected the movement. She would watch his finger moving and then represent his movements with her own, but the perfect match for which she was striving was slow to develop. Kenneth Kaye and Janet Marcus (1981) made similar observations of children who were still in their first year. The imitative motor acts of infants at this age gradually converged on their targets; they did not hit them immediately.

Although infants start to engage in goal-directed imitations toward the end of their first year, the goals they are pursuing are immediately present. That is, the model they are attempting to imitate is present, not absent. The end point in the development of infant imitative capacities will not be reached until infants demonstrate deferred imitation. Only this type of imitation requires a mental act to bridge the time between observation of the model and one's own imitation of the model. Piaget believed that the onset of this capacity occurs around 18 months, roughly the same age at which infants first begin to follow invisible displacements and solve sensorimotor problems through insight. Piaget's best known illustration of deferred imitation is his observation of his daugher Jacqueline who threw a play temper tantrum in clear imitation of a neighbor's real temper tantrum (Piaget, 1946/1962, p. 124). The neighbor had thrown his tantrum on the day before and was not present at the time that Jacqueline chose to imitate him.

One way to conceptualize the achievement marked by deferred imitation is to see it as a manifestation of the ability to observe a sensorimotor act that is performed by someone else in some other context and, then, to preserve that act in a context-free, person-free representation in one's own head. An example that illustrates this aspect of deferred imitations better than the tantrum example is Piaget's observation of Lucienne's behavior just after he had played an imitative game with her in which he got Lucienne to point to her own nose. Lucienne immediately went to get her doll and pointed to its nose. A comparable observation involves children who attempt to diaper their dolls. Such observations clearly suggest that actions are no longer just actions that occur in a fixed space and time. Instead, actions have a mental representation that frees them both spatially and temporally, allowing the child to recall actions, foresee actions, and generalize actions (for example, pointing to the doll's nose and diapering the doll, which were generalized from pointing to one's own nose and being diapered). The usefulness of this aspect of intelligence is not restricted to infancy. We use it the rest of our lives. Athletes and dancers use this ability to mentally correct deficiencies in their performance by comparing their own behavior to that of models, perhaps mental ones. The rest of us use it when performing activities as varied as building a birdhouse, repairing a flat tire, or planting the spring garden.

Critique and Evaluation

What is absolutely amazing about Piaget's descriptive account of infant development is that it has needed so little alteration. Piaget made most of the observations on which his account is based about 60 years ago, and he only had three subjects—his own children! Nonetheless, his account is still the definitive one, at least as regards the developments featured here (object knowledge, means–end behavior, and imitation). There are just two amendments that present-day researchers point to. One is general, the other is specific. The general amendment is that Piaget underestimated the competence of infants. The consensus among infant researchers today, for example, is that infants develop more rapidly along the Piagetian path than Piaget gave them credit for. Andrew Meltzoff (1985), the psychologist responsible for the claim that even neonates can imitate, now claims, for example, that 14-month-olds (and perhaps infants even younger) are capable of deferred imitation. Noted developmental scholar John Flavell believes that some (but not all) of the basic object knowledge that Piaget credited 18-month-olds with may in fact be available as early as 9 months. These general reservations notwithstanding, reviewers still concede that "Piaget's six stages of . . . sensory-motor development provide a fairly good, overall picture of how the human mind changes from birth to age 2 or so" (Flavell, 1985, pp. 44–45).

The one specific amendment has been with regard to Piaget's explanation for failures on the AAB task (see Figure 8-2). A failure on the AAB task occurs when infants find the object at location A when it is hidden there on the first two trials but then fail to find it at location B when it is hidden there on Trial 3. Instead of going to B, the correct hiding place, Stage-4 infants go back to A. Piaget ruled out a simple memory hypothesis as an explanation for this result (Piaget, 1936/1954, pp. 64-66). He claimed that infants made the AAB error because they believed that the existence of objects still depended on their actions toward them. Therefore, in the mind of a Stage-4 infant, acting on the object at A—its usual place—should be sufficient to make the object reappear. This interpretation of the AAB error (also called the "place error" and the "A not B error") seems to be incorrect. The major problem with it is that the usual hiding place does not have a great hold over infants. Errors at the usual hiding place are prominent only when there are just two places to choose from. Expand the number to five and errors are not made at the usual place; they are made at places adjacent to the correct place. For example, if there are five left-to-right positions labeled A, B, C, D, and E, moving an object to E that has been hidden at A will produce reaching errors to C and D but not A (Cummings & Bjork, 1981, 1983). Findings such as this make it appear likely that infants who make the AAB error are really trying to find the object at its present location and that they fail only because they have incredibly poor abilities to remember spatial information (even for just a 3-second delay). This is contrary to Piaget's explanation that Stage-4 infants have no idea where the object is presently located and that their purpose in reaching to A is to magically reproduce the object by reproducing a previously successful action. In all probability, however, the final word on the AAB error is yet to be written. You will recall, for example, that this error was discussed in Chapter 6 along with the line-of-sight error as evidence of immaturity in the frontal lobe of the brain (see Diamond & Goldman-Rakic, 1985). Therefore, AAB errors may signal more than just a poor memory for objects and their locations.

The Preoperational Period

By the end of infancy children are well on their way to formal thought in that they have taken the giant step from being just "actors" to being "thinkers." This has been made possible by the development of what Piaget called the *semiotic* or *symbolic function,* which is a label for the ability to represent reality to oneself or others using private symbols (such as mental images) or public ones (such as words). The emergence of this function accounts not only for deferred imitation, insightful problem solving, and success at following invisible displacements, but also for the rapid growth of language in the period 18 months to 2 years (see Chapter 11) and the sudden appearance of *make-believe play* in which children let one thing (a shell) stand for or represent something else (a hat, a cup, or a boat in the water). Exercise of the symbolic function dominates in the intellectual life of children aged 2 to 4.

The representational ability of 2-year-olds, which according to Piaget is a direct outgrowth of their sensorimotor development, is an ability of great breadth. With it children create images of objects and actions that they have experienced, and then they use these images in useful and valuable ways to locate objects, solve problems, and acquire new behaviors. Before long they begin to mix images of objects and actions in ways they have never in fact experienced. For example, they may imagine such events as a cow riding a bicycle, a thought that will strike them as very funny, or a shoe being used as a hammer, a thought that may strike them as very useful. Such common use of the imagination as this is a monumental achievement, and it could have become the focus for studies of cognitive development in the preschool period. In fact, however, until just recently (see Gelman,

Make-believe play requires symbolic thought.

1978), studies of the deficiencies and shortcomings of preschool thought far outnumbered studies of the positive factors that mark advances. Piaget was responsible for this.

For Piaget, preschool thought was identified solely by what it was not. In his mind, it was not operational (or logical), and thus he called it **preoperational.** Such thought has three primary characteristics. First, it is unstable and easily distracted by irrelevant aspects of a problem, a characteristic that merits it the label *intuitive*. Second, it is *egocentric* in the sense that the symbolic representations that preoperational children use when thinking are restricted to their own personal view. Third, preoperational thought is *centered,* which means that only one aspect of a problem is considered at a time. All of these characteristics can be viewed as deficiencies in the thought of children who otherwise are to be lauded in the fact that they are using their minds in creative and useful ways.

Intuitive Thought

If we present adults with the arrangement of lines below and ask whether line segment *A* or *B* is the longer, all will say that *A* is.

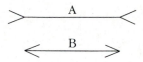

Imagine, however, that we change the procedure for presenting the problem. Rather than beginning with the fully developed illusion above, we build it up beginning with two lines that are equal in length.

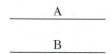

Presented side by side in this way, the equality of the lines is apparent. With this equality established at the outset, we now proceed to create the illusion of inequality by adding the line endings < > and > <.

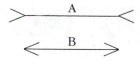

At this point, adults who have watched the illusion created would perceive the illusion, but they would be able to judge that the actual lengths of the two lines were still the same, despite appearances. Intuitive preoperational thinkers would not share in this judgment. In their view, adding the endings to the line segments might actually change the length of the lines (Cowan, 1978, p. 39). Such reasoning is intuitive because it is based purely on appearances. What seems to be the case at the moment is judged to be the case, even if this contradicts what one judged to be the case previously.

The intuitive thinker's response to the illusion presented above, the Müller–Lyer illusion, is a good one to begin with, because preschool children's responses to it represent the two essential features of intuitive thought. First, judgments are made on the basis of appearance and not logic. Second, successive judgments can be mutually contradictory (as in first saying that the lines are the same length but then saying they are different) without the child making any effort to reconcile the discrepant judgments.

The importance of appearances to the intuitive thinker can be illustrated in myriad ways, but the following is one of the more interesting. Preschool children commonly speak of the speed of moving objects and even of their relative speeds, but Piaget argued that their understanding of speed is purely perceptual, not logical. As evidence he set up arrangements, like those in Figure 8-3, in which two toy runners or cars would travel along tracks of varying lengths and shapes. His preschool-age subjects were very good at saying which one traveled faster if they could see that in the course of their travels one car or runner caught up to and passed the other. The

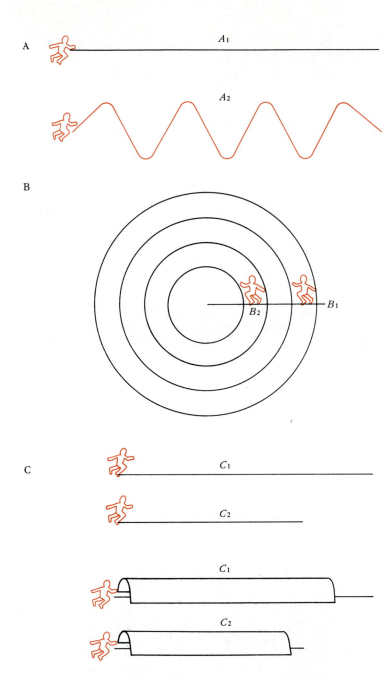

FIGURE 8-3

The Importance of Appearance in Intuitive Thought

Panel A: when two runners on the paths A_1 and A_2 move at the same speed, the runner on A_1 is judged to travel faster because he "passes" the runner on A_2, but if the runner on A_2 travels fast enough to "keep up" with the runner on A_1, both are said to travel the same speed. Panel B: when two runners B_1 and B_2 are moved 45 degrees along concentric paths, the two are judged to travel at the same speed if they start and stop together. The same judgment is made regardless of how the question is phrased (for example, "Which one had to hurry more?" or "Which one is more out of breath?"). Panel C: when the two runners are in plain view and their starting and stopping times are the same, then the runner on path C_1 (who goes farther) is correctly judged to have run faster. But when tunnels are used to hide the "passing" action, both runners—again with the same starting and stopping times—are said to travel at the same speed.

passing object was then said to have traveled faster. When Piaget took away this perception by having the toy cars or runners travel through tunnels that prohibited the child from seeing the act of passing, the children could not judge relative speed accurately. Moreover, if Piaget eliminated the perception of passing not by using a tunnel but by having one object's faster speed compensated for by a longer route, again children judged the objects to be traveling at the same speed. To quote Piaget on this subject,

> If the first object goes by a longer route without catching up to the second or goes backward or when the two follow two concentric circles, the child does not understand the inequality of speed even if there are great differences between the two routes. The intuition of speed thus reduces to the perception of objects overtaking one another and does not include an understanding of the relationship between time and distance covered. (1964/1968, pp. 31-32)

An observation by a French investigator, Françoise Frank (cited in Bruner, 1964), is pertinent to the discussion of the role of appearances in young children's judgments, because it clearly shows how appearances can overwhelm other bases children might have for making judgments. The problem that Frank gave to her subjects aged 4 to 7 was a variation of probably the most famous of Piaget's logic problems, the problem of *conservation of liquid amount*. To set up this problem, one begins with an equality—two containers of equal size that contain equal amounts of liquid. Then, just as we did for the Müller–Lyer problem above (which was in fact a problem in conservation of length), we transform the arrangement perceptually. In this case, we pour the liquid from one of the containers into a container of a different size and shape. We then ask whether the amount of liquid in this new container equals that in the original container. Frank's variation on this problem was to put a screen in front of the containers when she poured the liquid. Only the tops of the containers showed over the top of the screen, thus the children were unable to compare perceptually the relative heights of the columns of liquid in the new and old containers, but they were able to see that the new and old containers were a different size (see Figure 8-4). When children were not allowed to see the relative heights of the liquid, 50 percent of the 4-year-olds, 90 percent of the 5-year-olds, and 100 percent of the 6- and 7-year-olds said the amount of water had not changed. In contrast, when they were tested without the screen, none of the 4-year-olds, just 20 percent of the 5-year-olds, and just 50 percent of the 6- and 7-year-olds judged them to be equal. In the words of Jerome Bruner, "the perceptual display overwhelms them. . . ." (Bruner, 1964, p. 7).

The second aspect of intuitive thought, the general incoherence of successive judgments, is a quality that Piaget says "stands out in the thinking of the young child." It appears time and again when we ask children to reason in a logical way about familiar objects, actions, and their relationships. For example, if we ask the intuitive thinker to tell us, first, which objects in a collection of objects will float and, second, why they will float, we will find that the child will be satisfied with "multiple and often contradictory formulations" (Inhelder & Piaget, 1955/1958, pp. 21–22). The following is but one example. It is adapted from a data summary given by Inhelder and Piaget.

> A male, 5 years and 6 months of age is asked whether a small plank of wood will stay on top or go to the bottom when placed in a tub of water. "It goes to the bottom," reports the boy. "Why?" "Because it is heavy." The experimenter then demonstrates that it in fact stays on top. The boy is quick to explain this by saying that it stayed on top because ". . . there's too much water." When the boy tries to get the plank to stay on the bottom by pushing it there, he again finds that it comes back to the top. Why? "Because this plank is bigger . . ." A relatively small wooden ball he pushed to the bottom also came back up. Why? "Because it is smaller." When asked what would happen to a jar lid when pushed to the bottom, the child predicts "it will come back up . . . because it is smaller than this piece of wood." When the child tries it, it stays at the bottom which prompts the explanation, "It stayed down because I pushed too high up." (1955/1958, p. 26)

The mode of explanation that has been adopted by the boy in the example above is explanation by assertion rather than proof, and, as we have seen, the successive assertions do not need to fit with one another. Moreover, in keeping with the first aspect of intuitive thought, each assertion is based on some momentary perception that seems to strike the child as relevant. First it is the weight of the plank, then the amount of water, then the size of the objects (plank, ball, and lid), and then it is the manner in which he pushes the objects. Clearly the child is not at all opposed to contradicting himself.

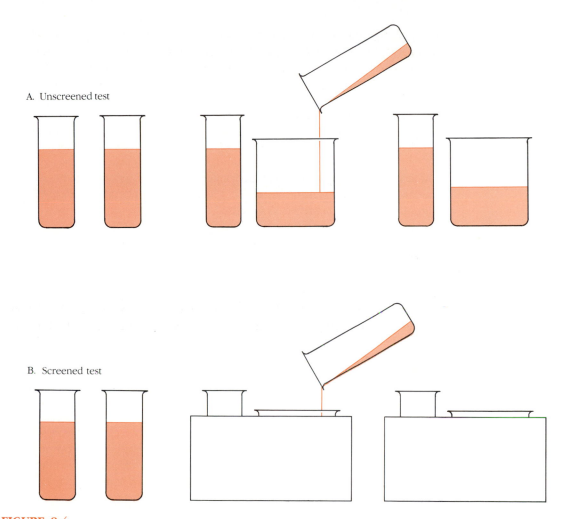

A. Unscreened test

B. Screened test

FIGURE 8-4

Frank's Conservation of Liquid Quantity Experiment

In the unscreened test for conservation of quantity (A), all of the 4-year-olds, 80 percent of the 5-year olds, and 50 percent of the 6- and 7-year-olds judged that the amount of water in the two containers was different following the transfer from the tall, thin container to the shorter, wider container. In the screened test (B), however, far fewer errors were made. This result can be explained by the different information available to children in the two test situations. When the perceptual information regarding relative heights of the liquid in the two containers is present, it overwhelms all else and becomes the intuitive basis for judgment. (After Bruner, 1966)

According to Piaget's theory, thought marked by the two features of intuitive thought—perceptual reasoning and contradictory judgments—inevitably appears in the period between sensorimotor thought and the type of thought we will discuss in the following section, concrete-operational thought. The usual ages given for this intuitive thinking are 4 to 7, with the ages for preoperational thought, in general, being 2 to 7.

Egocentric Thought

When Piaget described preoperational thought as egocentric, he did not mean that it was selfish. He chose the adjective egocentric purely for its literal meaning—centered on the self. Piaget felt the adjective was appropriate, because he found that preschool children's representations were limited to their own perspective. A quick illustration of this phenomenon is found in the interpretation of words. Many preschoolers misinterpret words like "front" and "back" or "right" and "left" because they falsely believe that these words should be defined relative to their own perspective. Seat a preschooler next to a television set, for example, and ask her to point to its front. She will probably point to the side facing her. If you stand across from her and ask her to indicate your right arm, she will point to your left because it is on her right side. In each case, she is making an egocentric interpretation.

If the negative implications of egocentric thought were limited just to the child's acquisition of certain vocabulary items, it would merit only minor consideration in the study of cognitive development. It turns out, however, that the limitations placed on cognitive ability by egocentrism are substantial. Egocentrism, for example, limits the ability to communicate effectively, because truly egocentric children fail to represent to themselves what their listeners know or need to know. Also, it limits social development, because egocentric children constantly confuse their own feelings, points of view, and thoughts with those of another, making it impossible to understand why other people might behave and feel as they do. Given the wide-ranging importance egocentrism has, it is not surprising that this aspect of preschool thought has been the subject of much research. As a result of the research, it now seems clear that egocentrism is a characteristic of preschoolers' reasoning, just as Piaget said it was. If you make the task simple enough, however, even preschoolers demonstrate an understanding that there are points of view other than their own. This means that their representations are not invariably egocentric, as we will see in the Critique and Evaluation section.

Judgments of What Another Person Sees   Tasks that require children to take the spatial perspective of another person provide one good measure of the egocentrism that is characteristic of preoperational thinkers. The most

famous example of such a task is Piaget's three-mountains problem (Piaget, Inhelder, & Szeminska, 1948/1960). The materials for the task consist of a three-dimensional set of pasteboard mountains that differ in size, color, and distinctive features (see Figure 8-5). The smallest mountain is green with a house on top; the next larger is brown with a cross on top; and the largest is grey with a snow-covered peak. In addition, there is a zigzag path down one side of the green mountain and a rivulet on one side of the brown mountain. The task is for children to be able to picture how the three mountains will appear to someone with a different spatial point of view than their own. To get children to answer questions regarding how the mountains would look to someone viewing them from a different perspective, Piaget moves a doll around the table on which the mountains are arranged and asks what the doll sees.

No matter how you have preoperational children indicate to you what the doll sees—whether by drawing it, constructing it, or selecting a picture that represents it—most of their answers will be wrong, and many of these wrong answers will be egocentric; that is, the children will indicate that the doll has the same perspective that they do. The conclusion Piaget drew from children's responses on his three-mountains task was, not surprisingly, that the type of wrong answer children give reflects their stage of cognitive development. The most primitive answer, developmentally, is the egocentric one that fails to distinguish between the child's point of view and that of the doll. Children who draw the mountains as they see them or select the picture that represents their own point of view, regardless of the doll's placement, are said to be at this level of development. Beyond this point, children come to recognize that the doll has a different view of the mountains than they do. Still, the view they draw or the picture they select will be wrong. The reason is that even though the children know that the doll's view is different, they are cognitively unable to construct the doll's point of

FIGURE 8-5

Piaget's Three-Mountain Problem

The three-mountain problem provides a good measure of the difficulty preoperational thinkers have in taking another person's spatial perspective. (After Piaget, Inhelder, & Szeminska, 1948/1960)

view through thought alone. Children move beyond this stage sometime after the age of 7. At this age, most children can accurately represent the doll's perspective.

Egocentrism in Referential Communication   Some of the very clearest evidence for egocentrism as a general characteristic of preschool thought comes from children's use of language when they try to tell others what they see, feel, or know—that is, when they engage in *referential communication*. This type of egocentrism leads to amusing episodes, like the case of a boy who held up a new toy truck while he was talking with a friend on the telephone and said "How do you like my new truck?" As you can guess, the presence of such egocentric use of language makes phone conversations a disaster when judged on the criterion of communicative effectiveness. In the defense of preschool children, we should note that accurate communication may not always be the goal when children converse. They may merely want to hold a type of conversation called a *collective monologue* (Piaget, 1923/1955) in which children take turns speaking but with each pursuing a topic of his or her own egocentric choosing. The following is one of the most delightful examples to appear in the literature:

JENNY: They wiggle sideways when they kiss.

CHRIS: (Vaguely) What?

JENNY: My bunny slippers. They are brown and red and sort of white. And they have eyes and ears and these noses that wiggle sideways when they kiss.

CHRIS: I have a piece of sugar in a red piece of paper. I'm gonna eat it but maybe it's for a horse.

JENNY: We bought them. My mommy did. We couldn't find the old ones. These are like the old ones. They were not in the trunk.

CHRIS: Can't eat the piece of sugar, not unless you take the paper off.

JENNY: And we found Mother Lamb. Oh, she was in Poughkeepsie in the trunk in the house in the woods where Mrs. Tiddywinkle lives.

CHRIS: Do you like sugar? I do, and so do horses.

JENNY: I play with my bunnies. They are real. We play in the woods. They have eyes. We all go in the woods. My teddy bear and the bunnies and the duck, to visit Mrs. Tiddywinkle. We play and play.

CHRIS: I guess I'll eat my sugar at lunch time. I can get more for the horses. Besides, I don't have no horses now. (Stone & Church, 1973)

When Piaget made a serious study of egocentrism in referential communication, he had children tell stories to other children so that he could observe egocentric errors such as the child's use of unspecified pronouns. Investigators since Piaget have developed methodologies that are even better at assessing egocentrism in referential communication. Sam Glucksberg of Princeton University, for example, had children communicate about the situation depicted in Figure 8-6. The boy in the left of this figure takes blocks in a fixed order from the block dispenser that is on his right and stacks them on the peg in front of him. Each block is marked with a unique

FIGURE 8-6
Glucksberg's Block-Stacking Task
Referential-communication tasks like this one can be used to assess children's ability to take another person's point of view. Young children frequently communicate in ways that are egocentric. (After Glucksberg, Krauss, & Weisberg, 1966)

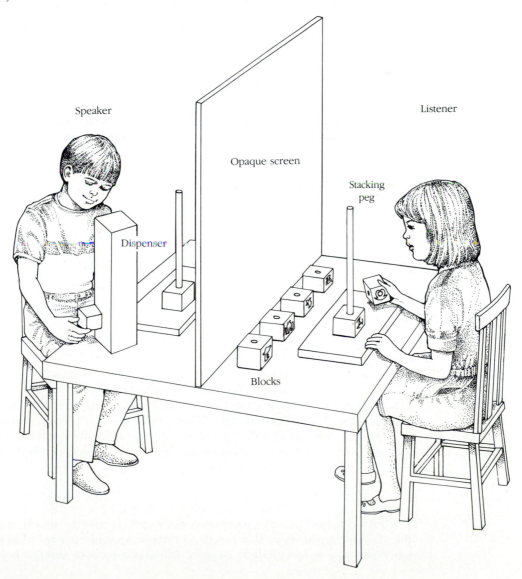

design. The designs on the girl's blocks correspond to those on the boy's. The goal in the task is for the boy and the girl to stack their blocks in the same order. To do this, the boy must successfully communicate to the girl which block is to be placed first, second, and so on. In having children of various ages perform this task, Glucksberg discovered that 4- and 5-year-olds were particularly likely to refer to the blocks in a highly idiosyncratic, egocentric way. For example, one child might tell the other, "Take the one that looks like Daddy's shirt," and then, "Now take the other one that looks like Daddy's shirt." One actual exchange went as follows:

> CHILD 1 (referring to one of the geometric figures): It's a bird.
> CHILD 2: Is this it?
> CHILD 1: No. (Glucksberg, Krauss, & Higgins, 1975, p. 321)

Glucksberg is not the only one to observe communications that are clearly egocentric. Phillip Cowan (1978), for example, used a task in which pairs of children were seated back to back in front of identical boards marked off with 16 squares (4 columns by 4 rows). The top 8 squares were all yellow and the bottom 8 were all red. Each child was given a set of 16 objects. The task for each pair of children was to agree where to place each object so that the boards would look the same when the game was finished. Reporting the results of his study, Cowan noted that

> in talking about where the object should be placed, the spatially egocentric children often gestured although their partners could not see them, or said, "Put it over there." Often they located a piece in only one spatial dimension, for instance "Put it in the bottom corner," when there were two bottom corners. (1978, pp. 219–20)

Moreover, Cowan noted—as did Glucksberg—that the egocentrism in referential communication was a two-way street in that the child receiving imprecise instructions did not question them. Rather, the second child went ahead and placed the object according to his or her own egocentric interpretation of what had been said. Such clear instances as these of egocentrism in the use of referential communication, when combined with evidence from spatial-perspective tasks, make it clear that egocentrism is a characteristic of preschool thought. Whether there is any validity, however, to the claim that preschool children are developmentally bound to their egocentrism is open to serious question, as will be pointed out in the Critique and Evaluation for this section.

Centered Thought

The final characteristic of preoperational thought in Piaget's theory is that the thought is *centered*. This serves to cripple a child's ability to reason whenever two or more factors must be taken into account simultaneously.

The reason is that the child focuses, or centers, on only one of the factors at a time. This means that arguments for a certain conclusion are not balanced with arguments against that conclusion. To illustrate this aspect of preoperational thought, we will consider some research done by Robert Siegler (1976) of Carnegie-Mellon University.

Among the problems Siegler has used with young children (ages 3 to 8) are the three problems illustrated in Figure 8-7. These are a balance-

FIGURE 8-7

Siegler's Three Tasks

Preoperational thinkers tend to make judgments based on the value of single variables. This aspect of preoperational thought is known as centering, and it can be revealed using tasks such as the balance-beam task, the projection-of-shadows task, and the probability task. (After Siegler, 1978)

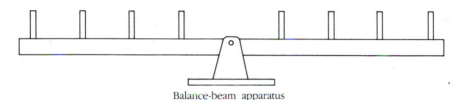

Balance-beam apparatus

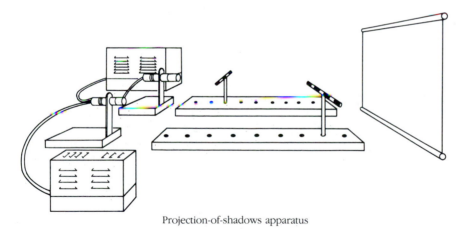

Projection-of-shadows apparatus

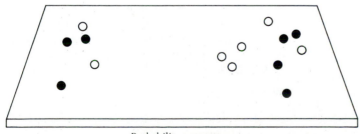

Probability apparatus

beam problem, a projection-of-shadows task, and a probability task. For the balance-beam task, children must predict which side of the beam will go down after varying numbers of weights are placed on the four pegs on either side of the fulcrum. In the projection-of-shadows task, children predict which of two bars will cast the longer shadow. In the probability task, they judge which of two collections of marbles a blindfolded child should pick from in order to have the best chance of getting a red marble. For each of these problems, children must reason about two variables simultaneously in order to be correct. For example, to judge which side of the balance beam will go down they need to relate the number of weights on each side to their distance from the fulcrum. Likewise, on the projection-of-shadows task, they must relate the length of the bar casting the shadow to the distance of this bar from the light source. Preschool children do not form these relationships in their thought. Nearly all of the balance-beam predictions made by Siegler's 5-year-old subjects, for example, were made on the basis of number of weights alone. Regardless of the distance of the weights from the fulcrum, the side with more weights on it was predicted—quite confidently—to go down. In the same manner, the longer bar, regardless of its distance from the light source, was predicted to cast the longer shadow; and the collection of marbles with more reds, regardless of the number of nonreds, was predicted to be the one that was most likely to yield a red marble when selection was made blind. In Piaget's terms, Siegler's young children answered in this way because their thought was centered on only one dimension at a time.

Do Siegler's results really support the concept of centering? The children might have answered as they did not because of the hypothesized centering in thought but rather because of sheer ignorance. They might have just thought that only one variable was important, so that even though they noted all the variables, they made their prediction on the basis of just one. Applying this reasoning to the balance-beam problem, we might hypothesize that the children knew perfectly well the relative distances of the weights from the fulcrum but ignored this information on the mistaken belief that it was irrelevant. This hypothesis is easily falsified, however, using what Siegler calls an *encoding task* in which children are presented with materials that differ on more than one variable to determine if they can accurately reconstruct what they have seen. If they succeed in reconstructing the arrangement according to only one variable, we can assume they in fact centered on this one variable when viewing the original arrangement.

Siegler's encoding task used the balance-beam problem: children had to reproduce the arrangement of weights they had seen on one balance beam by placing weights correctly on a second, identical beam. The result was that 5-year-olds and other children who had made their original judgments on the basis of number of weights alone were correct in reproducing the number of weights but incorrect in reproducing the distances of the weights from the fulcrum. Thus, it seems accurate to conclude that the root cause of the children's failure at the balance-beam task was that their thought centered on only one of the relevant variables. Not only was it the only variable they considered when making a prediction, it was the only variable available in thought. These data reveal, therefore, that even if all other aspects of reasoning were expert, these children would still fail in the balance-beam task for lack of sufficient information.

Additional evidence of preschool children's tendency to center their thought on only one perceptually salient variable at a time comes from work on what Piaget called *multiple-classification tasks* (Inhelder & Piaget, 1959/1964). These tasks, which are more commonly known as *matrix problems,* require the problem solver to pick the object or set of objects that belongs in a certain cell of a matrix. Figure 8-8 is a simple matrix problem that was used by Richard Odom and his colleagues at Vanderbilt University (Odom, Astor, & Cunningham, 1975) in a study of 4-year-old and 6-year-old

FIGURE 8-8

A Multiple-Classification Task

This matrix task is designed to measure the ability to think in terms of more than one variable at a time, which is the skill required for multiple classification. Subjects have to select one of the four cards at the bottom to fill the vacant spot in the matrix. Although the correct selection is Card 3, preoperational children may confidently choose another of the cards, particularly 1 or 4. (After Odom, Astor, & Cunningham, 1975, p. 761)

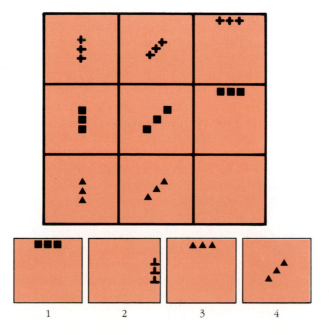

children. You will note that the matrix is defined by two variables—shape of the three figures in each cell and their position. Shape is the row variable and position, the column variable. Even on such a simple problem as this, preschool children are more often wrong than right, and their dominant error is to fill the empty spot with a card that matches either the row variable or the column variable but not both; that is, they tend to center on only one of the relevant dimensions. As always, they are quite confident in their choice; they appear to believe that the card they have picked is the one that truly "belongs" in the vacant spot.

Critique and Evaluation

Piaget's portrayal of preoperational thought as intuitive, egocentric, and centered has led to the unfortunate expectation that preschool children should invariably be intuitive, egocentric, and centered in their thinking. They are not; if you wish to find evidence of nonintuitive, nonegocentric, and noncentered thinking in the preschool period, you can certainly do so (Gelman & Baillargeon, 1983, p. 172). The most important amendment to Piaget's characterization of the cognitive abilities of preschoolers, therefore, is that Piaget's characterization has limited validity. Preschool children are frequently illogical in the way that Piaget said, but this does not mean that they lack the capacity for logical thought. This is quite clear in the case of egocentrism.

An abundance of research now shows that preschoolers are not invariably or even primarily egocentric in their thinking. Anyone who thinks so—and it is not clear that Piaget did—is wrong. Even 3-year-olds, for example, know that if they are looking at the cat side of a two-sided dog/cat card, then an adult sitting opposite them sees the dog side (Masangkay et al., 1974). They also know that white paper will look pink to someone wearing rose-colored glasses (Liben, 1978) and that closing one's own eyes does not cause a person to become invisible to others (Flavell, Shipstead, & Croft, 1978). Observations such as these clearly reveal that all 3-year-old children (and even about half of the 2-year-olds who have been studied) understand that other people have visual experiences that are different from their own. This makes it unlikely that children beyond age 2 are ever purely egocentric in the sense of not realizing that their own view is unique. Young children may slip up on occasion and forget this essential fact (as in their phone conversations and other referential communications), but when tested they show an awareness that people have different visual perspectives. Shortcomings appear primarily when children who know that others have a different perspective are called on to construct that perspective, but, even here, children show a rudimentary competence long before Piaget said they would.

Complete competence on perspective-taking tasks involves being able to accurately represent to oneself the exact spatial view of others. Piaget's three-mountains problem was a difficult test of this ability. When much simpler tests are used, 4- and 5-year-olds seem to be able to take another person's visual perspective. In one of the simplest tests of this competence (Masangkay et al., 1974), a picture of a turtle was laid down on a table and children were interviewed to see if they knew that a person opposite them would have an upside-down view of the turtle that they themselves could see from the right-side-up perspective. Most 3-year-olds, despite extensive practice, could not determine what the turtle would look like to a person opposite them, but almost all of the 4- and 5-year-olds could.

In another demonstration of perspective-taking ability in preschoolers, Martin Hughes and Margaret Donaldson used the task illustrated in Figure 8-9 (see Donaldson, 1978). The children's job in this task was to hide the figure representing a little boy behind one of the walls so that the policeman would not see him. Hughes and Donaldson found that children as young as 3½ could do this successfully, even though the task required that they ignore their own view and consider just that of the policeman. Even when there were two policemen whose views had to be coordinated, the vast majority of preschoolers were successful.

The important lesson to be derived from these amendments to the Piagetian view of egocentrism is that egocentrism is not an all-or-none quality of mind that one has for a period of time and then suddenly loses as a result of increasing maturity and knowledge. Egocentrism fades by degrees. This means errors can be induced on some problems but not others at most any age you choose in the preschool period. To find the errors, make the task complex, as Piaget did in the three-mountains problem with four points of view, three objects, and both left-to-right and front-to-back relations to be considered. To eliminate errors, simplify the task by eliminating variables, make the task less abstract (for example, having a child hide someone makes for a less abstract task than having a child draw what a doll "sees"), and give children practice. Observing children's responses in situations involving these manipulations leads to the conclusion that children are not invariably egocentric. They reveal instead that throughout the preoperational period, children gradually improve in their ability to construct another person's point of view and improve, too, in the reliability with which they do so. This amended view of egocentrism as a quality that one moves away from by degrees in development is true of intuitive thinking and centering as well. Children are no more purely centered or purely intuitive than they are purely egocentric. Nonetheless, centering, intuitive thinking, and egocentrism are important dimensions on which to measure the development of logical abilities, because on tasks of fixed difficulty, older children will show these characteristics less in their thinking than younger children.

FIGURE 8-9
A Simple Test of Perspective-Taking Ability
Children as young as 3 and 4 years of age were able to hide a figure representing a little boy behind a wall so that the policeman (or policemen) would not be able to see him. This demonstrates that young children are not invariably egocentric in all tasks that require them to take a perspective different than their own. (After Donaldson, 1978)

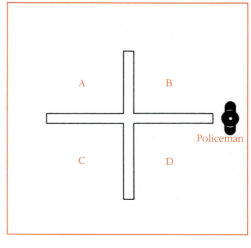

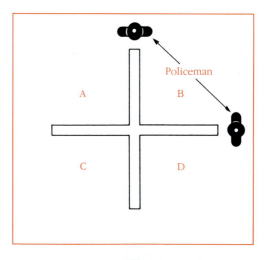

The Concrete-Operational Period

As we have just seen, entry into Piaget's third period of development, the **concrete-operational period,** cannot be judged by a *sudden* shift away from egocentrism, intuition, and centered thinking. How then are we to know when preoperational thought has ended and concrete-operational thought has begun? Many psychologists today would say that there is no sure way to know, because the distinction itself is artificial. What Piaget called concrete-operational thought, they argue, is really just a continuation of developments already begun in the preoperational period. This point will be discussed further in the section at the end of this chapter that discusses Piaget's theory of cognitive development.

Despite the difference of opinion over whether to characterize the move from preoperational to concrete-operational thought as a simple continuation of earlier developments or as a large-scale shift in the way one thinks, it is clear to all that the years from ages 5 to 7—the years that mark a transition from preoperational to concrete-operational thought in the Piagetian system—are important years in the development of children's thinking. Children may show the roots of logical thinking prior to this, perhaps even at the ages of 3 and 4, but this does not detract from the fact that after age 7 they are so much more consistently logical in so many different contexts that there really is the impression of a qualitative shift in behavior. In fact, even before Piaget's view on preoperational and concrete-operational thought had come into vogue in this country, American psychologists were talking about a *5-to-7 shift* (White, 1965). It seemed that regardless of the behavior that was examined—whether conditioning, rote learning, or problem solving—there was a shift in the way children performed between the ages of 5 and 7.

The advances in logical thought that occur in the years of middle and late childhood manifest themselves in at least three ways. These correspond to three aspects of concrete-operational thought that Piaget investigated: *classification, seriation,* and *conservation.* In the first, **classification,** children come to understand that one or more of the attributes of objects allows them to be grouped into conceptual classes. Furthermore, when objects are arranged in a hierarchy of classes, children can then reason about the quantitative relations among these classes. A second manifestation of concrete-operational thought involves **seriation.** This requires recognizing that objects can be arranged in a series according to their value on quantitative dimensions (for example, number, length, weight, and so forth) and recognizing, too, that there is a logic that governs the arrangement, called **transitivity.** Transitivity is the rule that if A is less than B, and B is less than C, then (by transitivity) A is less than C. The third manifestation of concrete-op-

erational thought, **conservation,** is achieved when children discover that there are attributes of objects that are invariant in the face of transformations of the object itself. For example, mashing down a ball of clay (the object) does not change the weight of the clay, the volume of the clay, or the color of the clay. These attributes are said to be invariant given the transformation described (mashing it down). Other attributes are not invariant under this transformation—for example, surface area. Collectively, the three mental activities of classification, seriation, and conservation mark the breadth of the child's cognitive growth during the concrete-operational period.

Classification: Forming Hierarchies and the Logic of Class Inclusion

Mature classification skills include the ability, first, to sort a set of objects into a number of mutually exclusive but hierarchically related classes and, second, to reason about the quantitative relationships among the classes. Carrying out the first of these skills is a common activity of school-age children. They engage in it whenever they impose a hierarchical order on collections.

Forming Hierarchies   The collections that children might arrange according to hierarchical relations could consist of any of the many things they collect, for example seashells, baseball cards, or pictures of prehistoric reptiles. The classification task that faces a child working with such collections is to break down the total into two or more parts that themselves can be decomposed into other parts. The best way to elicit this classificatory behavior in children is to indicate two or more boxes into which children should sort the materials. At the highest level of classification ability, children always sort the materials according to a principle of coequal classes. For example, if working with prehistoric reptiles they might group their reptiles into those that fly (pterodactyls) and those that walk (dinosaurs). If asked to further divide the dinosaurs, they might divide them into those that walk bipedally (on two legs) and those that walk quadrapedally (on four legs). At the lowest level of classificatory ability, children do not form classes at all. Instead they form what Piaget and Inhelder called *graphic collections* or what others call *thematic groupings* (Markman & Hutchinson, 1984, p. 3).

Graphic collections, or thematic groupings, are arrangements of objects that are based on perceptual or functional aspects of objects rather than on their class membership. Thus, if 4-year-old children are asked to arrange geometric forms into groups that belong together, they might put them together in designs such as are illustrated in Figure 8-10. If they are asked to divide a set of people and animals, they might put one of the people with the animals so that "the animals will have someone to take care of them." Delightful as this behavior is, it differs dramatically from the spontaneous behavior of older children, which is to form logical groupings based on some superordinate class relation that makes all the objects in one pile like one another but different from those in the other pile. For example, they might separate the geometric forms according to color, shape, and size, making piles of big blue triangles, small blue triangles, big red circles, small red circles, and so forth; and they might first arrange toy figures into animals and people and then subdivide these classes into babies and adults. The contrast between preschoolers, who think in terms of perceptual and functional relations, and school-age children, who think in terms of class relations, appears to be quite strong. Class membership is simply not a salient attribute of objects for preschoolers, and this is one of the factors that leads to their being labeled as preoperational by Piaget.

One observation that indicates the low salience of class membership for preoperational children is that they fail to take advantage of these memberships to aid in organizing material for later recall. For example, show preschoolers a group of 12 objects that they must later remember, and most will make no effort to form logical groupings among the objects as a mem-

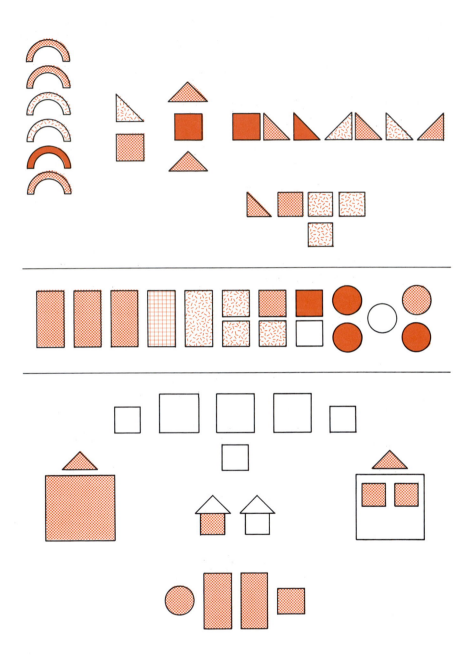

FIGURE 8-10
Graphic Collections
When preoperational children sort objects, they do not sort them according to class memberships, as concrete-operational children do. Their preference is to form graphic collections, as in these examples that involve block sorting. (After Inhelder & Piaget, 1964)

ory aid. In contrast, if older children are given a set of objects to recall, nearly all of them will spontaneously arrange the objects that are like one another together in their memory. Good evidence of this comes from a University of Minnesota study (Moely, Olson, Halwes, & Flavell, 1969). Children from 5 to 11 years of age were given a set of pictures to remember that included animals, furniture, vehicles, and articles of clothing. During the study period preceding the memory test, the pictures were arranged in a circle, but the children were told to regroup them if they thought that would help. The investigators found that the youngest children formed almost no categorical relations among the pictures. The oldest children, however, made extensive use of categorical organization by grouping pictures into the vehicles, clothes, animals, and furniture categories. The data that reflect this are given in Figure 8-11. Interestingly, the younger children could be trained to organize the pictures into categories, and this facilitated their recall. But the organizational strategy is one that they did not use spontaneously, whereas the older children did.

Observations of children playing the game of 20 Questions yield a second indication that young children do not spontaneously think of objects in terms of the category relationships that objects share. To illustrate, as-

FIGURE 8-11

Organization in Memory

These data show the increase with age in spontaneous use of categorical organization of memory material (lower curve) and the use of categorical organization following training (upper curve). The dependent variable in the study is a score that ranges from 0 (no organization) to 1.0 (complete organization) and reflects the extent to which the subjects in the study arranged pictures into categories (vehicles, furniture, clothes, and animals) while learning them. (After Moely, Olson, Halwes, & Flavell, 1969)

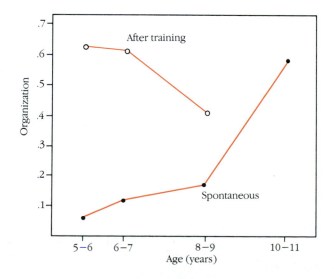

sume that the goal in a particular game of 20 Questions is to identify the item of clothing someone is thinking of. To do so in as few questions as possible, one must begin by conceptualizing a hierarchy of classes that includes individual items of clothes at its lowest level and larger groupings of clothes at its higher levels (for example, seasonal clothes and nonseasonal clothes, or clothes worn on the upper body, clothes worn on the lower body, and clothes worn around the waist.) Older children show a spontaneous appreciation for the need to think in terms of a classificatory scheme by asking their first questions about higher-level classes. Younger children do not. They ask all their questions at the lowest level. Thus, they begin with questions like, "Is it a pair of shoes?" rather than, "Do you wear it on your feet?"

Class Inclusion   The second of the mature classification skills—the ability to reason about the quantitative relations among classes—can be tested by having children compare the size of classes at different levels of a hierarchy. To do so, one asks what is called the *class-inclusion question*. An example appropriate for college students is the question of whether there are more coeds or more undergraduates. To test a child, the picture in Figure 8-12 could be used to ask whether there are more roses or more flowers. These are class-inclusion questions, because they ask for a size comparison among two classes, one of which includes the other. The logic of classification requires, of course, that the including class (called the *superordinate class*) be larger than the included class (called the *subordinate class*). This seems so terribly obvious that it comes as a surprise to learn that children do not answer class-inclusion questions correctly until age 8 or 9. For the class-inclusion problem given in Figure 8-12, most children under age 8 would tell us that there are more roses than flowers. Even if the children count the flowers to get eight and count the roses to get five, they will still say that there are more roses. Why should this happen, particularly when the children are quite adept at quantitative questions regarding size relations among classes that do not have the part–whole relation (for example, roses and petunias, boys and girls, or cars and trucks)? Piaget said that young children make the class-inclusion error because they cannot think simultaneously of a whole and its parts. When they have the parts in mind, the whole disappears, so it is impossible to compare them quantitatively. In Piaget's own words, when the child thinks of the whole, "he can envisage the parts which have not yet been dissociated, *but when he tries to dissociate one of the parts, he forgets the whole,* or disregards it, and mainly compares the part in question with the remaining part" (Piaget & Szeminska, 1941/ 1965, p. 1971; italics added). As amazing as this may seem, some parents find some appreciation for Piaget's explanation in the behavior of children who may reject the claim that they are Americans by responding that they are Minnesotans, or Mississippians. These children know full well that their

FIGURE 8-12
Class-Inclusion Problem
Are there more roses or more flowers? To answer this class-inclusion question correctly, one must be able to treat the roses as roses (the subordinate class) *and* as flowers (the superordinate class) simultaneously.

home states—Minnesota or Mississippi—are in America, but they find it impossible to think of themselves as a resident of both the country (the whole) and the state (the part) simultaneously.

Seriation: Constructing a Series and Transitive Reasoning

The second aspect of concrete-operational thought that becomes evident in the middle-childhood years is seriation. The term seriation as used by Piaget has two components. One is the ability to order a set of objects from least to most on a single dimension such as length or weight. The other is the ability to determine what the serial relation is between two objects in the series when the objects have not been compared directly. This second ability is called transitivity in that it requires children to make a *transitive inference*.

Constructing a Series   To test for the first ability, Piaget and his colleague Alina Szeminska (Piaget & Szeminska, 1941/1965) gave children ages 4 to 8 a set of ten rods that they were to arrange by length. The set was constructed so that adjacent rods in the completed series would differ only slightly in length (8 millimeters, a little over ¼ inch). The use of a large number of rods differing slightly in length was purposeful in that Piaget wanted to force children to reason about what they were doing rather than allow them to rely on perceptual intuition. In Piaget's words,

> we might have found a marked improvement in the seriation of length had we used fewer elements, or if there had been greater differences between the elements. But either of these variations would mean that we were measuring a perceptual adjustment to an intuitive whole instead of operational reasoning. (Inhelder & Piaget, 1959/1964, p. 251)

The experiments on serial ordering began with the experimenter constructing a "staircase" with the ten rods and then asking the child to do the same. When children succeeded on this seriation task they were then given an insertion task that consisted of fitting ten new sticks into the original series. The ten new sticks were size-graded to fit in between the elements of the original series, thus making for a 20-element series in which the rods differed by 4 millimeters.

The results of the Piaget and Szeminska study are given in Table 8-1. In the first "stage" of development on this problem, Stage 1A, children made no attempt to seriate the rods. In the next, Stage 1B, children ordered the sticks by pairs or triplets but could not put the whole together. In Stage 2, the children succeeded by trial and error on the seriation problem but could not perform the insertion task. Finally, in Stage 3, both the seriation and insertion tasks were performed with ease. These stages, beginning with 1B, are illustrated in Box 8-2.

To explain the conceptual advance that takes children from Stage 1 to Stage 3 on seriation tasks, Piaget focused on the need to understand that a given element in the series must be both larger than the preceding element

---

TABLE 8-1
Development of Seriation (in Percentage)

Age (Number of Subjects)	4 (15)	5 (34)	6 (32)	7 . (32)	8 (21)
Stage 1A No attempt at seriation	53	18	7	0	0
Stage 1B Small uncoordinated series	47	61	34	22	0
Stage 2 Success by trial and error	0	12	25	15	5
Stage 3 Success with operational method	0	9	34	63	95

SOURCE: From *The Early Growth of Logical Thinking from Childhood to Adolescence* (p. 250) by B. Inhelder and J. Piaget, 1959, New York: Harper & Row. Reprinted by permission.

BOX 8-2
Illustrative Behavior for a Seriation Task

The following quotes describe children's performance on David Elkind's replication of the seriation research that was conducted originally by Piaget and Szeminska (1941/1965); (see p. 420). Elkind used a "slats" task in which children arranged slats of wood differing by ½ inch in length. There were nine slats to be arranged, which Elkind refers to with capital letters A to I. The lower-case letters a to h are used to indicate the slats used on the insertion task.

Stage 1B

Bob (4 years, 7 months): On the seriation test, Bob arranged the slats in disconnected pairs: GE, HB, EA, etc. In other words, he made several seriations that lacked direction and exactness although the general idea of size differences was grasped. Bob was not able to seriate four slats, and seriation testing was stopped.

Hal (4 years, 6 months): On the seriation test, Hal put down CABEGFIH but arranged them so that the tops of the elements made a regular stepwise pattern. [The experimenter] then placed a straight-edge along the bottom of the series so that the elements were evenly aligned, but the tops of the elements no longer made a regular stepwise pattern. Immediately, Hal arranged the elements in the stepwise pattern again without regard to the size relations among them. Hal seriated four elements correctly and succeeded with seven elements after some trial and error. But when he had nine slats again, he once more ordered them by arranging the tops in a stepwise pattern.

Stage 2

Helen (5 years, 4 months): On the seriation test, Helen arranged the elements ABCDEGF and then recognized something was wrong and rearranged the elements several times until she got them right. Then she put H and I together on one side as if the other elements formed a completed series and as if she were starting a new one. When [the experimenter] asked: "Can you make these (H and I) into the stairway, too?" Helen added them but reversed the H and I and then got them correctly. When [the experimenter] produced five more slats from the second set, Helen attempted to build a second stairway alongside the first. After [the experimenter] demonstrated insertion with one element (c), Helen placed c in the stairway but removed C and then she put in f, but removed D. [The experimenter] said: "They are all supposed to fit in the stairway. Can you put these (the unseriated pieces) in?" This time Helen put them all in, but in egregiously wrong places, so that the series was AdBCgDcEFaGHIh. When she was asked: "Are they just right?" Helen replied, "Yes."

Stage 3

John (6 years, 4 months): On the seriation test, John started with the largest slat, I, and each time selected the largest of the remaining elements. He made no errors and the series was constructed in less than a minute. (Elkind, 1964) and smaller than those that follow it. Lacking this conceptual understanding, Stage-1 children and Stage-2 children can only represent a series as a perceptual arrangement with certain distinctive features. Stage-1 children (see Hal in Box 8-2), for example, because they work from a perceptual representation alone, commit the error of simply staggering the ends of the sticks without attending to the overall size relation of the sticks. Apparently, the overall size relation is not a feature retained in their representations. For Stage-2 children it is, because they are able to piece an original staircase back together in the way it was presented. Their trial-and-error approach, however, (see Helen in Box 8-2) implies that it is not logic that guides their actions but an image that they are trying to reproduce. This interpretation fits with their behavior on the insertion task. Insertion is no problem if one conceives of the original staircase as a rank ordering of elements. But if one conceives of it as just one distinct arrangement among many that are possible, then the problem of reconstructing the arrangement is, as David Elkind (1974) has suggested, a jigsaw puzzle in which the new elements clearly do not belong. Once one understands, however, that a series is an arrangement governed by a single logical principle, the task of reconstructing it and then inserting new elements becomes trivial (see John in Box 8-2).

Transitive Reasoning   Understanding the concept of a series also makes transitive inferences a trivial task. Once one has been shown that B is less than A and then, in a separate demonstration, that B is greater than C, one should be able to reason with no difficulty that A is greater than C. Piaget claimed that this type of inference, however, would be impossible for preoperational children to make.

One way of testing for transitivity is illustrated in Figure 8-13. On the left a boy is shown making a weight comparison among three balls that look identical but vary in weight by 50 grams each. On the right the boy compares the lengths of three dowels that differ by only ½ centimeter. After making the B-to-A comparison, the boy makes the B-to-C comparison and is then asked to infer the relation of A to C. The result of such tests is that most children do not answer the transitivity question correctly until middle childhood.

Conservation

The third aspect of concrete operations to develop in the middle-childhood years is conservation. Conservation, as Piaget used the term, refers to the knowledge that some property of an object has remained constant despite superficial transformations of the object itself. As was pointed out earlier, not all conservation requires reasoning. Recall, for example, the color, size, and shape constancies discussed in Chapter 7 on perceptual development. As a room grows darker at dusk, children do not perceive the colors of

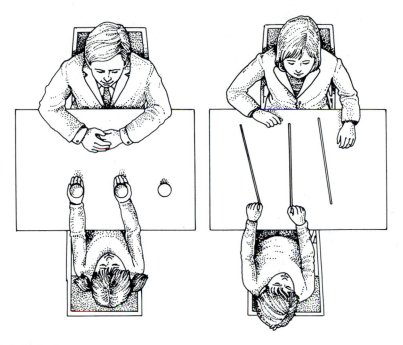

FIGURE 8-13
Tests for Transitivity
Concrete-operational thinkers can reason in terms of transitive relations. To the left, a girl is shown making the A-to-B comparison in a test of transitivity of weight. To the right, a boy is shown making the A-to-B comparison in a test of transitivity of length. Following the A-to-B comparison stage, the children are asked to make a B-to-C comparison and then infer what the relationship would be between A and C. (After Brainerd, 1973)

objects in the room to fade, nor do they judge that a change in the orientation and distance of objects signals a change in their shape or size. These are all conservations in the broad sense of the term, but they are not the sort of conservation that concerned Piaget in his studies of middle childhood. Piaget was concerned just with those conservations that were based on reason.

The following is a good example. What happens to sugar when you put some into a glass of water and stir? If you judge that the sugar is conserved, that there is the same amount after stirring as there was before, then you are either reciting something you have learned, or you are expressing a judgment based on reasoning that you yourself understand. Perception alone would be of no help to you in this matter. Of course, you could taste the water to discover that there was still sugar present, but this would not help you to know that the weight and the volume of the sugar had been conserved. This knowledge can be given to us only through reason.

When we say, therefore, that a child is able to conserve, we mean that the child, using principles of reason alone, is able to argue effectively that some property of an object remains unaltered despite transformations in the object's appearance. Prior to the middle-childhood years, children's judgments on Piaget's conservation tasks tend to be based not on reason but on perceptual factors. Frank's adaptation of Piaget's test for liquid conservation provided a good demonstration of this (see p. 399). In middle childhood, rather than use perceptual arguments ("There is more water in this one because it comes all the way up to here."), children appeal to

FIGURE 8-14
Tests for Assessing Whether Children Can Conserve Various Object Properties
(After Berger, 1980)

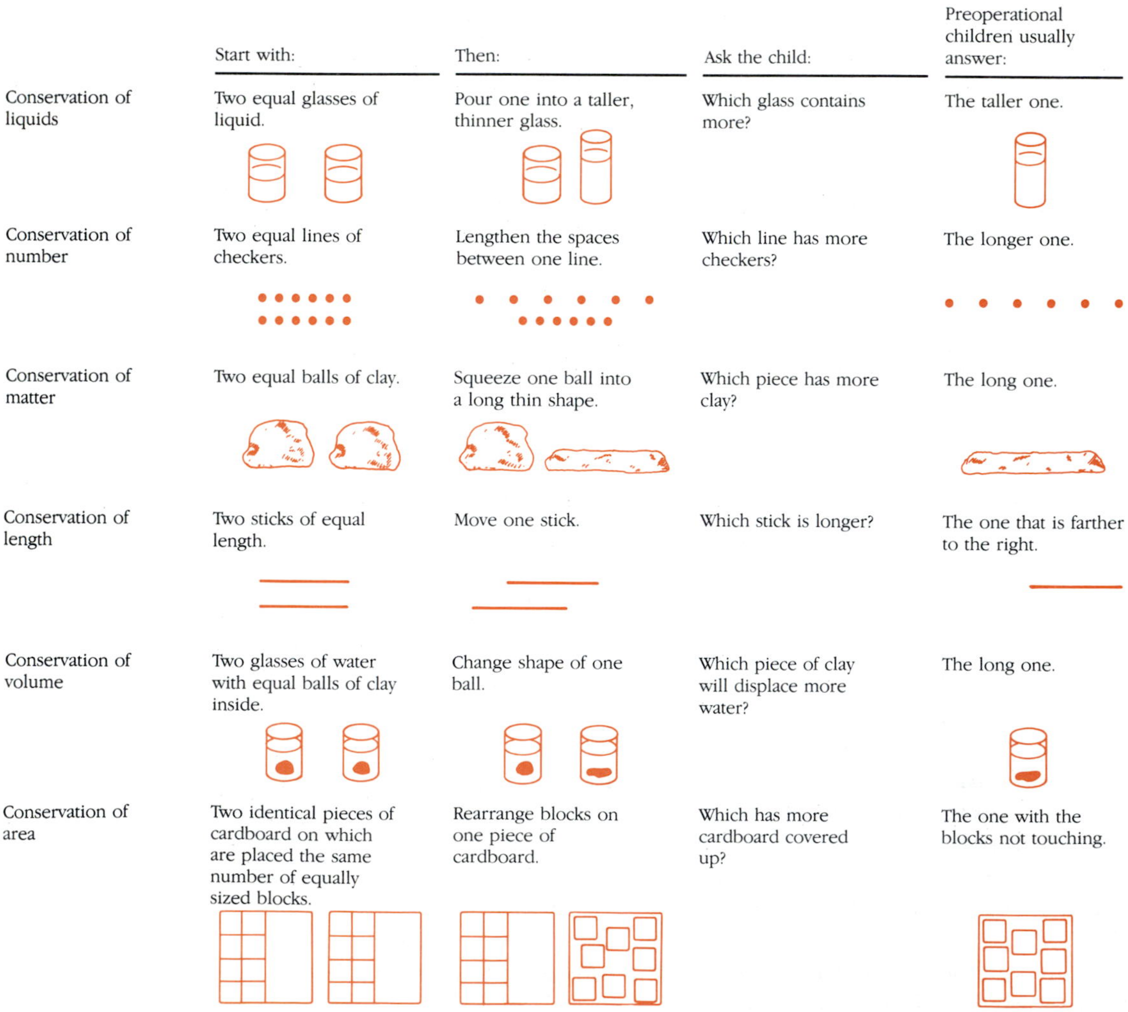

	Start with:	Then:	Ask the child:	Preoperational children usually answer:
Conservation of liquids	Two equal glasses of liquid.	Pour one into a taller, thinner glass.	Which glass contains more?	The taller one.
Conservation of number	Two equal lines of checkers.	Lengthen the spaces between one line.	Which line has more checkers?	The longer one.
Conservation of matter	Two equal balls of clay.	Squeeze one ball into a long thin shape.	Which piece has more clay?	The long one.
Conservation of length	Two sticks of equal length.	Move one stick.	Which stick is longer?	The one that is farther to the right.
Conservation of volume	Two glasses of water with equal balls of clay inside.	Change shape of one ball.	Which piece of clay will displace more water?	The long one.
Conservation of area	Two identical pieces of cardboard on which are placed the same number of equally sized blocks.	Rearrange blocks on one piece of cardboard.	Which has more cardboard covered up?	The one with the blocks not touching.

logical principles ("The amount of the water is the same because you did not add any or take any away when you poured."). Such reason is applied to many object properties that one might test for—number, amount, length, weight, area, volume, and so forth. Methods of testing for these are given in Figure 8-14. On each of these tests, Piaget and others have found a reliable developmental change from perceptual to logical arguments in support of one's judgments.

Interestingly, however, the logic of conservation emerges slowly, appearing first for judgments of overall amount, next for weight judgments, and last for volume judgments (see Box 8-3). This slow application of the principle of conservation to ever-new object properties is an instance of a general phenomenon in cognitive development that Piaget called **horizontal décalage.** As we will see at the end of the chapter, this phenomenon is quite important theoretically and, in fact, serves to challenge a key assumption in Piaget's theory.

Critique and Evaluation

One of the primary problems that has come to light regarding Piaget's analysis of development during the concrete-operational period regards what can be properly inferred from children's performance on his tasks. Though the tasks are supposed to be tests of children's understanding of the logic of classification, seriation, and conservation, they are not pure measures of these mental abilities (Kuhn, 1984, p. 154). This poses a problem for interpreting the results from children who fail Piaget's tasks. We can never be sure whether failure is due to deficits in logical ability or whether it is due to deficits in areas unrelated to logic per se. Take the transitivity test as an example. To answer the transitivity question correctly requires that a child remember the A-to-B and B-to-C relations that are needed to make the A-to-C transitive inference. The need to remember the A-to-B and B-to-C relations could be more a source of difficulty than the inference itself. This, at least, has been the argument of critics such as Peter Bryant (1974) of Oxford University in England, Charles Brainerd (1978) of the University of Alberta in Canada, and Tom Trabasso (1975) of the University of Minnesota. Indeed, it does turn out that when the memory requirement is reduced or eliminated, transitivity test performance improves (see review by Breslow, 1981). Thus, the memory requirement is part of what makes transitivity problems difficult. A similar analysis of other tasks used by Piaget reveals that other tasks, too, have accessory cognitive requirements unrelated to the actual logic of the situation. These accessory features might themselves be the source of difficulty or, at a minimum, might make it more difficult to apply the logic in question.

In addition to accessory cognitive requirements, the linguistic requirements of some of Piaget's tasks can serve to impede children's performance.

BOX 8-3
Piaget's Sugar-Conservation Task

The following passage (Piaget, 1964/1968) provides an illustration of the shift from perception to reason that occurs on conservation tasks. It concerns Piaget's research using the sugar-conservation task mentioned at the outset of this section (Piaget, 1964/1968). At first the children who were given this task judged that the sugar disappeared, because they could not see it any more. Their first judgment then was a perceptual judgment. But later, they *reasoned* that even though one could no longer see the sugar, it could still exist as invisible "little balls," which, if put back together, would add up to the original weight and volume. Their reasoning is a marvelous example of concrete-operational thought, because it involves mentally tearing down lumps of sugar and then putting them back together again, all with the goal of determining the effect of these actions on the conservation of a single property of the sugar (that is, its weight or volume). Needless to say, the symbolic and logical skills represented in this act are a far cry from those required for following invisible displacements and solving sensorimotor means–end problems through insight.

* * *

The . . . experiment . . . consists of presenting the child with two glasses of water of the same shape and size, filled three-quarters full. Two lumps of sugar are immersed in one glass, and the child is asked in advance if the water will rise. Once the sugar is immersed, the new water level is measured and the glass is weighed, so as to show that the glass containing the sugar weighs more than the other glass. While the sugar is dissolving, the following questions are asked:

1. Once the sugar is dissolved, will anything remain in the water?
2. Will the weight remain greater or become the same as the glass containing the clear water?
3. Will the level of the sugar water descend so as to become equal to the water level in the other glass or will it remain the way it is?

The child is asked to give reasons for all his replies. After the sugar has completely dissolved, the fact that the weight and volume (level) of the sugar water remain unchanged is pointed out and the discussion continues. The reactions observed at successive ages are so clear and regular that they can be used as a diagnostic procedure in

The typical conservation question is but one example. Here is a sample: "Do these two glasses have the same amount of water in them or does this one have more water in it, or does that one have more water in it?" Given the demands placed on children just to understand the question, it is not surprising that K. Wheldall and B. Poborca (1979) found that children were more likely to succeed at conservation tasks when they could indicate equality and inequality with a button push than when verbal answers had to be given to an experimenter's verbal questions.

the study of mental retardation. . . . To begin with, the child of less than seven years generally denies the conservation of any of the dissolved sugar and *a fortiori* that of the weight and volume associated with it. For him the fact that the sugar dissolves implies that it is entirely annihilated and no longer has any reality. It is true that the taste of the sugar water remains, but according to the very young child the taste, too, is destined for annihilation in a few hours or days in the same way that a smell or a shadow disappears. At about the age of seven, by contrast, the child understands that the dissolved sugar remains in the water, i.e., there is conservation of the substance. But in what form? For some subjects, it becomes transformed into water or liquefied into a syrup which mixes with the water; an explanation by transmutation. In the case of the more advanced child, something else is proposed. The child states that he can see the piece of sugar frittering into "little crumbs" in the course of dissolving. Once it is realized that these "little bits" become constantly smaller, it is easy to understand that the water still contains invisible "little balls." And, these subjects add: "That is what makes the sweet taste."

Thus atomism is born in the guise of a "metaphysics of dust" or powder, as a French philosopher has so wittily said. But it is still a qualitative atomism, since these "little balls" have neither weight nor volume and the child expects the weight to disappear and the level of the water to descend after the sugar has dissolved. At a later stage, which occurs at about nine years, the child reasons in the same way with respect to the substance but adds an essential element. Each small ball has its own weight, and if all the partial weights are added one will arrive at the weight of all the immersed sugar. By contrast, while he is capable of such a subtle *a priori* explanation for the conservation of weight, he is unable to do the same for volume and expects the level of the water to go down after the sugar has dissolved. Finally, at eleven to twelve years, the child generalizes his [explanation] to the volume itself and declares that, since each little ball occupies its own small place, the sum of these spaces will equal the space taken up by the immersed sugar so that the level of the water will not go down. (Piaget, 1964/1968, p. 43–45)

The task that is most often cited as linguistically confusing for children is the class-inclusion problem—which takes the form "Are there more X or more Y?"—where X is a class of objects subordinate to Y. Critics argue that this is such an odd question that children reinterpret it (see, for example, Siegel & Hodkin, 1982). Rather than interpret Y to mean all of Y, they interpret Y to mean just the part of Y that is not X. Thus the question, "Are there more boys or more children?" gets changed to the question, "Are there more boys or non-boys (that is, girls)?" Indeed many children do answer this way. When asked why they would say that there are more boys than children when referring to a collection of five boys and three girls, they might answer, "because there are just three girls." In and of itself, however, this does not contradict Piaget, because he, too, said that the boys-to-girls comparison is the one preoperational children would make. At issue is whether children make this comparison because it is the only quantitative comparison they are able to make (Piaget's position) or because they misinterpret the question (the critics' position).

Evidence that indicates that some children may misinterpret the traditional class-inclusion question comes from studies that have found that children's ability to answer the class-inclusion question varies with seemingly irrelevant circumstances. James McGarrigle and his colleagues at the University of Edinburgh (McGarrigle, Grieve, & Hughes, 1978), for example, increased the percentage of correct answers on class-inclusion problems when they did something to make the superordinate class as perceptually salient as the subordinate class. In one use of this technique, four toy cows—three black and one white—were laid on their sides, and children were asked, "Are there more black cows or more sleeping cows?" In a group of 48 6-year-olds, 23 were correct when the question was asked in this way, whereas only 12 were correct when the question was asked in the traditional way, "Are there more black cows or more cows?" Barbara Hodkin (1981) has shown that similar improvements in group performance can be obtained by inserting the word "all" in front of the superordinate class name. Thus, "Are there more roses or more of *all* the flowers?" is an easier class-inclusion question to answer than the standard, "Are there more roses or more flowers?" Such results do indicate that linguistic factors are important.

Linguistic confusions and accessory cognitive requirements do not exhaust the set of factors known to affect children's performance at Piaget's tasks. A third source of difficulty appears to be the social-psychological context created in Piaget's tasks. As critics Linda Siegel and Barbara Hodkin (1982) point out, studies of cognitive development involve "conversational interactions" between children and adults to which both children and adults bring certain expectancies and preconceptions. In these interactions, children are quite likely to be highly motivated to determine what the adult wants them to say and then say it. Demonstrating the potential validity of this argument are data from conservation tasks that show that when children are asked about an equality only after the transformation (rather than before and after as is usually the case), they perform better (Rose & Blank, 1974). A social-psychological explanation for this is that when adults ask children questions twice, as is the case in a conventional conservation task, it is usually because the first answer is wrong. In a conventional conservation task, therefore, once children have answered "yes" to the first equality question they may determine—for social-psychological reasons alone—that "no" must be the answer to the second. This is not the only social-psychological effect that critics have uncovered. James McGarrigle and Margaret Donaldson (1974) have pointed out, for example, that the mere fact that an adult acts so purposefully when transforming conservation-task materials might key children to think that something important has taken place. When McGarrigle and Donaldson compared transformations made to appear accidental to those made purposefully, they found that it did make a difference in performance. Children were more likely to conserve following accidental transformations.

As a result of the many studies that have been done on variations of Piaget's concrete-operational tasks, it is now quite clear that the percent of children who answer a classification, seriation, or conservation problem correctly—and the ages at which they first do so—is very much a function of the wording of the problems, the variables included, the social-psychological context, the memory demands, and other factors such as the degree of perceptual distraction and how meaningful the problem is made for children. But, still, even though this is clearly the case, two important points remain. First, no matter how you transform the problems, children still show a developmental progression on them. At the earliest ages tested, most children fail; at the later ages, most pass. Thus, even when troubling peripheral factors are eliminated, children still show an age-related progression in applying the core logic required in the modified Piagetian problems. This means that Piaget's ages for concrete operations may have been wrong, but his identification of at least some of the emergent skills was probably right.

The second major point to keep in mind is that altering Piaget's problems to show that children who fail the originals can pass an altered version does not answer the question of why they fail Piaget's tests. On this point, all are agreed: Piaget's observations are reliable. Showing that children can pass an altered version of a Piagetian test, therefore, still leaves us in the dark as to why they fail the original.

The Formal-Operational Period

With the achievements of middle childhood in the areas of classification, seriation, and conservation, children arrive at the brink of formal operations. Gone is their gross egocentrism, their centering on one dimension at a time, and their use of intuitive judgments. Now they can reason expertly about concrete situations involving the seriation or classification of objects and conservation of any of their properties. What remains for 11- or 12-year-olds to develop is the capacity to reason about abstractions that have no concrete representations. Along with this will come four additional aspects of formal-operational thought. These are *propositional logic, proportional reasoning, isolation of variables,* and *combinatorial reasoning.*

Reasoning About Abstractions

The hallmark of formal thought in everyone's definition is that it focuses on the possible, not just the real. This is the aspect that was emphasized at the outset of this chapter. One example given there showed how adolescents tend to represent a purely verbal expression such as, "Either the chip in my hand is green or it is not green" as a proposition that bears no necessary relation to the real world. In fact, for the formal thinker it should hardly matter at all if we changed the statement to read, "Either the chip in my hand is GLIP or it is not GLIP," because this proposition would be seen to be logically equivalent to the first one. The preadolescent concrete thinker, however, would either invent a concrete meaning for GLIP or express total bewilderment.

Reason about purely formal entities and their relations can be more than just a capacity that adolescents can call on when needed. For some it can become an obsession. These are the adolescents who bury themselves in thought by "thinking about thinking" or who trouble themselves by pondering the implications of the infinities of time and space or who become radicals, dreamers, idealists, zealots, and utopians, each with his or her own plan to save the world. Although not all adolescents will exhibit these symptoms, individuals who do are Piaget's prototypical adolescents, manifesting most clearly the change from the child who thinks concretely to the adolescent who thinks abstractly.

Propositional Logic

Propositions are common statements or assertions. Examples are, "All men are created equal," "Green dogs have bushy tails," and "Mississippians like grits." **Propositional logic** has to do with the truth value of combinations of such propositions in logical arguments. These arguments can take many forms. One frequently used form is the propositional argument known as the *conditional argument* ("If proposition P is true, then proposition Q is true"). Another is the *biconditional argument* ("Q is true if and only if P is true"). Yet another is the argument known as *exclusive disjunction* ("Either P is true or Q is true but not both"), which contrasts with *inclusive disjunction* ("Either P is true, Q is true, or both are true"). As may be apparent from these examples alone, propositional logic requires more than just dealing with abstractions (that is, propositions); it requires logically relating these abstractions and judging the truth value of the relation.

We have already seen one good example of a test for propositional logic in the nonsense-sentence test that required people to state what was wrong with statements such as, "I am very glad I do not eat onions, for if I liked them I would always be eating them, and I hate eating unpleasant things." Concrete thinkers, as we saw, did not object to this sentence on logical grounds. Formal thinkers did. They pointed out that the propositions composing the arguments were not logically connected; namely, the proposition "I hate eating unpleasant things" is an incompatible ending to the argument that begins "If I liked onions."

Another example of problems that require propositional logic for their solution are the liars-and-truth-tellers problems that are so popular with puzzle fans. You probably have heard one or more of these. They generally involve a traveler arriving at a fork in the road and having to get directions from a person who is either a truth-teller or a liar. Here is a variation on this type of problem that you may want to try. Note that the problem lists four propositions (the statements of Betty, Steve, Laura, and John). To solve the problem you must discover the condition under which one of the propositions is true and the other three false.

> The Nelsons have gone out for the evening, leaving their four children with a new babysitter, Nancy Wiggens. Among the many instructions the Nelsons gave Nancy before they left was that three of their children were consistent liars and only one of them consistently told the truth, and they told her which one. But in the course of receiving so much other information, Nancy forgot which child was the truth-teller. As she was preparing dinner for the children, one of them broke a vase in the next room. Nancy rushed in and asked who broke the vase. These were the children's statements:
>
> BETTY: Steve broke the vase.
> STEVE: John broke it.
> LAURA: I didn't break it.
> JOHN: Steve lied when he said I broke it.
>
> Knowing that only one of these statements was true, Nancy quickly determined which child broke the vase. Who was it?

The Nelsons' problem is quite difficult for people to solve when they have had no practice in setting up such problems in a way that the truth values of the statements can be simultaneously compared. Interestingly, when people fail to find a logical way to test the truth value of each child's statement, they fall back on concrete reasoning with statements like, "I think it was Laura because the guilty person will usually just deny it when they do something wrong." When prompted to use a more convincing form of logic with the question, "Can you prove it?" they are apt to say, "No, I just think it was her." Such reasoning is concrete, even if it does come from a junior in college, as the above response did. We should hasten to add, however, that failure to discover that John told the truth and Laura broke the vase does not necessarily mean that a person is an immature thinker. The key is in whether the person can understand an explanation of the answer once it is given, and then can generalize that explanation to other problems. In this case, the explanation is that there are three liars among the four children if and only if John told the truth.

In keeping with the Piagetian view of development, research has consistently shown that children show little to no success with propositional-reasoning tasks until they reach adolescence, when, for the first time, they begin to make progress. An illustration of this comes from research by Deanna Kuhn (1977), a major figure in the study of adolescent thought. She gave the following problem to a cross-sectional sample of children and adolescents in grades 2 through 8.

Mr. Jones was having trouble making his flowers grow. He thought there might be some bugs in his garden causing the trouble. He went out to his garden to investigate. He watched carefully and saw three kinds of bugs. This is what they looked like [A picture of a big striped bug, a small striped bug, and a small black bug was shown]. Later he was telling a friend about the bugs he saw in his garden. Which of the following sentences are true sentences that Mr. Jones might say about the bugs in his garden?

1. In my garden, if a bug is big, it is striped.
2. In my garden, if a bug is big, it is black.
3. In my garden, if a bug is small, it is striped.
4. In my garden, if a bug is small, it is black.
5. In my garden, if a bug is striped, it is big.
6. In my garden, if a bug is striped, it is small.
7. In my garden, if a bug is black, it is big.
8. In my garden, if a bug is black, it is small. (Kuhn, 1977, pp. 350–51)

If you take the time to work through this problem, you will see that only the conditional statements numbered 1 and 8 are true; the others are false. The only subjects in the study who were able to correctly judge the truth value of each of the eight statements were 20 of the 45 eighth graders (13 to 15 years of age). This 44-percent success rate among eighth graders was matched by a 0-percent success rate among the children at all the other grade levels. In the other grade levels, 83 percent of the second graders, 85 percent of the fourth graders, and 72 percent of the sixth graders misjudged four or more of the eight statements, a performance level that indicates absolutely no understanding of the logical implications of conditional statements. One might suspect that this low level of performance meant that the children were just guessing at truth values rather than reasoning about them. This was not the case. They were reasoning, but they were reasoning concretely. Thus, for a statement such as, "If a bug is small, it is striped," they would search through the pictures and answer true if they found a small striped bug and false if they did not. This strategy, as you can verify, leads to correct answers on exactly four of the eight statements, which is the reason we can say that unless one does better than this on Kuhn's test, there is no evidence that one understands the logical implications of conditionals.

Proportional Reasoning

Quantitative Proportions   When children become concrete operational in their thinking, they develop the ability to judge the absolute equality or inequality of concrete properties of objects and events. For example, using the form of reasoning that we labeled conservation, concrete-operational children discovered that a collection of 8 pennies was equal in number to another collection of 8 pennies, no matter how the two collections were arranged spatially. One could be spread out relative to the other or clumped up; it did not matter. The absolute equality of 8 = 8 was conserved. During the formal-operational period, children go beyond this achievement of judging numerical equivalence and acquire the concept of relative or proportional equivalence. To do so they need the aspect of formal-operational reasoning that Inhelder and Piaget (1955/1958) called **proportional reasoning,** through which ½ is found to be directly proportional to ¾ and inversely proportional to ⁴⁄₂. You might suspect that such reasoning would develop automatically with training in fractions in elementary school. There is good evidence, however, that proportional reasoning rests on an understanding of proportions that is independent of the mechanics of working with fractions, just as the logical understanding of number is independent of the mechanics of counting.

Determining equalities using proportional reasoning is a more advanced ability than determining equalities using conservation, for two reasons. First, proportional reasoning requires coordinating more factors. One has to attend not just to absolute quantities (for example, lengths, weights, and numbers) as in conservation tasks but to *relative* quantities that are themselves based on a relationship between absolute quantities (that is, the ratios of lengths, weights, and numbers). Take, for example, the probability task described on p. 408 in which a child is asked to judge which of two collections of marbles would yield the best chance of picking a red marble while blindfolded. If one attends only to the absolute numbers of red and non-red marbles, there is no adequate way to choose, because probability is not based on the number of red and non-red marbles per se but rather on the ratio of the one to the other. Likewise, in judging which side of a balance beam will go down when weights are put on both sides, one must not consider just the number of weights but their distances from the fulcrum as well. Two weights at four-units distance can compensate for four weights at two-units distance because of the inversely proportionate relationship between the numbers of weights and the positions of those weights on the two sides. Again, reasoning from the value of a single dimension alone will not yield consistently correct predictions.

The second reason that proportional reasoning is more advanced than conservation is the nature of the concepts to which proportional reasoning is addressed. On tests of conservation, children judge the equality of amounts, numbers, lengths, weights, and so forth, all of which are object properties that can be directly experienced. On proportional-reasoning tests, subjects judge the equality of such object and event properties as torque, probability, and density, none of which can be directly experienced. The concept of object density can be used to illustrate this. Object density— here on earth anyway—is the ratio of an object's weight to its volume. Both weight and volume can be experienced directly through sensory experiences of various sorts (for example, visual, kinesthetic, and tactile). Weight-per-unit volume, however, which is density, cannot be experienced directly through sensory channels. As applied to bits of cork or lead, therefore, density is a purely intellectual construction. This feature makes density and the other concepts to which we apply proportional reasoning higher-order properties of objects and events than the mind has dealt with thus far in development. In that these higher-order properties are invented through a mental manipulation of observable properties, we can see that they are formal as opposed to concrete properties.

When Inhelder and Piaget investigated proportionality, they did so by posing to children and adolescents a wealth of problems that involved either comparing probabilities (Piaget & Inhelder, 1951/1975) or discovering laws in the physical sciences (Inhelder & Piaget, 1955/1958). They concluded from these studies that the use of reasoning based on proportions did not develop until adolescence. In the words of Piaget (1957),

> We have been led to conclude from a large number of different kinds of experiments (dealing with motion, geometrical relations, probabilities, . . . proportions between the weights and distances on the two arms of a balance, etc.) that subjects from 8 to 10 are unable to discover the proportionalities involved. From 11 to 12 onward, on the average, the subject constructs a qualitative understanding of proportions that very quickly leads him on to metrical proportions, often without learning about these in school (p. 21).

An investigation by Gerald Noelting (1980) at the Université Laval in Quebec, Canada, strongly confirms the view that use of proportional reasoning does not emerge spontaneously until adolescence. In his research, Noelting gave children, who ranged in age from 6 to 16, the job of determining which mixtures of orange juice and water would result in a stronger orange taste (see Figure 8-15). When the mixtures to be compared were such that no form of reasoning other than proportional reasoning would yield a correct answer, the median age of success was 12 years and 2 months. An example of such a problem is one in which a pitcher with two measures of juice and one of water is compared to a pitcher with four measures of juice and three of water.

The developmental sequence that leads to the use of proportional reasoning begins with reasoning that is based on the value of a single dimension alone. An excellent example of such reasoning is provided in an article by Israeli psychologists Ruma Falk and her colleagues (Falk, Falk, & Levin,

FIGURE 8-15

Proportional Reasoning

Orange juice problems can be used to assess the ability to think in terms of proportions. Test takers are told that the dark glasses represent measures of orange juice, and the clear glasses represent measures of water. They are asked which combination will produce the stronger orange taste when combined in the pitcher. The two problems shown here are from a written version of the orange juice test. (After Noelting, 1980)

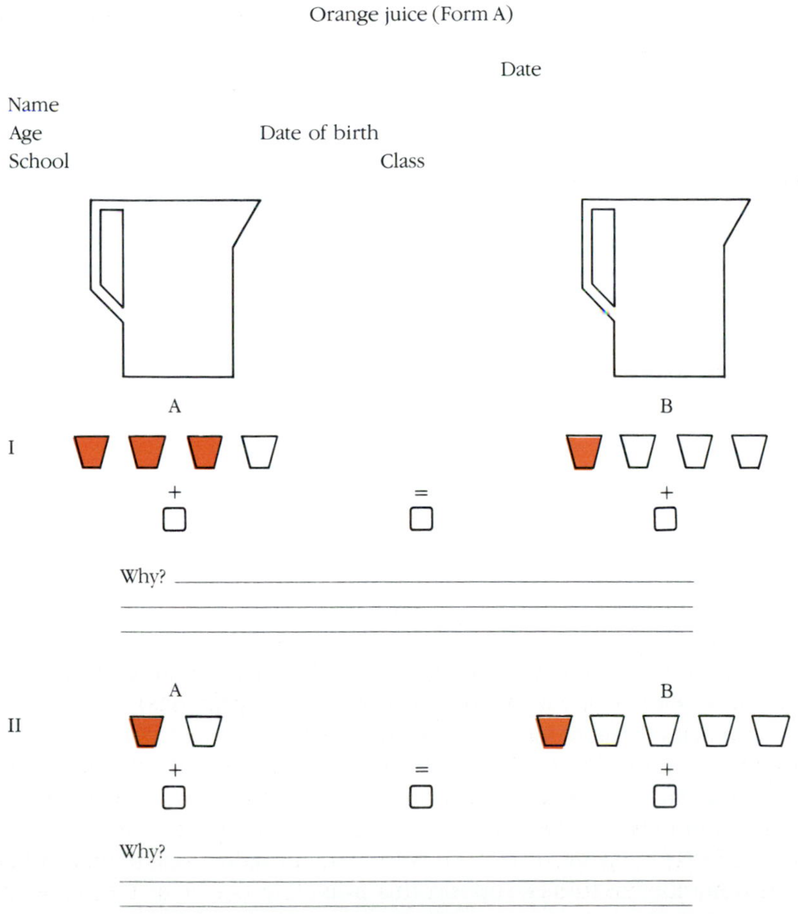

Orange juice (Form A)

Date

Name
Age   Date of birth
School   Class

Why? _____

Why? _____

1980). The problem was one of selecting which of two events was the more likely. The following interview with a girl named Gili shows that she based her probability predictions solely on the number of "payoff" events in the collections being compared. In this interview the acronym POC stands for payoff color.

> We presented the following choice problem (of beads in urns) to her [Gili]: (6 blues; 12 yellows) on the left versus (1 blue; 5 yellows) on the right with yellow as the POC. Gili selected the left-hand set and explained: "Here (on the left) there are more (yellow units), so I thought it would be easier for me to find a yellow one." When we told her that on the left there were also more blue beads, she answered: "This does not make any difference!" During the post-experimental interview, we started to construct a certain choice problem with beads in urns. Already upon putting in the urns the required numbers of blues (the POC of that task), before proceeding to fill in the yellows, she selected the urn containing more blue beads. We told her: "But we didn't put the yellow beads in yet, maybe you'd better wait and see how many yellow beads we put in each side" and she answered decisively: "That does not matter at all!" (Falk, Falk, & Levin, 1980, p. 195)

The next development occurs when children determine that reasoning about the value of a single dimension alone will not do, that the values of two dimensions need to be brought into relation. Rather than develop a ratio relation, however, their first attempt is with additive relations. Noelting (1980) illustrated this strategy with the responses of a 12-year-old girl Christiane. When she was asked which would have a stronger orange taste, a mixture of 2 glasses of juice with 3 glasses of water or 1 glass of juice with 2 glasses of water, she said they would both be the same, because "In both there is 1 glass of water more than of juice." In the final development, subjects detect the inadequacy of additive strategies and then hit upon the necessity of considering proportional values.

Semantic Proportions: The Logic of Analogy   An ability very closely related to the proportional reasoning we have been considering is the ability to comprehend analogies. Whereas reasoning correctly on orange juice and POC problems depends on establishing an equivalence of quantitative relations, reasoning using analogies depends on establishing an equivalence of *semantic relations* (that is, relations among word meanings). Thus, instead of dealing with quantitative relations like 1 is to 2 as 2 is to 4, we deal with semantic relations like *top* is to *bottom* as *head* is to *foot*. In both cases, a formal relation must be detected in the first pair of terms that is matched by a relation between the second pair. As with proportional reasoning, an ability to solve analogy problems does not normally appear until adolescence. A number of studies support this point.

Yale psychologist Robert Sternberg, for example, has been conducting research on children's and adolescents' understanding of analogies. In one study (Sternberg & Nigro, 1980), he presented subjects with incomplete analogies that they were to finish. One of the test items for instance was UNDER:BENEATH::PAIN: _____ (pleasure, doctor, feeling, hurt), with the four words in parentheses being the choices for filling in the blank in the analogy. This particular example involves a relationship of direct semantic equivalence (synonymous relation) in the two word pairs. Hence, the correct answer is "hurt." Other analogies employed other semantic relations such as antonymous relations (START:FINISH::FAR: _____ [near, away, travel, farther]), linear ordering (YESTERDAY:TODAY::BEFORE: _____ [now, when, after, time]), and category membership (NOON:TIME::WEST: _____ [direction, sunset, east, northwest]). Not all the relations were equally difficult, but, in general, Sternberg and Nigro concluded that there were two levels of performance on the problems, with the first level being characteristic of children in middle childhood and the second level being characteristic of adolescents. The first level was defined by use of either an associative strategy (that is, picking a term strongly associated with the third term regardless of the semantic relation) or an incomplete reasoning strategy, in which children did not "infer all possible relations between initial pairs of analogy terms . . ." (Sternberg & Nigro, 1980, p. 36). In the second level, the first half of the analogy was fully related to the second, so that solutions were the result of verbal reasoning rather than verbal association. These results are totally consistent with the view that analogical reasoning has some of the same cognitive requirements as proportional reasoning and that these abilities do not develop fully until adolescence.

Isolation of Variables

The third aspect of formal-operational thought to appear in adolescence is variously referred to as **isolation of variables,** separation of variables, and the strategy for making all else equal. What these terms refer to is the method for determining causality: one factor is varied while keeping all else constant in order to see if the one factor by itself makes a difference in the outcome. If it does, we judge the variable to be causal and *include* it in our explanation. If not, we judge it to be irrelevant and we *exclude* it from our explanation. Inhelder and Piaget's test for this form of reasoning (Inhelder & Piaget, 1955/1958) required subjects to design and conduct experiments to determine such things as what made a pendulum swing fast, what caused an object to sink in water, and what determined whether a rod would bend. Because the pendulum problem used by Inhelder and Piaget is simpler than the others, we will focus on this one to get a description of the development of isolation-of-variables reasoning.

In the pendulum problem (see Figure 8-16), subjects are given the materials necessary for discovering an interesting and somewhat unexpected fact: the period of the pendulum (that is, the time it takes to complete an oscillation) is determined only by the length of the pendulum. This is a good fact to have people discover, because it is counterintuitive. The intuitive expectation is that the weight of the bob or the height of the drop or the force of the push will affect how fast the pendulum swings, but this is not so. In that the result is counterintuitive, only isolation-of-variables logic can lead subjects to infer the true state of affairs.

To administer the pendulum problem, all you need are some different lengths of string, some different weights, and an apparatus from which you can hang the strings to allow them to swing freely. When you give these materials to preoperational preschool children and ask them to determine what makes the string swing faster or slower, you will find that they begin by conducting a few confounded experiments (simultaneously varying more than one thing at a time) and then, regardless of the outcome of these "experiments," they will announce the variable or variables that they believe are causal. Thus, a child might tie a light weight onto a long string and push it hard, then tie a heavy weight onto a short string and release it without a push. The second arrangement will result in more rapid oscillation, but the experiment does not give us the information needed for inferring why.

FIGURE 8-16
The Pendulum Problem
In order to discover that the length of the pendulum is the only variable that affects the time it takes to complete an oscillation, one must be able to isolate variables. (After Inhelder & Piaget, 1955/1958)

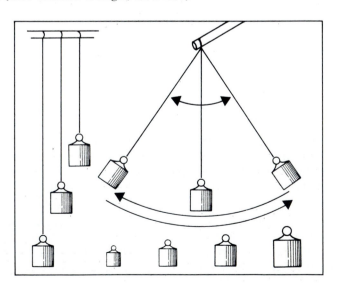

Nonetheless, the child might confidently announce that it is how hard you push it that makes a difference, a statement that is neither consistent with what was seen nor logically derived from it.

Concrete operational children will tend to design some useful experiments in that only one variable will be changed at a time, but they will not use this strategy exclusively. Thus, they may begin by comparing the different string lengths while keeping all else equal (that is, the same weight, same force, and same drop point), but then they will mix in some confounded tests (for example, varying weights and lengths simultaneously). After making a number of such observations in pretty much random order, they will reach a conclusion that will be subject to two errors of logic: one is *false inclusion;* the other, *false exclusion.* Both result from illogical reasoning regarding the outcome of confounded experiments. After varying both length and weight simultaneously, for example, a subject might conclude erroneously that the demonstration shows both weight and length to be important (false inclusion) or that it shows one but not the other to be important (false exclusion).

In contrast to the errors of preoperational and concrete-operational children on the pendulum problem, formal-operational thinkers begin by planning a set of observations that will yield valid information for confirming or disconfirming whatever hypothesis they hold, and, then, they draw the proper conclusions from the observations they make. Here, for example, is Inhelder and Piaget's description of the impeccable performance of an adolescent girl:

> [She] at first believes that each of the four factors is influential. She studies different weights with the same string length (medium) and does not notice any appreciable change: "That doesn't change the rhythm." Then she varies the length of the string with the same 200-gram weight and finds that "when the string is small, the swing is faster." Finally, she varies the dropping point and the impetus (successively) with the same medium length string and the same 200-gram weight, concluding for each one of these two factors: "Nothing has changed." (Inhelder & Piaget, 1955/1958, pp. 75–76)

In contemporary research on the isolation of variables, the developmental sequence first described by Inhelder and Piaget still holds. This is true even when the problem used to elicit isolation-of-variables reasoning is quite different from the ones used by Inhelder and Piaget. Deanna Kuhn, for example, has devised an isolation-of-variables problem that she calls the plant problem. On the surface it seems much easier than the pendulum problem because it deals with everyday matters of causality (the variables that affect the health of house plants), and it does not require subjects to generate their own data by designing a set of unconfounded experiments. In practice, however, it has proved to be somewhat more difficult than the pendulum problem (Kuhn & Brannock, 1977), a result that clearly indicates that the slow development of isolation-of-variables reasoning observed by Piaget was not a function of the unfamiliarity of the problems or the fact that subjects had to create their own data as well as reason from it.

For the plant problem, children are shown the four pictures in Figure 8-17, which are said to represent the outcomes that have resulted from using different combinations of food, water, and leaf lotion on a certain type houseplant. The experimenter then explains that there is another houseplant like those in the picture and that it will be given a little water, some light-colored plant food, and no leaf lotion. Children are asked first to state how they expect the plant to turn out and why (Question 1). Then they are asked whether the leaf lotion is important and why (Question 2).

Table 8-2 provides a description of the levels of reasoning that Kuhn and Brannock detected using the plant problem. The four levels are based on whether a subject was successful in isolating the relevant variable (plant food) when asked Question 1 and whether the subject was successful in

FIGURE 8-17
The Plant Problem

The different pictures in this figure show the results of four experimental conditions in which plant food, water, and leaf lotion served as variables. From these results, one can conclude that the only relevant variable is plant food. Plants that receive light-colored plant food are healthy; the others are not. Reaching this conclusion requires the ability to isolate variables in thought (After Kuhn & Brannock, 1977)

TABLE 8-2
Levels of Performance on Kuhn's Plant Problem

LEVEL	EXAMPLES OF RESPONSE
Level 0: No concept of variable isolation.	Question 1: First it's sick and then healthy. The last one was sick so this one will be healthy.
	Question 1: Not healthy, because leaf lotion and a small cup of water makes it grow good. My grandfather grows them. Leaf lotion and a small cup of water and if the sun shines, maybe it'll be healthy.
Level 1: Some concept of isolation of variables, although the correct variable is not isolated.	Question 1: Healthy, because it doesn't need plant lotion. Plant food is good enough with water.
	Question 1: Sick, because it doesn't have enough water. It depends on how much water.
Level 2: Partial success. Isolation of operative variable combined with failure to logically exclude alternative variables.	Question 2: Yes, because the third plant is in good health.
Level 3: Partial success. Failure to isolate the operative variable (in response to Question 1) combined with logical exclusion of an inoperative variable.	Question 1: Healthy, because it will get light powdery stuff and half a cup of water. (Does the lotion have anything to do with it?) No, because Number 1 didn't have any lotion and it still turned out healthy.
Level 4: Total success. Isolation of operative variable and logical exclusion of inoperative variables.	Question 2: No, because one of the plants with the lotion is sick and another with the lotion is healthy.
	Question 2: No, because it was healthy when you used it and didn't use it and sick when you used it and didn't use it.

SOURCE: Adapted from Kuhn, D. and Brannock, J. (1977), Table 1, pp. 12–13.

excluding the inoperative variable (leaf lotion) in answer to Question 2. Cross-sectional data indicated that there was a clear developmental progression in the use of the four "levels" of reasoning. Whereas 50 percent of the fourth and fifth graders used Level-0 or Level-1 reasoning, only 25 percent of the sixth graders did. Meanwhile, there was a steady increase in the percent of subjects at Level 4, with 15 percent of the fourth graders, 20 percent of the fifth graders, and 40 percent of the sixth graders reasoning at this fully mature level.

What is of principal interest in examining Table 8-2 is that even though Kuhn's plant problem was objectively very different from Inhelder and Piaget's problems in terms of what is required of subjects, the types of reasoning it elicited were very much the same. The first errors were to reason from intuition alone while showing little or no appreciation for the logic of isolation of variables (Levels 0 and 1). The next errors resulted from faulty inference. These were errors such as false inclusion, which is illustrated twice in the table. The first is the Level-2 response that the leaf lotion is important because the plant in Picture 3 was in good health, and the second is the Level-3 response in which water was included falsely as an operative variable. Level-4 responses in which both questions are correctly answered and justified corresponds to Piaget's final stage.

Before leaving the topic of isolation of variables, it is important to emphasize the everyday usefulness of this form of reasoning. It is not, as some tend to think, a rare form of thought restricted to scientific laboratories. Piaget's examples, all of which involved experiments in science, were misleading in this regard. Instead, isolation-of-variables logic is an essential component of adult human cognition. A passage from Robert Pirsig's *Zen and the Art of Motorcycle Maintenance* illustrates this point well.

> A motorcycle mechanic . . . who honks the horn to see if the battery works is conducting a true scientific experiment. He is testing a hypothesis by putting the question to nature. . . . If the horn honks, and the mechanic concludes that the whole electrical system is working, he is in deep trouble. He has reached an illogical conclusion. The honking horn only tells him that the battery and the horn are working. . . . To test [the electrical system] properly the mechanic removes the [spark plug] and lays it against the engine so that the base around the plug is electrically grounded, kicks the starter lever and watches the spark-plug gap for a blue spark. If there isn't any he can conclude one of two things: (a) there is an electrical failure or (b) his experiment is sloppy. If he is experienced he will try it a few more times, checking connections, trying every way he can think of to get that plug to fire. Then, if he can't get it to fire, he finally concludes that *a* is correct, there's an electrical failure, and the experiment is over. He has proved that his hypothesis is correct (Pirsig, 1975, pp. 102–3).

Pirsig's mechanic provides a marvelous example of isolation-of-variables logic in action. Some might think that the use of this logic is merely a matter of training. In this section, however, we have seen that there is a developmental course for isolation-of-variables logic and that most people do not use it easily and without error until adolescence. Even at this point in development, many may still fail to use it spontaneously when given one of Piaget's problems or even Kuhn's plant problem. In fact, in research we have already cited (Kuhn & Brannock, 1977), only 60 percent of the college students gave Level-4 responses to the plant problem. In subsequent research, however, Kuhn and her colleagues (Kuhn, Ho, & Adams, 1979) have shown that adolescents who fail to demonstrate the highest level of reasoning on the plant problem are still quite different from preadolescents who fail to show the highest form of reasoning. When exposed to exactly the same training program, the former group shows "immediate and substantial formal reasoning," whereas the latter group makes only "gradual, modest gains" (p. 1128).

Combinatorial Reasoning

At the outset of this section on formal operations, we stressed that the movement away from reality to possibility is a hallmark of the development of formal-operational thought. To reason about the possible rather than just the actual, however, one must be able to generate the possible. **Combinatorial reasoning**—the last of the four aspects of formal operations we are considering—contributes to this ability. It contributes by allowing us to take a set of elements and generate the total number of ways in which the set members can be combined. Thus, the three elements A, B, and C can be treated singly (A, B, C) or in pairs (AB, AC, BC) or as a triplet (ABC). This makes a total of seven possible combinations of three elements.

We have already seen one use of combinatorial reasoning. This was in the design of a set of unconfounded experiments that would lead to valid attributions of causality. In the pendulum problem, for example, one has to be at least implicitly aware of all the possible combinations of the four variables in order to reach a definitive conclusion regarding the causal variable. A more direct test of combinatorial reasoning, however—one that requires subjects to make explicit their ability to generate all possible combinations—is the chemicals problem shown in Figure 8-18 (Inhelder & Piaget, 1955/1958).

In the chemicals problem, subjects are shown that the liquid in a small container can be made to turn yellow by adding a combination of colorless liquids from other containers. The subject's job is to determine what that combination is. Because there are four substances to choose from, there are a total of 15 different possibilities made up of the one-way, two-way, three-way, and four-way combinations of the elements. The majority of adolescents can discover all of these by a systematic search procedure, whereas preadolescents tend to use a trial-and-error search strategy, which is not exhaustive of all the possibilities.

Piaget's discovery that the majority of adolescents succeed on problems that require subjects to generate all possible combinations of variables whereas preadolescents fail has been replicated a number of times, often

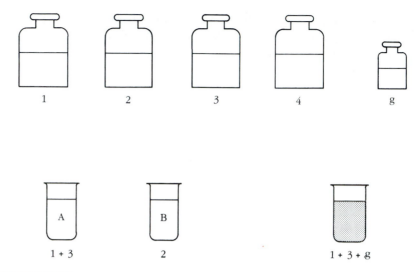

FIGURE 8-18
The Chemicals Problem
The bottles labeled 1 to 4 contain colorless liquids that in fact are different chemicals. The smaller bottle, *g*, contains potassium iodide. To test children for combinatorial reasoning, they are shown the flasks labeled A and B. These look identical, but one contains a combination of chemicals 1 and 3. The other contains just chemical 2. While the children watch, a few drops of *g* are added to the flasks. The result is that the liquid in Flask A turns yellow, whereas the liquid in Flask B remains colorless. The children are asked to reproduce this result, but to do so successfully they must be able to think in terms of all possible combinations of the four chemicals that they have to work with. (After Inhelder & Piaget, 1955/1958)

using tasks that are even more direct measures of combinatorial reasoning than Inhelder and Piaget's chemicals problem (see, for example, Neimark, 1975b; Roberge, 1976). We can safely say, therefore, that this form of formal operational reasoning does develop around adolescence and that it does so even in the absence of specific training. Nonetheless, as with all Piagetian problems we have seen so far, alteration of the task can produce somewhat earlier success. Marlene Scardamalia (1977), for example, has shown that many 9- and 10-year-olds can do well on combinatorial-logic problems when they involve fewer variables, and even adults have difficulty when a very large number of variables are used.

Critique and Evaluation

Piaget's descriptions of the cognitive abilities of infants and children are often criticized on the grounds that they underestimate the actual abilities of infants and children. Regarding his descriptions of adolescence, however, the criticism is reversed. Piaget is said to have overestimated the intellectual ability of typical adolescents. As Margaret Boden (1979/1980) is accurate in pointing out, Piaget writes on occasion as if adolescents should be "intoxicated with logic" and as if they are invariably capable of reasoning "in a way that would not disgrace a professor of formal logic" (pp. 74 and 75 respectively). In comparison with this impression that one gains from Piaget's writings, the data do not stack up. For example, even within Western, literate societies, many adolescents fail to use proportional reasoning or isolation-of-variables logic when these are clearly needed. Some studies using formal-reasoning tasks—including two of those presented in this chapter—show that only 30 to 40 percent of adolescents and adults succeed at formal reasoning when first tested (see Neimark, 1975a, p. 577). Also, data from cultures where schooling is not as extensive or common as in Western cultures often fail to show any evidence at all of formal thought (Dasen, 1977).

Though one frequently hears the criticism that Piaget either underestimated or overestimated the ability of some age group, this criticism is in fact not a substantial one. The reason is that Piaget did not put much stock in ages. His commitment was to stages, and one must never confuse the two. Thus, even though Piaget did give us the familiar ages of 0–2, 2–7, 7–11/12, and 12+ as the ages to be associated with his four major stages, he never intended for these ages to be taken as norms, and he certainly never intended that an age change be taken as a biological manifesto guaranteeing a stage advance. This means that criticizing Piaget's conception of a formal-operational stage on the basis of a relatively poor showing by a group of adolescents is misguided. His description of formal-operational thought as "adolescent" thought does not mean that all adolescents and adults must think that way. The fact that some do is sufficient to make the claim that, beginning in adolescence, there is a fourth stage of which humans are capable. (Some theorists are now claiming that there is even a fifth stage; see Commons, Richards, & Armon, 1985.) The consideration of species-typical capacities is far more relevant to the evaluation of Piaget's theory than is the consideration of species-typical performance.

A more relevant criticism of Piaget's formal-operational period focuses on the fact that formal thought should be immune to context effects, but it is not. Any number of studies show that the performance of adolescents is inconsistent across problems all of the same type. In one study of 13-year-olds, Stephen Pulos and Marcia Linn (1981) found that 92 percent of their subjects used the isolation-of-variables logic on at least one of a series of parallel problems, but only about 3 percent used this logic on all the problems. In a similar vein, P. C. Wason and J. N. Johnson-Laird have shown that a single propositional-logic problem can be solved by 98 percent of adolescents and adults or just 19.3 percent, depending on its content (see Wason,

1977). These results are contrary to Piaget's view that formal thought should be so abstract and free from concrete concerns that it can handle the term "GLIB" as easily as it handles the concrete term "green." In a 1972 article, Piaget acknowledged this problem with his theory, pointing out that the application of formal reasoning might only occur in familiar domains. The data conform to this revised version of the theory. Native navigators on the tiny South Pacific island of Puluwat do not appear to think abstractly on a problem involving the arrangement of colored chips into all possible combinations, but they do think abstractly on problems of navigation (Gladwin, 1970). The same can be said of Bushmen hunters (Tulkin & Konner, 1973), who are abstract reasoners when tracking game but not when solving standard Piagetian problems. Even for the people of a single culture, the application of formal-reasoning strategies varies by domain of expertise. Political-science, English, and physics students all demonstrate their most formal reasoning skills when working on problems within their domain of specialization (DeLiss & Staudt, 1980).

CONCLUSIONS

We now stand at the end of the long road to formal thought and it is time to look back over the developments along the way. The road began in infancy, when there is no thought, just action. By infancy's end, useful thought appears, and it begins to serve as a guide for action. At the outset, young children's logical thought is egocentric, intuitive, and centered. This makes it of limited use as an instrument of reason, but not so limited as Piaget implied. Researchers since Piaget have shown that preschool children are not invariably egocentric, intuitive, and centered. Given simplified problems to work on, they can be quite logical. Nonetheless, between the ages of 5 and 7, rapid developments take place that give the appearance of a qualitative change in reasoning ability. Children begin to perform logically on problems of classification, seriation, and conservation, even when they are posed in the complex, demanding ways characteristic of Piaget's tasks. Finally in adolescence, logical thought passes its ultimate milestone as children begin to take formal concepts (density, black holes, the proposition that X is bigger than Y) and not just concrete concepts (the length of a rod, the weight of a coin, the category memberships of elephants) as objects of thought. Thought of this sort enables them to perform propositional logic, combinatorial logic, and isolation-of-variables and proportional reasoning. It appears, however, that the ability to reason in a formal way is not as general as Piaget first thought. In fact, formal reasoning is domain-specific, and many adolescents show little evidence of it when they are tested in the domains most favored by Piaget—science and mathematics.

ESSENTIALS IN PIAGET'S THEORY OF COGNITIVE DEVELOPMENT

Though we have encountered some of Piaget's theoretical views already, we have yet to encounter Piaget's theory. The reason is that Piaget's theory really stands quite apart from the data he generated. This is an odd state of affairs, and it has been one of the most troubling aspects of Piaget's work for non-Piagetians to appreciate. The usual custom is for theories to be designed to fit the data.

The Assumptions Underlying Piaget's Theory

The best way to be introduced to Piaget's theory is via the assumptions that underlie it. We will take each in turn. Following their introduction, we will examine which of these assumptions are in trouble and why.

The Active-Organism Assumption

In the Piagetian view, the neonate, infant, child, and adolescent are perpetually active in trying to make sense of their world. To make cognitive advances, they act in effect as little scientists (Case, 1985, p. 22). They seek out stimulation, observe, manipulate, and test, all with a mind to "figuring things out." This view of what it takes to produce cognitive development is a far cry from the view fostered by early empiricist philosophers and by behaviorally oriented psychologists. According to these philosophers and psychologists, experience teaches; it imposes itself on the mind so reliably that all the teacher must do is ensure a proper sequence of instruction arranged with needed motivational elements. Learning and development follow directly on the heels of successful management of the learning environment. Jonas Langer (1969) has characterized this as the *mechanical-mirror view,* which he contrasts with Piaget's *organic-lamp view.* The metaphors are apt. In the first case we have a highly reactive organism that reflects the environment around it; in the second we have a highly active organism that illuminates the environment first through its infantile actions, later through its symbolic thought, later yet through its logically structured thought, and finally through its determination that existing reality is but one instance of what is possible.

Although there is undeniable merit in both the mechanical-mirror and organic-lamp views, the one a theorist adopts has important implications. It determines, for example, whether the developing child will serve as figure or as ground in the theory's picture of development. In Piaget's view, the child is undeniably the figure. This is manifest in the Piagetian view on "readiness," as described below.

From the mechanical-mirror view, the only child-based factor limiting development is maturational state. In the organic-lamp view, maturational state is important, of course; but beyond that the child must be cognitively ready, because experience "is always filtered through the child's current ways of understanding" (Miller, 1983, p. 37). Theorists such as Piaget pay far more attention, therefore, to children's "current way of understanding" as a predictor of what they are ready to learn than they pay to the specifics of the learning environment. The assumption is that once children are ready, they will discover for themselves what they next need to know, even in a relatively impoverished learning environment. This is a very child-based view of development.

The Constructivist Assumption

A second major assumption in Piaget's theory is that for children to know something, they must construct it themselves. There are two important implications for this assumption. The first involves instruction. According to the constructivist assumption, getting children to rote learn or to "repeat the little family lecture" will not lead to understanding, unless children succeed in integrating their rote learning and repetitions into their own growing world view. The second implication concerns the relationship of present knowledge to past knowledge. In the constructivist view, one's current level of understanding is an outgrowth of previous understanding, organized at a higher level perhaps but nonetheless linked to all that has gone before. Stated in this abstract way, this implication of the constructivist assumption is impossible to falsify; however, when applied to specific cases, it can be tested. On p. 451 we will apply it to Piaget's account of how an infant's initial understanding is constructed out of the sensorimotor actions of infancy.

The Assumption That Intelligence Functions like a Biological Structure

A third assumption regards the validity of an analogy that permeated all of Piaget's thought. The analogy was between the human intelligence and a biological system, such as the digestive or respiratory system. According to Piaget, there are important functional similarities between them. For example, they both work according to principles of assimilation and accommodation, and they serve the same overall purpose—adaptation of individuals to their environment. This analogy between an intelligence and a biological system is a surprising one for people who normally think of the mind and body as separate entities, but for Piaget—a biologist by training—the analogy made perfectly good sense.

The functional equivalence of biological systems and animal intelligence stems from the fact that both share the properties of assimilation and accommodation. These are quite easy to understand from the biological perspective. Taking the digestive system as an example, its role is to **assim-**

ilate nutrients into the body. It does so by extracting them from foods. But not all foods can be treated equally. This means that in order to assimilate the nutrients, the system must **accommodate** to the foods. Accommodations involve food-specific changes in the system. For example, fatty meats require somewhat different actions than pulpy, acidic fruits all the way from the process of chewing them in the mouth to digesting them in the gut. These different actions that are occasioned by the different foods are accommodations of the system to the food. Piaget argued that the same things occur in the use of intellectual structures. An intellectual structure such as the one that underlies the human ability to order things (seriation) is capable of assimilating a great many inputs, but in assimilating these inputs the intellectual system must invariably accommodate to them.

The Assumption of Holistic Structures

All cognitive psychologists refer to "thought structures" as a means of referring to what is stable and enduring in a person's response to different problem contents. The logic underlying isolation of variables, therefore, can be conceived of as a thought structure and so can the thought process that allows greater-than/less-than comparisons. Use of the word "structure" in this way is no more controversial (in the post-Piagetian days, at least) than saying that a calculator has a number of internal structures that correspond to its general ability to compute square roots or reciprocals. Piaget's assumption of **holistic structures** went far beyond this noncontroversial use of the structure concept. According to Piaget, all the specific structures, such as those used to isolate variables or make comparisons, emanate from a much more general framework for thought called a *structure d'ensemble,* which translates as "structure of the whole."

Although a structure d'ensemble may sound like a new concept, it is not. You are already familiar with the concept if you have ever thought of people as having personalities. The conceptualization we so readily accept as a personality is no less a structure d'ensemble than is Piaget's conceptualization of concrete- or formal-operational thought. The primary goal of Piaget as a theorist was to discover the nature of the holistic intellectual structures that he assumed to exist and then to find a way to represent them (see Flavell, 1963, p. 21). Just as personality theorists are not satisfied, therefore, with finding out about single values, attitudes or preferences of individuals, Piaget was not satisfied to discover single structures in thought. He wanted to be able to conceptualize the global unity linking them all.

The Assumption of Stagewise Development

A fifth important theoretical assumption is that cognitive development proceeds by a series of stages in which each stage is defined by a particular thought structure. In Piaget's application of this assumption, four major stages were postulated along with attendant structures: these were the sen-sorimotor stage, in which the relevant structures are not structures of thought at all but *schemes* for motor acts; the preoperational stage, in which the structures apply to thought, but haphazardly so; the concrete-operational stage, in which the structure of thought becomes organized for the first time into logical structures called *groupings;* and the formal-operational stage, in which human thought reaches its highest level of structural integration. Pi-aget's assumption of four stages with attendant structures has some very important and testable implications. One is that children, as they develop, should go through some relatively rapid periods of transition at the stage boundaries. Also, because stages are linked to Piaget's structures d'ensem-ble, we should be able to expect that when a stage change takes place, thought in the entire breadth of intellectual domains should shift from one level of maturity to a higher level. A contrary view to be considered below is that development is more continuous than Piaget portrayed it to be with progress being marked by small, domain-specific steps rather than by large leaps that have ramifications for thinking in all domains.

The Equilibration Assumption: Adaptive Responses to Disequilibrium

A final, crucial assumption in Piaget's theory is made in answer to the ques-tion: "What is the developmental force that drives children to become ever-more advanced in their ability to think and reason." Some psychologists might say the force is reinforcement; others might say it is maturation; and still others might say it is instruction. Piaget gives a different answer. He says that individual experience, maturation, and the social transmission of information are all prerequisite to intellectual advance, but the most impor-tant factor of all is an inherent biological propensity to respond to disequi-librium with adaptation. In technical terms, **disequilibrium** can be defined as a state in which the need to assimilate does not match the ability to accommodate.

To use a simple but effective example of how disequilibrium leads to adaptation in the intellectual realm, consider the case of children who de-fine birds as "animals that fly." This definition is a good start on an all-purpose definition, but it fails to fit all cases. In Piagetian terms, it assimi-lates both more and less than it should. There are, for example, flying ani-mals that are not birds, such as butterflies, and birds that do not fly, such as penguins. Encountering situations that force children to realize that their current bird concept is poorly adapted to the realities of the world leads to a state of disequilibrium. This leads automatically to efforts to adapt. Why? Simply because humans are naturally driven to have structures into which everything fits and which meet all their intellectual needs. On the surface, this may sound like no explanation at all because it is circular. If children advance, it is because they encountered disequilibrium; if they do not ad-vance, it is because they never encountered disequilibrium. The explanation gains strength, however, in that equilibration is a mechanism in biology that applies to evolutionary development, to homeostatic control, and to the way that ecologies manage to rebalance themselves after they have been upset by the draining of swamps, the building of roads, or the introduction of new predators. If one accepts the assumption, as Piaget does, that one's ability to reason is as biological a property as one's ability to digest food or to breathe, the equilibration mechanism gains in credibility.

From the six assumptions presented here we can piece together a reasonable picture of the process of cognitive development as viewed by Piagetians. Development is occasioned by the fact that children are constantly active in their efforts to make sense of the physical, linguistic, and social worlds into which they have been born. Through their own efforts at understanding, they construct ways of thinking and acting that can be represented as having some idealized, abstract structure. Individual structures are part of an overall pattern known as a structure d'ensemble. As the structures d'ensemble change, children advance in their stage of intellectual development, going from the sensorimotor stage to the preoperational stage to the concrete-operational stage and finally to the formal-operational stage. Progress through these stages depends on maturation, the child's own experiences, information the child gets from others, but most importantly it depends on the mechanism of equilibration. This mechanism is triggered whenever an existing structure proves inadequate. Recognizing the inadequacy puts the Piagetian child into a state of disequilibrium that is prerequisite to the constructive activities that will restore equilibrium and advance the child to a higher, more equilibrated stage of development.

Problems with Piaget's Theory

Though Piaget's theory is still of great interest today, three of its key assumptions have been seriously challenged. One is the assumption that the mental life and understanding of late infancy are constructed out of the sensorimotor actions of early infancy. The second is the assumption that there are holistic structures. The third is the assumption that there are definable periods or stages of development. In addition to problems with particular theoretical assumptions, there is a more general problem that was alluded to earlier: the theory is often quite distant from the observations on which it is based.

The Constructivist Assumption

A strict interpretation of the constructivist assumption leads to the prediction that the cognitive abilities of preoperational children will be constructed out of the sensorimotor actions of infancy (Piaget, 1936/1963). This would imply that sensorimotor actions are an absolute prerequisite to the rest of cognitive development. If infants were somehow barred from engaging in these actions, they would be cut off from any further mental advance—no object concepts, no mental problem solving, no symbolic ability. Unfortunately for this prediction, but fortunately for children, the absence of normal sensorimotor actions does not appear to limit the eventual development of purely cognitive abilities. This has been shown in research on thalidomide babies born without arms and legs (see, for example, Kopp & Shaperman, 1973), and it has been shown in one remarkable case of a girl with a normal-sized head but with a body of a neonate (Jordan, 1972). She was capable of no purposeful motor acts involving legs, arms, or hands. Nonetheless, she was quite normal in her cognitive development. Piaget, on being told of this case, responded that his emphasis on sensorimotor activity as a prerequisite to development should be taken in a very general sense, that he did not necessarily mean that cognitive development would be dependent on "using your hands, running around, etc." (in Jordan, 1972, p. 380). This is a weak response, however, because the implication in Piaget's writings is that sensorimotor actions, such as using one's hands and running around, *are* crucial. Certainly when Piaget used the term sensorimotor activity he had far more activity in mind than just thoughtful perception.

It seems, then, that the cognitive abilities of late infancy are not all constructed out of sensorimotor experiences as Piaget said they were. To deal with this flaw in Piaget's theory, future theories will either have to appeal more to maturation as an explanation for cognitive development (see Kohen-Raz, 1977) or to perceptual learning as a replacement for learning through sensorimotor action (Gibson & Spelke, 1983). Nonetheless, in defense of the constructivist assumption, we should note that the full weight of this assumption does not rest on the transition from sensorimotor actions to symbolic thought. It rests, too, on the more general proposition that learning, memory, and perception are not passive processes. In this regard, Piaget's assumption is quite widely accepted.

The Assumption of Holistic Structures

According to Bärbel Inhelder, even Piaget came to regret his use of the concept of holistic structures (Vuyk, 1981, p. 193). There is simply no evidence for them. Two primary pieces of evidence stand out against them.

The first is that children's performance on the various tasks that define a stage fail to correlate with one another as discussed below. If there in fact were a single structure d'ensemble that characterized children's thought at any one point in their development, we would expect correlated achievements across the entire breadth of whatever intellectual plane the children were on. In a single word we would expect synchrony. Instead what we find is asynchrony: children who do well on one task at a stage do not necessarily do well on the other tasks at that stage. More damaging yet, we find no clear order in children's progress across the breadth of accomplishments allegedly associated with each stage. Thus, whereas one child might be proficient at seriation tasks but not at classification tasks, another child might show evidence of concrete-operational thought first on classification tasks and only later on seriation tasks. Such findings do not fit with a belief that there are structures that are as broad and encompassing as Piaget said (see Case, 1985, p. 27; Kuhn, 1984, p. 153).

Equally damaging evidence against the belief that there are single structures that define intellectual advance in each of Piaget's stages comes from the widespread existence of the phenomenon known as horizontal décalage. Piaget himself invented this term and tried to deal with the phenomenon, but it still does unavoidable damage to a belief in the existence of general, all-purpose thought structures.

The literal meaning of décalage is "unwedging" or "uncoupling." Neither of these literal meanings is of help, however, in understanding the concept. A more useful definition for understanding what Piaget meant is "temporal displacement" (Flavell, 1963, p. 21n). A horizontal décalage is said to occur whenever use of a particular form of thought—whether conservation, seriation, classification, or some other—gets temporally displaced within a stage so that early in the stage it is applied to some tasks, and later in the stage it is applied to others. The most famous Piagetian example of this principle comes from the concrete-operational period during which Piaget reliably found that children demonstrated an ability to conserve amount before weight and weight before volume (see the reading in Box 8-3 for one example of this). Similar examples appear in the formal-operational stage, when adolescents can perform some forms of propositional logic (for example, exclusive disjunction) before others (for example, conditional reasoning) as shown by Roberge and Flexler (1979).

From a strict structuralist perspective, these time lags in the application of what is supposed to be a single unitary structure of thought should not occur. In principle, a structure should operate in an all-or-none fashion. That is, either the structure should be absent and unavailable for use on any problem—no matter how simple—or the structure should be present and available for use on any appropriate problem. Horizontal décalage, however, demonstrates that structures are gradually applied to ever-more varied contents. This might not be so bad if the variation in contents always involved differences as large as are involved in the case of amount, weight, and volume conservations. It turns out, however, that task alterations much smaller than this can disrupt the application of a "structure." Piaget himself had to deal with the fact that children who could answer the class-inclusion question about flowers (see Figure 8-12) might not be able to answer the same question when applied to birds (Vuyk, 1981, p. 193). Also, conservation judgments are upset by small task variations. The size of a transformation, for example, is a factor: children apply conservation arguments for small transformations before they apply them to large transformations. This means that if you proceed by degrees in rolling out a ball of clay to test for conservation of continuous substance (see Figure 8-14), you will observe that many children will "conserve" for small transformations but yield to perceptual judgments when the transformations become greater. One of the greatest transformations you can make is to break up one of the balls into small pieces of clay. Many children who will persist in their conservation judgments no matter how great your shape transformation will still regress to nonconservation when they see one fat ball of clay next to many little pieces of clay.

Whenever décalage occurs—whether within a given test context (such as amount) or across contexts (such as amount, weight, and then volume)—it implies that the "structures of thought," which should in principle be quite general, are in fact quite specific, at least at the outset. This fact forced Piaget's holistic-structuralist views to lose parsimony as he attempted to explain why structures develop slowly and why their application is a function of the context in which they are to be used. Today, neo-Piagetian theorists have abandoned the concept of holistic structures. Nonetheless, they retain the concept of structures in general, as we will see in the next chapter.

The Assumption of Stagewise Development

Because Piaget's stages were defined by the structures of thought that characterized them, falsification of the concept of structures d'ensemble does some initial damage to the concept of stages, at least those postulated by Piaget. But beyond this, there may be a problem with the view that cognitive development proceeds through a series of stages of any sort.

The concept of stages in development implies that there are definable jumps and pauses in the developmental sequence. There are problems with this view. One of the biggest problems with the jumps-and-pauses view is that décalage operates not only within stage boundaries, as discussed by Piaget; it acts across stage boundaries as well. The primary evidence has come from research on the competencies of preoperational children. As you will recall, Piaget focused on the incompetencies of these children. However, we saw in the Critique and Evaluation section to concrete operations that when you break down the tasks of the concrete-operational period (and, in fact, even those of the formal-operational period) into very fundamental, easily understood tasks with few elements and no distractors, children who are quite young can reveal some surprisingly good reasoning (surprising anyway in light of what Piaget led us to expect). This being the case, the stage concept ceases to have validity. Development appears to be far more of one piece than the stage concept implies. There may be periods of rapid development that look somewhat like "jumps," but there is little indication of true qualitative changes, and there is almost no indication of "pauses" in development, at least through the childhood years.

The Distance from the Data

A final problem with Piaget's theory is its distance from the data. Piaget talked of concepts such as assimilation, accommodation, and equilibration, but how is a teacher to translate these into the teaching of mathematics or science or social studies? And what does a structure of thought look like? Piaget's descriptions were in terms of formal logical systems that took the names of groupings and lattices. These were difficult to understand, impossible to apply to the activities of children as they worked at Piaget's tasks, and logicians have found all sorts of problems with them as formal structures (Ennis, 1982). In contrast to the great distance that Piaget maintained between his theoretical and empirical work, the neo-Piagetian theorists at work today are keeping their theories quite close to the data. This change will be quite apparent in the next chapter, which deals with the information-processing approach to cognitive development.

CONCLUSIONS

Although key aspects of Piaget's theory have been falsified, much that Piaget theorized continues to have heuristic value (see Gelman & Baillargeon, 1983, pp. 213-20). Because of Piaget, theorists today continue to think in terms of structures, though they are elementaristic structures, not holistic ones, and they continue to think in terms of stages, though often they are domain-specific stages rather than global ones. Another enduring legacy is the child-centeredness of Piaget's theory. This aspect has been retained in all the contemporary treatments of cognitive development, as has the general principle of constructivism (but not the specific principle of intellectual construction out of purely sensorimotor acts). Finally, although the concepts of equilibration, assimilation, and accommodation are too vague to serve as useful explanations, these terms are now widely used in a general, descriptive sense. Furthermore, theorists today are far more willing to view intellectual development as a problem in biological adaptation than they ever were before Piaget first offered his biological perspective on cognitive development.

SUMMARY

Because of their primary importance, the bulk of the chapter has dealt with Piaget's observations. We began with the developments of the sensorimotor period, which were divided up into observations on the development of object knowledge, imitation, and means–end behavior. Focusing just on the developments from 6 months to about 18 months (Stage 4 to Stage 6), we found that infants seem to move during this time from having no symbolic capacity to a point where objects, people, and the acts they perform can all be mentally represented in thought. This enables 18- to 24-month-olds to follow invisible-object displacements, defer imitations, and solve sensorimotor problems through insight. Piaget's descriptions of development in the sensorimotor period have been replicated by others. The only amendments to Piaget's descriptions are that, today, researchers believe infants to be somewhat more precocious in their development than Piaget thought, and they do not generally accept Piaget's account of the AAB error.

Piaget did not actually describe development in the preoperational period. Rather, the focus of his work was on the shortcomings of preoperational thought. He demonstrated the extent to which it could be egocentric, intuitive, and centered. One of the major contributions of researchers since Piaget has been to focus on the positive developments that take place in the preoperational period. These researchers point out convincingly that preschool children are capable of logical thought if problems are made simple and meaningful with few distracting elements and no extra cognitive requirements. Nonetheless, they acknowledge that children before the age of 5 and after the age of 7 are quite different.

In the concrete-operational period, children master the concepts of classification, seriation, and conservation. Mastery of the first of these is demonstrated when a child can form a hierarchy among classes and then reason about the class-inclusion relations existing within the hierarchy. Seriation is demonstrated in the ability to order objects on a single dimension, insert new objects into the series, and then infer the serial relation between two elements that have never been directly juxtaposed. Conservation is demonstrated in the ability to reason that some quantitative property of an object or a collection of objects (number, weight, volume, and so forth) does not change when deliberately misleading transformations have been carried out (such as spreading out the collection, reshaping an object, or breaking an object into pieces.) No one of these developments occurs at a single time, however. There are décalage patterns within each of the concepts, so that each is applied to some contents earlier than others. Conservation, for example, is applied to number before amount, amount before weight, and weight before volume. This fact serves to falsify Piaget's belief that holistic structures underlie development in the concrete-operational period. The fact that developments in classification, seriation, and conservation are not synchronous also serves to falsify the assumption of holistic structures.

 In early adolescence, many humans enter the last of Piaget's four stages—the stage of formal operations. The primary differences between this stage and the previous ones is that formal operational thinkers begin to consider possibility and not just reality. This is evident in new forms of logic such as proportional reasoning (both quantitative and semantic), propositional reasoning, combinatorial logic, and isolation of variables. The fact that not all adolescents manage to manifest these abilities on Piaget's tasks is not a challenge to his theory, but the fact that adolescents who manifest them on one of the tasks do not manifest them on superficially similar tasks is a challenge. The reason is that the structures of formal operations should be completely general and, therefore, immune to changes of problem content.

In addition to Piaget's extensive empirical contributions to the study of cognitive development, he made a major theoretical contribution. For the most part, the theory was too far removed from the data to be useful, and it employed concepts such as global stages and holistic structures that seem to have limited validity. Nonetheless, important aspects of the theory remain: the biological orientation to the study of development, the view of the child as actively constructing an understanding of the world, and the belief that a child's understanding and problem-solving abilities are limited by the thought structures available at the moment.

SUGGESTIONS FOR FURTHER READING

Boden, M. A. (1980). *Jean Piaget*. New York: Penguin Books. This brief work provides an intelligent summary of Piaget's theory coupled with fair criticism. The author is a philosopher as well as a psychologist.

Cowan, P. A. (1978). *Piaget with feeling: Cognitive, social, and emotional dimensions*. New York: Holt, Rinehart & Winston. A comprehensive guide to Piaget's theory and research. Although there are a number of such guides that have been published, Cowan's is among the very best.

Elkind, D. (1968, May 26). Giant in the nursery—Jean Piaget. *The New York Times Magazine*.

Evans, R. I. (1973). *Jean Piaget: The man and his ideas*. (E. Duckworth, Trans.). New York: E. P. Dutton & Co. This unique text includes an extensive dialogue between Piaget and the author, a summary of Piaget's theory, and an autobiography.

Piaget, J. (1970). *Genetic epistemology*. (E. Duckworth, Trans.). New York: Columbia University Press. This brief book, which is based on the Woodbridge lectures that Piaget gave at Columbia University in October 1968, gives a good introduction to the breadth of Piaget's theoretical thinking as well as to the intellectual style of the man himself.

CHAPTER OUTLINE

CHAPTER 9

Cognitive Development: Contributions from the Information-Processing Approach

Psychologists who take the information-processing approach to the study of cognitive development use the inner workings of computers as a model for conceptualizing the cognitive activities of human beings. This use of computers as a model for human information processing leads them to talk about memory in terms of buffers and storage devices, to use words like pattern recognition in place of perception, and to distinguish between hardware and software, input and output. The language of information-processing psychologists, however, is not what is most important about them. What is important is that their perspective has led to some major contributions in the study of cognitive development.

The first contribution of information-processing psychologists to the study of development has been to provide highly testable theories regarding the development of reasoning and problem-solving skills. The basis for this contribution is the precision with which information-processing psychologists describe the cognitive activities involved in problem solving. As so often happens in science, better descriptions of a phenomenon have led to better theories and applications. The second major contribution from the information-processing approach has been to make memory development central to cognitive development. In Piaget's view, memory development, as well as language development, is a secondary phenomenon (Piaget & Inhelder, 1973). If memory improved, it was because the structures of thought (operational structures and the structures d'ensemble) improved. Not so say many information-processing psychologists. If anything, the reverse is true. The ability to execute ever-higher forms of reasoning is in large part dependent on the development of memory (Brainerd, 1983; Case, 1985). The goal of this chapter is to demonstrate the value of these two contributions.

PROBLEM SOLVING AND THE DEVELOPMENT OF LOGICAL THOUGHT

The advances that information-processing psychologists have made in our understanding of the development of logical thought are based on improved descriptions of task performance. With better descriptions of children's actual thought processes at logical tasks such as those Piaget posed, we now have far more detailed descriptions of development on individual problems than Piaget ever provided. This advance on the descriptive side of cognitive science has made theoretical and applied advances possible. The theoretical advance is that we are better able to explain both why children fail and why they succeed at individual problems. The advance in applied cognitive science is that we are better able to instruct children.

Task Analysis

The goal in task analysis is to make explicit everything a child must know and do in order to solve a particular problem. People trained in computer programming are particularly good at this, because task analysis is the first job of any computer programmer. Programmers must break a task down into all of the little component steps that are required. Programmers, for example, cannot just tell their computers to arrange a set of numbers from largest to smallest. This is not explicit enough. Instead, they must tell the computer every step to make. To order numbers, this means they must first enter the numbers into the computer's memory. For the sake of an example, let us say that the programmer begins by entering three numbers into memory—5, 18, and 22. These are put in specific locations marked 1, 2, and 3, respectively. The next step is to tell the computer to take the number from location 1 and compare it to the number in location 2. If the location-1 number is larger, the computer is to leave it where it is. If it is smaller, the computer must transpose the numbers in locations 1 and 2. Transposing is itself not a simple operation, because a computer cannot simultaneously swap the information in locations 1 and 2. For this reason, the programmer tells the computer to take the number in location 1 and put it in a temporary location—call it 4. With location 1 cleared, the computer can now be instructed to take the number from location 2 and put it in the vacant location 1 and to transfer the number from the temporary location 4 into position 2. With all of this we have completed step 1 in our ordering task. Next, the number in location 2 must be compared to the number in location 3 and transposed if necessary. Then we must go through the whole process again before we can be sure of having the order right. Wow! You may never have thought the solution to a simple task could be so complex. It turns out, however, that cognitive acts—whether performed by people or computers—are exceedingly complex. By forcing ourselves to be perfectly explicit in representing this complexity, a lot can be learned about the problem-solving process.

Information-processing psychologists have a number of representational tools at their disposal to make explicit what we must know and do to solve a problem. One of the most useful is the *flow chart*. As an introduction to flow charts, Figure 9-1 has been included. It is a flow-chart representation of how a computer might go about the task, described above, of ordering three numbers from largest to smallest.

Flow charts are a good way to show the general outline of a problem-solving process. In addition to their use in making explicit what one must know and do to solve a problem, they can make explicit what one does not know or do in failing to solve a problem. For developmentalists, this aspect of programs is quite interesting, because developmentalists are not just concerned with descriptions of successful performance. In fact, they are often more interested in unsuccessful performance. Children fail before they succeed. To have an adequate descriptive science of cognitive development requires being able to describe the developmental progress of children as they proceed from unsuccessful problem-solving approaches to successful ones.

You will recall that Piaget's description of children's advances were frequently quite vague. He said, for example, that preoperational children failed at his tests of logical reasoning because they were intuitive, egocentric, and centered in their thinking. They later passed the tests when their thought became concrete operational. Because of the work of information-processing psychologists, we now have far more detailed descriptions of the developmental sequence for many of the concepts Piaget studied than we ever had before. An example is Robbie Case's (1978) information-processing description of four inadequate problem-solving procedures that children use on a proportional-reasoning test, Gerald Noelting's orange-juice problems (see Figure 8-15).

As we learned in the last chapter, Noelting's problems require stating which of two orange juice and water mixtures will have the stronger orange taste. The only adequate strategy is one based on the ratio of orange juice to water in the two mixtures. Prior to developing this strategy, however, children use others. Once identified, flow charts can make these strategies explicit, as demonstrated in Figure 9-2, which shows the four strategies identified by Case.

FIGURE 9-1
Sample Flow Chart
This is a flow-chart representation of how a computer could perform the task of putting three numbers in order from largest to smallest. (L1, L2, and so on stand for Location 1, Location 2, etc.) Rectangular boxes represent simple operations, and diamonds represent decisions. The variable A is used as a counter to keep track of the number of times the ordering procedure has been performed. In this case, it must be performed twice to ensure that three numbers are in order, which is why A must equal 2 before the program stops running.

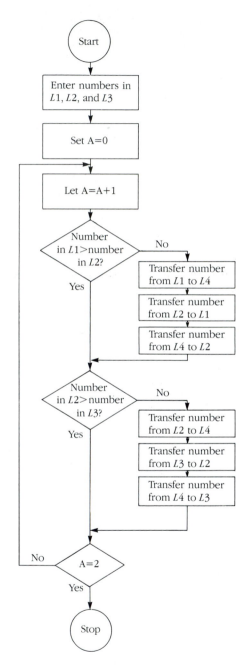

Case's first strategy, labeled *isolated centration,* is characteristic of children ages 3 to 4½. Children using this strategy determine first if there is any juice in mixture A and any juice in mixture B. If there is juice in one but not the other or if neither has juice, the procedure works; otherwise it fails. That is, if both mixtures have some juice, the isolated-centration procedure cannot distinguish them. *Unidimensional comparison* is the next strategy to develop. It is characteristic of children ages 4½ to 6. This is like Strategy 1 (isolated centration), except that the children count the number of measures of orange juice that go into each of the mixtures. With these two numbers held in short-term memory, they make a comparison and judge the mixture with more measures of juice to have the stronger orange taste. The next strategy to develop involves a *bidimensional comparison* and appears reliably in the years 7 to 8. To execute this strategy, children determine whether there is more juice or more water in both A and B. If one has more juice and the other more water, they are able to answer correctly. But if both have more juice than water or if both have more water than juice, they are unable to answer correctly. A fourth incorrect strategy, characteristic of 9- and 10-year-olds, involves the same bidimensional comparison as Strategy 3, except that now children determine and store information regarding the actual size of the water to juice difference. For this reason it is called *bidimensional quantitative comparison.* This strategy is adequate for any comparison in which the total amount of the mixtures A and B are the same. It only proves inadequate in cases where the total amount of A and B differ. For these cases, only a strategy that generates and stores ratio information is adequate.

The immediate value of Case's descriptions lies in their explicitness regarding the information-processing steps children are alleged to follow when solving, or failing to solve, orange-juice problems. The descriptions give us not only a child's *reasons* for a choice, but also the *reasoning* behind the choice. These descriptions specify what a child must know and do to execute the strategy and give what is in effect a map of the mental activities that intervene between the time the experimenter asks the question, "Which one has a stronger orange taste?" and the time the child provides an answer. As shown below, such precision has great value when it comes to developing theories.

How Task Analysis Leads to Testable Hypotheses

The theoretical value of the information-processing approach to the study of the development of logical thought is clearly illustrated in the work of Robert Siegler of Carnegie-Mellon University. Although Siegler has studied the development of logical thought in a wide variety of contexts (Siegler,

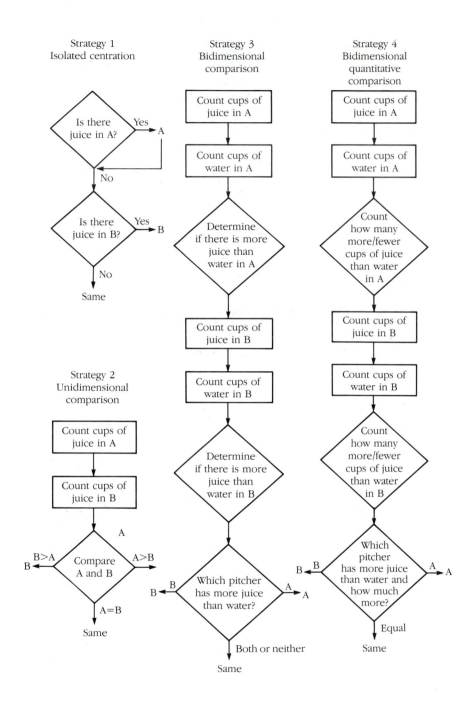

Strategy 1
Isolated centration

Strategy 2
Unidimensional comparison

Strategy 3
Bidimensional comparison

Strategy 4
Bidimensional quantitative comparison

SEQUENCE OF STRATEGIES OBSERVED ON NOELTING'S JUICE PROBLEM

Developmental Level	Age of Accession	Type of Item Passed	Global Description of Strategy
1	3 to 4	▼ ▽	Isolated centration
2	4 to 5	▼▼▼△▽ ▼▼▼△▽	Unidimensional comparison
3	7 to 8	 ▼▼△▽ ▼▼▼△△△▽	Bidimensional comparison
4	9 to 10	 ▼▼△△△▽ ▼▼▼△△△△△▽	Bidimensional comparison, with quantification

SOURCE: "Intellectual Development from Birth to Adulthood: A Neo-Piagetian Perspective" by R. Case, in *Children's Thinking: What Develops?* R. S. Siegler (Ed.)., 1978, Hillsdale, NJ: Lawrence Erlbaum.

FIGURE 9-2 (OPPOSITE AND ABOVE)
Strategies for Orange-Juice Problems
Robbie Case's analysis of the incorrect strategies that children of different ages use on orange-juice problems are represented in these flow charts on page 464. As shown in the table above, the strategies tend to appear in a fixed developmental order. Each strategy is successful in producing correct answers for some but not all of Noelting's orange-juice problems. (After Case, 1978)

1983b), his major theoretical work has been with data he obtained by analyzing what children need to know and do to solve Piaget's balance-beam problem (Siegler, 1976), a problem that requires children to predict how different arrangements of weights on the two sides of a balance beam will affect how the beam tips when it is released (see Chapter 8).

Siegler's Theoretical Analysis of Children's Reasoning About Balance-Beam Problems

Whereas Piaget proposed that failure on the balance-beam task could be attributed to the vague notion of preoperational or concrete-operational structures, Siegler formed a much more specific explanation. The explanation was that failure is due to a child having inadequate information about the problem and then processing that information with an inadequate rule. This explanation is not at odds with the one that Piaget offered, but it is more easily tested.

To understand Siegler's explanation, you need to know first that task analysis reveals a number of possible rules one could use to make a prediction on a balance-beam problem. The predictions stemming from four of these are given in Figure 9-3. The first, Rule 1, uses only the information

TYPE OF PROBLEM		PERCENT OF CORRECT ANSWERS			
		Rule 1	Rule 2	Rule 3	Rule 4
Balance		100	100	100	100
Weight		100	100	100	100
Distance		0^1	100	100	100
Conflict weight		100	100	33^3	100
Conflict distance		0^2	0^2	33^3	100
Conflict balance		0^2	0^2	33^3	100

[1]The incorrect answer given is that the balance beam is level.
[2]The incorrect answer given is that the beam tips to the right.
[3]The correct answer is given only by chance.

SOURCE: "How Knowledge Influences Learning" by R. S. Siegler, 1983, *American Scientist,*
    71(6), p. 632.

FIGURE 9-3
Predictions for Balance-Beam Task Performance
There are six different types of problems that can be posed using Siegler's balance-beam task. The names of the six types and an example of each are given on the left side of the table. The numbers entered in column 1 represent the percentage of correct answers that would be expected for each of the problem types using Rule 1. The numbers in column 2 are the percentage of correct answers that would be expected from someone using Rule 2, and so on. (After Siegler, 1983)

regarding the number of weights on each side. It predicts that when the weights are equal in number, the beam will stay in balance but that when the number of weights is unequal, the side with more weights will go down. As you can see in Figure 9-3, this rule would work perfectly for three of the six problems that Siegler devised. It leads to a correct prediction, for example, when the beam is balanced by having equal numbers of weights at equal distances (the balance problem) when the weights on the two sides are all at equal distances (the weight problem), and when more weights closer to the fulcrum serve to "outweigh" fewer weights far from the fulcrum (the conflict-weight problem). A second possible rule, Rule 2, would use weight information primarily, but in cases where the weights were equal it would check distance. Then the side with weights at the greater distance would be predicted to go down. Because of this, problem solvers who work with Rule 2 would be correct on the distance problem, as well as on the balance, weight, and conflict-weight problems. A third possible rule, Rule 3, would only solve problems in which there was no conflict, that is, problems in which the distances are the same or the weights are the same (namely, the balance, weight, and distance problems). For all others (different weights at different distances), a person operating with this rule could only guess. This is the reason Figure 9-3 shows Rule 3 leading to 33-percent correct answers. With three possible predictions—right side down, left side down, or neither side down—guessing alone would lead to 33 percent correct responses. Rule 4 is the only completely adequate rule in that it alone leads to correct predictions regardless of the arrangement of weights and distances.

In Siegler's information-processing view, the four possible rules become hypotheses about the way humans actually perform on balance-beam problems. The nature of these as hypotheses is best portrayed when the rules are turned into flow charts. As shown in Figure 9-4, a person operating with Rule 1 is predicted to enter information into memory regarding the number of weights on the two sides and then make a simple yes–no decision after comparing the numbers. A person operating with Rule 4 enters in weight information and compares, enters in distance information and compares, and then in the case of a weight–distance conflict, proceeds to enter new information into memory regarding the *cross products* of weight and distance (weight × distance yields a cross product).

Siegler's first test for his hypotheses was to determine if the rules adequately account for the predictions children actually make when solving balance-beam problems. The test was based on the fact that if some children use Rule 1, then there should be children who get all the balance, weight, and conflict-weight problems correct but miss the others. If Rule 2 is used, then some children should get all of the balance, weight, distance, and conflict-weight problems correct but miss the others. If Rule 3 is used, children should have chance performance on all the conflict problems, but be correct on the others. Rule 4 usage would be reflected in a perfect performance.

Not only did Siegler find that errors on balance-beam problems did indeed fall into the patterns he predicted from his various rules, but also the rules seemed to be used in a developmental sequence, so that children began with Rule 1, advanced first to Rule 2, and then to Rule 3 before attaining perfect performance with Rule 4. Siegler's four rules, then, seemed to provide a very concrete picture of the information-processing structures that underlie children's reasoning on balance-beam problems as the children develop. Unlike Piaget's much vaguer structures, Siegler's rules were open to tests.

One test for Rule 1 was based on the prediction that Rule-1 children would not have distance information in their memories when attempting to

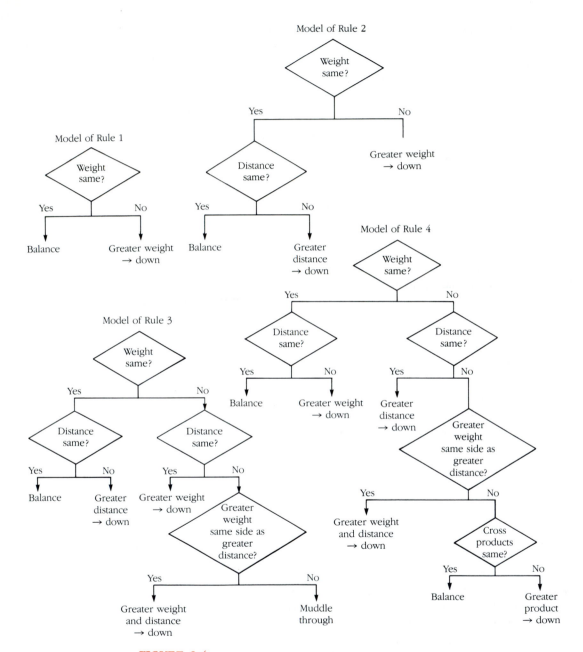

FIGURE 9-4
Siegler's Hypotheses Cast as Decision Trees
Flow charts represent the decisions made in executing each of the four rules that Siegler hypothesized children would use as they progress from preschool to adolescence. Excluded from these diagrams are the rectangles representing simple operations. Only the decisions are shown, thus Siegler calls these "decision-tree" representations of the children's rules. (After Siegler, 1978)

solve balance-beam problems. This prediction stems from the fact that Rule-1 children should only enter weight information into memory when shown a balance-beam problem. Siegler tested this using the "encoding test" mentioned in the previous chapter (p. 408). The test, as you may remember, required children to reconstruct an arrangement of weights on a balance beam. First they viewed a balance beam like one of those illustrated in Figure 9-3. Then it was covered, and they had to reproduce what they had seen. Siegler's data showed that contrary to what he expected, all Rule-1 children were not the same. In general, 5-year-old Rule-1 users performed on the encoding task according to predictions: they showed good recall for the number of weights on each side but very poor recall for the distances of the weights from the fulcrum. On the other hand, 8-year-old Rule-1 users were as accurate in recalling distance as in recalling weight. This means that Rule 1 as portrayed in Figure 9-4 is not a complete description of the information processing of these 8-year-olds. An extra step needs to be added in which they determine distance information. Even though they do not use this information in making their predictions, they still gather it.

The simple fact that Siegler was able to make a distinction in the thought processes of two groups of children, who otherwise appeared to be the same, turned out to be quite important theoretically. The reason has to do with an intriguing result Siegler obtained when he tried to teach his Rule-1 subjects through experience that Rule 1 was an inadequate rule.

The particular experience that Siegler gave his Rule-1 subjects (both 5-year-olds and 8-year-olds) was feedback on conflict problems for which Rule 1 was inadequate. The intriguing result was that the feedback experience was sufficient to get 8-year-olds but not 5-year-olds to move to Rule 2 or 3. That is, the same experience (exposure to conflict problems) that had a beneficial effect on the development of 8-year-olds had no effect on 5-year-olds. Actually, such a result is not uncommon in developmental psychology. Frequently it is found that older children profit from an experience that younger children do not profit from. The usual explanation is one of *readiness.* The older children are "ready" for the experience, and the younger ones are not. If you think about it though, you will realize that readiness is not a very powerful explanatory concept. Often it is purely circular, because our only evidence for readiness is the very data the concept is used to explain. The information-processing analysis of Siegler, however, gave a way of avoiding being caught in a circle.

To explain the fact that 8-year-olds learned from conflict problems while 5-year-olds did not, Siegler developed the hypothesis that the difference in readiness, or ability to learn, between 5- and 8-year-olds lay solely in the encoding difference between them. To test this hypothesis, Siegler trained a group of 5-year-olds to encode distance when they examined the balance-beam problems. This training by itself did not alter performance. The 5-year-olds continued to use Rule 1. But when they were then given feedback on the conflict problems, these 5-year-olds, who had been trained

Preschoolers encode information from just one dimension on the balance beam problem.

to encode distance, showed the same improvement as the 8-year-olds, who encoded distance without explicit training. They advanced to Rule 2 or Rule 3. Readiness in this case, therefore, consisted solely of having the distance information available to use when the weight information alone proved inadequate.

The General Importance of Encoding to Cognition

Could encoding differences among children and others frequently be the basis for differences in readiness to learn some cognitive act? Siegler's data imply that they are. In one separate demonstration of this, he has shown that 3-year-olds will perform like 5-year-olds on balance-beam problems if they are taught to encode the same information (Siegler, 1978). Also, he has shown that the failure to encode crucial information about start and stop times keeps some 11-year-olds from being able to answer a simple question about which of two trains running on parallel tracks runs for the longest time (Siegler, 1983a).

Research by other information-processing psychologists in the area of problem solving has shown that encoding differences may account for more than just developmental differences. In general, *novices* differ from *experts* in terms of the information they encode. Expert chess players, for example, take in information from the board that novice chess players do not, and the same is true for players in the Japanese game of go, a board game equally as complex as chess. Expert physicists and expert radiologists also differ from novices in their fields in terms of the information they extract from a problem setting (that is, a physics problem or an X ray).

To show you the general importance that encoding can have in problem solving, you might imagine that you have been given the problem of predicting heart disease from an EKG record like that in the top panel of Figure 9-5. As a novice dealing with this record you might note information about the relative heights of the wave peaks, the distance between them, and then something about the overall contour, like the fact that there are two low, fat waves separated by a tall, skinny one with two dips on either side. This novice encoding would leave out some information that would be vital to your diagnosis of potential heart disease. One bit of information

FIGURE 9-5

The Importance of Encoding

When electrodes are placed to get a measure of the heart muscle activity during a single contraction, they yield an electrical signal with a wave form like that in the top panel. (The particular wave form shown here is from what is known as a Lead I placement of electrodes.) Properties of this wave have proved to be diagnostic of certain heart conditions. One of these properties is the "T-intercept" (see lower panel). Because the T-intercept is not part of the information a novice would encode when examining the wave in search of diagnostic information, novices would be unable to solve prediction problems requiring this information.

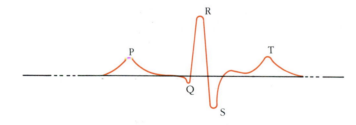

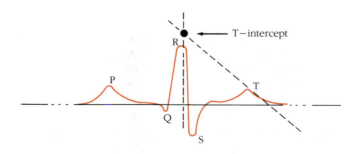

that is missing, for example, is what A. Djalaly (Djalaly, Hedayatti, & Zeigh-ami, 1977) calls the T-intercept (see the lower panel of Figure 9-5). Probably your representation of the information in the upper panel of Figure 9-5 was insufficient for you to be able to state where the T-intercept would fall on the portion of the tracing marked as R. Thus, when a prediction problem depended on this information, you would have been in the same situation as Siegler's 5-year-olds who had just been shown that their weight representation of the balance beam was inadequate. You would have known that your representation of the tracing was inadequate, but you would not have had the necessary information for making a prediction on any other basis.

In brief, then, the importance of the information-processing psychologists' attention to encoding in the study of cognitive development is the revelation that to explain some differences—not only between novices and experts but between children and adults as well—we may not need to appeal to structural qualities like general intelligence, ability to reason, or capacity to process information. We may be able to explain the difference with a far simpler construct—namely, the information problem solvers extract from problem statements.

The examples used thus far to demonstrate the theoretical advantages of the information-processing approach can be summarized in two points. One is that task analysis gives us a way of establishing hypotheses that can be tested about how children reason. We saw this process illustrated in Siegler's four-rule hypothesis for how children solve balance-beam problems. An explicit representation of the child's hypothesized reasoning process is drawn up, and then we observe children in problem settings where our observations will lead us to either confirm or deny the validity of the hypothesis. By following this *rule-assessment* methodology, procedural accounts can be developed for explaining developmental differences in problem solving. Such procedural accounts are far more revealing than are accounts that attribute differences in performance to stage differences. As Siegler (1978) points out, "It is difficult to infer from a stage classification just what a child knows; we lack detailed knowledge of what aspects of the child's performance caused him to be assigned to the particular stage" (p. 111).

The second general advantage illustrated here for the information-processing approach is that it makes an explicit distinction between two types of knowledge. One is *procedural knowledge,* which is the knowledge of how to do something; the other is *declarative knowledge,* which is the knowledge of certain facts (Mandler, 1983, pp. 423–24; Siegler, 1983c, p. 153). For the orange-juice and balance-beam problems, an important bit of procedural knowledge is knowing how to count. Declarative knowledge is reflected in knowing such things as the distances of weights from the fulcrum or the number of measures of orange juice that went into each of the containers. Declarative knowledge such as this can be gained either through encoding or retrieval from long-term memory. In the Piagetian approach, declarative knowledge is not explicitly represented. Rather, the emphasis is on procedural knowledge alone as it applies to reasoning about class inclusion, the invariance of object properties, or seriation. It is now clear, however, that declarative knowledge plays a crucial role in our ability to apply procedural knowledge. This was evidenced in Siegler's demonstration that the declarative knowledge of 5-year-olds and 8-year-olds accounts for differences in their ability to learn a new rule for solving balance-beam problems. In the last chapter we saw that Puluwat islanders could think abstractly about problems in navigation but not about a combinatorial problem involving unfamiliar colored chips. And in the upcoming section on memory in this chapter, we will see that the declarative knowledge children and adults have about chess affects their ability to store chess-player positions in memory. Given that declarative knowledge in these cases and many others appears to interact with our ability to perform the basic mental functions captured under the heading of procedural knowledge, only a theory that distinguishes procedural from declarative knowledge can adequately explain developmental differences in performance (see Glaser, 1984).

THE EDUCATIONAL VALUE OF THE INFORMATION-PROCESSING APPROACH

One of the most frequent questions that Piaget encountered was how children could be taught the mental concepts tapped by his tests. For example, how could they be taught to classify, to form transitive inferences, or to use combinatorial logic? Because Piaget got this question from American audiences more than any other, he came to call it the *American question*. His answer, basically, was that children cannot be taught these things directly. Rather, they must be placed in educational environments where they can discover these concepts for themselves. As Constance Kamii, an American educator who worked with Piaget, has expressed it,

> The role of the teacher . . . cannot be one of simply transmitting all types of knowledge to children. Her function is to help the child construct his own knowledge directly from feedback from objects and through his own reasoning with objects. In physical knowledge, for example, if the child believes that a block will sink, she encourages him to prove the correctness of his statement. If he predicts that chocolate pudding will turn into chocolate, she says, "Let's leave it here until tomorrow and find out what happens." (Kamii, 1972, p. 117, as quoted in Cowan, 1978, p. 140–41)

We can summarize Kamii's view, which is also Piaget's view, by saying that it is the teacher's role to put children into a state of cognitive *disequilibrium* (see Chapter 8, p. 450).

In general, the information-processing view of education does not alter this emphasis on creating situations that will promote conflict or disequilibrium. It does differ, however, in the specificity that it can employ in determining exactly which situations will create cognitive conflict or disequilibrium. Consider, for example, how specific you could now be in designing a program to teach children to solve orange-juice problems or balance-beam problems. In either case, your first step would be to establish the incorrect rule a child was currently using. Once the rule currently in use was established, you would be able to predict the judgment the child would make for every orange-juice and balance-beam problem you could design. For the purposes of educating the child, however, you would only want to select those problems that would put the child into conflict—that is, those problems on which the child's incorrect rule would lead to incorrect judgments. If a child used Strategy 2 on orange-juice problems, for example, you would need to present problems in which the total amount of the mixtures differed (regardless of the ratio of juice to water). Only in these situations could Strategy-2 children learn the error in their ways. Having children practice any other type of problems would be a waste of time, because Strategy 2 children would get them all right for the wrong reason. By the same token, for children who use Siegler's Rule 2 on balance-beam problems, it would do no good to present problems with equal weights on both sides. In brief, the information-processing approach has made it possible for teachers to pinpoint the exact cause of a child's difficulty for any number of tasks that have been analyzed. This diagnosis makes it possible to select the exercises and experiences that would be most beneficial in allowing children to advance their level of understanding. The Piagetian approach, on the other hand, has never been very helpful in this regard. Teachers knew they should challenge children's misconceptions, but they were never told how to diagnose the misconceptions or select experiences that would lead to disequilibrium.

Because of the specificity that the information-processing approach can bring to bear on questions of what experiences should produce conflict, there is hope that computers can be programmed to teach children some of the basic concepts they need to learn. A good start on such a program is one named BUGGY (Brown & Burton, 1978; Brown & Vanlehn, 1982); it diagnoses "bugs" or errors in children's rules for multidigit subtraction problems. Common errors that the program can diagnose are shown in Table 9-1. At present, BUGGY is only used to diagnose, but it could be made to teach if, after diagnosing a child's difficulty, it selected from its memory a set of problems that would conflict with the child's present rule. All that is required for the success of such programs is that children's errors be consistent rather than random. In one application of BUGGY, 43 percent of the primary-school students tested were found to perform consistently enough for BUGGY to make a diagnosis of their problem.

TABLE 9-1
Program for Diagnosing Children's Errors in Multidigit Subtraction Problems

NAME	EXAMPLE		DESCRIPTION
Borrow from zero	$\begin{array}{r} 103 \\ -\ 45 \\ \hline 158 \end{array}$	$\begin{array}{r} 803 \\ -508 \\ \hline 395 \end{array}$	When borrowing from a column whose top digit is 0, the student writes 9 but does not continue borrowing from the column to the left of the 0.
Smaller from larger	$\begin{array}{r} 253 \\ -118 \\ \hline 145 \end{array}$		The student subtracts the smaller digit in each column from the larger, regardless of which one is on top.
Zero minus a number equals the number	$\begin{array}{r} 140 \\ -\ 21 \\ \hline 121 \end{array}$		Whenever the top digit in a column is 0, the student writes the bottom digit as the answer.
Move over zero, borrow	$\begin{array}{r} 304 \\ -\ 75 \\ \hline 139 \end{array}$		When borrowing from a column whose top digit is 0, the student skips that column and borrows from the next one.
Zero minus a number equals the number *and* move over zero, borrow	$\begin{array}{r} 304 \\ -\ 75 \\ \hline 179 \end{array}$		Whenever the top digit in a column is 0, the student writes the bottom digit as the answer. When borrowing from a column whose top digit is 0, the student skips that column and borrows from the next one.

SOURCE: *Thinking, Problem Solving, Cognition* by R. E. Mayer, 1983, New York: W. H. Freeman.

Because of the advances that information-processing psychologists are making in studying the structure of complex thought and problem solving, some of these psychologists are hopeful that psychology might soon be able to make major contributions in teaching people how to think, reason, and solve problems. In an article expressing this view, Robert Glaser of the University of Pittsburgh noted that "Teaching thinking has been a long-term aspiration, and now progress has occurred that brings it into reach" (Glaser, 1984, p. 102). For this hope to be realized, however, psychologists must demonstrate that they can teach more than just specific problem-solving skills, such as how to solve an orange-juice or balance-beam problem. We know they can do this. What they must now demonstrate is that when children are taught to solve problems via conflict experiences, children then acquire new procedural knowledge general enough to be used on a host of problems. Clearly, teaching children to solve balance-beam or orange-juice problems is not an important goal in and of itself. What is important is that children learn such things as when to encode information about proportions and how proportions can be used procedurally to solve problems ranging from choosing the best buy in the grocery store to understanding buoyancy. Information-processing psychologists are hopeful that their general approach to the study of complex thinking and reasoning will lead us to a solution for this very important problem in education.

MEMORY DEVELOPMENT: THE INFORMATION-PROCESSING VIEW

Until now in the discussion of cognitive development, memory has not been featured at all. It has stayed in the background, as the storage site for declarative and procedural knowledge and as the source of infant difficulties on object-search tasks. In the eyes of many information-processing psychologists, memory deserves to be in the forefront rather than the background of any discussion of general cognitive development. The reason is that memory development is thought to play a key role in overall cognitive development. In a recent chapter addressed to this issue, Charles Brainerd wrote, "The underlying thesis of this chapter is that cognitive development can, in fact, be reduced to memory development" (1983, p. 168). In this section on memory development, we will focus on memory as the information-processing psychologists have, first, to see how memory development can be described and, second, to see what accounts for memory development.

The Computer Metaphor

Whenever one does not know what something actually is, the best way of grappling with it intellectually is to say what it is like. Beginning in the late 1960s with the work of Richard Atkinson and Richard Shiffrin, many psychologists found it useful to say that the processing and storage of information that takes place in human memories is like the processing and storage of information that takes place in computers. Atkinson and Shiffrin (1968), in fact, developed this metaphor in considerable detail by specifying a complete computer model of memory (see Figure 9-6). A key feature in this model was that it distinguished between memory structures and memory processes, each of which had some analog in computer memory systems.

The structural components of the still-popular Atkinson and Shiffrin memory model consist of three distinct storage devices—a **sensory store,** a **short-term-memory store,** and a **long-term-memory store.** The processes are information-management routines (called *control processes*) that are used to transform information, move information from one device to another, or maintain it where it is.

The sensory store holds raw sensory information for a brief time after the sensation itself ceases. You have consciously experienced visual memories from the sensory store whenever you have seen a point of rapidly mov-

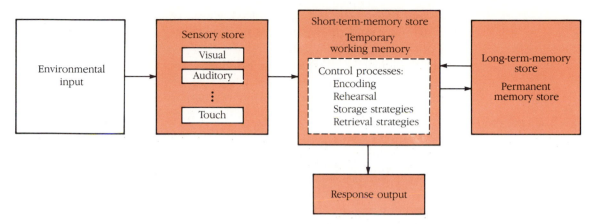

FIGURE 9-6
The Atkinson and Shiffrin Model of Memory
The Atkinson and Shiffrin model conceptualizes human memory as an information-processing system that is divisible into three distinct memory stores. A set of control processes serves to manage the information in memory, moving it along the paths indicated by arrows. Not represented in the Atkinson and Shiffrin model, but also important, is the memory component known as metamemory. If pictured, it would be represented as an executive control structure that would serve to direct the control processes. (After Atkinson & Shiffrin, 1971)

ing light at night, as when someone waves a sparkler or flashlight. As you know, you do not just experience the point of light under these circumstances. You experience a point of light (the current sensation) with a trail of light behind it. The trail is the sensory store's memory of the light's previous positions. Each of the senses has its own sensory-storage register to hold brief memories of the event itself (see Figure 9-6). Thus, there is a *visual* ("iconic") store, an *auditory* ("echoic") store and a *touch* ("haptic") store. None of these memories lasts long, but some last longer than others. Memories in the auditory store, for example, may last considerably longer than visual memories. We can be grateful for this. It enables us to retrieve bits of a conversation, even when we are justifiably charged with the social crime of not having heard a word that was said.

The short-term-memory store is the site where most information processing takes place. This store is frequently compared to a desk top, because like a desk top, we use it as the storage site for all the things we are currently working on. Furthermore, like a real desk top, our mental desk top is severely limited in size. Try to spread out too much at once and something will invariably fall off the edge.

Long-term memory, the third storage area in the Atkinson and Shiffrin tripartite division of memory, contains all the information available to us that is not being actively attended to at present. This could be information that we were exposed to just moments ago (such as the information in the previous paragraph) or information we were exposed to years ago (for example, the names of grade-school teachers). In contrast to the short-term-memory store, which is severely restricted in how much information it can hold, the long-term-memory store is limitless.

The control processes used to manage the information in human memory are executable in the short-term-memory store, which is why they are depicted there in the model shown in Figure 9-6. One control process is to consciously repeat information to oneself. This control process, known as *rehearsal*, is a way of maintaining information in the short-term-memory store. Rehearsal can also be used as a means of transferring information to long-term memory, but it is not a particularly effective process for doing this. A better way is to use a storage strategy that transforms and elaborates on the information to be stored. Imaging the information to be stored, or organizing it in some way, is effective in doing this. Once information is stored in the long-term-memory store, control processes are needed to get it back again. Such processes are called retrieval strategies.

Although there are details in the Atkinson and Shiffrin model that have proved controversial, psychologists have generally found the structure–process distinction made by the model to be useful. The structure-process distinction will be used here as a means of describing what takes place in memory development. Initially we will see that the vast majority of the memory development that gets noted by parents and teachers is due to developments on the processing side of the structure–process division. Processing developments alone, for example, can account for the fact that children go from being preschoolers who must practice and practice just to be able to recall their addresses and phone numbers, to being adolescents who in very short order can learn the principal exports of Argentina, six causes of the French Revolution, and the planets in their order of distance from the sun. People are apt to imagine that adolescents are better at remembering such things because of either general neurological development or specific brain developments that reflect on a person's structural capacity for storing and retaining information. In fact, the developments we are about to discuss—the ones that make for the most noticeable difference in memory abilities—are basically unrelated to physical maturation. Later we will see that there are apparently some maturational factors of importance, but they have a less noticeable impact on day-to-day behavior and, in fact, require careful measurement to detect.

Strategies and Metamemory: Nonmaturational Factors in Memory Development

Much of the story of memory improvement from the preschool years to adulthood is told by describing the age-related changes that are made, first, in how children encode, store, and retrieve information and, second, in what they know about these control processes. The first of these changes involves the development of strategies to use when trying to remember. The second involves the development of knowledge about memory and how it works, a type of knowledge known as *metamemory*.

Strategies for Deliberate Memory

In the late 1960s, thanks primarily to John Flavell (see Flavell and Wellman, 1977), we learned the extent to which memory development is dependent on the development of strategies for managing the contents of memory. Collectively, these strategies are all the active things one does to make information more memorable. They range from tying a string around a finger and underlining passages in a text to using memory tricks called **mnemonics** to remember such things as the 12 cranial nerves or the names of the months with just 30 days. As people develop more and more strategies for remembering, they become increasingly better at remembering.

The Importance of Strategies   The importance of memory strategies is nowhere better illustrated than in the case of people whose ability to remember is so remarkable that they can entertain audiences with their memory feats. One such person was the legendary Zerah Colburn (1833), who routinely performed a task that seemed to require a whole lot more short-term memory space than you or I have. He would multiply five-digit numbers times each other in his head (Smith, 1983). Another, the Russian S. V. Shereshevski (Luria, 1968), could store a meaningless mathematical equation like the one below in a matter of minutes and then remember it hours later.

$$N \cdot \sqrt{d^2 \times \frac{85}{vx}} \cdot \sqrt[3]{\frac{276^2 \cdot 86x}{n^2v \cdot \pi264}} \, n^2b = sv \frac{1624}{32^3} \cdot r^2s$$

He could also remember poems in a language he did not even know. Such feats, remarkable as they are, are not due to any special structural advantage in memory. These abilities, along with others like the alleged exceptional memory of *autistic savants* (Rimland, 1978), are based on the well-practiced use of some simple strategies. To give but one example, a college student from Pittsburgh can take an 80-digit string of random numbers and learn them in about 2 minutes (Ericsson, Chase, & Faloon, 1980). If this were all you knew about the student, you might think he was a freak of nature. In fact, the only truly exceptional thing about this student was that he was willing to work extremely hard to improve his memory span. For 1 hour a day, 3 to 5 days a week, for 20 months, this student practiced digit-span problems. The simple principle on which his improvement was based was chunking.

Chunking is a procedure for taking several discrete bits of information and lumping (or chunking) them together into just one unit. To remember the letters A-I-C, unless they happen to be the initials of your favorite uncle, would take up three bits of space in your short-term memory. If we turn them around, however, to make C-I-A, we have the familiar acronym for the Central Intelligence Agency, which is but one bit of information. By chunking three bits we get one bit. This is just what the student from Pittsburgh learned to do, but he did so on a grand scale. Most of his chunks were running times, because he happened to be an avid runner. So if the digits he was learning included the sequence 3492, he turned that into the running time of 3 minutes, 49.2 seconds, which is a world-class time for the mile run. This made them one chunk. By grouping these running-time chunks into larger chunks, he achieved his own world-class digit span of 82 digits.

Feats of memory like those of the state mnemonists and the student from Pittsburgh illustrate the power of strategies for enhancing our ability to recall information. These feats, however, only make the importance of strategies evident to us; they do not illustrate typical developmental change in memory abilities. For the normative picture of the development of memory strategies in twentieth-century children for whom formal schooling is an essential part of life, we can turn to a summary by Robert Kail and John Hagen (1982). To paraphrase these authors, strategies are seldom used to aid memory by preschoolers, they are occasionally used by children ages 7 to 10, and they are regularly used by children over age 10. The strategies included in this summary statement are storage and retrieval strategies.

Storage in Short-Term Memory   One of the common memory tasks that we assign to our short-term memories is the job of briefly retaining a few bits of information. The information will be some disposable bit of knowledge that we do not want to store away for a long period of time. For example, you might want to remember the catalog number for a book—BF721.P38—while you walk from the library's card catalog to the book's location in the stacks. To solve this simple memory problem, you could use *rehearsal*. Rehearsing the book's number would keep the number intact for the time it took to locate the book. If you discovered that you could no longer recall the number once you had the book off the shelf and in your hand, it would be clear evidence that you solved your memory problem using short-term memory alone.

As basic and fundamental a process as rehearsal may seem to be, children nonetheless "discover" rehearsal during their development. Kail and Hagen (1982, p. 351) put it quite simply, "Rehearsal is not a common cognitive activity prior to nine or ten years of age." What they mean by this is that when young children are given a short list of words or a small set of objects to remember, they do not use rehearsal as an aid to memory. In fact, preschoolers behave no differently when asked to remember a set of items than when asked just to look at them (Appel et al., 1972)! One concrete illustration of this comes from a study by John Flavell, David R. Beach, and Jack M. Chinsky (1966). When asked to remember sets of 3 pictures from a total set of 7, only 2 of the 20 preschoolers used rehearsal. In contrast, 13 of the 20 seven-year-olds and 19 of the 20 ten-year-olds did.

Given that children have poor short-term recall when they fail to rehearse, a natural question to ask is what would happen if they could be induced to rehearse. Would they, then, be as proficient at short-term recall as older children who use the rehearsal strategy? The answer is yes (see Keeney, Cannizzo, & Flavell, 1967). Use of the rehearsal strategy leads to an immediate improvement in memory. This means that we can characterize children's problem on tasks where rehearsal would be appropriate as a *production deficiency*—the failure to employ a demonstrably effective strategy. If children who were induced to use rehearsal failed to profit from the rehearsal procedure, their problem would be labeled a *mediation deficiency*. Mediation deficiencies occur when children use what should be an effective strategy but fail to benefit from it. As we are about to see, children's problems with storage and retrieval strategies of all types are best defined as production deficiencies. When an adult takes over the production function by suggesting or demonstrating effective strategies, age differences in memory performance can be made to disappear.

Storage in Long-Term Memory   When the goal is to store information over a long period of time, a strategy more effective than simple rehearsal is *elaborative rehearsal*. One case where this is true is in storing people's names for later retrieval. Repeating a name over and over to oneself is a poor way to carry out this particular memory chore. A better method is to think about the name and the person it goes with and try to find some meaningful connection between the sound of the name and something you know about the person. If you cannot find a ready-made meaningful connection (as in the fortuitous case where Mr. Armstrong happens to be a weight lifter), you can build in your own meaningful connection using an *imaging* process. Mr. Arbruster, for example, might be pictured with a set of ARtistic BRUises on his face. Caroline Lipsitt has something (a CAR perhaps) sitting on her LIP. Outrageous as such images may become, they are a definite aid to memory.

The particular technique of elaborating information with an image before storing it can hardly be said to be a typical skill for members of our species. A procedure that comes much closer to being species typical is *organization*. As a memory strategy, organization involves grouping together in memory those things that go together. One does this on the basis of discoverable or imposable relationships. Of interest to us here is the fact that there is a developmental shift in the types of relationships used in memory organization (Bjorklund, 1985).

Young children's preferred organizational scheme uses *functional* or *thematic* relations. We have already seen an example of the preference for thematic relations in Piaget's work on classification. As you will recall, preschoolers tended to form arrangements that Piaget called graphic collections (see Figure 8-10). The basis for these was some theme that children imposed. A house theme resulted in their putting together all the blocks that could be arranged into a houselike structure; a garden theme resulted in their putting together all the blocks that could be arranged like flowers in rows. A second example of the preference for thematic relations comes from research on the way in which children group words. Asked to select the best match among the words *needle, pin,* and *thread,* young children (in contrast to older ones) tend to pick *needle* and *thread* (Smiley & Brown, 1979). Why? Because they are related by a sewing theme.

Functional relations are quite similar to thematic relations, except that the "theme" relating objects is their shared function. Young children's preference for functional relations over alternatives is evident in their tendency to define words by function. They say, for example, that a shovel is to dig, a house is to live in, and a bike is to ride. This tendency, too, contrasts with that of older children who base object definitions on the object's category not its function (for example, a house is a structure, a bike is a vehicle, and a shovel is a tool).

There is nothing wrong with a function- or theme-based organizational system except that it overlooks one of the most powerful organizational tools available to humans—organization via categorical relations. If you are storing items in a shopping list or the names of heads of state, for example, you would be hard pressed to find any functional or thematic relations that would greatly aid memory. But if you were to group the items by category—vegetables, dairy products, and bakery items for the grocery list; royalty, elected officials, and self-appointed dictators for heads of state—memory for them would be enhanced.

Data from a wealth of studies show that young children do not tend to spontaneously impose categorical relations on to-be-remembered material. Between ages 6 and 9 they become ever-more likely to use categorical relations, but not until around 10 or 11 years of age do they do so routinely. You may recall that this is the case from Barbara Moely's research, which was presented in the last chapter—see p. 417 (Moely, Olson, Halwes, & Flavell, 1969). When children of different ages were shown some pictures that they were to try to remember, only the older children (fifth graders) reliably organized them into categorically related sets of pictures while learning them. Because of this they had superior recall for the pictures. However, when Moely and her colleagues arranged the pictures for the children and then labeled the categories, the memories of even the youngest children (kindergarteners) increased to nearly the level of the fifth graders. Third graders, in fact did better on average than the fifth graders. The conclusion is, then, that younger children can use categorical organization effectively when it is suggested to them, but they prefer not to (Smiley & Brown, 1979). The fact that children can use the organization strategy effectively when it is suggested to them but not otherwise leads to the conclusion that young children's problem on Moely's memory task, as on others, is a production deficiency.

Retrieval Strategies When you have used a particular strategy to store information, the information can be retrieved by simply recalling your strategy. Frequently, however, we seek to remember information that was not stored in a careful, deliberate way. Like the socks in a dresser drawer, this information just gets tossed into memory. When we are called on to pull this information out, we need a *cue* to aid retrieval. For example, if you were asked to remember where you left your sunglasses or umbrella, a good strategy would be to work back through your day, recalling each of the places you went. With a place in mind, you could generally cue your memory for whether you had the glasses or umbrella with you at the time. In trying to remember names of people, states, or countries you could cue your memory by simply working through the alphabet with "A" as the first cue, "B" as the second, and so on.

In keeping with the developmental trend we have seen throughout this section, preschool children do not use strategies that would produce the needed cues. Instead, they must depend on external cues to provide the means of retrieving whatever memories they have stored away. You and I, of course, use external cues as well, but we are not dependent on them to the extent that preschoolers are.

Two naturalistic studies support the generalization that young children recall information from their long-term memories only when external cues are available to jog their memories. In one, Hilary Ratner of the University of Chicago spent about 8 hours in the homes of 20 children ages 2½ to 3½. Her purpose was to record examples of the children's spontaneous use of past information during conversations with their mothers. One of the things Ratner found was that the children she observed did not produce their own cues to aid retrieval. In Ratner's words,

> Memory functioning did not appear to be greatly controlled by children even in more meaningful and familiar settings. Young children in this study . . . appeared to retrieve information with difficulty and to do little to help themselves remember during the retrieval process. (Ratner, 1980, p. 64)

In the second study of young children's spontaneous, real-life retrieval skills, Katherine Nelson and Gail Ross relied on mothers' diaries. The diaries covered a period of 3 months, and in them mothers were asked to record all instances of memories in their 2- to 2½-year-old children. Again there was no evidence of self-cued recall. According to the authors,

One striking finding of the study . . . is that there was no evidence from any report of a spontaneous (uncued) recall memory. In every case some recognizable external cue brought forth the verbalization or action that evidenced a memory. (Nelson & Ross, 1980, p. 95)

When we turn to laboratory studies for evidence of retrieval deficiencies, we find an even more surprising result. The evidence here indicates that even when children are given cues to use to aid retrieval, they may not take advantage of them without explicit instruction. One very convincing demonstration of this was provided by Akira Kobasigawa of the University of Waterloo. The task that Kobasigawa gave his subjects (Kobasigawa, 1974) was to remember the things that were depicted on each of 24 picture cards. After the children had named each of the cards, they were shown the cards once again. The procedure for showing the pictures this second time introduced the retrieval cue that would be used later. The procedure was to have the subjects complete a fill-in-the-blank sentence. Kobasigawa would point to one of the pictures in the series—for example, a bear—and then have the child complete the sentence, "In the zoo, you find a (bear)." This introduced "zoo" as a cue that could later help the child to recall the bear picture. Other cues for the pictured objects were a park, sink, road, room, fruit stand, baby, and music book. Once the 24 pictures had been introduced in this way, the children were shown pictures of the 8 cues. They were told that these pictures might help them recall the other pictures they had seen.

The statement that the 8 cue cards "might help their recall" was not explicit enough to suggest a retrieval strategy to the 6-year-old first graders in Kobasigawa's study. Of 12 first graders, 5 did not even look at the cue cards while trying to remember the pictures. Of the 7 who looked at the cards, only 2 used them to cue their memory for the pictures. Overall, the memory of the first graders for the pictures was no better with the cue cards than without them. The performance of the first graders in this case is a classic example of production deficiency, because when a separate set of 6-year-olds was given direction in using the cue cards, their memory was every bit as good as that of 12-year-old sixth graders. The directions were quite simple. Kobasigawa just showed the children a cue card (for example, the zoo card) and reminded them that three pictures went with that card (the bear and two others). When cue cards were presented in this way, the 6-year-olds used them effectively. Otherwise, however, they did not.

In contrast to the performance of the first graders in Kobasigawa's study, most of the third graders (9 out of 12) used the cue cards in their information retrieval. But they were ineffective in doing so. A retrieval cue is a powerful tool that can bring back a wealth of information. The 9-year-old third graders, however, only recalled about 1 picture per cue card. This is an abysmal performance as indicated by the fact that 9-year-olds who did not have the cue cards were able to remember as many pictures. Children in this age group had the form of a retrieval strategy, therefore, but not the substance. Only the 12-year-olds did a thoroughly adult job of using the cue cards as retrieval aids. This means that they began the recall task by looking at a card and then searched their memories exhaustively to remember all the pictures that had been associated with that cue. These results are summarized in Figure 9-7.

Thus far we have seen that the acquisition of memory strategies seems to account for major age-related improvements in short- and long-term memory that occur between the preschool and high-school years. We know this because when children with deficient memories are maneuvered into using an appropriate strategy, age-related differences in memory disappear. This confirms that children's failure to use the various strategies for infor-

FIGURE 9-7
The Use of Cues to Aid Retrieval
These data show how many of the 24 picture cards children from Grades 1, 3, and 6 could remember as a function of their experimental condition in Kobasigawa's study. The free-recall group was simply asked to recall the 24 pictures. The cued-recall group was given the set of 8 picture cues and reminded that the 24 pictures were associated with the 8 cues. The group receiving directive cues was asked to name the 3 pictures that went with each of the picture cues. (After Kobasigawa, 1974)

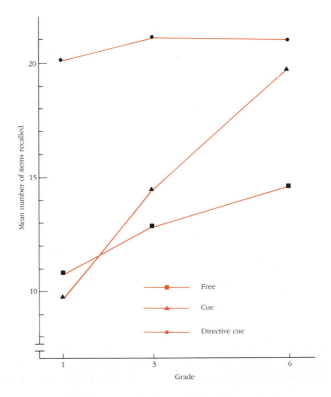

mation maintenance, storage, and retrieval is due not to a mediational but to a production deficiency. In everyday terms, their problem is that they just do not think to use the appropriate strategy. This fact has led researchers to ask why. Why should there be production deficiencies?

Metamemory

Many researchers believe that children's production deficiencies stem in part from their inadequate knowledge *about* memory and how it works (Flavell & Wellman, 1977). This means that their true problem might not be a memory problem per se but rather a *metamemory* problem.

The concept of metamemory was not part of Atkinson and Shiffrin's model, but it is obvious to researchers today that somewhere in the memory system there must be an executive control structure that has the responsibility for recognizing memory needs, choosing effective strategies, and monitoring the results (Kail, 1984). This control structure is **metamemory.** The knowledge that it uses to make decisions about information processing is known as metamemorial knowledge.

A considerable amount of research indicates that metamemory problems in young children may indeed be the primary source of their production deficiencies. One study, for example, has shown that young children tend to overestimate the amount of information they will be able to remember following a brief study period. Older children are far more accurate (see Figure 9-8). This indicates that older children are more aware of their own memory ability, as well as of the memory requirements posed by various tasks. These could be factors that contribute to their more frequent and more sophisticated use of strategies.

A second way in which gaps in metamemory might lead to production deficiencies is that children might overlook a particular strategy because they do not understand how it could be helpful. For example, even if children thought to use categorical organization, it might not be obvious to them that such organization would be a useful way to aid recall. Some evidence that this might be the case comes from attempts to train children to use memory strategies. These studies show that a child needs to be trained not only in the use of a strategy but trained, too, in the reason the strategy is effective (Kennedy & Miller, 1976). This is called *informed training* (Brown, Campione, & Day, 1981). The rationale for informed training is consistent with the finding that children do not routinely select a strategy until they have come to understand that the strategy is in fact effective (Moynahan, 1978). It is consistent, too, with the finding that getting children to attend to the strategies they use increases the likelihood that effective strategies will be reused (Lodico, Ghatala, Levin, Pressley, & Bell, 1983).

Despite the data that favor the causal hypothesis linking metamemory development to strategic development, correlational studies show little to no evidence that the children with the most metamemorial knowledge are

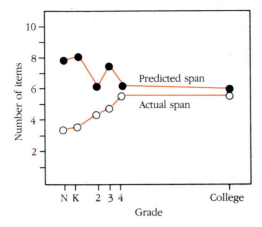

FIGURE 9-8

Inaccuracies in Predicting Memory Span

Children in nursery school (N) and kindergarten (K) show that they have very poor knowledge of what to expect from their memories. When they were shown sets of ten pictures and asked how many they would recall, these preschool children greatly overestimated their ability to recall. By late childhood, expectations were in line with ability. (After Flavell, Friedrichs, & Hoyt, 1970, and Yussen & Levy, 1975)

also the ones who are best at remembering. This runs counter to what we would expect. John Cavanaugh and Marion Perlmutter (1982) believe, however, that "the failure to find substantial correlations [between children's metamemorial knowledge and their ability to remember] is due more to bad research than flawed hypotheses" (p. 22). One of the problems in the correlational research may involve the failure to use memory tasks that are complex enough to force children to reflect on what they are doing (Borkowski, 1985). When tasks do not force reflection, children no less than adults are likely to make a strategy choice on the basis of ingrained habit alone. Tasks that allow children to execute memory acts without appealing to their metamemories would be expected, therefore, to produce the result that has in fact been obtained in studies of the relation between memory performance and metamemorial knowledge—namely, little to no correlation (Cavanaugh & Borkowski, 1980).

Maturational Developments Related to Capacity, Speed of Identification, and Retention

The discussion of strategies and metamemory makes it clear that a great deal of the improvement in memory from the preschool to adolescent years can be accounted for by development in these two domains alone. Because neither of these developments is directly related to maturational changes, however, one might well wonder whether maturation is at all relevant to memory development. Perhaps infants, from a neurological point of view at least, are as capable of storing, retaining, and retrieving information as are older children, adolescents, and adults. To conclude this chapter we will consider the evidence on this issue.

Can Maturational Developments in the Sensory Store Account for Aspects of Memory Development?

Because the sensory store stands at the start of the human information-processing system, it is possible that maturational changes here are the source of some part of the overall memory differences between infants and adults (Aslin, 1984). It is possible, for example, that the amount of information a sensory store can hold, or the length of time it retains the information, can change with age.

If there are changes in the amount of information held by the sensory store, they would be reflected in a measure known as the *span of apprehension,* which is a measure of the amount of information potentially available for processing. Methods do not exist for testing the spans of apprehension for neonates and young infants, but the results for preschoolers are clear. According to researchers who have tested the size of the visual memory in humans ages 5 to 18, there are "no age differences in the amount of information initially available for processing" (Morrison, Holmes, & Haith, 1974, p. 422). In brief, this means that from early childhood on, the amount of information available to the memory system from the sensory-input side is not a factor in development.

With regard to the duration of information in the sensory store, there is one known developmental change: infants retain information longer than adults in both their auditory and visual stores (Cowan, Suomi, & Morse, 1982; Lasky & Spiro, 1980). The implications of this for memory (and for perception) are not altogether clear, but they imply that infants cannot possibly process visual and auditory information at the same rate as older children and adults. The reason is that the sensory store must be cleared of previous sensations before new ones can be recorded. Nelson Cowan and his colleagues (1982) suggest, therefore, that the slower speech that parents universally use when talking to young infants is well adapted to the information-processing abilities of these infants. Insufficient research in this area, however, makes it impossible to speculate further on the consequences of maturational changes in sensory memories.

Short-term Memory and Maturation

You will recall from the brief description of short-term memory given earlier that one of the most interesting characteristics of short-term memory is its limited size. There is simply not room for a lot of information at any one time. Nonetheless, there is steady growth in short-term-memory storage capacity from about age 2 until adulthood. An important question to answer is whether this size increase has anything to do with maturation within the nervous system. Before answering it, we need to examine how the size of short-term memory is measured.

One way of measuring short-term-memory size is to take a measure of **memory span.** This is a measure of how much information people can passively retain in consciousness without the aid of rehearsal. You can obtain such a measure by presenting someone with a series of digits at a rate of one per second and then asking that all the digits be recalled in order. You can start with a series only a few digits long (for example, 9-3-8) and then build up to longer series by adding a digit at a time. The longest series correctly recalled is defined as the **digit span.** It serves as an estimate of the more general concept of memory span. (Measures of letter span and word span provide other estimates.) Normative studies in which digit-span measures have been taken lead to the conclusion that adult humans have room for only 5 to 9 digits in their short-term memories. The average adult span is just 7 digits (Miller, 1956).

Measures that tap what Juan Pascual-Leone calls **M-space** or *M-power* (Pascual-Leone, 1970) provide alternatives to memory-span measures for determining the capacity of short-term memory. The critical difference between M-space measures and simple span measures is that M-space measures require the execution of some mental act (for example, adding, comparing, integrating) rather than just passive storage. A good example, because it compares easily to digit span, is Robbie Case's *counting-span* measure of M-space (Case, Kurland, & Daneman, 1979). To obtain a measure of counting span, subjects are given cards with different numbers of dots on them. The dots must be counted and the total retained in memory as the next card is counted. Retaining the count from one card yields an M-space estimate of 1. Retaining the count from two cards yields an M-space estimate of 2, and so on.

One of the reasons that M-space measures have been developed as adjuncts to simpler memory-span tests is that information-processing psychologists today are more explicit than Atkinson and Shiffrin were in viewing short-term memory as not just a storage area but as a processing area (Dempster, 1985, p. 212). In keeping with this view, many information-processing psychologists prefer the term **working memory** (Baddeley & Hitch, 1974) to the term short-term store. The working-memory label captures more explicitly the notion that information in short-term memory is generally not just sitting there: rather it is being actively employed in some ongoing mental task. Thinking of short-term memory as having a dual processing–storage role leads to conceptualizations of short-term memory that allocate some portion of the total space to processing and some portion to storage. (Illustrations of such conceptualizations are shown in Figures 9-11 and 9-13.)

As indicated earlier, the fact of primary interest to developmentalists is that regardless of how you measure the storage capacity of short-term memory, whether using measures that stress both processing and storage (M-space measures) or those that stress primarily storage (memory-span measures), there is a reliable increase in storage capacity with age. Data from 13 studies using digit-span measures are summarized in Figure 9-9. These show that there is an increase from just better than two digits at age 2 to about seven digits for late adolescents and adults. M-space increases have not yet been studied normatively (Dempster, 1985), but the data in Figure 9-10 suggest that such changes occur. A very important question to be answered is whether these increases in apparent capacity imply a structural change in short-term-memory capacity itself or whether they imply that a storage area of fixed capacity is being used more efficiently. In either case, whether there is a capacity increase or just an efficiency increase, we need to consider whether maturation of the nervous system plays a role in the capacity or efficiency increase.

FIGURE 9-9

Developmental Differences in Memory Span

These data show how the digit-span size increases with age. The dashed lines show the total range in scores for a given age. The data on which this curve is based measured digit span by having subjects repeat a series of digits backwards. (After Dempster, 1981)

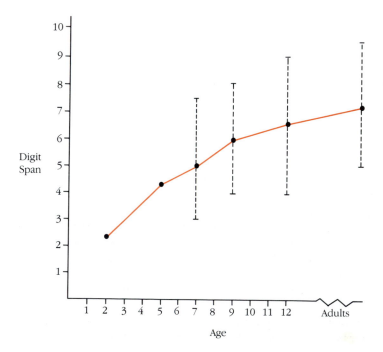

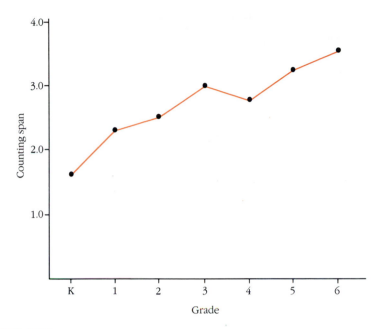

FIGURE 9-10
Developmental Differences in Counting Span
Normative data are not available on the growth of counting span, but these data, which come from a small-scale study, show a steady increase from preschool to late childhood. Advocates of M-space measures such as counting span argue that such measures are superior to memory-span measures because they reflect the trade-off that exists between processing space and storage space in the short-term store. The more space required for processing, the less space there is available for storage. Memory-span measures require no processing other than item identification and, so, fail to capture this dynamic aspect of working memory. (After Case, Kurland, & Goldberg, 1982)

Do Capacity Increases Underlie Span Increases? One structural change that would easily explain the increases in memory span would be an increase in the size of short-term memory. Juan Pascual-Leone has been a primary advocate for this hypothesis. In his view (see Figure 9-11), for example, maturation is said to produce M-space increases that amount to about one unit every 2 years from age 3 to midadolescence. Because these M-space increases correspond to increases in processing capacity, M-space growth in Pascual-Leone's theory is the basis for growth in cognitive abilities such as those outlined by Piaget. Pascual-Leone is not alone in holding this general view. According to Frank Dempster (1985), "One of the more pervasive theories in the field of cognitive development is that capacity increases throughout childhood and adolescence and that this increase is a major source of age-related changes in intellectual proficiency" (p. 222).

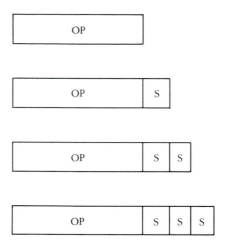

FIGURE 9-11

Pascual-Leone's Capacity-Increase Hypothesis

The capacity-increase hypothesis represented in this model holds that the number of slots available for memory storage (S) increases with age. The other section of short-term memory is the one in which mental operations (OP) are carried out— for example, item identification, counting, ordering, comparing, integrating, and so on. (After Case, 1985)

There are, however, some problems with the capacity-increase hypothesis, particularly when it is used to explain developmental differences in span from age 7 to adulthood (Dempster, 1981, p. 86). The principal problem is that the familiarity of the materials used in span tests can be easily shown to be a very important variable in determining the size of the span. One of the first experiments to demonstrate this was conducted by Michelene Chi of the University of Pittsburgh. The subjects in Chi's study (1978) were six 10-year-olds who were chosen because they were expert chess players and six nonexpert adults who, nonetheless, were familiar with the game. Chi found that when she compared the 10-year-old chess players to the adults on a digit-span task, the 10-year-olds appeared to have less storage space in their short-term memories. The adults could recall about eight digits on average; the 10-year-olds only recalled about six. But when the task was changed from recalling digits to recalling locations of chess pieces, the results were reversed (see Figure 9-12). The 10-year-old chess players could recall better than nine locations, but the non-chess-playing adults could recall only about six.

Chi's results show clearly that familiarity with the information to be retained in short-term memory can be a more important variable than age alone. Though this result is not a surprising one, it is quite important theoretically because it provides an exception to the general rule that capacity increases with age. Other results that prove an exception to this rule come

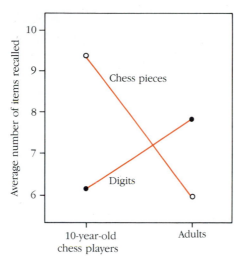

FIGURE 9-12
Familiarity Affects Memory Span
Judging from their digit-span performance alone, we would say that the 10-year-old chess players had less storage space than the adults; but judging from their memory for chess pieces, we would say they had more. Apparently, familiarity with test items to be recalled affects the size of a person's short-term memory span.

from studies in which children and adults have been equated in familiarity by giving them both some totally meaningless information to retain in memory. On tasks such as this, adults do just slightly better than children. Thus, whereas comparing adults to 5-year-olds on tasks using meaningful digits might produce an adult advantage on the order of 2 to 1, the advantage drops considerably on tasks using less meaningful materials (Chi, 1976; Dempster, 1981, p. 86). A capacity-increase hypothesis cannot account for these exceptions to the usual correlation between span and age without losing parsimony, because it must add the proviso that the hypothesis is only valid for certain stimuli. This is an untidy state of affairs, one that encourages good theoretical scientists to seek a single principle to account both for the familiarity data and for the usual span data. It turns out that there is such a principle. It is a measure of efficiency known as *speed of identification.*

Does Speed of Identification Account for Memory-Span Increases?   As explained by Frank Dempster (1981), the speed-of-identification hypothesis is that "an individual who has difficulty identifying items will have relatively less capacity left over for storing items and thus will have a shorter memory span than someone who identifies items with relative ease" (p. 79). According to this hypothesis, therefore, developmental differences in span—

whether conventional memory span, counting span, or span for chess-piece locations—are not due to capacity differences or even to age differences per se, they are due to differences in the speed with which people of various ages and knowledge states can identify the items used in the memory test. The hypothesis is depicted in Figure 9-13 to show how it contrasts with the capacity-increase hypothesis (compare with Figure 9-11).

The most common way of measuring speed of identification is to show visual representations of stimulus items (whether a digit, a word, or a picture) and have subjects name them as rapidly as possible. In complete agreement with the speed-of-identification hypothesis, there is a remarkable

FIGURE 9-13

Case's Speed-of-Identification Hypothesis

According to the speed-of-identification hypothesis, the overall capacity of short-term memory does not grow with age. What changes is the proportion of the total storage space that must be given over to processing (OP). With age and with familiarity, the space required for processing is reduced, thereby freeing up extra storage space (S). (After Case, 1985)

correlation between the speed with which people can name items and the number of those items that they can fit in their memory spans. Using children in the age range 3 to 6, for example, Robbie Case and his colleagues (Case, Kurland, & Goldberg, 1982, experiment 1) found a correlation of −.74 between identification speed and span length for sets of common words (star, ball, fish, tree, and so on). This means that children who took more time to identify the words used in the span test had the shorter memory spans, and those who took less time had larger memory spans. Case and his colleagues also showed that when the word-recognition times of adults were reduced to the level of 6-year-olds (an achievement brought about by giving the adults unfamiliar words like *dast, thaid, flim,* and *brup*), the adults had spans no greater than those of 6-year-olds. These observations tend to tie span length more closely to recognition speed than to age. Quite similar data exist for M-space measures. Namely, the speed with which a person can count seems to explain developmental differences in counting span better than a capacity-increase hypothesis.

The data supporting the counting-speed/counting-span relationship can be easily summarized. First (and not surprisingly), older children can count faster than younger children. Second, for children of a given age, those who count faster have the longer counting spans. Third, when the counting efficiency of older children and adults is handicapped by making them count in what is in effect a foreign language, their counting spans drop (Case, Kurland, & Goldberg, 1982, experiment 3). Interestingly, just as in the case of word spans, the adult counting spans drop to precisely the level that would be predicted given their counting speed. Namely, if their handicap reduces their speed level to that of a normal 6-year-old counting in English, the adults will have the counting span of 6-year-olds. Combining all this evidence makes it clear that counting speed is a major variable in determining counting span, and it makes it likely that age-related changes in speed underlie the age-related increase in counting span.

Because the data on counting speed and item-identification speed are so similar and because both are strongly correlated with measures of span, it is compelling to believe that increases in speed are the cause of increases in span. Furthermore, the speed-of-identification hypothesis, unlike the capacity-increase hypothesis, can account for the familiarity data without losing parsimony. Nonetheless, prudent observers of the theoretical debate over whether span increase is due to increased capacity or increased speed point out that there is absolutely no reason why there could not be some of both (Kail, 1984, p. 163). Speed does increase with age, and this could account for a great deal of the developmental difference. But capacity might also increase to some extent. If so, the increase is most likely to occur in the period from infancy to the end of early childhood. In this age range, age differences in span can be greatly reduced through manipulations involving familiarity, but they cannot be completely eliminated (Dempster, 1981, p. 86).

Are There Maturational Changes That Underlie the Structural Changes?
Regardless of whether a capacity increase, a speed increase, or both underlie the age-related changes in what people can achieve in their short-term memories, we are still faced with a problem of explaining how these structural changes come about. Both Case and Pascual-Leone appeal to myelinization within the nervous system as a possible mediating factor. As we saw in Chapter 6, this is a process that continues from birth through adolescence. Potentially, therefore, it could serve as the neurological basis for structural changes in short-term memory. Unfortunately, there are no data at all to directly link increased myelinization with memory-span or M-space increases. The myelinization hypothesis, therefore, is pure speculation even though some investigators do find it plausible (see particularly Case, 1985, pp. 377-81).

Automatization as an Alternative to a Maturational Hypothesis   It
might strike you that rather than go off in search of a maturational explanation within the nervous system for the increases that occur in working-memory capacity with age, there might be simpler explanations, ones that

do not involve maturational changes at all. One is automatization of processing. The simple hypothesis here would be that people perform mental operations (such as item identification and counting) more automatically with practice, thereby freeing up working-memory space for other storage or processing activities. This hypothesis works well for some sensorimotor activities. It explains how budding magicians and jugglers, with practice, can go from having to concentrate totally on their performances to having the extra memory capacity for telling jokes or conversing during their performances. But it does not work in all cases, particularly for nonsensorimotor mental tasks such as item identification and counting. In an important demonstration of the limitations on the automatization hypothesis, Midian Kurland (1981) had first graders practice counting for 15 to 25 minutes a day for 3 months. This practice had no impact on either their counting speeds or counting spans. We can conclude that the speed of processing for at least some mental acts will be impervious to practice, thus necessitating some other explanation—probably a maturational one—for the increase in speed that comes with age.

Chunking and Rehearsal Alternatives to a Maturational Hypothesis

Before settling on the need for a maturational hypothesis, there is yet another nonmaturational hypothesis to be considered for explaining age-related increases in working-memory capacity: namely, span increases may be due to the ever-more complete and sophisticated use of some of the control processes in the Atkinson and Shiffrin memory model. One control process that could affect span is chunking. Another is rehearsal.

The fact that young children fail to rehearse spontaneously (see p. 480) and the fact that they may lack the knowledge to form meaningful chunks of information provide a seemingly attractive alternative to a maturational explanation for age-related differences in memory and counting span. The explanation would be that, with age, children become ever-more likely to fill the interval between digits (or counts) with some rehearsal and to find chunkable sequences of numbers (9-7-5 perhaps). It turns out, however, that the strategic explanation is not sufficient to explain all the developmental differences that have been observed. Careful investigations reveal, for example, that despite the obvious importance of chunking and rehearsal on many short-term memory tasks, these strategies do not play much of a role on traditional tests of span (see Dempster, 1981, for a review). One of the reasons is that the tests of span are designed and administered in a way that reduces the opportunity for strategic activity. Thus, maturational hypotheses, such as the speed-of-identification and capacity-increase hypotheses discussed earlier, are still needed to explain the age-related differences in span. Processing improvements are certainly a factor in improved short-term memory in general, but they are not sufficient by themselves to explain the memory-span and counting-span data.

Long-term Memory and Maturation

Concern for the effects of maturation on long-term memory development have focused on the infancy period, with the first question being, "Do infants have the neural capacity for storing and retaining information over a long period of time?" One reason to think that they might not is the phenomenon of *infantile amnesia:* most people have no memory at all for the events of their first 2 to 3 years of life (Sheingold & Tenney, 1982; Spear 1984).

Do Infants Remember?

Do Infants Remember?   In order to determine whether young infants have long-term-memory storage ability, researchers have used *recognition* tests rather than recall tests. These assess the ability to distinguish the familiar from the unfamiliar. To conduct a recognition test, researchers begin by presenting an event that the subjects of the memory test have not experienced before. After establishing familiarity for this novel event, they then see how long it takes before the familiar event gets reduced to an unfamiliar one by forgetting. A specific instance of such a test—one that can be used even with very young infants—involves using the *habituation* method described in Chapter 7 (see p. 323).

As you will recall, habituation is reflected in a decline in attention to a previously novel stimulus, one that evoked a lot of attention when it was first presented. A test for habituation in infants involves a familiarization period that may take from 5 to 15 stimulus presentations over a 5- to 10-minute period. If habituation occurs, interest level as measured by fixation time or some other measure will decline to near zero with repeated presentations of the stimulus. This decline, when it is truly due to habituation and not just to fatigue, is evidence that the infant has a memory representation of the initial stimulus. Each time it is presented, infants recognize it; and with repeated presentations, they become disinterested in it. We can be sure that the decline is due to the presence of a memory and not just fatigue or some other transient state by observing what happens when a new stimulus is presented. If interest suddenly picks up again, the previous decline had to be due to habituation. Use of the habituation procedure has revealed that even neonates in their first hours can recognize prior visual experiences (Slater, Morison, & Rose, 1982).

Although habituation studies clearly show that even neonates can form memories, the evidence from these studies regarding the length of time young infants can retain a memory of the stimulus is less than impressive. Some studies show, for example, that in infants as old as 3 months of age, forgetting begins in less than 15 seconds and is complete in about 75 seconds (Stinson, 1973). Summing up this and other evidence, John Werner and Marion Perlmutter report that "there is little evidence that infants remember visual stimuli for more than a few minutes" (1979, p. 30). If we can generalize from visual memories to all memories and if we can take habituation data as a valid measure of the retentiveness of infant memories, it is no wonder that humans experience infantile amnesia. They experience amnesia because their memories of this period dissipate about as rapidly as they are formed.

Research by Carolyn Rovee-Collier (see review in Rovee-Collier, 1984), however, makes it quite clear that infant memories are not nearly as bad as habituation studies make them out to be. The problem with habituation tests, she says is that they test infants for memories of a basically meaningless event—the act of looking at some particular object or picture. Infants see novel things all day long. Why should the particular ones that psychologists use in habituation studies (see sample in Figure 9-14) have any special importance? To be truly meaningful, an event must be more than just a casual experience. Such, at least, is the thinking of Rovee-Collier and her colleagues, who believe that to obtain a valid measure of the retentiveness of young infant memories, researchers must first ensure that they have given infants something meaningful to remember.

The event that Rovee-Collier and her colleagues use in their research is one that involves learning as well as looking. An attractive mobile is hung over the cribs of infant subjects, and a ribbon is run from their ankles to the mobile (see Figure 9-15). In very brief order (usually in from 6 to 9 minutes), infants as young as 2 months of age learn the contingency between their own leg kicks and movements in the mobile (Davis & Rovee-Collier, 1983). They apparently find the contingency fascinating, because they will continue producing mobile movement for long periods of time,

FIGURE 9-14
Typical Habituation Stimuli
Stimuli such as these can be used in studies using the habituation method to demonstrate that neonates form memories for visual events.

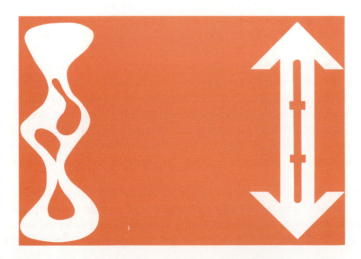

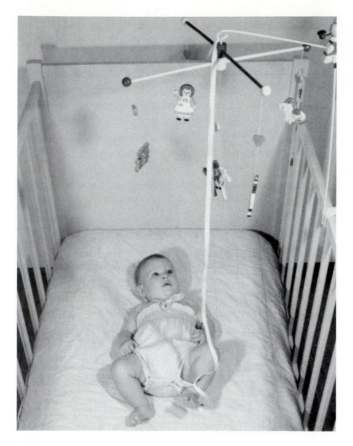

FIGURE 9-15
Establishing a Meaningful Memory
When ribbons are attached to their ankles, young infants learn to make a mobile move by kicking their legs. Infant's long-term memory for this learning has been the focus of research by Rovee-Collier and colleagues.

and when they look up to see the mobile, even when it is not attached to their legs, they will often smile (Rovee-Collier, 1984, p. 110). By all appearances then, the contingency between leg kicks and mobile movements is far more meaningful than just looking at something novel. The question then becomes how long the infants can retain this meaningful association of kicks and mobile movements. If they are put back in the cribs with the mobiles 1 day after learning, will they begin to kick again? How about 2 days later, and so on?

Rovee-Collier's data show that for infants who are just 12 weeks of age (see top curve in Figure 9-16), memory of how to make the mobile move will last for somewhere between 1 and 2 weeks. The evidence is that when

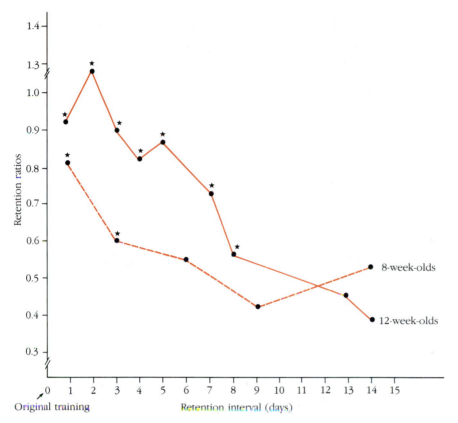

FIGURE 9-16

Measures of Long-term Memory Retention

The solid curve shows data for infants 12 weeks of age who were retested after 1, 2, 3, 4, 5, 7, 8, 13, or 14 days to see if they remembered the mobile and how to make it move. The frequency of leg kicks made during the retest was used as a sign of memory. If the kicks were as frequent during the retest as at the end of learning, the retention ratio (a measure of memory) was 1.00. The decline in frequency over time is a sign of forgetting (or retrieval failure). Statistical analysis showed that there was significant evidence of memory on every retest date from 1 to 8 days after training. This is indicated by the stars next to these data points. The dashed curve shows 8-week-olds who were retested after 1, 3, 6, 9, and 14 days. (After Earley, Griesler, & Rovee-Collier, 1985)

infants are put back in the test crib at any time from 1 to 8 days after the original training, they begin kicking at roughly the same rate as before. They recognize the mobile, therefore, and they also remember what to do to make it move. This is a far more impressive memory display than is obtained from habituation studies for infants the same age. Apparently, meaningfulness does enhance the memorability of events.

FIGURE 9-17
Reinstating Infant Memories
By putting an infant back in the context with all the necessary cues for reviving a memory, Rovee-Collier discovered that she could reinstate infant memories. Note that the infant does not have the ankle ribbon attached so no relearning can take place.

But is it in fact true that when infants cease to kick at the same rate as in the original training session their memory for what was learned in that session has faded? That is, can we interpret the absence of a high kick rate as evidence that the previous learning has completely disappeared from the long-term store? This, of course, is plausible. But it is also possible that the learning is still there in some sense but that it cannot be retrieved. Rovee-Collier and her colleagues have produced some interesting data that suggest that the second interpretation is the correct one. This means that we cannot even set 2 weeks as the upper limit on young infant memories.

The evidence that infants' long-term recognition problems might lie more in retrieval than in storage comes from the fact that a brief reminder (called a **reinstatement**) can make a memory retrievable once again, even after the memory is presumed to be gone. To produce reinstatement in Rovee-Collier's memory research, infants who have not seen the test mobile for a few weeks are shown the moving mobile again (see Figure 9-17). No further learning is involved, because the infants are sitting up and no ribbons are attached to their ankles. For just a brief time, their attention is drawn to the moving mobile (which previously they learned to move using leg kicks). If there were no memory of the mobile in storage at this time of reinstatement, the reinstatement would have no effect (and the reinstated event would be experienced not as a reinstatement but as a novel event.) But, in fact, reinstatement has a very dramatic effect. In one study, for example, a reactivated 13-day-old memory was just as strong on the day following reinstatement as was a 1-day-old memory on the day after learning (Rovee-Collier, Sullivan, Enright, Lucas, & Fagen, 1980, see Figure 9-18). Even when reinstatement came a month after the original learning, it served to reactivate the memory of the mobile (see lone point on far right in Figure 9-18). Obviously, therefore, the memory for the mobile was still stored long after the original training. It just had to be reactivated before becoming available for retrieval. This raises the intriguing possibility that infantile amnesia could be prevented through a plan of systematic memory reinstatement. We do not know this to be the case, however, because such an experiment has not been done.

Does Maturation Within the Nervous System Underlie Age Differences in the Retentiveness of Infant Memories? While Rovee-Collier's studies show considerable capacity for the long-term storage of information by young infants, her studies also show some age differences. In the absence of reinstatement, for example, 8-week-olds store information about the leg-kick/mobile contingency only for about 3 days (see lower curve in Figure 9-16) as compared with the 8+ days for infants just a month older. This raises the question of whether there might be neurological development within this period that enhances the long-term storage abilities of infants.

It turns out that neurological development in the period 8 to 12 weeks is a factor in explaining improved retention, but not in the way that you might think. You would think, for example, that the relevant neurological developments would have to do with the neural capacity to store information. In fact, the effect seems to be on encoding. The more-mature infants appear to acquire more information about the mobile and the surrounding context during their training sessions than do the younger infants (see Rovee-Collier, 1984, for a discussion). One of the neurological reasons that

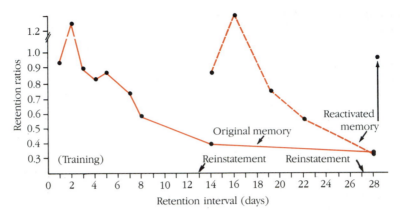

FIGURE 9-18
Reinstatement Protects Against Forgetting
Memories reinstated 13 days after learning could be recalled as well as memories only 1 day old. This is shown by comparing the Day-1 memories in the "original memory" group with the Day-14 memories in the "reactivated memory" groups. Note, too, that the forgetting curve for reactivated memories is very much like the forgetting curve for original memories. The single point at the far right shows the memory in the group of infants who were not retested until Day 28 after learning. Their reinstatement on Day 27 was sufficient to restore the memory to its full strength. (After Rovee-Collier, Sullivan, Enright, Lucas, & Fagen, 1980)

the older infants gather more information is that they have better visual acuity and contrast sensitivity. An even more important reason is that they are far more visually active in exploring the stimulus and the surrounding context. The younger infants, in contrast, seem to fixate on single aspects of the situation. This puts them at a disadvantage in the memory tests, because unless they again fixate on the same aspect of the situation, they will not recognize that they are back in a familiar situation. On the other hand, having encoded far more of the original context, older infants have a far greater probability of recognizing the familiarity of the situation. A fact consistent with the encoding hypothesis is that when training conditions are altered for 8-week-olds so that they are forced to encode more of the available information, their memories of the contingency last longer. Also consistent with this hypothesis are data on the value of reinstatement for 8-week-olds. Just as for 12-week-olds, reinstatement works. It prolongs memories for the contingency. This implies that the 8-week-old brain does not forget the contingency in just 3 days because of neurological immaturity in retaining the memory. Obviously the memory is there, because it can be brought back to life through reinstatement.

We can conclude from this section on long-term memory that long-term storage capacities are available in humans from birth; however, a number of variables determine whether a memory is stored over a long-term period as well as the length of time that the memory will be retrievable. One important variable is the meaningfulness of the event to be remembered. This can explain why visual stimuli used in habituation studies do not produce strong memories in infants younger than 6-month-olds and why the stimuli involved in more meaningful contingency learning do. Not until around 6 months does visual examination alone begin to produce stable, long-term recognition (Fagan, 1973); however, well before this, even at 2 months of age, infants can recognize the occasion for exercising some learned sensorimotor routine. In addition to meaningfulness, another variable affecting recognizability is the number of features encoded from the to-be-remembered event at the time the memory is formed. Younger infants encode fewer features, which means that they are less likely to find a feature in the test stimulus that reminds them of the original event. The importance of restricted encoding was illustrated in Rovee-Collier's research on the retention differences between 8- and 12-week-olds. The third important variable we have found to affect retention is the opportunity for reinstatement. Infant memories, like those of adults as well, can become more difficult to retrieve if they do not receive periodic reinstatement. The fact that reinstatement works so well is evidence that the memory failures on Rovee-Collier's tests are due to retrieval not storage errors.

SUMMARY

This chapter has served to demonstrate how the information-processing approach to the study of cognitive development has recently led to important advances in the descriptive, theoretical, and applied science of cognitive development. Now, more clearly than ever before, developmental psychologists can answer questions regarding what develops in cognitive development, why it develops, and how our knowledge of cognitive development can be used by educators. This approach has been particularly valuable in that it leads to theories that are testable and that include precise suggestions for teachers.

A major use of the information-processing approach has been to apply it to aspects of cognitive development that Piaget studied. Because this approach begins in task analysis, information-processing psychologists begin with detailed hypotheses of the flow of information that leads to a child's judgment in a Piagetian-type task. Flow charts make it possible to represent these hypotheses in precise ways. When tests show that a particular flow chart provides a valid representation of children's actual thought processes, the flow chart can then become a guide to educators who might want to alter those processes to achieve more effective problem solving.

Work by information-processing psycholoists such as Robert Siegler has led to the realization that differences in procedural knowledge emphasized by Piaget do not account for all of cognitive development. Differences in encoding and in the declarative knowledge available from long-term memory can be as important as procedural differences in creating performance differences on Piagetian tasks and other problem-solving tasks.

With regard to memory, information-processing psychologists have provided a structure–process distinction that provides an apt way of describing the major features of human memory. On the structure side there is a sensory store, a short-term-memory store (which many prefer to call a working memory), and a long-term-memory store. On the processing side, there are control processes that regulate the flow of information within memory. The one key aspect of the information-processing psychologist's current conception of memory not captured by the Atkinson and Shiffrin memory model is the concept of a metamemory that directs the usage of the many available control processes.

The development of memory includes both process and structural components, with some of the more dramatic memory improvements coming solely from improvements in processing. The general conclusion from a great deal of descriptive research is that 4- and 5-year-olds are nonstrategic on tasks requiring deliberate acts of encoding, storage, and retrieval. They do not rehearse, they do not use categorical relations to organize material, nor do they produce the kind of cues needed to aid retrieval. Children begin to use these processes in middle childhood, and by adolescence these processes are well-established, routine information-management techniques. One of the interesting findings regarding children's failures at strategy use is that the failures are due to production deficiencies, not mediation deficiencies. Given that this is the case, one would think that metamemory development would predict memory improvements. The reason is that understanding how memory works—an aspect of metamemory—should lead to better strategy deployment. The data to date do not show this relationship clearly, however.

In addition to the important age-related developments in control processes, there are important structural developments in memory. The most important involve the short-term memory store. As measured by digit-span and counting-span tests, which are memory-span and M-space measures respectively, the human capacity for retaining information in the short-term store increases gradually with age. One reason for this is an increase in processing efficiency as measured by increased speed of identification. It is possible, however, that there is also an increase in the actual size of the short-term-memory store, so that more information can be accommodated at one time. In either event, maturation within the nervous system seems to be a necessary component in explaining the increases. The reason is that automatization of processing and the use of strategies such as chunking and rehearsal are not sufficient to explain the span data.

If maturation affects memory performance that is mediated through the short-term store, one might also expect it to affect performance mediated by the sensory and long-term stores. In the case of the sensory store, however, there is no such evidence, at least for the period from early childhood to adolescence. In long-term memory, evidence from habituation studies shows that even neonates are sufficiently mature to store information for a long-term period. Rovee-Collier's research on memories for contingency learning shows that infant memories can be stored for a considerable length of time, but retrieval in the absence of reinstatement can be a problem. This evidence implies that errors in retrieval from long-term memory are not due to immaturity in the nervous system, except perhaps indirectly, as in the case of memories not retrieved because maturational immaturity led to poor encoding.

SUGGESTIONS FOR FURTHER READING

Kail, R. (1984). *The development of memory in children*. (2nd ed.). New York: W. H. Freeman. An excellent primer.

Siegler, R. S. (1978). *Children's thinking: What develops*. Hillsdale, NJ: Lawrence Erlbaum. This volume presents the views of participants at the 13th Annual Carnegie Cognition Symposium on the issue of what develops in cognitive development. Neo-Piagetian and information processing views are represented throughout, thus demonstrating the shift of focus that took place in cognitive studies in the mid- to late-1970s.

Siegler, R. S. (1983). Information processing approaches to development. In P. H. Mussen (Gen. Ed.) and W. Kessen (Vol. Ed.), *Handbook of child psychology, Vol. 1: History, theory, & methods*. New York: John Wiley.

Sternberg, R. J. (Ed.). (1985). *Human abilities: An information processing approach*. New York: W. H. Freeman. Human cognitive abilities ranging from language to problem solving are discussed from the information-processing perspective by leaders in the field.

CHAPTER OUTLINE

CHAPTER 10

Individual Differences in Intelligence

The last two chapters have dealt extensively with age differences in how people think, remember, and reason. In this chapter the focus will change from age differences to individual differences. Rather than study how and why people of one age differ in their cognitive abilities from those of another age, we will turn to an examination of the differences among individuals of a given age. In doing so, we will be concerned primarily with description. We want to be able to describe the differences that exist among people, state how these differences change over time, and determine whether there is any stability in the psychological trait known as individual intelligence. A second, related goal is to discuss issues in the diagnosis of retardation and giftedness.

DESCRIBING INDIVIDUAL DIFFERENCES IN INTELLIGENCE

Finding a measure of individual intelligence is the first task of describing individual differences in cognitive abilities and the changes in these differences over time. Psychology's quest for such a measure began in the latter half of the nineteenth century and continues today (McKean, 1985; Sternberg, 1985). Now, as then, the principal goal is to construct a measure that will meet the three primary criteria for descriptive science—objectivity, reliability, and validity (see Chapter 2). In addition, practical constraints necessitate an emphasis on ease and speed of administration as an additional requirement that measures of intelligence must meet. The psychologists responsible for creating measures that meet these criteria are known as **psychometricians.**

The tests that have been used by psychometricians throughout this century are quite different from the tests that a Piagetian or an information-processing psychologist would design. Psychologists from either the Piagetian or information-processing perspective would seek to measure something about the underlying process of thought. They would assess intelligence, for example, by determining the stage at which children think, the type of information they encode, or the speed at which they process information. The tests psychometricians in fact use do not attempt to diagnose process differences among children. Instead they focus on the products of thought. The tests consist of a great many questions (called *items* in the language of testmakers), and each item has acceptable and unacceptable answers. How children achieve their correct answers has no bearing on their test scores.

The definition of intelligence that is implicit in the standard, psychometric tests used today is that intelligence refers to an individual's potential for acquiring the knowledge and skills of the culture from which the test questions were derived, and then, perhaps, contributing something back to that culture in the way of art, science, or other skilled achievements. More briefly, intelligence refers to a person's potential for *scholastic achievement.* At the low end of the scholastic-achievement scale in contemporary society are people whose mastery of the culture goes no further than learning to tie their shoes, boil food on a gas stove, make change, or perhaps read a driver's-license manual. At the opposite end of the scale are people who acquire the most complex and historically recent technical skills and then use them to create, invent, and build.

Because the psychometric definition of intelligence equates intelligence with potential for scholastic achievement, many people feel dissatisfied with the definition. One reason is that scholastic achievement in contemporary society means doing well in school; yet schools do not tap the full range of human talent. The primary talents evaluated in schools are talents for logical, mathematical, verbal, and spatial reasoning. Restricting a definition of intelligence to potential in these areas alone results in a rather narrow definition that does not capture the full breadth of what most of us mean by intelligence. Most noticeably, this definition leaves out attributes of intelligence such as common sense, wisdom, and creativity. It also excludes from the definition of intelligence the set of human talents that underlies musical composition, interpersonal relations, dramatic interpretation, and athletic achievement (see Gardner, 1983). These shortcomings make it obvious that the psychometrician's definition of intelligence is quite narrow. But even though the psychometrician's definition of intelligence may seem at times maddeningly restricted, it is a definition with considerable practical value in some contexts. In fact, it was the need for a purely practical measure of intelligence that led to the development of psychology's first intelligence tests. Knowing the history of their development makes it easy to understand why intelligence came to be measured through tests of one's aptitude for scholastic achievement.

The Origin of the Psychometric Definition of Intelligence

In the latter half of the nineteenth century, universal education laws were becoming commonplace in the Western world. Whereas previously only the privileged few had attended private schools, now the masses were enrolled in public schools, at least through the primary years. Teachers found themselves with such a variety of children that they could not cope. Children in a single class were frequently of different ages (7 to 12), and they were always of different abilities. Some were exceptional students. Others were severely, moderately, or mildly retarded. It was imperative that these mentally defective students be separated from the others, because such children could not benefit from the regular lessons. For this reason, special-education classes were set up to handle the needs of slow children.

The appearance of special-education classes in the history of education brings us to the central problem that tests were designed to solve: How do we determine which children belong in which educational environment in a way that is fair to both children and society? In the late nineteenth and early twentieth centuries there were many "experts" around who were willing to voice an opinion. However, French psychologist Alfred Binet—the principal author of our first intelligence tests—scoffed at the thought of using the experts of the day. He cited one case in which a single child who was observed by four different doctors walked away with four different diagnoses. One labeled the child an *idiot,* which in the language of the time was the lowest category of retardation; the second labeled him an *imbecile,* which was a grade higher; the third labeled him a *moron,* which was the level of retardation next to normality; and the fourth labeled him as *degenerate,* which implied that the child's problem was more moral than mental.

If we agree that theoretical training alone does not qualify one to diagnose a child's level of scholastic aptitude, what other alternatives might there be for solving the classification problem? One possibility might be to ask the teachers. They, after all, have the most experience with the children. They should know clearly what students' scholastic potential is if anyone does. But the use of teachers' opinions did not provide a good measure either.

One problem with using teachers' opinions was that a child had to spend considerable time in the classroom before the child's retardation could be diagnosed. All of this time was lost time, full of frustration for the child, for the teacher, and for the other children in the classroom. Beyond this, it was not safe to assume that teachers had any clearer criteria for diagnosing retardation—or giftedness for that matter—than other experts. Binet cited the case of one "excellent teacher" who judged as the brightest student in her class a child who in fact was retarded by 2 years. The reason was that the teacher had not taken into account the age difference between this retarded child and the other children in the class, all of whom were younger (Binet & Simon, 1907/1914, p. 40).

The arbitrariness that was present in teachers' opinions was clearly evident to Binet when a commission of which he was a member sought statistics on the incidence of retardation in the public schools. Teachers supplied the estimates, which ranged from 0 to 25 percent, with the two extremes coming from neighboring schools that differed not at all in their student populations (Wolf, 1973, p. 169).

The disparity in teachers' opinions was due to many factors, not all of which were honorable. Some would judge a normal child as mentally deficient just to get the child—probably a troublemaker—out of the classroom. Others would judge deficient children as normal out of the conviction that their only problem was laziness.

This review of the historical context in which intelligence tests first evolved makes it clear that there was a tremendous need for a scientific means of discriminating among individuals in terms of their ability to master the curriculum taught in schools. Prior to the development of the first reasonable scientific instruments, decisions were being made about the differences that existed among children, but the decisions were often subjective, unreliable, invalid, and slow. A better means for assessing individual differences was needed.

The Binet–Simon Scale

Alfred Binet was not the first person to realize that there was a need for a means of distinguishing among the ability levels of children that would meet the scientific criteria for description. The need was clearly felt by everyone working on practical problems in education at the time. "All over the Western world," Theta Wolf reports, "men were trying to do something about the problem of determining degrees of retardation" (1973, p. 162). Wolf points out, for example, that in the United States, W. S. Munroe thought that a measure of facial dissymmetries might provide the speedy, objective, reliable, and valid measure that was needed. In California, investigators were using questionnaires that inquired into a child's behavior and family history. In Belgium, measures of attention were thought to provide the key.

Binet himself delved into measures of the skull *(cephalometry),* the study of handwriting *(graphology),* and psychological measures such as the *two-point tactile threshold* (this was the minimum distance between two legs of a compasslike instrument—called an esthesiometer—that could be felt as two points rather than one when it touched you). None of these measures, however, met the criteria for scientific description any better than a test based merely on "expert" opinion. The measures, though relatively quick and easy to take, suffered primarily from their lack of validity in diagnosing school difficulties.

As late as 1904, Binet despaired of being able to solve the measurement problem. In that year, however, the minister of public instruction in France asked Binet to assist in developing a "pedagogical and medical examination" that could be used in selecting children for experimental special-education classes then being set up in the Paris schools. This very practical and immediate need prompted Binet, along with his colleague Theodore Simon, to take a new approach to the measurement problem. Instead of persisting in the attempt to make socially important distinctions among children by measuring their differences on fundamental physical, sensorimotor, or physiological variables, they began to ask questions directed at children's understanding and judgment. For example, they asked them to point to their ears, or they asked them to tell why it would be silly to say such things as "I have three brothers—Jacques, Paul, and myself." They had them count and draw figures from memory. This approach paid off. In just one year's time, Binet and Simon had a 30-item test—the 1905 Binet–Simon Scale—that was quite good at distinguishing imbeciles (the mid degree of retardation) from normals and was reasonably good at distinguishing morons (the mildest degree of retardation) from normals. The test could be quickly administered, and the authors gave extensive instructions in how to score the test so that there would be little ambiguity about an individual child's performance.

By 1908 an improved version of the Binet–Simon Scale was complete—the **Binet–Simon Mental-Age Scale.** This version allowed examiners not only to diagnose retardation but also to assign a **mental age** to the children who were tested. The measurement of mental age was possible because the items on the test had been *standardized.* This meant that Binet and Simon had tried each of the items on a large enough sample of children so that they knew what the "normal" response would be for children of different ages. An item was assigned a year level equal to the age at which half or more of the children answered it correctly. As an example, we can take an item that required children to copy a picture of a diamond. This item was placed at the 6-year-old level because of the performance of children in Binet and Simon's *standardization sample.* Binet and Simon wrote, "At five years a child can draw a square, but it is not until seven years that he can draw a diamond; and even at seven years a fifth of them fail. At six

BOX 10-1

Items and Scoring Procedures for the 10-Year-Old Level on the 1911 Binet–Simon Mental-Age Scale

Ten Years

1. "You see these little boxes. They are not all the same weight. Some are heavy and some are light. Place the heaviest one here, and at its side the one which is a little less heavy, then the one still a little less, and finally the lightest of all."

The boxes in question weigh respectively 6, 9, 12, 15, and 18 grammes, and all look the same. They are placed in a pile before the child, and as the examiner gives the directions he indicates with his finger the place he appoints for each box. Three trials should be given, the boxes being mixed after each trial. In order to pass the child must be correct at least twice. The time should not exceed three minutes. The material for the test can be easily made from matchboxes.

2. "Now I am going to show you two drawings. You may look at them for ten seconds, which is a very short time. Then I will ask you to draw them from memory."[1]

For the drawings see [the drawings below]. The child is counted correct if he reproduces the whole of one drawing and half the other.

3. "I am going to read you some sentences, each of which contains something foolish. Listen attentively and tell me each time what is foolish."

The examiner reads the sentences impressively, but without any special emphasis on the part the child should comment on. Each time when he finishes he changes his tone, and demands, "What is foolish in that?"

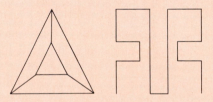

Sentences

(1) An unfortunate bicycle rider fell on his head and was killed instantly;

---

years half of the children fail" (1908/1916, p. 209). Thus, drawing a diamond was given a mental-age designation of 6 years.

In clear demonstration of the worldwide need that existed early in this century for a scientific means of assessing scholastic aptitude, the Binet–Simon test was quickly adapted for use in Canada, England, Australia, South Africa, Germany, Switzerland, Italy, Russia, China, Japan, Turkey, and the United States. In the U.S., the adaptation was called the **Stanford–Binet** in recognition of the fact that the preparation of the test for use with American schoolchildren was done at Stanford University. The adaptations of the Binet–Simon Mental-Age Scale for the various countries primarily involved restandardizing the test, but in the case of the Stanford–Binet, many new items were added as well.

he was taken to a hospital, and they fear he will not recover.

(2) I have three brothers, Paul, Ernest, and myself.

(3) The body of an unfortunate young girl, cut into eighteen pieces, was found yesterday on the fortifications. It is thought that she killed herself.

(4) There was a railway accident yesterday, but it was not a bad one; the number of dead is only forty-eight.

(5) Someone said: If I should ever grow desperate and kill myself, I will not choose Friday, because Friday is an unlucky day, and will bring me unhappiness.

Three satisfactory answers are required.

4. "What would you do if you were delayed in going to school?"— "What would you do before taking part in an important affair?"—"Why is a bad action done when one is angry more excusable than the same action done when one is not angry?"—"What would you do if you were asked your opinion of someone whom you did not know well?"—"Why should one judge a person by his acts rather than by his words?"

Three sensible answers must be given.

5. "I am going to read you three words, and I want you to make a sentence and use in it the three words. The words are Paris, fortune, stream."

The expression "make a sentence" must not be further explained, but the instructions may be repeated. The child is given a pencil and paper, and, if necessary, should be urged to write something. For a pass the sentence should be well co-ordinated. At this stage it may contain two distinct ideas, but not three; at the higher level it must contain only one idea. One minute is the time allowed for writing. (M. Drummond, 1914, pp. 154-56)

[1]The drawings shown here are not the same as those used on the original Binet–Simon test. Those drawings are still used on some tests today.

To this day, the Stanford–Binet is a widely respected test of intelligence still used for diagnostic purposes. It requires about an hour of time for a trained examiner to administer. The test was first made available in 1916 and has been revised and restandardized many times over the intervening years. The most recent revision and restandardization took place in 1972.

To give you a clearer idea of the type of items that Binet and Simon used to measure mental age, Box 10-1 presents all the 10-year-old items from the final version of the Binet–Simon Mental-Age Scale, a version that appeared in 1911, the year of Binet's untimely death. A summary of all the questions on the test is given in Box 10-2. Although you may be surprised by some of the items, you probably will judge most to be fairly legitimate

BOX 10-2
Summary of All the Items on the 1911 Binet–Simon Mental-Age Scale

Age III
1. Points to nose, eyes, and mouth.
2. Repeats two digits.
3. Enumerates objects in a picture.
4. Gives family name.
5. Repeats a sentence of six syllables.

Age IV
1. Gives own sex.
2. Names key, knife, and penny.
3. Repeats three digits.
4. Compares two lines.

Age V
1. Compares two weights.
2. Copies a square.
3. Repeats a sentence of ten syllables.
4. Counts four pennies.
5. Unites the halves of a divided rectangle.

Age VI
1. Distinguishes between morning and afternoon.
2. Defines familiar words in terms of use.

3. Copies a diamond.
4. Counts thirteen pennies.
5. Distinguishes pictures of ugly and pretty faces.

Age VII
1. Shows right hand and left ear.
2. Describes a picture.
3. Executes three commands given simultaneously.
4. Counts the value of six sous, three of which are double.
5. Names four cardinal colors.

Age VIII
1. Compares two objects from memory.
2. Counts from twenty to zero.
3. Notes omissions from pictures.
4. Gives day and date.
5. Repeats five digits.

Age IX
1. Gives change from twenty sous.
2. Defines familiar words in terms superior to use.
3. Recognizes all of the (nine)

measures of "intelligence"; but that is only because you have grown up with tests modeled on the Binet pattern. People at that time, however, were used to a totally different measurement approach. They expected intelligence to be measurable in physical traits such as skull size, or in variables such as attention span, reaction time, or sensitivity to touch. Binet and Simon's contemporaries, therefore, truly wondered whether the Binet–Simon Mental-Age Scales could possibly measure anything of importance. Henry Goddard (whom you will remember as the author of the Kallikak study; see Figure 5-5) was a principal in popularizing the use of the Binet–Simon test in this country, but when he first saw the test he was as critical as anyone. "It seemed impossible to grade intelligence in that way," Goddard (1916) said in an introduction to Binet and Simon's *The Development of Intelligence in Children*. The skeptics became convinced only when they discovered for themselves that the test was indeed easy to administer, reliable, and valid. Goddard said, for example, "Our use of the scale [at the Vineland Training

pieces of money.
4. Names the months of the year in order.
5. Answers or comprehends "easy questions."

Age X
1. Arranges five blocks in order of weight.
2. Copies two drawings from memory.
3. Criticizes absurd statements.
4. Answers or comprehends "difficult questions."
5. Uses three given words in not more than two sentences.

Age XII
1. Resists suggestion as to length of lines.
2. Composes one sentence containing three given words.
3. Names sixty words in three minutes.
4. Defines three abstract words.
5. Discovers the sense of a disarranged sentence.

Age XV
1. Repeats seven digits.
2. Finds three rimes for a given word in one minute.
3. Repeats a sentence of twenty-six syllables.
4. Interprets pictures.
5. Interprets given facts.

Adult
1. Solves the paper-cutting test.
2. Rearranges a triangle in imagination.
3. Gives differences between pairs of abstract terms.
4. Gives three differences between a president and a king.
5. Gives the main thought of a selection which he has heard read.

SOURCE: From *The Measurement of Intelligence* (pp. 37-39) by L. Terman, 1916, Boston: Houghton Mifflin.

School] was a surprise and a gratification. It met our needs. A classification of our children based on the Scale agreed with the Institution experience" (1916, p. 5).

Describing Individual Differences in Terms of the Ratio of Mental Age and Chronological Age

The 1908 and 1911 Binet–Simon tests were referred to as mental-age scales because they graded people according to their mental-age levels. On the basis of test results using these scales, examiners could say quite explicitly whether a person with a chronological age anywhere from age 3 to adulthood had responded at, beyond, or below age level. The mechanics of obtaining an actual mental-age score involved a scoring system that began with the assessment of a *basal mental age*. This was equal to the age level of the

TABLE 10-1
Calculating Mental Age Using the 1911 Binet–Simon Mental-Age Scale

AGE LEVEL OF ITEMS	NUMBER OF ITEMS PASSED	MENTAL-AGE CREDIT
VII	5/5	7.0 years (Basal mental age)
VIII	3/5	.6 years
IX	2/5	.4 years
X	1/5	.2 years
XI	0/5	.0 years (Ceiling age)

Total mental age = 8.2 years

highest test series in which all the items were answered correctly. Thus, if a person answered all the 10-year-old items from Box 10-1 correctly but missed one or more of the 11-year-old items, the person's basal mental age would be 10. With the basal mental age established at 10, the examiner would then add mental-age credit equal to one fifth of a year (because there were five questions per year) for any questions answered at a higher level. This scoring procedure is shown in Table 10-1.

The problem with the mental-age scheme for grading children was that mental age was not the sole factor to be considered in making a diagnosis. A 9-year-old who had a mental age of 7 was considered by the test to be retarded and perhaps in need of special education. A 7-year-old who performed the same was perfectly normal, and a 5-year-old at this level was gifted. Binet was happy to leave things in this state, because he thought of retardation as developmental arrest. Idiots, the lowest grade of intellect, did not develop beyond the 2-year-old level. Imbeciles stopped developing at the 5-year-old level, and morons, at the 9-year-old level.

When the test was adapted for use in America by Lewis Terman and his associates at Stanford, a suggestion by German psychologist William Stern to convert the mental-age/chronological-age relation into a single ratio number was adopted. Because ratios involve division, the resulting number was a quotient, hence the term **intelligence quotient** or **IQ.** The initial method of calculating IQs is given in Table 10-2.

Unlike the mental-age concept, an IQ does not indicate the level at which a person is "arrested," or even that there is developmental arrest. It merely indicates how well a person performs relative to people of the same age, whatever that age might be. A mental-age-to-chronological-age ratio of greater than 1 means that the person performed better than most people of the same age. A ratio less than 1 means the opposite. When mental age equals chronological age yielding a ratio of exactly 1.00, it means that the person is perfectly average. Because people early in this century did not like to deal with decimals and fractions any more than people do today, the

TABLE 10-2
Calculating IQ on the Stanford–Binet[1]

AGE LEVEL OF ITEMS	NUMBER OF ITEMS PASSED	MENTAL-AGE CREDIT
IV	6	4 years
IV-6[2]	5	5 months
V	4	8 months
VI	0	0 months

Total mental age = 5 years 1 month.
Chronological age of child = 6 years 2 months.

$$IQ = \frac{5 \text{ years } 1 \text{ month}}{6 \text{ years } 2 \text{ months}} \times 100 = \frac{61 \text{ months}}{74 \text{ months}} \times 100 = 82$$

[1]The procedure described here was only used for the 1916 and 1937 versions of the Stanford–Binet. After that a "deviation score" was used to calculate IQ.
[2]The Stanford–Binet divides the 4-year-level into two 6-month levels in order to increase the sensitivity of the test. This puts 12 items at the 4-year-level instead of the usual 6. Each item, therefore, is worth 1 month of mental-age credit.

actual mental-age-to-chronological-age ratio was multiplied by 100. This got rid of at least two decimal places, and beyond that no one cared anyway. Thus, an IQ of 100 is normal, or average. One thing to note here is that the IQ score, unlike the scores you get on finals or midterms, for example, has little to do with the actual number of test questions answered correctly. You should also note that in shifting from an absolute measure of aptitude (mental age) to a ratio measure (mental age/chronological age), the measurement of aptitude becomes age free, thus inviting cross-age as well as within-age comparisons of individuals.

The definition of IQ as an age-free measure of intelligence is still with us today; however, the method for calculating it is quite different. Beginning in 1960, the old ratio method was dropped in favor of a method based on **deviation scores.** These are measures of how far a person's individual test performance deviates from the average for that person's age group. The primary advantage of this approach is that it yields an identical meaning to IQ across all age groups. Under the old system, this was not the case. A child with an IQ of 110 at one age level might do as well relative to age-mates as a child with an IQ of 113 at some other age level. This was due to some distributional differences in scores at the two age levels. Because of these it might be easier to obtain a 113 at one age than at another. This created a real problem for longitudinal studies of intelligence. It made it difficult to say whether an increase in score was due to a real increase relative to one's peers or whether it was a meaningless increase due merely to changes in test difficulty. Under the new system, all cross-age inconsistencies have been eliminated. IQs have the same meaning at all age levels.

The Wechsler Tests

At present, the most widely used measures of IQ are the *Wechsler tests*. These tests were first developed when David Wechsler, who worked with adults at the Bellevue Hospital in New York, found the Stanford–Binet to be less than ideal for use in his clinical setting. One reason was that no one older than 18 years had been included in the standardization sample for the Stanford–Binet. Also, the content of the Stanford–Binet items was often inappropriate. As Wechsler put it, "Asking the ordinary housewife to furnish you with a rhyme to the words, 'day', 'cat', and 'mill', or an ex-army sergeant to give you a sentence with the words, 'boy', 'river', 'ball', is not particularly apt to evoke either interest or respect" (1944, p. 17).

In order to provide a more discriminating way of scaling the mental aptitude of adults, Wechsler developed a test that was first known as the *Wechsler–Bellevue Intelligence Scale* and later became known as the *Wechsler Adult Intelligence Scale,* or *WAIS*. The same test today is known as the **WAIS-R** (the R stands for "revised"). The WAIS and WAIS-R differ from the Stanford–Binet in that two scores are produced, not just one. One score is a largely *verbal* score; the other is a largely *nonverbal performance* score. Table 10-3 will give you some idea of the types of items that appear on these two subtests. The two scores are combined to get what is called a *full-scale IQ*. Success with the WAIS led Wechsler to develop similar tests for use with other age groups. The most widely used is the *WISC* (Wechsler Intelligence Scale for Children). Originally developed in 1949, the test was revised and restandardized in 1974 to become the **WISC-R.** The WISC-R can be used with children ages 6 to 17. For children of ages 4 to 6½, there is a separate test called the **WPPSI** (pronounced Wippsi). This stands for Wechsler Preschool and Primary Scale of Intelligence. Like the Stanford–Binet, all of these tests are designed for use by trained examiners in individual testing sessions lasting about an hour.

The Distribution of IQ Scores

If we gave either Stanford–Binet or Wechsler intelligence tests to large numbers of children sampled at random and then plotted the frequency of the various scores we obtained (that is, the number of 100s, 105s, 78s, and so forth), 100 would be the most frequent score. This is not a discovery. Rather, it is a sign that the children we are now testing are just like the children who were in our *standardization sample*. You can understand this if you recall that an IQ score is not an absolute measure of intelligence; it is a measure of intelligence relative to one's age-mates. The best estimate of how a person's age-mates would perform comes from the standardization sample. Thus, if a child is tested at age 10 and does as well as the 10-year-olds in the standardization sample, the result is an IQ of 100. Secular

TABLE 10-3
Sample Items from the WAIS-R

Verbal Subtests	Sample Items
Information	How many wings does a bird have? Who wrote *Paradise Lost?*
Digit Span	Repeat from memory a series of digits, such as 3 1 0 6 7 4 2 5, after hearing them once.
General Comprehension	What is the advantage of keeping money in a bank? Why is copper often used in electrical wires?
Arithmetic	Three men divided 18 golf balls equally among themselves. How many golf balls did each man receive? If two apples cost 15¢, what will be the cost of a dozen apples?
Similarities	In what way are a lion and a tiger alike? In what way are a saw and a hammer alike?
Vocabulary	This test consists simply of asking, "what is a _____?" or "what does _____ mean?" The words cover a wide range of difficulty or familiarity.

Performance Subtests	Description of Item
Picture Arrangement	Arrange a series of cartoon panels to make a meaningful story.
Picture Completion	What is missing from these pictures?
Block Design	Copy designs with blocks (as shown at right).
Object Assembly	Put together a jigsaw puzzle.
Digit Symbol	

1	2	3	4
X	III	I	0

Fill in the symbols:

3	4	1	3	4	2	1	2

SOURCE: From *Introduction to Psychology,* Third Edition, by D. Coon, 1983, St. Paul, MN: West.

changes in society can cause the age norms from a particular standardization sample to become outmoded. This explains in part why there have been revisions of the Stanford–Binet and of the Wechsler tests (see Table 10-4). Most of these revisions were occasioned by a need for restandardization. As you can well imagine, using age norms from 1916 to evaluate children in the 1980s would provide misleading estimates of IQ.

In addition to revealing that the average IQ score is 100, a frequency distribution of IQ scores would show that the scores on either side of 100 are distributed in a symmetrical, bell-shaped manner. The actual distribution of these scores—at least between the IQs of 60 and 150—would look very much like the distribution that statisticians call a *normal distribution.*

TABLE 10-4
A Chronology of Intelligence Tests

TEST	APPROPRIATE FOR ASSESSING	CONTRIBUTION
Binet–Simon Tests		
1905 Scale	Low-grade retardation	First useful test to assist in school placement.
1908 Scale	Age 3 to 13	Introduced concept of mental age.
1911 Scale	Age 3 to adult	Improved version of 1908 Scale.
Stanford–Binet		
1916	Age 3 to adult	An expanded version of Binet–Simon Scale, standardized for use with children in the U. S. This test introduced the concept of IQ.
1937	Age 2 to adult	Revised version of the original Stanford–Binet.
1960	Age 2 to adult	Revised version of the 1937 Stanford–Binet.
1972	Age 2 to adult	Revised version of the 1960 Stanford–Binet.
Wechsler Tests		
Wechsler–Bellevue Form 1, 1939 Form 2, 1946	Adult Adult	First tests designed for use with adults. Measured verbal IQ, and performance IQ, as well as full-scale IQ.
WAIS 1955 WAIS-R 1981	Adult Adult	Adult intelligence test designed to meet criticisms of the Wechsler–Bellevue.
WISC 1949 WISC-R 1974	Ages 6 to 17 Ages 6 to 17	Intelligence test for school-age children modeled after the Wechsler–Bellevue.
WPPSI 1967	Ages 4 to 6½	Intelligence test for preschool children modeled after the WISC and the WAIS.

The fact that the IQ scores on either side of 100 are distributed in a relatively normal way suits an important theoretical assumption that underlies the entire psychometric approach to the study of intelligence. The assumption is that intelligence is caused by a great number of factors, both genetic and environmental, which act independently. This assumption *requires* that intelligence be distributed in the bell-shaped, symmetrical manner known as normal. The reason has to do with the laws of probability.

Because of the close correspondence between an IQ distribution and the normal distribution, we can understand better than we otherwise could the actual meaning of an individual IQ score. We can state, for example, that in the long run approximately 16 children out of 100 will have a WISC-R IQ of 115 or above and that approximately 34 percent of the population will have a Stanford–Binet IQ between 84 and 100. We get this information simply from the knowledge that WISC-R IQs are normally distributed with a mean of 100 and a standard deviation of 15, while Stanford–Binet IQs are normally distributed with a mean of 100 and a standard deviation of 16. Figure 10-1 shows how this is done. The figure itself shows what a perfectly normal distribution of IQ scores would look like. Using this idealized distribution, you can read off the percent of people who will have any Stanford–Binet or Wechsler IQ you choose. Just refer to the Stanford–Binet and Wechsler scales on the x axis and then total all of the percents to the right of that score to determine the percent of people who would have that score or a higher one. Total the percents to the left to calculate the percent with a score this low or lower. To get the percent of people with IQs lying

FIGURE 10-1

The Distribution of IQ

Because IQ scores are approximately normally distributed, we can use a normal curve to estimate the percent of people in the population who will have IQs of different levels. (After Sattler, 1982)

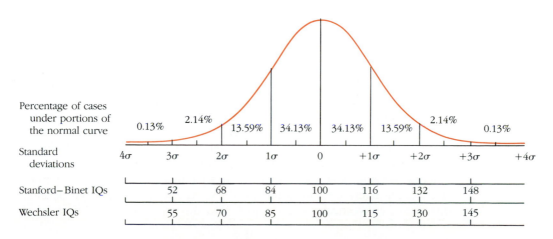

between two scores, just read off the percents associated with that particular sector of the normal distribution. This would not be possible to do unless IQ were distributed in a reasonably normal way.

Infant Tests

Historically, testing infants has been of less interest than testing school-age children, primarily because there are no important decisions to be made about the assignment of infants to educational environments. Infants are already in the one educational environment open to them—their own homes. Nonetheless, for a variety of both practical and theoretical reasons investigators as early as the 1920s (for example, Kuhlmann, 1922) began devising tests to measure individual differences in infants.

In 1927, pediatrician Arnold Gesell began a large-scale longitudinal study of infant behavioral development in New Haven, Connecticut. Gesell's careful observations of normal growth patterns in these infants resulted in the publication of the **Gesell Developmental Schedules,** an enormously popular instrument for assessing the developmental quotients of infants. According to Gesell, an infant **developmental quotient,** or **DQ,** "represents the proportion of normal development that is present at a given age" (Honzik, 1976, p. 62). Gesell's schedules measured a broad base of infant achievements including motor development, language development, social development, and general adaptive-behavior development.

The most widely used infant test at present is a test that Nancy Bayley began to develop in 1933 when she was working with the California Growth Studies. The current version of this test (Bayley, 1969) is an extremely well standardized test known as the **Bayley Scales of Infant Development.** The term "scales" in the title is plural because the test yields scores on both a mental scale and a motor scale. In addition, there is an infant behavior record that is completed by observing such things as the infant's attitude, emotions, and interests during the administration of the scales. The test, which draws heavily on much of the pioneering work by Gesell, can be used for assessing the developmental status of babies from 2 to 30 months of age. Table 10-5 gives a good idea of the types of items that are included on the two scales. The behavior record from the Bayley is used primarily to aid in interpreting the scale scores.

Despite the availability of such a well-standardized and reliable test as the Bayley, it is quite important to realize that an infant's developmental status, as assessed by the Bayley or any other infant test, is not a measure of IQ. Although many parents eager for some sign of their child's eventual intelligence will make IQ inferences from infant behaviors, these parents are making inferences unwarranted by the vast literature on child development. Every investigator ever to look into the relationship of infant devel-

TABLE 10-5
Illustrative Items on the Bayley Scales of Infant Development

AGE (months)	MENTAL SCALE	MOTOR SCALE
2	Visually recognizes mother	Elevates self by arms: prone
4	Turns head to sound of rattle	Head balanced
6	Looks for fallen spoon	Sits alone 30 seconds or more
8	Uncovers toy	Pulls to standing position
10	Looks at pictures in book	Walks with help
12	Turns pages of book	Walks alone
14	Spontaneous scribble	Walks sideways
16	Builds tower of 3 cubes	Stands on left foot with help
18	Initiates crayon stroke	Tries to walk on walking board
20	Differentiates scribble from stroke	Walks with one foot on walking board
22	Names 3 pictures	Stands on left foot alone
24	Names 3 objects	Jumps from bottom step
26	Train of cubes	Walks down stairs alone: both feet on each step
28	Understands 2 prepositions	Jumps from second step
30	Builds tower of 8 cubes	Walks on tiptoe, 10 feet

SOURCE: From *Assessment of Children's Intelligence and Special Abilities,* 2nd Edition (p. 254) by J. M. Sattler, 1982, Boston: Allyn & Bacon, Inc. Reprinted by permission.

opment and later childhood intelligence has walked away with the impression that there is little to no connection. There are two possibilities for explaining this: either there is no continuity in intelligence between infancy and later childhood, or the tests we use to measure continuity are in fact measuring different things. This will be a topic for discussion in the section that follows.

CHANGES IN INTELLIGENCE OVER TIME

In order to discuss the issue of whether there is continuity in intelligence between infancy and childhood, we need first to examine the question of continuity in childhood itself. Does intelligence change over time during this period? If so, a second question of developmental importance can be asked: What is the degree of change that occurs?

If by intelligence one means mental age, then quite obviously it does change over time. Older children know more on average than younger children, and their understanding and judgment are better. But what people generally mean in asking whether intelligence changes over time is whether a person's IQ remains stable. Before answering this question, we need to be clear on the meaning of the answer. A stable IQ would be a sign of normative stability as defined in Chapter 1 (see p. 40). Normative stability means that one's ranking on a trait relative to age peers remains relatively constant. A stable IQ would be indicative of such stability, because IQ, as we have seen, is a relative measure, not a measure of an absolute quality. Height is measured absolutely, and mental age is measured absolutely, but intelligence (as reflected in IQ anyway) is measured relatively. This means that any measure of stability in intelligence is automatically a measure of normative stability rather than absolute stability. Keeping in mind, then, that we are talking about the stability of one's ranking relative to age peers and not the stability of an absolute quality, we can proceed to the data on change in IQ over time.

Do IQ Scores Change?

For a long time after IQ tests were developed, many psychologists operated under the assumption that an IQ score, no matter at what age it was obtained, would be relatively stable. Some variability was expected because, after all, the test was not perfectly reliable. For this reason, the score on any one test administration was judged to be only a best guess of the actual score. The actual score (called a *true score*) was known to deviate as much as 5 points on either side of the obtained score. But this degree of instability was considered to be trivial, due simply to errors of measurement. When the results of longitudinal studies in which children had been repeatedly tested over a number of years began to come out, however, it was soon evident that there was a nontrivial source of instability in IQ scores. It appeared undeniable that there were changes in true scores.

In one major study of age-to-age variability in IQ (Honzik, Macfarlane, & Allen, 1948), it was found that approximately six out of every ten people had IQs that changed by as much as 15 points from age 6 to 16. A few individuals had scores that changed by as much as 30 points. Change as dramatic as this was completely incompatible with a belief in a fixed IQ. Some of the change could be explained as measurement error, and some could be attributed to age-to-age changes in IQs inherent in the old ratio scoring method, but the full extent of the change could not be explained without assuming that there were real changes in scholastic aptitude. Nancy Bayley clearly expressed the view of contemporary psychologists regarding the fact of true-score instability when she addressed the American Psychological Association in 1954:

> In a given character, such as height, or intelligence, a child may, over a period of years, shift from high to average, to low and back to average again, as compared with his age peers. The very frequency of these

shifts leads us to assume that, for the most part, they are normal and healthy patterns of growth. (1956, p. 45)

Thus, by the 1950s, thanks in part to longitudinal studies like the California Growth Studies of which Bayley was a part, psychologists had given up the notion of a fixed IQ.

Contemporary data demonstrating the general plasticity of IQ come from studies that have sought to stave off retardation in socially disadvantaged children through programs designed to compensate for the general impoverishment of their lives. A prime example of such a program is the Abecedarian Project discussed in Chapter 3. That project and others like it have routinely shown that education matters in the development of IQ. Thus, "If systematic education is provided, intellectual levels can be boosted by modest to quite dramatic amounts, depending primarily upon the intensity of the educational treatments" (Ramey, Bryant, & Suarez, 1985, p. 290). This conclusion was drawn after reviewing the results of a large number of preschool education programs designed to compensate children from socially deprived backgrounds for their educational impoverishment. The same conclusion comes from adoption studies in which children are moved from a less favorable to a more favorable educational environment. Such adoptions lead to IQs in the adopted children that are superior to what would have been expected had they remained in the homes of their biological parents (see Chapter 5, p. 227).

Changes in IQ as a Manifestation of Epigenesis in Intelligence

When Nancy Bayley and others were announcing to the psychological community at large that they had failed to find any evidence of a totally stable IQ in the school years, there were many psychologists who were disappointed. Their disappointment was due to the fact that they had hoped that psychologists might discover evidence of a fixed, native intelligence in each of us that would manifest itself continuously throughout our lives. In retrospect, this can be seen to be an unrealistic expectation, one that stands in contrast to an epigenetic view of development. From an epigenetic view, plasticity and potential for change should characterize the development of intelligence. Nonetheless, many psychologists over the years have held to a belief in a fixed intelligence. Sir Cyril Burt, for example, at the end of his life in 1971 still believed in the truth of what he had written in 1937 when he said that there is an inborn intelligence and "neither knowledge nor practice, neither interest nor industry, will avail to increase it" (p. 11).

The disappointment of nativists like Burt with the facts cited above from longitudinal studies, compensatory education programs, and adoption studies is certainly understandable. But as soon as one drops the nativist position, the facts become a source of encouragement. They imply that fluctuations in IQ can signal real changes in the aptitude of individuals for absorbing their culture and contributing back to it. This is encouraging because it denies once again the predeterminist position that there are things about ourselves that we just cannot change. Our intelligence relative to our peers, like every other developmental outcome, turns out to be a characteristic influenced by myriad factors (both genetic and nongenetic). These factors, which have acted in the past to put us at a certain IQ level, are continuously acting to either maintain or alter that level. In this context, you should recall what we learned in Chapter 2 about IQ in old age: it declines when people cease to perform intellectual tasks. If they remain intellectually active, however, their IQs will remain stable. For people who find themselves more intellectually stimulated later in life than they were earlier, IQs should even increase.

Instability of Individual Scores Does Not Imply a Lack of Continuity

In giving up the notion of a fixed IQ, psychologists concluded that IQ can definitely change over time. This, however, is not tantamount to the conclusion that there is no age-to-age continuity in IQ scores. That is, the admission of plasticity is not an admission of unconstrained possibility. To find whether some reasonable continuity accompanies the plasticity, we need to examine the age-to-age correlations for IQ in representative samples of people. This will tell us the degree to which the average person is likely to rise or fall in IQ relative to peers over time. If there is a 0 correlation across the period of time to be measured, then we can conclude that there is 0 continuity: scores at one age are totally unrelated to scores at the later age. A correlation of 1.00 would mean the opposite: scores at one age would predict perfectly the scores at the second age. Of course, we know already that the correlation could not possibly be 1.00. This would require completely stable scores, which we have already seen do not exist. But how far away from 1.00 does the correlation fall? This is what we need to know to be able to judge the extent to which scores at one age predict scores at later ages.

Calculating age-to-age correlations for the data in the California Growth Studies shows that even with all the shifting back and forth that was observed over the school years, IQ scores taken at age 6 are still fairly predictive of IQ scores at every later age. This is shown in the correlations of IQ at age 6 with IQ at ages 7, 8, 9, and so forth that are given in Figure 10-2. Furthermore, you can see in the individual curves of IQ change over time that are given in Figure 10-3 that IQs tend to get ever-more stable with age. Individuals who experience large changes generally experience the largest changes early in the school years, not late in the school years. The point to remember from this, therefore, is that even though IQs do change

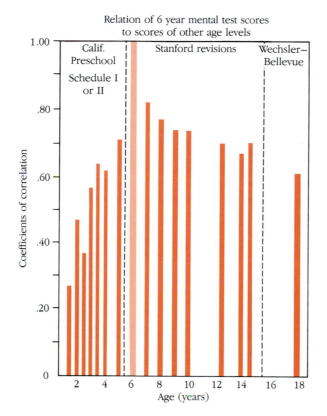

Figure 10-2

Relationship of IQ at Age 6 to IQ at Other Ages

The height of each bar in this figure represents the strength of the correlation between IQ at age 6 and IQ at other ages. A perfect relationship is reflected in a correlation of 1.00, which is the correlation shown for age 6 IQs when correlated with themselves (see the shaded bar in the figure). Other correlations are less. Note, however, that Stanford–Binet scores at age 6 correlated more highly with scores from ages 7 to 18 than with scores from early childhood and infancy. (All correlations come from a longitudinal study in which individuals were tested repeatedly from infancy to age 18. The Wechsler–Bellevue, used to test 18-year-olds, was a precursor to the WAIS and WAIS-R. The California Preschool Test, which was used with children from 1 to 5 years of age, was a precursor of the Bayley Scales of Infant Development.) (After Honzik, MacFarlane, & Allen, 1948)

for most people and can change for anyone, they only change because there are meaningful changes in the circumstances of people's lives. If a person's IQ did not change over the school years, it would only be because nothing dramatic had happened in that person's life to change the course of development in a way that affected IQ. In this regard, it may be helpful to think of IQ over the school years like wealth during adulthood. Your wealth relative to your peers once you begin working will be highly predictive of

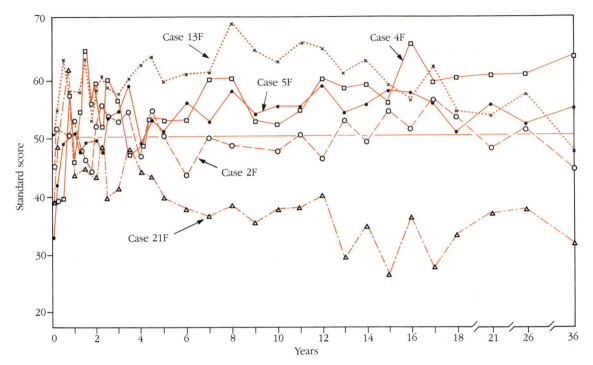

FIGURE 10-3
Longitudinal Changes in the IQs of Individuals

The ups and downs that occur in IQ across the life span can be gleaned from these data that show how five females in the Berkeley Growth Study changed relative to their peers over the years from birth to age 36. The scores reported (taken from Bayley, 1970) are not actual IQ scores, but they are related to them. For these data, the average score at each age level is 50 with a standard deviation of 10. The five individuals selected here represent the full range of aptitude levels found among females in the Berkeley Growth Study. Note that after age 6 the scores are more stable than they are prior to age 6. (After Bayley, 1970)

your wealth relative to them every year after that. The reason is not that wealth is a fixed entity that will stick with you no matter what. It is just that the factors that create wealth—job, family, motivation, and so forth—tend to go unaltered for most of us.

Are Intelligence Differences Later in Life Predictable in Infancy?

We noted earlier in this chapter that infant tests give us a way of assessing differences among infants in their rates of development. Thus, we can scale infants according to DQ just as we can scale older children according to IQ. A major question to be answered is whether there is any relationship between these two orderings: Do developmentally precocious infants always become intellectually gifted children? The answer is no.

As shown in data compiled by Robert McCall (1979) and reproduced in Table 10-6, infant tests during the first year have very little predictive value on the average. This situation improves somewhat in the second year, particularly after 18 months, but even then the degree of continuity from infancy to childhood is far less than the degree of continuity from, say, middle childhood to adolescence (see Figure 10-2). For this reason, McCall (1979, p. 715) comes to what he calls an "inescapable" conclusion: infant test performance in the first 18 months is a poor predictor of later intellectual differences. This conclusion applies to all the infant tests equally. It applies to Gesell's test, Bayley's test, and even some tests that assess Piagetian sensorimotor development. These are known as the Einstein Scales of Sensorimotor Intelligence (Escalona & Corman, 1969) and the Uzgiris–Hunt Assessment Scales (Uzgiris & Hunt, 1975).

Although investigators in general have not found DQ scores to predict IQ scores, there is one very important exception to this general conclusion: severe mental retardation is often detectable in infants. This fact provides infant tests with their greatest practical value. They allow us to screen for se-

TABLE 10-6
Median Correlations[1] Across Studies Between Infant Test Scores and Childhood IQ

AGE OF CHILDHOOD TEST (years)	AGE OF INFANT TEST (months)				
	1-6	7-12	13-18	19-30	
8-18	0.06 (6/4)	0.25 (3/3)	0.32 (4/3)	0.49 (34/6)	0.28
5-7	0.09 (6/4)	0.20 (5/4)	0.34 (5/4)	0.39 (13/5)	0.25
3-4	0.21 (16/11)	0.32 (14/12)	0.50 (9/7)	0.59 (15/6)	0.40
	0.12	0.26	0.39	0.49	

[1]Decimal entries indicate median correlation, the numbers in parentheses give the number of different r's and the number of independent studies used to calculate the median. In the case of more than one r per study, the median r for that study was entered into the calculation of the cell median. Marginal values indicate the average of the median r's presented in that row/column.

SOURCE: From R. B. McCall (1979), "The Development of Intellectual Functioning in Infancy and the Prediction of Later IQ." In J. D. Osofsky (Ed.), *Handbook of Infant Development*. New York: Wiley, p. 712. Reprinted by permission.

vere retardation early in life. You might think that an experienced pediatrician would hardly need a standardized test to be able to spot severe retardation, which in all likelihood would be associated with brain damage. Studies show, however, that this is not true. A test such as the Bayley given at 8 months of age can discriminate normal from abnormal children far better than experienced infant caretakers who do not use standardized tests to assist in making their assessments (Honzik, Hutchings, & Burnip, 1965). This does not mean the tests are foolproof. The best assessment is one that combines clinical judgment with a test score. Even then, if all signs point to brain damage, a child must not be pigeon-holed as a hopeless case. The whole purpose of early diagnosis of retardation is to trigger interventions that can facilitate development and overcome some of the expected handicap.

You might suspect that if severe retardation is diagnosable in infancy, genius might be also. But it is not. Robert McCall (1976, p. 102) cites data, for example, showing that 4-year-olds with IQs of 140+ were indistinct from normals when they were tested on the Bayley Scales at 8 months of age. Conversely, infants with high Bayley scores were apt to wind up as normals in IQ. Case histories do not allow us to induce general principles, but they do serve to underscore them: Albert Einstein, the most celebrated "genius" of the twentieth century, was retarded in learning to talk, and for this and other reasons his parents suspected that he was "subnormal" (Clark, 1973, p. 26). Thus, traditional infant tests diagnose severe mental retardation but, otherwise, are unrelated to eventual cognitive development.

One reason for the lack of continuity in individual differences from infancy to later childhood has to do with the plasticity of rates of development in infancy. As you will recall from Chapter 3, the pace of infant motor and mental development is highly susceptible to the effects of experience. Enrichment, for example, leads to significant advances in all the motor functions. Deprivation can lead to retardation. Parents can alter the rates at which their infants meet the various developmental milestones in the extent to which they enrich or deprive their infants' lives. Whichever parents do, however, there is no necessary carry-over from early stimulation to later intellectual achievement. In this regard, you might recall the children from San Marcos, Guatemala, who were studied by Jerome Kagan. They were severely retarded in their first year of development but then caught up nicely in childhood (Kagan & Klein, 1973). The same was true for the infants whom Wayne Dennis studied in the Iranian orphanage (Dennis & Najarian, 1957).

Aside from the fact that the rate of infant development is quite plastic, there is a second reason for the absence of a strong connection between DQ and IQ. This reason has nothing to do with development per se. It has to do with what the tests measure. Objectively there seems to be a distinction between the types of test items used to measure IQ and those used to measure DQ. You can see this for yourself if you compare the types of test items that appear on the Bayley mental and motor scales (Table 10-5) with items that appear on either the Binet–Simon Mental-Age Scale (Box 10-2) or the Wechsler tests (Table 10-3). To test the developmental status of infants we ask at what age they can perform certain simple sensorimotor functions (such as searching for a spoon, building a tower, or walking alone); to test the intelligence of older children we ask them questions requiring vocabulary skills and various bits of information that they should have learned. Also, we test their memories and require them to make comparisons and judgments. To even begin to justify the conceptual leap that both types of items measure "intelligence" would require data showing that infant DQs predict later IQs. As we have already seen, they do not—except in the case of severe mental retardation.

Is There a Discontinuity Between Infant and Childhood Intelligence?

The failure to find a link between the intelligence of the school years and the measurable attributes of infants has been frustrating to those who believe that there must be some basis for continuity. In the continuity view, individual differences in intelligence should not suddenly emerge in childhood. They should be based on some individual differences existing even in the early months of infancy. Recently, Joseph Fagan and his colleagues at Case Western Reserve University reported finding evidence of such continuity in a measure of infant behavior not included on any of the current infant tests. The measure is **recognition memory.** One of the interesting aspects of this measure is that it marks a return full circle in our assumptions regarding how intelligence can be measured. You will recall that Binet and his contemporaries in the late nineteenth century began their research on individual differences in intelligence by trying to gauge intelligence from individual differences in fundamental psychological functions. Failing at this they moved on to develop tests that measured high-level functions involving judgment, reasoning, and knowledge. Studies of recognition memory mark a return to the fundamental functions.

Fagan's Recent Research: Evidence for Continuity

Recognition memory, as you will recall from the previous chapter, contrasts with recall memory. Recall is an active process requiring a cue-driven search of memory. Recognition is passive. We either recognize an event as one we have experienced previously, or we do not. Recognition memory can be demonstrated in infants of any age, provided we use targets that are sufficiently distinct. Figure 10-4 shows pairs of visual targets that 5-month-olds are quite capable of discriminating on a recognition test.

A recognition test can be conducted in a variety of ways, but all depend on the same principle: infants will spend more time looking at novel, unfamiliar visual events than they will at familiar ones. This basic perceptual principle is referred to as *novelty preference*. Building on this basic princi-

FIGURE 10-4
Stimuli for a Recognition Memory Test
By 5 months of age, human infants can recognize which of the pictures in each pair they have seen before. They show this by ignoring the old, familiar picture when it is presented along with a somewhat similar picture. (After Fagan, 1982a)

ple, one can test for recognition of an old stimulus event by putting it in an attention-getting contest with some new event. The three basic means for doing this involve the visual-preference method, habituation method, and high-amplitude sucking procedure, all of which were discussed in Chapter 7. Fagan's preferred method is to use a visual-preference procedure (see Figure 10-5). He familiarizes his infant subjects with a single visual target for 20 seconds and then presents the familiar target along with a novel one for two 5-second viewing trials. The actual time spent looking at the novel target during the total 10 seconds of viewing time serves as the measure of preference.

Research by Fagan and others (see Fagan, 1984a) has shown that there is a strong association between novelty preference during the first year of infancy and later childhood IQ. The existence of this correlation means that, for the first time, there is a measure of first-year mental activity that serves to predict later intellectual functioning. The data are far from complete, but, to date, a reasonably strong association between infant novelty-preference scores and later childhood IQ has been found in 15 samples of children. The data from these samples are presented in Table 10-7. As you can see

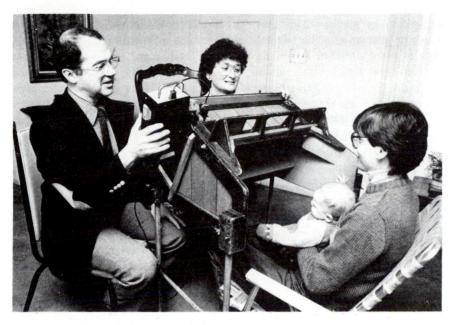

FIGURE 10-5
Visual-Preference Apparatus
This visual-preference apparatus was used by Joseph Fagan to obtain novelty-preference scores for young infants.

there, recognition memory tests that were given at ages ranging from 3 months to 1 year of age predicted IQs at ages ranging from 2 to 7½ years. The correlations ranged from .33 to .66. The overall correlation for the 15 samples reported by Fagan (1984a) is .45. Although this correlation is a far cry from perfect, it is a much better predictor of later IQ than measures taken on infants under 12 months of age using infant tests such as the Gesell or Bayley tests. There is reason to believe, moreover, that the current degree of prediction is an underestimate of the potential for prediction. One of the reasons is that many of the current correlations were obtained using novelty-preference scores that are relatively unreliable. By improving the reliability of the novelty-preference tests that are used, there is every reason to believe that we will improve the novelty-preference/IQ correlation.

As we all know, correlation does not necessarily imply an inherent, functional link between the measures that are correlated. For example, children's IQs may be correlated with the number of books in their homes without there being any necessary link between the two measures. That is, the books do not in any sense cause children to become intelligent, and, certainly, retarded children can develop in homes with many books, and geniuses can come out of homes with few. Much of the excitement sur-

TABLE 10-7
Correlations Between Tests of Visual Novelty Preference Given During Infancy and Later Tests of Intelligence

Sample Size	TEST 1 Age (months)	TEST 2 Age (years)	Correlation
57	3	2.0	.40
22	3	2.0	.52
39	6	3.0	.35
31	6	3.0	.42
16	7	3.0	.38
52	7	3.0	.44
35	7	3.8	.41
19	5	4.3	.33
36	7	5.0	.42
19	6	6.0	.56
21	12	6.0	.64
12	3	6.5	.50
20	4	6.5	.66
25	7	6.8	.36
19	5	7.5	.46

SOURCE: From J. F. Fagan, Early Novelty Preferences and Later Intelligence." In R. J. Sternberg (Chair), *Novelty As a Source of Developmental Continuity in Intelligence.* A symposium presented at the meeting of the Society for Research in Child Development, Toronto, April 1985. Reprinted by permission of the University of Chicago Press.

rounding Fagan's recent reports, therefore, stems not just from the existence of the correlations, but from the belief that these correlations do, in fact, signal an inherent functional link between the process of recognition memory and the process of later scholastic achievement. Fagan (1985b) has begun to theorize along these lines by suggesting that "the ability to detect similarities among otherwise diverse stimuli" is a basic intellectual process that underlies not only recognition memory but also analogical reasoning and the discovery of similarities and differences. This would make recognition-memory tests a direct measure of a fundamental intellectual ability. Future research will be needed to determine the merit of Fagan's theoretical claim. Meanwhile, there is a practical use to which the recognition-memory tests can be put: they can be used to predict retardation (Fagan, 1985a, 1985b).

As we discussed earlier, future retardation can be predicted fairly well using the standard tests of infant development. It turns out, however, that Fagan's test is better. This has been shown via direct comparison. In one sample of high-risk infants, for example, Fagan's infant test was correct in predicting 10 of 11 cases of retardation in children 3 years of age. Bayley's test, in contrast, predicted only 5 of these 11 cases.

To review briefly, this chapter began with a history of the Binet–Simon test in order to demonstrate how intelligence testing began. This historical perspective makes clear why psychometricians choose to define intelligence as the potential for scholastic achievement. The reason is that intelligence tests were developed for the purpose of aiding in decisions about academic placement. That was the original purpose, and it is still the chief use of intelligence tests today. The IQ score associated with these tests was originally defined as the ratio of mental age to chronological age (times 100), but today IQs are defined as deviation scores, not ratios. This makes the IQ a better number for judging the stability of one's intelligence relative to age-mates across time. Contrary to what psychologists from the nativist approach first believed, IQs are not fixed. Rather, IQ scores are apt to change considerably during a person's development, a fact that sits easily with one who has adopted the epigenetic view of development. Despite the frequent change in scores over time, some continuity remains, and this continuity increases with age. Although there have been tests available for measuring individual differences in the developmental status of infants since the 1920s, scores on these tests have never been meaningfully related to intelligence in later childhood. Recently, however, work by Joseph Fagan has led to the belief that individual differences in recognition memory in infants are predictive of later IQ. Now, to complete this chapter, we will consider issues related to the diagnosis of mental retardation and giftedness.

ISSUES IN THE DIAGNOSIS OF MENTAL RETARDATION

Mental Retardation as a Social Concept

A primary purpose for tests of individual differences in intelligence—whether in adults, children, or infants—is to diagnose retardation. Never, however, should a test score be the sole basis for a diagnosis. Other factors need to be considered also. For example, it is important to determine how well the child is getting along in his or her current nonacademic environment. Is the child in fact retarded relative to age-mates in everyday social skills and knowledge? The importance of this additional measure is made clear in the definition of mental retardation written by the American Association for Mental Deficiency, which emphasizes that "impairments in adaptive behavior" must exist along with subaverage intellectual functioning (Grossman, 1983, p. 11).

Measures of adaptive behavior take into account age-appropriate achievements in areas such as eating, dressing, toileting, communicating, and general social responsibilities. They measure whether a chld's low intelligence manifests itself in everyday activities. To measure adaptive behavior in a reasonably reliable way, a number of scales have been developed. One widely used measure is Jane Mercer's *Adaptive-Behavior Inventory for Children* (Mercer & Lewis, 1978). Another is the *Vineland Social-Maturity Scale* (Doll, 1965). As tests, these scales are not as reliable as IQ tests, but they do add important information for the purpose of diagnosis. The recommended order of testing (Helton & Workman, 1982) is that adaptive-behavior measures be given after IQ tests. If a child is known to fall into the retarded zone in IQ (an IQ of 69 or less), measures of adaptive behavior can then be used to confirm the diagnosis. If a child is found to be at age level in adaptive behavior but retarded on an intelligence test, the child is, by definition, *not* retarded. The usual recommendation would be that such a child's progress in school be monitored closely. The hope would be that with close monitoring and some remedial work the child could be restored to a normal level of mental functioning.

The emphasis on adaptive behavior in the definition of mental retardation makes clear that the concept of mental retardation is not synonymous with low IQ. A person can be of low IQ without being retarded. The reason is that retardation is a *social concept* (see Maloney & Ward, 1979, chap. 11). As the demands of society change, either a greater or lesser number of poeple will be able to meet the minimal requirements for coping in that society. This social relativity of the retardation concept is easily illustrated in the fact that the prevalence of retardation (that is, the number of people classified as retarded at any one time) changes as a function of age and culture.

The age change in the prevalence of retardation is graphically represented in Figure 10-6. As shown there, the prevalence of mental retardation is extremely low in infancy. It increases dramatically during the school years, peaking between ages 10 and 15. Then it declines again in adulthood. This developmental change in prevalence coincides directly with changes in adaptive-behavior requirements over these years (Zigler & Cascione, 1984, pp. 71-72). Specifically, far more people are able to function as competent infants and preschoolers than can function as competent elementary and junior-high students. There just are not the same intellectual demands in preschool tasks as there are in school tasks. By adulthood, it is again easier to be competent, primarily because people are free to choose their own niche in society. Thus, people who may need special-education classes in the schools may have no need at all for special work places or living arrangements.

Further illustrating the social relativity of the retardation concept are prevalence data in different countries. Some between-country data are given along with the age data in Figure 10-6. These serve to demonstrate some of the ups and downs in prevalence that occur as you move from one culture to another. An extreme case of cultural differences in prevalence is provided by the People's Republic of China, where, in 1977, the concept of mental retardation and special education did not exist in the schools. Ac-

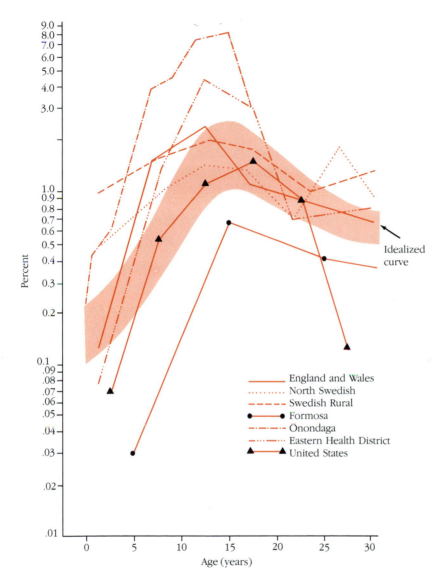

FIGURE 10-6
Age-Related Prevalence Rates for Mental Retardation in Different Cultures
The prevalence of mental retardation varies as a function of both age and culture.
The basic age-related pattern, however, which is indicated by the idealized curve in
the center of the figure, is present in all the cultures represented here. (After
Landesman-Dwyer & Butterfield, 1983)

cording to Nancy Robinson (1978), who reported on the state of special
education in China, the concept of mild retardation was not needed in the
schools at that time because the school curriculum was easy enough and

TABLE 10-8
Classification of Mental Retardation by IQ Level

LEVEL OF MENTAL RETARDATION	EDUCATIONAL- EQUIVALENT DESCRIPTION	RANGE IN STANDARD- DEVIATION VALUE
MILD	Educable	-2.01 to -3.00
MODERATE	Trainable	-3.01 to -4.00
SEVERE	Trainable (Dependent)	-4.01 to -5.00
PROFOUND	Custodial (Life Support)	< -5.00

SOURCE: From *Assessment of Children's Intelligence and Special Abilities* (p. 425) by J. M. Sattler, 1982, Boston: Allyn & Bacon, Inc. Reprinted by permission.

the students mutually cooperative enough that the slower children did not need to be segregated. We can be sure, however, that as China becomes a more modern society, one that demands that its citizens be able to compute and report taxes, negotiate insurance contracts, understand a complex legal system, navigate on freeway systems, and follow the directions for installing technologically advanced appliances, more of her citizens will fall into the retarded zone.

Determining Level of Retardation

In addition to determining whether a person merits the label "retarded," intelligence tests and measures of adaptive behavior are used to determine the level of retardation. Table 10-8 shows the IQ levels that are associated with the four levels of retardation recognized by the American Association of Mental Deficiency. You will note also that the labels *educable, trainable,* and *custodial* are listed next to the level designations *mild, moderate, severe,* and *profound.* The level designations are the terms that have been adopted to replace the unfortunately chosen terms: moron, imbecile, and idiot. The labels educable, trainable, and custodial refer to the level of adaptive behavior that people with each level of retardation can expect to attain. The educable mentally retarded (EMRs) will go on to master elementary-school subjects, and as adults they may be self-sufficient. The trainable mentally retarded (TMRs) are unlikely to ever be totally self-sufficient, primarily because they are not likely to be able to compete in the usual marketplace for jobs. For this reason, many will work in what are called *sheltered workshops,* which will give them a job they can handle and a small income. They

RANGE IN IQ FOR STANFORD–BINET, FORM L–M	RANGE IN IQ FOR WISC-R, WPPSI, AND WAIS-R[1]	APPROXIMATE MENTAL AGE AT ADULTHOOD	APPROXIMATE PERCENT IN THE POPULATION
67-52	69-55	8-3 to 10-9	2.7
51-36	54-40	5-7 to 8-2	0.2
35-20	39-25	3-2 to 5-6	0.1
<20	<25	<3-2	0.05

[1]The IQs shown for the severe and profound levels for the Wechsler tests are extrapolated.

may also live in group homes, where assistance in the chores of day-to-day living can be provided. Most of the custodial mentally retarded will be cared for as patients in state mental-retardation facilities. A more-complete description of the adaptive behaviors that are associated with the various degrees of retardation are given in Table 10-9.

Pathological Versus Cultural–Familial Retardation

Speaking of the mentally retarded as a single class of people is somewhat misleading, because there seem to be two reasonably distinct groups (Penrose, 1963; Zigler, 1967). One is the group of individuals with a known, specific defect. This is the **pathological** group, also known as the *organic* or *clinical* group. The second group consists of people having no specific, diagnosable defect. Retardation in this group is generally referred to as **cultural–familial retardation.**

Pathological Retardation

In all, about 250 specific pathologies have been identified that have moderate or severe retardation as a primary symptom (Maloney & Ward, 1979, p. 228). As you can imagine, they form a quite diverse group. Some of the pathologies have their onset prenatally. These include chromosomal and genetic conditions (see Chapter 5) as well as teratogenic effects on the developing brain and nervous system (see Chapter 4). Other pathologies can be created during or just after birth, because in this perinatal period, oxygen deprivation (known medically as *anoxia* and *hypoxia*) and infection are

TABLE 10-9
Levels of Adaptive Behavior for the Mentally Retarded

LEVEL	PRESCHOOL AGE (birth to 5 years)	SCHOOL AGE (6 to 21 years)	ADULT (over 21 years)
MILD RETARDATION	Can develop social and communication skills; minimal retardation in sensorimotor areas; rarely distinguished from normal until later age.	Can learn academic skills to approximately 6th-grade level by late teens; cannot learn general high-school subjects; needs special education, particularly at secondary-school age levels.	Capable of social and vocational adequacy with proper education and training; frequently needs guidance when under serious social or economic stress.
MODERATE RETARDATION	Can talk or learn to communicate; poor social awareness; fair motor development; may profit from self-help; can be managed with moderate supervision.	Can learn functional academic skills to approximately 4th-grade level by late teens if given special education.	Capable of self-maintenance in unskilled or semiskilled occupations; needs supervision and guidance when under mild social or economic stress.
SEVERE RETARDATION	Poor motor development; speech is minimal; generally unable to profit from training in self-help; little or no communication skills.	Can talk or learn to communicate; can be trained in elemental health habits; cannot learn functional academic skills; profits from systematic habit training.	Can contribute partially to self-support under complete supervision; can develop self-protection skills to a minimal useful level in controlled environment.
PROFOUND RETARDATION	Gross retardation; minimal capacity for functioning in sensorimotor areas; needs nursing care.	Some motor development present; cannot profit from training in self-help; needs total care.	Some motor and speech development; totally incapable of self-maintenance; needs complete care and supervision.

SOURCE: "A Rationale for Degrees of Retardation," 1955, *American Journal of Mental Deficiency, 60,* p. 262. Reprinted in *Assessment of Children's Intelligence and Special Abilities* (p. 426) by J. M. Sattler, 1982, Boston: Allyn & Bacon, Inc. Reprinted by permission.

possible. Either can lead to brain damage. Events can also occur in the postnatal period that will lead to retardation. These events include illnesses, head injuries, and dietary deficiencies.

In recent years medical and societal advances have given us the means to reduce the prevalence of pathological retardation. These advances in-

Many trainable mentally retarded individuals, although unlikely ever to be completely self-sufficient, may find work in sheltered workshops like the one pictured here.

clude such things as the establishment of genetic counseling as a medical specialty, better obstetrical care, the use of ultrasound and amniocentesis for detecting prenatal abnormalities, the control of infectious diseases, elimination of teratogenic hazards (for example, excess radiation, rubella, and certain drugs), and improved environmental controls on postnatal hazards ranging from child abuse to lead poisoning from paint.

The pathologically retarded differ from other retarded individuals in at least two ways. One is that they have lower IQs. The average IQ for the pathological group as a whole is about 32, and few individuals in this group have IQs above 50 (Dingman & Tarjan, 1960). A second distinguishing characteristic is that pathological retardation is not associated with any particular subgroup in society. For example, it is not associated with poverty or wealth, race, or any other general factor. This means that the causes of pathological retardation strike pretty much at random. There are a few exceptions to this general rule. For example, overall, males are more subject to pathological retardation than females. Also, maternal age is a predictor of certain chromosomal conditions that induce retardation (Ayme & Lippman-Hand, 1982). A well-known example is the relationship between maternal age and the incidence of Down's syndrome (see Table 10-10). These exceptions notwithstanding, however, we can conclude in general that the factors causing pathological retardation strike in an unpredictable way.

TABLE 10-10
Prevalence of Down's Syndrome as a Function of Maternal Age

MATERNAL AGE (years)	RATE OF DOWN'S SYNDROME AMONG LIVE BIRTHS
>20	1.46 per 1,000
20-24	1.40 per 1,000
25-29	1.76 per 1,000
30-34	2.57 per 1,000
35-39	7.32 per 1,000
40+	30.06 per 1,000

SOURCE: "Maternal-Age Effect in Aneuploidy: Does Altered Embryonic Selection Play a Role?" by S. Ayme and A. Lippman-Hand, 1982, *American Journal of Human Genetics, 34,* p. 561. Reprinted by permission of the University of Chicago Press.

Cultural–Familial Retardation

In strong contrast to the lack of predictability for pathologically based retardation, cultural–familial retardation is quite predictable. It occurs almost exclusively in the lower socioeconomic classes (see Figure 10-7). In this group, it is most prevalent in single-parent homes where the sole parent (almost invariably a woman) is retarded and unemployed. IQ level further distinguishes the pathologically retarded from the cultural–familially retarded. Cultural–familially retarded individuals tend to have scores in the IQ range from 50 to 70, whereas the pathologically retarded, as we have seen, generally have IQs below 50.

An interesting fact regarding the prevalence of the two types of retardation is that the prevalence of cultural–familial retardation is predictable based on the assumption that intelligence is normally distributed in the population. Thus, according to Haywood (1974), the actual number of people with IQs in the 50-to-70 range only exceeds the predicted number by just 1 percent. For IQs less than 50, however—that is, for the IQ group that includes most of the pathologically retarded—the normal curve predictions are greatly in error. In the IQ range from 20 to 50, for example, there are 125 percent more cases than would be expected. In the IQ range from 0 to 20, there are 175,339 percent more cases! To speak in terms of numbers of people rather than percentages, this last statistic means that if intelligence were normally distributed in a population of 240 million people, we would only expect to find 68 people in the IQ range from 0 to 20. In fact, however, we find approximately 119,000 people in this category. (This estimate is based on Haywood, 1974.)

Data of the sort just cited have given rise to a two-group theory of retardation. According to the theory, the pathological group makes up a distinct, qualitatively different population. We can assign IQs to people in this group, but that does not mean that an IQ of 45 or 50 has the same

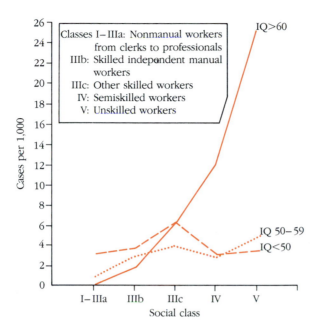

FIGURE 10-7

The Relationship Between Social Class and Degree of Retardation

In this figure, social class is scaled by the father's occupation from high (Class I) to low (Class V). As the figure shows, children with IQs less than 50 come from all social classes with equal frequency. But children with IQs between 50 and 59, and particularly retarded children with IQs of 60 or more, come primarily from lower-class families. (After Birch, Richardson, Baird, Horobin, & Illsley, 1970)

meaning for them as for someone who has no pathological condition. It also means that, in the pathological group, intelligence does not arise according to the probabilistic model in which many independent events collectively determine the IQ. Rather, in these pathological cases the outcome of one single event—for example, the chemical products of a particular gene, a chromosomal defect, the introduction of a teratogen—overwhelms all the others.

In contrast to the pathologically retarded, who are seen as a special population, the cultural–familially retarded are viewed as simply being the low end of the normal distribution of intelligence. This means that their intelligence is the end product of an essentially normal (though not necessarily desirable) developmental course. They are less intelligent than others, not because they are afflicted with a particular defect, but merely because the environmental and genetic factors involved in the development of intelligence conspired to make them less intelligent.

If we assume that a two-group structure in fact underlies the distribution of IQ in the retarded range, the actual distribution of IQ scores, with

FIGURE 10-8
The Two-Group Theory of
Mental Retardation
Panel A shows IQ distributed
in a perfectly normal way.
Panel B adds the
pathologically retarded as a
second, distinct group. Panel C
shows the distribution of IQs
that would result by
combining the IQs from the
normal and pathological
groups into a single frequency
distribution. This third
distribution reflects the actual
distribution that exists in our
society. (After Penrose, 1963)

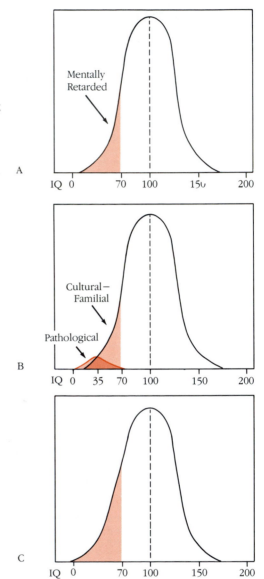

its excess of cases at the extreme low end, can be better understood. Figure
10-8 shows how. In this figure, two distributions are combined. One is the
distribution for normal intelligence, which includes cases of cultural–familial retardation in its tail. The other is the distribution of IQ for pathological
cases. Combining these distributions yields a single curve that diverges from
a perfectly normal curve in the same way as the actual IQ curve diverges
from a normal curve: namely, there is an excess of cases in the low end.

The two-group theory of retardation (Zigler, 1967) has received a good deal of support recently. Some of the strongest support comes from studies that show that the brothers and sisters of pathologically retarded individuals are quite normal in intelligence, whereas the brothers and sisters of the cultural–familially retarded are themselves subnormal. The most recent data of this sort come from a large-scale federal-government study of mental retardation (Nichols, 1984). As shown in Figure 10-9, the siblings of moderately and severely retarded individuals (those with IQs less than 50) have IQs that vary within the same range as members of the normal population, with an average IQ of 103. This average compares quite favorably to the expected value of 100. The same was not true for the brothers and sisters of mildly retarded individuals (that is, those with an IQ between 50 and 68). The mean for these children was 85, a value that is quite significantly lower than 100. Visually, it is apparent in Figure 10-9 that the two groups of siblings differ, and this difference is perfectly consistent with the view that the lowest levels of retardation are due to specific pathologies that have no relation to the intellectual status of other family members. The higher levels of retardation, however, are quite intimately connected to the intellectual status of other family members.

Family-study data such as those from Paul Nichols's study (see also Johnson, Ahern, & Johnson, 1976; Roberts, 1952) are important because they tend to validate the belief that pathological and cultural–familial retardation are indeed distinct categories with different developmental histories. Pathological retardation involves pathologies (over 250 different ones), hence the developmental course in this form of retardation is an abnormal course. Cultural–familial retardation, on the other hand, can be understood as the

FIGURE 10-9
IQ Distributions for the Siblings of Mildly and Severely Retarded Children
Support for the two-group theory of retardation is found in the fact that the brothers and sisters of mildly retarded children are themselves subnormal in intelligence. However, the brothers and sisters of severely retarded individuals are perfectly average in intelligence. These data are based on a family study involving 17,432 white children. Data from black families are not as supportive of the two-group theory as these data are. (After Nichols, 1984)

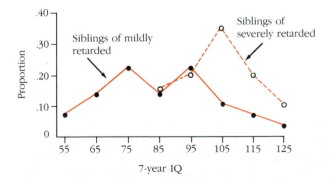

outcome of the normal interaction of genetic and environmental factors. Based on this interaction, some people wind up as gifted, some as retarded, and most wind up somewhere in the middle.

Calling the developmental history of cultural–familial retardation "normal" does not mean that nothing should be done to eliminate it. To the contrary, part of the heuristic value of the two-group theory is that it directs us to seek the causes of cultural–familial retardation in the cultural and familial situations of children and not in biomedical conditions per se (Zigler, 1978). Based on such research, intervention programs such as Head Start and the Abecedarian Project (see Chapter 3) will be better able to meet the goals of enhancing the adaptive behaviors and intelligence of high-risk children. Such programs will never eliminate low intelligence; there will always be a low end to the distribution of IQ. But given the plasticity of intelligence, this low end can be made high enough so that more of our citizens than at present will have the intellectual capacity to complete school and function independently in society.

ISSUES IN THE DIAGNOSIS OF GIFTEDNESS

Defining giftedness is a bit more of a problem than defining retardation. Retardation is a socially determined category that people fall into only if they prove unable to cope with the intellectual demands society places on them. An IQ level of 70 was set as a cutoff score for this category only because research and experience indicated that an IQ below 70 tends to correspond to a retarded level of functioning (Grossman, 1983, p. 23). But what will be the IQ and functional criteria for saying that a person is gifted?

If we take a purely statistical approach and define giftedness as the statistical opposite of retardation, we might set an IQ cutoff score of 130. With this score we will net about as many people in the upper reaches of intelligence as the cutoff score of 70 nets in the lower reaches of intelligence. This approach has some theoretical appeal in that it defines retardation and giftedness by the same criterion of statistical rarity. It labels the lower 2.3 percent or so as retarded and the upper 2.3 percent or so as gifted. This is symmetrical, neat, and in keeping with the theoretical view that intelligence is a normally distributed trait in the population. The one problem with the definition is that it is all too arbitrary. As we learned in the first section of this chapter—and again in the section on mental retardation—if we are to classify children, it must be done with a purpose.

The purpose in classifying children as gifted is for them to be able to receive the special-educational opportunities that have become increasingly available in our public schools since 1957. This was the year in which Russia's Sputnik was launched, setting off the fear in this country that we were not keeping up in science and technology. Before assigning children to the gifted classrooms of our schools, however, we need to identify in a way that is demonstrably reliable and valid those children who can best profit from a supplementary curriculum. This is the same measurement problem that Binet faced, but in reverse. So far there has been no contemporary Binet to come along and solve the problem for us. Although school systems generally employ a common verbal definition of giftedness, they differ greatly in their means of assessing it.

The verbal definition of giftedness that is most widely used is one that appeared in a report on education for the gifted by a former U.S. commissioner of education (Marland, 1972). The definition specifies six areas in which children could demonstrate their giftedness and, therefore, their need for special education. These were general intellectual ability, specific

Identifying creative potential in young children, such as this pianist, presents a serious challenge to researchers.

academic aptitude, creative or productive thinking, leadership ability, excellence in the visual and performing arts, and psychomotor ability. Since this definition was printed, the federal government has altered its definition to exclude psychomotor ability (The Gifted and Talented Children's Act, 1978, as cited in Callahan, 1981, p. 50). One thing to be gleaned from this definition is that the federal government thinks it would be in our best interest to offer special-educational opportunities to children who excel in ways other than those measured by IQ tests.

When it comes to deciding which children in a school are in fact covered by this definition, there is a problem, however. Schools have measures of *aptitude* (such as IQ tests) and *achievement* (such as the California Achievement Tests) that they can employ, and these provide reasonably reliable and valid assessments of two of the five areas of giftedness specified by the federal government. But measuring the potential for leadership ability, creativity, and excellence in the visual or performing arts is another matter altogether. How can these be assessed? An IQ test given to Einstein once he was into his school years would have detected his excellent intellect for abstract conceptual thinking. But could a leadership test have detected Churchill's potential? or Gandhi's? Could a test for potential in the visual or performing arts have identified the best of our contemporary artists? We should not rule out the possibility of finding reliable and valid aptitude tests for these areas of excellence, but if our experience with creativity tests (which we will cover in the following discussion) is any example, the measurement problem in the areas of the visual or performing arts and leadership may be insurmountable.

Problems in Measuring Creativity

If you search for tests that are called tests of creative potential you will find several. Paul Torrance, for example, has developed a widely used set of tests (Torrance, 1966) as have Michael Wallach and Nathan Kogan (1965). These are called the *Torrance Tests of Creative Thinking* and the *Wallach and Kogan Test* respectively. Although these tests are usually referred to as tests of creativity, they are better defined as tests of **divergent thinking,** or *ideational fluency* (Guilford, 1967). The reason is apparent if you examine the items that make up these tests.

A sample set of items from the Wallach and Kogan Test is given in Table 10-11. Each item requires the test taker to generate ideas rather than find answers. Finding answers, such as those to traditional IQ test items, is a process of **convergent thinking**—thinking that focuses on achieving a single product (Guilford, 1967). Divergent thinking on the other hand is the process involved in generating as many different ideas or thoughts as possible. The reliability with which an ability for divergent thinking can be measured is far less than the reliability for IQ, but there is some test-to-test

TABLE 10-11
Sample Items from Wallach and Kogan's (1965) Creativity Test

TYPE OF ITEM	EXAMPLE
I. Instances	Name as many things as you can that are round. Name as many things as you can that move on wheels.
II. Alternate Uses	Name as many uses as you can for a newspaper. Name as many uses as you can for a cork.
III. Similarities	Tell me as many ways as you can think of in which a cat and a mouse are similar.
IV. Pattern Meanings	Tell me all the things that these drawings might represent.

SOURCE: From *Modes of Thinking in Young Children: A Study of the Creativity–Intelligence Distinction* by M. A. Wallach and N. Kogan, 1965, New York: Holt, Rinehart, & Winston.

consistency in an individual's score. Thus, there is some reliability to our measurements. The real problem that we have with creativity tests like Torrance's or Wallach and Kogan's, however, is their validity. If by virtue of the test's reliability we grant that it is measuring something, we can still raise the question of whether that something has anything to do with the potential for making creative contributions in later life. Attempts to find this essential relation between divergent thinking and later creative products have largely failed (Kogan, 1983, p. 635). For example, if you ask architects to identify other architects whom they view as "creative," there will be little correlation between these rankings and the architects' scores on Wallach and Kogan's test. It turns out, therefore, that creativity tests like Wallach and Kogan's have only *face validity*. This means that superficially they seem to be measuring something we all would call creativity. But these measures in fact have little to do with the real-world criterion of creativity in the arts and sciences.

Given that we have no clear evidence that creativity tests measure potential for real-life creativity, is there any evidence that they measure anything that is really different from IQ tests? It could be that tests of divergent thinking are nothing but imperfect measures of IQ. If so, then there is surely no need for the extra test when IQ tests already do just fine. The answer to the question whether creativity tests measure anything different is both yes and no. The answer is yes for people with an IQ of about 120 or above and no for those below that level (Taylor, 1975, pp. 21-22). This means simply that we do not learn anything new about a person with an IQ under 120 by giving that person a creativity test. For people higher than that we do get some new information. We learn that not all high-IQ people are equally good at tests of divergent thinking. For this reason, some schools do include tests of divergent thinking among their tests for identifying the gifted. In 1972, however, the last year for which there were any data, only 14 percent of the schools with gifted classes used such tests (Marland, 1972).

At present, there are no tests that even purport to be tests of leadership or artistic potential. Schools, if they use measures of these, must rely on teacher judgment. It is quite problematic whether these judgments have any reliability or validity. Teachers quite understandably have no better grounds than the rest of us for judging potential in these areas. Their judgments, therefore, are liable to be highly idiosyncratic.

Because measuring anything other than IQ and academic achievement is such a problem, most schools rely heavily on these measures alone to identify the children they offer special classes to. Nonetheless, given the fact that IQ and achievement are about all we can measure with any reasonable accuracy, some experts are not at all sorry that the gifted tend to be identified by these tests alone. Kirk and Gallagher (1979), for example, believe that this system is the fairest because "even though superior intelligence is only one factor in determining success, achievement, or contribution to society, it still remains a basic ingredient of giftedness" (p. 71). Intellectual superiority, they hold, is the common denominator of all five forms of giftedness specified by the federal government. Thus, in the absence of any better measures, the best thing to do is to measure IQ and achievement.

Are the Gifted a Special Population?

We saw in the case of retardation that there are two groups of retarded individuals. One is the group of extremely retarded individuals, most of whom have some pathological condition that accounts for their retardation. The other is the group of mostly mildly retarded individuals whose familial background—both genetic and environmental—accounts for their retardation. This makes one wonder whether there might be a similar two-group structure that underlies intelligence at the upper end of the distribution—a highly intelligent group whose intelligence can be explained by the psychometrican's genes-and-environment, probabilistic model, and a second group whose high intelligence is in fact pathological.

A belief in pathologically based genius has been extended from the days of prescience up until the near present. This belief takes several forms, but all reduce to a belief in compensating factors. This means that if a person has great genius, he or she will also have great character flaws, physical deformities, or some other problem that will balance out the high intellect, making it clear that there is a price to be paid for genius. Madness, for example, is frequently linked to genius. As the poet John Dryden put it, "Great wits are sure to madness near allied / And thin partitions do their bounds divide." (From "Absalom and Achitophel," Part I [1681]) Another compensatory belief is that extreme precocity (like achieving a mental age of 12 at chronological age 7 or 8) can only be achieved at the expense of a premature decline. This is the "early ripe, early rot" hypothesis.

If one takes the compensatory view that some pathology is always linked—perhaps causally—to exceptionally high intellect, some confirmatory evidence can be found in case histories of demented genius. There are many such cases to be recounted. Psychotic depression, for example, frequently accompanies greatness in art, literature, and music (Karlsson, 1978, particularly chap. 18; Simonton, 1984, p. 55). But if one takes an unbiased sample of people with exceptionally high IQs and then looks for evidence to support a compensatory hypothesis, no evidence can be found. To the contrary, those gifted in intellect tend to have many other advantages in life as well. The evidence for this statement is quite clear. It comes from a massive, longitudinal study begun in 1922 involving approximately 1,500 children with 140+ IQs (the top 1 percent of the population). The study was conceived by Lewis Terman (see Terman, 1925; Terman & Oden, 1959; Terman, 1954; and Sears, 1977).

The initial results of Terman's study dealt with the characteristics of children with high IQs. In general, they were "appreciably superior to unselected children in physique, health, and social adjustment; markedly superior in moral attitudes as measured either by character tests or trait ratings; and vastly superior in their mastery of school subjects as shown by a three-hour battery of achievement tests" (Terman, 1954, p. 223). Teachers rated them as being leaders, well liked, and honest. In fact, the only trait on which they were not above average was manual dexterity, but even in this, they were hardly deficient.

According to the compensatory hypothesis, Terman's gifted subjects should have begun to pay the price of their intellects by adulthood. This, however, was not the case. Follow-up studies have been conducted periodically, with the most recent being reported by Robert Sears in 1977. These show that the incidence of mortality, ill health, insanity, and alcoholism among the gifted was less than would be expected in an unselected population of the same age; at the same time, the overall life satisfaction and social adjustment was greater. Also, the intelligence of the group remained superior, with 90 percent of the group showing increases in intelligence over time. As regards professional achievements, Terman (1954) estimated that the people in his gifted group were "from 10 to 20 to 30 times" more likely to achieve success in their fields than were people of the same age picked at random. Interestingly, however, it was not intellect that predicted which of the gifted would be most successful. Comparing the most success-ful of his adults with the least successful, Terman found them to be equal in IQ.

In addition to the fact that Terman's longitudinal study shows no evi-dence of any compensatory factors being associated with exceptionally high intelligence, there is further evidence in the brothers and sisters of gifted children to indicate that high intellect is not a sign of pathology, nor in any way necessarily linked to pathology. Instead, data on the siblings of the gifted make it appear that extreme intelligence is as cultural–familial in or-igin as is moderate to mild retardation. Leta Hollingworth (1929), for ex-ample, has reported that the siblings of children with genius-level IQs have above-average IQs themselves. In her particular sample, the siblings of chil-dren with an average IQ of 155 had an average IQ of 129. This is precisely what one would expect from the probabilistic model. Had there been some

FIGURE 10-10

IQ Distribution for the Offspring of Gifted Parents

The offspring of Terman's 1,525 gifted subjects had IQs that were normally distributed but well above average. These data support the view that extremes in intellectual giftedness do not occur at random in the population the way that extremes in retardation do. (After Jensen, 1980. The data are from Terman & Oden, 1959.)

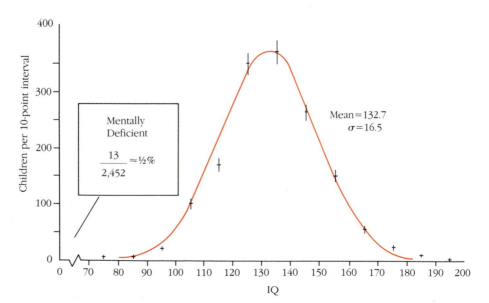

particular pathology, some fluke of nature, to account for the family member who ranked as exceptionally gifted, we would have expected the brothers and sisters to be more nearly normal in intelligence. Analyzing her data further, Hollingworth showed that the siblings of those with an IQ in excess of 150 were themselves superior in IQ to siblings with less-gifted brothers and sisters. Again, even in the upper reaches of the IQ distribution, we find that the brothers and sisters of the exceptionally intelligent are themselves above normal, more above normal in fact than children with less-distinguished but, still, gifted sibs.

A final contribution to the view that exceptional intelligence is cultural–familial in origin and not linked to or caused by any random pathologies are data on the offspring of Terman's gifted subjects. As shown in Figure 10-10, the scores of these children were normally distributed, but well above average. Again, high IQ seems quite predictable from a knowledge of a person's cultural–familial background. Extremely high intelligence, therefore, unlike extreme retardation, does not occur at random in the population.

SUMMARY

Unlike the previous two chapters, which dealt with descriptions and explanations of developmental differences in general cognitive processes, the present chapter has focused on individual differences in the products of cognition as they are manifested on intelligence tests. The psychometric definition of intelligence implicit in these tests is one that equates intelligence with scholastic aptitude. The reason for this is purely practical: when school attendance was made compulsory, societies needed a way to determine children's aptitude for profiting from the particular educational experiences that would be offered in the schools. They especially needed to know which children would be retarded in their learning, because it was in the best interest both of these children and of society that retarded children be placed in special-education classes. Selecting the children for these classes was never very scientific, however, until Binet and Simon developed a test that met better than any test before it the criteria for descriptive science. The test was easy and quick to administer, and it yielded a score that was objective, reliable, and valid.

When the Binet–Simon test was adapted for use in this country, it became the Stanford–Binet, which measured IQ rather than just mental age. IQ in its first usage was a true quotient, the ratio of mental age to chronological age, multiplied by 100. Today, however, it is a deviation score. The IQ variable is distributed in a reasonably normal way with a mean of 100 and a standard deviation of 15 or 16 depending on the test (Wechsler or Stanford–Binet). A number of infant tests exist for measuring individual differences in infant development.

Contrary to what psychometricians earlier in this century believed, IQ is not a fixed characteristic. One longitudinal study has shown that the average person changes by as much as 15 points in IQ over the school years alone. The lack of fixity in IQ does not imply, however, a complete lack of stability. In fact, when we examine the age-to-age correlations of IQ in samples of people, IQ beginning at age 6 is fairly reflective of IQ throughout the school years. Tests given earlier than age 6 show some correlation with school-age IQs, but they are not strong enough to provide much value as predictors. Overall, the least useful of the predictors are infant DQ test scores. The only value for these in predicting later IQ occurs in the case of moderate to severe retardation. But this in itself is quite a contribution, because early attention is necessary if retarded children are to receive the kind of training that will maximize their developmental potential.

One reason that traditional infant tests do not correlate well with later IQ measures seems be that they tap different aspects of development. A test that may correct this problem is Fagan's recognition-memory test. A number of studies show that measures of infant recognition memory taken at age 7 months correlate about .45 with IQ in the age range 3 to 6 years. In addition, recognition memory predicts retardation better than traditional tests. The theoretical and practical implications of the connection between infant recognition memory and later IQ are only now being developed.

To be diagnosed as retarded by an IQ test, children need to score at least two standard deviations below the mean. Assessing IQ, however, is only a first step in actually diagnosing retardation. The retarded must score low in adaptive behavior as well as IQ. In all, about 3 percent of the population meets the low-IQ criterion for retardation. This is more than we would expect if IQ were distributed in a perfectly normal way. The discrepancy can be explained by the two-group theory of retardation, which separates the pathologically retarded from the cultural–familially retarded.

Giftedness has a more variable definition than retardation. The gifted are defined not only by their scholastic aptitude and achievement but by their potential in leadership, the visual or performing arts, and creativity as well. Unfortunately, the only good tests that we have are for IQ and achievement; therefore, scores on these tests provide the primary basis by which children become eligible for gifted-child programs. Although many people have believed that genius generally bears with it some compensatory defect, scientific studies such as Terman's longitudinal study of genius show no evidence of this. To the contrary, those most gifted in IQ seem to be above average on most desirable traits. Unlike extreme pathological retardation, which is unpredictable in the population, genius is predictable on the basis of cultural and family background.

SUGGESTIONS FOR FURTHER READING

DuBois, P. H. (1970). *A history of psychological testing*. Boston: Allyn & Bacon. This short but comprehensive text provides an overview of the development of psychological tests and the field of psychometrics.

Edgerton, R. B. (1979). *Mental retardation*. Cambridge, MA: Harvard University Press. This is an extremely readable and interesting text appropriate for anyone with either practical or theoretical concerns regarding mental retardation.

Gardner, H. (1983). *Frames of mind*. New York: Basic Books. MacArthur Prize winner Howard Gardner expresses disenchantment with the view that intelligence is unidimensional. In his view, there are multiple intelligences.

Horowitz, F. D. & O'Brien, M. (Eds.). (1985). *The Gifted and talented: Developmental perspectives*. Hyattsville, MD: The American Psychological Association. This recent volume contains literature reviews, historical reviews, and discussions of issues that pertain to the portion of the population that can be identified as intellectually gifted and talented.

Jensen, A. R. (1982). *Straight talk about tests*. San Francisco: W. H. Freeman. Arthur Jensen holds some controversial views regarding the use and interpretation of mental test scores, but his scholarship is unsurpassed.

CHAPTER OUTLINE

CHAPTER 11

Language Development

If ontogeny was lawfully bound to recapitulate phylogeny, as developmentalists once thought (see Chapter 1), then a development so uniquely human as language should only come at the very end of our childhood. As you already know, however, language is not acquired at the end of our childhood but at its beginning. Before children have begun to think logically about concrete situations and before they have begun to use the simplest memory strategies, they have already mastered the essentials of their native language. This means that children learn the basic vocabulary and grammar of their native language without the aid of abstract reasoning abilities and without special memory aids. If you are currently struggling through a foreign-language course in college where you have at your disposal dictionaries and grammar books, it may amaze you to realize that preschool children playing in sandboxes can learn all that you are learning but without the effort and mental anguish. Not only can they learn *a* language this way, if they happen to live in a bilingual world, they will learn two languages with the same ease, and they will do so in no more time than it takes to learn one (Kessler, 1984). If you are amazed by this, you should be. It is a truly astonishing achievement.

To impress on you how much we should be in awe of preschool children's linguistic achievements, we will begin by learning what it means to know a *language*. Languages, as we will see, have certain structural and functional properties that are not completely shared by nonlanguage communication systems. By knowing more about these structural and functional attributes of language, you will be in a better position to appreciate the preschool child's achievement. Following this initial discussion of the structural and functional properties of language, we will proceed to a description of the language-acquisition process. The chapter will conclude with some theoretical considerations that lead us to believe that, even though language is obviously learned as a result of being exposed to it in a communicative social environment, the learnability of language rests ultimately on some special properties of the human brain.

WHAT IT MEANS TO KNOW A LANGUAGE

If you currently think that all communication requires the use of language, then you have a misconception. Language is, in fact, only one of many modes of communication. Observational studies of humans and other animals make this abundantly clear. There are many nonlinguistic methods by which humans and animals communicate. One method, common among insects (but not among humans), is to use chemical messages called *pheromones*. Another method is to use visual signals like tail wagging, arm waving, and gill flaring or acoustic signals such as songs, croaks, and hisses. Sometimes the communication system of which these signals are a part can become very sophisticated. Honeybees, for example, can communicate the location and distance of a food source (and something about its quality) using a dance that they perform in the hive (see Gould, 1982). Vervet monkeys even have what appears to be the start of a vocabulary (Struhsaker, 1967). If these East African monkeys are perched in a clump of trees when an eagle comes near, the first monkey to see the eagle will give a "rraugh" call and all the monkeys will move into the underbrush at the base of the trees. If it happens to be a leopard, a different cry will be given and the monkeys will move higher into the trees. If a venomous snake crosses the monkeys' territory, a third warning cry called a "snake chutter" is given (Seyfarth, Cheney, & Marler, 1980). Despite the cleverness of these communication systems, it is still helpful to distinguish them from language, the uniquely human communication system.

The communication systems of bees, vervet monkeys, and other animals fall short of being true languages because they have only *some* of the functional and structural properties of languages. We will begin this chapter with a brief overview to indicate what these functional and structural properties are. This will make clear that pheromone messages, bird cries, and monkey calls are really quite different from linguistic statements.

The Functional Properties of Language

Charles Hockett (1960) was the first to point out some of the interesting functional properties of language, most of which are absent from nonlanguage communication systems. Among the properties Hockett identified were *displaced reference, generativity,* and *prevarication.* Philosopher John Searle (1969), unlike the linguist Hockett, was not concerned with delineating between language and nonlanguage communication systems, but his analysis of the social functions of *speech acts* provides a second convenient means of making such a delineation. It turns out that a great many social functions can be performed via the speech acts of languages that cannot be performed by the communicative acts of nonlinguistic systems. (The act of promising is but one of many examples, see Table 11-1.) In addition, only in linguistic communication systems can social functions be performed through indirect, nonliteral means. By focusing on some of the differences that have been brought to light through Hockett's and Searle's analyses, we can begin to get an appreciation for the functional differences between languages and other communication systems.

Displaced Reference

Language is useful primarily because it allows us to communicate about objects and events that are not now present. This function—referring to objects and events in their absence—is known as **displaced reference.** To test whether a communication system is languagelike in this regard, you need only to ask whether it allows communication about the past and the future and the things that we cannot presently see, hear, taste, or touch. Most communication systems do not. When dogs bare their canines to make a threat, the threat is intended to be, and understood to be, a communication about the animal's present state. The same is true of the vervet monkey cries. They are symbolic vehicles for referring to the present only. Vervets do not use these cries for reminiscing over past attacks by predators, nor do they use them in planning for future ones. Human facial expressions and other aspects of "body language" also fall short on this criterion. Still, there are *some* nonlanguage communication systems that allow for displaced reference. The bee's communications about pollen sites and cavities in which a new hive could be built are prime examples.

Generativity

Generativity refers to the capacity of language for producing novel messages. Animal communication systems are, for the most part, closed systems allowing for no novel messages. Thus, vervet monkeys have cries for snakes, leopards, and eagles, but that is all (we think). Moreover, if these monkeys were introduced to a new environment with new predators, they would be unable (presumably) to vary their old cries in a way that would give them a means of referring to the new predators. Human languages are not restricted in this way. Given the generativity of language, we need never be at a loss for words. Not only can we create novel utterances to communicate novel messages, we create them so routinely that nearly every utterance we speak or hear is a novel one. And when new inventions come along like computers or new diseases like AIDS or new physical threats like acid rain, we find it quite easy to open up our language to encompass them. Language learners take at least partial advantage of this aspect of language from the very start by expressing themselves in unconventional but meaningful ways. To provide but a brief illustration, a young boy responded to harassment from another child who persisted in shoving a doll named Woodstock in his face by saying, "I'm going home so you won't Woodstock me" (Clark, 1982). Woodstock used as a verb was quite meaningful in this context, but if language lacked generativity, it would not have been.

Prevarication

Prevarication, or lying, is another function that is beyond the capacity of most communication systems to perform. Take, for example, the chemical messages that animals send each other. Because there is no voluntary control of scent glands, we can assume that no animal puts out a false scent message just for the fun of it. Therefore, if an ant lays down a pheromone trail on its return from a food site, other ants can trust that message to be true. Likewise, while it is amusing to imagine bees sending other bees off on their own version of a wild-goose chase, it is inconceivable that bees could have evolved to act so irresponsibly about such an important matter as food. The bee's dance, therefore, is another communication system that we can assume does not allow prevarication. Human body language also fails to meet the criterion of potential for prevarication. Even those who have not made a careful study of body language know that true feelings are hard to hide. People can say they are happy only to have their faces give them away.

Human languages differ from other communication systems in that with language, it is as easy to lie as not. All you have to do is negate the truth with a simple *no, nyet, nein,* or *non.* Children begin to use language in this way almost as soon as they acquire the negative. If you were to ask a young boy, for example, if he was the one who spilled milk on the floor, he would likely deny his obvious guilt with a *no.* Interestingly, chimpanzees who have acquired some of the rudiments of human sign language use their sign language to do the same thing. The chimp Lucy (see Temerlin, 1975), who lived in a human home in Oklahoma, was imperfectly toilet trained. As a consequence, she frequently left feces on the carpeted floors. When asked if she was responsible for the feces, however, she would routinely respond *no.* When asked who was responsible, she would pick any convenient adult and either point to the person or sign the person's name.

The Social Functions of Speech Acts

Most communicative acts (and all speech acts) are characterized by having a social function (Austin, 1962; Searle, 1969). They are designed to affect the behavior, knowledge, or attitude of another. A dog that wags its tail or bares its teeth at the approach of a stranger can be used to illustrate the concept of social function. The tail wagging and teeth baring serve the function of greeting in the one case and warning in the other.

Although nonlanguage communication systems can perform some small set of social functions—greeting and warning are two examples—no communication system compares to language in the wealth of functions that can be performed. Table 11-1 offers a quick introduction to the actual extent of that wealth. This wealth is realized in *all* human languages. One of the categories listed in Table 11-1 is declarations (after Searle, 1975). With this function, one can realize some rather amazing social acts. For instance, one can turn a bachelor into a married man and a free person into a prisoner. The words that perform this declarative function include performative verbs such as *decree, pronounce,* and *order* (often accompanied by *hereby,* as in "I hereby pronounce you man and wife"). Put into the right social context, these words work like magic wands to change the status quo into the status novo. Nonlanguage communication systems have nothing comparable to this. They even lack far more mundane capabilities. One of the most striking

TABLE 11-1
Categories of Speech Acts

Representatives	Speaker conveys his/her belief that a certain proposition is true (for example, assertions).
Directives	Speaker attempts to get the listener to do something (for example, ordering, commanding, begging, requesting).
Commissives	Speaker commits him/herself to a future action (for example, promises, vows, contracts).
Expressives	Speaker expresses his/her psychological state (for example, apologies, thanks, feelings, welcomes).
Declarations	Speaker's words bring about a change or a new state of affairs (for example, *You're fired*).

SOURCE: From "Language Acquisition: Linguistic Structure and Rule-Governed Behavior" by I. Brown, Jr. in *The Functions of Language and Cognition* (p. 170) by G. J. Whitehurst and B. J. Zimmerman (Eds.), 1979, New York: Academic Press, Inc. Reprinted by permission.

is their lack of a means for asking questions—a directive function known as *interrogation.*

Interrogation   One of the primary social functions of human languages is to serve as a vehicle for exchanging information. We make the exchange precise by asking questions and getting answers. Animal communication systems, however, seem to be devoid of means for asking questions. Given the potential value of being able to tap into another individual's knowledge bank to acquire information, one would think that if animals were given the linguistic means for asking questions that they would immediately begin to do so. Apparently, however, they do not. This, at least, is the conclusion to be drawn from research projects that have sought to bestow human languages on nonhuman primates.

The nonhuman primate research has been conducted with chimpanzees primarily. Thus far, these apes have succeeded in learning to communicate using gestural signs (Gardner & Gardner, 1969), plastic chips (Premack, 1976), and computer-linked buttons (Rumbaugh, 1977). But, interestingly, their communications—in whatever mode—do not involve questions. The chimpanzees command, make reference, and request, but they do not interrogate, except in the context of specific training activities. Thus, though they use the names of people, they do not routinely inquire the name of each new person they meet. Nor do they ask where things are, whose they are, or what they are. We can conclude that animals do not use the linguistic function of interrogation, regardless of whether they are communicating using a natural communication system or one that is man-made. Young children, on the other hand, make extensive use of this function from the very beginning. *Where, what,* and *why* are among the three most frequent words used in the vocabularies of 2- and 3-year-olds.

The Capacity for Nonliteral Illocutionary Acts   In addition to lacking the means to express the wide array of social functions expressible in language, nonlanguage communication systems are restricted by their being exclusively literal. Languages, on the other hand, can perform each of their social functions in nonliteral, indirect ways. To use John Searle's terminology, languages do not weld the **illocutionary** force (that is, social function) of speech to either its propositional content or to its grammatical structure. This means that language, unlike other communication systems, can function sarcastically ("Isn't this a lovely day?" a grammatical question used as a sarcastic reference to the fact that it is cold and dreary), indirectly ("It seems to be hot in here," used as an indirect request that someone, please, open a window), and metaphorically ("He's an old stick in the mud," "Life is a long hard road," "She's like a dream come true"). In communication systems other than human language, we do not find evidence for metaphor, sarcasm, or indirectness of any kind. This makes sense because nonlinguistic communication systems are dedicated to being literal rather than figurative and to being direct rather than indirect. Language, however, with its wider range of functions, has richer possibi 'ties.

The Structural Properties of Language

In addition to the functional properties that make human languages unique among communication systems, there are unique structural properties to human languages. This is indicated by the fact that linguistic communications can be broken down into a number of recombinable elements. Individual sentences, for example, can be broken down into constituents (noun phrase, verb phrase, and so forth), the constituents can be broken down into patterns of meaningful speech parts called *morphemes,* and the morphemes can be broken down into patterns of elementary speech sounds called *phonemes* (see Figure 11-1). Nonlinguistic communications cannot be broken down like this into a set of reusable parts. The messages that are part of nonlanguage communication systems are no more decomposable than a sneeze or a wave of the hand.

FIGURE 11-1
Structural Analysis of a Linguistic Communication
Communicative acts involving gestures, facial expressions, animal cries, or pheremones have no internal structure. This means that they cannot be analyzed into a collection of reusable parts. Linguistic communications, however, are quite clearly a collection of parts. As shown here, a single sentence can be analyzed into constituent phrases, phrases into syntactically ordered words, words into morphemes, and morphemes into phonemes. All human languages are structured in this same way. (After Gleitman, 1981.)

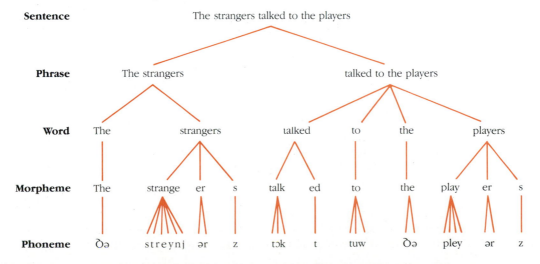

A more concise way of saying what is unique about the structure of human languages is to say that they have **grammar.** This is a set of rules for generating meaningful messages out of a set of elementary units—**phonemes**—which by themselves are no more meaningful than the letters of the alphabet. For human languages there are four types of rules in a grammar. There are **phonological rules,** which define allowable phoneme combinations; **morphological rules,** which govern the formation of words from morphemes; **syntactic rules,** which govern the arrangement of words in sentences; and **semantic rules,** which determine meaning.

Phonological Rules

You may have never heard of phonological rules before because they were not part of the "grammar" you studied in high school. Nonetheless, you are quite knowledgeable about the use of English phonology even though you have never made a formal study of it. You know, for example, that with the three phonemes [æ], [k], and [t] you can make three words consistent with English phonology. These are [ækt], [tæk], and [kæt] *(act, tack,* and *cat).* The

TABLE 11-2
Phonetic Symbols

CONSONANTS					
Stops			**Affricates**		
p	pig	[pɪg]	tʃ (tš, č)	choke	[tʃ ok]
b	big	[bɪg]	ǰ (dž, ǰ)	joke	[dʒ ok]
t	tip	[tɪp]			
d	dip	[dɪp]			
k	cap	[kæp]			
g	gap	[gæp]			
Nasals			**Liquids**		
m	sum	[sʌm]	l	led	[lɛd]
n	sun	[sʌn]	r	red	[rɛd]
ŋ	sung	[sʌŋ]			
Fricatives			**Glides**		
f	fan	[fæn]	w	wet	[wɛt]
v	van	[væn]	y (j)	yet	[yɛt]
θ	thigh	[θaɪ]			
ð	thy	[ðaɪ]			
s	sip	[sɪp]			
z	zip	[zɪp]			
ʃ (š)	shun	[ʃʌn]			
ʒ (ž)	vision	[vɪʒən]			
h	hat	[hæt]			

other three possible combinations ([ktæ], [tkæ], and [ætk]) are not English words, nor could they be. The reason is that each violates the phonological rules of English. They do not violate the phonology of all languages, however. The pattern of sounds in [ktæ], for example, would be acceptable in Arabic.

Each of the better than 5,000 human languages that currently exist around the globe has its own set of phonological rules that govern the way the phonemes of the language can be combined. Not only do these rules differ, but the sets of phonemes to which they are applied also differ. Altogether, there are about 90 phonemes used in the world's languages, but no one language uses them all. English, for example, uses the 38 phonemes listed in Table 11-2; other languages use as few as 20 phonemes or as many as 60. Because all languages sample from the same finite set of phonemes, there is considerable phonemic overlap from one language to another. For example the [m] and [a] (pronounced ah) sounds are present in all human languages as phonemes, and they are also among the first phonemes that children use in their *productive* (that is, nonimitative) speech. (No wonder, then, that *mama* is a common children's word in not only English but Jap-

VOWELS

Front			Central		
i	beet	[bit]	ə	above	[ˌəˈbʌv]
ɪ	bit	[bɪt]	ʌ	but	[bʌt]
e	bait	[bet]			
ɛ	bet	[bɛt]			
æ	bat	[bæt]			
Back			Diphthong		
u	boot	[but]	aɪ (ay)	bite	[baɪt]
ʊ	put	[pʊt]	aʊ (aw)	bout	[baʊt]
o	boat	[bot]	ɔɪ (oy)	boy	[bɔɪ]
ɔ	bought	[bɔt]			
a	pot	[pat]			

VARIOUS PHONETIC MARKINGS

- `:` indicates preceding sound is lengthened (e.g., [e:])
- `h` indicates preceding sound is aspirated (e.g., [tʰ])
- `~` indicates a nasalized vowel (e.g., [æ̃])
- `ʔ` indicates a glottal stop (e.g., *oh oh!* [oʔo])
- `ˈ` indicates the following syllable has primary stress (e.g., the first syllable of *eggplant* [ˈɛgˌplænt])
- `ˌ` indicates the following syllable has secondary stress (e.g., the second syllable of *eggplant* [ˈɛgˌplænt])

anese, Russian, and many other languages as well.) The English phonemes that distinguish our words *either* and *ether* ([ð] and [Θ]), on the other hand, are rarely found among the phonemes of other languages. Other languages might treat these as a single phoneme or perhaps not have a [th] sound at all. By the same token, whereas we have a single sound designated as [k], speakers of Arabic have two different phonemes: one is the [k] in *key;* the other is the [k] in *caw.* This distinction, too, is rare in the family of human languages.

With this very brief introduction to the intricacies of phonology, you can begin to see that there is a lot for children to learn. They must learn the sounds that are used in their target language (or native language) and then the rules for combining these in acceptable ways. Also, they must learn to produce subtle phonetic differences, like the difference between *either* and *ether* or between *pick* and *pig.* Nothing comparable to phonology exists in the structure of nonlanguage communication systems.

Morphological Rules

Morphological rules deal with the formation of words from morphemes. A **morpheme,** in the linguist's technical jargon, is the smallest sound or sound combination that has meaning. We can best define this term with examples. The sound combination [haʊz] is formed from three phonemes, but it could be either one or two morphemes depending on its usage. If we use this sound combination in the utterance "How's everybody doing?" it is two morphemes. The first is [haʊ], which is the phonetic transcription for the question word *how.* The second is the morpheme for the contraction of the verb *is.* If we use [haʊz] in the sentence "We need to house ten people," it is just one morpheme. If we use *house* again as a verb but this time make it past tense as in "Last night we housed ten people," we again have two morphemes, because the extra phoneme [d] in [haʊzd] carries the meaning of "occurring in the past." Linguists prefer the concept of a morpheme to that of a word, because in vocal speech there are no clear boundaries between one word and another. Only on a printed page do words appear in isolation.

The morphological rules that are most important in the study of language are the rules for using a set of morphemes known as *grammatical morphemes.* These morphemes, which consist of both free-standing words (for example, *the, and, at, more–than*) and word add-ons, or *affixes,* (for example, *-ed, -est, re-*), serve a number of purely grammatical functions. One of these is to alter the grammatical relations among words in a sentence. An example is the free morpheme *of,* which establishes a possessive relationship between *friend* and *Bill* in the phrase "friend of Bill." The affix *-s* can do the same thing as in "Bill's friend." Morphemes are used in similar ways in all the world's languages to specify the grammatical roles that words play.

In Japanese, for example, the morpheme *-wo* is added to nouns when they are the object of an action; the morpheme *-ni* is added when they are the recipient (or indirect object) of an action. To designate that Mr. Tanaka (Tanaka-*san* in Japanese) was the object of an action, one would say "Tanaka-san-*wo*." To designate that he was the recipient of an action, one would say "Tanaka-san-*ni*." English has a recipient marker but not an object marker. The recipient marker is the preposition *to*. Objects in English are understood from their position in the sentence.

When a grammatical morpheme is added to an utterance as a word affix, the morpheme is called an *inflection*. In English, inflections can be used to make verbs past tense *(work/worked)*, nouns plural *(book/books)*, and to do such things as turn adjectives into nouns *(good/goodness)* and adjectives into adverbs *(smooth/smoothly)*. Still, English uses inflections far less than some other languages. Japanese, as we have seen, uses inflections to mark objects as well as recipients. It also has an inflection (actually, there are two of them) to mark subjects. Using inflections to mark both subjects and objects is common among languages, as is the use of inflections to mark gender.

Syntactic Rules

Syntax involves the arrangement of words in sentences. If languages had no syntax, we could string the words of a sentence together as freely as we do the items in a shopping list. But languages are not this way. Thus, although it does not matter whether we shop for "Ajax, butter, apples, and noodles" or "butter, noodles, apples, and Ajax," it does matter whether we say *house light* or *lighthouse*. The last two contain different messages, and they do so because of a syntactic rule in English involving word order in modifier–noun relations. Syntax is probably the most complex aspect of language that children must learn. Consider, for example, all the syntactic knowledge required to transform a simple declarative sentence like "Cheryl jogs" into other sentence modalities: the negative is "Cheryl doesn't jog"; the future, "Cheryl will jog"; the past, "Cheryl jogged"; the emphatic declarative, "Cheryl does jog"; the interrogative, "Does Cheryl jog?"; the tag-question form of the interrogative, "Cheryl jogs, doesn't she?"; and the imperative, "Jog, Cheryl." These, of course, are just some of the possible syntactic variations one can make on the basic proposition that Cheryl jogs.

Semantic Rules

With just phonological rules, morphological rules, and syntactic rules you can make perfectly good sentences. What you cannot necessarily do with these rules alone, however, is make sense. To make sense, you must know the semantic rules of the language. These semantic rules make it incorrect and, therefore, ungrammatical to say such things as "The bald man parts his hair on the left." Without semantic rules, a lot of our language would be like Lewis Carroll's poem *Jabberwocky* (" 'Twas brillig, and the slithy toves   /   Did gyre and gimble in the wabe . . ."): it would sound like English but make no sense at all. Learning the semantic rules of language is primarily the job of mastering the meanings of the words in a language. This is the job linguists call acquiring the *lexicon*. Because semantics involves meaning, you might suspect that semantic development is tied to general cognitive development. As we will see, this is indeed the case.

This section has elaborated on the structural and functional aspects of human language so that you can better appreciate what children achieve when they learn a language. Unlike other communication systems that we know about, languages have a multitiered structure called a grammar, which consists of phonological, morphological, syntactic, and semantic rules. On the functional side, languages have the capacity to make an infinite number of both truthful and untruthful references to objects and events that can be either present or absent. These characteristics are reflected in what Charles Hockett calls the generativity of language and in its capacity for displaced reference and prevarication. From a separate functional perspective, one provided by John Searle's analysis of speech acts, linguistic communications can serve to fulfill a large number of social intentions, only a few of which can be fulfilled by nonlanguage communications. Also, languages allow users to express their social intentions in nonliteral ways through the use of indirect speech, metaphor, and sarcasm. The combination of functional and structural features that are present in every human language make it clear that linguistic communication is quite different from nonlinguistic communication. Although the communication systems used by other animals may share a few isolated features with human languages, to our knowledge none is even close to being completely languagelike.

LANGUAGE ACQUISITION

In one sense, language acquisition has an abrupt onset. It begins around 1 year of age, when children first begin to use isolated words from the linguistic code to achieve their social intentions (for example, requesting an object verbally rather than pointing and whining). In another sense, it has a gradual onset emerging out of prelinguistic motor, social, and cognitive achievements. To initiate our discussion of language development, we will take the gradualist view (which is also the connectionist view, see Chapter 1, pp. 39–41). In this view, prelinguistic developments play a direct role in the later onset and eventual mastery of the linguistic code.

Developmental Roots for Language

Although children do not begin to use language in earnest until they are well into their second year of life (with the first sporadically used words coming at about 12 months), many developmental psychologists hold that language development in the larger sense has been going on since birth. You will recall, for example, that there is a certain biological preparedness for language. By birth, the left hemisphere of the brain (in most infants) has already begun to differentiate in a way that specializes it for the reception and production of language (see Chapter 6, p. 305). The young infant brain also comes preequipped to make categorical discriminations among sound patterns that correspond to the phonemes of human languages (see Chapter 7, pp. 364–66). In addition to the linguistic preparedness of the infant brain, infants seem behaviorally predisposed toward language. For example, they seem to listen intently to speech signals and seem to enjoy it immensely when adults speak directly to them. Their joy is frequently expressed in a vocal response called *cooing* (a purely vocalic production). Later, in the second 6 months of life, infants will begin to take pleasure in peekaboo games and other turn-taking activities. The significance of these activities is that they have a distinctly conversational appearance, so that perhaps infants are getting their first lessons in how to initiate and maintain a social (and later, linguistic) interaction. (See the discussion of prelinguistic pragmatic training and formatting later in this chapter.) In brief, there are many indications even in the first year of life that human infants are firmly positioned on a language-learning track (see Anisfeld, 1984, chap. 10).

The development that might, on the surface, appear to be the most directly related to later language development is **babbling.** This is the label for the vocal play of infants that begins around 5 or 6 months of age. Babbling is easily distinguished from the cooing vocalizations that precede it by the fact that babbling is syllabic in structure. Reduplicated syllables like *ba-baba* or *gugugu* dominate among the babbling sequences of infants 6 to 10 months of age. *Variegated babbling,* which involves nonduplication such as *pataka* or *babi,* begins in the period 11 to 12 months (Oller, 1980).

Despite the apparently obvious connection between babbling and speech, conventional wisdom for many years held that the two were discontinuous (see, for example, McNeill, 1970, p. 1131). One of the arguments for a discontinuity between babbling and speech was a belief that the two failed to overlap in time. In fact, it was even held that a period of silence separated the two, such that there was a clear temporal boundary between a prolifically babbling 11-month-old and a much less loquacious though verbal 12-month-old (Velten, 1943, p. 281n). One got the impression that perhaps an old, phylogenetically primitive mechanism had been turned off, and a new, uniquely human one had been turned on much as might occur, say, when a vestigial reflex gives way to a voluntary motor act. In retrospect, the "discovery" of a clear temporal break between babbling and speech seems to be an event comparable to the sighting of homunculi in human sperm cells (see Figure 1-10): the discovery was due more to theoretical expectancies than to actual observations. The fact is that there is considerable overlap between babbling and speech (Clark & Clark, 1977, p. 390; Locke, 1983, pp. 52-53). First words are coincident with continued babbling.

A second argument for the discontinuity of speech and babbling, which turned out also to be based on an incorrect observation, held that there was a sharp phonetic contrast between babbling and speech (McNeil, 1970, p. 1131). The alleged contrast was between children who, as babblers, demonstrated a fluent capacity to produce any and all sounds of which the vocal tract is capable and children as language users who greatly narrowed their range of sounds down to just a few functional ones. H. V. Velten expressed the mistaken view that such a contrast exists when he wrote that "with the appearance of phonemes, the ability to produce a multitude of speech sounds seems to vanish overnight" (Velten, 1943, p. 281).

Contrary to the impression that Velten gives with this remark, the phonology of the first words does not contrast sharply with the phonology of babbling. In fact, in the view of the linguist John Locke, the sound patterns for children's first words are completely continuous with the sound patterns they use in babbling (Locke, 1983, p. 83). The continuity is evident first in that babbling does not sample from the full range of sounds available to the human vocal tract. Sounds that are rare in the languages of the world are rare in babbling (though occasionally a few of the rare sounds might be made). More important yet, the sounds that are most often used in babbling are the very ones that first appear in productive speech. This makes it apparent that there is actually far more continuity than discontinuity between the phonology of babbling and early speech. With few exceptions, the sounds for making children's first words come directly from their repertoire of most-frequently babbled sounds. The relationship is so good in fact that, in John Locke's opinion, it should be possible to predict individual differences in early phonemic development by knowing the frequency with which the various candidate sounds were exercised in the babbling period (Locke, 1983, p. 81). Quite clearly, then, the contemporary view is one of phonological continuity, not discontinuity between babbling and speech.

A third misconception regarding babbling, which has been corrected by recent research, held that the phonology of babbling, during the period 6 months to 1 year, gradually drifted toward the phonology of the target language. This belief was sparked by the observation that infants, late in the babbling period (that is, 9 to 12 months of age), often babbled sound sequences that had structural qualities similar to the target language of the babbler. The suspected reason was that infants who had previously babbled speech sounds at random were later being selective and babbling just those sounds that were phonemes-to-be. A falsification of the *babbling-drift hypothesis* comes in part from cross-linguistic studies (see Locke, 1983, pp 9-10). These show that the phonology of babbling changes over time, but in ways that are universal and not in ways peculiar to a language community.

What does change over time, however, are the prosodic aspects of babbling. (*Prosody* refers to aspects of an utterance such as the pattern of stress and intonation.) These prosodic features (also called *suprasegmental features*, because they operate at a level higher than the speech-sound segments) do become ever-more like the target language. In one demonstration of this, untrained listeners were able to distinguish the babbling of 8-month-old infants living in a French-speaking environment from the babbling of infants living in either a Cantonese- or Arabic-speaking environment (De Boysson-Bardies, Sagart, & Durand, 1984). Trained phoneticians could make the same distinction among infants just 6 months of age, the earliest age at which babbling is likely to begin. The observers did not make their distinctions by differentiating the actual speech sounds being produced from one another. Rather, the adult listeners found differences in the prosodic properties of babbling among the various language communities.

By correcting previous misconceptions regarding babbling drift and the discontinuity of babbling and speech, contemporary researchers have gradually revised the now dubious view that babbling is a vocal sidetrack having little to do with actual speech development. They hold, instead, that babbling has important links to language, links that go beyond whatever indirect benefit might be derived by exercise of the vocal musculature alone.

Acquiring the Lexicon and the Grammar

No matter how important prelinguistic motor, social, and cognitive development may prove to be in eventually mastering the structural features and functional uses of language, the start of language in most people's eyes is tied to use of the linguistic code itself—that is, to the comprehension and production of words. This is the aspect of language development that has a seemingly abrupt onset. It begins toward the end of the first year when parents initially detect some true linguistic understanding. The understanding is first evident in the fact that children respond appropriately to some words and phrases. Somewhat later, they start to use words in the referential way required of language. Mother appears and they say "Mama." The family dog arrives and they say "Doggie." More than just naming things, they also comment and request. For example, a child might hold up a sock and say "Mommy," indicating presumably that it is Mommy's sock. Or a child, after finishing a cookie, might request another cookie by pointing to the cupboard where cookies are kept and saying "More." Using words in this way marks the point at which we can begin to speak of children's phonological, syntactic, morphological, and semantic development.

Phonological Development

As was pointed out at the start of this chapter, the grammar of languages consists of phonological rules, as well as syntactic, morphological, and semantic rules. To know the phonological rules, children must first learn the sound system of their language. This means being able to both hear and produce all the phonemic contrasts ([t] versus [d], [l] versus [r], and so on) in the context of meaningful speech. In addition to knowing the sound system, children must also learn the rules for combining these sounds. This means knowing the difference between phonologically acceptable and unacceptable words.

You will recall from Chapter 7 that infants in their first 6 months can discriminate most, if not all, of the phonemic categories of human languages. This means that even the youngest infants know when a particular sound is just a variation on a single phoneme and when it is an altogether different phoneme. They show this in the habituation procedure by attending to the new phoneme but not to the altered phoneme. Such evidence might lead you to think that accurate phonemic perception is never a problem. This is not so. For some reason, when these distinguishable sounds are being used to discriminate meaningful messages, they can be confused. Evidence for this comes from research conducted by Olga Garnica at Stanford University (1973).

In her research, Garnica introduced children between 1 and 2 years of age to distinctive play figures who took on different names. They might be *Pok* and *Bok, Mik* and *Nik,* or *Zav* and *Chav.* Following the introduction, she asked the children to do something with one of the figures, like "Put Chav under the blanket" or "Take Zav for a ride in the car." It turned out that these children, who in the context of a habituation study could make all the required phonemic distinctions, were now confused. They did not know from the label alone which figure had been referred to. The problem was not one of making the proper association, because when distinctly contrasted labels were used (for example, *Zav* and *Bok*), the children performed well at the task. We can assume, therefore, that hearing a contrast in meaningful speech and knowing that it marks a semantic distinction is a different task from just being able to perceive sounds as discriminable.

Although children will have some difficulty at the start of speech development in hearing the phonemic contrasts that distinguish words, this discrimination task is still easier than the task of learning to produce all of the phonemic contrasts. For this reason, perhaps, we find that the ability to perceive a phonemic difference precedes the ability to produce the difference. Children will object, for example, if an adult speaks using the same incorrect pronunciation that they do. A child may say *wabbit,* but still expect an adult to say *rabbit.* David Palermo (1978, p. 96) has an anecdote to illustrate this point. A 3-year-old girl he was talking with was eating red candy fish from a bag. When Palermo asked her what she was eating she said, "Candy fis." "Candy fis?" Palermo asked. "No, fis," said the child. When Palermo told her he would like to have a candy "fis," the girl again corrected him. "No, not fis, fis!" "Oh, fish," said Palermo. "Yes, fis," said the child. Such stories are not hard to come by. Every parent has one. Thus, we must not judge children's knowledge of the phonemes in their language from their production alone.

What is particularly interesting about children's failure to pronounce words correctly even after they hear them correctly is that the mispronunciations are not due to the lack of motor control over the acoustic productions of the vocal tract. You might be inclined to think that this was the problem, that saying *wabbit* for *rabbit* or *fis* for *fish* was just a sign of the general motor clumsiness of young children—the verbal equivalent of "toddling" as opposed to walking. This, however, is not so. The vocal apparatus of children is capable of producing correct sounds long before children actually use them in their speech. We know this because during the period 6 months to 1 year, children's babbling is very rich in phonemic material. Though infants do not babble every sound used in every human language (Locke, 1983, pp. 3-7), they babble a great number of them. This means that children are better at sound production when they are not trying to speak than when they are. Many children, for example, do not make the [r] sound in their speech, but they are probably able to make a perfect [rrr] sound when imitating a car engine. This problem is further illustrated in the case of Amahl, the son of British linguist Nils Smith (1973, cited in de Villiers & de Villiers, 1978, p. 43). When Amahl tried to say *puddle* it came out as *puggle.* But when he tried to say *puzzle* it came out as a perfect *puddle.* He could say *puddle,* therefore, but only when he was not trying to.

One of the interesting things we will find to be true of children's early errors in speech production is that the errors are predictable, not random. This means that children's speech production is organized by a set of rules, albeit an incomplete or even inaccurate set. Knowing this, we can take special interest in errors, because they reveal what these rules are. This is as true for errors of pronunciation as for errors of syntax and semantics. Peter and Jill de Villiers (de Villiers & de Villiers, 1978) have employed this approach to deduce some of the pronunciation rules that children around the world use during the early stages of language acquisition (see also Locke, 1983, pp. 62-71). They have identified any number of them, all of which appear to have the quite reasonable goal of simplifying the pronunciation task that children face.

One of the universal simplification rules is **sound deletion.** Children learning English, for example, may handle the problem of consonant clusters at the start of a word by dropping one of the consonants. This means that *string* becomes *tring* and *stop* becomes *top*. Final consonants can also be dropped. Invoking this rule turns monosyllabic words like *duck* into *du*. For multisyllabic words, a second rule is used—reduplication. **Reduplication** results in productions such as *bubba* for *button, wawa* for *water,* and *dada* for daddy. A third simplification rule is **sound substitution.** An example of substitution in English is the tendency to voice initial consonants that should be voiceless. This produces the childlike *doe* for *toe* and *bie* for *pie*. Another common substitution involves devoicing final consonants, as in the substitution of *shoos* for *shoes*. In addition, children are likely to substitute a front consonant for a back one ([b], [p], [d], or [t] for [g] or [k]) when it is the first sound in a word and to substitute a glide ([w] or [y]) for a liquid ([l] or [r]) when the liquid precedes a vowel. These produce substitutions such as *dat* for *cat* and *wick* for *lick*. **Sound assimilation,** a fourth rule, refers to a tendency to form the vowels or consonants of a word all in the same place. By this rule, if a word has two consonants with separate points of articulation, the child might alter the word to have only one point of articulation. *Doggy* thus becomes either *doddy* or *goggy*. One consonant gets assimilated to the other. The four rules presented here are just some of the many rules that account for young children's baby talk.

The strategies for simplification reviewed above give way in an orderly manner as children gain the ability to reliably produce the various phonemes of their language. Although normative data are not available, small-scale studies of phonemic development have been conducted. Figure 11-2 shows the data from one such study that used a cross-sectional method of investigation (Prather, Hedrick, & Kern, 1975). The figure gives a general indication of the order of acquisition for the 24 consonantal phonemes of the English language. The order shown there supports a pattern that is true in all languages (see Ferguson & Macken, 1983, p. 238) of stops preceding fricatives (for example, [p], [t], [k], [b], [d], and [g] before [f], [s], [sh], [v], and [z]), labial consonants preceding alveolars (for example, [b] and [m] before [d] and [n]), and semivowels preceding liquids (for example, [y] before [r] and [l]). A universal in the development of vowels is that vowels made with the tongue placed low in the mouth precede vowels requiring higher tongue placement (for example, [o] before [i] and [u]).

FIGURE 11-2
Phonemic Development
Cross-sectional data give an indication of the general order of development for the consonantal phonemes of English. The left portion of a bar begins at the point where 50 percent of the children sampled were using the phoneme reliably when asked to produce the phoneme (as part of an object name). The right side terminates at the point where 90 percent of the children were producing the phoneme accurately. (After Shriberg's [1980] presentation of data from Prather, Hedrick, & Kern, 1975)

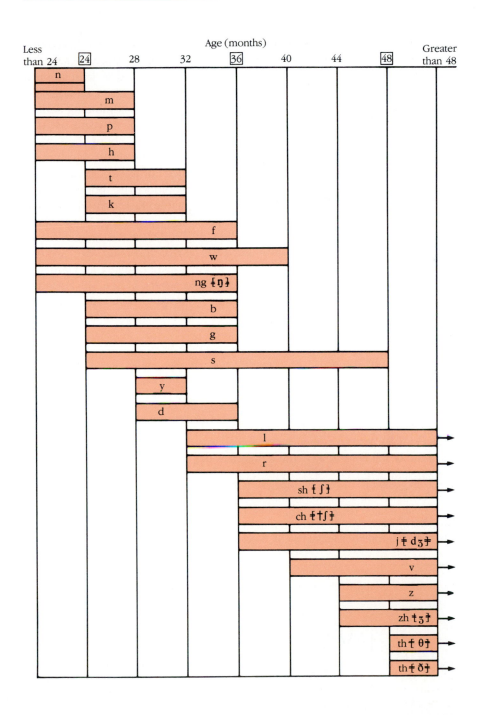

In addition to the tasks of accurate speech perception and production is the task of learning whether a given sound combination is acceptable or not in one's language. To make such judgments requires at least implicit knowledge of the rules that govern sound combinations in a language. Figure 11-3, which is a formal presentation of the rules for combining sounds in one-syllable English words, will give you an idea of the type of rules these are. Though you probably have never been told about these rules before, you nonetheless know them. You know them because you can make judgments completely in accord with the rules. If asked, for example, whether *srun* could be an English word, you would say no, but you would judge *grun, frun, shrun,* and *thrun* to be acceptable. Research on the topic of when children can make similar judgments is not extensive. Stanley Messer (1967), however, has shown that when children from 3 to 4 years of age are given word pairs such as *klek* and *dlek* or *frul* and *mrul,* they are reasonably accurate in indicating which is English in phonology and which is not. The mystery in this, for both children and adults, is how we learn the rules.

FIGURE 11-3

A Phonological Rule Used by Speakers of English

Benjamin Whorf's formula (1956) shows how to produce monosyllabic words that conform to the phonological rules of English. The formula is too complex to explain completely, but you can begin to see how it works if you focus first on the eighth term, which is V for vowel. This is a necessary item in all English syllables, and all the rest of the formula simply tells what sounds can precede or follow this vowel. It may be, for example, that no sound precedes the vowel, so the first term in the formula is O, which stands for nothing. Next, there is a comma indicating the word *or* followed by a C-. The C- indicates that any consonant can precede the vowel except one. This is the consonant [ŋ], which is the "ng" in *-ing*. Following this come columns that show some possible consonant and vowel combinations that could precede the vowel in the eighth term. Following the vowel, things are more complicated yet, so we will avoid the detail here. (For a detailed explanation, see Whorf, 1956, pp. 223–230.) The important point is that this formula describes the phonological knowledge that all native speakers of English have.

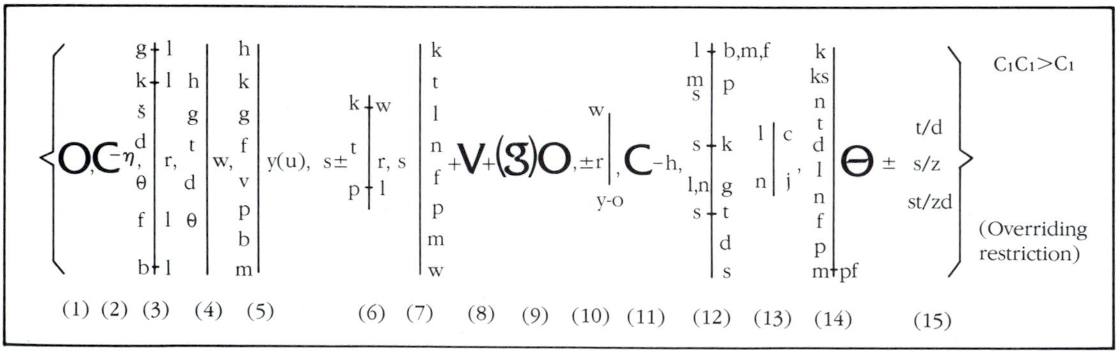

Syntactic and Morphological Development

As noted at the start of this section, children in their second year of life begin to use single words to name events and objects in their world. Naming, however, is a very simple linguistic function. Even chimpanzees are quite good at it (Gardner & Gardner, 1971). According to Patricia Greenfield and Joshua Smith (1976), however, children do much more with their one-word utterances than just name. They comment, request, and question as well. Using words in these ways is linguistically more advanced: it means that the word in the utterance is not just a label for some action or object (that is, a name); the word performs a speech act. For example, a child might point to the door, say "Door," and then look to the mother pleadingly. In this case it would be clear that the child was not just naming the door, but rather making a request such as "Please, open the door." In the jargon of linguists, using single words in this way constitutes a **holophrase,** because the one word is really just an abbreviated sentence. You use holophrases yourself sometimes—for example, when you let someone know that there is a phone call by getting the person's attention and then saying, "Telephone."

The use of holophrases is far more significant for language development than is the use of names because of the fact that a holophrase is a compressed sentence. Naming has no developmental future except for improved pronunciation and vocabulary. With holophrases, however, there is lots to learn—namely, how to expand a one-word utterance into a multiword utterance that is syntactically and morphologically correct. Syntactic and morphological development, therefore, can be viewed as learning the rules for expanding holophrases.

The first step in expanding holophrases emerges toward the end of the second year of life for most children. At this point they begin, for the first time, to put more than one word into a single utterance. The daughter of psychologist Marsha Walton made her first two-word utterance by combining the words *baby* and *juice* in a single utterance. She produced the utterance "Baby juice" as she plunged her baby doll into the water of the toilet bowl. This humorous incident marked the point at which the child took a giant step down the road toward adult use of English. She was beyond the one-word utterance and ready to master syntax and morphology.

To measure syntactic and morphological progress in language, psychologists have settled on a simple measure. It is called **MLU** for *mean length of utterance.* Actually the measure should be labeled MLU-M (Chabon, Kent-Udolf, & Egolf, 1982) to designate that it is the mean length in morphemes, not the mean length in words, that is measured. Roger Brown (1973) introduced the MLU measure to the study of language development because he found that it was a particularly good measure of overall language development, at least until around age 3½. Beyond that, the measure

TABLE 11-3
Speech Samples from Each of Brown's Five Stages of Syntactic and Morphological Development

STAGE	MLU	FOCUS	EXAMPLES
I	1.00-2.00	Basic Semantic and Grammatical Rules	
		Nominations	That ball
		Nonexistence	Allgone ball
		Recurrence	More ball
		Attribution	Big ball
		Possession	My ball, Adam ball
		Agent–action	Adam hit
		Agent–action–object	Adam hit ball
II	2.00-2.50	The Modulation of Meaning	
		Progressive aspect	I walk*ing.*
		in, on	*in* basket, *on* floor
		Plural	Two balls.
		Past irregular	It broke.
		Possessive inflection	Adam's ball.
		Uncontractible copula	There it *is.*
		Articles, *a, the*	That *a* book. That *the* dog.
		Past regular	Adam walk*ed.*
		Third person regular	He walks. She runs.
		Third person irregular	He *does.* She *has.*
		Uncontractible progressive auxiliary	This *is* going.
		Contractible copula	That's book.
		Contractible progressive auxiliary	I'*m* walking.
III	2.50-3.00	Modalities of the Simple Sentence	{Will Adam go?
		Yes-no questions	{Does Eve like it?

is not particularly reliable (Chabon, Kent-Udolf, & Egolf, 1982) nor is it particularly sensitive to advances in morphological and syntactic development. One reason is that past a certain stage of development, longer utterances are not necessarily more complex linguistically. You can make quite a long utterance, for example, through the use of the connector *and then.* Nonetheless, until the age of 3½, or the time when MLU reaches an average value of four morphemes per utterance, children with higher MLUs are reliably more sophisticated in their language use than children with lower MLUs. Brown (1973) has used MLU measures to divide the early period of language development into stages.

Brown's Stage I (MLU 1.00 to 2.00)   Brown's first stage is called the *telegraphic-speech stage* because the morphemes that children use in their speech include none of the essential grammatical morphemes. This means

STAGE	MLU	FOCUS	EXAMPLES
		Wh-questions	Where did Sarah hide? What did Eve see?
		Negatives	Adam can't go.
		Ellipsis of the predicate	Yes he can.
		Emphasis	He *does* want to go.
IV	3.00-3.50	Embedding One Simple Sentence Within Another Relative clauses	What is that playing the xylophone? You got a pencil in your bag.
		Various kinds of subordinate clause	I see what you made. I went where your office was. I want her to do it. You think I can do it.
V	3.50-4.00	Conjunction of One Simple Sentence with Another With no parts deleted	We can hear her and we can touch her. I did this and I did that too.
		With various redundant constituents deleted once Subject deleted Predicate deleted Predicate nominal deleted	He's flying and swinging. No, you and I had some. John and Jay are Boy Scouts.

SOURCE: From *Psychology* by R. Brown and R.J. Hernstein, 1975, Boston: Little, Brown. Reprinted by permission.

that there are no plural endings on nouns, no articles *(the, an, a),* and no verb endings—none which are productive anyway. The child's language consists primarily of the root forms of *contentives.* These are the major noun, adjective, and verb building blocks of sentences. Samples of this type of speech are given in Table 11-3.

The term telegraphic is a good descriptor for Stage-I speech because, as in a telegram, only a bare-bones message is communicated. Few, if any, grammatical morphemes are used. Still, this speech is far superior to holophrastic speech. Now instead of just saying "Kitty" or "Eat" or "Food" when pointing to the cat at its food bowl, the child might say "Kitty eat" (for "Kitty is eating") or "Kitty food" (for "It's kitty's food"). For all their simplicity, the latter utterances are an advance over their holophrastic versions, because the two-word utterances "Kitty eat" and "Kitty food" have syntax. The syntactical rules that these particular utterances obey are ones concerning word order: subject precedes predicate ("Kitty eat") and possessor precedes object possessed ("Kitty food"). All languages use word order to some extent to encode the grammatical roles of sentence elements (for example, subject, verb, or object), and children find this an easy syntactic feature to acquire (Slobin, 1966). Somewhat harder in most languages is learning to indicate grammatical roles using the host of grammatical morphemes that are added to subjects, objects, and verbs to mark their roles. This aspect of development is delayed until Stage II, at least in the learning of English.

Stage II (MLU 2.00 to 2.50)   Although children manage to communicate effectively using word order as a primary syntactic device, they soon begin to add to the quality of their speech by adding all the little words and inflections that constitute the grammatical morphemes of their language. "All these," Brown says, "like an intricate sort of ivy, begin to grow up between and upon the major construction blocks, the nouns and verbs, to which Stage I is largely limited" (1973, p. 249). This means that, semantically, there is no great advance when children move from the telegraphic speech of Stage I to the less-economical but more-precise speech of Stage II. They are still expressing basically the same semantic relations as before (for example, possession or subject–object relations). Now, however, they begin to mark these relations appropriately. An example is the change from the Stage-I utterance of "Kitty food" to the Stage-II utterance, "Kitty's food." Other examples of Stage-II speech are given in Table 11-3.

Gaining mastery over all of the grammatical morphemes in one's language is a slow process that may continue to age 4 or 5; so the development is hardly completed in Stage II. But it begins here. The most interesting aspect of the process is that speakers of all languages acquire use of the grammatical morphemes of their language in a relatively constant order. The usual order for 14 major grammatical morphemes in English is shown in Table 11-4. The relative reliability of this order seems to be due to several factors. One is the regularity of the morpheme. For example, *-ing* is always the same, whereas the plural morpheme can vary from [s] to [z] to [əz] depending on the word to which it is attached. Examples are *tacks* ([s]), *hills* ([z]), and *bushes* ([əz]). Sometimes, of course, the plural is marked by an absent morpheme (∅) as in deer.

A second factor predicting order of acquisition is the emphasis, or stress, given to a morpheme when it is vocalized as part of an utterance (see Gleitman & Wanner, 1985). In French, for example, to negate a verb you must put *ne* in front of the verb and *pas* after it. The *pas,* however, gets far more stress than the *ne,* so that French children learn to negate verbs with the post-verb *pas* alone. Some French children are not even aware of the existence of *ne* in the language until they begin reading.

Just as the lack of stress leads to delayed acquisition, the use of stress speeds it up. This is apparent from research on children learning Turkish.

TABLE 11-4
Usual Order for the Acquisition of 14 Major Grammatical Morphemes in English

FORM	MEANING	EXAMPLE
1. Present progressive: *-ing*	Ongoing process	He is sit*ting* down.
2. Preposition: *in*	Containment	The mouse is *in* the box.
3. Preposition: *on*	Support	The book is *on* the table.
4. Plural: *-s*	Number	The dog*s* ran away.
5. Past irregular: for example, *went*	Earlier in time relative to time of speaking	The boy *went* home.
6. Possessive: *-'s*	Possession	The girl*'s* dog is big.
7. Uncontractible copula be: for example, *are, was*	Number; earlier in time	*Are* they boys or girls? *Was* that a dog?
8. Articles: *the, a*	Definite/indefinite	He has *a* book.
9. Past regular: *-ed*	Earlier in time	He jump*ed* the stream.
10. Third-person regular: *-s*	Number; earlier in time	She run*s* fast.
11. Third-person irregular: for example, *has, does*	Number; earlier in time	*Does* the dog bark?
12. Uncontractible auxiliary be: for example, *is, were*	Number; earlier in time; ongoing process	*Is* he running? *Were* they at home?
13. Contractible copula be: for example, *'s, -'re*	Number; earlier in time	That*'s* a spaniel.
14. Contractible auxiliary be: for example, *-'s, -'re*	Number; earlier in time; ongoing process	They*'re* running very slowly.

SOURCE: After Brown 1973, cited in *Psychology and Language: An Introduction to Psycholinguistics* by H. H. Clark and E. V. Clark, 1977, New York: Harcourt Brace Jovanovich.

Like many other languages in the world, if you want to say "The boy kissed the girl" in Turkish, you must tack on inflections to the words boy and girl to indicate the roles that these two words play in the sentence. Because the roles here are agent and object respectively, a gramatically correct Turkish sentence would be "The boy-agent kissed the girl-object." Although many languages use agent and object case endings, these endings are generally somewhat less salient than the nouns to which they are appended. But in Turkish the case markings are a full syllable long and they are stressed. Because of this, young speakers of Turkish learn to use the Turkish case markings much earlier than do children learning a language with unstressed case endings such as those learning Serbo-Croatian in nearby Yugoslavia. One consequence of the fact that Turkish children learn the morphemes for agent and object so early is that these children do not go through a phase during which they use word order as a syntactic device for marking agents and objects, but children learning languages that mark agents and objects in less salient ways must go through such a phase (Slobin, 1982).

A third factor controlling order of acquisition is syntactic complexity. You might note in Table 11-4, for example, that the plural morpheme is used before the possessive morpheme, and the possessive morpheme, before the third-person-singular ending for regular verbs. What is interesting about this is that, objectively, the task is the same in each case—to add the [s], [z], or [əz] sound to the end of a word. According to former Harvard linguist Roman Jakobson, however, there is a progressive syntactic difficulty in applying these (cited in Moskowitz, 1978). In the case of plurals, the syntactic relation is simple: only a single word is involved. In the case of the possessive, the [s], [z], or [əz] ending marks the relation between two words in the same phrase. Thus, the relation between two words must be understood before the correct ending can be applied. In the case of the third-person singular, use of the [s], [z], or [əz] sound is dictated by the relation between the noun phrase in the subject position and the verb phrase in the predicate. Coordinating phrase relations would, on the surface, seem to be more complex than coordinating word relations.

A final factor that can be added to those controlling order of grammatical-morpheme acquisition is semantic complexity of the relation expressed by the morpheme. Just as there are words like *gravity* and *existentialism* that will not be added to a child's vocabulary until there is a need for these concepts, so there are grammatical morphemes that are not acquired until a child has need of the relation they express. An example is the form *as–as*. The as–as construction in English is regular, stressed, and syntactically simple, and yet it does not appear among the forms that English-speaking children use early in their language development. The reason, apparently, is that attribute comparisons in size (as big as), number (as many as), weight (as heavy as), and other dimensions are not a subject of children's thought when they are 2 and 3 years of age.

Stage III (MLU 2.50 to 3.00) and Beyond   The syntactic and morphological advances in Stage-III speech and beyond are captured by the child's gradual mastery of three major syntactic features of human languages. First is the Stage-III task of mastering what Brown has called the *modalities* of the sentence. In English, this means the ability to form negatives, questions, and imperatives. The Stage-IV task is to master the means of embedding one sentence in another, which in English is accomplished in large part through the use of *that, which,* and *who*. This is followed, finally, by the Stage-V task of coordinating the logical relations between simple sentences, which in English we accomplish through the use of the connectors called conjunctions (for example, *and, but, because, if-then, although, nevertheless,* and so forth). As you might expect, developments relative to all three of these syntactic achievements are spread throughout the language-learning period, so that assigning each to a particular MLU stage is really just a way of highlighting the developmental job that must be done. It is incorrect to think that each is begun and ended within its own "stage." A good example of this is the Stage-III task of mastering sentence modalities.

Children learning English are able to use the sentence modalities known as interrogation and negation as early as Stage I. The problem is that they do so in a way that is syntactically quite primitive. For a yes–no question, they simply use rising intonation at the end of an utterance (for example, "I have some?" "You like dis?" "We go home?"). For a Wh-question, they simply place the Wh-word at the start of the utterance (for example, "Where he can go?" "Why he do that?"). For a negative, they simply add a *no* or a *not* (for example, "No wipe finger," "Not fit," "Wear mitten no"). Correctly formed English negatives and questions require much more than the addition of a single element in order to be syntactically correct. First, verbs must be classed as auxiliary and main verbs. Then to form a negative, *not* must be placed between the auxiliary and main verb. To form a question, the subject must be placed between the auxiliary and the main verb. These are the kinds of rules that children with MLUs in the range of 2.50 to 3.00 (Stage III) can be expected to have mastered. Beyond this point, however, there are still some rules of syntax remaining. For example, once children begin to form questions correctly, they will overgeneralize their rule and say such things as "I know where did he go." Also, children will be in their school years before they master the rule in English for making *tag questions* such as "He won't take it, will he?" or "I'm tall enough, aren't I?" (Dennis, Sugar, & Whitaker, 1982). In short, as this one example of learning the modalities of the simple sentence shows, the language developments identified by Brown neither begin nor end precisely within the specific stage boundaries related to a child's MLU.

Semantic Development

In considering semantic development, we are concerned with the semantics of both words and word combinations. Development in the area of words is marked by the development of a **lexicon,** or vocabulary. The child's biggest problem in this area—apart from the problem of general cognitive development—is the problem of *overextending* and *underextending* the meanings of individual words. Development in the area of word combinations involves knowing how to interpret words in the context of a sentence. Thus, "Mindy delivered the Oxford Times" and "The Oxford Times was delivered by Mindy" are semantically equivalent though syntactically different. "Mindy is easy to please" and "Mindy is eager to please," on the other hand, have a superficial syntactic similarity that hides the fact that their meanings are quite different. In the one case Mindy is the one who will be pleased, and in the other she is the one who will do the pleasing. Learning to give proper semantic interpretations to such sentences is an aspect of semantic development that extends beyond the job of constructing a lexicon.

The problem of developing the lexicon was at one time thought to be synonymous with the development of language. People naively considered the size of a vocabulary to be an index of one's linguistic knowledge. Thus, studies of language development might consist of nothing more than a vocabulary count. One well-conducted count (Smith, 1926) revealed that children add about one and one-half words per day to their vocabulary during the years 2 to 5. The year-by-year growth as estimated cross-sectionally is given in Figure 11-4.

FIGURE 11-4

Growth of the Lexicon

This graph, based on a cross-sectional study, shows the changes in the size of children's vocabularies from 8 months of age to 6 years. (After Smith, 1926)

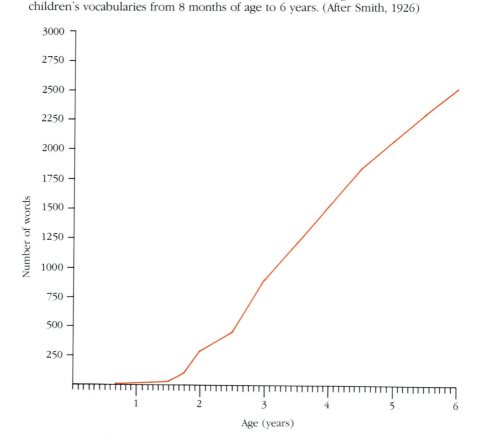

Today, we no longer see vocabulary counts as essential to the study of language development. First, as you know from the introduction to this chapter, which dealt with functional and structural properties of language, knowledge of words is not equivalent to knowledge of a language. Second, just because a child uses a word does not mean that the word is used correctly. Table 11-5, for example, lists some of the items from one child's vocabulary along with their apparent meanings. As you can see, these meanings diverge considerably from adult meanings. In this case, the divergence occurs in the direction of meaning too much, or **overextension.** In other cases, children might diverge in the direction of meaning too little, or **underextension.** A child might insist, for example, that a worm is not an animal, that a chicken is not a bird, and that a tree is not a plant.

Some overextensions appear to occur out of a failure to recognize the proper semantic borders for a word. This is a very honest kind of error that leads a child to call a butterfly a birdie or to refer to doorknobs and grapefruits as balls. Verbs also get overextended. One child used "open orange" to mean "peel the orange" and "open shoes" to mean "unlace my shoes" (Clark, 1977). To know, however, if the meaning of a word is truly overextended we need to test children for their comprehension. For example, we need to present pictures of objects of various shapes and ask which ones are balls. If they only point to actual balls and not to doorknobs or oranges, we can conclude that the overextensions in the child's productive speech are not due to a misunderstanding of the semantic boundaries. Instead, the overextensions are a second type of honest error, one that arises from the need to communicate in situations in which the child's vocabulary is inadequate.

According to Whitehurst (1979, p. 132), children who knowingly overextend the meaning of their few vocabulary words are like mechanics with insufficient tools; they are forced to use what they have even though they know it is not the right tool for the job. Tool selection in this case is guided purely by perceptual similarity, no matter how remote. The de Villiers (1978), for example, reported that their child, when he saw a black olive sitting atop a green salad, pointed to the olive and said "Nunu," which was the name of the family dog. To understand the appropriateness of this overextension you have to look at Nunu's picture (see Figure 11-5). Nunu's nose is indeed like a black olive. So for a child who lacked a word for olive and yet wanted to comment on it, overextending the word *Nunu* seems like a reasonable thing to do. It is probably not the case, however, that the child ever believed that *Nunu* was the proper label for this object, and, thus, overextensions of this sort are different from those based on a true conceptual misunderstanding.

When children develop the syntactic ability to make similes and metaphors using the words *like* and *as,* the need for overextensions due to a limited vocabulary declines, and so we find better overlap between the

TABLE 11-5
Examples of Semantic Overextension

SOME OVEREXTENSIONS BASED PRIMARILY ON SHAPE		
Lexical Item	First Referent	Domain of Application[1]
mooi	moon	cakes, round marks on windows, writing on windows and in books, round shapes in books, tooling on leather book covers, round postmarks, letter O
nénin	breast, food	button on garment, point of bare elbow, eye in portrait, face in portrait, face in photo
buti	ball	toy, radish, stone spheres at park entrance
ticktock	watch	clocks, all clocks and watches, gasmeter, fire hose wound on spool, bath scale with round dial
gumene	coat button	collar stud, door handle, light switch, anything small and round
baw	ball	apples, grapes, eggs, squash, bell clapper, anything round
kotibaiz	bars of cot	large toy abacus, toast rack with parallel bars, picture of building with columned facade
tee	stick	cane, umbrella, ruler, (old-fashioned) razor, board of wood, all sticklike objects
kutija	cardboard box	matchbox, drawer, bedside table
mum	horse	cow, calf, pig, moose, all four-legged animals

child's meanings for nouns and verbs and those in a dictionary. Substitute words like *thing, gizmo, make,* and *do* also help in this regard. But a problem that remains is the meaning of a whole host of terms for time, size, and number relations. Examples of these are *before* and *after, wide* and *narrow, tall* and *short,* and *more* and *less.* At one time it was thought that children would always learn the meaning of one of the pair members ahead of the other and that the one learned first would be predictable (see for example, Clark, 1973). Now, however, it is evident that no such general rule is possible for oppositional pair members (Whitehurst, 1982, p. 383). Children often learn what is called the "positive" pair member first, the one that is marked "plus" in meaning (for example, *big*) rather than "minus" (for example, *little*). It is by no means lawful, however, that children do this (see, for example, Kuczaj & Lederberg, 1977).

The development of a lexicon, important as it is, is only one aspect of semantic development. A second is the development of correct semantic interpretations of different syntactical arrangements of words. After all, as George Miller pointed out some time ago, a Venetian blind is altogether

SOME OVEREXTENSIONS BASED PRIMARILY ON MOVEMENT,
SIZE, SOUND, AND TEXTURE

Lexical Item	First Referent	Domain of Application[1]
sch	sound of train	all moving machines
ass	toy goat on wheels, with rough hide	animals, sister, wagon, all things that move, all things with a rough surface
fly	fly	specks of dirt, dust, all small insects, child's own toes, crumbs of bread, a toad
em	worm	flies, ants, all small insects, heads of timothy grass
bébé	baby (self)	other babies, all small statues, figures in small pictures and prints
fafer	sound of trains	steaming coffee pot, anything that hisses or makes a noise
sizo	scissors	all metal objects
va	white plush dog	muffler, cat, father's fur coat
wau-wau	dog	all animals, toy dog, soft house-slippers, picture of old man dressed in furs

[1] Words were overextended to other objects in the order listed.

SOURCE: From "Knowledge, Context, and Strategy in the Acquisition of Meaning" by E. V. Clark in D. P. Dato (Ed.), *Georgetown University Round Table on Languages and Linguistics 1975,* Washington, D.C.: Georgetown University Press.

different from a blind Venetian (Miller, 1965). In this case, the word order informs us of meaning. The first word is an adjective that denotes an attribute of the second word, which is a noun, so that in the former case we have a type of blind and in the latter, a type of Venetian. This particular semantic relation (attribute–object) is quite elementary, and children around the world achieve the syntactic means to express it very early in their language development. In fact, it is one of about eight basic semantic relations that collectively account for the majority of all Stage-I speech in whatever language you can imagine (see Table 11-6). This means that although the vocabularies of children differ, the semantic relations they can express using the words of their vocabularies tend to be the same.

The person responsible for the discovery that there is great semantic uniformity in the early language of children no matter where they live is Harvard psychologist Roger Brown (1973). He found, for example, that children around the world realize that a single noun from their vocabulary can be the agent of an action (the grammatical subject), the object of an action (the grammatical object), the recipient of an action (the indirect object), or

FIGURE 11-5
Nunu's Nose

even a location. Beyond that, they can treat the noun just as a name or a class ("This ball" or "Mommy lady"), and, as we have already seen, they can modify the meaning of nouns by using words that denote attributes. During Stage I of speech development, children indicate that they know all these things because in their speech they talk about agents and actions, actions and objects, possessors and possessions, locations, and object attributes. They also talk about the appearance ("Hi doggie," "More doggie") and disappearance of objects ("allgone sticky," "allgone ball").

Just as interesting as the fact that there is great uniformity in the semantic relations that children express is the fact that there is great uniformity in the semantic relations that they do not express. For example, children do not talk about event contingencies such as the one expressed in the adult utterance "If it rains, we will not go for our walk today." Stage-I children have the linguistic means of expressing such semantic relations, but they do not do so. They could say, for example, "Rain no walk." They could also make size or number comparisons (for example, "Doggie big me" for "The dog is as big as me" or "Not chairs" for "There aren't enough chairs"). The point is, however, that parents and psychologists who have listened very closely to the speech of children have found no evidence that they ever intend such meanings as these. They restrict themselves to the much more basic set of semantic relations described above. Why should this be true, and why should children around the world restrict themselves to the same set? Brown offers a very reasonable answer. Children express the same semantic relations because they are all basically the same in their level of cognitive development. "What the Stage I child talks about," Brown says, "is the sensori-motor world which he has organized in the first 18 months of his life" 1973, p. 182). Contingent relations, size and number relations, along with many other semantic relations are simply not yet a part of that world.

The knowledge that words can be made to express action–recipient relations, possessor–possession relations, agent–object relations, and so forth comes at the very start of language development. Children do not reliably detect these relations in sentences with somewhat atypical syntactic structures, however, until much later in their language development. One good example is the passive-sentence construction in English. In passive sentences, the agent and object reverse their normal positions. Rather than appearing in the pre-verb position as is usually the case, the agent in passive sentences comes in the post-verb position. This leads to semantic confusion, particularly when the only cues for the correct interpretation are syntactic. For example, children as old as 6 years of age are likely to misunderstand the passive sentence "Minerva was kicked by Beatrice." The reason is that either Minerva or Beatrice could logically be the one doing the kicking; therefore, we have only syntactic cues to guide us in knowing which was the actor and which the object. Had we said "The Ford station wagon was kicked by Beatrice," our knowledge that station wagons cannot kick people would assist us in choosing Beatrice as the subject.

Other syntactic structures that lead to misinterpretation of some basic semantic relations by children are also sentences in which the noun that immediately precedes a verb is not its subject. Consider, for example, the sentence "The doll is easy to see" and "John promised Bill to go." Operating under the usual rule that the agent of a verb will be the noun that precedes it, children will misinterpret these sentences to think that the doll will do the seeing and Bill the going. Such errors are made by children as old as 9 and 10 years of age, but the reason is simply that such sentences are syntactic rarities in English. The agent-before-verb rule works in most cases.

TABLE 11-6
Some Semantic Relations in Stage-1 Speech from Several Languages

Relation	English	German	Russian
Recurrence	more milk	mehr Milch (more milk)	yesche moloka (more milk)
Attributive	big boat	Milch heiss (milk hot)	papa bol-shoy (papa big)
Possessive	mama dress	Mamas Hut (mama's hat)	mami chashka (mama's cup)
Action–locative	walk street	Sofa sitzen (sofa sit)	
Agent–action	Bambi go	Puppe kommt (doll comes)	mamma prua (mama walk)
Action–object	hit ball		nasbla yaechko (found egg)
Question	where ball	wo Ball (where ball)	gdu papa (where papa)

SOURCE: Adapted from "Universals of Grammatical Development in Children," (tab. 1) by D. I. Slobin, in *Advances in Psycholinguistics* (pp. 178–79) by G. B. Flores d'Arcais and W. J. Levelt, 1970, Amsterdam: North-Holland.

THEORIES OF LANGUAGE DEVELOPMENT

Thus far we have dealt with many of the particulars of language development such as the phenomena of overextension, telegraphic speech, regularities in morphemic development, and the fact that children say *fis* before *fish*. But these particulars, though each requires an explanation, do not represent the facts about language development that are most demanding of an explanation. Far more central to theories of language development than these particulars are two primary facts. The first is that children are successful in deriving rules from the language that they hear (Chomsky, 1957, 1965). The second is that they are successful in assigning meanings to words, phrases, and sentences (Clark, 1977). We can refer to these two explanatory problems as the *rule-learning problem* and the *mapping problem* respectively.

In your foreign-language classroom neither the mapping problem nor the rule-learning problem poses difficulties, because you have a dictionary to solve the one and a grammar book to solve the other. In the native-language classroom, children have neither. They must learn from experience both the rules and the meanings. How they do so are the mysteries that theories of language acquisition seek to solve. The factor that compounds the mysteries is the general cognitive immaturity of the species-typical language learner. The typical learner is a child from ages 2 to 5

Finnish	Luo	Samoan
lisaa kakkua		
(more cake)		
rikki auto	piypiy kech	fa'ali'i pepe
(broken car)	(pepper hot)	(headstrong baby)
tati auto	kom baba	paluni mama
(aunt car)	(chair father)	(balloon mama)
viedaan kauppa	odhi skul	tu'u lala
(take store)	(he-went school)	(put down)
Seppo putoo	chungu biro	pa'u pepe
(Seppo fall)	(European comes)	(fall doll)
ajaa bmbm	omoyo oduma	
(drives car)	(she dries maize)	
missa pallo		fea Pupafu
(where ball)		(where Pupafu)

whose attention span is short, whose memory skills are few, and whose powers of inference are weak. Were the language learner an adult, the problem of explaining how someone could extract all the rules and meanings of language from limited experience would be difficult enough. The fact that language learners are preschool children makes the problem doubly great.

Explaining Language Development

In order to explain how preschool children extract meaning and rules from the diverse, unsystematic samples of speech that they hear, theorists appeal both to nature and to nurture. In fact, the interplay of nature and nurture, which we have seen to characterize the developmental process in general, is particularly well illustrated in the case of language development. Though we are still a long way from understanding all the variables involved in language acquisition, enough have come to light to make it clear that they derive from both the nature of humans and from their nurture in a linguistic environment. Any reasonable account of language development must appeal to both.

One way of capturing in a single phrase the dual roles of nature and nurture is to say that children's language learning depends on both a LASS and a LAD. The former term is an acronym for a *language-acquisition sup-*

port system and, as such, represents the environmental contribution to language learning. The term LAD is an acronym for a *language-acquisition device*. This is a nativist concept that derives from the belief that children come to the language-learning task with some language-specific learning abilities that are present neither in chimpanzees nor in the cleverest computers. There is good reason to believe that the two together—a specially prepared, linguistically inclined LAD that is nurtured in a social world offering some special support for the young language learner (that is, a LASS)—constitute the prerequisites for species-typical language acquisition.

The Language-Acquisition Support System

The most basic and fundamental component of a **language-acquisition support system (LASS)** is that it provides young language learners with the chance to use language to communicate. In addition to the support provided by this most basic component, LASS supports language acquisition through components that are labeled *prelinguistic pragmatic training, formatting, motherese,* and *expansions* and *recasts*. Collectively, these LASS components combine to create a very special language-learning environment, one that supports young humans as they make the transition from prelinguistic to linguistic communication.

Opportunity to Communicate

Only rarely do human beings fail to acquire language, but when there is a failure, there is a common cause: the absence of one-on-one communicative interactions between language users and the language learner. Autistic children provide one example of this general principle. These children, who are asocial by definition, shun physical and emotional contact with others. Their aversion to social interaction often extends to being "uncuddly" as infants. Also, as infants they fail to attend when their parents speak to them. This causes many parents to suspect a hearing problem. Despite their being so completely asocial, you might still think that autistic children would eventually learn language just by hearing it spoken around them. But they do not, unless special therapy is instituted. For autistic children, as for all children, language grows out of the social soil of human interaction, and when that is not present, neither is language (Caparulo & Cohen, 1983; Sugarman, 1984).

Further evidence that language development has social interaction as a prerequisite comes from children who fail to develop language because they are raised in total social isolation. Fortunately, there are not many such cases, but they do occur. The most recent is Genie, a child who was found at the age of 13 (Curtiss, 1977). Prior to this, she had been kept locked in a small room by her father. Genie had no language when she was found, but in 5 years of speech therapy (a key feature of which was the opportunity for communicative interactions), she made substantial progress (Curtiss, Fromkin, Krashen, Rigler, & Rigler, 1974). Even so, her speech never manifested the degree of morphological and syntactic mastery that would be expected of a 4-year-old, thus contributing to the suspicion that mastering the structural properties of language may be a sensitive-period phenomenon (Curtiss, 1982).

A more common case in which failure to establish communicative interactions leads to failure in language acquisition comes from children whose exposure to language is purely passive. For example, Dutch children who watch television programs in German do not learn German (Snow, 1977), and the hearing-children of deaf parents do not learn sign language unless the parents address their children in sign (de Villiers & de Villiers, 1979, p. 103). Not only do the hearing-children of deaf parents not learn sign, they will not learn a spoken language either unless there is someone to speak with them. One example of this is a child named Jim, whose only opportunity to learn English was through television and an occasional playmate until speech therapists began to give him his first one-on-one encounters with the language at age 4 (Sachs, Bard, & Johnson, 1981). Jim had had a lot of exposure to English prior to this, but it was not the sort of exposure that led to language acquisition.

We can conclude from the case of autistic children, socially isolated children, and children who are exposed to language passively that the opportunity to communicate is a component of LASS that is absolutely essential for language development. Social bystanders do not develop language. If we ask why communicative interactions are so important to a child's acquiring a first language, we are led to a second component of LASS—the opportunity to develop an understanding of pragmatics.

Prelinguistic Pragmatic Training

Pragmatics does not refer to language itself, at least not to the structural aspects of language such as phonology or syntax. *Pragmatics* refers to the rules for using language effectively and appropriately in social contexts. Children's understanding of this aspect of language is far in advance of all other areas throughout infancy. They know, for example, that vocalizing is an effective and appropriate way to get someone's attention and that pointing is an appropriate and effective way of shifting someone's attention. They also know about the role that turn-taking and eye-contact play in sustaining social interactions. Some of the elaborateness of young children's pragmatic knowledge is illustrated in their preverbal ability to make requests. Here is a typical example (Bates, 1976, p. 55). A 13-month-old girl vocalizes "Ha" to get her mother's attention. The mother comes over to her, and the child looks toward the kitchen, turning her upper body and shoulders to do so. The mother responds by picking her up and taking her to the kitchen. The child points to the sink. The mother pours her a glass of water and the thirsty child drinks it. This little communication had no phonemes, no morphemes, and no syntax, but pragmatically, it was linguistic. It performed what we earlier labeled as a speech act. In this case, the act was to make a request.

Confronted with the ability to perform speech acts through their knowledge of pragmatics alone, one is inclined to say that prelinguistic children have already mastered the hard part of language. All they have to do is learn to plug in words for gestures. They must learn to say "Mother" rather than "ha," to say "Go kitchen" rather than make a gestural gaze, and to say "Water" rather than point. This reduces language development to the task of "functional substitution" (Bruner, 1983a, p. 30). It implies that language development is basically the task of imposing the structural conventions of languages onto prelinguistic communications. Although this view trivializes the actual task of mastering the structural aspects of language, it is a view with considerable merit insofar as it hypothesizes that one must know how language is designed to be used before one can be expected to master the phonetic, syntactic, morphological, and semantic details of the design. In this light, the problem of autistic children can be said to be a problem that is more prelinguistic than linguistic. Not having learned the social uses of language, they can hardly be expected to attend to the structural features of language (Sugarman, 1984).

Formatting

Common interpersonal contexts in which children can learn the pragmatics of language are parent–child games that involve activities such as pointing, looking, vocalizing, tickling, or object sharing. Jerome Bruner calls these *formats,* which means that they are parent-child interactions involving separate but reversible roles (1983b, p. 120). A parent–child tickling game qualifies as a format because parent and child can swap the role of being the giver and receiver of tickles. Vocalizing games have the same structure in that parent and child swap the role of being talker and listener.

In the prelinguistic and early linguistic environment of most children, formats offer special support for the young language learner. In addition to the training the formats offer in pragmatic skills (for example, how to sustain an interaction, how to initiate a role swap, and how to terminate an interaction), the language that adults use in the formats seems ideally suited for offering a beginners' course in the meaning and structure of language. In Bruner's words, formats "frame the process of acquisition in a way that make it easier for the child to become an expert grammarian sooner" (1983a, p. 35).

Formatted activities such as this are an important part of LASS.

To see how helpful formats can be to someone attempting to master the meanings and structure of language, consider the format provided when parents and prelinguistic children "read" books together. In a typical situation observed by Bruner (1983a, p. 39) a mother pointed to a picture in a book and said "Oh look, Richard". This got the child to look at the object to which she was pointing. She then asked, "What's that?" If the child gave any vocalization in response, even if it was a babble, the mother responded, "Yes, it's an X." Then, once the child began to supply the correct labels, the mother fine tuned the format by moving it up a notch in syntactic complexity. Now she started the game not by asking "What's that?" with a rising intonation, but by asking "What's that" with a falling intonation. This was not a question but a friendly command. She smiled at Richard, knowing that he knew. When he gave his answer, she nodded and then asked "What's the X doing?"

Simple as this format is, it packages a great deal of pragmatic, semantic, and syntactic information. Moreover, it packages the information in a way that makes it highly accessible to the child. For example, the pointing and storybook elements in this format make it clear that language is used to make reference. Further, once reference has been established, language proceeds by making a comment. In this case the referent is X and the comment is what X is doing. The format reveals how language distinguishes new and old referents (by the use of *a* and *the* in English), it features the use of intonational change to alter the illocutionary force of an utterance, and it provides a meaningful context for the introduction of pronouns ("What's the X doing? *It's* _____ing"). Although as Bruner readily admits, formatted language games provide no explanation of how children acquire the rules of grammar, they do make us aware of the "considerable role" that adults can play in "scaffolding" a child's language learning. In Bruner's words, formatted linguistic exchanges between children and adults can supply "missing supports until the child can monitor his own performance" (1983a, p. 40) and in doing so, they seem to be an important part of the overall language-support system.

Motherese

A fourth component to the language acquisition support system is known as *motherese* (Newport, 1977). This refers to the special language that mothers and other caretakers use when addressing children. The special features of this language are that it is slower, better enunciated, and more grammatical than the speech that adults use with each other. Interestingly, it is not just adults who adjust their speech in this way when talking to infants: 4-year-olds who speak to 2-year-olds do the same thing (Shatz & Gelman, 1973).

It seems intuitively obvious that if children learn language from the input that they receive, then they should be at an advantage when that input is simplified. This is the reason motherese is included as a component of LASS: it ought to provide an assist to children learning language. Actually, however, there is some debate over whether motherese is essential or even especially helpful (Furrow, Nelson, & Benedict, 1979; Gleitman, Newport, & Gleitman, 1984). The outcome of the debate depends in part on how one states the "motherese hypothesis."

If the motherese hypothesis is interpreted to mean simply that children exposed to motherese will learn language more easily than those exposed to some other variant such as, perhaps, disc-jockeyese, then the hypothesis would surely be supported (though it has not been tested). But if one interprets the hypothesis to mean that one should learn best those aspects of language that are modeled most clearly in the actual motherese one hears, then the hypothesis seems to be incorrect (Gleitman, Newport, & Gleitman, 1984), with one exception. The exception is that mothers who employ a lot of yes-no questions ("Do you want to go outside?" "Can you help to put your hat on?") have children who are able to use the auxiliary verbs in English sooner than children whose mothers use yes-no questions less. The apparent reason is that in yes–no questions the auxiliary appears in the initial sentence position, which gives it salience. Also, the auxiliary in a yes–no question appears in an uncontracted form. Input that emphasizes the auxiliary verbs in this way seems to assist children in their task of isolating and analyzing the auxiliaries of English. This result notwithstanding, the more general conclusion is that so long as a mother is speaking in motherese of some kind, the structural details of her speech do not have much of an effect on the specifics of language development.

The Use of Expansions and Recasts

Expansions and recasts constitute the fifth component to LASS. Both offer children minilessons in aspects of the language that they do not yet use. The minilesson from an *expansion* is a lesson in how to transform telegraphic speech into conventional speech. Thus, if a child said, "Where shoe?" the expanding parent might say, "Where's the shoe?" thereby offering a conventional form for a telegraphic one. Recasts also involve some repetition of what a child has said, but to be a *recast* rather than an expansion, either new information must be added or the form of the utterance must be changed (Nelson, 1977). If a child said, "Truck, mommy," and the mother responded by saying "Yes, it's a big truck, isn't it?" then the mother would have not only added new information ("big") but also changed the form of the child's utterance from a declarative to a tag question (by adding "isn't it?"). These changes make the mother's utterance a recast version of the child's.

Just as in the case of motherese, one would surely think that expansions and recasts would be valuable assists to children learning language. The evidence on just how helpful they are is mixed, however. Keith Nelson (1977) has argued on the basis of experimental data that recasts are effective in adding to children's knowledge of language (Nelson, 1977). But when Elissa Newport and her colleagues (Newport, Gleitman, & Gleitman, 1977) looked to see whether there was a correlation between a mother's use of expansions and her children's linguistic development, the only effects they found were for auxiliaries. That is, just as in the case of yes-no questions, frequency of expansions and recasts predicted improved auxiliary use but little else.

Mixed results in the research literature are not particularly troubling if you take the approach of Roger Brown (1977). In his view, questions such as "Are expansions and recasts beneficial?" or "Does motherese facilitate language acquisition?" are rather unimportant questions to ask. As Brown points out, when parents use techniques such as expansions, recasts, and motherese, they do not do so in order to teach grammar; instead, they are trying to communicate. From this view, whatever importance expansions, recasts, and motherese have derives solely from the fact that they are among the devices frequently used by parents who are striving toward a higher linguistic purpose than training their children in grammar. Simply stated, that purpose is to communicate. Parents expand utterances to clarify meaning, they recast them to keep the conversational ball going, and they ask yes–no questions in meticulous motherese because they want to communicate effectively. Thus, to communicate well with someone who has marginal linguistic skills, all of these devices are used, but they are not the essential ingredient. That role is reserved for linguistic communication, no matter how it is effected. For this reason, Brown recommends to parents that they not try to practice expansions, recasts, yes–no questions, or any other training device per se. Rather, they should "seek, above all, to communicate" (Brown, 1977, p. 26). According to Brown, "If you concentrate on communicating, everything else will follow" (1977 p. 26). In Brown's view, then, communicating alone provides the premiere aspect of the language-acquisition support system.

Why LASS Is Not Enough

Given that children's social system is so supportive of their learning language, the task of explaining how children acquire language is simplified somewhat. At least children are not faced with the task of having to break a linguistic code while sitting on the linguistic sidelines listening to adults speak in the their usual rapid, poorly articulated, and often nonsensical ways ("Well, what I mean, you know, is that really it was kind of like . . ."). LASS then seems to be an important social contribution to the eventual achievement of species-typical language development. But is it enough? At one time psychologists thought so (see, for example, Mowrer, 1954; Skinner, 1957; Staats & Staats, 1963). Taking an extreme environmentalist view, these psychologists declared the assumption that humans had any special, inborn, language-specific talents to be unparsimonious. Language learning, they held, was no more a mystery than a pigeon's learning to peck keys in a Skinner box. The one was a case of instrumental learning and so was the other. Developmental psychologists today have rejected this extreme environmentalist view. We will see why this is the case by considering the mapping problem and the rule-learning problem at length.

The Mapping Problem

Children's introduction to the task of mapping linguistic units onto real-world meanings is simplified when it takes place in contexts such as mother-child formats that involve lots of pointing and concrete referents; but even in the simplified context of formats, the mapping problem does not go away entirely. Two problems stand out. The first is that even for concrete nouns in concrete contexts, there are always more possible match-ups for words and meanings than children ever seem to consider. This problem, which is present even in the simplest occasions for extracting meaning from context, becomes ever-more prominent as we move from concrete word–referent relations to abstract ones. The second overall problem is that when children encounter a new word in one specific context, they seem to know that the word's actual definition will extend beyond that specific context, and, more importantly, they seem to know which extensions of meaning are likely.

To illustrate the problem of there being more possible meanings for words than children ever consider, we will take one of the simplest vocabulary lessons possible, one that occurs in the mother-child picture-book format illustrated earlier. The mother points to a picture and says, "Look at the dog." In doing this, she assumes that the child will know that the referent for the word *dog* is a particular bounded, furry entity that is prominent in the picture and directly in line with her pointing finger. And she is right. That is what the child assumes. But perfectly logical language learners would have found the mother's vocabulary lesson to be ambiguous. In their minds, she might have been referring not just to a single bounded, furry entity but to the bounded, furry entity plus the rug it was standing on. Or perhaps the referent was a somewhat smaller segment of the total picture. Perhaps she meant to point out a bounded, furry entity minus legs, minus tail, and minus head. This would have led to the conclusion that *dog* meant animal midsection. What is interesting, then, is that even from the very start, children seem to share with their mothers some intuitions about what is reasonable and what is unreasonable in the way of word and meaning match-ups.

If you would agree that the mapping problem poses an explanatory problem even in the simplest of language-learning settings, then you can agree that the problem becomes even greater as we move from learning words with concrete referents to learning those with only abstract referents. As Barbara Landau and Lila Gleitman point out, "Whatever the basis for learning words that refer to rabbits, waistcoats, and watchfobs, much of the lexicon traffics in concepts that overreach in abstractness what any child can be expected to induce from immediate environmental cues" (1985, p. 5). Nonetheless, children succeed at the task of assigning abstract referents to words as if it required no explanation at all. They learn words such as *get* and *put, fun* and *pet, fair* and *good, pretty* and *please* just as easily as they learn *dog.* It seems obvious from this that children are able to arrive at correct, or at least approximate, meanings for all these terms only because they never entertain all of the many possible meanings. They begin the mapping task, then, with some restrictions that make the task far simpler than it otherwise would be. In the case of concrete nouns, they seem to restrict themselves to referents that have a holistic quality (see Quine, 1973, on the concept of body-mindedness, p. 54). Thus, children who hear the word *hot* said in conjunction with *stove* are apt to take *hot* as a name for stoves. Likewise, those who hear *No, No* every time they turn their attention to a houseplant are apt to decide that *No, No* means houseplant. One child heard the sentence "This team will start here" as his teacher spread out a blanket to mark the starting line in a game. He took the previously unknown word *team* to mean blanket (Clark & Clark, 1977, p. 486). In the case of abstract nouns and verbs, the restrictions children place on meanings are less obvious. All we can say is that children come to the language-learning task with what can best be described as good lexical sense. No one knows where this comes from except that children *do not* learn it in the way that a pigeon learns to peck keys (that is, instrumental conditioning). Thus, even the most carefully designed language-support system is not adequate to teach what children need to know to perform the mapping task successfully.

The good lexical sense that children use in solving the mapping problem does more than just restrict the set of possible word meanings in a particular context. It also informs children that they should generalize the meanings of words beyond the single contexts in which they are learned. Thus, once children learn a word for the bounded physical entity known as *father,* they extend this word for use with other adult males. Young word learners, if they were good theoreticians, would not do this. Their word meanings at any one time would be nothing more than parsimonious composites from their actual word–referent experiences. Thus, *father* would mean nothing more than the one person that [faðər] had been used to name. But children in fact operate from a totally different perspective. They generalize. Sometimes they underextend and sometimes they overextend, but—invariably—they extend.

Extension in and of itself is an interesting phenomenon, but it turns out that it is not a uniquely human characteristic. All animals generalize beyond the immediate learning context. Thus, a pigeon that has learned to peck a forest-green key will assume that a lime-green key should also be pecked. Vervet monkeys that have learned the "rraugh" call for eagles will initially apply it to non-eagle birds (Seyfarth, Cheney, & Marler, 1980). And chimpanzees that have learned to press a computer key to designate objects of a partiular class will press the same key for similar objects (Savage-Rumbaugh, Rumbaugh, Smith, & Lawson, 1980). Thus, the real explanatory problem for a theory of language acquisition is not so much the fact that learners generalize but how they know to restrict their generalizations to "reasonable" ones. How is it, then, that young word learners know to apply the label *dada* just to humans and just to males? If dad happens to be wearing glasses, why don't they extend it just to those humans wearing glasses, or perhaps to windows?

To see the enormity of the generalization problem, you might imagine the task of teaching a computer to form generalized meanings on the basis of particular experiences. First, you would have to instruct the computer to seek broader meanings than just the composite of all the concrete cases. Then, you would have to give it some general rules for making extensions. These add-ons for the computer learner come as original equipment in the human language learner. This realization is one of the factors that has driven developmental psychologists away from a purely environmentalist explanation for language development and toward an acknowledgment of at least some nativism.

The Rule-Learning Task

Although the mapping task poses problems for a theory of language, particularly a purely environmentalist theory, the task of rule learning poses even bigger problems. One reason is that the rules of language are exceedingly complex. This fact has been amply demonstrated by linguists who have made formal structural analyses of language (see, for example, Chomsky, 1957). They point out that languages have a great many interlinguistic rules that distinguish grammatical utterances from ungrammatical ones. These begin with such general rules as those for establishing agreements of number, gender, and tense among the elements in a sentence and proceed to the complexities of embedding one sentence within another and marking all the elements of a sentence for their grammatical roles (for example, subject, indirect object, direct object, and so on). From these already-complex beginnings, grammars must proceed to account for how identical phonological segments can have quite different meanings, as in the case of a man-eating fish (that is, a shark) and a man eating fish (that is, one who is consuming fish). They must also clear up some of the quirks in language where a seemingly grammatical sentence turns out to be ungrammatical. For example, why is it that in English "Bob is likely to go" is grammatical whereas "Bob is possible to go" is not (Maratsos, 1983, p. 770)? And why is it that you can pinch people on their noses but you cannot pull them on their noses? In brief, it is quite obvious that grammars are exceedingly complex sets of rules.

The unavoidable complexity of grammars leads to the second reason that rule learning poses such a problem for purely environmentalist theories. The reason is that children are the ones charged with the responsibility of mastering grammars. Although it is understandable how an adult, formally trained as a linguist, would be able to enter a foreign country and begin to infer the grammar of the language spoken there by simply talking with natives, one cannot understand how children can do the same thing. Not only do children lack a linguist's formal knowledge of languages, they are further handicapped by their generally poor cognitive skills in the areas of attention, memory, and inference. All in all, therefore, one might think that the intricacies of grammar would be no easier for children to figure out than the intricacies of advanced mathematics.

A third reason that rule learning is such a problem is essentially the same as the reason that mapping is a problem. Just as there are more possible language-to-meaning mappings than children ever in fact consider, so too there are more possible rules than children ever consider. According to linguists, in fact, if the grammars of languages were to be worked out by trial-and-error guessing based on linguistic exposure alone, it would take "more than a human lifetime" to acquire the grammar of any one language (Golinkoff & Gordon, 1983, p. 10). To explain language acquisition in humans, therefore, we must explain how a process, which in principle should take more than a lifetime, can be completed in just 3 years or so.

A fourth reason that rule learning is especially difficult to explain is that LASS does not contain a provision for routinely correcting children who apply incorrect rules (Grimshaw, 1981, p. 165). As Roger Brown and Camille Hanlon (1970) have pointed out, parents and others do not correct children for saying things that are ungrammatical; they correct them for saying things that are untrue or pragmatically inappropriate (such as not saying please when making a request). Were it the case that societies everywhere made a habit of stepping in to correct statements such as "I don't know where is it," then children would have a ready means of eliminating incorrect hypotheses about the grammar of their language. But the fact is that grammar lessons such as this are not part of LASS.

A fifth reason that rule learning is so hard to explain is that despite all of the apparent obstacles that face children trying to learn the grammar of a language, they nonetheless form and use grammatical rules from the very start. Whereas you might expect children to learn as parrots, at least for a while, they do not. A number of observations confirm this. In fact, when the words that would be parroted conflict with a rule, children follow their rules. This is evident in the observation that a normal part of language de-

TABLE 11-7
Imitations of Spoken Sentences[1]

MODEL SENTENCE	EVE, 25½ MONTHS	ADAM, 28½ MONTHS
I showed you the book.	I show book.	(I show) book.
I am very tall.	(My) tall.	I (very) tall.
It goes in a big box.	Big box.	Big box.
Read the book.	Read book.	Read book.
I am drawing a dog.	Drawing dog.	I draw dog.
I will read the book.	Read book.	I will read book.
I can see a cow.	See cow.	I want see cow.
I will not do that again.	Do again.	I will that again.
I do not want an apple.	I do apple.	I do a apple.
Do I like to read books?	To read book?	I read books?
Is it a car?	't car?	Is it car?
Where does it go?	Where go?	Go?
Where shall I go?	Go?	—

[1]( ) indicates uncertain transcription; – indicates no intelligible imitation was obtained; C indicates imitation was correct.

velopment involves replacement of linguistically correct language with incorrect language.

Phonemic substitutions provide the first evidence that a tendency to follow rules overrides a tendency to parrot. For example, a child who has learned to say the words *turtle* and *pretty* with perfect pronunciation may suddenly begin mispronouncing them, saying *kurka* and *biddy* instead (de Villiers & de Villiers, 1979, p. 25). Such regressions are common in language development and generally occur when a rule-derived utterance replaces one that was merely memorized. An example from the area of morphological development is the change from saying *brought* and *themselves* to saying *bringed* and *theirselves*. In syntactic development, a child might go from saying *Aren't I* to saying *Amn't I*. In the area of semantics, children might invent the words *nippled* to mean *nursed* or *tell-wind* to mean *weathervane* (see Clark, 1982). All of these developments reflect that the child's speech production is guided by a set of rules.

Further evidence that children's speech is rule driven from the very start comes from studies of the role of imitation in children's learning of language. Consider, for example, the results of a study by Roger Brown and Colin Fraser (1963) in which young children were asked to imitate simple sentences. The surprising results were that children's imitations seemed to be governed by the same language processor that produces their spontaneous speech. Table 11-7 gives some examples of this general principle. One might think that by presenting an example of well-formed speech, the language learners would immediately rise to the same level of well-formed-

HELEN, 30 MONTHS	IAN, 31½ MONTHS	JIMMY, 32 MONTHS	JUNE, 35½ MONTHS
C	I show you the book.	C	Show you the book.
I very tall.	I'm very tall.	Very tall.	I very tall.
In big box.	It goes in the box.	C	C
–	Read (a) book.	Read a book.	C
I drawing dog.	Dog.	C	C
I read the book.	I read the book.	C	C
C	Cow.	C	C
I do that.	I again.	C	C
–	I do not want apple.	I don't want a apple.	I don't want apple.
I read books?	I read book?	C	C
Car?	That a car?	Is it car?	C
Does it go?	Where do it go?	C	C
–	C	C	C

SOURCE: "The Acquisition of Syntax" by R. Brown and C. Fraser, in *Verbal Behavior and Learning: Problems and Processes* (1963), C. N. Cofer and B. Musgrave (Eds.), New York: McGraw-Hill.

ness in their imitative performance. One might even expect for them to use the opportunity to imitate a well-formed utterance as a springboard for language learning. But the evidence indicates that this is not the case. When some aspect of the grammar of a modeled utterance is novel, children follow their own rules in reproducing the utterance. They do not follow the rules modeled for them. To convince yourself of this, you might wait until you hear a child make a syntactic error and then try correcting the speech error by having the child repeat the correct form after you. Here is psychologist Martin Braine's report of what happened to him when he tried this method of instruction:

> I have occasionally made an extensive effort to change the syntax of my two children through correction. One case was the use by my two-and-a-half-year-old daughter of *other one* as a noun modifier. . . . I repeatedly but fruitlessly tried to persuade her to substitute *other* + N for *other one* + N . . . the interchange went somewhat as follows: "Want other one spoon, Daddy."—"You mean, you want THE OTHER SPOON"—"Yes, I want other one spoon, please, Daddy"—"Can you say 'the other spoon'?"—"other . . . one . . . spoon"—"Say . . . 'other' "—"Other"—" 'Spoon' "—"Spoon"—"Other . . . spoon' "— "Other spoon. Now give me other one spoon." Further tuition is ruled out by her protest, vigorously supported by my wife. (in Dale, 1976, p. 140)

The fact that children are so resistant to parents' well-intentioned language lessons may explain why LASS does not include grammatical instruction as one of the social supports for language learners.

Language Acquisition Device

Given that the mapping and rule-learning tasks are immense and the resources of the child small, many psychologists believe that no matter how important motherese, formatting, expansions, and an understanding of pragmatics might be as aids to learning, these alone are still not sufficient to explain a child's rapid learning of a complete language. These psychologists believe, therefore, that to explain language learning, one must assume that children come into life as prepared to learn language as a bird is to learn song. In Noam Chomsky's view, this assumption takes the form of a **language-acquisition device (LAD).** The device, according to Chomsky, embodies some a priori knowledge about the nature of language and the meanings to which it can be applied. Chomsky calls this knowledge *universal grammar* (Chomsky, 1980, p. 28). With this knowledge, children are able to make some reasonable inferences about the actual structure and meaning of language, whereas without the a priori knowledge, they would be led down so many blind alleys that they might not speak until sometime in adolescence. To make a simple but meaningful comparison, children who begin the language-learning task with LAD are like mystery readers who begin a ten-character murder mystery knowing already that eight of the ten are innocent. Having ruled out eight potential murderers, they can go through the story looking only for information implicating one of the two candidates who remain. The universal grammar to which LAD is privy puts the human language learner in the same enviable position. In brief, LAD accords them prior knowledge that greatly simplifies the task they face.

One bit of evidence, mentioned earlier in this chapter, that supports the view that language learners possess LAD-like a priori knowledge concerns the native capacity of the human auditory system to extract the phonemes of human languages from sounds that vary along continuous dimensions. This concrete example of what may be one small component of LAD tends to demystify somewhat the whole notion of a LAD. Just as there is prespecified knowledge regarding the potential phonemes in language, there could be prespecified knowledge regarding higher units of language (Gleitman & Wanner, 1985, p. 201). But the fact is that the proponents of LAD have never been able to describe in detail any of LAD's alleged knowledge. This means that people who believe in LAD do so primarily because they feel that LAD is a logical necessity. John Flavell, for example, has written that when the concept of LAD was first presented he felt it was farfetched, but that his current view is that "the various alternatives which have been put forward also seem implausible" so that "something like Chomsky's innatist position may well prove to be close to the truth" (1985, p. 268).

Arguments for LAD

Although the nativist position with regard to LAD has historically been based on logical arguments primarily, there are other arguments one can bring to bear. Two will be presented here. The first is that despite tremendous variability in the actual support individual children get for acquiring language, the language-learning process is remarkably stable. In fact, it is about as canalized a human development as, say, physical development or stereopsis. We will see how this is the case by considering data on language acquisition in the blind, the deaf, the retarded, and in children from cultures that use different language-support systems than are used in this country. These data lend support for the concept of LAD, because LAD provides a means of explaining how the course of human development could be buffered against such environmental diversity as in fact occurs. The second argument states that there are similarities in the linguistic intuitions of language inventors.

Language Learning in the Retarded

The language acquisition of retarded individuals differs from normal acquisition only in that it is delayed (Schiefelbusch & McCormick, 1981, p. 116). Otherwise, the course of development is quite normal. This means that a cognitively retarded person will be the linguistic equal of a person with a chronological age equal to the retarded person's mental age. Because non-retarded children have a nearly complete knowledge of the basics of language at a chronological age of just 4 or 5, even many severely retarded humans—ones who can learn no mathematics, no logical reasoning, and perhaps are not able to indicate what is wrong in a picture of a face with no nose—will, nonetheless, know the phonology, morphology, syntax, and semantic interpretations of their native language. The ability to learn the nuts and bolts of a human language, therefore, is in no way dependent on advanced conceptual abilities. Some recent case histories make this point quite well.

Susan Curtiss of the University of California has studied two individuals with mental ages at the 3- and 4-year level who nonetheless were quite skilled linguistically (Curtiss, 1982). One was a 6-year-old boy, Antony; the other was an adolescent girl, Marta. The quality of their language on a phonological, morphological, and syntactic level is illustrated by the sample of spontaneous utterances from these children that is given in Table 11-8. As a further illustration, here is the complete transcript of a dialogue involving Antony:

ANTONY: Do you got a brother?
ADULT: Uh huh. I have two brothers.
ANTONY: What's his names?
ADULT: My brothers' names are Stephen and Douglas. . . .
ANTONY: What's your sister's name?
ADULT: My sister's name is Heidi.
ANTONY: What's you other sister's name?
ADULT: I only have one sister. I have two brothers and one sister. How 'bout you?
ANTONY: I got two sisters. I got David and Vicky and Ann Margaret. (Curtiss, 1982, p. 296)

As the dialogue illustrates, Antony has remarkably good speech. All that is lacking is strict adherence to conventional mappings. In this dialogue, for example, Antony seems to have poor control over the fact that sisters are necessarily female, and he does not seem to have mastered the numerical concept of two. In other conversations reported by Curtiss, Antony uses the word *birthday* for *cake, that's* for *he's,* and *drum* for *horn.* But this semantic aspect of language is precisely the aspect of language in which we

TABLE 11-8
Speech Samples from Severely Retarded Children

ANTONY (age 6, IQ = 50 to 56)

I told somebody be quiet.
I would not have an ice cream.
Whyn't you make her hair like that.
Because I want to hate her.
I say you wash your face like that.
I don't got friends. I got by brother named David.
That clock says it's time to get some prizes.
Didn't ate this one.
I doed this already.

MARTA (adolescent, IQ = 44)

The police pulled my Mother an' so I said he would never remember them as long
    as we live.
I was like 15 or 19 when I started moving out o' home.
I haven't shown you my garage yet, but Dad would be really hard.
We should go out an, um go out, and do other things.
Maybe I could play with a friend.
I have like second friends.
. . . Somebody had his bangs trimmed in Iceland.

SOURCE: "Developmental Dissociations of Language and Cognition" by S. Curtiss, in
    Exceptional Language and Linguistics (1982), L. K. Obler and L. Menn (Eds.), New
    York: Academic Press.

would expect Antony to be deficient. Semantics, after all, is a conceptual
matter as much as a linguistic one. What is remarkable is that Antony's general cognitive deficit, which is clearly reflected in his failure to master some
elementary semantic matters, did not eliminate his ability to master language altogether.

Language Learning in the Deaf

Because of their inability to hear speech, deaf children cannot learn spoken
languages without extensive training. But if spoken language is replaced
with a sign language, the development of deaf children is normal. This is
quite an achievement when you realize that sign languages are real languages and not just Morse-code signaling systems like finger spelling. For
example, the widely used American Sign Language (ASL) is as much a language as Russian, English, or Chinese in that it meets all the structural requirements for a language (Stokoe, 1960, 1972). It also has all the functional
capabilities of human language (such as, generativity, displaced reference,
prevarication, interrogation, metaphoric reference, and sarcasm).

Children learn sign language as readily as they learn a spoken language.

One would think that shifting language functions over from the auditory–vocal mode of spoken languages to the visual–gestural mode for sign languages would at least slow deaf children down in their language acquisition. But it does not. The evidence to date, in fact, is that deaf children begin to use their first signs before normal children speak their first words (Bonvillian, Orlansky, & Novack, 1983; McIntire, 1977). Beyond that, the progress of deaf children is quite normal if they have the benefit of growing up in homes where the parents converse with them in sign (Schlesinger, 1978).

Language Learning in the Blind

One might suspect that blind children would experience a serious handicap in learning to map language onto objects and actions in the real world because they are unable to see objects and actions or to take advantage of all the pointing and gesturing that form part of early parent–child communications. In light of this expectation, the rapid linguistic progress of blind children is quite remarkable. They learn the same vocabulary items in about the same order and in about the same time as sighted children (Landau & Gleitman, 1985). A blind child, Kelli, for example, knew quite well that if she were asked to show someone a toy, she had to hold it up for them to see but that if she were to give someone the toy she had to carry it to them. She also distinguished looking from seeing (though when applied to herself, looking meant reaching out with her hands as shown in Figure 11-6).

FIGURE 11-6
Kelli's Meaning for "Look"
Sighted children, when blindfolded and asked to look up, tilt heads back (as shown on the left). A blind girl, Kelli, who was asked to look up, put her hands above her head because, when applied to herself, *look* meant *reach*. This self-adapted meaning for *look* preserves the active component to the meaning of *look* that is absent from the stative verb *see*. When the meaning of *look* was applied to other people, Kelli knew that they looked "with their eyes."

She even mapped the word *color* onto her conceptual world appropriately. Thus, she was able to figure out from her quite limited experience that objects could have color but that nonobjective entities (such as ideas) could not.

Language Acquisition in Other Cultures

Although it is probably true that all cultures make some special linguistic allowances for children learning language, the nature of that support can vary considerably. One quite radical departure occurs among Kaluli children of Papua, New Guinea. Adults in this jungle group believe that prior to 18 months of age, an infant has no understanding; hence, parents make no efforts to communicate. When prelinguistic infants are included in conversations, they play the same role as a rag doll; namely, someone will speak for them. Thus, if an older child addressed an infant brother, the mother would hold the infant facing the brother and then respond for the infant in a "high-pitched nasalized voice" (Schieffelin & Ochs, 1983, p. 122). These linguistic interactions offer a very different kind of social support for language than is offered to middle-class American children who get drawn into one-on-one interactive games and formats almost from birth.

Beyond the novelty of the way that preverbal infants are involved in social interactions by the Kaluli is the fact that Kaluli infants are not spoken to in motherese, at least not in a motherese that is overly simplified. Kaluli adults believe that using simplified language would handicap their children in learning to speak as adults.

In addition to lacking the formatting experiences and the extensive exposure to motherese that are both so commonplace among infants in this country, Kaluli infants are not exposed to expansions of their own speech. Instead, caretakers are likely to revamp the child's speech entirely and then ask the child to repeat. This is such a common practice in fact that there is even a special word in the vocabulary—*elema*—which means "Say it like this." Bambi Shieffelin, who is responsible for all the observations of the Kaluli, emphasizes that these requests to imitate are designed to impose adult ways of speaking on children and not to expand on the child's own utterances. As Schieffelin says, "caregivers will put words into the mouths of their children but these words originate from the caregiver" (Schieffelin & Ochs, 1983, p. 127).

The observations that the structure and nature of LASS need not always be what it is in middle-class America is further supported by Elinor Ochs's observations in Samoa (Ochs, 1982) where, again, significant variations in LASS have been observed. Despite these variations in LASS, however, children in one language community have no edge over those in another in acquiring language. Middle-class Americans, Kaluli, and Samoans all master their languages within the same period of childhood. Obviously, therefore, we are once again forced to believe that language development does not depend on specifics in the way in which infants are introduced to language.

Having determined that the essential facts of language development go unchanged even in the case of children with serious disabilities and even in the case of children living in vastly different language cultures, we have been led to conclude that the specifics of LASS are not what is most important about a child's linguistic environment. Surely these specifics account for some individual differences, as we have seen in the case of yes–no questioning having an effect on the acquisition of auxiliary verbs in English. But probably the effects are limited to fine touches in the areas of syntax, semantics, and pragmatics. The basic process itself of establishing a complete language goes on unabated in spite of local variations in the particular means and opportunities that children have for learning a language. This evidence is compatible with the belief that humans are equipped with a LAD that helps them make sense of the input from a rich or even not-so-rich LASS.

Similarities in the Linguistic Intuitions of Language Inventors

The support for Chomsky's concept of LAD thus far has derived from children learning a native language despite apparent obstacles and despite significant variations in the specifics of their language-acquisition support systems. But what would happen if LASS did not contain all the relevant information? And what if there were no LASS at all? Such cases do occur, and when they do, children do not seem to be totally at the mercy of their language (or, more accurately, nonlanguage) environment. Instead they seem to have some linguistic intuitions that serve them well. This is evident in two carefully studied case histories. One involves children who grow up learning a pidgin language. The other involves deaf children who have no one to teach them a sign language.

The Development of Creoles from Pidgins   Pidgin languages crop up in societies where two or more languages find themselves side by side, as occurred frequently during the period of European colonization in Africa and Asia. A **pidgin** is a rather anarchic blend of the languages and is devoid of syntactic and morphological complexity. It serves as a medium in which adults from the different language communities can conduct their commerce, but it is an impoverished language in terms of the actual speech functions it can fulfill. Over time, however, pidgins tend to go through a process of **creolization** whereby the marginally linguistic pidgin becomes a complete language. According to linguist Derek Bickerton, adults play no role in this creolization (Bickerton, 1981, 1984). Instead, children are the ones responsible for the syntactic inventions that turn pidgins into creoles.

The factor in the development of creoles that gives support to LAD is that the grammatical inventions that children use to expand pidgins are remarkably similar the world over. The overall similarity, Bickerton writes, is "too great to be attributed to chance" (1984, p. 173). It must come, he thinks, from what he calls a *language bioprogram,* which is very much the same thing as Chomsky's LAD. In Bickerton's own words, "the most cogent explanation of this similarity is that it derives from the structure of a species-specific program for language, genetically coded and expressed . . . in the structures and modes of operation of the human brain" (1984, p. 173).

The Development of Home Sign Among Deaf Children   Children who creolize pidgins are not the only ones to show signs of linguistic inventiveness. Some evidence exists, for example, that children from relatively normal language-learning environments may on occasion invent a private language. Technically, these communication systems are referred to as *autonomous speech.* Because identical twins are the most likely to invent such communication systems, the term *twin speech* is also used (Savic, 1980). To date there are no cases of twins inventing totally novel languages. Invariably, the invented language has been some idiosyncratic mixture of the languages to which the children have been exposed. In one recent case (Davis & Orange, 1978), for example, twin girls in California spoke a language that was an amalgam of German and English, the two adult languages spoken in their home. None of the adults understood the children, however, and the children were assumed to be retarded. Because the children had no playmates, their idiosyncratic language persisted until school age.

At present, there is insufficient data on the phenomenon of autonomous or twin speech for scientists to come to any conclusions regarding what it demonstrates or fails to demonstrate about native linguistic abilities in humans. The same is not true for deaf children who create what is called *home sign.* Two very thorough reports have been written on this phenomenon, and they allow us to draw conclusions relevant to the proposition that humans are imbued with native knowledge of how to construct a language.

The deaf children who create home sign grow up in environments where it is impossible to acquire a conventional sign language. The impossibility might exist because the parents do not know sign language or because they believe that sign language is an inferior language that should not be taught to children. In either case, the children have no model to follow in constructing their gestural communications.

Though understandably primitive, the home sign developed by deaf children who are isolated from conventional languages may nonetheless qualify as language (Goldin-Meadow & Mylander, 1984). The initial evidence for this claim came from work with six deaf children of hearing parents, all of whom developed their own versions of home sign. The psychologists who conducted this study—Heidi Feldman, Susan Goldin-Meadow, and Lila Gleitman (1978)—provided a careful analysis of the linguistic properties of the home sign that they observed. Rather than deal with the details of their linguistic analysis per se, however, the linguistic properties of home sign can be illustrated using a single example. The example comes from David, a 3½ year old whom Feldman and her colleagues referred to as the "William Shakespeare of home sign."

David's use of home sign in the example to be used here was triggered by his being shown a picture of a snow shovel. He responded by pointing to the shovel and then making a digging motion. Then he made a fluid series of gestures in which he pointed back to the shovel, made a gesture for putting on boots, pointed to the door (outside), pointed to the basement where the shovel was stored, pointed back to the shovel, made the digging motion, and then repeated the gesture for putting on boots. Next he pointed to himself. Then he repeated the digging motion, pointed to the outside, made a pantomime gesture for snow (by fluttering his fingers as he lowered them to his sides), pointed back to the shovel, and repeated the sign for snow.

To determine whether David's gesturing qualifies as language, we have to see whether it meets the criteria for language. It certainly seems to meet some of them. It is an open system that allows for displaced reference and could be easily used to lie or ask questions. There is a set of morphemelike units, and the way the morphemes are combined appears nonrandom; that is, there appears to be some syntactic constraint on their order. Beyond that, the communicative intent of the message as interpreted by Feldman and her colleagues is quite good for a 3-year-old. The message was: "The shovel is to dig with. I put on my boots and take the shovel from the basement and go outside and dig. Me! I dig when it snows outside and I shovel the snow." (Feldman, Goldin-Meadow, & Gleitman, 1978, p. 408). If the interpretation given to this utterance is correct, it shows evidence, too, of embedding, a procedure used by all languages to combine multiple propositions into one utterance frame (for example, "I dig when it snows"). Recent work with four profoundly deaf children in Chicago (Goldin-Meadow & Mylander, 1984) has further strengthened the claim that home sign has at least some of the essential features of language.

If it is the case that home sign has some of the essential features of language, we must ask where these come from. One likely source is a LAD or language bioprogram. With these in place, children faced with the common task of communicating come to common solutions. They use gestures as words, they use word order as a syntactic feature for encoding semantic relations, and they embed one proposition within another to gain economy of expression. Were a Martian to try to invent a language for communicating with humans, there is no guarantee that the Martian invention would have these properties. The data on home sign, therefore, augment those on creolization to suggest that humans begin language acquisition with good intuitions about the semantic and syntactic features that will be found in language. In the absence of an established language in which to discover these, they impose these features on their own mode of expression.

Combining all the evidence gives us substantial reason to believe, along with Noam Chomsky, that there is an innate, language-specific faculty in the human brain without which children would not learn language. In summary, the evidence for this claim is that young children, with their limited cognitive abilities, could not possibly solve the mapping and rule-learning problems without knowing in advance which solutions were likely. Second, a belief in language-specific abilities is supported by the fact that language acquisition in humans shows invariant properties despite wide variation in the cultures children grow up in and the cognitive, auditory, and visual capacities they bring to the task. Third, when the creoles from different cultures and the home sign from different children are compared, there are remarkable similarities that seem to indicate similarities in the linguistic intuitions that children bring to their task. These facts are ones that LASS alone cannot explain. Therefore, we are forced to appeal to LAD as well as LASS, even though the exact properties of LAD remain a mystery.

SUMMARY

In this chapter we have dealt with an aspect of development unique to humans—language development. Although other animals develop the ability to communicate, none do so using a communication system that has all the functional and structural features of language. On the functional side, language can be used to make displaced reference, to create new messages, to prevaricate, and to perform a number of speech acts. On the structural side, languages have grammars consisting of phonological, morphological, syntactic, and semantic rules. Any language act can be analyzed at any one of these levels. This is not true, however, of nonlinguistic communications. Such communications cannot be decomposed into parts as linguistic communications can.

Normal language development has important roots in the prelinguistic period. Children are born with a brain specialized for language, and they show strong interest in speech as a social signal. The formatted parent–child activities of the prelinguistic period may be instrumental in teaching children some of the rules for speech use (that is, pragmatics), and the vocal play called babbling prepares them motorically for speech. At one time babbling and speech were thought to be discontinuous, but this was a myth. Children continue to babble even after they start using words, and the sounds used in their early words are taken directly from their favored babbling repertoire. A second myth once held to be true was the belief that the repertoire of babbled sounds begins as a random collection of all sounds available to the human vocal tract but then gradually drifts toward just those phonemes to be used in the target language.

Children speak their first words, some of which are holophrases, around 1 year of age. Pronunciation in this period is fairly predictable in that children around the world use the same strategies for simplifying the adult phonology. By the end of the second year, children will have begun to string words together in their utterances. This is the point at which they begin to master the morphological and syntactic components of language.

Between the first two-word utterances and the point at around 3½ years of age when the MLU reaches 4.00 there are—according to Brown— five stages of language development. The first stage is a period of telegraphic speech in which grammatical morphemes are conspicuously absent from multiword utterances. Next is a period marked by the addition of grammatical morphemes, which, interestingly, are added in a predictable order. The next three stages feature developments that are not really restricted to the stage in question. The first is the job of mastering the essentials of forming questions, negatives, imperatives, and other simple sentence modalities. Next is the job of embedding one sentence within another through the use of devices such as relative clauses. The final job is that of connecting sentences and propositions using conjunctions.

The semantics of early child speech can be examined at the level of the lexicon or the utterance. Lexical items can be either overextended or underextended in meaning. The utterances in which these appear, at least during the telegraphic period, express one of just a small set of possible semantic relations. This has led to the generalization that children around the world all talk about the same things. Despite the fact that semantic relations such as agent and object are cognitively quite primitive, it takes English-speaking children a long time to be able to detect these relations in some relatively rare syntactic forms.

At present there is no good explanation for how children learn to speak a language in just 2½ to 3 years. All we can say for sure is that the eventual explanation will be one that draws both on environmental and native factors. On the environmental side, it is important to note that language learners are offered a rather exceptional language-support system (LASS), which seems to simplify their acquisition problem. The most fundamental component of this system is the communicative component, without which no one could learn a language. In addition there are components that serve to simplify the learner's task. Examples of these are prelinguistic pragmatic training, motherese, formatting, expansions, and recasts.

Although language learning is made possible by the communicative component of LASS and made easier by specific LASS components, psychologists today still believe that LASS is not enough to solve either the mapping problem or the rule-learning problem. For this reason, many contemporary psychologists resort to the nativist concept of a language-acquisition device (LAD), a concept first introduced by Noam Chomsky. The primary role of the device is to limit the hypotheses children might entertain about meanings and structures. With the set of hypotheses seriously constrained, children are then able to extract meanings and grammatical structure from the language that they hear. Indirect evidence for the existence of some LAD-like device in the brains of humans comes from the fact that despite tremendous variability in the actual support individual children receive for acquiring language, the language-learning process itself is remarkably stable. The blind and the deaf learn language at a normal rate despite their disabilities; the Kaluli learn language at a normal rate, as well, despite having a language-support system very different from that which is prevalent in middle-class America; and the severely retarded—though slow to learn language—make remarkable progress in learning grammar despite their severe conceptual limitations. In addition to these facts, the concept of LAD gains support from the fact that the process of creolization seems to be guided by linguistic intuitions shared by creolizers around the globe. Home signers, also, may share some of these same intuitions.

SUGGESTIONS FOR FURTHER READING

Fletcher, P., & Garman, M. (Eds.). (1986). *Language acquisition: Studies in first language acquisition* (2nd ed.). Cambridge, England: Cambridge University Press. This edited volume serves as an authoritative source book on all aspects of language acquisition.

Landau, B., & Gleitman, L. R. (1985). *Language and experience: Evidence from the blind child.* Cambridge, MA: Harvard University Press. A theoretically stimulating study of language acquisition in a blind child.

Reich, P. A. (1986). *Language development.* Englewood Cliffs, NJ: Prentice-Hall. This up-to-date introductory text is very comprehensive in its coverage. Undergraduates will find it to be very readable and interesting.

Smith, C. G. (1985). *Ancestral voices: Language and the evolution of human consciousness.* Englewood Cliffs, NJ: Prentice-Hall. Speculation on the evolutionary origins of human language is a topic of longstanding fascination. This text ties the evolution of language to the emergence of human consciousness.

Taeschner, T. (1983). *The sun is feminine: A study on language acquisition in bilingual children*. Berlin: Springer-Verlag. Lisa and Giulia grew up in Rome with an Italian father and a German mother. This account, written by the father, uses data from their language development to determine how children learning two languages differ from those learning just one.

CHAPTER OUTLINE

CHAPTER 12

Social Development Within the Family

Social development is the process whereby children acquire their social roles, values, and behaviors. A major factor in this process consists of the socializing forces that lie outside children themselves. These are the "others" in children's lives—parents, peers, teachers—each of whom consciously attempts to mold children socially.

Although outside forces have an undeniable impact on the direction that is taken in children's socialization, children themselves play a role as well. For one thing, children are different and do not all respond to socialization efforts in the same way. Furthermore, the shaping and molding process is not a one-way street. At the same time that outside forces are trying to shape children, children are trying to shape the outside forces. The bidirectional as opposed to unidirectional nature of social development will become a theme in this chapter, which deals with social development within the family. The chapter begins with a discussion of the event that commences social development in all humans—the formation of an attachment relationship.

ATTACHMENT

Students of animal behavior, known as *ethologists,* find it useful to categorize behaviors by their function. Thus, there are mating behaviors, nesting behaviors, play behaviors, and in all animals that have a period of mother dependency, there are *attachment behaviors*. These are behaviors, expressed by dependent juveniles, that serve the role of gaining or maintaining contact with an attachment figure, usually—but not necessarily—the mother.

In humans, the attachment behaviors expressed toward mother (or her surrogate) can include tracking her with the eyes, crawling to her, smiling at her, clinging to her, and crying when she is gone. Reciprocation of these attachment behaviors results in the establishment of an affectional bond between infants and their mothers known as **infant–mother attachment.** This attachment is the human equivalent of filial imprinting in precocial birds and mammals (see Chapter 4) in that it serves to establish a very special affectional relationship, which during infancy and later childhood can be a source of security and comfort, essential for normal development.

Attachment Versus Bonding

The process of attachment, which is our current focus, needs to be distinguished from the controversial process of bonding, which was discussed in Chapter 4. Though the two processes are similar in having as their goal the establishment of a parent–infant bond, they are otherwise quite different because they occur for different reasons, at different times, using different mechanisms. As defined by Marshall Klaus and John Kennell (1976), bonding is a biochemically assisted mother-to-infant process alleged to occur during a critical period shortly after birth. When bonding occurs, it serves as a biological guarantee that mothers will become fully committed to their offsprings' survival. The term bonding can be used more loosely than this to refer to the establishment of parent-to-child affections that are socially rather than biologically based, yet still the emphasis is on a parent-to-child process occurring during the first weeks of infancy (Konner, 1982, pp. 137, 153).

The process of attachment contrasts with bonding in that it is an infant-to-parent process that is protracted in time, requiring at least 6 months to complete in humans. The emphasis is on the infant's attachment behaviors and on the emotional security and comfort that infants derive from being with their attachment figures.

Using the single term bond to describe relationships that are established in different ways using different mechanisms at different times may lead to some unnecessary confusion; however, the fact is that no other word captures so well the nature of these relationships (Konner, 1982, p. 137). The bondlike nature of attachment is particularly striking when infants are separated from their mothers, because they behave as if an actual physical bond has been disrupted. The initial shock of separation produces strong protest and pain (Panksepp, Siviy, & Normansell, 1985). If the protest is unsuccessful in getting mother back, a period of despair and depression may ensue.

Protest at Separation

The protest and despair patterns caused by separation were first identified by John Bowlby (see Bowlby, 1973, pp. 26-27). They are as characteristic of other animals as they are of humans. Describing the protest in young sheep, Cairns (1979) wrote:

> The separation of young sheep from their mother is particularly striking. The extreme agitation and disorganization that result might lead one to believe that the young animals were enduring great pain or physical distress. These 20- to 30-pound animals run full speed around the isolation chamber. On occasion the circling pattern gives way to a line drive directed at the door or the wall. Finally, some lambs leap vertically upward. Others run head first into the ceramic tile wall. After recovering, the animals repeat the running and head-banging with groggy redundancy. Throughout, their activity is punctuated by distressful, plaintive, high-pitched "baa's." (p. 48)

Gordon Jensen and Charles Tolman (1962) of the University of Washington, who have reported on the separation of infant pigtail monkeys from their mothers, also note the violent protest that occurs. They say that separation is stressful not only for the monkeys but for the attendants and all others who "are within sight or earshot of the experience."

A period of separation protest marks the development of all mother-dependent animals.

Protest by human infants on separation occurs routinely somewhere in the period 6 months to 3 years (with the peak time being between 8 and 18 months). It is one of the milestones in human social and emotional development. The reaction is universal, occurring in infants of all cultures (see Figure 12-1). Most protest is quite mild, consisting of some crying and attempts to cling to the mother as she leaves. Occasionally, however, human protests can be as vigorous as those of sheep and monkeys. The severity seems to depend on how unusual the separation is (Spelke, Zelazo, Kagan, & Kotelchuck, 1973). If mother is just leaving to go to the store as she has often done in the past, the protest will be mild, but if the child is being left at a sitter's home for the first time, the protest could be far more severe. Historically, a cause for great protest has been the hospitalization of infants. In the interest of hospital efficiency, parents' visiting rights were restricted during the time their child was in the hospital. This practice was revealed, however, to be one that led to attachment-related emotional reactions that were strongly negative (Bowlby, Robertson, & Rosenbluth, 1952). Since the 1960s, therefore, hospitals have made it a practice to integrate the parents into the treatment program and, where possible, not to hospitalize infants at all.

FIGURE 12-1

Universality of Separation Protest

Regardless of the culture in which children develop, there is a rapid rise in separation protest beginning in the period 6 to 12 months. This is followed by a steady decline during the second year. (After Kagan, 1976)

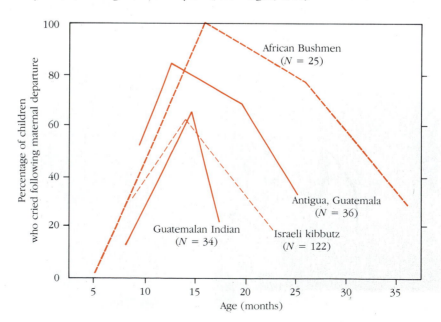

Postseparation Despair

Once the attachment bond established in infant humans or other animals is broken through separation, the infant often becomes quite depressed. It is as if an emotional lifeline had been severed. Without the lifeline intact, depression and despair set in. Describing a common "despair" reaction in an infant admitted to a hospital, Bowlby (1951) says,

> The active physical movements diminish or come to an end, and he may cry monotonously or intermittently. He is withdrawn and inactive, makes no demand on people in the environment, and appears to be in a state of deep mourning. (p. 27).

As with the protest reaction, humans are hardly unique in showing despair on separation. Other animals also become inactive and listless. Still photographs can capture quite well the state of these animals. Figure 12-2A shows, for example, the depressed, disinterested state of a pigtail monkey that has been separated from its mother. Figure 12-2B shows the depressed state of a chimpanzee named Merlin whose mother had died.

Although despair is indeed a common second-stage reaction to separation, it is not invariable. Whether despair in fact occurs seems to be dependent on the chance for substitute mothering. Imprinting relationships—like those between sheep—are usually exclusive, allowing no substitutes.

FIGURE 12-2
Depression in Monkeys and Apes
The body postures and facial expressions associated with depression are the same in monkeys (A) and apes (B) as in humans.

A   B

Humans, chimps, and monkeys, however, can establish new attachments when old ones fail. Leonard Rosenblum and I. Charles Kaufman (1968), for example, have shown that the opportunity for substitute mothering is the variable that determines how deep depression will be for infant monkeys separated from their mothers. In a species known as bonnet monkeys, there is seldom any depression at all if the infant is left with the bonnet social group it is accustomed to. Left with a familiar group, an abandoned infant will protest when its mother is removed, but then when the deprived infant approaches other females in the group, they provide the nurturance and contact that serve to protect the infant from despair. We know that the absence of despair is due to the nurturant response of females in the group because bonnet infants do become depressed when left in a group of familiar but nonnurturant monkeys, such as pigtail monkeys (Kaufman & Stynes, 1978). Not only do bonnet monkeys become depressed when left with pigtail monkeys, but motherless pigtail monkeys do as well—and for the same reason. Pigtails do not share their infants under normal group-living conditions, and so there is no tendency to adopt abandoned infants. Even in the pigtail species, however, substitute mothering is occasionally provided for the offspring of high-ranking, dominant females (Kaufman & Rosenblum, 1969). When it does occur, it has the same effect as for bonnets: it staves off severe depression.

Age of Onset

In humans, evidence that an infant–caretaker bond exists begins to appear around 6 or 7 months of age. Part of the evidence is that prior to this age, human infants are indiscriminate—one might even say promiscuous—in the use of their attachment behaviors. They will make eye contact with and smile at anyone. When a person comes close, they will reach out to grasp a nose, earlobe, or whatever else they can get their hands on. In short, any adult stimulates "approach" responses. After 6 months of age, there is a shift toward stranger wariness and fear, a reaction frequently referred to as *stranger anxiety.* Rather than seeking the contact of strangers, children will withdraw from them, at least initially. Prior to 6 months of age, therefore, infants do not respond to their mothers (or other attachment figures) in a way that is qualitatively different from the way they respond to strangers. Because attachment relations are by definition exclusive relations, we are not justified in saying an infant is attached until evidence of exclusivity appears.

A second bit of evidence for saying that human attachments do not form prior to 6 months of age is that infants separated from their mothers prior to this date show no signs of distress or protest. Only in the period 7 to 9 months does separation protest begin. During the time that there is no protest (the first 6 months or so), we can assume there is no attachment.

Ethological Considerations

The relatively late onset of human infant–mother attachment poses a slight problem. Why would a relationship that is so important for the survival of animals in the wild appear so late in the development of humans? Recognition of the mother, fear and wariness toward strangers, vigorous attempts to get mother back when she disappears—these would all seem to be characteristics important to survival and, indeed, in the precocial animals that imprint on their mothers, these characteristics develop in the first hours of life.

There are two explanations for the late appearance of attachment among humans: one has to do with the motoric immaturity of humans at birth; and the other, with their cognitive immaturity. On the motor side, human infants are not able to move about in their world independently until 6 months of age or later, at which time they begin to crawl. For animals such as humans whose newborns have no power of independent movement, attachment seems to be less critical than for animals whose young are precocious in their ability to walk about. This means that we would expect for attachments to form sooner for precocial animals, like ducks and deer, than for altricial animals, like rats and robins. The former animals have to be able to identify their mothers and follow them. The latter do not. Being helpless, the young in these and other altrical species can do nothing to ensure that their mothers will stay close or protect and feed them. Consequently, learning to recognize one's mother and forming an exclusive attachment with her seem less critical for altricial young than for the young of precocial species, particularly when you consider that the cost of an exclusive relationship is an unwillingness to accept nurturance from a stranger.

Aside from the fact that attachment may be delayed in humans because they have no locomotor ability at birth, it may also be delayed because of their immature cognitive state. To form an exclusive attachment with a single individual would seem to be dependent on the cognitive ability to conceive of that person as a unique individual, different from all others yet constant across time. In brief, the attachment figure must be a permanent entity in the child's mind. If you think back to what you learned about children's conceptions of objects in Chapter 8 (see pp. 384–90), you will remember that objects do not begin to attain any permanency in a child's conceptions until after 6 months of age. This means that mother, being a physical object as well as a mother, has no permanency in the minds of children under 6 months of age. When mother disappears from their sight, she disappears from their thoughts as well, and when she reappears, she is recognized as exceedingly familiar but not as the very same person who has disappeared and reappeared so often in the past. Though this view seems strange, there is evidence to support it. In research conducted by T. G. R. Bower (1971), for example, trick mirrors were used to make it appear that

FIGURE 12-3
The Effect of Multiple Mothers
Seeing three mothers simultaneously, an event made possible through the use of mirrors, is frightening for infants over 6 months of age, because they have developed a knowledge of what is normal in the world of objects (and people). Children under 6 months of age lack the concept of object permanency and, therefore, are not frightened by the multiple images.

there were three identical mothers smiling down at a seated infant (see Figure 12-3). The presence of three identical mothers delighted children under 6 months of age but frightened infants older than that. Apparently, the older children knew something the younger ones did not about what is normal and what is not in the world of objects.

Given that mother is one of the most familiar and interesting objects in a child's world, it is not surprising to learn that, for most children, mother permanency is a concept that develops earlier than general-object permanency (Bell, 1970). That is, in Piaget-type test situations children will search for their mothers before they search for toys. Nonetheless, the fact that it takes at least 6 months of cognitive development before mother can take on any conceptual permanency explains both the absence of attachment and the absence of protest in children under 6 months of age. A child cannot be attached to someone not known to exist on a permanent basis, because there is no *one* to be attached to. Also, a child cannot protest mother's absence so long as mother cannot be conceived of during her absence. In summary, the fact that human infants are both cognitively and motorically immature at birth offers a reasonable explanation for the relatively late onset of the infant-mother attachment bond.

Assessing the Quality of Attachment

If we are concerned with determining whether a 6- to 12-month-old has formed an attachment with a caretaker, we can determine whether the infant recognizes the caretaker, protests when he or she leaves, and shows some wariness or fear of noncaretakers. These observations would lead to a judgment that a child was either attached or not attached. More than this, if we observe closely how a mother's presence affects an infant's reactions to novelty, strangeness, and stress, we can learn something about the quality of the attachment relation as well. By taking quality-of-attachment measures, we can begin to assess individual differences in attachment.

To obtain quality-of-attachment ratings, a structured laboratory situation known as the **strange situation** is generally used (Ainsworth & Witig, 1969). It consists of eight staged "episodes" (see Table 12-1) involving mother–infant separation and reunion in a novel environment where there are attractive toys and strange adults (see Figure 12-4). During the approximately 20-minute session, observers score mother–child, child–stranger, and child–object interactions that have been found to reflect attachment

FIGURE 12-4
The Strange Situation
This figure illustrates a typical laboratory setting used to create the strange situation. (After Ainsworth & Witig, 1979)

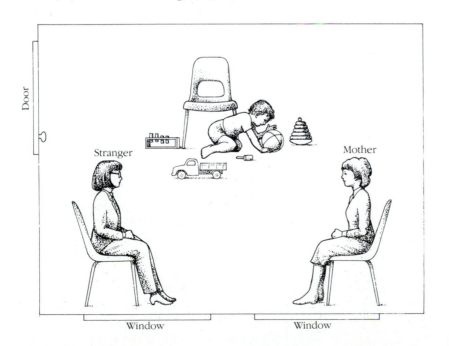

TABLE 12-1
Summary of Episodes of the Strange Situation

NUMBER OF EPISODE	PERSONS PRESENT	DURATION	BRIEF DESCRIPTION OF ACTION
1	Mother, baby, and observer	30 seconds	Observer introduces mother and baby to experimental room, then leaves.
2	Mother and baby	3 minutes	Mother is nonparticipant while baby explores; if necessary, play is stimulated after 2 minutes.
3	Stranger, mother, and baby	3 minutes	Stranger enters. First minute: stranger is silent. Second minute: stranger converses with mother. Third minute: stranger approaches baby. After 3 minutes mother leaves unobtrusively.
4	Stranger and baby	3 minutes or less[1]	First separation episode. Stranger's behavior is geared to that of baby.
5	Mother and baby	3 minutes or more[2]	First reunion episode. Mother greets and/or comforts baby, then tries to settle baby again in play. Mother then leaves, saying "bye-bye."
6	Baby alone	3 minutes or less[1]	Second separation episode.
7	Stranger and baby	3 minutes or less[1]	Continuation of second separation. Stranger enters and gears her behavior to that of baby.
8	Mother and baby	3 minutes	Second reunion episode. Mother enters, greets and picks up baby. Meanwhile stranger leaves unobtrusively.

[1]Episode is curtailed if the baby is unduly distressed.
[2]Episode is prolonged if more time is required for the baby to become reinvolved in play.

SOURCE: Patterns of Attachment: *A Psychological Study of the Strange Situation* (p. 37) by M. D. S. Ainsworth, M. C. Blehar, E. Waters, and S. Wall, 1978, Hillsdale, NJ: Lawrence Erlbaum.

differences among children. The scores they assign are based on such things as infants' willingness to play with the toys, their desire to be picked up or reluctance to be put down, their efforts to establish social interactions, their proximity to their mother, and so forth. Although infants show as much variability in their responses in the strange situation as they do in their responses to any other standard test situation, Mary Ainsworth and her colleagues (Ainsworth, Blehar, Waters, & Wall, 1978) have identified three distinct attachment patterns (along with some subpatterns). One of the major patterns reflects *secure attachment* and the others, *insecure attachment* (or anxious attachment).

Security of Attachment

When psychologists first began their attempts to measure individual differences in attachment, they focused on the intensity of infant reactions during separation (see, for example, Schaffer & Emerson, 1964). In general, they were concerned with quantifying the degree of disturbance, because they thought this would be a measure of the degree of attachment. Quite early in her studies, Mary Ainsworth came to the conclusion that the degree of disturbance observed in infants during separation does not directly reflect either security or insecurity (Ainsworth & Bell, 1970). Likewise, she determined that security of attachment is not reflected in the degree of clinging, touching, or smiling during nonseparation. In the strange situation as it is now employed, therefore, attachment ratings are based on *patterns* of interaction and not on quantitative measures of single behaviors (see Box 12-1).

Although a variety of observations from all eight strange-situation episodes contribute to the judgment that a baby is securely or insecurely attached, the key contrast is in the way the infants respond during the reunions with their mother (Episodes 5 and 8). Securely attached babies (labeled as Group B in the Ainsworth scoring system) want both contact and interaction with their mother at these times. Though the interaction may be limited to making eye contact, smiling, waving, or vocalizing, more often securely attached infants will want to make physical contact. When they obtain contact, they are reluctant to let go and, therefore, protest if put down. Insecurely attached infants, on the other hand, react differently. One type of insecure infant avoids the mother during reunions, and a second type is ambivalent toward her. Avoidant-type infants (labeled as Group A), instead of approaching their mother as securely attached infants would, turn away from her, move past her, or avert their gaze from her. If the mother picks up the avoidant infant (as in Episode 8), the infant does not cling or attempt to prolong the contact. During reunions, the second type of insecure infant (Group C) expresses an ambivalent attitude toward the mother. The ambivalence is captured in the seemingly contradictory acts of first seeking contact and then resisting it, often angrily. Secure and insecure in-

---

BOX 12-1
Ainsworth's Scoring System for Interaction Patterns in the Strange Situation

Group A: Avoidant

Conspicuous avoidance of proximity to or interaction with the mother in the reunion episodes. Either the baby ignores his mother on her return, greeting her casually if at all, or, if there is approach and/or a less casual greeting, the baby tends to mingle his welcome with avoidance responses—turning away, moving past, averting the gaze, and the like.

Little or no tendency to seek proximity to or interaction or contact with the mother, even in the reunion episodes.

If picked up, little or no tendency to cling or to resist being released.

On the other hand, little or no tendency toward active resistance to contact or interaction with the mother, except for probable squirming to get down if indeed the baby is picked up.

Tendency to treat the stranger much as the mother is treated, although perhaps with less avoidance.

Either the baby is not distressed during separation, or the distress seems to be due to being left alone rather than to his mother's absence. For most, distress does not occur when the stranger is present, and any distress upon being left alone tends to be alleviated when the stranger returns.

Group B: Secure

The baby wants either proximity and contact with his mother or interaction with her, and he actively seeks it, especially in the reunion episodes.

If he achieves contact, he seeks to maintain it, and either resists release or at least protests if he is put down.

---

fants also differ in their reactions to the stranger during Episodes 4 and 7 of the strange situation. Secure infants show a clear preference for their own mother and, therefore, when alone with the stranger, they respond differently than when alone with their own mother. The word most frequently used to describe their stranger reaction is "wary." Group A infants, on the other hand, are not usually distressed when left alone with a stranger, but if they are, they can be comforted as easily by the stranger as by their own mother. Group-C infants are conspicuous for their resistance to the stranger.

Correlates of Secure Attachment

The progress that Ainsworth and her coworkers have made in measuring individual differences in the security of attachment has led investigators to wonder what the correlates of this variable might be. How do securely at-

The baby responds to his mother's return in the reunion episodes with more than a casual greeting—either with a smile or a cry or a tendency to approach.

Little or no tendency to resist contact or interaction with his mother.

Little or no tendency to avoid his mother in the reunion episodes.

He may or may not be friendly with the stranger, but he is clearly more interested in interaction and/or contact with his mother than with the stranger.

He may or may not be distressed during the separation episodes, but if he is distressed this is clearly related to his mother's absence and not merely to being alone. He may be somewhat comforted by the stranger, but it is clear that he wants his mother.

Group C: Ambivalent

The baby displays conspicuous contact- and interaction-resisting behavior, perhaps especially in Episode 8.

He also shows moderate-to-strong seeking of proximity and contact and seeking to maintain contact once gained, so that he gives the impression of being ambivalent to his mother.

He shows little or no tendency to ignore his mother in the reunion episodes, or to turn or move away from her, or to avert his gaze.

He may display generally "maladaptive" behavior in the strange situation. Either he tends to be more angry than infants in other groups, or he may be conspicuously passive (Ainsworth, Blehar, Waters, & Wall, 1978).

tached children differ on average from insecurely attached children? A tremendous amount of research has been addressed to this issue (see Sroufe, 1985, p. 1), and the answer from it seems quite clear. Securely attached infants are better adjusted cognitively and socially than insecure infants. This overall relationship is found to hold between attachment measures and adjustment measures taken simultaneously at a single age and between attachment measures taken at one point in life and adjustment measures taken later in life. This means that attachment relates to adjustment both *concurrently* and *predictively.* Among the predictive relationships are the following: infants who are securely attached (Group B) at 1 year of age are found to be more competent with peers in the later preschool years (Waters, Wippman, & Sroufe, 1979). Also, securely attached infants have been shown to be better at problem solving at age 2 than insecurely attached infants (Matas, Arend, & Sroufe, 1978), and they have higher scores on tests of infant development (Main, 1983). At age 3, children who were securely attached at

12 months show rapid and smooth adjustments to strangers, and they respond well to feedback following failure (Lutkenhaus, Grossmann, & Grossmann, 1985). Alan Sroufe (1983) has reported that secure attachment at 12 months is even a good predictor of some factors related to overall personality at age 4. These were factors such as self-esteem, mood, independence, and social competence.

The Secure-Base Function of Attachment

From the theoretical perspective established by John Bowlby and Mary Ainsworth (Ainsworth, 1973; Bowlby, 1969), there is a good causal reason that secure attachment early in life predicts good adjustment later in life. The reason is that the attachment relation is said to provide infants with the emotional security they need to become independent. Ainsworth calls this the *secure-base* function of attachment. Without a secure base from which to operate, the world with all its objects and people can be too terrifying to explore. With a secure base, strange objects and people are interesting, and they lure the infant into investigating and examining. Bowlby and Ainsworth see this security-then-exploration sequence in evolutionary terms as the way the human behavior system is designed. As Ainsworth states it,

> It seems of obvious survival advantage in evolutionary terms for a species with as long and as vulnerable a period of infancy as that characteristic of humans to have developed an interlocking between the attachment system, whose function is protection, and exploratory . . . behavior, which promotes learning to know and to deal with . . . the environment. This . . . permits a situation in which an infant or young child is prompted by intriguing objects to move away from his "secure base" to explore them, and yet tend to prevent him from straying too far away or from remaining away for too long. (Ainsworth, Blehar, Waters, & Wall, 1978)

The concept of mother as a secure base, like the concept of attachment as a bond, can be taken quite literally. For securely attached infants in the strange situation, the mother indeed does seem to be a secure base. Occasionally the infant must come back to make contact with the mother, as if to get the "security batteries" recharged. Then the child can return to the toys and play. When the mother is away, play with the toys declines because a formerly secure, safe situation has turned into one that is potentially threatening. What we observe here in the case of securely attached human infants can also be observed in other animals. The richest set of observations of this sort on nonhumans comes from Harry Harlow's research with rhesus monkeys.

In Harlow's best-known research (Harlow & Zimmerman, 1959), infant rhesus monkeys were reared with either a terry-cloth-covered wire-mesh "mother" or a plain wire mother (see Figure 12-5). Both were called *surrogate mothers* because they served in place of real mothers. One of the discoveries of the research was that a cloth surrogate, although not in any way equivalent to a real mother, could, nonetheless, serve as a secure base. She (if we can personify the cloth surrogate) seemed to provide infant rhesus monkeys with the emotional wherewithal to begin exploring the rhesus-monkey world. Wire mothers were totally ineffective in providing this function, as is made evident in the series of photographs shown in Figure 12-6. These photographs were taken of the infant monkeys' responses to Harlow's own rendition of the strange situation, which involved exposing the rhesus monkeys either to novel stimuli like a toy drummer or to novel environments like a large toy-filled room. The reaction of the monkeys to these situations was very human. They ran to the surrogate who supplied a bit of security, and once reassured, they turned to investigate the strange object or environment, first visually and then by tentatively moving away from their base in order to examine things more closely.

FIGURE 12-5
Harlow's Cloth Mother and Wire Mother
Of these two surrogate mothers, only the terry-cloth mother on the right offered any emotional support for infant rhesus monkeys. This was true even when surrogate-reared monkeys were fed from a bottle mounted on the wire mother. Providing contact comfort is apparently a crucial component to successful mothering.

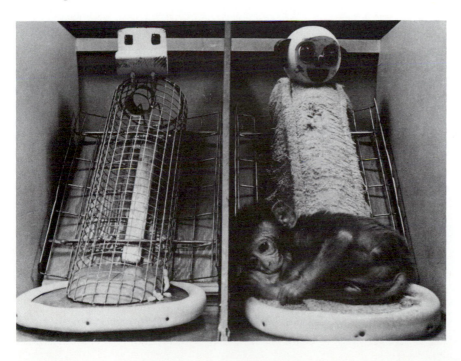

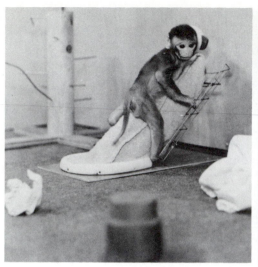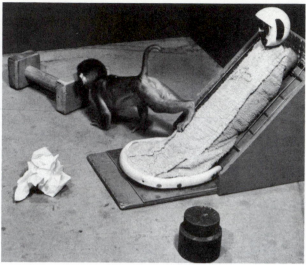

FIGURE 12-6
Exploration and the Secure-Base Function of Attachment
A rhesus monkey reared with a terry-cloth surrogate clings to its "mother" when placed in a novel environment. He is visually exploring the strange environment, however, and will soon have the courage to begin to explore it motorically. This is because his mother serves as a secure base.

Caretaker Variables: Contact Comfort and Sensitivity

The fact that a cloth-covered wire figure could become the object of a rhesus monkey's attachment raises the question of what it takes to be the object of attachment. A major factor is that the caretaker be available to the child. Beyond that, one must be an effective caretaker. A factor that makes cloth "mothers" more effective than wire ones (even if the wire one serves as a milk dispenser) is that the cloth mothers provide a degree of *contact comfort* essential to infant monkeys.

Contact Comfort

We have reason to believe that contact comfort is as important for humans as for monkeys. You may recall, for example, that one of the cases of deprivation dwarfism, cited in Chapter 3, was brought on when the mother ceased handling her infant daughter for fear that a surgically implanted tube in the child's stomach would be dislodged (see pp. 110–11). We know, too, from the security supplied by blankets and cloth dolls, that human needs in this domain are not very different from those of monkeys.

Because nursing requires frequent close contact between mother and infants, the development of humans and other mammals is tipped in the direction of making the mother the principal attachment figure. To the extent that father and older siblings are involved in the intimacies of child care, however, we can expect them to become secondary attachment figures. The basic rule seems to be that infants seek through their crying, smiling, and approach behavior to gain physical contact with some person in their social world. That person will probably be the mother, but if she is rarely available or if she is cold in her treatment of the infant, some other person in the social world could become the primary attachment figure. There is one case on record of six young girls who apparently became attached to one another. They spent the first years of their lives in a Nazi concentration camp. There they were separated from the care of any single adult, and they formed attachments to each other (Freud & Dann, 1951/1968). Harlow has raised some monkeys under similar conditions. The outcome can be seen in Figure 12-7.

The relationship of contact comfort to quality of attachment as assessed in the strange situation has been of special interest to Mary Main, one of Ainsworth's collaborators. In her original work on this topic, she and Ainsworth discovered that mothers of Group-B infants held their infants more carefully and tenderly and for longer periods of time during early infancy than non-B mothers did (Ainsworth, Blehar, Waters, & Wall, 1978, p. 150). Also, the mothers of infants with an avoidant Group-A attachment relation at 12 months had an aversion to physical contact when their infants were 3 months old. Their aversion was expressed in ways such as withdrawing from infant approach, becoming impatient while holding their babies, holding their babies in unnatural ways, and stating that holding "spoils"

FIGURE 12-7
Harlow's Peer-Reared Monkeys
Rhesus monkeys reared together with no adults become attached to each other.

babies. Main's more recent research (Main, 1981, in press) has confirmed these earlier observations. Providing contact comfort is important to the development of secure attachments, and when the contact comfort is deficient, the deficiency contributes to the development of an avoidant attachment.

Mother's Sensitivity

A second variable important in determining the type of attachment formed between infants and their mothers is mother's *sensitivity*. According to Ainsworth (Ainsworth, Blehar, Waters, & Wall, 1978), sensitive mothers have securely attached infants, and insensitive ones have insecurely attached infants. What Ainsworth means by sensitivity is defined in her statement that an "optimally sensitive mother is able to see things from her baby's point of view" (Ainsworth, Blehar, Waters, & Wall, 1978, p. 142). Such a mother is "alert to perceive her baby's signals, interprets them accurately, and responds appropriately and promptly." An insensitive mother, on the other hand, cannot read the baby's signals, and her responses to the baby's cries, facial expressions, and movements tend to be dictated by her own activities, states, and wishes.

Ainsworth found that the sensitive–insensitive difference was reflected in a host of specific maternal behaviors that she and her colleagues were able to observe on actual home visits with infants and mothers. These behaviors were ones that dealt with such things as when the mother picked up the infant, how she held the baby, how she acted and reacted when having face-to-face interactions with the baby, and how responsive she was to signals and communications regarding the baby's wants, needs, and intentions. Even in the first 3 months of the infant's first year, mothers of infants destined to become securely attached showed far greater sensitivity as reflected in the fact that there were significant differences on 13 of the 17 "sensitivity" measures taken in the home. Mothers of secure infants, for example, responded more frequently to crying, showed more affection while holding the infant, acknowledged the baby with a smile or conversation when entering the baby's room, and were better at feeding the baby because of their attention to the baby's signals.

Of the 13 sensitivity measures that separated the mothers of secure infants from the mothers of insecure infants, sensitivity during feeding was one of the best. The reason for this can be illustrated in an example given by Eleanor Maccoby (1980) showing all that can go wrong in a feeding episode. Maccoby's example features a 22-month-old girl and an aunt who has come to feed her. The aunt, because she is unfamiliar with the girl's feeding routine, has the kind of trouble during the feeding episode that one might expect from an insensitive mother. The aunt's insensitivity (which stems, of course, from ignorance) is contrasted with the highly sensitive behavior of the child's own mother.

The aunt prepared lunch and brought the child's highchair close to the table. She swung the highchair's tray into place and set out the child's utensils and bib on the tray. Then she lifted the little girl to put her into the highchair. The child stiffened her body, curled up her feet, and refused to be put into the highchair. The puzzled aunt set the child down on the floor. The child pointed to the tray of the highchair and cried. Finally the aunt held the child on her lap to feed her her lunch, but the child was clearly upset and the feeding did not go well. A few days later the aunt was present to watch the child's mother give her lunch. The mother brought out the highchair *without* setting the tray in place. The little girl lifted up her arms to be picked up. Her mother set her in the highchair. The child held her head back so the mother could swing the tray over her head into place. The child lifted her chin and the mother fitted the bib under it. The child leaned forward and put her head down on the tray while the mother tied the bib behind her neck. Then the child sat up with a big smile, banged the tray with her hand, and said, "Milk!" She was ready for lunch. (Maccoby, 1980, p. 66)

This example and Ainsworth's data indicate how well tuned sensitive mothers can be to all of a child's channels of communication. It also demonstrates that if investigators have just one opportunity to judge sensitivity, they could not choose a better activity to observe than feeding.

Ainsworth's data on the link between sensitivity and security have been widely replicated (Sroufe, 1985, p. 7). One recent replication was car-

Mealtime is a good time to assess a mother's sensitivity.

ried out in Germany by Karin and Klaus Grossmann (Grossmann, Grossmann, Spangler, Suess, & Unzner, 1985). Although their results shed some doubt on the cross-cultural validity of the strange situation as the best measure of attachment (see also Ainsworth, 1983, p. 49), the Grossmanns did find that the sensitivity measures assigned to mothers of infants under 6 months of age predicted the attachment-security ratings of those infants at 12 months. Byron Egeland and Ellen Farber (1984) of the University of Minnesota found the same thing to be true. They made in-home observations of mothers as they fed and played with their pre-6-month-old infants. At 12 months, the infants of the most sensitive mothers tended to be securely attached.

Although contact comfort and sensitivity are reliable predictors of attachment security, they are not infallible predictors. As Michael Lamb has painstakingly pointed out (Lamb, Thompson, Gardner, Charnov, & Estes, 1984), the relationships found between sensitivity and attachment are reliable but weak. We can only predict outcomes in groups of infant–mother pairs, not in individual cases. Even in families that show extreme deviation from societal norms for child care, it is impossible to make a confident prediction. For example, studies of abused and neglected children indicate an elevated risk for insecure attachment, but insecurity is not the exclusive outcome (Schneider-Rosen & Cicchetti, 1984; Schneider-Rosen, Braunwald, Carlson, & Cicchetti, 1985; Egeland & Sroufe, 1981a, 1981b). Somewhere around 30 percent of the infants with histories of severe maltreatment will be securely attached to their abusive or neglectful parents.

A second limitation in our ability to predict attachment outcomes from parental behavior is that we cannot predict whether the children of insensitive parents who provide little contact comfort will wind up in group A or C. Ainsworth has argued that mothers who are basically loving but insensitive will have infants who form Group-C attachments, whereas mothers with rigid, unloving, angry, and perfectionistic personalities will tend to have infants who form Group-A attachments (see, for example, Ainsworth, 1983, pp. 41-42). This is more on the order of a theoretical prediction than a confirmed fact, however. Again, to cite the literature on childhood abuse and neglect, 70 percent of maltreated children wind up in one of the insecure categories at 12 months, but there is no indication from their particular maltreatment histories (such as physical injury, neglect, emotional mistreatment, or other differentiating conditions) of why they would be in the one category rather than the other (see Schneider-Rosen, Braunwald, Carlson, & Cicchetti, 1985, p. 204).

Is Mother Alone Responsible for the Attachment Relation?

Concern about the relationship between maternal behavior and the quality of attachment is obviously motivated by the hypothesis that maternal behavior shapes the attachment relation. According to Mary Ainsworth, for example, specific behaviors such as the promptness and regularity with which mothers respond to an infant's crying will have an impact on the developing relationship. The fact is, however, that specific behaviors such as this are not reliably predictive of secure- or insecure-attachment outcomes (Lamb, Thompson, Gardner, Charnov, & Estes, 1984). Only global sensitivity measures provide replicable results. The failure to find stronger links to mother's behavior makes us wonder whether the quality of the infant–mother attachment can be attributed directly to the mother. Attachment theorists have implied that the answer is yes (see, for example, Sroufe, 1985). In their view, when infants wind up insecurely attached, it is the mother's fault. This appears to be a particularly one-sided view of development that overlooks the many ways in which infant characteristics might affect the relationship, either independently of what mother does or in interaction with it.

Later in the chapter, we will see that Ainsworth defends the one-sided approach by arguing that a mother's sensitivity, which is alleged to be the key factor in the development of secure attachments, reflects a mother's adjustments to her infant. Thus, even though the mother is unilaterally responsible for the security of the attachment, the unique characteristics of individual infants must still be taken into account. But first, we will take up another alleged instance of one-sided developmental causation in which differences in parenting styles appear to lead to differences in the overall cognitive, social, and emotional development of children. The primary data come from research by Diana Baumrind, a psychologist with the Institute of Human Development at the University of California, Berkeley.

PARENTING STYLES AS A FACTOR IN SOCIAL DEVELOPMENT

Like Mary Ainsworth, Diana Baumrind (1967, 1971, 1973) has been concerned with parents as factors in the social development of their children. She has worked, however, with children from an older age group—early to late childhood rather than infancy—and with different parent variables. The parent variables, moreover, are diverse, more diverse even than those that contribute to the "sensitivity" variable. Fortunately, however, we do not have to deal with them in all their diversity because they collapse fairly well into three **parenting styles** known as the *authoritarian style, authoritative style,* and *permissive style* (see Box 12-2).

Measuring Parenting Styles

To obtain her parent measures, Baumrind and her colleagues employed naturalistic observations in the home coupled with some structured laboratory observations. Measurements were taken as parents interacted with their

BOX 12-2
Baumrind's Three Parenting Styles

The Authoritarian Parent

[Attempts] to shape, control and evaluate the behavior and attitudes of the child in accordance with a set standard of conduct, usually an absolute standard, theologically motivated and formulated by a higher authority. She values obedience as a virtue and favors punitive, forceful measures to curb self-will at points where the child's actions or beliefs conflict with what she thinks is right conduct. She believes in inculcating such instrumental values as respect for authority, respect for work, and respect for the preservation of order and traditional structure. She does not encourage verbal give and take, believing that the child should accept her word for what is right.

The Authoritative Parent

[Attempts] to direct the child's activities but in a rational issue-oriented manner. She encourages verbal give and take, and shares with the child the reasoning behind her policy. She values both expressive and instrumental attributes, both autonomous self-will and disciplined conformity. Therefore, she exerts firm control at points of parent–child divergence, but does not hem the child in with restrictions. She recognizes her own special rights as an adult, but also the child's individual interests and special ways. The authoritative parent affirms the child's present qualities, but also sets standards for future conduct. She uses reason as well as power to achieve her objectives. She does not base her decisions on group consensus or the individual child's desires; but also, does not regard herself as infallible, or divinely inspired.

The Permissive Parent

[Attempts] to behave in a nonpunitive, acceptant and affirmative manner towards the child's impulses, desires, and actions. She consults with him about policy decisions and gives explanations for family rules. She makes few demands for household responsibility and orderly behavior. She presents herself to the child as a resource for him to use as he wishes, not as an active agent responsible for shaping or altering his ongoing or future behavior. She allows the child to regulate his own activities as much as possible, avoids the exercise of control, and does not encourage him to obey externally defined standards. She attempts to use reason but not overt power to accomplish her ends. (Baumrind, 1970).

children, primarily in situations requiring discipline. Home observations, therefore, included mealtime and bedtime—occasions that routinely require parents to exercise some authority. The structured laboratory observations were also rich in chances to observe how parents used their authority by having the parent teach the child a number concept, supervise the child's play, and get the child to help clean up. As you can well imagine,

Baumrind's data were rich in diversity, but she was able to find four general attributes on which parents could be compared. In her original formulation, these general attributes were parental control, maturity demands, parent–child communications, and nurturance (Baumrind, 1967).

To know what is meant by an authoritarian, authoritative, or permissive style, one must first know the meaning of the four parental attributes. What, then, is meant by *control?* Parents high in control give their children clear directives and consistently enforce these directives. Thus, when children are told to keep their toys off the floor (one of the laboratory tasks), they are expected to keep them off the floor. Parents low in control are apt to give in to their children's pressure. When children begin to beg, whine, or say "please," low-control parents capitulate.

Maturity demands can be understood by knowing that parents high in this attribute insist that their children be independent and that they not act in ways that could be considered babyish. Parents score high in this attribute if they frequently say things like "You are a big girl now and you can do that by yourself." Parents low in maturity demands say things like "You are such a baby I guess I'll have to do that for you."

To score high in *parent–child communications,* parents have to give their children reasons why they should comply with the parents' directives. The parents also have to listen to their children's opinions and evaluate them seriously. Thus, if a parent tells a child it is time to go to bed because the child has to get up early, that would be more communicative than if the parent simply told the child to go to bed. Communicative parents also listen when the child explains why he or she does not want to go to bed and acknowledge the child's argument ("I know you want to watch TV with mommy and daddy"). Low-communicative parents do not engage in a discussion of disciplinary matters and even cut off their child's attempts to argue with a curt command like "Do as you're told."

Nurturance in Baumrind's system refers to factors in the parent–child interaction that reflect warmth, nurturance, and love on the part of the parent. Thus, parents high in nurturance carry out their interactions in a warm and loving manner. Even "Do as you're told" can be said in a way that is nurturant. But nurturance as a general attribute amounts to more than just "tenderness of expression and touch" (Baumrind, 1967). It also refers to behaviors such as offering the child reinforcement, support, and encouragement.

By comparing parents simultaneously on the four attributes just listed (a comparison known as *profile analysis*), Baumrind was able to delineate the three parenting styles outlined in Box 12-2. Authoritative parents were high in control, high in communication, high in maturity demands, and high in nurturance. Authoritarian parents did not differ from authoritative parents in control or maturity demands, but they tended to be low in nurturance and communication. The permissive parents contrasted with the first two types by being low in control and maturity demands. In nurturance and communication, however, permissive parents were relatively high, thus forming a further contrast with authoritarian parents, but a similarity with authoritative parents.

Correlates of Baumrind's Parenting Styles

Although Baumrind's descriptive achievement in devising the means to measure differences in parenting behavior has proved to be a substantial contribution, her interest in parenting was not simply descriptive. Like Ainsworth, who wanted to know what the correlates of secure attachment might be, Baumrind wanted to know what correlates might exist for parenting style. What she found were concurrent and predictive relationships between parenting style and a measure of child development that she called *instrumental competence*.

The concept of instrumental competence, like the concept of parenting style, encompasses quite a wide range of specific behaviors. In Baumrind's own words, "Instrumental competence is defined by social responsibility, independence, achievement orientation, and vitality" (1973, p. 4). Instrumentally competent children are friendly, helpful, self-determined, and energetic. Instrumentally incompetent children are hostile, disruptive, aimless, and lacking in vigor. As you can gather, instrumental competence is as global a variable in the social sphere as intelligence is in the cognitive sphere. Nonetheless, Baumrind found that this variable, general as it was, related to her parenting-style measures. The concurrent relationship showed that parents who used an authoritative style with their children had the most-instrumentally-competent children. Parents who used permissive and authoritarian styles had less-instrumentally-competent children. The predictive relationship was the same. Followed longitudinally until ages 8 and 9, the children with the authoritative parents continued to show superiority on measures of instrumental competence (Baumrind, in preparation, cited in Maccoby & Martin, 1983).

Although there is much to be learned from Baumrind's correlation data, one of the most important lessons is that strong parental control is not incompatible with good socialization outcomes. This is apparent when you recall that high control is a hallmark of authoritative parents. They mix high control with high nurturance and communication. The fact that authoritative control is a correlate of instrumental competence serves to disconfirm the once popular belief that firm parental control could spoil children's independence and self-esteem (see, for example, Becker, 1964, p. 197). Author*itarian* control may have this effect, but Baumrind's data are clear proof that authori*tative* control does not.

Although the pattern of results relating an authoritative parenting style to developmental outcomes in children is clear, the results for children of

permissive and authoritarian parents are somewhat harder to report, primarily because there are some sex differences. In general, however, these parenting styles are associated with many undesirable outcomes in children. Drawing on a larger research base than that generated by Baumrind alone, Eleanor Maccoby and John Martin report, "Children of authoritarian parents tend to lack social competence with peers: They tend to withdraw, not to take social initiative, to lack spontaneity" (1983, p. 44). Overall, these negative characteristics are somewhat more pronounced in males than females. Summarizing the research on the offspring of permissive parents, Maccoby and Martin report, "[Permissive parenting] is associated with children's being impulsive, aggressive, and lacking in independence or the ability to take responsibility" (1983, p. 46).

THE INFLUENCE OF CONTROL PRACTICES

Baumrind is not alone in focusing on parenting styles as an important variable in socialization. Martin Hoffman (1983) is a second investigator who assigns a crucial role to parenting. However, his concern is with a narrower range of parenting behaviors and outcomes than those outlined by Baumrind. Whereas Baumrind linked parenting style to instrumental competence, Hoffman links a single component of parenting style to what is in effect a single component of instrumental competence. The competence-related outcome is best described as children's tendency to engage in the kinds of cooperative and helpful behaviors that are labeled as **prosocial** (to contrast with antisocial). The parental behaviors of interest are **control practices.** This reflects a narrower focus on parenting style than Baumrind's, because Baumrind included nurturance, maturity demands, and parent–child communications along with control as defining attributes.

Hoffman's study of parental control practices has led him to distinguish among three types of control (Hoffman, 1970). These are power assertion, love withdrawal, and induction. *Power assertion* is self-explanatory and is the favored practice of the parents whom Baumrind labels as authoritarian. It features the use of threat, physical force, and the withdrawal of privileges as the primary means of controlling a child's behavior. *Love withdrawal* does not involve threat or force. Instead, the parents choose to ignore, isolate, and refuse to speak to a child who is being bad. They are, in a sense, passively aggressive toward the child they are trying to discipline. The "silent treatment" is a control practice that merits the love-withdrawal label. In the control practice known as *induction* parents explain why a child's actions are considered to be bad. In particular, parents who use induction emphasize how a child's bad behavior has a negative impact on other people. A good synonym for induction is "reasoning." Induction is illustrated by indirect control messages such as "If you keep pushing him, he'll fall down and cry", or more direct messages such as "Don't yell at him; he was only trying to help" (Hoffman, 1985, p. 304). The common inductive component in these messages is that they draw the child's attention to the consequences for the victim. They are, therefore, victim-centered forms of control.

Correlates of Control Practices

The major relationship that has been found between parental control practices and children's socialization is that parents who use induction have children who are more prosocial than those who do not (Hoffman, 1975; Kuczynski, 1982, Zahn-Waxler & Radke-Yarrow, 1982). In one study, Hoffman (1975) had fifth graders rate each other for prosocial behavior using questions like "Which three children in your class are most likely to care about how other kids feel and try not to hurt their feelings?" and "Which three children are most likely to stick up for some kid that the other kids are calling names?" After taking this prosocial measurement on all of the 5th grade children, Hoffman interviewed the parents of 40 of the children about how they would handle certain disciplinary situations (for example, the parents' child has just destroyed another child's block house and has made the child cry, or the parents catch their child making fun of another child). Hoffman found that the children in his 40-child sample who were most often rated as being prosocial by their peers had parents who reported that they would use victim-centered discipline—an inductive technique. They said, for example, that they would have the child apologize and help build back the house, or they said they would have their child volunteer to play with the child who had been teased.

Carolyn Zahn-Waxler, Marian Radke-Yarrow, and Robert King (1979) have also found that parents who use inductive discipline techniques tend to have children who are prosocial in their response to the distress of others. Their study, like Hoffman's, involved naturalistic observations of children, who, at the time of the study, were just 2 to 2½ years old, much younger than in Hoffman's study. Nonetheless, in this study just as in Hoffman's, the mothers who used induction when controlling their children had children who were the most likely to behave prosocially. Prosocial behaviors in this study were defined as attempts by one child to soothe the distress of another—for example, by stroking the arm of a tearful friend and offering him a toy or by giving a playmate flower petals after hitting her and making her cry. The one proviso that Zahn-Waxler and her colleagues would add to Hoffman's recommendations regarding the use of induction is that effective induction may need to be mixed with strong emotion. As Zahn-Waxler and her colleagues wrote, "Effective induction [with 2-year-olds anyway] is not calmly dispensed reasoning, carefully designed to enlighten the child; it is emotionally imposed, sometimes harshly and often forcefully" (1979, p. 327), as in the case of a parent who gets visibly agitated and says, "Don't ever pull your sister's hair! Can't you see that you are hurting her?"

In addition to the positive relation between parental use of induction and prosocial development in children, there is a negative relation between the use of power assertion (in the absence of induction) and prosocial development. Children whose parents use power assertion predominantly (all parents, of course, use it on occasion) tend to be antisocial, less helpful, and less caring than children who are not controlled in this way (Brody & Shaffer, 1982). This is particularly true of the children who come from homes where power assertion yields to physical abuse. The children of child abusers tend to be unempathetic with others, sometimes disturbingly so.

Correlates of Child Abuse

The relative lack of empathy that has been found to characterize the victims of child abuse is vividly portrayed in research that Mary Main and Carol George conducted in day-care centers specializing in the care of children from stressed families (George & Main, 1979; Main & George, 1985). Two of the centers used in Main and George's research had abused children. Two other centers had children who had not been abused but were from similar home environments. Drawing on the resources of the four centers, Main and George conducted a naturalistic study in which they compared ten abused children to ten nonabused controls. At the time of the study, the children were from 2- to 3-years old. They were observed for their reactions to crying, pain, and other signs of distress in their age-mates. Would they show some sympathy and concern for the distressed peer or would they show indifference or some other response? Main and George found that the abused children showed no sympathy at all. Not once during the study did an abused child respond in a helpful, sympathetic way to the distress of another child. The nonabused control children responded to one third of the distress incidents with some prosocial action. This is a normal rate of empathetic response for children this age (Zahn-Waxler & Radke-Yarrow, 1982, p. 119).

More disturbing than the abused children's general lack of empathy for their distressed peers was the way they responded to the distress on the few occasions that a response was noted. Out of nine abused children who were exposed to distressed peers during the course of the study, eight responded on at least one occasion with some form of unusual behavior involving fear, anger, or aggression. Only one of the nine control children showed a similar response. Four of the abused children's bizarre responses involved a pattern of alternating comfort and attack, which is illustrated in the case of Martin.

> Martin (an abused child of 32 months) tried to take the hand of the crying . . . child, and when she resisted, he slapped her on the arm with his open hand. He then turned away from her to look at the ground and began vocalizing very strongly, "Cut it out! CUT IT OUT!" each time saying it a little faster and louder. He patted her, but when she became disturbed by his patting, he retreated, "hissing at her and baring his teeth." He then began patting her on the back again, his patting became beating, and he continued beating her despite her screams. (Main & George, 1985, p. 410)

This observation reveals a tendency for aggression in the abused children that was somewhat characteristic. George and Main (1979) observed, for example, that abused children, when interacting with their age-mates, were twice as likely to hit, kick, pinch, spit, slap, or grab as were the nonabused children in the same group. The abused children were also likely to attack caretakers, something nonabused children never did. Similar findings have been obtained with children older than George and Main's 2- and 3-year-olds (Parke & Slaby, 1983, p. 582). Overall, then, the results of research on the social behaviors of abused children are in line with the hypothesis that power assertion as a parental control tactic is associated with antisocial outcomes for children.

Explaining the Relationships

In order to explain the relationships that have been found between induction and empathy and between power assertion and a lack of empathy, Hoffman (1983, 1985) has proposed a causal theory that emphasizes the role of parental control practices in both the emotional and the cognitive lives of children. According to Hoffman, induction helps to put children's social development on a prosocial path, because induction is the only control technique that explicitly focuses children on the feelings and problems of others during control episodes. Other control techniques do the opposite. They focus children on themselves. Children being subjected to power-assertive control, for example, feel threatened, angry, afraid, and pained—all *self-focused* emotions. With all of their feelings and thoughts focused on their own pain and suffering, children cannot be expected to develop an appreciation for how their behavior affects others. According to Hoffman's theory, somewhat the same thing is true of children undergoing love withdrawal. They feel self-pity—another self-focused emotion. Therefore, only children who get their correction with a dose of induction have their attention focused less on self and more on the consequences of their actions for others. This helps those children in achieving the developmental step of being able to take the other person's point of view (see Chapter 14), to feel empathy with that person, and to feel guilt for one's own actions.

Hoffman's theory for relating parental control practices to prosocial development makes perfectly good sense, and—as we have seen—there is some support for it, at least insofar as it predicts a positive relation between prosocial behavior and the use of induction and a negative relation between prosocial behavior and the use of power-assertive techniques (see Radke-Yarrow, Zahn-Waxler, & Chapman, 1983). The data are less consistent, however, in showing a relationship between love-withdrawal and antisocial outcomes (Brody & Shaffer, 1982, p. 39; Hoffman, 1970, p. 300). In evaluating this less-than-perfect pattern in the data, one must keep in mind that research on parental control is nonexperimental and naturalistic. These facts make it very hard to establish what causal role any particular control practice might play. Also, assessment of Hoffman's hypothesis, or any other regarding parental influences, is made difficult by the fact that most parents—and certainly the parents who volunteer to participate in parenting studies—do not reflect extremes on any of the potentially negative dimensions of parenting. Thus, except when special populations, such as the population of abusive parents, become available for study, all inferences about the effects of parenting variables must be made from observations of parents who do not differ dramatically on these variables. Not surprisingly, then, it is difficult to adduce conclusive evidence to either support or refute theories regarding the causal relations among parenting variables and socialization outcomes. It is even more difficult when you consider that parents do not differ just in their parenting styles or just in their control practices. These specific parental differences are themselves associated with other variables—education, personal histories, number of previous children, genetics, values, and so forth—any one of which could be an important covariate in the determination of a child's socialization outcome. Also, in that we are only dealing with correlations in the first place, it is at least a logical possibility that parents do not really cause anything. If we are to be logical, we must at least entertain the notion that children cause parents to be as they are rather than vice versa (for example, certain types of children cause their parents to be abusive). Such thoughts lead us into the next section of this chapter in which we will begin to consider children's own contributions to their socialization as well as bidirectional effects (that is, reciprocal parent–child effects) on development.

ALTERNATIVES TO UNIDIRECTIONAL EXPLANATIONS

Thus far in our study of factors that affect the social development of children, we have focused on parenting. Attachment research has shown a relationship between the contact comfort and sensitivity that parents provide and the security of attachment in their offspring. Baumrind's research has shown that parenting style relates to instrumental competence. Other research relates parental inductive control techniques to the development of empathy and power-assertive techniques to a lack of empathy (as well as some disturbing antisocial tendencies.) By asking ourselves why these relationships between parenting behavior and developmental outcomes should exist, we are in a position to learn something about the epigenetic factors involved in social development.

Parent-to-Child Effects

The most popular explanation historically for parent–child correlations has been a unidirectional, parent-to-child causal explanation. You may recall that this was John B. Watson's environmentalist view of development, the view that parents can shape a child's development in whatever way they choose (see Chapter 3, p. 100). This environmentalist assumption underlies much of the research on correlates of parenting style. In introducing her original study, for example, Baumrind said that the research was conducted "with the assumption that the . . . social development of middle-class children is largely a function of parental childrearing practices. With varying degrees of consciousness and conscientiousness, parents *create* their children psychologically. . . ." (1967, p. 45; italics added). This underlying view leads to a number of specific hypotheses regarding how parents might create the psychological attributes of their children. For example, to explain why permissive and authoritarian parents have children lacking in instrumental competence, Baumrind hypothesizes that authoritarian and permissive parents tend to shield children from stress. Authoritarian parents do this by not giving their children adequate chances to take initiative. Permissive parents do it by not forcing children to confront the consequences of their own actions. In either case, the children wind up being overprotected and socially underdeveloped (Baumrind, 1973).

Although a unidirectional, parent-to-child causal hypothesis is one way to explain parent–child correlations, there are problems with this approach. Just to mention one of the most obvious, you will recall from the behavioral-genetics chapter (Chapter 5) that brothers and sisters can be quite different from one another, and adopted brothers and sisters can be extremely different. How are we to explain this within-family diversity if we assume that parents "create their children psychologically"? To explain the diversity and yet hold to a belief in a unidirectional, parent-to-child effect, we would have to argue that parents treat each child differently. But why should parents be authoritative with one and authoritarian with another? And why should a mother be sensitive with one child but not with another? Are parents in fact this fickle?

Child-to-Parent Effects

Given the problem that family-study and adoption-study data create for the unidirectional, parent-to-child hypothesis, you might want to consider an alternative means of explaining parent–child correlations. Equally plausible from a purely logical point of view is a unidirectional, child-to-parent causal hypothesis. From this point of view, children create certain characteristics in their parents. Pleasant, cooperative infants might create mothers who are sensitive to them, and instrumentally competent children might encourage an authoritative style in their parents. Richard Bell and Lawrence Harper have elaborated on this point of view in a book entitled *Child Effects on Adults* (Bell & Harper, 1977). In it they show that every putative parent-to-child effect in socialization could just as parsimoniously be explained as a child-to-parent effect. As an illustration, take the finding that parents who are "restrictive" of their children tend to have children who are more dependent than average (Maccoby & Masters, 1970, p. 143). The parent-to-child explanation for this relationship is that restrictive parents prevent their children from getting experience in physical and social situations where they could develop some independent coping skills. The child-to-parent explanation is the reverse: parents who perceive a lack of coping skills in their children respond by being restrictive of them. As Richard Bell points out, "such a reaction is not restricted to young children" (Bell & Harper, 1977, p. 73). When we, as adults, perceive our own parents becoming old and feeble, thereby losing some of their skills for coping, what is our natural response? We become protective and even restrictive of them. Restrictiveness, therefore, could just as easily be a consequence of poor coping skills as a cause of them.

Just as there are problems with the parent-to-child hypothesis, so, too, are there problems with the child-to-parent hypothesis. Aside from the fact that it defies common sense to believe that parents' behavior toward their children would be dictated solely by characteristics of the children, there are ample data to show that parents are not controlled by their children. Studies of quality of attachment, for example, show that a single child will often have attachment relationships that differ from the mother to the father (see Campos, Barret, Lamb, Goldsmith, & Stenberg, 1983, p. 868). If it were the child alone who dictated the relationship, the quality of attachment would be the same in both cases. By the same token, one parent might be permissive and the other authoritarian, both with the same child. Again, it is obvious that it is not the child who is in total control.

Bidirectional Effects in Socialization

By considering both parent-to-child and child-to-parent effects in development, we have opened the door to considering an interactional view of development. This view is commonly labeled the *bidirectional* view because it considers the mutual effects parents and children can have on each other or, in a broader context, the mutual effects that any two people can have on each other. From the bidirectional point of view, quality of attachment, parenting style, and the host of other variables that we could assess by viewing parent and child together are a joint function of the characteristics, beliefs, expectancies, and values of each of the two parties. Because young infants tend to be quite short on beliefs, expectancies, and values, you might think that the parents would still come out as the prime movers, even in a bidirectional process. To a large extent this is true. However, psychologists have discovered that there are a number of infant characteristics that can have a profound effect on shaping the parent–child interaction. One of the most important is temperament.

The Importance of Temperament

In the 1950s it was standard psychiatric lore that all childhood behavioral problems were due to inadequate parenting. In a clever play on words, the French term for "sea sickness" *(mal de mer)* was turned into "mother sickness" *(mal de mère)* to describe the developmental problem. Even psychotic disorders such as schizophrenia and autism were blamed on the parents. The belief that parents were unilaterally responsible for their children's outcomes ran contrary, however, to the experience of psychiatrists Alexander Thomas, Stella Chess, and Herbert Birch. Their clinical experience indicated quite clearly that parental practices that have one effect on one child can have an altogether different effect on another. For example, a domineering, authoritarian parenting style might result in either an anxious, submissive child or a defiant, antagonistic one. To explain the different outcomes, Thomas, Chess, and Birch (1968) argued that a child's temperament must be taken into account.

Temperament in its current use refers to characteristic styles of behavior—what Thomas, Chess, and Birch have called the "how" of behavior (see Figure 12-8). Emotionality, irritability, activity, and sociability are among the classic behavioral dimensions that are said to reflect one's temperament. (For a more elaborate but related list of temperament dimensions, see table in Box 12-3.) In illustration of the separability of temperament from other aspects of behavior, Thomas, Chess, and Birch point out that

> Two children may each eat skillfully or throw a ball accurately.
> . . . Yet, they may differ with respect to the intensity with which they
> act, the rate at which they move, the mood that they express, the
> readiness with which they shift to a new activity, and the ease with
> which they will approach a new toy, situation, or playmate (1968, p. 4).

Aside from being the "how" of behavior, temperaments are distinguished from other aspects of personality in that they are *constitutionally* based. This is a noncommittal way of saying that temperaments are somehow—and no one knows how—rooted in our biology. Given our ignorance regarding the roots of temperaments, the term constitutional has the advantage of allowing developmentalists to remain uncommitted regarding specific genetic, prenatal, or postnatal precursors to temperament while being quite committed on other points, such as the belief that temperaments are far more fixed and less subject to momentary influence than are nontemperamental aspects of personality. A second belief is that differences in temperament should be present from birth. To date, the first belief has not been completely validated (see Box 12-3), but the second has.

The New York Longitudinal Study   Although young infants do not have all of the cognitive and behavioral traits that are used in describing an adult personality, they do have temperaments. Thomas, Chess, and Birch hypothesized that differences in their temperaments might help to shape parent–child interactions during the early years of development in a way that would affect development over a long-term period. To test this hypothesis they began a longitudinal study in 1956, which they called the New York Longitudinal Study (NYLS). The study, which continues today, has focused pri-

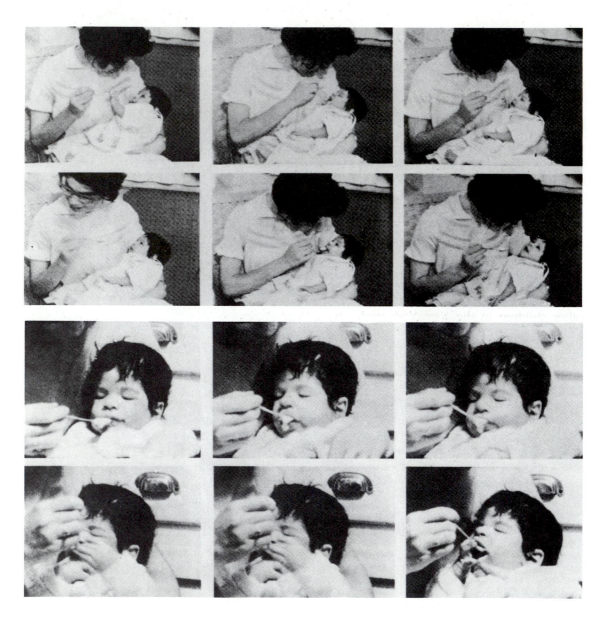

FIGURE 12-8
Differences in Adaptability
Differences in temperament are observable early in life. Here we see a difference in adaptability—one of the dimensions of temperament—between a brother and sister. Both were 3 months old when tested for their willingness to accept a new food. Hallie (top panel) is very accepting. Russ (bottom panel), however, rejects the new food. The difference between this pair of infants is not due to momentary factors; rather it is due to a relatively stable temperamental difference. Hallie adapts easily to almost all new aspects of the environment; Russ does not.

marily on 133 individuals and their families. These individuals entered the study at the age of 3 months and have now been followed into adulthood (Chess & Thomas, 1984). In addition to the 133 original subjects, a group of 97 Puerto Rican children and 52 mentally retarded children have been included along with their families. The primary reason for the additional samples was to enhance the generalizability of conclusions. The original sample of 133 children came from 84 families who were somewhat special by virtue of being predominantly Jewish, college-educated, middle- and upper-middle-class families. Because the samples of Puerto Rican and retarded children come from different ethnic, educational, and socioeconomic backgrounds, they provide useful comparison groups.

The major contribution that Thomas, Chess, and Birch have made lies in their conclusion that the results of parent–child interactions in development may be due more to the *goodness of fit* between infant temperaments and adult practices than to either one of these factors alone. A good example of the goodness-of-fit principle comes from the developmental history of a boy named Bobby (Thomas & Chess, 1977, p. 95), one of the original NYLS participants. Bobby was characterized, along with 25 percent of the other children in the New York study, as a *slow-to-warm-up* baby. This meant, in part, that he needed time to adapt to new people and situations. The parenting style of Bobby's parents was not well suited, however, for a child with Bobby's temperament. For slow-to-warm-up children, parents who are patient but encouraging provide the best fit. Bobby's parents were not this way. If he rejected some new food, they never served it to him again. When he was shy and fearful on the playground, his parents decided to keep him at home. The result of this poor fit was that at age 10 Bobby was a loner who lived on a diet of hamburgers, applesauce, and medium-boiled eggs.

In addition to the slow-to-warm up temperament, Thomas, Chess, and Birch identified two other temperament types that they labeled *easy* (40 percent of the sample) and *difficult* (10 percent of the sample). These types are identified by their scores on five behavioral dimensions: *rhythmicity* (for example, regularity in feeding, eating, and bowel movements), *intensity,* (for example, intensity of crying or laughing), *mood* (for example, tendency to smile or frown, fuss or show pleasure), *adaptability* (for example, ability to adjust to new routines), and *approach/withdrawal* (for example, tendency to seek or avoid new experiences). Easy babies, as you can guess from the label assigned to them, are regular, quick to adapt, pleasant in mood, low in the intensity of their reactions, and have a tendency to approach rather than withdraw when facing new experiences. This temperament seems to serve them well, because they adapt easily in a great variety of environments. Michael Rutter (1979), for example, has gone so far as to describe them as "invulnerable," able to go unaffected by all the family "flak." Difficult children, on the other hand, need very special care. This is reflected in the fact that difficulty of temperament, particularly when it exists

BOX 12-3
Measuring Temperament in Infants and Other Children

The clinician or researcher interested in measuring temperament in children can select from some 26 temperament measures currently in use (Hubert, Wachs, Peters-Martin, & Gandour, 1982). The great number is due to the fact that there is no consensus yet on just how we are to measure what Thomas, Chess, and Birch defined as the "how" of behavior. Some measures are based on interviews, others on observations, and others on questionnaires. These and other differences among the instruments, however, are not so important to us as the similarities. The major similarity is that all take measures on a number of specific dimensions of behavior that are thought to reflect overall temperament. For Thomas, Chess, and Birch (1968), these dimensions were activity, rhythmicity, adaptability, approach, threshold, intensity, mood, persistence, and distractibility. To get an idea of what

behaviors are included in each of these dimensions, examine the list of behavioral descriptions in the table below.

Because the original Thomas, Chess, and Birch procedure for measuring their nine dimensions of temperament was laborious and hard to use, there has since been some streamlining of measurement procedures. One example is the Perception of Baby Temperament Scales (PBT), a measure that was the source of all the behavioral descriptions in the table below. To get a temperament rating using this test, parents sort index cards with the nine behavioral descriptions into three piles that correspond to the perceptions "very much like my baby," "sometimes like my baby," and "not at all like my baby." Following this sorting, babies can be scored on each of the nine dimensions of the test (see Huitt & Ashton, 1982).

Perception of Baby Temperament Scales

I. Activity

1. During a bath, she kicks, splashes and wiggles. She is full of activity at these periods.
2. Her play with toys is active; she often kicks her legs and waves her arms.
3. During diapering and dressing, she squirms and kicks much of the time. She is so active that I sometimes have trouble doing these tasks.
4. She usually lies still during diapering and dressing. She rarely squirms and kicks during these activities.
5. She usually lies fairly still during sleep. She awakens in just about the same position as when she fell asleep.
6. When I feed her solid food, she tends to sit quietly, she rarely squirms or kicks.

II. Rhythmicity

1. She generally goes to sleep at about the same time each day for naps and nighttime sleep. She does not vary more than a half hour from one day to the next.
2. She generally takes about the same amount of food (milk) each day. It is not hard to anticipate how much she will eat.
3. She likes to be fed at about the same time each day. Hungry times do not vary more than a half hour from day-to-day.
4. She is unpredictable in when she likes to be fed. Hungry times vary by more than an hour from one day to the next.
5. She is unpredictable in the time when she will awaken from a nap or nighttime sleep. Awakening time may vary 1-2 hours from one day to the next.
6. The time when bowel movements occur shows no particular pattern from one day to the next.

III. Adaptability

1. When I changed her feeding schedule, she adjusted to the new routine within a day or two.
2. When we take her to a friend's house she doesn't seem to mind going to sleep in an unfamiliar bed or crib.
3. Usually when I interrupt her routine to change her diapers or clothes, she smiles or seems pleasant.
4. Usually she becomes a bit fussy when I interrupt her activities to change her diapers or clothing.
5. If I give her a food she doesn't like at first, she usually comes to accept it after one or two feedings.
6. She really doesn't like other people to feed or diaper her, even a familiar babysitter or grandparent.

IV. Approach

1. When I take her along on a shopping trip, she seems to enjoy the new sights and sounds.
2. When a visitor comes over and spends some time in our home, she shows a lot of interest in that person.
3. When I give her a new toy or other object to play with, she takes it right away and looks it over.
4. Often she doesn't play with a new toy or play object right away. She seems to warm up to new objects gradually.
5. When I give her a new food, she usually shows a little hesitation.
6. When I try out a new activity with her, such as swinging or using a jumper or walker, she is usually a little apprehensive at first.

BOX 12-3 Continued

V. Threshold

1. She rarely fusses when she has dirty diapers. It doesn't seem to bother her at all.
2. Loud or sudden sounds don't seem to bother her much. Often, she doesn't even notice them.
3. She does not show a strong reaction to the temperature of her food. She eats vegetables and cereal as readily whether they are cold or warm.
4. She reacts noticeably to the temperature of foods. If her vegetables or cereal are too cold, she will not eat them.
5. When she is asleep, loud sounds will often awaken her.
6. If I mix a food she doesn't like so well with one that she does like, she notices the difference right away.

VI. Intensity

1. At times when she is restless and nothing seems interesting to her, she usually lets me know by crying fairly loudly.
2. When I'm playing actively with her, she usually squeals and laughs vigorously.
3. When I'm feeding her and she is full, she lets me know in very active ways such as crying loudly, spitting out the food or pushing the spoon away.
4. When I'm feeding her and she is full, she lets me know in little ways by such things as letting food drool from her mouth or quietly turning away her head.
5. During feedings, she has a good appetite but she takes her time drinking or eating.
6. When she is upset because she has on a soiled diaper, she usually makes quiet or whimpering sounds to show her discomfort.

VII. Mood

1. When I bathe her, she usually smiles or laughs. She seems to enjoy bathing times.
2. Sometimes people come over whom the baby has been around fairly often. She generally is friendly and laughs or smiles at them.
3. When she wakes up from a nap, she almost always smiles and seems happy.
4. When she wakes up from a nap, she often is a bit fussy.
5. When I feed her and I need to interrupt the feeding for such things as burping, she seems to fuss for a bit when these interruptions occur.
6. She almost always has a fussy period each day.

VIII. Persistence

1. If I'm feeding her several foods and she likes one of them more than the others, she usually isn't happy unless I let her have all that she wants of her favorite food.

2. When I play a game with her like peek-a-boo, and we have to stop, she often expresses a wish to continue the game longer.

3. Once I get her settled in an interesting activity I can often count on having a half an hour while she plays by herself.

4. She doesn't like to spend more than about 10 minutes in one place or doing one thing without a change. She seems to like a lot of variety in her activities.

5. If a toy she wants gets out of reach, she usually will lose interest in it within a minute or two.

6. Her attention moves quickly from one to another. Usually she plays with even her favorite toy for only a few minutes, before moving on to another one.

IX. Distractibility

1. I can usually persuade her to stay in her crib a bit longer when she wants to get out by giving her a couple of toys to play with.

2. When she's upset by some caregiving procedure, for example, cutting her hair or nails, I can usually quiet her and continue if I give her something to play with.

3. If she's crying because she's hungry, I can often quiet her at least for a few minutes by picking her up or giving her a toy.

4. When she cries because she's hungry, nothing satisfies her until she gets fed. At these times, she is not easily distracted by a toy or cuddling.

5. When she's hungry, she really concentrates on eating or drinking. It takes a lot to draw her attention away from her meal.

6. If you take something away from her that she's interested in, she fusses and usually won't accept a substitute right away.

SOURCE: "Parents' Perception of Infant Development: A Psychometric Study" by W. G. Huitt and P. T. Ashton, 1982, *Merrill-Palmer Quarterly, 28,* pp. 95-109.

A second example of a streamlined temperament measure is the parent-interview scale called The Infant Behavior Questionnaire developed by Mary Rothbart (1981) at the University of Oregon. It takes only about 20 minutes to complete, and consists of items like the one below, which parents answer by circling a number from 1 (never) to 7 (always). They circle "X" when the item does not apply:

During the past week, when being undressed, how often did your baby:

Wave his/her arms and kick?

1   2   3   4   5   6   7   X

Cry?

1   2   3   4   5   6   7   X

Smile or laugh?

1   2   3   4   5   6   7   X

BOX 12-3 Continued

Rothbart's measure does not yield a score on exactly the same dimensions that Thomas, Chess, and Birch identified, but the dimensions are similar. You should note that although this measure relies on parents' retrospective memories, it reduces the chance for memory error by asking only about recent behavior. Also, by dealing with specific behaviors, it eliminates the chance for subjectivity, which would be present if we asked parents broad questions such as "How active is your child?"

One of the most crucial questions to be asked about temperament measures is whether they validate the assumptions that temperament is constitutionally based and relatively stable across time. The evidence is somewhat inconclusive at present, but most researchers are willing to blame the inconclusiveness on the inadequacy of our current tests rather than the inadequacy of the temperament concept itself. Evidence that temperament has a constitutional basis rests primarily on heritability studies employing twins. One encouraging result comes from the Lousiville Twin Study, in which an overall heritability coefficient of .44

was obtained for temperament-related behavioral differences among infants at 1 year of age (Matheny, Dolan, & Wilson, 1976). At the same time, other twin studies show impossibly large values for the heritability of temperament (for example, Plomin & Rowe, 1977), and still others show little to no heritability for key dimensions in the temperament concept such as activity (Matheny, 1980). As regards stability, additional data from the Louisville Twin Study provided the encouraging result that from 6 to 24 months of age the changes in children's temperament ratings were small (Matheny, Wilson, Dolan, & Krantz, 1981). A problem in interpreting these and similar data, however, is that they are based on mothers' reports of infant temperament. This makes it impossible to tell whether the stability exists because mothers' opinions are stable or because childrens' temperaments are stable (see Campos, Barrett, Lamb, Goldsmith, & Stenberg, 1983). The best evidence for the cross-situational consistency of temperament comes from a comparison of parents' responses to the various items on Rothbart's Infant Behavior Questionnaire. For

in the late preschool years, is predictive of later psychiatric problems. Thomas, Chess, and Birch found, for example, that 70 percent of their difficult children had some form of behavioral disorder by late childhood or adolescence.

In keeping with their goodness-of-fit theory of development, Thomas and Chess (1977) suggest that the enhanced risk of children with difficult temperaments is not due to the inherent bad character of these children;

example, there are 17 items on the scale that attempt to measure a child's overall acitivity level. Each deals with a different situation (for example, bathing, diapering, or feeding), yet parents report that children who are "active" in one situation tend to be "active" in the others as well. This result tends to validate the assumption that temperament is stable across situations. The problem is that so little research has addressed the issue of cross-situational consistency that there is a lack of corroborating evidence, making the results from Rothbart's questionnaire inconclusive as well.

The actual status that temperament eventually achieves as a developmental variable will depend largely on how well we are able to measure it. Thus far the measurements are good enough to show consistent evidence of individual differences in temperament and to delineate certain temperament types such as those of difficult, easy, and slow-to-warm-up children. Also, it has been possible to show that scores on some of the temperament dimensions have some predictive value. The most notable example is the relationship between difficult

temperament in the preschool years and later behavioral and psychiatric problems. Nonetheless, the concept of temperament—despite its clinical usefulness—is not yet a well-defined scientific concept. To the contrary, temperament is what researcher M. Berger (1982) has called a "fuzzy entity." This fuzziness has led to measurement problems that in turn have made it impossible to test conclusively the theoretical assumptions we have made. As the concept of temperament becomes better defined, however, tests will improve, and we can anticipate that the concept of temperament will then play a role in our understanding of a broader range of development than just normal and abnormal personality development. For example, it certainly seems reasonable to expect that the interaction of child temperament with the learning environment could have as large an effect on cognitive development as the interaction of temperament with parental rearing practices has on personality development. We can also expect a temperament–environment interaction in the establishment of the quality of infant–mother attachment.

rather, the risk is elevated because children with difficult temperaments, more so than any others, are likely to obtain a bad "fit" with their environment. Thomas and Chess counsel the parents of such children to be highly consistent in their upbringing, but also tolerant. To illustrate, they offer the case of Carl, one of their most "difficult" children, who as an adult was well adjusted. They attribute Carl's successful adjustment to the parents' understanding of his temperament. According to Thomas and Chess, the parents "knew that if they were patient, presented only one or a few new situations at a time and gave him the opportunity for repeated exposure, Carl would finally adapt positively" (1977, p. 166). And he did.

The goodness-of-fit hypothesis is supported not only by individual case-history data, but by group data as well. Group support, for example, comes from a comparison of the temperament-outcome relations in the sample of 133 middle-class children with the 97 children from Puerto Rican working-class backgrounds. In the Puerto Rican sample, low regularity and arrhythmicity in infant temperament did not predict later adjustment problems. In the primarily Jewish, middle-class sample it did—at least in the infancy and early-childhood years. Why the difference? The explanation, as presented by Richard Lerner (1983), has to do with cultural differences. Low regularity and arrhythmicity in the permissive Puerto Rican families did not cause any parent–child conflict. The reason was that these parents did not place demands on the sleep hours of their children, for example. In general, the Puerto Rican families allowed their children to go to bed and to awaken as they pleased. The same was true for meals. For an arrhythmic child, such a situation provides an obvious good fit. Arrhythmicity in the more-regimented, clock-based world of middle-class professional life was more of a problem, and so the arrhythmic children in this group started life with a poor fit. They were forced into a behavioral mold that ran counter to their temperaments. They adapted, but not without some problems that manifested themselves in the period of infancy and early childhood.

As a footnote to this discussion of different implications for arrhythmicity in different cultural groups, we might consider what happened later in life when the schools rather than the parents became the primary scheduling agents in these children's lives. At this point, the initially arrhythmic children who had been forced to adapt found themselves in good shape; they were temperamentally ready to fit with the school system. The Puerto Rican children were not. According to research by Sam Korn, "Their lack of a regular sleep pattern interfered with their getting sufficient sleep to perform well in school and, in addition, often caused them to be late for arrival to school" (Lerner, 1983, p. 283).

A separate example of group support for the goodness-of-fit hypothesis comes from examining the relationship of activity level to developmental outcomes in the NYLS children. Overall, there was a low incidence of behavioral problems in the Puerto Rican children in early childhood; but when there was a problem, it tended to be related to a high activity level. Problems related to high activity levels were not found in the children of middle- to upper-middle-class professional parents. The reason could again have to do with goodness of fit. The Puerto Rican families lived in smaller spaces with more people crowded into them than did the middle-class NYLS families. In the more-crowded conditions, a high activity level obviously would find a poorer fit than in the more-spacious surroundings of middle-class homes and playgrounds.

Other Evidence   Lest you get the impression that the NYLS is the only source of evidence for bidirectional effects involving infant temperaments and parental responses to differences in temperaments, we should focus briefly on other studies that lead to the same bidirectional conclusion. One particularly good example from the recent literature is Norwegian psychologist Dan Olweus's causal account for the development of aggression (Olweus, 1980). Working with early-childhood predictors of aggression in a set of 76 sixth-grade boys, Olweus discovered that a childhood temperament he labeled as "hot-headed and impetuous" went hand in hand with mothers' permissiveness for aggression. He reasoned that these were not independent events; more likely, hot-headed children wear their parents down, making the parents increasingly permissive of aggression in their children as they become ever-more habituated to having an aggressive child. If this scenario is correct, it provides another clear instance of a poor fit. Hot-headed children need parents who are especially vigilant in maintaining clear rules, not those who are especially permissive in allowing their children to break them.

Research from a new longitudinal study being conducted at Stanford University by Eleanor Maccoby comes to a conclusion regarding mother–child interactions that is quite similar to that of Olweus (see Maccoby, Snow, & Jacklin, 1984). Focusing on a mother's efforts to teach her child during a laboratory session, Maccoby and her colleagues found evidence between the ages of 12 and 18 months for what they call an "escalating cycle" of behavior. The cycle begins when mothers of difficult children withdraw from their efforts to influence their child's behavior (perhaps in anticipation of the uncooperativeness and degree of protest that will ensue). The withdrawal, however, only has the effect of increasing the very behaviors that led to the withdrawal in the first place (Maccoby, Snow, & Jacklin, 1984, p. 469). Quite interestingly, however, evidence for this cycle appeared only between mothers and sons, not mothers and daughters. In fact, mothers of difficult daughters tended not to withdraw from efforts to influence their daughters; instead, these mothers increased their efforts slightly.

Taken altogether, the work on the interactive dynamics of child–parent relations that was begun by the NYLS gives the impression that bidirectional theories may be better equipped than unidirectional theories to account for the data. This is certainly true for the data in this section, none of which can be accounted for by a purely unidirectional theory. The reason is that, for the cases presented here, neither parental behavior alone nor child temperament alone have much explanatory power. However, theories that integrate the two into a dynamic interactive picture seem to offer a very credible account. The same thing can be said for Gerald Patterson's coercion theory, a popular social-learning view of how families can foster the development of "out of control" children.

Patterson's Coercion Theory

Although many studies have been conducted that link individual parenting variables to aggression in children, it is generally acknowledged today that in order to understand the development of aggression within the family context (or the development of any other psychological attribute, for that matter), we need more than just a set of correlations between measured attributes of parents and their children. What we need are longitudinal studies that focus on the dynamic interactions of individuals. Such studies are beginning to appear. One of the most informative was the study by Daniel Olweus (1980), just cited, which showed that mothers became permissive over time in response to their children's aggressiveness. Research by Gerald Patterson (1982) has led to the development of a theory regarding family interactions over time that also relates parent and child characteristics in a causal way.

Patterson's coercion theory (see Patterson, 1982) has developed out of more than 30 years of experience in working with highly aggressive, "out-of-control" children and their families. The theory offers a dynamic, interactive account to explain how these overly aggressive children develop within a family context. The theory begins with the observation that when interacting with children—particularly preschool children—parents spend much of their time directing their children to behave in desired ways. Naturalistic observations show, for example, that parental direction occurs at a rate of once every 3 or 4 minutes (Patterson, 1980, p. 45). Statements such as "Don't touch that, Billy" or "Please don't talk when mother is talking" are characteristic of these directions. In the terminology of the theory, these parental directions are prompted by "low-key" aversive actions on the part of the child (for example, inappropriate reaching or talking). The parental directions, in turn, serve as low-key aversive stimuli for the child. The goal of effective parenting is to handle all conflicts at this low-key level. When parent and child fail to do so, a cycle of events begins that can lead to a pattern of family interactions involving constant bickering and frequent violent flare-ups. Whether this occurs depends largely on the events that immediately follow the minor aversive events.

Whenever a parent directs a child's behavior, the child has two choices: to either yield to the direction or to protest, perhaps by ignoring the parent, whining, or using some more direct form of aggression. What the child does and how the parent responds to the child's behavior is of crucial importance, according to coercion theory. If the child gives in to the parent's direction and the parent then positively reinforces the child for cooperating, then an interaction has occurred that shapes the child toward prosocial action in the future. But what if the child whines or otherwise fails to cooperate. Now, the parent has a choice: to back off, or to initiate coercion. Backing off is a bad strategy in the long run, but in the short run a parent might choose to back off, just to stop the aversive whining. In this case, the parent has again reinforced the child's behavior, but the reinforcement is for protesting and not for cooperating.

Because backing off has long-term negative consequences, a more far-sighted parent would choose to initiate coercion. Often at this stage a threat is offered. Again the child has a choice to comply or not. What if the child fails to comply and commences to whine, pout, or protest even more than before? Now the parent must decide whether to execute the threat or not. If the threat is one involving immediate, swift, irreversible consequences, then enforcing the threat will terminate the interaction and the child will have lost. But what if the parent is reluctant to execute the threat and, instead, opens the door to further whining and negotiating on the part of the child (for example, "Billy, you're going to clean up your room or else"). Now the interaction is back to where it began, except that both parties are operating at higher intensities. The threats are more aversive and so are the counterattacks. The level of intensity will make it ever-more attractive for parents just to back out of the episode. But to do this is to be inappropriately permissive. The alternative is to carry through with one of the stronger threats and thereby become power assertive in a physically abusive way. The parent is obviously in a bind. The longer the coercive cycle of threat and counterattack is allowed to continue, the worse the bind becomes.

At the end of a coercive episode, no matter how long it lasts, Patterson's theory focuses observers on two measures of outcome. First, did the parent win or the child? Second, how intense did the coercive attempts become until one side gave in? By taking these outcome measures and multiplying them across the episodes—which occur, as we have seen, at a rate of some 15 to 20 per hour of parent–child interaction—a rather important learning history is constructed. Children learn either that retaliation works or that it does not work, and they learn the levels to which coercive episodes must be raised before being resolved. This latter learning is quite important. Because both parties learn the level of escalation required to terminate the episodes, episodes tend to move quickly to that critical level. Thus, in families with a history of escalating coercive episodes, a conflict that begins with a very low-key parental direction ("Would you mind changing the channel?") can develop quickly into full-blown fights.

Patterson's theory has some very important implications for therapy in families where aggression has gotten out of hand. Patterson's primary interest in the theory, in fact, has been as a guide for therapeutic interventions.

For our purposes, we can put the theory to a different use: we can use it to give a developmental account of at least one of the reasons why nonnurturant, physically punitive parents are present in the same families as aggressive children. The explanation is that nonnurturant parents, through their inattention, generally do not reinforce their children for compliance and prosocial actions. On occasions when children are compliant, therefore, the parents fail to reinforce them for their compliance. Failing to get positive consequences for compliance, the children of nonnurturant parents will be more likely in the future to choose noncompliance. At least through noncompliance a child can get the attention of a nonnurturant parent. Thus, when a nonnurturant parent says "Go clean your room," the child becomes ever-more likely to say no.

Because an early history of nonreinforcement for cooperation tips children toward noncompliant behavioral choices, nonnurturant parents are faced with more instances of noncompliance than nurturant parents. With more instances of noncompliance, there are more occasions for punitive control. From the outset, then, we expect nonnurturant parents to come out higher on any measure of the frequency of punishment. They have to punish more frequently because they face noncompliance more frequently. But they do not have to be abusive in their punishment necessarily. How then can we account for the relationship between severity of punishment and aggressiveness in children? The answer comes from the theory's statement that coercive cycles escalate. As they escalate, the parent is threatening (and eventually having to carry out) increasingly severe punishments and the child is protesting ever-more aggressively. The severity of punishment relates to the aggressiveness of the child, therefore, because these two child and parent attributes grow in the same cycle of events.

Whether the causal picture for the development of aggressive interactions among parents and children occurs as Patterson's coercion theory specifies is not yet known. The answer will come from longitudinal studies, which provide the only means of knowing the actual relation among child noncompliance, aggression, and parental punitiveness. At present, one result that might cause us to wonder about the validity of the coercion theory as applied to the development of aggressive children is that normal children respond to punishment by ceasing to do whatever brought on the punishment. Highly aggressive, out-of-control children, however, respond in the opposite way (Patterson, 1982). Stepped-up punishment only works to increase the frequency of the aversive behavior. Might it be, then, that out-of-control children are just constitutionally different and that the punitiveness or permissiveness of their parents is a consequence, not a cause, of this difference? Longitudinal studies are clearly needed to know for sure the sequence of events, but in all likelihood Patterson will at least be correct in viewing both parental punitiveness and child aggressiveness as developing together through a mutually determining process.

UNIDIRECTIONAL MODELS RECONSIDERED

In light of the rich interactive views of development that are offered by bidirectional models, we need to reconsider the unidirectional models of Ainsworth, Baumrind, and Hoffman. What have the bidirectional models taught us about these as theories?

One thing we have learned is that unidirectional models are heuristically limiting. The limitation is created by the fact that unidirectional models spotlight caretaker variables as *the* variables of importance in child development. This tends to blind us to the many other factors that can play a part in the epigenetic equation. Development is a much more richly interactive process than unidirectional models lead us to appreciate.

The second thing we have learned is that there are alternative explanations for the parent–child correlations that have been used to give credibility to unidirectional accounts of developmental causation. Infant temperaments could account for some of the correlations; so could the cultural, historic, or even genetic context in which parents and children interact (see Chapter 5). As a result, the older unidirectional models of social development now face serious challenges from the newer bidirectional models. This theoretical competition is good for science because it leads to the consideration of new and different data. Recent research on the development of secure attachments illustrates the process.

Attachment theorists have claimed that parental sensitivity in early childhood determines the security of the attachment relationship as measured in the strange situation. This claim, which is backed up by a weak but reliable correlation between sensitivity and security of attachment, has been attacked on two grounds. One is that parental sensitivity may not be independent of the general characteristics of children, including their temperaments (Goldsmith & Campos, 1982). Some children, for example, might be so difficult in temperament that even skilled and loving mothers would appear insensitive when interacting with them. To the extent that temperament in general shapes sensitivity, then the actual causal model should be a three-part model that shows temperament leading to sensitivity and then sensitivity leading to security, rather than just the two-part, sensitivity-to-security model that was Ainsworth's original formulation. The second grounds for attacking Ainsworth's original causal model is that temperament might also play a role in the strange situation (Kagan, 1982). This test situation is designed to produce mild stress, and the way children handle that stress could be related to their temperaments. In fact, Jerome Kagan (1982) has suggested that the A, B, C groupings are nothing more than a sign of how children with different stress thresholds respond to strangers and maternal separation.

To deal with Kagan's hypothesis regarding what the strange situation in fact measures, researchers have examined how temperament relates to

Ainsworth's A, B, and C groupings. Contrary to what Kagan predicted, researchers have found temperament and the A, B, C classifications to be largely unrelated (Ainsworth, 1983; Bates, Maslin, & Frankel, 1985; Sroufe, 1985). Nonetheless, Alan Sroufe has acknowledged that temperament needs to be taken into account and has even suggested that there could be temperament-related variability within the A, B, and C classifications (Sroufe, 1985, p. 10). He has also acknowledged that considerations of temperament might help solve the problem of knowing why some children wind up with Group-A insecure attachments and others with Group-C ambivalent attachments, when the children's developmental histories alone would predict similar attachments.

The argument that temperament and other child characteristics affect sensitivity makes intuitive sense, but it has yet to receive any strong support. Ainsworth (1983), for example, reports having failed to find any evidence that differences in early infant behavior might predict later attachment. The only early-life predictor has been mother's sensitivity. Ainsworth argues that we should not be surprised by this once we realize that sensitivity is a measure of how well a mother has adjusted her behavior to fit her infant's moods and needs; it is not, therefore, just a measure of mother's behavior per se. This means that nothing in Ainsworth's approach denies the relevance of children's temperaments and other individual characteristics. These characteristics are relevant because mothers must adjust to them, just as Thomas, Chess, and Birch have said. But the sensitivity measure, in that it is a measure of the success of a mother's adjustments, tends to mask individual differences in infants. Only if there were some infants who were so difficult and trying that few mothers would be able to learn to anticipate their needs and moods would the temperament-causes-sensitivity argument have merit. Ainsworth and others (see, for example, Sroufe, 1985) have found no evidence that this is the case. Mothers who make the effort are able to adjust their behavior as needed to mesh with that of their infants, regardless of whatever highly individual characteristics infants might bring to the relationship.

In brief summary, then, Ainsworth's theory regarding mother's role in creating the groundwork for a secure attachment is still viable, even after one acknowledges that mothers do not behave in a vacuum. Surely it is easier to establish sensitive relations with some infants than with others; nonetheless, research to date indicates that the sensitivity that is found in caretaker–infant interactions is more a function of caretakers than of infants. To this extent, Ainsworth's parent-to-child, unidirectional model has held up well as an explanation for the correlation between sensitivity and later attachment. Whether Baumrind's and Hoffman's unidirectional theories will fare as well remains to be seen. The correlational data on which their theories are based have yet to be questioned from the bidirectional perspective in the way that Ainsworth's have. Regardless of the outcome of any specific theoretical debate, however, we will eventually understand children's social development within the family much better as a result of the challenge that bidirectional theories provide to unidirectional ones. They have provided us with new explanatory hypotheses and have forced us to think critically about existing theories.

SUMMARY

Social development for many animals, humans included, begins with the establishment of an infant–mother attachment. In humans this attachment first manifests itself around 6 months of age. Evidence comes from the fact that mother recognition, separation protest, and stranger anxiety all appear about this time. Although all infants form attachment relations with a mother figure, the quality of that attachment can vary. Measuring quality of attachment using Ainsworth's strange situation leads to the conclusion that there are at least three different types of attachment: secure attachment (Group B), avoidant attachment (Group A), and ambivalent attachment (Group C). According to Ainsworth, there are two primary antecedents to secure attachment. One is contact comfort and the other is the mother's sensitivity to her infant's needs. Ainsworth in fact postulates a causal chain of events that leads from mother's sensitivity to secure attachment to successful developmental outcomes.

Baumrind, like Ainsworth, sees the parents' behavior as crucial in determining their children's outcomes. In Baumrind's case, however, the concern is not with parental sensitivity and contact comfort in infancy but with parenting style in childhood. Based on measures of parental control, maturity demands, nurturance, and parent–child communication, Baumrind identified the authoritative, authoritarian, and permissive parenting styles. Of these, only the authoritative style was associated with consistently good outcomes in instrumental competence.

Hoffman is a third developmental psychologist who has proposed that parental behavior has important unidirectional effects in determining aspects of socialization. The aspect he is concerned with is prosocial behavior and empathy for others. He has found that most children who have these qualities come from homes where the parents tend to use inductive rather than power-assertive or love-withdrawal control practices. Induction, Hoffman argues, directs children's attention to the effects of their behavior for others. This has affective and cognitive consequences that contribute to prosocial development. Power assertion and love withdrawal, on the other hand, focus children's attention on themselves, thereby inhibiting their development of an understanding and concern for how their behavior affects others. Data show that the use of power assertion as a primary control tactic is found among the parents of nonempathetic and generally antisocial children. Abused children show this relationship quite strongly.

As theorists, Ainsworth, Baumrind, and Hoffman all share in their emphasis on the parents as the prime factors in children's socialization. In support of their parent-to-child causal hypotheses, however, they only have correlational data. Ainsworth, Baumrind, and Hoffman prefer to interpret these data using a unidirectional, parent-to-child causal hypothesis. In their view, the parents shape their children, not the other way around. Logically, however, a child-to-parent hypothesis is equally as plausible as a parent-to-child hypothesis for explaining parent–child correlations. A third alternative hypothesis is a bidirectional hypothesis that acknowledges child-to-parent as well as parent-to-child effects. The results of a number of contemporary investigations seem to be more readily interpretable from the bidirectional perspective than from any of the unidirectional perspectives.

The first investigation to argue strongly for a bidirectional interpretation of socialization outcomes was Thomas, Chess, and Birch's New York Longitudinal Study. Both the individual data and group data from this study suggest that outcomes are a function of the goodness of fit between children's temperaments and the social environments in which they develop. This study and others have defined temperaments as constitutionally based differences in the "how" of behavior. Measures of temperament yield temperament classifications such as easy, difficult, and slow to warm up.

Patterson's work on the development of "out of control" children has led to a coercion-theory explanation for how they develop. The coercion theory, like the goodness-of-fit theory, is based on a bidirectional model of parent–child influence. In this case, the interactions of interest begin with minor aversive events. How the parents handle the job of achieving control in these instances and how their children respond to the control techniques jointly determine the developmental outcome. If parents achieve control before events escalate, the outcome will be a well-controlled child. If events escalate to the point that parents must either capitulate in their demands or enforce a harsh punishment, out-of-control children will develop.

Despite the fact that bidirectional models seem to capture the interactive nature of epigenesis better than unidirectional models, the ultimate test for them as theories lies in whether they are better at accounting for the existing data. In the case of the correlational data dealt with by Ainsworth, the unidirectional model is still viable, because researchers have not yet shown that temperament is directly related to the security of attachment. No evaluation can be made of the relative merits of unidirectional and bidirectional models for explaining the correlational data relating parenting style to instrumental competence and relating control practices to prosocial development.

SUGGESTIONS FOR FURTHER READING

Baumrind, D. (1972). Socialization and instrumental competence in young children. In W. W. Hartup (Ed.), *The young child: Review of research* (Vol. 2). Washington, D.C.: National Association for the Education of Young Children. A useful introduction to the research and conclusions of Diana Daumrind regarding precursors to the development of competence in young children.

Belsky, J., Lerner, R. M., & Spanier, G. B. (1984). *The child in the family.* Reading, MA: Addison-Wesley. This is a general text that deals with many practical issues in child development not covered in the present chapter.

Chess, S. & Thomas, A. (1984). *Origins and evolution of behavior disorders: From infancy to early adult life.* New York: Brunner/Mazel. This volume offers a comprehensive treatment of findings from the New York Longitudinal Study along with interesting discussions of their implications.

Lamb, M. E., Thompson, R. A., Gardner, W., & Charnov, E. L. (1985). *Infant-mother attachment: The origins and developmental significance of individual differences in strange situation behavior.* Hillsdale, NJ: Lawrence Erlbaum. This text provides a thorough review of the literature concerning the origins, interpretation, and developmental significance of individual differences in early infant–mother attachment.

Patterson, G. R. (1982). *A social learning approach, Vol. 3: Coercive family process.* Eugene, OR: Castalia Publishing Co. An easy-to-read, informative presentation of Patterson's coercion theory.

CHAPTER 13

Social Development Beyond the Family

Although parents act as the primary agents of socialization during children's earliest years, the parental influence wanes as children gain autonomy and expand social contacts. This chapter will provide an introduction to some of the important topics in children's social development outside the family. The topics are autonomy, children's play, the development of prosocial and antisocial behavior, and the development of self-control.

BEYOND ATTACHMENT TO AUTONOMY

The sequel to the attachment phase of social development is a phase in which the infant achieves some autonomy, or independence (literally self-rule), for the first time. This notion originally comes from Sigmund Freud, who labeled the years from about age 2 to 4 as the *anal period,* a label that hides the fact that the basic developmental issue is whether the child can achieve some sense of self-control and control over the environment. Erik Erikson, an influential psychoanalytic theorist, was perfectly explicit in stating that the years from 2 to 3 are the years in which autonomy is the biggest developmental concern (Erikson, 1950). He believed, moreover, that the "trust" established during the attachment phase forms the basis for the achievement of autonomy. Margaret Mahler (1979), another psychoanalytic theorist, also put autonomy at the forefront in that she labeled the postinfancy years the "separation–individuation phase." Children at this time, she said, go through what is in effect a second birth as they are "hatched" from the "symbiotic mother–child common membrane" (Mahler, 1979, p. 110). Psychoanalytic theorists, therefore, are united in the view that the achievement of autonomy and some separation from the mother are basic goals for normal development in the postinfancy years.

The view of psychoanalytic theorists that children should seek autonomy and separation in the postinfancy years puts the mark of theoretical approval on what seems to be a fundamental pattern in the development of all initially dependent animals. Following a period of intense dependency comes a time for "leaving the nest" and "testing one's wings." A psychologist who has studied this process with particular care is Harry Harlow, formerly of the University of Wisconsin.

Harlow's observations were made on rhesus monkeys living in captivity (see Harlow & Harlow, 1965), but they seem to apply to free-living primates from other species as well (Hinde, 1983, p. 62). To make his observations of the normal process by which mother and infant achieve separation, Harlow housed his animals in a cage arrangement like that shown in Figure 13-1. The four large cages on the corners of the "playpen" field were living cages for mother–infant pairs. Figure 13-2 shows a mother and her infant together in one of the living cages. From the living cages there was access to the playpen area through small openings that only the infant rhesus monkeys could pass through. Doors between the individual playpen units enabled Harlow to control the time the infants got to spend in play with the neighboring infants.

FIGURE 13-1

Harlow's Cage Arrangement for Studying Mother–Infant Separation

This plan shows the arrangement of mother–infant cages and infant play areas used in Harlow's research on mother–infant separation. (After Harlow, 1962)

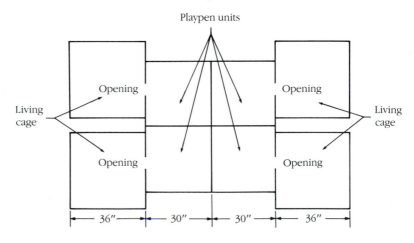

FIGURE 13-2
The Living Cage
Female rhesus monkey together with her infant in one of the living cages used in Harlow's study of normal mother–infant separation.

A not-too-surprising observation that Harlow made in this setting was that mother–infant separation was in part attributable to the infant. The infant sought ever-more separation. As Harlow said, "The outer-world lures of exploration and play are powerful forces acting to produce part-time maternal separation" (Harlow & Harlow, 1965, p. 298).

A more important observation, however, was that the mother participated in the separation. One sign of this, Harlow noted, was that in early infancy, if an infant began to wander off, the mother would retrieve it. If it attempted to wander into the playpen area, which was beyond mother's reach, the mother would block the way. Toward the end of infancy (age 3 months for rhesus monkeys), she no longer did so. Rather, "the mothers left the choice almost entirely to the infant, intervening only when disturbed by some fear-evoking stimulus" (Harlow & Harlow, 1965, p. 302). Moreover, if infants this age tried to nurse or climb on mother's back to be carried, they were likely to be rebuffed. The rebuffs might have consisted of a mother's "vigorously shaking the infant from her body or even stiff-arming the infant" (Harlow & Harlow, 1965, p. 305). Barring any rebuffs from the mother, infants were apt to continue clinging far longer than normal. The developmental history of peer-reared monkeys (see Figure 12-7) gives evidence of this.

In the case of peer-reared monkeys, the attachment figure never becomes rejecting or otherwise encouraging of independence. This produces an atypical developmental pattern. Normally, infant monkeys spend their time together in play, a vital activity for normal social learning (which we will discuss in the following section). Peer-reared monkeys are more likely to spend their time simply clinging to one another, thus depriving themselves of important playtime. Figure 13-3, for example, shows a group of normal, mother-reared 20-day-old rhesus monkeys interacting in play. Their play contrasts sharply with the clinging of peer-reared monkeys twice their age (Figure 13-4). This play deficit continues for some time. Writing of the peer-reared monkeys, Harlow said, "Even by the end of the first year of life, their play tended to be slow-motion, frequently interrupted, caricature of normal infant-monkey play" (Harlow & Harlow, 1965, p. 316).

FIGURE 13-3
Species-Typical Play
This photo shows 20-day-old rhesus monkeys engaging in active social play.

FIGURE 13-4
Species-Atypical Clinging
Two 40-day-old monkeys spend their time together clinging rather than playing.
These monkeys were reared together without mothers as part of Harlow's research
on peer-reared monkeys.

One reason to believe that these observations of monkeys are relevant
to human development as well is the intriguing similarity between the development of peer-reared monkeys and the development of the six children
who were reared in a Nazi prison camp (see pp. 637). The only attachments
these children developed were to each other because adults had been
moved in and out of the Nazi camp (a transit camp, not a death camp) so
quickly that no other relations had formed. When they were brought to
England after the war, the children were all 3 to 4 years old—an age by
which most children have achieved a sense of autonomy and have become
quite sociable, not only with adults but with other children. The six children
attached to each other were not this way.

The children's positive feelings were centered exclusively in
their own group. It was evident that they cared greatly for each other
and not at all for anybody or anything else. They had no other wish
than to be together and became upset when they were separated from

each other, even for short moments. No child would consent to remain upstairs while the others were downstairs, or vice versa, and no child could be taken for a walk or on an errand without the others. If anything of the kind did happen, the single child would constantly ask for the other children while the group would fret for the missing child. (Freud & Dann, 1951/1968, p. 169)

The behavior of these 3- to 4-year-old children, as described by Freud and Dann, sounds quite infantile. Without knowing their ages, one would predict from the intensity of their separation anxiety that the children were around 9 months of age. Obviously, then, the children were retarded socially, and one can only wonder whether this might not be due to a need in humans, like monkeys, for an adult attachment figure to encourage separation and independence.

To summarize this section, the development of autonomy in the postinfancy years is a development that is species typical not just of humans, but of all other animals that experience a dependent infancy. Psychoanalytic theorists focus on the achievement of this autonomy as a major step in normal development. Observations made by Harry Harlow have enhanced our knowledge of the mother–infant separation process by revealing that in rhesus monkeys, the separation is a result of behaviors on both the infant's and the mother's part. When the mother does not behave in the species-typical way to promote an infant's independence, autonomy may be achieved far later than normal.

SOCIAL PLAY

In their first year of life, children show an interest in each other. They look and smile at one another, for example, and when placed together, pairs of post-6-month-olds will make physical contact fairly often. But the interest they show in each other does not result in true interactions, because the overtures that one infant makes to another are generally ignored (Hartup, 1983, p. 114).

The one-sided nature of infant–infant interactions in the first year stands in sharp contrast to the two-sided, reciprocal exchanges that occur between parents and infants. These parent–infant exchanges, which include collaborative activities such as peekaboo, patty cake, and vocal imitation, can be sustained for quite some time. This is due, of course, to the skill of parents. Infants themselves are unskilled in sustaining social interactions unless someone else is actively guiding them (Hartup, 1983, p. 114). Because young infants do not know how to sustain interactions with each other, it is not surprising that they find other infants to be less interesting— and perhaps even less fun—than older children and adults.

Though it may sound subjective to say that infants do not find each other to be fun, the evidence in fact shows that there is a general lack of smiling and laughing among 1-year-olds when they interact (Ross & Goldman, 1976). Willard Hartup has described their interactions as "emotionally neutral" (1983, p. 115). This contrasts with the emotionally charged interactions that take place when 1-year-olds play with adults. Further evidence that adults are more fun comes from preference studies. Observations of infants in a day-care setting where the teacher to child ratio was one to three showed that 1-year-olds spent 42 percent of their time interacting with adults and only 6 percent with the other children (Finkelstein, Dent, Gallagher, & Ramey, 1978).

Much that is true of infant interactions in the first year of life remains true in the second year; however, by the end of the second year we begin to notice some changes. For one thing, infants who play in pairs in the presence of their mothers will spend an increasing amount of time in social proximity to each other and less and less time in proximity to their mothers over the course of the second year. Also, when the older infants interact, they are more likely than younger infants to show some sign that they enjoy the things they can do together. Hildy Ross and Barbara Goldman (1976), for example, found that positive affect was far more likely to accompany the interactions of 2-year-olds than 1-year-olds. There is even a glimmer of a beginning for sustained social interactions. Whereas an overture from one child to another often goes ignored during the first year, by the end of the second year, one child's overture is more likely to result in some form of reciprocation. Judith Rubenstein and Carollee Howes suggest that a basis for the increased peer contact is that older infants discover they share interests that are not shared by adults. Even the most devoted mother, they note, will not take pleasure in "jumping off a step 20 times and wearing pots as hats" (Rubenstein & Howes, 1976, p. 602). Other infants do take an interest in such activities, thereby providing a basis for interaction.

Beginning in the third year, the forms of social interactions among children become so numerous that we need a coding system to make developmental sense of them. Many coding systems for play behavior have been developed, but at their root are some distinctions set up long ago by Mildred Parten (1932). Parten's category system draws distinctions among unoccupied behavior, solitary play, onlooking behavior, parallel play, associative play, and cooperative play. The complete distinctions of play behavior are outlined in Box 13-1, but the basic distinction is in the nature and complexity of the social interactions involved. **Solitary play,** for example, which is quite characteristic of infants in their second year, requires no

---

BOX 13-1
Parten's Category System for Play Behavior

1. *Unoccupied behavior.* The child apparently is not playing, but occupies himself with watching anything that happens to be of momentary interest. When there is nothing exciting taking place, he plays with his own body, gets on and off chairs, just stands around, follows the teacher, or sits in one spot glancing around the room.

2. *Solitary play.* The child plays alone and independently with toys that are different from those used by the children within speaking distance and makes no effort to get close to other children. He pursues his own activity without reference to what others are doing.

3. *Onlooking behavior.* The child spends most of his time watching the other children play. He often talks to the children whom he is observing, asks questions, or gives

suggestions, but he does not overtly enter into the play himself. This type of behavior differs from the unoccupied behavior in that the onlooker is definitely observing particular groups of children, rather than anything that happens to be exciting. The child stands or sits within speaking distance of the group so that he can see and hear everything that takes place.

4. *Parallel play.* The child plays independently, but the activity he chooses naturally brings him among other children. He plays with toys that are like those which the children around him are using, but he plays with the toys as he sees fit and does not try to influence or modify the activity of the children near him. He plays *beside* rather than *with* the other children. There is no attempt to control the coming or going of children in the group.

social interaction. **Parallel play,** in which children play beside one another—often imitating one another without actually cooperating in their play—is mildly social (see Figure 13-5). More socially involved is **associative play,** in which children have a common play activity about which they converse. At the top of the social play scale is **cooperative play,** which involves a group activity in which each participant plays an essential role.

The primary finding from observational studies that have used Parten's coding system or a similar one to describe the interactions of preschool children in free-play settings is that the amount of associative and cooperative play increases dramatically during the preschool years. In Parten's own study, for example, associative play doubled and cooperative play quintupled over the ages 2 to 4 years. Contemporary studies of this same developmental period show similar change. In a recent longitudinal study, Beverly Fagot and Mary Leinbach (1983) found that 4- to 4½-year-olds spent

5. *Associative play.* The child plays with other children. The conversation concerns the common activity. There is a borrowing and loaning of play material, following one another with trains or wagons, and mild attempts to control which children may or may not play in the group. All the members engage in similar if not identical activity. There is no division of labor and no organization of the activity of several individuals around any material goal or product. The children do not subordinate their individual interests to that of the group; instead, each child acts as he wishes. By his conversation with the other children, one can tell that his interest is primarily in his associations, not in his activity. Occasionally, two or three children are engaged in no activity of any duration but are merely doing whatever happens to draw the attention of any of them.

6. *Cooperative organized play.* The child plays in a group that is organized for the purpose of making some material product, striving to attain some competitive goal, dramatizing situations of adult and group life, or playing formal games. There is a marked sense of belonging or of not belonging to the group. The control of the group situation is in the hands of one or two of the members who direct the activity of the others. The goal as well as the method of attaining it necessitates a division of labor, the taking of different roles by the various group members, and the organization of activity so that the efforts of one child are supplemented by those of another. (Parten, 1932)

FIGURE 13–5
Examples of Parallel Play
These children are engaged in a form of social play known as parallel play. The label indicates that the children are playing *beside* one another but not *with* each other.

one third of their free playtime engaged in associative and cooperative play and that children just 6 months older (that is, 4½ to 5) spent 40 percent of their time in these forms of play. This marked better than a fourfold increase over the amount of associative and cooperative play that was found among children at age 2 to 2½. Playing with others is obviously a preferred activity for children in their late preschool years.

At one time, investigators held that the increase in social forms of play during the preschool years was the culmination of an ontogenetic sequence that led from solitary, nonsocial activities to ones that were highly social and interactive. From this perspective, solitary play in group settings was taken as a sign of social immaturity (Parten, 1932). This turns out to be a gross misconception of how children's behavior develops in group-play settings. For one thing, children do not progress from solitary play into forms of play that require social participation (for example, parallel play, associative play, and cooperative play). Instead, the way children play alone and the way they play in groups tend to develop independently of each other. Thus, as social play evolves, so does solitary play. Support for their independence is found in data on how much time children spend at various activities when allowed to play freely in toy-filled rooms. It turns out that the children who spend large amounts of time playing alone in group settings may also spend a lot of time in cooperative play (Rubin, Maioni, & Hornung, 1976). Statistically, this fact is represented by the absence of a correlation between the amount of time that individual children spend in solitary play and the amount of time they spend in social play (Roper & Hinde, 1978). The fact that a child spends a lot of time in solitary play, therefore, tells us nothing about the child's social maturity.

A second problem with the once-popular conception that there is a natural developmental sequence that leads from parallel to cooperative play is that parallel play does not show any age-related increases or decreases. It appears about as frequently in the play of 2- and 3-year-olds as 5-year-olds. One reason may be that children of all ages frequently use parallel play as a way of easing into more social forms of play. When used in this way, parallel play is better characterized as a strategy than a stage (Bakeman & Brownlee, 1980; Fagot & Leinbach, 1983).

Beyond the preschool years, the most significant development in the way children interact when together in free-play settings is the increase in the frequency of a type of cooperative play called *games with rules*. In our culture, games such as tag, marbles, dodge ball, hopscotch, 20 questions, and jacks typify such games. A frequent, but not invariant, feature of these games is that they involve competition. In light of this, it is interesting that they should not become popular or pronounced until after about age 6.

Preschoolers, it turns out, do not have much of an appreciation for what it means to win or lose, and their games reflect this. Older children, on the other hand, find competition pleasurable. In a massive naturalistic study conducted among Israeli and Arab schoolchildren, Rivka Eifermann (1971) found that during free-play periods at school her subject population played some 2,000 different games with rules, and most were competitive games (see Figure 13-6A). Observations of children outside of school in the streets and on playgrounds reflected the same developmental trend (see Figure 13-6B).

Taken altogether, the first 10 years of life show substantial changes in how children interact with each other when placed together in free-play settings. Initially they show an interest in each other, but they do not engage each other in sustained interactions and do not seem to take much pleasure from the few interactions (most of which are one-sided) that they do have. In the preschool years, children's interactions become quite complex and they show a developmental progression away from social disinterest and onlooking toward ever-greater social participation. Play continues to be very social in the school years, with the major change being the increased interest in games with rules. Not until late childhood and early adolescence does social play decline in importance among the social activities of humans. This decline is depicted in the data from Eifermann (1971) that are given in Figure 13-6.

A Comparative Perspective on Social Play

The trend toward increased social play in the juvenile period that is characteristic of humans is characteristic of many animals, expecially those that are closest to us—the nonhuman primates. They, too, begin interacting extensively with peers as the period of intense attachment draws to a close. As in humans, many of these peer interactions are playful ones. They increase in frequency for a year or so and then begin to decline, thus following the same developmental pattern as with humans (Chalmers, 1984). Whenever we find similar developmental patterns and characteristics shared among species, we are led to believe—as in the case of attachment—that they may serve a common developmental purpose. Thus, even though some theorists in the past have flippantly dismissed play as the meaningless discharge of excessive energy (see, for example, Schiller, 1954), no theorist holds this view today. Sociologists, anthropologists, psychologists, primatologists, and all others who have occasion to make a serious study of this activity agree that play is developmentally vital. Russian psychologist Lev Vygotsky (1966/1976) called play "the leading source of development in the pre-school years." This leads us to ask why. Why should play be viewed as vital to the development of humans and other primates?

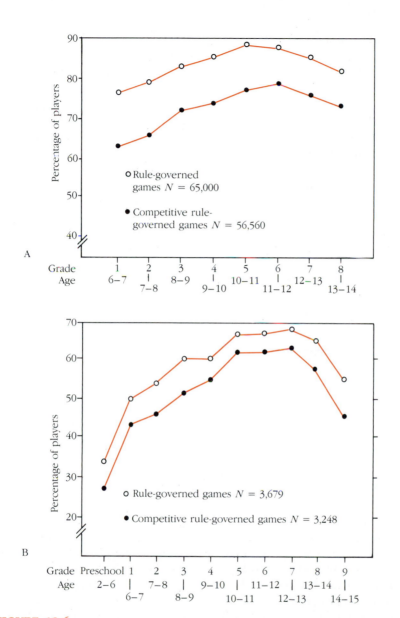

FIGURE 13-6

Developmental Changes in the Percent of Children Choosing Games with Rules
The data in graph A are based on observations of Israeli and Arab children playing
on school playgrounds during recess (*N* stands for sample size). They show the
general increase up until age 11 in the likelihood that children who were engaged
in play would be engaged in rule-governed play. Graph B shows data that were
obtained by observing children from preschool to postschool age in the streets and
on playgrounds. In both cases most of the rule-governed play involved competitive
games. (After Eifermann, 1971)

Social Play and Evolution

A first answer to the question of why play is considered vital comes from theorists who concern themselves with behavioral evolution. Their answer is that play must be vital because it has been selected through evolution. They arrive at this conclusion indirectly. They note, for example, that the young of almost every mammalian species spend some time and energy in social play. Stump-tailed macaque monkeys, who are hardly exceptional, are estimated to spend 10 percent of their time in vigorous social play (Bernstein, 1980). This play is quite costly in time and energy. Also, it enhances the chance for injury and makes animals obvious to predators. Such facts, when viewed from an evolutionary perspective, make it difficult to believe that play would have survived in the behavior of animals unless it conferred some substantial benefits. Hence, in the minds of behavioral evolutionists, the mere fact that social play has survived the evolutionary process argues for its importance.

Beyond simply asserting that survival argues for usefulness, theorists of behavioral evolution have put forward hypotheses to state precisely what the benefits of social play might be (see Bruner, Jolly, & Sylva, 1976; Fagen, 1981). Of all the evolutionary hypotheses, the one that seems to have the most merit is the *practice hypothesis*. As expressed by Peter Smith (1982), play is selected through evolution when it provides animals with a safe occasion to practice important skills, which if practiced directly, would be unsafe. Some of the skills that fall into this category are fighting, predation, and predator avoidance. The type of social play that provides training in all these skills is the vigorous *rough-and-tumble* play that characterizes so much of the social play in animals (Humphreys & Smith, 1984). In Smith's view such play is really mock combat, mock hunting, and mock escaping.

Along with the mock forms of fighting, predation, and predator avoidance, mock sexual activities (which involve mounting and thrusting) are frequent in animals' play (Smith, 1984). Whether these activities provide helpful practice is not clear, but it is interesting that in the absence of any peer contact during the juvenile period, young monkeys appear to be sexually inept. Stephen Suomi and Harry Harlow, for example, found that rhesus monkeys reared alone in wire-mesh cages, which allowed them to see but not to interact with other monkeys, did not know how to mate (see Suomi & Harlow, 1971/1976). Females reared in this way took off in fright when approached by sexually aroused males; males reared in this way were as apt to mount females from the front or side as from behind. Sometimes they would just sit down next to a female in estrus and masturbate. Though the social isolation imposed on the experimental monkeys deprived them of all social contact and not just of play, Suomi and Harlow concluded that the loss of play opportunities was particularly important because, in their words, "It is primarily through play that young monkeys learn to interact [sexually and otherwise] in a social world" (Suomi & Harlow, 1971/1976, p. 193).

Although the practice hypothesis appears reasonable, there is no direct evidence to support it at present (Martin & Caro, 1985). The hypothesis, therefore, is very speculative. Nonetheless, it does serve as a tentative answer for the question of why humans, along with almost all other animals in their mammalian class, would be motivated to engage in social play during their juvenile years. According to the hypothesis, they do so to practice social behaviors that will improve their fitness as adults. We must not think, however, that by explaining why social play might have evolved that we have "explained" the behavior. Evolutionary benefits are necessary if there is to be biological selection for a behavior. But once a behavior is in place, it can have many benefits that are completely incidental to its role in creating a selective advantage. This seems to be the case with social play, particularly in humans who have such extensive social-learning requirements. Humans must be able to read emotions and feelings, play social roles of extreme complexity, work in groups that have a common goal, regulate the behavior of group members using rules, and communicate about all of these with language. Social play may not have evolved to meet these needs, but it surely serves them. This is particularly evident when you observe children engaged in the form of cooperative play that is known as social pretend play (see Figure 13-7).

FIGURE 13-7
Social Pretend Play
These children are engaged in two forms of social pretend play. The play illustrated in the photo at left is best described as thematic fantasy play because it derives from pure fantasy. The play in the photo at right is best described as sociodramatic play because it deals with a real-life event. This distinction in the types of pretend play is occasionally useful.

Contemporary Benefits of Play

Social pretend play involves staging make-believe dramas in which children enact fictions that are based either on the real-life social world as they know it or on pure fantasy. The former enactments are known as *sociodramatic play*. The latter are called *thematic fantasy play* (see, for example, Saltz & Brodie, 1982). These forms of pretense may merge into one in some play episodes, but in pure form they differ in the extent to which the imaginary context for the play is divorced from reality. For example, enacting *Little Red Riding Hood* would be thematic fantasy play because the imagined context is that of "Once upon a time in a land far away." Such play suspends reality completely and, thereby, allows for such improbable characters as a talking wolf. In sociodramatic play (see Box 13-2), the goal is to enact a piece of real life. The characters then follow a script that is drawn from the domain of social experiences that are known to children. Playing fireman, grocery shopping, and taking a car trip would all involve sociodramatic pretense.

As modes of play unique to humans, the two types of social pretend play seem to offer a number of benefits to development (Athey, 1984; Christie & Johnsen, 1983). Psychoanalytic theorists, for example, have long emphasized that in pretend play children can safely express thoughts and feelings that are frightening and anxiety provoking ouside of play. To use an example from William Damon, a child who is angry with her father need not fear reprisal or loss of her father's love if she picks up a doll and says "Dolly has a nasty father; he never lets her play" (1983, p. 109). The child can even playfully make her father "go away." But these same thoughts expressed outside of play would be risky and frightening. Thus, pretend play gives children the chance to relieve the pressure from their unthinkable thoughts and anxieties by acting them out in situations of no consequence. A basic premise of the Freudian theory on which psychoanalysis is based is that opportunities such as this to express one's dangerous thoughts and feelings are necessary for mental health.

Cognitive psychologists emphasize different benefits of play. Namely, they see play as contributing to children's intellectual development by virtue of the opportunities pretend play offers for symbolic activity. Jean Piaget (1946/1962) held this view, of course, and so did the Russian psychologist Lev Vygotsky (1966/1976). William Damon has summarized Vygotsky's views by saying that Vygotsky believed pretend play to be the realm in which children acquire "the abilities to think symbolically, to reason about what is possible rather than what is merely real, and to examine the underlying meaning of their own social behavior" (Damon, 1983, p. 107). Other cognitively oriented psychologists (see, for example, Dansky, 1980; Pellegrini, 1985) believe that pretend play is also important in the development of children's problem solving and creativity.

BOX 13-2
Transcripts of Children Engaged in Sociodramatic Pretend Play

Playing in the corner of a preschool classroom, three 4-year-old girls take on the roles of *mother, mother's friend,* and *doctor.* The play begins with *mother* bringing in her sick baby (a doll).

MOTHER: Doctor, maybe you give her an injection?

DOCTOR: No need for injections, I will examine her.

MOTHER: (to child) There darling, the doctor is only examining you. Don't cry!

DOCTOR: (gives injection with some long object) I did it already, I finished the injection!

MOTHER'S FRIEND: You already did it?

DOCTOR: Give me some cotton, she is bleeding!

MOTHER: (as she hands cotton to doctor) There. Oh poor baby, she is bleeding. (to child) Sit nicely, I will change your cloth. (Forys & McCune-Nicolich, 1984)

Using the wooden stairs in a play area as a car, two 3-year-olds incorporated a traveling theme into much of their pretend play.

L: Get in the car.

A: Are we goin to the fancy meeting?

L: Yeah, but you havta get your fancy things.

A: My jewelry?

L: No. You havta get your brushes.

A: And my hat too? (Takes hat.)

L: No! That hat. (points to another hat) I havta put my hat on 'cause its raining.

A: Quick it's raining. Open the doors, get in the car. (Forys & McCune-Nicolich, 1984)

In this example of pretend play, a verbal 3-year-old girl serves as actor and director in a play sequence with a somewhat less verbal friend.

GIRL: Say, "Go to sleep now." (Girl is director)

BOY: Go sleep now.

GIRL: Why? (whining)

BOY: Baby.

GIRL: Why?

BOY: Because.

GIRL: No, say "Because." (emphatically) (Girl is director)

BOY: Because. (emphatically)

GIRL: Why? Because why?

BOY: Not good. You bad.

GIRL: Why?

BOY: Cause you spill your milk.

GIRL: No, cause I bit somebody. (Girl is director)

BOY: Yes, you did. (Boy slips out of role)

GIRL: And say, "Go to sleep, Put your head down." (sternly) (Girl is director)

BOY: Put your head down. (sternly)

GIRL: No.

BOY: Yes.

GIRL: No.

BOY: Yes, yes do . . . Okay, I will spank you. Bad boy. (spanks her)

GIRL: My head's up. (giggles)

BOY: (spanks her again)

GIRL: I want my teddy bear. (petulant voice)

BOY: No, your teddy bear go away. (sternly)

GIRL: Why?

BOY: Cause he does. (walks off with teddy bear)

GIRL: Are you going to pack your teddy bear? (Girl drops director and baby roles) (Garvey, 1979)

Psychologists whose concern is with social development emphasize yet other benefits of pretend play by focusing on the possibilities that it offers for either learning or practicing important social skills. Cooperation, leadership, and negotiation are among these. Cooperation is important to social pretense because, for the play to be fun, everyone must honor the common theme around which the play is organized. Children who do not cooperate are considered "no fun to play with." Leadership is required because someone must serve as the director for play episodes. Various people can assume this role during an episode. To do so, they step out of their play roles to offer direction to others involved in the play. Negotiation is such an integral part of social pretense that frequently the negotiation required to establish an agreed-on context may seem to be of more interest to children than the play itself.

Although it appears almost self-evident that engaging in social pretense is developmentally beneficial in some of the ways that psychoanalytic, cognitive, and socially oriented psychologists have suggested, they have been lax in actually testing the validity of their "self-evident" beliefs. In fact, only recently have studies been initiated that purport to test the hypothesis that social play involving pretense and cooperation is valuable (see Rubin, Fein, & Vandenberg, 1983, p. 751). To test the hypothesis, researchers measure the extent to which social play correlates with the general dimensions of social, emotional, and cognitive development. Studies to date yield some strong support that psychologists' long-standing faith in the developmental value of social pretend play is justified. One study cited by Rubin, Fein, and Vandenberg (1983), for example, showed that children who spent more of their playtime in social pretend play were more socially competent, more popular, and better at role-taking activities. These relationships held even when differences in IQ, sex, age, and nonsocial pretend play were taken into account.

In addition to correlational evidence, there is some experimental data to support the claim that social pretend play has substantial developmental benefits. In one experimental study, Eli Saltz, David Dixon, and James Johnson (1977) instituted training in pretend play as part of an ongoing preschool program for disadvantaged 3- and 4-year-old Detroit children. One group of children read and enacted a number of fairy tales (the thematic fantasy play group) as a regular activity for about 7 months. Another enacted real-life situations, like going to the store or flying airplanes (the sociodramatic play group). In addition to these groups that had social pretend play built into their regular school routine, there were two control groups. One control group read and talked about the fairy tales used for the thematic fantasy group. Another just interacted with the research staff at nonpretend activities like connect the dots or finger painting. The results of the study indicated that the social pretend activities, particularly when they involved thematic fantasy play, had substantial benefits. Social-pretend children had higher IQs at the end of the year, and their ability to resist temptation and to avoid behaving impulsively seemed to reflect that they had better mental control over their own behavior.

We can conclude from the available evidence that social games involving pretense may have a role in contemporary human development that transcends whatever evolutionary role social play alone may have had. Because of this, developmental psychologists who are concerned with the welfare of individual children have been eager to implement *play-tutoring* programs. Sara Smilansky (1968) was a pioneer in play tutoring, a role she attained after discovering large differences in the pretend play of children living in Israel. One clear result from play-tutoring programs is that they are successful in increasing the spontaneous use of pretense in children's play (Rubin, Fein, & Vandenberg, 1983, pp. 754-55). The study by Eli Saltz and his colleagues (1977) even showed that the use of fantasy as opposed to sociodramatic pretense could be selectively increased. If pretense in play is truly of cognitive, social, and emotional benefit to children, this demonstration that tutoring leads to increased spontaneous use of the tutored skill is one of substantial importance. It implies that intensive but brief training can alter behavioral tendencies with regard to an activity that is important to children's growth.

Individual differences in the tendency to engage in pretend play are an established fact. In Smilansky's case, and in most others, the particular children found to be low in pretend play were from the lower classes of society. One reason for this, it has been suggested, is that adults from the lower classes may be more likely than others to discourage children from engaging in make-believe. John and Elizabeth Newson (1970, 1978) conducted interviews in 700 families in Nottingham, England, and found that many of the working-class mothers tried to discourage pretend play because they associated it with lying. As one mother said of her son, "He'd make up stories. . . . It got so bad that I tried to stop it, because I didn't want him to go from an imaginary story to a downright lie—because there's not much difference between the two" (quoted in Dunn, 1985, pp. 79–80).

Because of the general finding that lower-class children are less likely on average to engage in social pretend play, play-tutoring programs have been recommended as a preschool activity for disadvantaged children (Feitelson & Ross, 1973; Smilansky, 1971). Where such programs have been instituted, they have led to relatively long-term increases in children's overall levels of social participation (Smith, Dalgleish, & Herzmark, 1981). Despite the apparent effectiveness of training programs, however, Helen Schwartzman (1984) has pointed·out that wide-scale implementation of play tutoring may be a bit premature, because the evidence for *reliable* social-class differences in play is still weak. Some studies, for example, do not agree that lower-class children are different from others in their use of sociodramatic and thematic fantasy play (McLoyd, 1985). Others wonder about the ecological validity of reports from laboratory studies where differences have been found (see Chapter 2, p. 64).

ANTISOCIAL AND PROSOCIAL BEHAVIOR

When children interact in social play and in other ways, it is interesting to watch for signs of antisocial and prosocial behavior. The former is evident in selfish, hurtful, and aggressive behavior; the latter, in cooperative, helpful, and altruistic behavior. Development of children's antisocial and prosocial tendencies are of particular importance because they serve as signs of whether children will fit in well in society and be liked by others or whether they will be outcasts.

In the discussion of antisocial and prosocial behavior that follows we will discuss a few of the factors that are related to individual differences in these dimensions of behavior. But first we will deal with the species-typical pattern of development.

Is There Any Developmental Priority for Antisocial Tendencies?

Intellectuals of the nineteenth century were quite taken by the idea that selfishness was in the natural order of things. Sigmund Freud, for example, thought that at birth, humans were motivated by a component of the human personality that was completely self-interested. This component was labeled the *id,* and it was thought to dominate children's social interactions during infancy. Only after infants learned that their crying and demanding would not always get them what they wanted would they begin to seek alternative means of satisfying their self-interests. Discovering these alternative means was the job of the *ego,* the rational component of the human personality.

One of the reasons that Freud and others were willing to accept the view that humans are initially inclined to act in purely self-interested ways was that this view of human nature seemed to be justified by evolutionary theory. As interpreted by social scientists, the essence of Darwin's theory of evolution was that development occurred when there was aggressive competition among individuals that led to what Darwin's contemporary, Herbert Spencer (1862), referred to as the "survival of the fittest." Competition, therefore, was nature's way of eliminating the weak, the inefficient, and the maladapted. This meant that competition was good, a part of the natural order. Cooperation, on the other hand, had to be taught. It could only be achieved, therefore, through the action of civilizing forces, such as parents who teach children to share, or through rational forces, such as Freud's ego. Without such forces to act as restraints on the more-fundamental aspects of human nature, life would be reduced to what the philosopher Thomas

Hobbes termed as a "war of all against all" in which the individual human life would be "solitary, poor, nasty, brutish, and short" (1651/1947).

Contemporary developmentalists vehemently object to the Hobbesian and Freudian view of what constitutes human nature. From the developmentalist's point of view, there is no human nature other than that realized in the course of development; and, Darwinian theory notwithstanding, there is no reason to believe that humans are inclined to be purely self-serving. In fact, contemporary interpreters of the data on evolution argue that prosocial, altruistic motives are as essential to evolution as any other. According to anthropologist Ashley Montagu, for example, "Cooperation, not conflict, was evidently the selectively most valuable form of behavior for man taken at any stage of his evolutionary history, and surely, quite as evidently never more so than today" (1965, p. 162). Recently, this argument for the biological advantages of cooperation has found a genetic basis. The argument is that of sociobiologists who hold that altruism is so much in our self-interest that the inclination to behave altruistically has become rooted in our genes (see Chapter 1, p. 43).

Regardless of whether altruism and other prosocial acts are in fact rooted in human genetic history, as sociobiologists claim, prosocial behaviors are quite typical of our species, making their first appearance early in human ontogeny. For example, 1-year-olds who are placed together to play with toys will spontaneously share, and if one of the children should become distressed and start to cry, the other will too. Crying at the distress of others is, in fact, a typical response for children from 10 to 12 months of age. Marian Radke-Yarrow and Carolyn Zahn-Waxler conducted a longitudinal study concerned with the roots of prosocial behavior and found the following reaction of an 11-month-old to be typical.

> Sari (on witnessing physical pain) looked sad, puckered up and burst out crying. She continued to cry intensely. She crawled over to her mother to be picked up. (1984, p. 89)

Such observations give weak confirmation to the ancient belief from Chinese philosophy that "All men have the mind which cannot bear to see the suffering of others" (quoted in Radke-Yarrow, Zahn-Waxler, & Chapman, 1983, p. 470).

Crying at the sight of pain in others, which occurs for about one third of the distress episodes viewed by 1-year-olds, gives way during the second year to real helping. Here, for example, is how an 18-month-old responded to the crying of a neighbor's baby.

> Jenny looked startled, her body stiffened. She approached and tried to give the baby cookies. She followed him around and began to whimper herself. She then tried to stroke his hair, but he pulled away. Later, she approached her mother, led her to the baby, and tried to put mother's hand on the baby's head. He calmed down a little, but

Jenny still looked worried. She continued to bring him toys and to pat his head and shoulders. (Radke-Yarrow & Zahn-Waxler, 1984, p. 89)

This example includes standard behaviors that are in most children's prosocial repertoire at this point. They include physical comfort through pats, hugs, or kisses, offering attractive objects, and seeking help from adults. Combining these prosocial response categories together with others, such as expressing verbal concern, revealed that better than 50 percent of the responses that 18- to 30-month-olds made to distress were prosocial (Radke-Yarrow & Zahn-Waxler, 1984, tab. 1).

The tendency of children 18 months and older to be helpful is not restricted to times of distress. According to Harriet Rheingold (1982), children this age are generally helpful, as is evident in their attempts to assist in common household chores. Even when an unfamiliar adult starts to perform some task such as pick up scattered pieces of paper, fold laundry, or set a table, children will spontaneously help. These many observations of children's behavior early in life argue strongly that humans do not develop out of selfishness. They have prosocial tendencies from the start. Parents may need to reinforce these response tendencies, but they hardly need to instill them.

In addition to the prosocial tendencies of infants, there are aggressive, self-serving tendencies as well. For example, even though the children over 18 months of age in Radke-Yarrow and Zahn-Waxler's study were predominantly prosocial in their reactions to distress, approximately 10 percent of their reactions were aggressive attempts to stifle or hurt the distressed child. You will recall that one of the nine control children in Mary Main and Carol George's (1985) study of abused children also responded aggressively to another child's crying (see Chapter 12, p. 648).

Because behavior reflecting the antisocial tendencies of children has historically been of greater interest to researchers than the prosocial tendencies, we have a generally better picture of this negative side to children's social development than we do of the positive side. Charlotte Patterson (1984) has provided a summary of this literature, which we will review shortly.

The type of aggression that is most common in infants and young children is what Willard Hartup (1974) has called **instrumental aggression.** This form of aggression consists of physical tussles and other aggressive acts that are designed to gain objects, privileges, or territory, but not necessarily to hurt people. For this reason, the aggression is labeled as instrumental rather than hostile. As Dale Hay and Hildy Ross have noted, instrumental aggression is "impersonally motivated and marked by limited attention to the peer" (1982, p. 105). Nonetheless, instrumental aggression is not socially blind, because toys are invariably made more attractive for children when someone else is playing with them (Eckerman, Whatley, & McGehee, 1979). Also, the object struggles of infants often show signs of

being motivated by selfishness and a desire to control peers. These motives are evident when children abandon their own toys to seize identical ones that are held by peers and when they give up newly seized toys in order to go after the next toys that peers pick up (Hay, 1984, p. 16). Still, as Patterson points out in her review, it is important to distinguish instrumental acts reflecting selfishness or a desire for control from acts that are truly hostile.

The absence of an intent to hurt that accompanies the physically rough interpersonal behavior of children in their second and third years gives way gradually to a social awareness of the effects of one's actions, and when it does we can find examples of truly hostile behavior. In Willard Hartup's study of children from 4 to 7 years of age, the incidence of true aggression (that is, acts specifically designed to hurt another person) was found to increase steadily over time. Hartup called intentionally hurtful aggression **hostile aggression.** Here's an example of the type of behavior that would be labeled hostile rather than instrumental aggression:

> Marian is complaining to all that David . . . had squirted her on the pants she has to wear tonight. She says, "I'm gonna do it to him to see how he likes it." She fills a can with water and David runs to the teacher and tells of her threat. The teacher takes the can from Marian. Marian attacks David and pulls his hair very hard. . . . Later, Marian and Elaine go upstairs and into the room where David is seated with a teacher. He throws a book at Marian. The teacher asks Marian to leave. Marian kicks David, then leaves. (Hartup, 1974, p. 339)

Although the above example illustrates a physically hostile act, Hartup determined that over the years from early to middle childhood, physically hostile acts decreased in frequency while verbally hostile acts increased. Thus, although hostile aggression increased over the years from 4 to 7, the use of physical violence declined. Such observations led Patterson to conclude her review of the literature on childhood aggression by saying that

"the major developmental achievement . . . appears to be an increasing ability to confine the use of physical violence to the pursuit of hostile aims and to develop alternative means of achieving other, non-hostile aims" (1984, p. 386).

The discussion of prosocial and antisocial tendencies in behavior so far has focused on species-typical patterns. Now we will turn to factors in the lives of individuals that may be influential in creating individual differences in these dimensions of behavior.

Sources of Individual Differences

The factors in development that lead one child to develop prosocial tendencies and another to develop antisocial tendencies are as diverse as those that affect intelligence or any other psychological trait. They include characteristics of individuals, characteristics of the environment in which they find themselves, and the interactions of the two. In the previous chapter, for example, we discussed factors such as parenting style, temperament, the use of induction, and the importance of achieving control over children before a cycle of coercion escalates. In this section we will focus on a limited number of other relevant factors. They are culture, social models, television, and gender.

Culture

Cultures vary in the extent to which they promote social competition and cooperation. There are societies such as that of the Arapesh in New Guinea (Mead, 1935), the Hopi of North America (Dennis, 1965), and even contemporary Soviet society (Bronfenbrenner, 1970) that quite self-consciously promote the mutual dependence of their members and the need for cooperation. Others such as the culture of the Mundugumor in eastern New Guinea (Mead, 1935) and the Ik in Uganda (Turnbull, 1972) seem designed to promote an opposite set of values—independence, competition, and individualism.

The clear differences that exist among cultures in the emphasis that they place on categories of behavior such as cooperation, altruism, aggression, and competition seem to have a strong impact on the developmental outcome of children growing up in those cultures. In a well-known cross-cultural study conducted by Beatrice and John Whiting (1975), for example, children from traditional, subsistence-farm settings in India, Kenya, Mexico, Japan, and the Philippines were compared on the trait of altruism to children from a nonagricultural community in the United States. Altruism was rated by scoring individual children on behaviors such as "offers help," "offers support," "seeks dominance," and "insults." The children were scored while they were engaged in play, work, learning, and casual social interactions. Combining scores on individual behaviors yielded a single altruism score. The results showed vast cultural differences. Whereas 100 percent of the Kenyans were above the median altruism score (the median is the middle score, the one that divides the top half of the group from the bottom half), only 8 percent of the U.S. children were above the median. In between were the Mexican children with 73 percent above the median, the Philippine children with 63 percent, the Japanese with 29 percent, and the Indians with 25 percent.

The results of the Whitings's field study, which employed naturalistic observations, are in close agreement with the results of laboratory studies. The method used to conduct cross-cultural laboratory studies is to have children from different cultures participate in a common activity under identical laboratory conditions. One of the most popular laboratory tasks has been a game played on what is known as the Madsen Cooperation Board (see Figure 13-8). The game, developed by Millard Madsen of UCLA, requires four players, all of whom can win if they cooperate. Failure to cooperate results in everyone losing. Although it makes no sense to compete at this game, many children do. The intensity of the competition is reflected in the fact that the original cotton strings on the apparatus had to be changed to nylon, and the experimenters frequently had to hold the board down to keep it from being yanked off its stand (Fishbein, 1984, p. 191). The research shows quite clearly that children from the United States (and other Western, industrialized societies) are more likely to compete— and less likely to cooperate—than children from rural, nonindustrialized societies (Madsen & Lancy, 1981).

To explain the cross-cultural differences in competitiveness and altruism that have been found in children, researchers have focused on the fac-

FIGURE 13-8
The Cooperation Board
Millard Madsen's Cooperation Board has been used in cross-cultural research as a standard means of measuring cultural differences in children's tendencies to compete or cooperate. At each corner of the board, there are eyelets through which strings pass. All the strings are attached to a pen and holder. The goal of the game is for children to mark through the circle in front of them with the pen, but to do that, all the players must be willing to cooperate.

tors that distinguish children's lives in traditional, rural, subsistence economies from the lives of children in affluent, urban economies. The reason is that research has consistently shown these cultural differences to covary with behavior. Even within a single country, for example, children from the rural, more-traditional areas are less competitive than those from the urban areas. In fact, there seems to be a direct connection between rural modes of life and cooperation in children and between urban modes of life and competition. This pattern appears in almost every cross-cultural study conducted using the Madsen game or a similar one. Just to illustrate the general finding, in studies conducted in Canada (Miller, 1973; Miller & Thomas, 1972), Blackfoot Indians from a nonintegrated rural school were compared to white urban Canadians. The urban Canadians were far more competitive. Blackfoot Indians and white Canadians who lived in the same community and attended the same school were alike in their competitiveness. In a separate study (Knight & Kagan, 1977), Americans of European descent were more competitive than third-generation Mexican American children, who in turn were more aggressive than second-generation Mexican Americans. Thus, even for children who were all living in this country, competitiveness at Madsen's game was directly related to the length of time the family had been part of this culture.

Though there is no way to know from the correlational data alone which particular variables are causal, the Whitings and others have put forth some interesting hypotheses. According to the Whitings, for example, one cultural factor of importance is the extent to which the child's cooperation in family activities is vital to the well-being of the family. A characteristic of traditional settings is that children are an important part of the family work force. They have chores, such as fetching firewood, caring for infants, tending animals, and cleaning, that are clearly related to the family's needs and well-being (see Figure 13-9). In the Whitings' judgment, such activities are a better school ground for learning to be cooperative and helpful than any other. When the Whitings examined the opportunities for affluent children from industrialized societies to learn these things through family chores, they found that the opportunities were lacking.

> In urban or semi-urban, nonagricultural communities . . . the tasks assigned to children are less clearly related to the economy and welfare of the child or the child's family and probably seem more arbitrary to the child. Picking up toys or making one's own bed are egoistic, for the benefit of the child. The need for having clothes hung up, bureau drawers tidy, or the bed smoothed out neatly is probably not immediately clear, nor are the consequences of negligence obviously serious. (Whiting & Whiting, 1975, p. 106)

If we ask what the principal work of childhood is in nontraditional, industrialized economies, we hit on the second of the Whitings' hypothesized factors of cultural importance: the training received in Western schools. While children in traditional, subsistence economies are contributing to the family's well-being, children in more affluent societies are going to school "to prepare for their futures." Just what that future is, they have no way of knowing. But in order to prepare for that future, they need to do as well as possible relative to their peers. This feature makes Westernized schools a breeding ground for competitiveness, at least in the Whitings' view. As they point out, "Schoolwork is egoistic and competitive. Academic success is individual and, although an educated person may be expected to help his or her family, this is probably not clear to [some children] and not expected [of others]" (Whiting & Whiting, 1975, pp. 106-107). Other students of intercultural differences agree that training in competition makes

FIGURE 13-9
Learning the Importance of Cooperation
In traditional cultures, children play vital roles in maintaining the family's well-being, as in this case of Bedouin children from the Musseina tribe of the Sinai who aid in building a stone house. This experience may be a basis for learning the importance of cooperation.

up part of the "hidden curriculum" in Western schools. Nancy and Theodore Graves (1978), for example, who have studied the impact of modernization on the cooperation and generosity of Cook Islanders found that the native children who had advanced farther in the Western schools were more competitive and less generous than children with less schooling.

Social Models

Humans, far more so than other animals, learn by observing others. A dog, for example, is unlikely to learn to roll over just by observing another dog get rewarded for this trick, but a child can easily learn the many ways of getting a teacher's attention by simply observing what works for others. This means that the *models* of social behavior that humans are exposed to are an important part of their social-learning environment. Presumably, if one is exposed to models of prosocial behavior, then one should learn the rewards and benefits of prosocial behavior; but if one is exposed to models of antisocial behavior, then the rewards and benefits of this form of behavior might be what one learns.

A great deal of research has gone into determining whether different social models in fact induce different social behaviors (see reviews by Parke & Slaby, 1983, and Radke-Yarrow, Zahn-Waxler, & Chapman, 1983). The conclusion to be drawn from this research is consistent with expectations: when cooperation, sharing, and other prosocial behaviors are modeled for children, the modeling leads to increases in the frequency of these socially positive behaviors. Likewise, modeling selfishness, aggression, and other antisocial behaviors leads to increases in the frequency of these socially negative behaviors. The effects, even in short-term experimental studies, are fairly long-lasting, and they generalize from modeled situations to other situations. More interesting than this result, however, is the result of studies that have focused on factors that optimize the effectiveness of models.

One clear result is that to be maximally effective, a model must have a nurturant relationship with the children who look to him or her as a model. The best, most compelling demonstration of nurturance as an interactive variable comes from an experiment conducted by Marian Radke-Yarrow, Phyllis Scott, and Carolyn Zahn-Waxler (Yarrow, Scott, & Waxler, 1973). In the study, two adults were introduced to a preschool setting, and, for a period of weeks, the children in the preschool were treated nurturantly by one of the adults and nonnurturantly by the other. (Each adult played both the nurturant and nonnurturant role, but with different children.) Nurturance was defined as offering help and support freely, initiating friendly interactions, sympathizing, protecting, and praising children, and expressing confidence in the children's abilities. In brief, the adults expressed nurturance by showing the children that they really liked them. They expressed nonnurturance by indifference.

Later in this study, the adults who had established either nurturant or nonnurturant relationships with particular children became models of prosocial behavior for these children. For example, they comforted an adult who had bumped her head or picked up things that had spilled from a cupboard. As models of prosocial behavior, they were effective in increasing prosocial behavior in both the nurtured and nonnurtured group of children, but they were most effective with the nurtured children. Only 24 percent of all the children acted prosocially on a pre-test that involved opportunities to spontaneously help or comfort someone in mild distress; however, the number of children acting prosocially increased to 84 percent on a post-test.

Given the relevance of nurturance to the developmental equation that relates modeling to the establishment of prosocial patterns of behavior, you might wonder why nurturance is not viewed as a factor in its own right. That is, it might be that nurturance alone is sufficient to promote prosocial behavior. This would make sense, because when one is being nurturant one is at the same time modeling a caring, other-directed attitude to the child. Although one might think that nurturance alone would be sufficient, research fails to support this view. Reviewers Paul Mussen and Nancy Eisenberg concluded some years ago that "simply giving a child warmth, support, and affection (even in fairly large doses) does not ensure that the child will become altruistic, kind, considerate, or generous" (1977, p. 92). The reason, according to Eisenberg (Moore & Eisenberg, 1984, p. 155), is that noncontingent warmth is interpreted as permissiveness, which, as we learned in Chapter 12, is a caretaker variable that fails to contribute to the social maturity of children. Thus, nurturance combined with modeling is effective in shaping children's behavior, as is nurturance combined with high maturity demands (see Chapter 12, pp. 643–44), but nurturance alone has no apparent effect on the direction social development takes. A nurturant relationship, therefore, is best seen as a facilitator of social influence but not as an influence in itself.

Television

Since television first became a national pastime in the 1950s, parents, educators, and government officials have been concerned about the impact it might be having on children. Because of the high incidence of violence on television (for example, according to Shaffer [1985] the average person has viewed 13,000 television deaths by the age of 16), one of the chief concerns has been with the impact of television viewing in the socialization of aggression. From the mass of research that has been conducted, one thing is quite clear: television viewing does predict aggressiveness in children. Some of the data supporting this view come from research by Leonard Eron at the Chicago Circle campus of the University of Illinois. In an initial study, Eron

and his colleagues (Eron, Huesmann, Lefkowitz, & Walder, 1972) tracked 475 children longitudinally from the third grade into adulthood. They took measures of aggressiveness, television viewing, and a host of other variables beginning in the third grade and then compared these ratings with similar ratings taken at a later time. The findings showed that the viewing of aggressive television programs at age 9 correlated with aggressiveness 10 years later at age 19. The cross-age correlation (that is, the correlation of television viewing at age 9 and aggression at age 19) was stronger in fact than either of the concurrent, or same-age, correlations (namely, the correlation of television viewing and aggression at age 9 and the correlation of television viewing and aggression at age 19).

A second study looked just at the younger years, first grade to fifth grade, the years that Eron assumed constituted a sensitive period for learning aggression via television. In all of these years, viewing violent television programs correlated with both self-reported and other-reported aggressiveness. This was true not only for a large sample of U.S. children, but it was true as well for children in Finland, Poland, and Australia. The correlations were not exceptionally strong (all in the .20 to .30 range), but they were consistent. They also tended to increase with time, which led Eron to believe that the effects of television viewing on aggressiveness are cumulative, at least across the early years.

The way in which television viewing and aggressiveness could increase together over time is outlined in Eron's hypothetical account of a case of television influence (Eron, 1982, p. 210). The account begins with a child whose use of aggression has made the child unpopular. Being unpopular, the child is now inclined to spend more time watching television. Seeing televised violence, the child is reassured that aggressive behavior is appropriate, and, at the same time, the child is taught new techniques for coercing others. Applying these techniques leads to continued unpopularity, and, so, the child is driven back to television.

In Eron's analysis of the role of television in the development of aggression, a great many variables other than just television viewing are considered. One of the most important of these is the person's perception of the reality of the social world as portrayed on television. Namely, does the child take television presentations to be a reasonable representation of the way things are? If so, television will have an important impact on the child's socialization. If not, television will have less of an impact.

Because television's credibility is a factor in judging its impact, it makes sense that television's influence would be restricted primarily to the early years, as Eron found. The reason is that young children have insufficient experience to know that the social world as portrayed on television is a highly intensified, dramatized, and violent version of the real social world. Young children, therefore, will tend to find television portrayals credible, and, thus, the programs will have a bigger impact on them than on older children who can better discriminate between "entertainment" and real life.

In addition to the many studies that have found viewing violent television programs to be associated with aggressive behavior, there is a second finding of importance that links television viewing to aggression. In this case, the relationship is between viewing violent television and children's judgment of what is "normal." Children who view more television are more tolerant of aggression. The interpretation of this relationship is that viewing television violence can desensitize people so that they are more accepting of violence in real life. This causal interpretation is backed up by research by Ronald Drabman and Margaret Thomas (1974). In their research, children monitors were asked to keep an eye on two preschoolers as they played together. The preschoolers were "in another room" but could be observed using a television surveillance system. The children serving as monitors were supposed to let a supervisor know if anything went wrong. As the monitors watched, the two children began to play ever-more aggressively. They wound up in a fight, knocking over the camera and eventually causing a total blackout of the television signal. Drabman and Thomas measured how long it took their subjects—the monitors—to make the judgment that "something was going wrong." Monitors who had seen a violent television Western just prior to the monitoring task were much more tolerant of aggression than were children who had not been "desensitized" in this way. Subsequent research even showed that children who had been desensitized did not become as physiologically aroused by watching the children fight as did children who had not been desensitized (Thomas, Horton, Lippincott, & Drabman, 1977). Though these studies only show short-term effects of television viewing on tolerance for aggression, it is reasonable to believe that television viewing could have long-term effects.

One might think that if the world as portrayed via standard television programs were more prosocial than the child's own world then we would find the same relationships for prosocial behavior and television viewing as are found for antisocial behavior and television viewing. Unfortunately, researchers have not investigated the relationships between television viewing and prosocial behavior as thoroughly as they have investigated the opposite. Concern for the antisocial content of programs began in the 1950s, but concern for the prosocial content dates only from the 1970s. According to reviewers Marian Radke-Yarrow, Carolyn Zahn-Waxler, and Michael Chapman (1983, p. 498), there is no evidence yet for either dramatic or long-lasting relationships between the viewing of prosocial television and subsequent prosocial behavior. One reason prosocial viewing may not be as potent a variable as the viewing of aggression is that prosocial behavior is far less salient and a good bit more subtle. The message, therefore, is low-key. Given this difference between prosocial and aggressive acts as portrayed on television, it may be unreasonable to expect that the learning would be parallel in the two cases. The more likely outcome is that for equal exposure to prosocial and aggressive acts on television, violent episodes will have a greater impact.

Gender

A final variable to be considered as a factor in the development of either prosocial or aggressive styles of interaction is a person's gender. Throughout the world, femaleness connotes caring, nurturing, and protecting more so than maleness does. Maleness connotes aggression, competitiveness, and independence (Ruble, 1984). Given that males and females are brought up in societies that almost universally uphold these sex-role stereotypes, we might expect for males and females to develop in ways that would validate the stereotypes through their own behavior. But do they?

With regard to aggression alone, it is quite clear that males are universally the more aggressive sex (Condry & Ross, 1985; Maccoby & Jacklin, 1980; Parke & Slaby, 1983). This conclusion applies to both physical and verbal aggression and to both instrumental and hostile aggression. Boys initiate more aggressive encounters, and they are more likely than females to counterattack aggressively when someone else "starts it." Not only are males consistently the more aggressive humans, they are the more aggressive, too, in the species closest to us, chimpanzees (Maccoby & Jacklin, 1980). We can conclude, then, that there is indeed a male–female difference in the tendency to respond aggressively in cases of social conflict.

How about prosocial behavior? Does the actual behavior of males and females again confirm the stereotype? Interestingly, it does not. Given the chance to act prosocially by sharing, helping, cooperating, or comforting, males are as likely as females to respond prosocially (Radke-Yarrow, Zahn-Waxler, & Chapman, 1983, pp. 518-23). Despite this similarity in behavior, there is a difference in the prosocial ratings of males and females. This means that if you ask people to rate their friends and acquaintances on prosocial dimensions (for example, who would be more likely to share crayons, to help an injured child to feel better, to look for a lost cat, and so forth), they perceive the females as being more prosocial on average (Zarbatany, Hartmann, Gelfand, & Vinciguerra, 1985). Behaviors and perception, therefore, do not match. Females are perceived as more likely to respond prosocially to the needs of others, even though that perception is not backed up in actual tests.

If males and females are equally likely to behave prosocially toward both peers and strangers, where does the difference in reputation come from? One possibility is that the reputation comes not from behavioral differences (which apparently do not exist) but from differences in the attitudes that accompany behavior. Marian Radke-Yarrow and her colleagues (Radke-Yarrow, Zahn-Waxler, & Chapman, 1983) argue that women are more likely than males to show concern and sympathy when behaving prosocially. Thus, even when men and women behave the same, women may appear to be the more caring, thereby earning their reputation as the more prosocially inclined of the two sexes.

A more pressing question than the one concerning sex differences (or their absence) in prosocial behavior is the question of why there would be differences in aggressive behavior. The cross-cultural and cross-species ubiquity of the sex difference in aggression leads many to believe that the difference must lie in some biological factor. The most likely candidate is hormones (see Parke & Slaby, 1983, p. 559).

One version of the hormone hypothesis is that aggression and testosterone go hand in hand. Although there is some very limited evidence showing an association between level of aggression among male prisoners and their blood levels of testosterone (see, for example, Ehrenkranz, Bliss, & Sheard, 1974), there is absolutely no evidence that male–female differences are related to testosterone levels. One strong piece of evidence against the testosterone hypothesis is that male–female differences in aggression show up in children ages 3 to 6, even though the circulating levels of testosterone (and other sex-related hormones, as well) do not differ at this age (Hoyenga & Hoyenga, 1979). Dramatic differences in levels of sex-related hormones do not appear until adolescence, and in adolescence, the sex differences in aggression are no greater (and perhaps even less) than earlier in life (Hyde, 1984).

A more reasonable hormone hypothesis for explaining male–female differences in aggression is Anke Ehrhardt's hypothesis that the differences are due to the effects that androgens in the prenatal period have on brain development. As you will recall from Chapter 4, this hypothesis is supported by experimental evidence in monkeys (p. 176) and correlational data on humans (p. 184). The data on monkeys show that females injected with testosterone during the period of prenatal brain development are more rough and tumble in their play than normal females (Goy, 1978). The data on humans show that prenatally androgenized females are more tomboyish than normal females (Money & Ehrhardt, 1972). In addition, their verbal reports support the view that they have a stronger aggressive tendency than other females. In a study that compared 17 prenatally androgenized women to their sisters (Ehrhardt & Baker, 1974), 11 reported being more likely than their sisters to start a fight. Although these data do fit Ehrhardt's hypothesis, some words of caution are in order.

An important point to remember from the discussion of sex differences in Chapter 4 is that hormones alone have never been shown to play a crucial causal role in any human behavior. The behavior of some animals may be directly manipulable through hormonal variations, but not human behavior. The most potent variables for humans are learning histories and cognitions. So, to explain differences in the aggressiveness of males and females, we should perhaps pay more attention to differences in their histories and their cognitions than their hormones. Eleanor Maccoby and Carol Jacklin (1980) have presented this view quite well. They note that biological differences—whether rooted in hormones, temperaments, or muscular physiques—may tip the developmental landscape a little, but this would hardly be important if there were no other factors around to ensure that the tipping resulted in a permanent incline. To conclude this section, we will consider how one of these other factors—societal expectations—might contribute.

It has been firmly established that adults treat children differently and have different expectations for them according to gender (Huston, 1983). This is evident even at birth. Babies labeled as girls are described as smaller, cuter, and more delicate than babies labeled as boys, and they are said to resemble their mothers (Rubin, Provenzano, & Luria, 1974). Babies labeled as boys are more likely to be described as strong and hardy. In interacting with babies, adults are more likely to give dolls to those babies labeled as girls. Babies labeled as boys are given male sex-typed toys such as hammers, and they get treated more vigorously with whole-body stimulation (Smith & Lloyd, 1978).

Given that boys and girls may be treated somewhat differently from birth, the treatment differences could quite plausibly become a wedge that would tend to separate the behavior of males and females in sex-typed ways that are expected of them by their parents and the rest of society. Evidence that differential treatment alone can produce dramatic effects comes from the case history described in Chapter 4 that involved twin boys, one of whom was surgically altered to be female following an accident that occurred during circumcision (see p. 177). Immediately following the sex-change operation, the mother began to treat her "daughter" differently from her son. The mother said, "I started dressing her not in dresses but, you know, in little pink slacks and frilly blouses . . . and letting her hair grow" (Money & Ehrhardt, 1972, p. 118). A year or so later the mother again commented on how she dressed her daughter. "I even made all her nightwear into granny gowns and she wears bracelets and hair ribbons" (Money & Ehrhardt, 1972, p. 118). Given the mother's special attention to her daughter's feminine appearance, it is not surprising to learn that the little girl began to prefer dresses and to take pride in her long hair. We can suppose that the mother's special attention to her daughter's clothes and hair helped shape her daughter's sex-typed preferences.

There is an even more vivid illustration of differential socialization practices in this same case history (Money & Ehrhardt, 1972, p. 120). When the mother caught her little boy urinating in a flower bed, she was amused. "I started laughing," she said, "and told daddy about it." But one day in the yard when her little girl took off her panties and threw them over the fence, the mother was not amused. She spanked the girl and "told her that nice little girls didn't do that." For somewhat similar behaviors, therefore, the two children were treated quite differently—but only because one was a boy and one was a girl.

Observations of parents with their own children indicate that the differential socialization practices illustrated in this case history are not uncommon. Even when parents are not fully aware of it, they tend to react differently to their children of different genders (Huston, 1983). This is particularly true of fathers.

The differential reactions that begin at birth tend to increase over time as children become sex-typed in their own behavior and attitudes. As sex-typing of behaviors and attitudes progresses through the preschool years, the children offer to their parents not just the physical appearance of a male or female, but the behavioral appearance as well. This can only feed further the tendency to treat one's children differently as a function of their sex, and that differential treatment can only feed further the tendency for children to differentiate from one another along sexual lines.

The potential for differential rearing to affect sex-role differentiation would be enhanced further if there were a correlation between some inherent constitutional factor and the rearing one receives (see Chapter 5, p. 251, on reactive genotype–environment correlation.) This could well be the case for the tendency of males to be more aggressive. If this tendency is begun by the effect of androgens on the developing brain, it is assisted by the way boys are treated postnatally. As we just discussed, even at birth they are given more vigorous stimulation. As infants they continue to be encouraged to engage in vigorous physical interactions, and they are often reinforced for their physically active play (Fagot, Hagan, Leinbach, & Kronsberg, 1985). Because males are expected to be more physically active and rough and tumble in their play, parents and teachers alike are liable to tolerate behavior in males that would be labeled as aggressiveness in females (Condry & Ross, 1985). In brief, expectations prevalent in the rearing environment seem to conspire from birth to keep male children on a developmental track that is compatible with their prenatal history. It conspires, at the same time, to keep females off this track. However, females exposed to androgens prenatally get caught somewhere in the middle, with the result that their initial behavioral tendencies may be somewhat at odds with societal expectations, thereby making behavioral outcomes a bit more problematic.

We have just reviewed data on culture, social models, television viewing, and gender that show that these factors are related to the development of prosocial and antisocial tendencies in individuals. The discovery of these relationships has made an important contribution to developmental psychology, but we must be careful not to infer too much from them. The first thing to remember is that the data are based primarily on correlational studies. Where this is true, we can only guess at the causal effects that created the correlations. Thus, although we may want to believe that correlations like those between degree of urbanization in a society and degree of competitiveness in children reflect a particular causal relationship, this inference goes beyond the data we have to support it.

A second thing to remember is that all the differences reported here are found in the averages for groups of individuals; they are not found in all individuals. On average, therefore, rural children are more prosocially inclined than urban ones, males are more aggressive than females, children imitate nurturant models more than nonnurturant ones, and 9-year-olds who watch aggressive acts on television are more likely to behave aggressively toward others in later adolescence. But these do not represent developmental certainties. There are too many other variables involved to be sure of the outcome in a single case. To make this point more vivid, we might consider just the case of male–female differences in aggressive behavior. The average difference, which has reliably appeared in almost every study ever conducted, is still a very small difference by absolute standards. In fact, it represents just 5 percent of the overall variation among humans in aggressiveness (Hyde, 1984). This leaves 95 percent to be explained by other factors. As a result, although the relationships we have been discussing are of practical and theoretical importance, we must be careful not to over interpret them.

SELF-CONTROL

Because humans live in such a highly interdependent social world, we must all count on each other to behave, to keep our social behavior in bounds, and to play by the rules. We have social institutions set up to assist in this (such as police forces and a judiciary), but the ultimate responsibility for control falls on the human conscience. The **conscience,** which is a popular way of referring to one's sense of moral responsibility, may be about as unique a human property as is language. According to primatologist R. E. Passingham, for example, "The difference between human and animal may be simply stated: a monkey may control its offspring by inducing fear, but a man can do so by instilling a conscience" (1982, p. 279).

The development of a conscience, or moral responsibility, is one of the most important outcomes of the socialization process, because it enables us to gain self-control. Were this essential quality absent in the members of a society, the society would fail for a lack of personal restraint on the one hand and a lack of interpersonal respect on the other. The development of a conscience, therefore, is a crucial part of our socialization process, and society has a tremendous investment in how the process turns out.

In addition to being one of the most important socialization outcomes, the development of conscience is one of the most interesting. At birth, as Freud noted long ago, we have not even the faintest glimmer of a conscience. Our behavior is totally unconstrained by any moral considerations. We sleep as much as we want, when in need we cry—even if it is 3:00 in the morning—and if we want something we just reach out and grab it. By adulthood, however, we are generally rather principled. We refuse ourselves the right to break in line, to park in handicapped-zones, and to take things from stores without paying for them. Also, if we cannot sleep at 3:00 A.M., we are sure to think it is wrong to wake the entire neighborhood to tell them about it. Obviously, then, we all go from being totally unrestrained to relatively restrained individuals. Because there often are no apparent external controls for our behaving in a restrained way, many psychologists have wondered how self-restraint develops. The general answer is that behavioral controls become internalized, but beyond that there are differences among the explanations offered by Freudian (or psychoanalytic) theory, social-learning theory, and attribution theory.

The Freudian View of Internalization

Historically, the most influential theoretical account of the development of conscience has been that of Freud who held that our principles of behavior are internalized versions of the external principles imposed on us by our parents. The parents' principles become an inner voice or conscience that speaks to the child even when the parents are not there. Freud explained how the **internalization** takes place by saying that it was the child's resolution of a universal developmental problem occurring between the ages of 3 and 5. The problem arises, according to Freud, because preschool-age children have a sexual attraction to the opposite-sex parent and hostility toward the same-sex parent of whom they are jealous. For males this attraction–hostility complex is called the *Oedipus complex*. In females it is called the *Electra complex*. In either case, the attraction–hostility complex creates a problem, because as long as the desire to possess one parent and displace the other persists, the child must live with fear of retaliation. This fear (called *castration anxiety* in males) serves as the motive for the eventual resolution of the Oedipus/Electra dilemma.

Motivated by fear, children are led, according to Freud, to *identify* with their same-sex parents. By identifying with the same-sex parent and striving to become like that parent, the preschool-age child no longer needs to fear. No longer a rival of the parent, the child perceives himself or herself to be a partner. Identification, therefore, is a convenient way out of the Oedipus/Electra dilemma. The part of the identification process of interest to us here is the internalization, or introjection, of the parent's values. In this way, all of the parent's specific rules for what the child can do, as well as the general rules for determining right from wrong, become the child's own rules. This means that proscriptions and rules that initially were external are now internal; they are part of the child's own being, a part that Freud called the **superego.**

Freud's theory of internalization, like the rest of his theory, is difficult to test because it is not written in a way that makes it falsifiable. However, as Martin Hoffman puts it: "Insofar as pertinent research exists, it tends to be nonsupportive" (1983, p. 237). Take, for example, the prediction that children of punitive parents should have more-punitive superegos than children of permissive parents. It turns out that the children of less-punitive parents show more self-control and more guilt than children with highly punitive parents (Hoffman, 1970). Results such as these have even led many psychoanalytic theorists to abandon Freud's view on the origins of the superego. Nonetheless, the fact that children in the preschool years come to have a conscience, which at the outset can be particularly severe and unyielding, is a developmental fact that must be dealt with. If this conscience is not literally the internalization of parental views, what is it?

Social-Learning Theory and the Development of Conscience

Social-learning theory is an extension of general-learning theory. The latter concerns learning in all animals, but **social-learning theory** is modified to make room for humans' greater symbolic and observational abilities (Bandura, 1977). A great strength of the social-learning theory's approach to the study of moral development is that it, above all others, has encouraged research on factors in development that have real implications for behavior. In fact, much of the research already reviewed in this and the previous chapter regarding the effects of modeling, television viewing, parent's choice of discipline techniques, and so forth was undertaken from a social-learning-theory point of view. We have even had a good example of a social-learning-theory explanation of behavior in Patterson's coercion-theory account of how parents and children learn to make life aversive for each other. Now, however, we want to divorce ourselves from considerations of the considerable heuristic value that social-learning theory has had in order to focus just on the theory's explanation for the development of conscience.

In the social-learning theorist's conceptualization, the problem in developing a conscience is one of learning to inhibit behaviors that are immoral and unwanted while learning to produce moral, desirable alternatives. According to the theory, children's success in doing this will be unrelated to their cognitive understanding of moral principles and unrelated as well to the specific instruction they have received from parents. It will be related only to their specific learning histories.

The term *learning history* provides a convenient way to refer, in general, to all of a person's past experiences with specific consequences that followed on the heels of specific behaviors. The aspect of these behavior–consequence relations that is of greatest importance is whether they are positive (leading to learning) or negative (leading to inhibition). Each behavior–consequence pairing—whether positive or negative—makes for what is called a *learning trial*.

Central to social-learning theory is the belief that the behavior–consequence pairings that make up the learning history do not all have to be direct, personal experiences. Many of the pairings, for example, will come by observing others. Other pairings will just be imaginatively experienced, perhaps through reading a story or even through thought alone. No matter what their source, direct and indirect experiences alike can all go into the learning history to affect the likelihood that a person will have "conscience" enough to inhibit unwanted behaviors.

The specifics of constructing a conscience out of behavior–consequence pairings rely on some principles from general-learning theory. One of these is the principle of *conditioned anxieties* (see Eysenck, 1970). The anxiety portion of a conditioned anxiety is easy to understand. This is the unpleasant, anxious feeling we get whenever we contemplate misbehaving. But the heart of the general-learning-theory account of conditioned anxiety lies in how we acquire these anxieties and what their consequences are. We acquire the anxieties, the theory holds, through a process of classical conditioning. The conditioning occurs when the behavior–consequence pairings just described involve punishments and other adverse consequences. An important aspect of the learning that takes place from behavior–punishment pairings is that the cognitive intents to behave (or, in this case, to misbehave) that precede the actual behavior serve as conditioned stimuli that arouse some of the punishment effects in anticipatory fashion. This means that on experiencing the intent to misbehave, there is an immediate anticipation of negative events. This anticipation is experienced as anxiety.

Once the anxiety is established, a "conscience" is in place, and children should learn to obey this conscience readily. The reason is that obeying one's conscience has an immediate positive effect: it alleviates the anxiety associated with thoughts of misbehaving. For reasons we need not be concerned with, the positive effect associated with inhibiting an intent to misbehave (that is, anxiety alleviation) is known as *negative reinforcement*. In the language of general-learning theorists, therefore, once a child has developed conditioned anxieties, choosing to obey leads to immediate negative reinforcement. And this leads to learning to obey, even when no one is around to force the child to inhibit undesirable behaviors.

Although the social-learning theory of conscience fits easily with the commonsense view that much of our moral behavior is motivated through guilt avoidance, it turns out that the conditioned-anxiety view of control is not completely satisfying. It fails as an adequate theory of how we achieve internal control of behavior, in fact, for some of the same reasons that the Freudian view of internalization fails. Along with Freudian theory, social-learning theory would predict that the most punitive parents would have children with the strongest internal control over their own behavior. The data, however, show an opposite relationship. Time and again, it has been found that a history of mild threats and punishments leads to greater self-control than does a history of strong threats and punishments. The final theory of internalization that we will review, attribution theory, has been specifically designed to account for this relationship.

Attribution Theory

Without any knowledge of the data from psychological research, most people—parents included—would judge that Freud and the social-learning theorists were probably right in predicting that there would be a direct connection between the strength of reinforcement or punishment that a person experiences and the strength of the person's resolve to behave or not behave in a given way. The premise that strong discipline leads to strong conscience does not turn out to be true, however. Correlational data show, for example, that frequent use of physical punishment is associated with low conscience development (Sears, Maccoby, & Levin, 1957). A more concrete illustration of the falsity of the premise than we have seen so far comes from work on children's ability to resist temptation. The research shows that children are more likely to resist temptation on their own if they have been previously induced to resist temptation through the use of mild rather than severe prohibitions.

One situation in which this has been observed experimentally involved the use of forbidden toys. Children were given either a mild or severe prohibition not to play with an attractive toy. Later, when these children were asked to play a rigged bowling game that could only be won by cheating, the children who had obeyed a mild prohibition not to play with the toy were more likely to avoid the temptation to cheat than children who had previously obeyed a severe threat not to play with the toy (Lepper, 1973). Attribution theory is alone among the internalization theories in being able to explain such a bizarre result.

The essence of **attribution theory,** which was first developed by Fritz Heider (1958), is that we are constantly trying to determine the causes of our behavior. When there is a salient consequence like severe punishment to deter us from misbehaving, we can explain our obedience in terms of the punishment. But how about when the threat is only mild? Now the potential punishment is not so great that it should deter us from doing what we want to do. If we nonetheless avoid misbehaving, the only way to explain our avoidance is to make what is called a *self-attribution*. This means that we judge the cause to be in our own personal characteristics (namely, our quality of obedience) rather than in characteristics of the environment (for example, reward or punishment). Applying this analysis to the forbidden-toy study above, we can reason that the children who obeyed mild threats were more likely to make the attribution that their obedience was due to the fact that they were "good children," the kind who obeyed adults (at least in the unusual context of a laboratory experiment conducted by adult psychologists). The children in the severe-threat condition were not required to make such an attribution to explain their behavior regarding the toy; therefore, they went into the bowling-game task with nothing other than their outside-the-laboratory rules of behavior to guide them.

Generalizing from this experiment and others, Mark Lepper (1983) has suggested that internalization of behavioral control can be best promoted by practicing a *minimal-sufficiency* rule in designing environmental controls on behavior. That is, if you want people to decide that they themselves are the cause of their own behavior, use minimal, not maximal, external control. In effect, you want to trick people into believing that the only reason they behave as they do is that they themselves choose to behave that way, or, stated another way, that it is their own consciences that control their behavior, not external contingencies. This bit of advice is far different from the advice originally given by social-learning theorists, which was to maximize the anxiety one would feel about misbehaving.

A second bit of advice that is derived from the attribution-theory approach to internalization is that intrinsic reasons for engaging in behaviors should be emphasized. This is the flip side of the minimal-sufficiency principle. Minimal sufficiency refers to minimizing the extrinsic reasons for engaging in an activity. The reverse is that one should maximize the intrinsic reasons for engaging in a behavior. This thought takes us back to a consideration of the role of inductive discipline in the moralization process. As we learned in the previous chapter, parents who use inductive techniques tend to have children with a more prosocial orientation. Hoffman reasoned that this was because other-oriented inductions promote empathy. But it is also true that inductive discipline techniques are associated with greater self-control. A field study showing this effect was conducted long ago by Robert Sears, Eleanor Maccoby, and Harry Levin (1957). These investigators related parental discipline techniques with children's strength of conscience in the late preschool years. They found that parents who were rated as high in their use of "reasoning" during discipline had children with stronger consciences than parents who used reasoning less often.

Laboratory studies have shown the same result as the Sears, Maccoby, and Levin field study. James Cheyne (1969), for example, measured the length of time kindergarten and third-grade children would resist playing with a forbidden toy as a function of the type of prohibition they had been given. One group was told "That's bad" when they picked up the toy that had been designated as the one they were not supposed to play with. Another group was told "That's bad; you shouldn't play with that toy." The third was told "That's bad; you should not play with that toy. That toy belongs to someone else." In Figure 13-10, these groups are labeled as no rule, simple rule, and rule and rationale, respectively. You can see there that children in the rule-and-rationale group were most able to refrain from playing with the forbidden toy and that this effect was even greater for third graders than for children in kindergarten.

The discovery that providing children with rationales for their behavior increases self-control fits with an attribution-theory explanation of internalization, because rationales make the intrinsic justifications for our behavior salient to us. By increasing the salience of intrinsic justifications, we automatically increase the probability of a self-attribution for behavior. The reason is that extrinsic and intrinsic reasons for behaviors will inevitably be present. They hang forever in a balance for the child to decide which is the weightier. When one is emphasized over the other, we increase the chance that the attribution of causality will focus on that factor. Thus, it is better to say to a child, "You picked up your toys in order to make mother feel better, didn't you?" than to say "You picked up your toys so that you wouldn't get a whipping, didn't you?"

Parenting experts who find both practical benefit and theoretical justification in communicating to children about the intrinsic reasons for their

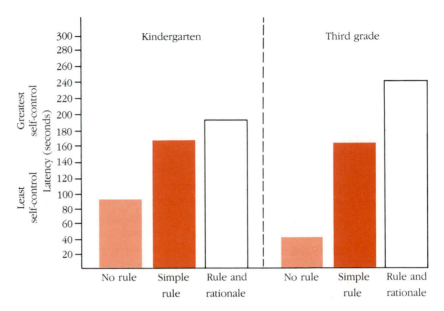

FIGURE 13-10

The Relationship of Rationales to Self-Control

These data show that when prohibited from using a "forbidden toy," both kindergarten and third-grade children were most likely to resist temptation if the prohibition given to them was coupled with a rationale, thereby leading to greater self-control. (After Cheyne, 1969)

behavior offer advice on how to make rationales most effective. One piece of advice is that the rationales should be kept short (Hetherington, 1975). In cases of discipline, for example, children do not need a lecture on ethics. They need only to be given enough information so that they can understand why the parent considers their behavior to be wrong. In giving this information, parents should keep in mind developmental level. For example, 3-year-olds have a poor appreciation for the abstract notion of property rights, but they know quite well that they are a danger to fragile objects. Therefore telling 3-year-olds that it is wrong to touch something because they might break it will have more impact than telling them that it is wrong to touch it because it belongs to someone else (Parke, 1977).

SUMMARY

This chapter began with the development of autonomy out of attachment, a development that occurs in the postinfant lives of all dependent animals. The move is occasioned not only by infants' increasing willingness to separate themselves from their mothers, but also by mothers' willingness to allow their infants to separate from them. Once infants achieve some autonomy, social play with peers becomes a major pastime.

After a beginning marked more by mutual interest than by interaction, children begin to play together in earnest in late infancy and early childhood. The frequency of associative and cooperative play increases throughout the preschool period. Games with rules, many of which involve competition, become popular in middle childhood before declining in interest in late childhood and early adolescence.

Evolutionary theorists and others hold that play is not just an idle recreation; it is a developmentally vital activity. For animals of all species, play is a safe occasion for practicing skills that will be useful in adulthood. In humans, play is more than just a safe means of practicing, it is also an occasion for developmental experiences that are of emotional, cognitive, and social importance. The benefits of play to social development are most evident in social pretend play. This has prompted some psychologists to suggest that play tutoring be instituted in preschool programs for children who do not already have a strong preference for pretend play.

When children play together or have other social interactions, it is interesting to look for signs of prosocial or antisocial behavior. Contrary to the belief that was popular in the nineteenth century, there is no evidence that antisocial tendencies have any priority in development. In fact, recent research has shown that infants are surprisingly prosocial. Nonetheless, aggressive tendencies are evident in most children at least some of the time. Hostile aggression as opposed to instrumental aggression does not appear until children can understand the consequences of their actions. From preschool to middle childhood, the frequency of physical hostility declines while verbal hostility increases.

A number of factors relate to the development of individual differences in prosocial and antisocial behavior. Cross-cultural research by the Whitings and others has consistently shown that children from urban, industrialized societies with Western-style schools are more competitive than children from traditional rural settings. One reason may be that families in traditional settings depend on mutual cooperation among family members more so than families in nontraditional cultures. Also, the system of schooling in traditional cultures does not promote interpersonal competition to the same extent as Western schooling.

Exposure to different social models is a second factor that is associated with individual differences in antisocial and prosocial behavior. Social models are effective in increasing the levels of both prosocial and antisocial behavior, with nurturant models being the ones who are most likely to be effective in prosocial development.

Television is a third factor of importance. Longitudinal research provides evidence of a link between the frequency with which children watch televised violence in middle childhood and their aggressive tendencies in adolescence. Leonard Eron interprets the evidence to mean that viewing violent television, particularly during a time of intellectual immaturity, can contribute to the development of individuals who choose aggressive solutions to interpersonal conflict. Viewing televised violence may also make people more tolerant of violence in general.

Gender relates to aggressive behavior but not to prosocial behavior. Nonetheless, females have a reputation for prosocial behavior that may be due to differences in verbal expressions and affect more than to actual behavior. With regard to the male–female difference in aggression, many assume that this difference must be related to the biological differences between the sexes. The biological difference that has been most strongly implicated is the difference in androgen levels that exist prenatally during the time of brain development. As Anke Ehrhardt and others have shown, there is some merit to this hypothesis; however, hormonal differences are not sufficient to explain behavioral differences in so complex an animal as humans. Studies of social expectations show that parents and other adults treat children of the two sexes differently from birth onward in ways that seem to reinforce the male propensity toward rough-and-tumble play and perhaps even toward aggression.

Given the social interdependence of humans, the development of self-control is essential to the well-being of social groups. The issue of how self-control develops has been addressed by Freudian theory, social-learning theory, and attribution theory. Freudian theory holds that the human conscience, or superego, emerges as the resolution to the Oedipus complex in males and the Electra complex in females. The conscience is the internalization of parental values and rules. According to social-learning theorists, conscience does not develop in one fell swoop as a resolution to a particular developmental crisis; rather, conscience develops through a slow, step-by-step learning history in which children learn to discriminate acceptable from unacceptable behavior and develop anxieties about behaving in unacceptable ways. A problem with the Freudian and social-learning views is that neither can account for the fact that parents who use mild threats and punishments have children with better self-control than parents who use stronger forms of control. Attribution theory provides a way of explaining this result. It does so through use of the minimal-sufficiency principle.

SUGGESTIONS FOR FURTHER READING

Harlow, H. F. & Mears, C. (1979). *The human model: Primate perspectives.* New York: John Wiley. In this volume Harlow brings together the major research papers from his long and illustrious research career.

Mussen, P. & Eisenberg-Berg, N. (1977). *Roots of caring, sharing, and helping: The development of prosocial behavior in children.* San Francisco: W. H. Freeman. A somewhat dated but still useful introduction to the field of prosocial development.

Whiting, B. B. & Whiting, J. W. M. (1975). *Children of six cultures: A psychocultural analysis.* Cambridge, MA: Harvard University Press. A report of data from the massive Six Culture Study.

Yawkey, T. D. & Pellegrini, A. D. (1984). *Child's play: Developmental and applied.* Hillsdale, NJ: Lawrence Erlbaum. A useful collection of descriptive and theoretical articles on the contributions of play to human development.

CHAPTER 14

Social Cognition

In the late 1960s, researchers began to broaden their studies of cognitive development. Whereas before they had focused primarily on the physical world of objects and events, increasingly they turned to the social world of people and interpersonal relations. Not too surprisingly, they found that young children were as immature in their reasoning about social concepts (for example, the self, morality, friendship, and intentions) as they were about purely physical concepts (for example, weight, classifications, and logical relations). Mature cognitions in the social realm of people and interpersonal relations, therefore, were found to be as dependent on abstract and decentered thinking as were mature cognitions in the nonsocial realm of objects and logical relations.

In this chapter we will discuss the development of self-awareness and self-understanding, the development of perspective-taking skills, and the development of moral reasoning. These three topics do not exhaust the field of social cognition (Shantz, 1983), but they are the three that have been most thoroughly researched. In presenting what we know about development in each of these areas, the primary goal will be to describe the typical pattern of development with a secondary emphasis on factors that contribute to it.

The ability to describe the ontogeny of social cognition is important to a science of development, because there is a firm conviction among researchers that how one conceptualizes oneself and one's relationships with others has major implications for one's ability to get along with oneself and with others. In fact, it is quite plausible that many of the factors we have previously seen to be related to social development—factors such as rural/urban life-style, authoritative parenting, social pretend play, and inductive discipline—may relate to social development because of the effect they have on the development of social cognition (Pellegrini, 1985).

THE DEVELOPMENT OF SELF-UNDERSTANDING

Becoming Aware of Oneself

The first step in self-awareness is to become aware of the I–other distinction. This is the quite elementary understanding that there is a boundary between all that is self and all that is nonself. At present, we can only guess how infants might come to realize that they are entities distinct from all others because we have no methodology for empirically determining when self-awareness first develops. Surprisingly, however, there is general agreement among psychologists on how self–other differentiation could rationally come about. It develops, they say, through a discovery of reliable if–then relationships that link one's own behavior to its consequences (Lewis & Brooks-Gunn, 1979; Watson, 1985). These if–then relationships, called *contingencies,* probably provide the earliest education in the distinction between self and other.

The I–Other Distinction

Most attempts to conceptualize the dawning of self-awareness in the consciousness of infant humans begin with the assumption that, initially, self and other are fused. Therefore, everything an infant senses or experiences is sensed or experienced merely as an extension of self. For example, the pacifiers on which infants suck no less than the thumbs on which they suck are sensed as a part of self. But through experience, the thumb becomes "self" and the pacifier "other." This occurs because there is a quite fundamental difference between the way the two are experienced. Specifically, each sucking movement is matched by a thumb sensation (a "me experience"), but not by a pacifier sensation. From this fundamental sensory–motor, action–reaction contingency, infants have the grounds for a far-reaching inference: thumb and mouth must be part of a single self-system, whereas pacifier and mouth must be part of separate systems. Such observations form the foundation not only for self-knowledge but for object knowledge as well (see Chapter 8).

The argument that our first awareness of self is constructed out of experiences of contingent action–reaction relations makes sense. The self, from this point of view, is a parsimonious hypothesis put forth by the infant brain to account for the contingencies. But is this reasonable account true? Does repeated exposure to action–reaction contingency information in fact lead to the mental construction of a self–other boundary? There is no way to know for sure, but observations of infants in their first months of life indicate that they have ample data to form the hypothesis of an integrated self that is separate from all other entities. Piaget noted, for example, that some action–reaction sequences that he called *primary circular reactions* dominate among infant behavior patterns in the period 1 to 4 months (Piaget, 1936/1963). Those behaviors involve actions such as sucking and looking that are focused primarily on one's own body. Michael Lewis and Jeanne Brooks-Gunn give a brief example of such actions:

> [Three-month-old Gregory is] awake, on his back, with his right hand extended above him and to the right; his head is turned toward his hand and he is watching his fingers move with considerable interest. He continues to do this for a while longer, then lowers his arm and finally gets the fingers of his right hand into his mouth. (1979, p. 2)

In this brief portrayal of infant experience we have two excellent examples (first visually observing the fingers and then sucking on them) of the sort of self-based, action–reaction contingencies that are constantly available to infants as a source of self-knowledge, the sort of contingencies that would lead to the inference that hand, fingers, arm, and mouth are all part of the same self-system. We find it reasonable to believe that infants in fact use such primitive, body-centered contingencies to construct their initial self-awareness.

Knowledge of Personal Agency

In addition to the contingencies that exist between self-based actions and reactions, there are contingencies between infants' actions and the actions of others—both objects and people. Continuing to think more as philosophers than as hard-nosed, objective scientists, we can conjecture that infants use these contingencies to further their knowledge of self by adding to their I–other knowledge—the knowledge that "I can make things happen." This knowledge of one's ability to produce and control events in the social and physical world is known as a knowledge of **personal agency.**

The first clear indication that infants know they can make things happen in the world outside themselves comes around the fourth month. At this age, infants kick, scream, reach, and grasp with apparent awareness of at least some of the causal connections between their own actions and the outcomes in the world around them. This is evident in the following example of an infant's actions relative to objects:

> [Four-month-old Susan] is lying on her back in her crib looking at a
> brightly colored mobile above her. She kicks her foot and the mobile
> rattles. Within seconds she kicks her foot again and again the mobile
> moves. She watches the moving objects with great interest without
> kicking. Finally, 20 seconds after the mobile is perfectly still, she kicks
> her foot again while watching it. (Lewis & Brooks-Gunn, 1979, p. 1)

Young infants seem to be as aware of their effects on other people as they
are of their effects on objects, as is illustrated in this report:

> Our 6-month-old has just learned that if she moves in her walker
> toward a large hanging plant and then screams, mom comes running
> in to move her away. We have enjoyed peeking in and watching her
> move across the room toward the plant, scream, and then sit and wait
> for mom to appear. (Edward Lonky, personal communication, June 30,
> 1985)

As these observations reveal, young infants have an apparent appreciation
for the role they play in controlling both the physical and social events that
occur around them.

According to Piaget (1936/1954), the awareness of personal agency that
is present in infants as young as 4 months of age is a mental construction
just as the I–other distinction is. Infants allegedly construct the personal-
agency hypothesis as a means of explaining the contingencies they observe
between their own actions and the actions of others. Piaget labeled the action sequences that could lead to a knowledge of personal agency as *secondary circular reactions*. They are secondary because they focus not on
self (which is primary) but on other (which is secondary). They are circular
because they are patterns of self–other interaction that are repeated again
and again.

When secondary circular patterns of behavior first appear (such as the
circular episodes involving kicking the feet and then watching a crib mobile
move), infants allegedly have no appreciation for the causal role they play.
But by virtue of maturation and the experience of frequently observing secondary contingencies, infants are able to determine that they play a role.
Grounds for inferring that infants do construct a belief in personal causality
is that they frequently misapply their learning, as when they kick their feet
on seeing a familiar mobile, even if it is located across the room (Piaget,
1936/1954).

Does Parental Sensitivity Help Create One's Sense of Personal Agency?

Although there are no differences among mobiles in the extent to which
they will respond contingently to an infant's kicks, there are differences
among parents in the extent to which they will behave contingently in re-

sponse to their infants' signals. As we learned in Chapter 12, the difference is in the parental variable known as *sensitivity*. Sensitive parents establish contingent, appropriate, and consistent responses to their infants' signals; insensitive parents do not. This raises the question of whether parental differences in sensitivity might create differences in personal agency among infants. Might it be that infants with insensitive parents develop a poorer sense of personal agency than infants with more-sensitive parents? The nearly unanimous answer from contemporary developmental psychologists is yes (Lamb & Easterbrooks, 1981, p. 147). Infants are liable to have a poor sense of personal agency, at least as regards their parents, if they do not have the privilege of experiencing such common child–parent contingencies as crying and being held or making eye contact and being talked to (or at least smiled at). As Michael Lamb and M. Ann Easterbrooks (1981) point out, this could affect the quality of their subsequent attachment. Infants with a Group C ambivalent attachment, for example, might have this form of attachment precisely because they have been unable to establish any clear expectancies for their parents' behavior. The infants are ambivalent because their parents have been ambiguous. An even greater fear is that the poor sense of agency would not be restricted just to the parents (Lamb & Easterbrooks, 1981). It might generalize into a condition that clinical psychologists refer to as *learned helplessness,* which refers to an invalid and maladaptive belief that one is powerless to control the events of one's life (Seligman, 1975).

Self-recognition

Whereas we have no clearly objective means of measuring infants' awareness of the I–other distinction or their own personal agency, we do have a means of measuring self-recognition, which is a third component to infants' awareness of self. The means is to provide infants with visual feedback that is in perfect synchrony with their own movements and then see if they can infer from this that they themselves are the source of movement in the synchronized image (Brooks-Gunn & Lewis, 1984).

Research with infants as young as 6 months of age shows that they respond differently to an image that is synchronized to their own movements than one that is not. Hans Papoušek showed this to be true of facial images (Papoušek & Papoušek, 1974), and John Watson showed it to be true even of televised views of one's feet and legs (Watson, 1985, see Figure 14-1). Interestingly, infants prefer watching *nonsynchronized* images, as if an "other" might be more interesting than self. Actually, however, the preference data alone do not argue for any awareness of self. They only show that the synchrony is noted. Before we can infer an awareness of self, we must show that infants become purposeful in their manipulation of their synchronized image. The most convincing way to do this is to use mirrors and look for signs of self-recognition.

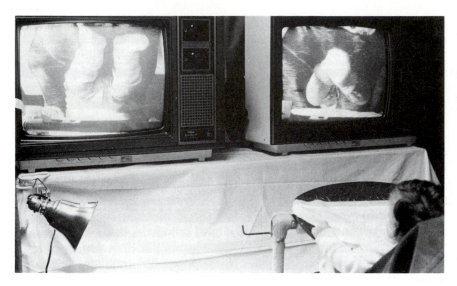

Figure 14-1
Preference for Nonsynchronized Movements
A visual preference test pits a live image of a 5-month-old's own feet and legs versus a taped image. Preferential looking to one image or the other indicates that infants detect the difference between an image that is contingent on their own movements and one that is not. This contingency recognition could be the basis of self-recognition.

Mirror Research   When humans or other animals have the experience of seeing themselves in a mirror, it creates an interesting experience. The mirror objectifies the self as if it were not self but other. It is not surprising, then, that when humans and other animals first see a self-image they react to it as if it were an "other." This is inferred from their image-directed behavior. For example, children reach out to the image and touch it (see Figure 14-2). In keeping with the "other" interpretation, many fish, birds, and mammals react aggressively when they see their image for the first time (Brooks-Gunn & Lewis, 1984). Apes and monkeys often look behind the mirror as if seeking some substantiation of the image.

Although treating a mirror image as if it were a stranger is an understandable reaction for an animal or human that is seeing a self-image for the first time, we might expect that both animals and humans would be able to figure out the meaning of a mirror image after some experience with mirrors. The reason lies in the synchrony of movements: image movements are perfectly contingent on self-movements. Twitch a facial muscle and there is a contingent change in the visual image of the face. Bob and turn the head and the same thing happens. Animals and humans that are able to infer from this contingency that "I am in control of the image" should come to realize that the person in the mirror is "me." An objective way of determining whether they do is to watch for self-directed behaviors to replace image-directed behaviors as a response to seeing one's mirror image. A more specific test is to surreptitiously place a bit of dye on an ear or above an eye. If this leads not just to self-directed but to mark-directed behaviors, we can be sure that the mirror image is interpreted to be self and not other.

Results from the mark-on-the-face test show that infants as young as 9 months of age engage in more self-directed behavior when looking at their marked rather than their unmarked image. There is no substantial evidence of self-recognition, however, until around 15 months of age. At this age, 20 percent of the infants studied by Michael Lewis and Jeanne Brooks-Gunn (1979) wiped their noses when they saw in a mirror that a bit of red rouge had been put there. Mark-directed behavior becomes typical of infants in the period between 18 to 24 months of age (Brook-Gunn & Lewis, 1984). Beyond 2 years of age, the mark-on-the-face test is no longer needed to assess self-recognition. You can just ask children who they see in the mirror. Most will be able to name themself (Gesell, 1928). This succession of ever-more explicit evidence for self-recognition probably reflects that the capacity we have been calling self-recognition "does not emerge suddenly with one particular behavior, but develops gradually through a succession of types of behaviors" (Bertenthal & Fischer, 1978, p. 44).

Of the many species of animals that have been observed in mirror tests, the only ones other than humans to react in a way that reflects self-recognition are chimpanzees (Gallup, 1970) and orangutans (Lethmate &

Figure 14-2
Self-recognition
One can infer that the image in a mirror is self from either the self-contingent movement in the image or from a recognition of one's unique facial features. Contingency information is thought to be primary in the development of self-recognition.

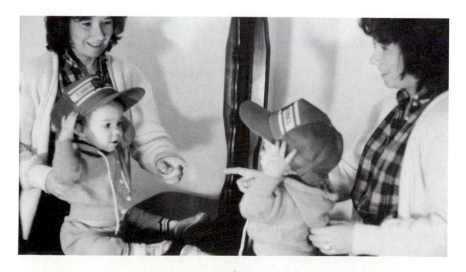

Ducker, 1973). They do so after relatively brief exposure to their mirrored images. In research by Gordon Gallup (1970), for example, full-length mirrors were set up in the cages of 4 chimpanzees for 10 days. Initially the chimps treated their mirror images as if they represented unfamiliar companions. They hooted at their images, threatened them, and made other social responses. But these social responses quickly waned, giving way on Days 3 through 10 to primarily self-directed behavior. For example, the chimps made faces at the mirror, blew bubbles, picked their teeth, and used the mirror to groom parts of their bodies that they could not otherwise see. In the acid test of self-recognition, the chimps responded as humans do to the mark-on-the-face test. The marks were applied while the animals were anesthetized. On waking they were shown their faces in a mirror. The chimps spent a lot more time than usual examining their faces, and they directed their attention to the mark, frequently rubbing it and then examining their fingers (Gallup, 1970).

In light of the animal data, the ability of 18-month-old humans to correctly interpret mirror images takes on new significance. The ability to infer that a contingently moving image is a reflection of oneself is not an ability that is duplicated in every creature with a brain for recording the contingency information. Though not completely unique in the animal kingdom, the human capacity for judging when image movements are self-reflections is a capacity we share only with those few animals that are most like us—the great apes.

In brief summary of the account of the development of self-awareness to this point, we can reason that awareness of self begins in body awareness, which arises, we believe, from self-based action–reaction sequences like those that Piaget identified as primary circular reactions. These experiences are sufficient for making the initial I–other distinction. In later infancy, self-knowledge is elaborated with knowledge of personal agency, the knowledge that "I" can act as a causal factor in both the physical and social world. The capacity to recognize oneself as the source of contingently moving images appears some time after this. The most rigorous test of self-recognition is the mark-on-the-face test that is passed by the majority of infants 18 months of age and older. However, self-directed movements in response to a mirror image are frequent among 1-year-olds, and even 6-month-olds discriminate images that are contingent on self-movements from those that are not.

Discovering One's Own Unique Attributes

As infants become aware of themselves as distinct entities, they also become aware of some of their defining characteristics. For example, they learn about their physical features (curly hair or floppy ears), their behaviors (rides a tricycle but cannot tie shoes), their social roles (oldest daughter and member of Brownies Troop No. 24), and their psychological traits (sociable and intelligent). The composite of such self-knowledge that one has at any given time constitutes one's knowledge of the *categorical self* (Lewis & Brooks-Gunn, 1979).

The earliest categorical knowledge involves appearance: infants learn what they look like and how their own appearance is different from that of others. You might think that the mirror data already presented make this point, but they do not. The reason is that mirrors confound contingent movement with physical features, so that we have no way to know which an infant is using to make the judgment that the mirror image is a self-image. They might recognize just their movements and not their features. To test for feature recognition alone, videotapes or photographs must be used. Tests using videotape presentations of self and a same sex, same age "other" show self-recognition by 15 months of age (Lewis & Brooks-Gunn, 1979). Test using photographs show self-recognition by 21 months of age (Lewis & Brooks-Gunn, 1979).

In addition to knowing their own unique features, children in late infancy are aware of some of their behavioral capacities. According to Jerome Kagan (1981), for example, children of 22 to 24 months of age will frequently cry if an adult demonstrates a simple action that the child is not competent to repeat. The alleged reason is that they immediately recognize the actions that fall within their competency to perform and the ones that do not. A more direct measure of 2-year-olds' awareness of what they can and cannot do comes from listening to them talk. "I can" and "I can't" are among the things they often say.

In addition to knowing what they themselves look like and what some of their behavioral limitations are, 2-year-olds are aware in a crude way of their age and gender. Both of these categorical aspects of self are of particular interest to infants, and, beginning in infancy, they form primitive conceptualizations of these dimensions of selfhood. Examing the nature of these conceptualizations will give us our first view of the intimate tie between social and nonsocial cognition.

Age

Studies of person perception using photographs and other stimuli show that infants make age discriminations quite easily. The first indication of age as an important social stimulus comes in early infancy when infants show a peculiarly strong interest in baby pictures. Later, they demonstrate the ability to discriminate baby pictures from adult pictures (Fagan, 1972), and by 3 years of age they can correctly sort pictures into the categories *little child, big child, parent, and grandparent* (Edwards, 1984; Edwards & Lewis, 1979). Data from children 4 and 5 years of age indicate that even at this point in social development, age remains a more salient personal attribute than any other except sex. It is even more salient, for example, than race (McGraw, Durm, & Patterson, 1983).

Children's precocious attention to the age variable is particularly interesting in light of the fact that infants and young children have little understanding of age as a quantitative concept (that is, number of years since birth). Lacking the quantitative understanding needed to conceptualize age properly, children generally use size as their primary cirterion. Bigger, they reason, is older. This was brought out clearly in some of Piaget's interviews in which children were quizzed about age relations among trees that grew at different rates (Piaget, 1946/1969). Young children invariably reported that a 4-year-old pear tree was older than a 5-year-old apple tree because it was taller. Twins, too, are judged to be different ages if one grows taller than the other, and "daddies" are older than "mommies" for the same reason. Children's use of size to define age serves to explain the commonly held childhood belief that once you are grown-up, you stop having birthdays. As psychologist David Elkind's child said to him: "Daddy, you don't need any more birthdays; you're all grown up already" (quoted in Formanek & Gurian, 1981, p. 95).

Gender

Even more important than age as a self-attribute is gender. In fact, the first thing people want to know about a new baby is its gender: "Is it a boy or a girl?" Later, they might inquire about the baby's birth weight, general health, and whether the baby was delivered in a normal, uneventful way; but first they want to know its sex (Intons-Peterson & Reddel, 1984). With others putting such emphasis on gender, it is not surprising that gender is one of the first things children learn about themselves.

By age 3, almost all children can identify themselves as a boy or girl. You might think that this knowledge is rote knowledge, memorized like one's own name. But one's gender is not just a memorized label. This is evident in the fact that children can identify the sex of others as easily as they identify their own sex. Research by Spencer Thompson (1975), for example, showed that children just 2 years of age could look at unfamiliar male–female picture pairs and indicate which of the two pictures was the boy–girl, man–woman, mommy–daddy, and so forth. The boy–girl label that children apply to themselves at this age, therefore, is not just a label; it is a concept. Children 2 and 3 years of age even know some of the implications of being male or female. For example, Thompson's 2-year-olds scored 61 percent correct on a test of their ability to sort pictures of sex-typed objects (for example, a necktie or tube of lipstick) into male and female categories. By 3 years of age they scored 86 percent correct.

Although children can label both self and other according to gender as early as 2 years of age, children have conceptual failings regarding the meaning of gender just as they do about the meaning of age. These conceptual failings are referred to as a lack of **gender stability** and a lack of **gender constancy.** The first reflects a failure to realize that one's own gender, and the gender of others, *does not* change over time. The second reflects a failure to realize that gender *cannot* change over time. These two failings may seem surprising until you consider that stability and constancy are uncommon characteristics for personal attributes. For example, age and strength will change, so why shouldn't sex?

Gender Stability   To assess knowledge of their own gender stability, children can be asked questions such as "When you were a little baby, were you a little boy or a little girl?" or "When you grow up, will you be a mommy or a daddy?" Children who give an answer to either question that is inconsistent with their current identity are judged to be unaware of the stability of gender as a personal characteristic (Slaby & Frey, 1975). To assess knowledge of gender stability for others, children can be shown a doll (Munroe, Shimmin, & Munroe, 1984) and then asked similar questions about the doll.

Gender Constancy   To assess knowledge of gender constancy, children are asked whether they themselves would become a member of the opposite sex if they were to begin playing opposite-sex games or wearing opposite-sex clothing. They are also asked whether they could become a member of the opposite sex "if they wanted to." Children who answer yes to these questions are judged to lack a belief in their own gender constancy. If they make similar judgments about dolls (see Box 14-1), they are said to lack a belief in the gender constancy of others.

Although you might think that children who realize gender to be a stable attribute would automatically believe in its constancy, this is not so. All children—even in cultures quite different from our own (Munroe, Shimmin, & Munroe, 1984)—believe in stability before constancy. This has been shown in both cross-sectional and longitudinal studies (Fagot, 1985). It is as if children recognize stability to be a *species-typical* characteristic of gender before they recognize it to be an *inevitable* characteristic. In the doll tests, for example, even if the dolls have genitals that remain constant (McConaghy, 1979), children who express a belief in stability will frequently say that changing the dolls' clothes or hair would change the dolls' gender. They will also say that if they themselves were changed in the way the dolls are changed (that is, a change of hair, clothes, or behavior), they too would undergo a sex change. This belief does not fade until around age 7, when children recognize that gender, unlike age and other personal characteristics, can never change. Their faith in this conclusion derives from the discovery that anatomy defines gender; clothes, hair, and the sex-typed activities one engages in (sewing or playing football) are irrelevant.

> **Box 14-1**
> **Sample Questions to Assess Gender Constancy**
>
>
>
> **Task 1: Girl stimulus**
>
> Item 1: If Janie really *wants to be* a boy, can she be?
>
> Item 2: If Janie *played with trucks and did boy things,* what would she be? Would she be a girl, or would she be a boy?
>
> Item 3: If Janie *puts on boy clothes* like this, what would she be? Would she be a girl, or would she be a boy?
>
> Item 4: If Janie has her *hair cut short* like this, what would she be? Would she be a girl, or would she be a boy?
>
> Item 5: If Janie has her *hair cut short* like this and *wears boy clothes* like this, what would she be? Would she be a girl, or would she be a boy?
>
> **Task II: Boy stimulus**
>
> Item 1: If Johnny really *wants to be* a girl, can he be?
>
> Item 2: If Johnny *played with dolls and did girl things,* what would he be? Would he be a boy, or would he be a girl?
>
> Item 3: If Johnny *puts on girl clothes* like this, what would he be? Would he be a boy, or would he be a girl?
>
> Item 4: If Johnny lets his *hair grow long* like this, what would he be? Would he be a boy, or would he be a girl?
>
> Item 5: If Johnny lets his *hair grow long* like this and *wears girl clothes* like this, what would he be? Would he be a boy, or would he be a girl. (Emmerich, W., Goldman, K.S., Kirsh, B., & Sharabany, R., 1976)

The Link Between Gender Concepts and General Cognition   Lawrence Kohlberg (1966) has related the development of gender constancy to the conceptual achievement of conservation. Conservation (whether of amount, weight, area, or volume) occurs when children realize that certain conceptual properties of objects remain constant despite superficial transformations (see Chapter 8). Achieving gender constancy requires a similar realization (Marcus & Overton, 1978). Children must realize that gender does not change just because a child grows longer hair, puts on pants or a skirt, engages in sex-typed activities. Preschool children are apt to think that gender does change under these circumstances just as they believe that changing the shape of a ball of clay changes its weight or changing the arrangement of pennies in a row changes their number.

Research on the acquisition of gender constancy has uncovered further correspondence between the development of a full understanding of the social concept of gender and other aspects of children's conceptual development. Like children's understanding of physical-world concepts, gender understanding develops according to the principle of *horizontal decalage* (see Chapter 8 p. 425). The understanding matures first for self-judgments, then for same-sex other judgments, and last for opposite-sex other judgments (Eaton & VonBargen, 1981; Gouze & Nadelman, 1980). This means that labeling accuracy, accuracy in the judgment of stability, and accuracy in the judgment of constancy will be achieved in the predictable self-before-other and same-sex-before-other-sex orders.

From Defining Self Physically to Defining Self Psychologically

The fact that preschool-age children define age using height and facial features and that they define gender using the criteria of hair, clothes, and behavior comes as no surprise given what we know about children's self-understanding in general. For not just gender and age, but for all social categories, the overt, external, physically present factors are the determining factors (see, for example, the discussion of *objective responsibility* later in this chapter). Because of this, a concept like gender identity (see Chapter 4), which refers to an inner definition of self, has no validity with preschoolers. The real self is the apparent self. If you look and act like a girl, you are a girl. If you are taller, you are older. In middle childhood, this view shifts. Physical displays of self-attributes are still important, but the real self is the thinking, psychological self that lies behind the outer facade. Thus, one can be afraid while acting brave, and one can be a girl even while doing "boy" things. One can also age—physically and emotionally—without necessarily growing.

The Private Psychological Self as Distinct from the Public Self

The developmental trend from physical to psychological self-definitions is present in all the work on children's conceptions of self (see Damon & Hart, 1982). In research by John Broughton, for example, a 10-year-old reported his inner distinctiveness this way: "I am one of a kind. . . . There could be a person who looks like me or talks like me, but no one who . . . thinks exactly like me" (1978, p. 86). Another example comes from research by Robert Selman (1980) in which children were told a story about a boy who had lost his dog. The boy in the story says that he is so distressed over the loss of his dog that he never wants to have another dog again. In interviews with children of different ages, Selman found that preschoolers took the boy at his word. According to the preschoolers, if the boy said he did not want a dog, then he did not want a dog. Thus, it would be a bad idea, the preschoolers thought, to buy him one for his birthday.

Unlike the preschoolers, whom Selman describes as being at Level 1 (see Box 14-2) in self-awareness, older children recognize that the boy in Selman's story might say he does not want a dog, even though he really does want one. These children might argue that it would be a good idea to buy another dog because—from their understanding of selves—"it's what the boy really wants." Such reasoning is at Level 2 in Selman's system. One of the children interviewed by Selman manifested his Level-2 understanding of selves when in answer to the question "Is there a kind of inside and outside to a person?" he said, "Yes. . . . if there was a brother and a sister, like the brother always says I can't stand you, but really inside, he really likes her" (Selman, 1980, p. 98). Older children recognize, therefore, that the real self and the apparent self may not coincide and that to know the real self one must know a person's private thoughts (see Box 14-2).

Reference to an Inner Psychological Self when Describing People

Believing that a person's true self is defined more by thoughts than acts is only half the evidence for a physical-to-psychological shift in middle childhood. Further evidence comes from the increased use of psychological constructs in the description of people. English psychologists W. J. Livesley and D. B. Bromley have reported, for example, that around age 7 or 8 "the child learns to take into account things other than a person's appearance, identity, and possessions" when describing that person (1973, p. 214). The things that are newly taken into account at this age are the person's habits, characteristics, and traits, all of which are attributes much closer to one's psychological self than are the temporary, superficial characteristics that children focus on earlier in development.

Livesley and Bromley's conclusion that there is a sudden increase after age 7 in the use of psychological features to describe people comes from research in which they asked children to describe some specific people whom they liked or disliked. At age 7, about half of the descriptive statements that children made referred only to external qualities of the person, as illustrated in the following description:

> He is very tall. He has dark brown hair, he goes to our school. I don't think he has any brothers or sisters. He is in our class. Today he has on a dark orange jumper and grey trousers and brown shoes. (Livesley & Bromley, 1973, p. 213)

By age 8, references to external qualities had fallen to about 15 percent of all statements. Use of psychological characteristics and other more permanent attributes had increased porportionately. The somewhat older descriptions sounded more like this:

> He smells very much and is very nasty. He has no sense of humour and is very dull. He is always fighting and he is cruel. He does silly things and is very stupid. He has brown hair and cruel eyes. He is sulky and 11 years old and has lots of sisters. I think he is the most horrible boy in the class. He has a croaky voice and always chews his pencil and picks his teeth and I think he is disgusting. (Livesley & Bromley, 1973, p. 217)

Research by Carl Barenboim (1981) of the University of Pittsburgh produced results similar to those of Livesley and Bromley. Barenboim asked children from 6 to 11 years of age to describe three people whom they knew well. At age 6, almost no children described other people using psychological constructs, other than constructs of the most general sort (for example, "He's nice" or "She's naughty"). Beginning at age 7, the use of such constructs began to climb steadily from a low of 2 percent at age 7 to a high of 26 percent at age 11. This indicates that people's stable, underlying

When school-age children describe their friends they will refer to qualities and characteristics that describe the stable inner self and not just the transitory public self.

attributes become quite salient for children in the years of middle child-hood. In Barenboim's data this was evident in the increasing importance that children gave to descriptors dealing with attributes such as bossiness ("Randy is always trying to boss other kids around"), generosity ("She's always giving things away"), or intelligence ("He's a real stubborn idiot"). Previously, the children had focused only on immediate and less-enduring attributes.

The Use of Comparative Information in Definitions of Self and Others

Apart from the physical-to-psychological shift, there is a second advance in self-understanding that occurs from the preschool to the middle- and late-childhood years. This advance consists of an increased tendency to define oneself in comparison with others rather than in absolute, noncomparative terms. Preschoolers, therefore, if given the task of assessing their own competence at a task, tend to ignore information about the competence of others. They judge their competence solely on their own success or failure at the task. The same information is used to judge task difficulty. Children beyond age 7, for the first time, compare their own performance to that of others in order to come up with competence and difficulty judgments (Aboud, 1985; Ruble, 1983). What applies to self applies to others as well. Around age 7, children begin to focus on behavioral comparisons to form their impressions of others. Carl Barenboim's research, just cited as evidence for the physical-to-psychological shift, also gives evidence of the increased attention to comparative information. In analyzing children's descriptions of friends, Barenboim looked for statements that employed behavioral comparisons. These were statements such as "Billy runs a lot faster than Jim" or "She draws the best in our whole class." The results showed that between ages 6 and 8, the use of such comparisons doubled.

The Use of Bipolar Information in Descriptions of Self and Other

When children first begin to describe themselves and others in terms of stable internal traits, they tend to view self and other in an all-or-none fashion. That is, they will say that a person is uniformly good, kind, and intelligent or uniformly bad, mean, and dumb (Harter, 1983b; Rogers, 1978). The self- and other-descriptions of preschoolers, therefore, tend to portray people as stock characters from a morality play rather than as real people who have conflicting positive and negative attributes. Older children, however, recognize that people can be both good and bad simultaneously. This means that older children have a capacity that may be lacking in younger children for considering the two sides to a single person simultaneously. They can simultaneously see both pros and cons.

The developmental shift from conceptualizations of people that include just unipolar information (that is, just pros or just cons) to conceptualizations that include bipolar information (both pros and cons) is perfectly matched by developmental data on children's understanding of internal emotional states. Initially, children believe that people can only experience one emotion at a time. By late childhood, however, they realize that multiple, contradictory emotions can be experienced simultaneously. For example, when Susan Harter (1983a) asked children under age 6 whether they could feel some other emotion at the same time they were feeling happy (or sad or scared or mad), they answered no. One child said quite explicitly, "You *can't* have more than one feeling" (Harter, 1983a, p. 164). Another explained that simultaneous emotions would be impossible to achieve because "You only have one mind." In contrast, 9-year-old children were able to provide many examples of experiencing two different emotions simultaneously. One child gave this example: "On my birthday I was really *happy* about going sledding but I was *scared* cause we were going down a really steep hill" (Harter, 1983a, tab. 6.1, p. 171). Another gave this example: "When I went horse-back riding by myself I was *glad* cause it was good to be away from my brothers and sisters but I was *lonesome* all by myself cause there was no one to talk to" (Harter, 1983a, tab. 6.1, p. 171). Children's awareness of the potential for multiple, contradictory emotions, therefore, develops at the same time as their awareness of the potential for conflicting traits, and both develop out of the awareness that inner psychological attributes are more relevant to self-descriptions than are physical attributes.

How Social Cognitive Changes Fit with General Cognitive Changes

We have just reviewed three changes in self- and other-awareness that occur in middle to late childhood—the change from defining people in terms of their transient physical attributes toward defining them in terms of their stable inner traits; the change from descriptions that use absolute terms to ones that use relative terms; and the change from simple unipolar descriptions to complex bipolar descriptions. These changes fit nicely with the cognitive advances identified by Piaget for children this age.

The tendency to characterize others by their enduring traits fits with other cognitive advances of the concrete-operational period, because during this period children become freed from the intuitive thinking that leads them to describe objects and events only according to present impressions (see Chapter 8, p. 396 ff). In the physical world, this advance is reflected in the ability to conserve physical properties; in the social world, it is reflected in the ability to conserve psychological properties. Thus, rather than conceptualize people in terms of their observable characteristics (for example, where they live, what they look like, what they know how to do, and so forth), there is a shift toward conceptualizing them in terms of the enduring traits that persist despite superficial changes in characteristics such as possessions, appearance, and habits.

The use of comparative information fits with development in the concrete-operational period because, as you will recall, children in their middle-childhood years begin to conceptualize the relationships among variables. Relational concepts are at the heart of the ability called *seriation,* and for children to become aware of serial relations between themselves and others (and simply between "others") is in complete keeping with their general cognitive development.

The fact that children in middle childhood appreciate that people (themselves included) can have conflicting attributes and emotions also fits with the cognitive advances of the concrete-operational period, because to represent the conflicting elements, children must *decenter.* Centering, you will recall, is characteristic of preschoolers who answer conservation or proportional-reasoning problems by focusing on information from just one variable (for example, height, length, or number) when information from two or more variables is needed. The tendency to portray people as all good or all bad and the tendency to deny they can have more than one emotion at a time are consistent with the general tendency toward centering. Perceiving people in terms of multiple variables simultaneously reflects decentering.

Self- and Other-awareness in Adolescence

As children enter adolescence they begin to think in the purely abstract and decentered way that Piaget identified as a key component to formal-operational thought (see Chapter 8, p. 429 ff). Because there is this change in general cognition during adolescence, you will not be surprised to learn that there is a change, too, in conceptions of self. In Selman's system, the advances constitute Levels 3 and 4 of self-awareness. The first of these advances involves a change in the conceptualization of the inner self. The second involves the recognition that there can be an unconscious as well as a conscious self. The differences between these and Selman's two previous levels are depicted in Box 14-2 and are discussed below. Both reflect a formal-operational level of thinking.

The Discovery of an Observing Ego

As discussed on p. 734, children in Level 1 of the development of self-awareness believe that the true self is apparent in what a person does and says. In Level 2, children become aware of the *psychological self* that is more real and more permanent than the *apparent self.* The Level-3 advance in-

Box 14-2
Selman's Levels of Self-awareness

Level 0:
The Undifferentiated Self

I am an undifferentiated physical entity. I make no distinctions between mind and body.

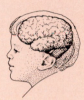

Level 1: The Superficial, Apparent Self

My mind and body are separate entities; thus, I have both an inner reality and an outer appearance. But to know my inner reality, all you have to do is look at me. I am what I say and do.

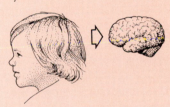

Level 2: The Thinking, Psychological Self

The real me lies behind the scenes. Sometimes what I say and do corresponds to the real me, but sometimes not. My mind is in control of my body.

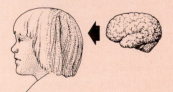

Level 3: The Self as Observing Ego

My thoughts and intentions are an important part of me, just as my behavior is, but the real me is the part of me that directs both thoughts and behavior. This is my observing ego. With it, I can deceive people through my behavior, and I can even deceive myself. That is, I can make myself think or believe something just by willing it.

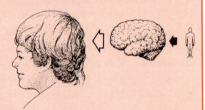

Level 4: The Conscious and Unconscious Self

Just as before, I believe that the observing ego monitors my inner reality and outer appearance. But I no longer believe that the conscious ego is totally in charge. In addition to the ego, which provides conscious control, there is an unconscious part to me that even the conscious ego cannot always fathom. Thus, it is possible that I will direct myself to behave in certain ways and to think certain thoughts and yet not truly be aware of why I have chosen to behave and think in this way.

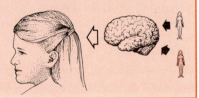

volves further differentiation of this psychological self. Already distinct from the body, the psychological self must now become distinct from the mind, which is to say distinct from the thoughts, motives, plans, and other cognitions that a person has. Thus, whereas self-awareness at Level 2 is reflected in knowing that one's thoughts may potentially differ from one's actions, a Level-3 self-awareness is reflected in knowing that one has control over one's own mind. The mystical entity that directs the thoughts is what Robert Selman has called an **observing ego** (1980, p. 104).

In that the observing ego is aware of what the mind is thinking, self-awareness at Level 3 includes an awareness of one's own thoughts and motives. This awareness represents a capacity known as *self-reflection*. One can reflect on one's own thoughts, and one can think about thinking. Given the presence of an **observing ego** with these capacities, it is no wonder that adolescents are routinely self-conscious.

In addition to allowing for self-reflection, the observing ego allows for purposeful manipulation of one's thoughts and motives. This adds an entirely new dimension to the sense of personal agency that first emerged in infancy. No longer is the self just an effector of events in the external world. Now the self is one that can control the inner psychological world, as well.

The concept of self as an active manipulator of thoughts stands in contrast to the Level-2 conception of a relatively passive self (as represented by an unmanipulable and uncontrollable mind). The Level-2 passive self can keep secrets, hide ideas, and sometimes forget unpleasant feelings, but it has no real control over these functions of self. The Level-3 conception differs in that the self is active. If it chooses to drive unpleasant thoughts from the mind, it can do so. If it chooses to hide feelings, it can do so. And if it chooses not to let anyone know what its plans are, it can do so. At this point, figures of speech such as "brainwashing" and "talking oneself into it" take on real meaning. One of Selman's subjects made up his own original means of expressing the power of the self to control thoughts and feelings. You (that is, "you" as represented in the observing ego) just keep on telling yourself something, he said, "until it just takes over your brain" (Selman, 1980, p. 104). Such expressions make it clear that the Level-3 self is conceived to have the power to manipulate and control the contents of consciousness.

The emergence in adolescence of the concept of a self that can observe and direct the mind is reflected in adolescents' responses to Selman's lost-dog story. For example, young adolescents might reason that the boy really wants a dog by saying that "the boy has only deceived himself into thinking that he doesn't want one." Self-deception of this sort would be inconceivable were mind and self indivisible, as they are in Level-2 conceptions. But now, the conceptualization of self is that there is one inner-psychological self (the ego) that is capable of deceiving another (the mind). This level of self-understanding is a clear advance beyond the purely superficial self-understanding of young children, or the shallow psychological reality attached to self in middle and late childhood.

Discovery of an Unconscious Self

Despite all the sophistication of a Level-3 self-understanding, there is still a further step that can be taken. This step involves adding the notion of an unconscious self to the active, observing ego (see Box 14-2). With this Level-4 self in place, adolescents have a means of explaining how a part of the true inner self can always remain hidden from the consciousness of the active, observing ego. They can also explain why it is that they may be unsuccessful in driving thoughts from their minds. Sometimes, no matter how hard one tries, the thoughts keep coming back. The explanation is that people are only *partly* in control of their own minds, not completely in control as they believed at Level 3.

Here is a transcript of a conversation with an adolescent who apparently understands that the true psychological self has both a conscious and an unconscious component:

INTERVIEWER: If Mike thinks about what he said, will he realize that he really would like another dog?

ADOLESCENT: Maybe, but maybe not. He might not be aware of his deeper feelings.

INTERVIEWER: How is that possible?

ADOLESCENT: He may not want to admit to himself that another dog could take Pepper's [his dog's] place. He might feel at some level that would be unloyal to Pepper to just go out and replace the dog. He may feel guilty about it. He doesn't want to face these feelings, so he says, no new dog.

INTERVIEWER: Is he aware of this?

ADOLESCENT: Probably not. (Selman, 1980, p. 106)

At the highest level of self-understanding, then, adolescents recognize an *unconscious* self lying behind the *conscious* self. With this level of self-understanding, adolescents have in effect a theory of self that demystifies much of what appears self-contradictory in people's actions, thoughts, and intents. Achievement of such a theory tops off development.

Additional Evidence for New Levels of Self-awareness in Adolescence

Selman is not the only investigator who has evidence that self-awareness makes important advances in adolescence. Some independent evidence for such an advance comes from research on the development of "psychological-mindedness" (Dollinger & McGuire, 1981). In this research (see also

Chandler, Paget, & Koch, 1978), children have been asked to explain behavior that has a surface meaning and a deep meaning that are quite different. The behavior is further distinguished in that it can be either consciously or unconsciously motivated. Here is an example:

> A group of Charley's classmates formed a club but they wouldn't let Charley join. When they started the club, Charley really wanted to be a member but they still wouldn't let him join. Later, Charley's sister asked if he was in the new club. And Charley said, "No. But I'm too busy already; with tennis and piano lessons, I'm too busy. So I didn't join the club." (Dollinger & McGuire, 1981, p. 120)

Charley's behavior in this case would be characterized by a psychologist as *defensive*. This means that the behavior (either becoming too busy or just thinking that one is too busy) serves as a self-defense. In Freudian terms, it protects the ego from some damaging and unpleasant self-revelations—namely, "I am not wanted." Children ages 10 to 14 who heard this story were able to explain Charley's statement that he was too busy in a way that revealed that they had some intuitive insight into the deep meaning of Charley's behavior. Younger children could not.

Because Dollinger did not interview his subjects in the same way as Selman, it is impossible to say whether his 10- to 14-year-old subjects had a Level-3 or a Level-4 understanding of defense mechanisms. The distinction would come from knowing whether they recognized that Charley might have behaved as he did *without necessarily being aware* of his true motivation (Level 4), or whether they just automatically assumed that Charley's ego had consciously directed him to become too busy in order to save face (Level 3). In either case, however, Dollinger's data do support the view that self-understanding does not end in middle childhood when one first begins to focus on the psychological self. The height of understanding can proceed one or two levels beyond this point.

To summarize briefly, the development of self-awareness in humans begins with the discovery of a self–other distinction. Contingency information seems to be the basis for infants' initial self-knowledge. By the end of infancy, children have a firm sense of self as a causal agent, and they have even begun to learn some of the differences between themselves and others. They know what they look like, and they know their gender and their age. These same attributes of others are part of their social awareness. As self-concepts emerge, they focus initially on physical aspects of self: people are what they appear to be, they mean what they say, and their intents can be judged from their actions. In later childhood, this view is amended to include the psychological, thinking self as the true self. In early adolescence, the conceptualization of an inner, psychological self becomes more complex with the realization that there is an inner self—the observing ego—

that directs one's thoughts. By the end of adolescence, there is a final advance in self-conceptualization with the realization that the observing ego is not totally in control; there is, in addition, an unconscious component to self. At this point, the entire self-system, consisting of physical attributes, mind, ego, and an unconscious self, is understood as an integrated whole.

BECOMING AWARE OF DIFFERENCES BETWEEN SELF AND OTHER

The Relationship of Self-knowledge to Other-knowledge

In describing the development of self-awareness from infancy through adolescence, it has been apparent that there are intimate links between knowledge of self and knowledge of others (Hart & Damon, 1985; Harter, 1983b). Children are not cognizant, for example, just of their own sex; they are cognizant of the sex of others as well. Nor do they think that they are the only ones who have an inner thinking self (Level 2) that is distinct from the outward behaving body. Although one might be inclined to think that knowledge of the properties of self would at least precede the same knowledge of others, there is only limited evidence for this conclusion. Personal agency for self may precede a belief in agency for others, and knowledge of one's own gender constancy may precede the same knowledge for others; but, for the most part, self- and other-understanding appear to develop in tandem. As John Flavell says: "The development of knowledge and cognition about the self closely parallels and overlaps the knowledge and cognition . . . about others" (1985, p. 154). Daniel Hart and William Damon concur (1985, p. 170). They point out that when young children, old children, and adolescents describe themselves and others, they focus on the same qualities, regardless of whether self or other is the object of the description.

The general assumption of self–other similarity works to the benefit of children in determining that others have the same attributes of self that they themselves have, but it works to their detriment when they try to judge others' thoughts, motives, and feelings. The danger is that children will assume similarity where it does not in fact exist. This is the error known as *egocentrism*(see Chapter 8). It manifests itself on inference tasks that bear the general name of *perspective-taking tasks.*

Perspective taking is a highly versatile and useful aspect of social cognition because it enables us to infer the feelings, motives, and thoughts of others. According to Selman (1976, p. 301), perspective taking is the basis of effective social problem solving (as is required, for example, in cooperative and competitive games such as hide-and-seek); it underlies effective communication, particularly persuasive communication; it is a cognitive prerequisite for feeling guilt over harm we have brought to others (Hoffman, 1983); and it is an essential basis for understanding fairness and justice. Others suspect that perspective-taking skills bear a relationship to how one settles interpersonal conflicts (Gurucharri, Phelps, & Selman, 1984). All in all, there appears to be no more important attribute of social cognition than the general ability to take another person's perspective on social issues and thereby infer that person's thoughts, motives, and feelings.

The ontogenetic sequence by which perspective-taking skills emerge is one that begins in the centered, egocentric thought of preschoolers and ends in the decentered, abstract thinking of adolescents.

Perspective Taking in Early Childhood: The Egocentrism Problem

Egocentric inferences regarding the thoughts, feelings, and motives of others are illustrated in the Freudian mechanism known as *projection,* which is the false assumption that others are experiencing the very same thoughts, feelings, and motives that we are experiencing. For example, if a person in business cheats a perfectly honest partner and then justifies the cheating by saying that "I only did it because it was obvious that you were out to cheat me, too," Freud would view this as a case of projection. One's own intent to cheat was projected onto the other. In one classic study of this phenomenon (Sears, 1936), fraternity members who were rated as stingy by their peers tended to give high stinginess ratings to others.

The fact that egocentrism can appear in the social judgments of college-age adults illustrates that the egocentric bias in other-perception is not restricted to childhood. Throughout life, there will be a tendency to assume that we can make inferences about others from a knowledge of ourselves. As Piaget was the first to recognize, however, the egocentric bias is never so acute as in the early years of childhood. Preschoolers are all too willing to believe that other people are just like them.

In Chapter 8, we investigated this claim with regard to pure perspective taking—the task of visually representing to oneself the world as another person sees it (see Figure 8-5, p. 403). Here we will deal with perspective taking in which the task is to infer another person's thoughts, feelings, and motives.

Egocentrism in Judging What Another Person Thinks

Preschool children's judgments about what another person is thinking, like their judgments about what others see, are not invariably egocentric. Nonetheless, preschool children are not nearly as good at inferring another's thoughts as one might expect. The type of test situation that brings out the deficiencies in preschool children's inferences about another's thoughts most clearly is one that requires children to infer the strategy of an opponent in a game. A good example comes from research by Robert Selman (1971).

In one version of a social-inference task that Selman used (see Figure 14-3), one child had to guess which of two choices another child might make in a guessing game. To begin the task, a child who was to play the role of the "observer" helped the experimenter hide a toy Indian on the end of one of two long sticks. The other ends of the sticks protruded through a wall into a room in which a second child (the "guesser") was located. In order to make reference to the sticks easy, a toy airplane was mounted on the far end of one of the sticks and a toy horse on the other. The observer's job was to predict which of the two sticks—the airplane stick or the horse stick—the guesser would select as the one on which the Indian was hidden.

Figure 14-3
Judging the Thoughts of Others
This figure illustrates the layout of a social-inference task devised by Selman. In this task, an "observer" is asked to predict the strategy another child (the "guesser") might use to select the stick on which the Indian is hidden. (After Selman, 1971)

Selman found that his subjects aged 4 to 6 gave answers reflecting four different levels of perspective-taking ability. The first three, which he labeled A, B, and C, showed varying degrees of egocentrism ranging from predictions that the other child would pick the horse or airplane stick because "that's where we put it" to predictions that he would pick the horse or airplane stick because "that's what I would do." Totally nonegocentric answers that reflected the independence of the other child's thought from the subject's own (Level-D answers) did not appear until age 6 when they were the dominant type of answer given (see Figure 14-4). Selman's data clearly support, therefore, the generalization that there is a shift at about the time children enter school from egocentric inferences about another's thinking to nonegocentric inferences.

Egocentrism in Judging How Others Feel

As we saw in Chapter 13, even infants will act prosocially toward others who are perceived to be in need. They might, for example, give their own toy to someone who is crying (Borke, 1971). Such acts give the impression that even very young children have an appreciation for how others feel. In fact, however, responding to another person's needs does not offer evidence of an ability to infer emotions. Emotional states are expressed overtly in tears, smiles, and angry looks; with these direct signals available, there is

Figure 14-4
The Emergence of Nonegocentric Reasoning on Selman's Social-Inference Task
Nonegocentric judgments (Level D) of what the "guesser" might be thinking in Selman's social-inference experiment did not appear until age 6. (From Selman, 1971)

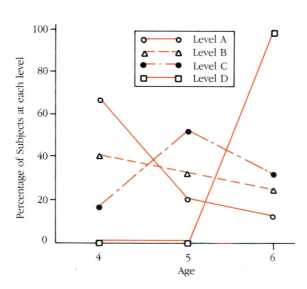

no need to draw an inference. For this reason, tests of children's ability to infer emotions have focused on their ability to infer emotions from story content alone.

Research on young children's ability to infer the emotional states of others began with research by Helen Borke (1971). The question Borke asked was whether young children could tell from a story alone the emotion that a storybook character would experience. The stories dealt with such topics as a child losing a toy, having to go to bed early, getting lost in the woods, or eating a favorite food. To make their judgments, children picked a facial expression (representing happiness, fear, sadness, or anger) that would be appropriate for the child in the story. Borke found that children as young as 3 years of age could select the happy face appropriately and by age 4 and 5 most could select the sad and angry faces appropriately.

Although Borke's research showed that even 3-year-olds can make accurate social judgments about the emotions of children in stories, the test is inadequate for testing children's ability to make nonegocentric judgments. The reason, as Michael Chandler and Stephen Greenspan pointed out, is that

> nonegocentric thought in the sense intended by Piaget . . . is not simply a synonym for accurate social judgment but implies the ability to anticipate what someone else might think or feel *precisely when those thoughts or feelings are different from one's own.* (1972, p. 105; italics added)

An adequate test of the ability to infer emotions, therefore, must involve people who are quite different from the children themselves.

In the case of very young children, there are some clear indications of a failure to appreciate that other people might have an emotional response to events that is different from the children's own. This is reflected in their egocentric expectations for the emotional impact of some actions. They seem to think, for example, that whatever would soothe their own distress would soothe that of someone else. Thus, children will go get their own mother to soothe a crying child rather than get the child's own mother, even if the child's mother is equally available (Hoffman, 1982, p. 287). Also, they offer toys to adults, as if the toys would have the same emotional value for adults as for children.

The same egocentric tendency that is present in the behavior of very young preschool children is present in the verbal statements of somewhat older preschoolers. In a study of children's understanding of parental emotions, for example, Susan Harter (1983a) asked children what would make their parents happy, sad, mad, or scared. In response to Harter's questions, 4- and 5-year-olds tended to project their own emotional experiences onto that of the parents (Harter, 1983a, p. 184). When asked, for example, what would make their parents happy, the young children suggested such things as "going to the circus" and "getting a new toy." In answer to questions about what would cause parental sadness, they said things like "going to bed when they wanted to watch television" and "losing a toy giraffe in the backyard." One suggestion for what would make a parent angry was having friends refuse to play. Interestingly, Harter even found some lingering egocentrism in children ages 6 to 8. Although these children reported events that were appropriate for adults, the events tended to be child centered. For example, one child said, "My mom gets mad when she has to tell me six times to pick up my room." Another said, "Mommy would be scared if I got lost." Not until late childhood, do children completely decenter from themselves and report emotion-producing events that are totally unrelated to self (for example, "Daddy would be mad if someone wrecked his new chiropractor's table" and "Mommy would be scared if she was home alone and she thought she heard a burglar").

Reasoning About Others' Motives

A final perspective-taking task that yields evidence of young children's egocentrism is the task of inferring another person's motives. We are called on to infer motives whenever we must determine the intent that lies behind another person's acts or words. For example, what if a person bumps into you, drops something, or knocks over a glass. Was the act intentional or not? Some interesting developmental research shows that children do not clearly discriminate between intentional and accidental acts until late in the preschool years. In fact, 4-year-olds are apt to think that people intend *all* their actions. Such judgments are egocentric because they are based on children's own perceptions. All the children can see is the overt act. When they are asked about an intention that might lie behind the act, they are being asked to fathom the other person's mind—something they cannot see. Thus, to answer the question about intentions, egocentric children simply tell us what they do see. Some typical data come from research by Michael Smith (1978).

The Assumption of Intent   In Smith's study, children from 4 to 6 years of age were shown videotapes of an actor performing 20 distinct acts. The first 12 included 4 voluntary acts (walking across a room, sitting down in a chair, doing some arm exercises, and chewing something), 4 involuntary acts involving reflexes (sneezing, yawning, saying "ow" when poked, and laughing when tickled), and 4 involuntary acts involving passive movement (an umbrella hooks onto a lady's arm and moves it, a lady is pushed across the floor by a file cabinet, a lady stumbles over a box, and a lady slips on a rug and falls into a chair). The last 8 involved a woman actor either picking up an object or knocking against it with her forearm. Sometimes she was looking at the object when she did this, and sometimes she was not. Also, the object sometimes landed in an appropriate place (for example, a piece of trash lands in the trash can) and sometimes in an inappropriate place (for example, the trash lands on the floor or a box of cookies lands in the trash can).

The results of Smith's study showed that 4-year-olds judged the sequence of 4 reflexes (sneezing, saying "ow", yawning, and laughing) to be just as intentional as the 4 truly voluntary acts. Even at 6 years of age, children were slightly more likely than adults to see these acts as intended. Moreover, it did not matter whether intentionality was judged by having children answer the question "Did the person want to do (whatever the act was)?" or "Did the person try to do (whatever the act was)?" In both cases, 4-year-olds almost invariably said yes. Even for the passive movements that were induced by objects (the umbrella, the file cabinet, the box, or the rug). four-year-olds judged 2.61/4.00 of the movements to be intentional. The results for the last 8 episodes paralleled those of the first 12. For example, 6-year-olds and adults used the information on whether the actor was looking to judge whether the actor was acting intentionally; 4-year-olds tended to ignore the "looking" information.

The results of research such as this are generally interpreted to mean that young children have a bias toward seeing all of other people's acts as intentional (Shantz, 1983, p. 502). This is curious in that children, having sneezed and giggled involuntarily themselves, should realize that the sneezes and giggles of others could also be involuntary. One would also think that having accidently bumped things themselves (perhaps, even, into the trash) they would recognize that others could be similarly victimized by bad luck. But although they are certainly aware of the relevance of intentions to their own behavior (Shultz, 1980), young children do not tend to put emphasis on the intentions of others. Thus, when children judge behavioral episodes like those used in Smith's research, they ignore differences in the actors' intentions that are obvious to older children and adults; when they recount stories they have heard, they tend to leave out information about the actors' intentions (Flapan, 1968); and when they evaluate behavior, they frequently base their evaluation much more on objective characteristics of the behavior than on the good or bad intentions and motives that might underlie it. This last point was first made in memorable fashion by Jean Piaget (1932/1965) in his research on the phenomenon of objective responsibility.

Piaget's Research on Objective Responsibility   First and foremost, a belief in **objective responsibility** implies that the consequences of an act are relevant to determining whether the act is good or bad. Beyond that, a belief in objective responsibility implies that the greater the consequences, the worse the act. Adults hold to this belief somewhat when they make distinctions between crimes such as petit larceny and grand larceny. The latter crime is judged to be worse than the first, and deserving of a greater punishment, solely because of the amount of money involved—for example, more than $50 versus less than $50. But even though adults acknowledge the relevance of considering the magnitude of the effects acts have, they do not weigh magnitude nearly as heavily as young children do.

The most famous illustration of the bias toward objective responsibility that exists among young children comes from the responses children give to a story in which they are asked to say who is the naughtier of two boys. One boy, John, was called to dinner, and when he opened the dining room door, the door struck a tray of 15 cups. This was not John's fault, but all 15 cups were broken. A second boy to whom John is compared is one who sneaked into the kitchen while his mother was out in order to get some jam from the cupboard. He knocked over and broke a single cup while climbing to get the jam. After hearing the stories and answering questions, which ensure that the stories have been understood, children are asked whether one of the boys is naughtier than the other. The typical response of children up to age 7 is that the boy who broke the 15 cups is the naughtier.

A second observation supporting the claim that children initially believe in objective responsibility as a criterion for blameworthiness is that they judge the seriousness of a lie by the magnitude of the discrepancy from the truth. Thus, if you say that $2 + 2 = 5$, it is judged to be a lie, but not so bad a lie as saying that $2 + 2 = 7$. Surprisingly, an inaccurate guess is also considered to be a lie, and the magnitude of the lie is a function of how far off the guess is from the true state of affairs. For example, if two people guess a person's age and both are wrong, then both have told lies, but the one who misses by the most has told the biggest lie. Piaget illustrates this aspect of the belief in objective responsibility with the transcripts of a number of interviews. The following is typical. It concerns the story of one child who got excited and described a dog to be as large as a cow and a second child who reported a different grade from the one she had in fact received.

INTERVIEWER: Which of the two children is the naughtiest?

CHILD: The little girl who said she saw a dog as big as a cow.

INTERVIEWER: Why is she the naughtiest?

CHILD: Because it could never happen.

INTERVIEWER: Why did she say that?

CHILD: To exaggerate.

INTERVIEWER: And why did the other one tell a lie?

CHILD: Because she wanted to make people believe that she had a good report.

INTERVIEWER: Did her mother believe her?

CHILD: Yes.
INTERVIEWER: Which would you punish most if you were the mother?
CHILD: The one with the dog because she told the worst lies
                   and was the naughtiest. (Piaget, 1932/1965, pp. 150-51)

Such observations lead to the conclusion that the absolute magnitude of one's "untruth," like the number of cups that are broken, plays a role in early-childhood thinking that it does not play in adult thought. For older children and adults, intentions matter most, but not for young children, at least not according to Piaget.

Although children under age 7 do tend to believe in objective responsibility, they do not invariably ignore the intents of actors when evaluating the extent to which their acts are meritorious or blameworthy (Karniol, 1978; Keasey, 1977). Thus, to claim that young children ignore intents is as incorrect as to claim that they are invariably egocentric (see Chapter 8, p. 410). Nonetheless, young children do give far more attention and importance to outcomes than do older children and adults. The tendency to do so is wholly consistent with young children's general tendency to focus on the physical, external, and observable aspects of people and their behavior rather than on the inner, psychological components.

Perspective Taking in Later Childhood and Adolescence

As emphasized at the start of this section, egocentrism as manifested in an inattention to other's motives, an inability to guess their thoughts, and a failure to know the unique events that make them happy or sad does not stem from a cognitive disorder that magically disappears with age. The egocentric bias in social reasoning is with us throughout life. We are able to overcome it, however, when we realize that others have a perspective equally as valid as our own and when we have the cognitive ability to create that perspective. Of these two components to nonegocentric thinking, creating the other person's perspective is the hard part. Who, for example, can truly take the social perspective of an Albert Schweitzer, a Mother Theresa, or an Adolph Hitler?

As regards children's ability to overcome the two components to egocentrism, you will recall from the original discussion of egocentrism in Chapter 8 that children know others have a unique visual perspective on the world well before they are able to create that perspective in their own minds. Because taking another person's perspective on social issues is even harder than creating another person's visual perspective, it is not surprising that developmentalists find evidence of improvements in perspective-taking ability occuring as late as adolescence. The improvements seem to be age related.

Using the Clinical Method to Uncover Further Development in Perspective Taking

All of the evidence for late-childhood and adolescent advances in perspective taking have come from research that employs the method of clinical interviews. This, of course, is the method that was pioneered by Piaget for use in studies of cognitive development. As used by researchers in the field of social cognition, the procedure involves telling a story that the interviewer and interviewee can discuss at length. Interviews can range from 20 minutes to 90 minutes depending on the age and perseverence of the child. Interviewers have a set of stock questions to ask, but they are free to probe for clarification.

Robert Selman has used a story known as the "Holly story" to assess perspective-taking skills (Selman & Byrne, 1974). What appears in the following extract is only a synopsis. The actual story was presented in more detail using a film strip.

> Holly is an 8-year-old girl who likes to climb trees. She is the best tree climber in the neighborhood. One day while climbing down from a tall tree she falls off the bottom branch but does not hurt herself. Her father sees her fall. He is upset and asks her to promise not to climb trees any more. Holly promises.
>
> Later that day, Holly and her friends meet Sean. Sean's kitten is caught up in a tree and cannot get down. Something has to be done right away or the kitten may fall. Holly is the only one who climbs trees well enough to reach the kitten and get it down, but she remembers her promise to her father. (Selman, 1980, p. 36)

After familiarizing them with the Holly story, Selman conducted interviews that called on the children to present the perspectives of the various protagonists and, more importantly, to coordinate these in various ways. Here are some of the questions he used for the Holly story: "Does Sean know why Holly cannot decide whether or not to climb the tree?" "How will Holly's father feel if he finds out she climbed the tree?" "What does Holly think her father will think of her if he finds out?" and "What would the Golden Rule (the rule that specifies that you should do unto others as you would have them do unto you) say to do in this situation?" Such questions are very demanding on people's social-reasoning abilities. They are much more demanding, for example, than questions about what a friend's strategy might be in a guessing game or about how an adult would feel if his or her new chiropractor's table was broken. Given the complexity of the questions and their apparent demand on abstract, formal-reasoning skills, interviewees of different ages tend to produce different types of answers. In fact, judging the answers purely on the basis of their form and not their content, Selman and his co-workers find evidence of five different types.

There is some evidence, moreover, that these five types constitute a developmental sequence, which is outlined in Table 14-1.

A Description of Selman's Perspective-Taking Stages

The best way to get an appreciation for the differences in the perspective-taking stages identified by Selman is to view children's answers in terms of five key issues, with each issue corresponding to a level of reasoning. The issues will be expressed as questions.

1. Do the children's answers demonstrate an appreciation for the fact that the various protagonists have different perspectives, motives, and values and that these create an inevitable conflict? (Do they know, for example, that if Holly does what she wants, her dad will be unhappy? Or do they assume that if Holly does what she wants, it will be okay with her dad?)
2. Can they keep the perspective of one protagonist in mind while taking the perspective of a second protagonist? (Do they know, for example, that Holly's dad knows that Holly would want to help her friend Sean?)
3. Do they know that each protagonist is aware of the other protagonists' points of view and can represent these in their own thinking? (Do they know, for example, that Holly knows that her Dad knows that Holly would like to help Sean?) This is the level of perspective-taking required to be able to apply the Golden Rule.
4. Can they create the perspective of a "generalized other" and thereby get out of the bind of having to reason via recursion as in the previous example? ("He knows that she knows that he knows that she knows; therefore. . . .") Recursive thinking in which one shifts from one person's point of view to another's often leads to poor social cognition as humorously shown in Figure 14-5. The more advanced ability requires decentering and taking a perspective not actually present in the story itself—that is, the perspective of the generalized other.
5. Can the generalized other who looks on the conflict from a third-person perspective take on multiple perspectives so that the other might represent the conflict as a representative of society at large, the legal profession, a developmental psychologist, or some other disinterested party who can view this one conflict as an instance of more-general principles.

Selman's claim that children's responses to the Holly story and other such dilemmas can be scored in a reliable way to reveal a structured, con-

TABLE 14-1
Selman's Five Stages in the Development of Perspective Taking

STAGE	AGE RANGE[1]	CHILD'S UNDERSTANDING
Stage 0 Egocentric Viewpoint	3–6 years	Child has a sense of differentiation of self and other but fails to distinguish between the social perspective (thoughts, feelings) of other and self. Child can label other's overt feelings but does not see the cause and effect relation of reasons to social actions.
Stage 1 Social-Informational Role Taking	6–8 years	Child is aware that other has a social perspective based on other's own reasoning, which may or may not be similar to child's. However, child tends to focus on one perspective rather than coordinating viewpoints.
Stage 2 Self-reflective Role Taking	8–10 years	Child is conscious that each individual is aware of the other's perspective and that this awareness influences self and other's view of each other. Putting self in other's place is a way of judging his intentions, purposes, and actions. Child can form a coordinated chain of perspectives,

sistent, and developmentally ordered perspective-taking ability is an exciting one. Some initial evidence to support the claim of developmental ordering comes from both cross-sectional (Selman & Byrne, 1974) and longitudinal research (Gurucharri & Selman, 1982; Gurucharri, Phelps, & Selman, 1984). Nonetheless, until more research has been done, we must leave open the possibility that the stages Selman has described lack validity. The factors underlying his stages may not be perspective-taking abilities per se; they may just be differences in intelligence, social experience, or verbal abilities. We will not know for sure for some years to come, but Selman's system acquires credibility from the fact that it is very similar to a descriptive system developed over 30 years ago by Lawrence Kohlberg (1958). Kohlberg's system has been widely validated, as we will see in the next section, which deals with the aspect of social cognition known as moral judgment.

STAGE	AGE RANGE[1]	CHILD'S UNDERSTANDING
		but cannot yet abstract from this process to the level of simultaneous mutuality.
Stage 3 Mutual Role Taking	10–12 years	Child realizes that both self and other can view each other mutually and simultaneously as subjects. Child can step outside the two-person dyad and view the interaction from a third-person perspective.
Stage 4 Social- and Conventional-System Role Taking	12–15+ years	Person realizes mutual perspective taking does not always lead to complete understanding. Social conventions are seen as necessary because they are understood by all members of the group (the generalized other) regardless of their position, role, or experience.

[1]Age ranges for all stages represent only an average approximation.

SOURCE: Based on R. L. Selman, "Social-Cognitive Understanding: A Guide to Educational and Clinical Practice" by R. L. Selman, in *Moral Development and Behavior: Theory, Research, and Social Issues,* T. Lickona (Ed.), (1976), New York: Holt, Rinehart, & Winston, p. 309. Reprinted with permission.

REASONING ABOUT RIGHT AND WRONG

At the outset of this chapter, studies of social cognition were said to constitute a recent development within the general field of cognitive development. Although this is true for the most part, there is one exception—the study of moral judgment. The relationship between moral development and general cognitive development was a matter of concern among psychologists and philosophers early in this century. John Dewey (Dewey & Tufts, 1932), James Mark Baldwin (1906), Emile Durkheim (1906), and Jean Piaget (1932) all addressed some of the central questions that still concern us today: for example, "How do children conceptualize individual rights and responsibilities?" and "How do these conceptualizations relate to their conception of the law, as enforced by parents, teachers, and courts?" Of all the

© 1962 United Features Syndicate, Inc.

Figure 14-5
An Example of Recursive Thinking

work that was done on moral development early in this century, the work of greatest historical importance has been Piaget's.

Piaget

Piaget's personal contribution to the study of moral development was completed in 1932 with the publication of a work that, in English, is titled *Moral Judgment in the Child*. Piaget never considered this work to be definitive, rather he called it a "scaffolding" from which others could "build an edifice" (1932/1965, p. 9). In testimony to his genius, however, Piaget's work is far more than scaffolding in that even today, reviewing his work is essential to presenting what we know.

In contrast to his views of cognitive development, Piaget did not believe that moral development proceeded by "stages properly so called" (1932/1965, p. 124). Nonetheless, there was a general shift in thought on moral issues from the preschool years to adolescence. According to Piaget, in the preschool years children's thought is dominated by what he called a **heteronomous morality.** Literally this means "other ruled" and is in opposition to an *autonomous* or self-ruled morality. The primary distinction lies in who is viewed as the authority for rules. Preschool children, not surprisingly, are apt to believe that rules exist solely by the will of God, political authority, or parents. What is surprising, however, is that they think this even of the rules for children's games. According to Piaget,

> . . . from the moment the child begins to imitate the rules of others, . . . he regards the rules of the game as sacred and untouchable; he refuses to alter these rules and claims that any modification even if accepted by general opinion, would be wrong. (Piaget, 1932/1965, p. 54)

Children, therefore, initially view rules to be very much outside themselves. Their developmental task is to realize that rules exist only so long as people choose to obey them or authorities choose to enforce them. By adolescence, they have made this discovery, at least as regards children's games (for example, marbles). Subsequently, they take the autonomous view that rules are of our own doing and for our own sake.

A second way to characterize the preschool child's thinking in the area of morality is to say the the preschooler is possessed of a **moral realism,** which will later be replaced by a **moral relativism.** Moral realism here captures the child's belief that moral laws, like physical laws, have an existence in their own right, independent of the will of the people. We cannot by vote suspend the law of gravity nor can we suspend the rules for capturing marbles. Only in adolescence will the child uniformly be of the opinion that the rules that societies institute for regulating the conduct of members of the society are quite different from the unalterable, inviolable physical laws. As we will see shortly, Kohlberg's research does not offer the same evidence for moral realism as does Piaget's, but then Kohlberg worked with children who, at their youngest, were 10 years of age. This age difference accounts for the fact that the least mature of Kohlberg's subjects do not believe in the sacredness of rules as entities in and of themselves.

Piaget's view that there is a developmental shift from moral realism to relativism and from heteronomy to autonomy only captures in part the change that takes place in the early years of moral development. There are four more specific characteristics that he observed when he interviewed children on either the game of marbles or one of the many made-up stories he used to elicit children's opinions. One of these characteristics—a belief in objective responsibility—has been reviewed already. The others are a belief that obedience is always good, a preference for expiative punishment, and a belief in immanent justice. These are all characteristics of immature, heteronomous moral thought that gradually disappear during the school years.

Obedience Is Right

The belief that obedience to authority is always good is evident in interviews dealing with stories in which authority figures behave unfairly. An example is the story of a mother who asked one of her daughters to do all the work about the house when the other daughter, who was supposed to be helping, went out into the street to play. When young children were asked if the mother's request was fair, a typical answer was that "It was fair because her mother had told her to" (Piaget, 1932/1965, p. 279). In one of his rare uses of group statistics to back up his conclusions, Piaget reported that 95 percent of the 6-year-olds he and his colleagues interviewed made the authority choice in stories such as this. This percent gradually declined to 0 by age 12.

Expiative Punishment Is Best

Another aspect of the heteronomous moral view is the belief that *expiative punishment* is best. From this view, punishments should be designed to inflict "upon the guilty a pain that will smart enough to make them realize the gravity of their misdeed" (Piaget, 1932/1965, p. 213). This is a boil-them-in-oil and beat-them-till-they-bleed view of punishment in which the goal is to make the person fearful of ever committing the same offense again. It is in contrast to the view that punishments should be designed to make amends or, in Piaget's words, to establish reciprocity. The contrast can be seen in the punishments children choose. For example, in designing a proper punishment for a boy who failed to go get bread for the family's supper, one 6-year-old said, "If I had a dark cupboard I'd put him in there till the evening and I'd give him a damn good box on the ear. And if I had a strap, I'd do nothing but beat him" (Piaget, 1932/1965, p. 211). The punishments suggested by older children were more in line with the actual offense. One boy said that since the boy in the story had not helped his family, his family might refuse him help when next he needed it. "He didn't help so they oughtn't to give him any help either" (Piaget, 1932/1965, p. 215). The latter punishment is clearly one regulated by a tit-for-tat reciprocity rule. The former is in no way regulated by this rule. The only rule is to make the person as sorry as possible.

The advance away from expiative punishment seems be tied to advances in perspective taking and self-understanding, because expiative punishment only makes sense so long as one sets oneself apart from the other, as if the other were inherently different and subject to different rules and regulations. For reciprocity to become the guiding principle, children must be able to reason in terms of the Golden Rule, which is a Stage-3 development in Selman's system.

Immanent Justice

The final characteristic of heteronomous morality is that it leads to a belief in *immanent justice,* which means that punishments inescapably follow misdeeds. This is a belief that there is a moral order operating in the universe to ensure that everyone gets their just desserts. When you tell children, for example, about a boy who stole some apples and who later fell into the water when a bridge collapsed under him, young children invariably link the two events. The one is thought to be a consequence of the other. For example, when one 6-year-old was asked why the bridge had cracked, he answered, "Because he had eaten the apples." "What if he had not eaten the apples?" the experimenter suggested. Then, said the boy, "the bridge would not have cracked" (Piaget, 1932/1965, p.253). An unfortunate corollary to this form of reasoning is that when some misfortune occurs, children may judge that the misfortune is a punishment for something bad that has been done. This can lead to inappropriate guilt. For example, young children are likely to view a nightmare as a sign that they have done something wrong. Having a nightmare, therefore, can make them feel guilty. To illustrate this general phenomenon, Piaget cites the case of a psychiatrist who recalled the guilt he had felt as a child when a picnic basket had inadvertently fallen shut on his hand as he reached for an apple. There was nothing wrong in reaching for the apple, but the psychiatrist, nonetheless, felt a strong guilt (Piaget, 1932/1965, p. 260).

Kohlberg

Along with the immense amount of research conducted in moral development using Piagetian-type tasks, a second tradition of empirical and theoretical research has developed around the work of Lawrence Kohlberg. In the 1950s, when Kohlberg was a graduate student at the University of Chicago, he set out to extend some of Piaget's research as part of his doctoral dissertation (see Kohlberg, 1982). The longitudinal-research project on moral judgments that he began at that time became the basis for a major descriptive elaboration and extension of Piaget's work on the sequence of changes that occur during human ontogeny. Structurally, the sequence is very much related to the stages that Selman has described for self-awareness and perspective taking. There is no surprise in this, because Selman modeled his system on Kohlberg's. The methods are Kohlberg's, the approach is Kohlberg's, and even some of the original data come from Kohlberg (see Selman, 1980, p. 35).

The data for Kohlberg's work on moral development have come from clinical interviews on a set of nine stories that pose moral dilemmas. To construct these, Kohlberg drew on issues that are traditional in the study of moral philosophy. These are issues relating human life to property, the boundaries of personal responsibility for the welfare of another, the meaning of rules and laws in society, the value of honesty, and the importance of one's contractual arrangements (in Damon, 1983, p. 273). The most famous of the dilemmas involves a man named Heinz who must decide whether to steal from a druggist the one drug that might save his wife's life. The entire story appears in Box 14-3, along with two of the other dilemmas that Kohlberg has used. You should take time to read these now in order to appreciate what follows.

For his inital work on moral reasoning, Kohlberg presented his dilemmas to 72 boys who ranged in age from 10 to 16. Subsequently, this same group of boys was followed longitudinally for 20 years, with follow-up interviews being given every 3 years. Analysis of the kinds of statements made by the boys when they were interviewed about the dilemmas led Kohlberg to two conclusions that were initially quite controversial (Kurtines & Greif, 1974). First, Kohlberg concluded that the great wealth and variety of statements that his subjects made during interviews could be scored as one of just six types. The second controversial claim was that these six types were arranged in an invariant developmental order. Because of this, Kohlberg assumed that there were six distinct stages of moral reasoning. The stages were claimed to form a universal order that was the same for Gentiles as for Jews, the same for Hindus as for Buddhists. That was because evidence for the stages was found not in people's judgments per se (that is, in whether they said that Heinz should or should not steal the drug), but in the structure of reasoning that underlay the judgments.

A Description of Kohlberg's Stages

A complete description of Kohlberg's six stages is given in Table 14-2. As you will note there, the stages are divided into three levels with two stages at each level. The levels bear the names *preconventional, conventional,* and *postconventional.* The major factor used in defining these levels and the stages that make them up is the *sociomoral perspective* that subjects take when discussing the particulars in a story such as that of Heinz. If they take a purely personal perspective, they are placed at either Stage 1 or 2. Arguments at this level would identify what Heinz should or should not do by taking note of the consequences—positive and negative—that might result from a particular course of action. There would be no reference to Heinz's duty, the rights of his wife, or the purpose of laws. All the discussion would

---

Box 14-3
Three Moral Dilemmas

Story 1

In Europe, a woman was near death from a kind of cancer. There was one drug that the doctors thought might save her. It was a form of radium that a druggist in the same town had recently discovered. The drug was expensive to make, but the druggist was charging ten times what the drug cost him to make. He paid $200 for the radium and charged $2,000 for a small dose of the drug. The sick woman's husband, Heinz, went to everyone he knew to borrow the money, but he could only get together about $1,000 which is half of what it cost. He told the druggist that his wife was dying and asked him to sell it cheaper or let him pay later. But the druggist said, "No, I discovered the drug and I'm going to make money from it." So Heinz gets desperate and considers breaking into the man's store to steal the drug for his wife.

Story 2

Heinz did break into the store and got the drug. Watching from a distance was an off-duty police officer. Mr. Brown, who lived in the same town as Heinz and knew the situation Heinz was in. Mr. Brown ran over to try to stop Heinz, but Heinz was gone by the time Mr. Brown reached the store. Mr. Brown wonders whether he should look for Heinz and arrest him.

Story 3

Joe is a fourteen-year-old boy who wanted to go to camp very much. His father promised him he could go if he saved up the money himself. So Joe worked hard at his paper route and saved up the $40 it cost to go to camp and a little more besides. But just before camp was going to start, his father changed his mind. Some of his friends decided to go on a special fishing trip, and Joe's father was short of the money it would cost. So he told Joe to give him the money he had saved from the paper route. Joe didn't want to give up going to camp so he thinks of refusing to give his father the money. (Kohlberg, 1958)

---

be from the more personal perspective of what is best for Heinz. At this level of reasoning—which is characteristic of most children under 9 years of age, many adolescents, and many adult criminal offenders—looting when the electricity goes off seems like a rational thing to do.

More-advanced levels of reasoning are marked by the achievement of ever-greater distance from the perspective of pure self-interest. At the conventional level of reasoning, for example, which is the level assigned to most older adolescents and adults, arguments stem from a societal perspective. This means that conventional-level thinkers would have Heinz do what is right in society's eyes: Heinz must do what society expects of him or what

TABLE 14-2
Kohlberg's Six Stages of Moral Judgment

Level and Stage	Content of Stage		Social Perspective of Stage
	What Is Right	Reasons for Doing Right	
LEVEL I— PRECONVENTIONAL Stage 1—Heteronomous Morality	To avoid breaking rules backed by punishment, obedience for its own sake, and avoiding physical damage to persons and property.	Avoidance of punishment, and the superior power of authorities.	*Egocentric point of view.* Doesn't consider the interests of others or recognize that they differ from the actor's; doesn't relate two points of view. Actions are considered physically rather than in terms of psychological interests of others. Confusion of authority's perspective with one's own.
Stage 2—Individualism, Instrumental Purpose, and Exchange	Following rules only when it is to someone's immediate interest; acting to meet one's own interests and needs and letting others do the same. Right is also what's fair, what's an equal exchange, a deal, an agreement.	To serve one's own needs or interests in a world where you have to recognize that other people have their interests too.	*Concrete individualistic perspective.* Aware that everybody has his own interest to pursue and these conflict so that right is relative (in the concrete individualistic sense).
LEVEL II— CONVENTIONAL Stage 3—Mutual Interpersonal Expectations, Relationships, and Interpersonal Conformity	Living up to what is expected by people close to you or what people generally expect of people in your role as son, brother, friend, etc. "Being good" is important and means having good motives, showing concern about others. It also means keeping mutual relationships, such as trust, loyalty, respect, and gratitude.	The need to be a good person in your own eyes and those of others. Your caring for others. Belief in the Golden Rule. Desire to maintain rules and authority which support stereotypical good behavior.	*Perspective of the individual in relationships with other individuals.* Aware of shared feelings, agreements, and expectations which take primacy over individual interests. Relates points of view through the concrete Golden Rule, putting yourself in the other guy's shoes. Does not yet consider generalized system perspective.
Stage 4—Social System and Conscience	Fulfilling the actual duties to which you have agreed. Laws are to be upheld except in	To keep the institution going as a whole, to avoid the breakdown in the system "if	*Differentiates societal point of view from interpersonal agreement or motives.*

Level and Stage	Content of Stage		Social Perspective of Stage
	What Is Right	Reasons for Doing Right	
	extreme cases where they conflict with other fixed social duties. Right is also contributing to society, the group, or institution.	everyone did it," or the imperative of conscience to meet one's defined obligations (easily confused with Stage 3 belief in rules and authority).	Takes the point of view of the system that defines roles and rules. Considers individual relations in terms of place in the system.
LEVEL III— POSTCONVENTIONAL or PRINCIPLED Stage 5—Social Contract or Utility and Individual Rights	Being aware that people hold a variety of values and opinions, that most values and rules are relative to your group. These relative rules should usually be upheld, however, in the interest of impartiality and because they are the social contract. Some nonrelative values and rights like *life* and *liberty,* however, must be upheld in any society and regardless of majority opinion.	A sense of obligation to law because of one's social contract to make and abide by laws for the welfare of all and for the protection of all people's rights. A feeling of contractual commitment, freely entered upon, to family, friendship, trust, and work obligations. Concern that laws and duties be based on rational calculation of overall utility, "the greatest good for the greatest number."	*Prior-to-society perspective.* Perspective of a rational individual aware of values and rights prior to social attachments and contracts. Integrates perspectives by formal mechanisms of agreement, contract, objective impartiality, and due process. Considers moral and legal points of view; recognizes that they sometimes conflict and finds it difficult to integrate them.
Stage 6—Universal Ethical Principles	Following self-chosen ethical principles. Particular laws or social agreements are usually valid because they rest on such principles. When laws violate these principles, one acts in accordance with the principle. Principles are universal principles of justice: the equality of human rights and respect for the dignity of human beings as individuals.	The belief as a rational person in the validity of universal moral principles and a sense of personal commitment to them.	*Perspective of a moral point of view from which social arrangements derive.* Perspective is that of any rational individual recognizing the nature of morality or the fact that persons are ends in themselves and must be treated as such.

SOURCE: From "Moral Stages and Moralization" by L. Kohlberg, 1976, in T. Lickona (Ed.), *Moral Development and Behavior: Theory, Research and Social Issues* (pp. 34-35), New York: Holt, Rinehart & Winston.

it is his duty to do. When considering right and wrong from this perspective, what is best for Heinz himself becomes irrelevant. Heinz has two roles in society—as a husband and as a citizen subject to the law. These roles take precedence over his self-interest. Heinz's behavior is right if he fulfills societal expectations and wrong if he does not. Social expectations, therefore, provide the arbiters of morality.

The sociomoral perspective associated with the postconventional level of reasoning is labeled the *prior-to-society perspective* because it holds that there are duties and responsibilities inherent in being human that take precedence over any duties and responsibilities that are associated with societal membership and roles. Someone with this perspective might argue that the lawfulness of what Heinz decided to do would be irrelevant, because Heinz's decision could not be made on the basis of law. Thus, issues of theft, punishment, and what people might think of Heinz should not be central to his decision. People operating at the postconventional level would be expected to make the same judgments of right and wrong regardless of whether they lived in a prison-free or a prison-filled society and regardless of whether they were praised or ostracized for their decisions. Given that this highest sociomoral perspective is well beyond the pale of self-interest and local norms, it is not surprising that only a minority of the adults Kohlberg has interviewed demonstrate this perspective consistently in their thinking. Those that do have all been placed in Stage 5. In his many years of research, Kohlberg has yet to find a Stage-6 individual, even though he theorizes that champions of civil disobedience such as Mahatma Gandhi, Henry David Thoreau, and Martin Luther King, Jr., probably operated at this level (Damon, 1983, p. 279).

Evaluating Kohlberg's Stages from the Perspective of Science

Thus far, the developmental sequences of first Selman and now Kohlberg have been presented without any appeal to the scientific data that are needed to justify them as objectively measured, reliably observed, and valid sequences. There is a reason for that. Raising the issues of science with Selman's work would have been premature, because his work is modeled so closely after the work of Kohlberg. Also, there are far more data available for evaluating the scientific merit of Kohlberg's descriptions. Therefore, Kohlberg's work provides the better test case. If his work can be shown to have scientific merit, then it is reasonable to expect that Selman's will too.

To document from a scientific point of view that there are in fact stages in moral development, Kohlberg's data must manifest three essential features of stagewise development. First, development must be a one-way street without regression. This means that individuals must go ever-upward and never backward through his six stages. Second, individuals must go through all the stages in order, without skipping any. Third, a person who is classed as thinking at a particular stage level must show some overall pattern of moral thinking that distinguishes this person sharply from a person classed at any other stage. It would not do to have people classed as Stage 3, for example, if they were only 40 percent Stage 3 and 60 percent Stage 2 and 4.

Until recently, there was serious reason to doubt whether Kohlberg could validate his developmental sequence scientifically. Particularly damaging was a critique by William Kurtines and Esther Greif (1974) that challenged the reliability and the validity of the evidence Kohlberg and his colleagues had produced to that point. In response to his critics, Kohlberg has come back with new and better evidence (Colby, Kohlberg, Gibbs, & Lieberman, 1983). This evidence makes the stage view credible once again. It is based on a reanalysis of old data using a new and improved procedure for measuring stages of moral development. The procedure used today is called Standard Issue Scoring (see Cortese, 1984, for an evaluation). As a result of this new scoring procedure, which is carefully described in a 1200-page manual (Colby & Kohlberg, in press), there is better data than ever before to substantiate the claim that the six stages of reasoning provide a valid description of a developmental course common to all humans, regardless of the society in which they develop.

According to the new data (Colby, Kohlberg, Gibbs, & Lieberman, 1983), Kohlberg's stages do represent distinct types of thinking. Multiple raters were able to reliably assign stage ratings to the statements individuals made during moral-judgment interviews. In addition, there was very little scatter in the stage scores assigned to single individuals across the different dilemmas. In fact, about two thirds of the subjects gave all their responses at a single stage level. The bulk of the rest gave responses at just two adjacent stage levels. This means that the Standard Issue Scoring of the moral-dilemma interviews yielded a measure of moral maturity that was internally consistent. Scores on the nine dilemmas tended to agree with one another. This would not have occurred if individuals tended to think first one way and then another.

Further supporting the validity of the stage-theory explanation of Kohlberg's data is the fact that there was no stage jumping (for example, going from Stage 2 to Stage 4) in Kohlberg's longitudinal data; also, only about 3 percent of the longitudinal subjects ever showed a stage decline from one testing session to the next. (Because no psychological measurement procedure is ever exact, we can accept a 3-percent finding as due simply to measurement error.) Finally, the moral-maturity scores using Standard Issue Scoring procedures appeared to be clearly tied to development because they climbed steadily with age (see Figure 14-6). Moreover, the stages defined by these moral-maturity scores showed a waxing and waning effect that was also developmentally appropriate (see Figure 14-7): they appeared and disappeared in a developmentally ordered way.

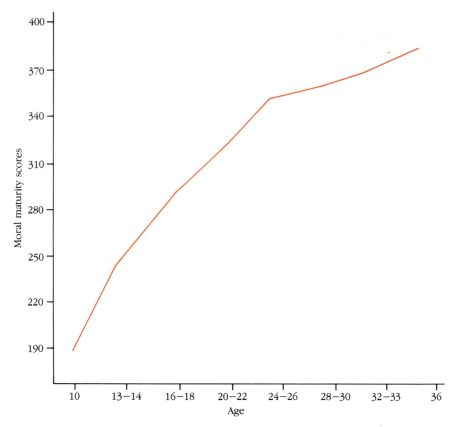

Figure 14-6
Relationship of Age to Moral Maturity
Moral-maturity scores, which are derived from the stage scores with Stage 1 = 100 and Stage 5 = 500, increased steadily with age in Kohlberg's longitudinal study. (After Colby, Kohlberg, Gibbs, & Lieberman, 1983)

Altogether, then, the evidence is quite impressive in supporting a stage-theory explanation for the individual differences among subjects in Kohlberg's longitudinal sample of subjects: there is consistency across dilemmas in the scores of individuals, no stage jumping, little-to-no stage regression, and stage-level increases with age. Not only do the data from Kohlberg's U.S. subjects support his claims, but so do the data from subjects in other countries. John Snarey conducted a massive review of 45 cross-cultural studies and discovered "striking support for the underlying assumptions" of Kohlberg's model (1985, p. 202). Nonetheless, Snarey did find reason to question the universality of Kohlberg's system for scoring development at the postconventional level (that is, Stages 5 and 6). At this level, there is an apparent bias in the current scoring system that favors urban societies and middle-class populations.

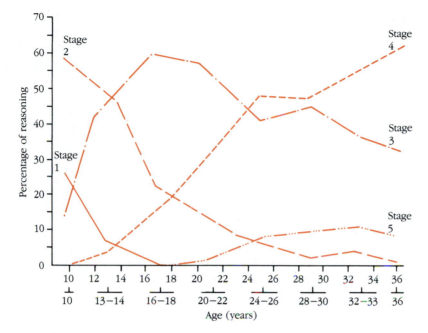

Figure 14-7
The Rise and Fall of Stages of Moral Reasoning
Averaging across all the subjects in Kohlberg's longitudinal study shows that the forms of reasoning designated by the stage labels rise and fall with age, just as the theory says they should. (After Colby, Kohlberg, Gibbs, & Lieberman, 1983)

The Relationship of Moral Reasoning to Behavior

One of the reasons that studies of moral judgment have attracted as much attention as they have is that moral judgment is thought to relate to moral behavior: people who conceptualize moral issues from a societal or a pre-societal point of view should be better citizens than those who conceptualize them from a purely personal point of view. At the same time, however, everyone acknowledges that there will be a highly imperfect relationship between thought and behavior if for no other reason than the fact that people often do not behave as they think they should. Pressures to conform, for example, can lead people to act in ways they are not proud of. Also, people frequently behave on impulse without analyzng issues as carefully as they do in a moral-judgment interview.

The best evidence for a link between moral judgment and behavior comes from studies of juvenile delinquents (see, for example, Hudgins & Prentice, 1973; Kohlberg & Freundlich, 1977). There is a definite relationship between lower-level moral reasoning (usually Stage 2) and a record of juvenile offenses against society. This led reviewer Augusto Blasi (1980) to

Adolescents who can reason at the conventional level have a cognitive buffer against the temptation to commit antisocial acts.

conclude that "moral reasoning is an important aspect of delinquency," though he hastens to add that the reasoning–delinquency relationship is hardly a perfect one.

The theoretical link between moral reasoning and delinquency has been spelled out by John Gibbs and his colleagues (1984) at Ohio State University. In their view, conventional-level thinking serves as a "cognitive buffer" against the temptations and opportunities that adolescents have for vandalism, theft, and more-serious crimes. Adolescents lacking this buffer are at greater risk, therefore, for using their newfound physical strength, size, and autonomy in self-serving, antisocial ways. According to Gibbs and his colleagues, most children have developed to at least the conventional level of thinking by the time they enter adolescence because they have had adequate role-taking opportunities in their homes and schools. But when children grow up in authoritarian homes and schools and when they fail to get the benefit of inductive discipline, their general role-taking abilities can be retarded. The reason is that authoritarian social systems and power-assertive discipline techniques promote unilateral, self-focused views of human relations that impede the development of empathy and mutual understanding (see Hoffman, 1982, 1985; see also Chapter 12 in this text).

Although the link between authoritarian environments, low-level interpersonal perspective-taking ability, and delinquent behavior is a plausible one, there is no experimental evidence to support it at present. Nonetheless, a number of programs have been initiated to remediate the retarded moral reasoning of delinquents and others. The programs show that the use of small-group discussions of moral issues (Gibbs, Arnold, Ahlborn, & Chessman, 1984) and the formation of what Kohlberg calls "just communities" (Muson, 1979) can advance the sociomoral perspective of individuals who participate in them.

Gilligan's Criticism of Kohlberg's Stage Model

Although Kohlberg has parsimoniously captured key aspects of the developmental changes that occur in moral reasoning, one of his colleagues, Carol Gilligan, feels that he has missed a very important element. In Kohlberg's scoring systems, both past and present, greatest weight is given to arguments based on preserving abstract, individual rights. Gilligan claims that this overlooks the fact that high-level moral arguments can be made on the basis of grounds other than the preservation of abstract individual rights; they can be made on the basis of preserving individual relationships.

The most eloquent statement of Gilligan's claim comes in a book titled *In a Different Voice* (Gilligan, 1982). In the book, she presents many examples of moral arguments that do not fit well within Kohlberg's system. They do not fit well because Kohlberg's system gives credit to those who treat moral dilemmas as "human math problems." Not everyone, Gilligan argues, is inclined to treat dilemmas this way. Illustrative evidence comes from a girl named Amy. For this girl, the job in reasoning about Kohlberg's dilemmas was not to determine who was right (which is what Kohlberg would want her to do); the job was to determine how this human conflict could be solved in a way that enabled everybody to get along. For example, when asked if Heinz should steal the drug, Amy said, "I think there might be other ways besides stealing it, like if he could borrow the money or make a loan or something, but he really shouldn't steal the drug—but his wife shouldn't die either" (Gilligan, 1982, p. 28). From her answer, Amy appears confused. But this is only because she is not thinking in terms of awarding justice to the party representing the highest human right. She is thinking of ways to work out the problem to everyone's satisfaction. Thus, she suggests that Heinz and the druggist might get together and work out a payment plan. The whole conflict has arisen, she insists, because Heinz and the druggist "haven't talked it out long enough."

Using Kohlberg's scoring system, Amy would not score well relative to a boy, Jake, who grasped immediately that the issue in the Heinz dilemma concerned the conflict between two human rights—the right to property and the right to life. To decide the dilemma, all one has to do is establish an ordering of the two rights so that one can take priority over the other. Jake does so in a particularly mercenary way: "A human life," Jake explains, "is worth more than money, and if the druggist only makes $1,000, he is still going to live, but if Heinz doesn't steal the drug, his wife is going to die" (Gilligan, 1982, p. 26). Ergo, Heinz should steal the drug; it is the only logical (and economical) thing to do.

Gilligan's major point is that Kohlberg's scoring system only has room for Jake's reasoning. There is no place for arguments such as Amy's—arguments that are based more on the need to preserve relationships than the need to preserve rights. Therefore, Jake, who argues as an ethical logician, would get substantial credit for his answer, but Amy, who argues as a caring person who does not want to see anyone hurt, would get little credit for hers. Her argument "falls through the sieve" created by the scoring system, even though, according to Gilligan, there is development within arguments based on the need for caring and the maintenance of relationships just as there is development in the arguments based on abstract individual rights. If there really is a regular advance on this second dimension of moral reasoning, we must wonder why Kohlberg missed it. Why would he not have seen that children have arguments based on human relations that advance in the same regular way as arguments based on human rights?

Gilligan's answer for why Kohlberg missed the human relations arguments is that his theory was constructed from data collected on males. The alleged importance of the all-male data set is that it kept Kohlberg from hearing "the different voice" of women. Males, Gilligan argues, are not as strongly socialized as women to think in terms of interpersonal relationships and responsibilities. Had Kohlberg included women, he would have heard this voice, along with the voice of abstract, impersonal principles and found a place for it in his scoring system. As it is, only the male voice is represented.

Despite Gilligan's claim of a male bias in Kohlberg's scoring system, the evidence to date shows that, on average, the Amys of the world do not score lower than the Jakes (Walker, 1984). Apparently, even if Gilligan is right and women are indeed inclined to think and speak in a somewhat different voice, this difference does not lead to a sex difference in level of moral reasoning. Apparently, women can reason about rights as well as men when pressed to do so in actual test situations. Despite this fact, if there really is development in how children reason about the need to preserve human relations, this aspect of moral development should be reflected in our measures of moral development.

SUMMARY

The development of social cognition, like the development of cognition itself, stretches from the earliest days of infancy well into adolescence. In this chapter we covered the developments that take place in self-awareness, perspective taking, and moral reasoning.

Infants develop their initial sense of self out of the sensory–motor contingencies that are part of every infant's early experiences. These enable infants to make the I–other distinction, and they also provide a basis for the sense of personal agency that is captured in the belief that "I can make things happen." The contingencies that train this sense of self are available in the physical world where infants engage in primary and secondary circular reactions. They are also available in the social world, but in varying degrees. Sensitive parents provide the best training in personal agency.

In later infancy, infants will recognize themselves in mirrors, videotapes, and photographs. As early as 6 months of age, they distinguish contingent from noncontingent movement in these mirror and televised images, but not until 18 months of age does the mark-on-the-face test give definitive evidence of self-recognition. Humans and apes are the only animals that develop this capacity for self-recognition.

Research has shown an uncanny sensitivity on the part of infants and young children to both gender and age as aspects of their categorical selves. Even infants can make some age and gender discriminations, and by 3 years of age, the discrimination skills of all children are extremely acute. Interestingly, however, children's concept of age and gender are both deficient. Age is conceptually confused with size, and gender is confused with clothes, hairstyle, and behavior. Children's beliefs about gender, moreover, reflect a lack of gender stability and a lack of gender constancy. Not until age 6 or 7 will children have a purely quantity-based understanding of age and a purely anatomy-based understanding of gender.

In the years of early childhood, children's concept of self is based on physical attributes primarily, just as their concepts of age and gender are. If asked to describe a friend or family member, they rely almost exclusively on superficial, temporary characteristics such as where they live, the clothes they wear, or the color of their hair. If asked to interpret what someone wants, they focus on what they say they want. Around age 7, children's descriptions become much more psychological as they focus on traits, personality, and habitual behaviors. Also, children indicate for the first time that what a person thinks can be different from what that person says or does. Children at this time also begin to include comparative information in their self-definitions. This is a recognition that the self must be defined relative to others. Both these advances in self-understanding are consistent with general cognitive advances for the early school years. In terms of Selman's five-leveled system for describing advances in self-awareness, the preschool to school-age shift is a shift from Level 0 (undifferentiated self) to Level 1 (mind and body are separate aspects of self). Level-2 understanding is based on the realization that minds direct bodies and that one cannot automatically infer the inner reality of a person from the person's outer appearance. A Level-3 understanding comes when children attribute an active, observing-ego status to inner consciousness. Level-4 understanding includes the belief that people's thoughts and behavior do not always arise from a conscious self.

Children's knowledge of other people can be tested by determining how well they can predict other people's feelings, thoughts, and motives. The usual procedure has been to tell children stories and have them answer questions from the perspective of different people in the story. In early childhood, interpersonal understanding is limited by the egocentric perspective that children tend to take when judging others. True perspective taking in which the child acknowledges that the other person's point of view may differ from the child's own does not begin until the school years. Selman found that perspective taking advances by levels, or stages, just as self-awareness does. Purely egocentric views are designated at Stage 0 with Stages 1 to 4 indicating advances in nonegocentric thought. These culminate in the ability to reason about interpersonal relations from all points of view simultaneously (Stage 3) and in a way that acknowledges the impact of historical and societal factors in creating the different perspectives (Stage 4).

Selman's work on interpersonal perspective taking is based on Kohlberg's earlier work on the development of moral reasoning. Using clinical interview data and a longitudinal sample of males who were followed from age 10 to adulthood, Kohlberg found that there are six stages in the development of moral judgment. His claims have scientific merit in that they have been shown to be objective, reliable, and valid interpretations of the development-related statements made by his subjects. Kohlberg's stages are divided into three levels: the preconventional, conventional, and postconventional. These differ primarily in terms of sociomoral perspective.

Gilligan has argued that Kohlberg's scoring system favors those who are more concerned with human rights than with human relationships. She believes that moral arguments based on the need to preserve relationships are not developmentally inferior to arguments based on rights, and that Kohlberg's scoring system should be adjusted to reflect this fact.

Long before Kohlberg began his work on moral reasoning, Piaget was investigating the moral judgments of children from preschool age to adolescence. He found a general shift from heteronomous reasoning to autonomous reasoning and from moral realism to moral relativism. Associated with the immature views are a belief in objective responsibility, expiative punishment, immanent justice, and the rights of authorities to impose whatever rules they choose to impose.

SUGGESTIONS FOR FURTHER READINGS

Damon, W. (1983). *Social and personality development: Infancy through adolescence.* New York: W. W. Norton.

Gilligan, C. (1982). *In a different voice: Psychological theory and women's development.* Cambridge, MA: Harvard University Press.

Higgins, E. T., Ruble, D. N., & Hartup, W. W. (Eds.). (1983) *Social cognition and social development.* New York: Cambridge University Press. Leading researchers present their data and theories.

Piaget, J. (1932/1965). *The moral judgment of the child.* New York: The Free Press. This classic study provides an excellent introduction to Piaget as both scientist and philosoper.

Shantz, C. (1983). Social cognition. In J. H. Flavell & E. M. Markman (Vol. Eds.), and P. H. Mussen (Gen. Ed.), *Handbook of child psychology: Vol. 3. Cognitive development.* New York: Wiley. This chapter is an updated version of Shantz's 1975 review of research in the area of social cognition which appeared in E. M. Hetherington (Ed.), *Review of child development research,* Vol. 5.

Glossary

accommodation 1. In perception, the eye's ability to bring objects located at different distances into focus by changing the shape of the lens; 2. In Piaget's theory, the process by which people adapt their cognitive structures (or schemes) in order to be able to cope with new information or realizations.

accretion and deletion of texture A dynamic cue that provides information about the relative distance of objects. The cue is created whenever objects move relative to their background.

adoption studies Studies in which adopted children are compared to members of their adopted families and members of their biological families for the purpose of assessing the relative importance of genes and the environment in creating individual differences.

adrenocortical hyperplasia An inherited metabolic disorder that results in an excessive production of androgens by the adrenal cortices. During the prenatal period, this condition can cause masculinization of the developing genitals and brain.

affective disorders A group of mental disorders in which there is a prolonged, pervasive disturbance of mood (either depression or elation). One well-known subtype is the bipolar manic-depressive disorder that is characterized by mood swings from extreme elation and optimism to extreme depression.

allele Any one of two or more variants of a gene that can occur at a given chromosomal site.

analogy Similarity that derives from having a common function or structure without regard to evolutionary origins. Contrasts with **homology.**

androgen insensitivity An inherited condition that results in a failure of androgens to have their usual masculinizing effects on developing tissues.

associate play Play that involves a common activity (for example, making mudpies) but that does not require cooperation among the children other than perhaps sharing materials or conversing. The children involved in associative play work independently of each other toward goals of their own choosing.

attribution theory A theory that deals with the process by which people assign causes to their own behavior and that of others.

babbling Meaningless vocalizations that have a syllabic structure (that is, consonant + vowel structure); babbling occurs universally among humans beginning around 6 months of age.

Bayley Scales of Infant Development A well-standardized set of measures for assessing both mental development and psychomotor development during the period 2 months to 2½ years. The test also includes a behavior record that is useful for some evaluative purposes.

Binet-Simon Mental Age Scales A 1908 psychometric instrument that proved to be the world's first reliable and valid means of determining objectively when children were in need of special education. The test was widely interpreted to be a measure of individual differences in intelligence.

binocular cues Visual cues to depth that are created because our two eyes view the world from slightly different perspectives.

biogenetic law See **law of recapitulation.**

biological fitness In evolutionary theory, the reproductive success of individual animals.

birth catch-up The very rapid human growth that occurs just after birth. Tanner assumes that this rapid growth represents catch-up for growth that was denied during the fetus's last weeks in the uterus.

bonding The process by which a mother develops a strong attachment to her newborn. This process is alleged to occur in humans and some other mammals and is thought to involve hormonal events that are stimulated through sight, hearing, touch, and smell.

carrier In genetics, a person who carries an unexpressed recessive gene. Carriers do not have the trait associated with the recessive gene, but they are responsible for transmitting it.

case study A report of a unique event usually based on observations that are made of a single individual.

cephalocaudal From head to tail along the central axis of the body. A cephalocaudal gradient is evident in neuromuscular maturation in all vertebrates.

cerebral cortex The gray matter that forms the outer layer of the cerebral hemispheres.

cerebrum The portion of the brain that includes the left and right cerebral hemispheres. In vertebrates, the cerebrum constitutes the largest part of the brain.

child-study movement The 19th century scientific movement that promoted the collection of normative data on the growth and development of children.

chromosomal anomaly A species-atypical chromosomal condition. Possible anomalies include trisomies, monosomies, translocation, and breakage.

chronological age Age since birth. Contrasts with **conceptual age.**

chunking The process of making one memory unit out of several units. Chunking provides one way of expanding the absolute amount of information that can be stored in short-term memory.

classification The process of ordering a collection of objects into a set of mutually exclusive and exhaustive classes. The ability to construct such an ordering mentally, and then to reason about the quantitative relation between classes and their subclasses, first develops in the concrete operational period.

clinical interview A technique pioneered by Piaget for discovering what children know and think and, thereby, studying their cognitive development. A primary characteristic is that the interviewer has some freedom to probe and question.

cognitive development The development of mental processes such as perception, problem solving, reasoning, and memory, and the development of knowledge in general.

cohort A group of individuals sharing the same birth year.

cohort effect A cohort difference that shows up as an age difference in a cross-sectional research design.

cohort sequential research design A design first used by Schaie that enables developmentalists to separate cohort effects from true developmental changes. To execute the design, one must collect longitudinal data on multiple cohorts.

combinatorial reasoning The mental process whereby one creates the set of all possible combinations of existing elements. The ability to perform this mental act is associated with formal operational thought.

competence The ability one actually has as opposed to the ability that one succeeds in demonstrating. Contrasts with **performance.**

conceptual age Age since conception. This age provides a more reliable index of developmental status than does chronological age for infants in their first year.

concrete operational period In Piaget's theory, the period from about age 7 to about age 11 or 12 during which children discover the processes known as classification, seriation, and conservation, which they apply to real objects and their concrete properties.

confluence model Zajonc and Markus's model for predicting characteristics of one's intellectual growth curve from knowledge about family size, birth order, and spacing.

conscience A sense of moral responsibility that many believe to be uniquely human. In Freudian theory, the human conscience is represented by the superego.

conservation The process of reasoning that some property of an object has remained invariant despite a superficial change in the object's appearance. The ability to conserve object properties such as number, weight, area, and volume first develops in the concrete operational period.

continuous trait A trait that can be measured in degrees, such as height or intelligence. Contrasts with **threshold trait.**

control The hallmark of any experiment. To conduct an experiment one must be able to control the independent variable (by manipulating it at will) and all extraneous variables (by holding them at some constant value).

control practices Procedures parents use to exert their will in situations of parent–child conflict. General categories for control practices include power assertion, love withdrawal, and induction.

control processes In the Atkinson and Shiffrin memory model, the processes used to transfer, store, and retrieve information.

controlled breeding studies Studies that use inbreeding or selective breeding in order to determine the relative roles of heredity and environment in creating individual differences.

convergent thinking Thinking that is directed at producing a single, correct answer to a problem. Contrasts with **divergent thinking.**

cooing A meaningless vocalization that is purely vocalic (that is, consists of vowel-like sounds).

cooperative play Play that is organized for some specific purpose and that requires a division of labor. Players are easily distinguished from non-players in cooperative play.

correlation coefficient A statistic designated by the letter r that indicates the degree of linear relationship that exists between two variables. The statistic ranges in value from $+1.00$ to -1.00. It equals 0.00 when there is no relationship.

correlational studies Studies in which investigators are able to investigate the statistical relationship that exists between two variables. Investigators must remember that a statistical relationship is not proof of causality. See **experiment.**

creole A pidgin language that has become the mother-tongue of a speech community. The process of creolization expands the structural and stylistic range of the pidginized language.

critical period A period of fixed length during which developmental events can have a permanent effect on some characteristic of the developing organism. Outside of the period the same events have either no effect or a different effect.

cross-sectional research design A design that measures age-related changes by studying the differences between individuals of different ages. Contrasts with **longitudinal research design.**

cultural familial retardation Retardation that has its origins in the general genetic and cultural conditions of families and not in any single isolatable cause.

declarative knowledge The knowledge of facts and specific bits of information. Contrasts with **procedural knowledge.**

dependent variable The variable in an experiment that is observed and measured. Compare **independent variable.**

deprivation dwarfism Severely retarded growth that is due to parental neglect or emotional upset. See also **failure-to-thrive syndrome.**

developmental psychology The scientific discipline concerned with describing age-related changes in the behavior and mental processes of both humans and animals and then explaining how nature and nurture through their interaction produce these changes.

developmental quotient (DQ)   A measure of development that reflects one's performance on a standardized test of infant development relative to same age peers. DQ is not a good predictor of IQ.

deviation score   A score that indicates the extent to which one deviates from the average for one's age group on a test. Deviation scores are derived from raw scores using a simple statistical transformation.

digit span   The maximum number of digits that can be retained in short-term memory following the oral presentation of a series of digits at the rate of one per second.

disequilibrium   In Piaget's theory, a state in which one's available schemes (or mental structures) are discovered to be inadequate. This state is prerequisite to cognitive advance.

displaced reference   A capacity shared by all languages for referring to objects and events that are distant in either time or space.

divergent thinking   Thinking that is directed at producing as many novel but appropriate ideas as possible. Contrasts with **convergent thinking.**

dominant gene   A gene (or allele) that expresses itself in the phenotype regardless of the gene (or allele) with which it is paired.

Down's syndrome   The physical and mental condition that results from having three 21st chromosomes rather than the usual two. Also called **trisomy 21** and formerly called *mongolism.*

dynamic cues   Visual cues to depth that are created by movements either of the viewer or of the objects in the visual field of the viewer.

ego   In Freudian theory, the component to the human personality that is dominated by reason.

embryo   The developing human organism from the 2nd to the 8th week of gestation, which is the period during which primary tissues differentiate and organs develop.

environmentality   The proportion of the variance in a trait that is attributable to the differences in the environments in which people develop.

epigenesis   The view that development is characterized by the emergence of new properties that are neither predestined nor predetermined. In biology, epigenesis stands in contrast to the preformationist view. In psychology, it stands in contrast to the view that knowledge of either nature or nurture alone is sufficient to predict developmental outcomes.

ethology   A branch of psychology that is dedicated to the naturalistic study of animal behavior and to the interpretation of animal behavior in terms of its evolutionary significance.

evoked potential   A specific, event-related response that can be detected in the brain using an electroencephalograph or EEG.

evolutionism   A concern for understanding the origins and development of natural phenomena.

experiment   A procedure for making causal inferences from observations of the relationships that exist among variables.

expiative punishment   Punishment that is designed not to rectify a wrong but to gain revenge on the guilty.

extraversion   The tendency to seek out stimulation from the world of people and things; characterized by a preference for novelty and variety; high sociability. Contrasts with **introversion.**

failure-to-thrive syndrome   A childhood condition characterized by a severely retarded growth rate. The condition can occur as a result of parental neglect and emotional upset. See also **deprivation dwarfism.**

falsifiability   One of the criteria for evaluating the scientific merit of theories. A theory is falsifiable when it is stated in such a way that it can be disproved.

family studies   Studies that determine the extent to which family members resemble one another on a trait. Family studies are conducted to determine whether a trait might be heritable.

fetus   The developing human organism from the end of the 8th week of gestation until birth.

field studies   See **naturalistic studies.**

formal operational period   In Piaget's theory, the period from about age 11 or 12 to late adolescence during which children develop the ability to think and reason about abstractions. As part of this process, they become capable of propositional logic, proportional reasoning, isolation of variables, and combinatorial reasoning.

foundational period A period during ontogenesis when certain experiences must occur to provide the developmental foundation for later experiences. Should the initial experiences not occur at their customary time, the developmental loss can be corrected by having a person go back to make up for the missed experience.

frontal lobe The part of each cerebral hemisphere that is in front of the central sulcus; the forwardmost portion of the brain.

gender constancy The belief that gender is a constant, inalterable attribute of people that persists no matter how they might change their appearance or behavior.

gender identity A person's own private sense of being male or female.

gender role The public expression of one's gender through activities and preferences that can be sex-typed as male or female.

gender stability The belief that gender is a stable attribute of people but that it can nonetheless change if people choose to dress or behave like a member of the opposite sex.

generativity A capacity shared by all languages for creating novel messages from a number of reusable linguistic units.

genetic epistemology Piaget's name for the branch of cognitive science that concerns itself with the ontogenetic origins and development of the human ability to know and to reason.

genotype A person's total genetic makeup as represented by the sum of the genetic information in all the chromosomes or some particular aspect of this genetic makeup, such as the genotype for baldness or the genotype for albinism.

Gesell Developmental Schedules One of the earliest instruments for assessing individual differences in the behavioral development of infants.

glial cells Nonneuronal cells in the brain and spinal cord that provide structural and functional support for the neurons of the central nervous system.

grammar A structural characteristic of all languages; the grammars of human languages include phonological, morphological, syntactic, and semantic rules.

habituation A process that manifests itself in a loss of attention to previously novel stimuli when these stimuli are presented repeatedly.

habituation method A procedure that is widely used in infant research to investigate the discriminatory and memory abilities of infants.

heritability The proportion of the variance in a trait that is attributable to the genetic differences that exist among individuals. Compare **environmentality.**

heterochrony A change in the normal temporal sequence for the development of tissues, organs, and other animal parts. Such changes are thought to have played a role in the origins of some species.

heteronomous mortality The developmental precursor to autonomous morality; it is characterized by a belief in moral realism, expiative punishment, objective responsibility, and obedience to authority.

heterozygote An individual differing with respect to the alleles at one or more gene loci.

heuristic value One of the criteria for evaluating the scientific merit of theories. A theory has heuristic value if it proves to be useful either as a stimulus for new scientific discoveries or as a guide for practical applications.

high-amplitude sucking method (HAS) A procedure for investigating infant cognition that takes advantage of infants' willingness to work to make interesting spectacles last. Infants are able to maintain a stimulus at an optimal level of intensity by sucking on a nipple that is electronically connected to an apparatus such as a slide projector or tape recorder.

holophrase A one-word utterance, which is to say an utterance in which a single word carries the meaning of an entire sentence.

home sign An idiosyncratic sign language spontaneously invented by deaf children who have not had the opportunity to learn a conventional sign language.

homology Similarity that derives from having a common structure and evolutionary origin. Compare **analogy.**

homozygote An individual with identical alleles at one or more gene loci.

horizontal decalage A developmental principle that is characteristic of cognitive development in the domain of thinking and problem solving. The principle is that mental structures will be applied to some problem contents before others. For example, children can conserve number before weight and weight before volume even though all three types of problems—number, weight, and volume—require what seems to be identical logic.

hostile aggression Aggression that is designed to harm or injure. Contrasts with **instrumental aggression.**

id In Freud's theory, the component to the human personality that is directed by basic biological cravings.

illocutionary force The social function that an utterance is intended to perform, which may differ from the grammatical function. For example, the utterance "How are you doing?" which is a question from the point of view of grammar, generally has the illocutionary force of a greeting, not a question.

imaging The process of picturing information in order to enhance its memorability.

immanent justice A belief that bad acts are invariably tied to punishments, with the result that one cannot have the one without the other.

imprinting The process by which infant–mother attachments are formed in many precocial species.

inbreeding Any breeding program in which relatives mate with relatives. Inbreeding, even in just one generation, increases the incidence of homozygosity in offspring and, if continued long enough, can result in the absence of any genetic variability at all.

independent variable The variable in an experiment that is manipulated under the control of the experimenter for the purpose of discovering how changes in this one variable affect some other variable or variables.

induction 1. In embryology, the process by which the developmental fate of undifferentiated cells and tissue is determined; the fate is in-duced through the effects of chemical substances released by neighboring cells and tissues. 2. As a parental control practice, the practice of informing children about the effect of their behavior on others.

infant–mother attachment The special affectional relationship that connects infants to their mothers and provides infants with the emotional security and comfort necessary for normal development.

inflection A morpheme placed at the end of a word that alters the word's semantic or syntactic interpretation. In English, the past tense of verbs, the plural of nouns, and possession are all marked through the use of inflections.

instrumental aggression Acts that are aggressive in form (for example, pushing, grabbing, or hitting) but that are designed to achieve a goal rather than to hurt someone.

instrumental competence A term that encompasses a wide range of specific behaviors, most notably behaviors that reflect social responsibility, independence, achievement orientation, and vitality.

instrumental learning Learning that occurs because a person's response is instrumental in producing a reinforcer. Rats that learn to press bars in order to produce food pellets provide the usual textbook illustration of instrumental learning.

intelligence quotient (IQ) A measure of intelligence that reflects one's performance on an intelligence test relative to peers. Formerly IQ was calculated using the formula MA/CA × 100, but today deviation scores are used to compute IQ.

intersensory knowledge Knowledge that leads one to know how an object will appear to one sense (for example, touch) after having experienced the object via another sense (for example, vision).

introversion The tendency to avoid the stimulation provided by novel people and things; low sociability. Contrasts with **extraversion.**

ipsative stability Stability that is achieved by maintaining constancy in some trait or tendency over time. Compare **normative stability.**

isolation of variables The mental operation that allows one to know which observations carry the implication that one variable is causally related to another and which do not.

Klinefelter's syndrome The set of distinctive physical and mental characteristics that result from having an XXY genotype rather than the usual XX or XY.

language acquisition device (LAD) Chomsky's name for the innate knowledge that humans appear to have regarding the possible rules and meanings of language; the availability of the "device" makes it possible for two-year-olds to infer the grammar of whatever human language they are exposed to.

language acquisition support system (LASS) The special features in the linguistic environments of children that serve to facilitate the process of language acquisition.

law of recapitulation The principle that ontogeny recapitulates phylogeny, which was widely held as a general developmental principle in the late 19th century; also called the **biogenetic law.**

lexicon The vocabulary of a language or of a language user.

longitudinal research design A design that measures age-related change by following a single group of individuals over time. Contrasts with **cross-sectional design.**

long-term memory store In the Atkinson and Shiffrin model of memory, a storage area that is distinct from the short-term store and that serves to retain an unlimited amount of information indefinitely.

M-space Term used by Pascual-Leone to label the storage capacity of short-term memory.

masculinization The process by which sex-neutral tissues and organs in the embryo become masculine in their structure and function.

mean length of utterance (MLU) The average length of a child's utterances as measured in morphemes.

mediation deficiency An inability to use a strategy or procedure that would improve learning and memory.

memory span A general term for referring to the amount of information that can be held in short-term or working memory at one time. Measures of memory span include tests of digit span and counting span.

menarche The onset of menstruation in females; the date of the first menstrual period.

mental age A measure of intellectual development that reflects the age-level of one's performance on a standardized test of intelligence.

metamemory The knowledge one has about memory and how it works.

minimal sufficiency principle A principle derived from attribution theory that holds that self-control can be instilled most readily by deemphasizing the external controls on behavior. Thus, parents wishing to promote self-control in their children would be advised to use rewards and punishments that are low key and minimally sufficient to obtain the desired behavior.

monogenic trait A trait that is controlled by a single gene.

moral realism The belief that the rules that govern human social behavior are as fixed and inalterable as the laws of physics. Contrasts with **moral relativism.**

moral relativism A belief that the rules that govern social behavior are arbitrary conventions adopted by societies for the mutual benefit of their members. Contrasts with **moral realism.**

morpheme A word or word part that has meaning and that cannot itself be further divided into other meaningful elements; the most fundamental linguistic element that has meaning.

morphological rules Those grammatical rules that deal with combining morphemes into words.

motherese The special language that mothers and other caretakers use when addressing children.

motion parallax A dynamic cue to depth created by the fact that the visual images of distant objects are displaced less than the visual images of near objects when the objects themselves or their observer moves.

motor development Development of behaviors that are effected through the use of motor neurons and skeletal muscles. Examples of such behaviors are walking, grasping, climbing, and throwing.

Müllerian inhibiting substance (MIS)   A hypothetical substance secreted by the fetal testes that serves to inhibit the development of the Müllerian structure.

Müllerian structure   The initial embryonic structure from which the female fallopian tubes and uterus will develop.

myelinization   The process by which nerve axons develop a white, fatty coating of myelin, which serves to speed nerve transmission.

natural experiments   Naturally occurring situations that allow investigators to determine whether variation in one variable is causally related to variations in another variable.

naturalistic studies   A noninvasive, nonexperimental study conducted under naturally occurring conditions (for example, an ethologist's study of the behavior of chimpanzees or a psychologist's study of aggressive episodes on a children's playground). Also known as **field studies.**

nature–nurture issue   The issue that concerns the relative roles of hereditary and environmental factors in determining the course of development.

neoteny   The retention of juvenile features of ancestral species in the adult features of derived species.

nerve growth factor   A chemical substance that is sought out by developing nerve cells as they establish their connections with muscles, organs, and other neurons during development.

neuromuscular maturation   Maturation that involves the muscles of the skeletal system, the nerves that innervate them, and the motor areas of the brain that control voluntary motor acts.

neurons   Individual nerve cells, each of which consists of a cell body, an axon, dendrites, and axonal branches.

normative stability   Stability that is achieved when one maintains over a period of time a constant ranking relative to one's peers in some trait or tendency.

objective responsibility   A belief that the magnitude of an offense can be judged solely by the magnitude of its consequences regardless of the offender's intentions.

objectivity   One of the criteria for evaluating the scientific merit of observations. It requires that one avoid subjective judgments and restrict all descriptive statements to those that are objectively verifiable.

observing ego   In Selman's theory of the development of a sense of self, the observing ego represents a view of self that is characteristic of late childhood and early adolescence when children think of themselves as having an inner, hidden self that is in charge of both their behavior and their thoughts.

ontogenesis   The development of an individual member of a species. Compare **phylogenesis.**

organogenesis   The process by which the different animal organs form and develop. The bulk of this process occurs during the embryonic period; however, the process continues during the fetal period and even after birth for organs of the sensory system and the central nervous system.

overextension   The young child's tendency to use a rather specific word to refer to a wide class of referents (for example, using the word daddy to refer to men in general).

ovum   The female sex cell or egg; the complement to the male sperm cell. The period of the ovum refers to the initial stage of human development, which includes fertilization, implantation of the fertilized egg, and the initial stages of tissue differentiation.

parallel play   Play that occurs beside rather than with other children.

parenting styles   Styles identified as characteristic of the ways parents interact with their children. Using measures of parental control, nurturance, maturity demands, and communication it is possible to define the authoritarian, authoritative, and permissive styles.

parsimony   One of the criteria for evaluating the scientific merit of theories. A parsimonious theory is one that explains a large set of observations using relatively few explanatory principles.

pathological retardation   Retardation that can be attributed to specific pathologies such as those that result from disease, injury, metabolic errors, and chromosomal abnormalities.

pedigree studies   A type of family study appropriate for determining whether the appearance of some threshold trait (for example, stuttering, schizophrenia, or PKU) in members of a family could be attributable to the transmission of a single gene to children within that family.

perception   The meaningful interpretation of a sensory event such as a sight, sound, pain, and so on.

performance   The ability that one demonstrates as opposed to the actual ability one might have. Contrasts with **competence.**

period of the ovum   See **ovum.**

personal agency   The ability one has to produce and control events in the social and physical world.

phenotype   The total of the measurable aspects of an organism. The phenotype consists of the observable consequences of the interactions of heredity and environment in development.

phonemes   Individual sounds, meaningless in themselves, that are used to make up linguistic utterances.

phonological rules   The rules in a language that deal with which sound combinations are allowable and which are not.

phylogenesis   The development of species. Compare **ontogenesis.**

pictorial cues   Distance cues that are present in static visual images. Examples are shading, texture density gradients, and overlay.

pidgin   A language with a markedly reduced grammatical structure and lexicon. Pidgins develop when two speech communities attempt to communicate by employing obvious features of the two languages. Pidgins become creolized when they become the mother-tongue of a community.

plasticity   Capacity for being molded or shaped; designates a developmental state in which there is potential for change.

pleiotropy   The multiple effects of a single gene on different aspects of the phenotype.

polygenic trait   A trait that is determined by the actions of many genes whose individual effects are not discernible.

pragmatics   The rules for using language effectively and appropriately in social contexts.

precedence effect   The experience of hearing but one sound—the one with precedence—when two identical sounds are presented laterally with a time separation of from 7 to 50 milliseconds.

preference method   A method used in infant research to determine which of two stimuli infants prefer. The method is used to gain knowledge about the perceptual abilities of preverbal infants.

prehension   Act of taking hold, seizing, or grasping.

preoperational period   In Piaget's theory, the period from about age two until seven, during which time children tend to reason in an intuitive, centered, and egocentric way.

preparedness   The principle used to explain the fact that some intersensory associations are acquired far more readily than others. According to advocates of the principle, the associations that are acquired most easily are those that we have been prepared to form through evolution.

prevarication   A functional characteristic shared by all languages for representing what is not true, or real.

proband   In a pedigree study, the first person in the family to be identified as having the trait of interest.

procedural knowledge   How-to knowledge such as the knowledge of strategies, procedures, and skills. Contrasts with **declarative knowledge.**

production deficiency   A failure to employ spontaneously the strategies and procedures that would improve learning and memory.

projection   In Freudian theory, a mechanism for expressing one's own hidden and, perhaps, dangerous thoughts by attributing them to other people. Projection is egocentric in the sense that it attributes one's own inner motives and feelings to others.

proportional reasoning The mental operation needed to make quantitative comparisons of proportions.

propositional logic The logic needed to judge the truth value of arguments that combine propositions, as in the case of if-then arguments (conditionals), both-and arguments (biconditionals), and either-or arguments (disjunctives).

proprioceptive sense The sense of body movement and position. Proprioceptive information is derived from nerve endings and organs in the muscles, tendons, joints, and the labyrinth of the ear.

prosocial behavior Helpful, cooperative behavior that benefits others. Comforting, sharing, and altruism are specific prosocial acts.

prosody The speech features of pitch, loudness, tempo, and rhythm.

proximodistal From near to far; a proximodistal gradient is evident in neuromuscular maturation in that maturation proceeds from the central nervous system out into the limbs.

psychogenesis The formation of the psychological attributes of animals. Contrasts with **organogenesis.**

psychometrician A psychologist who specializes in the construction, administration, and interpretation of standardized tests that are designed to measure individual differences in psychological functions such as intelligence, creativity, or sociability.

recessive gene A gene that only expresses itself in the phenotype when it is paired with a second gene of the same type; that is, a gene that expresses itself only in the homozygotic state.

recognition memory The capacity to discriminate new from old information, a capacity that can be tested even in very young infants and that seems to relate to eventual intelligence as assessed by IQ tests.

reduplication One of the ways young children simplify the phonology of a language. It involves repeating a single syllable from the word in order to represent the whole word as in saying **baba** for **bottle.**

referential communication Communication that makes reference to objects or events that one cannot experience directly.

regulatory genes Genes that serve to regulate the activity of other genes through the synthesis of a repressor substance. Contrasts with **structural genes,** which are genes that direct the production of proteins.

reinstatement A procedure for stimulating the retrieval of a memory without offering an occasion for relearning.

reliability A criterion for assessing the scientific merit of observations; science admits as fact only those observations that are reliable in the sense that they can be replicated (test-retest reliability) and that they are agreed on by multiple observers (interobserver reliability).

retinal expansion A dynamic cue that signals when objects are approaching and when they are receding; hence, a dynamic cue to depth.

retrospective research design A design that measures age-related change by using people's memory for events as data.

scatterplot A graphic representation of the relationship that exists between two variables.

secular trend A systematic change in some characteristic of a population that is due to social changes, not genetic changes.

selective breeding A controlled breeding program in which mating pairs are selected on the basis of a shared phenotypic trait.

semantic rules Rules in a grammar that have to do with meaning.

semiotic function The ability to represent aspects of one's experience either in private images or public codes. Also referred to as **symbolic function.**

sensation The conscious experience of a sensory event such as a sight, sound, pain, and so on.

sensitive period A period during development when an organism is particularly and, perhaps, uniquely susceptible to the effects of specific experiences. In contrast to developments that occur during critical periods, sensitive period developments can be altered by later events. Also, the time period for sensitive periods is not so rigid as for critical periods.

sensorimotor period In Piaget's theory, the period from birth to about 2 years during which time infants go from a cognitive state in which they can only experience the world through their sensory and motor actions to a state in which they can experience the world through their own symbolic representations.

sensory store In the Atkinson and Shiffrin model of memory, a store that retains raw sensory information for a very brief period of time; the first stage of information processing.

seriation The process of arranging objects in a series according to their value on a single dimension. The ability to construct a series mentally and then to reason about the transitive relations among objects in the series first develops in the concrete operational period.

sex-limited trait A trait that expresses itself in only one sex. Baldness, for example, is usually limited to males and breast development to females even though individuals of both genders carry genes for these traits.

sex-linked trait A trait that is determined by a gene on one of the sex chromosomes.

shape constancy The perception that the shape of objects remains constant despite changes in the angle from which they are viewed.

short-term memory store In the Atkinson and Shiffrin model of memory, the store that holds the information being processed at the moment. It is severely limited in size. In the absence of rehearsal, information cannot be retained in the short-term store for more than about 30 seconds.

size constancy The perception that the size of objects remains the same despite changes in the distance from which they are viewed.

skeletal age Age as determined through a comparison of a person's bone development relative to norms for people the same age.

socialization The process by which people acquire the roles, behavior, and attitudes that are expected of them by society.

social learning theory An extension of general learning theory that emphasizes the role of imitation and observation in human learning.

social pretend play Cooperative play that follows a make-believe format. *Sociodramatic play*

deals with real-life events like shopping and visiting the doctor. *Thematic fantasy play* takes children out of the realm of real-life into pure fantasy and imagination.

social referencing The use of the emotional expressions of others to resolve the meaning of otherwise ambiguous situations.

sociobiology The study of the biological basis for social behavior in humans and other animals.

solitary play Play that has no social component, not even to the extent of seeking proximity to others while playing.

sound assimilation One of the ways young children simplify the phonology of a language. It involves changing one of the sounds in a word to make it more like some other sound.

sound deletion One of the ways young children simplify the phonology of a language. An example is the deletion of unstressed syllables as occurs when *away* is pronounced as '*way* and *tomato* as '*mado*.

sound substitution One of the ways young children simplify the phonology of a language. It involves substituting a sound that is easy to produce for one that is difficult.

species-typical behavior A term that should be substituted for the term *instinct* because it avoids the misleading implication that some behaviors are predetermined and not subject to the usual epigenetic process in development.

Stanford-Binet The American version of the mental age scale developed in France by Binet and Simon. It is called the Stanford-Binet in recognition of the fact that it was developed by psychologists at Stanford University, most notably Lewis Terman.

strain A population of animals produced through a prolonged inbreeding program that has virtually no genetic variability and no heterozygotic gene loci.

strange situation Mary Ainsworth's procedure for assessing the quality of attachment in 1- to 2-year-old infants.

stranger anxiety The species-typical response of human infants to strangers in the period from about 6 months until late infancy or early childhood. The period from 8 to 10 months is the peak period for stranger anxiety in the children of all cultures.

structures d'ensemble Literally, structures of the whole; Piaget's term for hypothetical holistic structures that are available to children in each of the four major periods of development. Each period is characterized by a different *structure d'ensemble*.

superego In Freudian theory, the component to mind that represents the human conscience.

symbolic function See **semiotic function.**

syntactic rules The rules in a grammar that deal with word order and how one marks words so that they will play a particular grammatical role (for example, as a subject, object, or recipient).

target seeking James Tanner's conceptualization of the mechanism that controls growth. In his view, the mechanism monitors actual growth relative to an idealized growth plan so that when actual growth deviates from the plan, actions are triggered that help to get growth back on target.

temperament A person's characteristic style of behavior, as measured by behavioral dimensions such as emotionality, irritability, activity, and sociability. Many believe that there is a genetic component to temperament and that temperaments remain relatively stable throughout life.

teratogen Any agent that can cause abnormalities in physical development during the prenatal period.

threshold trait A trait that can be judged to be either present or absent (for example, blue eyes or schizophrenia). Contrasts with **quantitative trait.**

tonic-neck reflex A postural reflex present in neonates and very young infants which is characterized by limb extension on the side to which the head is turned and limb flexion on the opposite side.

transitivity In Piaget's theory, an aspect of the mental operation known as seriation. Transitivity enables one to discover through reason alone the relationship that exists between two series members such as *A* and *C* from the knowledge of the relationship between series members *A* and *B* and *B* and *C*.

trisomy A chromosomal abnormality in which there are three chromosomes of a single type rather than the usual two. It is usually caused by an error in cell division called nondisjunction.

trisomy 21 See **Down's syndrome.**

Turner's syndrome The set of physical and mental characteristics associated with the monosomic X0 genotype.

twin studies Studies that use data from DZ twins, MZ twins, and the families of twins in order to answer questions regarding the relative importance of heredity and environment in creating individual differences.

underextension The young child's tendency to limit the meaning of a word to fewer referents than an adult would (for example, using the word *shoes* just for bedroom slippers).

validity A criterion for measuring the scientific value of the statements used when describing or interpreting observations. Internally valid statements are true with regard to what was observed, externally valid statements are true in general, and ecologically valid statements are true for the real-world in which people live (rather than for just the special worlds that scientists might have created for the purpose of making the observations.)

variance A statistic that is a measure of how spread out the scores in a distribution are. For any normally distributed variable, the greater the range in scores, the greater the variance.

vestigial reflexes Reflexes that are present at birth but that disappear over the first few months of life.

visual-cliff apparatus An apparatus used to determine whether infants and young animals can interpret the visual cues that signal a drop-off.

WAIS-R Wechsler Adult Intelligence Scale—Revised. The revised version of the WAIS (originally the Wechsler-Bellevue) which is a standardized test for measuring adult intelligence. Like all the Wechsler tests, the WAIS-R yields a verbal score, a performance score, and a full-scale IQ with a mean of 100 and a standard deviation of 15.

WISC-R Wechsler Intelligence Scale for Children—Revised. A standardized test of intelligence appropriate for children from 6 to 17 years of age.

WPPSI Wechsler Preschool and Primary Scale of Intelligence. A standardized test of intelligence appropriate for children from 4 to 6½ years of age.

Wolffian structure The initial embryonic structure from which the internal reproductive anatomy of males develops. The mature male structures that develop from the Wolffian structure include the vas deferens, epididymis, and seminal vesicles.

working memory An alternative label for short-term memory, one that emphasizes that the information in short-term memory is not just being stored, it is being processed.

X-linked gene A gene that is known to be located on the X chromosome.

zygote The fertilized ovum prior to the onset of cell division. The zygote is formed when an ovum and a sperm unite.

References

Aboud, F. E. (1985). Children's application of attribution principles to social comparisons. *Child Development, 56,* 682–688.

Abravanel, E. & Sigafoos, A. D. (1984). Exploring the presence of imitation during early infancy. *Child Development, 55,* 381–392.

Acredolo, L. P., Adams, A., & Goodwyn, S. W. (1984). The role of self-produced movement and visual tracking in infant spatial orientation. *Journal of Experimental Child Psychology, 38,* 312–327.

Acredolo, L. P. & Hake, J. L. (1982). Infant perception. In B. B. Wolman (Ed.), *Handbook of Developmental Psychology.* Englewood Cliffs, NJ: Prentice Hall.

Agassiz, L. (1849). *Twelve lectures on comparative embryology.* Boston: Henry Flanders.

Agassiz, L. (1857). Essay on classification. In *Contributions to the natural history of the United States,* Vol. 1. Boston: Little, Brown & Co. (Reprinted 1962, ed. E. Lurie. Cambridge, MA: Harvard University Press.)

Ainsworth, M. D. S. (1973). The development of infant-mother attachment. In B. M. Caldwell & H. N. Ricciuti (Eds.), *Review of child development research* (Vol. 3). Chicago: University of Chicago Press.

Ainsworth, M. D. S. (1983). Patterns of infant-mother attachment as related to maternal care. In D. Magnusson & V. Allen (Eds.), *Human development: An interactional perspective.* New York: Academic Press.

Ainsworth, M. D. S. & Bell, S. M. (1970). Attachment, exploration, and separation: illustrated by the behavior of one year-olds in a strange situation. *Child Development 41,* 49–67.

Ainsworth, M. D. S., Blehar, M. C., Waters, E., & Wall, S. (1978). *Patterns of attachment: A psychological study of the strange situation.* Hillsdale, NJ: Lawrence Erlbaum.

Ainsworth, M. D. S. & Witig, B. A. (1969). Attachment and the exploratory behavior of one-year-olds in a strange situation. In B. M. Foss (Ed.), *Determinants of infant behavior* (Vol. 4) London: Methuen.

Aitken, S. & Bower T. G. R. (1982). Intersensory substitution in the blind. *Journal of Experimental Child Psychology, 33,* 309–323.

Altmann, S. A. (1973). Primate communication. In George A. Miller (Ed.), *Communication, language, and meaning.* New York: Basic Books.

Ambrose, J. A. (1963). The concept of a critical period for the development of social responsiveness in early infancy. In B. M. Foss (Ed.), *Determinants of infant behavior II.* London: Methuen.

Anderson, J. E. (1956). Child development: An historical perspective. *Child Development, 27(2),* 181–196.

Anisfeld, M. (1984). *Language development from birth to three.* Hillsdale, NJ: Lawrence Erlbaum Associates.

Appel, L. F., Cooper, R. G., McCarrell, N., Sims-Knight, J., Yussen, S. R., & Flavell, J. H. (1972).

The development of the distinction between perceiving and memorizing. *Child development, 43,* 1365–1381.

Arey, L. B. (1974). *Developmental anatomy* (8th ed.) Philadelphia: W. B. Saunders Co.

Aries, P. (1962). *Centuries of childhood: A social history of family life.* New York: Vintage Books.

Arnold, A. P. (1980). Sexual differences in the brain. *American Scientist, 68,* 165–173.

Aronson, E. & Rosenbloom, S. (1971). Space perception in early infancy: Perception within a common auditory-visual space. *Science, 172,* 1161–1163.

Aslin, R. N. (1977). Development of binocular fixation in human infants. *Journal of Experimental Child Psychology, 23,* 133–150.

Aslin, R. N. (1984). Sensory and perceptual constraints on memory in human infants. In R. Kail and N. E. Spear (Eds.), *Comparative perspectives on the development of memory.* Hillsdale, NJ: Lawrence Erlbaum.

Aslin, R. N., Alberts, J. R., & Petersen, M. R. (1981). *Development of perception: Psychobiological perspectives (Vol. 2). The visual system.* New York: Academic Press.

Aslin, R. N., Pisoni, D. B., & Jusczyk, P. W. (1983). Auditory development and speech perception in infancy. In M. M. Haith & J. J. Campos (Vol. eds.), and P. H. Mussen (General ed.), *Handbook of child psychology: Infancy and developmental psychobiology* (Vol. 2). New York: Wiley.

Athey, I. (1984). Contributions of play to development. In T. D. Yawkey & A. D. Pellegrini (Eds.), *Child's play: Developmental and applied.* Hillsdale, NJ: Lawrence Erlbaum Associates.

Atkinson, J. & Braddick, O. (1981). Acuity, contrast sensitivity, and accommodation in infancy. In R. N. Aslin, J. R. Alberts, & M. R. Petersen, *Development of perception: Psychobiological perspectives (Vol. 2). The visual system.* New York: Academic Press.

Atkinson, R. C. & Shiffrin, R. M. (1968). Human memory: A proposed system and its control processes. In K. W. Spence & J. T. Spence (Eds.) *The psychology of learning and motivation* (Vol. 2). New York: Academic Press.

Atkinson, R. C. & Shiffrin, R. M. (1971). The control of short-term memory. *Scientific American, 225,* 82–90.

Aubenque, M. (1957). Note documentaire sur la statistique des tailles des etudiants au cours de ces dernieres annees. *Biotypologie, 18,* 202–214.

Austin, J. L. (1962). *How to do things with words.* Cambridge, MA: Harvard University.

Ayme, S. & Lippman-Hand, A. (1982). Maternal-age effect in aneuploidy: Does altered embryonic selection play a role? *American Journal of Human Genetics, 34,* 558–565.

Baddeley, A. D. & Hitch, G. (1974). Working memory. In G. Bower (Ed.), *The psychology of learning and motivation* (Vol. 8). New York: Academic Press.

Bahrick, L. & Watson, J. S. (1985). Detection of intermodal proprioceptive-visual contingency as a potential basis of self-perception in infancy. *Development Psychology, 21,* 963–973.

Bakeman, R. & Brownlee, J. R. (1980). The strategic use of parallel play: A sequential analysis. *Child Development, 51,* 873–878.

Baldwin, J. M. (1906). *Social and ethical interpretations in mental development.* New York: Macmillan.

Balinsky, B. I. (1970). *An introduction to embryology* (3rd ed.). Philadelphia: W. B. Saunders.

Ball, W. & Tronick, E. (1971). Infant responses to impending collison: Optical and real. *Science, 171,* 818–820.

Bandura, A. (1977). *Social learning theory.* Englewood Cliffs, NJ: Prentice-Hall.

Banks, M. S. & Salapatek, P. (1978). Acuity and contrast sensitivity in 1-, 2-, and 3-month-old human infants. *Investigative Opthalmology and Visual Science, 17,* 361–365.

Banks, M. S. & Salapatek, P. (1983). Infant visual perception. In M. M. Haith & J. J. Campos (Vol. eds.), and P. H. Mussen (General ed.), *Handbook of child psychology: Infancy and developmental psychobiology* (Vol. 2). New York: Wiley.

Barenboim, C. (1981). The development of person perception in childhood and adolescence: From behavioral comparisons to psychological constructs to psychological comparisons. *Child Development, 52,* 129–144.

Bates, E. (1976). *Language and context: The acquisition of pragmatics.* New York: Academic Press.

Bates, J. E., Maslin, C. A., & Frankel, K. A. (1985). Attachment security, mother-child interaction, and temperament as predictors of behavior-problem ratings at age three years. In I Bretherton & E. Waters (Eds), Growing points of attachment theory and research. *Monographs of the Society for Research in Child Development, 50,* (1–2, Serial No. 209).

Bateson, P. (1979). How do sensitive periods arise and what are they for? *Animal Behaviour, 27,* 470–486.

Baumrind, D. (1967). Child care practices anteceding three patterns of preschool behavior. *Genetic Psychology Monographs, 75,* 43–88.

Baumrind, D. (1970). Socialization and instrumental competence in young children. *Young Children 26 (2),* 104–119.

Baumrind, D. (1971). Current patterns of parental authority. *Developmental Psychology Monograph, 4* (1, Pt. 2).

Baumrind, D. (1973). The development of instrumental competence through socialization. In A. D. Pick (Ed.), *Minnesota Symposium on Child Psychology* (Vol. 7). Minneapolis: University of Minnesota Press.

Bayley, N. (1933). *The California first-year mental scales.* Berkeley: The University of California Press.

Bayley, N. (1949). Consistency and variability in the growth of intelligence from birth to 18 years. *Journal of Genetic Psychology, 75,* 165–196.

Bayley, N. (1956). Individual patterns of development. *Child Development, 27,* 45–74.

Bayley, N. (1968). Cognition in aging. In K. W. Schaie (Ed.), *Theory and methods of research on aging.* Morgantown West Virginia University Library.

Bayley, N. (1969). *The Bayley scales of infant development.* New York: Psychological Corporation.

Bayley, N. (1970). Development of mental abilities. In P. H. Mussen (Ed.), *Carmichael's manual of child psychology* (Vol. 1). New York: Wiley.

Becker, W. C. (1964). Consequences of different kinds of parental discipline. In M. L. Hoffman & L. W. Hoffman (Eds.), *Review of child development research* (Vol. 1). New York: Russell Sage Foundation.

Bell, R. Q. & Harper, L. V. (1977). *Child effects on adults.* Hillsdale, NJ: Lawrence Erlbaum Associates.

Bell, S. M. (1970). The development of the concept of the object and its relationship to infant-mother attachment. *Child Development, 41,* 291–312.

Belmont, L. & Marolla, F. A. (1973). Birth order, family size, and intelligence. *Science, 182,* 1096–1101.

Belsky, J., Lerner, R. M., & Spanier, G. B. (1984). *The child in the family.* Reading, MA: Addison-Wesley.

Berbaum, M. L., Markus, G. B., & Zajonc, R. B. (1982). A closer look at Galbraith's "closer look." *Developmental Psychology, 18,* 174–180.

Berger, K. S. (1980). *The developing person.* New York: Worth.

Berger, M. (1982). Personality development and temperament. In *Ciba Foundation Symposium 89, Temperamental differences in infants and young children,* London: Pitman.

Berlin, B. & Kay, P. (1969). *Basic color terms: Their universality and evolution.* Berkeley: University of California Press.

Bernstein, I. S. (1980). Activity patterns in a stumptail macaque group. *Folia Primatologica, 2,* 50–63.

Bertenthal, B. I., Campos, J. J. & Barrett, K. C. (1984). Self-produced locomotion: An organizer of emotional, cognitive, and social development in infancy. In R. N. Emde & R. J. Harman (Eds.), *Continuities and discontinuities in development.* New York: Plenum Press.

Bertenthal, B. I., Campos, J. J. & Haith, M. M. (1980). Development of visual organization: The perception of subjective contours. *Child Development, 51,* 1072–1080.

Bertenthal, B. I. & Fischer, K. W. (1978). Development of self-recognition in the infant. *Developmental Psychology, 11,* 44–50.

Bickerton, D. (1981). *Roots of language.* Karoma.

Bickerton, D. (1984). The language bioprogram hypothesis. *The Behavioral and Brain Sciences, 7,* 173–221.

Billow, R. M. (1981). Observing spontaneous metaphor in children. *Journal of Experimental Child Psychology, 31,* 430–445.

Binet, A. & Simon, T. (1907/1914). *Les enfants anormaux.* Paris: Armand Colin, 1907. Translated by W. B. Drummond, *Mentally defective children.* London: Edward Arnold, 1914.

Binet, A. & Simon, T. (1908/1916). Le développement de l'intelligence chez les enfants. *L'année psychologique,* 1908, *14* 1–94. Reprinted in E. S. Kite (translator), *The development of intelligence in children.* Baltimore: William & Wilkins Co., 1916.

Birch, E. E., Shimojo, S., & Held, R. (1985). Preferential-looking assessment of fusion and stereopsis in infants aged 1–6 months. *Investigative Ophthalmology and Visual Science, 26,* 366–370.

Birch, H. G., Richardson, S. A., Baird, D. Horobin, G., & Illsley, R. (1970). *Mental subnormality in the community: A clinical and epidemiologic study.* Baltimore: Williams & Wilkins.

Bjorklund, D. F. (1985). The role of conceptual knowledge in the development of organization in children's memory. In C. J. Brainerd & M. Pressley (Eds.), *Basic processes in memory development.* New York: Springer-Verlag.

Blakemore, C. & Cooper, G. F. (1970). Development of the brain depends on the visual environment. *Nature, 228,* 477–478.

Blakemore, C. & Mitchell, D. E. (1973). Environmental modification of the visual cortex and the neural basis of learning and memory. *Nature, 241,* 467–468.

Blasi, A. (1980). Bridging moral cognition and moral action: A critical review of the literature. *Psychological Bulletin, 88,* 1–45.

Blauvelt, H. (1955). Dynamics of the mother-newborn relationship in goats. In B. Schaffner, Ed., *Group processes. Transactions of the first conference.* New York: Josiah Macey, Jr. Foundation.

Blommers, P. & Lindquist, E. F. (1960). Elementary statistical methods in psychology and education. Boston: Houghton Mifflin.

Bloom, L., Hood, L., & Lightbower, P. (1974). Imitation in language development: If, when, and why. *Cognitive Psychology, 6,* 380–420.

Boden, M. (1979/1980). *Jean Piaget.* New York: Penguin Books.

Bohman, M. (1978). Some genetic aspects of alcoholism and criminality. *Archives of General Psychiatry, 35,* 269–276.

Bohman, M., Sigvardsson, S., & Cloninger, C. R. (1981). Maternal inheritance of alcohol abuse. *Archives of General Psychiatry, 38,* 965–969.

Bolton, T. L. (1982). The growth of memory in school children. *American Journal of Psychology, 4,* 362–380.

Bonvillian, J. D., Orlansky, M. D., & Novack, L. L. (1983). Developmental milestones: Sign language acquisition and motor development. *Child Development, 54,* 1435–1445.

Borke, H. (1971). Interpersonal perception of young children: Egocentrism or empathy? *Development Psychology, 5,* 263–269.

Borke, H. (1975). Piaget's mountains revisited: Changes in the egocentric landscape. *Developmental Psychology, 11,* 240–243.

Borkowski, J. G. (1985). Signs of intelligence: Strategy generalization and metacognition. In S. R. Yussen (Ed.), *The growth of reflection in children.* Orlando: Academic Press.

Bornstein, M. H. (1976). Infants are trichromats. *Journal of Experimental Child Psychology, 21,* 425–445.

Bornstein, M. H., Kessen, W., & Weiskopf, S. (1976). The categories of hue in infancy. *Science, 191,* 201–202.

Bower, T. G. R. (1971). The object in the world of the infant. *Scientific American, 225,* 30–38.

Bower, T. G. R. (1974). *Development in infancy.* San Francisco: W. H. Freeman & Co.

Bower, T. G. R. (1979). *Human development.* San Francisco: W. H. Freeman & Co.

Bower, T. G. R. (1982). *Development in infancy* (2nd ed.). San Francisco: W. H. Freeman & Co.

Bower, T. G. R., Broughton, J. M., & Moore, M. K. (1970a). Infant responses to approaching objects: An indicator of response to distal variables. *Perception and Psychophysics, 9,* 193–196.

Bower, T. G. R., Broughton, J. M., & Moore, M. K. (1970b). Demonstration of intention in the reaching behaviour of neonate humans. *Nature, 228,* 679–681.

Bower, T. G. R., Broughton, J. M., & Moore, M. K. (1970c). The coordination of visual and tactual input in infants. *Perception & Psychophysics, 8(1),* 51–53.

Bowlby, J. (1951). *Maternal care and mental health.* Geneva: World Health Organization.

Bowlby, J. (1969). *Attachment and loss: Vol. 1. Attachment.* New York: Basic Books.

Bowlby, J. (1973). *Attachment and loss: Vol. 2. Separation.* New York: Basic Books.

Bowlby, J., Ainsworth, M., Boston, M., & Rosenbluth, d. (1956). The effects of mother-child separation:

A follow-up study. *British Journal of Medical Psychology, 29,* 211–247.

Bowlby, J., Robertson, J., & Rosenbluth, D. (1952). A two-year-old goes to the hospital. *Psychoanalytic Study of the Child, 7,* 82–94.

Boyd, E. (1980). *Origins of the study of human growth.* University of Oregon Health Sciences Center Foundation.

Brackbill, Y. & Nichols, P. L. (1982). A test of the confluence model of intellectual development. *Developmental Psychology, 18,* 192–198.

Brainerd, C. J. (1973). The origin of number concepts. *Scientific American, 228(3),* 101–109.

Brainerd, C. J. (1978a). *Piaget's theory of intelligence.* Englewood Cliffs, NJ: Prentice Hall, Inc.

Brainerd, C. J. (1978b). The stage question in cognitive-developmental theory. *Behavioral and Brain Science, 1,* 173–182.

Brainerd, C. J. (1983). Working-memory systems and cognitive development. In C. J. Brainerd (Ed.), *Recent advances in cognitive-developmental theory.* New York: Springer-Verlag.

Brazier, M. A. B. (1959). The historical development of neurophysiology. In M. A. B. Brazier (Ed.), *Handbook of Physiology: Neurophysiology* (Vol. 1), Washington, DC: American Physiological Society.

Bready, J. W. (1926). *Lord Shaftesburg and social-industrial progress.* London: G. Allen & Unwin Ltd.

Breslow, L. (1981). Reevaluation of the literature on the development of transitive inferences. *Psychological Bulletin, 89,* 325–351.

Brimmer, J. L. (1962). Strange little world of the hoatzin. *National Geographic, 122,* 399.

Brody, G. H. & Shaffer, D. R. (1982). Contributions of parents and peers to children's moral socialization. *Developmental Review, 2,* 31–75.

Bronfenbrenner, U. (1970). *Two worlds of childhood.* New York: Russell Sage Foundation.

Brooks-Gunn, J. & Lewis, M. (1984). The development of early visual self recognition. *Developmental Review, 4,* 215–239.

Broughton, J. (1978). Development of concepts of self, mind, reality, and knowledge. *New Directions for Child Development, 1,* 75–100.

Brown, A. L., Campione, J. C., & Day, J. D. (1981). Learning to learn: On training students to learn from texts. *Educational Researcher, 10,* 14–21.

Brown, A. L. & Scott, M. S. (1971). Recognition memory for pictures in preschool children. *Journal of Experimental Child Psychology, 11,* 401–412.

Brown, I. (1979). Language acquisition: Linguistic structure and rule-governed behavior. In G. J. Whitehurst & B. J. Zimmerman (Eds.) *The functions of language and cognition.* New York: Academic Press.

Brown, J. S. & Burton, R. B. (1978). Diagnostic models for procedural bugs in basic mathematical skills. *Cognitive Science, 2,* 155–192.

Brown, J. S. & Vanlehn, K. (1982). Towards a generative theory of "bugs." In T. A. Romberg, T. D. Carpenter, & J. M. Moser (Eds.), *Addition and subtraction: A cognitive perspective.* Hillsdale, NJ: Erlbaum.

Brown, R. (1973). *A first language: The early states.* Cambridge, MA: Harvard University Press.

Brown, R. (1977). Introduction. In C. E. Snow & C. A. Ferguson, *Talking to children: Language input and acquisition.* Cambridge: Cambridge University Press.

Brown, R., Cazden, C. B., & Bellugi, U. (1969). The child's grammar from I to III. In J. P. Hill (Ed.), *Minnesota symposium on child psychology* (Vol. 2). Minneapolis: University of Minnesota Press.

Brown, R. & Fraser, C. (1963). The acquisition of syntax. In C. N. Cofer & B. Musgrave (Eds.), *Verbal behavior and learning: Problems and processes.* New York: McGraw-Hill.

Brown, R. & Fraser, C. (1964). The acquisition of syntax. In U. Bellugi & R. Brown (Eds.), The acquisition of language. *Monographs of the Society for Research in Child Development, 29,* (Serial No. 92).

Brown, R. & Hanlon, C. (1970). Derivational complexity and order of acquisition. In J. R. Hayes (Ed.), *Cognition and the development of language.* New York: Wiley.

Brown, R. & Hernstein, R. J. (1975) *Psychology.* Boston: Little, Brown & Co.

Bruce, E. J. & Ayala, F. J. (1978). Humans and apes are genetically very similar. *Nature, 276,* 264–265.

Bruce, H. A. (1914). *The education of Karl Witte.* New York: Thomas Crowell.

Bruner, J. S. (1964). The course of cognitive growth. *American Psychologist, 19,* 1–15.

Bruner, J. S. (1966). On the conservation of liquids. In J. S. Bruner, R. Olver, & P.M. Greenfield (Eds.), *Studies in cognitive growth*. New York: Wiley.

Bruner, J. S. (1983a). The acquisition of pragmatic commitments. In R. M. Golinkoff (Ed.), *The transition from prelinguistic to linguistic communication*. Hillsdale, NJ: Lawrence Erlbaum Associates.

Bruner, J. S. (1983b). *Child's talk: Learning to use language*. New York: Norton & Co.

Bruner, J. S., Jolly, A., & Sylva, K. (1976). *Play: Its role in development and evolution*. London: Penguin.

Brunn, K., Markkanen, T. & Partanen, J. (1966). *Inheritance of drinking behavior, a study of adult twins*. Helsinki: The Finnish Foundation for Alcohol Research.

Bryant, P. (1974). *Perception and understanding in young children: An experimental approach*. New York: Basic Books.

Bullough, V. L. (1981). Age at menarche: A misunderstanding. *Science, 213,* 365–366.

Burnham, W. H. (1893). Individual differences in the imagination of children. *Pedagogical Seminary, 2,* 204–225.

Burt, C. (1937). *The backward child*. New York: D. Appleton-Century Co.

Busnel, M. C. & Granier-Deferre, C. (1983). And what of fetal audition? In A. Oliverio & M. Zappella (Eds.), *The behavior of human infants*. New York: Plenum.

Buss, A. H. & Plomin, R. (1984). *Temperament: Early developing personality traits*. Hillsdale, NJ: Erlbaum.

Cairns, R. B. (1979). *Social development: The origins of plasticity of interchanges*. San Francisco: W. H. Freeman.

Callahan, C. M. (1981). Superior abilities. In J. M. Kauffman & D. P. Hallahan (Eds.), *Handbook of special education*. Englewood Cliffs, NJ: Prentice-Hall.

Campos, J. J., Barret, K. C., Lamb, M. E., Goldsmith, H. H., & Stenberg, C. (1983). Socioemotional development. In M. M. Haith & J. J. Campos (Vol. eds.), and P. H. Mussen (General ed.), *Handbook of child psychology: Infancy and developmental psychobiology* (Vol. 2). New York: Wiley.

Campos, J. J., Hiatt, S., Ramsay, D., Henderson, C., & Svejda, M. (1978). The emergence of fear on the visual cliff. In M. Lewis & L. A. Rosenblum (Eds.), *The development of affect* (Vol. 1). New York: Plenum.

Campos, J. J., Langer, A., & Krowitz, A. (1970). Cardiac responses on the visual cliff in prelocomotor human infants. *Science, 170,* 196–197.

Campos, J. J. & Stenberg, C. R. (1981). Perception, appraisal and emotion: The onset of social referencing. In M. E. Lamb & L. R. Sherrod (Eds.), *Infant social cognition: Empirical and theoretical considerations*. Hillsdale, NJ: Lawrence Erlbaum Associates.

Campos, J. J., Svejda, M., Bertenthal, B., Benson, N., & Schmid, D. (1981). *Self-produced locomotion and wariness of heights: New evidence from training studies*. Paper read at the meeting of the Society for Research in Child Development, Boston, April.

Caparulo, B. K. & Cohen, D. J. (1983). Developmental language studies in the neuropsychiatric disorders of childhood. In K. E. Nelson (Ed.), *Children's Language,* Vol. 4. Hillsdale, NJ: Lawrence Erlbaum Associates.

Caplan, F. (1977). *The parenting adviser*. Garden City, NY: Anchor Press.

Carmichael, L. (1926). The development of behavior in vertebrates experimentally removed from the influence of external stimulation. *Psychological Review, 33,* 51–58.

Carmichael, L. (1946). *Manual of Child Psychology*. New York: John Wiley & Sons.

Carmichael, L. (1954). *Manual of Child Psychology,* (2nd ed.) New York: John Wiley & Sons.

Carter-Saltzman, L. (1980). Biological and sociocultural effects on handedness: Comparison between biological and adoptive families. *Science, 209,* 1263–1265.

Caruso, D., Taylor, J. J., & Detterman, D. K. (1982). Intelligence research and intelligent policy. In D. K. Detterman & R. J. Sternberg (Eds.), *How and how much can intelligence be increased*. Norwood, NJ: Ablex.

Case, R. (1978). Intellectual development from birth to adulthood: A neo-Piagetian interpretation. In R. S. Siegler (Ed.), *Children's thinking: What develops?* Hillsdale, NJ: Lawrence Erlbaum Associates.

Case, R. (1985). *Intellectual development: Birth to adulthood.* Orlando: Academic Press.

Case, R., Kurland, M., & Daneman, M. (1979). *Operational efficiency and the growth of M-space.* Paper presented at the meeting of the Society for Research on Child Development, San Francisco.

Case, R., Kurland, M., & Goldberg, J. (1982). Operational efficiency and the growth of short-term memory span. *Journal of Experimental Child Psychology, 33,* 386–404.

Cavanaugh, J. C. & Borkowski, J. G. (1980). Searching for metamemory-memory connections: A developmental study. *Developmental Psychology, 16,* 441–453.

Cavanaugh, J. C. & Perlmutter, M. (1982). Metamemory: A critical examination. *Child Development, 53,* 11–28.

Chabon, S. S., Kent-Udolf, L., & Egolf, D. B. (1982). The temporal reliability of Brown's mean length of utterance (MLU-M) measure with post-Stage V children. *Journal of Speech and Hearing Research, 25,* 124–129.

Chalmers, N. (1984). Social play in monkeys. Theories and data. In P. K. Smith (Ed.), *Play in animals and humans.* Oxford, England: Basil Blackwell.

Chandler, M. J. & Greenspan, S. (1972). Ersatz egocentrism: A reply to H. Borke. *Developmental Psychology, 7,* 104–106.

Chandler, M. J., Paget, K. F., & Koch, D. A. (1978). The child's demystification of psychological defense mechanisms: A structural and developmental analysis. *Developmental Psychology, 14,* 197–205.

Chess, S. & Thomas, A. (1982). Infant bonding: Mystique and reality. *American Journal of Orthopsychiatry, 52,* 213–222.

Chess, S. & Thomas, A. (1984). *Origins and evolution of behavior disorders: From infancy to early adult life.* New York: Brunner/Mazel.

Cheyne, J. A. (1969). *Behavioral and physiological reactions to punishment: Attention, anxiety, and the timing of punishment hypothesis.* Paper presented at the biennial meeting of the Society for Research in Child Development, Santa Monica.

Chi, M. T. H. (1976). Short-term memory limitations in children: Capacity or processing deficits? *Memory and Cognition, 4,* 559–572.

Chi, M. T. H. (1978). Knowledge structures and memory development. In R. S. Siegler (Ed.), *Children's thinking: What develops?* Hillsdale, NJ: Lawrence Erlbaum.

Chomsky, N. A. (1957). *Syntactic Structures.* The Hague: Morton.

Chomsky, N. A. (1965). *Aspects of the theory of syntax.* Cambridge: MIT Press.

Chomsky, N. A. (1980). *Rules and representations.* New York: Columbia University Press.

Chomsky, N. A. (1983). Interview with Noam Chowsky. *Omni, 6(2),* 113–118, 171–174.

Chrisman, O. (1893). The hearing of children. *The Pedagogical Seminary, 2,* 397–441.

Christie, J. F. & Johnsen, E. P. (1983). The role of play in social-intellectual development. *Review of Educational Research, 53(1),* 93–115.

Clark, E. V. (1975). Knowledge, context, and strategy in the acquisition of meaning. In D. P. Dato (Ed.), *Georgetown University round table on languages and linguistics,* 1975. Washington, D.C.: Georgetown University Press.

Clark, E. V. (1977). Strategies and the mapping problem in first language acquisition. In J. MacNamara (Ed.), *Language learning and thought.* New York: Academic Press.

Clark, E. V. (1982). The young word maker: A case study of innovation in the child's lexicon. In E. Wanner & L. R. Gleitman (Eds.), *Language acquisition: The state of the art.* Cambridge: Cambridge University Press.

Clark, H. H. (1973). Space, time, semantics, and the child. In T. E. Moore (Ed.), *Cognitive development and the acquisition of language.* New York: Academic Press.

Clark, H. H. & Clark, E. V. (1977). *Psychology and language: An introduction to psycholinguistics.* New York: Harcourt Brace Jovanovich, Inc.

Clark, R. W. (1973). *Einstein: The life and times.* London: Hodder & Stoughton.

Clarke, A. D. B. & Clarke, A. M. (1981). "Sleeper effects" in development: Fact or artifact? *Developmental Review, 1,* 344–360.

Clarke, A. M. & Clarke, A. D. B. (1976). *Early experience: Myth and evidence.* New York: The Free Press.

Clifton, R., Morrongiello, B., Kulig, J., & Dowd, J. (1981). Developmental changes in auditory localization in infancy. In R. Aslin, J. Alberts, & M.

R. Petersen (Eds.), *The development of perception: Psychobiological perspectives (Vol. 1). Audition, somatic perception, and the chemical senses.* New York: Academic Press.

Cloninger, C. R. (1983). Genetic and environmental factors in the development of alcoholism. *Journal of psychiatric treatment and evaluation, 5,* 487–496.

Cloninger, C. R., Bohman, M., & Sigvardsson, S. (1981). Inheritance of alcohol abuse: Cross-fostering analysis of adopted men. *Archives of General Psychiatry, 38,* 861–868.

Coghill, G. E. (1929). *Anatomy and the problem of behavior.* Cambridge: University Press, New York: MacMillan.

Cohen, L. B., DeLoache, J. S., & Strauss, M. S. (1979). Infant visual perception. In J. D. Osofsky (Ed.), *Handbook of infant development.* New York: John Wiley.

Cohen, L. B. & Gelber, E. R. (1975). Infant visual memory. In L. B. Cohen & P. Salapatek, (Eds.), *Infant perception: From sensation to cognition* (Vol. 1). New York: Academic Press.

Colburn, Z. (1833). *A memoir Zerah Colburn: Written by himself.* Springfield: G. & C. Merriam.

Colby, A. & Kohlberg, L. (in press). *The measurement of moral judgment, Vol. 2: Standard issue scoring manual.* New York: Cambridge University Press.

Colby, A., Kohlberg, C., Gibbs, J., & Lieberman, M. (1983). A longitudinal study of moral judgment. *Monographs for the Society for Research in Child Development, 48* (1,2).

Collias, N. E. (1956). The analysis of socialization in sheep and goats. *Ecology, 37,* 228–238.

Collins, R. L. (1968). On inheritance of handedness. I. Laterality in inbred mice. *Journal of Heredity, 59,* 9–11.

Collins-Ahlgren, M. (1975). Language development of two deaf children. *American Annals of the Deaf, 120,* 524–539.

Colombo, J. (1982). The critical period concept: Research, methodology, and theoretical issues. *Psychological Bulletin, 91(2),* 260–275.

Commons, M. L., Richards, F. A., & Armon, C. (1985). *Beyond formal operations: Late adolescent and adult cognitive development.* New York: Praeger.

Condry, J. C. & Ross, D. F. (1985). Sex and aggression: The influence of gender label on the perception of aggression in children. *Child Development, 56,* 225–233.

Conel, J. L. (1939–1963). *The postnatal development of the human cerebral cortex.* Vols. I–VI. Cambridge: Harvard University Press.

Conger, J. J. & Petersen, A. C. (1984). *Adolescence and youth: Psychological development in a changing world.* New York: Harper & Row.

Cooper, W. E. & Ross, J. (1975). Word order. In R. Grossman, L. San, & T. Vance (Eds.), *Papers from the parasession on functionalism.* Chicago: Chicago Linguistic Society.

Coren, S., Porac, C., & Duncan, P. (1981). Lateral preference behaviors in preschool children and young adults. *Child Development, 52,* 443–450.

Cortese, A. J. (1984). Standard issue scoring of moral reasoning: A critique. *Merill-Palmer Quarterly, 30,* 227–246.

Cotman, C. W. & McGaugh, J. L. (1980). *Behavioral neuroscience: An introduction.* New York: Academic Press.

Cowan, N., Suomi, K., & Morse, P. A. (1982). Echoic storage in infant perception. *Child Development, 53,* 984–990.

Cowan, P.A. (1978). *Paiget with feeling.* New York: Holt Rinehart, & Winston.

Cowan, W. M. (1979). The development of the brain. *Scientific American, 241(3),* 112–133.

Cowan, W. M., Fawcett, J. W., O'Leary, D. D. M., & Stanfield, B. B. (1984). Regressive events in neurogenesis. *Science, 225,* 1258–1265.

Crnic, L. S. (1984). Nutrition and mental development. *American Journal of Mental Deficiency, 88(5),* 526–533.

Cronbach, L. J. (1960). *Essentials of psychological testing* (2nd ed.) New York: Harper & Brothers.

Cummings, E. M. & Bjork, E. L. (1981). The search behavior of 12 to 14 month-old infants on a five-choice invisible displacement hiding task. *Infant Behavior and Development, 4,* 47–60.

Cummings, E. M. & Bjork, E. L. (1983). Perseveration and search on a five-choice visible displacement hiding task. *Journal of Genetic Psychology, 142,* 283–291.

Curtiss, S. (1977). *Genie: A psycholinguistic study of a modern-day "wild child."* New York: Academic Press.

Curtiss, S. (1982). Developmental dissociations of language and cognition. In L. K. Obler & L. Menn (Eds.), *Exceptional language and linguistics.* New York: Academic Press.

Curtiss, S., Fromkin, V., Krashen, S., Rigler, D., & Riglen, M. (1974). The linguistic development of Genie. *Language, 50,* 528–554.

Dale, P. S. (1976). *Language development: Structure and function* (2nd ed.). New York: Holt, Rinehart, & Winston.

Daly, M. & Wilson, M. I. (1981). Abuse and neglect of children in evolutionary perspective. In R. D. Alexander & D. W. Tinkle (Eds.), *Natural selection and social behavior.* New York: Chiron Press.

Damon, W. (1983). *Social and personality development: Infancy through adolescence.* New York: W. W. Norton & Co.

Damon, W. & Hart, D. (1982). The development of self-understanding from infancy through adolescence. *Child Development, 53,* 841–864.

Dansky, J. L. (1980). Make believe: A mediator of the relationship between play and associative fluency. *Child Development, 51,* 576–579.

Darwin, C. (1872/1965). *The expression of the emotions in man and animals.* New York: D. Appleton and Co. (Reprinted Chicago: University of Chicago Press, 1965)

Darwin, C. (1859). *The origin of species.* London: John Murray.

Dasen, P. R. (1977). *Piagetian psychology: Cross-cultural contributions.* New York: Gardner Press.

Davis, F. & Orange, J. (1978). The strange case of the children who invented their own language. *Redbook, 150(5),* 113.

Davis, J. M. & Rovee-Collier, C. K. (1983). Alleviated forgetting of a learned contingency in 8-week-old infants. *Developmental Psychology, 19,* 353–365.

Dawkins, R. (1976). *The selfish gene.* New York: Oxford University Press.

Day, R. H. & McKenzie, B. E. (1981). Infant perception of the invariant size of approaching and receding objects. *Developmental Psychology, 17,* 670–677.

DeBoysson-Bardies, B., Sagart, L., & Durand, C. (1984). Discernible differences in the babbling of infants according to target language. *Journal of Child Language, 11,* 1–15.

DeCasper, A. J. & Fifer, W. P. (1980). Of human bonding: Newborns prefer their mothers' voices. *Science, 208,* 1174–1176.

DeFries, J. C., Johnson, R. C., Kuse, A. R., McClearn, G. E., Polovina, J., Vandenberg, S. G., & Wilson, J. R. (1979). Familial resemblance for specific cognitive abilities. *Behavior Genetics, 9,* 23–43.

DeFries, J. C., Kuse, A. R., & Vandenberg, S. G. (1979). Genetic correlations, environmental correlations, and behavior. In J. R. Royce & L. P. Mos, *Theoretical advances in behavior genetics.* Alphen aan den Rijn: Sijthoff & Noordhoff.

DeFries, J. C. & Plomin, R. (1978). Behavioral genetics. *Annual Review of Psychology, 29,* 473–515.

DeFries, J. C., Vandenberg, S. G., & McClearn, G. E. (1976). Genetics of specific cognitive abilities. *Annual Review of Genetics, 10,* 179–207.

Delacato, C. H. (1966). *Neurological organization and reading.* Springfield, IL: Charles C. Thomas.

DeLiss, R. & Staudt, J. (1980). Individual differences in college students' performance on formal operational tasks. *Journal of Applied Developmental Psychology, 1,* 201–208.

Delprato, D. J. (1980). Hereditary determinants of fears and phobias: A critical review. *Behavior Therapy, 11,* 79–103.

DeMause, L. (1974). *The history of childhood.* New York: The Psychohistory Press.

Dempster, F. N. (1981). Memory span: Sources of individual and developmental differences. *Psychological Bulletin, 89,* 63–100.

Dempster, F. N. (1985). Short-term memory development in childhood and adolescence. In C. J. Brainerd & M. Pressley (Eds.), *Basic processes in memory development.* New York: Springer-Verlag.

Dennis, M., Sugar, J., & Whitaker, H. A. (1982). The acquisition of tag questions. *Child Development, 53,* 1254–1257.

Dennis, M. & Whitaker, H. A. (1976). Language acquisition following hemidecortication: Linguistic superiority of the left over the right hemisphere. *Brain and Language, 3,* 404–433.

Dennis, W. (1934). Congenital cataract and unlearned behavior. *Journal of Genetic Psychology, 14,* 340–351.

Dennis, W. (1935). The effect of restricted practice upon the reaching, sitting, and standing of two infants. *Journal of Genetic Psychology, 47,* 17–32.

Dennis, W. (1940). The effect of cradling practices upon the onset of walking in Hopi children. *Journal of Genetic Psychology, 56,* 77–86.

Dennis, W. (1960). Causes of retardation among institutionalized children: Iran. *Journal of Genetic Psychology, 96,* 47–59.

Dennis W. (1965). *The Hopi child.* New York: Science Editors, Wiley.

Dennis, W. (Ed.) (1972). *Historical readings in developmental psychology.* New York: Appleton-Century-Crofts.

Dennis, W. & Najarian, P. (1957). Infant development under environmental handicap. *Psychological Monographs, 71* (7, Whole No. 436).

de Villiers, J. G. & de Villiers, P. A. (1978). *Language acquisition.* Cambridge, MA: Harvard University Press.

de Villiers, P. A. & de Villiers, J. G. (1979). *Early language.* Cambridge, MA: Harvard University Press.

Dewey, J. (1909). *Moral principles in education.* Boston: Houghton Mifflin Co.

Dewey, J. & Tufts, J. H. (1932). *Ethics.* New York: Holt.

Diamond, A. (1981). Retrieval of an object from an open box: The development of visual-tactile control of reaching in the first year of life. *Society for Research in Child Development Abstracts, 3,* 78.

Diamond, A. (1985). Development of the ability to use recall to guide action, as indicated by infants' performance on AB. *Child Development, 56,* 868–883.

Diamond, A. & Goldman-Rakic, P. S. (1985). *Evidence that maturation of the frontal cortex of the brain underlies behavioral changes during the first year of life: II. Object retrieval.* Presented at the biennial meeting of the Society for Research in Child Development, Toronto.

Diamond, M. (1982). Sexual identity, monozygotic twins reared in discordant sex roles and a BBC follow-up. *Archives of Sexual Behavior, 11,* 181–186.

Dingman, H. F. & Tarjan, G. (1960). Mental retardation and the normal distribution curve. *American Journal of Mental Deficiency, 64,* 991–994.

Djalaly, A., Hedayatti, H. A., & Zeighami, E. (1977). Screening capabilities of the Lead I electrocardiogram. *Journal of Electrocardiology, 10,* 245–250.

Dobbing, J. & Sands, J. (1973). Quantitative growth and development of the human brain. *Archives of Diseases in Childhood, 48,* 757–767.

Doll, E. A. (1965). *Vineland social maturity scale: Manual of directions* (rev. ed.). Educational Test Bureau. (Available from Circle Pines, MN: American Guidance Service.)

Dollinger, S. J. & McGuire, B. (1981). The development of psychological-mindedness: Children's understanding of defense mechanisms. *Journal of Clinical Child Psychology,* 117–121.

Donaldson, M. (1978). *Children's minds.* New York: Norton.

Dorner, G. (1976). *Hormones and brain differentiation.* Amsterdam: Elsevier Scientific Publishing.

Douglas, J. W., Ross, J. M., & Simpson, H. R. (1968). *All our future.* London: Peter Davies.

Drabman, R. S. & Thomas, M. H. (1974). Does media violence increase children's toleration of real-life aggression? *Developmental Psychology, 10,* 418–421.

Drummond, M. (1914). An appendix containing the Binet-Simon tests of intelligence. In W. B. Drummond, translator, *Mentally defective children.* A translation of A. Binet & T. Simon, *Les enfants anormaux.* Paris: Armand Colin, 1907.

Duke, P. M., Carlsmith, J. M., Jennings, D., Martin, J. A., Dornbusch, S. M., Gross, R. T., & Siegel-Gorelick, B. (1982). Educational correlates of early and late sexual maturation in adolescence. *The Journal of Pediatrics, 100,* 633–637.

Dunn, J. (1985). Pretend play in the family. In C. C. Grown & A. W. Gottfried, *Play interactions: The role of toys and parental involvement in children's development.* Johnson and Johnson Baby Products Co.

Dunn, L. M. (1973). Children with moderate and severe general learning disabilities. In L. M. Dunn

(Ed.), *Exceptional children in the schools: Special education in transition* (2nd ed.). New York: Holt, Rinehart, & Winston.

Durkheim, E. (1906/1953). *Sociology and Philosophy.* Glencoe, IL: Free Press, 1953. (Originally published 1906).

Earley, L., Griesler, P., & Rovee-Collier, C. (1985). *Ontogenetic changes in retention in early infancy.* Paper presented at the meeting of the Society for Research in Child Development, Toronto.

Eaton, W. D. & Von Bargen (1981). Asynchronous development of gender understanding in preschool children. *Child Development, 52,* 1020–1027.

Eckerman, C. O., Whatley, J. L., & McGehee, L. J. (1979). Approaching and contacting the object another manipulates: A social skill of the one-year old. *Developmental Psychology, 15,* 585–593.

Edwards, C. P. (1984). The age group labels and categories of preschool children. *Child Development, 55,* 440–452.

Edwards, C. P. & Lewis, M. (1979). Young children's concepts of social relations: Social functions and social objects. In M. Lewis and L. A. Rosenblum (Eds.), *The child and its family.* New York: Plenum.

Egeland, B & Farber, E. A. (1984). Infant-mother attachment: Factors related to its development and changes over time. *Child Development, 55,* 753–771.

Egeland, B. & Sroufe, L. A. (1981a). Attachment and early maltreatment. *Child Development, 52,* 44–52.

Egeland, B. & Sroufe, L. A. (1981b). Developmental sequelae of maltreatment in infancy. In R. Rizley & D. Cicchetti (Eds.), *Developmental perspective in child maltreatment.* San Francisco: Jossey-Bass.

Ehrenkranz, J., Bliss, E., & Sheard, M. H. (1974). Plasma testosterone: Correlation with aggressive behavior and social dominance in man. *Psychosomatic Medicine, 36,* 469–475.

Ehrhardt, A. A. & Baker, S. W. (1974). Fetal androgens, human central nervous system differentiation, and behavioral sex differences in behavior.

In R. C. Friedman, R. M. Richart, & R. L. Van de Wiele (Eds.), *Sex differences in behavior.* New York: John Wiley & Sons.

Ehrhardt, A. A. & Meyer-Bahlburg, H. F. L. (1981). Effects of prenatal sex hormones on gender-related behavior. *Science, 211,* 1312–1318.

Ehrman, L. & Parsons, P. A. (1981). *Behavior genetics and evolution.* New York: McGraw-Hill.

Eicher, W. (1984). *Transexualismus.* Stuttgart and New York: Gustav Fischer Verlag.

Eifermann, R. (1971). Social play in childhood. In R. E. Herron & B. Sutton-Smith (Eds.), *Child's play.* New York: John Wiley.

Eimas, P. D. (1975). Auditory and phonetic coding of the cues for speech: Discrimination of the [r-l] distinction by young infants. *Perception and psychophysics, 18,* 341–337.

Eimas, P. D., Siqueland, E. R., Jusczyk, P. & Vigorito, J. (1971). Speech perception in infants. *Science, 171,* 303–306.

Ekman, P. (1973). Cross-cultural studies of facial expression. In P. Ekman (Ed.), *Darwin and facial expression: A century of research in review.* New York: Academic Press.

Ekman, P. (1982). *Emotion in the human face* (2nd ed.). Cambridge, MA: Cambridge University Press.

Elkind, D. (1964). Discrimination, seriation, and numeration of size and dimensional differences in young children: Piaget replication study VI. *Journal of Genetic Psychology, 104,* 275–296.

Emlen, S. T. (1975). The stellar-orientation system of a migratory bird. *Scientific American, 233(2),* 102–111.

Emmerich, W. Goldman, K. S., Kirsh, B., & Sharabany, R. (1976). *Development of gender constancy in economically disadvantaged children.* Report of the Educational Testing Service, Princeton, NJ.

English, H. B. (1929). Three cases of the "conditioned fear response." *Journal of Abnormal and Social Psychology, 24,* 221–225.

Ennis, R. H. (1982). Children's ability to handle Piaget's propositional logic: A conceptual critique. In S. Modgil & C. Modgil (Eds.), *Jean Piaget: Consensus and controversy.* Suffolk, England: Praeger Publishers.

Enoch, J. M. & Rabinowicz, I. M. (1976). Early surgery and visual correction of an infant born with unilateral eye lens opacity. *Documenta Opthalmologica, 41(2),* 371–382.

Ericsson, K. A., Chase, W. G., & Faloon, S. (1980). Acquisition of a memory skill. *Science, 208,* 1181–1182.

Erikson, E. H. (1950). *Childhood and society.* New York: W. W. Norton and Co.

Eron, L. D. (1982). Parent-child interaction, television, violence, and aggression of children. *American Psychologist, 37,* 197–211.

Eron, L. D., Huesmann, L. R., Lefkowitz, M. M., & Walder, L. O. (1970). Does television violence cause aggression? *American Psychologist, 27,* 253–263.

Ervin-Tripp, S. (1964). Imitation and structural change in children's language. In E. H. Lenneberg (Ed.), *New directions in the study of language.* Cambridge, MA: MIT Press.

Escalona, S. K. & Corman, H. (1969). *Albert Einstein scales of sensori-motor development.* New York: Albert Einstein College of Medicine of Yeshiva University.

Evans, D., Bowie, M. D., Hansen, J. D. L., Moodie, A. D. & van der Spuy, H. I. J. (1980). Intellectual development and nutrition. *The Journal of Pediatrics, 97(1),* 358–363.

Evans, R. I. (1973). *Jean Piaget: The man and his ideas.* New York: E. P. Dutton.

Eysenck, H. J. (1956). The inheritance of extraversion-introversion. *Acta Psychologica, 12,* 95–110.

Eysenck, H. J. (1970). *The structure of human personality* (3rd ed.). London: Methuen.

Fagan, J. F. (1972). Infant's recognition memory for faces. *Journal of Experimental Child Psychology, 14,* 453–476.

Fagan, J. F. (1973). Infant's delayed recognition memory and forgetting. *Journal of Experimental Child Psychology, 16,* 424–450.

Fagan, J. F. (1982a). Infant memory. In T. Field (Ed.). *Review of Human Development.* New York: Wiley

Fagan, J. F. (1982b). New evidence for the prediction of intelligence from infancy. *Infant Mental Health Journal, 3,* 219–228.

Fagan, J. F. (1984a). The intelligent infant: Theoretical implications. *Intelligence, 8,* 1–9.

Fagan, J. F. (1984b). Recognition memory and intelligence. *Intelligence, 8,* 31–36.

Fagan, J. F. (1985a). A new look at infant intelligence. In D. K. Detterman (Ed.), *Current topics in human intelligence, Vol. 1: Research Methodology.* Norwood, N. J.: Ablex Publishing Corp.

Fagan, J. F. (1985b). Early novelty preferences and later intelligence. In R. J. Sternberg (Chair), *Novelty as a source of developmental continuity in intelligence.* A symposium presented at the meeting of the Society for Research in Child Development, Toronto.

Fagen, R. M. (1981). *Animal play behavior.* New York: Oxford University Press.

Fagot, B. I. (1985). Changes in thinking about early sex role development. *Developmental Review, 5,* 83–98.

Fagot, B. I., Hagan, R., Leinbach, M. D. & Kronsberg, S. (1985). Differential reactions to assertive and communicative acts of toddler boys and girls. *Child Development, 56,* 1499–1505.

Fagot, B. I. & Leinbach, M. D. (1983). Play styles in early childhood: Social consequences for boys and girls. In M. B. Liss (Ed.), *Social and cognitive skills: Sex roles and children's play.* New York: Academic Press.

Falconer, D. S. (1960). *Introduction to quantitative genetics.* New York: The Ronald Press.

Falk, R., Falk, R., & Levin, I. (1980). A potential for learning probability in young children. *Educational Studies in Mathematics, 11,* 181–204.

Family Economics Review. (1985). No. 4. Published by United States Department of Agriculture: Agricultural Research Service, 26.

Fantz, R. L. (1961). The origin of form perception. *Scientific American, 204,* 66–72.

Fantz, R. L. (1963). Pattern vision in newborn infants. *Science, 140,* 296–297.

Fantz, R. L. & Fagan, J. F. (1975). Visual attention to size and number of pattern details by term and preterm infants during the first six months. *Child Development, 46,* 3–18.

Faraone, S. V. & Tsuang, M. T. (1985). Quantitative models of the genetic transmission of schizophrenia. *Psychological Bulletin, 98,* 41–66.

Farber, S. L. (1981). *Identical twins reared apart.* New York: Basic Books.

Faust, M. S. (1960). Developmental maturity as a determinant in prestige of adolescent girls. *Child Development, 31,* 173–184.

Feitelson, D. & Ross, G. S. (1973). The neglected factor—play. *Human Development, 16,* 202–223.

Feldman, D. H. (1980). *Beyond universals in cognitive development.* Norwood, NJ: Ablex.

Feldman, H., Goldin-Meadow, S., & Gleitman, L. (1978). Beyond Herodotus: The creation of language by linguistically deprived deaf children. In A. Lock (Ed.), *Action, gesture and symbol: The emergence of language.* London: Academic Press.

Ferguson, C. A. & Macken, M. A. (1983). The role of play in phonological development. In K. E. Nelson (Ed.), *Children's language,* Vol. 4. Hillsdale, NJ: Lawrence Erlbaum.

Field, T. M., Woodson, R., Greenberg, R., & Cohen, D. (1982). Discrimination and imitation of facial expressions by neonates. *Science, 218,* 179–181.

Finkelstein, N. W., Dent, C., Gallagher, K. & Ramey, C. T. (1978). Social behavior of infants and toddlers in a daycare environment. *Developmental Psychology, 14,* 257–262.

Fishbein, H. D. (1984). *The psychology of infancy and childhood.* Hillsdale, NJ: Lawrence Erlbaum.

Flapan, D. (1968). *Children's understanding of social interaction.* New York: Teachers College Press.

Flavell, J. H. (1963). *The developmental psychology of Jean Piaget.* New York: D. Van Nostrand.

Flavell, J. H. (1970). Developmental studies of mediated memory. In H. W. Reese & L. P. Lipsitt (Eds.), *Advances in child development and behavior* (Vol. 5). New York: Academic Press.

Flavell, J. H. (1985). *Cognitive development* (2nd ed.) Englewood Cliffs, NJ: Prentice-Hall.

Flavell, J. H., Beach, D. R. & Chinsky, J. M. (1966). Spontaneous verbal rehearsal in a memory task as a function of age. *Child Development, 37,* 283–299.

Flavell, J. H., Friedrichs, A. G., & Hoyt, J. D. (1970). Developmental changes in memorization processes. *Cognitive Psychology, 1,* 324–340.

Flavell, J. H., Shipstead, S. G. & Croft, K. (1978). Young children's knowledge about visual perception: Hiding objects from others. *Child Development, 49,* 1208–1211.

Flavell, J. H. & Wellman, H. M. (1977). Metamemory. In R. V. Kail & J. W. Hagen (Eds.), *Perspectives on the development of memory and cognition.* Hillsdale, NJ: Lawrence Erlbaum.

Florderus-Myrhed, B., Pederson, N., & Rasmuson, I. (1980). Assessment of heritability for personality based on a short form of the Eysenck Personality Inventory: A study of 12,898 twin pairs. *Behavior Genetics, 10,* 153–162.

Følling, A., Mohr, O. L., & Rudd, L. (1945). Oligophrenia phenylpyrouvica, a recessive syndrome in man. Norske Videnskaps/Akadem: I Oslo, Matematisk-Naturvidenskapelig Klasse, 13, 1–44.

Formanek, R. & Gurian, A. (1981). *Charting intellectual development* (2nd ed.) Springfield, IL: Charles C. Thomas.

Forys, S. K. S. & McCure-Nicolich, L. (1984). Shared pretend play: Sociodramatic play at 3 years of age. In I. Bretherton (Ed), *Symbolic play: The development of social understanding.* Orlando, FL: Academic Press.

Fox, R. (1981). Stereopsis in animals and human infants: A review of behavioral investigations. In R. N. Aslin, J. R. Alberts, & M. R. Petersen (Eds), *Development of perception: Psychobiological perspectives (Vol. 2). The visual system.* New York: Academic Press.

Fox, R., Aslin, R. N., Shea, S. L., & Dumais, S. T. (1980). Stereopsis in human infants. *Science, 207,* 323–324.

Frank, F. (1966). Perception and language in conservation. In J. S. Bruner (Ed.), *Studies in cognitive growth.* New York: Wiley.

Frankenburg, W. K. & Dodds, J. B. (1967). The Denver developmental screening test. *The Journal of Pediatrics, 71,* 181–191.

Freeman, R. D., Mitchell, D. E., & Millodot, M. (1972). A neural effect of partial visual deprivation in humans. *Science, 175,* 1384–1386.

Freeman, R. D. & Thibos, L. N. (1975a). Contrast sensitivity in humans with abnormal visual experience. *Journal of Physiology,* London, *247* 687–710.

Freeman, R. D. & Thibos, L. N. (1975b). Visual evoked responses in human with abnormal visual experience. *Journal of Physiology,* London, *247,* 711–724.

Freud, A. (1968). James Robertson's A two-year-old goes to hospital film review. In *The writings of Anna Freud,* Vol. IV. New York: International Universities Press.

Freud, A. & Dann, S. (1951/1968). An experiment in group upbringing. Psychoanalytic study of the child. 1951, 8, 127–168. Reprinted in *Indications for child analysis and other papers 1945–1956: The writings of Anna Freud,* Vol. IV. New York: International Universities Press, 1968.

Freud, S. (1909/1955). Analysis of a phobia in a five-year-old boy. In J. Strachey (Ed.), *The standard edition of the complete psychological works of Sigmund Freud,* Vol. 10. London: The Hogarth Press.

Freud, S. (1938a). The interpretation of dreams. In A. Brill (Ed.), *The writings of Sigmund Freud.* New York: The Modern Library.

Freud, S. (1938b). Three contributions to the theory of sex. In A. A. Brill (Ed.), *The basic writings of Sigmund Freud.* New York: Modern Library.

Freud, S. (1949a). *An outline of psychoanalysis.* Translated by J. Strachey. London: Hogarth Press.

Freud, S. (1949b). *Introductory lectures on psychoanalysis.* London: George Allen & Unwin, Ltd.

Freud, S. (1963). *The standard edition of the complete psychological works of Sigmund Freud. 16, Introductory lectures on psycho-analysis,* Part III (1916–17), J. Strachey & A. Tyson (Eds.). London: The Hogarth Press.

Fuller, J. L. & Thompson, W. R. (1978). *Foundations of behavior genetics.* St. Louis: C. V. Mosby.

Furrow, D., Nelson, K., & Benedict, H. (1979). Mothers' speech to children and syntactic development: Some simple relationships. *Journal child language, 6,* 423–442.

Furth, H. G. (1966). *Thinking without language.* New York: Free Press.

Galbraith, R. C. (1982). Sibling spacing and intellectual development: A closer look at the confluence model. *Developmental Psychology, 18,* 151–173.

Galbraith, R. C. (1983). Individual differences in intelligence: A reappraisal of the confluence model. *Intelligence, 7,* 185–194.

Gallup, G. G., Jr. (1970). Chimpanzees: Self-recognition. *Science, 167,* 86–87.

Gallup, G. G. (1977). Self-recognition in primates: A comparative approach to the bidirectional properties and consciousness. *American Psychologist, 32,* 329–338.

Galton, F. (1876). The history of twins as a criterion of relative powers of nature and nurture. *Royal Anthropological Institute of Great Britain and Ireland Journal, 6,* 391–402.

Galton, F. (1881). *Hereditary genius.* New York: D. Appleton & Co.

Garcia, J. & Koelling, R. A. (1966). Relation of cue to consequence in avoidance learning. *Psychonomic Science, 4,* 123–124.

Gardner, B. T. & Gardner, R. A. (1971). Two-way communication with an infant chimpanzee. In A. M. Schrier & F. Stollnitz (Eds.), *Behavior of non-human primates.* New York: Academic Press.

Gardner, H. (1983). *Frames of mind.* New York: Basic Books.

Gardner, L. I. (1972). Deprivation dwarfism. *Scientific American, 227(1),* 76–82.

Gardner, R. A. & Gardner, B. T. (1969). Teaching sign language to a chimpanzee. *Science, 165,* 664–672.

Garner, J. & Plant, E. L. (1972). On the measurement of egocentrism: A replication and extension of Aebli's findings. *British Journal of Educational Psychology, 42,* 79–83.

Garnica, O. K. (1973). The development of phonemic speech perception. In T. E. Moore (Ed.), *Cognitive development and the acquisition of language.* New York: Academic Press.

Garvey, C. (1974). *Some properties of social play.* Merrill-Palmer Quarterly, 20(3), 164–180.

Garvey, C. (1979). Communicational controls in social play. In B. Sutton-Smith (Ed.), *Play and learning.* New York: Gardner Press.

Gelman, R. (1978). Cognitive development. *Annual Review of Psychology, 29,* 297–332.

Gelman, R. & Baillargeon, R. (1983). A review of some Piagetian concepts. In J. H. Flavell & E. M. Markman (Vol. eds.), and P. H. Mussen (General ed.), *Handbook of child psychology: Cognitive development* (Vol. 3). New York: John Wiley.

George, C. & Main, M. (1979). Social interactions of young abused children: Approach, avoidance and aggression. *Child Development, 50,* 306–318.

Gesell, A. (1928). *Infancy and human growth.* New York: MacMillan Co.

Gesell, A. (1933). Maturation and the patterning of behavior. In C. Murchison (Ed.), *A handbook of child psychology* (2nd ed.) Worcester, MA: Clark University Press.

Gesell, A. & Thompson, H. (1929). Learning and growth in identical infant twins. *Genetic Psychology Monographs, 6,* 1–124.

Gesell, A. & Amatruda, C. S. (1947). *Developmental diagnosis: Normal and abnormal child development* (2nd ed.). New York: Hoeber.

Getzels, J. W. & Jackson, P. W. (1963). The highly intelligent and the highly creative adolescent. In C. W. Taylor and F. Barron (Eds.), *Scientific creativity: Its recognition and development.* New York: Wiley.

Gibbs, J. C., Arnold, K. D., Ahlborn, H. H., & Cheesman, F. L. (1984). Facilitation of sociomoral reasoning in delinquents. *Journal of Consulting and Clinical Psychology, 52,* 37–45.

Gibson, E. J. (1980). Eleanor J. Gibson. In G. Lindzey (Ed.), *A history of psychology in autobiography* (VII). San Francisco: W. H. Freeman.

Gibson, E. J. & Spelke, E. S. (1983). The development of perception. In J. H. Flavell & E. M. Markman (Vol. eds.), and P. H. Mussen (General ed.), *Handbook of child psychology: Cognitive development* (Vol. 3). New York: John WIley.

Gibson, E. J. & Walk, R. D. (1960). The "visual cliff". *Scientific American, 202,* 64–71.

Gibson, E. J. & Walker, A. S. (1984). Development of knowledge of visual-tactual affordances of substance. *Child Development, 55,* 453–460.

Gibson, J. J. (1966). *The senses considered as perceptual systems.* New York: Houghton Mifflin.

Gilligan, C. (1982). *In a different voice: Psychological theory and women's development.* Cambridge, MA: Harvard University Press.

Gladwin, T. (1970). *East is a big bird: Navigation and logic on Puluwat Atoll.* Cambridge, MA: Harvard University Press.

Glaser, R. (1984). Education and thinking. *American Psychologist, 39,* 93–104.

Gleitman, L. R., Newport, E. L., & Gleitman, H. (1984). The current status of the motherese hypothesis. *Journal of Child Language, 11,* 43–79.

Gleitman, L. R., Wanner, E. (1985). Current issues in language learning. In M. H. Bornstein & M. E. Lamb, (Eds.), *Developmental psychology: An advanced textbook.* Hillsdale, NJ: Lawrence Erlbaum.

Glucksberg, S., Krauss, R., & Higgins, E. T. (1975). The development of referential communication skills. In F. D. Horowitz (Ed.), *Review of child development research* (Vol. 4). Chicago: University of Chicago Press.

Glucksberg, S., Krauss, R. M., & Weisberg, R. (1966). Referential communication in nursery school children: Method and some preliminary findings. *Journal of Experimental Child Psychology, 3,* 333–342.

Goddard, H. H. (1912). *The Kallikak family: A study in the heredity of feeble-mindedness.* New York: Macmillan.

Goddard, H. H. (1916). An introduction in E. S. Kite (translator), *The development of intelligence in children.* Baltimore: Williams & Wilkins Co.

Goldin-Meadow, S. & Mylander, C. (1984). Gestral communication in deaf children: The effects and noneffects of parental input on early language development. *Monographs of the Society for Research in Child Development, 49(3–4),* Serial No. 207.

Goldsmith, H. H. & Campos, J. J. (1982). Toward a theory of infant temperament. In R. N. Emde & R. Harmon (Eds.), *The development of attachment and affiliative systems.* New York: Plenum.

Goldstein, A., Aronow, L., & Kalman, S. M. (1974). *Principles of drug action* (2nd ed.). New York: John Wiley.

Goldstein, E. B. (1984). *Sensation and Perception* (2nd ed.). Belmont, CA: Wadsworth Publishing Co.

Golinkoff, R. M. & Gordon, L. (1983). In the beginning was the word: A history of the study of language acquisition. In R. M. Golinkoff (Ed.), *The transition from prelinguistic to linguistic communication.* Hillsdale, NJ: Lawrence Erlbaum.

Gollin, E. (1981). Development and plasticity. In E. S. Gollin, (Ed.), *Developmental plasticity: Be-*

havioral and biological aspects of variations in development. New York: Academic Press.

Gombrich, E. H. (1961). *Art and illusion: A study in the psychology of pictorial presentation.* Princeton, NJ: Princeton University Press.

Goodwin, D. W. (1979). Alcoholism and heredity. *Archives of General Psychiatry, 36,* 57–61.

Gorski, R. A. (1979). Hormonal modulation of neuronal structure. In F. O. Schmitt & F. G. Worden (Eds.), *The neurosciences: Fourth study program.* Cambridge, MA: MIT Press.

Gottesman, I. I. (1963). Genetic aspects of intelligent behavior. In N. Ellis (Ed.), *Handbook of mental deficiency: Psychological theory and research.* New York: McGraw-Hill.

Gottesman, I. I. & Shields, J. (1977). Twin studies and schizophrenia a decade later. In B. A. Maher (Ed.), *Contributions to the psychopathology of schizophrenia.* New York: Academic Press.

Gottesman, I. I., & Shields, J. (1982). *Schizophrenia: The epigenetic puzzle.* Cambridge, MA: Cambridge University Press.

Gottlieb, G. (1970). Conceptions of prenatal development. In L. R. Aronson, E. Tobach, D. S. Lehrman, & J. S. Rosenblatt (Eds.), *Development and evolution of behavior: Essays in memory of T. C. Schneirla.* San Francisco: Freeman.

Gottlieb, G. (1981). The role of early experience in species-specific perceptual development. In R. N. Aslin, J. R. Alberts, & M. R. Petersen (Eds.), *Development of perception: Psychobiological perspectives (Vol. 1). Audition, somatic perception, and the chemical senses.* New York: Academic Press.

Gould, J. L. (1982). *Ethology: The mechanisms and evolution of behavior.* New York: W. W. Norton and Co.

Gould, S. J. (1977). *Ontogeny and phylogeny.* Cambridge, MA: The Belknap Press.

Gould, S. J. (1981). *The mismeasure of man.* New York: Norton.

Gouze, K. R. & Nadelman, L. (1980). Constancy of gender identity for self and others in children between the ages of three and seven. *Child Development, 51,* 275–278.

Goy, R. W. (1978). Development of play and mounting behavior in female rhesus monkeys virilized prenatally with esters of testosterone or dihydrotestosterone. In D. J. Chivers & J. Herbert (Eds.), *Recent advances in primatology* (Vol. 1). New York: Academic Press.

Goy, R. W. & McEwen, B. S. (1980). *Sexual differentiation of the brain.* Cambridge, MA: The MIT Press.

Granrud, C. E. & Yonas, A. (1984). Infants' perception of pictorially specified interposition. *Journal of Experimental Child Psychology, 37,* 500–511.

Granrud, C. E., Yonas, A., Smith, I. M., Arterberry, M. E., Glicksman, M. L., & Sorknes, A. C. (1984). Infants' sensitivity to accretion and deletion of texture as information for depth at an edge. *Child Development, 55,* 1630–1636.

Gratch, G. (1972). A study of the relative dominance of vision and touch in six month old infants. *Child Development, 43,* 615–623.

Gratch, G., Appel, K. J., Evans, W. F., LeCompte, G. K., & Wright, N. A. (1974). Piaget's stage IV object concept error: Evidence of forgetting or object conception. *Child Development, 45,* 71–77.

Graves, N. B. & Graves, T. D. (1978). The impact of modernization on Polynesian personality, or how to make an up-tight, rivalrous Westerner out of an easy-going, generous Pacific Islander. *Human Organization, 37,* 115–135.

Gray, P. H. (1958). Theory and evidence of imprinting in human infants. *Journal of Psychology, 46,* 155–166.

Green, W. H., Campbell, M., & David, R. (1984). Psychosocial dwarfism: A critical review of the evidence. *Journal of the American Academy of Child Psychiatry, 23(1),* 39–48.

Greenberg, J. H. (1963). Some universals of grammar with particular reference to the order of meaningful elements. In J. H. Greenberg, (Ed.), *Universals of language.* Cambridge, MA: M.I.T. Press.

Greenberg, M., Rosenberg, I., & Lind, I. (1973). First mothers rooming-in with their newborns: Its impact on the mother. *American Journal of Orthopsychiatry, 43,* 783–788.

Greenfield, P. M. & Smith, J. H. (1976). *The structure of communication in early language development.* New York: Academic Press.

Greenough, W. T. & Green, E. J. (1981). Experience and the changing brain. In L. McGaugh & B. Kiesler (Eds.), *Aging: Biology and behavior.* New York: Academic Press.

Greulich, W. W. & Pyle, S. I. (1959). *Radiographic atlas of skeletal development of the hand and wrist* (2nd ed.). Stanford, CA: Stanford University Press.

Grier, J. W. (1984). *Biology of animal behavior*. St. Louis: Times Mirror/Mosby.

Griffin, D. R. (1977). Expanding horizons in animal communication behavior. In T. A. Sebeok (Ed.), *How animals communicate*. Bloomington, IN: Indiana University Press.

Grimshaw, J. (1981). Form, function, and the language acquisition device. In C. L. Baker & J. J. McCarthy (Eds.), *The logical problem of language acquisition*. Cambridge, MA: MIT Press.

Grossman, H. J. (1973). *Manual on terminology and classification in mental retardation. 1973 Revision*. American Association on Mental Deficiency. Baltimore: Garamine/Pridemank Press, 1973.

Grossman, H. J. (1983). *Classification in mental retardation*. Washington DC: American Association on Mental Deficiency.

Grossmann, K., Grossmann, K. E., Spangler, G., Suess, G., & Unzner, L. (1985). Maternal sensitivity and newborn's orientation responses as related to quality of attachment in Northern Germany. In I. Bretherton & E. Waters (Ed.), Growing points of attachment theory and research. *Monographs of the Society for Research in Child Development, 50* (1–2, Serial No. 209).

Grotevant, H. D., Scarr, S., & Weinberg, R. A. (1977). Intellectual development in family constellations with adopted and natural children: A test of the Zajonc and Markus model. *Child Development, 48,* 1699–1703.

Grusec, J. E. & Kuczynski, L. (1980). Directions of effect in socialization: A comparison of the parent's versus the child's behavior as determinants of disciplinary techniques. *Developmental Psychology, 16,* 1–19.

Gubernick, D. J. (1981). Mechanism of maternal "labeling" in goats. *Animal Behavior, 29,* 305–6.

Guilford, J. P. (1967). *The nature of human intelligence*. New York: McGraw-Hill.

Guillaume, P. (1926/1971). *Imitation in children*. Chicago: University of Chicago Press.

Guiton, P. (1966). Early experience and sexual object choice in the brown leghorn. *Animal Behavior, 14,* 534–538.

Gump, P. V. & Kounin, J. S. (1959–1960). Issues raised by ecological and "classical" research efforts. *Merrill-Palmer Quarterly, 6,* 145–152.

Gump, P. V. & Sutton-Smith, B. (1955). The "it" role in children's games. *The Group, 17,* 3–8.

Gurucharri, C. & Selman, R. L. (1982). The development of interpersonal understanding during childhood, preadolescence, and adolescence: A longitudinal follow-up study. *Child Development, 53,* 924–927.

Gurucharri, C. & Selman, R. L. (1984). The development of interpersonal understanding: A longitudinal and comparative study of normal and disturbed growth. *Journal of Consulting and Clinical Psychology, 52,* 26–36.

Haldane, J. B. S. (1928). *Possible worlds and other papers*. New York: Harper & Brothers.

Halford, G. S. (1984). Can young children integrate premises in transitivity and serial order tasks? *Cognitive Psychology, 16,* 65–93.

Hall, G. S. (1883). The contents of children's minds. *Princeton Review, 11,* 249–272.

Hall, G. S. (1904). *Adolescence: Its psychology and its relations to physiology, anthropology, sociology, sex, crime, religion, and education* (Vol. 1). New York: D. Appleton & Co.

Hall, G. S. (1910). The national child welfare conference: Its works and its relations to child study. *The Pedagogical Seminary, 17,* 497–504.

Hamer, B. (1982). All in the family. *Science 82, 3,* 88–89.

Hancock, J. A. (1894). A preliminary study of motor ability. *Pedagogical Seminary, 3,* 9–29.

Harlow, H. F. (1962). Development of the second and third affectional systems in macaque monkeys. In T. T. Tourlentes, S. L. Pollack, & H. F. Himwich (Eds.), *Research approaches to psychiatric problems*. New York: Grune & Stratton.

Harlow, H. F. (1965). Total social isolation: Effects on macaque monkey behavior. *Science, 148* (Whole No. 3670), 666.

Harlow, H. F., Dodsworth, R. O., & Harlow, M. K. (1965). Total social isolation in monkeys. *Proceedings of the National Academy of Sciences, 54,* 90–96.

Harlow, H. F. & Harlow, M. E. (1965). The affectional systems. In A. M. Schrier, H. F. Harlow, &

F. Stollnitz (Eds.), *Behavior of nonhuman primates* (Vol. 2). New York: Academic Press.

Harlow, H. F., Harlow, M. K., & Suomi, S. J. (1971). From thought to therapy: Lessons from a primate laboratory. *American Scientist, 59,* 538–549.

Harlow, H. F., & Mears, C. (1979). *The human model: Primate perspectives.* Washington, D.C.: V. H. Winston & Sons.

Harlow, H. F. & Zimmerman, R. R. (1959). Affectional responses in the infant monkey. *Science, 130,* 421–432.

Harper, J. F. & Collins, J. K. (1972). The effects of early or late maturation on the prestige of the adolescent girl. *Australian and New Zealand Journal of Sociology, 8,* 83–88.

Harris, P. L. (1983). Infant cognition. In M. M. Haith & J. J. Campos (Vol. eds.), and P. H. Mussen (General ed.), *Handbook of child psychology: Infancy and developmental psychobiology* (Vol. 2). New York: Wiley.

Hart, D. & Damon, W. (1985). Contrasts between understanding self and understanding others. In R. L. Leahy (ed.), *The development of self.* Orlando, FL: Academic Press.

Harter, S. (1983a). Children's understanding of multiple emotions: A cognitive-developmental approach. In W. F. Overton, (Ed.), *The relationship between social and cognitive development.* Hillsdale, N. J.: Lawrence Erlbaum.

Harter, S. (1983b). Developmental perspectives on the self-system. In E. M. Hetherington (Vol. ed.) and P. H. Mussen (General Ed.), *Handbook of child psychology: Socialization, personality, and social development* (Vol. 4). New York: Wiley.

Hartlage, L. C. (1970). Sex-linked inheritance of spatial ability. *Perceptual Motor Skills, 31,* 610.

Hartup, W. W. (1974). Aggression in childhood: Developmental perspectives. *American Psychologist, 29,* 220–226.

Hartup, W. W. (1976/1983). Peer interaction and the behavioral development of the individual child. In W. Damon (Ed.), *Social and personality development: Essays on the growth of the child.* New York: W. W. Norton. Reprinted from E. Schopler & R. J. Reichler (Eds.), *Psychopathology and child development.* New York: Plenum, 1976.

Hartup, W. W. (1983). Peer relations. In E. M. Hetherington (Vol. ed. and P. H. Mussen (General Ed.), *Handbook of child psychology: Socialization, personality, and social development* (Vol. 4). New York: Wiley.

Hasler, A. D., Scholz, A. T., & Horrall, R. M. (1978). Olfactory imprinting and homing in salmon. *American Scientist, 66,* 347–355.

Hay, D. F. (1984). Social conflict in early childhood. In G. J. Whitehurst (Ed.), *Annals of child development: A research annual* (Vol. 1). Greenwich, CT: JAI Press, Inc.

Hay, D. F. & Ross, H. S. (1982). The social nature of early conflict. *Child Development, 53,* 105–113.

Haynes, H., White, B. L., & Held, R. (1965). Visual accommodation in human infants. *Science, 148,* 528–530.

Haywood, H. C. (1974). Distribution of intelligence. In *Encyclopedia Britannica* (15th ed.). Chicago: Benton. (Macropedia Vol. 9, 672–677).

Heath, P. (1960). Translator of M. Von Senden's *Space and Sight* (1932). Methuen: London.

Heider, F. (1958). *The psychology of interpersonal relations.* New York: Wiley.

Held, R. & Hein, A. (1963). Movement-produced stimulation in the development of visually guided behavior. *Journal of Comparative and Physiological Psychology, 56,* 872–876.

Helmholtz, H. Von (1925). *Handbuch der physiologischen optik.* Hamburg: Verlag von Leopold Voss, 1910. Translated by P. C. Southall as *Helmholtz's treatise on psychological optics,* Vol. 3. Menasha, WI: Optical Society of America.

Helton, G. B. & Workman, E. A. (1982). Considerations in assessing the mildly handicapped. In T. L. Miller & E. E. Davis (Eds.), *The mildly handicapped student.* New York: Grune & Stratton.

Herbert, W. (1982). Treatment for brain damage under fire. *Science News,* Dec. 4.

Hersher, L., Richmond, J. B., & Moore, A. U. (1963). Maternal behaviour in sheep and goats. In H. L. Rheingold (Ed.), *Maternal behaviour in animals.* New York: Wiley.

Heston, L. L. (1966). Psychiatric disorders in foster home reared children of schizophrenic mothers. *British Journal of Psychiatry, 112,* 819–825.

Hetherington, E. M. (1975). *Children of divorce.* Paper presented at the Biennial Meetings of the

Society for Research in Child Development, Denver.

Hinde, R. A. (1983). Ethology and child development. In M. M. Haith & J. J. Campos (Vol. eds.), and P. H. Mussen (General ed.), *Handbook of child psychology: Infancy and developmental psychobiology* (Vol. 2). New York: Wiley.

Hines, M. (1982). Prenatal gonadal hormones and sex differences in human behavior. *Psychological Bulletin, 92,* 56–80.

Hines, M. & Shipley, C. (1984). Prenatal exposure to diethylstilbestrol (DES) and the development of sexually dimorphic cognitive abilities and cerebral lateralization. *Developmental Psychology, 20,* 81–94.

Hobbes, T. (1651/1962). *Leviathan.* Originally published in 1651. Edited edition by M. Oakeshott, with an introduction by R. S. Peters. New York Collier Books.

Hockett, C. F. (1960). The origin of speech. *Scientific American, 203(3),* 89–96.

Hodkin, B. (1981). Language effects in assessment of class-inclusion ability. *Child Development, 52,* 470–478.

Hoenig, J. (1985). Etiology of transsexualism. In B. W. Steiner (Ed.), *Gender dysphoria.* New York: Plenum.

Hofer, M. A. (1981). *The roots of human behavior: An introduction to the psychobiology of early development.* San Francisco: W. H. Freeman.

Hoff-Ginsberg, E. & Shatz, M. (1982). Linguistic input and the child's acquistion of language. *Psychological Bulletin, 92,* 3–26.

Hoffman, M. L. (1970). Moral development. In P. H. Mussen (Ed.), *Carmichael's manual of child psychology* (Vol. 3). New York: John Wiley.

Hoffman, M. L. (1975). Altruistic behavior and the parent-child relationship. *Journal of Personality and Social Psychology, 31,* 937–943.

Hoffman, M. L. (1978). Toward a theory of empathic arousal and development. In M. Lewis & L. A. Rosenblum, (Eds.), *The development of affect.* New York: Plenum.

Hoffman, M. L. (1982). Development of prosocial motivation: Empathy and guilt. In N. Eisenberg-Berg (Ed.). *The development of prosocial behavior.* New York: Academic Press.

Hoffman, M. L. (1983). Affective and cognitive processes in moral internalization. In E. T. Higgins, D. N. Ruble, & W. W. Hartup (Eds.), *Social cognition and social development.* Cambridge, MA: Cambridge University Press.

Hoffman, M. L. (1985). Moral development. In M. H. Bornstein & M. E. Lamb, (Eds.), *Developmental psychology: An advanced textbook.* Hillsdale, NJ: Lawrence Erlbaum.

Hollingworth, L. S. (1929). *Gifted children, their nature and nurture.* New York: The Macmillan Co.

Honzik, M. P. (1957). Developmental studies of parent-child resemblance in intelligence. *Child Development, 28,* 215–228.

Honzik, M. P. (1976). Value and limitations of infant tests: An overview. In M. Lewis (Ed.), *Origins of intelligence.* New York: Plenum.

Honzik, M. P., Hutchings, J. J., & Burnip, S. R. (1965). Birth record assessments and test performance at eight months. *American Journal of Diseases in Children, 109,* 416–426.

Honzik, M. P., Macfarlane, J. W., & Allen, L. (1948). The stability of mental test performance between two and eighteen years. *Journal of Experimental Education, 17,* 309–324.

Horn, J. M., Loehlin, J. C., & Willerman, L. (1979). Intellectual resemblance among adoptive and biological relatives: The Texas adoption project. *Behavior Genetics, 9,* 177–207.

Howard, D. (1983). *Cognitive psychology.* New York: MacMillan Publishing Co.

Hoyenga, K. B., & Hoyenga, K. T. (1979). *The question of sex differences.* Boston: Little, Brown & Company.

Hrdlicka, A. (1931). *Children who run on all fours.* New York: McGraw-Hill.

Hubel, D. H. & Wiesel, T. N. (1962). Receptive fields, binocular interaction and functional architecture in the cat's visual cortex. *Journal of Physiology, 160,* 106–154.

Hubel, D. H. & Wiesel, T. N. (1965). Binocular interaction in striate cortex of kittens reared with artificial squint. *Journal of Neurophysiology, 28,* 1041–1059.

Hubert, N. C., Wachs, T., Peters-Martin, P., & Gandour, M. J. (1982). The study of early temperament: Measurement and conceptual issues. *Child Development, 53.* 571–600.

Hudgins, W. & Prentice, N. M. (1973). Moral judgment in delinquent and nondelinquent adolescents and their mothers. *Journal of Abnormal Psychology, 82,* 145–152.

Huitt, W. G. & Ashton, P. T. (1982). Parents' perception of infant temperament: A psychometric study. *Merrill-Palmer Quarterly, 28,* 95–109.

Humphreys, A. P. & Smith, P. K. (1984). Rough-and-tumble in preschool and playground. In P. K. Smith (Ed.), *Play in animals and humans.* Oxford, England: Basil Blackwell.

Hunt, M. (1982). *The universe within.* New York: Simon & Schuster.

Huston, A. C. (1983). Sex-typing. In M. E. Hetherington (Vol. ed.) and P. H. Mussen (General Ed.). *Handbook of child psychology: Socialization, personality, and social development* (Vol. 4). New York: Wiley.

Huttenlocher, P. R. (1984). Synapse elimination and plasticity in developing human cerebral cortex. *American Journal of Mental Deficiency, 88(5),* 488–496.

Hyde, J. S. (1984). How large are gender differences in aggression? A developmental meta-analysis. *Developmental Psychology, 20,* 722–736.

Imamoglu, E. O. (1975). Children's awareness and usage of intention cues. *Child Development, 46,* 39–45.

Immelmann, K. (1972). Sexual and other long-term aspects of imprinting in birds and other species. In D. S. Lehrman, R. A. Hinde, & E. Shaw, (Eds.), *Advances in the study of behavior* (Vol. 4). New York: Academic Press.

Immelmann, K. & Suomi, S. J. (1981). Sensitive phases in development. In K. Immelmann, G. W. Barlow, L. Petrinovich, & M. Main, *Behavioral development.* Cambridge, MA: Cambridge University Press.

Imperato-McGinley, J., Peterson, R. E., Gautier, T., & Sturla, E. (1979). Androgens and the evolution of male-gender identity among male pseudohermaphrodites with 5α-reductase deficiency. *New England Journal of Medicine, 300,* 1233–1237.

Inhelder, B. & Piaget, J. (1955/1958). De la logique de l'énfant à la logique de l'adolescent. Paris: Presses Universitaires de France, 1955. *The growth of logical thinking from childhood to adolescence.* New York: Basic Books. 1958.

Inhelder, B. & Piaget, J. (1959/1964). La genese des structures logiques elementaires. Neuchatel: Delachaux & Niestle, 1959. *The early growth of logic in the child: Classification and seriation.* New York: Harper & Row. (Originally published in 1959).

Intons-Peterson, M. J. & Reddel, M. (1984). What do people ask about a neonate? *Developmental Psychology, 20,* 358–359.

Itard, J. M. (1806/1972). A Report to his Excellency the Minister of Interior. In W. Dennis (Ed.), *Historical readings in developmental psychology.* Appleton-Century-Crofts.

Iwanaga, M. (1973). Development of interpersonal play structures in 3, 4, and 5-year-old children. *Journal of Research and Development in Education, 6,* 71–82.

Izard, C. (1978). On the ontogenesis of emotions and emotion-cognition relationships in infancy. In M. Lewis & L. A. Rosenblum (Eds.), *The development of affect.* New York: Plenum Press.

Izard, C. E., Kagan, J., & Zajonc, R. B. (1984). *Emotions, cognition, and behavior.* Cambridge, England: Cambridge University Press.

Jacob, F. & Monod, J. (1961). Genetic regulatory mechanisms in the synthesis of proteins. *Journal of Molecular Biology, 3,* 318–356.

Jacobson, M. (1978). *Developmental neurobiology* (2nd ed.). New York: Plenum Press.

James, W. (1890). *Principles of psychology* (2 vols). New York: Holt.

Jensen, A. (1969). How much can we boost IQ and scholastic achievement. In *Environment, heredity, and intelligence* (reprint series No. 2). *Harvard Educational Review, 39,* 1–123.

Jensen, A. R. (1980). *Bias in mental testing.* New York: The Free Press.

Jensen, A. R. (1981). Raising the IQ: The Ramey and Haskins study. *Intelligence, 5,* 29–40.

Jensen, G. D. & Tolman, C. W. (1962). Mother-infant relationship in the monkey, Macaca Nemestrina: The effect of brief separation and mother-infant specificity. *Journal of Comparative and Physiological Psychology, 55,* 131–136.

Johnson, C. A., Ahern, F. M., & Johnson, R. C. (1976). Level of functioning of siblings and parents of probands of varying degrees of retardation. *Behavior Genetics, 6,* 473–477.

Jones, H. E. (1971). Physical maturing among girls

as related to behavior. In M. C. Jones N., Bayley, J. W. Macfarlane, & M. P. Honzik (Eds.), *The course of human development*. Waltham, MA: Xerox College Publishing.

Jones, M. C. (1965). Psychological correlates of somatic development. *Child Development, 36,* 899–911.

Jones, M. C. & Bayley, N. (1950). Physical maturing among boys as related to behavior. *Journal of Educational Psychology, 41,* 129–148.

Jones, M. C., Bayley, N., Macfarlane, J. W., & Honzik, M. P. (1971). *The course of human development*. Waltham, MA: Xerox College Publishing.

Jordan, N. (1972). Is there an Achilles' heel in Piaget's theorizing? *Human Development, 15,* 379–382.

Kagan, J. (1976). Emergent themes in human development. *American Scientist, 64,* 186–196.

Kagan, J. (1980). Perspectives on continuity. In O. G. Brim, Jr. & J. Kagan (Eds.), *Constancy and change in human development*. Cambridge, MA: Harvard Univ. Press.

Kagan, J. (1981). *The second year*. Cambridge: Harvard University Press.

Kagan, J. (1982). *Psychological research on the human infant: An evaluative summary*. New York: W. T. Grant.

Kagan, J. (1983). Developmental categories and the premise of connectivity. In R. M. Lerner (Ed.), *Developmental psychology: Historical and philosophical perspectives*. Hillsdale, NJ: Lawrence Erlbaum Associates.

Kagan, J. (1984a). Continuity and change in the opening years of life. In R. N. Emde & R. J. Harmon (Eds.), *Continuities and discontinuities in development*. New York: Plenum Press.

Kagan, J. (1984b). *The nature of the child*. New York: Basic Books, Inc.

Kagan, J. & Klein, R. E. (1973). Cross cultural perspectives on early development. *American Psychologist, 28,* 947–961.

Kaij, L. (1957). Drinking habits in twins. *Acta Genetica et Medica, 7,* 437–441.

Kail, R. (1979). *The development of memory in children*. San Francisco: W. H. Freeman & Co.

Kail, R. (1984). *The development of memory in children* (2nd ed.). New York: W. H. Freeman.

Kail, R. & Hagen, J. W. (1982). Memory in child-

hood. In B. B. Wolman (Ed.), *Handbook of developmental psychology*. Englewood Cliffs, NJ: Prentice-Hall.

Kamii, C. (1972). An application of Piaget's theory to the conceptualization of a preschool curriculum. In R. F. Parker (Ed.). *The preschool in action: Exploring early childhood programs*. Bosten: Allyn and Bacon.

Kamin, L. J. (1974). *The science and politics of I.Q.* Potomac, MD: Lawrence Erlbaum Associates.

Kandel, E. R. (1981). Synapse formation, tropic interactions between neurons, and the development of behavior. In E. R. Kandel & J. H. Schwartz, (Eds.). *Principles of neural science*. New York: Elsevier/North-Holland.

Kandel, E. R. & Schwartz, J. H. (1981). Principles of neural science. New York: Elsevier/North-Holland.

Karlsson, J. L. (1978). *Inheritance of creative potential*. Chicago: Nelson-Hall.

Karniol, R. (1978). Children's use of intention cues in evaluating behavior. *Psychological Bulletin, 85,* 76–85.

Katchadovrian, H. (1977) *The biology of adolescence*. San Francisco: W. H. Freeman.

Kaufman, I. C. & Rosenblum, L. A. (1967). The reaction to separation in infant monkeys: Anaclitic depression and conservation-withdrawal. *Psychosomatic Medicine, 29,* 648–675.

Kaufman, I. C. & Rosenblum, L. A. (1969). The waning of the mother-infant bond in two species of macaque. In B. M. Foss (Ed.), *Determinants of infant behavior,* (Vol. 4). London: Methuen.

Kaufman, I. C. & Stynes, A. J. (1978). Depression can be induced in a bonnet macaque. *Psychosomatic Medicine, 40,* 71–75.

Kaufmann, R., Maland, J., & Yonas, A. (1981). Sensitivity of 5- and 7-month-old infants to pictorial depth information. *Journal of Experimental Child Psychology, 32,* 162–168.

Kay, L. (1974). A sonar aid to enhance spatial perception of the blind: Engineering design and evaluation. *The Radio and Electronic Engineer, 44,* 605–627.

Kay, L. (1984). Learning to use the ultrasonic spatial sensor by the blind infant: Comments on Aitken and Bower. *Journal of Experimental Child Psychology, 37,* 207–211.

Kaye, K. & Marcus, J. (1981). Infant imitation: The

sensorimotor agenda. *Developmental Psychology, 17,* 258–265.

Keasey, C. B. (1977). Children's developing awareness and usage of intentionality and motives. In C. B. Keasey (Vol. ed.). and H. E. Howe (Series ed.), *Nebraska Symposium on Motivation 1977: Social Cognitive Development.* Lincoln, Nebraska: University of Nebraska Press.

Keeney, T. J., Cannizzo, S. R., & Flavell, J. H. (1967). Spontaneous and induced verbal rehearsal in a recall task. *Child Development, 38,* 953–966.

Keeton, W. T. (1981). The ontogeny of bird orientation. In K. Immelmann, G. W. Barlow, L. Petrinovich, & M. Main (Eds.), *Behavioral development: The Bielefeld interdisciplinary project.* Cambridge, MA: Cambridge University Press.

Kendler, K. S. & Gruenberg, A. M. (1984). An independent analysis of the Danish Adoption study of Schizophrenia VI. The relationship between psychiatric disorders as defined by DSM III in the relatives and adoptees. *Archives of General Psychiatry, 41,* 555–564.

Kennedy, B. A. & Miller, D. J. (1976). Persistent use of verbal rehearsal as a function of information about its value. *Child Development, 47,* 566–569.

Kenney, M. D., Mason, W. A., & Hill, S. D. (1979). Effects of age, objects, and visual experience on affective responses of rhesus monkeys to strangers. *Developmental Psychology, 15,* 176–184.

Kessler, C. (1984). Language acquisition in bilingual children. In N. Miller, (Ed.), *Bilingualism and language disability.* San Diego: College Hill Press.

Kessler, J. W. (1966). *Psychopathology of childhood.* Englewood Cliffs, NJ: Prentice-Hall.

Kinsbourne, M. & Hiscock, M. (1983). The normal and deviant development of functional lateralization of the brain. In M. M. Haith & J. J. Campos (Vol. eds.), and P. H. Mussen (General ed.), *Handbook of child psychology: Infancy and developmental psychobiology* (Vol. 2). New York: Wiley.

Kinsey, A. C., Pomeroy, W. B., & Martin, C. E. (1948). *Sexual behavior in the human male.* Philadelphia: W. B. Saunders.

Kirk, S. A. & Gallagher, J. J. (1979). *Educating exceptional children.* Boston: Houghton Mifflin Co.

Klahr, D. & Wallace, J. G. (1976). *Cognitive development: An information processing view.* Hillsdale, NJ: Lawrence Erlbaum.

Klaus, M. H. & Kennell, J. H. (1976). *Maternal-infant bonding: The impact on early separation or loss on family development.* St. Louis: Mosby.

Klaus, M. H., & Kennell, J. H. (1982). *Parent-infant bonding.* St. Louis: Mosby.

Klein, D. B. (1970). *A history of scientific psychology.* New York: Basic Books.

Klopfer, P. H. (1971). Mother love: What turns it on? *American Scientist, 59,* 404–407.

Knight, G. P. & Kagan, S. (1977). Acculturation of prosocial and competitive behaviors among second and third generation Mexican-American children. *Journal of Cross-Cultural Psychology, 8,* 273–284.

Kobasigawa, A. (1974). Utilization of retrieval cues by children in recall. *Child Development, 45,* 127–134.

Kohen-Raz, R. (1977). *Psychobiological aspects of cognitive growth.* New York: Academic Press.

Kohlberg, L. (1958). *The development of modes of moral thinking and choice in the years ten to sixteen.* Unpublished doctoral dissertation, University of Chicago.

Kohlberg, L. (1963). The development of children's orientations toward a moral order: I. Sequence in the development of moral thought. *Vita Humana, 6,* 11–33.

Kohlberg, L. (1966). A cognitive-developmental analysis of children's sex-role concepts and attitudes. In E. E. Maccoby (Ed.), *The development of sex differences.* Stanford: Stanford University Press.

Kohlberg, L. (1976). Moral stages and moralization: The cognitive-developmental approach. In T. Lickona (Ed.), *Moral development and behavior.* New York: Holt, Rinehart & Winston.

Kohlberg, L. (1982). Moral development. In J. M. Broughton & D. J. Freeman-Moir (Eds.), *The cognitive-development psychology of James Mark Baldwin: Current theory and research in genetic epistemology.* Norwood, NJ: Ablex.

Kohlberg, L. & Freundlich, D. (1977). *Moral judgment in youthful offenders.* Unpublished manuscript, Harvard University.

Kohnstamm, G. A. (1967). *Teaching children to solve a Piagetian problem of class inclusion.* Amsterdam: North Holland Publishing Co.

Kogan, N. (1983). Stylistic variation in childhood

and adolescence: Creativity, metaphor, and cognitive styles. In J. H. Flavell & E. M. Markman (Vol. eds.), and P. H. Mussen (General ed.), *Handbook of child psychology: Cognitive development* (Vol. 3). New York: Wiley.

Kolata, G. (1984). Studying learning in the womb. *Science, 225,* 302–303.

Kolb, B. & Whishaw, I. Q. (1980). *Fundamentals of human neuropsychology.* San Francisco: W. H. Freeman.

Koluchova, J. (1976). A report on the further development of twins after severe and prolonged deprivation. In A. M. Clarke & A. D. B. Clarke, *Early experience: Myth & evidence.* London: Open Books.

Konner, M. (1982). Biological aspects of the mother-infant bond. In R. N. Emde & R. J. Harmon, *The development of attachment and affiliative systems.* New York: Plenum Press.

Kopp, C. B. & Shaperman, J. (1973). Cognitive development in the absence of object manipulation during infancy. *Developmental Psychology, 9,* 430.

Krashen, S. D. (1973). Lateralization, language learning, and the critical period: Some new evidence. *Language Learning, 23(1),* 63–74.

Kreutzer, M. A. & Charlesworth, W. R. (1973). *Infants reactions to different expressions of emotions.* Paper presented at the biennial meeting of the Society for Research in Child Development, Philadelphia.

Kroodsma, D. E. & Pickert, R. (1980). Environmentally dependent sensitive periods for avian vocal learning. *Nature, 288(4),* 477–479.

Kuczaj, S. A. & Lederberg, A. R. (1977). Height, age, and function: Differing influences on children's comprehension of "younger" and "older." *Journal of Child Language, 4,* 395–416.

Kuczynski, L. (1982). Intensity and orientation of reasoning: Motivational determinants of children's compliance to verbal rationales. *Journal of Experimental Child Psychology, 34,* 357–370.

Kuhl, P. & Miller, J. (1975). Speech perception by the chinchilla: Voiced-voiceless distinctions in alveolar plosive consonants. *Science, 190,* 69–72.

Kuhl, P. K., & Meltzoff, A. N. (1982). The bimodal perception of speech in infancy. *Science, 218,* 1138–1141.

Kuhlmann, F. (1922). *A handbook of mental tests.* Baltimore, Md.: Warwick & York.

Kuhn, D. (1977). Conditional reasoning in children. *Developmental Psychology, 13,* 342–353.

Kuhn, D. (1984). Cognitive development. In M. H. Bornstein & M. E. Lamb (Eds.), *Developmental psychology: An advanced textbook.* Hillsdale, NJ: Lawrence Erlbaum.

Kuhn, D. & Brannock, J. (1977). Development of the isolation of variables scheme in experimental and "natural experiment" contexts. *Developmental Psychology, 13,* 9–14.

Kuhn, D., Ho, V., & Adams, C. (1979). Formal reasoning among pre- and late-adolescents. *Child Development, 50,* 1128–1135.

Kuo, Z. Y. (1921). Giving up instincts in psychology. *Journal of Philosophy, 18,* 645–664.

Kuo, Z. Y. (1922). How are instincts acquired? *Psychological Review, 29,* 334–365.

Kuo, Z. Y. (1930). The genesis of the cat's response toward the rat. *Journal of Comparative Psychology, 15,* 1–15.

Kuo, Z. Y. (1938). Further study on the behavior of the cat towards the rat. *Journal of Comparative Psychology, 25,* 1–8.

Kuo, Z. Y. (1967). *The dynamics of behavior development.* New York: Random House.

Kurent, J. E. & Sever, J. L. (1977). Infectious diseases. In J. B. Wilson & F. C. Fraser (Eds.), *Handbook of Teratology,* Vol. 1. New York: Plenum.

Kurland, D. M. (1981). *The effect of massive practice on children's operational efficiency and memory span.* Unpublished doctoral dissertation, University of Toronto (OISE).

Kurtines, W. & Greif, E. B. (1974). The development of moral thought: Review and evaluation of Kohlberg's approach. *Psychological Bulletin, 81,* 453–470.

LaCoste-Utamsing, de C., Holloway, R. L. (1982). Sexual dimorphism in the human corpus callosum. *Science, 216,* 1431–1432.

Lamb, M. E. & Campos, J. J. (1982). *Development in infancy: An introduction.* New York: Random House.

Lamb, M. E., & Easterbrooks, M. A. (1981). Individual differences in parental sensitivity: Origins, components, and consequences. In M. E. Lamb & L. R. Sherrod (Eds.), *Infant social cognition: Empirical and theoretical considerations.* Hillsdale, NJ: Lawrence Erlbaum Associates.

Lamb, M. E., & Hwang, C. P. (1982). Maternal attachment and mother-neonate bonding: A critical review. In M. E. Lamb, & A. L. Brown (Eds.), *Advances in developmental psychology* (Vol. 2). Hillsdale, NJ: Lawrence Erlbaum Associates.

Lamb, M. E., Thompson, R. F., Gardner, W., & Charnov, E. L. (1985). *Infant-mother attachment.* Hillsdale, NJ: Lawrence Erlbaum.

Lamb, M. E., Thompson, R. A., Gardner, W. P., Charnov, E. L., & Estes, D. (1984). Security of infantile attachment as assessed in the "strange situation": Its study and biological interpretation. *The Behavioral and Brain Sciences, 7,* 127–171.

Landau, B. & Gleitman, L. R. (1985). *Language and experience. Evidence from the blind child.* Cambridge, MA: Harvard University Press.

Landesman-Dwyer, S. & Butterfield, E. C. (1983). Mental retardation. In M. Lewis (Ed.), *Origins of intelligence* (2nd ed.) New York: Plenum.

Langer, J. (1969). *Theories of development.* New York: Holt, Rinehart, & Winston.

Langlois, J. H. & Stephan, C. W. (1981). Beauty and the beast: The role of physical attractiveness in the development of peer relations and social behavior. In S. S. Brehm, S. M. Kassin, & F. X. Gibbons (Eds.), *Developmental social psychology.* New York: Oxford University Press.

Lasky, R. E. & Spiro, D. (1980). The processing of tachistoscopically presented visual stimuli by five-month-old infants. *Child Development, 51,* 1292–1294.

Lasky, R. E., Syrdal-Lasky, A., & Klein, R. E. (1975). VOT discrimination by four- to six-and-a-half-month-old infants from Spanish environments. *Journal of Experimental Child Psychology, 20,* 215–225.

Lazar, I., Darlington, R., Murray, H., Royce, J., & Snipper, A. (1982). Lasting effects of early education: A report from the Consortium for Longitudinal Studies. *Monographs of the Society for Research in Child Development, 47,* (2–3, Serial No. 195).

Leiderman, P. H. (1981). Human mother-infant social bonding. In K. Immelmann, G. W. Barlow, L. Petrinovich, & M. Main (Eds.), *Behavioral development.* Cambridge: Cambridge University Press.

Lenneberg, E. (1967). *Biological foundations of language.* New York: Wiley and Son.

Lepper, M. R. (1973). Dissonance, self-perception, and honesty in children. *Journal of Personality and Social Psychology, 25,* 65–74.

Lepper, M. R. (1983). Social control processes, and the internalization of social values. In E. T. Higgins, D. N. Ruble, & W. W. Hartup (Eds.), *Social cognition and social behavior: A developmental perspective.* San Francisco: Jossey-Bass.

Lerner, R. M. (1976). *Concepts and theories of human development.* Reading, MA: Addison-Wesley.

Lerner, R. M. (1978). Nature, nurture, and dynamic interactionism. *Human Development, 21,* 1–20.

Lerner, R. M. (1983). A "goodness of fit" model of person context interaction. In D. Magnusson & V. L. Allen, *Human development: An interactional perspective.* New York: Academic Press.

Lerner, R. M. (1984). *On the nature of human plasticity.* New York: Cambridge University Press.

Lethmate, J. & Ducker, G. (1973). Untersuchungen zum selbsterkennen in spiegel bei orang-utans und einigen anderen affenarten. *Zeitschrift fur Tierpsychologie, 33,* 248–269.

Lewis, M. (1981). Self-knowledge: A social cognitive perspective on gender identify and sex-role development. In M. E. Lamb & L. R. Sherrod (Eds.), *Infant social cognition: Empirical and theoretical considerations.* Hillsdale, NJ: Lawrence Erlbaum.

Lewis, M. & Brooks-Gunn, J. (1979). *Social cognition and the acquisition of self.* New York: Plenum Press.

Lewis, M. & Michalson, C. (1983). *Children's emotions and moods: Developmental theory and measurement.* New York: Plenum.

Lewontin, R. C., Rose, S., & Kamin, L. J. (1984). *Not in our genes.* New York: Pantheon.

Liben, L. S. (1978). Perspective-taking skills in young children: Seeing the world through rose-colored glasses. *Developmental Psychology, 14,* 87–92.

Livesley, W. J. & Bromley, D. B. (1973). *Person per-*

ception in childhood and adolescence. New York: Wiley.

Locke, John L. (1983). *Phonological acquisition and change.* New York: Academic Press.

Lodico, M. G., Ghatala, E. S., Levin, J. R., Pressley, M., & Bell, J. A. (1983). The effects of strategy-monitoring training on children's selection of effective memory strategies. *Journal of Experimental Child Psychology, 35,* 263–277.

Loehlin, J. C. (1984). Familial correlations and X-linked genes: A comment. *Psychological Bulletin, 95,* 332–333.

Loehlin, J. C., Horn, J. M., & Willerman, L. (1981). Personality resemblance in adoptive families. *Behavior Genetics, 11,* 309–330.

Loehlin, J. C. & Nichols, R. (1976). *Heredity, environment, and personality: A study of 850 sets of twins.* Austin: University of Texas Press.

Loehlin, J. C., Willerman, L., & Horn, J. M. (1982). Personality resemblances between unwed mothers and their adopted-away offspring. *Journal of Personality and Social Psychology, 42,* 1089–1099.

Loftus, E. (1980). *Memory: Surprising new insights into how we remember and why we forget.* California: Addison-Wesley Publishing Company.

Lorenz, K. (1955). Morphology and behavior patterns in closely allied species. In B. Schaffner (Ed.), *Group processes.* New York: Macy Foundation.

Lorenz, K. (1935/1970). The conspecific as the eliciting factor for social behavior patterns. Originally published in 1935 as *Der Kumpan in der Umwelt des Vogels (Journal für Ornithologie, 80, Heft 2)* appears in translation in K. Lorenz, *Studies in animal and human behavior,* Vol. 1. Cambridge, MA: Harvard University Press.

Lorenz, K. (1971/1976). *Studies in animal and human behavior* (Vol. 2). Cambridge, MA: Harvard University Press. 1971. Excerpted in J. Bruner, A. Jolly, & K. Sylva (Eds.), *Play: Its role in development and evaluation.*

Lorenz, K. (1981). *The foundations of ethology.* New York: Springer-Verlag.

Luria, A. R. (1968). *The mind of a mnemonist.* Avon, New York: Basic Books.

Lütkenhaus, P., Grossmann, K. E. & Grossmann, K. (1985). Infant-mother attachment at twelve months and style of interaction with stranger at the age of three years. *Child Development, 56,* 1538–1542.

Lyell, C. (1830–1833). *Principles of geology, being an attempt to explain the former changes of the earth's surface by reference to causes now in operation.* 3 vols. London: John Murray.

Maccoby, E. E. (1980). *Social development.* New York: Harcourt Brace Jovanovich, Inc.

Maccoby, E. E. & Jacklin, C. N. (1980). Sex differences in aggression: A rejoinder and reprise. *Child Development, 51,* 964–980.

Maccoby, E. E. & Martin, J. A. (1983). Socialization in the context of the family: Parent-child interaction. In E. M. Hetherington (Vol. ed.) and P. H. Mussen (General Ed.), *Handbook of child psychology: Socialization, personality, and social development* (Vol. 4). New York: Wiley.

Maccoby, E. E. & Masters, J. (1970). Attachment and dependency. In P. H. Mussen (Ed.), *Carmichael's manual of child psychology* (Vol. 2) (3rd ed.). New York: Wiley.

Maccoby, E. E., Snow, M. E., & Jacklin, C. N. (1984). Children's disposition and mother-child interaction at 12 and 18 months: A short-term longitudinal study. *Developmental Psychology, 20,* 459–472.

MacFarlane, A. (1977). *The psychology of childbirth.* Cambridge, MA: Harvard University Press.

MacFarlane, J. A. (1975). Olfaction in the development of social preferences in the human neonate. In M. A. Hofer (Ed.), *Parent-infant interaction.* Amsterdam: Elsevier.

Macfarlane, J. W. (1971). The impact of early and late maturation in boys and girls: Illustrations from life records of individuals. In M. C. Jones et al., (Eds.), *The course of human development.* Waltham, Mass.: Xerox College Publishing.

Macintyre, R. J. (1982). Regulatory genes and adaptations: Past, present, and future. In M. K. Hecht, B. Wallace, and G. T. Prance, (Eds.), *Evolutionary biology,* Vol. 15. New York: Plenum.

Madsen, M. C. & Shapira, A. (1970). Cooperation and competitive behavior of Afro-American, Anglo-American, and Mexican Village children. *Developmental Psychology, 3,* 16–20.

Madsen, M. C. & Lancy, D. F. (1981). Cooperative and competitive behavior. *Journal of Cross-Cultural Psychology, 12,* 389–408.

Mahler, M. S. (1979). *The selected papers of Margaret S. Mahler, M.D., Vol. 1.: Infantile psychosis and early contributions.* New York: Jason Aronson.

Main, M. (1981). Avoidance in the service of attachment: A working paper. In K. Immelmann, G. Barlow, L. Petrinovich, & M. Main (Eds.), *Behavioral development: The Bielefeld interdisciplinary project.* New York: Cambridge University Press.

Main, M. B. (1983). Exploration, play, and cognitive functioning related to mother-infant attachment. *Infant Behavior Development, 6,* 167–174.

Main, M. (in press). Parental observed aversion to physical contact with the infant: Stability, consequences, and reasons. In T. B. Brazelton & Barnard (Eds.), *Touch.* New York: International Universities Press.

Main, M. & George, C. (1985). Responses of abused and disadvantaged toddlers to distress in agemates: A study in the day care setting. *Developmental Psychology, 21,* 407–412.

Malina, R. M. (1979). Secular changes in size and maturity: Causes and effects. In A. F. Roche (Ed.), Secular trends in human growth, maturation, and development. *Monographs of the Society for Research in Child Development, 44,* 59–102.

Maloney, M. P. & Ward, M. P. (1979). *Mental retardation and modern society.* New York: Oxford University Press.

Mandler, J. M. (1983). Representation. In J. H. Flavell & E. M. Markman (Vol. eds.) and P. H. Mussen (General ed.), *Handbook of child psychology: Cognitive development* (Vol. 3). New York: Wiley.

Maratsos, M. (1983). Some current issues in the study of the acquisition of grammar. In J. H. Flavell & E. M. Markman (Vol. eds.) and P. H. Mussen (General ed.), *Handbook of child psychology: Cognitive development* (Vol. 3). New York: Wiley.

Marcus, D. E. & Overton, W. F. (1978). The development of cognitive gender constancy and sex role preferences. *Child Development, 49,* 434–444.

Markman, E. M. & Hutchinson, J. E. (1984). Children's sensitivity to constraint on word meaning: Taxonomic vs thematic relations. *Cognitive Psychology, 16,* 1–27.

Markman, E. M. & Seibert, J. (1976). Classes and collections: Internal organization and resulting holistic properties. *Cognitive Psychology, 8,* 561–577.

Marland, S. P., Jr. (1972). *Education of the gifted and talented: Report to the Congress of the United States by the U. S. Commissioner of Education.* Washington, D.C.: U.S. Government Printing Office.

Marshall, W. A. (1974). Interrelationships of skeletal maturation, sexual development and somatic growth in man. *Annals of Human Biology, 1,* 29–40.

Martin, P. & Caro, T. M. (1985). On the functions of play and its role in behavioral development. In J. S. Rosenblatt, C. Beer, M. C. Busnel & P. J. B. Slater (Eds.), *Advances in the study of behavior* (Vol. 15). Orlando, FL: Academic Press.

Masangkay, Z. S., McCluskey, K. A., McIntyre, C. W., Sims-Knight, J., Vaughn, B. E., & Flavell, J. H. (1974). The early development of inferences about the visual precepts of others. *Child Development, 45,* 357–366.

Mason, W. A., & Kenney, M. D. (1974). Redirection of filial attachments in rhesus monkeys: Dogs as mother surrogates. *Science, 183,* 1209–1211.

Matheny, A. P., Wilson, R. S., Dolan, A. B., & Krantz, J. Z. (1981). Behavioral contrasts in twinships: Stability and patterns of differences in childhood. *Childhood Development, 52,* 579–588.

Matas, L., Arend, R., & Sroufe, L. (1978). Continuity of adaptation in the second year: The relationship between quality of attachment and later competence. *Child Development, 49,* 547–556.

Matheny, A. P. (1980). Bayley's infant behavior record: Behavioral components and twin analyses. *Child Development, 51,* 1157–1161.

Matheny, A. P., Dolan, A., & Wilson, R. S. (1976). Twins: Within-pair similarity on Bayley's infant behavior record. *Journal of Genetic Psychology, 128,* 263–270.

Matheny, A. P., Wilson, R. S., Dolan, A. B., & Krantz, J. Z. (1981). Behavioral contrasts in twinships:

Stability and patterns of differences in childhood. *Child Development, 52,* 579–588.

Maurer, D., Salapatek, P. (1976). Developmental changes in the scanning of faces by young infants. *Child Development, 47,* 523–527.

Mayer, R. E. (1983). *Thinking, problem solving, cognition.* New York: W. H. Freeman and Co.

Mayr, E. (1982). *The growth of biological thought.* Cambridge, MA: Belknap Press.

McBride, W. G. (1961). Thalidomide and congenital abnormalities. *Lancet, 2,* 1358.

McCall, R. B. (1976). Toward an epigenetic conception of mental development in the first three years of life. In M. Lewis (Ed.), *Origins of intelligence.* New York: Plenum Press.

McCall, R. B. (1977). Challenges to a science of developmental psychology. *Child Development, 48,* 333–344.

McCall, R. B. (1979). The development of intellectual functioning in infancy and the prediction of later IQ. In J. D. Osofsky (Ed.), *Handbook of infant development.* New York: John Wiley & Sons.

McCall, R. B. (1984). Developmental changes in mental performance: The effect of the birth of a sibling. *Child Development, 55,* 1317–1321.

McClearn, G. E. (1976). Experimental behavioural genetics. In D. Barltrop (Ed.), *Aspects of genetics in paediatrics.* London: Fellowship of Postdoctorate Medicine.

McConaghy, M. J. (1979). Gender permanence and the genital basis of gender: Stages in the development of constancy of gender identity. *Child Development, 50,* 1223–1226.

McCullers, J. C. (1969). G. Stanley Hall's conception of mental development and some indications of its influence on developmental psychology. *American Psychologist, 24,* 1109–1114.

McCullers, J. C. & Love, J. M. (1976). The scientific study of the child. In B. J. Taylor & T. J. White, (Eds.), *Issues and ideas in America.* University of Oklahoma Press.

McEwen, B. S. (1981). Neural gonadal steroid actions. *Science, 211,* 1303–1311.

McGarrigle, J. & Donaldson, M. (1974). Conservation accidents. *Cognition, 3,* 341–350.

McGarrigle, J., Grieve, R., & Hughes, M. (1978). Interpreting inclusion: A contribution to the study of the child's cognitive and linguistic development. *Journal of Experimental Child Psychology, 26,* 528–550.

McGee, M. G. (1979). Human spatial abilities: Psychometric studies and environmental, genetic, hormonal, and neurological influences. *Psychological Bulletin, 86(5),* 889–918.

McGlone, J. (1980). Sex differences in human brain asymmetry: A cortical survey. *Behavioral and Brain Sciences, 3,* 215–227.

McGraw, K. O., Durm, M. W., & Patterson, J. N. (1983). Concept discrimination learning by preschool children using facial stimuli differing in age, sex, race, and eyeglasses. *The Journal of General Psychology, 108,* 193–202.

McIntire, M. L. (1977). The acquisition of American Sign Language hand configurations. *Sign Language Studies, 16,* 247–266.

McKean, K. (1985, October). Intelligence: New ways to measure the wisdom of man. *Discover,* pp. 25–41.

McKenzie, B. & Over, R. (1983). Young infants fail to imitate facial and manual gestures. *Infant Behavior and Development, 6,* 85–95.

McKenzie, B. E., Tootell, H. E., & Day, R. H. (1980). Development of visual size constancy during the 1st year of human infancy. *Developmental Psychology, 16,* 163–174.

McKeown, T. & Record, R. G. (1952). Observations on foetal growth in multiple pregnancy in man. *Journal of Endocrinology, 8,* 386–401.

McKusick, V. A. (1978) *Mendelian inheritance in man.* Baltimore: Johns Hopkins Univ. Press.

McKusick, V. A. (1983). *Mendelian inheritance in man: Catalogs of autosomal dominant, autosomal recessive, and X-linked phenotypes.* (6th ed.). Baltimore: The Johns Hopkins University Press.

McLaughlin, B. (1982). Current status of research on second-language learning in children. *Human Development, 25,* 215–222.

McLoyd, V. C. (1982). Social class differences in sociodramatic play: A critical review. *Developmental Review, 2,* 1–30.

McLoyd, V. C. (1985). Social class and pretend play. In C. C. Brown & A. W. Gottfried (Eds.). *Play interactions: The role of toys and parental involvement in children's development.* Johnson and Johnson Baby Products Co.

McNeill, D. (1970). The development of language. In

P. H. Mussen (Ed.), *Carmichael's manual of child psychology,* Vol. 1 (3rd ed.). New York: Wiley.

Mead, G. H. (1934). *Mind, self, and society.* Chicago: University of Chicago Press.

Mead, M. (1935). *Sex and temperament in three primitive societies.* New York: Morrow.

Meltzoff, A. N. (1985). Immediate and deferred imitation in fourteen- and twenty-four-month old infants. *Child Development, 56,* 62–72.

Meltzoff, A. N. & Moore, M. K. (1977). Imitation of facial and manual gestures by human neonates. *Science, 198,* 75–78.

Meltzoff, A. N. & Moore, M. K. (1983). The origins of imitation in infancy: Paradigm, phenomena, and theories. In L. P. Lipsitt & C. K. Rovee-Collier (Eds.), *Advances in infancy research,* Vol. 2. Norwood, NJ: Ablex.

Mendlewicz, J. & Rainer, J. D. (1977). Adoption study supporting genetic transmission in manic-depressive illness. *Nature, 268,* 327–329.

Mercer, J. R. & Lewis, J. F. (1978). *System of multi-cultural pluralistic assessment.* New York: Psychological Corporation.

Merriman, C. (1924). The intellectual resemblance of twins. *Psychological Monographs, 33,* 1–58.

Messer, S. (1967). Implicit phonology in children. *Journal of Verbal Learning & Verbal Behavior, 6,* 609–613.

Miller, A. G. (1973). Integration and acculturation of cooperative behavior among Blackfoot Indians and non-Indian Canadian children. *Journal of Cross-cultural Psychology, 4,* 374–380.

Miller, A. G. & Thomas, R. (1972). Cooperation and competition among Blackfoot Indian and urban Canadian children. *Child Development, 43,* 1104–1110.

Miller, G. A. (1956). The magical number seven, plus or minus two: Some limits on our capacity for processing information. *Psychological Review, 63,* 81–87.

Miller, G. A. (1965). Some preliminaries to psycholinguistics. *American Psychologist, 20,* 15–20.

Miller, J. A. (1982). Cell death: Sculptor of development and disease. *Neuroscience Commentaries, 1(2),* 33–38.

Miller J. F. & Chapman, R. S. (1981). Research note: The relation between age and mean length of utterance in morphemes. *Journal of Speech and Hearing Research, 24,* 154–161.

Miller, P. H. (1983). *Theories of developmental psychology.* San Francisco: W. H. Freeman.

Milner, B. (1963). Effects of brain lesions on card sorting. *Archives of Neurology, 9,* 90–100.

Milner, B. (1964). Some effects of frontal lobectomy in man. In B. Milner (Ed.), *The frontal granular cortex and behavior.* New York: McGraw-Hill.

Ministry of Health, Standards of normal weight in infancy (1959). *Minister of Health Report on Public Health No. 99.* London: His Majesty's Stationary Office.

Miyazaki, J. M. & Mickevich, M. F. (1982). Evolution of Chesapecten (Mollusca, Bivalvia, Miocene—Pliocene) and the Biogenetic Law. In M. K. Hecht, B. Wallace, & G. T. Prance (Eds.), *Evolutionary Biology,* Vol. 15. New York: Plenum.

Moely, B. E., Olson, F. A., Halwes, T. G., & Flavell, J. H. (1969). Production deficiency in young children's clustered recall. *Developmental Psychology, 1(1),* 26–34.

Molfese, D. L. (1977). Infant cerebral asymmetry. In S. J. Segalowitz & F. A. Gruber (Eds.), *Language development and neurological theory.* New York: Academic Press.

Monaghan, F. V. & Corcos, A. F. (1985). Mendel, the empiricist, *Journal of Heredity, 76,* 49–54.

Money, J. & Ehrhardt, A. E. (1972). *Man & woman, boy & girl.* Baltimore: Johns Hopkins Univ. Press.

Money, J., Hampson, J. G., & Hampson, J. L. (1955). Hermaphroditism: Recommendations concerning assignment of sex, change of sex, and psychologic management. *Bulletin of the Johns Hopkins Hospital, 97,* 284–300.

Money, J. & Tucker, P. (1975). *Sexual signatures: On being a man or a woman.* Boston: Little, Brown.

Montagu, A. (1965). *The human revolution.* New York: World Publishing.

Moody, E. A. (1972). William of Ockham. In P. Edwards (Ed.), *The encyclopedia of philosophy,* Vol. 7 (Reprint ed.). New York: Macmillan Publishing Co., Inc. & The Free Press.

Moore, B. S. & Eisenberg, N. (1984). The development of altruism. In G. J. Whitehurst (Ed.), *Annals of child development,* Vol 1. Greenwich, CT: JAI Press.

Moore, K. L. (1977). *The developing human* (2nd ed.). Philadelphia: W. B. Saunders.

Morehead, D. M. (1971). Processing of phonological

sequences by young children and adults. *Child Development, 42,* 279–289.

Morrison, F. J., Holmes, D. L., & Haith, M. M. (1974). A developmental study of the effect of familiarity on short-term visual memory. *Journal of Experimental Child Psychology, 18,* 412–425.

Morrongiello, B. A., Kulig, J. W., & Clifton, R. K. (1984). Developmental changes in auditory temporal perception. *Child Development, 55,* 461–471.

Morse, P. A. (1972). The discrimination of speech and nonspeech stimuli in early infancy. *Journal of Experimental Child Psychology, 14,* 477–492.

Moskowitz, B. A. (1978). The acquisition of language. *Scientific American, 239* (5), 92–108.

Mosley, J. L. & Stan, E. A. (1984). Human sexual dimorphism: Its costs and benefits. In H. W. Reese, *Advances in child development and behavior,* Vol. 18. Orlando, FL: Academic Press.

Mowrer, O. H. (1954). The psychologist looks at language. *American Psychologist, 9,* 660–694.

Moynahan, E. (1978). Assessment and selection of paired-associate strategies: A developmental study. *Journal of Experimental Child Psychology, 26,* 257–266.

Muir, D. & Field, J. (1979). Newborn infants orient to sounds. *Child Development, 50,* 431–436.

Muir, D., Abraham, W., Forbes, B. & Harris, L. (1979). The ontogenesis of an auditory localization response from birth to four months of age. *Canadian Journal of Psychology, 33,* 320–333.

Muir, D. W. & Mitchell, D. E. (1973). Visual resolution and experience: Acuity deficits in cats following early selective visual deprivation. *Science, 180,* 420–422.

Munroe, R. H., Shimmin, H. S. & Munroe, R. C. (1984). Gender understanding and sex role preference in four cultures. *Developmental Psychology, 20,* 673–682.

Mussen, P. H. (1970). Preface to the *Manual of child psychology* (3rd ed.). (Vols. 1 & 2). P. H. Mussen, (Ed.) New York: John Wiley & Sons, Inc.

Mussen, P. H. (1983). Preface to the *Handbook of child psychology* (4th ed.). (Vols. 1–4). P. H. Mussen (Gen. Ed.). New York: John Wiley & Sons.

Mussen, P. H. & Eisenberg-Berg, N. (1977). *Caring, sharing and helping.* San Francisco: W. H. Freeman.

Myers, B. J. (1984). Mother-infant bonding: The sta-

tus of this critical-period hypothesis. *Developmental Review, 4,* 240–274.

Nash, J. (1978). *Developmental psychology: A psychobiological approach* (2nd ed.). Englewood Cliffs, NJ: Prentice-Hall, Inc.

Neimark, E. D. (1975a). Intellectual development during adolescence. In F. D. Horowitz (Ed.), *Review of child development research,* (Vol. 4). Chicago: University of Chicago Press.

Neimark, E. D. (1975b). Longitudinal development of formal operations thought. *Genetic Psychology Monographs, 91,* 171–225.

Nelson, K. E. (1977). Facilitating children's syntax acquisition. *Developmental Psychology, 13,* 101–107.

Nelson, K. E. & Ross, G. (1980). The generalities and specifics of long-term memory in infants and young children. In M. Perlmutter (Guest Ed.), *New directions for child development* (No. 10). San Francisco: Jossey-Bass.

Nesselroade, J. R. & Baltes, P. B. (1974). Adolescent personality development and historical change: 1970–1972. *Monographs of the Society for Research in Child Development, 39* (1, Serial no. 154).

Newport, D. L., Gleitman, H., & Gleitman, L. R. (1977). Mother, I'd rather do it myself: Some effects and noneffects of maternal speech style. In C. Snow & C. A. Ferguson (Eds.), *Talking to children: Language input and acquisition.* Cambridge, England: Cambridge University Press.

Newport, E. L. (1977). Motherese: The speech of mothers to young children. In N. J. Castellan, D. Pisoni, & G. Potts (Eds.), *Cognitive theory* (Vol. 2). Hillsdale, NJ: Erlbaum.

Newsom, J. & Newsom, E. (1970). *Four years old in an urban community.* Harmondsworth, England: Pelican Books.

Newsom, J. & Newsom, E. (1978). *Seven years old in the home environment.* Harmondsworth, England: Pelican Books.

Newsweek. (1985, July 15). *Playing both mother and father.* pp. 42–43.

Nichols, P. L. (1984). Familial mental retardation. *Behavior Genetics, 14,* 161–170.

Nichols, R. C. (1978). Heredity and Environment: Major findings from twin studies of ability, personality and interests. *Homo, 29,* 158–173.

Noelting, G. (1980). The development of proportional reasoning and the ratio concept: Part I-Differentiation of stages. *Educational Studies in Mathematics, 11,* 217–253.

Nottebohm, F. (1969). The "critical period" for song learning. *Ibis, 111,* 386–387.

Ochs, E. (1982). Talking to children in western Samoa. *Language in Society, 11,* 77–104.

Odom, R. D., Astor, E. C., & Cunningham, J. (1975). Effects of perceptual salience on the matrix task performance of four- and six-year-old children. *Child Development, 46,* 758–762.

Ohno, S. (1979). Major sex-determining genes. *Monograph of Endocrinology, 11,* 1–140.

Oller, D. K. (1980). The emergence of the sounds of speech in infancy. In G. H. Yeni-Komshian, J. F. Kavanagh, & C. A. Ferguson, *Child Phonology,* Vol. 1. New York: Academic Press.

Olweus, D. (1979). Stability of aggressive reaction pattern in males: A review. *Psychological Bulletin, 86* (4), 852–875.

Olweus, D. (1980). Familial and temperamental determinants of aggressive behavior in adolescent boys: A causal analysis. *Developmental Psychology, 16,* 644–666.

Osherson, D. & Markman, E. (1975). Language and the ability to evaluate contradictions and tautologies. *Cognition, 3,* 213–226.

Oster, H. (1975). *Color perception in ten-week-old infants.* Paper presented at the meeting of the Society for Research in Child Development, Denver.

Oster, H. (1981). "Recognition" of emotional expression in infancy? In M. E. Lamb & L. R. Sherrod (Eds.), *Infant social cognition: Empirical and theoretical considerations.* Hillsdale, NJ: Lawrence Erlbaum.

O'Sullivan, C., Fouts, R. S., Hannum, M. E., & Schneider, K. (1982). Chimpanzee conversations: Language, cognition, and theory. In S. A. Kuczaj, II, *Language development* (Vol. 2). Hillsdale, N.J.: Lawrence Erlbaum Associates.

Owens, W. A. (1966). Age and mental abilities: A second adult follow-up. *Journal of Educational Psychology, 57,* 311–325.

Oyama, S. (1979). The concept of the sensitive period in developmental studies. *Merrill-Palmer Quarterly, 25,* 83–103.

Palermo, D. S. (1978). *Psychology of language.* Glenview, Ill.: Scott, Foresman, and Co.

Panksepp, J., Siviy, S. M. & Normansell, L. A. (1985). Brain opioids and social emotions. In M. Reite & T. Field (Eds.), *The psychobiology of attachment and separation.* Orlando, FL: Academic Press.

Papoušek, H. & Papoušek, M. (1974). Mirror image and self recognition in young human infants: I. A new method of experimental analysis. *Developmental Psychobiology, 1*(2), 149–157.

Parke, R. D. (1977). Punishment in children: Effects, side effects and alternative control strategies. In H. L. Hom and P. A. Robinson (Eds.), *Psychological processes in early education.* New York: Academic Press.

Parke, R. D. & Slaby, R. G. (1983). The development of aggression. In E. M. Hetherington (Vol. ed.) and P. H. Mussen (General Ed.), *Handbook of child psychology: Socialization, personality, and social development* (Vol. 4). New York: Wiley.

Parker, S. T. (1977). Piagetian sensorimotor series in an infant macaque: A model for comparing unstereotyped behavior and intelligence in human and nonhuman primates. In S. Chavalier-Skolnikoff & F. E. Poirier (Eds.), *Primate bio-social development: Biological, social, and ecological determinants.* New York: Garland.

Parten, M. B. (1932). Social play among pre-school children. *Journal of Abnormal and Social Psychology, 27,* 243–269.

Pascual-Leone, J. (1970). A mathematical model for the transition rule in Piaget's developmental stages. *Acta Psychologica, 32,* 301–345.

Passingham, R. E. (1982). *The human primate.* Oxford: W. H. Freeman.

Passow, A. H. (1981). The nature of giftedness and talent. *Gifted Child Quarterly, 24,* 5–10.

Patel, A. J. (1983). Undernutrition and brain development. *Trends in NeuroScience, 58,* 151–154.

Patterson, C. J. (1984). Aggression, altruism, and self-regulation. In M. H. Bornstein & M. E. Lamb, *Developmental psychology: An advanced textbook.* Hillsdale, NJ: Lawrence Erlbaum Associates.

Patterson, F. (1978a). Conversations with a gorilla. *National Geographic, 154*(4), 438–465.

Patterson, F. (1978b). The gestures of a gorilla: Language acquisition in another pongid. *Brain and Language, 5,* 72–97.

Patterson, G. R. (1980). Mothers: The unacknowledged victims. *Monographs of the Society for Research in Child Development, 45* (5), Whole no. 186.

Patterson, G. R. (1982). *A social learning approach, Vol. 3: Coercive family process.* Eugene, OR: Castalia Publishing Co.

Peeples, D. R. & Teller, D. Y. (1975). Color vision and brightness discrimination in two-month-old human infants. *Science, 189,* 1102–1103.

Peeples, D. Y. & Teller, D. Y. (1978). White-adapted photopic spectral sensitivity in human infants. *Vision Research, 18,* 49–53.

Pelligrini, A. D. (1984). The effects of exploration and play on young children's associative fluency: A review and extension of training studies. In T. D. Yawkey & A. D. Pelligrini (Eds.), *Child's play: Developmental and applied.* Hillsdale, NJ: Lawrence Erlbaum.

Pellegrini, D. S. (1985). Social cognition and competence in middle childhood. *Child Development, 56,* 253–264.

Penrose, L. S. (1963). *The biology of mental defect.* London: Sidgwick and Jackson.

Perret, E. (1974). The left frontal lobe of man and the suppression of habitual responses in verbal categorical behavior. *Neuropsychologica, 12,* 323–330.

Peskin, H. (1967). Pubertal onset and ego functioning: A psychoanalytic approach. *Journal of Abnormal Psychology, 72,* 1–15.

Petersen, A. C. (1980). Biopsychosocial processes in the development of sex-related differences. In J. E. Parsons (Ed.), *The psychobiology of sex differences and sex roles.* Washington, DC: Hemisphere Publishing Corp.

Petterson, G. & Bonnier, G. (1937). Inherited sex mosaic in man. *Heriditas, 23,* 49–69.

Pettersen, L., Yonas, A., & Fisch, R. O. (1980). The development of blinking in response to impending collision in preterm, full-term, and postterm infants. *Infant Behavior and Development, 3,* 155–165.

Pfeiffer, C. A. (1936). Sexual differences of the hypophyses and their determination by the gonads. *American Journal of Anatomy, 58,* 195–226.

Piaget, J. (1929). *The child's conception of the world.* New York: Harcourt, Brace, & World, Inc.

Piaget, J. (1936/1954). *La construction du réel chez l'enfant.* Neuchâtel: Delachaux & Niestlé, 1936. *The construction of reality in the child.* New York: Basic Books, 1954

Piaget, J. (1923/1955). *Language and thought of the child.* Cleveland: The World Publishing Co.

Piaget, J. (1957). *Logic and psychology.* New York: Basic Books.

Piaget, J. (1946/1962). *La formation du symbole chez l'enfant.* Neuchâtel: Delachaux & Niestlé, 1946. *Play, dreams, and imitation in childhood.* New York, Norton, 1962.

Piaget, J. (1936/1963). *La naissance de l'intelligence chez l'enfant.* Neuchâtel: Delachaux & Niestlé, 1936. *The origins of intelligence in the child.* New York: Norton, 1963.

Piaget, J. (1932/1965). Le jugement moral chez l'enfant. Paris: Librairic F. Alcan, 1932. *Moral judgment of the child.* New York: Free Press, 1965.

Piaget, J. (1964/1968). *Six études de psychologie.* Geneva: Edition Gonthier, 1964. *Six psychological studies.* New York: Vintage Books, 1968.

Piaget, J. (1946/1969). *Le développement de la notion de temps chez l'enfant.* Paris: Presses Universitaire de France, 1946. Translated as *The child's conception of time.* London: Routledge & Kegan Paul, 1969.

Piaget, J. (1969). Genetic epistemology. *Columbia Forum, 12 (3),* 4–11.

Piaget, J. (1968/1970). *Le structuralisme.* Paris: Presses Universitaires de France, 1968. *Structuralism.* New York: Basic Books, 1970.

Piaget, J. (1970). *Genetic epistemology.* New York: Columbia University Press.

Piaget, J. (1972). Intellectual evolution from adolescence to adulthood. *Human Development, 1972, 15,* 1–21.

Piaget, J. & Inhelder, B. (1948/1956). *La représentation d'espace chez l'enfant.* Paris: Presses Universitaires de France, 1948. *The child's conception of space.* London: Routledge & Kegan Paul, 1956.

Piaget, J. & Inhelder, B. (1951/1975). *La genèse de l'idée de hasard chez l'enfant.* Paris: Presses Universitaires de France, 1951. *The origin of the idea of chance in children.* New York: Norton, 1975.

Piaget, J. & Inhelder, B. (1973). *Memory and intelligence.* New York: Basic Books, 1973.

Piaget, J., Inhelder, B., & Szeminska, A. (1948/1960).

The child's conception of geometry. New York: Basic Books, 1960.

Piaget, J. & Szeminska, A. (1941/1965). *La genèse du nombre chez l'enfant*. Neuchâtel: Delachaux & Niestlé, 1941. *The child's conception of number*. New York: Norton, 1965.

Piers, M. W. (1978). *Infanticide: Past and present*. New York: Norton.

Pirchio, M., Spinelli, D., Fiorentini, A., & Maffei, L. (1978). Infant contrast sensitivity evaluated by evoked potentials. *Brain Research, 141*, 179–184.

Pirsig, R. M. (1975). *Zen and the art of motorcycle maintenance*. New York: Bantam Books.

Plomin, R. (1981). Ethological Behavioral Genetics and Development. In K. Immelmann, G. W. Barlow, L. Petrinovich & M. Main (Eds). *Behavioral development*. London: Cambridge University Press.

Plomin, R. (1983). Developmental behavioral genetics. *Child Development, 54*, 253–259.

Plomin, R. (1983). Childhood temperament. In B. B. Lahey & A. E. Kazdin, *Advances in clinical child psychology* (Vol. 6). New York: Plenum.

Plomin, R., DeFries, J. C. & Loehlin, J. C. (1977). Genotype-environment interaction and correlation in the analysis of human behavior. *Psychological bulletin, 84*, 309–322.

Plomin, R. DeFries, J. C., & McClearn, G. E. (1980). *Behavioral genetics: A primer*. San Francisco: W. H. Freeman & Co.

Plomin, R. & Rowe, D. (1977). A twin-study of temperament in young children. *Journal of Psychology, 97*, 107–113.

Popper, K. R. (1968). *Conjectures and refutations*. New York: Harper & Row.

Prader, A., Tanner, J. M., & Von Harnack, G. A. (1963). Catch-up growth following illness or starvation. *Journal of Pediatrics, 62*, 646–659.

Prather, E. M., Hedrick, D. L. & Kern, C. A. (1975). Articulation development in children aged two to four years. *Journal of Speech and Hearing Disorders, 40*, 179–191.

Premack, D. (1976). *Intelligence in ape and man*. Hillsdale, NJ: Lawrence Erlbaum Associates.

Premack, A. J. & Premack, D. (1972). Teaching language to an ape. *Scientific American, 227*, 92–99.

Pulos, S. & Linn, M. C. (1981). Generality of the controlling variables scheme in early adolescence, 1(1), 26–37.

Purves, D. & Lichtman, J. W. (1985). *Principles of neural development*. Sunderland, MA: Sinauer Associates, Inc.

Quine, W. V. O. (1973). *The roots of reference*. La-Salle, IL: Open Court.

Radke-Yarrow, M. & Zahn-Waxler, C. (1984). Roots, motives, and patterns in children's prosocial behavior. In E. Staub, D. Bar-Tel, J. Karylowski & J. Reykowski (Eds.), *Developmental and maintenance of prosocial behavior: International perspectives or positive morality*. New York: Plenum.

Radke-Yarrow, M. Zahn-Waxler, C. & Chapman, M. (1983). Children's prosocial dispositions and behavior. In E. M. Hetherington (Vol. ed.) and P. H. Mussen (General Ed.), *Handbook of child psychology: Socialization, personality, and social development* (Vol. 4.). New York: Wiley.

Rakic, P. (1985). Limits of neurogenesis in primates. *Science, 227*, 1054–1055.

Rakic, P. & Riley, K. P. (1983). Overproduction and elimination of retinal axons in the fetal rhesus monkey. *Science, 219*, 1441–1444.

Ramey, C. T., Bryant, D. M., & Suarez, T. M. (1985). Preschool compensatory education and the modifiability of intelligence: A critical review. In D. K. Detterman (Ed.), *Current topics in human intelligence. Vol. 1: Research methodology*. Norwood, NJ: Ablex Publishing Corp.

Ramey, C. T. & Campbell, F. A. (1984). Preventive education for high-risk children: Cognitive consequences of the Carolina Abecedarian Project. *American Journal of Mental Deficiency, 88* (5), 515–523.

Ramey, C. T. & Haskins, R. (1981). The modification of intelligence through early experience. *Intelligence, 5*, 43–57.

Ramey, C. T., MacPhee, D., & Yeates, K. O. (1982). Preventing developmental retardation: A general systems model. In L. Bond & J. Joffe (Eds.), *Facilitating infant and early childhood development*. Hanover, NH: University Press of New England.

Ramey, C. T., Yeates, K. O., & Short, E. J. (1984). The

plasticity of intellectual development: Insights from preventive intervention. *Child Development, 55,* 1913–1925.

Rampling, D. (1980). Abnormal mothering in the genesis of anorexia nervosa. *The Journal of Nervous and Mental Disease, 168,* 501–504.

Ramsay, D. S. (1980a). Onset of unimanual handedness in infants. *Infant behavior and Development, 3,* 377–385.

Ramsay, D. S. (1980b). Beginnings of bimanual handedness and speech in infants. *Infant Behavior and Development, 3,* 67–77.

Rank, O. (1929). *The trauma of birth.* New York: Harcourt, Brace.

Rasch, E., Swift, H., Riesen, A. H., & Chow, K. L. (1961). Altered structures and composition of retinal cells in dark-reared mammals. *Experimental Cell Research, 25,* 348–363.

Rathbun, C., McLaughlin, H., Bennett, O., & Garland, J. A. (1965). Later adjustment of children following radical separation from family and culture. *American Journal of Orthopsychiatry, 35,* 604–609.

Rathbun, C., Di Virgilio, L. & Waldfogel, S. (1958). The restitution process in children following radical separation from family and culture. *American Journal of Orthopsychiatry, 28,* 408–15.

Ratner, H. H. (1980). The role of social context in memory development. In M. Perlmutter (Guest Ed.), *New directions for child development,* (No. 10). San Francisco: Jossey-Bass.

Raup, D. M. (1962). Computer as aid in describing form in gastropod shells. *Science, 138,* 150–152.

Razran, G. (1971). *Mind in evolution.* New York: Houghton Mifflin.

Reaney, M. J. (1914). The psychology of the Boy Scout movement. *Pedagogical Seminary, 21,* 407–411.

Record, R. G., McKeown, T., & Edwards, J. P. (1970). An investigation of the difference in measured intelligence between twins and single births. *Annals of Human Genetics, 34,* 11–20.

Reese, H. W. & Lipsitt, L. P. (1970). *Experimental child psychology.* New York: Academic Press.

Reinisch, J. M. (1981). Prenatal exposure to synthetic progestins increases potential for aggression in humans. *Science, 211,* 1171–1173.

Rensberger, B. (1981). Facing the past. *Science 81, 2,* 51.

Ressler, R. H. (1962). Parental handling in two strains of mice reared by foster parents. *Science, 137,* 129–130.

Ressler, R. H. (1963). Genotype-correlated parental influences in two strains of mice. *Journal of Comparative and Physiological Psychology, 56,* 882–886.

Ressler, R. H. (1966). Inherited environmental influences on the operant behavior of mice. *Journal of Comparative and Physiological Psychology, 61,* 264–267.

Rest, J. R. (1983). Morality. In J. H. Flavell & E. M. Markman (Vol. Eds.), and P. H. Mussen (General Ed.). *Handbook of child psychology: Cognitive development* (Vol. 3). New York: Wiley.

Restak, R. M. (1984). *The brain.* Toronto: Bantam Books.

Rheingold, H. (1982). Little children's participation in the work of adults, a nascent prosocial behavior. *Child Development, 53,* 114–125.

Riesen, A. H. (1950). Arrested vision. *Scientific American, 183,* 16–19.

Rimland, B. (1978). Inside the mind of the autistic savant. *Psychology Today, 12*(3), 68–80.

Ristau, C. A. & Robbins, D. (1979). A threat to man's uniqueness? Language and communication in the chimpanzee. *Journal of Psycholinguistic Research, 8,* 267–300.

Robbins, L. C. (1963). The accuracy of parental recall of aspects of child development and of child rearing practices. *Journal of Abnormal and Social Psychology, 66,* 261–270.

Roberge, J. J. (1976). Developmental analyses of two formal operational structures: Combinational thinking and conditional reasoning. *Developmental Psychology, 12,* 563–564.

Roberge, J. J. & Flexler, B. K. (1979). Proportional reasoning in adolescence. *Journal of Genetic Psychology, 100,* 85–91.

Roberge, J. J. & Flexler, B. K. (1980). Control of variables and propositional reasoning in early adolescence. *Journal of General Psychology, 103,* 3–12.

Roberts, J. A. F. (1952). The genetics of mental deficiency. *Eugenics Review, 44,* 71–83.

Robinson, N. M. (1978). Mild mental retardation:

Does it exist in the People's Republic of China? *Mental Retardation, 16,* 295–299.

Roffwarg, H. P., Munzio, J. N. & Dement, W. C. (1966). Ontogenetic development of the human sleep-dream cycle. *Science, 152,* 604–619.

Rogers, C. (1978). The child's perception of other people. In H. McGurk (Ed.), *Issues in childhood social development.* London: Methuen.

Roper, R. & Hinde, R. A. (1978). Social behavior in a play group: Consistency and complexity. *Child Development, 49,* 570–579.

Rose, R. J., Harris, E. L., Christian, J. C., & Nance, W. E. (1979). Genetic variance in nonverbal intelligence: Data from the kinships of identical twins. *Science, 205,* 1153–1154.

Rose, S. A. & Blank, M. (1974). The potency of context in children's cognition: An illustration through conservation. *Child Development, 45,* 499–502.

Rosenblatt, J. S. & Lehrman, D. S. (1963). Maternal behavior of the laboratory rat. In H. L. Rheingold (Ed.), *Maternal behavior in mammals.* New York: Wiley.

Rosenblatt, J. S. & Siegel, H. I. (1981). Factors governing the onset and maintenance of maternal behavior among nonprimate mammals: The role of hormonal and nonhormonal factors. In D. J. Gubernick & P. H. Klopfer (Eds.), *Parental care in mammals.* New York: Plenum.

Rosenblith, J. F. & Allinsmith, W. (1966). *The causes of behavior II: Readings in child development and educational psychology* (2nd ed.). Boston: Allyn and Bacon, Inc.

Rosenblum, L. A. & Kaufman, I. C. (1968). Variations in infant development and response to maternal loss in monkeys. *American Journal of Orthopsychiatry, 38,* 418–426.

Rosenthal, D. (1963). *The Genain quadruplets.* New York: Basic Books.

Rosenthal, D. (1970). *Genetic theory and abnormal behavior.* New York: McGraw-Hill.

Rosenzweig, M. R. (1984). Experience, memory, and the brain. *American Psychologist, 39*(4), 365–376.

Rosenzweig, M. R. & Bennett, E. L. (1978). Experiential influences on brain anatomy and brain chemistry. In G. Gottlieb (Ed.), *Early influences: Studies on the development of behavior and the*

nervous system, Vol. 4. New York: Academic Press.

Rosenzweig, M. R., Krech, D., Bennett, E. L., & Diamond, M. C. (1962). Effects of environmental complexity and training on brain chemistry and anatomy: A replication and extension. *Journal of Comparative and Physiological Psychology, 55,* 429–437.

Ross, H. S. & Goldman, B. M. (1976). Establishing new social relations in infancy. In T. Alloway, L. Krames, & P. Pliner (Eds.), *Advances in communication and affect* (Vol. 4). New York: Plenum Press.

Rothbart, M. K. (1981). Measurement of temperament in infancy. *Child Development, 52,* 569–578.

Rovee-Collier, C. K. (1984). The ontogeny of learning and memory in human infancy. In R. Kail & N. E. Spear (Eds.), *Comparative perspectives on the development of memory.* Hillsdale, NJ: Lawrence Erlbaum.

Rovee-Collier, C. K., Sullivan, M. W., Enright, M., Lucas, D., & Fagen, J. W. (1980). Reactivation of infant memory. *Science, 208,* 1159–1161.

Rowe, D. C. & Plomin, R. (1981). The importance of nonshared (E1) environmental influences in behavioral development. *Developmental Psychology, 17,* 517–531.

Rubenstein, J. L. & Howes, C. (1976). The effects of peers on toddler interaction with mothers and toys. *Child Development, 47,* 597–605.

Rubin, J. Z., Provenzano, F. J., & Luria, Z. (1974). The eye of the beholder: Parents' views on sex of newborns. *American Journal of Orthopsychiatry, 44,* 512–519.

Rubin, K. H., Fein G. G., & Vandenberg, B. (1983). Play. In E. M. Hetherington (Vol. ed.) and P. H. Mussen (General Ed.), *Handbook of child psychology: Socialization, personality, and social development* (Vol. 4). New York: Wiley.

Rubin, K. H., Maioni, T. L., & Hornung, M. (1976). Free play behaviors in middle-and lower-class preschoolers: Parten and Piaget revisited. *Child Development, 47,* 414–419.

Rubin, R. T., Reinisch, J. M., & Haskett, R. F. (1981). Postnatal gonadal steroid effects on human behavior. *Science, 211,* 1318–1324.

Ruble, D. N. (1983). The development of social-comparison processes and their role in achievement-related self-socialization. In E. T. Higgins, D. N. Ruble, & W. W. Hartup (Eds.), *Social cognition and social development*. Cambridge, MA: Cambridge University Press.

Ruble, D. N. (1984). Sex-role development. In M. H. Bornstein & M. E. Lamb (Eds.), *Developmental psychology: An advanced textbook*. Hillsdale, NJ: Lawrence Erlbaum Associates.

Ruff, H. A. (1980). The development of perception and recognition of objects. *Child Development, 51,* 981–992.

Ruff, H. A. & Kohler, C. J. (1978). Tactual-visual transfer in six-month-old infants. *Infant Behavior and Development, 1,* 259–264.

Rumbaugh, D. M. (Ed.) 1977. *Language learning by a chimpanzee: The Lana project*. New York: Academic Press.

Rutter, M. (1972). Parent-child separation: Effects on the children. *Journal of Child Psychiatry, 6,* 71–83.

Rutter, M. (1979). Maternal deprivation, 1972–1978: New findings, new concepts, new approaches. *Child Development, 50,* 283–305. *Applied Psycholinguistics, 2,* 33–54.

Sachs, J., Bard, B., & Johnson, M. L. (1981). Language learning with restricted input: Case studies of two hearing children of deaf parents. *Applied Psycholinguistics, 2,* 33–54.

Sackett, G. P. (1966). Monkeys reared in isolation with pictures as visual input: Evidence for an innate releasing mechanism. *Science, 154,* 1468–1473.

Saltz, E., Dixon, D. & Johnson, J. (1977). Training disadvantaged preschoolers on various fantasy activities: Effects on cognitive functioning and impulse control. *Child Development, 48,* 367–380.

Saltz, E. & Brodie, J. (1982). Pretend play training in childhood: A review and critique. In D. J. Pepler & K. H. Rubin (Eds.), *The play of children: Current theory and research*. Basel: Karger.

Salzen, E. A. & Meyer, C. C. (1968). Reversibility of imprinting. *Journal of Comparative and Physiological Psychology, 66,* 269–275.

Samelson, F. (1980). J. B. Watson's Little Albert, Cyril Burt's twins, and the need for a critical science. *American Psychologist, 35,* 619–625.

Sander, L. W. (1969). The longitudinal course of early mother-child interaction: Cross-case comparison in a sample of mother-child pairs. In B. M. Foss (Ed.), *Determinants of infant behavior* (Vol. 1). New York: Wiley.

Sarnat, H. B. (1978). Olfactory reflexes in the newborn infant. *The Journal of Pediatrics, 92(4),* 624–626.

Sattler, J. M. (1982). *Assessment of children's intelligence and special abilities* (2nd ed.). Boston: Allyn & Bacon, Inc.

Savage-Rumbaugh, E. S., Rumbaugh, D. M., Smith, S. T., & Lawson, J. (1980). Reference: The linguistic essential. *Science, 210,* 922–924.

Savic, S. (1980). *How twins learn to talk: A study of the speech development of twins from 1 to 3.* London: Academic Press.

Scammon, R. E. (1930). The measurement of the body in childhood. In J. A. Harris, C. M. Jackson, D. G. Paterson, & R. E. Scammon. *The measurement of man*. Minneapolis: University of Minnesota.

Scammon, R. E. (1942). Developmental anatomy, reprint of section I. In H. Morris (Ed.), *Morris' human anatomy* (10th ed.). New York: The Blakiston Company.

Scardamalia, M. (1977). Information processing capacity and the problem of horizontal decalage: A demonstration using combinational reasoning tasks. *Child Development, 48,* 28–37.

Scarr, S. (1981). Genetics and the Development of Intelligence. In S. Scarr, *Race, social class, and individual differences in I. Q.* Hillsdale, N. J.: Lawrence Erlbaum Associates.

Scarr, S. (1985). Constructing psychology: Making facts and fables for our times. *American Psychologist, 40,* 499–512.

Scarr, S. & Kidd, K. K. (1983). Developmental behavior genetics. In P. H. Mussen (Ed.), *Handbook of child psychology,* Vol. 2 (4th ed.). New York: John Wiley & Sons.

Scarr, S. & McCartney, K. (1983). How people make their own environments: A theory of genotype—>environment effects. *Child Development, 54,* 424–435.

Scarr, S., Webber, P. L., Weinberg, R. A., & Wittig, M.

A. (1981). Personality resemblance among adolescents and their parents in biologically related and adoptive families. *Journal of Personality and Social Psychology, 40,* 885–898.

Scarr, S. & Weinberg, R. A. (1976). IQ test performance of black children adopted by white families. *American Psychologist, 31,* 726–739.

Scarr, S. & Weinberg, R. A. (1977). Intellectual similarities within families of both adopted and biological children. *Intelligence, 1,* 170–191.

Scarr, S. & Weinberg, R. A. (1978). The influence of "family background" on intellectual attainment. *American Sociological Review, 43,* 674–692.

Scarr, S. & Weinberg, R. A. (1983). The Minnesota adoption studies: Genetic differences and malleability. *Child Development, 54,* 260–267.

Scarr, S. & Yee, D. (1980). Heritability and educational policy: Genetic and environmental effects on IQ, aptitude, and achievement. *Educational Psychologist, 15,* 1–22.

Schacher, S. (1981). Determination and differentiation in the development of the nervous system. In E. R. Kandel & J. H. Schwartz (Eds.), *Principles of neural science.* New York: Elsevier North Holland, Inc.

Schaeffer, J. P. (Ed.). (1942). *Morris anatomy.* Philadelphia: W. B. Saunders.

Schade, J. P. & van Groenigen, W. B. (1961). Structural organization of the human cerebral cortex: Maturation of the middle frontal gyrus. *Acta Anatomica, 47,* 74–111.

Schaffer, H. R. & Emerson, P. (1964). The development of social attachments in infancy. *Monographs of the Society for Research in Child Development, 29* (3, Serial No. 94).

Schaie, K. W. (1965). A general model for the study of developmental problems. *Psychological Bulletin, 64,* 92–107.

Schaie, K. W. (1975). Age changes in adult intelligence. In D. S. Woodruff & J. E. Birren (Eds.), *Aging: Scientific perspectives and social issues.* New York: D. Von Nostrand Co.

Schaie, K. W. (1983). Age changes in adult intelligence (2nd edition.). In D. S. Woodruff and J. E. Birren (Eds.), *Aging: Scientific perspectives and social issues.* Belmont, CA: Wadsworth, Inc.

Schaie, K. W. (1983). The Seattle Longitudinal Study: A twenty-one year exploration of psychometric

intelligence in adulthood. In K. W. Shaie (Ed.), *Longitudinal studies of adult psychological development.* New York: Guillford.

Schaie, K. W. & Hertzog, C. (1983). Fourteen-year cohort-sequential analyses of adult intellectual development. *Developmental Psychology, 19,* 531–543.

Schaie, K. W. & Strother, C. R. (1968). A cross-sequential study of age changes in cognitive behavior. *Psychological Bulletin, 70,* 671–680.

Schallenberger, M. E. (1894). A study of children's rights, as seen by themselves. *Pedagogical Seminary, 3,* 87–96.

Schell, R. E. & Hall, E. (1983). *Development psychology today* (4th ed.). New York: Random House.

Schiefelbusch, R. L. & McCormick, L. P. (1981). Language and speech disorders. In J. M. Kauffman & D. P. Hallahan (Eds.), *Handbook of special education.* Englewood Cliffs, N.J.: Prentice-Hall.

Schieffelin, B. B. (1982). *How Kaluli children learn what to say, what to do, and how to feel: An ethnographic study of the development of communicative competence.* New York: Cambridge University Press.

Schieffelin, B. B. & Ochs, E. (1983). A cultural perspective on the transition from prelinguistic to linguistic communication. In R. M. Golinkoff (Ed.), *The transition from prelinguistic to linguistic communication.* Hillsdale, NJ: Lawrence Erlbaum.

Schiller, F. (1954). *On the aesthetic education of man.* New Haven, CT: Yale University Press.

Schlesinger, H. (1978). The acquistion of signed and spoken language. In L. Liben (Ed.), *Deaf children: Developmental perspectives.* New York: Academic Press.

Schmidt, J. (1909). *Das biogenetische Grundgesetz Ernst Haeckels und seine Gegner.* Frankfurt: Neuer Frankfurter Verlag.

Schneider-Rosen, K., Braunwald, K. G., Carlson, V., & Cicchetti, D. (1985). Current perspectives in attachment theory: Illustration from the study of maltreated infants. In I. Bretherton and E. Walters (Eds.), Growing points of attachment theory and research. *Monographs of the Society for Research in Child Development, 50,* (1–2, Serial No. 209).

Schneider-Rosen, K. & Cicchetti, D. (1984). The relationship between affect and cognition in maltreated infants: Quality of attachment and the development of visual self-recognition. *Child Development, 55,* 648–658.

Schneirla, T. C. & Rosenblatt, J. S. (1961). Animal research panel 1960. *American Journal of Orthopsychiatry, 31,* 223–253.

Schoenfeldt, L. F. (1968). The hereditary components of the Project TALENT two-day test battery. *Measurement and Evaluation in Guidance, 1,* 130–140.

Schuster, C. S. & Ashburn, S. S. (1980). *The process of human development: A holistic approach.* Boston: Little, Brown, and Co.

Schwartz, B. (1984). *Psychology of learning and behavior* (2nd ed.). New York: W. W. Norton & Co.

Schwartzman, H. B. (1984). Imaginative play: Deficit or difference. In T. D. Yawkey & A. D. Pelligrini (Eds.), *Child's play: Developmental and applied.* Hillsdale, NJ: Lawrence Erlbaum.

Scott, J. P. (1962). Critical periods in development. *Science, 138,* 949–958.

Scott, J. P. & Fuller, J. L. (1965). *Genetics and the social behavior of the dog.* Chicago: University of Chicago Press.

Scott, J. P., Stewart, J. M., & De Ghett, V. J. (1974). Critical periods in the organization of systems. *Developmental Psychobiology, 7(6),* 489–513.

Searle, J. R. (1969). *Speech acts: An essay in the philosophy of language.* London: Cambridge University Press.

Searle, J. R. (1975). Speech acts and recent linguistics. In D. Aaronson & R. Rieber (Eds.), *Developmental psycholinguistics and communication disorders.* New York: New York Academy of Sciences.

Sears, R. R. (1936). Experimental studies of projection: I. Attribution of traits. *Journal of Social Psychology, 7,* 151–63.

Sears, R. R. (1975). Your ancients revisited: A history of child development. In E. M. Hetherington (Ed.), *Review of child development research.* Chicago: The University of Chicago Press.

Sears, R. R. (1977). Sources of life satisfactions of the Terman gifted men. *American Psychologist, 32,* 119–128.

Sears, R. R., Whiting, J. W. M., Nowlis, V., & Sears,

P. S. (1953). Some child-rearing antecedents of aggression and dependency in young children. *Genetic Psychology Monographs, 47,* 135–234.

Sears, R. R., Maccoby, E. E., & Levin, H. (1957). *Patterns of child rearing.* Evanston, Illinois: Row, Peterson, & Company.

Seay, B., Hansen, E., & Harlow, H. F. (1962). Mother-infant separation in monkeys. *Journal of Child Psychology and Psychiatry, 3,* 123–132.

Seitz, V. (1984). Methodology, In M. H. Bornstein & M. E. Lamb (Eds.) *Developmental psychology: An advanced textbook.* Hillsdale, NJ: Lawrence Erlbaum Associates.

Seligman, M. E. P. (1971). Phobias and preparedness. *Behavior Therapy, 2,* 307–321.

Seligman, M. E. P. (1975). *Helplessness.* San Francisco: Freeman.

Seligman, M. E. P. & Hager, J. L. (1972). *Biological boundaries of learning.* New York: Appleton-Century Crofts.

Selman, R. L. (1971). Taking another's perspective: Role-taking development in early childhood. *Child Development, 42,* 1721–1734.

Selman, R. L. (1976). Social-cognitive understanding: A guide to educational and clinical practice. In T. Lickona (Ed.), *Theory, research, and social issues.* New York: Holt, Rinehart, Winston.

Selman, R. L. (1980). *The growth of interpersonal understanding.* New York: Academic Press.

Selman, R. L. & Byrne, D. F. (1974). A structural developmental analysis of levels of role taking in middle childhood. *Child Development, 45,* 803–806.

Senden, M. von (1960). *Space and sight.* Translated by P. Heath. London: Methuen & Co., Ltd.

Seyfarth, R. M., Cheney, D. L. & Marler, P. (1980). Monkey responses to three different alarm calls: Evidence of predator classification and semantic communication. *Science, 210,* 801–803.

Shaffer, D. R. (1985). *Developmental psychology: Theory, research, and applications.* Monterey, CA: Brooks/Cole.

Shantz, C. (1983). Social cognition. In J. H. Flavell and E. M. Markman (Vol. eds.), and P. H. Mussen (General ed.), *Handbook of child psychology: Cognitive development* (Vol. 3). New York: Wiley.

Shatz, M. & Gelman, R. (1973). The development of

communication skills: Modifications in the speech of young children as a function of the listener. *Monographs of the Society for Research in Child Development,* (38, Serial No. 152).

Sheingold, K. & Tenney, Y. J. (1982). Memory for a salient childhood event. In U. Neisser (Ed.), *Memory observed: Remembering in natural contexts.* San Francisco: W. H. Freeman, 1982.

Shepard, R. N. (1978). The mental image. *American Psychologist, 33,* 129.

Shirley, M. M. (1933). The first two years: A study of twenty-five babies and locomotor development. *Institute of Child Welfare monograph* (1, No. 6). Minneapolis: University of Minnesota Press.

Shore, E. R. (1984). The former transexual: A case history. *Archives of sexual behavior, 13,* 277–285.

Shriberg, L. D. (1980). Developmental phonological disorders. In T. J. Hixon, L. D. Shriberg, & J. H. Saxman (Eds.), *Introduction to communication disorders,* Englewood Cliffs, NJ: Prentice Hall.

Shultz, T. R. (1980). Development of the concept of intention. In W. A. Collins (Ed.), *Minnesota symposia on child psychology* (Vol. 13). Hillsdale, NJ: Lawrence Erlbaum Associates.

Siegel, A. & White, S. H. (1982). The child study movement: Early growth and development of the symbolized child. In H. W. Reese (Ed.), *Advances in child development and behavior,* Vol. 17. New York: Academic Press.

Siegel, L. S. & Hodkin, B. (1982). The garden path to the understanding of cognitive development: Has Piaget led us into the poison ivy? In S. Modgil and C. Modgil (Eds.), *Jean Piaget: Consensus and controversy.* New York: Praeger.

Siegler, R. S. (1976). Three aspects of cognitive development. *Cognitive Psychology, 8,* 481–520.

Siegler, R. S. (1978). The origins of scientific reasoning. In R. S. Siegler (Ed.), *Children's thinking: What develops.* Hillsdale, NJ: Lawrence Erlbaum.

Siegler, R. S. (1983a). Five generalizations about cognitive development. *American Psychologist, 38,* 263–277.

Siegler, R. S. (1983b). How knowledge influences learning. *American Scientist, 71,* 631–638.

Siegler, R. S. (1983c). Information processing approaches to development. In W. Kessen (Vol. ed.) and P. H. Mussen (General ed.), *Handbook of child psychology: History, theory, and methods* (Vol. 1). New York: Wiley.

Simonton, D. K. (1984). *Genius, creativity, and leadership.* Cambridge, MA: Harvard University Press.

Siqueland, E. R. & DeLucia, C. A. (1969). Visual reinforcement of nonnutritive sucking in human infants. *Science, 165,* 1144–1146.

Skeels, H. M. (1966). Adult status of children with contrasting early life experiences. *Monographs of the Society for Research in Child Development, 31*(3) (Serial No. 105).

Skinner, B. F. (1957). *Verbal behavior.* New York: Appleton-Century-Crofts.

Skodak, M. & Skeels, H. M. (1949). A final follow-up of one hundred adopted children. *Journal of Genetic Psychology, 75,* 85–125.

Slaby, R. G. & Frey, K. S. (1975). Development of gender constancy and selective attention to same-sex models. *Child Development, 46,* 849–856.

Slater, A., Morison, V., & Rose, D. (1982). Visual memory at birth. *British Journal of Psychology, 73,* 519–525.

Sloan, W. R. & Walsh, P. C. (1976). Familial persistent Müllerian duct syndrome. *The Journal of Urology, 115,* 459–461.

Slobin, D. (1966). The acquisition of Russian as a native language. In F. Smith & G. A. Miller (Eds.), *The genesis of language: A psycholinguistic approach.* Cambridge, MA: MIT Press.

Slobin, D. I. (1979). *Psycholinguistics,* (2nd ed.). Glenview, IL: Scott, Foresman, & Co.

Slobin, D. I. (1982). Universal and particular in the acquisition of language. In E. Wanner & L. R. Gleitman (Eds.), *Language acquisition: The state of the art.* Cambridge: Cambridge University Press.

Sluckin, W. (1965). *Imprinting and early learning.* Chicago: Aldine.

Sluckin, W., Herbert, M. & Sluckin, A. (1983). *Maternal bonding.* Oxford, England: Basil Blackwell Publisher Limited.

Smilansky, S. (1968). *The effects of sociodramatic play on disadvantaged preschool children.* New York: Wiley.

Smilansky, S. (1971). Can adults facilitate play in

children? Theoretical and practical considerations. In *Play: The child strives toward self realization*. Washington, DC: National Association for the Education of Young Children.

Smiley, S. S. & Brown, A. L. (1979). Conceptual preference for thematic and taxonomic relations: A nonmonotonic age trend from preschool to old age. *Journal of Experimental Child Psychology, 28,* 249–257.

Smith, C. & Lloyd, B. (1978). Maternal behavior and perceived sex of infant: Revisited. *Child Development, 49,* 1263–1266.

Smith, D. W. & Bierman, E. L. (1973). *The biologic ages of man*. Philadephia: W. B. Saunders.

Smith, J. D. (1985). *Minds made feeble*. Rockville, MD: Aspen Systems Corp.

Smith, L. B. (1983). Development of classification: The use of similarity and dimensional relations. *Journal of Experimental Child Psychology, 36,* 150–178.

Smith, M. (1978). Cognizing the behavior stream: The recognition of intentional action. *Child Development, 49,* 736–743.

Smith, M. E. (1926) An investigation of the development of the sentence and the extent of vocabulary in young children. *University of Iowa Studies in Child Welfare, 3*(5), 241–243.

Smith, P. K., Dalgleish, M. & Herzmark, G. (1981). A comparison of the effects of fantasy play tutoring and skills tutoring in nursery classes. *International Journal of Behavioral Development, 4,* 421–441.

Smith, P. K. (1982). Does play matter? Functional and evolutionary aspects of animal and human play. *The Behavioral and Brain Sciences, 5,* 139–184.

Smith, P. K. (Ed.) (1984). *Play in animals and humans*. Oxford, England: Basil Blackwell.

Smith, S. B. (1983). *The great mental calculators*. New York: Columbia University Press.

Snarey, J. R. (1985). Cross-cultural universality of social-moral development: A critical review of Kohlbergian research. *Psychological Bulletin, 97,* 202–232.

Snow, C. E. (1977). Mothers' speech research: From input to interaction. In C. E. Snow & C. A. Ferguson, (Eds.), *Talking to children: Language input and acquisition*. Cambridge: Cambridge University Press.

Soltz, E., Dixon, D. & Johnson, J. (1977). Training disadvantaged preschoolers on various fantasy activities: Effects on cognitive functioning and impulse control. *Child Development, 48,* 367–380.

Sorce, J. F., Emde, R. N., Campos, J., & Klinnert, M. D. (1985). Maternal emotional signaling: Its effect on the visual cliff behavior of 1-year-olds. *Developmental Psychology, 21,* 195–200.

Sorrells-Jones, J. (1983). *A comparison of the effects of Leboyer delivery and modern "routine" childbirth in a randomized sample*. Unpublished doctoral dissertation. University of Chicago.

Spear, N. E. (1984). Ecologically determined dispositions control the ontogeny of learning and memory. In R. Kail & N. E. Spear (Eds.), *Comparitive perspectives on the development of memory*. Hillsdale, NJ: Lawrence Erlbaum.

Spelke, E. (1976). Infants' intermodal perception of events. *Cognitive Psychology, 8,* 553–560.

Spelke, E. (1979). Perceiving bimodally specified events in infancy. *Developmental Psychology, 15,* 626–636.

Spelke, E. & Cortelyou, A. (1981). Perceptual aspects of social knowing: Looking and listening in infancy. In M. E. Lamb & L. R. Sherrod (Eds.), *Infant social cognition: Empirical and theoretical considerations*. Hillsdale, NJ: Lawrence Erlbaum Associates.

Spelke, E., Zelazo, P., Kagan, J., & Kotelchuck, M. (1973). Father interaction and separation protest. *Developmental Psychology, 9,* 83–90.

Spemann, H. (1938). *Embryonic development and induction*. Yale University Press, New Haven.

Spencer, H. (1862). *First principles*. London: Williams & Norgate.

Spitz, R. A. (1945). Hospitalism: An inquiry into the genesis of psychiatric conditions in early childhood. *Psychoanalytic Study of the Child, 1,* 53–74.

Spitz, R. A. & Wolf, K. M. (1946). The smiling response: A contribution to the ontogenesis of social relations. *Genetic Psychology Monographs, 34,* 57–125.

Springer, S. P. & Deutsch, G. (1981). *Left brain, right brain*. New York: W. H. Freeman.

Sprott, R. L. & Staats, J. (1975). Behavioral studies using genetically defined mice—a bibliography. *Behavior Genetics, 5,* 27–82.

Sprott, R. L. & Staats, J. (1978). Behavioral studies using genetically defined mice—a bibliography (July 1973–July 1976). *Behavior Genetics, 8,* 183–206.

Sprott, R. L. & Staats, J. (1979). Behavioral studies using genetically defined mice—a bibliography (July 1976–August 1978). *Behavior Genetics, 9,* 87–102.

Sprott, R. L. & Staats, J. (1981). Behavioral studies using genetically defined mice—a bibliography (August 1979–July 1980). *Behavioral Genetics, 11,* 73–83.

Sroufe, L. A. (1979). Socioemotional development. In J. D. Osofsky (Ed), *Handbook of infant development.* New York: John Wiley.

Stroufe, L. A. (1983). Infant-caregiver attachment and patterns of adaptation in preschool: The roots of maladaptation and competence. In M. Perlmutter (Ed.), *Minnesota symposium in child psychology* (Vol. 16). Hillsdale, NJ: Lawrence Erlbaum.

Sroufe, L. A. (1985). Attachment classification from the perspective of infant-caregiver relationships and infant termperament. *Child Development, 56,* 1–14.

Sroufe, L. A. & Waters, E. (1977). Attachment as an organizational construct. *Child Development, 48,* 1184–1194.

Staats, A. W. & Staats, C. K. (1963). *Complex human behavior.* New York: Holt.

Stafford, R. E. (1961). Sex differences in spatial visualization as evidence of sex-linked inheritance. *Perceptual Motor Skills, 13,* 300–308.

Stanley, S. M. (1981). The new evolutionary timetable. New York: Basic Books.

Steiner, J. E. (1979). Human facial expressions in response to taste and smell stimulation. In H. W. Reese & L. P. Lipsitt (Eds.), *Advances in child development and behavior* (Vol. 13). New York: Academic Press.

Stephan, C. W. & Langlois, J. H. (1984). Baby beautiful: Adult attributions of infant competence as a function of infant attractiveness. *Child Development, 55,* 576–585.

Sternberg, R. J. (1985). Human abilities: An information-processing approach. New York: W. H. Freeman.

Sternberg, R. J. & Nigro, G. (1980). Developmental patterns in the solution of verbal analogies. *Child Development, 51,* 27–38.

Sternberg, R. J. & Powell, J. (1983). The development of intelligence. In J. H. Flavell & E. M. Markman (Vol. eds.), and P. H. Mussen (General ed.), *Handbook of child psychology: Cognitive development* (Vol. 3). New York: Wiley.

Stevenson, H. W. (Ed.). (1966). Concept of development: A report of the conference commemorating the 40th anniversary of the Institute of Child Development, University of Minnesota. *Monographs of the Society for Research in Child Development, 31* (5), (Serial No. 107).

Stinson, F. S. (1973). Visual short-term memory in four-month infants. *Dissertation Abstracts International, 33,* 3998–3999B. (University Microfilms No. 73–2340).

Stokoe, W. C. (1960). Sign language structure: An outline of the visual communication of the deaf. *Studies in Linguistics, Occasional Paper 8.* Buffalo, NY, University of Buffalo.

Stokoe, W. C. (1972). *Semiotics and human sign languages.* The Hague: Mouton.

Stone, L. J. & Church, J. (1973). *Childhood and adolescence: A psychology of the growing person* (3rd ed.). New York: Random House.

Stott, D. H. (1983). Brain size and "intelligence". *British Journal of Developmental Psychology, 1,* 279–287.

Struhsaker, T. (1967). Auditory communication among vervet monkeys. In S. A. Altmann (Ed.), *Social communication among primates.* Chicago: University of Chicago Press.

Sugarman, S. (1984). The development of preverbal communication. In R. L. Schiefelbusch & J. Pickar (Eds.), *The acquisition of communicative competence.* Baltimore: University Park.

Sulloway, F. (1979). *Freud, biologist of the mind: Beyond the psychoanalytic legend.* New York: Basic Books.

Suomi, S. J. & Harlow, H. F. (1971/1976). Monkeys without play. In J. S. Bruner, A. Jolly, & K. Sylva (Eds.), *Play—Its role in development and evolution.* New York: Basic Books, 1976. Reprinted from *Natural History Magazine,* special supplement, Dec. 1971.

Suomi, S. J. & Harlow, H. F. (1972). Social rehabilitation of isolate-reared monkeys. *Developmental Psychology, 6,* 487–496.

Svanum, S., & Bringle, R. G. (1980). Evaluation of confluence model variables on IQ and achievement test scores in a sample of 6- to 11-year-old children. *Journal of Educational Psychology, 72,* 427–426.

Tanner, J. M. (1970) Physical growth. In P. H. Mussen (Ed.), *Carmichael's manual of child psychology,* Vol. 1. New York: John Wiley.

Tanner, J. M. (1978). *Foetus into man: Physical growth from conception to maturity.* Cambridge, MA: Harvard University Press.

Tanner, J. M., Taylor, G. R., & the editors of Life (1965). *Growth.* New York: Time.

Tanner, J. M. (1963). The regulation of human growth. *Child Development, 34,* 817–848.

Tanner, J. M. (1962) *Growth at Adolescence.* (2nd ed.). Oxford: Blackwell Scientific Publications. Philadelphia: Davis.

Tanner, J. M., Whitehouse, R. H., & Takaishi, M. (1966). Standards from birth to maturity for height, weight, height velocity, and weight velocity: British children. *Archives of Diseases in Childhood, 41,* 454–471; 613–635.

Taylor, G. R. (1979). *The natural history of the mind.* New York: E. P. Dutton.

Taylor, I. A. (1975) A retrospective view of creativity investigation. In I. A. Taylor & J. W. Getzels, *Perspectives in creativity.* Chicago: Aldine.

Taylor, J. (Ed.). (1958). *Selected writings of John Hughlings Jackson.* New York: Basic Books.

Temerlin, M. K. (1975). *Lucy: Growing up human.* Palo Alto, CA: Science and Behavior Books.

Terman, L. M. (1905). A study in precocity and prematuration. *The American Journal of Psychology, 16,* 145–183.

Terman, L. M. (1916). *The measurement of intelligence.* Boston: Houghton Mifflin Co.

Terman, L. M. (1925). *Genetic studies of genius: Mental and physical traits of a thousand gifted children* (Vol. 1). Stanford, CA: Stanford University Press.

Terman, L. M. (1954). The discovery and encouragement of exceptional talent. *American Psychologist, 9,* 221–230.

Terman, L. M. & Oden, M. H. (1959). *Genetic studies of genius, V: The gifted group at mid-life: Thirty-five years' follow-up of the superior child.* Stanford, CA: Stanford University Press.

Terrace, H. S. (1981). A report to an academy, 1980. In T. A. Sebeok & R. Rosenthal (Eds.), The clever Hans phenomenon: Communication with horses, whales, apes, and people. *Annals of the New York Academy of Science, 364,* 94–114.

Thelen, E. & Fisher, D. M. (1982). Newborn stepping: An explanation for a "disappearing" reflex. *Developmental Psychology, 18,* 760–775.

Thomas, A. & Chess, S. (1977). *Temperament and development.* New York: Bruner/Mazel.

Thomas, A., Chess, S., & Birch, H. G. (1968). *Temperament and behavior disorders in children.* New York: New York University Press.

Thomas. H. (1983). Familial correlational analyses, sex differences, and the X-linked gene hypothesis. *Psychological Bulletin, 93,* 427–440.

Thomas, M. H., Horton, R. W., Lippincott, E. C., & Drabman, R. S. (1977). Desensitization to portrayals of real-life aggression as a function of exposure to television violence. *Journal of Personality and Social Psychology, 35,* 450–458.

Thompson, D. W. (1917). *On growth and form,* Vol. II. Cambridge: Cambridge University Press. (Reprinted 1959.)

Thompson, R. & Hoffman, M. L. (1980). Empathy and the arousal of guilt in children. *Developmental Psychology, 15,* 155–156.

Thompson, R., Lamb, M., & Estes, D. (1982). Stability of infant-mother attachment and its relationship to changing life circumstances in an unselected middle-class sample. *Child Development, 53,* 144–148.

Thompson, R. F. (1975). *Introduction to physiological psychology.* New York: Harper & Row.

Thompson, S. K. (1975). Gender labels and early sex role development. *Child Development, 46,* 339–347.

Thompson, W. R. & Grusec, J. E. (1970) Studies of early experience. In P. H. Mussen (Ed.), *Carmichael's manual of child psychology,* Vol. I. New York: John Wiley.

Tieger, T. (1980). On the sociobiological basis of sex differences in aggression. *Child Development, 51,* 943–963.

Time (1982, Oct. 4). The seniors' slump may be over, p. 87.

Toran-Allerand, C. D. (1976). Sex steroids and the development of the newborn mouse hypothalamus and preoptic area *in vitro:* Implications for sexual differentiation. *Brain Research, 106,* 407–412.

Torrance, E. P. (1966). *Torrance tests of creative thinking.* Princeton, NJ: Personnel Press.

Trabasso, T. (1975). Representation, memory, and reasoning: How do we make transitive inferences? In A. D. Pick (Ed.), *Minnesota Symposium on Child Psychology,* Vol. 9. Minneapolis: University of Minnesota Press.

Trabasso, T., Isen, A. M., Dolecki, P., McLanahan, A., Riley, C., & Tucker, T. (1978). How do children solve class inclusion problems? In R. S. Siegler (Ed.), *Children's thinking: What develops?* Hillsdale, NJ: Lawrence Erlbaum.

Tracy, F. (1893). The language of children. *American Journal of Psychology, 6,* 107–138.

Trevarthen, C. (1974). Cerebral embryology and the split brain. In M. Kinsbourne & L. Smith (Eds.), *Hemisphere disconnection and cerebral function.* Springfield, IL: Charles C. Thomas.

Trivers, R. L. (1974). Parent-offspring conflict. *American Zoologist, 14*(1), 249–264.

Tryon, R. C. (1940). Genetic differences in maze-learning ability in rats. *Yearbook of the National Society for the Study of Education,* 39, 111–119.

Tryon, R. C. (1942). Individual differences. In F. A. Moss (Ed.), *Comparative psychology.* New York: Prentice-Hall.

Tulkin, S. R. & Konner, M. J. (1973). Alternative conceptions of intellectual functioning. *Human Development, 16,* 33–52.

Turnbull, C. M. (1972). *The mountain people.* New York: Simon & Schuster.

U.S. NCHS (1980). Advance report: Final mortality statistics, 1978. *Monthly Vital Statistics Report 29,* No. 6, supplement 2.

Uzgiris, I. C. & Hunt, J. McV. (1975). *Assessment in infancy.* Urbana, IL: University of Illinois Press.

Vaillant, G. E. (1977). *Adaptation to life.* Boston: Little, Brown.

Vale, J. R., Vale, C. A., & Harley, J. P. (1971). Interaction of genotype and population number with regard to aggressive behavior, social grooming, and adrenal and gonadal weight in male mice. *Communications in Behavioral Biology, 6,* 209–221.

Valetine, C. W. (1930). The innate bases of fear. *Journal of Genetic Psychology, 37,* 394–420.

Vandenberg, S. G. & Kuse, A. R. (1979). Spatial ability: A critical review of the sex-linked major-gene hypothesis. In M. A. Wittig & A. C. Petersen (Eds.), *Sex-linked differences in cognitive functioning.* New York: Academic Press.

Vasta, R. (1982). Child study: Looking toward the eighties. In R. Vasta (Ed.), *Strategies and techniques of child study.* New York: Academic Press.

Vaughn, B., Egeland, B., Sroufe, L. A., & Waters, E. (1979). Individual differences in infant-mother attachment at twelve and eighteen months: Stability and change in families under stress. *Child Development, 50,* 971–975.

Velten, H. V. (1943). The growth of phonemic and lexical patterns in infant language. *Language, 19,* 281–292.

Vuyk, R. (1981). *Overview and critique of Piaget's genetic epistemology 1965–1980,* Vols. 1 and 2. London: Academic Press.

Vygotsky, L. S. (1966/1976). Play and its role in the mental development of the child. Originally published in *Soviet Psychology, 12,* 1966, 62–76. Reprinted in J. S. Bruner, A. Jolly, and K. Sylva, (1976) *Play—Its role in development and evolution.* New York: Basic Books.

Waddington, C. H. (1957). *The strategy of genes.* London: Allen and Unwin.

Walk, R. D. (1981). *Perceptual development.* Monterey, CA: Brooks/Cole.

Walker, J. F., Gilbert J. H. V., Humphrey, K. & Tees, R. C. (1981). Developmental Aspects of Cross-Language Speech Perception. *Child Development, 52,* 349–355.

Walker, L. J. (1984). Sex differences in the development of moral reasoning: A critical review. *Child Development, 55,* 677–691.

Walker-Andrews, A. S. & Lennon, E. M. (1985). Auditory-visual perception of changing distance by human infants. *Child Development, 56,* 544–548.

Wallach, M. A., & Kogan, N. (1965). *Modes of thinking in young children: A study of the creativity-intelligence distinction.* New York: Holt, Rinehart, & Winston.

Walters, R. H., Leat, M., Mezei, H. (1963). Response inhibition and disinhibition through empathic learning. *Canadian Journal of Psychology, 17,* 235–243.

Warren, N. (1973). Malnutrition and mental development. *Psychological Bulletin, 80*(4), 324–328.

Wason, P. C. (1977). The theory of formal operations: A critique. In B. A. Geber (Ed.), *Piaget and knowing: Studies in genetic epistemology.* London: Routledge, Kegan Paul.

Waters, E. (1978). The reliability and stability of individual differences in infant-mother attachment. *Child Development, 49,* 483–494.

Waters, E., Wippman, J., & Sroufe, L. A. (1979). Attachment, positive affect and competence in the peer group: Two studies in construct validation. *Child Development, 50,* 821–829.

Watson, J. B. (1924/1930). *Behaviorism.* New York: Norton.

Watson, J. B. (1928). *Psychological care of infant and child.* New York: Norton.

Watson, J. B., & Rayner, R. (1920). Conditioned emotional reactions. *Journal of Experimental Psychology, 3,* 1–14.

Watson, J. S. (1985). Contigency perception in early social development. In T. M. Field & N. A. Fox (Eds.), *Social perceptions in infants.* Norwood, NJ: Ablex.

Watts, E. S. & Gavan, J. A. (1982). Postnatal growth of nonhuman primates: The problem of the adolescent spurt. *Human Biology, 54,* 53–70.

Wechsler, D. (1944). *The measurement of adult intelligence,* (3rd ed.). Baltimore: The Williams & Wilkins, Co.

Weisfeld, G. E. & Berger, J. M. (1983). Some features of human adolescence viewed in evolutionary perspective. *Human Development, 26,* 121–133.

Werker, J. F., Gilbert, J. H. V., Humphrey, K., & Tees, R. C. (1981). Developmental aspects of cross-language speech perception. *Child Development, 52,* 349–355.

Werner, H., & Kaplan, B. (1967). *Symbol formation.* New York: John Wiley.

Werner, J. S. & Perlmutter, M. (1979). Development of visual memory in infants. In H. W. Reese & L. P. Lipsitt (Eds.), *Advances in child development and behavior,* Vol. 14. New York: Academic Press.

Wertheimer, M. (1961). Psycho-motor coordination of auditory-visual space at birth. *Science, 134,* 1692.

West, M. J., King, A. P., & Eastzer, D. H. (1981). The cowbird: Reflections on development from an unlikely source. *American Scientist, 69,* 56–66.

Wheldall, K. & Poborca, B. (1980). Conservation without conversation? An alternative, non-verbal paradigm for assessing conservation of liquid quantity. *British Journal of Psychology, 71,* 117–134.

White, B. L. (1971a). An analysis of excellent early educational practices: Preliminary report. *Interchange: A Journal of Educational Studies, 2,* 71–88.

White, B. L. (1971b). *Human infants: Experience and psychological development.* Englewood Cliffs, N.J.: Prentice-Hall.

White, B. L., Castle, P., & Held, R. (1964). Observations on the development of visually directed reaching. *Child Development, 35,* 349–364.

White, B. L., & Held, R. (1966). Plasticity of sensorimotor development in the human infant. In J. F. Rosenblith & W. Allinsmith (Eds.). *The causes of behavior II.* Boston: Allyn and Bacon.

White, S. H. (1965). Evidence for a hierarchical arrangement of learning processes. In C. P. Lipsitt & C. C. Spiker (Eds.), *Advances in child development and behavior* (Vol. 2). New York: Academic Press.

Whitehurst, G. J. (1979). Meaning and semantics. In G. J. Whitehurst & B. J. Zimmerman, (Eds.), *The functions of language and cognition.* New York: Academic Press.

Whitehurst, G. J. (1982). Language development. In B. B. Wolman (Ed.), *Handbook of developmental psychology.* Englewood Cliffs, NJ: Prentice-Hall.

Whiting, B. B. & Whiting, J. W. M. (1975). *Children of six cultures: A psychocultural analysis.* Cambridge, MA: Harvard University Press.

Wickelgren, L. W. (1967). Convergence in the human newborn. *Journal of Experimental Child Psychology, 5* 74–85.

Wickelgren, L. W. (1969). The ocular response of human newborns to intermittent visual movement. *Journal of Experimental Child Psychology, 8,* 469–482.

Widdowson, E. M. (1951). Mental contentment and physical growth. *The Lancet, 260*(1), 1316–1318.

Wiesel, T. N., & Hubel, G. H. (1965). Comparison of the effects of unilateral and bilateral eye closure on cortical unit responses in kittens. *Journal of neurophysiology, 28,* 1029–1040.

Wiggam, A. E. (1923) *The new decalogue of science.* Indianapolis: Bobbs, Merrill.

Willems, E. P. & Alexander, J. L. (1982). The naturalistic perspective in research. In B. B. Wolman (Ed.), *Handbook of developmental psychology,* Englewood Cliffs, NJ: Prentice-Hall.

Wilson, E. O. (1975). *Sociobiology.* Cambridge, MA: Belknap Press.

Wilson, J. D., George, F. W., & Griffin, J. E. (1981). The hormonal control of sexual development. *Science, 211,* 1278–1284.

Wilson, R. S. (1983). The Louisville twin study: Developmental synchronies in behavior. *Child Development, 54,* 298–316.

Wiltse, S. E. (1894). A preliminary sketch of the history of child study in America. *Pedagogical Seminary, 3,* 189–212.

Winchester, A. M. (1977). *Genetics: A survey of the principles of heredity* (5th ed.). Boston: Houghton Mifflin.

Winick, M. (1980). Nutrition and brain development. *Natural History, 89*(12), 6–13.

Wishart, J. G. & Bower, T. G. R. (1984). Spatial relations and the object concept: A normative study. In L. P. Lipsitt & C. Rovee-Collier, *Advances in infancy research,* Vol. 3. Norwood, NJ: Ablex.

Wolf, T. H. (1973). *Alfred Binet.* Chicago: University of Chicago Press.

Wolff, P. (1963). Observations on the early development of smiling. In B. Foss (Ed.), *Determinants of infant behavior* (Vol. 2). London: Methuen.

Wolman, B. B. (Ed.). (1982). *Handbook of developmental psychology.* Englewood Cliffs, NJ: Prentice-Hall.

Woods, B. T. (1983). Is the left hemisphere specialized for language at birth? *Trends in Neurosciences, 6*(4), 115–117.

Yarrow, M., Campbell, J., & Burton, R. (1970) Recollections of childhood: A study of the retrospective method. *Monographs of the Society for Research in Child Development, 35*(5, Serial No. 138).

Yarrow, M. R., Scott, P. M., & Waxler, C. Z. (1973). Learning concern for others. *Developmental Psychology, 8,* 240–260.

Yonas, A. (1981). Infants' responses to optical information for collision. In R. N. Aslin, J. R. Alberts, & M. R. Petersen (Eds.), *Development of perception: Psychobiological perspectives (Vol. 2). The visual system.* New York: Academic Press.

Yonas, A., Bechtold, A. G., Frankel, D., Gordon, F. R., McRoberts, G., Norcia, A., & Sternfels, S. (1977). Development of sensitivity to information for impending collision. *Perception & Psychophysics, 21*(2), 97–104.

Yonas, A., Cleaves, W. T., & Pettersen, L. (1978). Development of sensitivity to pictorial depth. *Science, 200,* 77–79.

Yonas, A., Granrud, C. E., & Pettersen, L. (1985). Infants' sensitivity to relative size information for distance. *Developmental Psychology, 21*(1), 161–167.

Yonas, A., Pettersen, L., & Granrud, C. E. (1982). Infants' sensitivity to familiar size as information for distance. *Child Development, 53,* 1285–1290.

Yonas, A., Pettersen, L., & Lockman, J. J. (1979). Young infants' sensitivity to optical information for collision. *Canadian Journal of Psychology, 33,* 268–276.

Yussen, S. R. & Levy, V. M. (1975). Developmental changes in predicting one's own span of short-term memory. *Journal of Experimental Child Psychology, 19,* 93–100.

Zahn-Waxler, C., Radke-Yarrow, M., & King, R. A.

(1979). Child rearing and children's prosocial initiations toward victims of distress. *Child Development, 50,* 319–330.

Zahn-Waxler, C. & Radke-Yarrow, M. (1982). The development of altruism: Alternative research strategies. In N. Eisenberg (Ed.), *The development of prosocial behavior.* New York: Academic Press.

Zajonc, R. B. (1976). Family configuration and intelligence: Variations in scholastic aptitude scores parallel trends in family size and the spacing of children. *Science, 192* (4236), 227–236.

Zajonc, R. B. (1983). Validating the confluence model. *Psychological Bulletin, 93,* 457–480.

Zajonc, R. B., & Bargh, J. (1980). Birth order, family size, and decline of SAT scores. *American Psychologist, 35*(7), 662–668.

Zajonc, R. B., & Markus, G. B. (1975). Birth order and intellectual development. *Psychological Review, 82,* 71–88.

Zajonc, R. B., Markus, H. B., & Markus, G. B. (1979).

The birth order puzzle. *Journal of Personality of Social Psychology, 37,* 1325–1341.

Zarbatany, L., Hartmann, D. P., Gelfand, D. M. & Vinciguerra, P. (1985). Gender differences in altruistic reputation: Are they artifactual? *Developmental Psychology, 21,* 97–101.

Zelazo, P. R., Zelazo, N. A., & Kolb, S. (1972). "Walking" in the newborn. *Science, 176,* 314–315.

Zelazo, P. R. (1976). From reflexive to instrumental behavior. In L. P. Lipsitt (Ed.), *Developmental psychobiology: The significance of infancy.* Hillsdale, NJ: Lawrence Erlbaum.

Zigler, E. (1967). Familial mental retardation: A continuing dilemma. *Science, 155,* 292–298.

Zigler, E. (1978). National crisis in mental retardation research. *American Journal of Mental Deficiency, 83,* 1–8.

Zigler, E. & Cascione, R. (1984). Mental retardation: An overview. In E. S. Gollin, (Ed.), *Malformations of development.* New York: Academic Press.

Copyrights and Acknowledgments

ILLUSTRATION CREDITS

Chapter 1

1-1 Courtesy Shakespeare Centre Library, Stratford-upon-Avon; **1-4** Gould, Stephen Jay (1977). *Ontogeny and phylogeny.* Cambridge, MA: Harvard University Press. Reprinted by permission; **1-5** Ostrom, John (1979, Jan.-Feb.). Bird Flight: How Did It Begin? *American Scientist.* Reprinted with permission; **1-6a** *Scientific American* (11 May, 1889). San Francisco: W. H. Freeman, Co.; **1-6b & c.** Lennart Nilsson; **1-7** Hrdlicka, Ales (1931). *Children who run on all fours.* New York: McGraw-Hill; **1-8a** Art Resource; **1-8b** From Albrecht Dürer, *De symmetria human ovum corporum.* Nuremberg, 1532; **1-9** left, after Hartsoeker, 1694; right, after Dalempatius; **1-10,** Children's Employment Commission. First report of the Commissioners: Mines. (House of Commons Sessions Papers, 1842, XV); courtesy H. M. Stationery Office; **1-11** top, © Diane Koos Gentry/Black Star; bottom © Black Star.

Chapter 2

2-1 Bower, T. G. R. (1974). *Development in infancy.* San Francisco: W. H. Freeman, 1982; **2-2** and **2-3** Adapted from Blommers, P., and Lindquist, E. F. (1960). *Elementary statistical methods in psychology and education.* Boston: Houghton Mifflin; **2-4** Wechsler, David (1944). *The measurement of adult intelligence.* (3rd ed.) Baltimore: The William & Wilkins. © 1944; **2-5** Nesselroade, J. R. & Baltes, P. B., *Adolescent personality development and historical change. 1970-1972* (Monographs of the Society for Research in Child Development, 39, 1 (serial no. 154); **2-7,** Belmont, Lillian, and Marolla, Francis (1973) Birth order, family size, and intelligence. *Science,* 182, pp. 1096-1107. Copyright 1973 by the AAAS; **2-8** Zajonc, R., Markus, H., and Markus, G. (1979). The birth order puzzle. *Journal of Personality and Social psychology, 37.* Copyright 1979 by the American Psychological Association, Inc. Reprinted with permission; **2-11** Zajonc, R. B. (1976) Family configuration and intelligence: Variations in scholastic aptitude scores parallel trends in family size and the spacing of children. *Science, 192.* © 1976 by the AAAS.

Chapter 3

3-1 adapted from Waddington, C. H. (1957). *The strategy of the genes.* New York: Allen & Unwin; **3-3** ©. UPI/Bettmann Newsphotos; **3-4,** Gardner, Lyatt (1972, July). Deprivation dwarfism. © by *Scientific American,* p. 102; **3-5** Widdowson, E. M. (1951). Mental contentment and physical growth. *The Lancet, 260;* **3-6** adapted from Shirley, Mary M., The first two years; A study of twenty-five babies. (*Child Welfare Monograph* No. 7, Vol. II.) Minneapolis: University of Minnesota Press, copyright 1933; **3-7,** Coghill, G. E. (1929) *Anatomy and the problem of behavior.* New York: Macmillan; **3-8** © John Running; **3-9** courtesy Dr. Burton L. White; **3-11** courtesy Mead Johnson Nutritional Group. Evansville, IN 47721; **3-12** Zelazo, P., Zelazo, N., and Kolb, S. (1972) 'Walking' in the Newborn. *Science, 176.* © 1972 by the AAAS; **3-13,** Ramey, C. T. et al. (1985). Preschool compensatory education and the modifiability of intelligence: A critical review. In D. K. Detterman (Ed), *Current topics in human intelligence. Vol. 1: Research methodology.* Norwood, N.J.: Ablex; **3-14** courtesy NIMH and Edna Morlock.

Chapter 4

4-1 T. H. Shepard as modified from Wilson, J. G., *Environment and Birth Defects.* Philadelphia: Academic Press, 1973; **4-2** adapted from Moore, K. L. (1973). *The developing human.* Philadelphia: W. B. Saunders; **4-3** © Black Star; **4-4** Goldstein, A., Aronow, L., and Kahlman, S. M. (1974). *Principles of drug action* (2nd ed.). New York: John Wiley & Sons, Inc. © 1974 Reprinted with permission; **4-5a,** Thomas McAvoy, *Life* © 1955, Time Inc.; **4-5b & c,** Salzery, E. A., and Meyer, C. E. (1968). Reversibility of imprinting. *Journal of Comparative and Physiological Psychology, 66,* © 1968 by the APA; **4-6** Scott, J. P. (1962). Critical periods in behavioral development. *Science, 138,* © 1962 by the AAAS; **4-7** Klopfer, P. H. (1971). Mother Love: What turns it on? *American Scientist, 59.* Reprinted with permission; **4-8** Emlen, S. (1975). The stellar-orientation system of a migratory bird. © *Scientific American, 233;* **4-9** Mason, W. A., & Kenney, M. D. (1974). Redirection of filial attachments in rhesus monkeys: Dogs as mother surrogates. Science, *183.* © 1974 by the AAAS; Photo by Jeff Fricker; **4-11** © E. D. Fawcett/Photo Researchers, Inc.; **4-12** © Photo Researchers; **4-13** & **4-14** Wilson, J. O., George, F. W., and Griffin, J. E. (1981). The hormonal control of sexual development. *Science 211,* © 1981 by the AAAS; **4-15** & **4-17** Money, John, and Ehrhardt, Anke (1972). *Man & woman, boy & girl.* Baltimore: Johns Hopkins University Press.

Chapter 5

5-1 Reproduced with permission from the Institute of Psychiatry, University of London; courtesy of Dr. H. Gurling on behalf of James Shields; **5-2** adapted from Lerner, I. Michael, *Heredity, evolution and society.* San Francisco: W. H. Freeman and Company, copyright © 1968; **5-3** Tryon, R. C. (1942). Individual differences, in F. A. Moss (Ed.) *Comparative psychology.* New York: Prentice-Hall; **5-4** adapted from Plomin, R., DeFries, J. C., and McClean, F. E. (1980) *Behavioral genetics: A primer.* San Francisco: W. H. Freeman and Company; **5-5** Goddard, H. H. (1913). *The Kallikak family: A study in the heredity of feeblemindedness.* New York: Macmillan; **5-6** © Blair Irwin; **5-7** Stern, Curt (1973). *Principles of human genetics* (3rd ed.). San Francisco: W. H. Freeman; **5-8** Ehrman, L, and Parsons, P. A. (1981). *Behavior, genetics and evolution.* New York: McGraw-Hill; **5-10** © AP/Wide World Photos; **5-11** adapted from Rose et al. Genetic Variance in nonverbal intelligence: Data from the kinships of identical twins. (1979). *Science, 14,* © 1979 by the AAAS; **5-12** Wilson, R. S. (1983). The Louisville twin study. *Child Development, 54;* **5-13** Houzik, M. P. (1957). Developmental studies of parent-child resemblance in intelligence. *Child Development, 24;* **5-14a** © Science Source/Photo Researchers; **5-14b** © R. A. Boolootian, Box 5-1, Stern, Curt. (1973). *Principles of human genetics* (3rd ed.). San Francisco: W. H. Freeman and Co.

Chapter 6

6-1 Duke, P. M. (1982). Educational correlates of early and late sexual maturation in adolescence. *The Journal of Pediatrics, 100;* **6-2** Tanner, J. M. (1975). Growth & endocrinology of the adolescent. In L. Gardner (Ed.), *Endocrine & genetic diseases of childhood* (2nd ed.). Philadelphia: W. B. Saunders; **6-3** Tanner, J. M. (1978). *Fetus into man.* Cambridge: Harvard University Press; **6-4** Marshall, W. A. (1974). Interrelationships of skeletal maturation, sexual development and somatic growth in man. *Annals of Human Biology 1;* **6-5** Fantz, R. et al. (1975). Visual attention to size and number of pattern details. *Child Development, 46;* **6-6** Tanner, J. M. (1970). Physical growth. In *Carmichael's Manual of child psychology* (3rd ed.) Vol. 1. New York: John Wiley & Sons, Inc. © 1970; **6-7**, Robbins, W. J. et al, *Growth.* New Haven: Yale University Press, copyright 1929; **6-8** Tanner, J. M. (1970). Physical Growth. In Carmichael's *Manual of child psychology* (3rd ed) Vol 1. New York: John Wiley & Sons, Inc. © 1970; **6-9** adapted from Thompson, R. F. (1975). *Introduction to physiological psychology.* New York: Harper and Row; **6-10** & **6-11**, Tanner, J. M. (1970). Physical Growth. In Carmichael's *Manual of child psychology* (3rd ed.). Vol. 1. New York: John Wiley & Sons, Inc. © 1970; **6-12** Gardner, Lytt (1972). Deprivation Dwarfism. © 1972 *Scientific American, 227* (1); **6-13** Tanner, J. M. (1970). Physical Growth. In Carmichael's *Manual of child psychology* (3rd ed.). Vol. 1. New York: John Wiley and Sons, Inc. © 1970; **6-14** Tanner, J. M. (1962) *Growth at*

adolescence. Oxford: Blackwell Scientific Publications. With permission of Blackwell Scientific Publications; **6-15** Lewontin, R. C. (1978). Adaptation. In *Evolution: A scientific American book.* San Francisco: W. H. Freeman & Co.; **6-16** Adapted from Forbes, J. L., & King, J. C. (Eds.). *Primate behavior.* New York: Academic Press, 1982; **6-17** Cowan, W. M. (1979). The Development of the Brain. In *Scientific American, The brain: A Scientific American book,* San Francisco: W. H. Freeman & Co.; **6-18** Adapted from Trevarthen, C. Cerebral embryology and the split brain. In *Hemisphere disconnection and cerebral function,* M. Kinsbourne and L. Smith, Eds. Springfield: Charles C. Thomas, Publisher. © 1974; **6-19** Adapted from Munn, N. L., *The evolution of the human mind.* Boston: Houghton Mifflin Co., 1971; **6-20** Reprinted from Jastrow, Robert, *The enchanted loom.* New York: Simon & Schuster, © 1981 Reader's Library; **6-21** Lindsay, P. H. and Norman, D. A. (1977). *Human information processing.* New York: Academic Press; **6-22** From Gorski, R. A., Hormonal modulation of neuronal structure. In F. O. Schmitt and F. G. Worden (Eds.) *The Neurosciences: Fourth study program.* Cambridge: MIT Press, 1979; **6-23** From Jastrow, Robert, *The Enchanted Loom.* New York: Simon & Schuster, © 1981 Reader's Library; **6-24a** From Hubel, D. H., and Wiesel, T. N. (1962) Receptive fields, binocular interaction and functional architecture in the cat's visual cortex. In *Journal of Physiology, 160.* Copyright by the *Journal of Physiology;* **6-24b** From Wiesel, T. N., and Hubel, D. H. (1965). Comparison of the effect of unilateral and bilateral eye closure on cortical unit responses in kittens. In *Journal of Neurophysiology, 28.* Copyright 1965 by the American Physiological Society; **6-25** From Blakemore, C., and Cooper, G. F. (1970). Controlled visual environment. *Nature, 228;* **6-26** Rosenzweig, M. R., Bennett, E. L., and Diamond, Marion C. (1972, February). Brain changes in response to experience. © 1972 by *Scientific American;* **6-27** © Pellacan Graphics; **6-28** Eibl-Eibesjeldt, Irenaus (1975). *Ethology: The biology of behavior.* New York: Holt, Rinehart & Winston, Inc.; **6-29** Diamond, Adele (1985). The development of the ability to use recall to guide action, as indicated by infants' performance on AB. *Child Development, 56,* 868–883; **6-30** Diamond, Adele (1981). Retrieval of an object from an open box: The development of visual-tactile control of reaching in the first year of life. *Society for Research in Child Development Abstracts, 3.*

Chapter 7

7-1 From Shepard, Roger N. (1978). The mental image. *American Psychologist, 33* © 1978 by the APA; **7-2** Fantz, R. L. (1961). The origin of form perception. © 1961 by *Scientific American, 204;* **7-3** Goldstein, E. B. (1984). *Sensation and perception.* (2nd ed.) Belmont: Wadsworth Publishing Co. © 1984; **7-4** Steiner, J. E. (1979). Human facial expressions in response to taste and smell stimulation. In *Advances in child development and behavior, vol 13.* New York: Academic Press; **7-5** Goldstein, E. B. (1984). *Sensation and perception.* (2nd ed.) Belmont: Wadsworth Publishing Co. © 1984; **7-6** Ginsburg, A. P. (1978). Visual information processing based on spatial filters constrained by biological data. Doctoral dissertation, Cambridge University. Photos courtesy Dr. Arthur P. Ginsburg, Vision Research Laboratory Vistech Consultants, Inc.; **7-7** Tevor-Roper, P., *The world through blunted sight.* Indianapolis: Bobbs-Merrill, 1970; **7-8** Bornstein, M. H. (1976). Infants are trichromats. *Journal of Experimental Child Psychology, 21;* **7–9** Granrud, Carl E. (1984). Infants' sensitivity to accretion and deletion of texture as information for depth at an edge. *Child Development, 55,* p. 1631; **7–10** Adapted from Gibson, J. J. (1950). *The perception of the visual world.* p. 179. © 1950, renewed 1978 by Houghton-Mifflin Co.; **7–12** Coren, S., Porac, C., & Ward, L. (1979). *Sensation and perception* (2nd ed.). New York: Academic Press; **7–13** Gibson E., and Walk, R. D. (1960). The visual cliff. *Scientific American, 202.* Photos by William Vandivert; **7–14** Held, R. and Hein, A. (1963). Movement produced stimulation. *Journal of Comparative and Physiological psychology, 56* © 1963 by the APA; **7–15** top, Yonas, A., Cleaves, W., and Pattersen, L. (1978). Development of sensitivity to pictorial depth. *Science, 200* © 1978 by the AAAS; bottom, adapted from Kaufmann, R. et al. (1981). Sensitivity of 5- and 7-month-old infants to pictorial depth information *Journal of Experimental Child Psychology. 32;* **7–16** © Blair Irwin; **7–18** Ekman, Paul (1973). *Cross cultural studies of facial expression.* New York: Academic Press; Photos courtesy Dr. Ekman; **7–19** Mauer, D., and Salapatek, P. (1976). Developmental changes in scanning of faces by young infants. *Child Development, 47,* 523–527; **7–21** Gerber, S. E. (1974). *Introductory hearing science.* Philadelphia: W. B. Saunders; **7–22a** Meltzoff, A. N., and Moore, M. K. (1983). Newborn infants imitate adult facial gestures, *Child Development, 54,* 702–709; **7–22b,** Field, Tiffany M. et al. (1982). Discrimination and imitation of facial expressions. *Science, 218* © 1982 by the AAAS; **7–23** Bower, T. G. R. (1977). Blind babies see with their ears. *New Scientist. 73.* Photos © Ric Gemmel.

Chapter 8

8–1 Courtesy Professor Adele Diamond; **8–2** Wishart, J., and Bower, T. G. R. "Spatial relations and the object concept: a normative study." In L. P. Lipsitt and C. Rovee-Collier (Eds.) (1984). *Advances in infancy research, Vol. 3.* Norwood, NJ: Ablex; **8–4** Adapted from Bruner, J. S. (1972). In P. C. Wason and P. N. Johnson-Laird (Eds.). *Thinking and reasoning.* New York: Penguin Books; **8–5** Piaget, J., and Inhelder, B. (1956). *The child's conception of space.* London: Routledge & Kegan Paul. Atlantic Highlands, NJ: Humanities Press, 1963; **8–6** Glucksberg, S., Krauss, R. M., and Weisberg, R. (1966). Referential communication in nursery school children: method and some preliminary findings. *Journal of Experimental Child Psychology, 3,* 333–342; **8–7** Siegler, R. S. (1978). The origins of scientific thinking. In R. S. Siegler (Ed.). *Children's thinking: What develops?* Hillsdale, NJ: Erlbaum, © 1978; **8–8** Odom, R. D. et al. (1975). Effects of perceptual salience on the matrix task performance of four- and six-year-old children. *Child Development, 46,* 758–762; **8–9** Donaldson, M. (1978). *Children's minds.* New York: W. W. Norton; **8–10** Inhelder, B., and Piaget, J. (1969). *Early growth of logic in the child.* New York: W. W. Norton; **8–11** Data from Moely, Barbara E. et al. (1969). Production deficiency in young children's clustered recall. *Developmental Psychology,* Vol. 1, pp. 26–34 © 1969 by the APA; **8–13** Brainerd, Charles J. (1979). *The origins of number concepts.* New York: Praeger; **8–14** Berger, Kathleen S. (1980). *The developing person.* New York: Worth Publishers, Inc.; **8–15** Noelting, G. (1980). The development of proportional reasoning and the ratio concept: Part I Differentiation of stages *Educational Studies in Mathematics, 11,* pp. 217–253; **8–16,** Inhelder, B., and Piaget, J. (1958). *The growth of logical thinking from childhood to adolescence.* New York: Basic Books; **8–17** Kuhn, D., and Brannock, J. (1977). Development of the isolation of variables scheme in experimental and "natural experiment" contexts. *Developmental Psychology, 13,* pp. 9–14 © 1977 by the APA; **8–18** Inhelder, B., and Piaget, J. (1958). *The growth of logical thinking from childhood to adolescence.* New York: Basic Books.

Chapter 9

9–2a, Mayer, R. E. (1983). *Thinking, Problem Solving, Cognition.* New York: W. H. Freeman; **9–2b,** Case, R. (1978). Intellectual development from birth to adulthood: A neo-piagetian perspective. In *Children's thinking: What develops?* R. S. Siegler (Ed.), Hillsdale, NJ: Erlbaum; **9–3** Siegler, R. S. (1983). How knowledge influences learning. *American Scientist, 71,* p. 632; **9–4** Siegler, R. S. (1978). The origins of scientific reasoning. In R. S. Siegler (Ed.), *Children's thinking: What develops?* Hillsdale, NJ: Erlbaum; **9–5** Lockheed, J. and Clement, J. (Eds.) (1979). *Cognitive process instruction.* Philadelphia: The Franklin Institute Press; **9–6** Atkinson, R. C., and Shiffrin, R. M. (1971). The control of short-term memory. © 1971 by *Scientific American, 225,* pp. 82–90; **9–7** Kobasigawa, A. (1974). Utilization of retrieval cues by children in recall. *Child Development, 45,* pp. 127–134; **9–8** Kail, R. (1984). *The development of memory in children* (2nd ed.). San Francisco: W. H. Freeman; **9–9** Dempster, F. N. (1981). Memory span: Sources of individual differences. *Psychological Bulletin, 89;* **9–10** Case R. et al. (1982) Operational efficiency and the growth of short-term memory span. *Journal of Experimental Child Psychology, 33;* **9–11** Case, R. (1985) *Intellectual development.* Orlando: Academic Press; **9–12** Chi, M. T. H. Knowledge structures and memory development. In R. Siegler (Ed.), *Children's thinking: What develops?* Hillsdale, NJ: Copyright 1978 by Lawrence Erlbaum Associates, Inc. Reprinted by permission; **9–13** Case, R. (1985). *Intellectual development.* Orlando: Academic Press; **9–14** Slater, A. et al. (1982). Visual memory at birth, *British Journal of Psychology, 73;* **9–15, 9–17, 9–18** Rovee-Collier, Carolyn et al. (1980). Reactivation of infant memory, *Science, 208.* © 1980 by the AAAS Courtesy of Carolyn Rovee-Collier, photographed by Breck P. Kent; **9–16** Earley, L. et al. Ontogenetic changes in retention in early infancy. Presented at meeting of the Society for Research in Child Development, Toronto.

Chapter 10

10–1 Sattler, J. M. (1982). *Assessment of children's intelligence and special abilities* (2nd ed.) Boston: Allyn & Bacon, Inc.; **10–2,** Honzik, M. P. (1948). The stability of mental test performance between two and eighteen years. *Journal of Experimental Education, 17,* pp. 309–324; **10–3** Bayley, N. (1970). Development of mental abilities. In Paul H. Mussen (Ed.), *Carmichael's manual of child psychology,* Vol. 1 (3rd ed.). New York: John Wiley and Sons, Inc. © 1970; **10–4** Fagan, J. F. (1982). Infant memory. In T. Field (Ed.) *Review of human development.* New York: John Wiley and Sons, Inc. © 1982; **10–5** Fagan, J. (1985). A new look at infant intelligence. In D. K. Detterman (Ed.), *Current topics in human intelligence,* Vol. 1. Norwood, NJ: Ablex Publishing Corp. Reprinted with permission; **10–6** Landesman-Dwyer, S., and Butterfield, E. C. (1983). Mental retardation. In M. Lewis (Ed.) *Origins of intelligence* (2nd ed.) New York: Plenum Publishing Corp.; **10–7** Achenbach, T.

(1982). *Developmental psychopathology* (2nd ed.) New York: John Wiley and Sons, Inc. © 1982; **10–8** Zigler, E. (1967). Familial mental retardation: a continuing dilemma. *Science, 155* © 1967 by the AAAS; **10–9** Nichols, P. L. (1984). Familial mental retardation. *Behavior Genetics, 14.* Plenum Publishing Corp.; **10–10** Reprinted with permission of The Free Press, a division of Macmillan Inc. from *Bias in Mental Testing* by Arthur R. Jensen. © 1980.

Chapter 11

11–1 Gleitman, Henry (1981). *Psychology.* New York: W. W. Norton & Co.; **11–2** Locke, John (1983). *Phonological acquisition and change.* New York: Academic Press; **11–3** Wharf, B. (1956). *Language, thought and reality.* Cambridge: MIT Press; **11–4** Smith, M. E. (1926). An Investigation of the development of the sentence and the extent of vocabulary in young children. University of Iowa Studies in Child Welfare, 3; **11–5** DeVilliers & DeVilliers (1979). *Early language.* Cambridge: Harvard University Press. Reprinted with permission; **11–6** Landau, B., and Gleitman, L. (1985). *Language and experience.* Cambridge: Harvard University Press.

Chapter 12

12–1 Kagan, Jerome (1974). Discrepancy, temperament and infant distress. In M. Lewis & L. Rosenblum (Eds.), *The origins of fear.* New York: John Wiley and Sons, Inc. © 1974; **12–2a** Kaufman, I. C., and Rosenblum, L. A. (1967). The reaction to separation in infant monkeys. *Psychosomatic Medicine. 24,* (6); **12–2b** after Van-Lawick Goodall, Jane (1971). *In the shadow of man.* Boston: Houghton-Mifflin Co. Photo copyright National Geographic Society; **12–3** Bower, T. G. R. (1979). *Human development.* San Francisco: W. H. Freeman & Co.; **12–4** Ainsworth, Mary et al. (1978). *Patterns of attachment.* Hillsdale, NJ: LEA; **12–5, 12–6 & 12–7** Courtesy of Harlow Primate Laboratory, University of Wisconsin; **12–8** Thomas, Alexander et al. (1970, August). The origin of personality. © 1970 by *Scientific American.*

Chapter 13

13–1, 13–2, 13–3, & **13–4** Courtesy of Harlow Primate Laboratory, University of Wisconsin; **13–5** © Elizabeth Crews; **13–6** Eifermann, R. (1971). Social play in childhood. In R. E. Herron & B. Sutton-Smith, *Child's play.* New York: John Wiley and Sons, Inc.; **13–7a** © J. Berndt/Stock, Boston; **13–7b** © Elizabeth Crews; **13–8** Madsen, M. C., and Connor, C. (1973). Cooperative and competitive behavior of retarded and nonretarded at two ages. *Child Development, 44.* © The Society for Research in Child Development; **13–9** © R. Ingo Riepl/Anthro Photo; **13–10** Cheyne, J. A., and Walters, R. H. (1970). Punishment and prohibition: Some origins of self-control. In *New directions in psychology 4.* New York: Holt, Rinehart & Winston.

Chapter 14

14–1 Bahrick, L. E., and Watson, J. S. (1985). Detection of intermodal proprioceptive-visual contingency as a potential basis of self-perception in infancy. In *Developmental Psychology, 21,* pp 963–973 © 1985 by the APA; **14–2** courtesy Dr. Kenneth McGraw; **Box 14–1** Emmerich, W. et al. (1976). Development of gender constancy in economically disadvantaged children. Report of the Educational Testing Service, Princeton, NJ; **14–3** & **14–4** After Selman, R. L. (1971). Taking another's perspective: Role-taking development in early childhood, *Child Development 42,* pp. 1721–1734; **14–6** & **14–7** Colby, A. et al. (1983) A longitudinal study of moral development. *Monographs of the Society for Research in Child Development, 48,* (1–2) Serial no. 200, p. 46.

TEXT CREDITS

Box 8–2 Elkind, D. (1964). Discrimination, seriation and numeration of size and dimensional differences in young children: Piaget replication study VI. *Journal of Genetic Psychology, V,* 104. Reprinted with permission of the Helen Dwight Reid Educational Foundation. Copyright 1964.

Box 8–3 Piaget, J. (1968). *Six psychological studies,* 43–44. (D. Elkind, Ed., A. Tenzer, Trans.). New York: Random House, Inc. Reprinted by permission.

Box 12–1 Ainsworth, M. D. S., Blehar, M. C., Waters, E., & Wall, S. (1978). *Patterns of attachment: A psychological study of the strange situation,* 37. Hillsdale, NJ: Lawrence Erlbaum Associates, Inc. Reprinted by permission.

Box 12–2 Baumrind, D. (1970, December). Socialization and instrumental competence in young children. *Young Children, 26(2).* Copyright 1970 by the National Association for the Education of Young Children, 1834 Connecticut Ave., Washington, DC, 20009.

Box 12–3 Huitt, W. G., & Ashton, P. T. (1982). Parents' perception of infant development: A psychometric study. *Merrill-Palmer Quarterly, 28,* pp. 95–109. Reprinted by permission.

Box 14–1 Emmerich, W., Goldman, K. S., Kirsh, B., & Sharabany, R. (1977). Evidence for a transitional phase in the development of gender constancy. *Child Development, 48,* pp. 930–936. Reprinted by permission of Educational Testing Service.

Box 14–3 Kohlberg, L. (1958). *The development of moral thinking and choice in the years ten to sixteen.* Unpublished doctoral dissertation, University of Chicago.

Name Index

Subject Index

Page references in *italics* indicate figures, tables, and other illustrative material.